P9-BHU-270

Nineteenth-Century Literature Criticism

Guide to Gale Literary Criticism Series

For criticism on	Consult these Gale series
Authors now living or who died after December 31, 1959	*CONTEMPORARY LITERARY CRITICISM (CLC)*
Authors who died between 1900 and 1959	*TWENTIETH-CENTURY LITERARY CRITICISM (TCLC)*
Authors who died between 1800 and 1899	*NINETEENTH-CENTURY LITERATURE CRITICISM (NCLC)*
Authors who died between 1400 and 1799	*LITERATURE CRITICISM FROM 1400 TO 1800 (LC)* *SHAKESPEAREAN CRITICISM (SC)*
Authors who died before 1400	*CLASSICAL AND MEDIEVAL LITERATURE CRITICISM (CMLC)*
Black writers of the past two hundred years	*BLACK LITERATURE CRITICISM (BLC)*
Authors of books for children and young adults	*CHILDREN'S LITERATURE REVIEW (CLR)*
Dramatists	*DRAMA CRITICISM (DC)*
Hispanic writers of the late nineteenth and twentieth centuries	*HISPANIC LITERATURE CRITICISM (HLC)*
Native North American writers and orators of the eighteenth, nineteenth, and twentieth centuries	*NATIVE NORTH AMERICAN LITERATURE (NNAL)*
Poets	*POETRY CRITICISM (PC)*
Short story writers	*SHORT STORY CRITICISM (SSC)*
Major authors from the Renaissance to the present	*WORLD LITERATURE CRITICISM, 1500 TO THE PRESENT (WLC)*

ISSN 0732-1864

Volume 61

Nineteenth-Century Literature Criticism

Criticism of the
Works of Novelists, Poets, Playwrights,
Short Story Writers, Philosophers, and Other
Creative Writers Who Died between 1800
and 1899, from the First Published Critical
Appraisals to Current Evaluations

Gerald R. Barterian
Denise Evans
Mary L. Onorato
Editors

GALE

DETROIT · NEW YORK · TORONTO · LONDON

STAFF

Gerald R. Barterian, Denise Evans, Mary L. Onorato, *Editors*

Jelena Krstović, James E. Person, Jr., *Contributing Editors*

Aarti D. Stephens, *Managing Editor*

Susan M. Trosky, *Permissions Manager*
Kimberly F. Smilay, *Permissions Specialist*
Sarah Chesney, *Permissions Associate*
Steve Cusack, Kelly A. Quin, *Permissions Assistants*

Victoria B. Cariappa, *Research Manager*
Michele P. LeMeau, *Research Specialist*
Laura C. Bissey, Julia C. Daniel, Tamara C. Nott,
Tracie A. Richardson, Cheryl L. Warnock, *Research Associates*

Mary Beth Trimper, *Production Director*
Deborah L. Milliken, *Production Assistant*

Gary Leach, *Desktop Publisher*
Randy Bassett, *Image Database Supervisor*
Robert Duncan, Michael Logusz, *Imaging Specialists*
Pamela A. Reed, *Photography Coordinator*

This book is printed on acid-free paper that meets the minimum requirements of American National Standard for Information Sciences—Permanence Paper for Printed Library Materials, ANSI Z39.48-1984.

Library of Congress Catalog Card Number 84-643008
ISBN 0-7876-1127-1
ISSN 0732-1864
Printed in the United States of America

10 9 8 7 6 5 4 3 2 1

Contents

Preface vii

Acknowledgments xi

Preface

S ince its inception in 1981, *Nineteenth-Century Literature Criticism* has been a valuable resource for students and librarians seeking critical commentary on writers of this transitional period in world history. Designated an "Outstanding Reference Source" by the American Library Association with the publication of its first volume, *NCLC* has since been purchased by over 6,000 school, public, and university libraries. The series has covered more than 300 authors representing 29 nationalities and over 17,000 titles. No other reference source has surveyed the critical reaction to nineteenth-century authors and literature as thoroughly as *NCLC*.

Scope of the Series

NCLC is designed to introduce students and advanced readers to the authors of the nineteenth century, and to the most significant interpretations of these authors' works. The great poets, novelists, short story writers, playwrights, and philosophers of this period are frequently studied in high school and college literature courses. By organizing and reprinting commentary written on these authors, *NCLC* helps students develop valuable insight into literary history, promotes a better understanding of the texts, and sparks ideas for papers and assignments. Each entry in *NCLC* presents a comprehensive survey of an author's career or an individual work of literature and provides the user with a multiplicity of interpretations and assessments. Such variety allows students to pursue their own interests; furthermore, it fosters an awareness that literature is dynamic and responsive to many different opinions.

Every fourth volume of *NCLC* is devoted to literary topics that cannot be covered under the author approach used in the rest of the series. Such topics include literary movements, prominent themes in nineteenth-century literature, literary reaction to political and historical events, significant eras in literary history, prominent literary anniversaries, and the literatures of cultures that are often overlooked by English-speaking readers.

NCLC continues the survey of criticism of world literature begun by Gale's *Contemporary Literary Criticism (CLC)* and *Twentieth-Century Literary Criticism (TCLC),* both of which excerpt and reprint commentary on authors of the twentieth century. For additional information about *TCLC, CLC,* and Gale's other criticism series, users should consult the Guide to Gale Literary Criticism Series preceding the title page in this volume.

Coverage

Each volume of *NCLC* is carefully compiled to present:

- criticism of authors, or literary topics, representing a variety of genres and nationalities
- both major and lesser-known writers and literary works of the period
- 5-8 authors or 4-6 topics per volume
- individual entries that survey critical response to an author's work or a topic in literary history, including early criticism to reflect initial reactions, later criticism to represent any rise or decline in reputation, and current retrospective analyses.

Organization

An author entry consists of the following elements: author heading, biographical and critical introduction, list of principal works, excerpts of criticism (each preceded by a bibliographic citation and an annotation), and a bibliography of further reading.

- The **Author Heading** consists of the name under which the author most commonly wrote, followed by birth and death dates. If an author wrote consistently under a pseudonym, the pseudonym will be listed in the author heading and the real name given in parentheses on the first line of the biographical and critical introduction. Also located at the beginning of the introduction to the author entry are any name variations under which an author wrote, including transliterated forms for an author whose language uses a nonroman alphabet.

- The **Biographical and Critical Introduction** outlines the author's life and career, as well as the critical issues surrounding his or her work. References are provided to past volumes of *NCLC* in which further information about the author may be found.

- Most *NCLC* entries include a **Portrait** of the author. Many entries also contain reproductions of materials pertinent to an author's career, including manuscript pages, title pages, dust jackets, letters, and drawings, as well as photographs of important people, places, and events in an author's life.

- The list of **Principal Works** is chronological by date of first publication and identifies the genre of each work. In the case of foreign authors with both foreign-language publications and English translations, the English-language version is given in brackets. Unless otherwise indicated, dramas are dated by first performance, not first publication.

- **Criticism** in each author entry is arranged chronologically to provide a perspective on changes in critical evaluation over the years. All titles of works by the author featured in the entry are printed in boldface type to enable the user to easily locate discussion of particular works. Also for purposes of easier identification, the critic's name and the publication date of the essay are given at the beginning of each piece of criticism. Unsigned criticism is preceded by the title of the journal in which it appeared. Publication information (such as publisher names and book prices) and some parenthetical numerical references (such as page and line references to specific editions of works) have been deleted at the editors' discretion to provide smoother reading of the text. Footnotes that appear with previously published pieces of criticism are reprinted at the end of each essay or excerpt. In the case of excerpted criticism, only those footnotes that pertain to the excerpted text are included.

- A complete **Bibliographic Citation** provides original publication information for each piece of criticism.

- Critical excerpts are prefaced by **Annotations** providing the reader with a summary of the critical intent of the piece. Also included, when appropriate, is information about the critic's reputation, individual approach to literary criticism, and particular expertise in an author's works, as well as information about the relative importance of the critical excerpt. In some cases, the annotations cross-reference excerpts by critics who discuss each other's commentary.

- An annotated list of **Further Reading** appearing at the end of each entry suggests secondary sources on the author. In some cases it includes essays for which the editors could not obtain reprint rights.

Cumulative Indexes

- Each volume of *NCLC* contains a cumulative **Author Index** listing all authors who have appeared in Gale's Literary Criticism Series, along with cross-references to such biographical series as *Contemporary Authors* and *Dictionary of Literary Biography*. Useful for locating authors within the various series, this index is particularly valuable for those authors who are identified with a certain period but who, because of their death dates, are placed in another, or for those authors whose careers span two periods. For example, Fyodor Dostoevsky is found in *NCLC*, yet Leo Tolstoy, another major nineteenth-century Russian novelist, is found in *TCLC* because he died after 1899.

- Each *NCLC* volume includes a cumulative **Nationality Index** which lists all authors who have appeared in *NCLC*, arranged alphabetically under their respective nationalities.

- Each new volume in Gale's Literary Criticism Series includes a cumulative **Topic Index**, which lists all literary topics treated in *NCLC, TCLC, LC 1400-1800*, and the *CLC* Yearbook.

- Each new volume of *NCLC*, with the exception of the Topics volumes, contains a **Title Index** listing the titles of all literary works discussed in the volume. In response to numerous suggestions from librarians, Gale has also produced a **Special Paperbound Edition** of the *NCLC* title index. This annual cumulation lists all titles discussed in the series since its inception. Additional copies of the index are available on request. Librarians and patrons have welcomed this separate index: it saves shelf space, is easy to use, and is recyclable upon receipt of the following year's cumulation. Titles discussed in the Topics volume entries are not included in the *NCLC* cumulative index.

Citing *Nineteenth-Century Literature Criticism*

When writing papers, students who quote directly from any volume in Gale's Literary Criticism Series may use the following general forms to footnote reprinted criticism. The first example pertains to material drawn from periodicals, the second to material reprinted from books:

[1]T.S. Eliot, "John Donne," *The Nation and Athenaeum*, 33 (9 June 1923), 321-32; excerpted and reprinted in *Literature Criticism from 1400-1800,* Vol. 10, ed. James E. Person, Jr. (Detroit: Gale Research, 1989), pp. 28-9.

[2]Clara G. Stillman, *Samuel Butler: A Mid-Victorian Modern* (Viking Press, 1932); excerpted and reprinted in *Twentieth-Century Literary Criticism,* Vol. 33, ed. Paula Kepos (Detroit: Gale Research, 1989), pp. 43-5.

Suggestions Are Welcome

In response to suggestions, several features have been added to *NCLC* since the series began, including annotations to excerpted criticism, a cumulative index to authors in all Gale literary criticism series, entries devoted to criticism on a single work by a major author, more illustrations, and a title index listing all literary works discussed in the series.

Readers who wish to suggest authors, single works, or topics to appear in future volumes, or who have other suggestions, are cordially invited to write: The Editors, *Nineteenth-Century Literature Criticism,* 835 Penobscot Bldg., 645 Griswold St., Detroit, MI 48226-4094; call toll-free at 1-800-347-GALE; or fax to 1-313-961-6599.

Elizabeth Barrett Browning

1806-1861

English poet and translator.

For additional information on Barrett Browning's life and works, see *NCLC,* Volumes 1 and 16. A single-work entry on *Aurora Leigh* (1856) is planned for an upcoming *NCLC* volume.

INTRODUCTION

Elizabeth Barrett Browning, whose accomplishments were such that she was for a time considered for the post of Britain's poet laureate, is best remembered for her *Sonnets from the Portuguese* (1850), among the most beautiful love cycles in English literature. Beloved by many readers, her poetry has nevertheless been consistently criticized for technical carelessness; recent critics, however, contend that her unconventional rhymes and loose diction were neither negligent nor haphazard, but deliberate experiments by a conscientious student of prosody. But scholars generally concur that Browning's poetry is flawed by her emphasis on passionate emotion over clear expression, and most agree that she achieved her highest poetic expression in the sonnet, whose formal structure restrained her effusiveness.

Biographical Information

The oldest of eleven children, Elizabeth Barrett was raised by an overbearing father who forbade his daughters to marry. However, he encouraged their scholastic achievement and was so proud of Elizabeth's writing ability that he privately published her first book of poetry, *The Battle of Marathon*, in 1820. Around this time, Elizabeth injured her spine in a riding accident and seemed doomed to a life of infirmity and confinement. The drowning death several years later of her favorite brother sent her into a deep depression that made her condition worse. Despite these adversities, she continued to study and write. In 1826 she published *An Essay on Mind, with Other Poems*, followed by a translation of Aeschylus' *Prometheus Bound* in 1833, both of which appeared anonymously; and in 1838, she published *The Seraphim, and Other Poems*, her first signed volume. All three attracted much favorable attention, and she was regarded as a serious and talented poet. From her sickroom in the family home on Wimpole Street in London, Elizabeth dedi-

cated herself to a literary life, receiving special guests, notably Mary Russell Mitford, and corresponding frequently with various literati, among them Edgar Allan Poe, James Russell Lowell, and Thomas Carlyle, all of whom sent flattering appraisals of her poetry.

Robert Browning joined these correspondents after Elizabeth admiringly mentioned his name in a poem entitled "Lady Geraldine's Courtship." Deeply moved by this tribute from a recognized poet, he responded in a letter, "I love your verses with all my heart, dear Miss Barrett," and a few lines later, "I love you, too." Robert Browning became a frequent visitor to Wimpole Street. In 1846, ignoring Elizabeth's poor health and the disapprobation of her father, the poets eloped to Italy and settled in Pisa. Although she remained somewhat frail, Barrett Browning was invigorated by her love for her husband and for her adopted homeland, and began writing with a new passion, completing the *Poems* of 1844, *Sonnets from the Portuguese*, and *Aurora Leigh* (1856), among other works. Barrett Browning's triumphant emergence from the sick room, in addition to her son's birth in 1849 and the stimulating presence of her husband, inspired in her a creative energy that did not wane until her death at age fifty-five.

Major Works

Although Barrett Browning's earlier works attracted some favorable attention, *The Seraphim, and Other Poems* was her first work to draw a wide readership. This early period was followed by the prolonged composition of *Poems* and *Sonnets from the Portuguese*, which records the growth of love between Elizabeth Barrett and Robert Browning. She expressed her political passion for Italian liberal causes in *Casa Guidi Windows* (1851) and *Poems before Congress* (1860), but critics generally dismiss this fervent verse as reckless and overly emotional. Barrett Browning made a gentler statement in *Aurora Leigh*, an ambitious novel in blank verse; but, while praising the power of many passages, critics have pointed out the didacticism of her social criticism. Nevertheless, *Aurora Leigh* is widely read and admired and remains one of Barrett Browning's most characteristic creations, embodying both her strengths and weaknesses.

Critical Reception

In the lavish eulogies that appeared at the time of her death, Barrett Browning was called England's greatest woman poet. While her reputation has faltered somewhat over the years, she is still revered as a sonneteer and also considered a literary heroine. It has been suggested, in fact, that the overpowering Browning legend—the brilliant invalid fleeing from tyrannical father to poet-lover—has distracted critics from the merits of her work. Her unorthodox rhyme and diction, often scorned, have been cited as daring experiments that prefigured the techniques of George Meredith, Gerard Manley Hopkins, and, through them, modern poets. Her candid treatment of political and social issues, too, was bold for her time. While her talent is perhaps best revealed within the confines of the sonnet, there is much to be appreciated in Browning's unrestrained poetic imagination.

PRINCIPAL WORKS

An Essay on Mind, with Other Poems (poetry) 1826
Prometheus Bound, Translated from the Greek of Aeschylus and Miscellaneous Poems by the Translator [translator] (poetry) 1833
The Seraphim, and Other Poems (poetry) 1838
Poems (poetry) 1844; published in the United States as *A Drama of Exile, and Other Poems*, 1844

*Poems (new edition) (poetry) 1850
Casa Guidi Windows (poetry) 1851
Aurora Leigh (poetry) 1856
Poems before Congress (poetry) 1860
Last Poems (poetry) 1862

*This is a new and enlarged edition of the 1844 *Poems*, and contains *Sonnets from the Portuguese*.

CRITICISM

Helen Cooper (essay date 1979)

SOURCE: "Working into Light: Elizabeth Barrett Browning," in *Shakespeare's Sisters: Feminist Essays on Women Poets*, edited by Sandra M. Gilbert and Susan Gubar, Indiana University Press, 1979, pp. 65-81.

[*In the essay that follows, Cooper considers Browning's portrayal of the patriarchal literary tradition and her criticisms of women's complicity in their own oppression.*]

A year after the publication of Elizabeth Barrett Browning's **Poems of 1844,** which established her as Britain's foremost woman poet, she was painfully aware of the absence of foremothers:[1]

> . . . England has had many learned women, not merely readers but writers of the learned languages, in Elizabeth's time and afterwards—women of deeper acquirements than are common now in the greater diffusion of letters; and yet where were the poetesses? The divine breath . . . why did it never pass, even in the lyrical form, over the lips of a woman? How strange! And can we deny that it was so? I look everywhere for grandmothers and see none. It is not in the filial spirit I am deficient, I do assure you—witness my reverent love of the grandfathers![2]

Chaucer, Spenser, Shakespeare, Milton, Pope, Wordsworth: British poetry embodied four hundred years of male practice of the art. Unlike Arthur Quiller-Couch, who describes how Britain nurtured the men who became its major poets—claiming a university education as a virtual prerequisite for "poetical genius"—Barrett Browning never formulated a penetrating political or social analysis of the factors contributing to the absence of great women poets.[3] However, in letters of 1845 she demonstrates some ambivalence over this issue. To Robert Browning she confesses:

> . . . let us say & do what we please & can . . there *is* a natural inferiority of mind in women—of the intellect . . not by any means, of the moral nature—

& that the history of Art . . & of genius testifies to this fact openly. . . .

Seeming "to justify for a moment an opposite opinion," her admiration for George Sand undercuts this:

> Such a colossal nature in every way—with all that breadth & scope of faculty which women want—magnanimous, & loving the truth & loving the people—and with that "hate of hate" too. . . .[4]

In the same year she admits to a Miss Thompson, who had solicited some classical translations for an anthology:

> Perhaps I do not . . . partake quite your 'divine fury' for converting our sex into Greek scholarship. . . . You . . . know that the Greek language . . . swallows up year after year of studious life. Now I have a 'doxy' . . . that there is no exercise of the mind so little profitable to the mind as the study of languages. It is the nearest thing to a passive recipiency—is it not?—as a mental action, though it leaves one as weary as ennui itself. Women want to be made to *think actively:* their apprehension is quicker than that of men, but their defect lies for the most part in the logical faculty and in the higher mental activities.[5]

It is not women's "natural inferiority of mind" that hinders them, but their training into a "passive recipiency." Such a mental state is incompatible with the active thinking necessary for a poet.

Deprived of "grandmothers," Barrett Browning energetically explored what it meant to be a woman poet writing out of a male tradition, in which she was thoroughly self-educated. In 1857 she formulated a clear statement of the material appropriate to the woman poet when she challenged the critical reception to her discussion of prostitutes in *Aurora Leigh:*

> What has given most offence in the book . . . has been the reference to the condition of women in our cities, which a woman oughtn't to refer to . . . says the conventional tradition. Now I have thought deeply otherwise. If a woman ignores these wrongs, then may women as a sex continue to suffer them: there is no help for any of us— let us be dumb and die.[6]

The "conventional tradition" allowed to early nineteenth-century women poets is exemplified by the works of two of the most popular of them, Felicia Hemans (1793-1835) and Letitia Landon (1802-1838). In the preface to *The Venetian Bracelet* (1829), Landon justifies "Love as my source of song":

> I can only say, that for a woman, whose influence and whose sphere must be in the affections, what subject can be more fitting than one which it is her peculiar province to refine, spiritualise, and exalt? I have always sought to paint it self-denying, devoted, and making an almost religion of its truth. . . .[7]

Hemans's rage at the condition of women's lives is carefully controlled. Writing on "Evening Prayer at a Girls' School," she encourages the girls to enjoy the present, for

> Her lot is on you—silent tears to weep,
> And patient smiles to wear through
>   suffering's hour,
> And sumless riches, from affection's deep,
> To pour on broken reeds—a wasted shower!
> And to make idols, and to find them clay,
> And to bewail that worship,—therefore pray!
>
> . . . . .
>
> Meekly to bear with wrong, to cheer decay,
> And oh! to love through all things,—
>   therefore pray!

Hemans's advice bristles with ambivalence. The contempt surfacing for "broken reeds" and "clay idols" that waste women's energy is undercut by the resignation of the last two lines. Landon and Hemans see self-denial and suffering, a woman's natural duty, as their subject matter. Barrett Browning grew to realize the abuse of women as her material, believing that the world may be made finer for women through their unflinching concern for one another. Refusing to be contained within boundaries prescribed as "woman's sphere," she interpreted the woman poet's special subject matter as being anything and everything which honestly illuminates her life.

Not only did Barrett Browning reject any limitation on the content of women's poetry, she also insisted on a rigorous assessment of women's work:

> The divineness of poetry is far more to me than either pride of sex or personal pride. . . . And though I in turn suffer for this myself—though I too . . . may be turned out of "Arcadia," and told that I am not a poet, still, I should be content, I hope, that the divineness of poetry be proved in my humanness, rather than lowered to my uses.[8]

This standard is revolutionary, for the "poetesses" had always been judged by very different criteria from their male counterparts. H. T. Tucker aptly demonstrates this:

> The spirit of Mrs. Hemans in all she has written
> is essentially feminine. . . . She has thrown over
> all her effusions, not so much the drapery of
> knowledge or the light of extensive observation,
> as the warm and shifting hues of the heart.[9]

Tucker exemplifies a criticism purporting to speak
highly of women's work while in fact condemning it.
To avoid recognizing her language as overly sentimental and vague as he would that of a male poet, he
praises the "warm and shifting hues of the heart" and
exonerates her from lacking "the drapery of knowledge or the light of extensive observation."

To realize her aesthetic Barrett Browning took the
idea of excellence from, yet resisted the domination
of, the male poetic tradition. Increasingly she absorbed a woman's culture: her letters are peppered
with references to Hemans, Landon, and other women
poets, to Jane Austen, Charlotte Brontë, George Eliot,
George Sand, Mrs. Gaskell, and Harriet Beecher
Stowe, to Harriet Martineau and Margaret Fuller, and
to the young American sculptor Harriet Hosmer. She
probes their work, their assessment of themselves,
their strengths and weaknesses, creating for herself
a network of support while systematically breaking
through the limiting proprieties ascribed to women
poets.

Informing this sense of community was the memory
of the love between herself and her mother, who died
suddenly away from home in 1828 when Barrett Browning was twenty-two. Three years later she records in
her diary:

> How I thought of those words *"You will never
> find another person who will love you as I love
> you"*—And how I felt that to hear again the
> sound of those beloved, those ever ever beloved
> lips, I wd barter all other sounds & sights—that
> I wd in joy & gratitude lay down before her my
> tastes & feelings each & all, in sacrifice for the
> love, the exceeding love which I never, in truth,
> can find again.[10]

The relationship between Barrett Browning and Edward Moulton Barrett, her father, has become legend,
but the love between the poet and Mary Graham-Clarke,
her mother, has been ignored by critics. Certainly her
father educated her from the full bookcases in his
study and was intensely a part of her adult life. However, the education the young poet received from her
mother about the nurturing power of love between
women also needs exploration and documentation, for
it is this that resonates through such poems as her
sonnets to George Sand and *Aurora Leigh*.

By the age of twelve Barrett Browning had read Mary
Wollstonecraft's *A Vindication of the Rights of Woman*.

Taplin, her biographer, records her reading in 1828 in
The Literary Souvenir:

> . . . a sentimental poem by Miss Landon called
> "The Forsaken," which represented the lament of
> a country girl whose lover had left her to look for
> city pleasures. Elizabeth thought the verses were
> "beautiful and pathetic." She was also much
> affected by a poem by Mrs Hemans—it "goes to
> the heart," she wrote—describing the death of a
> mother and her baby in a shipwreck.[11]

Yet her second book, *An Essay on Mind,* privately
published in the same year, bears the unmistakable
imprint of Pope's style:

> Since Spirit first inspir'd, pervaded all,
> And Mind met Matter, at th' Eternal call—
> Since dust weigh'd Genius down, or Genius gave
> Th' immortal halo to the mortal's grave;

and so on for more than a thousand lines.

The Seraphim and Other Poems (1838) and *Poems
of 1844* were Barrett Browning's first widely published volumes and the first in which a new sense of
herself as a woman poet emerged. The latter especially brought good reviews:

> Mr. Chorley, in the "Athenaeum," described the
> volume as "extraordinary," adding that "between
> her poems and the slighter lyrics of the sisterhood,
> there is all the difference which exists between
> the putting-on of 'singing robes' for altar service,
> and the taking up lute or harp to enchant an
> indulgent circle of friends and kindred."[12]

"The Seraphim" (1838) and "The Drama of Exile"
(1844) are both long dramatic poems, influenced by
Milton's work. "A Vision of Poets" (1844) and "Lady
Geraldine's Courtship" (1844), both about poets,
seem traditional because the writers are male. In each
case, however, the writer's vision is clarified through
interaction with a strong and intelligent woman. In the
former the woman specifically instructs the poet as to
his true function. Although the poet is not yet identified as a woman, as she will be ten years later in
Aurora Leigh (1856), this is a radical departure from
male tradition, where the woman's function is not to
know about poetry but to "inspire" the poet from afar
through her beauty or to seduce him away from his
work.

Barrett Browning was certain of her dedication to
poetry:

> I cannot remember the time when I did not love
> it—with a lying-awake sort of passion at nine
> years old, and with a more powerful feeling

since. . . . At this moment I love it more than ever—and am more bent than ever, if possible, to work into light . . not into popularity but into expression . . whatever faculty I have. This is the object of the intellectual part of me—and if I live it shall be done. . . . for poetry's own sake . . . for the sake of my love of it. Love is the safest and most unwearied moving principle in all things—it is an heroic worker.[13]

To this poet love is not self-denial and resignation, but a powerful energy source for the transformation of vision into poetry. Sloughing off the male mask in **"The Soul's Expression"** (1844), she describes forcefully her own creative process:

> With stammering lips and insufficient sound
> I strive and struggle to deliver right
> That music of my nature, day and night
> With dream and thought and feeling
>   interwound,
> And inly answering all the senses round
> With octaves of a mystic depth and height
> Which step out grandly to the infinite
> From the dark edges of the sensual ground.
> This song of soul I struggle to outbear
> Through portals of the sense, sublime and
>   whole,
> And utter all myself into the air:
> But if I did it,—as the thunder-roll
> Breaks its own cloud, my flesh would perish
>   there,
> Before that dread apocalypse of soul.

Her determination to "work into light" necessitates the "stammering lips and insufficient sound" with which she struggles to "deliver right / That music of my nature." Her vision comes through her senses, as she seeks transcendence to "step out grandly to the infinite / From the dark edges of the sensual ground." As a woman trained to a "passive recipiency," she experiences the active energy of creativity as potentially destructive. Compelled to deliver the "music of my nature," she fears to give herself totally to her imagination "and utter all myself into the air," fears "my flesh would perish there, / Before that dread apocalypse of soul." And yet it was through the power of her imagination that she created her identity and her ability to deal with her eight-year "captivity" as a Victorian female invalid, as **"The Prisoner"** (1844) reveals:

>   . . . Nature's lute
> Sounds on, behind this door so closely
>   shut,
> A strange wild music to the prisoner's ears,
> Dilated by the distance, till the brain
> Grows dim with fancies which it feels too
>   fine:

"Behind this door" she responded passionately to George Sand's novels, and her sonnet **"To George Sand: A Recognition"** (1844) contains a clear statement about the special nature of a woman's voice writing of women's concerns:

> True genius, but true woman! dost deny
> The woman's nature with a manly scorn,
> And break away the gauds and armlets
>   worn
> By weaker women in captivity?
> Ah, vain denial! that revolted cry
> Is sobbed in by a woman's voice forlorn,—
> Thy woman's hair, my sister, all unshorn
> Floats back dishevelled strength in agony,
> Disproving thy man's name: and while
>   before
> The world thou burnest in a poet-fire,
> We see thy woman-heart beat evermore
> Through the large flame. Beat purer, heart,
>   and higher,
> Till God unsex thee on the heavenly shore
> Where unincarnate spirits purely aspire!

The male mask can never hide the "revolted cry . . . sobbed in by a woman's voice forlorn." She implies no woman can "break away the gauds and armlets worn / By weaker women in captivity." Barrett Browning recognized that if women generally are exploited and oppressed, then all women as a class suffer, no matter any individual woman's apparent privilege. She identifies herself here as part of a community of women, "we," as opposed to "the world" of men.

In *Poems of 1844* there is a strongly evolving consciousness of herself as a woman poet and of her belief that the "sole work" of the poet "is to represent the age," as **"The Cry of the Children"**—about child factory-workers—shows.[14] But this new voice and subject matter were not supported by nor obvious to all of her old friends. In September 1843 she articulates to an early mentor, Hugh Boyd, her belief in this new poetry:

> Will you see the **'Cry of the (Children)'** or not? It will not please you, probably. It wants melody. The versification is eccentric to the ear, and the subject (the factory miseries) is scarcely an agreeable one to the fancy. Perhaps altogether you had better not see it, because I know you think me to be deteriorating, and I don't want you to have farther hypothetical evidence of so false an opinion. Frankly, if not humbly, I believe myself to have gained power since . . . the **'Seraphim'**. . . . I differ with you, the longer I live, on the ground of what you call the 'jumping lines' . . . and the tenacity of my judgement (arises) . . . from the deeper study of the old master-poets—English poets—those of the Elizabeth and James ages, before the corruption

of French rhythms stole in with Waller and Denham, and was acclimated into a national inodorousness by Dryden and Pope.[15]

Barrett Browning asserts her "power," the "tenacity of her judgement," and her defiance of both her critics and the established poetic tradition. In the following year, August 1844, she explains to John Kenyon:

> I wish I could persuade you of the rightness of my view about 'Essays on Mind' and such things, and how the difference between them and my present poems is not merely the difference between two schools, . . . nor even the difference between immaturity and maturity; but that it is the difference between the dead and the living, between a copy and an individuality, between what is myself and what is not myself.[16]

She grew increasingly convinced that women writers should actively concern themselves with social conditions. In 1853 she exhorts the art critic and her lifelong correspondent, Mrs. Jameson:

> Not read Mrs. Stowe's book! But you *must*. Her book is quite a sign of the times, and has otherwise and intrinsically considerable power. For myself, I rejoice in the success, both as a woman and a human being. Oh, and is it possible that you think a woman has no business with questions like the question of slavery? Then she had better use a pen no more. She had better subside into slavery and concubinage herself, I think, as in the times of old, shut herself up with the Penelopes in the 'women's apartment,' and take no rank among thinkers and speakers.[17]

"A Curse for a Nation" confirms Barrett Browning's refusal to "subside into slavery and concubinage." Written for the abolitionist movement in America and published in *Poems Before Congress* (1860), the poem incurred the wrath of critics disturbed by her interference in politics. Tough poetry results from her conviction that this is precisely her role:

> 'Therefore,' the voice said, 'shalt thou write
>   My curse to-night.
> Because thou hast strength to see and hate
> A foul thing done *within* thy gate.'
>
> 'Not so,' I answered once again.
>   'To curse, choose men.
> For I, a woman, have only known
> How the heart melts and tears run down.'
>
> 'Therefore,' the voice said, 'shalt thou write
>   My curse to-night.
> Some women weep and curse, I say
> (And no one marvels), night and day.

> 'And thou shalt take their part to-night,
>   Weep and write.
> A curse from the depths of womanhood
> Is very salt, and bitter, and good.'

Barrett Browning specifically repudiates her assigned role as "lady" who knows only "How the heart melts and tears run down." She designates herself as spokesperson for those less-privileged women who "weep and curse, I say / (And no one marvels), night and day," thereby defying patriarchy's division of "ladies" from working-class women.

Her anger against critics who disavowed her right to step beyond the limits laid down for "lady poets" had been revealed some years earlier in a fascinating discussion of Florence Nightingale, whom she came to see as performing an age-old role, that of angel on the battlefield:

> I know Florence Nightingale slightly. . . . I honour her from my heart. . . .
>
> At the same time, I confess to be at a loss to see any new position for the sex, or the most imperfect solution of the 'woman's question,' in this step of hers. . . . Since the seige of Troy and earlier, we have had princesses binding wounds with their hands; it's strictly the woman's part, and men understand it so. . . . Every man is on his knees before ladies carrying lint, calling them 'angelic she's,' whereas, if they stir an inch as thinkers or artists from the beaten line (involving more good to general humanity than is involved in lint), the very same men would curse the impudence of the very same women and stop there. . . . For my own part (and apart from the exceptional miseries of the war), I acknowledge to you that I do not consider the best use to which we can put a gifted and accomplished woman is to *make her a hospital nurse*. If it is, why then woe to us all who are artists![18]

Barrett Browning wants to start healing the wounds of women by naming them. She writes of the Crimean War:

> War, war! It is terrible certainly. But there are worse plagues, deeper griefs, dreader wounds than the physical. What of the forty thousand wretched women in this city? The silent writhing of them is to me more appalling than the roar of the cannons.[19]

The "homely domestic ballad" which Chorley sees as being purified on "passing into female hands" is subverted by Barrett Browning to condemn men's seduction and exploitation of women.[20] **"The Rhyme of the Duchess of May"** (1844), a long ballad-poem set in the Middle Ages, tells of an orphaned girl betrothed by her guardian at twelve to his son. Grown into womanhood, she refuses this marriage, having chosen her own lover. The viewing of women as a commercial commodity is pointed up by her guardian's response to her decision:

> 'Good my niece, that hand withal looketh
>   somewhat soft and small
> For so large a will, in sooth.'

To which the niece astutely replies:

> 'Little hand clasps muckle gold, or it were
>   not worth the hold
> Of thy son, good uncle mine!'

The duchess secretly marries her lover. When her uncle's soldiers try to reclaim his "property," even her husband intends to kill himself on the assumption that his wife will be forgiven. She refuses to see herself as property and dies with her chosen husband to avoid life with a man she detests.

The finely honed ballad **"Amy's Cruelty"** (1862) hinges on the ironic observation that what seems to be a woman's cruelty to her lover is in fact her only defense against exploitation:

> Fair Amy of the terraced house,
>   Assist me to discover
> Why you who would not hurt a mouse
>   Can torture so your lover.
>
>   . . . . .
>
> But when *he* haunts your door . . . the
>   town
>   Marks coming and marks going . . .
> You seem to have stitched your eyelids
>   down
>   To that long piece of sewing!

Amy's life is circumscribed. She sits daily in the "terraced house" fulfilling her sewing duties. Yet she has the power to protect herself and the insight to know the dangers of love:

> He wants my world, my sun, my heaven,
>   Soul, body, whole existence.
>
>   . . . . .
>
> I only know my mother's love
>   Which gives all and asks nothing;
> And this new loving sets the groove
>   Too much the way of loathing.
>
> Unless he gives me all in change,
>   I forfeit all things by him:

> The risk is terrible and strange—
>   I tremble, doubt, . . . deny him.

The "risk is terrible": in **"Void in Law"** (1862) a court finds a marriage void because only one witness was competent. The husband can now marry another woman, approved by society, one whose:

> . . . throat has the antelope curve,
> And her cheek just the color and line
>   Which fade not before him nor swerve.

The first wife and child are legally abandoned.

"Bianca Among the Nightingales" (1862), one of Barrett Browning's most technically exciting ballad-poems, opens with a frank celebration of sexuality. Bianca remembers embracing her lover in the Italian moonlight:

> And *we,* too! from such soul-height went
>   Such leaps of blood, so blindly driven,
>
>   . . . . .
>
> The nightingales, the nightingales!
>
> We paled with love, we shook with love,
>   We kissed so close we could not vow. . . .

The nightingales, whose singing "throbbed" in Italy with the passion of their love, haunt Bianca in "gloomy England," where she follows her lover who has abandoned her to pursue a woman of great beauty: "These nightingales will sing me mad." Bianca delineates the difference between his love for her and for the other woman:

> He says to her what moves her most.
>   He would not name his soul within
> Her hearing,—rather pays the cost
>   With praises to her lips and chin.

She is physically to be praised as ritualistically as any sonneteer's mistress. She has a "fine tongue" and "loose gold ringlets," but to Bianca she is "mere cold clay / As all false things are." The only person who will know this woman's soul is Bianca: "She lied and stole, / And spat into my love's pure pyx / The rank saliva of her soul." Barrett Browning explores the reality that a woman who truly wishes to be herself, to experience her sexuality and some kind of fruitful relationship with the male world will be challenged by the more acceptable norm of the woman who has learned to remain all beautiful surface, hidden both from herself and from the men she must please. The refrain "The nightingales, the nightingales" moves relentlessly from an affirmation of love to a taunting that drives Bianca to madness. In the last stanza the extended refrain and repetition enact her frenzy:

—Oh, owl-like birds! They sing for spite,
   They sing for hate, they sing for doom,
They'll sing through death who sing
   through night,
   They'll sing and stun me in the tomb—
The nightingales, the nightingales!

Bianca knows she can never be like the other woman, but neither can she bear the ostracism attendant on being different.

The woman who is not abandoned is just as easily prey to exploitation. **"Lord Walter's Wife"** (1862) sets her husband's friend straight when he is horror-stricken at her suggestion of an affair—the logical conclusion to his flirtatious innuendoes:

'A moment,—I pray your attention!—I
   have a poor word in my head
I must utter, though womanly custom
   would set it down better unsaid.

     . . . . .

'You did me the honour, perhaps to be
   moved at my side now and then
In the senses—a vice, I have heard, which
   is common to beasts and some men.

     . . . . .

'And since, when all's said, you're too
   noble to stoop to the frivolous cant
About crimes irresistible, virtues that swindle, betray, and supplant,

'I determined to prove to yourself that,
   whate'er you might dream or avow
By illusion, you wanted precisely no more
   of me than you have now.'

This poem caused Thackeray much embarrassment when it was submitted to him for publication in the *Cornhill Magazine* in 1861:

. . . one of the best wives, mothers, women in the world writes some verses which I feel certain would be objected to by many of our readers. . . . In your poem, you know, there is an account of unlawful passion, felt by a man for a woman, and though you write pure doctrine, and real modesty, and pure ethics, I am sure our readers would make an outcry, and so I have not published this poem.[21]

Barrett Browning replies in no uncertain terms:

I am not a 'fast woman.' I don't like coarse subjects, or the coarse treatment of any subject. But I am

deeply convinced that the corruption of our society requires not shut doors and windows, but light and air: and that it is exactly because pure and prosperous women choose to *ignore* vice, that miserable women suffer wrong by it everywhere. Has paterfamilias, with his Oriental traditions and veiled female faces, very successfully dealt with a certain class of evil? What if materfamilias, with her quick sure instincts and honest innocent eyes, do more towards their expulsion by simply looking at them and calling them by their names?[22]

This strong conviction in the last year of her life that the responsibility of the woman poet was to confront and name the condition of women had manifested itself in her poetry from the *Seraphim* on, as she sought to delineate the complexity of female experience. She wrote powerfully about the institution of motherhood in patriarchy, and the experience of biological motherhood. **"The Virgin Mary to the Child Jesus"** (1838) is a meditation in Mary's voice. She begins poignantly, unsure what name she can call this child who is both of her flesh and also her Lord. She watches Jesus sleeping, imagines he dreams of God his father, whereas the best she can give him is a mother's kiss. Patriarchal Christian tradition exalts Mary as most honored; a woman writes of the pain Mary would experience mothering a child simultaneously hers and not hers:

        Then, I think aloud
The words 'despised,'—'rejected,'—every
   word
Recoiling into darkness as I view
   The DARLING on my knee.
Bright angels,—move not—lest ye stir the
   cloud
Betwixt my soul and his futurity!
I must not die, with mother's work to do,
   And could not live—and see.

The implications of the poem point beyond the immediate meditation to a consideration of how patriarchy always destines its sons for a life beyond their mothers. Another early poem, **"Victoria's Tears"** (1838), explores how the young woman is jolted from her childhood into mothering her country as its queen (when women were not even enfranchised). Barrett Browning contrasts the grandiose coronation with her sense of what the young woman has lost:

   She saw no purples shine,
     For tears had dimmed her eyes;
She only knew her childhood's flowers
     Were happier pageantries!
And while her heralds played the part,
     For million shouts to drown—
'God save the Queen' from hill to mart,—
She heard through all her beating heart,

And turned and wept—
She wept, to wear a crown!

Both poems pinpoint the isolation of the "token woman," whose position of supposed privilege is actually one of loneliness and confusion.

In **"The Cry of the Children"** (1844), she exposes how hopeless it is for the child factory workers to cry to mothers powerless to alleviate their suffering:

Do ye hear the children weeping, O my
     brothers,
     Ere the sorrow comes with years?
They are leaning their young heads against
     their mothers,
     And *that* cannot stop their tears.

. . . . .

But the young, young children, O my
     brothers,
     Do you ask them why they stand
Weeping sore before the bosom of their
     mothers,
     In our happy Fatherland?

The capitalization of "Fatherland" but not of "mothers" underlines the power structure: the natural flesh bond between the child and mother is helpless before the demands of patriarchy. The children mourn Alice, who died from the brutal working conditions: "Could we see her face, be sure we should not know her, / For the smile has time for growing in her eyes. . . ." That it is a girl who dies from such work in a society that draped its middle-class women with prudery, passivity and sentimentality should not go unnoticed. Repetition creates the delirium of these children's exhaustion, pulling us into their experience:

'For all day the wheels are droning, turning;
     Their wind comes in our faces,
Till our hearts turn, our heads with pulses
     burning,
     And the walls turn in their places:
Turns the sky in the high window, blank
     and reeling,
     Turns the long light that drops adown
     the wall,
Turn the black flies that crawl along the
     ceiling:
     All are turning, all the day, and we with
     all.
And all day the iron wheels are droning,
     And sometimes we could pray,
"O ye wheels" (breaking out in a mad
     moaning),
     "Stop! be silent for to-day!"'

Victimization is again exposed in **"The Runaway Slave at Pilgrim's Point"** (1850), spoken in the voice of a young black woman slave being flogged to death where the pilgrims landed. On the plantation she had loved a black male slave. The white overseers, learning of this love, beat the man to death and, seeing her grief, her owner rapes her. Her initial response to the child born of this rape is love:

Thus we went moaning, child and mother,
One to another, one to another,

but

. . . the babe who lay on my bosom so,
     Was far too white, too white for me;
As white as the ladies who scorned to pray
Beside me at church but yesterday.

Soon she cannot look at her son and strains a handkerchief over his face. He struggles against this, wanting his freedom: "For the white child wanted his liberty—/ Ha, Ha! he wanted the master-right." The dichotomies her son represents overwhelm her. She loves him but hates that, being male and white, he will grow up with the right to violate a woman as her rapist, his father, did. She loves him but:

Why, in that single glance I had
     Of my child's face, . . . I tell you all,
I saw a look that made me mad!
     The *master's* look, that used to fall
On my soul like his lash . . . or worse!
And so, to save it from my curse,
     I twisted it round in my shawl.

She strangles her son so she will neither have to repudiate him later, nor experience her rape reenacted every time she looks into his face. She runs from the plantation holding the child to her for many days before burying him. Her owner catches her and flogs her to death. Taplin's dismissal of the poem as "too blunt and shocking" only underscores the poem's explosive exposure of racism and sexism.[23]

Barrett Browning had four pregnancies in the four years after her marriage. Only the third ended with a birth, that of her son, Robert Wiedeman ("Penini") in 1849. The experience of childbirth and biological motherhood informs **"Only a Curl"** (1862), written on receiving a lock of hair from the parents of a dead child unknown to the poet. In language movingly reminiscent of **"The Soul's Expression,"** written twenty years earlier about the creative process, Barrett Browning comforts by saying how once a mother has known her power in childbirth her child is always in some way part of the mother's experience:

> . . . I appeal
> To all who bear babes—in the hour
> When the veil of the body we feel
> Rent round us,—while torments reveal
>   The motherhood's advent in power,
>
> And the babe cries!—has each of us known
>   By apocalypse (God being there
> Full in nature) the child is our own,
> Life of life, love of love, moan of moan,
>   Through all changes, all times,
>   everywhere.

She records in her letters what a powerful and health-giving experience childbirth was. Even today, forty-three is considered "late" for giving birth to a first child. For Barrett Browning, almost given up as dead three years earlier, to have that much physical power was exhilarating.

One of her last poems, **"Mother and Poet"** (1862), confronts, like **"The Virgin Mary to the Child Jesus,"** the conflict between a mother's relationship with her sons and their destiny within patriarchy. It is spoken in the voice of Laura Savio, an Italian poet and patriot dedicated, as was Barrett Browning, to the unification of Italy. Savio's two sons were killed fighting for "freedom." The poet reconsiders the meaning of both motherhood and patriotism after their deaths:

> To teach them . . . It stings there! I made
>   them indeed
>   Speak plain the word *country.* I taught
>   them, no doubt,
> That a country's a thing men should die for
>   at need.
>   *I* prated of liberty, rights, and about
>   The tyrant cast out.

She imagines the victory celebrations:

> Forgive me. Some women bear children in
>   strength,
>   And bite back the cry of their pain in
>   self-scorn;
> But the birth-pangs of nations will wring us
>   at length
>   Into wail such as this—and we sit on
>   forlorn
>   When the man-child is born.
>
> Dead! One of them shot by the sea in the
>   east,
>   And one of them shot in the west by the
>   sea.
> Both! both my boys! If in keeping the feast
>   You want a great song for your Italy
>   free,
>   Let none look at *me!*

To Barrett Browning, whose son had grown up listening to her passionate political talk and at twelve spoke eagerly of his own desire to fight for freedom, this is an assessment of great integrity about her own complicity in patriarchy. She understands that the energetic womanhood manifest in the bearing of children is undermined by mothers, like herself, who incorporate patriarchal values into their own consciousness and become breeders of cannon fodder. Taplin brushes the poem off as "devoid of inspiration," quite missing the poet's sophisticated insight into women's contribution to their own oppression.[24]

"Mother and Poet" fuses three of Barrett Browning's preoccupations in her writing—art, politics, and motherhood—as a manifestation of powerful womanhood. "What art's for a woman?" she has Laura Savio ask. In her own career she was increasingly convinced that women as "artists and thinkers" must be concerned with social interaction, social conditions, and political events. Realizing that the "personal is the political," she used her physical and emotional experiences as a woman to illuminate the public sphere. In doing so she created a voice and vision for herself as a woman poet and became truly our "grandmother." Like many grandmothers, she has been unjustly ignored; like many grandmothers, she has healing wisdom to share. As early as 1845 she believed:

> . . . we should all be ready to say that if the
> secrets of our daily lives & inner souls may instruct
> other surviving souls, let them be open to men
> hereafter,even as they are to God now. Dust to
> dust, & soul-secrets to humanity—there are
> natural heirs to all things.[25]

Notes

[1] Christened Elizabeth Barrett Moulton Barrett, the poet shortened her maiden name to Elizabeth Barrett Barrett—E.B.B. These initials remained unchanged when she took her husband's name in 1846. Half her work was published under the name Elizabeth Barrett Barrett, half under Elizabeth Barrett Browning. I have decided to use the latter name throughout this discussion of her work, as it is the one she herself adopted.

[2] *The Letters of Elizabeth Barrett Browning,* ed. Frederic G. Kenyon. (New York: Macmillan, 1897), I, 231-32.

[3] Sir Arthur Quiller-Couch, *The Art of Writing.* Quoted in Virginia Woolf, *A Room of One's Own* (New York: Harcourt, Brace and World, 1929), pp. 111-12.

[4] *The Letters of Robert Browning and Elizabeth Barrett Barrett,* 1845-1846, ed. Elvan Kintner (Cambridge, Mass.: Harvard University Press, 1969), I, 113-14.

[5] *Letters of EBB,* I, 260-61.

[6] Ibid., II, 254.

[7] Quoted in *Poetical Works of Letitia Elizabeth Landon* (London: Longman, Brown, Green, and Longmans, 1850), I, xiv.

[8] *Letters of EBB,* I, 232.

[9] *Poems by Felicia Hemans,* ed. Rufus Griswold (Philadelphia: John Ball, 1850), p. x.

[10] *Diary by E.B.B.,* ed. Philip Kelley and Ronald Hudson (Athens, Ohio: Ohio University Press, 1969), p. 88.

[11] Gardner B. Taplin, *The Life of Elizabeth Barrett Browning* (New Haven: Yale University Press, 1957), p. 21.

[12] *Letters of EBB,* I, 180. Editor's note.

[13] *Elizabeth Barrett to Miss Mitford,* ed. Betty Miller (London: John Murray, 1954), p. 102.

[14] *Aurora Leigh,* Fifth Book, 202.

[15] *Letters of EBB,* I, 153-56.

[16] Ibid., I, 187.

[17] Ibid., II, 110-11.

[18] Ibid., 189.

[19] Ibid., 213.

[20] Henry F. Chorley, *Memorials of Mrs. Hemans* (Philadelphia: Carey, Lea & Blanchard, 1836), p. 56.

[21] *Letters of EBB,* II, 444.

[22] Ibid., 445.

[23] Taplin, p. 194.

[24] Ibid., p. 397.

[25] *Letters of RB and EBB,* I, 469.

Sandra M. Gilbert (essay date 1984)

SOURCE: "From *Patria* to *Matria*: Elizabeth Barrett Browning's Risorgimento," in *PMLA,* Vol. 99, No. 2, March, 1984, pp. 194-211.

[In the following essay, Gilbert claims that Browning's "visions of Italia Riuníta had more to do with both her

femaleness and her feminism than is usually supposed," and served as a vehicle for establishing her own poetic identity.]

> Then Lady Reason . . . said, "Get up, daughter! Without waiting any longer, let us go to the Field of Letters. There the City of Ladies will be founded on a flat and fertile plain. . . ."
>
> Christine de Pizan,
> *The Book of the City of Ladies* 16

> Our lives are Swiss—
> So still—so Cool—
> Till some odd afternoon
> The Alps neglect their Curtains
> And we look farther on!
>
> *Italy* stands the other side!
> While like a guard between—
> The solemn Alps—
> The siren Alps
> Forever intervene!
>
> Emily Dickinson, no. 80

> Our insight into this early, pre-Oedipus phase in the little girl's development comes to us as a surprise, comparable in another field with the discovery of the Minoan-Mycenaean civilization behind that of Greece.
>
> Sigmund Freud, "Female Sexuality" 195

> And now I come, my Italy,
> My own hills! Are you 'ware of me, my
>   hills,
> How I burn toward you? do you feel to-
>   night
> The urgency and yearning of my soul,
> As sleeping mothers feel the sucking babe
> And smile?
>
> *Aurora Leigh* 5. 1266-71[1]

When in 1860 Elizabeth Barrett Browning published **Poems before Congress,** a frankly political collection of verses that was the culmination of her long commitment to Italy's arduous struggle for reunification, English critics excoriated her as unfeminine, even insane. "To bless and not to curse is woman's function," wrote one reviewer, "and if Mrs. Browning, in her calmer moments, will but contrast the spirit which has prompted her to such melancholy aberrations with that which animated Florence Nightingale, she can hardly fail to derive a profitable lesson for the future" ("Poetic Aberrations" 494). Interestingly, however, the very first poem in the volume depicts Italy as a friendless, powerless, invalid woman, asking if it is " . . . true,—may it be spoken,—" that she is finally alive

> . . . who has lain so still,
> With a wound in her breast,

And a flower in her hand,
And a grave-stone under her head,
    While every nation at will
Beside her has dared to stand,
And flout her with pity and scorn. . . .
                    (**"Napoleon III in Italy"** 111-18,
                        Poetical Works 412)

Creating an ostensibly "unfeminine" political polemic, Barrett Browning consciously or unconsciously seems to adopt the persona of a nurse at the bedside of an imperiled relative, almost as if she *were* a sort of literary-political Florence Nightingale. Putting aside all questions about the inherent femininity or unfemininity of political poetry, I will argue that this English expatriate's visions of *Italia Riunita* had more to do with both her femaleness and her feminism than is usually supposed. In fact, where so magisterial a reader as Henry James believed that Barrett Browning's commitment to "the cause of Italy" represented a letting down of "her inspiration and her poetic pitch" (quoted by Markus, in **Casa Guidi Windows** xvi-xvii), I believe instead that, as Flavia Alaya has also observed, Italy became for a complex of reasons both the embodiment of this woman poet's inspiration and the most vivid strain in her "poetic pitch."[2]

Specifically, I will suggest that through her involvement with the revolutionary struggle for political identity that marked Italy's famous risorgimento, Barrett Browning enacted and reenacted her own personal and artistic struggle for identity, a risorgimento that was, like Italy's, both an insurrection and a resurrection. In addition, I will suggest that, by using metaphors of the healing and making whole of a wounded woman/land to articulate both the reality and fantasy of her own female/poetic revitalization, Barrett Browning figuratively located herself in a re-creative female poetic tradition that descends from Sappho and Christine de Pizan through the Brontës, Christina Rossetti, Margaret Fuller, and Emily Dickinson to Renée Vivien, Charlotte Perkins Gilman, H. D., and Adrienne Rich. Infusing supposedly asexual poetics with the dreams and desires of a distinctively sexual politics, these women imagined nothing less than the transformation of *patria* into *matria* and thus the risorgimento of the lost community of women that Rossetti called the "mother country"—the shadowy land, perhaps, that Freud identified with the mysterious "Minoan-Mycenaean civilization behind that of Greece." In resurrecting the *matria,* moreover, these women fantasized resurrecting and restoring both the *madre,* the forgotten impossible dead mother, and the *matrice,* the originary womb or matrix, the mother-matter whose very memory, says Freud, is "lost in a past so dim . . . so hard to resuscitate that it [seems to have] undergone some specially inexorable repression" ("Female Sexuality" 195).[3]

Not surprisingly, then, Barrett Browning begins her covertly political 1857 *Kunstlerroman, Aurora Leigh,* with a meditation on this lost mother, using imagery that dramatically foreshadows the figure with which the poet opens her overtly political **Poems before Congress**. Gazing at a portrait of her mother that was (significantly) painted after the woman's death, young Aurora sees the maternal image as embodying in turn all the patriarchal myths of femaleness—muse, Psyche, Medusa, Lamia; "Ghost, fiend, and angel, fairy, witch, and sprite" (1.154). But most heartrendingly she sees her as "Our Lady of the Passion, stabbed with swords / Where the Babe sucked" (1.160-61): the only *maternal* image of the lost mother dissolves into the destroyed woman/country from **Poems before Congress,** "who has lain so still, / With a wound in her breast" while "every nation" has flouted her "with pity and scorn."[4]

Among eighteenth-, nineteenth-, and early twentieth-century English and American writers, tropes of Italy proliferated like flowers in Fiesole, so much so that the country, as its nationalist leaders feared, would seem to have had no reality except as a metaphor. As far back as the sixteenth but especially in the late eighteenth century, English romancers had exploited what Kenneth Churchill calls "the violence-incest-murder-prison paradigm of Gothic Italy" (66). More seriously, from Gibbon to Byron and Shelley to John Ruskin, George Eliot, Henry James, Edith Wharton, and D. H. Lawrence, English-speaking poets and novelists read the sunny, ruin-haunted Italian landscape as a symbolic text, a hieroglyph, or, perhaps more accurately, a palimpsest of Western history, whose warring traces seemed to them to solidify in the stones of Venice and the bones of Rome. Shelley, for instance, reflecting on the ancient city where Keats died seeking health, sees it both as "that high Capital, where kingly Death / Keeps his pale court in beauty and decay" and as "the Paradise, / The grave, the city, and the wilderness" ("Adonais" 55-56, 433-34)—a place whose ruins, building on and contradicting one another, suggest the paradoxical simultaneity of the originary moment (paradise) and the fall from that moment (the grave), the invention of culture (the city) and the supervention of nature (the wilderness). In "St. Mark's Place," Samuel Rogers is less metaphysical, but he too elaborates a vision of Italy as text, asserting that "Not a stone / In the broad pavement, but to him who has / An eye, an ear for the Inanimate World, / Tells of past ages" (301), and George Eliot develops a similar perception when she writes in *Middlemarch* of "the gigantic broken revelations" of Rome (bk. 2, ch. 15). Finally, emphasizing the dialectic between culture and nature that, as Shelley also saw, underlies all such statements, Edith Wharton summarizes the point most simply: Italy, she writes, is "that sophisticated landscape where the face of nature seems moulded by the passions and imaginings of man" (3).

Interestingly, however, as post-Renaissance Italy sank ever further into physical decay and political disarray, lapsing inexorably away from the grandeur that was imperial Rome and the glory that was fourteenth-century Florence, both native and tourist poets increasingly began to depict "her" as a sort of fallen woman. In Byron's famous translation, for example, the seventeenth-century Florentine patriot Vincenzo da Filijaca imagines "Italia" as a helpless naked seductress, while Byron himself writes of Venice as "a sea Cybele" and Rome as the "Lone mother of dead Empires," "The Niobe of nations!" (*Childe Harold's Pilgrimage*, canto 4, sts. 2, 78, 79).[5] Similarly, Ruskin, who sees Venice as "the Paradise of cities," the positive of Shelley's more equivocal Rome, hints that "her" charm lies in her seductive femininity (*Diaries* 1: 183, *Letters* 128), and the expatriate novelist Ouida writes of her adopted city that "in Florence [the past is] like the gold from the sepulchres of the Aetruscan kings that shines on the breast of some fair living woman" (*Pascarel,* quoted in Churchill 163).[6] The trope of Italy or of one of "her" city-states as a living, palpable, and often abandoned woman had become almost ubiquitous by the time Barrett Browning began to write her poems about the risorgimento, and of course it derived from a traditional grammatical convention that tends, at least in most Indo-European languages, to impute metaphorical femaleness to such diverse phenomena as countries, ships, and hurricanes. As applied to Italy, however, this metaphor of gender was often so intensely felt that, most notably for women writers, it frequently evolved from figure to fantasy, from speculation to hallucination. Thus Italy as art object "moulded by the passions and imaginings of man" becomes Italy as Galatea and, worse still, a Galatea seduced and betrayed by her creator,[7] while Italy as destroyed motherland becomes Italy as wounded mother, Madonna of the sorrows whose restored milk and honey might nourish errant children, and especially daughters, of all nations. Ultimately, then, such women writers as Christina Rossetti and Elizabeth Barrett Browning revise and revitalize the dead metaphor of gender that is their literary and linguistic inheritance, using it to transform Italy from a political state to a female state of mind, from a problematic country in Europe to the problem condition of femaleness. Redeeming and redeemed by Italy, they imagine redeeming and being redeemed by themselves.

More specifically, as artists like Rossetti and Barrett Browning (and Emily Dickinson after them) struggle to revive both the dead land of Italy and the dead metaphor of "her" femaleness, they explore five increasingly complex but always interrelated definitions of this lost, fragmented woman-country: (1) Italy as a nurturing mother—a land that feeds, (2) Italy as an impassioned sister—a land that feels, (3) Italy as a home of art—a land that creates, (4) Italy as a magic paradise—a land that transforms or integrates, and (5) Italy as a dead, denied, and denying woman—a land that has been rejected or is rejecting.

Christina Rossetti's ostensibly religious lyric "Mother Country" is the most visionary statement of the first definition, for in it this poet, who was (paradoxically enough) fully Italian only on her father's side, mourns her exclusion from a dreamlike, distinctively female Mediterranean queendom:

> Not mine own country
>   But dearer far to me?
> Yet mine own country,
>   If I may one day see
> Its spices and cedars
>   Its gold and ivory.
>
> (245)

Glamorous, rich, and giving, such a maternal paradise is opposed to *this* (implicitly patriarchal) country, in which "All starve together, / All dwarfed and poor" (245), and the metaphorical climates of the two locales strongly suggest that the luxurious mother country is Italy while the impoverished fatherland—"here"—is England. As if to support such an interpretation with matter-of-fact reportage, Elizabeth Barrett Browning writes countless letters from Pisa and Florence, praising the nurturing maternal land to which she has eloped with Robert Browning after her perilous escape from the gloomily patriarchal household at 50 Wimpole Street. Food, in particular, seems almost eerily ubiquitous. Barrett Browning never tires of describing great glowing oranges and luscious bunches of grapes; the Italian landscape itself appears largely edible, the scenery deliciously beautiful. As for "real" meals, they continually materialize at her table as if by magic. In Florence, she reports that "Dinner, 'unordered,' comes through the streets and spreads itself on our table, as hot as if we had smelt cutlets hours before," while more generally, in another letter, she observes that "No little orphan on a house step but seems to inherit naturally his slice of watermelon and bunch of purple grapes" (*Letters* 1: 341, 343).[8]

This land that feeds is also a land that feels. As both a mother country and, again in Rossetti's words, a "sister-land of Paradise" (377), female Italy neither contains nor condones the superegoistic repressions that characterize patriarchal England. Literary visions of Italy had always emphasized the passion and sensuality of "her" people, but where Renaissance playwrights and Gothic romancers had dramatized the stagey strangeness of violent Italians, women writers like Barrett Browning, Rossetti, and later Dickinson wistfully set the natural emotiveness of this mother country against the icy artifice of the Victorian culture in which they had been brought up. Indeed, from Barrett Browning's Bianca in "Bianca among the Nightingales," who freely expresses her fiery rage at the cold Englishwoman who has stolen her lover away (**Poetical Works** 428-30), to Rossetti's Enrica, who "chill[s]" Englishwomen with "her liberal glow" and "dwarf[s]" them "by her ampler scale" (377-78), the women who represent Italy in women's writing increasingly seem like ennobled versions of *Jane Eyre*'s Bertha Mason Rochester: large, heated, dark, passionate foreigners who are wholly at ease—even at one—with the Vesuvius of female sexual creativity that Dickinson was later to find *un*easily "at home" in her breast (no. 1705).

Together, in fact, such heroines as Barrett Browning's Bianca, her Laura Savio of **"Mother and Poet"** (**Poetical Works** 446-48), and Rossetti's Enrica seem almost to propose an ontology of female power as it might be if all girls were not, in Rossetti's words, "minted in the selfsame [English] mould" (377). That most of these women are in one way or another associated with a violent uprising against the authoritarian rule of Austria and the patriarchal law of the pope, with Enrica (according to William Michael Rossetti) based on a woman who knew both Mazzini and Garibaldi, further cements their connection with Brontë's rebellious Bertha, but with a Bertha revised and transformed so that she, the alien, is free, and English Jane is trapped. As if to demonstrate this point, Christina Rossetti was "en route" to Italy ("Italy, Io Ti Saluto") when she imagined herself as "an 'immurata' sister" helplessly complaining that

> Men work and think, but women feel,
>   And so (for I'm a woman, I)
>   And so I should be glad to die,
> And cease from impotence of zeal. . . .
>
>   (380)

For, as Barrett Browning (and Charlotte Brontë) also knew, that "Italian" speech of feeling was only "half familiar" and almost wholly inaccessible to Englishwomen.

What made the inaccessibility of such speech especially poignant for poets like Rossetti and Barrett Browning, besides Italy's role as a feeding, feeling mother-sister, was "her" special status as the home, even the womb, of European art; this mother-sister became a muse whose shapes and sounds seemed to constitute a kind of primal aesthetic language from which no writer should allow herself to be separated. In Florence, Barrett Browning imagines that she is not only in a city that makes art, she is in a city that *is* art, so much so that, as in some Edenic dream, the solid real and the artful unreal merge uncannily: "The river rushes through the midst of its palaces like a crystal arrow, and it is hard to tell . . . whether those churches . . . and people walking, in the water or out of the water, are the real . . . people, and churches" (**Letters** 1: 332). That the art of Florence is almost entirely male—

Michelangelo's monuments of unaging intellect, Ghiberti's doors—appears oddly irrelevant, for living in Florence Barrett Browning begins to believe, if only briefly, that she might live in, even inherit, this art; insofar as art is Italy's and Italy might be her lost and reclaimed self, art itself might at last be her own.

In allowing herself such a dream, the author of **Aurora Leigh** was tacitly acknowledging the influence of a foremother she greatly admired, Mme de Staël, whose *Corinne ou l'Italie* was "an immortal book" that, said Barrett Browning, "deserves to be read three score and ten times—that is, once every year in the age of man" (**Elizabeth Barrett** 176). For not only is *Corinne,* in the words of Ellen Moers, "a guidebook to Italy," it is specifically a guidebook to an Italy that is the nurturing *matria* of a "woman of genius," the enchanting *improvisatrice* Corinne, whose brilliant career provided a paradigm of female artistry for countless nineteenth-century literary women on both sides of the Atlantic.[9] Like Aurora Leigh, Staël's poetic heroine is the daughter of an Italian mother and an English father, and, like Barrett Browning herself, she transforms the Italy dominated by relics of such great men as Michelangelo and Ghiberti into a land of free women, a female aesthetic utopia. Corinne herself, writes Staël, is "l'image de notre belle Italie" (bk. 2, ch. 2., p. 50). Triumphing as she improvises on the theme of Italy's glory, dances a dramatic tarantella, and translates *Romeo and Juliet* into "sa langue maternelle" (bk. 7, ch. 2, p. 183), Corinne becomes not only a symbol of redemptive Italy but also a redemptive emblem of the power of symbolization itself, for, observes Staël, "tout étoit langage pour elle" (bk. 6, ch. 1, p. 141). No wonder, then, that Barrett Browning, *Corinne*'s admirer, seems secretly to imagine an Italian heaven of invention whose speech constitutes a different, mystically potent language, a mother tongue: as if to balance Rossetti's remark that "our [English] tongue grew sweeter in [Enrica's] mouth," she writes wistfully of the way in which "the Tuscan musical / Vowels . . . round themselves as if they planned / Eternities of separate sweetness" (**Casa Guidi Windows** 1.1188-90).

Such a sense that even Italian speech encompasses "eternities of . . . sweetness" inevitably translates itself into a larger vision of Italy as earthly paradise, a vision that brings us back to the "green golden strand" of Rossetti's mother country and the vehement "*Italy*" of Dickinson's "Our lives are Swiss—." In this fourth incarnation, however, Italy is not just a nurturing mother country, she is a utopian motherland whose glamour transforms all who cross her borders, empowering women, ennobling men, and—most significantly—annihilating national and sexual differences. Describing the hopeful celebration of Florentine freedom that miraculously took place on the Brownings' first wedding anniversary in 1847, Barrett Browning writes about a jubilant parade: "class after class" took part, and "Then too, came the foreigners, there was a place for them" (*CGW* 66). She notes that "the people were *embracing* for joy" (*CGW* 66) and expressing "the sort of gladness in which women may mingle and be glad too" (*CGW* 67). In this setting, both sexes and all nationalities become part of the newer, higher nationality of Florence, so that expatriation turns, magically, into expatriotism. Less mystically and more amusingly, Virginia Woolf makes a similar point about Italy as utopia in *Flush,* her biography of the Brownings' dog. Arriving in Pisa, this pedigreed spaniel discovers that "though dogs abounded, there were no ranks; all—could it be possible?—were mongrels." At last inhabiting a classless society, he becomes "daily more and more democratic. . . . All dogs were his brothers. He had no need of a chain in this new world" (75, 78-79).

Finally, however, as Rossetti's "Mother Country," "Enrica," and "An 'Immurata' Sister" suggest, women writers from Barrett Browning to Dickinson are forced to admit that the nurturing, utopian, artful, feelingful, female land of Italy is not their own. Bred in what Barrett Browning and, after her, Rossetti call "the rigid North," such writers are forever spiritually if not physically excluded from "the sweet South," forever alienated from Italy's utopian redemption, if only by symbolic windows like those of Casa Guidi, which mark Barrett Browning's estrangement from Florence's moment of regeneration even while they allow the poet to view the spectacle of that rebirth.[10] As the poets make this admission, maternal Italy, guarded by the intervention of the "solemn Alps" and "the bitter sea," lapses back into the negated and negating woman whose image opens both *Poems before Congress* and *Aurora Leigh*. Dead, she is denied and denying: as Aurora leaves for England, her mother country seems "Like one in anger drawing back her skirts / Which suppliants catch at" (1.234-35), and Christina Rossetti, exclaiming "Farewell, land of love, Italy, / Sister-land of Paradise,", summarizes the mingled regret and reproach with which these English daughters respond to the drastic loss such denial enforces:

> Wherefore art thou strange, and not my
> mother?
> Thou hast stolen my heart and broken it:
> Would that I might call thy sons 'My
> brother,'
> Call thy daughters 'Sister sweet':
> Lying in thy lap, not in another,
> Dying at thy feet.

("**En Route,**" *Works* 377)

For Rossetti, the despair these lines express becomes a characteristic gesture of resignation; the mother country is not to be found, not in this world at any rate, and so she immures herself in the convent of her soul, for "Why should I seek and never find / That something which I have not had?" (380). For Barrett Browning, however, the struggle to revive and reapproach, rather than reproach, the lost mother country of Italy becomes the narrative project to which she devotes her two major long poems, *Casa Guidi Windows* (1851) and *Aurora Leigh*.

Though explicitly (and successfully) a political poem that mediates on two carefully defined historical occasions, *Casa Guidi Windows* is also a preliminary working through of important psychological materials that had long haunted Barrett Browning; as such, it is a crucial preface to the poet's more frankly confessional *Aurora Leigh*. To be specific: even while Barrett Browning comments in part 1 on the exuberant 1847 demonstration with which the Italian and "foreign" citizens of Florence thanked Duke Leopold II for granting them the right to form a militia, and even while she mourns in part 2 the temporary failure of the risorgimento when in 1849 the Austrians defeated the Italians at Novara, she tells a more covert story—the story of Italy's and her own seduction and betrayal by the brutality, indifference, and greed of patriarchal history. From this betrayal, this fall into the power of powers not her own, Italy/Barrett Browning must regenerate herself, and she can only do this, the poet's metaphors imply, through a strategic deployment of female, especially maternal, energies. By delivering her children both to death (as soldiers) and life (as heirs), she can deliver herself into the community of nations where she belongs.

For Barrett Browning this plot had distinctively personal overtones. "After what broke [her] heart at Torquay"—the drowning of her beloved alter ego, "Bro"—she herself, as she later told her friend Mrs. Martin, had lived for years "on the outside of my own life . . . as completely dead to hope . . . as if I had my face against a grave . . ." (*Letters* 1: 288). Immuring herself in her room at 50 Wimpole Street, she had entrusted her future entirely to the will and whim of her notoriously tyrannical father, so much so that, as she also told Mrs. Martin, employing a strikingly political metaphor, "God knows . . . how utterly I had abdicated myself. . . . Even my poetry . . . was a thing on the outside of me . . . [a] desolate state it was, which I look back now to [as] one would look to one's graveclothes, if one had been clothed in them by mistake during a trance" (*Letters* 1: 288). Clearly, in some sense, the drowning of the younger brother who was Barrett Browning's only real reader in the family and for whose death she blamed herself, caused a self-alienation so deep that, like Emily Brontë's Catherine Earnshaw Linton mourning the absence of *her* male alter ego, Heathcliff, she felt the world turn to "a mighty stranger." Invalid and isolated, she herself became a figure like Italy in part 1 of *Casa Guidi Windows,* who

> Long trammeled with the purple of her
> youth
> Against her age's ripe activity,
>   Sits still upon her tombs, without death's
>   ruth,
> But also without life's brave energy.
>
> (171-74)

Yet just as the Italy of *Casa Guidi Windows,* part 1, trusts "fathers" like Leopold II and Pio Nono to deliver "her" from her living death, Barrett Browning expected her father to care enough to cure her illness; and just as Italy is duped by "her" faith in these patriarchs, Barrett Browning was deceived by her faith in her father, who refused to send her south (significantly, to Italy) for her health, so that she was "wounded to the bottom of my heart—cast off when I was ready to cling to him" (*Letters* 1: 291). But the plot thickens as the poet quickens, for, again, just as in Barrett Browning's own life a risorgimento came both from another younger brother figure—Robert Browning—and from the female deliverance of motherhood, so, in *Casa Guidi Windows,* promises of resurrection are offered wounded Italy both by the hope of a sturdy male leader who will "teach, lead, strike fire into the masses" and by the promise of "young children lifted high on parent souls," children whose innocence, fostered by maternal grace, may unfold "mighty meanings" (2.769, 741).

Given the personal politics embedded in this story, it is no wonder that Barrett Browning prefaces the first edition of *Casa Guidi Windows* with an "advertisement" in which she takes especially intense "shame upon herself that she believed, like a woman, some royal oaths"; that in part 2 she reproaches herself for her "woman's fault / That ever [she] believed [Duke Leopold] was true" (64-65); and that she also asks "what woman or child will count [Pio Nono] true?" (523). It is no wonder, either, that, in aligning herself with the revolutionary cause of Italy, Barrett Browning aligns herself against the strictures and structures of her fatherland, England, whose "close, stifling, corrupt system," like her imprisoning room in Wimpole Street, "gives no air nor scope for healthy . . . organization" (*Letters* 2: 190), a country for which "nothing will do . . . but a good revolution" (*Letters* 2: 193). As magisterial and patriarchal as Edward Moulton Barrett, England has "No help for women, sobbing out of sight / Because men made the laws" and "no tender utterance . . . For poor Italia, baffled by mischance" (*CGW* 2.638-39, 649-51). What is more remarkable in *Casa Guidi Windows,* however, and what more directly foreshadows the Italian dream of *Aurora Leigh* is the way in which Barrett Browning, dreaming behind the mediation of her windows, imagines Italy

ultimately redeemed by the voices and visions of mothers and children: part 1 begins, after all, with "a little child . . . who not long had been / By mother's finger steadied on his feet" (11-12), singing *"O bella libertà, O bella,"* and part 2 ends with the poet's "own young Florentine, not two years old," her "blue-eyed prophet," transforming society with a clear, unmediated gaze not unlike Wordsworth's "eye among the blind." In between these epiphanies, Miriam the prophetess appears, clashing her "cymbals to surprise / The sun" (1.314-16), and Garibaldi's wife outfaces "the whistling shot and hissing waves, / Until she [feels] her little babe unborn / Recoil within her" (2.679-83).

But what is finally perhaps most remarkable and, as Julia Markus points out, "most daring" about *Casa Guidi Windows* is the way in which, as Barrett Browning meditates on the plight of wounded "Italia," the poet finally presents herself, against the weight of all the literary history she dutifully recounts throughout the work, as "the singer of the new day":

> And I, a singer also, from my youth,
> Prefer to sing with those who are awake,
>   With birds, with babes, with men who will
>   not fear
> The baptism of the holy morning dew . . .
>
>   . . . . .
>
> Than join those old thin voices with my
> new. . . .
>
> (1.155-62)

Crossing the Anglo-Italian frontier represented by Casa Guidi windows, Barrett Browning gains her strongest voice in Italy and regains, as we shall see, a vision of her strengthened self from and as Italy, for the female artistic triumph that this passage describes points directly to the triumphant risorgimento of the woman poet that *Aurora Leigh* enacts.

As its title indicates, *Aurora Leigh* is a mythic narrative about "the baptism of the holy morning dew" that Barrett Browning proposed to sing in *Casa Guidi Windows*. But before she and her heroine can achieve such a sacrament or become true singers of "the new day" and of the renewed *matria/matrice* that day implies, both must work through precisely the self-division that left "Italia" (in *Casa Guidi Windows*) and Barrett Browning (in Wimpole Street) living "on the outside" of their own lives. Significantly, therefore, the tale of the poet-heroine's risorgimento, which parallels the plot of the poet-author's own insurrection-resurrection, begins with a fragmentation of the self that is both symbolized and precipitated by a shattering of the nuclear family, a shattering that leads to a devastating analysis of that structure. Just as significantly, the story ends with a reconstitution of both self and family that provides a visionary new synthesis of the relationships among men, women, and children.

As if to emphasize the larger political issue involved in these emotional dissolutions and resolutions, the heroine's self and family are defined by two *paysages moralisés,* her mother country of Italy and her father-land of England, between which (although at one point Aurora claims that "a poet's heart / Can swell to a pair of nationalities, / However ill-lodged in a woman's breast" [6.50-52]) she must ultimately choose. Both in its theatrical, sometimes hectically melodramatic, plot, then, and in its intensely symbolic settings, *Aurora Leigh* continually reminds us that it is not only a versified *Kunstlerroman* which famously aims to specify the interaction between an artist and the particular "full-veined, heaving, double-breasted Age" (5.217) that created her, it is also an "unscrupulously epic" (5.215) allegory of a woman artist's journey from disease toward what Sylvia Plath once called "a country far away as health" ("Tulips," *Ariel* 12).[11]

Not surprisingly, given these geographical and dramatic imperatives, *Aurora Leigh* begins and ends in Italy, the lost redemptive land that must be redeemed in order for both poet-heroine and poet-author to achieve full selfhood. Here, in book 1, Aurora encounters and is symbolically rejected by her dead mother, "a Florentine / Whose rare blue eyes were shut from seeing me / When scarcely I was four years old" (29-31), and here, even as she comes to terms with "a mother-want about the world" (40), her father dies, leaving her suddenly awake "To full life and life's needs" (208-10). While the mother seems irremediably gone, however, the father, "an austere Englishman" (65), is quickly replaced by "A stranger with authority" (224) who tears the child so abruptly from the land which has come to represent her mother that, watching "my Italy, / Drawn backward from the shuddering steamerdeck, / Like one in anger drawing back her skirts" (232-34), she is uncertain whether the mother country has been rejected ("drawing back") or is rejecting ("drawing back").

This violent, neo-Wordsworthian fall into division from the mother and into "my father's England," home of alien language and orphanhood, is followed by a more subtle but equally violent fall into gender. Arriving in patriarchal England at the crucial age of thirteen, Aurora discovers that she is a *girl,* destined to be brought up in "A sort of cage-bird life" (1.305) by a new and different "mother"—her "father's sister," who is her "mother's hater" (1.359-60), for "Italy / Is one thing, England one" (1.626-27); inexorably parted, the two nations are irrevocable emblems of separation. Hence, as many feminist critics have pointed out, the girl is coerced into (at least on the surface) accepting a typical Victorian education in "femininity," reading "a score

of books on womanhood / To prove, if women do not think at all, / They may teach thinking" (1.427-29), learning "cross-stitch," and so forth. That she has "relations in the Unseen" and in Nature, which romantically persist and from which she draws "elemental nutriment and heat . . . as a babe sucks surely in the dark" (1.473-75), and that she darkly remembers "My multitudinous mountains, sitting in / The magic circle, with the mutual touch / Electric . . . waiting for / Communion and commission" (1.622-26)—another striking image of the mother's nurturing breasts—are the only signs that somewhere in the shadows of her own psyche her mother country endures, despite the pseudo-oedipal wrenching she has undergone.

As Aurora grows into the fragmentation that seems to be (English) woman's lot, things go from bad to worse. Exiled from the undifferentiated unity of her mother country, the girl discovers that her parents have undergone an even more complicated set of metamorphoses than she at first realized, for not only has her true dead southern mother been replaced by a false and rigid northern stepmother—her "father's sister"—but her true dead father, after being supplanted by "a stranger with authority," has been replaced by a false and rigid northern stepfather, her cousin Romney Leigh, who, upon her father's death, has become the putative head of the family. To be sure, as Aurora's cousin, Romney has the potential for becoming a nurturing peer, an empowering "Bro" rather than a debilitating patriarch. But certainly, when the narrative begins, he is a symbolic father whose self-satisfied right and reason represent the masculine "head" that inexorably strives to humble the feminine "heart."

"I am not very fond of praising men by calling them *manly;* I hate and detest a masculine man," Barrett Browning told one correspondent (*Letters* 1: 134), and clearly by "masculine" she did not mean "virile" but "authoritarian." Yet such (implicitly patriarchal) authoritarianism is exactly what characterizes Romney Leigh at the cousins' first meeting, for his, says Aurora, was "The stranger's touch that took my father's place / Yet dared seem soft" (1.545-46), and she adds "A godlike nature his" (1.553). That Aurora has evidently been destined to marry this man makes the point even more clearly. Drawn away from the natural lore and lure of the mother, she has been surrendered to what Lacan calls the law of the father, inscribed into a patrilineal kinship system where she is to be doubly named by the father, both as daughter-Leigh and as wife-Leigh, just as Elizabeth herself was originally named Elizabeth Barrett Barrett. That Romney refuses to read her poetry, claiming that her book has "witchcraft in it" (2.77), clarifies the point still further. Her work is either "mere" or "magical" "woman's work" (2.234) because she exists "as the complement / Of his sex merely" (2.435-36), an (albeit precious) object of exchange in a network of marital transactions that must by definition deprive her not only of her autonomy but, more importantly, of her desire.

Nevertheless, Aurora insists on continuing to transcribe the texts of her desire, poems whose energy is significantly associated with her inner life, her "relations in the Unseen," and her mother country. At the same time, because she has been exiled in her fatherland, she must inevitably write these works in her father tongue. Inevitably, therefore, because she is struggling to find a place in traditions created by that masculine (and masculinist) language, she must study her father's books. Creeping through the patriarchal attic "Like some small nimble mouse between the ribs / Of a mastodon" (1.838-39), she finds a room "Piled high with cases in my father's name" (1.835) and "nibbles" fiercely but randomly at what amounts to a paradigmatic library of Western culture. Most inevitably, however, this furtive self-education, which both parallels and subverts her aunt's effort to educate her in "femininity," leads to further self-division. She can and does reject both Romney's offer of marriage and the financial legacy he tries with magisterial generosity to bestow on her, but once she has internalized—nibbled, devoured—the texts that incarnate patriarchal history, she is helplessly implicated in that history, so that even her "own" poetry is tainted, fragmented, impure.

How, then, is Aurora to rectify and clarify both her art and her self? Barrett Browning's "unscrupulous" epic seeks to resolve this crucial issue, and, perhaps paradoxically, the author begins her curative task by examining the ways in which her other major characters are just as fragmented and self-alienated as her heroine. To start, for instance, she shows that, despite (or perhaps because of) his superegoistic calm, Romney too is self-divided. This "head of the family," she quickly suggests, is no more than a "head," abstractly and, as his abortive wedding to Marian Erle will prove, ineffectually espoused to "social theory" (2.410). In fact, he is not just a false father because he has replaced Aurora's "true" father, he is a false father because, as Barrett Browning decided after her long imprisonment in Wimpole Street, all fathers are in some sense false. Indeed, the very idea of fatherhood, with its implications of social hierarchy and psychic fragmentation ("man with the head, woman with the heart" [Tennyson, *The Princess* 5.439]), is dangerously divisive, not only for women but for men. As a brother like her own "Bro," Romney might be able to "read" (and thus symbolically unite with) the texts of female desire that transcribe Aurora's otherness, but as a father he is irremediably blind to them. As a brother, moreover, he might more literally unite himself to the social as well as sexual others from whom his birth and breeding separate him, but as a father or "head," he is, again, hopelessly estranged from most members of the "body" politic.

Daguerreotype, c. 1848.

That Romney craves a union with both social and sexual others is, however, a sign that, like Aurora, he is half consciously struggling toward a psychic reunification which will constitute as much of a risorgimento for him as it will for her. His ill-fated and "mis-conceived" proposal to Aurora suggests his intuition of his own need, even while the fact that she "translates" him "ill" emphasizes the impossibility of communion or communication between them. In addition, his eagerness to go "hand in hand" with her among "the arena-heaps / Of headless bodies" (2.380-81) till, through her "touch," the "formless, nameless trunk of every man / Shall seem to wear a head with hair you know, / And every woman catch your mother's face" (2.388-90) implies that, at least metaphorically, he understands the self-division that afflicts both him and his cousin, even while Aurora's reply that since her mother's death she has not seen "So much love . . . / As answers even to make a marriage with / In this cold land of England" (2.398-400) once again outlines the geography of "mother-want" in which both characters are situated. Similarly, his subsequent plan to "take [a] wife / Directly from the people" (4.368-69) reveals once more his yearning to heal in his own person the wounds of the body politic, even while Aurora's recognition that his scheme is both artificial and divisive, "built up as walls are, brick by brick" (4.353), predicts the project's failure. For Romney, who feels himself "fallen on days" when marriages can be likened to "galley-couplings" (4.334), redemption must come not from the outward ceremony of marriage but from an inward metamorphosis that will transform him from (false) father to (true) brother, from (false) "god" to (true) groom.

Despite its misguided formulation, however, Romney's impulse to wed Marian Erle does begin the crucial process of metamorphosis, for this "daughter of the people" (3.806), an "Erle" elf of nature rather than an "earl" of patriarchy, has a history that parallels his and Aurora's history of fragmentation at the same time that she is an essential part of the reunified family/being he and Aurora must become.[12] Ignored and emotionally abandoned by a drunken father who beat her and a bruised mother who tried to prostitute her to a local squire, this "outcast child . . . Learnt early to cry low, and walk alone" (3.874-77). Her proletarian education in alienation offers a darkly parodic version of Aurora's bourgeois education in femininity. Reading the "wicked book" of patriarchal reality (3.952) with the same fervor that inspired Aurora's studies of her father's patriarchal texts, Marian imagines a "skyey father and mother both in one" (3.899) just as Aurora imagines inscribing her desire for her motherland in her father's tongue. Finally, too, the shriek of pain Marian utters when her mother tries to sell her to the squire—"God, free me from my mother . . . / These mothers are too dreadful" (3.1063-64)—echoes and amplifies Aurora's impassioned protest against the "Keeper's voice" (2.561) of the stepmother-aunt, who tells her that she has been "promised" to her cousin Romney: "I must help myself / And am alone from henceforth" (2.807-08). Repudiating the false mothers of patriarchal England, both these literally or figuratively orphaned daughters cry out, each in her own way, the intensity of the "mother-want" that will eventually unite them, along with Romney and with Marian's child, in the motherland of Italy, where each will become a nurturing mother country to the other.

When Marian and Aurora first meet, however, both are stranded in the alienating cityscape of nineteenth-century London, where each lives in an attic that seems to symbolize her isolation from world and self alike. Though Aurora has ostensibly become a successful poet, her ambition continually reminds her of her failure, since it constantly confronts her with fragmented verses whose "heart" is "Just an embryo's heart / Which never yet had beat" (3.247-48), while Marian, though her "heart . . . swelled so big / It seemed to fill her body" (3.1083-85), lives up a "long, steep,

narrow stair, 'twixt broken rail / And mildewed wall" (3.791-92). Parts of a scattered self—the one heartless, the other too great-hearted—this pair of doubles must be unified like the distant and dissonant city-states of Italy, and ultimately, of course, the two are brought together by Romney's various though similar desires for them. To begin with, however, they are united by the visits of yet another potential wife of Romney's—Lady Waldemar—to their parallel attics.

Voluptuous and vicious, the figure of Lady Waldemar offers a further comment on nineteenth-century ideals of "femininity." In fact, as we shall see, she is the (false) wife/mother whose love the (false) father must reject if he is to convert himself into a (true) brother. At the same time, though, her beckoning sexuality both initiates and instigates the "plot" proper of *Aurora Leigh,* emblematizing a fall into heterosexual desire with which Aurora and Marian must variously struggle before they can become whole. Almost at once, Aurora perceives this fashionable aristocrat as a male-created, socially defined "lady"—"brilliant stuff, / And out of nature" (3.357-58)—a perception Lady Waldemar's name reinforces with its reminiscences of generations of Danish kings. But even while Aurora defines her as "out of nature" in the sense that she is an antinatural being, a cultural artifact, this "fair fine" lady defines herself as being "out of nature" in the sense that she is *from* nature, nature's emissary. For, confessing that she has "caught" love "in the vulgar way" (3.466), Lady Waldemar instructs the poet-heroine that "you eat of love, / And do as vile a thing as if you ate / Of garlic" (3.450-52) since "love's coarse, nature's coarse" (3.455). Two books later, when she reappears at a party Aurora attends, the very image of Lady Waldemar's body reiterates her "natural" sexuality. Gorgeously seductive, "the woman looked immortal," (5.618), her bare breasts splitting her "amaranth velvet-bodice down / To the waist, or nearly, with the audacious press / Of full-breathed beauty" (5.622-24).

As emblems of nurturing maternity, breasts have obsessed both author and heroine throughout *Aurora Leigh,* but this is the first time their erotic potential is (quite literally) revealed, and tellingly the revelation is associated with Aurora's growing sense of artistic and sexual isolation: "Must I work in vain, / Without the approbation of a man?" (5.62-63); with her confession of "hunger . . . for man's love" (5.498); and, most strikingly, with her feeling that her "loose long hair [has begun] to burn and creep, / Alive to the very ends, about my knees" (5.1126-27). Furthermore, Lady Waldemar's eroticism is associated with—indeed, causes—Marian's betrayal into sexuality, a betrayal that leads to both a "murder" and a rebirth, while Aurora's mingled fear of and fascination with Lady Waldemar's erotic presence finally drive the poet back to her motherland of Italy, where she is ultimately to be reunited with both Marian and Romney. In fact, what have often been seen as the awkward or melo-dramatic turns of plot through which Barrett Browning brings these three characters back together in a sort of Florentine paradise are really important dramatic strategies by which the author herself was trying to work out (and out of) the "problem" of female sexuality by first confronting the engendered world as it is and then reengendering and reconstituting it as it should be.

Trusting the duplicitous Lady Waldemar, who "wrapped" the girl in her arms and, ironically enough, let her "dream a moment how it feels / To have a real mother" (6.1001-03), Marian is treacherously brought to France by the servant of this false "mother," placed in a brothel where she is drugged and raped, and thereby sold into sexual slavery—a deed that, as Marian herself notes, was "only what my mother would have done" (7.8-9). At the same time, Aurora—missing her "woodland sister, sweet maid Marian" (5.109), and convinced that Romney is about to marry the "Lamia-woman," Lady Waldemar (7.152)—finally decides to return to the Italy that she has long heard "crying through my life, / [with the] piercing silence of ec-static graves" (5.1193-94). Not coincidentally, she plans to finance her trip by selling the "residue / Of my father's books" (5.1217-18), a crucial first step in what is to be a definitive renunciation of the power of the fatherland. Her journey to the mother country, however, is impelled as much by desire as by denial, for, in the passage I have used as an epigraph to this essay, she "burns" toward her "own hills" and imagines that they desirously reciprocate her "yearning . . . As sleeping mothers feel the sucking babe / And smile" (5.1268-71). Thus, when en route she encounters the lost Marian in a Paris flower market, she begins the process of reunification that will regenerate both these wounded daughters. For the "fallen" Marian, whose face haunts Aurora like the face of a "dead woman," has become a mother whose assertion of what J. J. Bachofen was later in the century to call "mother right"—"I claim my mother-dues / By law"—proposes an empowering alternative to "the law which now is paramount," the "common" patriarchal "law, by which the poor and weak / Are trodden underfoot by vicious men, / And loathed for ever after by the good" (6.665-69). Becoming such a powerful figure, moreover, she has become a creative authority whose maternal eroticism speeds the two women toward the unfallen garden of female sexuality that they will plant in the richly flowering earth of Florence. There Marian's "unfathered" child will "not miss a . . . father," since he will have "two mothers" (7.124), there Aurora will set Marian like a "saint" and "burn the lights of love" before her pure maternity (7.128), and there, in a revision of her own eroticism, Aurora will exorcise the haunting vision of what she now comes to see as Lady Waldemar's distorted (Lamia-like) sexuality.

For when she returns to her motherland with Marian as her sister/self, Aurora returns transformed. No longer merely an aching outcast daughter crying her inchoate "mother-want," she has become herself, symbolically at least, a mother, since she is one of the "two mothers" of Marian's child. In addition, transformed into a hierophant of "sweet holy Marian" (6.782), she has learned to devote herself to the specifically female theology of the Madonna, the Queen of Heaven whom the Florentine women worship and whose rituals facilitate Aurora's increasing self-knowledge. Finally, she has become a poet, an artist-heroine who can not only weep but word her desire, in a language that through her interaction with Marian she has begun to make into a mother tongue. In fact, as she learns some weeks after her arrival in Florence, people in England have finally begun to "read" her. Her new book, writes her painter friend Vincent Carrington, "Is eloquent as if you were not dumb" (7.553), and his fiancée, who has Aurora's verses "by heart" more than she has her lover's words (7.603), has even insisted on having a portrait painted with "Your last book folded in her dimpled hands / Instead of my brown palette as I wished" (7.607-08).

That Marian's child is "unfathered" contributes in yet another way to the regenerative maternity both women now experience, for after all, the baby is only figuratively unfathered; literally, he was fathered by some nameless customer in a brothel. To call him "unfathered," therefore, is to stress the likeness of his mother, Marian, not only to the fallen woman Mary Magdalen but also to the blessed Virgin Mary, whose immaculate conception was the sign of a divine annunciation. That Barrett Browning surrounds Marian's maternity with the rhetoric of Mariolatry implies the theological force she wants to impute to this "maiden" mother's female energy. As opposed to the often sentimentally redemptive power ascribed to such Victorian "mothers' boys" as Gaetano (in Browning's *The Ring and the Book*), Leonard (in Mrs. Gaskell's *Ruth*), or Paul Dombey (in Dickens' *Dombey and Son*), Marian's son has an austerely religious significance. Nameless but beautiful, he is hardly ever characterized as a real child might be. Rather, when Marian explains that, in her despair after her rape, "I lived for him, and so he lives, / And so I know, by this time, god lives too" (7.112-13), the ambiguity of her language—does she believe that he is the "God" who "lives" or does his survival mean that "God lives"?—argues that he is in some sense a divine child, a baby god whose sacred birth attests to the divinity of his mother. Thus, even while she revises the story of the annunciation to question the brutality of a male God who uses women merely as vessels for his own ends, Barrett Browning suggests that the female creativity "holy" Marian and reverent Aurora share can transform the most heinous act of male sexual brutality, a rape, into a redemption. At the same time, by demonstrating the self-sufficient strength of Marian and Aurora's mutual maternity, she interrogates the idea that there is anything more than a momentary biological need for fathers or fatherhood.

It is noteworthy, then, that when she returns to Italy Aurora keeps reminding herself that she has returned to the land where her father is buried, the land of her mother's birth and her father's tomb, her "father's house / Without his presence." Though both her parents are buried near Florence, it is, curiously enough, evidence of only her father's disappearance that Aurora seeks and finds; when she revisits "the little mountain-house" where she had lived with him, she discovers that it has been effaced by female fertility symbols—"lingots of ripe Indian corn / In tessellated order and device / Of golden patterns" (7.1124-26)— so that "not a stone of wall" can be seen, and a black-eyed Tuscan girl sits plaiting straws in the doorway, as if forbidding entrance. While Aurora's mother lives on in the Italian motherland, her father is as irretrievably dead as Marian's child's father is nonexistent.

But how are both Aurora and Barrett Browning to deal with the wished-for but unnerving fate of the dead father? Freud famously argued that anxiety about the murder of this mythic figure ultimately constituted a social order in which "his" absent will was internalized as the superego that creates the law (see *Totem,* esp. 915-19). Barrett Browning, however, as if responding in advance to Freud's hypothesis, implicitly suggests that man as father must be exorcised rather than internalized and that, in a risorgimento of matriarchal law, he must be replaced with man as brother or man as son. For, unlike such a precursor as Christine de Pizan (in *City of Ladies*) or such a descendant as Charlotte Perkins Gilman (in *Herland*), Aurora does not envision an all-female paradise. Rather, she longs for a mother country or "sisterland to Paradise" in which women *and* men can live together free of the rigid interventions and interdictions of the father.

Thus, even when she and Marian and Marian's child have been securely established in "a house at Florence on the hill / Of Bellosguardo" (7.515-16), from which, like goddesses surveying past and future, they can see sunrise and sunset, "morn and eve . . . magnified before us" (7.525-26)—a scene that recalls Marian's "skyey father and mother both in one"—Aurora yearns obsessively for Romney. "Like a tune that runs / I' the head" (7.960-61), the erotic longing for her cousin that was first signaled by the appearance of Lady Waldemar has made her, she admits at last, just what Lady Waldemar confessed herself—a "slave to nature" (7.967). In addition, that longing reveals Aurora's radical sense of incompleteness, a feeling of self-division which suggests that, for Barrett Browning as for her heroine, a *matria* without men might become madly and maddeningly maenadic. As she sinks into a sort of

sexual fever, Aurora notes that even her beloved Florence "seems to seethe / In this Medæan boil-pot of the sun" (7.901-02) and ruefully confesses that, in the absence of the consort whom she desires because his presence would complete the new configuration of humanity toward which she aspires, even her old "Tuscan pleasures" seem "worn and spoiled" (7.1041).

In endowing a woman named *Aurora Leigh* with such erotic feeling for a cousin whom she wishes to remake in the image of a brother, however, Barrett Browning must at least half consciously have understood that her wish to provide her protagonist with a fraternally understanding and erotically egalitarian lover might oblige her to risk retracing the outlines of the nineteenth century's most notorious brother-sister incest plot: Byron's affair with his half-sister, *Augusta Leigh*. Unlike such "realistically" depicted sister-brother pairs as Tom and Maggie Tulliver in *The Mill on the Floss,* but like Romney and Aurora, Byron and Augusta rarely met until they were young adults, when both couples discovered and resisted similar mutual attractions. To be sure, the socially illicit Byronic duo made a far weaker effort at resistance than Barrett Browning's socially "legitimate" pair of cousins. Nevertheless, what Leslie Marchand says of Byron and Augusta is equally true of Romney and Aurora: "in their formative years they had escaped the rough familiarity of the brother-sister relationship," so that "consanguinity," with all the equality it might imply for peers of the same generation, was "balanced by the charm of strangeness" (1: 396). But Barrett Browning, who as a girl had dreamed of dressing in boy's clothes and running away to be Lord Byron's page, grew up to become, if not as censorious as her friend Carlyle was toward the hero of Missolonghi, at least ambivalent toward him. Even while insisting that her "tendency" was "not to cast off my old loves," she wrote that Byron's poems "discovered not a heart, but the wound of a heart; not humanity, but disease" (for EBB's ambivalent feelings toward Byron, see Taplin 15, 103). In addition, she was close to both the "wronged" Lady Byron's friend Anna Jameson and to Harriet Beecher Stowe, author of *Lady Byron Vindicated,* both of whom would have reminded her of the masculine exploitativeness involved in Byron's sexual exploits.

Simultaneously inspired and exasperated by the Byron story, therefore, Barrett Browning had to rewrite it to gain strength from it. Thus the seductive and antipoetic Augusta Leigh becomes the pure poet Aurora Leigh, and the morally corrupt but sexually devastating and romantically self-dramatizing Byron becomes the morally incorruptible but physically devastated and romantically diffident Romney. Furthermore, the sexual inequities implied by Byron's sordid secret affairs and by Romney's one-time authority as "head" of the Leigh family are eradicated both by Aurora's purity and by her recently achieved matriarchal strength. Newly defined "brother" and "sister" can unite, and even unite erotically, because the Byron episode has been reenacted on a "higher" plane, purged of social disorder and sexual disease.

The humbled Romney's arrival in Florence does, then, complete both the reconfiguration of the family and the regeneration of the motherland that poet-author and poet-heroine have undertaken. Blinded in a fire that recalls yet another famous nineteenth-century plot—the denouement of *Jane Eyre*—this former patriarch seems to have endured the same punishment that Brontë's Bertha dealt Rochester, although in personality Romney is closer to Jane Eyre's austere cousin St. John Rivers than to that heroine's extravagant "master." Significantly, however, Barrett Browning—who seems vigorously to have repressed her memory of the *Jane Eyre* episode, no doubt so she could more freely revise it[13]—swerved from Brontë in having Romney's injury inflicted not by a mad wife but by a bad father: William Erle, the tramp and poacher who began his career of destructiveness by bruising and abusing his daughter, Marian. Women do not need to destroy the fatherland, Barrett Browning implies by this revision, because it will self-destruct. Again, Barrett Browning swerves from Brontë in allowing her disinherited patriarch to rescue one item from the house of his fathers—a portrait of the lady from whom Aurora inherited her mouth and chin. A woman, she implies by this revision, may be an inheritor. In the end, therefore, as Romney describes "the great charred circle" where his ancestral mansion once stood with its "one stone stair, symbolic of my life, / Ascending, winding, leading up to nought" (8.1034-35), his saving of the picture suggests also that the power of the Leighs has not been destroyed but instead transferred to "a fairy bride from Italy" (9.766), who has now become the true heir and "head" of the family.

That Aurora has successfully become a "head" of the family, the figure both Romney's father, *Vane* Leigh, and Romney himself only vainly strove to be, is made clearest by her blinded cousin's revelation that he has at last really read and recognized her work. Seeing through and because of his blindness, like wounded father figures from Oedipus and Gloucester to Rochester, Romney receives and perceives Aurora's prophetic message—"in this last book, / You showed me something separate from yourself, / Beyond you, and I bore to take it in / And let it draw me" (8.605-08)—and that message, "Presented by your voice and verse the way / To take them clearest" (8.612-13), elevates her to the "dearest light of souls, / Which rul'st for evermore both day and night!" (9.831-32). Finally too, therefore, he has become, as both "Bro" and Robert Browning were for Barrett Browning herself, a "purely" attentive brother-reader who can at last comprehend the revisionary mother tongue in which the woman

poet speaks and writes. It is no coincidence, surely, that Barrett Browning has Aurora, who never before associated Romney with the ocean, envision her lost lover as arising from beneath the bitter waters that had engulfed her lost brother and standing before her like a "sea-king" while "the sound of waters" echoes in her ears (8.59-60).[14] Deciphering the texts of Aurora's desire, Romney has accomplished his own transformation into an ex-patriarch who entrusts himself and his sister-bride to the "one central Heart" (9.890) of love that may ultimately unify all humanity by eradicating the hierarchies and inequities of patriarchy. At the same time, emigrating from the rigid north of the Leighs to the warm south ruled by his "Italy of women" (8.358), he has become both an expatriate and an ex-patriot, a dweller in the new *matria* where, in a visionary role reversal, the empowered Aurora will "work for two" and he, her consort and cohort, "for two, shall love" (9.911, 912).

Romney's violent metamorphosis reminds us of Barrett Browning's implicit belief that, as in ***Casa Guidi Windows*** (where the poet advocates the self-sacrifice of Italian men), only the devastation of the fatherland can enable the risorgimento of the mother country.[15] Both Marian and Aurora too, however, have experienced violent metamorphoses, Marian literally, in the rape she describes as a "murder," and Aurora figuratively, in her passionate struggle to come to terms with the eroticism Lady Waldemar incarnates and with the murderous rage "the Lamia-woman" evokes. Now, though, after all this violence, these characters are brought together in a symbolically reunified family of brother/husband and sister/wife and mother and son. Is Aurora the dawn in which Marian and Romney can be reborn? Is Marian the womb that gives new life to Aurora's and Romney's light? Is Romney the lover who can read their new roles rightly in the "bittersweet" darkness of his visionary blindness? Is Marian's child the redemptive son whose coming signals a new day? There is certainly a temptation to define each member of this prophetic quartet allegorically. But even without stipulating meanings that the epic "unscrupulously" leaves in shadow, it is clear that in its final wholeness this newly holy family integrates what the writer called "Philosophical Thought" with what she called "Poetical Thought" and unifies both with the powerful dyad of mother and child, womb and womb fruit (see **"A Thought on Thoughts,"** *Complete Works* 6: 352-59). Eastering in Italy, moreover, these four redeemed beings begin to make possible the "new day" that their author imagined in, for, and through the country she chose as her *matria*. For among themselves they constitute—to go back to the qualities women writers have sought in Italy—a land that feels, that feeds, that makes art, and that unmakes hierarchies. In mythologizing them as she does, Barrett Browning sets against the exhaustion of belatedness that she thought afflicted contemporary (male) poets "who scorn to touch [our age] with a finger tip" a matriarchal future that she hoped would be sacramentally signaled by "the holy baptism of the morning dew."

In its ecstatic delineation of a female risorgimento, the redemption of Italy that Barrett Browning began to imagine in **Casa Guidi Windows** and fully figured in **Aurora Leigh** was both predictable and precarious. Given the long history of Italy as a literary topos, together with the country's personal association for this woman poet, it is not surprising that that embattled nation would come to incarnate both a mother's desire for *bella libertà* and a daughter's desire to resurrect the lost and wounded mother. Certainly Barrett Browning's American contemporary Margaret Fuller imagined the country in a similar way. "Italy has been glorious to me," she wrote Emerson in 1847, explaining that her expatriate experience had given her "the full benefit of [a] vision" of rebirth "into a state where my young life should not be prematurely taxed." In an 1848 dispatch to the *Tribune,* she added that in Rome "the sun and moon shine as if paradise were already re-established on earth. I go to one of the villas to dream it is so, beneath the pale light of the stars" (quoted in Chevigny 435, 453).

Part of this visionary passion no doubt arose from Fuller's revitalizing and egalitarian romance with Angelo Ossoli, in whom, as one observer put it, she loved "an imagined possibility in the Italian character" much as Aurora, in loving Romney (and Elizabeth Barrett, in loving Robert Browning), loved "an imagined possibility" in the English character.[16] At the same time, however, Fuller's dream of an Italian paradise was not just energized by her hope for a utopian future that the risorgimento might make possible; it was also shaped by her sense that behind Italy's "official" history of popes and patriarchs lay another history, the record of a utopian, and specifically matriarchal, past. Visiting "an Etrurian tomb" in 1847, she noted that "the effect . . . was beyond my expectations; in it were several female figures, very dignified and calm . . . [whose] expression . . . shows that the position of women in these states was noble." Later, passing through Bologna, she remarked that "a woman should love" that city "for there has the spark of intellect in woman been cherished with reverent care," and she made similar points about Milan, as well as, more generally, about the Italian "reverence to the Madonna and innumerable female saints, who, if like St. Teresa, they had intellect as well as piety, became counsellors no less than comforters to the spirit of men" (Chevigny 427-28).[17]

But in particular Fuller's analysis of Etruscan tomb paintings, like the novelist Ouida's apparently casual likening of Florence's past to "gold from the sepulchres of the Aetruscan kings . . . on the breast of some fair living woman," should remind us that as early as the 1840s, in just the years when both Fuller and Barrett Browning were imagining the risorgimento of an Italian *matria,* the Swiss jurist J. J. Bachofen was visiting Etruscan tombs outside Rome, where his discovery of a painting depicting "three mystery eggs" led him to speculate that in "Dionysian religion . . . the supreme law governing the transient world as a *fatum* [is] inherent in feminine matter" and that "the phallic god striving toward the fertilization of matter" stands merely "as a son" to "the maternal womb" (28-29). This speculation, published only two years after **Aurora Leigh** in Bachofen's 1859 *Essay on Mortuary Symbolism,* led in turn to the even more radical hypotheses of his *Mother Right* (1861), in which he presented the first strong argument that matriarchy was the primordial form of social organization.

In visiting, studying, and "reading" Etruscan tombs (as Freud too would do some fifty years and D. H. Lawrence some eighty years later), Bachofen was in one sense "reading" the palimpsest of Italy the way travelers like Shelley, Rogers, and Ruskin did in the archaeological metaphors I quoted earlier. Unlike them, however, and like both Fuller and Barrett Browning, he was "reading" beyond or beneath the patriarchal history Western tourists had always expected to find among the ruins of Rome and the monuments of Florence and interpreting his reading as Freud did his reading of the "Minoan-Mycenaean" age. Thus Bachofen too was preparing at least his female audience to resurrect the old lineaments of a "new, near Day" (**Aurora Leigh** 9.956) just as the newly matriarchal Aurora does at the end of Barrett Browning's epic when, in a revisionary swerve from Shelley and Ruskin, Barrett Browning has her "read" an Italian sunrise for Romney in the language of Apocalypse: "Jasper first . . . And second, sapphire; third, chalcedony; / The rest in order:—last, an amethyst" (9.962-64). Through such revisionary readings, moreover, both writers (along with Fuller) were preparing the way for such a descendant as H. D.: her *Tribute to Freud* ends with a reading of Goethe's "Kennst du das Land," the German poet's vision of Italy as sister land to paradise, a vision that makes the American modernist think of "the *Ca d'Oro,* the Golden House on the Grand Canal in Venice . . . the *domus aurea* of the Laurentian litany" (111). That it was Goethe who sought also to understand the *Ewige Weibliche* and whose injunction to "go down to the Mothers" deeply influenced Bachofen (see *Faust* 2.1.6215-21) would have surely given extra richness to the regenerated Italy of his (and H. D.'s) "Land wo die Zitronen blühn. . . ." Guarded by siren mountains and a bridge of clouds, as Emily Dickinson also believed, the regenerated *matria* of Italy stands "on the other side" of patriarchal history.

Yet both Goethe's poem and H. D.'s *Tribute* end with Mignon's equivocal plea: "o Vater, lass uns ziehn!"

For both the female poet and her German precursor, the journey to the magic land can only be accomplished with the guidance of the father. If he permits, the *matria* will be revealed; if not, the Alps and clouds, emblems of despair as well as desire, must, in Dickinson's words, "forever intervene." Similarly, Barrett Browning's visions of female regeneration are subtly qualified, for even while the plots and characters of *Aurora Leigh* and *Casa Guidi Windows* propose matriarchal apocalypses, the poet acknowledges that such consummations, though devoutly wished, require (in this world) male cooperation—Romney's abdication, the sacrifices of Italian men—and (in heaven) the grace of God the Father, who, with masculine wisdom, will build into "blank interstices" (*CGW* 2.776) and "make all new" (*AL* 9.949). By the time she wrote *Poems before Congress,* Barrett Browning's quasi-feminist vision had darkened even further. In just the poem whose image of Italy as an invalid woman echoes and illuminates Aurora's vision of her dead mother as "Our Lady of the Passion, stabbed with swords," the author imagines the redemption of her *matria* by, and only by, the grace of the French ruler Louis Napoleon, whose feats of male military bravery will make him "Emperor/Evermore." And, in fact, Italy's risorgimento was finally achieved only by the maneuvers of traditionally masculine "heroes" like Louis Napoleon, Mazzini, Garibaldi, Victor Emmanuel, Charles Albert, and—most of all—the Machiavellian statesman Cavour.[18] Thus the specifically matriarchal risorgimento of *Aurora Leigh* is ultimately almost as momentary and provisional as the brief hopeful revelation of the "mercy Seat" behind the "Vail" that ends *Casa Guidi Windows*. For inevitably the reality of patriarchal history, with its successes and successions, obliterated Barrett Browning's implicit but impossible dream of a *matria*.

Though Barrett Browning was disturbed by the unfavorable comparison one English reviewer made between her and Florence Nightingale, then, she might have sympathized with the view that unfairly stereotyped "lady with a lamp" expressed in a book the author of *Aurora Leigh* probably never read. As if commenting on the marriage of true minds Barrett Browning's epic envisions at its close, Nightingale argued in *Cassandra* (written in 1852 and privately printed in 1860) that "the true marriage—that noble union, by which a man and woman become together the one perfect being—probably does not exist at present upon earth" (44). Indeed, this woman, whose Christian name—Florence—was intended to honor the very city in which Barrett Browning found a modicum of *bella libertà* and who hoped that the "next Christ" might be, like the redemptive Aurora, a "female Christ," used a specifically Italian metaphor to describe the enchained reality of nineteenth-century woman: "She is like the Archangel Michael as he stands upon Saint Angelo at Rome. She has an immense provision of wings . . . but when she tries to use them, she is petrified into stone" (50).

Perhaps, given the power and pressure of history, a woman who is "nobody in the somewhere of patriarchy" can only, as Susan Gubar has observed, be "somebody in the nowhere of utopia" (140), for even a land like Italy, with all the metaphorical possibilities that give it strength as a matriarchal topos, is inextricably part of the larger topos of European time. As such, it is a text whose usefulness to women can be countered by masculinist rereadings that redeem it for both the father and the phallus. Even Bachofen, the theorist of matriarchy, was to argue that "mother right" must historically be transformed and transcended by "father right," and sixty years after Barrett Browning imagined Italy as a *matria,* D. H. Lawrence claimed the land as a metaphorical *patria,* asserting that "To the Italian the phallus is the symbol of individual creative immortality, to each man his own Godhead" (44). Even the word *matria,* moreover, which I have used throughout this essay to describe the visionary country sought by women like Fuller, Rossetti, Barrett Browning, and Dickinson, is nonexistent. The real Italian word for "motherland" is *madrepatria,* a word whose literal meaning—"mother-fatherland"—preserves an inexorably patriarchal etymology. In Italian linguistic reality, there is no matriarchal equivalent to patriarchal power: one can only imagine such an antithetical power in the "nowhere" of a newly made vocabulary.

It is no wonder, then, that Barrett Browning appointed Louis Napoleon "Emperor/Evermore" and that in the last poem she ever wrote, entitled **"The North and the South,"** she came full circle back to Aurora's self-divided beginnings, admitting the dependence of the matriarchal south on the patriarchal language of the rigid north. While the north sighs for the skies of the south "that are softer and higher," the south sighs. "For a poet's tongue of baptismal flame, / To call the tree or the flower by its name!" (*Poetical Works* 450).[19] Though she had enacted and examined a vision of female redemption far more radical than any Rossetti had allowed herself to explore, Barrett Browning would have conceded that, along with Rossetti, she was chained like Nightingale's angel to the rock of patriarchal Rome, and, along with Rossetti, she finally had to bid farewell to the Italy both had dreamed might be a sister land to paradise. As Christine de Pizan and Charlotte Perkins Gilman knew, in the world as it is, the City of Ladies can only be built on "the Field of Letters."

Notes

[1] All the quotations from *Aurora Leigh* in this essay come from the edition introduced by Cora Kaplan. All references to *Casa Guidi Windows* are to the edition by Julia Markus.

I am deeply grateful to Elliot Gilbert for critical insights that have been helpful throughout this essay. In addition, I am grateful to Susan Gubar and Dorothy Mermin for useful comments and suggestions. Finally, I want to thank my mother, Angela Mortola, for inspiring me to think about Italy. This paper is dedicated to her, with love.

2 In a brilliant essay on the Brownings and Italian politics, Flavia Alaya notes the connections among the regeneration of Aurora Leigh, the reunification of Italy, and EBB's personal sense of rebirth after her flight with Browning from England to Italy. But Alaya's study emphasizes the literary dialectic between two major poets who were, as she puts it, "quite literally political bedfellows," for she shows through a close reading of *The Ring and the Book* how Browning's Pompilia constitutes a re-vision of both Elizabeth and Italy, so that the husband's complex set of dramatic monologues is in some sense a response to the wife's earlier, apparently more naive and personal epic of a heroine's risorgimento. In addition, through close readings of Barrett Browning's letters and some of her poems, Alaya vigorously defines and defends this woman poet's often misunderstood (and frequently scorned) political stance.

3 Though Alaya sees Browning/Romney as the "father" of Elizabeth/Aurora's reborn self, an opinion I disagree with, she does also suggest that "a mother-quest played a much more dominant role in [Barrett Browning's] psychic life" than is usually thought (30, n. 18).

4 For a discussion of Aurora's vision of her mother's portrait, see Gilbert and Gubar 18-20.

5 Alaya also discusses this pervasive trope of Italy as a tragic woman and the political function of the image in the risorgimento (14-16).

6 Significantly, Ruskin describes the way the pillars of the porches of San Marco "half-refuse and half yield to the sunshine, Cleopatra-like, 'their bluest veins to kiss' . . ." (*Letters* 128).

7 For a discussion of woman as Galatea, see Gilbert and Gubar 12-13.

8 Elsewhere, Barrett Browning remarks that "[we] can dine our favorite way . . . with a miraculous cheapness . . . the prophet Elijah or the lilies of the field took as little thought for their dining, which exactly suits us" (*Letters* 1: 303).

9 For an extraordinarily useful analysis of *Corinne*'s significance to nineteenth-century women writers, and especially to EBB, see Ellen Moers 173-210. On *Corinne*'s Italy as a "land of women," see Madelyn

Gutwirth 208-15 and Ellen Peel, esp. 34-64. I am grateful to Ellen Peel for sharing this material with me.

10 For "the rigid North," see "Enrica" and *Casa Guidi Windows* 1.1173; it is possible, even likely, that Rossetti borrowed the phrase from Barrett Browning. For "the sweet South," see Rossetti's "Italia, Io Ti Saluto," 378-79.

11 Until recently, few critics have dealt directly with *Aurora Leigh;* major modern writers on the subject include Virginia Woolf, *"Aurora Leigh"*; Ellen Moers, esp. 201-07; Helen Cooper; Cora Kaplan, introd., *Aurora Leigh*; Barbara Gelpi; Virginia Steinmetz; and Dolores Rosenblum.

12 The name Marian Erle evokes Goethe's "Erlkönig," the uncanny and elfish forest spirit who is a manifestation of nature rather than of culture.

13 See Kaplan 23-24, in *Aurora Leigh*. Dorothy Mermin has pointed out to me the resemblances between Romney Leigh and St. John Rivers, a likeness Taplin also takes up (316-17). Interestingly, as Romney becomes more like Rochester, he also becomes, in a sense, more Byronic; at the same time, however, his kinship to St. John Rivers mutes (and thus makes acceptable) his Byronic qualities.

14 Immersed in Browning's very name is a wordplay on "Bro's" fate: "Browning" suggests a conflation of "Bro" and "drowning."

15 See *Casa Guidi Windows* 2.399-405:

> I love no peace which is not fellowship,
>   And which includes not mercy. I would
>   have
> Rather, the raking of the guns across
>   The world, and shrieks against Heaven's
>   architrave;
> Rather the struggle in the slippery fosse
>   Of dying men and horses, and the wave
> Blood-bubbling. . . .

16 Chevigny ascribes this comment to W. H. Hurlbut, who thought Ossoli an "underdeveloped and uninteresting Italian" (see Chevigny 375). In any case, the parallels between Barrett Browning and Fuller are interesting. Although Barrett Browning makes Romney older than Aurora, both Ossoli and Browning were considerably younger than their mates, as though Fuller and Barrett Browning had each half-consciously decided that in a utopian rearrangement of the relationship between the sexes men should be younger than their wives in order symbolically to free women from the bonds of daughterhood. In addition, both Fuller and Barrett Browning, quite late in life and rather unexpectedly, had children in Italy, and the private

experience of maternity may well have reinforced their mutual hopes for a public experience of matriarchy.

[17] As Susan Gubar has pointed out to me, the conclusion of George Eliot's *Romola* (1863) imagines a kind of private matriarchy secretly existing behind the patriarchal facade of fifteenth-century Florence.

[18] As Chevigny notes, Fuller's experiences during the risorgimento were marked by similar—and more dramatically personal—ambiguities, for motherhood simultaneously empowered and weakened her. While Ossoli was fighting in Rome, she was in Rieti, absorbed in child care, and "in their letters [during this period] they came near assuming conventional sex roles" (385).

[19] It is interesting that she wrote this poem to honor a literary man, Hans Christian Andersen, who had produced such visions of redemptive (but self-renouncing) femaleness as "The Snow Queen" and "The Mermaid."

Works Cited

Alaya, Flavia. "The Ring, the Rescue, and the Risorgimento: Reunifying the Brownings' Italy." *Browning Institute Studies* 6 (1978): 1-41.

Bachofen, J. J. "The Three Mystery Eggs." In *Myth, Religion, and Mother Right: Selected Writings of J. J. Bachofen.* Trans. Ralph Manheim. Bollingen Series. Princeton: Princeton Univ. Press, 1967, 24-30.

Browning, Elizabeth Barrett. *Aurora Leigh and Other Poems.* Introd. Cora Kaplan. London: Women's Press, 1978.

————. *Casa Guidi Windows.* Ed. Julia Markus. New York: Browning Institute, 1977.

————. *The Complete Works of Elizabeth Barrett Browning.* Ed. Charlotte Porter and Helen A. Clarke. 6 vols. New York: Crowell, 1900; facsim., New York: AMS, 1973.

————. *Elizabeth Barrett to Mr. Boyd.* Ed. Barbara McCarthy. New Haven: Yale Univ. Press, 1955.

————. *The Letters of Elizabeth Barrett Browning.* Ed. Frederic G. Kenyon. 2 vols. New York: Macmillan, 1899.

————. *The Poetical Works of Elizabeth Barrett Browning.* Ed. Harriet Waters Preston. Cambridge Edition. 1900; rpt. with introd. by Ruth M. Adams, Boston: Houghton, 1974.

Chevigny, Bell Gale. *The Woman and the Myth: Margaret Fuller's Life and Writings.* Old Westbury, N. Y.: Feminist, 1976.

Churchill, Kenneth. *Italy and English Literature 1764-1930.* London: Macmillan, 1980.

Cooper, Helen. "Working into Light: Elizabeth Barrett Browning." In *Shakespeare's Sisters: Feminist Essays on Women Poets.* Ed. Sandra M. Gilbert and Susan Gubar. Bloomington: Indiana Univ. Press, 1979, 65-81.

Dickinson, Emily. *Complete Poems of Emily Dickinson.* Ed. Thomas Johnson. Boston: Little, 1960.

Freud, Sigmund. "Female Sexuality." Trans. Joan Riviere. In his *Sexuality and the Psychology of Love.* Ed. Philip Rieff. New York: Collier, 1963, 194-211.

————. *Totem and Taboo.* In *The Basic Writings of Sigmund Freud.* Trans. and ed. A. A. Brill. New York: Modern Library, 1938, 807-930.

Gelpi, Barbara. "*Aurora Leigh*: The Vocation of the Woman Poet." *Victorian Poetry* 19.1 (1981): 35-48.

Gilbert, Sandra M., and Susan Gubar. *The Madwoman in the Attic: The Woman Writer and the Nineteenth-Century Literary Imagination.* New Haven: Yale Univ. Press, 1979.

Gilman, Charlotte Perkins. *Herland.* 1915; rpt. New York: Pantheon, 1979.

Gubar, Susan. "*She* in *Herland*: Feminism as Fantasy." In *Coordinates: Placing Science Fiction and Fantasy.* Ed. George E. Slusser, Eric S. Rabkin, and Robert Scholes. Carbondale: Southern Illinois Univ. Press, 1983, 139-49.

Gutwirth, Madelyn. *Madame de Staël, Novelist: The Emergence of the Artist as Woman.* Urbana: Univ. of Illinois Press, 1978.

H. D. [Hilda Doolittle]. *Tribute to Freud: Writing on the Wall, Advent.* New York: McGraw-Hill, 1975.

Lawrence, D. H. "The Lemon Gardens." In *D. H. Lawrence and Italy.* New York: Compass-Viking, 1972, 32-54.

Marchand, Leslie. *Byron: A Biography.* New York: Knopf, 1957.

Moers, Ellen. *Literary Women.* New York: Doubleday, 1976.

Nightingale, Florence. *Cassandra.* Old Westbury, N. Y.: Feminist, 1979.

Peel, Ellen. "Both Ends of the Candle: Feminist Narrative Structures in Novels by Staël, Lessing, and Le Guin." Diss. Yale Univ. 1982.

Pizan, Christine de. *The Book of the City of Ladies*. Trans. Earl Jeffrey Richards. New York: Persea, 1982.

Plath, Sylvia. *Ariel*. New York: Harper, 1965.

"Poetic Aberrations." *Blackwood's* 87 (1860): 490-504.

Rogers, Samuel. *The Complete Poetical Works of Samuel Rogers*. Ed. Epes Sargent. Boston: Phillips, Sampson, 1854.

Rosenblum, Dolores. "Face to Face: Elizabeth Barrett Browning's *Aurora Leigh* and Nineteenth-Century Poetry." *Victorian Studies* 26.3 (1983): 321-38.

Rossetti, Christina Georgina. *The Poetical Works of Christina Georgina Rossetti*. Ed. William Michael Rossetti. London: Macmillan, 1928.

Ruskin, John. *The Diaries of John Ruskin*. Ed. J. Evans and J. H. Whitehouse. Oxford: Oxford Univ. Press, 1956.

————. *Ruskin's Letters from Venice 1851-1852*. Ed. J. L. Bradley. New Haven: Yale Univ. Press, 1955.

Staël, Mme de. *Corinne ou l'Italie* (1807). Ed. Claudine Herrman. Paris: Des Femmes, 1979.

Steinmetz, Virginia. "Beyond the Sun: Patriarchal Images in *Aurora Leigh*." *Studiés in Browning and His Circle* 9.2 (1981): 18-41.

Taplin, Gardner B. *The Life of Elizabeth Barrett Browning*. New Haven: Yale Univ. Press, 1957.

Wharton, Edith. "An Alpine Posting Inn." In her *Italian Backgrounds*. New York: Scribners, 1905, 3-14.

Woolf, Virginia. "*Aurora Leigh*." In her *The Second Common Reader*. New York: Harcourt, 1932, 182-92.

————. *Flush: A Biography*. New York: Harcourt, 1933.

Angela Leighton (essay date 1986)

SOURCE: "'No name . . . My father! more belov'd than *thine*!': The Daughter's First Muse," in *Elizabeth Barrett Browning*, edited by Sue Roe, Harvester Press, 1986, pp. 23-54.

[In the following essay, Leighton examines the role of Browning's father in both her early poetry, in which he is a central figure, and her mature poetry, in which he is conspicuously absent.]

> For 'neath thy gentleness of praise,
> My Father! rose my early lays!
> And when the lyre was scarce awake,
> I lov'd its strings for *thy* lov'd sake;
> Woo'd the kind Muses—but the while
> Thought only how to win thy smile—

('To My Father on His Birthday', 33-8)[1]

The story of Mr Barrett's emotional and financial domination of his family is well known. It was not only his favourite oldest daughter, but all his eleven children who suffered from the extraordinary rigidity of his rule against marriage. There was, Elizabeth reports, a regular 'setting forth of the whole doctrine', which was a doctrine of ' "passive obedience, & particularly in respect to marriage" '. This uncompromising 'monomania' ([*The Letters of Robert Browning and Elizabeth Barrett: 1845-1846*, 2 vols., ed. Elvan Kintner (Cambridge, Mass.: Harvard University Press, 1969); hereafter *Letters: 1845-1846*], I, 408) forced her, at the age of forty, into a secret marriage with Robert Browning, and subsequent escape from her father's house to Italy. Her worst fears about his reactions were well founded. Mr Barrett refused to communicate further with his once best-loved daughter. He had all her belongings removed from the house, and years later returned her many pleading letters, unopened. He died in 1857, apparently unrepentant of this strange rule of law, and unshaken by the fact that three of his children, Elizabeth, Henrietta and George, had eloped and been disinherited in his lifetime.

The psychological and emotional explanations for this story have long been the material of biographies, and the reputation of Barrett Browning in the twentieth century rests largely on the intriguing resonances of this story. Thus, for instance, *The Barretts of Wimpole Street* relishes the idea of an incestuous element in the relationship of father and daughter, and finds piquant evidence for it in their shared night prayers, as well as in that prolonged invalidism which made Elizabeth so flatteringly dependent. Virginia Woolf endorses such an interpretation in *Three Guineas*, where she describes Mr Barrett as the worst example of the 'infantile fixation'[2] of many Victorian fathers, of whom her own father, of course, provided another powerful example. More recent biographies have tried to find extenuating reasons for this obsessive despotism, in Mr Barrett's acute loneliness after the death of his wife,[3] for instance, and in the possibility that he turned wholly to his young, adoring children for emotional compensation.[4] That he was much loved and admired seems indisputable, and the many birthday odes written for him with playful grandiloquence by his children are a sign of it. One of Elizabeth's own tributes, **'To My Father on His Birthday'** (1826), amply acknowledges his power to inspire her love and to make all other loves seem poor by comparison. The 'name' of that father was, from an early age, more 'belov'd' than any other.

But the poem also acknowledges his power to inspire her writing. The emotional domination of the father was inseparable from his imaginative attraction and authority. The young poet remembers how she 'Woo'd the kind Muses', but in reality 'Thought only how to win thy smile.' The traditional female sources of inspiration were early supplanted by the figure of her uniquely adored father. The power of that father's 'smile' did not then lessen with time, but continued to be, throughout the poet's life, a figure for the only imaginative reward she cared to seek and feared to lose. Consequently, it is important to recognise that the other side of the story of Mr Barrett's 'infantile fixation' and quirks of tyranny is to be found in some profound and lasting need in the daughter for that very paternal power which he exercised with such convinced righteousness. Her poetry registers the strength of that need almost to the end of her life.

However, Barrett Browning's private emotional and literary dedication to her father must also be seen in the context of a larger seductive ideology of fatherhood, which predominated in the nineteenth century, and which was particularly strong in the writings of Victorian women. As Elaine Showalter points out, a common trait among women writers of the century was their 'identification with, and dependence upon, the father; and either loss of, or alienation from, the mother.'[5] By contrast to the mother's constant association with childbearing and death, the father's free physical strength must have seemed enviably the superior lot. Furthermore, as de Beauvoir notes, the father's access to a life outside the home gave him a 'mysterious prestige',[6] a glamour of freedom and worldly wisdom, in the emulous imagination of the daughter.

As a result, there develops round the figure of the father in nineteenth-century literature a very persuasive myth of power, knowledge and reliability. It is a myth which the socially dependent but ambitious daughter has her reasons to perpetuate. The father's superior education and freedom of movement are both privileges which she desires for herself, if not literally, at least imaginatively. He is the sign of a power to be envied, courted and gained. However, the social and moral authority of the father is also a force which prohibits the daughter from seeking too much knowledge, freedom or power of her own. While he is, on the one hand, a sign of what the daughter desires for herself, he is also, on the other hand, a sign that restricts her desires. This contradiction forcefully shapes her attitude to him.

Elizabeth Barrett would have found corroboration for her own emotional idealisation of her father in a book she read many times and which profoundly influenced her poetry. 'I have read *Corinne* for the third time . . . It is an immortal book' ([**Elizabeth Barrett to Mr. Boyd: Unpublished Letters of Elizabeth Barrett Browning to Hugh Stuart Boyd,** ed. Barbara P. McCarthy (London: John Murray, 1955)], p. 176), she wrote at the age of twenty-six. Madame de Staël's *Corinne,* as Ellen Moers has shown,[7] influenced a whole generation of women, and encouraged a widespread fantasy of the woman as dedicated artist who forfeits love for her ambition. However, there is another aspect of *Corinne* which might have endeared it to the female imagination at this time: namely, its consciousness of the power of the father. Madame de Staël's attitude to her own father was one of curiously uninhibited sentimental and sexual attraction. 'Of all the men in the world it is he I would have wished for a lover,'[8] she declared at the age of nineteen, and after his death, she lamented him in equally passionate terms: 'I was to lose my protector, my father, my brother, my friend, he whom I would have chosen to be the only love of my life if fate had not cast me in a generation other than his.'[9]

The strange fact behind this lifelong adoration is that de Staël's father disapproved of her writing. *Corinne* was written immediately after his death, and is, on the one hand, a loving commemoration of him. But it is also, on the other hand, a guilt-ridden story of betrayal. The hero, Lord Nelvil, is haunted by the memory of his dead father's wish that he should marry, not the passionate, artistic, Italian Corinne, but the quiet, domesticated, English Lucile. His love for Corinne therefore carries a disproportionate and irredeemable load of guilt, that is not only guilt of betraying the beloved father, but of betraying a whole array of powers which the father represents: 'j'avais trahi sa tendresse, et . . . j'étais rebelle à ma patrie, à la volonté paternelle, à tout ce qu'il y a de sacré sur la terre'[10] (I had betrayed his tender love, and . . . I was a rebel against my country, against the paternal will, against everything that is sacred on earth). Although *Corinne,* on the one hand, shows the triumph of the woman as artist, it also, on the other hand, shows the triumph of the paternal will and of filial love. 'Je n'ai jamais rien aimé plus profondément que mon père'[11] (I have loved nothing more deeply than my father), the hero declares. That love is the real emotional centre of the novel. It is as if de Staël were expiating her own guilt of writing against her father's will by having her hero finally adhere to his dead father's wishes. However, the fact that the two themes of woman's ambition and of filial love are separated in the novel betrays the extent to which they represent a contradiction of purpose in the author. De Staël's insistence on passive obedience to the father on the one hand and total independence for the woman artist on the other reveals her essentially female conflict of desire.

The enormous popularity of *Corinne* among nineteenth-century women writers may have derived, not only from its celebration of the woman as artist and its eulogies of Italy as the place of artistic and sexual freedom, but also from its troubled portrayal of the power of the dead father. The time-honoured story of romantic love as an escape from parental tyranny is complicated, here, by a rival love between father and son. That it is really a love between father and daughter is a secret that the novel fails to keep. It seems unlikely that Elizabeth Barrett, who marked all those passages in her copy of *Oedipus at Colonus,* for instance, where Antigone warmly declares her love for her father,[12] did not note and appreciate the powerful myth of the father which broods through *Corinne* and determines, both emotionally and literally, the outcome of its plot.

> My beloved father has gone away . . . His tears fell almost as fast as mine did when we parted . . . I never told him of it, of course, but, when I was last so ill, I used to start out of fragments of dreams, broken from all parts of the universe, with the cry from my own lips, 'Oh, Papa, Papa!' I could not trace it back to the dream behind, yet there it always was very curiously, and touchingly too, to my own heart, seeming scarcely *of* me, though it came *from* me, at once waking me with, and welcoming me to, the old straight humanities. ([*The Letters of Elizabeth Barrett Browning to Mary Russell Mitford: 1860-1854,* 3 vols., ed. Meredith B. Raymond and Mary Rose Sullivan (The Browning Institute and Wellesley College, 1983); hereafter *MRM*], I, 104)

Elizabeth Barrett wrote this while recuperating in Torquay in 1838. She was thirty-two years old. Such expressions of demonstrative reliance on her father recur throughout her early letters. Although probably exaggerated by illness, her automatic call for '"Papa"' from the midst of her hectic dreams shows how deeply her consciousness has imbibed the idea of his moral dependability. Simply the invocation of his name can banish the terrors of her sleep. He is a source of sanity and restraint, and a reminder of 'the old straight humanities.' This myth of protectiveness and moral authority which her imagination builds round the name of her father draws on a strong and uninhibited emotional connection between them: 'His tears fell almost as fast as mine did . . .' The myth is strengthened by the emotional intensity of a relation which often seems to poach the language of sexual love without any sense of indecorum. The 'beloved father' weeps almost as unrestrainedly as his daughter at parting.

Certainly, Elizabeth Barrett would not have been surprised at the sentiments voiced by George Eliot about nursing her father through his last illness. The young Marian Evans wrote that 'these will ever be the happiest days of life to me. The one deep strong love I have ever known has now its highest exercise and fullest reward.' In another letter she goes on to stress the moral security offered by her father: 'What shall I be without my Father? It will seem as if a part of my moral nature were gone. I had a horrid vision of myself last night becoming earthly sensual and devilish for want of that purifying restraining influence.'[13] In both passages, the daughter's emotionally demonstrative love for the father is closely linked with a sense of his moral authority. The father is a rescue from a state of encroaching mental confusion or moral anarchy. He saves his daughter from the terrors of her own dreams or from the terrors of her own dangerous proclivities to be 'earthly sensual devilish'. It is as if the figure of the father, by freeing and then channelling the daughter's expressions of love towards himself, thus protects her from the alternative forbidden expression of her feelings. This law of the father is one which prohibits the daughter's desires precisely by permitting her 'one deep strong love' for himself.

The association of the father's emotional accessibility with a moral law is evident in Barrett Browning's writing as it is in de Staël's and George Eliot's. The consequence, however, is that the father saves his daughter not only from herself, but also from the moral threat that comes from other men. The sense of him as an alternative is still strong in those letters Barrett Browning wrote after her marriage. 'Always he has had the greatest power over my heart,' she wrote some weeks after her arrival in Italy—not of Robert but of her father—'because I am of those weak women who reverence strong men. By a word he might have bound me to him hand and foot' ([*The Letters of Elizabeth Barrett Browning,* 2 vols., ed. Frederic G. Kenyon (London, 1897); hereafter *Kenyon*], I, 291). She admits here, startlingly, that if her father had returned her love, she could not have left him. He alone possessed a natural 'power' over her 'heart'. Even after the romance and happiness of her marriage, the idea of that 'power' continued to press upon her imagination with the force, not only of a tyrannical rule which she had shed, but also of a love which she had lost.

Simone de Beauvoir, in *The Second Sex,* might be commenting on Barrett Browning in particular when she writes: 'If her father shows affection for his daughter, she feels that her existence is magnificently justified . . . she is fulfilled and deified. All her life she may longingly seek that lost state of plenitude and peace.'[14] The father appears in Barrett Browning's poetry as the object of that quest for inspiration and power which all her life she pursues. But he also represents a 'power' which can bind her 'hand and foot'. To seek the father 'longingly,' as she might the 'lost state of plenitude and peace' that womanhood has forgone, is also to seek, however, a crippling dependence and powerlessness for herself. Her theory of creativity is one which, throughout her life, is closely implicated with the power of the father as something she desires to keep, but needs to repudiate. The emotional attraction and the ideological danger of that power are the contradictory but linked aspects of the figure whose 'smile' supplants all the other 'kind Muses'.

In **'To My Father on His Birthday'** the young poet had written:

> But still my Father's looks remain
> The best Maecenas of my strain;
> My gentlest joy, upon his brow
> To read the smile, that meets me now—
>
> (43-6)

Nearly twenty years later, Elizabeth Barrett, at the age of thirty eight, lovingly dedicated her 1844 collection of poetry to her father. She invoked his attention and his approval with the words: *'it is my fancy thus to seem to return to a visible personal dependence on you, as if indeed I were a child again; to conjure your beloved image between myself and the public, so as to be sure of one smile . .'.*[15] This Dedication was Elizabeth's last to her father. A month or so after its publication she received her first letter from Robert Browning. Nonetheless, the thought of that potent 'smile' continued to haunt her for the rest of her life. Two years after her marriage, for instance, and after the disappointment of another miscarriage, she wrote to Miss Mitford that 'perhaps after all . . . I should choose the smile of my own father to that of my own child . . . oh yes, I should & would' (*MRM,* III, 234). That her father might smile on her was still the goal of her ambition and the end of her desires.

This lifelong and single-minded courtship of the figure of her father neatly endorses recent feminist descriptions of the woman poet's relation to her muse. While the task of 'the strong poet', according to Harold Bloom, is to '"rescue" the beloved Muse from his precursors',[16] the task of the strong female poet, as Gilbert and Gubar emphasise,[17] must be different. This difference is persuasively analysed by Joanne Feit Diehl, who argues that poets like Christina Rossetti, Barrett Browning and Emily Dickinson do not distinguish between precursor and muse in this way, but rather look back to a single, composite precursor-muse figure which is male.[18] This general father-lover then stands in a difficult, exclusive relation to the female poet. He is both desired and threatening—desired like the muse, but threatening because he wields a power the daughter desires for herself. Thus the very fact of courting the father's appreciation risks upsetting the natural hierarchy of their relation. For Barrett Browning, the contradiction which informs her imagination's myth of the father is the contradiction of wanting to

be to him both a daughter and a strong poet; of wanting, as she writes in the 1844 Dedication, *'to satisfy my heart while I sanctify my ambition'*. The many poems that invoke the presence of the father reveal the extent to which this contradiction shaped her identity as a poet.

'A Romance of the Ganges' (1838) is one of a number of ballads which Elizabeth Barrett wrote in response to a demand in the 1830s and 1840s for morally educative poems, which were published in illustrated annuals and were directed towards a primarily female readership. Her own contributions were generally highly-coloured tales of tragically thwarted romantic love, ending in death or suicide. But the moral of these, however coy and high-minded it might sound, is often curiously obfuscated by the presence of a father or a mother. It is this confusion of purpose which makes these early ballads unexpectedly interesting.

'A Romance of the Ganges' was written to illustrate a picture of '"a very charming group of Hindoo girls floating their lamps upon the Ganges'" (*MRM,* I, 37, note 2), as Miss Mitford explained, and was published in the annual which she edited, and which carried the alluring title of *Findens' Tableaux of the Affections: a Series of Picturesque Illustrations of the Womanly Virtues.* It tells the story of two girls, Luti and Nuleeni. Luti has lost her lover to Nuleeni, and as proof of it the lamp on her boat goes out. In anger, she exacts from the younger girl a vow that, once married, she will remind her husband of his faithlessness to her friend. So far, it is a picturesque tale of spoilt love. But there is a third presence in the poem, for which there is no original in Miss Mitford's '"charming'" picture.

Luti remembers that by this same river of love she had sat with her dying father. Furthermore, she remembers the highly suggestive fact that '"on my childish knee was leaned / My dying father's head'" (75-6).[19] This memory provides Luti with a strong alternative to the love she has lost. She declares: '"I weep no faithless lover where / I wept a loving father'" (88-9). As in *Corinne,* the figure of the dead father exerts a compelling emotional hold over the actions of his child. Faithful paternal love is contrasted with faithless romantic love, and Luti determines, therefore, to be constant to the first.

However, the troubling fact remains that the father is dead. He is faithful but lost, so that the daughter's choice of romantic or paternal love involves a choice of life or death. The poem's finale has all the narrative predictability of a tale of thwarted love. But the moral is confusing. Luti drowns herself, not because the lover was treacherous, but because the father was constant. The adult daughter kills herself in order to be faithful to the memory of the father's love which she had known as a child. It is to the poem's credit, at least, that in the end it remains unclear which of *'the Womanly Virtues'* is being illustrated.

In fact, **'A Romance of the Ganges'** is not about womanly virtues at all. It is about an emotional rivalry that looms large in the consciousness of the daughter. Father and lover are forces that contend for her love, and of the two she chooses her father. However, the poem also subtly undermines the validity of this choice. The father offers a secure primal faithfulness, but he offers it in death. The picture of the child nursing and supporting her dying father suggests a connection which is not just the connection of a somehow acceptable emotional and even erotic experience—the experience George Eliot described as the 'highest exercise and fullest reward' of her 'one deep strong love'. There is another more sinister connection in this picture, which will haunt Barrett Browning's imagination throughout her life. This connection becomes clear in a subsequent ballad, written a year later, in 1839.

Elizabeth Barrett sent **'The Lay of the Brown Rosary'** (1844), which she termed a 'Patagonian ballad', and an 'ichthyosaurus of a ballad' (**MRM,** I, 135), with some justified trepidation to Miss Mitford. The poem is a female re-working of the Faust myth. Onora, the heroine, sells her soul to the ghostly nun of the brown rosary in order to repeal a divine decree that she must die. Thus she hopes to be able to marry her betrothed. This queer moral premise purports to show Onora foolishly bartering immortal life for earthly love. But punishment is exacted on the very altar steps at her wedding, when her lover falls dead at her feet. After this, Onora herself pines away and dies. However, Elizabeth Barrett brings to this improbable Gothic tale an idea which radically confuses the romantic impulse of the story. This is, once again, the idea of the dead father.

Onora, we are told, consorts with the ghost of a nun who was '"buried alive"' (46)[20] for some sin against her vow; of course, her vow of chastity. But unlike *Villette,* where the nun will represent Lucy's bid for freedom and sexual love, here the nun is an evil spirit who has designs on the heroine's immortal soul. What is strange, however, is that there is no social or even religious basis for the divine decree that Onora should die rather than marry. The lover is approved of by her family, and he is honourable. Thus the usual justifications for a social or familial prohibition are missing. This is not a case of illicit or immoral love, from which Onora might be protected by authoritative moral forces. It is simply a case of her not being permitted to love at all. The reasons for this ruthlessly prohibitive story are to be found in a third shadowy presence in the poem.

At one point Onora has a dream. 'I only walk among the fields, beneath the autumn-sun, / With my dead father, hand in hand, as I have often done' (137-8), she relates. Against the powers of evil, represented by the nun and the earthly lover, there are ranged the powers of good, represented by Onora's family, and especially by her dead father. This distribution of moral forces in the poem means that the family is on the side of God's decree that Onora must die, unwed. However, the absurdity of this moral alignment is blurred by something else in the poem: 'And then he calleth through my dreams, he calleth tenderly, / "Come forth, my daughter, my beloved, and walk the fields with me!"' (144-5). Onora's dreams of her good father are dreams that reveal an alternative motive for the poem's odd construction. With the figure of the father, there is introduced an emotional charge which radically displaces the moral of the story. '"Come forth, my daughter, my beloved, and walk the fields with me!"' is a call that sounds as emotionally compelling as any earthly lover's. The father calls his daughter, like Solomon calling his '"beloved"'. It is this connection between the dead father and the unwed daughter that carries the conviction which is plainly missing from the narrative and moral structure of the poem. God's decree is justified by the dead father's infinitely compelling and desirable love.

However, in her response to that father's lover-like call, Onora implicitly acknowledges the conditions of that love:

> Have patience, O dead father mine! I did not
>   fear to die—
> I wish I were a young dead child and had
>   thy company!
> I wish I lay beside thy feet, a buried three-
>   year child,
> And wearing only a kiss of thine upon my
>   lips that smiled!
>
>   (162-5)

These lines are like Elizabeth Barrett's own words of Dedication to her father: *'it is my fancy thus to seem to return to a visible personal dependence on you, as if indeed I were a child again.'* Onora's dream of being a child again is also, however, a dream of being dead. It is as if Elizabeth Barrett were here obscurely remembering another 'three-year child' who stayed faithful by dying: the child Lucy. Wordsworth's desire to retain his imagination's 'memory of what has been, / And never more will be' (41-2)[21] requires the sacrifice of Lucy to nature's amorous but deadly ways. Onora's reply suggests that the crime from which she must be saved is not that of over-reaching Faustian desire, nor of illicit love, nor of consorting with evil spirits; her crime is simply the fact of having become a woman, and of having betrayed the father's love with other kisses on her lips. This is the reason why she must die, and why she herself really wishes to have died. She imagines staying in a prelapsarian world of childhood, and walking with her father there, 'hand in hand'. But it is not just childhood which this belated, post-Romantic daughter desires; it is a permanent childhood, and therefore a childhood sealed by death. Onora's strange concealed guilt, in this poem, is the guilt of having lived on.

The figure of the dead father, then, is the key to the hidden message of these confused and precipitate ballads. The father is dead, not by some sad chance, but *because* the daughter lives. The connection between the father's death and the daughter's life is a profoundly suggestive and influential one, which in both poems sanctions the suicidal direction of the ending. The daughter forgoes earthly love in order to answer the more seductive call of the dead father who offers her, instead, a lasting security and dependency. He offers her her childhood once again. Such a call implicitly, therefore, requires the daughter to deny her adult self; it requires a permanent stalling of her development into womanhood. To be *'as if indeed . . . a child again'* is the main emotional impetus behind these surprising romances.

It is possible to detect in these poems the beginning of a contradiction in Elizabeth Barrett's attitude. The father's emotional attraction is one which distorts all morality and all logic. In **'The Lay of the Brown Rosary'** it is he who gives emotional validity to the decree that Onora must not live on and love, and who thus sides with God in making her other desires sinful. The idea that the father is a source of moral security and constancy entails the idea that he prohibits the daughter's own chaotic or sensual desires. But to prohibit them entirely is to command the daughter's suicide. '"Come forth, my daughter, my beloved, and walk the fields with me!"' is tender only to disguise a paternal fiat that is, like God's, tyrannically absolute for the daughter's death.

These poems seem to proclaim that the father's love triumphs over all others, and that the daughter finds the 'lost state of plenitude and peace' of her childhood's dependence on him, by dying before being wed. Nonetheless, they also proclaim that to reach such love and such emotional plenitude the daughter must no longer live or love others. The unmentioned third prohibition, implicitly commanded by the father's otherworldly possessiveness, is that she should no longer write either. That both ballads end in the daughter's suicide or death is a comment which cannot entirely ride on the justification of emotional constancy. To die still a child to the father is to renounce more than the loves which threaten his; it is to renounce the power of writing also. It is that consciousness of power which is indicatively lacking in these ballads, but which, when

it is present, creates a conflict of purpose that lies at the heart of Barrett Browning's father-centred poetics.

'But dear Papa's wishes w.ᵈ be consulted more tenderly, if his commands were less straight & absolute' (**MRM,** III, 129), Elizabeth wrote in 1845, with a noticeable new uncertainty in her tone. Throughout the letters written to Robert in 1845 and 1846 it is possible to detect a struggle to believe still in the old cherished ideal of her father. But while she had once proclaimed that 'my poor most beloved Papa's *biases* are sacred to me' (**MRM,** I, 226), she now tells Robert of how every member of her family, except herself, is humiliatingly 'dependent in money-matters on the inflexible will'. That 'will', which she had once looked to as a moral authority, and which she had deified as near to God's, now comes to seem 'inflexible'. But, she adds anxiously, 'what you do NOT see what you *cannot* see, is the deep tender affection behind & below all those patriarchal ideas of governing grownup children' (**Letters: 1845-1846,** I, 169). Her faith in that 'deep tender affection' might still excuse and mitigate her father's 'patriarchal ideas of governing'.

But it is evident in these letters that the dear ideal of her father is under threat from two figures associated with it. Just as in **'The Lay of the Brown Rosary'** the father sides with the divine decree that the daughter must die, so in these letters the father's will seems sometimes harsh as God's. He is the 'High priest' (**MRM,** III, 127) and 'grand Signor' (**MRM,** III, 129) of the household, and, as Elizabeth knew well, his 'principle of passive filial obedience' was 'held . . drawn (& quartered) from Scripture' (**Letters: 1845-1846,** I, 408). Mr Barrett ruled his children with the convinced authority of a Jehovah.

But there was another figure which Elizabeth came to associate, however reluctantly, with her father. 'I belong to a family of West Indian slaveholders, and if I believed in curses, I should be afraid' (**Kenyon,** II, 220), she once reported. Mr Barrett owned sugar plantations in Jamaica until the Abolition in 1833, when he lost much of his wealth. The idea of slavery is one which creeps into Elizabeth's descriptions of her father's rule, though she never accuses him directly of using the tactics of a slave-owner. His 'principle of passive filial obedience,' for instance, is one which encourages in his children that 'disingenuousness' and 'cowardice' which she calls the '"vices of slaves"' (**Letters: 1845-1846,** I, 169). Elsewhere, she describes to Robert one of those domestic scenes in which all the children 'walked out of the room' leaving only the suitor of Henrietta to hear the end of the lecture on '"passive obedience."' She reports, without comment, that at the end Captain Surtees Cook asked '"if children were to be considered slaves"'

(*Letters: 1845-1846,* I, 408-9). That the 'essential features' of the patriarchal family are 'the incorporation of unfree persons and paternal power'[22] was a knowledge stressed by the facts of the family inheritance, but also by Elizabeth's own reluctant perceptions. It was only after her marriage in 1846 that she was able to write a poem which powerfully repudiates the authority which had so magisterially dominated her own life.

'The Runaway Slave at Pilgrim's Point' (1850) tells the story of a nameless female slave, who has seen her black lover killed by white masters, and who has herself been raped by them. To her horror, she subsequently bears a white child. The language of the whole poem is marked by the ideological division of black and white: black slaves and white masters, black mother and white child, black earth and white heaven. There is no moral authority which can be exempted from this stark new relativism of a world seen black or white. Even the authority of God is implicated, for he comes with incriminatingly 'fine white angels' (157).[23] In spite of all its heightened melodrama and carrying rhetoric, **'The Runaway Slave'** is still a startlingly iconoclastic poem. This is because it breaks with two sacred myths of English Victorian society: the myths of motherhood and fatherhood.

At one point the slave looks on her child and sees that he is white:

> My own, own child! I could not bear
>   To look in his face, it was so white;
> I covered him up with a kerchief there,
>   I covered his face in close and tight:
> And he moaned and struggled, as well might be,
> For the white child wanted his liberty—
>   Ha, ha! he wanted the master-right.
>
> (120-6)

The new moral order is simply one of white and black, and even the prototypically innocent child cannot escape it. The imperialism of whiteness is a hereditary one, and the child's desire for liberty is a desire already corrupted by the assumption of 'master-right'. Because the system of master and slave is based on an original birthright, there is only one course of defiance for the female slave:

> Why, in that single glance I had
>   Of my child's face, . . . I tell you all,
> I saw a look that made me mad!
>   The *master's* look, that used to fall
> On my soul like his lash . . . or worse!
> And so, to save it from my curse,
>   I twisted it round in my shawl.
>
> (141-7)

The easiness of this last verb neatly avoids any note of tragedy or sentimentality. The logic of killing the child comes as naturally as wrapping it in a shawl for protection. Simply by the fact of its colour, and to some extent, one imagines, of its sex, the white child inherits the *'master's* look'. The only way to break this imperial lineage is quietly to kill him, and the poem accomplishes the black slave's revolt with persuasive moral conviction.

However, this is a poem which protests not only at the domination of black races by white, but also at the domination that is carried out in the name of the *father*. The rape of the black slave is an outrage which is perfectly consistent with the myth of power that supports the rule of the white masters. The child inherits the father's look as well as the master's. The mystique of the father's line and of the father's name is one which the poem questions and defies. It shows fatherhood in complicity with racial power, and the sign of both lies in the authority of the 'name'. That 'name' stands for mastery, and its repetition creates in the poem a linguistic line of descent which links fathers of all kinds in a league of power which naturally excludes the nameless female slave herself.

At the start, she kneels where the first Pilgrim Fathers landed and where they thanked their God 'for liberty' (4):

> O pilgrims, I have gasped and run
> All night long from the whips of one
>   Who in your names works sin and woe!
>
> (12-14)

The 'names' of those first Fathers are the origin of a long history of 'sin and woe'—a history which leads logically to the act of violent fathering that is perpetrated in the poem's story. Along this route is to be found also *God the Father:*

> Indeed we live beneath the sky,
>   That great smooth Hand of God stretched out
> On all His children fatherly . . .
>
> (43-5)

This divine father is soon found to be partisan for the white man. He has thrown the black race 'Under the feet of His white creatures' (26), and he comes equipped with his own 'fine white angels' (157). This patrilineal succession is a white succession, and it is one that links all white fathers both divine and human.

However, there is an alternative name in the poem, which the black slave chants like a spell. It is the name of her black lover:

I sang his name instead of a song,
   Over and over I sang his name,
Upward and downward I drew it along
   My various notes,—the same, the same!
                            (78-81)

Significantly, this is the 'name' of what might be a different succession—a line fathered by love and rebellion rather than hatred and domination. But such a 'name' cannot belong to the white child: 'I dared not sing to the white-faced child / The only song I knew' (132-3). The white child already carries in the colour of his skin the 'name' of his authority and mastery. There is no humanitarian solution in this poem to the system of power by birthright. There is only the possibility of breaking the system, by killing the child who will bear the name of a long line of fathers: the first Pilgrim Fathers and 'their hunter sons' (204). Such language is explicit. This is a rule of fathers and sons, and the black woman can only refuse to perpetuate it. She buries the white child in the black earth, and immediately she is free again to sing the other 'name': 'I sate down smiling there and sung / The song I learnt in my maidenhood' (188-9).

The name of the father is thus, on the one hand, the sign of inherited right to power. But it is also, on the other hand, a principle of inspiration. The slave sings her black lover's 'name instead of a song', and it remains, behind all her 'various notes,' simply 'the same, the same!' This idea of the name as an external source of creative power is one which recurs in Barrett Browning's verse, and in **'The Runaway Slave'** it glancingly suggests a theory of poetry in which the man's name is needed to steady the woman's words. The name of the lover is the *raison d'être* of the woman's love-song, but it remains secret in order that the song should go on. This need for the one name behind all common names is expressed in one of the **Sonnets from the Portuguese,** for instance, where Elizabeth Barrett writes:

And this . . . this lute and song . . . loved
   yesterday,
(The singing angels know) are only dear
Because thy name moves right in what they
   say.

                      (Sonnet VII)[24]

Poetry is authorised by the one 'name' which might put an end to all naming if it were spoken, but which, unspoken, is like a muse, drawing the poet's words in desire towards itself.

However, in Barrett Browning's imagination, the name which holds her in its power and which she more often sings is that of the father. **'The Runaway Slave'** rejects the name of the line of white fathers, and would supplant it with the name of the lover, thus

implicitly reversing the romance of the earlier ballads. But in many other poems, which have not the political guilt and the personal freedom of this one, the daughter's creativity needs the name of the father to give authority to her verse. 'No name can e'er on tablet shine, / My father! more belov'd than *thine*!' (11-12). This early personal declaration of dependence in **'To My Father on His Birthday'** is never fully revoked. But it is never again so gladly celebrated. That fatherhood is a sign which supports a religious and political imperialism is a fact which Barrett Browning knows and forcefully condemns. But that it is a sign of creative power which the daughter admires and envies is a fact with which she must continue to struggle.

'Papa would laugh at me if he stood near; he who always laughs whenever I say "I am busy,"—laughs like Jove with superior amusement. As if people could possibly be busy with rhymes . . .' ([**Letters to Elizabeth Barrett Browning Addressed to Richard Hengist Horne**, 2 vols., ed. R. S. T. Mayer (London, 1876-77)], II, 284). Although she courted her father's attention and her father's smile as the reward of her writing, it seems that Mr Barrett had little appreciation of his daughter's poems, and that he was often inclined to laugh at her. Yet, that he 'laughs like Jove' suggests something also of the attraction of his power. He remains a high god in his very aloofness and mockery. He is the philistine and thunderous Jove, who must be continually supplicated and won. Like some authoritarian, unbending muse, he inspires constant effort in order to be moved. His smile is hard to gain. But more often than his smile, it is that other characteristic of his nature which awaits the daughter poet: his thunder.

'Only one person holds the thunder—& I shall be thundered at; I shall not be reasoned with' (**Letters: 1845-1846,** I, 318-19), Elizabeth wrote in trepidation to Robert, on hearing his proposal to confront her father with the truth about his love for her. On another occasion her fear of that thunder proved justified when Mr Barrett, discovering that Robert's visit had been prolonged during a storm, furiously admonished his daughter, and looked, to her, all the time 'as if the thunder had passed into him' (**Letters: 1845-1846,** II, 922). He could seem the very incarnation of that elemental energy to which she was so nervously sensitive. 'I never wait to enquire whether it thunders to the left or the right, to be frightened most ingloriously' (**Letters: 1845-1846,** I, 119), she confided to Robert. One of her rare memories of her mother is of a 'sweet, gentle nature, which the thunder a little turned from its sweetness' (**Letters: 1845-1846,** II, 1012). The high prerogative of Jove is not only to laugh at small things 'with superior amusement', but also to spoil or destroy them with his thunderbolt.

Yet, in spite of her constitutional terror of storms and in spite of her abhorrence of the moral violence of her father, Barrett Browning, as a poet, is intrigued and envious of the power he wields. His name and his thunder are signs of an authority which, imaginatively, she desires to make her own. The power of the creator-god is like the power of the Romantic poet. In both cases, it is associated with the thunder and lightning of the storm. The daughter poet's desire for her father is not only a desire to court his smile or speak his name; it is also a desire to overcome her fear and steal his thunder.

'**The Tempest**' (1833) is an early poem, based on an actual storm which occurred in 1826. Elizabeth Barrett wrote it in her twenties. However, the differences between the storm which she describes in a letter and the events of the poem are interesting. In the original storm, the young poet stood transfixed at the window, from where she witnessed the lightning strike a large old tree, 'within two hundred yards' of where she was standing. Some time later, news reached her of the deaths of 'two young women' (*Letters: 1845-1846,* I, 119-20) who had also been struck. In '**The Tempest**', however, she makes some strategic changes. First, the speaker goes out into the storm and rejoices in its violence; secondly, the two women are replaced by a single male character; and thirdly, this victim becomes mysteriously known to the speaker. There is thus an emotional nexus in the poem which is new, and which is both startlingly intimate and tantalisingly unspecific. This has led critics to suggest that '**The Tempest**' is a highly autobiographical poem, and that the male victim of the storm is Elizabeth's beloved brother Edward,[25] or else her father.[26] The theme and imagery point strongly to the latter. It was her father's fanciful, metal-spired house, Hope End, which seemed to Elizabeth designed to attract all the lightnings of heaven. She associated that father, throughout her life, with the thunderous and violent god Jove. Furthermore, it was that same father who looked with scorn and impatience on her own fear of storms, and who thus seemed to put into question her Romantic 'pretension to poetry' (*Letters: 1845-1846,* I, 119). The evidence of the letters suggests that the imagery of thunder and lightning was often linked in Elizabeth's mind with the thought of her godly, authoritative father.

However, '**The Tempest**' is interesting, not just because it seems to enact a private drama of revenge, but because it enacts an early version of the literary drama which becomes peculiarly Barrett Browning's own. Its uncanny confusion of the sources of literal and creative power, of domination and inspiration, makes it the first of many poems in which she both acknowledges and repudiates the heritage of her fathers—her real father and her Romantic 'grandfathers'. It is impossible to separate the poem's intriguingly private and autobiographical elements from its public and literary ostentation.

'**The Tempest**' begins like a showy poetical exercise. The high-sounding, derivative rhetoric of the first lines presents a contrast between the brooding silence of Nature and the incipient violence of the storm. Within this strained register, however, there develops a gender distinction that is crucial. 'Nature', which is 'All dumb' (21), is presented as female, while the thunder is described as 'martial' (24) and male. The one is fearful, inarticulate and passive, while the other has a violent, sounding power. This contrast is then offered as a choice to the speaker. To be 'dumb' like Nature or to rage like the storm is a choice which places the poem in the tradition of the Romantic ode, and immediately turns the narrator into a would-be poet. 'Writing poetry', Margaret Homans suggests, 'would seem to require of the writer everything that Mother Nature is not.'[28] The speaker of '**The Tempest**' duly rejects the example of 'dumb' Nature, and invokes the Romantically expressive force of 'the martial thunder'.

The advent of the storm is then greeted in an enthusiastic and lofty poetical address:

> Was not my spirit gladden'd, as with wine,
> To hear the iron rain, and view the mark
> Of battle on the banner of the clouds?
> Did I not hearken for the battle-cry,
> And rush along the bowing woods to meet
> The riding Tempest—skyey cataracts
> Hissing around him with rebellion vain?
> Yea! and I lifted up my glorying voice
> In an 'All hail;' when, wildly resonant,
>   . . . the thunder cried . . .
>
>   (37-45, 48)

This embarrassment of Romantic voices at the climax of the poem betrays the creative anxiety that lies behind its composition. The thunder does not intimidate, but inspires speech equal to its own. Like Shelley, in the 'Ode to the West Wind', this speaker goes out to meet and match the power of the elements. 'Yea! and I lifted up my glorying voice' is an ambitious attempt to rival the earlier poet's sublime inspiration. That Elizabeth Barrett's is all a storm of words might be excused by her relative youth and immaturity. Nonetheless, the engagingly derivative poeticisms in which she confidently relates this alternative story of the storm are themselves a witness to the element of creative competition in the poem. It was, after all, as she admitted many years later, precisely her fear of thunder which threatened to undermine her high 'pretension to poetry'.

The elevated address '"All hail"' mimics the moment of inspiration in the Romantic ode, when collaboration with some external power proves inner imaginative potential. The rhetoric of this passage rides exuberantly on the *idea* of such a collaboration. However, the interest of **'The Tempest'** lies not so much in its cheerful appropriation of Romantic voices to proclaim its success, as in the way that its brave energy fails. Having triumphantly asserted the right to speak with a voice of 'thunder', the narrator does not experience the inner ebbing of energy which afflicts Shelley, but a starkly literal confrontation:

> All hail unto the lightning! hurriedly
> His lurid arms are glaring through the air,
> Making the face of heav'n to show like hell!
> Let him go breathe his sulphur stench
>   about,
> And, pale with death's own mission, lord
>   the storm!
> Again the gleam—the glare: I turn'd to hail
> Death's mission: at my feet there lay the
>   dead!
> The dead—the dead lay there!
>
>   (52-9)

There is a hint of moral accountability here, which is unlike anything that has gone before. The Wordsworthian 'gleam' does not turn to sad vanishings, but to a destructive 'glare', the effect of which is mercilessly literal: 'The dead—the dead lay there!'

In one sense, this is just queasily melodramatic. But in another sense, the catastrophe follows a sinister logic which cannot easily be dispelled. The consequences of daring to dissociate oneself from Nature and share the power of the storm, it seems, are death. Such heavy consequences necessarily comment on the magnitude of the act of speaking in this poem. 'Mother Nature is hardly powerless', writes Margaret Homans, 'but, enormous as her powers are, they are not the ones that her daughters want if they are to become poets.'[29] The sheer weight of the penalty that comes of speaking betrays the sex of the anonymous narrator: 'at my feet there lay the dead!' Just as she turns to hail the lightning, the *furor poeticus* of her Romantic predecessors, this speaker finds that the human consequences are laid at her feet. The storm of creativity, for Elizabeth Barrett, kills.

The melodramatic crisis of the poem clearly derives from a subtle association of two kinds of power in the poet's consciousness: the power to speak and the power to destroy. Her own youthful 'anxiety of authorship'[30] is one which recognises a strangely literal threat in the desire for creative power. The reason why Elizabeth Barrett's early attempt at the grand style of Romanticism ends in this human disaster is to be found in the unspoken fact that, for all its rhetorical derivativeness, the speaker of this poem is still a woman. This woman's 'pretension to poetry' has to overcome certain internal and external obstacles, which the poem then strangely and frighteningly realises.

The power of speech, however, does not bring down some random victim; it brings down one who is intimately known to the speaker:

> Albeit such darkness brooded all around,
> I had dread knowledge that the open eyes
> Of that dead man were glaring up to mine,
> With their unwinking, unexpressive stare;
> And mine I could not shut nor turn away.
> The man was my familiar.
>
>   (85-90)

The significance of this movement from a public drama of literary ambition to a private drama of intimate emotional recognition is supplied by the suppressed idea of the father. While the thunder in one sense suggests the voices of the Romantic poets, with whom Elizabeth Barrett would compete, it is also, confusingly, the sign of one particular male presence, with whom it is dangerous and unnatural to compete: 'Only one person holds the thunder.' The new and tortured logic of this would-be Romantic poem links the poetic ambition to speak with a private drama in which the heart cannot afford to rival, in power, the object of its *'tenderest and holiest affection'* (Dedication to *Poems,* 1844).

'The Tempest' thus enacts the female poet's struggle to speak with a power that is not naturally her own. She refuses to be like Mother Nature, 'All dumb'. Instead, she chooses to share the thunder of the fathers: the father god, the father poets, and also, the father himself—the 'familiar'. However, to win this struggle for speech is to know, at the very moment of triumph, the cost too dear. It is this 'dread knowledge' which the poem betrays. The speaker, in the end, is shown to have harboured a death-wish towards her victim in the very act of stealing the thunder for her speech. The idea of her guilt then comes brilliantly and nightmarishly true in the figure of the dead man at her feet. Such guilt, the poem tells, is the inevitable concomitant, for the female poet, of desiring to *say* so much.

In **'The Tempest'** the threat to the power of the father comes not from any rival lover, as it does in the ballads, but from poetry. Yet the drama of influence which it expresses is similarly triangular. At about the same time that she wrote **'The Tempest'** Elizabeth Barrett also composed a poem which she, fortunately, never published, called **'Leila: A Tale'**. It tells the story of a girl, Leila, who falls in love with a dying minstrel boy. His last request to her, before his death, is that she should use her influence to free his imprisoned father. She does so; but the shocking and unexpected outcome of this generous deed is that the boy's father acts out some ancient vow of revenge against Leila's own father, and kills him. Curiously, however, the guilt remains entirely the daughter's: 'For still her wandering lips distracted say / "He died—I murdered him"' (p. 111).[31]

The emotional logic of the poem is clear. By desiring a rival love, Leila has betrayed her father. But there is another implication to the story. By desiring a minstrel boy, Leila reveals a wish for something else which subtly threatens her father: a wish for the boy's art of song. Behind the unconvincing melancholy tale of misplaced honour, there is an undercurrent message of literary betrayal which **'The Tempest'** then develops and exaggerates.

In both poems, the father is killed by some subtle volition in the daughter who has pretensions to art. The connection is obscure, but it recurs with the force of a conviction in Barrett Browning's work. From her earliest poems to ***Aurora Leigh,*** the figure of the father is imagined as dead. But the timing of his death is one which resonantly implicates the daughter. He is dead, because the daughter is no longer a child, because she desires a rival lover and, finally, because she seeks the power of speech. To be a woman and a poet is to threaten the father's power. As a result, the very condition of the poem's writing is the realisation of that threat: '"He died—I murdered him."'

In a passage from a much later work, ***Casa Guidi Windows*** (1851), which was written after Elizabeth's escape to Italy, the connection between literary influence and lost paternal love is made nostalgically obvious. Barrett Browning writes:

> Could I sing this song,
>   If my dead masters had not taken heed
> To help the heavens and earth to make me strong,
>   As the wind ever will find out some reed
> And touch it to such issues as belong
>   To such a frail thing? None may grudge the Dead
> Libations from full cups. Unless we choose
>   To look back to the hills behind us spread,
> The plains before us sadden and confuse;
>   If orphaned, we are disinherited.
> (Part I, 432-41)[32]

What begins as a tribute to her 'dead masters' turns into a quiet commemoration of her own father, from whom she fears to be 'orphaned' and thus 'disinherited'. Masters and father are subtly confused in the motif of inspiration: 'the wind' which will fill the 'reed' of poetry. The speaker's fear of being an orphan is in one sense confirmed in the statement that the 'full cups' of her imagination's offerings are for 'the Dead'.

But it is to be 'orphaned' *even* of 'the Dead' that Barrett Browning fears. For as long as those 'Dead' are still present to her imagination, the landscape of her future will keep its gladness and its meaning. The idea of 'the Dead' protects her from being quite alone in landscapes which 'sadden and confuse'; in landscapes which have no direction and no residing spirit. If the daughter loses that sense of 'dead masters', and particularly the sense of one, the 'familiar', she will be disoriented and sad in her literary endeavours. Her imagination needs the spirits of 'the Dead' if the world is not to appear forlorn and empty. If they are absent, she is 'orphaned' in the imagination; she is left without an external source of power—a muse.

Paradoxically, however, it is this very sense of being imaginatively 'disinherited' which will gave to Barrett Browning's later poetry its distinctive tone. To be fatherless, or to be without a beloved object for her poetry's 'Libations from full cups', is to be in a place which is deserted and senseless. Whereas the absence of the mother will be a cause for indifference in the child poet who can be sufficient to herself, the absence of the father will be a cause of desolation and uncertainty. It is this sense of absence, of having been both 'orphaned' and 'disinherited', which marks Barrett Browning's mature poems, and which marks especially the long, daughterly quest of ***Aurora Leigh***. Here, the father comes to seem, not seductively faithful and dead, as in the ballads, but simply absent. Barrett Browning's most important and most successful poem commemorates the figure of a father whom, in the end, she knows she does not need. From this harsh disinheritance comes her woman's strength.

Notes

[1] Elizabeth Barrett Browning, 'To My Father on His Birthday', in [*The Complete Works of Elizabeth Barrett Browning,* 6 vols., ed. Charlotte Porter and Helen A. Clarke (New York: Thomas Y. Crowell, 1900)] 1, 100-1.

[2] Virginia Woolf, *Three Guineas* (1938; Harmondsworth, Penguin Books, 1977), p.149.

[3] Dorothy Hewlett, *Elizabeth Barrett Browning: A Life* (1952; New York, Octagon Books, 1972), p.47.

[4] Gardner B. Taplin, *The Life of Elizabeth Barrett Browning* (London, John Murray, 1957), p.19.

[5] Elaine Showalter, *A Literature of Their Own: British Women Novelists from Brontë to Lessing* (London, Virago, 1978), p.61.

[6] Simone de Beauvoir, *The Second Sex* (1949; Harmondsworth, Penguin Books, 1972), p.314.

[7] Ellen Moers, *Literary Women* (London, The Women's Press, 1978), pp. 173-210.

[8] See Madelyn Gutwirth, *Madame de Staël, Novelist: The Emergence of the Artist as Woman* (Urbana, Chicago and London, University of Illinois Press, 1978), p.43.

[9] Ibid., p.42.

[10] Madame de Staël, *Corinne ou L'Italie* (Paris, 1845), p.13.

[11] Ibid., p.259.

[12] Michael Meredith, 'The Wounded Heroine: Elizabeth Barrett's Sophocles', *Studies in Browning and His Circle,* 3 (1975), 1-12, p.8.

[13] *The George Eliot Letters,* ed. Gordon S. Haight (9 vols, London, Oxford University Press, 1954-78), I, 283-4.

[14] Simone de Beauvoir, op. cit., p.315.

[15] Elizabeth Barrett Browning, 'Dedication: To My Father', in *Complete Works,* II, 142-3.

[16] Harold Bloom, *The Anxiety of Influence: A Theory of Poetry* (London, Oxford University Press, 1973), p.63.

[17] Sandra Gilbert and Susan Gubar, *The Madwoman in the Attic* (New Haven and London, Yale University Press, 1979), p.47.

[18] Joanne Feit Diehl, ' "Come Slowly—Eden": An Exploration of Women Poets and their Muse', *Signs,* 3 (1978), p.576.

[19] Elizabeth Barrett Browning, 'A Romance of the Ganges', in *Complete Works,* II, 29-37.

[20] Elizabeth Barrett Browning, 'The Lay of the Brown Rosary', in *Complete Works,* II, 254-75.

[21] William Wordsworth, 'Three years she grew . . .', in *Wordsworth: Poetical Works,* ed. Thomas Hutchinson, rev. Ernest de Selincourt (London, Oxford University Press, 1936), p.148.

[22] Frederick Engels, *The Origin of the Family: Private Property and the State,* intro. Eleanor Burke Leacock (London, Lawrence & Wishart, 1972), p.121.

[23] Elizabeth Barrett Browning, 'The Runaway Slave at Pilgrim's Point', in *Complete Works,* III, 160-70.

[24] Elizabeth Barrett Browning, *Sonnets from the Portuguese,* in *Complete Works,* III, 227-48.

[25] Betty Miller, *Robert Browning: A Portrait* (London, John Murray, 1952), p.92.

[26] Alethea Hayter, *Mrs Browning: A Poet's Work and its Setting* (London, Faber, 1962), p.26.

[27] Elizabeth Barrett Browning, 'The Tempest', in *Complete Works,* I, 122-8.

[28] Margaret Homans, *Women Writers and Poetic Identity* (Princeton, N.J., Princeton University Press, 1980), p.17.

[29] Ibid., p.16.

[30] Gilbert and Gubar, op. cit., p.51.

[31] Elizabeth Barrett Browning, 'Leila: A Tale', in *New Poems by Robert Browning and Elizabeth Barrett Browning,* ed. Frederic G. Kenyon (London, 1914), pp. 83-111.

[32] Elizabeth Barrett Browning, *Casa Guidi Windows: A Poem, in Two Parts,* in *Complete Works,* III, 249-313.

Deborah Byrd (essay date 1987)

SOURCE: "Combating an Alien Tyranny: Elizabeth Barrett Browning's Evolution as a Feminist Poet," in *Browning Institute Studies,* Vol. 15, 1987, pp. 23-41.

[*In the essay that follows, Byrd explores Browning's poetry as a protest against patriarchy and an attempt to establish a feminist literary community.*]

> The drama of woman lies in this conflict between the fundamental aspirations of every subject (ego)—who always regards the self as the essential—and the compulsions of a situation in which she is the inessential. (Simone de Beauvoir xxxiv)

> The name [of poet]
> Is royal, and to sign it like a queen
> Is what I dare not,—though some royal blood
> Would seem to tingle in me now and then,
> With sense of power and ache.
> (*Aurora Leigh* I. 934-38)

> 'Tis Antidote to turn—
> To Tomes of solid Witchcraft—
> (Emily Dickinson, #593)

"Speed and energy, forthrightness and complete self-confidence—these are the qualities that hold us enthralled" as we read Elizabeth Barrett Browning's *Aurora Leigh,* wrote Virginia Woolf in 1932 (I. 212).

Robert Browning.

poems, it is important to identify the experiences that furthered her development of a feminist consciousness and aesthetic. Foremost among these experiences were the poet's encounters with literary texts.[1] Aware of Barrett Browning's erudition, numerous scholars have drawn attention to specific ways in which the poet draws upon or swerves from male writers, especially the acknowledged "masters" of European verse.[2] But with the exception of a few studies of Barrett Browning's debts to Sand, DeStaël, Gaskell, and Charlotte Brontë, surprisingly little has been written about the poet's artistic interaction with women authors, particularly women poets.[3]

It is quite true that Barrett Browning's favorite poets were men. She believed that England had produced no "poetess before Joanna Baillie [1762-1851]—poetess in the true sense," and she regarded no nineteenth-century woman poet as highly as she did Wordsworth, Byron, Browning, and Tennyson; (Kenyon 1:30). Barrett Browning's dissatisfaction with English women poets does not mean, however, that she did not participate in a female poetic tradition.[4] As numerous scholars have shown, the nineteenth-century woman writer generally searched for and was empowered by her discovery of literary foremothers and sisters. Even when she chose to modify or depart from the practices of her female predecessors and contemporaries, she often defined herself in relation to other literary women—attempting to avoid making their mistakes, trying to accomplish where they had failed.[5]

Barrett Browning was no exception. She was an avid reader of poems, essays, and fiction by women and took a keen interest in the lives of other professional women writers.[6] Moreover, as a poet she frequently imitated or responded critically to literary texts by other women, regarding such "Tomes of solid Witchcraft" as sources of sustenance as well as instruction. The women poets of her own century and country played a particularly crucial role in Barrett Browning's development, for when she began emulating these poets in the late 1830s she took the first step towards transforming herself into a woman-identified poet.[7]

Throughout her career Barrett Browning engaged in conversations with writers of both sexes, particularly other poets. Identifying the texts she read and chose to respond to is important, for it can help account for the marked changes in style and vision that characterize each distinctive stage of her career. I cannot in short compass describe all the ways in which this self-proclaimed "book-ferret" was influenced by other writers (Raymond and Sullivan 1:117). But I will provide an overview of Barrett Browning's poetic evolution, drawing attention to the ways in which her aesthetic principles and practices change as her reading habits and literary tastes alter.

As Woolf points out, these qualities emanate not so much from Aurora as from her creator, whose strong and lively presence so pervades the poem that "Again and again . . . Aurora the fictitious seems to be throwing light upon Elizabeth the actual. . . . [making it] impossible for the most austere of critics not sometimes to touch the flesh when his [*sic*] eyes should be fixed upon the page" (212). And as Woolf observes, the "flesh" the critic touches is that of a woman who knows that the royal blood of poets flows through her veins. "Elizabeth the actual" is a subject, speaking boldly of the world as she perceives and experiences it.

Wit and verve, directness and energy, an authorial voice radiating a firm sense of self and a firm sense of purpose—these are the salient characteristics not only of *Aurora Leigh* but of most of the poems that Barrett Browning wrote after 1845. In such works the poet "use[s] the woman's figures naturally" and often is "plain at speech, direct in purpose" when critiquing patriarchy (*AL* 8. 1127-31); in some instances, she even transforms poetic forms that her contemporaries considered the exclusive province of men into vehicles for the expression of female and feminist concerns. Since Barrett Browning's reputation as a major Victorian poet rests primarily on these late woman-centered

Initially imitating women novelists, then treading closely in the footsteps of her poetic forefathers, in the late 1830s Barrett Browning turned her attention once again to women writers, this time to women poets. In this transitional stage of her career, she sometimes modeled her poetic efforts on those of other women; at other times she attempted, not always successfully, to synthesize aspects of the two distinct (though of course related) poetic traditions to which she was heir. At the height of her powers, Barrett Browning came to view her task as that of writing as "a woman & man in one," a feat she believed her friend Mary Russell Mitford and her idol George Sand had accomplished. She brings into harmony the potentially discordant elements of her dual literary heritage, writing authentically of her own and other women's experiences with the "forthrightness and self-confidence" she considered to be more characteristic of male than of female writers.[8]

Surprising as it may seem, the first stage of this precocious poet's literary career spans the brief period from 1814 to 1817, ending when the eleven-year-old became the pupil of Daniel McSwiney. In 1814, at the age of eight, Barrett Browning was designated by her father "Poet-Laureat [*sic*] of Hope End" (Kelley and Hudson 1:10), a position she took seriously for years, considering it her duty to compose poems on birthdays and other important family occasions. Yet it was not until the age of eleven that the Poet Laureate exhibited a decided preference for composing in verse. The longest and most ambitious works of her childhood are written in prose, not surprisingly, for once she had outgrown her taste for fairy tales, reading and "studying" novels became Elizabeth's "most delightful" pastime (Kelley and Hudson 1:349-50). Significantly, the novels that she knew and liked best (novels generally selected by her mother) were by women authors such as Maria Edgeworth, Charlotte Smith, and Amelia Opie. Barrett Browning particularly admired the fiction of Edgeworth, in which the woman who gives free rein to her passions and "forgets womanly duties in the personality of a man" is criticized, and the young woman who exhibits "too much sense" to be considered a "heroine" is presented as a character worthy of emulation (Kelley and Hudson 1:33-34).[9]

As long as she sought to emulate women novelists, and as long as she wrote for as well as about women (most of these early works were directed to Elizabeth's mother or other female relatives), Barrett Browning could write with both authenticity and confidence. Without anxiety she could imagine the kind of woman she would like to become, could attempt to write her own story, to chart the course her future would take. But in 1817 she suddenly began to regard novels as a form of light entertainment and decided to seek her fame as a writer of poems and essays (Kelley and Hudson 1:33, 350).

Had she begun to read and imitate poems and nonfiction prose by women, Barrett Browning night have continued to assert her subjectivity and might not have suffered—or suffered as intensely—from that female malady that Sandra Gilbert and Susan Gubar term "the anxiety of authorship" (*Madwoman* 48-49). But internalizing the patriarchal standards of literary excellence espoused by McSwiney, she began to study and imitate her poetic forefathers—only to feel "the whole extent of my own immense & mortifying inferiority" (Kelley and Hudson 1:351). Essentially, Barrett Browning began to undergo the process that Judith Fetterley calls "immasculation," began to experience

> not simply the powerlessness which derives from not seeing one's experience articulated, clarified, and legitimized in art, but more significantly, the powerlessness which results from the endless division of self against self, the consequence of the invocation to identify as male while being reminded that to be male—to be universal— . . . is to be *not female* (xiii).[10]

Thus during the second stage of her literary career, which roughly spans the years 1818 to 1838, Barrett Browning writes as a divided self. The fragmentary **"Essay on Woman"** (ca. 1822) shows that she was quite capable of identifying and criticizing writers who espoused partriarchal values. Writing as a disciple of Mary Wollstonecraft, she openly reproaches poets who depict women as timid and subservient creatures, poets who "Paint . . . The trembling, melting voice of tenderness, / And all that Mother, Sister, Wife impart / To nurture, solace and subdue the heart" of man.[11] Proclaiming that her goal is "To bend to nobler thoughts the British fair" by "Found[ing] the proud path, where . . . [Woman] stands the equal of her Master Man," Barrett Browning leads us to expect that henceforth she will present women as resourceful and self-reliant beings.

Yet it was not until the late 1830s that Barrett Browning began to compose poems in which female characters act assertively and independently. Indeed, most of the poems she wrote before 1838 center on the experiences of men. When the poet does write about real or imaginary women, she generally depicts them as relative creatures, as associates of men of courage and nobility of character. For example, she praises Riego's widow for behaving in a way that enhances our appreciation of her patriot husband's integrity and valor, urges a young girl to heed the advice her father gives her as she sits meekly at his feet, and tells Bettine, "The Child-Friend of Goethe," that having her existence acknowledged by a man of genius should adequately compensate her for any suffering she has experienced or any sacrifices she has made as the poet's worshiper.[12] Moreover, in the few poems in which men are criticized for treating women like chattel or for being fickle or self-serving, women tend to die of grief or passively bemoan their fate; the poet regards such characters sympathetically, but she presents them as helpless victims rather than as active combatants of patriarchy.[13]

Most of these poems about women are sentimental, lacking the emotional power that comes from writing authentically out of one's own experience of the world. Barrett Browning had written elsewhere that she spurned "that subserviency of opinion which is generally considered necessary to feminine softness" and regarded as the most "odious" of creatures "a damsel famed in story for a superabundance of sensibility" (Kelley and Hudson 1:354-55). Moreover, she did not sit humbly at the feet of her own father, nor was she content to achieve fame as the adoring child-friend of the classical scholars Boyd and Price.[14]

To understand why it took Barrett Browning over three decades to write poems that reflect the reality of her own and other women's lives, one must turn once more to **"Essay on Woman."** Despite its overtly feminist themes, the poem suggests that henceforth Barrett Browning often will write as a male-identified poet. Indeed, she does so to a certain extent in this poem, for although she refutes Pope's belief in woman's inferiority, she feels compelled to demonstrate that she has mastered "Pope's" verse form, the heroic couplet. In other words, Barrett Browning seems to assume that to be a great poet she must compete with male predecessors on their terms, must excel in the poetic modes that men have considered most valuable. Accepting the patriarchal notion that some verse forms are inherently more noble than others, she apparently does not realize that the idea of a hierarchy of literary forms historically has been used to disparage and to exclude from the literary canon much of the verse written by women.

Or perhaps Barrett Browning did realize that women poets do not fare well when judged by patriarchal standards of literary excellence. Perhaps she failed to finish **"Essay on Woman"** because as a teenager, she was incapable of positing critical standards that would allow her to argue persuasively that the accomplishments of her poetic foremothers were as significant as those of her forefathers. After all, of the four women authors cited in the poem only Anne Dacier and Hannah More wrote in verse, and evidence suggests that Barrett Browning considered both to be second-rate authors.[15] Moreover, if the poet truly believed More and Dacier to be women of genius (as the final stanza of the poem implies), why does she describe her own task as that of *founding*—rather than treading in or enlarging—the poetic path in which woman stands the equal of man? And why did she not complete the poem, giving her predecessors the opportunity to reply to the charge that women, including women poets, are doomed to sigh in obscurity?

I believe that Barrett Browning failed to finish **"Essay on Woman"** because in the process of writing the poem, she came to the dismal and frightening conclusion that none of her literary foremothers had been a poet of major stature and that therefore the burden of proving that women could excel in poetic composition rested squarely on her own shoulders. Convinced that poets could learn much from imitating their precursors but not wanting to follow in the footsteps of poets whose works she regarded as second-rate, until the late 1830s Barrett Browning equated poetic excellence with and measured her own progress as a poet in terms of her ability to equal or best the literary efforts of the male poets whose artistic achievements she most admired. Not surprisingly, she found it almost impossible to depict women as fully autonomous beings and to express authoritatively her own vision of the world while drawing upon and responding almost exclusively to poetic texts by men, texts that generally convey the authors' assumption that the perspective, concerns, and experiences of men are central and quintessentially human.

At the height of her powers Barrett Browning was to rewrite in original and daring ways and from a woman's point of view some of the "masterpieces" of the Western European poetic tradition. But as works such as *The Battle of Marathon, An Essay on Mind,* and *The Seraphim* reveal, the poet's earliest attempts to write long poems led her to ignore, marginalize, or trivialize the experiences of women.[16] The fact that Barrett Browning wrote such poems at all, however, testifies to her audacity and rebelliousness. For in composing epics, verse dramas, and long philosophical-didactic poems, the poet was deliberately violating the existing norms governing the relationship between gender and genre. Refusing to restrict herself to the portrayal of domestic life and the expression of the affections, she insisted on being read and judged as a poet rather than as a "poetess"—insisted on writing about subjects that interested her, even if these subjects were ones about which a middle-class Victorian woman was supposed to be uninformed.[17]

In the third stage of her literary career, represented primarily by the two-volume collection of 1844, Barrett Browning continues to allude and respond to her poetic forefathers. But having discovered and begun to participate in a female poetic tradition, she no longer is so overwhelmed by the influence of male precursors that she adopts a male perspective on reality. On the contrary, she generally writes as a woman-identified woman, proclaiming that her central subject—the consciousness of woman—is a subject "more expressible by a woman than a man."[18]

"An Island," one of the best poems of the *Seraphim* volume, helps to account for Barrett Browning's transition from an immasculated to a woman-identified poet. In this poem a woman dreams of escaping from the violent and hierarchically-ordered world of patriarchy; she longs to settle with a few select others on an island which has neither weapons nor rulers. This peaceful and egalitarian island is clearly a motherland: it is a realm reserved for "Those who would [ex]change man's voice and use / For [a female] Nature's way and tone," a land of undulating, breast-like hills where maternal cows gaze approvingly upon "The warm mouths milking them for love" (111-112, 72). If she lived in this nurturing environment, the speaker proclaims, she could compose poems freely and easily, almost "Unconsciously" (143). She predicts that in the sweetness of their music her songs would rival those of Pindar, Æschylus, and Homer; indeed, she avers that her poetry would be superior to that of her forefathers because she would depict a world of harmony rather than one of strife and discord. In the concluding stanzas, however, the woman not only sadly acknowledges that her "island-place" does not exist, but she also expresses her fear that her fantasy of a world in which women's creativity is valued and nurtured is the product of a sinful mind, the dream of a woman who should be content to accept the world and the role that God has chosen for her.

Despite its ambiguous conclusion, **"An Island"** reveals that by 1836 Barrett Browning longed to ally herself with "two or three" who shared both her utopian dreams and the dissatisfaction with patriarchy that had prompted them. Fortunately, at about the time she composed **"An Island"** the poet found such an ally in Mary Russell Mitford, a writer who played an essential role in Barrett Browning's evolution as a feminist poet. For although she was to remark in 1850 that she could "never *count* upon her [Mitford] in poetry, of which, in my mind, she does not apprehend the essential qualities," it certainly was Mitford who urged Barrett Browning to study and consider emulating such popular and prolific poets as Letitia Landon, Felicia Hemans, Ann Barbauld, Mary Howitt, Joanna Baillie, Eliza Cook, Fanny Kemble Butler, Sara Clarke Lippincott, Anna Seward, Caroline Norton, Georgiana Bennet, and Maria Jane Jewsbury—poets from whose failures as well as successes Barrett Browning was to learn a great deal (Heydon and Kelley 20).[19] Moreover, it was in the pages of *Findens' Tableaux,* which Mitford edited in the late 1830s and early 1840s, that Barrett Browning first seems to have experimented self-consciously with the literary modes and devices that characterize some of the best and most representative poems by late eighteenth- and early nineteenth-century women writers.[20]

It is important to note, however, that Barrett Browning's debts to these poets are quite different in kind from her debts to her poetic forefathers. For rather than borrowing details from a particular poem or entering into a dialogical relationship with a specific female precursor, Barrett Browning writes about the subjects which interested her literary sisters and does so by using the tropes, imagery, and rhetorical strategies that distinguish much of the poetry written by women of the period 1780-1850 from that composed by men of the age. When drawing upon English women poets Barrett Browning generally responds not to particular texts but to an entire body of poetry, working within the confines of and expanding the possibilities of recognizable and distinctively female *types* of poems.

The female poetic tradition in which Barrett Browning began to participate is one in which authors take as their central subject matter and draw their metaphors from the lives of women. It is a tradition in which authors attempt to define the rights and duties of the Christian woman, portray the struggles and accomplishments of women artists, evaluate heterosexual relationships, depict the benefits of sisterhood, examine the process of female socialization, and ponder the degree to which women do and should participate in the economic and political life of the country. In addition, it is a tradition in which authors sometimes demonstrate their awareness that the fabric of Western society is woven of the intertwined threads of sexism, racism, and imperialism. Most English women poets of the period 1780-1850 write not only of the subjection of women, but also—and sometimes simultaneously—of the plight of Blacks, Native Americans, Irish Catholics, the poor, and politically-oppressed nations of the past and present.

To be sure, none of the poets mentioned above was a consistently vocal critic; in fact, each wrote a number of poems in which woman is presented as fragile and pure, as the obedient helpmate or helpless victim of man. Yet each also wrote a number of "protest poems" in which patriarchal values and institutions are criticized, though usually in indirect and covert rather than explicit ways. For example, these poets generally attribute heroic stature not to their English contemporaries, but to individuals of distant times or places who attempt to subvert existing power structures. In other poems, particularly those with contemporary settings, they encode rebellious sentiments in seemingly conventional texts; in such works, statements that seem to endorse patriarchal ideology are voiced ironically or ambiguously or are called into question by the poem's imagery or structure.

As is revealed by such explicitly topical protest poems as **"The Cry of the Children"** and **"Lady Geraldine's Courtship,"** both of which appeared in the 1844 *Poems,* Barrett Browning soon was to become dissatisfied with such a palimpsestic method of recording her own and other women's concerns. Concluding that "puckerings in the silk," even when stitched by clever literary seamstresses, were more imprisoning than liberating, by late 1844 she was declaring to friends that in the future she was going to meet "face to face & without mask the Humanity [or Inhumanity?] of the age" (Kintner 1:31).[21] But in many of the poems published in the 1844 collection she uses the strategies of indirection as well as the tropes that characterize much of the verse of her poetic sisters and foremothers.

For example, these poets write frequently of a young girl's joyous appreciation of or an older woman's nostalgia for time spent alone—and usually creatively—in a bower, garden, or other spot in nature.[22] In such poems, the youthful female is not, like Tennyson's Lady of Shalott, "half sick of shadows" (71); on the contrary, she finds her privacy and her escape from social and domestic duties delightful. And the older woman does not, like the persona of Wordsworth's "Intimations Ode," celebrate and yearn for a time of "obstinate questionings / Of sense and outward things" (142-143). She *is* nostalgic, but what she laments is the loss of her belief that as an adult she could engage in meaningful, personally-chosen activities. Moreover, unlike the male personae of many of Wordsworth's poems, this middle-aged woman does not believe that she has received "Abundant recompense" for her loss ("Tintern Abbey" 88), nor does she characterize her experience as an inevitable and universal (that is, genderless) one. In **"The Lost Bower"** and **"The Romance of the Swan's Nest"** (1844), and **"Hector in the Garden"** (1846) Barrett Browning carries on this female tradition of articulating in a metaphorical and somewhat veiled way the sadness a woman experiences when she realizes that for women, the transition from childhood to adulthood generally entails a loss of hope, self-esteem, and imaginative freedom.

Similarly, in poems like **"The Romaunt of the Page"** and **"The Rhyme of the Duchess May,"** Barrett Browning follows her poetic sisters into the Middle Ages, often envisioned by female poets as a time in which at least some women had control over their property and destiny and the courage to venture into the "male" arenas of politics and war.[23] In such poems, Barrett Browning, like other women poets, uses an historical setting, the romance form, and in the case of **"The Romaunt of the Page,"** ambiguous wording to hide from the unsympathetic reader the fact that she is protesting against middle-class Victorian definitions of the good wife and good daughter. In these poems the poet urges her female readers, as Carlyle had urged male readers of *Sartor Resartus* and *Past and Present,* to cast off their ill-fitting clothes and to benefit from both the wisdom and the mistakes of their forebears, in this case foremothers.

Countless other poems in the 1844 collection—**"A Soul's Expression," "The Seraph and the Poet,"** **"Work and Contemplation," "The Lay of the Early Rose," "Wine of Cyprus,"** and the two sonnets to George Sand, for example—reveal that as Barrett Browning began to view herself as carrying on a female as well as male poetic tradition her conception of God and of the poet began to change, to become more woman-centered. Perhaps the poem that best reveals the poet's growing determination to assert her independence from her poetic forefathers is *A Drama of Exile.*

A poetic drama that depicts the frame of mind of Adam and Eve immediately after they have been expelled from the Garden of Eden, *A Drama of Exile* is far from being a consummate artistic whole. Yet it is an unsuccessful poem precisely because the poet is determined to wrestle with the massive figure of Milton, with whom she closely identifies as a Christian but whose view of woman's subordinate status she wishes to refute. The product of this struggle is a poem that contains conflicting views of woman's rights and duties, a drama in which characters lack internal consistency, and a work in which passages vary greatly in poetic power, fluidity and grace. But though *A Drama of Exile* is riddled with the kind of ambiguity that detracts from rather than contributes to a poem's artistic success, it is a key text in Barrett Browning's poetic evolution and a poem that gives us great insight into the anxieties suffered by the woman poet working in a patriarchal society and within a male-dominated literary tradition. The same can be said of **"The Lay of the Brown Rosary,"** a poem in which Barrett Browning unsuccessfully tries to fuse aspects of the female Gothic tradition with technical and thematic elements of poems by Keats, Wordsworth, and Coleridge.

If *Poems* of 1844 is the volume of a woman who is still suffering from anxieties of influence and who finds it somewhat "easier to gaze . . . On mournful masks and sad effigies / Than on real, live, weak creatures crushed by strong" (*Casa Guidi Windows* 1:46-48), *Poems* of 1850 is the volume of a poet who is drawing in a sophisticated way upon her dual poetic heritage, the work of a feminist who can be witty and playful as well as express righteous indignation. In **"The Runaway Slave at Pilgrim's Point"** Barrett Browning not only vehemently protests against slavery but also clearly spells out the connections between racism and sexism; in the companion poems **"A Woman's Shortcomings"** and **"A Man's Requirements,"** she humorously but with equal directness and artistic skill exposes inequities in relationships between Victorian women and men. Moreover, having married a man who shared her desire to identify and combat the evils of patriarchy, she has the courage to make public *Sonnets from the Portuguese,* a poem in which she honestly recounts the vacillation between feelings of fear and joy, self-abasement and self-worth, that she experienced when she began to fall in love with Browning.

Reaffirming in another 1850 poem that the reed rather than the trumpet is her emblem, Barrett Browning announces that henceforth she will be the voice of women, children, and the common man rather than blast forth the "hollow" sounds of "priest or king" (**"A Reed"** 3-4). Pan, whom the poet associates with freedom, eroticism, and egalitarianism, is not so dead as the last poem of the 1844 collection seems (but only seems) to declare him to be. Moreover, by re-adopting as her symbol the reed of Pan, the playmate of nymphs who was bested by the more aloof and refined Apollo, Barrett Browning prepares us for her attempt to "blow all class-walls level as Jericho's" (*Aurora Leigh* 9.932) and for the literal and meta-phorical union of female and male, pagan and Chris-tian, that is at the heart of her subsequent and greatest poems.

One of these poems is *Casa Guidi Windows*. Writing with confidence about contemporary European poli-tics, Barrett Browning unabashedly stakes her claim to a land into which most of her poetic foremothers had feared even to tread. In so doing, the poet weaves an ornate tapestry out of the three thematic strands that so frequently appear in her earlier poetry: the duties of the artist, the responsibilities of the Christian, and the rights of the oppressed. Having learned to value the wisdom and strength of mothers and to discriminate between good and bad fathers, in this poem Barrett Browning frankly and gratefully acknowledges her lit-erary debts to "dead masters" yet proclaims: "We do not serve the dead" (1.217). Similarly, Barrett Brown-ing the Christian invokes the aid of Christ and the Virgin Mary but castigates a Pope who has betrayed his charges, and Barrett Browning the citizen defends the dedicated freedom fighters of her adopted mother-land while exposing the cowardice of a "paternal Duke" and the hypocrisy and crass materialism of her pow-erful fatherland. Finally, Barrett Browning the feminist praises the Italian women and men who are working together to combat their oppressors, but bitterly notes that in "liberal nations" there is "No help for women sobbing out of sight / Because men made the laws" (2.638-39). Almost succumbing to despair at the poem's conclusion, she recovers faith in the possibil-ity of constructive change only when she remembers that some children, among them her own son, are being reared by parents committed to the establish-ment of a more egalitarian and just society.

In *Aurora Leigh,* an even more ambitious work, the formal and thematic characteristics of both male and female predecessors are welded into a unique, mag-nificent structure. A "verse novel" that owes much to the author's extensive reading of poems, fiction, and non-fiction prose by women; a first-person account of

the growth and development of a woman poet's mind; "a Don Juan, without the mockery & impurity" of Byron, "admitting of much philosophical dreaming & digression" but "having unity, as a work of art" (Raymond and Sullivan 3:49); and a distinctively fe-male envisioning of the kind of personal and societal paradise that has been lost and the means by which it may be regained, *Aurora Leigh* is certainly one of the most important long poems of the Victorian pe-riod. It also is one of the major works of the female literary tradition in English, for in *Aurora Leigh* the poet demonstrates that the epic mode can accommo-date the experiences, language, and viewpoint of women.

Having proclaimed in *Aurora Leigh* that it is the task of great poets to represent both the glory and the corruption of "this live, throbbing age" (5.203), Barrett Browning continues in *Poems Before Congress* to write openly about the controversial social and political events of her time. But rather than sharing with her readers the observations and meditations of a woman safely ensconced in a Florentine apartment, the poet ventures into the more public arenas of "Italy and the World" and explicitly directs her comments to those who have the power to shape world affairs. Praising rulers who are helping to "deliver" Italy from the womb of a nation that has failed to nurture her, paying tribute to one Italian woman who nurses with equal tenderness dying freedom fighters of varying nationalities, and praising another who not only makes French soldiers regard Italian women with respect but who also cre-ates an atmosphere in which French and Italian sol-diers are moved to kiss one another "mouth to mouth," in *Poems Before Congress* Barrett Browning boldly advances a notion that had been covertly suggested in the political poems of many of her poetic foremothers and sisters: that the "mother-want about the world" (*Aurora Leigh* 1.40) can be eliminated only if indi-viduals and nations become more womanly.[24] No longer asking—as she had in *Casa Guidi Windows*—to be absolved of an ardent idealism and emotionalism that she explicitly had labeled female, she firmly declares her belief that "A curse from the depths of woman-hood / Is . . . good," essential to the apocalyptic transformation of society ("Prologue" to **"A Curse for a Nation"** 47-48).

Cursing of the power-hungry, apathetic, and cowardly is less evident, however, in the verses on Italy that appear in the posthumously published *Last Poems* (1862). The change in tone is due in part to the poet's belief that the Italian struggle for independence was succeeding, but even more to her growing awareness of the tragedy of war, even one fought for noble ends. Not surprisingly, the horrors of war are most power-fully depicted in poems that focus on the experiences of Italian women, the poet suggesting in both **"Part-ing Lovers"** and **"Mother and Poet"** that "daughters give up more than sons" when nations experience their "birth-pangs" (**"PL"** line 52, **"MP"** line 93).

But it is not just sympathy for the women of Italy that produces the best poems of Barrett Browning's last years; it is compassion for all women living in patriarchy. For example, in **"Where's Agnes?"** and **"Lord Walter's Wife,"** the poet criticizes men who cannot or will not regard women as autonomous human beings and who therefore view women either as angelic creatures who "scarcely tread the earth" or as harlots, "mere dirt" (**"Agnes"** 86-87). And in poems such as **"Void in Law," "Bianca Among the Nightingales,"** and **"Amy's Cruelty,"** she openly characterizes men as selfish, untrustworthy, and exploitative, warning women that unless they use great caution when selecting a mate they may "forfeit all things" by loving (**"Amy's Cruelty"** 34). Thus Barrett Browning concludes her poetic career by firmly rejecting the notion that she had challenged only tentatively in *A Drama of Exile*: the notion that women, including women poets, must passively endure the "pressures of an alien tyranny / With its dynastic reasons of larger bones / And stronger sinews" (lines 1865-67).

Notes

1 Throughout her life Barrett Browning believed that emulating authors one admired benefited rather than harmed a writer. "There is no vanity, but rather wisdom, in following humbly [in] the footsteps of perfection," the poet announces in the preface to *The Battle of Marathon* (Porter and Clarke 1:9). She expresses the same sentiment thirty years later in *Casa Guidi Windows,* claiming that she could not "sing this song, / If my dead masters had not taken heed / To help the heavens and earth to make me strong" (1:432-34).

2 See, for example, Kaplan; Gilbert and Gubar, esp. 70, 189, 391, 547; Cooper, "Theory"; Zimmerman; Rosenblum; Mermin; and Hayter.

3 EBB's debts to women prose writers are explored in Kaplan; Donaldson; Hickok, "'New Yet Orthodox'"; Holloway; Thomson; and Moser. Cooper comments on EBB's artistic interaction with other nineteenth-century women poets in Chapter 2 of her dissertation and discusses ways EBB's poetry differs from that of her literary sisters in "Working into Light."

4 As Showalter remarks, a woman writer "confronts both paternal and maternal precursors and must deal with the problems and advantages of both lines of inheritance. . . . The female tradition can be a positive source of strength and solidarity as well as a negative source of powerlessness; it can generate its own experiences and symbols which are not simply the obverse of the male tradition" (265).

5 See, for example, Miller's discussion of Emily Dickinson's revisions of the poems of her female contemporaries, especially Chapter 9.

6 For the most part, Barrett Browning shared her interest in the lives and writings of women authors with other women—initially with her mother, later with friends such as Anna Jameson, Mary Russell Mitford, Harriet Martineau, and Eliza Ogilvy. The influence that female relatives and friends exerted on Barrett Browning's development is a subject that needs to be explored further, particularly since Kelley and Hudson have demonstrated that it was Mary Moulton-Barrett rather than the poet's father who was "the prime motivator in EBB's early poetic development" (1: xxxiv).

7 To date, the only book-length study of early nineteenth-century English women's poetry (much of which is out of print) is Hickok's *Representations of Women*. My own study of the poetry women published in England during the period 1780-1850 was made possible by a grant from the Committee on Advanced Study and Research of Lafayette College, to whom I express my appreciation.

8 The phrase "a woman & man in one" appears in an 1844 letter to Mitford in which EBB notes that it is "a hard & difficult process for a woman to get forgiven for her strength by her grace. . . . [E]very woman of letters knows it is hard" (Raymond and Sullivan 3:38). In this paragraph I am not arguing that to be a great poet a woman *must* draw upon the works of predecessors of both sexes, but I believe that EBB held this view and that in many of her finest poems she works out of both a female and a male poetic tradition.

9 Although the phrase "forgets womanly duties in the personality of a man" is applied by EBB to Scott's Diana Vernon, it also describes the behavior of many of the female characters Edgeworth criticizes in her novels. For a thoughtful analysis of the way Edgeworth responds as a writer to her father's literary productions and views of women, see Hawthorne.

10 For other discussions of "immasculation" see Gilbert and Gubar; Cooper's "Theory"; Homans; Diehl; and Flynn and Schweickart, especially the essays by Schweickart, Schibanoff, and Fetterley (31-62, 83-106, 147-64).

11 A transcription of EBB's manuscript poem "Fragment of an 'Essay on Woman'" appears in *SBHC* 12 (1984), along with Moser's discussion of the ways EBB drew on *A Vindication of the Rights of Woman* when writing this poem.

12 The poems referred to are "On a Picture of Riego's Widow," "The Little Friend," and "To Bettine." The

first was published with *An Essay on Mind* in 1826; the others appeared in the *Seraphim* volume. See also "To a Poet's Child" and "Isobel's Child," published in the collections of 1833 and 1838 respectively.

[13] Among the poems in this category are "The Poet's Vow," "The Romaunt of Margaret," and "A Romance of the Ganges."

[14] EBB's ambivalent feelings about her father are conveyed particularly well in a poem addressed to him on his thirty-third birthday (in which she subtly compares him to Pitt, "who made blest freedoms weep / His name") and in an untitled essay of 1827, written after her father had called her latest production "most wretched" (Kelley and Hudson 1.59-60, 361). The poet had no need to abase herself before Uvedale Price, who treated her with respect, but she had to actively combat the temptation to become the docile handmaiden of Hugh Stuart Boyd, who often behaved selfishly and maliciously. EBB's hostility towards Boyd is recorded frequently in her diary of 1831-32; see, for example, pp. 39 and 148 (Kelley and Hudson *Diary*).

[15] In "The Book of the Poets" (1842), More is one of the writers EBB cites when arguing that during the second half of the eighteenth century England produced no great poets (Porter and Clarke 6:298). Similarly, in a letter of December 1842 EBB asserts that Dacier was "a learned writer" but not "a woman of genius" (Raymond and Sullivan 2:136).

[16] In *The Battle of Marathon* (1820), Barrett Browning praises the Athenian warriors who defended their city-state against the Persians; the fact that the rights and privileges of Athenian democracy did not extend to women does not seem to disturb her. Moreover, the Greek commander, whom the poet repeatedly and without irony terms "sage," responds scornfully to the rousing speech of a patriotic Greek matron and steels his warriors for battle by proclaiming that the Persians "not as heroes, but as women fight; / Grovelling as proud, and cowardly as vain" (756-60, 977-78). Women are totally excluded from *An Essay on Mind* (1826), a work in which Barrett Browning pays tribute to countless males who have furthered the intellectual development of Western "man," and issues of gender are avoided in *The Seraphim* (1838), the poet viewing the crucifixion through "seraphic" rather than human eyes.

[17] In Book 2 of *Aurora Leigh,* Barrett Browning vehemently protests against those who urge women poets to limit themselves to expressing emotions with grace and delicacy and who then argue that poetry by women is inherently inferior to that by men.

[18] In the preface to the 1844 *Poems* EBB claims that Eve's state of mind after the fall is "more expressible by a woman than a man"; however, the phrase applies equally well to the other poems about women that appear in this collection.

[19] As the poem "Felicia Hemans" reveals, before meeting Mitford EBB was familiar with the verse of Hemans and Letitia Landon, the two most highly regarded English women poets of the 1820s and 1830s. But she does not seem to have read extensively or attentively poetry by other nineteenth-century women writers, most likely because she had internalized her male contemporaries' disparaging view of the productions of poetesses. Women poets are a frequent topic of discussion in EBB's letters to Mitford, however.

[20] EBB published the following poems in *Findens' Tableaux*: "A Romance of the Ganges," "The Romaunt of the Page," "The Dream" (later entitled "A Child Asleep"), and "Legend (later "The Lay") of the Brown Rosary."

[21] Although the second quotation comes from a February 1845 letter to Browning, EBB expresses the same desire to approach "the conventions of vulgar life . . . & touch this real everyday life of our age" in a December 1844 letter to Mitford (Raymond and Sullivan 3:49). The phrase "puckerings in the silk" is one spoken by Aurora Leigh, who frequently uses sewing as a metaphor for composing poetry. Aurora tells Romney: "I'm plain at speech, direct in purpose; when / I speak, you'll take the meaning as it is, / And not allow for puckerings in the silk / By clever stitches" (8.1127-30).

[22] Following is a partial list of this kind of "nature poem": Eliza Cook's "The Waters," "The Old Water-Mill," "The Old Mill Stream," "The Forest Brake," "When I Wore Red Shoes," and "Stanzas by the Sea-Side"; Maria Jane Jewsbury's "I am Come Back from my Bower," "A Remembered Scene," and "A Summer Eve's Vision"; Felicia Hemans' "To the Mountain Winds"; Letitia Landon's "Erinna," "A History of the Lyre," and "The Enchanted Island"; and Anna Barbauld's "Verses Written in an Alcove." The bower motif appears frequently in women's fiction as well as in women's poetry, as is demonstrated by Annis Pratt and her co-authors.

[23] The idea that women poets often wrote of the Middle Ages and were particularly fond of presenting female characters who disguised themselves as male pages was so common a notion that Frances Trollope could mock the phenomenon in her satirical *The Mother's Manual; or, Illustrations of Matrimonial Economy. An Essay in Verse* (64). Examples of this kind of poem include Landon's "The Vow of the Peacock," "Inez," and "The Castilian Nuptials," and Sara Clarke Lippincott's [alias Grace Greenwood] "Dreams." For other depictions of women of the Middle Ages see

Hemans' "The Abencerrage," "The Widow of Crescentius," "Woman on the Field of Battle," "The Effigies," and "The Lady of Provence."

[24] References are to these poems: "Napoleon III. in Italy," "A Court Lady," and "The Dance."

Works Cited

Cooper, Helen. "Working Into Light: Elizabeth Barrett Browning." *Shakespeare's Sisters: Feminist Essays on Women Poets*. Ed. Sandra Gilbert and Susan Gubar. Bloomington: Indiana UP, 1979. 65-81.

Cooper, Helen Margaret. "Elizabeth Barrett Browning: A Theory of Women's Poetry." Diss. Rutgers U, 1982.

de Beauvoir, Simone. *The Second Sex*. Ed. and trans. H.M. Parshley. New York: Random House, 1952.

Dickinson, Emily. *The Complete Poems of Emily Dickinson*. Ed. Thomas H. Johnson. Boston: Little, Brown, 1960.

Diehl, Joanne Feit. "'Come Slowly—Eden': An Exploration of Women Poets and Their Muse." *Signs* 3 (1978): 572-87.

Donaldson, Sandra M. "Elizabeth Barrett's Two Sonnets to George Sand." *SBHC* 5 (1977): 19-22.

Fetterley, Judith. *The Resisting Reader: A Feminist Approach to American Fiction*. Bloomington: Indiana UP, 1978.

Flynn, Elizabeth A., and Patrocinio P. Schweickart, eds. *Gender and Reading: Essays on Readers, Texts, and Contexts*. Baltimore: Johns Hopkins UP, 1986.

Gilbert, Sandra, and Susan Gubar. *The Madwoman in the Attic: The Woman Writer and the Nineteenth-Century Literary Imagination*. New Haven: Yale UP, 1979.

Hawthorne, Mark D. *Doubt and Dogma in Maria Edgeworth*. U of Florida Monographs, The Humanities, 25. Gainesville: U of Florida P, 1967.

Hayter, Alethea. "'These Men Over-Nice': Elizabeth Barrett Browning's 'Lord Walter's Wife'." *BSN* 8 (1978): 5-7.

Heydon, Peter N., and Philip Kelley, eds. *Elizabeth Barrett Browning's Letters to Mrs. David Ogilvy 1849-1861*. New York: Quadrangle and The Browning Institute, 1973.

Hickok, Kathleen. *Representations of Women: Nineteenth-Century British Women's Poetry*. Westport, CT: Greenwood, 1984.

Hickok, Kathleen K. "'New Yet Orthodox': The Female Characters in *Aurora Leigh*." *International Journal of Women's Studies* 3 (1980): 479-89.

Holloway, Julia Bolton. "*Aurora Leigh* and *Jane Eyre*." *Brontë Society Transactions* 17 (1977): 126-32.

Homans, Margaret. *Women Writers and Poetic Identity: Dorothy Wordsworth, Emily Brontë, and Emily Dickinson*. Princeton: Princeton UP, 1980.

Kaplan, Cora. Introduction. *Elizabeth Barrett Browning: Her Novel in Verse Aurora Leigh with Other Poems*. London: The Women's P, 1978.

Kelley, Philip, and Ronald Hudson, eds. *The Brownings' Correspondence*. 4 vols. Winfield, KS: Wedgestone Press, 1984-.

———. *The Unpublished Diary of Elizabeth Barrett Barrett, 1831-1832*. Athens: Ohio UP, 1969.

Kenyon, Frederic G., ed. *The Letters of Elizabeth Barrett Browning*. 2 vols. New York: Macmillan, 1899.

Kintner, Elvan, ed. *The Letters of Robert Browning and Elizabeth Barrett Barrett 1845-1846*. 2 vols. Cambridge, MA: Harvard UP, 1969.

Mermin, Dorothy. "The Female Poet and the Embarrassed Reader: Elizabeth Barrett Browning's *Sonnets from the Portuguese*." *ELH* 48 (1981): 351-67.

Miller, Ruth. *The Poetry of Emily Dickinson*. Middletown, CT: Wesleyan UP, 1968.

Moser, Kay. "Elizabeth Barrett's Youthful Feminism: Fragment of 'An Essay on Woman'." *SIB* 12 (1984): 13-26.

Porter, Charlotte, and Helen A. Clarke, eds. *The Complete Works of Elizabeth Barrett Browning*. 6 vols. New York: Thomas Y. Crowell, 1900.

Pratt, Annis, and others. *Archetypal Patterns in Women's Fiction*. Bloomington: Indiana UP, 1981.

Raymond, Meredith B., and Mary Rose Sullivan, eds. *The Letters of Elizabeth Barrett Browning to Mary Russell Mitford 1836-1854*. 3 vols. Winfield, KS: Armstrong Browning Library of Baylor University, The Browning Institute, Wedgestone Press, and Wellesley College, 1983.

Rosenblum, Dolores. "Face to Face: Elizabeth Barrett Browning's *Aurora Leigh* and Nineteenth-Century Poetry." *VS* 26 (1983): 321-38.

Showalter, Elaine. "Feminist Criticism in the Wilderness." *The New Feminist Criticism: Essays on Women, Literature, and Theory*, New York: Pantheon, 1985.

Thomson, Patricia. *George Sand and the Victorians: Her Influence and Reputation in Nineteenth-Century England.* New York: Columbia UP, 1977.

Trollope, Frances. *The Mother's Manual: or, Illustrations of Matrimonial Economy. An Essay in Verse.* London: Treuttel and Würtz, 1833.

Woolf, Virginia. "*Aurora Leigh.*" *Collected Essays of Virginia Woolf.* Ed. Leonard Woolf. New York: Harcourt, Brace and World, 1953.

Wordsworth, William. *The Poetical Works of Wordsworth.* Ed. Paul D. Sheats. Boston: Houghton Mifflin, 1982.

Zimmerman, Susan. "*Sonnets from the Portuguese*: A Negative and a Positive Context." *Mary Wollstonecraft Newsletter* 2 (1973): 1-11.

Helen Cooper (essay date 1988)

SOURCE: "The Angel: *The Seraphim, and Other Poems* (1838)," in *Elizabeth Barrett Browning, Woman and Artist,* University of North Carolina Press, 1988, pp. 12-45.

[*In the following chapter from her* Elizabeth Barrett Browning, Woman and Artist, *Cooper surveys Browning's early literary influences and how she transformed them to establish an original voice in* The Seraphim, and Other Poems.]

> *Heaven is dull,*
> *Mine Ador, to Man's earth.*
> —"**The Seraphim**"

The reviewer in *Blackwood's Edinburgh Magazine* who asked, "What other pretty book is this?" discovered it to be *The Seraphim, and Other Poems* (1838) by Elizabeth Barrett Browning.[1] Barrett was thirty-two; she had already written an autobiography, *Glimpses Into My Own Life and Literary Character* (1820),[2] and published three volumes of poetry, *The Battle of Marathon* (1820), *An Essay on Mind, With Other Poems* (1826), and *Poems, 1833. The Seraphim,* however, was her first work both to receive a wide readership and extensive critical response, and also to represent "with all its feebleness and shortcomings and obscurities . . . the first utterance" of her "own individuality" ([*The Letters of Elizabeth Barrett Browning*; hereafter, *L* followed by volume and page], 1:188). But the expression of that "individuality" was achieved through years of reading and imitating the male masters and of recognizing the relationship of gender to her determination to be a poet.

Her autobiography is a precocious, ebulliently self-confident document, in which the adolescent Barrett recorded her self-conscious training to be a poet. At age seven she "began to think of 'forming [her] taste' . . . *to see what was best to write about and read about*" ([*Elizabeth Barrett Browning: Hitherto Unpublished Poems and Stories with an Inedited Autobiography*; hereafter *A*], 8-9). As a consequence:

> I read the History of England and Rome; at eight I perused the History of Greece and . . . first found real delight in poetry. "The Minstrel," Pope's "Illiad" [*sic*], some parts of the "Odyssey," passages from "Paradise Lost" selected by my dearest Mama and some of Shakespeare's plays among which were, "The Tempest," "Othello" and a few historical dramatic pieces. . . .

> At nine . . . Pope's "Illiad" [*sic*] some passages from Shakespeare and Novels which I enjoyed to their full extent. . . . At ten my poetry was entirely formed by the style of written authors and I read that I might write. Novels were still my most delightful study, combined with the sweet notes of poetic inspiration! At eleven I wished to be considered an authoress. Novels were thrown aside. Poetry and Essays were my studies and I felt the most ardent desire to understand the learned languages. To comprehend even the Greek alphabet was delight inexpressible. Under the tuition of Mr. McSwiney I attained that which I so fervently desired. . . .

> [At twelve] I read Milton for the first time thro' together with Shakespeare and Pope's Homer. . . .

> I perused all modern authors who have any claim to superior merit and poetic excellence. I was familiar with Shakespeare, Milton, Homer and Virgil, Locke, Hooker, Pope. I read Homer in the original with delight inexpressible, together with Virgil.

> [*A*, 9-15]

This astonishing record indicates that, even as a young girl, Barrett appreciated both the tradition she hoped to appropriate and also the crucial importance of the classics in the education of an English poet. That formal education she was denied by virtue of gender she sought to gain for herself. As an adolescent, she received permission to study with her brother's tutor, Mr. Mc-Swiney. Then, as a young woman, she acted as an amanuensis to Hugh Boyd, a blind, rather pedantic, and second-rate Greek scholar, who lived near the Barrett house at Hope End, Malvern, and had written to the young poet in 1826 after the publication of *An Essay on Mind.* This educational history was not the equivalent of Eton and Oxbridge, but it demonstrates Barrett's understanding of the apprenticeship necessary for a poet.

Years later she reevaluated the time spent pondering the minutiae of Greek grammar and working on a study of the Greek Christian poets with Boyd, recognizing it as wasted labor. In 1845 she wrote to a Miss Thompson, who had requested some translations from the Greek for an anthology: "Perhaps I do not . . . partake quite your 'divine fury' for converting our sex into Greek scholarship. . . . You . . . know that the Greek language . . . swallows up year after year of studious life. Now I have a 'doxy', . . . that there is no exercise of the mind so little profitable to the mind as the study of languages. It is the nearest thing to a passive recipiency—is it not?—as a mental action, though it leaves one weary as ennui itself. Women want to be made to *think actively*" (*L*, 1:260-61). Barrett never analyzed why Greek scholarship induces a "passive recipiency" in woman, precluding her need to "think actively." It is tempting to infer her conviction that study of the classics forces woman to read herself always as the object of male narrative, while to "think actively" necessitates claiming herself as subject of experience and discourse. However valid this mature evaluation of classical study for women may be, Barrett was wise to immerse herself in such study as a young poet. It gave her the credentials to be taken seriously by the critics and enabled her as a poet to engage in the epic terms she would finally realize in *Aurora Leigh,* not merely in the lyrical verse of the affections associated with the popular "poetesses."

The young Barrett, to use de Beauvoir's terms, "play[ed] at being a man" by linguistically "dress[ing] up in men's clothes" ([*The Letters of Elizabeth Barrett Browning to Mary Russell Mitford, 1836-1854*; hereafter, *MRM* followed by volume and page], 2:7). At fourteen, in her Preface to *The Battle of Marathon,* she declared Homer as the model for her epic poem based on the Greek defense against Persian invaders on the plains of Marathon in 490 B.C.: "It would have been both absurd and presumptuous, young and inexperienced as I am, to have attempted to strike out a path for myself" ([*Complete Works*; hereafter, *W* followed by volume and page] 1:9). Yet even in this work, Barrett demonstrated strategies for appropriating the "path" that this literary father had walked. She assumed a male identity: "He who writes an epic poem must transport himself to the scene of action; he must imagine himself possessed of the same opinions, manners, prejudices, and belief; he must suppose himself to be the hero he delineates" (*W,* 1:7-8). Yet earlier she had revealed the poem's true hero: "Who can be indifferent, who can preserve his tranquillity, when he hears of one little city rising undaunted, and daring her innumerable enemies, in defense of her freedom?" (*W,* 1:6). The epic poet she designated, according to con-

vention, as "he," and yet the "little city rising" she designated, again according to convention, as female. Naming her poetic self as male while creating the epic hero with whom "he" must identify not as a brave male but as a courageous female both located Barrett within a tradition and also subverted it by elevating a rebellious woman who is acting "in defense of her freedom" as subject of the story to be told.

Barrett studied Homer not only in the original but also in Pope's translation. This informed her imitation of Pope in *An Essay on Mind* (1826), a poem remarkable only for demonstrating Barrett's erudition in philosophy. Barrett then returned to classical sources, and in 1833 she published her first translation of Aeschylus's *Prometheus Bound,* a Romantic endeavor that assumes an added dimension for a woman whose disobedient act of writing resonated to Prometheus's theft of fire from the gods. In her Preface to the translation, reworked and published with her *Poems of 1850,* she described a kinship with Aeschylus as one of the "ancient Greeks [who] . . . felt passionately, and thought daringly" (*W,* 6:83). Barrett did not attempt a Shelleyan revision of the Prometheus myth, but her translation exhibited her classical credentials and also linked her with a writer who represented her own ambitions as woman and poet to feel passionately and be daring in thought. She recognized that "sometimes [Aeschylus's] fancy rushes in, where his judgment fears to tread" (*W,* 6:84), as she would later determine that the poem which eventually became *Aurora Leigh* would "rush into drawing-rooms & the like 'where angels fear to tread'" ([*Letters of Robert Browning and Elizabeth Barrett Barrett*; hereafter cited as *RB & EBB* followed by volume and page], 1:31). Certainly Barrett's intentions from an early age were infused with entrepreneurial energy. Whereas Tennyson's early poems had languid heroines, Barrett boldly walked where women had for too long feared to tread; her early publications demonstrate how centrally she wished to locate herself in English poetic tradition.

She conformed to the apprenticeship of imitating the fathers, yet she was also aware very early that her gender necessitated comment:

> My mind is naturally independant [*sic*] and spurns that subserviency of opinion which is generally considered necessary to feminine softness. But this is a subject on which I must always feel strongly, for I feel within me an almost proud consciousness of independance [*sic*] which prompts me to defend my opinions and to yield them only to conviction!!!!!!!

> My friends may differ from me: the world may accuse me but this I am determined never to retract!!

Better, oh how much better, to be the ridicule of mankind, the scoff of society, than lose that self respect which tho' this heart were bursting would elevate me above misery—above wretchedness and above abasement!!! These principles are irrevocable! It is not—I feel it is not vanity that dictates them! it is not—I know it is not an encroachment on Masculine prerogative but it is a proud sentiment which will never, never allow me to be humbled in my own eyes!!! [*A,* 24]

Aware that "subserviency of opinion" is conventionally demanded of women, she determined to nurture her right to an independent mind. The style, with all its exclamation points and exaggerated language, is adolescent in expression, yet it reveals Barrett's understanding that the independent thinking demanded of a poet would render women the "ridicule of mankind, the scoff of society." Although many poets have suffered such scorn, the young Barrett was aware that she would be ridiculed, not as men are for the content of their thought, but as women are, for the act of thinking at all.

She evidences how hard it was to sustain her commitment to the intellectual life in her surviving diary (June 1831 to May 1832).[3] When Boyd wrote to her after reading *An Essay on Mind,* inviting her to visit him and his family in nearby Malvern, Barrett's father forbade the visit: "as a *female,* and a *young* female" such a visit would be overstepping the established observances of society ([*Elizabeth Barrett to Mr. Boyd. Unpublished Letters of Elizabeth Barrett Browning to Hugh Stuart Boyd*; hereafter, *HSB*] 11). Even when the friendship was finally established and Barrett visited Boyd as often as possible to work at Greek, her aunt "Bummy" (who cared for the family of ten after their mother's death in 1828) and her sister Henrietta frowned on this transgression of woman's social norm:

This evening, Henrietta proposed inviting Mrs. Griffith to drink tea here tomorrow,—upon which, Bummy insisted on my returning from Malvern sooner than I shd otherwise do!! I was annoyed & said so—& even refused going at all, in the case of my being obliged to come back, by anything else than darkness. Henrietta need not have asked Mrs. G tomorrow,—nor, if she had asked her, need *I* have been forced to receive her company. But the point was yielded at last—of course by *me!* [*Diary by E.B.B.: The Unpublished Diary of Elizabeth Barrett Browning*; hereafter, *D*], 131]

Her family was distressed at the "impropriety" of her feeling "*more friendship for Mr. Boyd than for the Martins!* . . . They have, as most people have, clearer ideas of the aristocracy of rank & wealth, than of the aristocracy of mind" (*D,* 104). How different must

intellectual life have been for Tennyson in the company of the Apostles at Cambridge, or for Robert Browning in the home that his parents provided when he determined to be a poet, where his friendship with Carlyle developed. Her relationship with Boyd was analogous to the one Eliot imagined between Dorothea Brooke and Mr. Casaubon: "My dear friend Mr. Boyd!—If he knew how much it gratifies me to assist him in any way (I wish I cd do so in *every*way) all his '*drudgeries*' wd devolve upon me" (*D,* 44). Although Boyd encouraged Barrett's studies, he also trivialized her:

[Mr. Boyd] asked me to talk to Mr. Spowers at dinner: "on *his* account, he thought I ought to do it." I promised to do my best; and as I went out of the room, he said that I must remember what I had promised, & that he wd ask Mrs. Boyd if I had been "naughty or good." I in a panic of course. . . . Down to dinner. I impelled myself to talk, whether I had anything to say or not—to talk about the country, & the newspaper, & the raven, & Joanna Baillie & Lord Byron. So that when I had to answer Mr. Boyd's "naughty or good," I could say "good." [*D,* 58]

It is hard to imagine Tennyson, Browning, or Arnold accused of valuing intellect more than afternoon tea, of being called "naughty" at twenty-five. Yet these comparisons reveal the very different issues at the heart of creative composition for men and women bound by such cultural conventions. As surely as Dickens's childhood experiences—the blacking factory and his parents' imprisonment for debt—defined the nature of his fiction, so Barrett's experience of growing up female while determining to be a poet defined the form of her poetry. Only when the basic issue for a woman is understood to be "dare she write" (what Gilbert and Gubar refer to as the "anxiety of authorship") as much as "what to write" (the "anxiety of influence") can she be appreciated on her own terms. Whereas in her intellectual life Barrett was studying and imitating the classics, emotionally she recognized the discrepancy between the world expressed in male poetry and that inhabited by middle-class woman.

Many women and men exhorted middle-class woman to her role of wife and mother: the sentiments of Sarah Stickney Ellis (whose *Women of England* was published in the same year as *The Seraphim, and Other Poems*) were typical:

Women, considered in their distinct and abstract nature, as isolated beings, must lose more than half their worth. They are, in fact, from their own constitution, and from the station they occupy in the world, strictly speaking, relative creatures. If, therefore, they are endowed with only such faculties as render them striking and distinguished in themselves, without the faculty of instrumentality, they are only as dead letters in the volume of human life, filling what would otherwise be a blank space, but doing nothing more.[4]

Barrett, in a letter to Kenyon about *The Seraphim, and Other Poems,* insisted that the expression of her own "individuality" represented "maturity" and belonging to the "living" (*L,* 1:187). Conversely, Ellis exhorted women to remember that because by nature they are "relative creatures" to their parents, husbands, and children, "individuality" renders them "dead letters." Ellis's rather than Barrett's convictions informed the work of the two most popular nineteenth-century "poetesses," Letitia Landon and Felicia Hemans.

Landon in her Preface to "The Venetian Bracelet" identifies love as her "source of song": "For a woman, whose influence and whose sphere must be in the affections, what subject can be more fitting than one which it is her peculiar province to refine, spiritualize, and exalt? I have always sought to paint it self-denying, devoted, and making an almost religion of its truth." In the "Immolation of a Hindoo Widow" Landon takes such self-denial to its extreme in her depiction of suttee:

> The red pile blazes—let the bride ascend,
> And lay her head upon her husband's heart,
> Now in a perfect unison to blend—
> No more to part.

Hemans equally defines woman as a relative creature. Unlike Barrett who admired de Stael's poet heroine, Corinne, Hemans (recalling a scene in the novel in which Corinne receives the poet's laurel) concludes "Corinne at the Capitol" as follows:

> Happier, happier far than thou,
> With the laurel on thy brow,
> She that makes the humblest hearth
> Lovely but to one on earth!

For the poetesses, woman's role was usually accompanied by suffering in the wake of betrayal, loss, and rejection. In "Madeline," from *Records of Woman,* Hemans describes woman's destiny as being to "suffer and be still." Sarah Stickney Ellis endorsed Hemans's attitude, taking those words as the epigraph for *Women of England.*

In the "Indian Woman's Death-Song" (*Records of Woman*), however, Hemans has a mother drown herself and her daughter after her husband deserted them:

> "And thou, my babe! though born, like me,
> for woman's weary lot,
> Smile!—to that wasting of the heart, my
> own! I leave thee not;

> Too bright a thing art *thou* to pine in
> aching love away—
> Thy mother bears thee far, young fawn!
> from sorrow and decay."

Hemans's recognition that "woman's weary lot" is intolerable represents a rage against the very condition she attempts to support. This rage, rumbling under the sentimental, domestic surface of both her work and Landon's, is portrayed as violence that is inflicted on women by themselves or others, and ultimately expressed as death. The anger, which cannot be turned on the men who make them suffer, destroys the devoted "angels" themselves. If the frequent deaths of women in the poetesses' work are viewed not only as a morbid or sentimental strain but also as an expression of this anger inflicted by robust women writers on their long-suffering heroine victims, then such deaths can be seen as a strategy to exalt suffering woman while desiring to kill her off as an image of womanhood. It was a strategy Barrett inherited.

Although Barrett's record of her early reading focused on male writing, certainly by her late teens she was familiar with the work of the poetesses. The two poems she most liked in *The Literary Souvenir; or, Cabinet of Poetry and Romance* for 1826 were Landon's "The Forsaken" and Hemans's "The Wreck."[5] She eulogized both poets after their deaths in **"Felicia Hemans"** (*W,* 2:83) and **"L.E.L.'s Last Question"** (*W,* 3:117), revealing thorough knowledge of their work. Yet, although their verse engaged her and often found echoes in the choice, if not the treatment, of her own subject matter, Barrett recognized the limitations of both Hemans and Landon as poets as she assessed them to her friend, Mary Russell Mitford:

> If I had those two powers to choose from . . Mrs. Hemans's & Miss Landon's . . I mean the *raw* bare powers . . I wd choose Miss Landon's. I surmise that it was more elastic, more various, of a stronger web. I fancy it wd have worked out better—had it *been* worked out—with the right moral & intellectual influences in application. As it is, Mrs. Hemans has left the finer poems. Of that there can be no question. But perhaps . . & indeed I do say it very diffidently . . there is a sense of sameness which goes with the sense of excellence,—while we read her poems—a satiety with the satisfaction together with a feeling "this writer has written her best,"—or "It is very well— but it can never be better." [*MRM,* 1:235]

Barrett never placed Hemans and Landon in the same class as Homer, Aeschylus, Milton, Pope, or Wordsworth—the class to which she aspired. Nevertheless, they offered her a valuable model of women whose lives had been devoted to writing poetry. Even though they wrote of women analogous to Milton's Eve, they modeled woman actively describing herself rather than being passively described. It is qualitatively different to "suffer and be still" and to suffer and write about it. Yet at best, Hemans, Landon, and their like offered Barrett problematic models: patronized by the critics; committed to the notion that it was better for a woman to "make the humblest hearth" than to "wear the laurel on [her] brow"; and diligent in their portrayal of woman's acceptance of her "weary lot." Lacking the stature of the revered and envied precursors by which male poets were nurtured, they did not challenge the privileged male voice of English poetry.

Women prose writers pioneered an alternative image of womanhood for the young Barrett: "I read Mary Wolstonecraft when I was thirteen: no twelve! . . and, through the whole course of my childhood, I had a steady indignation against Nature who made me a woman, & a determinate resolution to dress up in men's clothes as soon as ever I was free of the nursery, & go into the world 'to seek my fortune.' *'How,'* was not decided; but I rather leant towards being poor Lord Byron's PAGE" (*MRM,* 2:7). Her "steady indignation against Nature" was Barrett's protest against woman as long-suffering relative creature. Wollstonecraft emphasized learning and education for women, even while stressing the importance of her role as educated wife and mother. However, by the time she wrote *The Seraphim, and Other Poems* Barrett had read Madame de Stael's *Corinne* three times. Here for the first time was woman, in her own "clothes," represented as a poet. De Stael juxtaposed the freedom possible in Italy for woman's artistic endeavors and sexual passion with a passive servitude and repression she depicted as required of English women. The Italian landscape and sensibility provided Barrett with a metaphor for artistic freedom (even before she lived there), which she later exploited fully in *Aurora Leigh*. These literary mothers, while not being precursors held in general esteem, provided models for Barrett's task of creating an image of woman from her felt reality. She was aware that it was in *The Seraphim, and Other Poems* that such a "reality" began to take shape.

Barrett's awareness that this volume revealed an original poetic voice was shared by reviewers whose responses appeared in many journals, including the *Examiner,* the *Athenaeum, Blackwood's Edinburgh Magazine,* the *Quarterly Review,* the *North American Review,* and the *English Review.*[6] They paid unusually serious attention to this unknown woman poet, placing her in a male tradition, yet treating her as a woman poet.

Echoing Barrett's sense of her "own individuality," the *Athenaeum* found *The Seraphim* "an extraordinary volume" (466), while the *Quarterly Review,* in a discussion of nine women poets, was representative in recognizing that Barrett both stood out "as well for

her extraordinary acquaintance with ancient classic literature, as for the boldness of her poetic attempts," and failed to achieve a "success . . . in proportion to her daring" (382-83). However, the *North American Review,* like her mentors, Boyd and Kenyon (but unlike Robert Browning), lamented that as Barrett progressed from her early male imitations into a more original voice, she violated poetic decorum. In *The Seraphim,* which "contains more of original poetry" than both her former volumes, the reviewer found that "her mind has gone through essential changes, which are not in all respects for the better. . . . Her great defect is a certain lawless extravagance" (207).

In their discussion of the title poem, **"The Seraphim,"** reviewers saw Barrett as heir to a poetic tradition epitomized in their minds by Milton. Barrett talked of Aeschylus as her inspiration for this poem, but its focus on the Crucifixion evoked Milton's earlier treatment of the Fall. The *Examiner* felt that "sacred subjects" were "not fit for poetry," that even "Milton degraded the Deity" and "the presumption of Dante is at least equal to his genius" (387). The *Quarterly Review* judged that **"The Seraphim"** was "a subject from which Milton would have shrunk." However, the *English Review* allowed the poem almost unqualified approval and, without "quot[ing] Milton in defense of our author," judged Barrett fully "justified in approaching such a theme" (264).

Dante, Milton. The reviewers sensed in Barrett a poet who deserved mention with pillars of the male tradition. Yet in *Aurora Leigh* Romney argues against Aurora's being a poet:

> You never can be satisfied with praise
> Which men give women when they judge a book
> Not as mere work but as mere woman's work,
> Expressing the comparative respect
> Which means the absolute scorn.

> [2.232-36]

This double standard was widespread, as confirmed by the reviewers' treatment of Barrett as a woman poet.[7]

In *Blackwood's,* "Christopher North" admired Barrett's work. Yet he typifies those reviewers who in a patronizing tone created a halo round the smiling face of "our fair author," the "fair Elizabeth." He questioned, "What other pretty book is this? *The Seraphim, and other Poems,* by Elizabeth Barnett [*sic*], author of a Translation of *Prometheus Bound.* High adventure for a Lady—implying a knowledge of Hebrew—or if not—of Greek. No common mind displays itself in this Preface pregnant with lofty thoughts. Yet is her heart humble withal." Placing Barrett in a tradition of women poets—of Mary Tighe, Felicia Hemans ("that other Sweetest Singer")—and Letitia Landon—North queried, "Surely Poetesses (is there such a word?) are very happy, in spite of all the 'natural sorrows, griefs, and pains,' to which their exquisitely sensitive being must be perpetually alive" (281). He dismissed the tensions manifest in Barrett's work: "And our Elizabeth—she too is happy—though in her happiness she loveth to veil with a melancholy haze the brightness of her childhood—and of her maidenhood."

This sentimentality also informed the *Quarterly Review*'s discussion of Barrett among nine women poets:

> We feel that we never did a bolder thing than now we do, in summoning these nine Muses to our Quarter Sessions. The very ink turns blue with which we write their names.

> It is easy to be critical on men; but when we venture to lift a pen against women, straightway *apparent facies;* the weapon drops pointless on the marked passage; and whilst the mind is bent on praise or censure of the poem, the eye swims too deep in tears and mist over the poetess herself in the frontispiece, to let it see its way to either. [375]

The review is, in fact, quite rigorous and insightful, but the reviewer adopted rhetoric associated with the female poet, making her a quite different species from the male. Detracting from a focus on her poetry, the *North American Review,* placing Barrett as one of the "tuneful tribe" (206), lamented, "In regard to this lady . . . [we] are ignorant of her lineage, her education, her tastes, and (last not least, where a lady is concerned,) her personal attractions" (202). Only the *English Review* addressed the issue of male prejudice against women writers: "her scholarship, solid and genuine, can defy the charge of female pedantry: that jealous cant of ignorant men is now, indeed, almost exploded; and women may not only cultivate high knowledge, but confess, and dare to show it, without disparagement to womanhood" (264).

Overall the reviewers preferred to imagine Barrett as a poetess; if, by invoking Milton's name, they saw **"The Seraphim"** as the quintessentially male poem of the volume, they found **"Isobel's Child"** the quintessentially female one—such that it was mentioned and quoted in almost every journal. Clearly they felt comfortable with that most feminine icon—mother and child. The poem is a dialogue between a mother who is willing her sick infant to live and the infant who is desiring to die, to escape earth's suffering. The *Athenaeum* devoted two sentimental columns to quoting from and summarizing the poem. "Christopher North"

found that "the workings of a mother's love through all the phases of fear, and hope, and despair, and heavenly consolation, are given with extraordinary power" (279-80). The *Quarterly Review* considered this "somewhat fantastic poem . . . a fair specimen of Miss Barrett's general manner and power" (388). The *North American Review* acknowledged that it was a "poem of singular originality of conception and impassioned depth of feeling . . . suggested by an infant sleeping upon its mother's arm" (209). The *English Review* chose **"Isobel's Child"** as its "favorite . . . tender, thoughtful, and imaginative, the poem flows naturally on, developing with fine pathos the meaning of its text." The reviewers did not wholeheartedly endorse the poem. But neither coincidence nor aesthetics determined so many to discuss **"Isobel's Child"**: it was surely the fact that only this poem depicted woman in her "natural role," as a mother with her baby.

To the reviewers Barrett's gender was a crucial issue, provoking both patronizing condescension and startled admiration. Either way they recognized in this volume representing her "own individuality" an original poetic voice: it was neither familiarly male nor, alarmingly and refreshingly, did it speak as a woman should.

The reviewers' recognition of Barrett both as heir to a male tradition and also as poetess dramatically presents the dialectic that operated throughout her career until she achieved her synthesis of these two roles in **Aurora Leigh**. In particular, two pairs of poems in **The Seraphim, and Other Poems** reveal this dialectic as Barrett simultaneously presents and challenges traditional literary images of woman: Barrett's revisionary reading of Aeschylus in **"The Seraphim"** and her "tender" **"Isobel's Child"**; her revisionary reading of Wordsworth in **"The Poet's Vow"** and her heroine of the affections in **"The Romaunt of Margret."**

In the Preface to the title poem, **"The Seraphim,"** Barrett evoked a male precursor; she revealed her "thought, that had Aeschylus lived after the incarnation and crucifixion of our Lord Jesus Christ, he might have turned . . . from the solitude of Caucasus to the deeper desertness of that crowded Jerusalem where none had any pity" (*W,* 1:164). **"The Seraphim,"** not one of Barrett's enduring achievements, is ostensibly an orthodox Christian celebration of divine love made manifest through the Crucifixion. However, her "vision of the supreme spectacle" from "a less usual aspect" (*W,* 1:167), namely that of two angels, covertly, if not self-consciously, allowed Barrett to create a narrative strategy both for presenting woman's relationship to public events and also for analyzing her subjective experience of that relationship.

In Aeschylus, Prometheus and those who visit him speak; Milton's narrative allowed for extensive dialogue between the principals of the action. Barrett, although following epic tradition in designating her angels male, chose an "aspect" for them suggestive of women's relation to public events; her protagonists are spectators of, not actors in, the public drama. How consciously Barrett at this stage linked woman and angel it is impossible to know, but it was certainly an established connection after Coventry Patmore published "The Angel in the House" (1854-62).

Using the "less usual aspect" of the angels, Barrett decentered the male narrative; however, she did not allow woman's subjective experience to replace it:

> A woman kneels
> The mid cross under,
> With white lips asunder.
> And motion on each.
> They throb, as she feels,
> With a spasm, not a speech.
>
> [2.476-81]

The Crucifixion could not be viewed from Mary's point of view—an equally "less usual aspect"—because as woman she had to "suffer and be still," to feel with "a spasm, not a speech."

In **"The Seraphim,"** however, Jesus, recognized by Zerah and Ador, the two angels, as both "man's victim" and "his deity" (1.248), suggests the paradox of Victorian middle-class woman's being viewed both as powerless "relative creature" in a society venerating masculine industrial power and also as "angel" worshipped for her moral integrity. Jesus thereby dramatizes woman's position, creating an analogy between the divine Jesus's assuming the human condition and woman's entering male public life. The poem's fascination with dangerous public events of earth rather than with the safe security of the angels' Heaven serves as a metaphor for female desire to be included in such events, whatever the cost.

The angels assess this public life on earth, comparing it with their protected home, Heaven. Zerah, convinced that "Heaven is dull, / Mine Ador, to man's earth" (2.596-97), describes the former:

> The light that burns
> In fluent, refluent motion
> Along the crystal ocean;
> The springing of the golden harps between
> The bowery wings, in fountains of sweet
>   sound,
> The winding, wandering music that returns
> Upon itself, exultingly self-bound
> In the great spheric round
>   Of everlasting praises.
>
> [2.597-605]

In spite of these sensuous qualities, Zerah yearns for involvement in earthly "dust and death" (2.612): the "fluent, refluent" Heaven with its "winding, wandering music" cloys beside earth's harsher realities. Far from having "bowery wings," nature is destructive: "The yew-tree bows its melancholy head / And all the undergrasses kills and seres" (1.146-47); and, as Ador recognizes, humans are greedy: "having won the profit which they seek, / Men lie beside the sceptre and the gold / With fleshless hands that cannot wield or hold" (1.151-53). Zerah contrasts Heaven, where "seraphic faces" continually grow more "beautiful with worship and delight" (2.608-10) with earth, where the three who are crucified hang "'Ghast and silent to the sun. / Round them blacken and welter and press / Staring multitudes" (2.460-62). Barrett conveys the horror of the Crucifixion by the crowd's reaction to it as they push and shove to watch rather than by Jesus's suffering. Whereas in Heaven "light . . . burns . . . Along the crystal ocean" and the air is filled with "the springing of the golden harps," on earth light and sound reveal suffering and cruelty:

> Can these love? With the living's pride
> They stare at those who die, who hang
> In their sight and die. They bear the streak
> Of the crosses' shadow, black not wide,
> To fall on their heads, as it swerves aside
>   When the victims' pang
>   Makes the dry wood creak.
>
> [2.469-75]

Like the Lady of Shalott, the angels desire to be on earth, with all its suffering. Barrett fuses these male angels with female spectators desirous of some involvement in public events.

In the male world of patriarchal struggle enacted at the Crucifixion women have no part. With "a spasm, not a speech" the woman is a powerless and silent observer to the public world of male decision making (God, Herod, Pilate, Judas, Jesus, Peter, the soldiers). Barrett as a woman and a poet partially circumvents this: she assumes the persona of the powerless observer, but gives the angels (closer to androgyny than to traditional masculinity) the right to speech rather than spasm. Zerah identifies himself as "tearless" (2.514) because he is nonhuman, in contrast to Mary who weeps. This links the Miltonic angel as poet interpreter between God and man, and the notion of woman as angel so prevalent in nineteenth-century rhetoric. Fusing here her two traditions—male and female—Barrett, however consciously, dramatizes her desire to engage in activities hitherto reserved for men. It is not an easy task: the angels are fearful of leaving their sheltered domain. They experience "the fear of earth" and understand postlapsarian corruption. Nevertheless, whatever their hesitations while still in Heaven, they find earth preferable to their earlier protected existence. Their reasoning is not persuasive. There is nothing in the language that convinces us earth is a better place. The preference results merely from a belief that Christ/God, taking on human form, makes heaven dull in comparison with "man's earth" for all its corruption, suffering, and death. Such fear, yet determination, suggests the nineteenth-century "angels'" fear of leaving the male-sheltered house for creative combat in a world that denied them place.

Barrett fuses here a woman's desire to engage in the public concerns of humanity with her conviction that such an engagement is the poet's task. She embraces a poetic creed that provides an aesthetic cover for legitimizing her woman's desire for involvement in public concerns, not just domestic issues.

In the epilogue, when the speaker touches on the blasphemy of her enterprise in writing of a sacred subject, Barrett implies the parallel blasphemy of "counterfeiting" male texts by transforming the angels into female speakers whose "language [has] never [been] used or hearkened":

> And I—ah! what am I
> To counterfeit, with faculty earth-darkened,
>   Seraphic brows of light
> And seraph language never used nor
>   hearkened?
> Ah me! what word that seraphs say, could
>   come
> From mouth so used to sighs, so soon to
>   lie
> Sighless, because then breathless, in the
>   tomb?

[3]

> Forgive me, that mine earthly heart should
>   dare
> Shape images of unincarnate spirits
> And lay upon their burning lips a thought
> Cold with the weeping which mine earth
>   inherits.

[4]

The female mouth is "so used to sighs," rather than to the transcendental male privilege of speech, that, having accomplished her task of "shap[ing] images" and "lay[ing] . . . a thought," the speaker asks forgiveness for her daring.

In contrast to the external, male-dominated setting of **"The Seraphim,"** **"Isobel's Child"** is set indoors and the protagonists are a mother, her infant son, and his nurse. There is one brief mention of the child's father. A three-month-old dying child is brought by the night-time ministrations of his nurse and his mother, the Lady Isobel, back to health. Smiling over his recovery, his mother is oblivious to the ominously raging

storm outside. The tempestuous "external nature" that "broke / Into such abandonment" mysteriously (and repressively) transforms its energies into "A sense of silence and of steady / Natural calm" when it enters the "human creature's room" (5). Here the mother, praying for her child's life, compares herself to "Mary mild" who was not denied "mother-joy" but was "blessèd in the blessèd child" (10). The boy lives, but after the storm mysteriously dies down, the infant loses his "baby-looks" for the "earnest gazing deep" (26) of an old man and precociously tells his mother of his desire for death. This "dark . . . dull / Low earth, by only weepers trod" (27) cannot compare to his knowledge of the "happy heavenly air" (27) seen in a Wordsworthian "vision and a gleam":

> "I saw celestial places even.
> Oh, the vistas of high palms
>   Making finites of delight
>   Through the heavenly infinite,
> Lifting up their green still tops
>   To the heaven of heaven!"

[29]

He challenges the efficacy of poetry to provide him with a comparable vision:

> "Can your poet make an Eden
>   No winter will undo,
> And light a starry fire while heeding
>   His hearth's is burning too?
> Drown in music the earth's din,
> And keep his own wild soul within
>   The law of his own harmony?"

[31]

He longs for the "little harp . . . whose strings are golden" (31) that waits for him in heaven. The mother, in her happy acceptance of her child's wish, seems unnatural. As Sandra Donaldson points out, the "theme of Christian consolation . . . seems almost formulaic" as the childless Barrett demonstrates how mothers "should be grateful their child is now in heaven. . . . By asking the mother why she would want him to live, the child pushes the theme of Christian consolation to its logical but deadly conclusion."[8]

Obviously, **"The Seraphim"** and **"Isobel's Child"** can be seen as exercises in orthodox religious thought— God's great love manifest in the Incarnation and Crucifixion, and the consolation of heaven. But what concerns me is the opposing visions these two poems represent in the context of their settings. The public male drama, played out at the Crucifixion at which Mary is speechless and powerless, makes heaven seem dull and earth, if not exciting or attractive, at least appealing in its dynamic energy. On the other hand the private female drama, enacted in the domestic interior of the Lady Isobel's castle, around which a turbulent external world whirls, exhibits only "dreary earthly love" in a world of "weepers." In comparison, the open spaces of heaven, offering "vistas of high palms" and the "sweet life-tree that drops / Shade like light across the river" (29), promise a more enticing vision to the infant, one of a future not spent with women in the castle but outside in highways of heaven bustling with a "thousand, thousand faces," where he can play his harp "tuned to music spherical, / Hanging on the green life-tree / Where no willows ever be" (31). Whereas the woman in **"The Seraphim"** is silent and powerless, the male infant of **"Isobel's Child"** convinces his mother his words should be privileged.

"The Seraphim" stresses the desire for involvement in the turmoil and joy of humanity, thereby privileging the public world, which is associated with men. **"Isobel's Child"** sees in the domestic world of the female only suffering on earth and finds death and heaven to be preferable states. While Christian consolation may be the overt message of both poems, covertly they repudiate the claustrophobia perceived in female-dominated internal space and endorse the attraction of "man's earth," male-dominated external space.

"The Romaunt of Margret" and **"The Poet's Vow"** should also be viewed as companion poems. Barrett's acknowledged intention was to show in **"The Romaunt of Margret"** that the "creature cannot be *sustained* by the creature," and in **"The Poet's Vow"** to "enforce a truth—that the creature cannot be *isolated* from the creature" (*W*, I:168). However, at the same time she also challenges cultural assumptions about woman and the male poet. In **"The Romaunt of Margret"** woman, identified purely as a relative creature, dies. The male poet in **"The Poet's Vow"** is deluded when he imagines he can retreat from human interaction and substitute maternal nature for woman.

"The Romaunt of Margret" is a ballad. The poetesses had already appropriated the revived form by introducing issues of domesticity. Landon's "Song of the Hunter's Bride" (from *The Troubadour*) is a conventional tale of a woman anxiously awaiting her husband's return from hunting. As it grows late she fears he has been hurt, then complains,

> Why stays he thus?—he would be here
>   If his love equall'd mine;—
> Methinks had I one fond cage dove,
>   I would not let it pine.

This complaint is undercut by her joy at her husband's eventual return, "My Ulric, welcome home." But the image of woman as analogous to a "fond cage dove" lingers. In Hemans's "Troubadour Song" a warrior fights valiantly in a grisly battle. His life of external masculine activity is juxtaposed with the feminine passivity of the woman left behind in her "smiling home." The warrior survives the "thousand arrows" to return, but the woman meanwhile had "died as roses die, / That perish with a breeze." Although the poem stereotypes the knight and lady, its final question, "There was death within the smiling home— / How had death found her there?" suggests a murderous idle domesticity.

Barrett takes this fatal domesticity to its extreme in **"The Romaunt of Margret."** A fairly conventional ballad narrative, in which Margret dies because she has lost her love, reveals a domestic subtext dramatizing the killing of the Angel in the House. In *Professions for Women* Virginia Woolf records how, as a writer, she had to do battle with a phantom, suggestive of Ellis's "woman of England":

> She was intensely sympathetic. She was immensely charming. She was utterly unselfish. She excelled in the difficult arts of family life. She sacrificed herself daily. If there was chicken, she took the leg; if there was a draught she sat in it—in short she was so constituted that she never had a mind or a wish of her own, but preferred to sympathize always with the minds and wishes of others. Above all—I need not say it—she was pure. . . . Had I not killed her she would have killed me. She would have plucked the heart out of my writing.

Woolf knew that to write demands "having a mind of your own, . . . expressing what you think to be the truth about human relations, morality, sex. And all these questions, according to the Angel in the House, cannot be dealt with freely and openly by women; they must charm, they must conciliate, they must—to put it bluntly—tell lies if they are to succeed." Woolf battled this image of woman, consuming time better spent on "roaming the world in search of adventures." She recognized that "killing the Angel in the House was part of the occupation of a woman writer."[9]

Barrett's 1838 and 1844 ballads evoke a figure like Woolf's Angel. Alethea Hayter describes "Mrs. Browning's Ideal Woman, noble, constant, self-sacrificing, and all blushes, tears and hair down to the ground" as a "tiresome creature." While Hayter's sense that she is "a perfectly nineteenth-century figure" may be accurate, I would argue that it is the age's rather than Barrett's "Ideal Woman."[10] However unconsciously, **"The Romaunt of Margret"** reveals a narrative desire to "kill off" this "tiresome creature," not endorse her; Margret dies because she fulfilled her female duty to tend to others and it proved insufficiently life-sustaining.

Certainly Margret is a "relative creature": she embroiders her brother's "knightly scarf," attends his animals, waits at home for his return, sings "hunter's songs" to him, and pours him his "red wine"; she combs her sister's hair, gives her her own special bird, shares flowers with her, and rears her in Godliness. She is also her father's special handmaiden (more favored than the "hundred friends" in his court); denying herself the delight of watching the knights at tournament, she reads him a "weary book" and cherishes "his blessing when [she's] done." When not caring for her family, she sits by the river thinking of her "more than a friend / Across the mountains dim." She wears his "last look in [her] soul, / Which said, *I love but thee!*" Margret is indeed an ideal daughter of England, a veritable Angel in the House. Why does she die? Ellis would say that such unrequited love as Margret gives to her family and the suffering engendered by the separation from her lover merely require her to "suffer and be still." Margret dies because her daemon, the shadow that rises from the water and sits beside her, engages Margret in dialogue, confronting her with a subversive message. The narrator's response is to lament that earthly love will not last: "O failing human love! . . . O false, the while thou treadest earth!" But the daemon suggests that an existence predicated entirely on Ellis's notion of the "faculty of instrumentality," of being identified as always in a serving relationship to others, kills women. The daemon challenges the idea that the self-identified woman, with "faculties [that] render her striking and distinguished" in herself, is merely a "dead letter in the volume of human life"; she implies that the "relative creature" cannot sustain her own life. Margret's main fantasies focus on her absent lover, but it is not, as Gardner Taplin asserts, merely his death that kills her:[11] it is the gradual recognition of the murderous instrumentality of her existence. As the daemon asserts that her brother, her sister, and her father love their material possessions more than they love Margret, the physical environment around her withers, representing the withering of her own life:

> The sounding river which rolled, for ever
>   Stood dumb and stagnant after.
>
>   [14]
>
> You could see each bird as it woke and
>   stared
>   Through the shrivelled foliage after.
>
>   [17]
>
> And moon and stars though bright and far
>   Did shrink and darken after.
>
>   [20]

Margret exists solely in her serving relation to others and on the fantasy of a lover: when that role proves to be futile, she dies. The daemon asphyxiates the angel.

The narrator, a troubadour, begins her singing of the "wild romaunt" in the present tense as though describing a scene unfolding before her. This continues until the daemon ("the lady's shadow") leaves the water: "It standeth upright in the cleft moonlight, / It sitteth at her side." The narrator now addresses Margret, forcing her to look at the daemon, her own death: "Look in its face, ladye." At this the narrator seems frightened by her own tale for she removes herself from the action, changes to the past tense, and the rest of the tale is a record of, rather than an involvement with, Margret's story.

Whereas in the first stanza the narrator knows her tale is of death—"The yew-tree leaf will suit"—by the last stanza she feels inadequate to telling her tale: "I have no voice for song. / Not song but wail, and mourners pale, / Not bards, to love belong." Her exclamatory ending shifts from narration to rhetorical chant and her lament certainly lends credence to the notion of the poem as one of transitory love:

> O failing human love!
>   O light, by darkness known!
> O false, the while thou treadest earth!
>   O deaf beneath the stone!

But she feels that "mourners" not "bards" belong to love (echoing Mary's feeling with "a spasm, not a speech" in "**The Seraphim**"). Does this imply that the poet's function is not to tell the story of "failing human love," but to indict a society that suggests that its middle-class women can and must survive only on love?

The confused relationship of the narrator to her tale suggests an anxiety about the implications of her subject matter, determined to an extent by the autobiographical impulse informing this poem. Dwelling on Barrett's invalidism, Porter and Clarke focus on such an impulse: "Elizabeth must have been the painter's manikin, serving as first model for Margret. . . . The hold on life through the love of others in life,—for the sake of a peculiarly loved brother's love, a cherished little sister's, a fondly proud father's,—these are all longing snatches at the life about to elude Margret which must have quivered through the outstretched fingers of her own actual experience" (*W,* 2:vii-viii). What Porter and Clarke fail to recognize is that life is only about to elude Margret because she realizes that her love is not returned and that she is a drudge.

Much of the autobiographical significance lies not in Barrett's precarious health (as Porter and Clarke imagine), but in the relationship between Barrett and her mother. The narrator offers no explanation for the missing mother, but the implication is that she died in the same way as Margret dies, through unrequited self-sacrificing love. It is also ominously suggested that Margret's younger sister, who "wears / The look our mother wore" (15) will die this inevitable female death. Margret, successfully educated to be womanly, has taken on her mother's role: she is sister/lover to her brother, sister/mother to her sister, and daughter/wife to her father. The poem, therefore, repeats Barrett's own family situation with her brothers, younger sisters, and her father.

Through study and invalidism, Barrett had sought to avoid the female occupations, thereby incurring the wrath of her sister, Henrietta. She was subject to the departures and returns of her favorite brother, Edward, whose masculine freedom she envied in her youth. And, although he encouraged her writing, her father was peremptory, authoritarian, and emotionally contained. In 1828, when Barrett was twenty-two, her mother died, having given birth to twelve children (one died). Barrett wrote about her to Browning: "Scarcely was I woman when I lost *my* mother—dearest as she was & very tender, . . . but of a nature harrowed up into some furrows by the pressure of circumstances. . . . A sweet, gentle nature, which the thunder a little turned from its sweetness—as when it turns milk—One of those women who never can resist,—but, in submitting & bowing on themselves, make a mark, a plait, within, . . a sign of suffering. Too womanly was she—it was her only fault" (*RB & EBB,* 2:1012). Barrett describes her mother in language analogous to Woolf's angel, "A sweet, gentle nature. . . . One of those women who can never resist . . . submitting and bowing." To Barrett being such a woman was a "fault." The angel cannot sustain her sweet submissive nature because the "thunder" (Mr. Barrett?) "a little turned [her] from its sweetness—as when it turns milk." Barrett is ambivalent in both admiring and condemning her mother for being such a woman; yet she attributes her mother's death to embracing that role. It was not a role her eldest daughter intended to assume. And, as though dramatizing these responses to her mother's life, in **"The Romaunt of Margret"** she examines the fate of a woman who was "too womanly . . . it was her only fault."[12] However, the narrator never spells out the implications of her tale, that a woman who refuses to see herself as the relative creature Margret is, and who realizes herself through "such faculties, as render [her] striking and distinguished" in herself, will survive. Such a woman could be a poet.

Barrett's early resistance to marriage and her suspicion of romantic love are dramatized by Margret's death when the lover across the "mountains dim" (was he ever real?) dies. Romantic love is unreliable. Margret's death then is not merely a melancholy repetition of ballad conventions, but a questioning of their assumptions. The poem annihilates woman's self-annihilative role. The heroine's death, which we expect to mourn, becomes in fact a liberating act, freeing Barrett from the "Ideal Woman's" fate.

The protagonist's death is an equally sorrowful yet liberating act in **"The Poet's Vow,"** Barrett's revisionary reading of Wordsworth and of Romantic ideology about Nature. Barrett's overt admiration of and covert entrapment by Wordsworth as a precursor are revealed in **"The Book of the Poets,"** her critical essay on the history of English poetry published in the *Athenaeum* (1842). She laments how the followers of Dryden and Pope reduced poetry to "the trick of accoustical mechanics," how in their writings "thought had perished . . . and we had the beaten rhythm without the living footstep." In their work Nature had been "expelled" (*W,* 6:299). But Cowper, Burns, and Coleridge heralded a change consummated by Wordsworth, "the chief of the movement." These poets allowed "Nature, the long banished, [to redawn] like the morning." To accomplish this they abandoned, after a hard struggle, the "conventional dialects" of poets, conventional words, attitudes, and manners, consecrated by "wits." Wordsworth "in a bravery bravest of all . . . to the actual scandal of the world which stared at the filial familiarity, . . . threw himself not at the feet of Nature, but straightway and right tenderly upon her bosom . . . trustfully as child before mother" (*W,* 6:300). Barrett cites Wordsworth as the primary poet of Nature, suggesting that he and his rhetoric of Nature had a much stronger influence on her than other Romantic poets. Indeed, she outgrew her adolescent fervor for Byron, admired Keats, but found Shelley too cold and distant as a poet.

Wordsworth was spokesman for a literary tradition that posited Nature as a maternal figure. A psychoanalytic scenario of this would, thereby, have the male precursor poet as the father, and the female presence in Romantic poetry as Mother Nature, the silent other, the woman. The son, the young poet, engages in a struggle of desire for and separation from her, and is both subject to and yet controls her power.[13] In **"The Poet's Vow"** Barrett dramatizes the dilemma Wordsworth's representation of nature posed for her as a daughter poet.

The poem tells of an unnamed male poet who rejects his fellow human beings in order to live with the "touching, patient Earth" (1.12) to "feel [her] unseen looks / Innumerous, constant, deep" (1.19):

> "And ever, when I lift my brow
>   At evening to the sun,
> No voice of woman or of child
>   Recording 'Day is done.'
> Your silences shall a love express,
>   More deep than such an one."

[1.20]

Barrett portrays a clichéd Romantic poet for whom nature, assuming female qualities, is preferable to a wife welcoming him home. But a new aspect of man's relationship to and exploitation of "Earth" is presented by this poet. He believes that, while God created a "very good" earth, man made it "very mournful," a violently crazed place instead of a calm and silent haven:

> "Poor crystal sky with stars astray!
>   Mad winds that howling go
> From east to west! perplexèd seas
>   That stagger from their blow!
> O motion wild! O wave defiled!
>   Our curse hath made you so."
>
> [1.13]

To restore the paradisal bond between man and nature (son and mother's breast), the poet breaks his bonds with other people. Forsaking adult concerns, he hopes again (as a child fantasizes) to control this mother turned madwoman, this woman who is neglecting his needs.

The narrator, however, establishes the error of his vision:

> This poet daringly,
>   —The nature at his heart,
> And that quick tune along his veins
>   He could not change by art,—
> Had vowed his blood of brotherhood
>   To a stagnant place apart.
>
> He did not vow in fear, or wrath,
>   Or grief's fantastic whim,
> But, weights and shows of sensual things
>   Too closely crossing him,
> On his soul's eyelid the pressure slid
>   And made its vision dim.
>
> [1.9-10]

What he sees as a "touching, patient Earth," the narrator views as a "stagnant place apart." What he feels to be the "dessicating sin" of human involvement, she describes as the "weights and shows of sensual things / Too closely crossing him." Nature is not a maternal figure to the narrator, but a mere stagnant place unless populated by human intercourse.

In Part 2 ("Showing to Whom the Vow was Declared"), the poet assigns all his silver and gold to his "crowding friends." The narrator tellingly describes how the friends are "solaced" by "clasping bland his gift,—his hand / In a somewhat slacker hold" (2.1-2). Only his friend, Sir Roland, and his fiancée, Rosalind (his childhood companion), remain, and he dismisses them to marry each other, with his lands as Rosalind's dowry. Rosalind refuses to be so assigned, and, although she describes herself as "half a child" and the poet as "very sage" (2.8), it is she who will eventually

demonstrate how fallacious is his romance with nature. She learns from his face the "cruel homily" of "the teachings of the heaven and earth" (2.8-9). Preferring to remain "untouched, unsoftened" by their beauty, she dissociates her female identity from "the senseless, loveless earth and heaven" (2.9). Sir Roland also tries to persuade the poet that his understanding of the relationship between people and the earth is destructive. The poet's response reveals a masochistic vision of his desired natural environment:

> "I go to live
>   In Courland Hall, alone:
> The bats along the ceilings cling,
> The lizards in the floors do run,
> And storms and years have worn and reft
> The stain by human builders left
>   In working at the stone."
>
> [2.22]

His "touching, patient Earth" is destructive. His retreat, a cobwebby squalor, undercuts his notion of nature's "unseen looks / Innumerous, constant, deep," and her "silences" that "love express" (1.19-20). In his male hands domestic space resembles an unfeminized gothic interior.

In Part 3 ("Showing How the Vow was Kept") Barrett wrote an uncanny counterpoint to Tennyson's "The Lady of Shalott." Although critics commented on certain similarities of style between Barrett and Tennyson, neither had read the other's work at this stage.[14] A comparison between the two is, however, illuminating. In Tennyson's poem the woman inside the tower knows only that a curse of unknown origin is on her. This confines her inside, prohibiting her from looking through her window. She longs to go outside—"I am half sick of shadows"—but remains the artist, weaving representations of the images from outside reflected in her mirror. Love finally compels her to look at the handsome Sir Lancelot, but such engagement in the world causes her death. Tennyson, the male poet who is free, whatever his psychopathology, to move in the world beyond his house and engage in its activities, projects a fantasy of escape from the public world onto a female artist whom he condemns to stay removed from the world and its destructive energies.

Barrett, a woman writer confined to a domestic sphere, transforms such domestic enclosure into the gothic habitat of a male poet who deliberately turns from love and the world, and chooses to stay within his tower. To the narrator this is a curse: "a lonely creature of sinful nature / It is an awful thing" (3.2). Unlike the Lady of Shalott, who only saw shadowy reflections in her mirror yet longed to look out, this "poet at his lattice sate, / And downward looked he" (3.4). Free to look down and walk about, he only peered through his window at the churchgoers, the bridal party, and the child who "Stood near the wall to see at play / The lizards green and rare" (3.6). The poet neither joined them nor blessed them, but purposely withdrew. This brought him not solace but fear:

> He dwelt alone, and sun and moon
> Were witness that he made
> Rejection of his humanness
> Until they seemed to fade;
> His face did so, for he did grow
> Of his own soul afraid.
>
> The self-poised God may dwell alone
> With inward glorying,
> But God's chief angel waiteth for
> A brother's voice, to sing;
> And a lonely creature of sinful nature
> It is an awful thing.
>
> An awful thing that feared itself;
> While many years did roll,
> A lonely man, a feeble man,
> A part beneath the whole,
> He bore by day, he bore by night
> That pressure of God's infinite
> Upon his finite soul.
>
>   [3.1-3]

The psychic disturbance caused by denial of "his humanness," defined as involvement in the world outside the home, turns the poet into an "awful thing that feared itself."

Part 4 ("Showing How Rosalind Fared by the Keeping of the Vow") evokes Keats's "La Belle Dame Sans Merci." If the knight's encounter with "La Belle Dame" leaves him wasted and aimless, so Rosalind's rejection by the poet leaves her wasted: "In deathsheets lieth Rosalind / As white and still as they" (6.1). His devotion to nature makes Rosalind turn from her "rival" and, in an exaggerated reaction to the poet's own behavior, she insists that the windows in her room be closed so she hears nothing from outside and sees none of God's "blessed works" (4.3). When she is dead, she wants her corpse carried to Courland Hall via the natural landscape of her childhood—the long church grass, the river bank, the brook, the hill, the "piny forest still" and the "open moorland" (4.9-10). Nature, instead of fulfilling its promise ("the brook with its sunny look / Akin to living glee"), has been used against her; only as a corpse will she traverse it again.

In Part 5 ("Showing How the Vow was Broken") the poet (on the day Rosalind dies) revels alone in the beauty of the stars at midnight:

> They shine upon the steadfast hills,
> Upon the swinging tide,

> Upon the narrow track of beach
> And the murmuring pebbles pied:
> They shine on every lovely place,
> They shine upon the corpse's face.
>
>   [5.2]

The poet learns that Rosalind is dead; his "touching, patient Earth" cannot preserve him from human interaction. The sterility of his aesthetic is now challenged by a woman poet: attached to Rosalind's corpse is a scroll. Written before her death, the poem is in the Hemans-Landon tradition of love-laments: "'I have prayed for thee with bursting sob / When passion's course was free.'" She suffered silently and tearfully the years without him. Her poem, however, effects change. Rosalind insists that nature is not a substitute for woman: "'I tell thee that my poor scorned heart / Is of thine earth.'" Dead, she can no longer pray for him:

> "The corpse's tongue is still,
> Its folded fingers point to heaven,
> But point there stiff and chill."

Like the ancient mariner, the poet's only salvation lies with himself:

> "I charge thee, by the living's prayer,
> And the dead's silentness,
> To wring out from thy soul a cry
> Which God shall hear and bless!"

"Triumphant Rosalind" awakens his "long-subjected humanness," manifest as a "lion-cry" (5.6), and he weeps. Their roles reversed now, Rosalind, the "half-a-child," is a wise poet, and the male poet reveals "That weeping wild of a reckless child / From a proud man's broken heart" (5.7). The man "who so worshipped earth and sky" (5.8) is "found too weak / To bear his human pain" (5.9), and he too dies.

Sir Roland, years later, brings his little son to the grave. When the boy, like the poet before him, turns "upward his blithe eyes to see / The wood-doves nodding from the tree," his father, echoing Rosalind, tells him:

> "Nay, boy look downward, . . .
> Upon this human dust asleep.
> And hold it in thy constant ken
> That God's own unity compresses
> (One into one) the human many,
>
>   . . . . .
>
> If not in love, on sorrow then,—
> Though smiling not like other men,
> Still, like them we must weep."
>
>   [5.10]

The religious overtones of Barrett's aesthetic creed matured as her poetry became boldly feminized through her understanding that her responsibility was to speak for those women who "suffer wrong . . . everywhere" (*L,* 2:445). She was convinced that the real work of poets is the work women have always been rooted in—human suffering and joy—but without its attendant self-abnegation.

Barrett's conviction that the poet must engage with social and political issues had its terrors and burdens for her, a woman imagining herself as a descendent of the great male poetic tradition, as the "fear of earth" had for the angels in **"The Seraphim."** She suggests such anxiety in her dramatization of other prominent women in **"The Virgin Mary to the Child Jesus,"** **"Victoria's Tears,"** and **"The Young Queen."** In the first of these, Mary's meditation over her sleeping son, Mary knows that future generations will say of her, "Thou art / The blessedest of women!" (6), but Barrett examines the practical implications of this status. Mary feels that her pure son was "created from my nature all defiled" (7) and recognizes that:

No small babe-smiles my watching heart has
  seen
To float like speech the speechless lips
  between,
No dovelike cooing in the golden air,
No quick short joys of leaping babyhood.

                                              [9]

Barrett imagines that Mary, knowing her son's destiny, will have painfully ambivalent feelings about the "majestic angel whose command / Was softly as a man's beseeching said" (1) naming her as the chosen mother of Jesus. When she thinks of "the drear sharp tongue of prophecy, / With the dread sense of things which shall be done," of how her son will be called "despised" and "rejected," she feels: "I must not die, with mother's work to do, / And could not live—and see" (10).

In **"Victoria's Tears"** Barrett imagines how this eighteen-year-old girl, "Maiden! heir of kings," must feel as a woman leading a country (in which women were disenfranchised) when she can "no longer lean" on her "mother's breast." The contrast between the adult woman with a public function—whether queen or poet—deprived of such maternal nurturance, and Barrett's sense of Wordsworth as one who "threw himself right tenderly upon [Nature's] bosom" is a poignant one. Barrett stresses the great pomp of the coronation, but

    She saw no purples shine,
      For tears had dimmed her eyes;
    She only knew her childhood's flowers
      Were happier pageantries!

And while her heralds played the part,
  For million shouts to drown—
"God save the Queen" from hill to mart,—
She heard through all her beating heart,
  And turned and wept—
  She wept, to wear a crown!

Barrett suggests that token women who attain public prominence feel ambivalent about their status. As she reveals her own anxiety as a woman measuring her feet inside the shoes of her dead literary fathers, so she imagines Victoria to be similarly unnerved at her sudden power. In **"The Young Queen,"** she delineates how "Her palace walls enring / The dust that was a king—/ And very cold beneath her feet, she feels her father's grave." At fourteen Barrett had felt some comfort in walking in Homer's footsteps and not striking out a path for herself; now she imagines in chilling terms a severance from the father as woman appropriates power traditionally reserved for him. Instead of guiding her feet the precursor now numbs them with cold. It is a statement of loss; but it also determines the daughter to walk her own path.

The first tentative steps along such a path resulted from the "individuality" represented in *The Seraphim, and Other Poems,* in Barrett's conviction that in this "age of steam" the poet had to embrace the world "of dust and death" and "human pain." By taking Jesus, "man's victim" and "his deity"—with his engagement in human concerns—rather than God, the divine creator, as her model for the poet, Barrett legitimized her desire that woman engage in art and politics.

In *The Seraphim, and Other Poems* Barrett initiated her departure both from the "frustration" of the male poetic tradition, which privileged the male voice as subject of poetic discourse with woman as object and other, and from the "delusion" of following the poetesses who overtly advocated resignation to woman's "weary lot" even while covertly transgressing their own dictum. She began in these poems to place woman as the subject of her own discourse. When Kenyon expressed fond nostalgia for her early poems, Barrett dismissed *The Battle of Marathon* and *An Essay on Mind* as a "girl's exercise," convinced that "the difference between them and my present poems is not merely the difference between . . . immaturity and maturity; but that it is the difference between the dead and the living, between a copy and an individuality, between what is myself and what is not myself" (*L,* 1:187-88). Far from lamenting the past, she eagerly anticipated fashioning the "new manners" of the discourse expressing that subjectivity; her *Poems of 1844* represented a decisive challenge to the "old manners" she was outgrowing.

Notes

[1] Wilson, "Christopher in His Cave," p. 279.

[2] Barrett Browning, *Autobiography* (hereafter cited in the text as *A* followed by page).

[3] Barrett Browning, *Diary*, p. xix (hereafter cited in the text as *D* followed by page).

[4] Ellis, *Women of England*, pp. 149-50.

[5] Watts, *Literary Souvenir*. Barrett's comments on the poems are in an unpublished pocket notebook in Wellesley College Library (from Sotheby Lot 110—Barrett's pocket diary for 1823 and notebook for 1824-25).

[6] *Examiner*, pp. 387-88; *Athenaeum*, pp. 466-68 (the reviewer was probably Henry Fothergill Chorley); Wilson, "Christopher in His Cave," pp. 279-84; *Quarterly Review*, pp. 382-89; *North American Review*, pp. 201-18 (George S. Hillard was probably the reviewer); Warburton, *English Review*, pp. 259-73. Reviews also ran in the *Sunbeam*, p. 243; *Metropolitan Magazine* (London), pp. 97-101; *Monthly Review*, pp. 125-30; *Monthly Chronicle* (London), p. 195; *Atlas*, p. 395; *Literary Gazette*, pp. 759-60; *Arcturus, A Journal of Books and Opinions* (U.S.), pp. 171-76.

[7] For a discussion of how this was also true for women novelists see Showalter, *Literature of Their Own*, chap. 3.

[8] Donaldson, "Motherhood's Advent in Power," pp. 52-53.

[9] Woolf, "Professions for Women," pp. 237-38.

[10] Hayter, *Mrs. Browning*, pp. 82-83.

[11] Taplin, *Life of Elizabeth Barrett Browning*, p. 62.

[12] This theme of the womanly woman dying is taken up twenty years later in *Aurora Leigh*, when Aurora's aunt who "liked a woman to be womanly" (1:443) educated Aurora to understand woman's "Potential faculty in everything/ Of abdicating power in it" (1:441), so that Aurora feels her aunt has "dried out from [Aurora's] drowned anatomy / The last sea-salt left in [her]" (1:383-84) such that visitors worry that "she will die" (1:498).

[13] Margaret Homans delineates this scenario in her discussion of the difficulties confronting Dorothy Wordsworth, Emily Brontë, and Emily Dickinson as writers. Homans, *Women Writers and Poetic Identity*.

[14] See Hayter, *Mrs. Browning*, p. 31:

> The 1838 volume first started the charge, so often brought against her, of imitating Tennyson—in "The Romaunt of Margret" said the *Atlas*; in "Isobel's Child" said the *Quarterly*. "It always makes me a little savage when people talk of Tennysonianisms!" she told Browning. "I have faults enough as the Muses know,—but let them be *my* faults! When I wrote the 'Romaunt of Margret,' I had not read a line of Tennyson.". . . . "Nearly everything in the 'Seraphim' was written before I ever read *one* of his then published volumes," she told Horne in 1844.

Bibliography

WORKS BY ELIZABETH BARRETT BROWNING

Aurora Leigh and Other Poems. Introduced by Cora Kaplan. London: Women's Press, 1978.

Casa Guidi Windows. Edited by Julia Markus. New York: Browning Institute, 1977.

The Complete Works of Elizabeth Barrett Browning. Edited by Charlotte Porter and Helen A. Clarke. 6 vols. New York: Thomas Y. Crowell & Co., 1900. Reprint. New York: AMS Press, 1973.

Diary by E. B. B.: The Unpublished Diary of Elizabeth Barrett Barrett, 1831-1832. Edited by Philip Kelley and Ronald Hudson. Athens: Ohio University Press, 1969.

Elizabeth Barrett Browning: Hitherto Unpublished Poems and Stories with an Inedited Autobiography. Edited by H. Buxton Forman. Boston: Bibliophile Society, 1914.

Elizabeth Barrett to Mr. Boyd. Unpublished Letters of Elizabeth Barrett Browning to Hugh Stuart Boyd. Edited by Barbara P. McCarthy. London: John Murray, 1955.

The Letters of Elizabeth Barrett Browning. Edited by Frederic C. Kenyon. 2 vols. New York: Macmillan Co., 1897.

The Letters of Elizabeth Barrett Browning to Mary Russell Mitford, 1836-1854. Edited by Meredith B. Raymond and Mary Rose Sullivan. 3 vols. Armstrong Browning Library of Baylor University, Browning Institute, Wedgestone Press, and Wellesley College, 1983.

WORKS BY ELIZABETH BARRETT BROWNING AND ROBERT BROWNING

The Letters of Robert Browning and Elizabeth Barrett Barrett, 1845-1846. Edited by Elvan Kintner. 2 vols.

Cambridge: Harvard University Press, Belknap Press, 1969.

SECONDARY SOURCES

Donaldson, Sandra M. "Motherhood's Advent in Power: Elizabeth Barrett Browning's Poems about Motherhood." *Victorian Poetry* 18, no. 1 (Spring 1980): 51-60.

Ellis, Sarah Stickney. *The Women of England.* London: Fisher, Son & Co., 1838.

Hayter, Alethea. *Mrs. Browning: A Poet's Work and Its Setting.* London: Faber & Faber, 1962.

Hemans, Felicia. *The Poetical Works.* London: Peacock, Mansfield & Co.

Homans, Margaret. *Women Writers and Poetic Identity.* Princeton: Princeton University Press, 1980.

Landon, Letitia. *The Poetical Works of L. E. L. Landon.* Boston: Phillips, Sampson and Co., 1853.

Showalter, Elaine. *A Literature of Their Own.* Princeton: Princeton University Press, 1977.

Taplin, Gardner B. *The Life of Elizabeth Barrett Browning.* New Haven: Yale University Press, 1957.

Watts, Alaric A., ed. *The Literary Souvenir; or, Cabinet of Poetry and Romance.* London, 1825.

Woolf, Virginia. "Professions for Women." In *The Death of the Moth and Other Essays.* 1942. Reprint. New York: Harcourt Brace Jovanovich, Harvest Books, 1974.

REVIEWS

Reviews of *The Seraphim, and Other Poems*

Arcturus, a Journal of Books and Opinions (U.S.) 1 (February 1841): 171-76.

Athenaeum, July 7, 1838, 466-68.

Atlas, June 23, 1838, 395.

Examiner, June 24, 1838, 387-88.

Literary Gazette, December 1, 1838, 759-60.

North American Review 55 (1842): 201-18.

Metropolitan Magazine (London), August 22, 1838, 97-101.

Monthly Chronicle (London) 2 (1838): 195.

Monthly Review, n.s. 3 (1838): 125-30.

Quarterly Review 66 (1840): 382-89.

Sunbeam, September 1, 1838, 243.

Warburton, [?]. *English Review,* December, 1845, 259-73.

Wilson, John [Christopher North, pseud.]. "Christopher in His Cave." *Blackwood's Edinburgh Magazine* 44 (1838): 279-84.

Marjorie Stone (essay date 1995)

SOURCE: "A Cinderella Among the Muses: Barrett Browning and the Ballad Tradition," in *Elizabeth Barrett Browning,* St. Martin's Press, 1995, pp. 94-133.

[*In the following essay, Stone evaluates the poetic innovations of Browning's ballads in the context of the Romantic ballad revival and its tradition in Victorian England.*]

In their 1867 edition of Bishop Percy's folio of ballads, John H. Hales and Frederick J. Furnivall picture the ballad before the Romantic revival as a 'Cinderella' among the Muses:

> She had never dared to think herself beautiful. No admiring eyes ever came near her in which she might mirror herself. She had never dared to think her voice sweet. . . . She met with many enemies, who clamoured that the kitchen was her proper place, and vehemently opposed her admission into any higher room. The Prince was long in finding her out. The sisters put many an obstacle between him and her. . . . But at last the Prince found her, and took her in all her simple sweetness to himself.[1]

Some readers might pause over the class- and gender-inflected assumptions in this ingenuous fairy story of a gallantly patronizing 'Prince' taking a low-born maiden 'to himself'. But few would dispute the importance of the union Hales and Furnivall fancifully describe. Every student of Romantic poetry recognizes the profound significance of the ballad revival, reflected in Bishop Percy's *Reliques of Ancient English Poetry* (1765), in Sir Walter Scott's 'minstrelsy', and above all in the *Lyrical Ballads* published by Wordsworth and Coleridge in 1798.

Yet the ballad is seldom recognized as an important Victorian genre, even though it attracted major and minor poets throughout the nineteenth century. G. Malcolm Laws' catalogue of literary ballads in the Victorian period (1832-90) is longer than his catalogue for the Romantic period. As Laws' survey suggests, the ballad was held in particular esteem by the Pre-Raphaelite poets.[2] Tennyson, like Hardy after him, also employed innovative variants of the form throughout his long career, in works such as 'The Sisters', with its refrain 'O the Earl was fair to see!', 'The Lady of Shalott', the immensely popular 'Lady Clare Vere De Vere', 'Edward Gray', 'Lady Clare', 'Locksley Hall', 'The Revenge: A Ballad of the Fleet', and 'Rizpah'. Ballads are particularly numerous in his 1842 *Poems,* reflecting their prominence in a period marked by the success of Macaulay's *Lays of Ancient Rome* (1842) and the continuing popularity of Sir Walter Scott's ballads and narrative poems.

Although Elizabeth Barrett was no 'Prince', she too took that 'Cinderella' among the Muses, the ballad, to herself—not so much because the form was simple and sweet, but because its energy, its strong heroines, its elemental passions of love and revenge, its frank physicality and its sinewy narrative conflicts allowed her to circumvent the ideologies of passionless purity and self-sacrifice confining middle-class Victorian women. Ballads have an even higher profile in her 1844 *Poems* than in Tennyson's 1842 *Poems.* Moreover, her 'peculiar skill' in 'this species of poetry' was frequently praised (*BC* 9:341, 365).

In our own century, however, popular Victorian ballads and Barrett Browning's ballads in particular have been underappreciated for a number of reasons, among them the intersecting ideologies of gender and genre. In short, the marriage celebrated by Hales and Furnivall seems to have ended in divorce, with Cinderella dismissed to her proper place in the kitchen. Ironically, despite Wordsworth's subversion of genre and his democratizing aims in the *Lyrical Ballads,* most reconstructions of the nineteenth-century ballad tradition have been informed by prescriptive categorical distinctions separating the ballad from the romance, 'serious' poetry from popular verse, literary from authentic folk ballads, Romantic from Victorian poets, and female from male traditions. These critical ideologies have had especially unfortunate consequences in the case of Barrett Browning. Even recent feminist critics disparage her ballads, ironically by placing them in the context of a separate 'feminine genre' of popular ballad-writing which is, in Dorothy Mermin's words, 'sentimental' and 'retrogressive' (91).

By considering the intertextuality of a number of Barrett Browning's ballads and by reconstructing the horizon of expectation against which they were written and read, I hope to show that her innovations can be better appreciated when we approach poems like **'The Poet's Vow'**, **'The Romaunt of Margret'**, **'A Romance of the Ganges'** and **'The Romaunt of the Page'** in the context of the Romantic ballad revival and the tradition it produced. In many cases, Barrett Browning refashioned motifs and conventions from folk ballads and

Romantic narrative verse in ways that anticipate the ballads of the Pre-Raphaelite poets. At the same time, however, her handling of the form differs from that of many other poets working in the tradition because of the distinctively gynocentric focus of her Romantic revisionary impulse. In her appropriations of the 'Cinderella' among the muses, the ballad is used to subvert the conventional inscriptions of sexual difference the genre appears to confirm.

The originality of Barrett Browning's ballads is particularly apparent in her modification of what Nancy K. Miller terms 'female plots'—that is, the plots that 'culture has always already inscribed' for women, plots reinscribed in 'the linear time of fiction'.[3] Like Charlotte Brontë, Barrett Browning has often been faulted for her handling of plot. Even Mermin generally observes that it was fortunate Barrett Browning did not write novels because she 'had no gift for inventing plots' (186) and the stories in her ballads are 'invariably silly', if 'entertaining' (90). But in many instances the 'silly' stories that Mermin objects to in Barrett's 1838 and 1844 ballads are no more absurd than the plots they play against in the traditional ballads collected by Percy, such as 'Child Waters', and in the ballads and narratives written in the Romantic revival by the German poet Gottfried Bürger, by Scott, and by Wordsworth and Coleridge.

The substantial revisions Barrett Browning made in her ballads, both at the manuscript stage and after they had appeared in periodicals and annuals, further illumine her complex adaptation of plots and motifs in precursor texts. These modifications also call in question the common view that she wrote her ballads quickly and did not take them very seriously. In **'The Poet's Vow'**, Barrett Browning appropriates elements in the anonymous ballads of the Percy collection to carry out a critique of Wordsworth and Coleridge—a critique she extends in the many revisions she made in the poem after its initial publication. In **'The Romaunt of the Page'**, she subverts the gender-inflected plots in certain of the Percy ballads themselves. Significantly, the most substantial revisions in **'The Romaunt of the Page'** expand the role and motivation of the poem's male protagonist, revealing how Barrett Browning progressively complicated her 'female plots' by portraying their intersections with the social systems that create and encompass them. The changes in **'The Romaunt of the Page'** thus look forward to *Aurora Leigh,* where Barrett Browning shows how the 'female plots' shaping Aurora's existence are inseparable from the gender plots of Romney and his society.

'The Poet's Vow' and **'The Romaunt of Margret'**, both published in 1836 in the *New Monthly Magazine,* were the first ballads by Barrett to attract the interest of readers. These were followed by **'A Romance of the Ganges'**, **'The Romaunt of the Page'**, and **'The**

Legend of the Brown Rosarie', published in the 1838, 1839 and 1840 editions of the annual edited by Mary Mitford, *Findens' Tableaux*. The 1844 **Poems** brought substantially revised versions of **'The Romaunt of the Page'** and **'The Legend of the Brown Rosarie'** before a wider public, along with several new poems identified as 'ballads' by contemporary reviewers: most notably **'Rhyme of the Duchess May'**, **'Bertha in the Lane'**, **'The Romance of the Swan's Nest'**, and **'Lady Geraldine's Courtship'**. Barrett Browning's ballads were acclaimed by general readers as well as critics, and remained among her most popular works until the end of the century. They were often reprinted in selected editions of her poems, while particular favourites, such as **'Rhyme of the Duchess May'** and **'Lady Geraldine's Courtship'** were republished separately in illustrated editions until well past the turn of the century.

The vogue for ballads in the mid-Victorian period inevitably led to parodies like those in the frequently reprinted 'Bon Gaultier' *Ballads* (1845), which included in one of its later editions a parody of **'Rhyme of the Duchess May'** entitled 'The Rhyme of Lancelot Bogle'. Such parodies no doubt contributed to the relatively low profile of the ballad in modern constructions of the Victorian poetical canon—and, in Barrett Browning's case, to the disappearance of her ballads from literary history altogether. The assumption that a popular *literary* work is of little artistic value has lingered longer in the case of Victorian poets than in the case of novelists such as Dickens or Wilkie Collins.

Paradoxically, in the case of popular literary ballads, the effects of this assumption have been exacerbated by narrow definitions of the genre that privilege the anonymous or 'authentically' popular folk ballad over equally popular literary 'imitations'. J. S. Bratton shrewdly notes some of the limitations of such constraining definitions in the case of Francis J. Child's enormously influential collection, *The English and Scottish Ballads,* and detects the 'same assumption of the innate superiority of the traditional ballad' in studies of the literary ballad by Albert B. Friedman and Anne Ehenpreis.[4] Barrett Browning's ballads have particularly suffered from definitions of the genre privileging the 'authentic' folk form because they move farther away from this model than literary ballads like Keats' 'La Belle Dame Sans Merci' and D. G. Rossetti's 'Sister Helen'.

These general assumptions about the popular literary ballad underlie Alethea Hayter's dismissal of Barrett Browning's ballads in 1962 as 'synthetic' confections with a 'certain narrative sweep and excitement' appealing to 'people who did not normally read poetry at all' (81). Hayter adds in extenuation that Barrett Browning 'never really took them seriously', supporting this conclusion with the well-known lines in *Aurora Leigh*:

> My ballads prospered; but the ballad's race
> Is rapid for a poet who bears weights
> Of thought and golden image.
> (Book 5:84-6)

Traces of Hayter's disparaging tone persist in recent feminist reinterpretations. Kathleen Hickok dismisses **'The Lay of the Brown Rosary'** as 'an uninspired jumble', **'The Romaunt of Margret'** as completely conventional, and **'Rhyme of the Duchess May'** as a 'Spasmodic' poem (173-5). Leighton approaches **'A Romance of the Ganges'** and **'The Lay of the Brown Rosary'** as 'confused and precipitate' ballads 'which Elizabeth Barrett wrote in response to a demand . . . for morally educative poems' directed towards 'a primarily female readership' (1986, 32). Although Leighton has more recently acknowledged the 'modern sexual politics' in **'The Romaunt of the Page',** she still describes it as 'an awkward, pseudo-Spenserian ballad' written in 'quirky archaic registers' (1992, 82-3).

In a series of articles subsequently incorporated into *Elizabeth Barrett Browning: The Origins of a New Poetry*, Mermin was the first to reinterpret Barrett Browning's ballads as poems providing 'a covert but thorough-going reassessment, often a total repudiation, of the Victorian ideas about womanliness to which they ostensibly appeal' (71). 'Beneath their apparent conventionality,' Mermin argues, the ballads sceptically examine 'the myths and fantasies of nineteenth-century womanhood', including 'the virtues of self-repression and self-sacrifice' they seem to affirm (90-1). At the same time, Mermin doubts that the poet herself was very aware of the subversiveness of her own poems (90). 'Almost all of her ballads cry out to be read as feminist revisions of old tales', but 'Elizabeth Barrett told the old stories in a style and tone that gave no hint of revisionary intention, and she discarded the ballad form without discovering how to use it effectively against itself' (95). Detecting a more consistently subversive dimension in Barrett Browning's medieval ballads, Helen Cooper reads them as an examination of 'the sexual economy of courtship and marriage' (70), and Glennis Stephenson analyses their critique of 'chivalric conventions' and gender roles (29). Like Mermin, however, they emphasize the limits of Barrett Browning's revisionism, and approach it within the context of a 'female genre' (Cooper 70) of ballad writing which is 'squarely in the tradition of' Letitia Landon (Mermin 107). In keeping with this compartmentalization, Mermin and Cooper separate **'The Poet's Vow'** with its male protagonist from the 'romantic ballads' with female protagonists—even though **'The Poet's Vow'** more clearly employs the ballad form than a poem like **'The Lay of the Brown Rosary'**.

Resituating Barrett Browning's ballads within the context of the Romantic ballad revival requires an approach wary of retrospectively imposed compartmentalizations by gender, genre, period and popularity. Early Victorian conceptions of the ballad seem to have been remarkably broad and inclusive, both in terms of gender and in terms of genre. While some of Barrett Browning's ballads particularly appealed to women, neither the poet herself nor the majority of her readers approached them in the context of a separate feminine tradition. A relatively inclusive generic definition is also in order because assumptions about the ballad form were more amorphous in the early Victorian period than they became after Child's collection of 'authentic' folk ballads appeared.

Like **'The Lay of the Brown Rosary'**, many of the works described by Barrett's reviewers as ballads might more probably be classified as romances or romantic tales today. In fact, **'Lady Geraldine's Courtship'** bore the subtitle **'A Romance of the Age'**, yet was still referred to as a ballad by early Victorian reviewers. Albert Friedman and Hermann Fischer acknowledge the difficulty of distinguishing between ballad and romance forms in nineteenth-century narrative verse, and trace the developments that contributed to the mixing of the two modes. Fischer notes that when Scott attempted to describe the new genre of '"romantic poetry"' or romantic verse narrative in 1813, he did 'not distinguish between [sic] ballads, lays and romances'; moreover, Scott's own poetical works reflect an 'eclectic mixture' of conventions from 'the ballad and romance traditions'. Friedman's more condemnatory approach to the 'intrusion of romance' into nineteenth-century 'ballad poetry' reflects the genre ideologies that contributed to the neglect of Barrett Browning's ballad-romances, along with Scott's.[5]

Barrett Browning's titles for her 'ballads' ('romaunt', 'lay', 'rhyme', 'romance') and her references to these works in her letters suggest that for her, as for many of her contemporaries, all of these terms were loosely synonymous. Harriet Martineau's reference to Barrett's ballads as her 'Rhyme, Romaunt, lay-style of poem' is indicative (*BC* 9:141). I therefore use the term 'ballad' here as Barrett Browning and other Victorians used it, to refer to all of her narrative poems with clear affinities either with the characteristic features of the ballad form (the ballad stanza, the use of dialogue and the refrain, tragic and/or topical subject matter, narrative compression and intensity) or with the larger tradition of 'minstrelsy' and Romantic narrative verse. The principal exception to this rule is the group of narrative poems with dramatized speakers, including **'Catarina to Camoens'**, **'Bertha in the Lane'**, **'Lady Geraldine's Courtship'**, **'The Runaway Slave at Pilgrim's Point'**, **'Void in Law'**, and **'Mother and Poet'**. These works were often described as 'ballads' and they share many characteristics with both folk ballads and the ballads of the Romantic revival: there are clear echoes of the old Scottish ballad 'Lady

Bothwell's Lament' in 'Void in Law', for example. But since this group of poems displays even stronger affinities with the developing form of the dramatic monologue, I have chosen to treat them as such elsewhere and to make only passing reference to their ballad traits below.

Barrett Browning often expressed her love for 'the old burning ballads, with a wild heart beating in each!' (*BC* 6:268). She also probably thought of ballad writing as a natural preparation for the writing of an epic, a mode of thinking subsequently borne out by her own career as she moved from writing simpler to more elaborate ballads and narratives between 1836 and 1844, culminating in **'Lady Geraldine's Courtship'**, which she clearly saw as the germ of her novel-epic *Aurora Leigh* (*LMRM* 3:42). As Barrett observed in her 1842 essay, **'The Book of the Poets'**, the ballad is 'a form epitomical of the epic and dramatic' (6:296). Thus it seems unlikely that she saw her ballads as mere diversionary exercises in a 'feminine' genre or that she devalued her *Findens'* ballads, as Stephenson suggests (24). On the contrary, her plans for her 1844 volumes reflect the prominence she wished her ballads to have (*BC* 6:260).

Unfortunately, space did not permit Barrett to include a survey of the 'anonymous & onymous ballads' in **'The Book of the Poets'**, as she explained to Mitford (*BC* 6:7). Nevertheless, she revealed her enthusiastic appreciation of the Romantic ballad revival and the innovations it fostered. 'We must not be thrown back upon the "Ballads," lest we wish to live with them for ever', she fondly observes as she passes them by (*CW* 6:296). She does find room to allude to 'the *réveillé* of Dr. Percy's "Reliques of English Poetry"', which sowed 'great hearts' like Wordsworth's with 'impulses of greatness' (298), and to the '"Scottish Minstrelsy"' inspired by the *Reliques* (299-300).

Scott's epic narrative *Marmion* (1808) is one product of the Romantic ballad revival that enters into the intertextuality of Barrett's 1844 ballads, contributing to the resonance of her depiction of a woman disguised as a page and a nun buried alive in **'The Romaunt of the Page'** and **'The Lay of the Brown Rosary'**. The pronounced Gothic strain in the **'The Lay of the Brown Rosary'** also owes something to Scott, although it reflects more closely the lingering influence of 'Lenora', the immensely popular German ballad by Gottfried Bürger that was so important a prototype for Wordsworth, Coleridge, Scott and Southey in the 1790s, as Mary Jacobus and Stephen Parrish have shown.[6]

Barrett's readers and reviewers up to 1844 were quick to link her ballads to such precursors in the larger ballad tradition. Responding to **'The Poet's Vow'** in 1836, Mitford wrote to Barrett, 'I have just read your delightful ballad. My earliest book was "Percy's Reliques," the delight of my childhood; and after them came Scott's "Minstrelsy of the Borders," the favorite of my youth; so I am prepared to love ballads' (***BC*** 3:195). Reviewers similarly viewed **'The Romaunt of the Page'** and **'The Lay of the Brown Rosary'** as 'revivals of the old English ballad, to which Miss BARRETT appears to be extremely partial' (***BC*** 9:370, 326). John Forster compared **'Rhyme of the Duchess May'** to the Scottish border ballad 'Edom o'Gordon' in Percy's *Reliques,* while Sarah Flower Adams observed of the same poem, 'it has all the rapidity of action of "Lenore", [and] the descriptive power of Scott and Campbell, united with the deep pathos of the earlier Scottish ballads' (***BC*** 9:347, 376).

Nevertheless, Scott and company were not the most important precursors for Barrett the balladist; Wordsworth and Coleridge were. Her focus on abandoned or betrayed women in early ballads such as **'The Romance of the Ganges'** has reinforced the assumption that she was writing primarily in a sentimental female tradition. But such figures were a staple in traditional ballads such as 'Lady Bothwell's Lament', in German ballads by Bürger like 'The Lass of Fair Wone', and in lyrical ballads by Wordsworth, such as 'The Mad Mother' and 'The Thorn'. **'The Runaway Slave at Pilgrim's Point'**, which Barrett Browning referred to as a 'long ballad' (***LMRM*** 3:310), adapts motifs from 'The Lass of Fair Wone' and the 'The Thorn' (the mother's act of infanticide and burial of her child beneath the roots of a tree), as well as from 'The Mad Mother'.

Barrett was also drawn to Coleridge's 'Christabel', with its sinister symbolic mother-daughter relationship and its innovative irregular metre. Jacobus observes that many of the *Lyrical Ballads* are like 'Christabel' in releasing 'subconscious impulses' in 'dramatic confrontation' (225). Much the same can be said of two of Barrett Browning's ballads that echo 'Christabel', **'The Lay of the Brown Rosary'**, and **'Isobel's Child'**. The latter, published in 1838, resembles Coleridge's poem in its loose ballad form, in its Gothic imagery and setting, and in its symbolically indirect treatment of the dark undercurrents in a mother's possessive love for her dying infant. Sara Coleridge was one Victorian reader who noticed that **'Isobel's Child'** was 'like "Christabel" in manner' (***BC*** 8:333).

The poems with female protagonists in the *Lyrical Ballads* seem to be those which most directly influenced Barrett Browning's choice of subject matter and perspective in many of her ballads. In representing female subjects, however, Wordsworth remained a 'man speaking to men', to cite his famous 'Preface', whereas she increasingly wrote as a woman speaking to women. William Herridge observed in 1887 that her ballads 'appeal with an especial force to the author's own sex, and strike almost every note in the scale of woman's thought and emotion' (612-13). **'The Poet's Vow'** and **'Lady Geraldine's Courtship'** with their male protagonists skilfully combine an appeal to both male and female readers. But in each of these works, the female characters who seem to be secondary become the centre of interest by the end of the poem.

The impact of the *Lyrical Ballads* is also apparent in Barrett Browning's use of the ballad form throughout her career to extend the social consciousness of a community of readers. Noting the conflation of the traditional ballad and the topical broadside ballad in Wordsworth's use of the form, Tilottama Rajan describes his interest in the genre as 'social not antiquarian'.[7] Barrett Browning was similarly interested in the power of the ballad to appeal to common human sympathies: 'all the passion of the heart will go into a ballad, & feel at home', she observed (cited Mermin 90). As **'The Runaway Slave at Pilgrim's Point'** indicates, she turned to a variant on the ballad form to cut across class barriers and, in this case, sexual and racial divisions as well.

In her later career, however, Barrett Browning was inclined to be more radically polemical than Wordsworth in appropriating the ballad for political purposes, following Shelley's example more than Wordsworth's. In the 1854 political poem, **'A Song for the Ragged Schools of London',** she writes in the tradition of the topical broadside ballad, using the form as Shelley had used it in 'Song to the Men of England' and 'The Mask of Anarchy', and as it was widely used by the Chartists in England during the 1840s. As I have argued elsewhere, **'A Song for the Ragged Schools'** adapts and strategically revises Shelley's rhetorical tactics in 'A Mask of Anarchy' to reach an audience more female than male ('Cursing', 161-2). This highly political 'Song' was written to help raise money not for the Ragged Schools in general, but for a refuge for young destitute girls that Barrett Browning's sister Arabella helped to establish, one of the first of its kind. Moreover, in a female appropriation of the broadside ballad tradition, it was first published in a pamphlet sold at a charity bazaar.

If Barrett Browning departs from Wordsworth's example in making directly political use of the ballad, she also differs from both Scott and Wordsworth in her handling of narrative. Like the traditional ballads in the Percy collection, her ballads typically exhibit a strong narrative propulsion, despite the fact that she herself did not value narrative as the highest element in poetry (***BC*** 4:109). 'It is the *story* that has power with people', she recognized (***LEBB*** 1:247). She was strongly influenced by Wordsworth's focus on the psychological complexities of dramatized speakers, but she was equally drawn to the narratives of human conflict in the old anonymous ballads—conflict that Wordsworth tended to avoid in lyricizing the form. Rajan rightly detects an 'elision' of political and social concerns in Wordsworth's reduction of 'narrative to a lyric tableau that constructs the world in terms of feeling rather than events or situations' (145). The result is an apolitical 'hermeneutics of sentimentalism' that privileges archetypal and universal feeling over political, social, and gender differences.

Barrett Browning's focus, on the contrary, is on configurations of plot and character that foreground ideologically grounded gender differences in their intricate intersections with other hierarchies of power: man over Nature, God over man, knight over page, parent over child, priest over nun, and, in **'The Runaway Slave',** master over slave. In many cases, these configurations create ironies intensified by her revisionary echoes of earlier texts and her appropriations of common ballad motifs. Rajan points out that, because the ballad is a 'cultural palimpsest inhabited by traces of more than one ideology', it 'functions as a psychic screen on which desires having to do with ideological authority and hermeneutic community are projected and analysed' (141-2). Barrett Browning's ballads function in precisely this way. When we appreciate their allusive intertextuality, we can read them not only as inscriptions of resistance to Victorian ideologies of womanhood, but also as subversive transformations of texts and conventions familiar to early Victorian readers.

In many cases, the convolutions and excesses that disrupt the narrative propulsion of Barrett Browning's ballads embody her critique of the 'plausible' plots encoding woman's lives in earlier ballads, both 'anomymous & onymous'. As Nancy Miller points out, such plots seem 'plausible' because they embody the assumptions of the dominant ideologies promoting their constant reiteration.[8] Like Hardy in the 'The Ruined Maid', Barrett Browning undermines such plausibility and the ideologies that sustain it. Most notably, in her ballads of the 1830s and 40s, she employs the starker power structures of medieval society to foreground the status of women as objects in a male economy of social exchange, and to unmask the subtler preservation of gender inequities in contemporary Victorian ideology. Thus, like some of the 'honey-mad' women writers Patricia Yaeger discusses, she engages in 'a form of textual violation that . . . overgoes social norms by doubling them, by making them visible'.[9]

'The Poet's Vow', the 1836 ballad in which Barrett Browning most noticeably echoes the *Lyrical Ballads,* illustrates the striking differences between her handling of the ballad form and Wordsworth's. It also reveals her artful use of folk ballad conventions to carry out a revision of both Wordsworth and Coleridge. As Cooper suggests, **'The Poet's Vow'** is a critique of the Romantic ideology positing Nature as female,

'the silent other' (37). Possessed by the conviction that mankind has afflicted Earth with the curse of the fall, the nameless and representative poet referred to in the poem's title vows to forswear contact with humanity, consecrating himself to communion with Nature instead. Publicly declaring his vow, he bestows his 'plighted bride' Rosalind upon his 'oldest friend' Sir Roland, offering his own lands as Rosalind's dower (ll. 136-40).

Declining to be the object in this male exchange, the betrayed Rosalind, still 'half a child', rejects the 'cruel homily' the poet has found in 'the teachings of heaven and earth' (ll. 165-72). Years later, after the poet alone in his hall has withered within from 'rejection of his humanness' (1.266), Rosalind dies and instructs that her bier be placed before his 'bolted door': '"For I have vowed, though I am proud, / To go there as a guest in shroud / And not be turned away"' (ll.371-5). On her breast, like a Lady of Shalott who refuses to be judged merely by her 'lovely face', she bears a scroll:

> 'I left thee last, a child at heart,
>   A woman scarce in years.
> I come to thee, a solemn corpse
>   Which neither feels nor fears.
>
>   . . . . .
>
> Look on me with thine own calm look:
>   I meet it calm as thou.
> No look of thine can change *this* smile,
>   Or break thy sinful vow:
> I tell thee that my poor scorned heart
> Is of thine earth—thine earth, a part:
>   It cannot vex thee now.'
>
>   (ll.416-29)

As Mermin notes (65-6), the 'unmistakable' echoes in these lines of Wordsworth's famous Lucy poem, 'A Slumber Did My Spirit Seal', reflect Barrett's recognition of the 'unprivileged position of woman' in the Romantic myth of a female Nature. To speak with the voice of Nature is to speak with the voice of the dead—or, as in Wordsworth's poem, with the voice of the male poet who chooses to commingle with Nature and the dead. In either case, the individual woman is buried.

The crucial difference, of course, in Barrett Browning's rewriting of the Romantic man-Nature love relationship is that in **'The Poet's Vow'** we *do* hear the voice of the still unburied Rosalind speaking from the scroll as an individual woman, not as a mythic female force articulated by the male poet. Rosalind speaks, moreover, with all of the passion and bitterness of the betrayed women in the old anonymous ballads published by Percy. She bears a particularly striking resemblance to the dead Margaret in 'Margaret's Ghost', who appears at her lover's bedside to indict him for betraying his plighted troth.[10] By superimposing a traditional ballad plot of human love and betrayal on Wordsworth's lyrical ballad of fusion with Nature, Barrett Browning foregrounds the conflicts he elides in identifying Lucy with the earth, thereby disrupting his focus on apparently universal feeling.

In substantially revising **'The Poet's Vow'**, first for her 1838 volume *The Seraphim, and Other Poems,* and then for her 1850 *Poems,* Barrett Browning intensified both the narrative conflicts between the poet and Rosalind, and the passion and forcefulness of her ballad heroine. In the process, she extended her critique of Wordsworth. For instance, in both the *New Monthly Magazine* and the 1838 versions of poem, the section entitled **'The Words of Rosalind's Scroll'** begins with, '"I left thee last, a feeble child / In those remembered years"'. In revising, Barrett Browning removed the emphasis on her heroine's feebleness, and made it clear that, though Rosalind was '"a woman scarce in years"' (l.147) like Wordsworth's Lucy when her lover consigned her to her fate, she speaks now with a woman's desires and a woman's strength. The revisions also intensify Rosalind's bitter scorn for the poet's '"sinful vow"' (l.426). In the two earliest versions, the second stanza of Rosalind's scroll ends with the lines, '"My silent heart, of thine earth, is part— / It cannot love thee now"'—not with the forceful declaration cited above, '"I tell thee that my poor scorned heart / Is of thine earth—thine earth, a part: / It cannot vex thee now."' The syntactic doubling in 'of thine earth—thine earth' undoes Wordsworthian ideology by simultaneously exaggerating and contradicting the identification of woman and Nature he assumes in the Lucy poems. Moreover, by intensifying Rosalind's bitterness, Barrett Browning forces the reader to distinguish between the betrayed feelings of an individual woman and Nature as mythic female presence.

'The Poet's Vow' provides a further critique of Wordsworth in demonstrating the limited redemptive influence of recollections of early childhood and in ironically subverting Wordsworth's own teaching. Additional revisions in the poem emphasize the redeeming memories the poet *should* have shared with Rosalind—memories he has apparently forgotten.[11] Meanwhile, the epigraph from 'Lines Left upon a Seat in a Yew Tree' added in 1838 implies that Wordsworth himself should have followed his own instruction. 'O be wiser thou, / Instructed that true knowledge leads to love', the epigraph reads. In Wordsworth's poem, this advice from the moralizing poet is prompted by the example of a hermit who withdrew from the world and died in the pride of his solitude. But in **'The Poet's Vow'**, it is the Wordsworthian poet himself who withdraws into the pride of solitary communion with Nature and who therefore needs instruction. Barrett

Browning thus turns Wordsworth's teaching back on his own example.

Still other revisions in **'The Poet's Vow'** emphasize the ironic contradictions between the poet's 'vow' to mate himself with the 'touching, patient Earth' (1.68) and his broken vow to Rosalind. Moreover, in the 1850 version Barrett Browning added explicit reference to *her* vow ('"For I have vowed . . ."'). This revision foregrounds both the ambiguities of the title and the narrative doublings the ballad's convoluted plot enacts. Not only is the poet's vow itself doubled, given that the poet breaks his vow to Rosalind in making his vow to Earth. The figure of the poet is also doubled, as Rosalind uses her scroll to publish her vow. In implying that the representative poet of the title may be female, Barrett Browning subverts the universalizing assumption that the poet is male. More tellingly, of the two poets in **'The Poet's Vow'**, Rosalind speaking from her scroll seems to be the stronger. In the poem's words, she is 'Triumphant Rosalind!', as the words of her text and the text of her body combine to 'wring' a cry from the 'long-subjected humanness' (ll.458-66) of the poet who has 'vowed his blood of brotherhood / To a stagnant place apart' (ll.53-4).

Such passages in **'The Poet's Vow'** point to its parallels with Tennyson's 'The Palace of Art', where the proud and sinful soul of the speaker who withdraws from human contact becomes 'a spot of dull stagnation'. The Victorian critic Peter Bayne aptly described Barrett Browning's poem as 'the ethical complement of Tennyson's' in its treatment of 'the cardinal sin of isolation from human interests' (38). But of the two, **'The Poet's Vow'** is the more pertinent and telling critique, since Barrett Browning makes her representative male poet a lover of Nature, whereas Tennyson makes his sterile aesthete a lover of art, a type that less often appears in Romantic poetry.

Barrett Browning's representation of the poet's love of Nature in **'The Poet's Vow'** incorporates a critique of Coleridge along with Wordsworth. This critique is accomplished principally through an echo of 'The Rime of the Ancient Mariner' that ironically questions Coleridge's vision of the mariner's redemption. In a passage of **'The Poet's Vow'** anticipating the ending of Tennyson's 'The Two Voices', Barrett Browning describes her solitary poet looking down from his lattice to see 'Three Christians' going by to prayer, then a bridal party, and finally a little child watching the 'lizards green and rare' playing near the wall. But the poet remains unmoved, even by the child, who remains 'Unblessed the while for his childish smile / Which cometh unaware' (ll.301-2). Thus the spontaneous release that comes to the Ancient Mariner when, 'unaware', he blesses the watersnakes does not come to Barrett Browning's poet. The child's spontaneous response to Nature's beauty cannot undo the effects of a crime against the poet's own humanity originally motivated by a misplaced love of Nature.

This ironic echo of 'The Rime of the Ancient Mariner' emphasizes the revisionary intent of Barrett Browning's poem and points to her reasons for making her alienated figure a poet who sins against his 'humanness', rather than a man who sins against the natural order, as in Coleridge's poem. Despite its use of supernatural rather than natural incidents, 'The Ancient Mariner' powerfully reinforces the idea expressed elsewhere in the *Lyrical Ballads* by Wordsworth: that Nature and natural feeling, defamiliarized by the poet, offer sinful man redemption. But the poet's feeling of fusion with Nature that brings redemption in the *Lyrical Ballads* of Wordsworth and Coleridge becomes the very source of alienation in Barrett Browning's poem.

This alienation is only overcome in **'The Poet's Vow'** when the 'wail' of the poet's 'living mind' fuses with Rosalind's 'senseless corpse' (ll.462-3). While 'earth and sky' look on 'indifferently', God smites the poet with his own 'rejected nature' (ll.478-83) and he joins his fellow poet Rosalind in death, much as William finally joins the ghost of Margaret in her grave in the Percy ballad: 'They dug beneath the kirkyard grass / For both one dwelling deep' (ll.491-2). Despite the tone of reconciliation in these lines, the note of revenge more obviously pervades the conclusion to **'The Poet's Vow'**. This feature again links the poem to the old folk tradition, in which revenge is as common a motif as betrayal. In Barrett Browning's rewriting of the male Romantic communion with Nature, the Supernatural assists 'Triumphant Rosalind' in achieving her revenge, as she recalls the arrogant male poet to a recognition of his humanness as well as his.

The focus on female subjectivity in the second half of **'The Poet's Vow'** intensifies in Barrett Browning's other ballads of the 1830s: **'A Romance of the Ganges'**, **'The Romaunt of Margret'** and **'The Romaunt of the Page'**. The first of these has much in common with the exotic poems of 'psuedo-Oriental sentimentalism' popular in the early nineteenth century: poems such as London's 'The Hindoo Girl's Song' (Hickok 172). But **'A Romance of the Ganges'** has even closer affinities with the traditional ballad. Although the poem was written to accompany an illustration in the 1838 *Findens' Tableaux: A Series of Picturesque Scenes of National Character, Beauty, and Costume,* Barrett Browning downplays the exotic elements of costume, setting and nationality. Instead, as in **'The Poet's Vow'**, she focuses on the burning passions of love and revenge so pervasive in the Percy ballads.

In **'A Romance of the Ganges'**, however, these passions are exclusively female, as the male lover becomes no more than an absent catalyst for the narrative conflict between the betrayed Luti and her unwitting rival Nuleeni. With a further twist, Barrett Browning transforms the two women of **'A Romance of the Ganges'** from rivals in love into accomplices in revenge, much as Tennyson does in 'The Sisters', a ballad which she later praised (*BC* 6:212). Thus Luti leads the child-like Nuleeni to vow to '"whisper"' to her bridegroom on her wedding day, '"*There is one betrays / While Luti suffers woe*"' (ll.161-2). And to her '"little bright-faced son"' when he asks '"What deeds his sire hath done"', Nuleeni vows to whisper, '"*There is none denies, / While Luti speaks of wrong*"' (ll.171-2). When Nuleeni, in wondering innocence, softly asks why Luti would wish to defile a '"bride-day"' with a '"word of *woe*"' and a sinless child's ear with a '"word of *wrong*"', her fellow maiden cries out:

> 'Why?' Luti said, and her laugh was dread,
> And her eyes dilated wild—
> 'That the fair new love may her bridegroom prove,
> And the father shame the child!'
>
> (ll.174-85)

In **'A Romance of the Ganges'** we begin to see the 'strong, angry heroine who dominates' most of Barrett Browning's ballads (Mermin 72). Indeed, Luti's cry for revenge registers an unrepentant excess that is formal as well as emotional, for her fierce declaration appears in four extra lines that spill over the limits of the eight-line ballad stanza employed throughout **'A Romance of the Ganges'**. It is as if the river flowing in insistent monotone through the poem's constant refrain, 'The river floweth on'—resisting as well as marking each stanza's containment—has suddenly risen in angry overflow. As the refrain implies and the narrative makes clear, Luti's bitterness and grief flow from herself to Nuleeni. Thus the curious use of the female pronoun without a clear referent in the first stanza proves justified: 'The wave-voice seems the voice of dreams / That wander through her sleep: / The river floweth on.' (ll.7-9). The pronoun in the final line—'She weepeth dark with sorrow'—is similarly ambiguous in its possible reference to both Luti and Nuleeni. Luti could be any woman, the poet implies, and her sorrow every woman's.

In the earlier 1836 ballad **'The Romaunt of Margret'**, the 'running river' in which the protagonist enounters the shadow of her own darkest fears murmurs a parallel story of betrayal and 'failing human love' (ll.39,240). The shade that rises from the river to confront Margret torments her with the thoughts that the love of her brother, her father, her sister, and her lover—all, all, will prove inconstant. The poem derives some of its power from the haunting effect of its relentlessly darkening images: the sound of 'silent forests' growing between the pauses of the shade's voice (68); the recurrent trembling of the shade's movement on the grass 'with a low, shadowy laughter'; the shadows falling 'from the stars above, / In flakes of darkness' on Margret's face (11.204-6). Margret finally drowns herself in despair, fusing with her dark double and, ironically, with the inconstancy of the river in death.

The spell-binding effect of **'The Romaunt of Margret'** is deepened by the ambiguities that Barrett Browning subtly develops. Were Margret's dark doubts justified or not? Does she suffer from the inconstancy of others' love, or the inconstancy of her own faith in love? Is the love of the knight who has given her no sign but an apparently heartfelt 'look' a 'transient' love because he is unfaithful or because he is dead (11.197,210)? '"The wild hawk's bill doth dabble still / I' the mouth that vowed thee true"' (11.211-12), the shade whispers with grisly relish. Lines such as these give **'The Romaunt of Margret'** 'the true sadness of the old ballads' and their 'genuine cold grue' (Hayter 32).

The narrative frame of the poem, presenting an anonymous minstrel singing the 'wild romaunt' of Margret to the accompaniment of a harp, suggests how closely and consciously Barrett Browning was writing within the tradition revived by Percy's *Reliques*. Indeed, she may have felt particularly drawn to the minstrel tradition because, although Bishop Percy declared in the first edition of the *Reliques* that no 'real Minstrels were of the female sex', by the fourth edition if not before, the preface acknowledged that there were women minstrels who accompanied their ballads with the music of the harp.[12] In **'The Romaunt of Margret'**, the minstrel's sex is not revealed. But the intensity of the narrator's response to Margret's fate— 'Hang up my harp again / I have no voice for song' (11.236-7)—may imply that the minstrel too is a woman.

Cooper suggests that the minstrel's apparent identification with Margret manifests the 'confused relationship of the narrator to her tale' (34) and her inadequacy to conclude her story. The minstrel's cry is a conventional framing device, however. More importantly, it marks the poem's movement into a deliberately ambiguous coda in which Barrett Browning develops the *Doppelgänger* motif at a meta-narrative level. The minstrel concludes but is unable to resolve the tale of Margret's dark inner conflicts. Her final series of laments (11.240-4) can be read either as her response to the 'failing human love' that has betrayed Margret, or as her condemnation of Margret's own failing love. In effect, then, the minstrel mirrors the division within Margret herself embodied in the refrain, 'Margret, Margret'. In its subtle double depiction of the dialogue of the mind with itself, **'The Romaunt of Margret'** justifies Cornelius Mathews' observation that Barrett's handling of the ballad form is 'subjective' (*BC* 9:342).

'The Romaunt of the Page' is a less 'subjective' ballad than **'The Romaunt of Margret'**, yet ultimately a more complex one that achieves its effects by subtly adapting the conventional figure of the woman-page so prevalent in the drama, in ballads and in Romantic narrative verse. As Dianne Dugaw suggests in *Warrior Women and Popular Balladry,* the female page has many features in common with the transvestite heroine who appears in the 'Female Warrior' ballads popular throughout the seventeenth and eighteenth centuries, in which a woman disguised as a man follows her lover to war or to sea. Barrett Browning was undoubtedly familiar with one of the most famous of the Female Warrior ballads, the variant on 'Mary Ambree' included in Percy's *Reliques*. By illuminating the social and historical conditions that explain the immense popularity of the 'Female Warrior' ballads among diverse social classes, Dugaw's study indirectly suggests why a literary ballad like 'The Romaunt of the Page' had such a widespread appeal at a time when popular ballads like 'Mary Ambree' were dying out because of an increasingly inflexible 'semiotics of gender'.[13]

Mitford revealed her critical acumen in making **'The Romaunt of the Page'** the lead poem in the 1839 *Findens' Tableaux of the Affections: A Series of Picturesque Illustrations of the Womanly Virtues*. She also singled it out in the 'Preface' and praised it privately to Barrett as 'by far the finest thing that you have ever written' (*BC* 5:135). Reviews of the 1839 *Findens'*, with the exception of *The Literary Gazette*, were equally laudatory, describing **'The Romaunt of the Page'** as 'a poem with the spirit of the elder and better day of poetry in every line of it', 'dipped in the hues of ballad minstrelsy' and 'full of the early spirit of English poetry' (*BC* 4:405-6).

As these comments suggest, readers clearly linked **'The Romaunt of the Page'** to the ballads recovered in the Romantic revival. Henry Chorley was atypical in relating the poem to the exclusively female tradition of 'Records of Woman' by Hemans and other 'songstresses' in his reviews of *Findens'* (*BC* 4:409) and of the 1844 *Poems* (*BC* 9:320). Chorley's association of **'The Romaunt of the Page'** with Hemans is justified in one respect: the poem's conclusion does echo certain details in Hemans' ballad 'Woman on the Field of Battle' (which appeared in *Songs of the Affections,* not *Records of Woman*). But the differences between Hemans' ballad and **'The Romaunt of the Page'** are much more striking than the parallels, and again they help to reveal the distinctive features of Barrett Browning's ballad-writing.

Chalk drawing by Field Talfourd, 1859.

Whereas Hemans presents a static, sentimental tableau of womanly sacrifice in 'Woman Slain on the Field of Battle', showing no interest in the narrative that leads up to it, Barrett Browning develops an ironic series of narrative conflicts in which a knight and a lady are both victimized by a system of gender relations treating women as objects of exchange. Much as Barrett Browning's woman-page is slain by the Saracens, Hemans pictures a 'gentle and lovely form' with 'golden hair' slain on the battlefield: an image that appears in the manuscript version of **'The Romaunt of the Page'**, though not in the published version. In Hemans' ballad, however, only one motive could have led a woman to such a death, the poet declares: not glory, but love, which 'Woman's deep soul too long / Pours on the dust'.[14]

Love is also a force contributing to the fate of Barrett's heroine, but in this case it is only one element in a subtle mix of circumstances, motives, and passions. **'The Romaunt of the Page'** begins *in medias res,* with a knight and a page returning from 'the holy war in Palestine' (1.2), where the page has saved the knight's life 'once in the tent, and twice in fight' (1.11). As thoughts of home fill the minds of both, the page recalls the dying prayer of his mother, while the

knight points out to the page that, although he has proven himself in battle, he is too silent to serve well in the bower of the knight's lady. The page leads the knight to speak more of his lady: is she 'little loved or loved aright' (1.100)? Gloomily, the knight explains that he doesn't even know what his lady looks like since he married her in haste and darkness before leaving for Palestine. Moreover, he makes it clear that he married her out of a sense of obligation to his friend Earl Walter, who lost his life in avenging the honour of the knight's own dead father. On her death-bed, the Earl's wife sent for the knight and asked him to marry her daughter, the 'sweet child' made 'an orphan for thy father's sake' (11.162-3). Bitterly the knight recalls how his bride rose from the ceremony '[a]nd kissed the smile of mother dead, / Or ever she kissed me' (11.180-1).

In revising the *Findens'* version of **'The Romaunt of the Page'** for its reissue in her 1844 *Poems,* Barrett Browning made the narrative fuller, more complex, more ironic, and more conflicted in developing the psychology of the knight and the page. Most notably, she greatly expanded the knight's inset narrative of the marriage forced on him by circumstance and the chivalric code—a narrative reversing the conventional plot in which a knight or a 'stranger (to all save the reader)', as Robert Browning facetiously remarked, wins a bride because the father owes his life or some other debt to him (*RB-EBB* 2:881). Barrett's additions create sympathy for the knight and develop his passions with psychological depth as he declares that it would have been better if he had avenged his own father and died, rather than have 'murdered friend and marriage-ring / Forced on [his] life together' (11.146-7).

Responding with tears of grief to the knight's tale, the page explains that his own sister was married as the knight's lady was, but that she 'laid down the silks she wore' and followed her new husband to the 'battle-place', '[d]isguised as his true servitor'. The knight reacts with a 'careless laugh':

> 'Well done it were for thy sister,
>   But not for my ladye!
> My love, so please you, shall requite
> No woman, whether dark or bright,
>   Unwomaned if she be.'

> (11.191-6)

In this case again, Barrett's revisions intensify the conflict between her two characters. In the manuscript the knight simply laughs 'loudly'; while in *Findens'* his laugh is 'gay', not 'careless', and the last three lines of his declaration are briefer and less unequivocal.

As the page passionately defends his hypothetical sister's actions to the scornful knight, Barrett presents her ironically paradoxical vision of the 'womanly virtues' the 1839 *Findens'* was meant to celebrate:

> 'Oh, womanly she prayed in tent,
>   When none beside did wake!
> Oh, womanly she paled in fight,
>   For one beloved's sake!—
> And her little hand, defiled with blood,
> Her tender tears of womanhood
>   Most woman-pure did make!'
>
>   (11.207-13)

Such a combination of heroic valour 'in fight' and womanly devotion is also quite typical of the 'Female Warrior' ballads that Dugaw explores, but in early nineteenth-century variants on these, as in **'The Romaunt of the Page'**, insistent 'gender-markers' like Barrett's phrase 'little hand' became much more common.[15]

Little hand or not, such a woman-servitor is wholly unacceptable in the eyes of Barrett's knight, who reiterates his belief in a more conventional type of womanly virtue that hides behind a veil. '"No casque shall hide her woman's tear"' (1.220), he declares in an ironically prophetic, punning line that does not appear in the manuscript. According to the knight, womanly virtue is '"[s]o high, so pure, and so apart"' from the world that it shines like '"a small bright cloud / Alone amid the skies!"' (11.230-3). If his own lady so '"mistook"' his mind as to follow him disguised into battle, the knight asserts that he '"would forgive"' her, and '"evermore / Would love her as my servitor / But little as my wife"' (11.223-9). As the little cloud that provokes the knight's comparison disappears behind a blacker one, the page sees the Saracens approaching. But while 'the page seeth all, the knight seeth none' (1.241), presumably because his eyes are still dazzled by what Barrett Browning scornfully referred to as the 'cloud-minding theory' of idealized womanhood (*LMRM* 3:81). As Stephenson notes (29-32), Barrett thought this chivalric theory was as perniciously confining for women as the 'pudding-making and stocking-darning' theory. 'Twas a stroke of policy in those ranty-pole barons of old to make their lady-loves idols, and curb their wives with silken idleness', another Victorian woman astutely remarked.[16]

Barrett Browning dramatically reveals the sterility of the chivalric ideal of womanhood in the hauntingly anticlimactic ballad, **'The Romance of the Swan's Nest'**, in many ways the counterpart of **'The Romaunt of the Page'**. In this depiction of a young girl's fantasies, the female who opts for the conventional lady's role of inspiring rather than following her knight—of being his idol rather than his disguised page and 'servitor'—is as bitterly betrayed as her more active opposite. As Cooper observes (97), Little Ellie's fate in **'The Romance of the Swan's Nest'** shows how

'dreaming courtly fantasies . . . gnaws at women's energy, sexuality, and identity' as insidiously as the rat gnaws at the reeds surrounding the empty swan's nest in the poem's ending.

'The Romaunt of the Page' concludes with the page sending the blind knight on before to safety, while the loyal 'servitor' drops her disguise, and the embittered wife exclaims,

> 'Have I renounced my womanhood
>   For wifehood unto *thee,*
> And is this the last, last look of thine
>   That ever I shall see?
>
> Yet God thee save, and mayst thou have
>   A lady to thy mind,
> More woman-proud and half as true
>   As one thou leav'st behind!'
>
>   (11.276-83)

Disillusioned by earthly love, Earl Walter's daughter turns to God's love and faces the Saracens, a '"Christian Page"' who taunts the enemy as boldly as any knight might do (1.301). 'False page, but truthful woman' (1.227), she dauntlessly dies beneath the scimitar, meeting its downward sweep '[w]ith smile more bright in victory / Than any sword from sheath' (11.225-6).

Mermin observes of this conclusion that the protagonist of **'The Romaunt of the Page'** 'succumbs to an ideal of "womanly virtues" that the poet both scorns and shares' because her page chooses 'a woman's fate—unrecognizing, self-sacrificing death' (91-2). Hickok similarly views the poem as 'a sentimental tale of extreme wifely devotion and self-sacrifice' (173). What such readings do not address, however, is the fact that Barrett Browning's heroic page never acts more like a man, in conventional terms, than when she is 'truthful woman'. Even her smile flashes like a sword. Moreover, her motives are mixed rather than 'pure' in that, like so many folk ballad heroines, she is driven as much by revenge as by devotion.

In revising **'The Romaunt of the Page'** Barrett Browning intensified the woman-page's more vindictive motives. For example, in the manuscript, the page wishes her knight may find another lady 'More woman-proud, yet all as true / As one thou leavest behind'. In *Findens'* she wishes he may find a lady 'More woman-proud, not faithfuller / Than one thou leav'st behind!' The change from 'all as true' to 'half as true' is startling, bringing out the anger in the page's comment to her departing master, 'ride on thy way' (1.250), altered from the more tender address of 'my master dear' in the *Findens'* version. The page's pledge to be near to her master as 'parted spirits cleave / To mortals too beloved to leave' (11.259-60) has a rather ominous note to it as well. Does the outraged wife plan to bless him from above, like the dying Catarina in 'Catarina to Camoens'? Or does she plan to haunt him? Perhaps the thought of her will indeed haunt him when he arrives home and realizes that the page who sacrificed himself for him was also the wife he so fiercely resented—a quite probable narrative extrapolation that is not considered in interpreting the page's sacrifice as unrecognized. He may be 'a knight of gallant deeds' (1.1), but how will he feel when he discovers, as the reader already has, that in this particular 'romaunt', the page and not the knight performs with greatest gallantry?

The ironies permeating **'The Romaunt of the Page'** are intensified when Barrett Browning's representation of the lady-page figure is read against its prototypes in ballads like 'Child Waters' and 'A Not-browne Mayd' and in Scott's *Marmion*. The immediate inspiration of **'The Romaunt of the Page'** was the illustration Mitford supplied Barrett with, picturing a woman disguised as a page, wearing a very short skirt and hiding behind a tree in the foreground, while a knight rides away from her in the background (**BC** 4:192). But it is clear that the conventions of the old ballads and 'Child Waters' in particular were in Barrett's mind when she composed the poem. Apologizing to Mitford for the length of her 'long barbarous ballad', she quips, 'I ought to blush—as ladyes always do in ballads—"scarlet-red" . . . By the way, the pictured one pretty as she is, has a good deal exaggerated the ballad-receipt for making a ladye page—Do you remember?—"And you must cut your gown of green / An *INCH* above the knee"! She comes within the fi fa fum of the prudes, in consequence' (**BC** 4:33, 38). The 'receipt for making a ladye page' Barrett cites is Child Waters' own, in the ballad of the same title in Percy's *Reliques*.

The frankly physical treatment of the heroine's ordeals in 'Child Waters' supplies an interesting subtext to the declaration of Barrett Browning's knight that, if his lady followed him as his page, he would love her as his 'servitor' but not as his wife. Hardly the conventional model of chivalry, Child Waters instructs his female companion Ellen, swollen with child by him, to cut off her skirt and her hair and run barefoot as his foot-page by his side. In this state, she must run to the north country, swim a swollen river, stable and feed his horse, find him a paramour to spend the night with (while she lies at the foot of the bed), and then feed his horse again. Finally, as she is moaning with labour pains in the stable, Child Waters' mother hears her, the gallant knight arrives to see the babe born, and like Griselda, Ellen is rewarded. Child Waters tells her to be of good cheer: he will marry her. But the ballad ends before the marriage takes place.

'The Romaunt of the Page' clearly echoes 'Child Waters' but also reverses its plot by making marriage the beginning and cause of the page's ordeals, not the end. Moreover, Barrett Browning shifts the focus of her ballad, both in its title and its narrative perspective, to the woman-page rather than the knight. In her ballad, it is the knight who is tested and found wanting, not the woman who is tested and rewarded. A testing of woman's devotion similar to that in 'Child Waters' appears in another Percy ballad Barrett Browning particularly liked, 'The Not-browne Mayd' (**BC** 7:266). The revisionary narrative of **'The Romaunt of the Page'** is therefore written against a standard ballad plot of 'plausible' female constancy, as much as against a particular ballad.

Several textual echoes and parallels also connect **'The Romaunt of the Page'** to Scott's epic romance *Marmion,* which more directly suggests the perils that attend the woman who proves her love by following her knight as his page.[17] When Constance breaks her religious vows to follow Marmion disguised as a horseboy in his train, he treats her as such, making her not only his servitor but also his whore. Betraying his promise to marry her, he pursues the wealthy young Clara instead, while Constance is buried alive in the walls of a monastery dungeon for breaking her religious vows. *Marmion* indicates why, in the more prudish 1830s, Barrett was careful to have her heroine marry her knight before following him as her page, and like 'Child Waters', it illumines the narrative innovations in **'The Romaunt of the Page'**. Whereas Scott depicts the old story of women suffering from male falsehood, Barrett Browning's ballad shows both sexes suffering from an oppressive ideology.

Barrett Browning's adaptation of elements in *Marmion* is also apparent in the long Gothic ballad-romance, **'The Legend of the Brown Rosarie'**, retitled **'The Lay of the Brown Rosary'** in her 1844 *Poems*. Anticipating Charlotte Brontë in *Villette,* Barrett appropriates the figure of the buried nun popularized by Scott's *Marmion* and other works to represent intense psychic conflicts. Whereas Scott's central focus in *Marmion* is male and military, Barrett Browning's, like Brontë's after her, is on the conflicts of female desire with institutionalized repression that speak so powerfully in the interstices of his narrative. The *Doppelgänger* motif linking Onora, the heroine of **'The Lay of the Brown Rosary'**, with the defiant cursing nun who is buried alive for her sins makes this poem a 'subjective' ballad like **'The Romaunt of Margret'**, but it is a more daring work, too complex in its play of intertextual allusions to consider fully here. Along with *Marmion*, **'The Lay of the Brown Rosary'** also seems to draw on *Faust*, 'Christabel', Gottfried Bürger's 'Lenora', and possibly some of the Percy ballads, fusing elements from these texts in a highly original way with Barrett's own innovations, among them the heroine's dream, which she herself thought of as 'rather original in its manner' (*BC* 6:276). Any analysis of **'The Lay of the Brown Rosary'** is further complicated by the extensive revisions made in the poem after its initial publication in the 1840 *Findens'*, including the change of the heroine's name from Lenora (a direct link with Bürger's ballad) to Onora.

'Rhyme of the Duchess May' also reflects Barrett's adaptation of motifs from Bürger's 'Lenora', in this case, as we have seen, creating a connection readily detected by the *Westminster* reviewer Sarah Flower Adams. By echoing Lenora's swift, dark gallop to the bridal bed of the grave with the ghost of her slain lover, Barrett subtly foreshadows the fate of the orphan Duchess May and her newly wed husband Sir Guy of Linteged as they flee to his castle, evading her guardian, the Earl of Leigh and the cousin whose hand in marriage she spurns: 'Fast and fain the bridal train along the night-storm rod [sic] amain' (1.89). Reminiscent of 'Lenora' too, **'The Duchess May'** depicts what one reviewer aptly described as a 'dark bridal' concluding with a 'double death-ride'.[18] Facing certain defeat after a fourteen-day siege by the Leighs in which his castle has 'seethed in blood' (1.43), the anguished Sir Guy seeks to save the lives of his loyal men by riding from his castle tower to a sacrificial death. Against his will, he is accompanied by his young bride, who leaps into the saddle with him at the last minute. Reviewers were especially taken by this spectacular and novel climax, which Mermin astutely interprets as 'in effect a bold, bizarre sexual consummation' (93)— even if it does occur three months after the Duchess' actual marriage to Sir Guy.

'Rhyme of the Duchess May' adapts situations and scenes from the old Scottish ballad 'Edom o'Gordon' as well as Bürger's 'Lenora', although its sacrificial death leap was probably suggested by Benjamin Haydon's painting, 'Curtius Leaping Into the Gulf' (*BC* 6:208-9). The hero of 'Edom o'Gordon' is not the brutal border-raider referred to in the title, but the fiercely loyal wife of a Scottish lord who takes a stand on the castle walls and valiantly resists Gordon and his men in her husband's absence. The traces of 'Edom o'Gordon' in **'Rhyme of the Duchess May'** thus once again reveal Barrett Browning's interest in the 'warrior women' heroines of the 'old burning ballads'. As in the case of **'The Romaunt of the Page'**, however, she once again significantly revises the ballad plot she most conspicuously echoes in **'Rhyme of the Duchess May'**. Most notably, she rejects the futile and passive sacrifice that occurs in 'Edom o'Gordon' when the Scottish lord's daughter is lowered over the walls in a sheet and spitted on Gordon's spear. Instead, she depicts a more active and heroic sacrificial leap on the part of the Duchess May, whom she made more forceful and wilful in revising the manuscript draft of the poem. Other significant revisions in the

draft intensify and complicate the psychological and narrative conflict between the Duchess May and Sir Guy in ways that make Sir Guy a prototype of Romney in *Aurora Leigh*.

Deborah Byrd suggests that Victorian women poets like Barrett Browning turned to the Middle Ages because it was envisioned 'as a time in which at least some women had control over their property and destiny and the courage to venture into the "male" arenas of war and politics' (33). There is much truth in this. The women Barrett Browning encountered in the Percy ballads and even in Scott's romances were not yet confined by what Mary Poovey identifies as the cult of the 'proper lady'.[19] In fact, in its frankly physical depiction of strong, heroic, passionate heroines, the traditional ballad, that 'Cinderella' among the Muses, very often was not the bashful maiden Hales and Furnivall quaintly imagined.

Nevertheless, Barrett Browning was no celebrator of the often brutal and violent gender and human relations that prevailed in the Middle Ages when a 'black chief' was 'half knight, half sheep-lifter'—like Edom o'Gordon and his kind—and a 'beauteous dame' was 'half chattel and half queen' (*Aurora Leigh* 5:195-6). In medieval ballads like **'The Romaunt of the Page'**, and **'Rhyme of the Duchess May'**, she dramatizes the crudely overt power structures of the society that also produced the chivalric idealization of women. Thus the younger Lord Leigh threatens to take the Duchess May in marriage over the 'altar' of her husband's corpse, seizing her hand and the gold it brings just as he seizes the sword in order to prevail.

Barrett Browning's ballads after 1844 represent contemporary rather than medieval scenes. Her often noted progression from medieval to modern subjects is manifested not only in **'Lady Geraldine's Courtship'**, but also in the unfinished ballad, **'The Princess Marie'** in the 'Sonnets Notebook' in the Armstrong Browning Library. **'The Princess Marie'** focuses on the daughter of King Louis Philippe of France. Phillip Sharp, who supplies a helpful account of this ballad's historical context, along with a rather unreliable transcription of the manuscript, describes **'The Princess Marie'** as a 'domestic poem about a head of state' (169). But what really seems to have aroused Barrett Browning's interest in the Princess Marie was not her relation to Louis Philippe, but her skill in sculpture and the human cost of her devotion to her art. **'The Princess Marie'** is thus not only a ballad in which Barrett turns to contemporary subjects, but also one anticipating her focus on the woman-artist in *Aurora Leigh*.

Although they move farther away from their prototypes in the old English and Scottish ballads and the narrative verse of the Romantic revival, most of Barrett Browning's later ballads continue to exhibit the distinguishing features I have dwelt upon in this chapter: the ironic manipulation of traditional ballad plots and motifs (often through narrative reversals or doublings); the focus on female subjectivity and on the conflicts created by female desire; and the exploration of connections between the 'female plots' shaping women's lives and the gender plots of encompassing ideologies. The female perspective, complicated by lingering ironies, is apparent in the deceptively simple **'Amy's Cruelty'**, for instance, where Barrett Browning explores female as well as male possessiveness in love. The manipulation of traditional ballad conventions is perhaps most evident in the often praised **'Lord Walter's Wife'**. Like 'The Not-browne Mayd', 'Lord Walter's Wife' contains elements of the traditional debate or flying match concerning female constancy. Yet typically, Barrett Browning subverts conventional expectations by dramatizing the contradictions and sexual double standard in male perceptions of women and by showing a man tested and found wanting, not the woman he flirts with and condemns.

In their representation of strong, transgressive women and their paradoxical combination of the medieval and the modern, Barrett Browning's ballads contributed to the nineteenth-century ballad tradition in ways that remain largely unexplored today. Several Victorian critics noted the impact of her medieval ballads on Pre-Raphaelite poets like D. G. Rossetti. In 1900, Charlotte Porter and Helen Clarke similarly observed that 'Rossetti and others of the pre-Raphaelite brotherhood' had followed Barrett Browning in writing 'modern ballads', 'archaic in diction and suggestion' yet striking 'new themes'. 'But her ballads were first', Porter and Clarke remind us. 'They are miracles of sympathetic reproduction of an old *genre* in new substance' (*CW* 2:xiii). Hayter suggests one reason why the influence of Barrett Browning on the Pre-Raphaelites was 'forgotten' in noting how critics after 1900 repeatedly apologized for or dismissed the many traces of Mrs Browning in the works of D. G. Rossetti and William Morris (231-2).

As long as this subtle work of cultural 'forgetting' remains unanalysed and unresisted, and as long as Barrett Browning's ballads continue to be excluded from standard anthologies and surveys of Victorian poetry, there will be a missing link in the history of the ballad revival—that movement that continues to shape the work of many poets and singers in our own century. Bob Dylan, whose 'Desolation Row' is now studied alongside T. S. Eliot's 'The Waste Land', seems very unlike Elizabeth Barrett Browning. Yet Dylan and his many followers seem drawn to the ballad form for some of the same reasons she was. Like Barrett Browning, Dylan recognizes the power of ballad stories with the people. Like her, he

has often written in the tradition of the politicized broadside ballad. Like her, he exploits ironic twists in plotting ('twists of fate') as sites for exploring psychological and ideological conflict. And like Barrett Browning, Dylan—as 'Desolation Row' evinces—transforms the ballad form into a cultural palimpsest by intensifying its intertextuality. All of these features of Barrett Browning's balladry helped to prepare her for the writing of *Aurora Leigh*.

Notes

Parenthetical documentation is used for all works listed in the Selected Bibliography. Other sources are identified in the footnotes. The following abbreviations are used:

AL—*Aurora Leigh,* ed. Margaret Reynolds (Athens, Ohio, Ohio University Press, 1992).

BC—*The Brownings' Correspondence,* ed. Philip Kelley and Ronald Hudson, 11 vols (Winfield, Kan., Wedgestone Press, 1984-).

CW—*The Complete Works of Elizabeth Barrett Browning,* ed. Charlotte Porter and Helen A. Clarke, 6 vols (1900; New York, AMS rpt, 1973).

LEBB—*The Letters of Elizabeth Barrett Browning,* ed. Frederic G. Kenyon, 2 vols (New York, Macmillan, 1897).

LMRM—*The Letters of Elizabeth Barrett Browning to Mary Russell Mitford 1836-1854,* ed. Meredith B. Raymond and Mary Rose Sullivan, 3 vols (Winfield, Kan., Armstrong Browning Library of Baylor University, Browning Institute, Wedgestone Press & Wellesley College, 1983).

RE-EBB—*The Letters of Robert Browning and Elizabeth Barrett Browning 1845-1846,* ed. Elvan Kintner, 2 vols (Cambridge, Mass., Bellknap Press of Harvard University Press, 1969).

[1] *Bishop Percy's Folio Manuscript: Ballads and Romances,* vol. 2, part I (London, N. Trubner & Co., 1867) pp. xviii-xix.

[2] Malcolm Laws, Jr, *The British Literary Ballad: A Study in Poetic Imitation* (Carbondale, Southern Illinois University Press, 1972) pp. 151-8, 89-93.

[3] Nancy K. Miller, *Subject to Change: Reading Feminist Writing* (New York, Columbia University Press, 1988) p. 208.

[4] *The Victorian Popular Ballad* (London, Macmillan, 1975) pp. 4-7.

⁵ Hermann Fischer, *Romantic Verse Narrative: The History of a Genre,* trans. Sue Bollans (Cambridge, Cambridge University Press, 1991) pp. 24-35, 53, 90; Albert B. Friedman, *The Ballad Revival: Studies in the Influence of Popular on Sophisticated Poetry* (Chicago, University of Chicago Press, 1961) p. 298.

⁶ Stephen Parrish, *The Art of the Lyrical Ballads* (Cambridge, Mass., Harvard University Press, 1973) pp. 86-90; Mary Jacobus, *Tradition and Experiment in Wordsworth's 'Lyrical Ballads' (1798)* (Oxford, Clarendon Press, 1976) pp. 209-32, 277-83.

⁷ Tilottama Rajan, *The Supplement of Reading: Figures of Understanding in Romantic Theory and Practice* (Ithaca & London, Cornell University Press, 1990) p. 140.

⁸ *Subject to Change,* p. 208.

⁹ [Patricia Yaeger, *Honey-Mad Women: Emancipatory Strategies in Women's Writing,* Gender and Culture Studies (New York, Columbia University Press, 1988), p. 117].

¹⁰ Thomas Percy, *Reliques of Ancient English Poetry, Consisting of Old Heroic Ballads, Songs, and other Pieces of our Earlier Poets, Together with some few of later Date* (London, J. Dodsley, 1765) vol. 3, pp. 310-13.

¹¹ For a more detailed analysis of revisions and textual echoes in 'The Poet's Vow' and 'The Romaunt of the Page', see the version of this chapter published in *Victorian Literature and Culture,* 21 (1993).

¹² See *Reliques of Ancient English Poetry,* 1765 edn, vol. 3, p. xviii. Barrett acquired the 5th edition of Percy's *Reliques* in 1826; see Kelley and Coley, p. 156.

¹³ *Warrior Women and Popular Balladry 1650-1850,* Cambridge Studies in Eighteenth-Century Literature and Thought (Cambridge, Cambridge University Press, 1989) pp. 146, 172, 164.

¹⁴ *The Poetical Works of Mrs. Hemans,* ed. W. M. Rossetti (New York, Hurst & Co., n.d.) p. 235.

¹⁵ *Warrior Women and Popular Balladry,* p. 149.

¹⁶ Cited by Mary Poovey, *Uneven Developments: The Ideological Work of Gender in Mid-Victorian England* (Chicago, University of Chicago Press, 1988) p. 147.

¹⁷ Leighton notes the probable influence of Byron's *Lara* as well (1992, 81).

¹⁸ 'Last Poems and Other Works of Mrs. Browning', *North British Review,* 36 (1862) p. 527.

¹⁹ *The Proper Lady and the Woman Writer: Ideology as Style in the Works of Mary Wollstonecraft, Mary Shelley, and Jane Austen* (Chicago, Chicago University Press, 1984).

Selected Bibliography

Bayne, Peter, *Two Great Englishwomen: Mrs. Browning & Charlotte Brontë, with an Essay on Poetry, Illustrated from Wordsworth, Burns, and Byron* (London, James Clarke, 1881).

Byrd, Deborah, 'Combating an Alien Tyranny: Elizabeth Barrett Browning's Evolution as a Feminist Poet', *Browning Institute Studies,* 15 (1987) 23-41.

Cooper, Helen, *Elizabeth Barrett Browning: Woman and Artist* (Chapel Hill, University of North Carolina Press, 1988).

Hayter, Alethea, *Mrs. Browning: A Poet's Work and Its Setting* (New York, Barnes & Noble, 1963).

Herridge, William T. 'Elizabeth Barrett Browning', *Andover Review,* 7 (1887) 607-23.

Hickok, Kathleen, *Representations of Women: Nineteenth-Century British Women's Poetry* (London, Greenwood Press, 1984).

Leighton, Angela, *Elizabeth Barrett Browning,* Key Women Writers Series (Brighton, Harvester Press, 1986).

Leighton, Angela, *Victorian Women Poets: Writing Against the Heart* (Charlottesville, University Press of Virginia, 1992).

Mermin, Dorothy, *Elizabeth Barrett Browning: The Origins of a New Poetry,* Women in Culture and Society Series (Chicago, University of Chicago Press, 1989).

Sharp, Phillip D., 'Poetry in Process: Elizabeth Barrett Browning and the Sonnets Notebook', Diss. Lousiana State University, 1985.

Stephenson, Glennis, *Elizabeth Barrett Browning and the Poetry of Love* (Ann Arbor, UMI Press, 1989).

Stone, Marjorie, 'Cursing as One of the Fine Arts: Elizabeth Barrett Browning's Political Poems', *Dalhousie Review,* 66 (1986) 155-73.

FURTHER READING

Bibliography

Donaldson, Sandra. *Elizabeth Barrett Browning: An Annotated Bibliography of the Commentary and Criticism, 1826-1990.* New York: G. K. Hall & Co., 1993, 642 p.

    Bibliography of Browning scholarship from 1826-1990, including commentary written in English, French, and Italian.

Biography

Hewlett, Dorothy. *Elizabeth Barrett Browning: A Life.* New York: Octagon Books, 1972, 388 p.

    Detailed biography of Browning, with extensive critical discussion of her poetry.

Criticism

Cunliffe, John W. "Elizabeth Barrett's Influence on Browning's Poetry." *Publications of the Modern Language Association of America* XXIII, No. 2 (1908): 169-83.

    Argues that Elizabeth Barrett Browning's "most enduring contributions to literature were not direct but indirect—through the influence she exerted on her poet-husband."

Donaldson, Sandra M. "Elizabeth Barrett's Two Sonnets to George Sand." *Studies in Browning & His Circle* V, No. 1 (Spring 1977): 19-22.

    Examines Browning's portrayal of the "ideal person" as an androgynous combination of the masculine and the feminine.

———. "'Motherhood's Advent in Power': Elizabeth Barrett Browning's Poems About Motherhood." *Victorian Poetry* XVIII, No. 1 (Spring 1980): 51-60.

    Compares Browning's early portrayal of motherhood with her later poems, after she had miscarried and borne a son.

Falk, Alice. "Elizabeth Barrett Browning and Her Prometheuses: Self-Will and a Woman Poet." *Texas Studies in Women's Literature* VII, No. 1 (Spring 1988): 69-85.

    Considers Browning's attempt to fuse classical scholarship with a burgeoning feminism, especially in her translation of *Prometheus Bound.*

Radley, Virginia L. "A More Vigorous Voice: The *Poems of 1844.*" In her *Elizabeth Barrett Browning,* pp. 57-71. New York: Twayne Publishers, Inc., 1972.

    Evaluates the poetry in Browning's *Poems* (1844).

Stedman, Edmund Clarence. "Elizabeth Barrett Browning." In his *Victorian Poets,* pp. 114-49. Boston: Houghton, Mifflin and Company, 1893.

    Surveys Browning's work as it relates to her developing character, and considers her "as the representative of her sex in the Victorian era."

Stephenson, Glennis. "The Vision Speaks: Love in Elizabeth Barrett Browning's 'Lady Geraldine's Courtship'." *Victorian Poetry* XXVII, No. 1 (Spring 1989): 17-31.

    Explores "Lady Geraldine's Courtship" as an attempt by Browning to create the picture of a successful romantic relationship.

Aleksandr Ivanovich Herzen

1812-1870

(Also transliterated as Alexander; also Hérzen, Hertzen, Gertsen; also wrote under pseudonym of Iskander) Russian novelist, essayist, autobiographer, and short story writer.

For further discussion of Herzen's life and works, see *NCLC,* Volume 10.

INTRODUCTION

Herzen is recognized as one of nineteenth-century Russia's preeminent revolutionary thinkers. His writings provide a perceptive view of the Russian intellectual climate in the mid-nineteenth century, most notably in his extensive memoirs, *Byloye i dumy* (*My Past and Thoughts*; 1854). A progressive thinker throughout his life, Herzen ultimately espoused an agrarian socialist philosophy that combined Slavophile and Western ideals. While he admired the Western values of individual freedom and progress, he argued that a new social order, based on the peasant commune championed by the Slavophiles, should replace the bourgeois capitalist society that he believed had corrupted Europe. This socialist philosophy formed the ideological basis for most of Russia's revolutionary activity in the 1850s. Though Herzen had fallen into disfavor at the time of his death, critics today cite him as one of the most significant figures in Russia's literary and political history.

Biographical Information

Herzen's parents, the prosperous nobleman Ivan Yakovlev and a young German woman named Luise Haag, lived together in the Yakovlev family homes but never formally married under Russian law. When Aleksandr was born, his father—apparently reluctant to give him the family name—gave him the surname Herzen, from the German "herz," or heart. Guided by his father, Herzen studied world literature and developed an intense interest in Russian history. When he was thirteen he witnessed the Decembrist uprising— an attempt by the Russian nobility to compel from Czar Nicholas I a more democratic form of government—and its aftermath. The insurgents were hanged, becoming martyrs in the eyes of many Russian young people, including Herzen. With his friend Nikolai Ogarev, he vowed allegiance to the defeated rebels and their ideals. In 1829 Herzen entered the University of Moscow, where he became the leader of a small group of students interested in radical politics and philosophy. While at the university, he studied the works of the French philosophers Claude Henri de Rouvroy Saint-Simon and Charles Fourier, whose political theories instilled in Herzen a great desire for political change. In particular, Herzen admired Saint-Simon's desire to end the exploitation of the individual by government institutions. From his study of Fourier, Herzen derived an interest in cooperative societies that could accommodate the economic and personal needs of each group member.

In 1833, the year after Herzen's graduation, he and Ogarev were arrested and charged with subversion; their political views, actively voiced in many venues, appeared threatening to the Czarist regime. Consequently, the two young men were exiled to the far provinces of Russia. During his confinement, Herzen turned to the works of the German philosopher Georg Wilhelm Friedrich Hegel, whose writings on dialectics influenced many revolution-minded Europeans in the mid-nineteenth century, including Karl Marx. When

Herzen returned from exile, he married and settled in Moscow, where he attended literary salons and took part in the debates between advocates of Western and Slavophile revolutionary thought. He began voicing his opinion in local journals, publishing essays that attempted to balance the Western primacy of the individual with the Slavophile ideal of the commune.

Herzen spent the early years of the 1840s between prison and Moscow's intellectual community. In 1847, he published his novel *Kto vinovat?* (*Who Is to Blame?*). Despite his growing status in Russia, supported by the positive reception of his novel, Herzen decided that it was time to leave Russia soon after his father's death in 1847. Aided by the large fortune he had inherited, Herzen settled his family in Paris. Despite his years of admiration for French philosophy, Herzen soon grew disillusioned with the radical political climate in France. The bourgeoisie that dominated France's economic and political system struck him as a class little different from the Russian aristocracy he despised. His disappointment deepened with the failure of the European revolutions of 1848. Motivated by this discontent, Herzen wrote *Vom andern Ufer* (*From the Other Shore;* 1850), a series of dialogues and essays in which he shared the lesson he had drawn from European life: that the failure of revolutions indicated a general moral decline of Western ideals. As a result, he now believed Russia to be far more vigorous than any European nation. At the same time, however, his radical activities enraged the authorities in his native country, making it more difficult for him to return.

In 1852, Herzen moved to London, after his dissatisfaction with life on the European continent had been compounded by his wife's affair with the German revolutionary poet Georg Herwegh. He responded to this upheaval in his personal life with painstakingly detailed introspection, all recorded in his journals. Herzen's marital problems were still unresolved when, shortly after his move to England, his wife, mother, and son all died within weeks of one another. In response to his grief, Herzen undertook several projects, working on his memoirs and using his inheritance to develop the first Russian free press abroad. Initially Herzen utilized the press to appeal for the emancipation of the serfs and to foster the spread of socialism. His first journal, *Polyarnaya Zvezda* (*The Polar Star*), was devoted to Russian reform; in 1857, he founded *Kolokol* (*The Bell*), a weekly newspaper that became a primary political force in Russia even though it had to be smuggled into the country. Herzen's Russian success is thought to be due to his political tact: though he refused to surrender his socialist tenets, he was willing to accept a monarchy if its intentions for reform seemed well founded. His office became well known and attracted a number of famous visitors, including the Russian novelists Ivan Turgenev and Leo Tolstoy and English author Thomas Carlyle. Dedicated

to "the liberation of Russia," *The Bell* is now considered to have been a major impetus in the liberation of the serfs in 1861. The papers also allowed Herzen a vehicle for the highly personal essays he had been writing since the time of his wife's infidelity. Beginning with *The Polar Star* and continuing in *The Bell*, Herzen published these self-analyses, which would later come together in separate volumes and ultimately as his collected memoirs, *My Past and Thoughts*.

Herzen moved to Geneva, where he sporadically published issues of *The Bell*. The journal's popularity had waned, however, after the failure of the Polish-Russian uprising of 1863. Herzen's pro-Polish position alienated more conservative followers and appeared outmoded to younger radicals who felt that more violent measures were needed to bring about social change in Russia. The journal's reputation declined irreparably, the size of his following continued to dwindle, and in 1868, *The Bell* ceased publication. Two years later, Herzen died of pneumonia.

Major Works

All of Herzen's writings—creative as well as polemical—endure as theoretical revolutionary documents. His ideas survive in many forms, including short fiction, articles, and extensive journals, but the two works that stand out from his corpus are the novel *Who Is to Blame?* and the completed volume of his memoirs. The protagonist of *Who Is to Blame?*, Vladimir Beltov, typifies the brooding, independent hero who would become a standard character in Russian literature known as the "superfluous man." Beltov and the other main characters are caught in a romantic entanglement, influenced by larger social forces, that ends catastrophically, leaving the reader with the question posed by the novel's title. Since its initial release, the novel has received praise for Herzen's ability to embody his social concerns in psychologically well-rounded characters. A similar quality distinguishes his memoirs, *My Past and Thoughts*, which combine political discourse with personal anecdotes in detailing Herzen's coming of age under the reign of Nicholas I and his observations of the 1850s. The author apparently sought to combine these elements—the personal and the political—in such a way that his own minutely recorded emotional experiences bodied forth the historical forces bearing on his generation.

Critical Reception

Although Herzen's earliest writings betrayed his interest in German Romanticism, his more mature efforts quickly shifted to the "naturalist" style that became predominant in the latter part of the nineteenth century. This quality has since prompted much of the praise for his work, initiated by the immediate popularity of *Who Is to Blame?* At the time of its publication, several critics lauded the novel; Vissarion Belinski, who was in effect Herzen's first literary promoter, embraced the novel for its ability to promote ideas through its "natural" style. That style, which emphasizes psychological verisimilitude, has also won considerable acclaim for *My Past and Thoughts*. Commentators have consistently praised the memoirs as one of the great works of nineteenth-century Russian literature, ranking them alongside the novels of such luminaries as Tolstoy and Dostoyevski. The common view of *My Past and Thoughts*—as the most accurate and evocative portrait of Russian social and cultural history in the first half of the nineteenth century—exemplifies the valuation of Herzen's works as significant historical texts as well as finely crafted pieces of literature.

Given the general consensus about the quality of Herzen's writing and his unambiguous political agenda, there has been little room for critical debate. One approach focuses on his depiction of human agency. In general, critics have seen in his portrayal of social issues a tendency to determinism: human action is of little consequence against larger social forces. Soviet critics, who embraced Herzen as a Russian literary and political figure, saw in his combination of psychological detail and social awareness an indictment of bourgeois values. A few critics, however, including Lydia Ginzburg, have argued instead that Herzen challenges the reader to place responsibility on individual human action despite apparently overwhelming odds. Either way, critics always find in his work a finely-wrought portrayal of and love for humanity.

PRINCIPAL WORKS

Kto vinovat? [as Iskander] (novel) 1847
　　[*Who Is to Blame?*, 1978]
*Vom andern Ufer (essays) 1850
　　[*From the Other Shore*, 1956]
Le peuple russe et le socialisme (letter) 1852
　　[*The Russian People and Socialism*, 1855]
Byloye i dumy (memoirs) 1854
　　[*Memoirs of Alexander Herzen* (partial translation), 1923; also published as *My Past and Thoughts*, 6 vols., 1924-27]
Prison and Exile (memoirs) 1854
Polnoe sobranie sochinenii [*Collected Works*] 22 vols. (novel, short stories, essays, and memoirs) 1919-25
Sobranie sochinenii [*Collected Works*] 30 vols. (novels, short stories, essays, and memoirs) 1954-64
Selected Philosophical Works (essays) 1956

*Also published as *S togo berega* in 1855.

CRITICISM

P. V. Annenkov (essay date 1880)

SOURCE: "Chapter XVII," in *The Extraordinary Decade: Literary Memoirs*, by P. V. Annenkov, edited by Arthur P. Mendel, translated by Irwin R. Titunik, University of Michigan Press, 1968, pp. 86-91.

[*Annenkov, a Russian of aristocratic background, was a member of the same intellectual circles as Herzen, and he later proved to be a faithful recorder of his colleagues' thoughts and manners. In the following excerpt, Annenkov sketches Herzen's multifaceted character.*]

In the early days of my acquaintance with [Herzen], I must admit, I was stunned and nonplussed by that extraordinarily mobile intellect which ranged from one subject to another with inexhaustible wit, brilliance, and incomprehensible rapidity, and which was able to grasp, be it in the case of someone's speech or some simple happening from current life or any abstract idea, the one telling detail that gave it its distinctive shape and vital expression. Herzen had an unusually well-developed talent for making, on the spur of the moment, and one after another, parallels between heterogeneous things, a talent which was sustained, first, by his power of subtle observation and, second, by the formidable capital of his encyclopedic knowledge, and which was so well-developed that it ended up by wearying his listeners. The inextinguishable fireworks of his speech, his inexhaustible imagination and inventiveness, a sort of reckless intellectual prodigality—these things constantly aroused his conversation partners' astonishment. After the always impassioned, but not always strictly consecutive, speech of Belinsky, Herzen's tortuous, endlessly mutating, often paradoxical and irritating, but invariably intelligent talk required of his conversation partners, aside from strenuous attention, also the necessity of always being on guard and armed with an answer. For all that, however, no banality, no flabby thinking could withstand even a half-hour's confrontation with him, and pretentiousness, pomposity, and pedantic conceit simply fled from him or melted before him like wax before a fire. I knew people, people predominantly from among those called serious and competent, who could not abide Herzen's presence. On the other hand, there were people, even foreigners during the period of his life abroad, for whom he quickly became not only an object of wonder but of passionate and blind devotion.

His literary and publicistic activity produced practically the same results. Herzen very early—from his first appearance in the social world—revealed the qualities of a first-class Russian writer and thinker, and he retained these qualities throughout the course of his life, even when he suffered from delusions. Generally speaking, few are the people to be encountered in the world who could maintain, as he did, their rights to attention, respect, and study at the very same time as being in the throes of some obsession. His mistakes and delusions bore the imprint of thought of the kind impossible to dismiss merely with an expression of scorn or rejection. In this aspect of his career, he resembled Belinsky, but Belinsky, constantly soaring in the region of ideas, had none of that ability to discern people's characters on first meeting and possessed none of that wicked humor of a psychologist and observer of life. Herzen, on the contrary, seemed to have been born with a critical bent of mind, with aptitudes for exposing and hounding out unwholesome aspects of existence. This became evident in him from the very earliest times, from as far back as the Moscow period of his life about which we are now talking. Even then Herzen's was an indomitable and uncompromising intellect with innate, organic abhorrence for everything made to appear the established rule, glossed over with general silence, concerning some unverified truth. In such instances, all the, so to speak, predatory aptitudes of his mind arose and issued forth en masse, astounding people with their acerbity, cunning, and resourcefulness. A resident of Sivtsev-Vrazhek in Moscow and still a figure unknown to the public, he had already acquired a reputation in his own circle as a clever and dangerous observer of the surrounding milieu. Of course, he did not always manage to keep secret those dossiers, those service records about people near and far which he kept in his head and to himself. People who took their friendship with him for granted could not help being astonished and, at times, becoming angry when some portion or other of this automatic activity of his temperament came out in the open. Surprisingly enough, this existed side by side in him with the most tender, almost loving, regard for special friends, who were not exempt from his analysis. But for an explanation of this matter, we must go to another side of his character.

As if to restore some equilibrium to his moral makeup, Nature had taken measures to implant in his soul one indomitable belief, one invincible proclivity: Herzen believed in the noble *instincts* of the human heart; his analysis would fade away and stand in awe before the instinctive promptings of the moral organism, as before the single, indubitable truth of existence. He had a high regard for noble-minded, deeply felt obsessions in people no matter how out of place they may have been, and never made fun of them. This dualistic, contradictory play of his nature—suspicious negativism, on the one hand, and blind belief, on the other—caused frequent difficulties between himself and his companions, and led to quarrels and confrontations; but it was in the fire of just these altercations that, until the very moment of his departure for abroad, people's devotion to him, instead of disintegrating, was

tempered even harder than before. The reason why is clear: in everything Herzen did and thought then, there was not the slightest trace of falsehood, secretly nurtured bad feeling, or self-minded calculation; on the contrary, he was always his whole self in every single word and act. And there was still another reason that made people forgive him, even his insults, sometimes—a reason that may seem incredible to people who did not know him.

For all his staunch, proud, and energetic intellect, his was an utterly soft, kindly, almost feminine character. Under the severe exterior of skeptic and epigrammatist, under the camouflage of a humor virtually without scruple and anything but timid, there lived within him a child's heart. He had the ability to be somehow ungainly tender and delicate, and should he deal an opponent too harsh a blow, he had a way of instantly making obvious, though only implicit, apologies. Particularly beginners, people still searching for their way and still sounding themselves out, found sources of encouragement and strength in his advice: he would bring them directly into full communion with himself, with his thought, which did not prevent his anatomizing analysis from conducting, at times, very painful psychological experiments and operations on them. Should one speak of some peculiar anomaly? He himself was sensible of this note of kindliness in him, and he took measures to keep it from ringing out too clearly. It was as if his pride was offended at the thought that people might also notice, aside from his intelligence and talents, that he had kindness of heart. On occasion he would do deliberate violence to his natural character in order to appear for a time, not the man he was created, but one of truculent mold. But these caprices did not last long. Matters changed when he arrived abroad and secured his position in the party movements: he undertook a very serious overhaul of his character then. It was not possible to remain in the midst and at the head of European democrats and keep the same candor in his ways of living and conducting himself as in Moscow. That in itself could have ruined a man in the eyes of the clubbist and socialist assembly, who willingly made use of good-naturedness but valued it very cheaply. Herzen began to groom himself for his new public as a man bearing on his shoulders the weight of an enormous political mandate and mission, whereas what occupied his interest were all the extremely diverse ideas of science, art, European culture, and poetry, for Herzen was also, in his way, a poet. Indications of this unseemly operation on himself came to the fore especially after his first attempts to aid Russian society in its task of divesting itself of the garb of *archaic* man met with general sympathy: he contrived to make himself over into an unrecognizable type of person. What readiness to trample on all old ties and remembrances, all old sympathies, in the interests of abstract liberalism! What arrogant credulity in accepting reports flattering to his personal outlook and merely echoing him! And what a perpetual standing on guard lest any feeling of his own, any personal or national trait, distort the majestic image of the impassive man incarnating the fate of nations! However, it must be added that Herzen never did fully attain the goal of his strivings. He did not succeed in turning himself inside out; he only succeeded in ruining himself. He succeeded also in one other thing—in bringing down misery on himself from which there was no escape; and if anyone's fate can be called tragic, then it is, of course, his fate toward the end of his life.

With his unusually inquiring and penetrating mind, he discerned down to the last speck the paltriness, the banal and comic side of the majority of the coryphaei of European propaganda, and, nevertheless, he followed them. With that vital moral sense which he shared in common with Belinsky, Granovsky and the whole Russian epoch of the 1840's, he felt indignation at the shamelessness, the cynicism of thought, and action among the *free* people who banded together under the same banner with him, and he carefully concealed his revulsion. For all his efforts, his comrades, governed by a sense of self-preservation, descried in him an enemy and turned on him their usual weapons—calumny, libel, defamation, lampoon. Herzen remained alone. But all of this was still far away. When I got to know him, Herzen was in the full bloom of youth, filled with high hopes for himself, and was the pride and consolation of his circle. . . .

Isaiah Berlin (essay date 1968)

SOURCE: Introduction to *My Past and Thoughts: The Memoirs of Alexander Herzen,* translated by Constance Garnett, revised by Humphrey Higgens, introduction by Isaiah Berlin, University of California Press, 1982, pp. xix-xliii.

[*Berlin is a noted twentieth-century critic of Russian literature. The essay that follows—written in 1968—presents an overview of Herzen's biography, personality, and political commitment. Berlin stresses in particular Herzen's talents as a writer and an intellectual.*]

Alexander Herzen, like Diderot, was an amateur of genius whose opinions and activities changed the direction of social thought in his country. Like Diderot, too, he was a brilliant and irrepressible talker: he talked equally well in Russian and in French to his intimate friends and in the Moscow salons—always in an overwhelming flow of ideas and images; the waste, from the point of view of posterity (just as with Diderot) is probably immense: he had no Boswell and no Eckermann to record his conversation, nor was he a man who would have suffered such a relationship. His

prose is essentially a form of talk, with the vices and virtues of talk: eloquent, spontaneous, liable to the heightened tones and exaggerations of the born storyteller, unable to resist long digressions which themselves carry him into a network of intersecting tributaries of memory or speculation, but always returning to the main stream of the story or the argument; but above all, his prose has the vitality of spoken words—it appears to owe nothing to the carefully composed formal sentences of the French *'philosophes'* whom he admired or to the terrible philosophical style of the Germans from whom he learnt; we hear his voice almost too much—in the essays, the pamphlets, the autobiography, as much as in the letters and scraps of notes to his friends.

Civilised, imaginative, self-critical, Herzen was a marvellously gifted social observer; the record of what he saw is unique even in the articulate nineteenth century. He had an acute, easily stirred and ironical mind, a fiery and poetical temperament, and a capacity for vivid, often lyrical, writing—qualities that combined and reinforced each other in the succession of sharp vignettes of men, events, ideas, personal relationships, political situations and descriptions of entire forms of life in which his writings abound. He was a man of extreme refinement and sensibility, great intellectual energy and biting wit, easily irritated *amour propre* and a taste for polemical writing; he was addicted to analysis, investigation, exposure; he saw himself as an expert 'unmasker' of appearances and conventions, and dramatised himself as a devastating discoverer of their social and moral core. Tolstoy, who had little sympathy with Herzen's opinions, and was not given to excessive praise of his contemporaries among men of letters, especially when they belonged to his own class and country, said towards the end of his life that he had never met anyone with 'so rare a combination of scintillating brilliance and depth.' These gifts make a good many of Herzen's essays, political articles, day-to-day journalism, casual notes and reviews, and especially letters written to intimates or to political correspondents, irresistibly readable even to-day, when the issues with which they were concerned are for the most part dead and of interest mainly to historians.

Although much has been written about Herzen—and not only in Russian—the task of his biographers has not been made easier by the fact that he left an incomparable memorial to himself in his own greatest work—translated by Constance Garnett as **My Past and Thoughts**—a literary masterpiece worthy to be placed by the side of the novels of his contemporaries and countrymen, Tolstoy, Turgenev, Dostoyevsky. Nor were they altogether unaware of this. Turgenev, an intimate and life-long friend (the fluctuations of their personal relationship were important in the life of both; this complex and interesting story has never been adequately told) admired him as a writer as well as a revolutionary journalist. The celebrated critic Vissarion Belinsky discovered, described and acclaimed his extraordinary literary gift when they were both young and relatively unknown. Even the angry and suspicious Dostoyevsky excepted him from the virulent hatred with which he regarded the pro-Western Russian revolutionaries, recognised the poetry of his writing, and remained well-disposed towards him until the end of his life. As for Tolstoy, he delighted both in his society and his writings: half a century after their first meeting in London he still remembered the scene vividly.[1]

It is strange that this remarkable writer, in his lifetime a celebrated European figure, the admired friend of Michelet, Mazzini, Garibaldi and Victor Hugo, long canonised in his own country not only as a revolutionary but as one of its greatest men of letters, is, even to-day, not much more than a name in the West. The enjoyment to be obtained from reading his prose—for the most part still untranslated—makes this a strange and gratuitous loss.

Alexander Herzen was born in Moscow on the 6th April, 1812, some months before the great fire that destroyed the city during Napoleon's occupation after the battle of Borodino. His father, Ivan Alexandrovich Yakovlev, came of an ancient family distantly related to the Romanov dynasty. Like other rich and well-born members of the Russian gentry, he had spent some years abroad, and, during one of his journeys, met, and took back to Moscow with him, the daughter of a minor Württemberg official, Luiza Haag, a gentle, submissive, somewhat colourless girl, a good deal younger than himself. For some reason, perhaps owing to the disparity in their social positions, he never married her according to the rites of the Church. Yakovlev was a member of the Orthodox Church; she remained a Lutheran.[2] He was a proud, independent, disdainful man, and had grown increasingly morose and misanthropic. He retired before the war of 1812, and at the time of the French invasion was living in bitter and resentful idleness in his house in Moscow. During the occupation he was recognised by Marshal Mortier, whom he had known in Paris, and agreed—in return for a safe conduct enabling him to take his family out of the devastated city—to carry a message from Napoleon to the Emperor Alexander. For this indiscretion he was sent back to his estates and only allowed to return to Moscow somewhat later. In his large and gloomy house on the Arbat he brought up his son, Alexander, to whom he had given the surname Herzen, as if to stress the fact that he was the child of an irregular liaison, an affair of the heart. Luiza Haag was never accorded the full status of a wife, but the boy had every attention lavished upon him. He received the normal education of a young Russian nobleman of his time, that is to say, he was looked after by a host of nurses and serfs, and taught by private tutors, German and French, carefully chosen by his neurotic, irritable, devoted, suspicious father. Every care was taken to develop his gifts. He was a lively and imaginative child and absorbed knowledge easily and eagerly. His father loved him after his fashion: more, certainly, than his other son, also illegitimate, born ten years earlier, whom he had christened Yegor (George). But he was, by the eighteen-twenties, a defeated and gloomy man, unable to communicate with his family or indeed anyone else. Shrewd, honourable, and neither unfeeling nor unjust, a 'difficult' character like old Prince Bolkonsky in Tolstoy's *War and Peace,* Ivan Yakovlev emerges from his son's recollections a self-lacerating, grim, shut-in, half-frozen human being, who terrorised his household with his whims and his sarcasm. He kept all doors and windows locked, the blinds permanently drawn, and, apart from a few old friends and his own brothers, saw virtually nobody. In later years his son described him as the product of 'the encounter of two such incompatible things as the eighteenth century and Russian life'—a collision of cultures hat had destroyed a good many among the more sensitive members of the Russian gentry in the reigns of Catherine II and her successors. The boy escaped with relief from his father's oppressive and frightening company to the rooms occupied by his mother and the servants; she was kind and unassuming, crushed by her husband, frightened by her foreign surroundings, and seemed to accept her almost Oriental status in the household with uncomplaining resignation. As for the servants, they were serfs from the Yakovlev estates, trained to behave obsequiously to the son and probable heir of their master. Herzen himself, in later years, attributed the deepest of all his social feelings (which his friend, the critic Belinsky, diagnosed so accurately), concern for the freedom and dignity of human individuals, to the barbarous conditions that surrounded him in childhood. He was a favourite child, and much spoiled; but the facts of his irregular birth and of his mother's status were brought home to him by listening to the servants' gossip and, on at least one occasion, by overhearing a conversation about himself between his father and one of his old army comrades. The shock was, according to his own testimony, profound: it was probably one of the determining factors of his life.

He was taught Russian literature and history by a young university student, an enthusiastic follower of the new Romantic movement, which, particularly in its German form, had then begun to dominate Russian intellectual life. He learned French (which his father wrote more easily than Russian) and German (which he spoke with his mother) and European, rather than Russian, history—his tutor was a French refugee who had emigrated to Russia after the French Revolution. The Frenchman did not reveal his political opinions, so Herzen tells us, until one day, when his pupil asked him why Louis XVI had been executed; to this he replied in an altered voice, 'Because he was a traitor to his country', and finding the boy responsive, threw off his reserve and spoke to him openly about the liberty and equality of men. Herzen was a lonely child, at once pampered and cramped, lively and bored; he read voraciously in his father's large library, especially French books of the Enlightenment. He was fourteen when the leaders of the Decembrist conspiracy were hanged by the Emperor Nicholas I. He later declared that this event was the critical turning point of his life; whether this was so or not, the memory of these aristocratic martyrs in the cause of Russian constitutional liberty later became a sacred symbol to him, as to many others of his class and generation, and affected him for the rest of his days. He tells us that a few years after this, he and his intimate friend Nick Ogarëv, standing on the Sparrow Hills above Moscow, took a solemn 'Hannibalic' oath to avenge these fighters for the rights of man, and to dedicate their own lives to the cause for which they had died.

In due course he became a student in the University of Moscow, read Schiller and Goethe, and somewhat later the French utopian socialists, Saint-Simon, Fourier and other social prophets smuggled into Russia in defiance of the censorship, and became a convinced and passionate radical. He and Ogarëv belonged to a group of students who read forbidden books and discussed dangerous ideas; for this he was, together with most other 'unreliable' students, duly arrested and, probably because he declined to repudiate the views imputed to him, condemned to imprisonment. His father used all his influence to get the sentence mitigated, but could not save his son from being exiled to the provincial city of Vyatka, near the borders of Asia, where he was not indeed kept in prison, but put to work in the local administration. To his astonishment, he enjoyed this new test of his powers; he displayed administrative gifts and became a far more competent and perhaps even enthusiastic official than he was later prepared to admit, and helped to expose the corrupt and brutal governor, whom he detested and despised. In Vyatka he became involved in a passionate love affair with a married woman, behaved badly, and suffered agonies of contrition. He read Dante, went through a religious phase, and began a long and passionate correspondence with his first cousin Natalie, who, like himself, was illegitimate, and lived as a companion in the house of a rich and despotic aunt. As a result of his father's ceaseless efforts, he was transferred to the city of Vladimir, and with the help of his young Moscow friends, arranged the elopement of Natalie. They were married in Vladimir against their relations' wishes. He was in due course allowed to return to Moscow and was appointed to a government post in Petersburg. Whatever his ambitions at the time, he remained indomitably independent and committed to the radical cause. As a result of an indiscreet letter,

opened by the censors, in which he had criticised the behaviour of the police, he was again sentenced to a period of exile, this time in Novgorod. Two years later, in 1842, he was once more permitted to return to Moscow. He was by then regarded as an established member of the new radical intelligentsia, and, indeed, as an honoured martyr in its cause, and began to write in the progressive periodicals of the time. He always dealt with the same central theme: the oppression of the individual; the humiliation and degradation of men by political and personal tyranny; the yoke of social custom, the dark ignorance, and savage, arbitrary misgovernment which maimed and destroyed human beings in the brutal and odious Russian Empire.

Like the other members of his circle, the young poet and novelist Turgenev, the critic Belinsky, the future political agitators Bakunin and Katkov (the first in the cause of revolution, the second of reaction), the literary essayist Annenkov, his own intimate friend Ogarëv, Herzen plunged into the study of German metaphysics and French sociological theory and history—the works of Kant, Schelling, and above all, Hegel; also Saint-Simon, Augustin Thierry, Leroux, Mignet and Guizot. He composed arresting historical and philosophical essays, and stories dealing with social issues; they were published, widely read and discussed, and created a considerable reputation for their author. He adopted an uncompromising position. A leading representative of the dissident Russian gentry, his socialist beliefs were caused less by a reaction against the cruelty and chaos of the *laissez-faire* economy of the bourgeois West—for Russia, then in its early industrial beginnings, was still a semi-feudal, socially and economically primitive society— than as a direct response to the agonising social problems in his native land: the poverty of the masses, serfdom and lack of individual freedom at all levels, and a lawless and brutal autocracy.[3] In addition, there was the wounded national pride of a powerful and semi-barbarous society, whose leaders were aware of its backwardness, and suffered from mingled admiration, envy and resentment of the civilised West. The radicals believed in reform along democratic, secular, Western lines; the Slavophils retreated into mystical nationalism, and preached the need for return to native 'organic' forms of life and faith that, according to them, had been all but ruined by Peter I's reforms, which had merely encouraged a sedulous and humiliating aping of the soulless, and, in any case, hopelessly decadent West. Herzen was an extreme 'Westerner', but he preserved his links with the Slavophil adversaries—he regarded the best among them as romantic reactionaries, misguided nationalists, but honourable allies against the Tsarist bureaucracy—and later tended systematically to minimise his differences with them, perhaps from a desire to see all Russians who were not dead to human feeling ranged in a single vast protest against the evil régime.

In 1847 Ivan Yakovlev died. He left the greater part of his fortune to Luiza Haag and her son, Alexander Herzen. With immense faith in his own powers, and burning with a desire (in Fichte's words that expressed the attitude of a generation) 'to be and do something in the world,' Herzen decided to emigrate. Whether he wished or expected to remain abroad during the rest of his life is uncertain, but so it turned out to be. He left in the same year, and travelled in considerable state, accompanied by his wife, his mother, two friends, as well as servants, and, crossing Germany, towards the end of 1847 reached the coveted city of Paris, the capital of the civilised world. He plunged at once into the life of the exiled radicals and socialists of many nationalities who played a central role in the fermenting intellectual and artistic activity of that city. By 1848, when a series of revolutions broke out in country after country in Europe, he found himself with Bakunin and Proudhon on the extreme left wing of revolutionary socialism. When rumours of his activities reached the Russian government, he was ordered to return immediately. He refused. His fortune in Russia and that of his mother were declared confiscated. Aided by the efforts of the banker James Rothschild who had conceived a liking for the young Russian 'baron' and was in a position to bring pressure on the Russian government, Herzen recovered the major portion of his resources, and thereafter experienced no financial want. This gave him a degree of independence not then enjoyed by many exiles, as well as the financial means for supporting other refugees and radical causes.

Shortly after his arrival in Paris, before the revolution, he contributed a series of impassioned articles to a Moscow periodical controlled by his friends, in which he gave an eloquent and violently critical account of the conditions of life and culture in Paris, and, in particular, a devastating analysis of the degradation of the French bourgeoisie, an indictment not surpassed even in the works of his contemporaries Marx and Heine. His Moscow friends for the most part received this with disfavour: they regarded his analyses as characteristic flights of a highly rhetorical fancy, irresponsible extremism, ill suited to the needs of a misgoverned and backward country compared to which the progress of the middle classes in the West, whatever its shortcomings, was a notable step forward towards universal enlightenment. These early works—*The Letters from Avenue Marigny* and the Italian sketches that followed—possess qualities which became characteristic of all his writings: a rapid torrent of descriptive sentences, fresh, lucid, direct, interpersed with vivid and never irrelevant digressions, variations on the same theme in many keys, puns, neologisms, quotations real and imaginary, verbal inventions, gallicisms which irritated his nationalistic Russian friends, mordant personal observations and cascades of vivid images and incomparable epigrams,

which, so far from either tiring or distracting the reader by their virtuosity, add to the force and swiftness of the narrative. The effect is one of spontaneous improvisation: exhilarating conversation by an intellectually gay and exceptionally clever and honest man endowed with singular powers of observation and expression. The modd is one of ardent political radicalism imbued with a typically aristocratic (and even more typically Muscovite) contempt for everything narrow, calculating, self-satisfied, commercial, anything cautious, petty or tending towards compromise and the *juste milieu,* of which Louis Philippe and Guizot are held up to view as particularly repulsive incarnations. Herzen's outlook in these essays is a combination of optimistic idealism—a vision of a socially, intellectually and morally free society, the beginnings of which, like Production, Marx, and Louis Blanc, he saw in the French working class; faith in the radical revolution which alone could create the conditions for their liberation; but with this, a deep distrust (something that most of his allies did not share) of all general formulae as such, of the programmes and battle cries of all the political parties, of the great, official historical goals—progress, liberty, equality, national unity, historic rights, human solidarity—principles and slogans in the name of which men had been, and doubtless would soon again be, violated and slaughtered, and their forms of life condemned and destroyed. Like the more extreme of the left wing disciples of Hegel, in particular like the anarchist Max Stirner, herzen saw danger in the great magnificent abstractions the mere sound of which precipitated men into violent and meaningless slaughter—new idols, it seemed to him, on whose altars human blood was to be shed tomorrow as irrationally and uselessly as the blood of the victims of yesterday or the day before, sacrificed in honour of older divinities—church or monarchy or the feudal order or the sacred customs of the tribe, that were now discredited as obstacles to the progress of mankind. Together with this scepticism about the meaning and value of abstract ideals as such, in contrast with the concrete, short-term, immediate goals of identifiable living individuals—specific freedoms, reward for the day's work—Herzen spoke of something even more disquieting—a haunting sense of the ever widening and unbridgeable gulf between the humane values of the relatively free and civilised élites (to which he knew himself to belong) and the actual needs, desires and tastes of the vast voiceless masses of mankind, barbarous enough in the West, wilder still in Russia or the plains of Asia beyond. The old world was crumbling visibly, and it deserved to fall. It would be destroyed by its victims—the slaves who cared nothing for the art and the science of their masters; and indeed, Herzen asks, why should they care? Was it not erected on their suffering and degradation? Young and vigorous, filled with a just hatred of the old world built on their fathers' bones, the new barbarians will raze to the ground the edifices of their oppressors, and with them all that is most sublime and beautiful in Western civilisation; such a catalystm might be not only inevitable but justified, since this civilisation, noble and valuable in the eyes of its beneficiaries, has offered nothing but suffering, a life without meaning, to the vast majority of mankind. Yet he does not pretend that this makes the prospect, to those who, like him, have tasted the riper fruits of civilisation, any less dreadful.

It has often been asserted by both Russian and Western critics that Herzen arrived in Paris a passionate, even utopian idealist, and that it was the failure of the Revolution of 1848 which brought about his disillusionment and a new, more pessimistic realism. This is not sufficiently borne out by the evidence.[4] Even in 1847, the sceptical note, in particular pessimism about the degree to which human beings can be transformed, and the still deeper scepticism about whether such changes, even if they were achieved by fearless and intelligent revolutionaries or reformers, ideal images of whom floated before the eyes of his Westernising friends in Russia, would in fact lead to a juster and freer order, or on the contrary to the rule of new masters over new slaves—that ominous note is sounded before the great débâcle. Yet, despite this, he remained a convinced, ultimately optimistic revolutionary. The spectacle of the workers' revolt and its brutal suppression in Italy and in France, haunted Herzen all his life. His first-hand description of the events of 1848-9, in particular of the drowning in blood of the July revolt in Paris, is a masterpiece of 'committed' historical and sociological writing. So, too, are his sketches of the personalities involved in these upheavals, and his reflections upon them. Most of these essays and letters remain untranslated.

Herzen could not and would not return to Russia. He became a Swiss citizen, and to the disasters of the revolution was added a personal tragedy—the seduction of his adored wife by the most intimate of his new friends, the radical German poet Georg Herwegh, a friend of Marx and Wagner, the 'iron lark' of the German Revolution, as Heine half ironically called him. Herzen's progressive, somewhat Shelleyan, views on love, friendship, equality of the sexes, and the irrationality of bourgeois morality, were tested by this crisis and broken by it. He went almost mad with grief and jealousy: his love, his vanity, his deeper assumptions about the basis of all human relationships, suffered a traumatic shock from which he was never fully to recover. He did what few others have ever done: described every detail of his own agony, every step of his altering relationship with his wife, with Herwegh and Herwegh's wife, as they seemed to him in retrospect; he noted every communication that occurred between them, every moment of anger, despair, affection, love, hope, hatred, contempt and agonised, suicidal self-contempt. Every tone and *nuance* in his own moral and psychological condition are raised to high

relief against the background of his public life in the world of exiles and conspirators, French, Italian, German, Russian, Austrian, Hungarian, Polish, who move on and off the stage on which he himself is always the central, self-absorbed, tragic hero. The account is not unbalanced—there is no obvious distortion—but it is wholly egocentric. All his life Herzen perceived the external world clearly, and in proportion, but through the medium of his own self-romanticising personality, with his own impressionable, ill-organised self at the centre of his universe. No matter how violent his torment, he retains full artistic control of the tragedy which he is living through, but also writing. It is, perhaps, this artistic egotism, which all his work exhibits, that was in part responsible both for Natalie's suffocation and for the lack of reticence in his description of what took place: Herzen takes wholly for granted the reader's understanding, and still more, his undivided interest in every detail of his own, the writer's, mental and emotional life. Natalie's letters and desperate flight to Herwegh show the measure of the increasingly destructive effect of Herzen's self-absorbed blindness upon her frail and *exalté* temperament. We know comparatively little of Natalie's relationship with Herwegh: she may well have been physically in love with him, and he with her: the inflated literary language of the letters conceals more than it reveals; what is clear is that she felt unhappy, trapped and irresistibly attracted to her lover. If Herzen sensed this, he perceived it very dimly. He appropriated the feelings of those nearest him as he did the ideas of Hegel or George Sand: that is, he took what he needed, and poured it into the vehement torrent of his own experience. He gave generously, if fitfully, to others; he put his own life into them, but for all his deep and life-long belief in individual liberty and the absolute value of personal life and personal relationships, scarcely understood or tolerated wholly independent lives by the side of his own; his description of his agony is scrupulously and bitterly detailed and accurate, never self-sparing, eloquent but not sentimental, and remorselessly self-absorbed. It is a harrowing document. He did not publish the story in full during his lifetime, but now it forms part of his Memoirs.

Self-expression—the need to say his own word—and perhaps the craving for recognition by others, by Russia, by Europe, were primary needs of Herzen's nature. Consequently, even during this, the darkest period of his life, he continued to pour out a stream of letters and articles in various languages on political and social topics; he helped to keep Proudhon going, kept up a correspondence with Swiss radicals and Russian *émigrés,* read widely, made notes, conceived ideas, argued, worked unremittingly both as a publicist and as an active supporter of left wing and revolutionary causes. After a short while Natalie returned to him in Nice, only to die in his arms. Shortly before her death, a ship on which his mother and one of his children, a deaf-mute, were travelling from Marseilles, sank in a storm. Their bodies were not found. Herzen's life had reached its lowest ebb. He left Nice and the circle of Italian, French and Polish revolutionaries to many of whom he was bound by ties of warm friendship, and with his three surviving children went to England. America was too far away and, besides, seemed to him too dull. England was no less remote from the scene of his defeats, political and personal, and yet still a part of Europe. It was then the country most hospitable to political refugees, civilised, tolerant of eccentricities or indifferent to them, proud of its civil liberties and its sympathy with the victims of foreign oppression. He arrived in London in 1851.

He and his children wandered from home to home in London and its suburbs, and there, after the death of Nicholas I had made it possible for him to leave Russia, his most intimate friend, Nicholay Ogarëv, joined them. Together they set up a printing press, and began to publish a periodical in Russian called *The Pole Star*—the first organ wholly dedicated to uncompromising agitation against the Imperial Russian régime. The earliest chapters of **My Past and Thoughts** appeared in its pages. The memory of the terrible years 1848-51 obsessed Herzen's thoughts and poisoned his blood stream: it became an inescapable psychological necessity for him to seek relief by setting down this bitter history. This was the first section of his Memoirs to be written. It was an opiate against the appalling loneliness of a life lived among uninterested strangers[5] while political reaction seemed to envelop the entire world, leaving no room for hope. Insensibly he was drawn into the past. He moved further and further into it and found it a source of liberty and strength. This is how the book which he conceived on the analogy of *David Copperfield* came to be composed.[6] He began to write it in the last months of 1852. He wrote by fits and starts. The first two parts were probably finished by the end of 1853. In 1854 a selection which he called **Prison and Exile**—a title perhaps inspired by Silvio Pellico's celebrated *Le Mie Prigioni,* was published in English. It was an immediate success; encouraged by this, he continued. By the spring of 1855, the first five parts of the work were completed; they were all published by 1857. He, revised part IV, added new chapters to it and composed part V; he completed the bulk of part VI by 1858. The sections dealing with his intimate life—his love and the early years of his marriage—were composed in 1857: he could not bring himself to touch upon them until then. This was followed by an interval of seven years. Independent essays such as those on Robert Owen, the actor Shchepkin, the painter Ivanov, Garibaldi (*Camicia Rossa*), were published in London between 1860 and 1864; but these, although usually included in the Memoirs, were not intended for them. The first complete edition of the first four parts appeared in 1861. The final section—part VIII and almost the whole of part

VII—were written, in that order, in 1865-7. Herzen deliberately left some sections unpublished: the most intimate details of his personal tragedy appeared posthumously—only a part of the chapter entitled **"Oceano Nox"** was printed in his lifetime. He omitted also the story of his affairs with Medvedeva in Vyatka and with the serf girl Katerina in Moscow—his confession of them to Natalie cast the first shadow over their relationship, a shadow that never lifted; he could not bear to see it in print while he lived. He suppressed, too, a chapter on 'The German Emigrants' which contains his unflattering comments on Marx and his followers, and some characteristically entertaining and ironical sketches of some of his old friends among the Russian radicals. He genuinely detested the practice of washing the revolutionaries' dirty linen in public, and made it clear that he did not intend to make fun of allies for the entertainment of the common enemy. The first authoritative edition of the Memoirs was compiled by Mikhail Lemke in the first complete edition of Herzen's works, which was begun before, and completed some years after, the Russian Revolution of 1917. It has since been revised in successive Soviet editions. The fullest version is that published in the new exhaustive edition of Herzen's works, a handsome monument of Soviet scholarship—which at the time of writing is still incomplete.

The Memoirs formed a vivid and broken background accompaniment to Herzen's central activity: revolutionary journalism, to which he dedicated his life. The bulk of it is contained in the most celebrated of all Russian periodicals published abroad—*Kolokol—The Bell*—edited by Herzen and Ogarëv in London and then in Geneva from 1857 until 1867, with the motto (taken from Schiller) *Vivos voco. The Bell* had an immense success. It was the first systematic instrument of revolutionary propaganda directed against the Russian autocracy, written with knowledge, sincerity and mordant eloquence; it gathered round itself all that was uncowed not only in Russia and the Russian colonies abroad, but also among Poles and other oppressed nationalities. It began to penetrate into Russia by secret routes and was regularly read by high officials of State, including, it was rumoured, the Emperor himself. Herzen used the copious information that reached him in clandestine letters and personal messages, describing various misdeeds of the Russian bureaucracy to expose specific scandals—cases of bribery, miscarriage of justice, tyranny and dishonesty by officials and influential persons. *The Bell* named names, offered documentary evidence, asked awkward questions and exposed hideous aspects of Russian life Russian travellers visited London in order to meet the mysterious leader of the mounting opposition to the Tsar. Generals, high officials and other loyal subjects of the Empire were among the many visitors who thronged to see him, some out of curiosity, others to shake his hand, to express sympathy or admiration. He reached the peak of his fame, both political and literary, after the defeat of Russia in the Crimean War and the death of Nicholas I. The open appeal by Herzen to the new Emperor to free the serfs and initiate bold and radical reforms 'from above,' and, after the first concrete steps towards this had been taken in 1859, his paean of praise to Alexander II under the title of 'Thou hast Conquered, O Galilean,' created the illusion on both sides of the Russian frontier that a new liberal era was at last dawning, in which a degree of understanding—perhaps of actual cooperation—could be achieved between Tsardom and its opponents. This state of mind did not last long. But Herzen's credit stood very high—higher than that of any other Russian in the West: in the late fifties and early sixties, he was the acknowledged leader of all that was generous, enlightened, civilised, humane in Russia. More than Bakunin and even Turgenev, whose novels formed a central source of knowledge about Russia in the West, Herzen counteracted the legend, ingrained in the minds of progressive Europeans (of whom Michelet was perhaps the most representative), that Russia consisted of nothing save only the government jack-boot on the one hand, and the dark, silent, sullen mass of brutalised peasants on the other—an image that was the by-product of the widespread sympathy for the principal victim of Russian despotism, the martyred nation, Poland. Some among the Polish exiles spontaneously conceded this service to the truth on Herzen's part, if only because he was one of the rare Russians who genuinely liked and admired individual Poles, worked in close sympathy with them, and identified the cause of Russian liberation with that of all her oppressed subject nationalities. It was, indeed, this unswerving avoidance of chauvinism that was among the principal causes of the ultimate collapse of *The Bell* and of Herzen's own political undoing.

After Russia, Herzen's deepest love was for Italy and the Italians. The closest ties bound him to the Italian exiles, Mazzini, Garibaldi, Saffi and Orsini. Although he supported every liberal beginning in France, his attitude towards her was more ambiguous. For this there were many reasons. Like Tocqueville (whom he personally disliked), he had a distaste for all that was centralised, bureaucratic, hierarchical, subject to rigid forms or rules; France was to him the incarnation of order, discipline, the worship of the state, of unity, and of despotic, abstract formulae that flattened all things to the same rule and pattern—something that had a family resemblance to the great slave states—Prussia, Austria, Russia; with this he constantly contrasts the decentralised, uncrushed, untidy, 'truly democratic' Italians, whom he believed to possess a deep affinity with the free Russian spirit embodied in the peasant commune with its sense of natural justice and human worth. To this ideal even England seemed to him to be far less hostile than legalistic, calculating France: in such moods he comes close to his romantic

Slavophil opponents. Moreover, he could not forget the betrayal of the revolution in Paris by the bourgeois parties in 1848, the execution of the workers, the suppression of the Roman Revolution by the troops of the French Republic, the vanity, weakness and rhetoric of the French radical politicians—Lamartine, Marrast, Ledru-Rollin, Félix Pyat. His sketches of the lives and behaviour of leading French exiles in England are masterpieces of amused, half-sympathetic, half-contemptuous description of the grotesque and futile aspects of every political emigration condemned to sterility, intrigue and a constant flow of self-justifying eloquence before a foreign audience too remote or bored to listen. Yet he thought well of individual members of it: he had for a time been a close ally of Proudhon, and despite their differences, he continued to respect him; he regarded Louis Blanc as an honest and fearless democrat, he was on good terms with Victor Hugo, he liked and admired Michelet. In later years he visited at least one Paris political salon—admittedly, it was that of a Pole—with evident enjoyment: the Goncourts met him there and left a vivid description in their journal of his appearance and his conversation.[7] Although he was half German himself, or perhaps because of it, he felt, like his friend Bakunin, a strong aversion from what he regarded as the incurable philistinism of the Germans, and what seemed to him a peculiarly unattractive combination of craving for blind authority with a tendency to squalid internecine recriminations in public, more pronounced than among other *émigrés*. Perhaps his hatred of Herwegh, whom he knew to be a friend both of Marx and of Wagner, as well as Marx's onslaughts on Karl Vogt, the Swiss naturalist to whom Herzen was devoted, played some part in this. At least three of his most intimate friends were pure Germans. Goethe and Schiller meant more to him than any Russian writers. Yet there is something genuinely venomous in his account of the German exiles, quite different from the high-spirited sense of comedy with which he describes the idiosyncrasies of the other foreign colonies gathered in London in the fifties and sixties—a city, if we are to believe Herzen, equally unconcerned with their absurdities and their martyrdoms. As for his hosts, the English, they seldom appear in his pages. Herzen had met Mill, Carlyle and Owen. His first night in England was spent with English hosts. He was on reasonably good terms with one or two editors of radical papers (some of whom, like Linton and Cowen, helped him to propagate his views, and to preserve contact with revolutionaries on the continent as well with clandestine traffic of propaganda to Russia), and several radically inclined Members of Parliament, including minor ministers. In general, however, he seems to have had even less contact with Englishmen than his contemporary and fellow exile, Karl Marx. He admired England. He admired her constitution; the wild and tangled wood of her unwritten laws and customs brought the full resources of his romantic imagination into play. The entertaining passages of *My Past and Thoughts* in which he compared the French and the English, or the English and the Germans, display acute and amused insight into the national characteristics of the English. But he could not altogether like them: they remained for him too insular, too indifferent, too unimaginative, too remote from the moral, social and aesthetic issues which lay closest to his own heart, too materialistic and self-satisfied. His judgments about them, always intelligent and sometimes penetrating, are distant and tend to be conventional. A description of the trial in London of a French radical who had killed a political opponent in a duel in Windsor Great Park is wonderfully executed, but remains a piece of *genre* painting, a gay and brilliant caricature. The French, the Swiss, the Italians, even the Germans, certainly the Poles, are closer to him. He cannot establish any genuine personal relationship with the English. When he thinks of mankind he does not think of them.

Apart from his central preoccupations, he devoted himself to the education of his children, which he entrusted in part to an idealistic German lady, Malwida von Meysenbug, afterwards a friend of Nietzsche and Romain Rolland. His personal life was intertwined with that of his intimate friend Ogarëv, and of Ogarëv's wife who became his mistress; in spite of this the mutual devotion of the two friends remained unaltered—the Memoirs reveal little of the curious emotional consequences of this relationship.[8]

For the rest, he lived the life of an affluent, well born man of letters, a member of the Russian, and more specifically, Moscow gentry, uprooted from his native soil, unable to achieve a settled existence or even the semblance of inward or outward peace, a life filled with occasional moments of hope and even exultation, followed by long periods of misery, corrosive self-criticism, and most of all overwhelming, omnivorous, bitter nostalgia. It may be this, as much as objective reasons, that caused him to idealise the Russian peasant, and to dream that the answer to the central 'social' question of his time—that of growing inequality, exploitation, dehumanisation of both the oppressor and the oppressed—lay in the preservation of the Russian peasant commune. He perceived in it the seeds of the development of a non-industrial, semi-anarchist socialism. Only such a solution, plainly influenced by the views of Fourier, Proudhon and George Sand, seemed to him free from the crushing, barrack-room discipline demanded by Western communists from Cabet to Marx; and from the equally suffocating, and, it seemed to him, far more vulgar and philistine ideals contained in moderate, half-socialist doctrines, with their faith in the progressive role of developing industrialism preached by the forerunners of social democracy in Germany and France and of the Fabians in England. At times he modified his view: towards the end of his life he began to recognise the historical significance of the organised urban workers. But all in all, he remained faithful to his belief in the Russian peasant commune as an embryonic form of a life in which the quest for individual freedom was reconciled with the need for collective activity and responsibility. He retained to the end a romantic vision of the inevitable coming of a new, just, all-transforming social order.

Herzen is neither consistent nor systematic. His style during his middle years has lost the confident touch of his youth, and conveys the consuming nostalgia that never leaves him. He is obsessed by a sense of blind accident, although his faith in the values of life remains unshaken. Almost all traces of Hegelian influence are gone. 'The absurdity of facts offends us . . . it is as though someone had promised that everything in the world will be exquisitely beautiful, just and harmonious. We have marvelled enough at the deep abstract wisdom of nature and history; it is time to realise that nature and history are full of the accidental and senseless, of muddle and bungling.' This is highly characteristic of his mood in the sixties; and it is no accident that his exposition is not ordered, but is a succession of fragments, episodes, isolated vignettes, a mingling of *Dichtung* and *Wahrheit,* facts and poetic licence. His moods alternate sharply. Sometimes he believes in the need for a great, cleansing, revolutionary storm, even were it to take the form of a barbarian invasion likely to destroy all the values that he himself holds dear. At other times he reproaches his old friend Bakunin, who joined him in London after escaping from his Russian prisons, for wanting to make the revolution too soon; for not understanding that dwellings for free men cannot be constructed out of the stones of a prison; that the average European of the nineteenth century is too deeply marked by the slavery of the old order to be capable of conceiving true freedom, that it is not the liberated slaves who will build the new order, but new men brought up in liberty. History has her own tempo. Patience and gradualism—not the haste and violence of a Peter the Great—can alone bring about a permanent transformation. At such moments he wonders whether the future belongs to the free, anarchic peasant, or to the bold and ruthless planner; perhaps it is the industrial worker who is to be the heir to the new, unavoidable, collectivist economic order.[9] Then again he returns to his early moods of disillusionment and wonders whether men in general really desire freedom: perhaps only a few do so in each generation, while most human beings only want good government, no matter at whose hands; and he echoes de Maistre's bitter epigram about Rousseau: 'Monsieur Rousseau has asked why it is that men who are born free are nevertheless everywhere in chains; it is as if one were to ask why sheep, who are born carnivorous, nevertheless everywhere nibble grass.' Herzen develops this theme. Men desire freedom no more than fish desire to fly. The fact that a few flying fish exist does not demonstrate that fish in general were created to fly, or are not fundamentally quite content to stay below the surface of the water, for ever away from the sun and the light. Then he returns to his earlier optimism and the thought that somewhere—in Russia—there lives the unbroken human being, the peasant with his faculties intact, untainted by the corruption and sophistication of the West. But this Rousseau-inspired faith, as he grows older, grows less secure. His sense of reality is too strong. For all his efforts, and the efforts of his socialist friends, he cannot deceive himself entirely. He oscillates between pessimism and optimism, scepticism and suspicion of his own scepticism, and is kept morally alive only by his hatred of all injustice, all arbitrariness, all mediocrity as such—in particular by his inability to compromise in any degree with either the brutality of reactionaries or the hypocrisy of bourgeois liberals. He is preserved by this, buoyed up by his belief that such evils will destroy themselves, and by his love for his children and his devoted friends, and by his unquenchable delight in the variety of life and the comedy of human character.

On the whole, he grew more pessimistic. He began with an ideal vision of human life, largely ignored the chasm which divided it from the present—whether the Russia of Nicholas, or the corrupt constitutionalism in the West. In his youth he glorified Jacobin radicalism and condemned its opponents in Russia—blind conservatism, Slavophil nostalgia, the cautious gradualism of his friends Granovsky and Turgenev, as well as Hegelian appeals to patience and rational conformity to the inescapable rhythms of history, which seemed to him designed to ensure the triumph of the new bourgeois class. His attitude, before he went abroad, was boldly optimistic. There followed, not indeed a change of view, but a cooling-off, a tendency to a more sober and critical outlook. All genuine change, he began to think in 1847, is necessarily slow; the power of tradition (which he at once mocks at and admires in England) is very great; men are less malleable than was believed in the eighteenth century, nor do they truly seek liberty, only security and contentment; communism is but Tsarism stood on its head, the replacement of one yoke by another; the ideals and watchwords of politics turn out, on examination, to be empty formulae to which devout fanatics happily slaughter hecatombs of their fellows. He no longer feels certain that the gap between the enlightened élite and the masses can ever, in principle, be bridged (this becomes an obsessive refrain in later Russian thought), since the awakened people may, for unalterable psychological or sociological reasons, despise and reject the gifts of a civilisation which will never mean enough to them. But if all this is even in small part true, is radical transformation either practicable or desirable? From this follows Herzen's growing sense of obstacles that may be insurmountable, limits that may be im-

passable, his empiricism, scepticism, the latent pessimism and despair of the middle sixties. This is the attitude which some Soviet scholars interpret as the beginning of an approach on his part towards a quasi-Marxist recognition of the inexorable laws of social development—in particular the inevitability of industrialism, above all of the central role to be played by the proletariat. This is not how Herzen's Russian left wing critics interpreted his views in his lifetime, or for the half century that followed. To them, rightly or wrongly, these doctrines seemed symptomatic of conservatism and betrayal. For in the fifties and sixties, a new generation of radicals grew up in Russia, then a backward country in the painful process of the earliest, most rudimentary beginnings of slow, sporadic, inefficient industrialisation. These were men of mixed social origins, filled with contempt for the feeble liberal compromises of 1848, with no illusions about the prospects of freedom in the West, determined on more ruthless methods; accepting as true only what the sciences can prove, prepared to be hard, and if need be, unscrupulous and cruel, in order to break the power of their equally ruthless oppressors; bitterly hostile to the aestheticism, the devotion to civilised values, of the 'soft' generation of the forties. Herzen realised that the criticism and abuse showered upon him as an obsolete aristocratic dilettante by these 'nihilists' (as they came to be called after Turgenev's novel *Fathers and Sons,* in which this conflict is vividly presented for the first time) was not altogether different from the disdain that he had himself felt in his own youth for the elegant and ineffective reformers of Alexander I's reign; but this did not make his position easier to bear. What was ill-received by the tough-minded revolutionaries pleased Tolstoy, who said more than once that the censorship of Herzen's works in Russia was a characteristic blunder on the part of the government; the government, in its anxiety to stop young men from marching towards the revolutionary morass, seized them and swept them off to Siberia or prison long before they were even in sight of it, while they were still on the broad highway; Herzen had trodden this very path, he had seen the chasm, and warned against it, particularly in his 'Letters to an Old Comrade.' Nothing, Tolstoy argued, would have proved a better antidote to the 'revolutionary nihilism' which Tolstoy condemned, than Herzen's brilliant analyses. 'Our young generation would not have been the same if Herzen had been read by them during the last twenty years.' Suppression of his books, Tolstoy went on, was both a criminal, and from the point of view of those who did not desire a violent revolution, an idiotic policy. At other times, Tolstoy was less generous. In 1860, six months before they met, he had been reading Herzen's writings with mingled admiration and irritation: 'Herzen is a man of scattered intellect, and morbid *amour-propre,*' he wrote in a letter, 'but his breadth, ability, goodness, elegance of mind are Russian.' From time to time various correspondents record the fact that Tolstoy read Herzen, at times aloud to his family, with the greatest admiration. In 1896, during one of his angriest, most nati-rationalist moods, he said, 'What has Herzen said that is of the slightest use?'—as for the argument that the generation of the forties could not say what it wanted to say because of the rigid Russian censorship, Herzen wrote in perfect freedom in Paris and yet managed to say 'nothing useful.' What irritated Tolstoy most was Herzen's socialism. In 1908 he complained that Herzen was 'a narrow socialist,' even if he was 'head and shoulders above the other politicians of his age and ours.' The fact that he believed in politics as a weapon was sufficient to condemn him in Tolstoy's eyes. From 1862 onwards, Tolstoy had declared his hostility to faith in liberal reform and improvement of human life by legal or institutional change. Herzen fell under this general ban. Moreover, Tolstoy seems to have felt a certain lack of personal sympathy for Herzen and his public position—even a kind of jealousy. When, in moments of acute discouragement and irritation, Tolstoy spoke (perhaps not very seriously) of leaving Russia forever, he would say that whatever he did, he would not join Herzen or march under his banner: 'he goes his way, I shall go mine.' He seriously underrated Herzen's revolutionary temperament and instincts. However sceptical Herzen may have been of specific revolutionary doctrines or plans in Russia—and no-one was more so—he believed to the end of his life in the moral and social need and the inevitability, sooner or later, of a revolution in Russia—a violent transformation followed by a just, that is a socialist, order. He did not, it is true, close his eyes to the possibility, even the probability, that the great rebellion would extinguish values to which he was himself dedicated—in particular, the freedoms without which he and others like him could not breathe. Nevertheless, he recognised not only the inevitability but the historic justice of the coming cataclysm. His moral tastes, his respect for human values, his entire style of life, divided him from the tough-minded younger radicals of the sixties, but he did not, despite all his distrust of political fanaticism, whether on the right or on the left, turn into a cautious, reformist liberal constitutionalist. Even in his gradualist phase he remained an agitator, an egalitarian and a socialist to the end. It is this in him that both the Russian populists and the Russian Marxists—Mikhaylovsky and Lenin—recognised and saluted.

It was not prudence or moderation that led him to his unwavering support of Poland in her insurrection against Russia in 1863. The wave of passionate Russian nationalism which accompanied its suppression, robbed him of sympathy even among Russian liberals. *The Bell* declined in circulation.[10] The new, 'hard' revolutionaries needed his money, but made it plain that they looked upon him as a liberal dinosaur, the preacher of antiquated humanistic views, useless in the violent social struggle to come. He left London in the late sixties and attempted to produce a French edition of *The Bell* in Geneva. When that too failed, he visited his friends in Florence, returning to Paris early in 1870, before the outbreak of the Franco-Prussian War. There he died of pleurisy, broken both morally and physically, but not disillusioned; still writing with concentrated intelligence and force. His body was taken to Nice, where he is buried beside his wife. A life-size statue still marks his grave.

Herzen's ideas have long since entered into the general texture of Russian political thought—liberals and radicals, populists and anarchists, socialists and communists, have all claimed him as an ancestor. But what survives to-day of all that unceasing and feverish activity, even in his native country, is not a system or a doctrine but a handful of essays, some remarkable letters, and the extraordinary amalgam of memory, observation, moral passion, psychological analysis and political description, wedded to a major literary talent, which has immortalised his name. What remains is, above all, a passionate and inextinguishable temperament and a sense of the movement of nature and of its unpredictable possibilities, which he felt with an intensity which not even his uniquely rich and flexible prose could fully express. He believed that the ultimate goal of life was life itself; that the day and the hour were ends in themselves, not a means to another day or another day or another experience. He believed that remote ends were a dream, that faith in them was a fatal illusion; that to sacrifice the present, or the immediate and foreseeable future to these distant ends must always lead to cruel and futile forms of human sacrifice. He believed that values were not found in an impersonal, objective realm, but were created by human beings, changed with the generations of men, but were nonetheless binding upon those who lived in their light; that suffering was inescapable, and infallible knowledge neither attainable nor needed. He believed in reason, scientific methods, individual action, empirically discovered truths; but he tended to suspect that faith in general formulae, laws, prescription in human affairs was an attempt, sometimes catastrophic, always irrational, to escape from the uncertainty and unpredictable variety of life to the false security of our own symmetrical fantasies. He was fully conscious of what he believed. He had obtained this knowledge at the cost of painful, and, at times, unintended, self-analysis, and he described what he saw in language of exceptional vitality, precision and poetry. His purely personal credo remained unaltered from his earliest days: 'Art, and the summer lightning of individual happiness: these are the only real goods we have,' he declared in a self-revealing passage of the kind that so deeply shocked the stern young Russian revolutionaries in the sixties. Yet even they and their descendants did not and do not reject his artistic and intellectual achievement.

Herzen was not, and had no desire to be, an impartial observer. No less than the poets and the novelists of his nation, he created a style, an outlook, and, in the words of Gorky's tribute to him, 'an entire province, a country astonishingly rich in ideas,'[11] where everything is immediately recognisable as being his and his alone, a country into which he transplants all that he touches, in which things, sensations, feelings, persons, ideas, private and public events, institutions, entire cultures, are given shape and life by his powerful and coherent historical imagination, and have stood up against the forces of decay in the solid world which his memory, his intelligence and his artistic genius recovered and reconstructed. ***My Past and Thoughts*** is the Noah's ark in which he saved himself, and not himself alone, from the destructive flood in which many idealistic radicals of the forties were drowned. Genuine art survives and transcends its immediate purpose. The structure that Herzen built in the first place, perhaps, for his own personal salvation, built out of material provided by his own predicament—out of exile, solitude, despair—survives intact. Written abroad, concerned largely with European issues and figures, these reminiscences are a great permanent monument to the civilised, sensitive, morally preoccupied and gifted Russian society to which Herzen belonged; their vitality and fascination have not declined in the hundred years that have passed since the first chapters saw the light.

Notes

[1] P. Sergeyenko, in his book on Tolstoy, says that Tolstoy told him in 1908 that he had a very clear recollection of his visit to Herzen in his London house in March 1861. 'Lev Nikolaevich remembered him as a not very large, plump little man, who generated electric energy. "Lively, responsive, intelligent, interesting", Lew Nikolaevich explained (as usual illustrating every shade of meaning by appropriate movements of his hands), "Herzen at once began talking to me as if we had known each other for a long time. I found his personality enchanting. I have never met a more attractive man. He stood head and shoulders above all the politicians of his own and of our time."' (P. Sergeyenko, *Tolstoi i ego sovremenniki,* Moscow, 1911, pp. 13-14.)

[2] There is evidence, although it is not conclusive, that she was married to him according to the Lutheran rite, not recognised by the Orthodox Church.

[3] The historical and sociological explanation of the origins of Russian socialism and of Herzen's part in it cannot be attempted here. It has been treated in a number of (untranslated) Russian monographs, both pre-and post-revolutionary. The most detailed and original study of this topic to date is *Alexander Herzen and the Birth of Russian Socialism, 1812-1855* (1961) by Professor Martin Malia.

[4] The clearest formulation of this well-worn and almost universal thesis is to be found in Mr. E. H. Carr's lively and well documented treatment of Herzen in his *The Romantic Exiles* and elsewhere. Mr Malia's book avoids this error.

[5] Herzen had no close English friends, although he had associates, allies, and admirers. One of these, the radical journalist W. J. Linton, to whose *English Republic* Herzen had contributed articles, described him as 'short of stature, stoutly built, in his last days inclined to corpulence, with a grand head, long chestnut hair and beard, small luminous eyes, and rather ruddy complexion. Suave in his manner, courteous, but with an intense power of irony, witty, . . . clear, concise and impressive, he was a subtle and profound thinker, with all the passionate nature of the "barbarian," yet generous and humane.' (*Memories,* London, 1895, pp. 146-7.) And in his *European Republicans,* published two years earlier, he spoke of him as 'hospitable and taking pleasure in society, . . . a good conversationalist, with a frank and pleasing manner,' and said that the Spanish radical Castelar declared that Herzen, with his fair hair and beard, looked like a Goth, but possessed the warmth, vivacity, 'verve and inimitable grace' and 'marvellous variety' of a Southerner. Turgenev and Herzen were the first Russians to move freely in European society. The impression that they made did a good deal, though perhaps not enough, to dispel the myth of the dark 'Slav soul,' which took a long time to die; perhaps it is not altogether dead yet.

[6] 'Copperfield is Dickens's *Past and Thoughts,*' he said in one of his letters in the early sixties; humility was not among his virtues.

[7] See entry in the *Journal* under *8th February* 1865—'Dinner at Charles Edmond's (Chojecki) . . . A Socratic mask with the warm and transparent flesh of a Rubens portrait, a red mark between the eyebrows as from a branding iron, greying beard and hair. As he talks there is a constant ironical chuckle which rises and falls in his throat. His voice is soft and slow, without any of the coarseness one might have expected from the huge neck; the ideas are fine, delicate, pungent, at times subtle, always definite, illuminated by words that take time to arrive, but which always possess the felicitous quality of French as it is spoken by a civilised and witty foreigner.

'He speaks of Bakunin, of his eleven months in prison, chained to a wall, of his escape from Siberia by the Amur River, of his return by way of California, of his arrival in London, where, after a stormy, moist embrace, his first words to Herzen were "Can one get oysters her?".'

Herzen delighted the Goncourts with stories about the Emperor Nicholas walking in the night in his empty palace, after the fall of Eupatoria during the Crimean War, with the heavy, unearthly steps of the stone statue of the Commander in 'Don Juan.' This was followed by anecdotes about English habits and manners—'a country which he loves as the land of liberty'—to illustrate its absurd, class conscious, unyielding traditionalism, particularly noticeable in the relations of masters and servants. The Goncourts quote a characteristic epigram made by Herzen to illustrate the difference between the French and English characters. They faithfully report the story of how James Rothschild managed to save Herzen's property in Russia.

[8] See chapters 8 and 12 of E. H. Carr's *The Romantic Exiles* for what the Memoirs don't reveal, which is a lot. Carr's account draws largely on Natalie Ogarëv's unpublished diaries. Similarly, Carr uses papers made available to him by Herwegh's son—his fascinating little book is in the Herzen style: as much novel as history—"to correct the serious omission and inaccuracies of the Herzen version" of the liaison between the German radical poet and Herzen's wife. For the Herzen version, see pp. 840-920 and 932-50 of the complete Garnett-Higgens edition (Knopf, 1968), which unhappily had to be omitted in this politically oriented abridgment. I think, myself, that the Herzen version is closer to the truth, and farther from the facts, than the Carr version. (*D.M.*)

[9] This is the thesis in which orthodox Soviet scholars claim to discern a belated approach to those of Marx.

[10] Herzen's lifelong enemy, the reactionary Pan-Slavic journalist, M. N. Katkov, came out strongly for "national unity" against the Polish rebels—and against Herzen. Russian opinion was overwhelmingly on his side. A public subscription was raised for Katkov. "He has rendered us great service!" exclaimed a Moscow nobleman. "He has crushed the serpent's head! He has broken Herzen's authority!" When a rash of incendiary fires broke out (cf. Dostoevsky's *The Possessed*), Katkov charged they were the work of a vast conspiracy organized by the Polish rebels, "Herzen and his scoundrels," and various persons in Paris, London, and Geneva including the Duc d'Harcourt. . . . By the end of that year *Kolokol*'s circulation had dropped from 2500 to 500. (*D.M.*)

[11] *Istoriya Russkoy Literatury,* p. 206 (Moscow, 1939).

Edward Acton (essay date 1979)

SOURCE: Introduction to *Alexander Herzen and the Role of the Intellectual Revolutionary,* Cambridge University Press, 1979, pp. 1-24.

[*Acton portrays Herzen's life as the negotiation of his philosophical, activist, and private selves. In the essay that follows, Acton focuses specifically on how these three aspects interacted to position Herzen in Russian society before his emigration in 1847.*]

In 1847 Alexander Herzen left Russia for western Europe, never to return. 'I found everything I sought—yes, and more,' he would write later, after his first five years abroad, 'ruin, the loss of every blessing and every hope, blows from behind my back, sly treachery, desecration . . . and moral corruption of which you can have no conception' (VIII, 398).[1] Although the west did not give Herzen what he wanted, it did provide the richest personal and political contrast and drama. The product of autocratic, serf-ridden, agricultural Russia, he was to spend the rest of his life in the west, witnessing revolution, parliamentary government and industrailisation. Born into a cosmopolitan generation he was to confront the growing nationalist current in Europe. Having developed, under the influence of the romantics, an overweening self-confidence, he was to undergo the most devastating blows to his ego. And maturing with the euphoric expectations of utopian socialism, he was to suffer the shock of 1848 and live his most productive years in the calm of Victorian England. He stood at a central crossroad of mid-nineteenth century European history. And he had the attributes to make him an unusually sensitive barometer of the period. He had the intellectual power and insight to form a coherent world-view on which the developments he witnessed made a definite and measurable impact. He had the ability—and the capital—to create an important journalistic role for himself on the political scene in Russia. He had the personality to develop a full private life which played an integral part in what he saw as the series of disillusionments he underwent in the west.

What set his experience apart, in terms both of interest and of complexity, was the sheer range of new events and ideas which impinged upon him, and his responsiveness to them. Political, social and ideological developments in Russia, France, Italy and England, as well as the dramatic events in his own life, affected him intimately. And he was ready, while retaining the same values, to reappraise his assumptions and his role when experience seemed to challenge them. Moreover, the different facets of his life—his political philosophy, his practical activity and his private life—conditioned each other directly. Changes in one facet had immediate repercussions on the others. The development of each facet cannot, in fact, be explained satisfactorily in isolation. And it is only in studying their interaction that something of the man himself may be recaptured.

The nodal point from which their interaction may best be seen is that of Herzen's changing concept of his

A lithograph of Herzen in his earlier years.

role. What role did he wish to play and how did his view of that role change and develop? It is a question that might lead to a better understanding of many historical figures: in the case of the author of ***My Past and Thoughts*** it is crucial. He was led by both temperament and social and intellectual environment to a remarkably self-conscious approach towards the events of his day—as was demonstrated by his life-long penchant for autobiography skilfully woven into the social and political background.[2] Well aware that he was an outstandingly gifted man within a minute elite, he felt himself born to a role on the grand historical scene. And this role demanded that he be fully in tune with the times, with change—'In history,' he wrote, 'the worst crime is to be uncontemporary' (XIV, 104). From early youth he understood this role in terms of protest against oppression and commitment to an approaching socialist millennium. The content of his socialism was not precisely spelt out when he left Russia, but it involved every aspect of life. He sought to be the personification of the future society. For him this meant both to work for the socialist utopia and to affirm in his own private life the values he hoped to see embodied socially. It was therefore here, in his view of his role, that his experiences, public and private, were most clearly registered. The changes involved were striking. From preoccupation with inter-

preting the direction of contemporary history, he was led by the triumph of reaction in 1848 to primary emphasis on a private life true to the ideals he now feared he might never see generalised; personal catastrophe drove him from this to the desire for immediate involvement in practical political affairs. And the combination of personal and political disillusionment transformed the historico-philosophical assumptions in terms of which he saw his role.

To understand Herzen's experience in the west in the period from the 1840s to the 1860s, it is necessary first to establish his stance when he left Russia in 1847. This requires an outline of the social context from which he sprang, and of his development within it. Herzen was born into the wealthy ranks of the Russian landowning class. Peter the Great had moulded this class into a nobility, formalised by the Table of Ranks, to serve the state. The army and bureaucracy were to draw on western experience, and the nobility were accordingly forcibly westernised in dress, custom, language and culture. This process cut them off from the illiterate and enserfed mass of the Russian peasantry. And the demands of state service prevented them establishing firm provincial ties of the sort that integrated the contemporary British landowning classes into the society around them.[3] The humiliation of the Church by Peter weakened the ideological hold of Orthodoxy on the better educated and more reflective members of the nobility. And at the same time the insensitive bureaucratic machine which evolved from Peter's initiative destroyed for many the sense of personal loyalty and duty to the Tsar. When, in the course of the latter part of the eighteenth century, the compulsory nature of their state service was gradually eroded, a number of noblemen became professionally as well as ideologically cut off from the Russian state. It was among these elements that radical criticisms of the establishment took root, and that European ideas and the European tour exercised their chief attraction. Catherine II herself enjoyed the attention and stimulation of the *philosophes,* and though she took fright at the implications of the French Revolution, she could not prevent Russia from being drawn into the ensuing war. The march to Paris at the end of the Napoleonic Wars stimulated the hopes and imagination of a broad section of the nobility still within the fold of state service. Six hundred men, some from the very highest families, went on trial for the Decembrist rising of 1825—the rising which was to provide a sense of revolutionary heritage and a source of inspiration for Herzen throughout his life.

It was to the less heroic majority of the Decembrist generation that Herzen's father belonged. He had enjoyed the European tour, brought back Herzen's German mother, preferred French to Russian and owned a thoroughly western library. An unhappy figure, he personified the political and intellectual impasse created for his kind by a Russia still dominated by autocracy and Orthodoxy. Without himself going beyond cynicism, Iakovlev nevertheless bequeathed a rationalist irony to his son which could be put to more radical purposes.

Herzen was born in 1812, the year in which Alexander I dismissed his reforming minister, Speransky, and faced Napoleon's invasion. The political atmosphere in which he matured was one of almost unrelieved gloom. The ruthless Arakcheev dominated the last years of Alexander's reign, and Nicholas's ascent to the throne in 1825, ushered in with the suppression of the Decembrists, was characterised by an even more stagnant, unimaginative conservatism. The Third Section of His Majesty's Personal Chancellery, the proliferating secret police, epitomised the regime that took as its slogan 'Orthodoxy, Autocracy and Nationality'—the last merely implying the natural loyalty of Russians to the former concepts. Independent thought and initiative were in effect discouraged by a government which adopted the military approach towards every sphere of national life. As a result, those who began to find fault with the Russian *status quo* were provoked to more and more revulsion. Herzen's generation were even more responsive to progressive political and humanitarian principles than his father's most enterprising contemporaries. They were further estranged from the Russian state. Where the Decembrists had for the most part been officers in the Tsar's army, the men of the forties were outside the army and the bureaucracy, and those who had the option—which by no means all the 'gentry' generation of intelligentsia did—rejected the role of serf-owning farmers. Frustrated by an environment which in relative terms was becoming more and more backward socially, politically and economically, they were driven to intransigent denial. Moreover, they had the Decembrist example before them. To some extent they could draw progressive ideas from Russian poets and writers. And their political impotence, borne in upon them by the hopeless failure of the Decembrists, attracted them to an approach towards political and social progress which stressed ideas and philosophy at the expense of more tangible levers of change. Both the intensity and the nature of Herzen's approach must be seen in this context.

The particular features of Herzen's outlook derived from his personal experience of Russia. At home he was the emotional focus of his father, his mother, and to some extent the household serfs. Quick and attractive, he aroused near adulation as a child. At university he was a centre of attention and he was the acknowledged heart of his circle of friends in the thirties and forties. He developed an enormous, ebullient ego. In the poet Ogarev he found, while they were still boys, a kindred spirit with a similarly romantic though less egocentric view of life. The friendship they developed

seemed to Herzen the epitome of what life could offer. Perhaps most important of all was his relationship with Natalie, which evolved from cousinly affection to the most intense romance. Natalie's devotion played a vital part in heightening his self-esteem, and in creating the exalted view of life with which he came to the west. For while in exile in the provincial town of Vyatka (1835-8) he underwent a crisis of confidence which shook him deeply. Cut off from his university friends, and bored by his job in the local administration, he felt corrupted by the 'vulgar remarks, dirty people, mean ideas and coarse feelings' which surrounded him (*Past*, 232).[4] He was humiliated in his own eyes by his petty interests and above all by what he saw as a sordid affair with a woman whom he felt he deceived since he had no desire to marry her. His dishonourable intentions were clearly exposed by the untimely death of her husband. Natalie appeared as his Beatrice leading him back to the heights his ego demanded. Their courtship was carried on in the most heady, romantic correspondence of the period. Encouraged by his fiancée and A. L. Vitberg, the mystical Russian architect with whom he was living at the time, Herzen passed through a religious period during which he saw their relationship as symbolic of the regenerative power that love would soon exercise over the world.[5] Although the religious mood would fade, and their marriage (1838) would suffer some strain during the forties, Natalie's devotion remained a cornerstone of his self-esteem. When he came to write his memoirs it was his early married life which evoked his most lyrical and self-confident lines. 'There was not the shadow of a sad memory, not the faintest dark foreboding; it was all youth, friendship, love, exuberant strength, energy, health and an endless road before us' (*Past*, 392). His romantic image of their love, their relationship and his consciousness of the envy of others for their idyllic home cast a glow over his whole view of life. He developed and left Russia with what he called 'an overweening confidence in life' (*Past*, 1859). His ego, his extraordinarily gifted and vibrant personality gave him a sense of the richness and beauty of life unusual among his contemporaries and reminiscent rather of the receding age of Pushkin. It would be tested by experience, but when he emigrated, this sense, this sheer *joie de vivre* inspired an intense personal aspiration to lead the full life.

Herzen's lofty image of what life could be chafed against the interference of authority to produce a sweeping denial of the real in the name of the ideal. The oppressive cossetting of a morose and hypochondriac father served as a foretaste of political constrictions to follow.[6] He recalled identifying with his father's oppressed serfs and believed that the sight of their treatment sparked off his lifelong commitment to liberty. His discovery that in the eyes of the Russian state he was illegitimate, since his father had not married his mother in the Orthodox Church, gave Herzen a sense of independence and defiance of that state. The young Ogarev developed a similar protest against the *status quo*. They shared a heady view of their own historical mission in the name of this protest. They identified with the heroes of December 1825. The romantic, idealistic atmosphere they breathed is captured by the scene of their famous vow, on the Sparrow Hills overlooking Moscow, to dedicate themselves to the struggle for freedom. 'Flushed and breathless we stood there mopping our faces,' recalled Herzen. 'The sun was setting, the cupolas glittered, beneath the hill the city extended farther than the eye could reach; a fresh breeze blew on our faces, we stood leaning against each other and, suddenly embracing, vowed in the sight of all Moscow to sacrifice our lives to the struggle we had chosen. This scene may strike others as very affected and theatrical, and yet twenty-six years afterwards I am moved to tears as I recall it; there was a sacred sincerity in it' (*Past*, 69). Their feeling of isolation, both now and in the circles of the thirties and forties, increased their sense of their own historical importance.[7] Political opposition never seemed more noble and glamorous than in the Russia of the 'remarkable decade'. The articulate opposition was so small, the odds so overwhelming, the future promise so great.

The point is not to imply an element of posturing, of insincerity in Herzen's social and political crusade: the everpresent offence of serfdom, on which he knew his own privileged opportunities had depended, guaranteed against that. In any case, as a young man he felt the direct impact of government interference in his own life. He was accused of sedition, imprisoned and suffered two intensely frustrating periods in provincial exile (II, 212-13). Political conditions in Russia made it impossible for him to separate his private life from political questions, even if such separation had been theoretically possible. Herzen in fact did not see it as possible even in theory. In his view, sheer lack of social involvement was the cause of Natalie's tendency to morbid introspection, which at times seemed to mar their married life. And the example of his father's generation convinced him that, without social and political commitment, the 'superfluous man's' life is bound to be aimless and distorted. Both his novels, *Who Is to Blame?* and *Duty before All* (the latter written after he emigrated) illustrated how one-sided characters were destroyed by the narrowness of their purely personal interests. The point that must be made is, rather, that the socio-political crusade in the name of freedom for all, for the mass of the peasantry, was not set over against but was part of his aspiration to the full life. His literary heroes, such as Schiller's Karl Moor, 'did not cut themselves off by love from general interests of citizenship, art, science; on the contrary, they brought all its animation, all its ardour into

these spheres, and, on the other hand, they carried the breadth and scale of these worlds into their love' (H, 68).

Herzen's personal experience of Russia under Nicholas moulded the three central features of his outlook in the forties. In the first place, he saw the overriding problem facing contemporary thinkers and society as the reconciliation of the individual and the community. The free individual and the just and cohesive society were his supreme ideals. And his conception of man as inherently social and political, his view that a satisfying private life implies involvement in 'general interests', not only removed any fundamental contradiction between the two, but made them complementary. The second point is that his outlook was imbued with optimism. He confidently expected the 'future reformation' which would resolve the problem. Finally, the balanced and rich individual life was not merely the end product of this socialist regeneration: he aspired to it himself. Even if the political dimension of his life was to be lived in working towards utopia and not enjoying it, even if appalling social injustice and oppression of the individual continued, he wanted the full life himself, now. It is in terms of these three points that the controversial question of his attitude to western thought and society in the forties may best be understood.

Herzen was brought up on thoroughly western intellectual fare. He was given private lessons in history and language by western tutors. Like many of his peers he was at ease in French and German. Lonely and intelligent, as a boy he enjoyed reading and made full use of his father's library. He tasted Pushkin and Ryleev, but his childhood favourites were Schiller, Voltaire and Rousseau;[8] he greatly admired Shakespeare and Goethe; as a young man he encountered many of the ideas of Schelling and soon after leaving university he discovered the Saint-Simonists; during the thirties and forties he read Blanc, Fourier, Proudhon, Sand and Considérant, among other French authors of the left;[9] he was delighted by Feuerbach and made a close study of Hegel.[10] He was in a position from his earliest youth to draw on the western classics and on the great romantics, socialists and philosophical idealists of the period. That they interacted with his environmentally shaped preoccupations and figured in his thought and work throughout his life was readily acknowledged by Herzen himself. He paid particular tribute to Schiller, Saint-Simon, Proudhon and Hegel. Their ideas offered positive attraction as well as compensation for the frustrations of Russian life. Yet it does not follow that his ideas were a mere reflection of western thought. The Russian intelligentsia as a whole would draw from foreign thinkers those elements which helped them to solve their own problems. When they were enamoured of a whole body of ideas, they interpreted them in accordance with their own predilections. The particular impact on Herzen of western philosophical idealism and western socialism must be seen in this light.[11]

He was fully involved in the philosophical debates which characterised the first half of the nineteenth century in Russia. The outlook with which he came to the west was informed by his reading in pure philosophy, and he always considered a knowledge of Hegelianism, 'the algebra of revolution', essential for a man to be 'modern' (*Past*, 402-3). But concentration on pure philosophy was engendered by political impotence and censorship, and in Herzen's case at any rate, once out of this rarefied atmosphere, his primary social and personal interests asserted themselves explicitly. 'An exclusively speculative tendency,' he later remarked, 'is utterly opposed to the Russian temperament' (*Past*, 397). The story of his development after his emigration to the west in 1847 did not involve any shift in his basic philosophical values, and the changes in his concept of his role did not follow from purely philosophical insights.[12] However, in 1840 when he returned from exile to Moscow, he found Hegel in vogue. He had not abandoned his sense of being more concerned with real life and social problems than the Stankevich and early Slavophile circles, but since the German philosopher dominated the field of intellectual debate, he now plunged into the study of his thought.

In **'Dilettantism in Science'** (1842-3) and **'Letters on the Study of Nature'** (1845) he made the most important critique of Hegel from the Russian left. His approach to Hegel has generally been seen as a search for philosophical guarantees of the socialist utopia for which he yearned.[13] The philosophy of history, an interpretation of history which would bolster their rejection of the Russian *status quo,* was a primary concern of both Westerners and Slavophiles. And in so far as he accepted Hegel's system, he did see in the dialectic an explanation for the vicissitudes of an historical process which could be seen to be moving forward—and forward far beyond the realm of ideas and the contemporary Prussian state into a utopian future uniting thought and action, the individual and society. He could enthuse over the prospect of the Ideal realising itself (III, 64-88). But Hegel did not create his optimism, and even in the mid-forties his system could provide only qualified support for it in Herzen's eyes. For Herzen questioned the pantheist implications of Hegel's philosophy. Rather than agonising over the rival claims of materialism and idealism, he rejected an Absolute dominating human development because of his prior affirmation of the individual.[14] Moreover, personal experience made him question any rational principle at all in history: the uphill work of restoring Natalie's morale was destroyed by sheer ill-fortune—their son Sasha's illness (II, 316-17). An alarming storm made him ponder, in his diary,

the helplessness of man amidst 'the terrible vortex of chance' (II, 370). The discovery that individual men are subject to chance and guaranteed nothing, whatever capacities they may feel in themselves, led him to question any purpose, any definite direction, in history in general. It is comforting 'to think that the fate of man, for example, is secretly preordained, to try to unravel this mystery, to grasp something', but in reality 'there is no concealed secret about the life of each man' (II, 286). He was struck by the earth's dependence on arbitrary developments in the solar system: the whole world, animals, plants, and man could be instantly destroyed—'It is a terrible thing, but undeniable' (II, 369). He warned against relying on 'a dream about the future which will never be realised in line with our thought' (II, 346). This scepticism prevented Herzen from imbibing deeply a rationally constructed philosophy of history which saw an idea being inevitably realised—and by 1847 he had rejected Hegel's system. But his optimism was intact. Its source lay deeper than any logical justification drawn from western philosophy—it lay primarily in the conjuncture of his personality and Russian reality. Only political and personal blows could undermine what was essentially an emotional assumption.

If Herzen rejected the structure of Hegelian idealism while deriving a certain encouragement from it, his debt to western socialist thought was of a rather similar kind. As with Hegel, however, he was at first very impressionable. The Saint-Simonists, Blanc, Fourier and Proudhon, he believed, were working on the same problem as he was. They were not isolated malcontents nor impotent speculators, but confident prophets and analysts of an impending reformation. He approached their work with the question 'how will it be?' rather than 'will it be?' or 'how can we help to bring it about?' Indeed during the early forties he seemed at times to adopt wholesale their prescriptions for the future. He was attracted by their critique of the political and economic domination of the bourgeoisie, and was excited by their vision of total transformation, economic equality, true republican freedom, feminine emancipation and the overthrow of religion. 'In the future epoch,' he would write with enthusiasm after reading George Sand, 'there will be no marriage, the wife will be free from slavery . . . Free relationships of the sexes, public education of children and the organisation of property. Morality, conscience and not the police or public opinion will determine the details of relationships' (II, 290). And in 1843 he recorded the general impression he had formed: 'Events will show the form, the flesh, the strength of the reformation. But its general sense is clear: the public control of property and capital, communal living, the organisation of labour and of wages and the right to private property placed on different foundations' (II, 266).

Western authors and his view of western society thus reinforced his concern for social solidarity, but now for the sake of the masses rather than for the individual personality, for economic rather than primarily aesthetic reasons. From the books and articles of men of industrialising countries he learned of the sense of social dissolution particularly acute in France after the Napoleonic wars. He was made conscious of the injustice and wretched poverty which characterised early capitalism, and of the unbridled individualism to which it might be attributed. For a period this western concern increased his consciousness of the claims of the Russian peasant masses *as opposed* to those of individuals like himself. And this led him to see on the 'banner' of the coming epoch, 'not the individual but the commune, not liberty but fraternity, not abstract equality but the organic division of labour' (II, 336). It is symptomatic of the broad spectrum of concern for social cohesion in the west which affected Herzen that it should have been a conservative baron from Germany who drew his attention to the Russian peasant commune as a possible answer to the problem. Both socialist and conservative protests were initially very similar in the west, seeking a replacement for communal religion and liberal optimism as a foundation for social solidarity.[15] The sympathy between Herzen and the Slavophiles over the commune reflected a similarly widespread concern within Russia to avoid western atomisation. At any rate, for a while Herzen did toy with the commune as the solution. But while still in Russia he rejected it. Both his prior commitment to the free flowering of the individual, and his optimism limited the influence that western anxiety could bring to bear upon him. In the later forties his aspiration to the full life was at its most intense. And he could not overcome his sense that the commune absorbed, limited, constricted the individual.[16] During his final two years in Russia he left little comment on the commune and the whole thrust of his thought was towards a total reconciliation for which it was inadequate. His optimism led him to seek a higher ideal: the individual and the community, freedom and fraternity were compatible to the very full.

On reflection Herzen was inclined to modify radically the predictions he had at first taken almost uncritically from western authorities—he quickly came to see the forced removal of children from their mothers as barbaric. In part his more critical attitude reflected growing independence of judgement. But basically the influence of western socialists on the content of his socialism was not more positive because their preoccupations and approach were not the same as his. In common with other members of the intelligentisa, he showed a remarkable lack of interest in the economic and industrial aspects of their thought, considering how central these were to western socialists.[17] He did not see economic inequality as the greatest evil, and economic forces played a subsidiary role to that of

ideas among his interests and in his understanding of the development of social and political life. The rigid conservatism of the Russian state ensured that his vision soared not only beyond such mundane steps as the abolition of serfdom but beyond the concrete organisation of a socialist society. Whether it was their failure to integrate philosophy into their analyses, or the constriction on the individual that he detected in their programmes, he found something lacking in all western socialists.

To depict Herzen's outlook as the passive creation of western ideas, is, then, clearly false. Yet his interest in and debt to western thinkers and western society was extremely deep. The point that must be made in placing him on the Westerner-Slavophile spectrum is not that he was intellectually uncritically receptive, but that he was emotionally involved. He identified with western strivings, and specifically with those of France. This is in no way to deny that his first love was Russia, that his pride in her had been nourished since boyhood by tales of Borodino, the defeat of Napoleon and the march to Paris. He could enthuse over the potential in the Russian peasant (II, 217) and speculate on the possibility of the Slavs solving the problem of contemporary man (II, 336). To see socialism realised in Russia would be for him the highest reward. Nor is it to deny his early interest in the commune, and his emphasis that the Slavophiles were exaggerating the hope rather than inventing the possibility.[18] But in the mid-forties he rejected the commune, and for all his love of Russia he could not overlook the unfavourable contrast with Europe in terms of past achievements and imminent prospects of progress towards freedom. It was because of this that he became so caught up in the future of the west. The twin ideals which lay at the root of his outlook—his socialism and his personal aspiration to the full life—not only permitted but made necessary a profoundly cosmopolitan approach rather than preoccupation with Russia's claims. For the conditions of Russia, the oppressive sense of stagnation, the smallness, helplessness and isolation of his 'circle', the evident strength of the regime and the passivity of the masses presented an overwhelming denial of these ideals. And Herzen often voiced the deep gloom this could induce: 'Our position is hopeless,' he would write in his diary, 'because it is false, because historical logic shows that we are outside the needs of the people and our fate is desperate suffering' (II, 278). The fact that he did not despair but, more than any of his contemporaries, maintained a sweeping optimism about the 'future regeneration' and a determination himself to find 'a wide arena' must be seen in the context of the European dimension.

The west, and above all France, was the home of revolution; it was there that concrete steps had been taken in the past, it was there that the best work was being done on the approaching millennium, and it was

France which offered the greatest hope of an imminent sequel in the direction of socialism. From boyhood he had identified with the heroes of 1789 and 1793. He was fully involved in the hopes and disappointments of 1830. His diary of the 1840s reflects his cosmopolitanism, his delight at events infinitely distant from Russia. He was thrilled by the release, in the face of the wishes of the British establishment, of the Irish nationalist O'Connell. 'This event is universal,' he wrote in 1844, 'its importance is incalculable . . . the poor petty Slavophiles! . . . The soil of Europe is holy, blessings on it, blessings!' (II, 380-1). Progress towards liberty in Europe provided his utopian hopes with support at a level incomparably deeper than the logical constructs of Hegel. Victory there was his victory—both his own and Natalie's reactions to the events of 1848 would prove the point. And even before the great transformation began, while the bourgenisie still dominated the west, he saw there the relative freedom which could enable him to lead an integrated public and private life himself. He did not wish to accept the fate of a victim of Russia's backwardness: his order of priorities was not such that he would be a stocial martyr for Russia's future. He wanted to take part in the vibrant intellectual and social search he saw in the west. Long before the opportunity to emigrate arose, he yearned to take Natalie there to begin a free and rich life (II, 211). And when the chance at last arrived, he seized upon it, took no trouble to keep the road home open, and quickly adopted western customs and friends. To overlook this emotional cosmopolitanism, to see his development in terms of a dominant nationalism which took precedence over his humanist ideal and personal aspiration to the full life would be to distort his outlook and make his subsequent experience incomprehensible.[19]

His yearning to believe in an approaching millennium, then, interacted with the evidence and hope which Europe seemed to offer. Without building up too detailed a picture of the structure and operation of socialist society, he was able to associate the tone, the extremism of western schemes with his own far more psychological approach to the changes required. Annenkov has left a slightly jaundiced but useful first-hand account of the socialism of Herzen and his friends during the forties. It consisted in 'more or less fortuitously combined and coordinated collections of starling, stupefying and imperious aphorisms'. Citing several examples, including those of Proudhon and Weitling, he concluded that 'The strength of these thunder-bearing postulations lay not in their logical inevitability but in the fact that they heralded some new order of things and seemed to throw beams of light into the dark vista of the future, making discovery there of unknown and felicitous domains of work and pleasure about which each person judged according to the impressions he received in the brief instant of one or another such flash of light'.[29] The irony is

excessive, at any rate where Herzen's knowledge of the works of socialist thinkers is concerned. But even he did not gain a concrete and consistent picture of socialist society but rather an insubstantial vision and a strong sense of movement into which he could project his own preoccupations.

In the forties Herzen equated his role with that of socialist writers in the west. Like them he would analyse the basis of the change society must and will undergo. This was the role in 'general affairs' with which he began his European adventure. But the terms in which he approached the central problem of reconciling the free individual with social cohesion reflected the Russian socio-political air he breathed. Ideas were the most visible area of exhilarating change, and it was to ideas rather than to economics or institutions, that he looked for the dynamics of change. He sought a psychological liberty not to be enjoyed in splendid isolation but as the basis for social transformation. It was from this viewpoint that he would analyse western society when he emigrated. And during the forties it was friction over this approach which constituted a central cause of the rift in his circle—the rift which finally precipitated his emigration. Both he and Natalie felt themselves driven to confrontation with their friends by the conviction that they had 'with great labour worked out for themselves an inward liberty', and by frustration that the others should refuse to see the light. Their friends objected because, as Natalie reported N. M. Satin's opinion, they found her 'cold, hard and completely under the influence of Alexander, who was spreading a theory of false self-sufficiency and egoism' (*Past*, 1007).[21]

What Satin called a theory was not in fact something external to Herzen, a mere thing to be juggled with. It informed the very structure of his thought and derived from his most basic assumptions. The point of departure was his profoundly optimistic view of human nature. 'The egoism of the developed, thinking man,' he believed, 'is noble' (II, 97). His contemporaries were struck by this straightforward faith.

> As if to restore some equilibrium in his moral make-up, Nature had taken measures to implant in his soul one indomitable belief, one invincible proclivity: Herzen believed in the noble *instincts* of the human heart; his analysis would fade away and stand in awe before the instinctive promptings of the moral organism, as before the single, indubitable truth of existence.[22]

In fact, one source of the tension in his later work was that he was led to question precisely this. But when he left Russia, this faith was crucial to his approach. His early romantic and idealist reading and his relationships with Ogarev and Natalie, the warmth of friendship that characterised his close-knit, isolated circle, and his intuitive faith in the simple nobleness of the peasants, which was derived in part from pity, may be cited as contributing to this confidence. A lofty evaluation of his own nature and instincts—and, despite the proportions of his self-esteem, he does appear to have been a warm, generous and self-controlled man—was probably central. He was himself the prototype of what men could and, unfettered, would be. Boldly and clearly he declared his faith in the potential harmonious, free and uncoerced cohesion of men:

> To be humane in a human society is certainly not a burdensome obligation, but the simple development of an internal need; no one would say that a bee has a bounden duty to make honey; it makes it because it is a bee . . . To do nothing anti-human is natural to every human nature, for this not even much intelligence is necessary; I don't give anyone the right to demand from me heroism, lyrical poetry etc., but everyone has the right to demand that I do not insult him and that I don't insult him by insulting others.
>
> (II, 94)

Does this faith in man, asked Herzen rhetorically, imply that 'all passions, debauchery, gluttony are fully justified?' Not at all. Only 'a degraded man has degraded desires . . . The more developed a man, the purer his breast becomes and the harder it becomes for him to believe that white is black, that everything natural is a crime, that everything giving real pleasure must be shunned.' Passions regarded as base are not base in themselves—'in themselves they are good, but debased by repression' (II, 395).

It was this repression, perpetuated by laziness and habit, which Herzen blamed for the fact that man had never achieved the desirable state he believed to be natural. And the source of this repression he saw not in economic 'alienation' or political oppression, but in the internal, psychological state of man. Man repressed his own yearnings because he imbibed ideas which made him distrust his passion, his instincts, his conscience, his reason, ideas, in short, which humiliated him. Religion had been a prime source of this humiliation, preaching dualism, the divorce of body and soul, the struggle between instincts and conscience, man's duty to crush his evil urges. In the Middle Ages,

> man was ashamed of his thoughts and feelings, and afraid of them . . . of course he abandoned himself to joys and pleasures even then, but he did so with the feeling with which a Moslem drinks wine, yielding to an indulgence which he had renounced. Giving way to his yearnings, he felt humiliated because he could not resist a desire which he could not deem just.
>
> (III, 241)

Ashamed, men accepted the authority of external rules and directives from the church. It is only because they are deceived and humiliated in their own eyes that men's moral perception becomes distorted, and it is only because it is distorted that they accept external guidance, external domination. There is one escape from this vicious circle—developed egoism. Man must trust his unfettered nature, he must believe in his natural goodness, and thereby he will free himself from the 'slanders' which he has accepted and which perpetuate his subservience.

Herzen saw definite political implications in this analysis. If only they could respect their true nature men would at once see they had no need of external constraint, religious or secular, and would reject it. He saw an historical development towards this liberation. When man became conscious, he inevitably developed 'the need to save *something of his own* from the vortex of chance', to attach supreme value to something (II, 154). But 'they always respect something outside themselves—father and mother, superstitions of their family, the morals of their country, science and ideas, before which they are completely effaced . . . It never enters their heads that inside them is something worthy of respect which, without blushing, bears comparison with everything they do respect' (II, 93). In his essay **'Some Observations on the Historical Development of Honour',** he gave an account of the various idols which have been accepted as of superior value and wisdom to that of the individual—family, tribe, custom, tradition, one man's god against his neighbour's. But there had been progress. Before the classical period there was no concept at all of individual dignity. In Greece and Rome men were at least respected as citizens, though not as individuals and not for their inherent nature. Christianity revealed man's dignity to himself, and the collapse of the Roman state opened the way to a higher concept than that of the citizen. The feudal knights, in fact, provided, in a one-sided form, the prototype of the future universal transformation. They developed 'an unlimited self-assurance in the dignity of their personality, and of course the personalities of their neighbours, acknowledged as equal according to the feudal concept' (II, 162). Respecting themselves they acquired dignity and automatically respected their equals, not because they were ordered to do so, but because this was the inherent consequence of their own respect for themselves. Within the 'Gothic brotherhood', the result was a fusion of individual freedom and social cohesion. But the knights were no more than a prototype. 'A great step had been taken since the ancient world—what was honoured, inviolable, holy was understood to be inside one's breast, and not in the city; but for the full development of the human personality, moral independence was lacking' (II, 167). The knight's respect for himself was based on a one-sided, physical concept of his honour, and not simply on his human nature. This made possible on the one hand, the oppression of the vast mass of the population, excluded from a brotherhood which still did not respect man as such. On the other, knights shook from fear before moral injunctions since they still did not have faith in their own instincts and judgement. The feudal world was therefore corrupted. The modern revolution, Herzen believed, started from the premise of the inviolability of the personality, but in fact elevated the republic above the personality, removed its rights for the good of the republic, and thus again placed an idol above the human individual. 'The dignity of a man is measured by his part in the *res publica,* his significance is purely as a citizen in the ancient sense. The revolution demanded selflessness, self-sacrifice to the one and indivisible republic' (II, 174).[23] Once again men accepted their inferiority. The escape from this continual sacrifice and humiliation was for Herzen the key to the social problem. A man who has thrown aside moral and social idols and attained full consciousness of his own inherent dignity will act 'humanely, because for him to act thus is natural, easy, automatic, pleasant, reasonable' (II, 94). Inwardly liberated men would combine in the social context they needed—but it would be a fully free society.

The links between these two processes—the inward liberation of respect for self and the external political, social and economic liberation—were left undefined. His expectation of a creative, purifying 'revolution' was as near as Herzen came, in 1846, to bridging the gap between the two. The practical elaboration was not his role in the forties. His role was to grasp the underlying basis of the impending transformation. And he approached this in psychological terms. He believed man cannot be liberated more in his outward, social life than he is liberated within. In **'New Variations on an Old Theme'** (1846), in which he expressed this outlook, he explicitly stated that he was talking 'not at all about external constraints, but about the timorous, theoretical consciences of people, about constraints of the interior, of the free will, of the warmth within one's own breast, of fear before the consequences, of fear before the truth'. When he asserted that 'authority [is] based on self-contempt, on the annihilation of one's dignity', he was not using 'Aesopian' symbols to incite the few sympathetic readers among the minute Russian educated elite to stage an armed uprising. He was attacking this 'self-contempt' for creating the vacuum into which authority had stepped. 'The responsibility of independence frightens people,' he wrote. 'External authority is far more comfortable' (II, 90-3).

This then was what Satin called Herzen's 'theory of false self-sufficiency and egoism'. And it was in large measure over this that his dispute with his circle developed. Where Herzen was intrigued and excited by the heralded upheaval of socialism in Europe, and

equated it with his own view of liberation, the others were less positive and the spectre of destructive revolution appalled one of his closest friends, the historian Granovsky. Granovsky's studies in history may have encouraged a moderation which stressed the difficulty of constructing conditions of freedom—precisely the kind of doubt and scepticism in man to which Herzen was objecting. Annenkov believed that explicit differences between the two men over western socialism and the significance of the bourgeoisie played the central role in the rift, but other ramifications of Herzen's 'egoism' played a comparable part. Soon after his emigration, he gave his Moscow friends his extremely hostile account of the French bourgeoisie. Granovsky replied that he had no inclination to discuss the real meaning of the bourgeoisie—'I say enough about that in the lecture theatre'—and that what he treasured were his personal relationships. He was offended that in Herzen's letters 'There is a kind of secret reproach . . . an unfriendly *arriére pensée* that threatens every moment to make its way into the open' (*Past*, 1784-5). The condemnation of the bourgeoisie was hardly an '*arriére pensée*', and this may have referred to the fact that Herzen's critique of the bourgeoisie was cast in exactly the same mould as his earlier criticisms of his Moscow friends.

The demands he made of the French, and his analysis of their short-comings in terms of dualism and contempt for human nature, echoed his previous strictures on his friends. It was in fact a metaphysical dispute which Herzen recalls bringing the rift into the open. One of the most pernicious sources of 'self-contempt' was in Herzen's view, as we have seen, a religious concept of man which divided him into a soul and body locked in moral conflict. He recalls Granovsky emotionally denying the implications. 'I shall never accept your dry, cold idea of the unity of soul and body, for with it the immortality of the soul disappears. You may not need it, but I have buried too many [friends] to give up this belief' (IX, 209). It has been argued that Herzen's account, written between 1856 and 1857, was distorted and that he wanted to gloss over the painful memory that Granovsky defended the bourgeoisie.[24] There may be some truth in this, though Granovsky was as disgusted as Herzen by the bourgeois reaction of 1848, and in the summer of 1849 told Herzen, 'If we could meet now, probably, we would no longer differ in ideas.'[25] Natalie, writing in her diary at the time of the dispute, cited their friends' refusal to abandon 'prejudices' such as belief in an after-life as a cause of the estrangement (*Past*, 1007-8).

For Herzen, of course, not only were there no supernatural truths which would—as he saw it—impose limits on the grandeur and moral autonomy of man, but ideally there should be no subservience to any external value which would stultify the full expression of each individual's being. People 'do not understand,' he insisted, 'that if a man, while despising himself, respects anything else, he surely reduces himself to dust before the object, becomes its slave' (II, 93). But whereas in his view this 'egoism' was compatible with, was in fact the necessary corollary of social harmony, freedom and mutual respect and equality, the idea struck many of his friends as self-indulgent and irresponsible. These early Russian intellectuals were not morbidly guilt-stricken;[26] the champagne flowed freely enough during their philosophical feasts, and their concern was with truth and thought rather than external political action. But their sense of historical mission easily turned into an obligation for self-sacrifice, and during Herzen's last years in Russia this became the vogue. They nurtured a profound sense of duty, of being the conscious part of the nation and therefore bound to sacrifice themselves to Russia and the Russian people. In his memoirs Annenkov recalled the pervading atmosphere among Herzen's friends before he emigrated. 'Control of oneself, relinquishment of certain impulses of heart and nature as of some pernicious element, constant practice of the same ritual of duty, responsibilities and lofty ideals—all this resembled a kind of strict monastic initiation.'[27] The portrait may be too colourfully drawn; the manifestations of this sacrifice were largely verbal or negative—the refusal to work for and cooperate with the regime. But there is no reason to doubt the sincerity and intensity of the feeling of constraint evoked in both Herzens. For Natalie the circle may have been partly the scapegoat for her frustrated longing for the romantic euphoria which had surrounded her courtship and early married life.[28] But doubtless she and Alexander discussed the constriction they felt, and Annenkov recalls Natalie on arrival in Paris emotionally condemning 'the eternal glorification of the sacrifices, labours and voluntary deprivations which were constantly borne before her eyes to the altars of various more or less honourable Molochs which went, in her opinion, under the name of ideas'.[29] Herzen had repeatedly expressed in his diary his rebellion against self-sacrifice. Though he felt himself committed to social transformation, he rejected the sacrifice of the present, of himself, to a utopian vision of the future. 'If one looks deeply into life, indeed,' he wrote in June 1842, 'one sees that the highest good is existence itself, whatever the external circumstances may be. When people understand this they will understand that there is nothing stupider than to ignore the present in favour of the future. The present is the real sphere of existence . . . the aim of life—is life' (II, 217). It was his own experience of personal happiness which brought out his greatest cascades of enthusiasm and his most impassioned protest. Just before Christmas, 1844, Natalie bore him a girl. He was sure the baby would live, Natalie was happy, he was ecstatic. 'Such days, periods in a man's life must be cherished; our cursed lack of attention to the present makes us only able to remember what we

have lost . . . Everything beautiful is delicate . . . life in its highest manifestations is weak . . . Such are the blessings of love—one must revel in them, give oneself up to them, live in them, seize and cherish every moment.' For him the ideal was 'To grasp the present, to activate in oneself all the possibilities for bliss—by this I mean both general activity, and the bliss of knowledge, as well as the bliss of friendship, of love, of family feeling' (II, 393-5).

For Herzen, apart from emigration itself, the obvious practical manifestation of this full, 'egotistical' life, was the fortune he inherited from his father shortly before the rift. There is evidence that some members of the circle felt uneasy amidst this new degree of affluence, and that Herzen was annoyed by what he took for envy. Herzen saw the injustice of wealth amidst abject poverty, but he was not plagued by guilt. He would yield to none in his compassion for the impoverished peasantry. But central to his view of his role was the affirmation of the full life, balancing love and poetry with social and political involvement—that life which was itself at once the means and purpose of social transformation. And financial independence made this affirmation possible.[30]

The friction in the circle was in part due to causes which were petty and are now untraceable. Natalie was at odds with almost all the women. And Herzen was later conscious that he might have argued with conceit, intolerance and sarcasm. But his own account of the intense emotion aroused by differences on specific ideas rings true. When Herzen and Ogarev insisted that belief in immortality was an escapist 'fairy-tale', Granovsky, 'turning pale and assuming the air of a disinterested outsider', replied:

> 'You will truly oblige me if you never speak to me on these subjects again; there are plenty of interesting things to talk about with far more profit and pleasure.'

> 'Certainly. With the greatest pleasure,' I said, feeling a chill on my face. Ogarev said nothing; we all looked at one another and that glance was quite enough; we all loved one another too much not to gauge to the full by our expressions what had happened . . . Ogarev and I had expected that we should come to an agreement . . . We were as sad as though someone near and dear had died.

> (*Past*, 586-7)

Herzen's commitment to his convictions was too deep to leave personal friendships unaffected.[31]

During 1846 his relationship with Granovsky, Korsh, Ketscher and the others was strained and for a while even cold. Ogarev was himself restless and Belinsky was away in St Petersburg. At the same time his frustration with censorship and with the improbability of any tangible political progress in Russia intensified throughout the forties. Unsuccessful arguments within a small group of men utterly divorced from power and cramped by a hostile and, for the foreseeable future, unshakeable regime felt increasingly limited. He yearned for the full life the west seemed to promise. His friends' strictures on his 'egoism' only made more urgent his desire to use his inheritance 'to go away, far away, for a long time' (**Past**, 589).

Notes

[1] This form will be used throughout for reference to A. I. Gertsen, *Sobranie sochinenii* (30 vols., Moscow, 1954-65).

[2] It was in his mid-twenties that Herzen made his first attempt at an autobiography.

[3] On the eighteenth-century background, see M. Raeff, *Origins of the Russian Intelligentsia* (New York, 1966).

[4] This form will be used throughout for reference to *My Past and Thoughts. The Memoirs of Alexander Herzen,* translated by Constance Garnett, revised by Humphrey Higgens (4 vols., New York, 1968). I have used this translation for the 4 volumes of Herzen's works covered except when I have preferred my own translation, where reference is made to A. I. Gertsen, *Sobranie sochinenii* (30 vols., Moscow, 1954-65).

[5] On Herzen's ordeal in the 1830s, see F. F. Seeley, 'Herzen's "Dantean" Period', *Slavonic and East European Review,* XXXIII (1954), 44-74.

[6] The view that his home life was a crucial factor provoking Herzen's rebellion against authority has been argued in detail by M. Malia, *Alexander Herzen and the Birth of Russian Socialism, 1812-1855* (Cambridge, Mass., 1961), pp. 13-24.

[7] See I. Berlin, 'A Marvellous Decade, 1838-1848', *Encounter* (June 1955), 34-5, and P. Shashko, 'Unity and Dissent among the Russian Westerners' (Ph.D. Dissertation, University of Michigan, 1969), Chapters I-VI, on the atmosphere of the circles. M. Perkal', *Gertsen v Peterburge* (Leningrad, 1971), brings out Herzen's personal acquaintance with major establishment figures in Russian society, which doubtless increased this sense of importance.

[8] Malia, *Alexander Herzen,* and R. Labry, *Alexandre Ivanovic Herzen* (Paris, 1928), give detailed treatment of Herzen's early intellectual mentors. Labry provides a table of the works read by Herzen between 1842 and 1845, pp. 307-11. On Schiller's influence, see also M. Malia, 'Schiller and the Early Russian Left', in H.

McLean, M. Melia, G. Fischer eds., *Russian Thought and Politics* (The Hague, 1957), pp. 169-200.

[9] On Proudhon's influence, see R. Labry, *Herzen et Proudhon* (Paris, 1928), and M. Mervaud, 'Herzen et Proudhon', *Cahiers du Monde Russe et Soviétique,* XII (1971), nos. 1-2, 110-88, which includes their correspondence.

[10] On Hegel's influence, see M. Mervaud, 'Herzen et la Pensée Allemande', *Cahiers du Monde Russe et Soviétique,* V (1964), 32-73.

[11] Recently there has been a reaction against the view, epitomised by Malia, that Herzen's generation of intellectuals were 'alienated' from Russian society, and that this is the basic explanation for their political ideals. V. C. Nahirny, 'The Russian Intelligentsia: from Men of Ideas to Men of Convictions', *Comparative Studies in Society and History,* IV (1962), no. 4, 403-35; J. L. Scherer, 'The Myth of the "Alienated" Russian Intellectuals' (Ph.D. Dissertation, Indiana University, 1968). While Herzen later certainly exaggerated his reaction to his environment before 1842, he did withdraw, emigrate, engage in revolutionary activity and become estranged from most of his Russian friends. However inherently attractive the intellectual currents from the west, the source and nature of his receptivity to them lay in a growing reaction against his Russian environment.

[12] See E. Lampert, *Studies in Rebellion* (London, 1957), on Herzen's philosophical development. Lampert concludes that his philosophical views were fully formed by the time he left Russia, p. 198.

[13] See, for example, A. I. Volodin, *V poiskakh revoliutsionnoi teorii (A. I. Gertsen)* (Moscow, 1962), Chapter 2.

[14] Herzen did not settle in his own mind the dispute between materialism and idealism. See Lampert, *Studies in Rebellion,* pp. 198-205; Volodin, *V poiskakh revoliutsionnoi teorii,* pp. 31-43.

[15] See G. Lichtheim, *Marxism* (London, 1971), on the consciousness of this problem in mid-nineteenth-century Europe, pp. 25-6.

[16] Herzen expressed these criticism even during 1844, the year in which he took the commune most seriously while still in Russia (II, 334).

[17] Analysing Herzen's political thought before he left Russia is of course complicated by the restrictions of censorship, though such works as his novel *Who is to Blame?* (1844) expressed clearly enough his hostility to the existing social and political structure, his sympathy for the peasantry, and his frustration at the

helplessness of men of his own stamp. But in fact even in the privacy of his diary his properly political and economic analyses did not go beyond the kind of brief formula quoted above.

[18] 'Our Slavophiles talk about the communal basis, about how we have no proletariat, about the sharing of the land—these are all good germs . . . but they forget, on the other side, the absence of any respect for self, the stupid endurance of every oppression, in a word, the [im]possibility of living in such conditions' (II, 288).

[19] The point entails a basic corrective to the widespread interpretation which portrays Herzen in terms of a life-long messianic and revolutionary nationalism. A. Koyré, *Etudes sur l'historie de la pensée philosophique en Russie* (Paris, 1950); Malia, *Alexander Herzen.*

[20] P. V. Annenkov, *The Extraordinary Decade,* translated by I. R. Titunik (Michigan, 1968), p. 141.

[21] In her memoirs T. A. Astrakova, another member of the circle, recalled finding Herzen spoilt and wanting adulation. *Literaturnoe nasledstvo,* 63 (1956), 547-54.

[22] Annenkov, *The Extraordinary Decade,* p. 87. It was the whole moral organism, reason and conscience as well as passion and instinct, in which Herzen placed such faith.

[23] Malia cites this paragraph to demonstrate Herzen's approval of involvement in the *res publica* being the measure of a man's worth (*Alexander Herzen,* p. 317). Herzen's *disapproval* of such a standard, of the implied superiority of the *res publica* over the individual, of any external and not intrinsic value-measurement of man, is central to his argument in the essay, and important in understanding his rejection of the commune in this period precisely because it committed a similar crime against the individual.

[24] See Ia. Z. Cherniak's essay in *Literaturnoe nasledstvo,* 62 (1955), 86-92.

[25] *Ibid.* 94.

[26] See Berlin, *Encounter* (June 1955) 27-39.

[27] Annenkov, *The Extraordinary Decade,* p. 188. The picture Herzen left of what perhaps had been the atmosphere in his circle in the earlier forties, has been too readily accepted for the whole decade. 'Feasting,' he said, 'goes with fullness of life; ascetic people are usually dry and egoistical . . . We were not like the emaciated monks of Zurbaran; we did not weep over the sins of the world—we only sympathised with its

suffering, and were ready with a smile for anything, and not depressed by a foretaste of our sacrifices to come' (*Past,* 491). The reaction of both Herzen and Natalie against a vogue of self-sacrifice later in the forties was an important factor in their attitude to their escape abroad.

[28] See E. H. Carr, *The Romantic Exiles* (London, 1968), pp. 22-4.

[29] Annenkov, *The Extraordinary Decade,* p. 190.

[30] Later Herzen also justified his inheritance as the means for more concrete political action: 'Money is independence, power, a weapon; and no-one flings away a weapon in time of war, though it may have come from the enemy and even be rusty' (*Past,* 757). Apart from financing the Free Russian Press during the fifties and sixties, he subsidised many political refugees.

[31] See Nahirny, 'The Russian Intelligentsia', for a very different interpretation. Nahirny draws a sharp line between Belinsky, as the prototype of those Russians totally and intensely committed to ideas, on the one hand, and Granovsky, Herzen and the others as too cultured and independent to be absorbed by an 'ism' or to allow differences of opinion to affect friendship. Whatever the merits of the argument generally, it is misleading in regard to Herzen. His commitment was to a vision rather than to an 'ism', but it was none the less the guiding principle of his life. And though he was a more gregarious, less thorny character than Belinsky, his description of his break with Granovsky precisely over differences of opinion could not be more poignant.

Michael R. Katz (essay date 1984)

SOURCE: Introduction to *Who Is to Blame?: A Novel in Two Parts,* by Alexander Herzen, translated by Michael R. Katz, Cornell University Press, 1984, pp. 15-39.

[*In the following essay, Katz places his synopsis of the novel* Who Is to Blame? *between a discussion of its literary precedents and a review of the critical evaluations it has received since its publication.*]

Intellectual Ferment

During the decade that followed the abortive Decembrist Rebellion of 1825, Russia was a bleak and hostile place. Tsar Nicholas's official policy of repressive measures had resulted in complete political stagnation and produced, particularly among the educated gentry, a feeling of intense isolation and an atmosphere of mutual suspicion. Only a few serious journals were allowed to be published and circulated among a coterie of devoted readers. With most channels for expression virtually closed, the intellectual community was forced inward upon itself. Comradeship and companionship, sought in private encounters and intimate circles, created an environment conducive to intellectual ferment and political debate.

In the fall of 1836 the enforced official silence was abruptly shattered. In the September issue of the *Telescope,* there appeared a document entitled *First Philosophical Letter,* by Petr Chaadaev (ca. 1793-1856). Signed and dated "Necropolis, December 1, 1829," this letter contained a sweeping and passionate rejection of Russia. Chaadaev argued that his country's past was empty, its present intolerable, and that there was no hope whatever for its future. He attributed this national tragedy to Russia's geographical and historical position between East and West—thus, to its isolation from the cultural heritage of either world. As a result Russia had developed not one "single spiritual idea" that might have served as the basis for an independent national character. It was a country "untouched by the universal education of mankind"; its national tradition was "devoid of any powerful teaching"; its inhabitants were "like children who had never been made to think for themselves."[1]

Alexander Herzen (1812-70), who was to emerge as one of the most outstanding and outspoken members of the Russian intelligentsia, describes in his memoirs the public commotion occasioned by the virulence of Chaadaev's unexpected attack: "The *Letter* was in a sense the last word, the limit. It was a shot that rang out in the dark night; whether it was something foundering that proclaimed its own wreck, whether it was a signal, a cry for help, whether it was news of the dawn or news that there would not be one—it was all the same: one had to wake up."[2]

Chaadaev's accusations outraged and embarrassed the already suspicious and anxious autocracy. The author of the letter was proclaimed insane and placed under police surveillance and medical supervision. The publication of the *Telescope* was discontinued and its editor exiled to a remote village in northern Russia. Chaadaev was forbidden to publish any further philosophical letters or, for that matter, anything else.

Chaadaev's *First Letter,* which Herzen later described as "a merciless cry of pain and reproach against Petrine Russia," brought into clearer focus the intellectual unrest among the educated gentry. Herzen's memoirs, *My Past and Thoughts* (1854-66), in addition to providing a poignant portrait of the author's own intellectual development, present a detailed picture of Russian intellectual life during this period. Herzen describes in considerable detail the emergence of the circles

(*kruzhki*), their ideologies and leading personalities during the 1830s, and he sheds considerable light on his own evolution as a serious thinker, a persuasive writer, and an ardent advocate of change.

These circles, which predated the Decembrist Rebellion as centers of liberal opposition to the autocratic regime, consisted of diverse groups of intellectuals united by a profound feeling of alienation from official Russia and by an overwhelming desire to alter the status quo. At the center of each group there usually stood some strong, charismatic figure. One of the most outstanding was Nikolai Stankevich (1813-40), subsequently characterized by Herzen as "a poet and a dreamer." He was actually a philosopher, a disciple and proponent of German idealism, especially that of Schelling and Hegel, and he served to popularize their ideas among young, enthusiastic Russian intellectuals. Stankevich wrote little, yet managed to breathe life into a set of ideas that inspired a generation of writers, critics, and revolutionaries. He argued that history should be seen as the development of humanity as a whole and that each nation was capable of expressing some single aspect of the life of mankind. He predicted that Russia was also destined to achieve greatness in philosophy, art, and literature.[3] In the wake of Chaadaev's gloom and despondency, Stankevich's optimistic fervor aroused, inspired, and kindled many youthful romantic dreams and ideals.

According to Herzen's testimony, the "most active, impulsive, and dialectically passionate, fighting nature" belonged to yet another major figure—the young critic Vissarion Belinsky (1811-48). Belinsky, who had considerable contact with the members of Stankevich's circle, served as translator and critic of the *Telescope* until that journal was suppressed. His political views and aesthetic criteria changed rapidly, but during the late thirties and early forties his literary criticism was firmly based on two assumptions. First, he demanded that literature should express *ideas*—that is, it should emphasize moral, social, and political values and should advocate positive ideals and progressive tendencies. Second, he argued that literature should be *natural* in its expression—it should aim to be faithful to life, "realistic."

It was on this basis that Russia's leading critic heralded the appearance of a major new talent. In 1846, from the pages of the *Contemporary,* Belinsky hailed **Who Is to Blame?** as a work of great social importance, in spite of what he perceived as its artistic shortcomings. And, in a personal letter dated April 6, 1846, Belinsky warmly welcomed its young author into the ranks of Russian men of letters: "I am completely convinced that you are a major figure in our literature, not a dilettante, not a partisan, not an amateur equestrian who has nothing better to do."[4] Clearly

Belinsky viewed Herzen's novel as the embodiment of his own critical principles. *Who Is to Blame?* was first and foremost a novel of ideas, and, as a work of literature, it was completely natural in its expression.

Biographical Sketch

Alexander Herzen was born on April 6, 1812, the illegitimate son of Ivan Yakovlev, a wealthy nobleman from an ancient Russian family, and Luiza Haag, the daughter of a minor German official.[5] Herzen's mother remained a Lutheran all her life, never marrying his father according to the rites of the Orthodox church and hence never accorded the legal or social status of a wife. The child was given the invented surname Herzen [from *Herz,* "heart"] as if to stress the fact that he was the product of an unusual liaison, an affair of the heart.

His upbringing took place in a large and gloomy house on the Arbat in the center of Moscow. The boy's father loved him after a fashion, but the father's presence was always somewhat frightening and oppressive. The lad sought refuge in his mother's rooms and in the servants' quarters: Luiza was a model of uncomplaining acceptance and stoic resignation, while the servants were appropriately obsequious in the performance of their duties. Herzen's concern for the freedom and dignity of the individual may well have had its origins in the inequitable conditions that surrounded him during his childhood.

He received the normal education for a wealthy young Russian nobleman of his day. Since he was a lively and imaginative child, much care was taken to develop his intellectual gifts. Attention was lavished on him by nurses, serfs, and private tutors. He was taught Russian literature and history by a young university student who was an enthusiastic follower of the Romantic movement, especially in its German manifestation. He learned French, German, and some European history from a tutor who had escaped the aftermath of the French Revolution and who held deep convictions regarding the liberty and equality of men. The young pupil read voraciously in his father's sizable library, taking a special interest in French books of the Enlightenment.

When Herzen was only fourteen, the leaders of the Decembrist Rebellion were hanged by Nicholas I as the initial act of the reactionary policy that was to follow. Herzen was subsequently to recall the solemn "Hannibalic" oath to avenge these martyrs that he and his young friend Nikolai Ogarev (1813-77) swore as they stood on the Sparrow Hills overlooking Moscow. The memory of these aristocratic conspirators became a source of inspiration for Herzen's later revolutionary activity.

In 1829 he enrolled as a student at Moscow University, where he encountered the works of Schiller and Goethe, and later those of the French utopian socialists, including Saint-Simon and Fourier. It was during his university days that Herzen became a confirmed and passionate radical. He and Ogarev organized a circle parallel to that of Stankevich but more oriented toward French thought (politics and progress) than German metaphysics. Forbidden books were read; "dangerous ideas" were discussed. Herzen was duly arrested and condemned to imprisonment. Perhaps as a result of his father's intervention, his sentence was commuted to internal exile. In 1834 Herzen left for the town of Vyatka at the eastern edge of European Russia, where he went to work for the local administration. There, somewhat unexpectedly, he enjoyed his tasks and succeeded in exposing the corruption of the local governor. He read Dante and went through a short-lived religious phase. He also became involved with two women: he had an affair with one, a married woman, P. P. Medvedeva, after which he suffered agonies of contrition, and he began a long and passionate correspondence with the other, his first cousin Natalya Aleksandrovna Zakharina (1817-52), who, like himself, was also illegitimate, and had lived as a companion in the house of a rich, despotic relative.

In 1838 Herzen was transferred to Vladimir, not far from Moscow. There, with his friends' help, but against the wishes of both their families, he arranged to elope with Natalya Aleksandrovna. In 1840 he was allowed to return to Moscow with his wife, and soon after he was appointed to a government post in Petersburg. He remained deeply committed to the cause of radical reform and was sent into exile again, this time to Novgorod, for writing an indiscreet letter that criticized the police. By 1842, the year in which he returned from exile to Moscow, Herzen was regarded as an established member of the new radical intelligentsia and as an early martyr to its cause. He began to study German metaphysics, as well as French sociological theory and history; he published historical and philosophical essays in various progressive journals; and he composed a number of short stories on social and political themes that were widely read and discussed.

In 1847 Herzen's father died and left a substantial fortune to his widow and his son. Herzen decided to leave for Europe. Accompanied by his wife, his mother, two friends, and some servants, Herzen departed from his homeland, traveled across Germany, and finally arrived in Paris, the center of the civilized world. There he plunged into the life of exiled radicals and socialists. By the time of the revolutions of 1848, Herzen stood on the extreme left wing of revolutionary European socialism. Although ordered to return to Russia, he flatly refused. His fortune was confiscated, but with expert legal assistance he was able to recover most of it, thus ensuring his financial independence.

Whether or not he intended that outcome, Herzen's departure from Russia was to be permanent.

Early Literary Endeavors

Herzen's earliest forays into literature were made during the summer of 1833.[6] In a conscious attempt to imitate the German Romantics (especially Schiller, Jean Paul, and Hoffmann), he wrote **"A Tale about Myself"** in an autobiographical mode, combining a romantic style with elevated literary language. Another surviving fragment that dates from 1836, **"A Legend,"** consists of a lyrical-philosophical meditation incorporating some of Saint-Simon's ideas on "New Christianity"—that is, "practical" Christian humanism—in a somewhat obscure allegorical form. Nevertheless, this early piece reveals something of what the genuine writer would become both in its directness of expression and in its depth of feeling.

Following his stay in Vyatka (which included both his affair with Medvedeva and his romance with Natalya), Herzen began work on yet another autobiographical tale, entitled **"There"** (later renamed **"Elena"**). This piece is a remarkable literary hybrid: while the beginning is controlled, realistic, ironic, even Gogolian, the conclusion is melodramatic, sentimental, and exalted.

In 1840 Herzen tried his hand at autobiography again, this time employing a more documentary approach. He wrote **Notes of a Young Man,** an autobiography in prose, based on his own letters to Natalya Aleksandrovna. The structure of this work is clearly episodic, the style often witty, the tone detached. In the continuation, **Further Notes of a Young Man** (1841), Herzen's satire took an even sharper turn.

His works of the early 1840s bear witness to the author's gradual evolution away from Russian romanticism and toward the so-called natural school. In all of his writings dating from the middle of this decade, Herzen adopted a new, more realistic world view, searching for objective forms of expression for his own experience and that of his contemporaries. He put aside his lyrical, autobiographical hero and instead created a new prose genre that embraced social commentary, psychological analysis, philosophical inquiry, and publicistic oratory, all unified by the author's intelligent consciousness. It is in these years immediately preceding his departure from Russia that Herzen produced his most important contribution to Russian fiction, the novel **Who Is to Blame?** (published 1845-46) and two tales, **"Dr. Krupov"** (1847) and **"The Thieving Magpie"** (1848).

In **"The Thieving Magpie,"** Herzen treats the same theme twice, first discursively, then allegorically. The tale consists of a dialogue between a Slavophile and a Westernizer on the subject of why Russia fails to produce women who are outstanding in the arts; this intellectual debate is then followed by a pathetic tale of the brilliant serf-actress Aneta. In **"Dr. Krupov,"** Herzen combines both autobiography and the case study method to develop the theme of a sick society by juxtaposing a variety of human types and revealing his own differing attitudes toward them.

When Belinsky responded to the publication of **Who Is to Blame?** with the announcement that a new, "major figure" had appeared in Russian literature, he had no inkling that Herzen's first novel would also be his last. Ths author was to find his mature voice in essays, articles, letters, and in his monumental memoirs, which have aptly been called "a literary masterpiece worthy to be placed by the side of the novels of his contemporaries and countrymen, Tolstoy, Turgenev, Dostoevsky."[7]

Who Is to Blame?

In addition to the sweeping indictment of Russia, Chaadaev's *First Letter* also succeeded in conveying the predicament of the individual Russian intellectual who is at a loss to find any useful employment for his talents: "It is a trait of human nature that a man gets lost when he can find no means to bind himself to what has come before him and what will follow after him. Then all consistency, all certainty escapes him. Lacking the guiding sense of continuous duration, he finds himself lost in the world."[8] Although Chaadaev acknowledged that there were "lost souls" in every country, he sadly asserted that in Russia the condition had become "a general characteristic." It was just such a "lost soul" that Herzen attempted to depict in **Who Is to Blame?**

In a letter to Natalya Aleksandrovna dated April 1, 1836, the author recorded an idea for a new hero: "a man endowed with a noble soul" but who possesses a "weak character."[9] Several years later, after having begun serious work on the tale, Herzen noted in his diary, "I am pleased with my article on dilettantism—very pleased. But not with my tale. The [genre of the] tale is not my métier; I know this [for a fact] and should renounce tales [in general]."[10] In spite of this and similar disclaimers, chapters 1 through 4 of part I of a new "tale," appeared in A. A. Kraevsky's journal *Notes of the Fatherland* in 1845, under the signature "I." (i.e., Iskander [Alexander]). Herzen's original working title, "The Adventures of a Teacher," had been replaced by the question **Who Is to Blame?** The epigraph chosen to introduce the novel had mysteriously been omitted.

The author was extremely eager to gauge the reactions of his readers and critics. It was their enthusiasm, in particular Belinsky's favorable response, that encouraged him to continue working on the novel. In April

1846, chapters 5 through 7 of part I were published in the same journal under the title **"Vladimir Beltov."** The appearance of this second installment brought Herzen considerable recognition and earned Belinsky's generous pronouncement. The critic urged the young author to write more. Herzen briefly interrupted work on the novel to complete the two stories mentioned above; then he resumed work on *Who Is to Blame?* and finished part II in the autumn of 1846.

After lengthy negotiations, Belinsky managed to persuade Herzen to break with Kraevsky and to publish parts I and II of the novel together as a supplement to Belinsky's own journal the *Contemporary*. Thus in 1847 the complete text of *Who Is to Blame?* appeared; it included a dedication to Natalya Aleksandrovna, and the epigraph was restored to its rightful place.

Herzen's depiction of the hero, Vladimir Beltov, as a "lost soul" was influenced by previous efforts of Russian writers to explore those "traits of human nature" that in Chaadaev's words, had become a "general characteristic" in Russian culture.[11] Chatsky, the hero of Aleksandr Griboedov's comedy *Woe from Wit* (1822-24), who bids an angry farewell to his former beloved Sofya and to the world that produced her, stands as the progenitor of a long line of heroes from which Beltov was descended.

Herzen paid tribute to another of the sources of his own inspiration in one of a series of articles entitled **"On the Development of Revolutionary Ideas in Russia"** (1850): "The image of [Pushkin's] Onegin is such a national one that it is encountered in every novel and poem that receives recognition in Russia, not because [everyone] wants to imitate it, but because we constantly find it alongside us or inside us."[12] In addition, Pushkin's novel in verse, *Eugene Onegin* (1823-31), raised the fundamental issue of culpability: is it the individual or his environment that is to be held responsible for the hero's tragedy?

Herzen's debt to Gogol is evident in the colorful "biographies" that he provides throughout *Who Is to Blame?* (particularly in part I), which are influenced by the satirical portraits of landowners and bureaucrats in Gogol's comedy *The Government Inspector* (1836) and his novel *Dead Souls* (1842). Lermontov's novel, *Hero of Our Time* (1840), presented Herzen with a model of an integrated cycle of tales depicting a central character who lives out his life under the rule of very powerful passions. Finally, in an article on the works of Turgenev written subsequently and entitled **"Bazarov, Once Again"** (1868), Herzen locates his own protagonist in a distinguished genealogy of Russian heroes:

> The Onegins and the Pechorins begot the Rudins and the Beltovs; the Rudins and the Beltovs—

Bazarov. The Onegins and Pechorins are past; the Rudins and Beltovs are passing; the Bazarovs will pass—even very soon.[13]

Part I of *Who Is to Blame?* contains a series of "biographies" of primary and secondary characters. Just before "digressing" on the life-history of a minor figure, the elder Beltov's eccentric uncle, the author defends his unusual artistic method:

> There is nothing on earth more individual and more diversified than the biographies of ordinary people, especially where no two people ever share the same idea, where each person develops in his own way without either looking back or worrying about where it will lead. . . . For this reason I never avoid biographical digressions. They reveal the full splendor of the universe. The reader who so wishes may skip over these episodes, but in so doing he will miss the essence of the story.

Indeed, it is through these "biographical digressions" that the author conveys the essence of his story. More than any of its predecessors in nineteenth-century Russian fiction, *Who Is to Blame?* is a novel of ideas and issues that are given artistic form through the medium of vivid and elaborate characterizations. An examination of the most important portraits that Herzen draws in the novel will therefore illustrate his principal themes and reveal his underlying intentions.

The novel begins with a portrait of a patriarchal landowner, Aleksei Abramovich Negrov, and his corpulent wife Glafira Lvovna. A retired major general, Negrov lives in the country, where he follows one golden rule: he never allows mental exertion to upset his digestion. Negrov is Herzen's principal representative of the rural aristocracy, dragging out its "overstuffed life" in an empty, boring, and useless manner. He is a vulgar and tyrannical patriarch both in his family circle and on his estate; however, Negrov is never condemned as an evil man. Herzen goes to great lengths to remind his readers that "life had destroyed more than one potentiality in him"; that he possessed "genuine abilities, first suppressed, then destroyed by life"; that since he had never become "accustomed to any activity," he could not possibly "imagine what to do." In fact, Negrov suffers from a strain of the very same nineteenth-century disease that afflicts Beltov, the hero of this novel—namely, "spleen" (*khandra*). Since there was no occupation for which Negrov was suited or even inclined, he did nothing at all. He lived out an endless succession of days with no activity, no purpose, no aspiration. Moreover, Herzen insists that Negrov was a "typical" representative of his class: his neighbors are described as "Negrov with a different last name"; a portrait of the household of Karp Kondratich, another local aristocrat, is included as an example of a family that, in all respects is much worse than the Negrovs.

Herzen's satiric gift is seen at its best in his detailed descriptions of the Negrov's entourage and their way of life. The master's inhuman treatment of his serfs (including, of course, his debauched affair with the lovely Avdotya Barbash); his self-assurance and vulgar "wit"; his obsession with food, drink, and carriages; his enjoyment of the pitiful "sponger" Eliza Avgustovna's scandalous accounts of aristocratic life— all serve to emphasize Negrov's complete lack of spiritual and intellectual depth.

His corpulent and soporific spouse, Glafira Lvovna, is an ideal mate for the general. She is the offspring of a debauched nobleman and a merchant's daughter. She was reared by an egotistical old maiden aunt, and her cheerless childhood and monotonous youth resulted in no development whatever of her character. She married Negrov to escape from her oppression, "adopted" his illegitimate daughter Lyubonka in a surge of romantic ecstasy, and then treated the child cruelly and callously, with no understanding whatever of her sensitive soul. In a splendid scene that culminates in pure bathos, Glafira falls in love with her son's innocent young tutor Dmitry and assumes the role of "conqueror and seducer," while the tutor plays the part of unsuspecting, chaste maiden. But just as Herzen points to Negrov's suppressed potential and destroyed abilities, so too he "explains" Glafira Lvovna's existence by the detailed account of her upbringing and steadfastly refuses to pass final judgment on her decision to adopt and rear Negrov's daughter.

While the Negrov family enables the author to present his views on the rural aristocracy, Lyubov Aleksandrovna (Lyubonka) is Herzen's contribution to the so-called woman question. The illegitimate child of a landowner father (Negrov) and a serf mother, she suffers the torments of her awkward predicament. She retreats into silence and broods over the incongruity of her ambiguous position in the Negrov household. The oppressiveness of her surroundings, the harsh treatment that she receives, her virtual isolation from meaningful human contact—all result in an extraordinary and seemingly inexplicable development of her soul and her spirit. Significantly, it is not the heroine's reading that provokes or promotes her growth; she does read, but with no great passion; she finds *even* Sir Walter Scott's romanticism boring at times! Instead, Lyubonka takes refuge in her thoughts and dreams: "she dreamed in order to relieve her spirit and thought in order to understand her dreams." Through her diary entries, recorded in both parts I and II, Herzen permits his readers to observe the intimate development of Lyubonka's character. In part I we come to appreciate her total alienation from the

Negrovs, her insightful critique of their way of life, her genuine love of nature, and her empathy with the oppressed peasants. And Herzen gives a poignant account of her growing affection for the young tutor Dmitry, their mutual confessions of love, and their subsequent departure from the Negrovs' household in order to establish their own family based on mutual respect and deep devotion. In part II Herzen describes Lyubonka's married life and continues the account of her intellectual and spiritual development. With the introduction of Beltov into their happy family circle, the heroine moves beyond her kind, sweet, but limited spouse. The author reveals her strength and vigor, her wideranging intellect, her simple, natural manner, her profound understanding of the hero's plight, and her deep sympathy for him. Once again through the medium of her diary, Herzen documents Lyubonka's personal growth: the new questions that she raises and the problems that she faces, her involvement with abstract ideas and the world outside her family, her reflections on the themes of freedom and fate, and ultimately the startling recognition that she loves two men, both her husband and Beltov, but in different ways.

Lyubonka is a powerful portrait of the "new woman"— descended in part from Pushkin's Tatyana and the heroines of George Sand[14] and in part from the author's own experience and that of his beloved wife Natalya Aleksandrovna. Lyubonka is presented as an intelligent, compassionate, independent person who discovers the contradictions inherent in her position in mid-nineteenth-century Russian society. The institutions of marriage and family are called into question, the themes of upbringing and education are examined and criticized; the "trade-off" between happiness and development is presented and explored. Lyubonka emerges as a noble character, morally superior even to the hero; she aspires to knowledge and activity; she sympathizes with the victims of the system from the oppressed peasants to the repressed hero; and she is ultimately destroyed by the results of her own development. At the end of the novel Lyubonka has lost both of her loves and is sinking rapidly into a state of physical and spiritual decline. The "new woman" has emerged, but she is as yet incapable of overcoming the enormous obstacles in her path.

The young tutor with whom Lyubonka first falls in love, Dmitry Krutsifersky, is Herzen's primary representative of the new breed of intellectual called *raznochintsy,* "men of various origins and classes," those who did not belong to the nobility or to the gentry.[15] This group was to come of age during the decade of the 1860s and would engage the literary talents of Turgenev, Chernyshevsky, and Dostoevsky, among others. But in the person of Krutsifersky Herzen provides Russian literature with an early and compassionate portrait of a "commoner," emphasizing his humble origins, his modest aspirations, and his limited spiritual horizons.

The young man is introduced into the novel as a gentle, bashful soul, eager to learn, hopelessly romantic, and naively idealistic—lacking any experience whatever in the real world. The son of a district physician and a German pharmacist's daughter, his early life consisted of a humiliating struggle against poverty. He was born prematurely, grew into a weak and nervous lad, and was rescued from a conventional future only by the intervention of "fate" in the form of a philanthropic privy counsellor from Moscow who "adopted" him as a ward. Thus was Dmitry able to leave the local gymnasium and receive a decent education at Moscow University, where his love of knowledge and persistent application, rather that any unusual ability, resulted in the awarding of his degree. Fate intervened in his life once again, this time in the form of Dr. Krupov, and Dmitry gratefully accepted a tutoring post in the Negrovs' household secured for him by the doctor. There he promptly fell in love with Lyubonka, united with her at once by the common bond of their aversion to the general's tyranny; by the end of part I, Dmitry offers to marry Lyubonka and to accept a position in the civil service.

At the beginning of part II, Dmitry is shown at the peak of happiness. He and his wife have created a family founded on mutual love and are pursuing a modest life-style based on common sense. Krutsifersky's pure, gentle, loving soul is at peace with the world. As an unforseen consequence of his happy marriage and satisfying career, however, his intellect stagnates; he resides happily in a world of romantic dreams and melancholic ecstasy.

When Beltov enters the Krutsiferskys' household and gradually wins Lyubonka's heart and mind, Dmitry is almost totally destroyed. Characteristically, he admits to having come "almost to love Beltov himself"; his tragic recognition and poignant reaction to the bitter truth are portrayed pathetically, as are his rapid decline into vulgar drunkenness and his desperate attempts at prayer. His simple nature cannot accommodate such extraordinary events; he is ultimately overcome by grief.

The person who first introduces Beltov into the Krutsiferskys' household and who presides over the tragic denouement is the curious figure of Dr. Krupov. He stands outside the class structure of the novel and intervenes in the action to utter prophesies, make predictions, move the plot along, and then cope with the consequences. He appears initially as a cheerful, healthy man of epicurean composure and good nature. As he comments on the action and the characters' motivations, he represents the voice of reason, common sense, and medical science. But we soon learn that as a result of his own bitter experience—primarily his long years

as a physician—he has become thoroughly disillusioned with life and love and has retreated into cynicism, unabashed egoism, and complacent materialism.

At the beginning of part II, Dr. Krupov has been incorporated into the Krutsiferskys' happy family circle. He who had warned Dmitry against marrying the "young tigress" Lyubonka now acknowledges his error, modifies his cynical views, and becomes an integral part of their household. All the more ironic, then, that it is Krupov who introduces them to Beltov. By the end of part II, it falls to him to summarize the unhappy consequences of their new friendship with Beltov. Krupov admits that, like Dmitry, he too has come to "love Beltov," even though Beltov has destroyed the Krutsifersky family and made four people miserably unhappy. Reluctantly he banishes the hero, while he himself retreats into gloomy cynicism.

The protagonist, Vladimir Beltov, is Herzen's brilliant portrait of the "lost soul" about whom Chaadaev had written in his *First Letter*. There Chaadaev had defined the essence of that character: "the flightiness of a life totally lacking in experience and foresight . . . which results simply from the ephemeral existence of an individual detached from the species. Such a life holds dear neither the honor nor the progress of any community of ideas or interests, not even a traditional family outlook or that mass of prescriptions and perspectives which compose . . . both public and private life."[16] A wealthy landowner and intellectual of noble birth, Beltov is introduced into the novel late and indirectly—through rumors, gossip, and paradoxes. Even his appearance presents contrasts that tend to heighten the mystery: he is good-natured, but supercilious; a gentleman, but a rake; melancholy, but passionate. Beltov is a figure who arouses both intellectual curiosity and emotional anxiety.

Herzen describes and analyzes the hero's origins, upbringing, and education at great length, obviously in order to explain the formation of his character and world view. His father was a dissolute nobleman, a gambler, and a drunkard, an inveterate womanizer who shamelessly flirted with one of his aunt's serfs (Sofya). An educated girl, Sofya succeeds in buying her freedom in order to escape to Petersburg, where she suffers from economic hardship and psychological humiliation. Finally she writes a scathing letter to the elder Beltov that causes him to repent his sins and to marry her; during their brief married life together she succeeds in discovering the "nobility of his true nature" under the "dross of his surroundings." Beltov dies shortly after his son's birth, but Sofya never fully recovers from the series of traumas that she has endured. She becomes pensive and withdrawn, concentrating her morbid sensibilities on the upbringing of her son. Thus, from an early age, the young Vladimir is separated from his peers, isolated from reality, and reared by an overprotective, *exaltée* mother whose entire existence revolves around her offspring.

In addition to having such an extraordinary mother, Vladimir was educated by an equally extraordinary Swiss tutor named Monsieur Joseph, a forty-year-old "youth," well educated in the works of Rousseau and Romanticism, an "inveterate dreamer," a "child," and a "madman." The environment that he structures for his pupil is compared to a "hothouse;" the education that he provides introduces Vladimir to abstract ideas, noble ideals, and beautiful dreams but seems to be designed to keep him from understanding reality in general, and Russian reality in particular. The author writes with unusually deep conviction: "Education must be climatological: for every age, as for every country, even more so for every class, and perhaps even for every family, there exists a particular kind of education." It was precisely this that Monsieur Joseph never learned and consequently was never able to convey to the young Beltov.

After such an inappropriate early education, his development continues at Moscow University, where, in a close and intimate circle, Beltov discovers the warmth of friendship, his own relative merit, and the value of learning. He graduates full of grand plans and noble goals and then moves to Petersburg, where he enters the civil service and makes his debut in high society. But neither is able to satisfy him: in possession of too great an intelligence, he finds life in the bureaucracy devoid of interest and soon retires. Thus begins a prolonged period of disillusionment. Beltov spends the next ten years "doing everything" but "accomplishing nothing." He tries his hand at medicine, painting, romance, and travel—but the result is always the same: ·boredom. Beltov, like Negrov, suffers from "spleen." At the end of part I he returns to Russia in order to take part in the local elections in the provincial town of N., hoping to find there some suitable employment for his talents.

However, the events that occasion his greatest crisis are his failure to gain elected office, the news of the death of his beloved Monsieur Joseph, and his acquaintance with the Krutsifersky family. Beltov comes to recognize that he is a useless creature, one who has surrendered to external circumstances; consequently he is without hope, searching for diversion. It is at this moment of spiritual nadir that he wins Lyubonka's love and discovers her strength, intelligence, and sympathy. When Dr. Krupov arrives at Beltov's hotel to upbraid him for destroying so much happiness and to banish him, he discovers that the hero has already composed a farewell letter to his love; however, as in so many previous instances, Beltov had been incapable of carrying through his intentions. The doctor acts as a catalyst yet again; after a poignant final meeting with Lyubonka, Beltov leaves the town of N. to continue his aimless travels—"a wanderer in Europe, a stranger abroad and at home."

Beltov's predicament has been succinctly summarized by Isaiah Berlin in one of his many essays on the life and works of Alexander Herzen: "[The hero is] too idealistic and too honest to accept the squalor and the lies of conventional society, too weak and too civilized to work effectively for their destruction, and consequently displaced from his proper function and doomed to poison his own life and the lives of others."[17] Who (or what) is to blame for Beltov's predicament? Once again, Isaiah Berlin: "Everything is partly the fault of the individual character, partly the fault of circumstance, partly in the nature of life itself."[18] Herzen seems to be affirming the complexity and insolubility of life's fundamental problems and consequently can offer no definitive answer to the question raised by the title of his novel.

Clearly in one sense Beltov's tragedy is indeed a deeply personal one and derives from his "individual character," his own human nature. And in another sense, Beltov's tragedy is a social one, inasmuch as he is the product of his circumstances: his family background and upbringing (especially the influence of his mother Sofya); his early education (especially the teaching of Monsieur Joseph); his later education (Moscow University); his class (landed gentry) and its way of life; and his society, with its fundamental institutions (autocracy, bureaucracy, marriage, "illegitimacy," and serfdom, to name but a few). But in the final sense, Beltov's tragedy is an existential one, which results from the "nature of life" itself—the will of fate, chance, accident. Herzen's question remains unanswered because the author has no answer, at least no simple one. Russian writers and critics would subsequently discover their own answers to Herzen's question; they would even go so far as to pose another, more practical question, one demanding immediate action: what is to be done? Herzen's novel, however, suggests that in spite of its author's own convictions and predilections, in spite of his passionate wish to assign blame and to discover a solution, no solution exists.

The artistic complexity of Herzen's novel has not always been fully appreciated.[19] In addition to the breadth of his characters and the depth of his ideas, he employs a rich assortment of literary techniques with great success: the "biographical" method that gives the novel its structural unity; the omnipresence of the author's voice—introducing, describing, and evaluating his characters—digressing, interrupting, commenting, and apostrophizing to his readers; the striking contrast between the author's empathetic and compassionate attitude toward the victims of the tragedy and his ironic and satiric treatment of the victimizers; his intelligence—sharp powers of observation, penetrating insights, and impressive erudition, evident particularly in the wealth of literary and historical allusions contained in the text; his stylistic range—including the broad comedy of the scenes describing the Negrovs' family life, the confessional sincerity of Lyubonka's diaries, the naturalism of the "physiological sketch" describing Sofya's life in Petersburg, and the abstract philosophical discourse on Beltov's upbringing and education.

After Herzen's emigration and his involvement with the revolutionary movements in Europe, when his name was banned from the Russian periodical press, writers and critics were forced to resort to periphrasis to refer to him. The one most frequently encountered is "the author of *Who Is to Blame?*." This serves as a clear indication that the novel was so popular that the author's name had become synonymous with the title, and as a testimony to the work's importance in the history of Russian literature and thought.[20]

The Critical Reaction

When Belinsky wrote to Herzen shortly after the publication of *Who Is to Blame?* and welcomed him into the ranks of Russian writers, he was in effect initiating the chorus of critical acclaim that was to surround the novel. Belinsky's review of part I in his "Survey of Russian Literature in 1845" was the first to be published (1846) and was more an appreciation of the author's literary talent than an analysis of his novel: "The author of *Who Is to Blame?* was somehow miraculously able to bring intelligence to poetry, to transform thought into real characters, the fruits of his observation into action full of dramatic movement."[21] In other words, Belinsky praised Herzen's synthesis of art and idea: the author had successfully combined imagination with thought. The critic continued, in his characteristic declamatory style: "What striking fidelity to reality, what profound thought, what unity of action, how it's all so much in proportion—nothing superfluous, nothing left unsaid; what originality of words, so much intelligence, humor, wit, soul, feeling!"[22] This was certainly an encouraging review of a young author's first serious attempt at writing fiction.

Belinsky's contemporaries were in general agreement about the worth of part I. Both in their published reviews and in their unpublished letters, there was almost universal recognition of the author's intelligence and the profundity of his philosophical approach to the contemporary scene. Thus the aspiring young writer Dostoevsky wrote to his brother, "There has appeared a whole host of new writers. Some are my rivals. Particularly noteworthy among them is Herzen (Iskander)."[23]

In 1847, after parts I and II were published together, critics acclaimed the novel as a triumph of the "natural school." *Who Is to Blame?* was said to be the first literary work that depicted contemporary life as it really was; therefore it could serve as convincing proof of the maturity of Russian letters. Even one of Herzen's so-called opponents, the Slavophile Ivan Aksakov (1823-86), wrote a moving tribute in a letter to his father: "It is not an artistic work, perhaps—but, aside from a morbid desire to be witty at all times, there are many wonderful things in it. When I read it I felt such a deep sense of oppression and melancholy, all the more so as it is a contemporary work, of the nineteenth century, with whose ills we all sympathize more or less."[24]

Belinsky finally addressed himself to the text of *Who Is to Blame?* in his "Survey of Russian Literature in 1847," published in *Contemporary* in 1848.[25] Here he seems to have retreated somewhat from his main thesis in his earlier review; he insists that it is Herzen's "thought" and "intellect," rather than his "creativity" or "artistry" that merit the attention of Russian readers. He sees the main interest of the novel not in an implied answer to the title question or in the character of the main hero, Beltov, but rather in the spiritual development of the heroine, Lyubonka. He dismisses Beltov as someone whose nature was spoiled by wealth, upbringing, and education and who gradually came to resemble Lermontov's Pechorin. Clearly Belinsky would have preferred more emphasis on the hero's external circumstances in conformity with his own changing attitudes toward the nature and function of literature.

Indeed, the figure of Beltov provoked considerable controversy among critics and writers in the second half of the nineteenth century. To some extent this divergence of opinion was foreshadowed in correspondence between the author and his close friend and fellow publicist, Nikolai Ogarev, in 1847.[26] Ogarev characterized the hero as "artificial," "romantic and pseudo-strong" and described his portrait in the novel as a "psychic study" of a "sick personality." Herzen replied with a more sympathetic reading of his protagonist's predicament, but he himself remained dissatisfied with Beltov's response to the problems of Russian society.

The writings of the radical critics in the late 1850s and early 1860s reflect Belinsky's reservations, Ogarev's criticisms, and Herzen's dissatisfaction. In their attempt to construct a genealogy of the Russian hero, they all assigned to Beltov his legitimate place in the pantheon. In so doing, they defined and redefined him, categorized and recategorized him, in order to fit him into various typologies. N. G. Chernyshevsky (1828-89), in an article entitled "The Verse of N. Ogarev" (1856), explained that "Onegin was replaced by Pechorin, [and] Pechorin by Beltov and Rudin."[27] N. A. Dobrolyubov (1836-61) developed this same theme. In a review ostensibly treating Goncharov's novel

Oblomov, entitled "What Is Oblomovitis?" (1859), he describes the tradition of the Russian hero as that of "strong natures crushed by unfavorable environments."[28] He compares Pushkin's Onegin, Lermontov's Pechorin, Herzen's Beltov, and Turgenev's Rudin as characters who all manifested early symptoms of the disease. He identifies the common themes uniting these "natures": their writing, reading, civil service, domestic life, attitudes toward women, and tendency toward self-humiliation. He acknowledges that while differences exist among their respective temperaments, they all share astonishing similarities. Most important, Dobrolyubov exonerates each individual from any responsibility for his unfortunate predicament. Under different circumstances, in some other society, these characters would have been entirely different. But in mid-nineteenth-century Russia they all suffer from the same barren striving for activity and from a painful awareness that while they *could* do a great deal, in fact, they will achieve nothing. Herzen's protagonist, although said to be the "most humane among them," belongs nevertheless to this unfortunate group.

On the other hand, in an article devoted to "I. S. Turgenev and His Novel *Nest of the Gentry*" (1859), Apollon Grigoriev (1822-64) distinguishes Beltov from Oblomov and argues that the moral position of Herzen's hero is far superior to that of Goncharov's.[29] Instead, Grigoriev groups Beltov together with Griboedov's Chatsky as a "fighter" and with Turgenev's Lezhnev and Lavretsky as men whose "ideals . . . cannot be reconciled with practice."

It is D. I. Pisarev (1840-68) who finally makes clear the purpose of all these typologies—the dethronement of the liberal aristocratic hero and the coronation of an altogether new character. In an article dealing with Turgenev's *Fathers and Sons,* entitled "Bazarov" (1862), Pisarev establishes a hierarchy of heroes to explain the emergence of Turgenev's young nihilist. The first stage, "will without knowledge," includes Onegin and Pechorin—men who are young, clever, and capable but who suffer from "spiritual hunger, boredom and disenchantment." Beltov and Rudin comprise the second group, "knowledge without will"—gloomy, frustrated idealists who aspire to do good but never archieve anything. Finally there is Bazarov, the representative of "knowledge and will," who unites "thought and deed" into "one solid whole."[30]

One year after Pisarev's review, Chernyshevsky published his revolutionary novel *What Is to Be Done?* (1863). The author intended it to be a direct and complex response in prose fiction to Herzen's **Who Is to Blame?** as well as to Turgenev's *Fathers and Sons.* The title itself dramatizes the move from the mere assigning of responsibility to the question of practical activity, while the subtitle, "Tales about New People," indicates that Chernyshevsky's characters belong to

yet another, more radical type of Russian hero—beyond Bazarov's combination of "knowledge and will." A full discussion of the polemical relationship between these novels lies outside the scope of this introduction; suffice it to say that Chernyshevsky's heroes Kirsanov and Lopukhov, his heroine Vera Pavlovna, and his "superhero" Rakhmetov focused the attention of readers and critics alike on the new generation, on the men and women of the sixties, on their aspirations and achievements.

Soviet criticism of **Who Is to Blame?** has, not unexpectedly, tended to concentrate on the assignment of culpability to the conditions of mid-nineteenth-century Russia. As one recent Soviet critic put it, Herzen intended to demonstrate "how the milieu disfigures the consciousness and lives of people at every level of the social hierarchy."[31] Lenin himself led the field in reductive conclusions when he declared that all the issues that Herzen raises in the novel (the nature of family, the institution of marriage, the status of women, the emergence of the intelligentsia, the origins of personality) are subordinate to one main problem: "all social questions are fused in the struggle against serfdom and its remnants."[32]

The purpose of all subsequent Soviet criticism of Herzen was clearly articulated by V. A. Putintsev in his major study, *Herzen: The Writer* (1963): "Reactionary and liberal-bourgeois critics have expended considerable effort to muffle the passionate protest in Herzen's fiction against the autocratic order and against serfdom. The task of Soviet literary criticism is to restore the importance of Herzen's novel as the highest artistic manifestation of Russian democratic thought in the 1840s."[33]

In fact, "reactionary and liberal-bourgeois" critics have not always done what they are accused of. Martin Malia, in his book entitled *Alexander Herzen and the Birth of Russian Socialism* (1965), comes close to repeating the "party line" on the novel. He argues that no one is to blame, that the question itself is false, and that the answer lies in the defects of Russian society. Thus it is the "alienations imposed by 'cursed Russian reality' that are to 'blame' for this triple failure of human promise."[34]

On the other hand, Nicholas Rzhevsky, in his recent study *Russian Literature and Ideology* (1983), asserts that Herzen does not view his characters as social victims but rather as individual heroic beings and that the "particular moral-fictional stance" that a character assumes is more significant in determining his or her life than class or social position. Rzhevsky concludes therefore, that Beltov and Lyubonka "are at fault much more than the society they inhabit because they allow themselves to be victimized by the social institution of marriage instead of asserting the moral prerogative of their love. The absence of such assertion lies at the heart of their tragic separation and indicates that 'blame' and responsibility, in Herzen's view, must rest finally with the individual, his internal make-up, and his ethical choices."[35] From Lenin's polemic assertion ("serfdom and its remnants") to Rzhevsky's "blaming the victim" ("they allow themselves to be victimized"), all Soviet and some Western critics have conspired to oversimplify the subtle and complex message of Herzen's novel. This new transition of ***Who Is to Blame?*** is offered in the hope that it may serve as something of a corrective to the excesses of both radical and reactionary zeal and that it may restore Herzen's novel to its rightful and distinguished place in the history of Russian letters.

Notes

[1] Peter Yakovlevich Chaadayev, *"Philosophical Letters" and "Apology of a Madman,"* trans. M.-B. Zeldin (Knoxville, 1969), 31-51.

[2] *My Past and Thoughts: The Memoirs of Alexander Herzen,* trans. Constance Garnett, translation revised by Humphrey Higgins, abridged by Dwight MacDonald (New York, 1973), 292-93.

[3] See Edward J. Brown, *Stankevich and His Moscow Circle, 1830-1840* (Stanford, 1966), 4-17.

[4] Vissarion Belinsky, *Polnoe sobranie sochinenii* (Moscow, 1953-59), XII, 270-71.

[5] This brief account of Herzen's life is summarized from Isaiah Berlin's introduction to Herzen's *My Past and Thoughts,* xix-xliii.

[6] For further details, see Monica Partridge, "Herzen's Changing Concept of Reality and Its Reflection in His Literary Works," *Slavonic and East European Review,* 46 (1968), 397-421.

[7] Berlin, "Introduction," xx.

[8] Chaadayev, *Philosophical Letters,* 39.

[9] G. N. Gai, *Roman i povest' A. I. Gertsena 30-40-kh godov* (Kiev, 1959), 48.

[10] Ibid.

[11] See Ellen Chances, *Conformity's Children: An Approach to the Superfluous Man in Russian Literature* (Columbus, Ohio, 1978), 53-56, for a discussion of Western influences on Herzen's fiction (esp. Hoffmann, Saint-Simon and Fourier, Balzac and Eugène Sue).

[12] D. D. Blagoi, "Znachenie Gertsena v razvitii russkoi literatury," in *Problemy izucheniya Gertsena,* ed. Yu. G. Oksman (Moscow, 1963), 328.

[13] A. G. Rozin, *Gertsen i russkaya literatura* (Krasnodar, 1976), 163. Pechorin is the protagonist of Lermontov's *Hero of Our Time* (1840), Rudin, of Turgenev's novel of the same name (1856), and Bazarov, of Turgenev's *Fathers and Sons* (1862).

[14] See Richard Stites, *The Women's Liberation Movement in Russia: Feminism, Nihilism, and Bolshevism, 1860-1930* (Princeton, 1977), 20-22.

[15] See Marshall Berman, *All That Is Solid Melts into Air: The Experience of Modernity* (New York, 1982), 212-15.

[16] Chaadayev, *Philosophical Letters,* 39.

[17] Introduction to Herzen, *From the Other Shore* (London, 1966), ix.

[18] "Alexander Herzen," in Isaiah Berlin, *Russian Thinkers* (New York, 1978), 202.

[19] See Gai, *Roman i povest',* 101-21, for a detailed analysis of Herzen's style.

[20] G. G. Elizavetina, "*Kto vinovat?* Gertsena v vospriyatii russkikh chitatelei i kritiki XIX v." in *Literaturnye proizvedeniya v dvizhenii epokh,* ed. N. V. Os'makov (Moscow, 1979), 41.

[21] *A. I. Gertsen v russkoi kritike,* ed. V. A. Putintsev (Moscow, 1953), 63.

[22] Ibid.

[23] Elizavetina, "*Kto vinovat?*" 42.

[24] Ya. El'sberg, *Gertsen* (Moscow, 1956), 163-64.

[25] *Belinsky, Chernyshevsky, and Dobrolyubov; Selected Criticism,* ed. R. E. Matlaw (New York, 1962), 35-45.

[26] See E. N. Dryzhakova, "Problema 'russkogo deyatelya' v tvorchestve Gertsena 40-kh godov," *Russkaya literatura,* 5 (1962) 2, 41-42.

[27] Elizavetina, "*Kto vinovat?*" 65.

[28] *Belinsky, Chernyshevsky, and Dobrolyubov: Selected Criticism,* 133-75.

[29] Elizavetina, "*Kto vinovat?*" 69.

[30] In Putintsev, *A. I. Gertsen v russkoi kritike,* 132-38.

[31] V. A. Putintsev, *Gertsen-pisatel'* (Moscow, 1963), 73.

[32] Ibid., 70.

[33] Ibid.

[34] *Alexander Herzen and the Birth of Russian Socialism* (New York, 1965), 270.

[35] Nicholas Rzhevsky, *Russian Literature and Ideology: Herzen, Dostoevsky, Leontiev, Tolstoy, Fadeyev* (Urbana, Ill., 1983), 59. Cf. Chances, *Conformity's Children*, 57-60: "It is not society's fault that Beltov cannot put his talents to work. It is not society which is to blame for his not fitting into Russian life." (58)

Martin A. Miller (essay date 1986)

SOURCE: "The World of Emigration in Nineteenth-Century Europe," in *The Russian Revolutionary Emigres: 1825-1870,* Johns Hopkins University Press, 1986, pp. 3-31.

[*In the excerpt that follows, Miller examines both how Herzen affected the emigrant circles in which he moved in the 1850s and how that context shaped him. Miller concludes with a look at the considerable success of Herzen's newspaper* The Bell.]

Alexander Herzen, an aristocrat whose name is synonymous with the development of Russian socialism, arrived in Western Europe on the eve of the outbreak of revolution in France in 1848. Herzen's role abroad, where he spent the most creative years of his life, was so overwhelming that he has come to be seen as the epitome of the entire Russian emigration during the nineteenth century. In the world of emigration, Herzen assumed a multidimensional role among the exiles of Europe. This role was appreciated in particular by later Russian émigrés, who worked in the same cities and for many of the same causes that Herzen had proclaimed as so necessary decades before. Plekhanov, who as an émigré conceptualized for the first time the fusion of Russian radicalism and European Marxism, spoke most knowingly of Herzen when he wrote that Herzen could never have achieved what he did had it not been for the "free conditions of West-European life" and the "rich supply of impressions that he received in the West."[30] Herzen's role was formed gradually during his years abroad, not suddenly upon his arrival. Once he did come to a coherent formulation, it was both specific and complex. He became, in the words of one of the most perceptive commentators on Herzen's career, "the first and as yet unsurpassed mediator between democratic Europe and the Russian intelligentsia."[31]

Herzen achieved this significance because of his unusual personal gifts and because he arrived in Western Europe at a critical moment in the separate but interacting histories of Russia and Europe. Herzen left Russia voluntarily, but the circumstances of his life made it imperative that he abandon his homeland if he was to continue to think, write, and act in the manner he had chosen. As is well known from the many studies of his pre-émigré career, Herzen had, on unsubstantiated charges, been exiled to Viatka, near the Urals, during his student years, had begun writing articles critical of the autocratic regime under Nicholas I, and had, since his childhood, looked to the West as a source of inspiration in studying the kind of political and social change he believed to be necessary in his own country.[32]

Herzen's first years abroad were shattering, disruptive, stimulating beyond even his own wildest dreams, and also depressing in a way he had not anticipated. He arrived in Paris as the revolution broke out, and made his initial contacts with friends and comrades as well as opponents and enemies in the context of this upheaval. He had come from a country where critical thought and action were severely restricted, and found himself suddenly thrust into a world where boundaries of all kinds were being broken down and redefined. Thus, not only was he experiencing the impact of the historic difference between "backward" Russia with its enserfed peasantry, entrenched aristocracy, and exclusive autocracy, and the "modern" West with its political pluralism, industrialized capitalist economy, and rich culture which set standards of quality and excellence for the rest of the world; he was also encountering the cracking apart of a historical paradigm that had dominated Europe and Russia since the defeat of Napoleon. The conservative structure of traditional Europe, fashioned out of the Congress of Vienna in 1814 and watched over by the Holy Alliance, had undergone many challenges in the ensuing decades. It was not until the outbreak of revolutions across the continent of Europe in 1848, however, that the extent to which the Old Order and its values had been undermined by the opposition currents of the preceding years was fully realized.

Herzen's involvement with the revolution in France is told in great detail in his own memoir and has been discussed by the historians who have written about him. There is no doubt that the revolution left him profoundly disturbed about Europe, Russia, and his own future. Because the revolution was defeated—and because of the particularly violent way in which it was—Herzen left Paris for Switzerland and Italy. He knew only that he could not return to Russia, and that fact, combined with the revolutionary failure in France, forced him to begin to evaluate his entire system of values and convictions. He has left a lengthy record of this process of self-discovery and self-redefinition in his many writings from this period.[33]

During the years of his wandering from France to Switzerland and Italy before finally settling in London, Herzen met some of the most prominent members of

A photograph taken in Herzen's later years.

nationality of humanity. This sense of a new and higher kind of national identity oriented around a radical vision of the future order was symbolized by the expressions often used in the letters the émigrés wrote to each other. Hugo, for example, addressed Herzen as "Dear Fellow Citizen" because of their shared desire for a society based on "the unity of humanity" rather than the divisive aspects of contemporary governments.[35] In a sense, Herzen played a role among the émigrés at this time not unlike that of Alexander I at the Congress of Vienna. He brought the reality of Russia to the consciousness of Europe by his presence, his involvement, and his activities. He became, through his writings and his wide-ranging contacts among the émigrés of Europe, a participant on the "general staff of the European revolution," and the "representative of Russian democracy" abroad.[36]

As Herzen compared and contrasted Russia and the West in his writings, which were, to a large extent, reflections of the struggle he was undergoing to establish a role and a new identity as an émigré, he observed with a penetrating eye the exiles around him whose difficult situation so resembled his own. No one has expressed the anguish and the significance of emigration as eloquently as Herzen did. After leaving Paris, Herzen went to Geneva, "the old haven of refuge for the persecuted." "Switzerland," he wrote, "was at this time the meeting place in which the survivors from European political movements gathered together from all parts. Representatives of all the unsuccessful revolutions were shifting about between Geneva and Basle, crowds of militiamen were crossing the Rhine, others were descending the St. Gothard or coming from beyond the Jura."[37] As for the émigrés themselves, he was painfully aware of the influence of the circumstances of their lives. Exile, he wrote,

> checks development and draws men away from the activities of life into the domain of fantasy. Leaving their native land with concealed anger, with the continual thought of going back to it once more on the morrow, men do not move forwards but are continually thrown back upon the past; hope prevents them from settling down to any permanent work; irritation and trivial but exasperated disputes prevent their escaping from the familiar circle of questions, thoughts and memories which make up an oppressive, binding tradition. . . . All emigres, cut off from the living environment to which they belonged, shut their eyes to avoid seeing bitter truths, and grow more and more acclimatized to a closed, fantastic circle consisting of inert memories and hopes than can never be realized.[38]

Herzen's portraits of individual émigrés reacting to these stresses and strains are both scathingly critical[39] and uncritically admiring.[40] He was also aware of the difficulties these émigrés placed upon the governments

the European exile community. These included Mazzini, Felice Orsini (who later gained notoriety in 1858 when he attempted to assassinate Napoleon III), Aurelio Saffi (a member of the ruling Triumvirate in revolutionary Rome during 1848 and later a literature professor at Oxford), and Garibaldi among the Italians, Proudhon, Victor Hugo, Louis Blanc, and Ledru-Rollin among the French, as well as Arnold Ruge and Georg Herwegh from Germany, Louis Kossuth from Hungary, Worcell and Edmund Chojecki (Charles Edmond) from Poland, and numerous others who are described in depth in Herzen's memoir.[34] Herzen mentions in passing that he also met three Russian émigrés in this period—Michael Bakunin, Nikolai Sazonov, and Ivan Golovin—but he has little to say about them, for reasons we shall examine shortly. In his own individualistic and somewhat removed manner, Herzen was, for the moment, at one with the cosmopolitan and internationalist mood, movement, and emerging vocabulary being generated among the exiles. These émigrés, "colonies of compatriots in an alien land," were seeking to transcend their national differences by inventing a new international that accepted them. In Geneva, for instance, exiles streamed in because the government was under the control of James Fazy, who had for years been involved with radical causes in Switzerland. The émigrés, Herzen wrote, "tormented Fazy and poisoned his existence. . . . The passions loosed during revolutionary movements had not been appeased by failure and, having no other outlet, expressed themselves in an obstinate restiveness of spirit. These men had a mortal longing to speak just when they should have held their tongues, retired into the background, effaced themselves and concentrated their forces." Instead, out of necessity and desperation, they produced inflammatory pamphlets, held public meetings, and "frightened the foolish governments with impending insurrections."[41] Herzen knew about this firsthand. He himself had been expelled from Nice less than a month after the demonstration of 19-20 May 1851, which terrified local government officials blamed on radical exiles.[42]

The émigrés, according to Herzen, could not immediately find a way to direct their energies into effective paths of action. They became "absorbed in wrangling among themselves, in personal disputes, in melancholy self-deception, and, consumed by unbridled vanity, they kept dwelling on their unexpected days of triumph" in "the revolution of the past." They then broke into small groups dominated less by principles than by petty hostilities. As they retreated more and more into their own exclusive camps and became more obsessed with the glories and the mistakes of the past, they began to express themselves—to dress and to act—in a distinct manner that, according to Herzen, created "a new class, the class of refugees."[43] Although Herzen himself did not express all these traits and moods, he did undergo a period in which his personal life overwhelmed his political concerns. This was the time he considered his greatest tragedy—the loss of his mother and son at sea, and the discovery of his wife's affair with his friend Herwegh.[44]

Herzen came to London in the summer of 1852 to begin what became the first stable period of his émigré years. Many of the émigrés whom he had seen and known on the Continent also had come to London around the same time. He still saw many of the problems that had riddled the émigré communities in Italy and Switzerland in the aftermath of 1848. "Meeting the same men, the same groups, in five or six months, in two or three years, one becomes frightened: the same arguments are still going on, the same personalities and recriminations; only the furrows drawn by poverty and privation are deeper; jackets and overcoats are shabbier; there are more grey hairs, and they are all older together and bonier and more gloomy . . . and still the same things are being said over and over again."[45] He also admitted his own state of confusion. Thinking at first that he would stay in London only briefly, "little by little I began to perceive that I had

absolutely nowhere to go and no reason to go anywhere."[46] He reestablished contact with his émigré comrades from the Continent—Mazzini, Ledru-Rollin, Kossuth, and others. Now, however, he began to ask himself, "Are not these men becoming the sorrowful representatives of the past, around whom another life and different questions are boiling up?"[47] After meeting with Worcell, whom he continued to respect, he nevertheless wondered, "How could he imagine that England would incite Poland to rise, that France of Napoleon III would provoke a revolution? How could he build hopes on the Europe which had allowed Russia into Hungary and the French into Rome? Did not the very presence of Mazzini and Kossuth in London loudly remind one of the decline of Europe?"[48] The absurdities of this fading mode of existence struck Herzen as well. He noted that Ledru-Rollin and Kossuth, who had friends and a general cause in common, had lived in London for over three years before meeting personally because it could not be decided to their satisfaction which of them should visit the other according to the dictates of émigré protocol!

Herzen was determined not to become part of this ossifying generation. He therefore began to turn his attention more directly to his homeland as he made plans to set up an émigré printing press in London. He was aided in this process of reestablishing his identity as a Russian in an émigré context by the curious manner in which he was treated in his new milieu. The English regarded Herzen with both more respect and greater distance than he was accustomed to experiencing since his departure from Russia. He made a great and lasting impression on some English radical figures, particularly W. J. Linton and Ernest Jones, who helped him gain entrée into the world of British publishing. Linton wrote in his memoir that Herzen "was short of stature, stoutly built, in his last days inclined to corpulence, with a grand head, long chestnut hair and beard, small, luminous eyes, and rather ruddy complexion. Suave in his manner, courteous, but with an intense power of irony, witty, choice as well as ready in speech, clear, concise and impressive, he was a subtle and profound thinker, with all the passionate nature of the 'barbarian,' yet generous and humane."[49]

During the 1850s, Herzen reached the height of his fame. His home became a visiting site for streams of people from Russia, from Western Europe and from London. This is how Herzen's home was described by one of his comrades:

> The visitor to London generally informed Trübner [Herzen's London publisher] of his desire to have the honor of making Herzen's acquaintance. Trübner would give him the address and offer to write a note. In answer to this note, Herzen would arrange a meeting, either at his place or at that of the visitor, if the latter for some reason did not want to be seen in Herzen's house. Such cases

were very frequent. . . . People did not use their real names in Herzen's house, or used them very rarely. Whoever did not wish to conceal his visits gave his own name; with those who were uncertain or asked that their names not be given out, we either changed them (which, incidentally, happened rarely) or dealt with indiscreet questions by saying that we didn't remember, didn't know, it was a difficult name, etc. And in fact it was hard to remember all those who came to worship, there were so many of them. They flashed by, one after the other; they came in, trembling with reverence, heard every word of Herzen and engraved it in their memory; they gave him information, either orally or in the form of prepared notes; they expressed their sympathy to him and the sympathy of their acquaintances; they thanked him for the benefits conferred upon Russia by his unmasking and for the fear which the *Bell* inspired in everything dishonest and unclean; then they took their leave and disappeared. Whom did I not see at Herzen's in my time! There were governors, generals, merchants, litterateurs, ladies, old men and old women—there were students. A whole panorama of some kind passed before one's eyes, really a cascade—and all this without taking into account those whom he saw *tête á tête*. Many a time, standing at the fireplace in his study in Fulham, I laughed inside to hear some retired captain, who had travelled to London expressly to see Herzen from some backwater like Simbirsk or Vologda, declare his sympathy, explain that he was not a reactionary.[50]

With the death of Nicholas I in 1855, the arrival of his close friend Nicholas Ogarev, and the creation of his Russian Free Press, Herzen achieved an international reputation. He still believed the was acting in concert with progressive opponents of reactionary regimes everywhere, but now he had found an appropriate instrument through which to act on his principles. He had become, as he said, Russia's "free, uncensored voice," which only an émigré could raise and transmit.[51]

Herzen's influence not only coincided with, but was integrally related to, the decidedly changed atmosphere under the new regime in Russia, that of Alexander II. For the first time, a commitment to abolish serfdom was made publicly and the process of how to work out the least disruptive manner of emancipation was set in motion. Hopes for change were aroused on many levels throughout Russian society, and the demand for an open discussion of the issues intensified. Nowhere, at least in the Russian language, was the problem of peasant emancipation and a variety of associated problems as freely discussed as they were in Herzen's émigré press, particularly in his newspaper, *Kolokol (The Bell)* . . . Herzen's place and authority in the wide-ranging currents of reform that swirled during the late 1850s and early 1860s were solidified through the prestige

of his *Kolokol*. Herzen found himself in indirect contact with his country through the vast number of letters he received for his paper, and through the large number of visitors who came to his door with information about the hidden and horrible events that lay behind the official shadows of the autocracy. As a prominent writer of the time put it, not only was Herzen's paper "read in Russia by people of all social grades, from the Winter Palace to the smallest police official," but Herzen was the person "who gave the chief impulse to political and social radicalism in Russia."[52] . . .

Notes

[30] G. V. Plekhanov, "Gertsen-emigrant," *Sochineniia*, vol. 23 (Moscow-Leningrad: Gosizdat., 1926), p. 414.

[31] M. Gershenzon, "Gertsen i zapad," *Obrazy proshlogo* (Moscow: Levenson, 1912), p. 176.

[32] For Herzen's life during these years, see Martin Malia, *Alexander Herzen and the Birth of Russian Socialism* (Cambridge: Harvard University Press, 1961); Franco Venturi, *Roots of Revolution* (New York: Knopf, 1960), pp. 1-35; Isaiah Berlin, "Alexander Herzen," *Russian Thinkers* (New York: Viking Press, 1978), pp. 186-209.

[33] See the recent analysis of these writings in Edward Acton, *Alexander Herzen and the Role of the Intellectual Revolutionary* (Cambridge: Cambridge University Press, 1979), pp. 40-82, and also the discussion in Franco Venturi, "Russians, French, and Italians in Nice, Genoa, and Turin after the Revolution of 1848," *Studies in Free Russia,* pp. 140-86.

[34] One of the earliest and still eminently readable discussions of Herzen's relationships with Western exiles is Gershenzon's essay, "Gertsen i zapad," pp. 175-280. For a good treatment of the émigré circles around Herzen in Nice, see Venturi, *Studies in Free Russia,* pp. 148-76.

[35] Gershenzon, pp. 180-81.

[36] The quoted phrases are from ibid., p. 184.

[37] Herzen, *My Past and Thoughts,* trans. Constance Garnett, 4 vols. (New York: knopf, 1968), 2:684.

[38] Ibid., p. 686.

[39] As in the case of Karl Peter Heinzen; see ibid., pp. 688-93.

[40] As with Saffi; see ibid., pp. 706-8.

[41] Ibid., p. 733.

[42] On this incident, see Venturi, *Studies in Free Russia,* pp. 158-61.

[43] Herzen, *My Past and Thoughts,* 2:741-42. The kind of émigré Herzen had in mind in this analysis was Arnold Ruge, who was politically destroyed by the 1848 defeat. Herzen poignantly describes how the progressive Paris editor of the 1840s tried to regain his place in London a decade later by giving a series of lectures on contemporary German philosophical movements and their political implications. Ruge stood before an empty hall, a lonely, embittered, and forgotten man, delivering his prepared talks to only Herzen and Worcell, who comprised the audience. Afterwards, he reacted in anger and irrationally. Seeing nations instead of people before him, he said: "Poland and Russia have come, but Italy is not here; I shant's forgive Mazzini or Saffi for this when there's a new people's rising" (ibid., 3:1157).

[44] On this, see E. H. Carr, *The Romantic Exiles* (Boston: Beacon Press, 1961), pp. 47-121, and also Acton, pp. 83-104.

[45] Ibid., p. 1046.

[46] Ibid., pp. 1023-24.

[47] Ibid., p. 1044.

[48] Ibid., p. 1140.

[49] William James Linton, *Memoirs* (London: Lawrence and Bullen, 1895), p. 146. On Herzen's English relations, see Monica Patridge, "Alexander Herzen and the English Press," *Slavonic and East European Review* 36, no. 8 (1958): 453-70, and idem, "Aleksandr Gertsen i ego angliiskie sviazi," in *Problemy izucheniia Gertsena,* ed. B. P. Volgin (Moscow: Akademiia nauk, 1963), pp. 348-69. In the latter article, Partridge argues with a wealth of evidence that Herzen was not nearly as isolated from British society as he suggests in his memoir. When he wrote his memoir, he did not mention individuals in politics whom he knew, such as Charles Bradlough and Joseph Cowan, for reasons that still remain unclear. Partridge suggests that he feared compromising their reputations by writing of them in his memoir, but there may have been other reasons. Isaiah Berlin argues that in spite of Herzen's wide contacts within British society—which included dining with Robert Owen, Charles Darwin, and the Carlyles, among others—he never had truly close friends in London. England provided Herzen with the liberty to operate as a successful émigré writer and thinker, but he never felt at home there in the way he did in Nice, for example, where he clearly developed warmer relationships. See Isaiah Berlin, "Herzen and His Memoirs," *Against the Current* (New York: Viking Press, 1980), pp. 199-200.

[50] V. I. Kel'siev, "Ispoved," *Literaturnoe nasledstvo* 41-42 (1941): 273-74, quoted in Abbot Gleason, *Young Russia: The Genesis of Russian Radicalism in the 1860s* (New York: Viking Press, 1980), pp. 96-97.

[51] A. I. Herzen, *Sobranie sochinenii,* 30 vols. (Moscow: Akademiia nauk, 1954-65), 12:64.

[52] Boborykin, "Nihilism in Russia," p. 126. All of the major studies of Herzen have discussed his vast influence. For a recent analysis of one of the lesser-known areas of Herzen's impact in Russia, see T. S. Vlasenko, "O revoliutsionnoi deiatel'nosti 'Biblioteki Kazanskikh studentov'," in *Epokha Chernyshevskogo,* ed. M. V. Nechkina (Moscow: Nauka, 1978), pp. 89-90.

Judith Zimmerman (essay date 1989)

SOURCE: "Conclusion," in *Mid-Passage: Alexander Herzen and European Revolution, 1847-1852,* University of Pittsburgh Press, 1989, pp. 221-28.

[*The following chapter, which reviews Herzen's reaction to the failed European uprisings of 1848, culminates in a comparison of Herzen's thought with that of Karl Marx.*]

Historians have perceived the revolutions of 1848 as paradoxical defeats for the revolutionary ideal. The dreams of political romanticism died on the barricades in Paris in June, or in Vienna in October; the makers of the revolution went to prison, or to exile, or to their deaths. The age of generous ideals and of simple, clear visions of political morality came to an end, to be succeeded by a new "toughness" and "realism." Yet within a quarter century, the victors had put into place many of the reforms the vanquished had fought for; the radical and democratic exiles were amnestied and could come home to a world of civil liberties, parliamentary government, and national unification. But if the victory of the government forces was paradoxical, so too was the ultimate vindication of the revolutionaries. The worlds to which they could return at the end of their lives were arenas of business as usual. Constitutions and broad suffrage did not translate into the virtuous republicanism that had been their sustaining vision, and the new national, constitutional states had as little use for their exalted political dreams as had the reactionary regimes of 1847.

The fate of the revolutionaries' political vision reflects their own strengths and failings. For years before the revolution, they had worked to develop and propagandize their programs. Occasionally, they fought and died for their views, and if each individual revolutionary effort failed, the series of noble failures created a mythology and martyrology for radicalism. The heroic legends and the noble ideals were made known to the public at large through journalism, art, public demonstrations, and manipulation of the establishment media. The methods of political propaganda developed by this generation of radicals would last for well over a century and are not yet completely out of date.

Through their efforts the revolutionaries had put the program of democratic and socialist reform on the agenda. Their success as propagandists meant that in most of Europe their ideals had become so entrenched in the awareness of politically active sectors of the population that it had become almost impossible to repudiate them. Thus, their programs were enacted by the governments that defeated them.

But although they succeeded in setting the political agenda, the radicals had no mechanism for translating their ideas into political reality. Revolutionary processes brought many of them close to governmental power in 1848, but they proved to be incapable of holding on to it and using it creatively. Once the revolution was over, they were reduced to squabbling over the mistakes of 1848 and plotting futile armed insurgencies. In the decades to come it would be men who could command the political power of the state and who were not afraid to use this power for change rather than cautious retrenchment—men like Cavour, Bismarck, and even Alexander II—who were able to set their imprint on political events, not small bands of dedicated souls acting out of love for ideals and the people.

Alexander Herzen's mature life was shaped by his response to the European radicals, just as his youthful social vision had owed much to their propaganda. His expectations of the West had been formed by reading radical critics—Blanc, Proudhon, and George Sand being the most important—and linking their denunciations of European conditions to his left-Hegelian radicalism. He had therefore been expecting to find an imperfect and unjust social order, with a dominant bourgeoisie unworthy of its power and influence, when he came to Western Europe in 1847. But reality exceeded all his expectations; he was shocked and appalled by what he perceived as the corruption, vulgarity, and hypocrisy in the Bourgeois Monarchy of Louis Philippe. New acquaintances among the French and émigré radicals, whom he met after his arrival in Paris, helped him sharpen his analysis of the failings of European society.

The outbreak of revolution found Herzen in Italy. He was entranced by the revolutionary process in its operatic Italian form, and his respect for the Italian heroes of the *Risorgimento* would last the rest of his life. But revolution in Italy was not powerful enough to break the strength of the Hapsburg monarchy. The movement was doomed without outside help, and

Herzen appears to have been aware of this by the time he left the peninsula to follow events farther north.

The Paris uprising and the establishment of the republic drew Herzen back to France. He arrived too late for the ebullience of February and found, instead, the first stages of reaction; even the moderate policies of the Provisional Government were repudiated by the conservative National Assembly. Herzen's response was critical and his view of the revolutionary movement complex. He now differentiated between the crowds who had made the revolution and the opposition politicians who has emerged with governmental power. It was the inadequacy, the timidity, and the fundamental conservatism of the politicians that had held them back from joining with the Paris populace to make a clean sweep of the old order. Forced into confrontation with revolutionary forces, they had lost their democratic veneer altogether. The French revolutionary government had been unable to take the measures necessary for victory, and Herzen had arrived in Paris just in time to see its defeat. This was registered by the election of the conservative National Assembly, followed soon after by the bloody defeat of the revolutionary Paris crowd.

The more radical leaders, who had never held power, might be admirable and heroic, and Herzen often could admire them as human beings; however, their theories and programs could no longer attract him. His political disillusionment was complete. Herzen perceived the exploited and oppressed Paris workers, and eventually the Russian peasants, as truly revolutionary forces and thought they might well ultimately win; but he also felt that these forces were themselves indifferent to the values of individual freedom that he cherished. There seemed no way of linking the call for freedom and individual autonomy of the middle-class radicals with the urgent demand for social justice that animated the Paris workers.

Despite his disenchantment with the revolution, Herzen renewed and extended his acquaintance with French and exiled radicals in Paris, as well as socialist politicians and journalists. If he could no longer admire them as leaders, he could still appreciate them as potential colleagues and friends. He entered into the world of political action with his move to Geneva in the summer of 1849. Soon, he was involved in the collaboration with Proudhon on *La Voix du Peuple* and in addition was developing networks of contacts among the Italian and German exile colonies. He began to write extensively for French and German audiences, thus discovering his dual Western journalist's role as gadfly of the radical movement on the one hand, and as the interpreter of Russia to the Western left on the other.

Throughout his first years in the West Herzen appears to have been seeking a community in which he could find both liberty and fraternity—the individualism lacking in Russia combined with the harmonious friendship of his old Moscow circle. Constitutionalism, revolution, and the Geneva exiles all failed to satisfy his political demands, and by 1852 the circle itself was irrevocably lost, not only by his emigration, but also by his friends' repudiation of his work. Finally, he attempted to create his own little high-minded commune on the narrowest conceivable scale—his family and the Herweghs, living in relative isolation from the mainstream of exile life. The family crisis shattered this dream forever, and his faith that private life offered a sanctuary for his values was destroyed once and for all.

Nor was there any hope of going back, retreating to a pre-European innocence. From the latter part of 1848 onward, nostalgia for friends and youthful memories in Russia became a major motif; it inspired many of the best pages of *Byloe i dumy*. But Herzen never entertained the slightest illusion that he could return in fact to his homeland.[1] (In the memoris of Herzen's Russian acquaintances, he is frequently portrayed as expressing a painful homesickness and fantasizing about going back, but it is unlikely that he ever believed this was a possible option. More often than not, the fantasy revolved around his children returning to Russia after his own death.) Russia was more repressive, politically more hopeless than the West. Emigration offered the only practical way to work for radical change in Russia.

Herzen retained his illusions about the circle for a longer time; the reality of his isolation from the friends he had loved so much and trusted so long was unbearable. His emotional disengagement from the circle, to the extent it ever took place, came only in 1855-1856. First Granovskii died, leaving the circle without its most important member, and then Ogarev joined him in London, and the two men were able to recreate in part the world of friendship.

Yet, even as Herzen lost his youthful idealism, he became a tougher, more realistic, and more effective political figure. He rejected grand theoretical schemes and dismissed socialist panaceas, but he established the press and edited his journals, and thereby did provide a vehicle for uncensored Russian thought. In the short run he had some influence on the reform effort of Alexander II, and in the long run he helped shape Russian revolutionary thought. During his career as a journalist, he kept his sights fixed on his goals; and like Proudhon in 1849, he was willing to find short-term alliances wherever possible, from the provincial estate to the Winter Palace, and was also willing to give up his stake in revolution for the sake of meaningful reform in the present.

He also found a community in which he could function—the world of exile as it crystallized in London during the 1850s. He often found the émigrés naive or foolish. The controversies that periodically tore the community apart seemed futile and pointless to him, and the tactics even of the men he most admired he found unacceptable. Nonetheless, he joined them, and found in their midst sociability, if not the profound affection he had earlier sought from his friends. The exiles also provided a set of moral and cultural standards that helped give shape to a life that was otherwise threatened by a loss of all values. On a more practical level, the revolutionary community provided Herzen with legitimation of his own activity and with practical experience in publishing and disseminating émigré literature.

Always, however, he remained something of an outsider, the stranger, the Russian "barbarian," observing even the most sympathetic men with the unsentimental gaze of one who was not himself involved. Since he had not been a participant himself, he did not need to rationalize or defend the measures taken during the revolutionary struggle. The very absence of a Russian émigré community helped him in this; there was no "party" to establish a "party line" in interpreting events; there was no revolutionary strategy that could be harmed by a misplaced word or a too harsh and too public assessment of an ally. This disengagement from the revolutionary milieu enabled Herzen to write one of the best analyses of the French revolution of 1848, that contained in the *Pis'ma* series, as well as the frequently mordant portraits of the members of the international revolutionary community found in *Byloe i dumy*.

One Western 1848 revolutionary politician stood at least as far from his fellow exiles as did Herzen—Karl Marx. Even before revolution broke out in 1848, Marx had separated himself from the community of middle-class intellectual radicals and journalists in order to build a modern political movement. He sought primarily working-class groups,[2] which he then attempted to forge into obedient executors of his commands. He was uninterested in working with other middle-class theorists; they were potential rivals, and at best they confused the drive for action by offering alternative strategies and visions. We have seen that even before 1848 Marx was more likely to drive such intellectuals out of his organization than deal with them.

In Cologne during the revolutionary period, Marx's special style had matured. He had attempted, ultimately successfully, to seize control of the workers' movement from the more popular and more responsive Andreas Gottschalk, at considerable cost in bitterness. He had also insisted on complete tactical flexibility, attempting to forge an alliance with non-working class radicals and rejecting the demands from his own constituency for revolutionary purity. Ultimately he alienated not only the Cologne organization and his would-be liberal-democratic allies, but also even his own lieutenants who had come from London to work with him. The cost, by 1851, was the dissolution of the Communist League, the arrest of the Cologne leadership, and the splitting of the London communist organization. The same pattern would be repeated later on, most spectacularly in the case of the First International.

Marx thus failed as dismally in 1848 as all the other revolutionaries. However, he had begun the process of creating a modern, working-class party. Social Democracy, once Marx had forged it, would understand power and would be able to utilize the new political structures to organize a strong constituency and wield very considerable influence. By the time Marx died, such a party would have been created in Germany, and by the end of the nineteenth century parties heavily influenced by the Marxist and German Social Democratic example would have been established throughout Western Europe. To be sure, the socialist parties did not develop as Marx had predicted, and their very success in organizing and representing the workers may well have been a factor in the exhaustion of the revolutionary impulse in Europe. Nonetheless, it is Marx's imprint that the modern socialist movement bears.

Herzen and Marx—this unbalanced pair continues to force comparisons. Both lived for over a decade in London, at times not more than a mile or two apart. Both stood apart from the enthusiasms and the squabbles of the main émigré groups. Both also stood apart from Mazzini's attempts to establish émigré organizations, and they both rejected the Italian's old-fashioned liberal nationalism. Both saw the motive force of revolutionary change coming from the exploited depths of society. And they refused to have anything to do with each other. Marx charged that Herzen was a Russian nationalist who called for European revitalization through a barbarian Russian invasion. On at least one occasion, he refused to share a speaker's podium with the Russian, and he was not at all pleased that his English ally Ernest Jones was also an ally of Herzen.[3] Herzen charged that Marx purposely fomented the rumors that Bakunin was a Russian agent[4] and undermined his socialist credibility by allying himself with the conservative Russophobe David Urquhart. Herzen's portrait of Marx's followers is the most biting in **Byloe i dumy**. One has the sense that the mutual antipathy between these two men was fueled by the fact that each felt that the other presented an alternative vision of socialist organization.

What was Herzen's alternative? Like Marx, he turned away from the maneuvering within the radical exile community; however, instead of seeking a different constituency and a more modern type of organization, as had Marx, he turned back to Russia. His mission became the one that the first wave of exiles had carried out well in the period preceding the outbreak of revolution. Fröbel had established a press to smuggle forbidden work into Germany; the poetry of Herwegh had had pride of place in this activity. Herzen's press made available to Russian readers the poetry of Pushkin and other classic writers which for political or moral reasons could not pass the censors, as well as that of his friend Ogarev. Herwegh and Ruge had attempted to create written symposia to expose the viewpoints of a variety of political thinkers who could not publish in their homeland; Herzen would accomplish this goal for Russia with *Poliarnaia zvezda*. The Poles and Germans in Paris had popularized their respective causes among the French politicians and journalists; Herzen did the same in London. In general, the pre-1848 emigrations had established the legitimacy of demands for democratic and socialist change in their homelands; Herzen did the same for his. In so doing, he implicitly asserted the validity of the program of middle-class, intellectual revolutionaries, while Marx's entire career repudiated that program.

The Russian dimension to his work made it unnecessary for Herzen to involve himself too deeply in émigré life. But, unlike Marx, his avoidance of the squabbles did not constitute a condemnation of the men and women who made up the exile community. On the contrary, he continued in his personal life to be a traditional middle-class intellectual radical who operated through the written word and social interaction, not political organization. He shunned hierarchical organizations, seeking instead egalitarian communities. He acknowledged the norms of the radical subculture and contributed to elaborating the sense that this culture possessed its own mores and values that were more rational and humane than those of surrounding Victorianism. Russian backwardness meant that there was a fruitful field of work for a tough-minded survivor who retained the ideals of a gentler, more romantic age.

Notes

[1] In 1861, Tolstoi told Proudhon of Herzen's desire to return; Herzen responded, "I do not think at all about going into the bear's mouth. Probably Count Tolstoy has taken my castles in Spain for castles on the banks of the Volga" (Herzen to Proudhon, in Mervaud, "Six Letters," p. 314).

[2] I am deliberately avoiding the term *proletariat*. Marx, of course, believed that revolution would come from the organized industrial workers, whom he called the proletariat. There are two problems with this usage. First, it appears to be a rather idiosyncratic definition used by some Saint-Simonians and by Marx, but not

generally accepted. For other socialist thinkers of the time, the word meant the poorest and most oppressed of the poor, without regard to the source of their income; in actual fact, these would more likely be artisans, especially in decaying crafts, than industrial workers. Marx's *Lumpenproletariat* seems rather closer to the contemporary meaning of *proletariat*. (On the Saint-Simonian use of *proletariat* to mean industrial workers, see James Briscoe, "The Unfinished Revolution: The Saint-Simonians and the Social Question—Origins of Socialist Debate in the July Monarchy," The Consortium on Revolutionary Europe, *Proceedings* [1984], pp. 235-37.) Second, Marx's own groups were more often made up of artisans than of industrial workers.

[3] It is a measure of the hostility of Marx and Engels toward Herzen that Engels felt one of their friends had failed in his responsibility by allowing an article of Herzen's to be published in an English newspaper. Marx did not argue with Engels's desire for censorship, but pointed out that the friend in question worked for a different newspaper, and thus was not to blame for the article appearing (Engels to Marx, April 21, 1854; Marx to Engels, April 22, 1854, in Marx and Engels, *Werke* 28:344-46).

[4] *Sobranie sochinenii* 11:158-60, recalls an episode in 1853; see also Marx to Engels, September 3 and 28, 1853, in Marx and Engels, *Werke* 28:280-84, 295. There was another episode in 1862.

FURTHER READING

Biography

Carr, Edward Hallett. *The Romantic Exiles: A Nineteenth-Century Portrait Gallery.* New York: Frederick A. Stokes Co., 1933, 391 p.

An account of Herzen's life after he left Russia. Carr focuses on the personal aspects of those years and extensively discusses Herzen's wife's affair with the German poet Georg Herwegh.

Herzen, Alexander. *My Past and Thoughts: The Memoirs of Alexander Herzen.* Trans. Constance Garnett. Berkeley and Los Angeles: University of California Press, 1973, 684 p.

Herzen's own account of his life, considered by scholars to be an important historical and literary document.

Malia, Martin. *Alexander Herzen and the Birth of Russian Socialism: 1812-1855.* Cambridge, Mass.: Harvard University Press, 1961, 486 p.

A biography of Herzen's life until the death of Czar Nicholas I in 1855. In addition to analyzing Herzen's political philosophy, Malia explores three topics in early nineteenth-century Russian intellectual history: the emergence of socialism, the influence of romantic idealism on socialism, and the development of ideological nationalism.

Criticism

Chances, Ellen B. "On the Road to Ideology: Herzen, Turgenev, and Goncharov." In her *Conformity's Children: An Approach to the Superfluous Man in Russian Literature*, pp. 50-90. Columbus, Ohio: Slavica Publishers, Inc., 1978.

Examines *Who Is to Blame?* as a study of character formation, deeming it "almost . . . a documentary tracing the emergence of a social type."

Dryzhakova, Elena. "Herzen's *Past and Thoughts: Dichtung und Wahrheit.*" In *The Golden Age of Russian Literature*, pp. 115-37. Ed. Derek Offord. New York: St. Martin's Press, 1990.

Emphasizing the influence of Goethe, chronicles Herzen's autobiographical writings.

Frank, Joseph. "Alexander Herzen: *Who Is to Blame?*" In his *Through the Russian Prism: Essays on Literature and Culture*, pp. 213-24. Princeton: Princeton University Press, 1990.

A brief summary of the novel and its place in Russian literature.

Ginzburg, Lydia. "Herzen's *My Past and Thoughts* and Historical Identity." In *On Psychological Prose*, translated and edited by Judson Rosegrant, pp. 195-217. Princeton, N.J.: Princeton University Press, 1991.

An in-depth analysis of Herzen's memoirs, looking specifically at the interplay of individual psychological detail and the broad social forces that Herzen wished to document.

Grenier, Svetlana. "Herzen's *Who Is to Blame?*: The Rhetoric of the New Morality." *Slavic and East European Journal* 39, No. 1 (Spring 1995): 14-28.

Reads Herzen's novel against the conventional interpretation, contending instead that it makes an argument for human agency above social forces.

Hecht, David. "The American 'Exceptionalism': Alexander Herzen." In his *Russian Radicals Look to America, 1825-1894*, pp. 16-40. Cambridge, Mass.: Harvard University Press, 1947.

Through an examination of references to America in Herzen's works, argues that he viewed the country as a possible utopia, but also as too young culturally to give birth to extensive social revolution.

Herzen, Aleksandr. Essay in *The Pole Star,* 1855. Reprinted in *My Past and Thoughts: The Memoirs of Alexander Herzen.* Trans. Constance Garnett, revised by Humphrey Higgens, introduction by Isaiah Berlin, pp. v-vi. Berkeley and Los Angeles: University of California Press, 1973.

> From an essay originally published in the newspaper *The Pole Star* in 1855. Herzen comments on the value of personal memoirs and discusses one of his reasons for writing his memoirs.

Kelly, Aileen. "Irony and Utopia in Herzen and Dostoevsky: *From the Other Shore* and *Diary of a Writer.*" *The Russian Review* 50 (October 1991): 397-416.

> While investigating Herzen's influence on Dostoevsky, argues that both writers presented an unprecedented critique of post-revolutionary European culture.

Lampert, E. "Alexander Herzen (1812-1870)." In his *Studies in Rebellion,* pp. 171-260. London: Routledge and Kegan Paul, 1957.

> Discusses Herzen's role in the history of Russian revolutionary thought during the second quarter of the nineteenth century.

Partridge, Monica. *Alexander Herzen: Collected Studies.* Cotgrave, England: Astra Press, 1988, 157 p.

> An anthology of essays on many aspects of Herzen's life and work, including his significance as a literary and journalistic figure.

Schapiro, Leonard. "Turgenev and Herzen: Two Modes of Russian Political Thought." In his *Russian Studies,* pp. 321-37. Ed. Ellen Dahrendorf. London: Collins Harvill, 1986.

> Places Herzen in the context of the debate over Russia's cultural and political backwardness relative to Western Europe, embodied in his disagreements with Turgenev. Schapiro portrays Herzen as Russia's champion against Turgenev's idealization of Western Europe.

Stites, Richard. "Women and the Russian Tradition." In his *The Women's Liberation Movement in Russia: Feminism, Nihilism, and Bolshevism, 1860-1930,* pp. 3-25. Princeton, N. J.: Princeton University Press, 1978.

> Sketches Herzen's viewpoint on female emancipation, presenting his sometimes inconsistent support for liberation as exemplary of nineteenth-century progressive thought.

Venturi, Franco. "Herzen." In his *Roots of Revolution: A History of the Populist and Socialist Movements in Nineteenth-Century Russia,* pp. 1-35. Trans. Francis Haskell. New York: Alfred A. Knopf, 1960.

> Studies Herzen's role in the development of Populism in Russia during the reign of Czar Nicholas I.

Winegarten, Renee. "The Parting of the Ways." *Writers and Revolution: The Fatal Lure of Action,* pp. 146-53. New York: New Viewpoints, 1974.

> Locates Herzen in the post-revolutionary ebb of 1850. Includes a lengthy comparison with anarchist Mikhail Bakunin.

Zenkovsky, V. V. "A. I. Herzen." In his *A History of Russian Philosophy.* Vol. I, pp. 271-98. Trans. George L. Kline. New York: Columbia University Press, 1953.

> Discusses Hegel's influence on Herzen's thought.

Additional coverage of Herzen's life and career is contained in the following source published by Gale Research: *Nineteenth-Century Literature Criticism,* Volume 10.

Richard Monckton Milnes

1809–1885

English politician, poet, biographer, and essayist.

INTRODUCTION

Both a poet and a longtime member of Parliament, Milnes is largely remembered for his biography *Life, Letters, and Literary Remains of John Keats* (1848), the first life of Keats and a work responsible for bringing about a favorable reassessment of the Romantic poet's merits. A social dilettante who held numerous dinner parties and gatherings for the intellectual and social elite at Fryston, his country home in Yorkshire, Milnes is also known for his association with several major figures of nineteenth-century English literature, including Thomas Carlyle and Algernon Charles Swinburne. The former was one of his lifelong friends—Milnes recorded some of their conversations in his day books—while the latter was allowed to browse Milnes' vast library of continental erotica and received assistance from his friend in publishing some of his earliest poems.

Biographical Information

Milnes was born in Mayfair, London, on 19 June 1809 to Maria Monckton Milnes and Robert Pemberton Milnes, a distinguished member of Parliament. His early education consisted of both private instruction and formal schooling at Hundhill Hall, until he entered Trinity College, Cambridge in 1827. While there Milnes came into contact with such figures as Arthur Hallam and Alfred Tennyson, and published his first work, *The Influence of Homer,* an essay that earned him the university's English Essay Prize in 1829. He graduated several years later and began to travel throughout the European continent, particularly in Germany, Italy, and Greece; one result of these travels was his first collection of poetry, *Memorials of a Tour in Some Parts of Greece, Chiefly Poetical* (1834). Having spent some three years abroad, Milnes returned to London in 1836, and almost immediately became a familiar sight in the city's elite social circles. The following year he was elected to the House of Commons as a Conservative in his father's old district, Pontefract. As the result of further travels he produced several more collections of poetry, the last of which was *Palm Leaves* (1844). He published his most important book of criticism, *Life, Letters, and Literary Remains of John Keats,* in 1848. Three years later he married Annabel Crewe; by this time he had ceased to com-

pose poetry, having turned his attention instead to political matters, though he continued to expand his rare book collection. Among these books were several by the infamous Marquis de Sade which significantly influenced the young poet Swinburne after he was shown them in 1861. Two years later Milnes was named Lord Houghton and appointed to the House of Lords; during the remaining decades of his life he spent most of his time serving as a statesman—entertaining foreign dignitaries and speaking at public events, such as the opening of the Suez Canal in 1869 and the unveiling of Samuel Taylor Coleridge's bust at Westminster Abbey. He died in Vichy, France, on 11 August 1885.

Major Works

Milnes' early works include five collections of poetry as well as several essays and speeches delivered before Parliament. Of his poems, most are lyrics or ballads, elegiac or sentimental in tone. Some are occasional poems, written to commemorate specific events, and many of these are included in *Memorials of a Tour in Some Parts of Greece, Chiefly Poetical* and *Memorials of a Residence on the Continent, and Historical Poems* (1838), Milnes' first two collections. Both are conventional in nature and evoke Milnes's reminiscences of excursions in Europe during the 1830s. *Poems of Many Years* (1838) and *Poetry for the People* (1840) contain simple ballads, lyrics, didactic verse, and two narrative poems, "Venus and the Christian Knight" and "The Northern Knight in Italy"—the first retellings of the tragic Tannhäuser legend in English. *Palm Leaves* comprises Milnes' poetic observations of Egypt and the Middle East, and his admiration for Islamic culture. *One Tract More, by a Layman* (1841) is characteristic of his political writings, demonstrating Milnes' defense of the Oxford Movement and maintaining traditional practices in the Church of England. Of far greater significance to critics than his poetry, Milnes' biography *Life, Letters, and Literary Remains of John Keats* represented a turning point in the reputation of the romantic poet, who, before Milnes, was typically reviled by or unknown to critics. In the biography Milnes incorporated letters and other forms of primary information from close friends of Keats in order that the poet might speak for himself in the work. The publication of his Keats biography in 1848 also marked a change in Milnes's own oeuvre, away from original verse and into other avenues. Political topics predominate among his later writings, though

Milnes also produced two essays of specialized interest: *Another Version of Keat's "Hyperion"* (1856) and *A Discourse of Witchcraft* (1858), written for the Philobiblon Society—an organization Milnes' cofounded to satisfy his interest in collecting rare books and manuscripts. Another of his notable later works is the children's nursery rhyme *Good Night and Good Morning* (1859).

Critical Reception

While popular in his day, Milnes' poetry has received little serious attention by modern scholars. His contemporary Walter Savage Landor once called him "the greatest poet now living in England," but this unconditional praise was far from the norm. Elizabeth Barrett observed that, as a poet, Milnes "perceives and responds rather than creates." Most of his verse has since been forgotten, though in 1915, Lafcadio Hearn called the poem "Strangers Yet" Milnes' best, and praised his work overall. By the mid twentieth century, Milnes had come to be known primarily for his literary influence and ability to discern poetic talent in others rather than for his own literary skill. The inspiration and assistance he provided to Swinburne has been noted by biographers of both men. Likewise, his biography of Keats—long since replaced as the standard on the subject—has nevertheless been lauded for its incipient perception of Keats as one of the greatest nineteenth-century English poets.

PRINCIPAL WORKS

The Influence of Homer (essay) 1829
Memorials of a Tour in Some Parts of Greece, Chiefly Poetical (poetry) 1834
Memorials of a Residence on the Continent, and Historical Poems (poetry) 1838
Poems of Many Years (poetry) 1838
A Speech on the Ballot, Delivered in the House of Commons (speech) 1839
Poetry for the People, and Other Poems (poetry) 1840
One Tract More, by a Layman (essay) 1841
Thoughts on Purity of Election (essay) 1842
Palm Leaves (poetry) 1844
The Real Union of England and Ireland (essay) 1845
Speech of R. Monckton Milnes, esq. in the House of Commons, March 11, 1847, on Mr. Hume's Motion Respecting the Suppression of the Free State of Cracow and the Payment of the Russian-Dutch Loan (speech) 1847
Life, Letters, and Literary Remains of John Keats (biography) 1848
The Events of 1848, Especially in Their Relations to Great Britain. A Letter to the Marquis of Lansdowne (essay) 1849

Answer to R. Baxter on the South Yorkshire Isle of Axholme Bill (essay) 1852
Speech of Richard Monckton Milnes in the House of Commons, April 1, 1852. Extracted from Hansard's Parliamentary Debates (speech) 1852
Another Version of Keats's "Hyperion" (essay) 1856
A Discourse of Witchcraft (essay) 1858
Good Night and Good Morning: A Ballad (poetry) 1859
Address on Social Economy (speech) 1862
Selections from the Poetical Works (poetry) 1863
Monographs: Personal and Social (essays) 1873
The Poetical Works of (Richard Monckton Milnes) Lord Houghton (poetry) 1876
Some Writings and Speeches of Richard Monckton Milnes in the Last Year of His Life (essays and speeches) 1888

CRITICISM

R. H. Horne (essay date 1844)

SOURCE: "Richard Monckton Milnes and Hartley Coleridge," in *A New Spirit of the Age*, Oxford University Press, London, 1907, pp. 187-96.

[*Although it was not publicly known at the time, Elizabeth Barrett collaborated extensively with Horne in the production of his collection of essays on contemporary poets. Evidence from their correspondence indicates that the essay from which this excerpt is taken was primarily the work of Barrett. In the following, originally published in 1844, Horne describes Milnes' poetic style, calling it subdued, graceful, lyrical, and spiritual.*]

The poetry of Richard Monckton Milnes has met with considerable praise in many quarters, yet hardly as much as it deserves; and it has met with peculiar dispraise, more than it deserves, either in kind or degree. A common case enough. . . .

Mr. Milnes has been accused of a want of the divine fire of imagination and passion; and he has, moreover, been accused of merely thinking that he thinks,—or of imitating the tone and current of other men's minds, and mistaking that for the original impulse and production of his own. Not any of these broad accusations are justifiable, and in some respects they are demonstrably unfounded.

Mr. Milnes does not appear to possess the least *dramatic* passion, nor does he display much impulse or energy in his poetry. There is no momentum in the progress of his lines; and the want is conspicuously betrayed in his blank verse, because, of all other forms,

Milnes as sketched by Charles Martin in 1845.

that is the one which absolutely requires the most genuine, thought-sustained, and unflagging energies. We are almost tempted to hazard the opinion that fine blank verse requires great material stamina; in fact, a powerful internal physique, to carry on the burden and purpose of the soul. We think that the psychological history of nearly every one of our great poets who wrote in blank verse will bear us out in the opinion. Several exceptions are undoubtedly against this; and the greatest of them would be Keats; yet here the exception would tend to prove the rule, as he died soon after the production of his only poem in blank verse, which is, moreover, unfinished. How far this latter speculation—which indeed may be of sound value—would be applicable or inapplicable to the poet at present under discussion, need not be considered, because he seldom writes in blank verse; he is essentially a lyrical poet; but to his occasionally attempting the former may be attributed some of the accusations of want of passion and impulsive energies.

But the most ostensible is not always the most forcible; there is latent fire as well as palpable combustion; and the effect of genuine elements, though always proportionate to its cause, must seem inadequate, in all cases of very refined or quiet development, except to those who are prepared with a ready sympathy, and can recognize the deepest source from the least murmuring that rises up to the surface. A poet should be judged by the class to which he belongs, and by the degree of success he attains in his own favourite aim. Mr. Milnes, regarding poetry as 'the gods' most choicest dower', says of it, in his **'Leucas'**,—

> Poesy, which in chaste repose abides,
> As in its atmosphere; that placid flower
> Thou hast exposed to passion's fiery tides,
> &c.

Here, at once, we discover Mr. Milnes's theory, and the chief aim of his muse. Sappho is blamed for steeping her verse in 'passion's fiery tides', because poesy is said to abide 'in chaste repose', as its proper atmosphere. By this standard then, is the poetry of Richard Monckton Milnes to be measured; it is a standard of inherent beauty; and he will be found to attain it most completely. A short extract from one of the earliest poems in his collection, published ten years ago, will suffice to illustrate this.

> But when in clearer unison
> That marvellous concord still went on;
> And *gently as a blossom grows*
> A frame of syllables uprose;
> With a delight akin to fear
> My heart beat fast and strong, to hear
> Two murmurs beautifully blent
> As of a voice and instrument,
> A hand laid lightly on low chords,
> A voice that sobbed between its words.
> Stranger! the voice that trembles in your ear
>   You would have placed had you been
>   fancy-free
> First in the chorus of the happy sphere,
>   The home of deified mortality.
>
>   . . . . .
>
> Stranger, the voice is Sappho's—weep; oh!
>   weep,
> That the soft tears of sympathy may fall
> Into this prison of the sunless deep,
>   Where I am laid in miserable thrall.[1]—
>   **'Leucas'.**

It is as a lyric and elegiac poet (in the ancient sense of elegy), with a temperament rather elegiac than lyric, that Mr. Monckton Milnes takes his place among the distinguished writers of his age and country. Notwithstanding that he has written *Poetry for the People,* neither in the work in question nor in any other, has he given evidence of a genius calculated for popular appeals. He might have called his work 'Poetry for the Philosophers'; but the very philosophers should be of the upper House and accustomed to tread softly upon Plato's carpets, or they would be found inevitably defective, now and then, in their range of sympathies. In style he is clear and concise, almost familiar, and in his blank verse he too often indulges in a commonplace colloquialism; but the impulses of mind and heart, although abundantly human and true, are surrounded by so definite a circle of intellectual habit, that they cannot or, at least, do not cast themselves beyond it; and it gives a fine and recondite colour to his simplest forms of expression. . . .

                    . . . . .

Mr. Milnes's earlier poems are more individual in expression and ideal in their general tone, and probably contain more essential poetry and more varied evidence of their author's gifts, than the writings which it has since pleased him to vouchsafe to the public. He has since divested himself of the peculiarities which offended some critics, and has more studiously incar-

nated himself to the perception of readers not poetical. The general character of his genius is gentle and musing. The shadow of an academical tree, if not of a temple-column, seems to lie across his brows, which are bland and cheerful none the less. He has too much real sensibility, too much active sympathy with the perpetual workings of nature and humanity, to have any morbid moaning sentimentality. Beauty he sees always; but moral and spiritual beauty, the light kernelled in the light, he sees supremely. Never will you hear him ask, with a great contemporary poet, if there is 'any moral shut within the bosom of a rose', because while he would eschew with that contemporary the vulgar utilitarianism of moral-drawing, he would perceive as distinctly as the rose itself, and perhaps more distinctly, the spiritual significance of its beauty. His philosophy looks upward as well as looks round—looks upward because it looks round: it is essentially and specifically Christian. His poetry is even ecclesiastical sometimes; and the author of *One Tract More,* and his tendency towards a decorative religion, are to be recognized in the haste with which he lights a taper before a picture, or bends beneath a **'Papal Benediction'**. For the rest, he is a very astringent Protestant in his love for ratiocination— and he occasionally draws out his reasons into a fine line of metaphysics. He sits among the muses, making reasons; and when Apollo plucks him by the ear to incite him to some more purely poetic work,— then he sings them. With every susceptibility of sense and fancy, and full of appreciations of art, he would often write pictorially if he did not nearly always write analytically. Moreover, he makes sentiments as well as reasons; and whatever may be the nobility of sentiment or thought the words are sure to be worthy of it. He has used metres in nearly every kind of combination, and with results almost uniformly, if not often exquisitely, harmonious and expressive. There may be a slight want of suppleness and softness in his lighter rhythms, and his blank verse appears to us defective in intonation and variety, besides such deficiencies as we have previously suggested; but the intermediate forms of composition abundantly satisfy the ear. With all this, he is quite undramatic; and, in matters of character and story, has scarcely ever gone the length, and that never very successfully, even of the ordinary ballad-writer. His poems, for the most part, are what is called 'occasional',—their motive—impulse arising from without. He perceives and responds, rather than creates. Yet he must have the woof of his own personality to weave upon. With the originality which every man possesses who has strength enough to be true to his individuality, his genius has rather the air of reflection than of inspiration; his muse is a Pythia competent to wipe the foam from her lips—if there be any foam. Thoughtful and self-possessed instead of fervent and impulsive, he is tender instead of passionate. And when he rises above his ordinary level of philosophy and tenderness, it is into a still air of rapture instead of into exulting tumults and fervours. Even his love poems, for which he has been crowned by the critics with such poor myrtle as they could gather, present a serene transfiguring of life instead of any quickening of the currents of life: the poet's heart never beats so tumultuously as to suspend his observation of the beating of it.

The last publication of this poet is entitled **Palm-Leaves,** and is a valuable gift to the public, not only for its poetical beauties, but for the enlarged toleration of its views and teachings. So that a religion be sincerely felt, whether Mahommedan, or of ancient Egypt, he regards even its fragmentary forms of truth with reverence;—

> —though a gleam,
> Not less a portion of the fires that steep
> Mankind's brute matter in the heavenly
>   stream,
> And lead to waking life, through mazy
>   modes of dream.
>   **'The Burden of Egypt.'**

Palm-Leaves departs from the old conventionalisms of fiction as to the manners, customs, and religion of the East, and sets the truth before us in a light which, in this instance, is far more delightful to contemplate. The poems will not be found the less poetical, in the hands of Mr. Milnes, on this account. The **'Hareem'** is as beautiful as it is new in poetry and true in sentiment. The **'Mosque'** and **'Mahommedanism'** are deeply interesting; and the Arabian legend entitled **'Mahommed and the Assassin'** is simple, brief, and sublime, uplifting the heart and soul with magnanimity and devotion. Nor is the book wanting in abundance of graceful thoughts and pleasing fancies, albeit their general tenor is grave and subdued.

The general estimate of Richard Monckton Milnes is a thinking feeling man, worshipping and loving as a man should—gifted naturally, and refined socially; and singing the songs of his own soul and heart, in a clear sweet serenity which does not want depth, none the less faithfully and nobly, that he looks occasionally from the harp-strings to the music-book. His **'Lay of the Humble'**, **'Long Ago',** and other names of melodies, strike upon the memory as softly and deeply as a note of the melodies themselves—while (apart from these lyrics) he has written some of the fullest and finest sonnets, not merely of our age, but of our literature. . . .

Notes

[1] *Memorials of a Tour in Greece,* by R. M. Milnes. 1834.

Fraser's Magazine (essay date 1847)

SOURCE: "Mr. R. Monckton Milnes," in *Fraser's Magazine for Town & Country*, Vol. XXV, No. CCX, June, 1847, pp. 722-26.

[*In the following excerpt, the anonymous critic evaluates Milnes's strengths and weaknesses as a politician.*]

It is very rarely that we find men successful in the House of Commons who have made any reputation for themselves in other pursuits. Such men form the exception, indeed, rather than the rule. Distinguished barristers are almost invariably bad parliamentary orators. Lord Brougham and Sir William Follett were, no doubt, brilliant exceptions; but they, therefore, serve to make the failures of others more remarkable. Literary men, too, seldom make a great figure in the House of Commons. Neither Sir Edward Bulwer, nor his brother Henry, ever commanded much attention there; and although Mr. Disraeli is now one of the acknowledged orators of the day, it has only been after a long course of self-tuition that he has succeeded in obliterating the traces of his early failures. Poets have been the most unfortunate of all. Mr. Serjeant Talfourd occurs at once as an instance. With all his admitted talent, and despite some brilliant orations he delivered on more than one important question, he could never attain parliamentary influence. His tone was too *exalté*, his language too good for the average comprehension: the very same composition which as an essay would have been admired, was as a speech voted a bore.

We cannot except Mr. Monckton Milnes from this unlucky category. Considering his unquestionable abilities, remembering the evidences of determination of purpose which he has displayed since he has been in parliament, and looking back at some of the speeches he made in the earlier part of his career, we cannot but feel surprised that he has not taken a more decided position. But he has now been ten years a member of parliament, without having achieved a single decisive success as a legislator or as an orator, without having succeeded in attaching that weight or interest to his opinions or conduct, which have been secured by men far his inferiors in ability. The names of some mere men of business are familiar with the public, and they are themselves in the way to high official promotion, while Mr. Milnes is never spoken of as a man likely to rise in the State, or to render himself permanently useful or important. On the other hand, there is the brilliant example of Mr. Smythe to shew that the imputation of the possession of talents, of being addicted to literary pursuits, and above all, of being a poet— dangerous though such imputations may be in this commercial country—is no bar to either popular esteem or official promotion. Mr. Milnes ought long since either to have been a member of some administration, or, at least, to have stood high among those who might be called upon to serve the State. But he is in no such condition. He has no direct party ties, yet has not made for himself a strong independent position. It would be difficult to persuade any one who has attentively observed the honourable gentleman's career, that this proceeds from any indifference to public honour, or any want of personal ambition. He has wilfully neglected opportunities, and having done so, he has been unable to make new ones, when caprice or a sudden fit of activity has led him to desire to do so.

But do we, therefore, undervalue the abilities of Mr. Milnes? Would we assume that non-success in the House of Commons is any proof of inferiority? Do we even assert that Mr. Milnes could not attain that success, and triumphantly too, if he were so minded? By no means. When all the visible evidences of success,—applause, and official promotion, are attainable by the mere red-tape men, it would be unfair to try a man of originality and unusual intellectual powers like Mr. Milnes by any such standard. It would be equally unfair in his case to say that he could not easily shoot far ahead of this class of politicians, and beat them on their own ground. Then how to account for his anomalous position? Why do we find a man like Mr. Disraeli (who grossly failed on his first appearance, which Mr. Milnes never did), one of the leaders of a party; or a man like Mr. Smythe, who has only been half the time he has been in parliament, having held an under-secretaryship, and likely hereafter to be still further promoted; and yet see Mr. Milnes lagging behind in the race, with no defined position and no apparent probability of his taking any? The only explanation we can give is, that he labours under some constitutional tendency to indolence, which prevents him from vigorously following up any particular object; unless, indeed, the imaginative faculty be too strong in him to allow of his sufficiently identifying himself with the more commonplace realities of political affairs. That he would succeed were he resolutely to persevere, we do not hesitate to affirm.

Another reason why he has not long since taken a higher position may have been that his mind is so much elevated above political passions, that he cannot be an efficient ally of party. In this respect he differs from Mr. Disraeli and others, who have displayed superior parliamentary talents. As a politician, he may be described as a liberal Conservative; one who would, perhaps, be prepared to go further than even the professed Liberals themselves. Thinkers of his class would realise all the pleasures of legislation, without incurring its responsibilities; they deal profusely in proposition, which, however well they may read in a speech, would be very dangerous if embodied in an act of parliament. Mr. Milnes usually deals, from preference, in the abstract truths of political science, and does not shew a disposition to make compromises of details. Hence, he is not so much in favour with statesmen as are men of a more plastic, or, as they have it, of a more practical nature. Mr. Milnes has been so far a party-man, that he has supported, with tolerable consistency, the politics of Sir Robert Peel; but he seems to have done so rather because the liberal tendency suited his own views, than from any special obligation of fealty to a leader.

The speeches of Mr. Milnes are always distinguished by much thought, often by great vigour and originality. At times they have been so good, they have arrived so near the point of excellence, as to make one regret, that a little more pains should not have been bestowed on them, so as to render them more perfect. But even with their occasional looseness, both of thought and phraseology, they are still superior to the majority of the speeches delivered in parliament. Many a wordy and tedious harangue of pompous placemen, which is reported with a slavish accuracy of word-catching, might be dispensed with in favour of a speech from Mr. Milnes, who only receives abbreviated honours. One of the best speeches he ever made was one of his earliest. It was delivered in 1839, against a motion for the Ballot. Besides being a most able argument on the question, it contained some passages worthy of being remembered. Speaking of the constitution of this country, he said that ours was not a written charter—that our political system was the offspring of time, and the disciple of necessity. The nationality of ages and the habits of generalising were not to be merged in the most ingenious ballot-box of which philosophers or mechanicians ever dreamed. It was no commonplace cant to call the ballot-box un-English. It was "un-English," not with reference to any fanciful analysis of national character, not as inconsistent with a traditionary ideal of what Englishmen ought to be rather than what they are, but un-English so far (and this was all they had to do with) as to prevent the powers of it from working harmoniously and co-ordinately with the other parts of our social and political organisation. Again, in reference to the cry that the ballot should be tried as an experiment only, he said that there was no such thing in political science as a pure and simple experiment. If an experiment failed, there was no going back. Every act of legislation went far beyond what was apparent at the time of its enactment. If the ballot were granted and it failed, there would then be a cry for universal suffrage. Thus we should go on, from change to change, from disease to remedy and remedy to disease, until all that was vigorous and stable in our social institutions was exhausted, until all natural influences or lawful rights be distorted or destroyed, and nothing be left us but that unmitigated discontent which is at once the child and the parent of revolution. These passages are vigorously put, and the whole speech is powerfully argued and full of apt illustrations.

In 1840, he supported Sir Robert Inglis in his motion for Church Extension, upon the broad ground that the voluntary system was totally inadequate to supply the spiritual wants of the community. There were evils, he said, in our social system, with which the voluntary system was totally incompetent to grapple. The defect of that system was, that when in our social state we were going on from bad to worse, the voluntary system took no notice of it. Mr. Milnes also supported the measure for National Education under the guidance of the Church. He supported Sir R. Peel's Income-tax, and his liberal measures towards Ireland, especially the Maynooth-bill and the Colleges-bill. In supporting the former, he made a bold defence of the principle of acting on expediency—that bugbear of old-fashioned politicians. He openly avowed his belief that expediency was the best principle of political action, and defended his opinion on good philosophical grounds. His speeches on the subject of the Roman Catholics have always been remarkably liberal and bold. He deserves the more credit for them, because they were made against the bigoted prejudices of a large portion of his constituents. In supporting the Maynooth-bill, he declared that he was ready to lose his seat if that was to be the consequence of his supporting a liberal policy towards the Roman Catholics. And he soon after went down to his constituents at Pontefract, that they might bite if they chose, having shewn their teeth. However, they did not think proper to call on him to resign. He was for a Ten-hours'-bill, and when Sir R. Peel's government was shaken by the adverse vote of the House of Commons on that question, he was one of those Conservative members who had the courage to refuse to stultify themselves by rescinding their former votes. He supported Sir R. Peel's Corn-bill of 1846, but avowing his belief that he was not the man to propose it. It was only because Lord J. Russell had refused to take the government that he considered Sir R. Peel justified.

In questions of foreign policy Mr. Milnes takes great interest. Having travelled much in various parts of the world, he has studied such subjects in their true aspects. He often takes part in debates on foreign policy, and almost invariably throws a new light, derived from his personal experience, on the topics discussed. Here, as in home politics, Mr. Milnes is always found to be on the side of human advancement and freedom. Yet he is no mere theorist. He would not sacrifice the solid advantages of established government, however imperfect, to vague aspirations after an unattainable liberty. With the cause of Poland, however, he has always sympathised. Whenever there have been debates in the House of Commons on the affairs of that country, Mr. Milnes has been among the loudest and boldest of those who have protested against the conduct of the despotic powers; nor has he been the least eloquent of those able advocates of the Poles who have been called into activity in this country by the spirit of freedom. On the other hand, he has always desired to see peace maintained on the Continent; and he was very earnest in deprecating Lord Palmerston's diplomatic evolutions some years since, by which that great benefit to the world was perilled. Speaking on that subject on one occasion, he put his case tersely and forcibly when he said that "an armed peace is a peace without its profits,—a war without its stimulants, or any of those concomitant circumstances that make it endurable."

Mr. Milnes sometimes makes speeches so superior in quality, as to make it more to be regretted that he should not have assumed a higher position in the House of Commons. Whatever subject he takes up he regards it philosophically. He does not drag it down to the level of the party passions of the hour, but rather seeks to lift up his auditors to the full height of which the argument is capable. In common with many of the younger members of the House, he chafes under the sublimated mediocrity which rules in contemporary politics. He would wish to see our statesmen take a firmer grasp of their position, knowing the true situation of things better, and being inspired by loftier aims. He would rather that they left off timidly paddling along the shore of legislative discovery, and struck boldly out into the open sea, with science for their guide and the compass of good intentions. He is, to some extent, imbued with the Continental doctrines of centralisation, but without going the full length of our economists. He has not yet been able to bring himself to deny the common claims of human nature. It is very fortunate for him that his party have for some years been more or less in a transition state, and that he has been able to speak his mind with a freedom which a few years ago might have been dangerous to the general union. For, accident made him a Tory,—sentiment, a Liberal. All that is comprehensive and statesmanlike in the old creed of his party he adopts with avidity, but always with a lurking preference for some of the most cherished opinions of those to whom he has been nominally opposed. He was at one time put forward by Sir Robert Peel as a pawn, to indicate his game; and a more favourable specimen of an enlightened Conservative could not be found. At another period, he allowed himself to be partially identified with the Young England party; and, in point of talent, the association was a natural one; but his opinions and their's could not long amalgamate. There was too decided a tendency to absolutism in their ulterior views. He found it more in accordance with his opinions and predilections to follow Sir Robert Peel; and, as we have said, he gave that statesman a general, though not an invariable support. But the original leaven of Liberalism became apparent when Lord John Russell came into power. He immediately published a declaration, which had some effect at the time, that he was prepared to "give the Whigs a fair trial."

The fault of Mr. Milnes' speeches is their inconclusiveness. With the exception of the speech on the Ballot, already referred to, we do not remember one address of his, on a great topic, which is thoroughly well argued from beginning to end, or which, from any sustained declamatory power or careful use of oratorical art, was calculated to produce a permanent effect. It may be an erroneous impression, but he appears to us, of late years, to have been too indolent to perfect any thing. His speeches abound in the raw material both of statesmanship and eloquence. They display a thorough comprehension of the subject, and occasionally present brilliant passages; but as a whole they want coherency, and there is none of that symmetry which so charms in the perusal of a speech by Mr. Smythe or Mr. Macaulay, and which allies the argument to the sympathies and the memory by a new tie, independent of the reasoning faculty. There are constantly provoking evidences of carelessness. He allows himself to be drawn aside from the course of his argument by irrelevant matter. A paradox is to him an irresistible temptation; and, although he has a considerable command of humour, his attempts to be comic usually fail, simply because he will not take the pains to make his sallies neat and pungent. Any one to whom reputation was precious, and fame agreeable, might secure both by going over Mr. Milnes' speeches, and recasting the ideas in a more attractive form. There is the stuff of an orator in h:m were he only in earnest. The worst part of the affair is, that Mr. Milnes seems to be growing less careful of the conditions of success every year. He has rather declined than advanced in the opinion of the House since his first efforts secured him respect and attention. Yet it ought not to be so, for his mind has not retrograded. Nor was he an impostor in the first instance, like some of those distinguished-extinguished, who come out with a flash and go in again ingloriously.

Mr. Milnes, like Mr. Macaulay, at first sight disappoints you. In his physical aspect he belies his reputation as a poet and a man of intellect,—a reputation in his case well-deserved. Personally, he is by no means distinguished. Scarcely above the middle height, too stout for his size, and rather heavy in his aspect and gait, he would be overlooked at first, in an assembly where there are so many men of a commanding exterior as in the House of Commons. Nor, at a glance, do the face and head, as with Mr. Macaulay, correct the first impression. But they improve on examination. Although the features are irregular,—the nose too prone on the lips, which are disproportionably large, the chin very massive, till the whole face approaches somewhat to that which, if we are to judge from their sculpture, would seem to have been the Egyptian ideal,—and although there is generally a heaviness in the aspect, it is all re-

deemed when you contemplate the broad, high, intellectual forehead, and the full deep eye, which tells of habitual thought. An expression of sternness prevails in the countenance; but it is a habit of the features, rather than of the mind. The little unconscious actions, which often betray the character, confirm the tale told by his speeches. Careless, even almost to slovenliness in his dress, he looks and acts like a man to whom it is too much trouble to make up for the world. He moves indolently; lounges, as if without a purpose; has brief fits of activity, and long intervals of quiescence; in short, looks like one who might be happy, if he had only something to do. That delightful dreaminess of existence which is part of the poet's birthright, no one would deprive him of; but when a recluse chooses to be a member of parliament, new duties are imposed on him, especially if Nature has blessed him with unusual talents. He must be an active, working man, in direct relations with the world, however mechanical and common-place it may seem. As a speaker, Mr. Milnes fully bears out this suspicion of habitual indolence. Whether the defect be within or external, whether it be want of earnestness or want of self-training, the effect is the same. He never exercises half the influence he desires to have, or a tithe of what he is capable of. The word slovenly would be scarcely too strong as applied to some of his speeches. His voice is thick and monotonous, only because he will not take the trouble to modulate it; his action is either ungainly or ungraceful, when it is not wholly nugatory, because he will not study the graces of personal delivery. The best proof of his short-comings in these respects is, that in spite of his deficiencies and wilful negligence of the little arts which are due, as a matter of courtesy even, to an audience, he sometimes produces, by detached portions of his speeches, powerful effects.

Of Mr. Milnes' productions as a poet we could speak at length, were this a fitting place, and should not fear having to use terms of qualified praise, still less of dispraise. Some of them have already been noticed in this periodical. They abound in beauties of the highest order. Mr. Milnes *is* a poet. That is the best and truest criticism we can give.

As a public man, Mr. Milnes may yet do much more than he has done. He has not fulfilled his mission. His talents were not given him to be frittered away, or to be allowed to rust in inglorious idleness. These are not times when such men as he can be dispensed with. The reign of the placeman will not last forever. More powerful and comprehensive minds are wanted to grapple with the difficulties and dangers which the future already shadows forth. Mr. Milnes will have to bear his share of the general burden. As yet, he has not fulfilled his early promise. But there is still time.

James Robinson Planché (poem date 1863)

SOURCE: "A Literary Squabble," in *A Century of Humorous Verse, 1850-1950*, edited by Roger Lancelyn Green, J. M. Dent & Sons Ltd., 1959, pp. 3-4.

[*In the following poem, composed in 1863, Planché makes a humorous commentary on Milnes' adoption of the name Lord Houghton.*]

A Literary Squabble

The Alphabet rejoiced to hear
That Monckton Milnes was made a Peer;
For in this present world of letters
But few, if any, are his betters:
So an address by acclamation,
They voted of congratulation,
And H, O, U, G, T, and N,
Were chosen the address to pen;
Possessing each an interest vital
In the new Peer's baronial title.
'Twas done in language terse and telling,
Perfect in grammar and in spelling:
But when 'twas read aloud, oh, mercy!
There sprang up such a controversy
About the true pronunciation
Of said baronial appellation.
The vowels O and U averred
They were entitled to be *heard*;
The consonants denied their claim,
Insisting that they *mute* became.
Johnson and Walker were applied to,
Sheridan, Bailey, Webster, tried too;
But all in vain, for each picked out
A word that left the case in doubt.
O, looking round upon them all,
Cried, 'If it be correct to call,
T H R O U G H, *throo,*
H O U G H, must be *Hoo,*
Therefore there can be no dispute on
The question, we should say, "Lord
  *Hoo*ton." '
U brought 'bought,' 'fought,' and 'sought,'
  to show
He should be doubled and not O,
For sure if 'ought' was '*awt,*' then 'nought'
  on
Earth could the title be but '*Haw*ton,'
H, on the other hand, said he,
In 'cough' and 'trough,' stood next to G,
And like an F was thus looked soft on,
Which made him think it should be '*Hof*ton.'
But G corrected H, and drew
Attention other cases to,
'Tough,' 'rough,' and 'chough' more than
  'enough'
To prove O U G H spent '*uff,*'
And growled out in a sort of gruff tone,

They must pronounce the title '*Huff*ton.'
N said emphatically 'No!'
There is D O U G H '*doh,*'
And *though* (look here again) that stuff
At sea, for fun, they nicknamed 'duff,'
They should propose they took a vote on
The question, 'Should it not be *Hot*on?'
Besides in French 'twould have such force,
A lord was of 'Haut ton,' of course.
Higher and higher contention rose,
From words they almost came to blows,
Till T, as yet who hadn't spoke,
And dearly loved a little joke,
Put in his word and said 'Look there!
"Plough" in this *row* must have its *share.*'
At this atrocious pun each page
Of Johnson whiter turned with rage,
Bailey looked desperately cut up,
And Sheridan completely shut up,
Webster, who is no idle talker,
Made a sign indicating 'Walker'!
While Walker, who had been used badly,
Just shook his dirty dog's ears sadly.
But as we find in prose or rhyme
A joke made happily in time,
However poor, will often tend
The hottest argument to end,
And smother anger in a laugh,
So T succeeded with his chaff
(Containing, as it did, some wheat)
In calming this fierce verbal heat.
Authorities were all conflicting,
And T there was no contradicting;
P L O U G H was *plow,*
Even 'enough' was called '*enow,*'
And no one who preferred 'enough'
Would dream of saying 'Speed the Pluff!'
So they considered it more wise
With T to make a compromise,
And leave no loop to hang a doubt on
By giving three cheers for 'Lord {Hough
  How} ton!'

Richard Monckton Milnes (essay date 1876)

SOURCE: Preface to *The Poetical Works of (Richard Monckton Milnes) Lord Houghton*, Vol. I, John Murray, 1876, pp. v-xiv.

[*In the following preface to his collected poems, Milnes comments on the geographical, intellectual, and personal sources of his poetry.*]

The Grecian poems have their date in that period of life which, in a cultivated Englishman, is almost universally touched and coloured by the studies and memories of the classic world; and the scenes and personages they commemorate are, as it were, the most natural subjects of his poetic thought and illustration. They were accompanied, as first given to the public, with a considerable amount of prose narration and some antiquarian research; but the country has since then been so thoroughly explored by travellers and archæologists, that I am glad to avoid what would be a profitless repetition. There were, too, at that time, earnest expectations of a regenerated Greece, to which not only the visionary poet, but the sober politician must now look back with disappointment; and the agreeable associations of a glorious ideal past, with an approximate interesting future, may be said to have passed away. Greece may, indeed must, have its part in the important political changes that overhang the east of Europe, but there will be never again an untoward battle of Navarino, or a Poet-hero of Missolonghi.

The majority of the Italian poems were inspired by a long residence in Venice, the delightful city whose special historical interests may perhaps be weakened by that regeneration of Italy, which I am thankful to have lived to witness; and whose "ruins without antiquity," as described by a cynical German, may lose something of their picturesqueness in a revival of material prosperity. My experience belongs to the period when the traveller only saw in the sad beauties of the present the monuments of a past magnificence of civic and artistic life. I have purposely omitted some Roman poems, published in previous editions, not in disregard of the thoughts and feelings they might record, but because they seemed to invest a transitory state of mind with more meaning than it deserved. The personal inclinations of the moment are no fit themes for verse.

It is otherwise with the poems on Oriental subjects. There the Western writer can only be the interpreter of thoughts and feelings historically alien to his own civilisation, and to which his subjective relation can be but imperfect and accidental. The translation, indeed, may exhibit as wide a variety of excellence and worth as an original production; its merit may range from the shadowy infidelity of Moore's "Lalla Rookh," to the truth and power of Goethe's "Westöestliche Divan;" but no skill or ingenuity can impart to it the full satisfaction of the poetry of Western life. In the East unconscious passion, undoubted duty, unchallenged faith, complete the history of humanity;—there the reality of objects has remained unquestioned, and mankind is, as it were, a portion of eternal nature, with but higher faculties and a larger destiny. There have, indeed, been mystics in the East, asserting the right and power of spiritual intuition above the restriction of positive ordinance; but the motive forces of that world have ever been Facts, and not Ideas, thus accounting for the absence of, and even animosity to, the forms of Art, and the habitual confusion between the notions of truth and power.

In my attempt to delineate the great theistic religion which Christianity so long persisted in confounding with Paganism, and which Roman Catholic dogmatists have lately defined as the most extensive Protestant heresy, I was perhaps somewhat in advance of the present state of opinion, both with regard to the genius of the faith and the character of the Prophet. There is not perhaps much merit in the recognition of Mohammed as other than an impostor or fanatic, for Mr. Carlyle's Lectures on Hero-Worship had made that vulgar estimate no longer possible; but it is to the more elaborate work of such writers as Sprenger and Muir that we must look for the investigation of that devious path which led the simple positive reformer and worshipper of the Unseen into those mystic regions where reality compromises with imagination, and where the insincerity of the Seer towards himself impels him irresistibly into untruth to others. In my poem on Mohammedism I have adhered with scrupulous fidelity to that wonderful book which is read at first with difficulty, but afterwards with reverence, and which presents with vivid power what is now the life-belief of two hundred millions of men, and substantially at this time the only progressive religion upon earth.

I have also felt the embarrassment of writing with apparent knowledge of the inner habits of Eastern peoples. Travellers see so small a portion even of the surface, and are not only so ignorant of what lies below it, but have so misapprehended and falsified even the external relations of social existence in those countries, that anyone may be almost afraid to conjecture where so many have been so grossly deceived.

Yet I believe that I have given true delineations of the two inviolate sanctuaries of family and faith, the one, including all we call Home, and the other what we mean at once by Church and Society; and though alien fashions have now invaded the Hareem, and booted infidels parade about the Mosque, it may be well that the old sense of these institutions should not be forgotten. The strange re-appearance in the distant West of the Prophet-rule, accompanied by the revival of that primæval form of marriage with which we are familiarised from our childhood by the patriarchal traditions that form so large a part of Protestant teaching, but which we believed to have been obliterated in that "Orbis Romanus" of law and language to which we and our cognate peoples belong, reminds us that no lapses of time or intervals of space can destroy the old affinities of mankind, or prevent the birth of analogous institutions under certain similar conditions of nature and mind.

The **"Poems of Sentiment and Reflection"** are mainly the product of that lyrical faculty of early years which, in its spontaneous effluence, apart from external circumstance and even from intellectual qualification, has been, and ever will be, one of the most interesting and at the same time, inexplicable, of mental phenomena. It has occurred to me in my literary pursuits to have been especially impressed with this form of genius in a striking contrast—in the poet Keats, where the power, though prominently instinctive, was soon fostered by sympathetic culture and genial associations, and in the weaver-boy of Glasgow, David Grey, where it rose among the harshest and commonest surroundings, which would have rendered the acquisition of ordinary literature difficult, and its finer development apparently impossible. But the connection of the human imagination with the assonance of words lies deeper than psychology can penetrate, and thus it is that the rudest efforts often impress the producer with a sense of wonder and delight that partakes of the sense of inspiration. Let no one deal harshly with the rhymester, in whom there is any faculty beyond mere imitation, but let him be told to read and learn till he finds that he is only one among many, and that his gift, small or great, is not the especial miracle he may justly at first believe it to be. For it is in truth the continuance and sustenance of the poetic faculty, which is the test of its magnitude: when it grows with a man's growth in active life, when it is not checked or smothered by the cares of ordinary existence or by the successes or failures of a career, when it derives force and variety from the experiences of society and the internal history of the individual mind, then, and then only, can it be surely estimated as part of that marvellous manifestation of Art and Nature, the Poetry of the world.

On the other hand, it is equally true that, while the more subtle imaginations and noblest cadences often fail to obtain recognition and audience till the heart of the poet fails within him, and delay seems the forerunner of oblivion, not only have single poems, rising out of the very dearth and desert of imagination, given delight to mankind and lasting honour to names otherwise unknown—but casual phrases that touch the unconscious fancy, and refrains that are no more than accidental melodies struck out by the finger on an instrument, have captured the public ear and become parts of the musical language of a people. It is a good example of this odd felicity that the burthen of **"Beating of my own Heart,"** written by me in a moonlight drive to visit Miss Edgeworth, in 1830, and thought unworthy of print by myself and others, should, within ten years after, have been heard by a traveller parodied in a chorus of slaves singing in the cotton-fields of Western America.

I have sometimes thought that I should like to review my own poems, as I have done those of others, conscious that the distances of time and the alterations of temperament qualify me to do so with perfect impartiality: but if I do not do this, I think I can judge them, so far as to see that, whatever little hold they may

have taken on their time, is owing to their sincerity of thought and simplicity of expression.

The more purely sentimental are the earliest, and a fantastic gloom is permitted to that period of life, as tears to childhood, which, in later years, would imply weakness or incapacity. Thus, such poems as **"The Flight of Youth," "The Weary Soul," "The Palsy of the Heart,"** are but the expression of the curious introspection with which vigour and vitality meet the coming possibilities of a world of change and decay, and in which fancy often misrepresents the past as much as it misapprehends the future. They can only be acceptable to certain casual moods and temperaments, while **"The Long-ago," "The Men of Old," "The Worth of Hours," "Happiness," "Domestic Fame," "Never Return," "Requiescat in Pace,"** and **"Strangers Yet,"** standing on a firm, ethical basis, and aiming at an apt and melodious representation of conditions of thought and emotion which men do not willingly surrender or forget, may hope to interest a wide circle of humanity. . . .

Saintsbury on Milnes's talents:

[Richard Monckton Milnes] was of the golden age of Trinity during this century, the age of Tennyson, and throughout life he had an amiable fancy for making the acquaintance of everybody who made any name in literature, and of many who made none. A practical and active politician, and a constant figure in society, he was also a very considerable man of letters. His critical work (principally but not wholly collected in **Monographs**) is not great in bulk but is exceedingly good, both in substance and in style. His verse, on the other hand, which was chiefly the produce of the years before he came to middle life, is a little slight, and perhaps appears slighter than it really is. Few poets have ever been more successful with songs for music: the **"Brookside"** (commonly called from its refrain, "The beating of my own heart"), the famous and really fine **"Strangers Yet,"** are the best known, but there are many others. Lord Houghton undoubtedly had no strong vein of poetry. But it was always an entire mistake to represent him as either a fribble or a sentimentalist, while with more inducements to write he would probably have been one of the very best critics of his age.

George Saintsbury, in A History of Nineteenth Century Literature (1780-1895), *Macmillan and Co., 1896.*

T. Wemyss Reid (essay date 1890)

SOURCE: "Literary and Personal Characteristics," in *The Life, Letters, and Friendships of Richard Monckton Milnes, First Lord Houghton*, Vol. II, by T. Wemyss Reid, Cassell & Company, Limited, 1890, pp. 437-67.

[In the following excerpt, Reid recounts Milnes' publications of poetry and surveys the contemporary criticism of these works.]

To the present generation the poetry of Lord Houghton is practically known only in connection with one or two brief pieces, of unimpeachable grace and melody, which have attained a popularity that is literally worldwide. His more important works, as well as many shorter poems that are in every way equal in merit to those that have secured a lasting popularity, are but little known to the readers of to-day. The changes of fashion, which are as marked in literature as in dress, account in part for a fact of which no one was more conscious than Lord Houghton himself. In part, too, we may attribute it to the undisputed pre-eminence in the world of poetry of the great singer who had been Houghton's friend at college, and whose rapid growth in power and fame none had watched with greater pleasure than he had done. Nowadays it may seem strange, almost unintelligible to the ordinary reader, that there was a time when Monckton Miles was looked upon as the destined successor to the premiership in English poetry. I have mentioned how, at a breakfast at Rogers's, Landor stoutly maintained that he was the greatest poet then living and writing in England; and there were many who shared Landor's opinion. No such estimate of himself was ever made by Milnes, nor will it be set forth here; but this, at least, is certain, that if an opinion which exalted him to such a pinnacle was exaggerated, the comparative neglect into which his poetry has of late years fallen is entirely undeserved. A great singer he may not have been; a sweet singer with a charm of his own he undoubtedly was; nor did his charm consist alone in the melody of which he was a master. In many of his poems real poetic thought is linked with musical words; whilst in everything that he wrote, whether in verse or in prose, one may discern the brightest characteristics of the man himself—the catholicity of his spirit; the tenderness of his sympathy with weakness, suffering, mortal frailty in all its forms; the ardour of his faith in something that should break down the artificial barriers by which classes are divided, and bring into the lives of all a measure of that light and happiness which he relished so highly for himself. Like all other men who write much, he was unequal in his work; and, at times, in his poetry the tricks of conventionalism, alike in substance and in form, were plainly to be seen. But there were other times when it was clear that the song sprang from the singer's heart, and that he had poured forth in it the real inspiration of a soul which could rise above the sordid commonplaces of life.

One of his friends used to tell in later years how, chancing to sit beside Houghton in a company of which Tennyson happened to be a member, the former said, pointing to the Poet-Laureate, "A great deal of what he has done will *live;*" and then added, half, as it were, to himself, "and some things that I have done should live too." It was no overweening estimate of his own merit. Some of the verses he has added to English literature will not easily lose their place in it. The reader in this story of his life has seen Monckton Milnes chiefly as the busy man of society, the ambitious politician in his younger days, the leisured literary expert of his maturity, the kindest of friends both in youth and in age—and perhaps this was all that the later generation saw in him. But nothing could be more unjust than to forget that—at any rate, until he reached middle life—he held a high place in the estimation of his contemporaries as a poet, and that great hopes were cherished for his future by a wide circle of men and women throughout Europe. The season of his activity in the production of poetry was comparatively brief. He first made his appearance before the public, with his *Memorials of a Tour in Greece,* in 1834; and it was just ten years later, in 1844, that he published *Palm Leaves*. In these ten years he brought forth a remarkable quantity of verse; and though, as I have said, his productions were of unequal merit, it may be confidently affirmed that in the work of these ten years there was much that no lover of English poetry would willingly let die. *The Memorials of a Tour in Greece* were followed in 1838 by *The Memorials of a Residence on the Continent, and Historical Poems,* and *The Poems of Many Years,* printed in the first instance for private circulation only. In 1840 appeared another volume of poetry collected from the magazines, to which he was then a regular contributor, and including his *Poetry for the People*; whilst four years later appeared his *Poems: Legendary and Historical,* which included several pieces published in former volumes, and his little volume of *Palm Leaves*. After that date, which coincides with the commencement of his serious political career, he wrote but little poetry, though many of the pieces which subsequently appeared from his pen had all the charm that belonged to his work in his earlier days. He had always maintained that to write poetry was an admirable preparation for the writing of prose; and after 1844 it was in prose, rather than in verse, that he gave his thoughts to the world. He had already, in his remarkable *One Tract More,* published in 1841, given proof of the fact that he was the master of an admirable style. He was even then writing regularly in the *Quarterly* and *Edinburgh* reviews, and was doing much to create the taste of that generation for the writings of those younger men upon whom the elder reviewers had frowned persistently. Let it always be remembered to his credit that he was one of the first to tender, through the pages of a great review, the full acknowledgment of the genius of Tennyson. In later years it was his happy lot to make another great poet—Algernon Swinburne—similarly known to the outer world; and again and again, in the course of those critical writings of his, he gave proof of the keenness of his perception where genius was concerned, and of the absolute freedom from jealousy which characterised his critical utterances when he was helping to introduce a new writer to the world of letters.

One Tract More was followed in 1842 by his pamphlet entitled *Thoughts on Purity of Election.* Two or three years after that time he devoted himself with great thoroughness to a more serious task, the writing of that *Life of Keats* which still maintains its place as a standard biography. This appeared in 1848, and in 1849 came the pamphlet on *The Events of 1848,* to which I have referred at length elsewhere. There was a long interval after this, during which his literary labours were almost wholly anonymous, though they comprised many pieces of work of rare merit, such as the short poem on **"Scutari"** published in the *Times,* the lines on Thackeray which appeared after the death of the great novelist in the *Cornhill Magazine,* the sympathetic notice of David Gray prefixed to his poem "The Luggie," and many articles on the chief books of the time in the *Edinburgh* and *Quarterly* reviews. In 1866 a volume of selections from his poetry appeared, and this revived for a time the poetic fame of his earlier years. Seven years later came the best of his prose works, his volume of **Monographs,** a work which in the fulness of its knowledge, derived almost entirely from personal experiences, in the soundness of its critical judgment, and in the charm of its style, has an excellence that is almost unique. In 1876 the collected edition of his poems appeared, and enjoyed a considerable popularity. In addition to his writings in the two great quarterlies, he contributed largely to the *Fortnightly Review,* under the editorship of Mr. Morley, and to the *Pall Mall Gazette,* under that of Mr. Greenwood, whilst in later years he took a warm interest in the *Academy,* and was a not infrequent writer in its pages. One cannot but regret that he never set himself to a task for which he was so well fitted, the writing of a book in which we should have had something like a complete picture of the society of his own time, a picture for which the **Monographs** might well have been regarded as preparatory sketches. Such a work from such a pen would have had an altogether exceptional interest and value; but that inability to make any prolonged or continuous effort from which he suffered in his later days stayed his hand, and although more than once he seriously contemplated a book of this kind, his intentions remained unfulfilled, and not even a fragment of the promised memoirs was discovered after his death. But even as it is, the volume of his literary labours was large, and the substance of undoubted merit.

It is hardly the part of a biographer to assume the critic, and it will perhaps be more to the purpose if I record here rather the judgment of the best critics of his own day upon his writings than attempt to pass any verdict of my own. So far back as 1838 the *Quarterly Review* devoted a long article to the poems

of Trench and Milnes, in which full justice was done to the merits of the latter, though the writer was not blind to the desultoriness of his mind, and concluded his review by expressing the earnest hope that he would yet give his talents fair play by devoting himself of set purpose to some serious labour. In the same year another *Quarterly* reviewer rebuked him for having allowed himself to be led astray by the new lights of the hour:

> We are quite sure [said this critic, who accurately represented the standard of critical judgment in his time] that Monckton Milnes will hereafter obey one good precept in an otherwise doubtful Decalogue,
>
> "Thou shalt believe in Milton, Dryden, Pope,"
>
> and regret few sins of his youth more bitterly than the homage he has now rendered at the fantastic shrines of such baby-idols as Mr. John Keats and Mr. Alfred Tennyson.

Perhaps, after quoting this remarkable passage, I am hardly doing a service to the subject of my memoir when I say that the critic announced, in conclusion, that "in spite of all their weaknesses and affectations, Milnes's poems contain better English verses than have as yet been produced to the public by any living writer not on the wrong side of the Mezzo Cammin."

Some years later, in 1843, he was again the subject of serious attention from the critics.

> Milnes [said a writer in one of the leading magazines] is a true poet for the people, though not of them. He is a scholar, a gentleman, and a Tory of the Coleridgian school. An old *Quarterly* reviewer, in a notice of his poetry, speaks of him as "a leading pupil of that school, which embraced some of the most intelligent politicians and best instructed of the nobility of England. . . . We may add, though it may be considered somewhat irrelevant, that Milnes is besides a poet for the scholar. He has a fine antique imagination of the past, and reverence for the memorials and monuments of national and personal greatness, that cannot fail to awaken the sympathies of the retired student, who knows nothing of political distinctions, but worships all of the remnants of every faded glory. Our poet has a fine chivalry of nature that by no means unfits him for the advocacy of the rights of his fellows, yet which adds an additional grace to the manliness of his thoughts and style, rendering him an attractive author to those who might be repulsed by the homeliness of one class of his productions.

It was in the same year that Christopher North, in *Blackwood,* devoted a pleasant article to his verse, quoting as worthy of special commendation that poem on **"The Flight of Youth"** which Milnes himself always regarded as his best.

We read these lines [said Christopher] without fearing to let all their pathos fall upon our spirits, for into its depths, should that pathos sink, it will find there a repose it cannot disturb, or a trouble it cannot allay. The truths they tell have been so long familiar there, that we seem to hear but our own voice again, giving utterance to thoughts that for many years have lain silent, but alive, in their cells, like slumberers awakened at midnight by solemn music, lifting up their heads for a while to listen, and then laying them down to relapse into the same dreams that had possessed their sleep. But ye who are still young, yet have begun to experience how sad it is and mournful exceedingly to regret, perhaps to weep over, the passing away of the past, because that something *was* that never more *may be,* ponder ye on the strain, and lay the moral, the religious lesson, it teaches within your hearts. So may the sadness sanctify, and the spirits that God sends to minister unto us children of the dust find you willing to be comforted, when Youth has left you heedless if to despair—for, angel though he seemed, he is not of Heaven; but of Heaven are they, and therefore immortal."

After an exordium such as this, from one who was by no means the kindliest of critics, it is only fair that the reader should have the opportunity of judging Milnes's more serious verse for himself, and I therefore quote his lines on **"The Flight of Youth"** as being those which not only received the unstinted commendation of the ablest men among his contemporaries, but which, as I have said, seemed in his own opinion to be the best that he had written.

THE FLIGHT OF YOUTH.

No, though all the winds that lie
In the circle of the sky
Trace him out, and pray and moan,
Each in its most plaintive tone,—
No, though Earth be split with sighs,
And all the Kings that reign
Over Nature's mysteries
Be our faithfullest allies,—
All—all is vain:
They may follow on his track,
But he never will come back—
Never again!

Youth is gone away,
Cruel, cruel youth,
Full of gentleness and ruth
Did we think him all his stay;
How had he the heart to wreak
Such a woe on us so weak,
He that was so tender-meek?

How could he be made to learn
To find pleasure in our pain?
Could he leave us, to return
Never again!

Bow your heads very low,
Solemn-measured be your paces,
Gathered up in grief your faces,
Sing sad music as ye go;
In disordered handfuls strew
Strips of cypress, sprigs of rue;
In your hands be borne the bloom,
Whose long petals once and only
Look from their pale-leavèd tomb
In the midnight lonely;
Let the nightshade's beaded coral
Fall in melancholy moral
Your wan brows around,
While in very scorn ye fling
The amaranth upon the ground
As an unbelievèd thing;
What care we for its fair tale
Of beauties that can never fail,
Glories that can never wane?
No such blooms are on the track
He has past, who will come back
Never again!

Alas! we know not how he went,
We knew not he was going,
For had our tears once found a vent,
We' had stayed him with their flowing.
It was as an earthquake, when
We awoke and found him gone,
We were miserable men,
We were hopeless, every one!
Yes, he must have gone away
In his guise of every day,
In his common dress, the same
Perfect face and perfect frame;
For in feature, for in limb,
Who could be compared to him?
Firm his step, as one who knows
He is free, where'er he goes,
And withal as light of spring
As the arrow from the string;
His impassioned eye had got
Fire which the sun has not;
Silk to feel, and gold to see,
Fell his tresses full and free,
Like the morning mists that glide
Soft adown the mountain's side;
Most delicious 'twas to hear
When his voice was trilling clear
As a silver-hearted bell,
Or to follow its low swell,
When, as dreamy winds that stray
Fainting 'mid Æolian chords,
Inner music seemed to play

Symphony to all his words;
In his hand was poised a spear,
Deftly poised, as to appear
Resting of its proper will,—
Thus a merry hunter still,
And engarlanded with bay,
Must our Youth have gone away,
Though we half remember now,
He had borne some little while
Something mournful in his smile—
Something serious on his brow:
Gentle Heart, perhaps he knew
The cruel deed he was about to do!

Now, between us all and Him
There are rising mountains dim,
Forests of uncounted trees,
Spaces of unmeasured seas:
Think with Him how gay of yore
We made sunshine out of shade,—
Think with Him how light we bore
All the burden sorrow laid;
All went happily about Him,—
How shall we toil on without Him?
How without his cheering eye
Constant strength embreathing ever?
How without Him standing by
Aiding every hard endeavour?
For when faintness or disease
Had usurped upon our knees,
If he deigned our lips to kiss
With those living lips of his,
We were lightened of our pain,
We were up and hale again:—
Now, without one blessing glance
From his rose-lit countenance,
We shall die, deserted men,—
And not see him, even then!

We are cold, very cold,—
All our blood is drying old,
And a terrible heart-dearth
Reigns for us in heaven and earth:
Forth we stretch our chilly fingers
In poor effort to attain
Tepid embers, where still lingers
Some preserving warmth, in vain.
Oh! if Love, the Sister dear
Of Youth that we have lost,
Come not in swift pity here,
Come not, with a host
Of Affections, strong and kind,
To hold up our sinking mind,
If She will not, of her grace,
Take her Brother's holy place,
And be to us, at least, a part
Of what he was, in Life and Heart,
The faintness that is on our breath
Can have no other end but Death.

A criticism upon some of his later poems appeared in the *Quarterly Review* from the pen of his friend Mr. W. D. Christie. In this criticism Milnes was compared favourably with any of the young writers of his day. The melody of his verse, we are told, was perfect, "his language chaste, correct, and nervous. Thought, feeling, and fancy abound in his poems; and there are not a few, especially in the earlier volumes, which prove him capable of the highest efforts of 'shaping imagination.'"

I have given these brief extracts from contemporary criticism in order to show how Milnes struck the men of his own day at the time when he was bringing forth his poetry. In later years, when a generation had arisen which knew him well as a social favourite, but hardly knew him at all as a poet, there were still those who maintained the accuracy of the judgment they had pronounced many years before. Among these was Mr. Christie, who, writing in *Macmillan's Magazine,* said:—

> If Richard Monckton Milnes had not been a man of the world, and a busy politician, and if he had been able to concentrate his energies on poetry, and gird himself to the building up of some great poem, none who know what poetry he has written can doubt that it was in him to be a great poet; and none who know his *Life of Keats,* or any of his many pamphlets and articles in reviews and magazines, will deny that he presents another example of what he himself has lately proclaimed and supported by much good proof, that a good poet makes himself a good prose writer.

A still later critic, [in The *World,* August 22nd, 1883.] after quoting Landor's estimate of Milnes, "the greatest poet now living in England," added some words of genuine critical insight:—

> Startling as this opinion may sound now, there would have seemed nothing surprising in it when it was originally uttered. There were many competent critics who held that you were appreciably Tennyson's superior in the chosen walk of his genius; nor is it inconceivable that if your destiny had been different, you would have done poetic work of imperishable calibre. As it is, you have written much which will always have a place in every anthology of English verse. The originality of your genius declared itself in the extreme freshness, the keen insight, and the vivid truth of your productions. You were as anxious to show men Nature, and as successful in showing it, as was Wordsworth himself. The form taken by your interpretation of the Universal Mother was all your own. When it is recollected that the age in which you accomplished this was wedded to literary artificiality, that it was the epoch of false sentiment, tawdry rhetoric, and spurious imagery, it must be allowed to constitute a considerable achievement. Much indeed that you wrote does not rise above the level of the best album

epigraphs of the period; while many of your most exquisite compositions have been set to music, and are cheapened by their associations with importunate piano strummings. But when all deductions on these grounds have been made, there is yet enough in your public writings to vindicate your claim to a respectable niche in the shrine of the Muses. You were the poet of society; you did not, indeed, write in the accepted sense of the term "society verses," but every verse which came from your pen was primarily intended for polite minds. A little more zeal and enthusiasm, a little more of that fire which would have burned less fitfully in a different social atmosphere, would have saved you from that tendency to desultoriness and trifling which was ever your besetting sin. The true charm of your poems is that they furnish those who read them carefully with something like a philosophy of existence; but the philosophy is only partially revealed. You give us glimpses of every kind of life and character, but they are glimpses only. When you touch a deep chord, you suddenly withdraw your hand as if you had been guilty of some breach of good taste. There is something tantalising in the way in which you play with profound problems, and dally with dark enigmas. What is probably your most familiar poem, **"Strangers Yet,"** is also your most characteristic, and in it I read as follows:—

"Oh, the bitter thought to scan
All the loneliness of man!
Nature, by magnetic laws,
Circle unto circle draws;
But they only touch when met,
Never mingle—strangers yet."

To some these lines may seem commonplace because of their familiarity. As a matter of fact there is nothing commonplace about them. They belong to an extremely high order of poetic thought and feeling; but they bear the impress of a hand which, qualified as it is to lift the curtain on the mysteries and contradictions of life, will not do so because it would be a work of some trouble.

When Mr. Forster wrote to a friend describing his first meeting with Milnes, he spoke of him as a man "with some small remnant of poetry left in his eyes, and nowhere else;" but in later years, when Forster knew his friend better, he would not have repeated that superficial judgment, the first which naturally occurred to the man who met the poet for the first time, and who judged from the outward side of things only. It is true that as the years passed, and the constant strain of social life, mingled with those demands of duty and ambition which he never forgot, pressed upon Milnes, the poetic side of his nature was driven from the surface, showing itself outwardly at all events "only in his eyes"; but, as to the last day of his life he

continued to write verse, so to the end, deep down in his soul, was a well of pure poetic thought. Its existence, unsuspected by the multitude, hidden with care from ordinary society, was known to those who knew him best, and to the last in their eyes he was not merely the man who had written poetry, but the poet who could still judge the world around him from a different and a higher standpoint than that of his ordinary fellow-creatures. But to what purpose do we dwell here upon what might have been in the case of a man like Lord Houghton? Of what avail are regrets for that which never came to pass? Doubtless these questions occur to the mind of the reader; but no picture of Milnes's life and character would be complete which did not show how, as in his college days his old friend Stafford O'Brien had prophesied would be the case, he came "near something very glorious, though he never reached it." . . .

Lafcadio Hearn (essay date 1915)

SOURCE: "A Poem by Lord Houghton," in *Interpretations of Literature*, Vol. I, by Lafcadio Hearn, edited by John Erskine, Dodd, Mead and Company, 1915, pp. 300-03.

[*In the following essay, Hearn analyzes Milnes's poem "Strangers Yet," calling it his best and one of the few possessing "that rare quality which appeals to the universal human experience."*]

Among many English noblemen who have figured in Victorian literature with more or less credit to themselves, there was perhaps nobody who could write more hauntingly at times than Lord Houghton. He did not write a great deal, but a considerable proportion of the few pieces which he did write have found their way into anthologies, and are likely to stay there. I shall quote and comment upon only one of these, which I think to be the best—not, perhaps, as mere verse, but as a bit of emotional thinking. The subject is a curious one, a subject which has driven some men almost mad. It was this subject which especially tormented the matchless French story-teller, Guy de Maupassant, shortly before he lost his reason; and he wrote a terrible essay about it. Very young men never think of the matter at all, but few men of intelligence reach middle life without having thought about it. I mean this fact,—that no one human being can ever really understand another human being. We think we know a great deal about our friends, or about our enemies—at least we think so while we are young. But later on we discover that there are depths or abysses in every human character, which we can not know anything about. A character is really like the sea. ·When we look at the sea we observe only the surface,—the changes of colour, the motion of waves and the foam. When we look at our friends it is really much the same; we can see the surface only, the mood of the moment, the aspect of kindness or gratitude or sympathy passing over that other life as waves or colours play over the surface of the water. But the profundities are beyond our vision. Really the father does not know his child, nor the husband his wife, nor the wife her husband. There is always a something hidden in the frankest child which the most loving mother can not discern. Naturally it must be so, because every individual has something of the infinite within him; because also the feelings and tendencies of millions and millions of past lives are stored up in every present life. When you come to think about it, either from the scientific point of view or from the purely metaphysical point of view, you will perceive that it could not be otherwise. But the first time that a man learns this fact, it comes like a great shock to him. It is really a very terrible thing, and requires a little philosophical coolness to consider it. Here is what Lord Houghton said about it:

STRANGERS YET

Strangers yet!
After years of life together,
After fair and stormy weather,
After travel in far lands,
After touch of wedded hands,—
Why thus joined? Why ever met,
If they must be strangers yet?

Strangers yet!
After childhood's winning ways,
After care and blame and praise,
Counsel asked and wisdom given,
After mutual prayers to Heaven,
Child and parent scarce regret
When they part—are strangers yet!

Strangers yet!
After strife for common ends—
After title of "old friends,"
After passions fierce and tender,
After cheerful self-surrender,
Hearts may beat and eyes be met
And the souls be strangers yet.

Strangers yet!
Oh! the bitter thought to scan
All the loneliness of man!
Nature, by magnetic laws,
Circle unto circle draws,
But they only touch when met—
Never mingle—strangers yet!

The comparison of each life to a complete circle or sphere, which may touch another sphere but never penetrate it, is not new, but it is used here with great force. This problem is the same thing to which of later years French psychologists have been giving so much attention under the title of Multiple Personality. It is not that there is really a hidden man within the man; it is that every personality is extraordinarily complex and that this complexity is perpetually changing, so that the individual is not really the same at all times and places in his relation to other individuals. Viewed scientifically, the fact seems to be a natural result of evolution, but that does not make it less wonderful, nor, in a certain sense, less awful.

This is the best poem that Lord Houghton ever wrote in his long life, and he wrote a great deal of fairly good poetry. But he wrote nothing else quite so good as this; it has that rare quality which appeals to universal human experience. I often fancy that the condition of his own life must have been particularly likely to inspire him with reflections upon this subject. He lived really a double existence; but the principal part of his life was given—like that of another remarkable English nobleman, the younger Lord Lytton—to diplomacy, an occupation which certainly keeps minds out of sympathy with each other. He was born in 1809, and died in 1885. After leaving the university he almost immediately entered public life, became within a few years a member of Parliament, and remained a prominent figure in politics for more than a generation. He was known only as Richard Monckton Milnes before he was raised to the peerage. You would scarcely suppose that such a man could have found time to devote to poetry and song. But he was really double-natured. He had a great vein of sentiment, and such a love of literature that he sought out and made friends with almost every literary person of the time. At Cambridge he had been the friend of Tennyson and Hallam and other brilliant men, but these acquaintances among the aristocracy of literature did not have the effect of making him at all exclusive. Even while a distinguished statesman, he would go out of his way to find some poor student poet and offer his friendship and assistance. Thus he became the helper of many struggling geniuses, and was looked up to by hundreds of young men with gratitude and esteem. However, once outside of the literary circle, the man was hard and cold as steel, keen as the edge of a sword. Had it been otherwise he could not have fulfilled the double duties of his life. And yet perhaps it was owing to this very fact—that he had to be one person in his literary friendship and a totally different person in his diplomatic and political sphere of action—that he began to feel at last that weird lonesomeness which inspired his little poem **"Strangers Yet."**

J. R. MacGillivray (essay date 1949)

SOURCE: Introduction to *Keats: A Bibliography and Reference Guide with an Essay on Keats' Reputation*, University of Toronto Press, 1949, pp. l-liv.

[In the following excerpt, MacGillivray examines how Milnes sought to vindicate Keats' sullied reputation in his 1848 biography Life, Letters, and Literary Remains of John Keats.*]*

Milnes' book [*Life, Letters, and Literary Remains of John Keats*] was certainly not a biography of the first rank, but it would be difficult to name one that was better designed "for the purpose of vindicating the character and advancing the fame" of its subject. Falsehoods and half-truths about Keats had been in circulation for thirty years, some inspired by enemies, others by well-meaning friends, and all accepted indiscriminately by the reading public. In the Preface (pp. xvi-xvii) the biographer gives an account of his first and general problem.

> I had else to consider what procedure was most likely to raise the character of Keats in the estimation of those most capable of judging it. I saw how grievously he was misapprehended even by many who wished to see in him only what was best. I perceived that many, who heartily admired his poetry, looked on it as the production of a wayward, erratic, genius, self-indulgent in conceits, disrespectful of the rules and limitations of Art, not only unlearned but careless of knowledge, not only exaggerated but despising proportion. I knew that his moral disposition was assumed to be weak, gluttonous of sensual excitement, querulous of severe judgment, fantastical in its tastes, and lackadaisical in its sentiments. He was all but universally believed to have been killed by a stupid, savage, article in a review, and to the compassion generated by his untoward fate he was held to owe a certain personal interest which his poetic reputation hardly justified.

So well had *Blackwood's* persuaded the predisposed of a generation to believe that "Johnny Keats" was an ignorant anarchist in literature and morals; so well had Shelley and others popularized the opposing myth of the crime of the *Quarterly* and the fading of the pale flower. Given these established misconceptions, the question of procedure was particularly important. There was no scarcity of biographical material, especially letters and unpublished reminiscence, but a too unrestrained use of them would offend Victorian propriety and would probably give a new lease of life to *Blackwood's* damaging accusation that Keats and his friends were not gentlemen. On the other hand, a carefully selective biography, with all the subject's most private thoughts and feelings suppressed or decently obscured by polite generalities, would fail both to satisfy the friendly and to win over the hostile. Milnes decided that in order to substitute a true picture for the false ones current he would have to produce much of the first-hand evidence in his possession, quoting letters at length, and introducing the trivialities

of reminiscence, even at the risk of a breach of decorum. He eventually went further. The book, he determined, would be largely the work of Keats and his friends, a "compilation" rather than a biography, and he would "act simply as editor of the Life which was, as it were, already written." Or as he explained his function at the beginning of the memoir which was afterwards published in numerous editions of the poems: "The Editor had little more to do than to arrange and connect the letters freely supplied to him by kinsmen and friends, and leave them to tell as sad, and, at the same time, as ennobling a tale of life as ever engaged the pen of poetic fiction."

Milnes' modesty may be commended but we need not believe that he had so little to do with the influential biography—or "compilation"—which appeared in 1848. To be sure, one does often get the impression that it is only an extensive collection of poems and letters, arranged chronologically, and loosely connected by the running comments of the editor-biographer. But to be distracted by the curious form may be to miss the good sense and shrewdness of the general design. A selection of the poems in order of composition is for the first time made to show Keats' extraordinary growth as an artist in the three or four years which separated the beginning and the end of his literary life. The large group of letters not only throws much additional light on the poems, but (again for the first time) reveals an eager, intelligent, and subtle mind, richly stored with a new-found wealth of experience from life and from books, keenly aware of the problems of poetry, gaining much from the society of his friends but finding his own way toward early and splendid maturity as a man and an artist. The letters which Milnes published destroyed forever what remained of the *Blackwood's* legend of the fatuous bard of Cockaigne. They showed, to use George Keats' words, that "John was . . . as much like the *Holy Ghost* as [like] *Johnny Keats*."[1] As for Shelley's legend, Milnes never missed a chance to illustrate Keats' courage, his good sense, his lack of concern, at least in 1818, about the campaign of vilification against him. In both cases novel truth was more readily acceptable because the reader was allowed to draw his own conclusions from a mass of plain evidence. The self-effacing editor was more persuasive than any biographer could be.

Less ingenuous, but mildly entertaining to the reader of a century later, is Milnes' apparent concern to suggest that if Keats was not quite a gentleman in the strict sense of the term he fell not far short, and his friends were eminently respectable people. Keats' maternal uncle who "had been an officer in Duncan's ship in the action off Camperdown," his parents' mere consideration of the possibility of sending their sons to Harrow, and his own early association with Mr. Felton Mathew, "a gentleman of high literary merit, now employed in the administration of the Poor Law," were all intended to shed some glory on the poet. Milnes' gracious patronage of the whole Keats circle was enough to guarantee its respectability. What a spacious sense of wealth and aristocratic leisure devoted to the arts is conveyed by the first sentence of the Preface: "It is now fifteen years ago that I met, at the villa of my distinguished friend Mr. Landor, on the beautiful hill-side of Fiesole, Mr. Charles Brown, a retired Russia-merchant, with whose name I was already familiar as the generous protector and devoted Friend of the Poet Keats." The "retired Russia-merchant" had actually returned unsuccessful and bankrupt from his adventure abroad at the age of twenty-four (several years before Keats knew him) and thereafter lived thriftily on a legacy from his brother.[2] This occasional tendency to improve on the facts reappears in Milnes' later memoir in preface to the poems, where we are told that Keats was born "in the upper rank of the middle-class," and the livery-stable is never mentioned. The explanation of these polite obfuscations is that it never seemed more important for a man to be a gentleman, in the hereditary and economic sense, than in the mid-years of the nineteenth century when new wealth advanced many new and questionable candidates for that honour. (Witness the anxieties of both Dickens and his characters on this score.) The decorum of the age also required the frequent suppression of names in the published letters and a very general reference to the love-affair. It is extraordinary, with all the information at his command, that Milnes did not know about Fanny Brawne, or rather that he believed that "the lady . . . [who] inspired Keats with the passion that only ceased with his existence" was Reynolds' wealthy Anglo-Indian cousin, the Charmian with "a rich eastern look." Yet even this misconception, in a way, served Milnes' purpose: it must have been gratifying to be able to indicate that Keats' love was returned by the grand-daughter and heiress of a nabob.

The *Life, Letters, and Literary Remains* was widely reviewed, often at considerable length, and with few exceptions favourably.[3] Milnes' social prestige, his array of evidence, his reasonableness, his elaborately courteous manner which did not fail him even when he was commenting on Keats' former detractors, all served to persuade, to gain goodwill, and to turn away wrath. Although Croker, Lockhart, and Wilson were still active, *Blackwood's* and the *Quarterly* ignored the book. In any event it was far too late to hope to rouse the old antagonism of the days of Gifford. Some traces of former political alignments in literary criticism may be observed in the comparative hostility of the conservative *Gentleman's Magazine* and the friendliness of the *Athenaeum,* the *Edinburgh Review,* and the *Westminster Review.* Hereafter political feeling ceases to influence criticism of Keats; in fact, the time had come when that literary veteran, Leigh Hunt, late of Horsemonger Lane Jail, for libelling his Prince, could be considered

as a not impossible candidate for the office of Poet Laureate.[4] His successful rival was one of the few who expressed a strong distaste for Milnes' work, in his angry lines *To——, After Reading a Life and Letters.* Tennyson's youthful delight in the newfound poetry of Keats is not open to question. His occasional and general commendations in later years ("there is something magic and of the innermost soul of poetry in almost everything he wrote") were sincere. But he was shocked in 1848, not so much by any revelations in the published letters of Keats' failure to conform to a strict Tennysonian ideal of reticence, but by the suggestion that a poet's private life should be exposed to throw light on his art. First it was Currie's *Burns,* then Milnes' *Keats,* and one day, if he were not careful, there might be a similar life of Tennyson.

> For now the Poet cannot die
> Nor leave his music as of old,
> But round him ere he scarce be cold
> Begins the scandal and the cry:
>
> "Proclaim the faults he would not show:
> Break lock and seal: betray the trust:
> Keep nothing sacred: 't is but just
> The many-headed beast should know."

Notes

[1] *The Poetical Works and Other Writings,* IV, p. 404; in a letter of April 20, 1825.

[2] *Letters,* p. xlix.

[3] For a much longer list than I have included, see J. P. Anderson's bibliography at the end of Rossetti's *Keats.*

[4] Edmund Blunden, *Leigh Hunt* (London, 1930), pp. 305-6.

James Pope-Hennessy (essay date 1949)

SOURCE: "1837-1840" and "1848," in *Monckton Milnes: The Years of Promise, 1809-1851,* Constable, 1949, pp. 98-120, 272-96.

[*In the following excerpt, Pope-Hennessy studies the contemporary critical response to Milnes' Grecian poems and his biography of Keats.*]

The discussion of Milnes' poetry by Samuel Rogers and Gladstone was no doubt caused by the simultaneous appearance of two volumes of his verse. These successors to the Grecian pieces of five years before were entitled *Memorials of a Residence on the Continent* and *Poems of Many Years.* Privately printed in

1838 for circulation amongst the poet's friends, they were published and put on sale later the same year. The twin volumes were well and prominently reviewed, praised for 'the equable tone of sound, unaffected sensibility which pervades them,' but declared to be out of keeping with the times. Quoting **"The Flight of Youth,"** with its melancholy little metre:

> Yes, he must have gone away,
> In his guise of every day,
> In his common dress, the same
> Perfect face and perfect frame
>
> . . . . .
>
> In your hands be borne the bloom
> Whose long petals once and only
> Look from their pale-leavéd tomb
> In the midnight lonely;
> Let the nightshade's beaded coral
> Fall in melancholy moral
> Your wan brows around,
> While in very scorn ye fling
> The amaranth upon the ground
> As an unbelievéd thing.

The Sun suggested that twenty years earlier these lines would have excited general attention—'but the present age has no great relish for pure, abstract poetry; it is essentially practical and utilitarian in its predilections. . . . Mr. Milnes . . . cannot hope to be extensively read.' The majority of Milnes' poems were probably too slight and too personal to become popular at that epoch, and there was in any case only a limited demand for poetry. Milnes noted a story of Murray the publisher speaking to a lady novelist of the moment: 'You think, ma'am, that the public don't like poetry. You're wrong, ma'am. They hate it.'

Extensively read or not, these two small, neat octavo volumes achieved a *succès d'estime.* They were bound in the dark cloth with a white label habitual to the Dover Street publishing house of Edward Moxon, the young publisher who had produced **Memorials of a Tour in Greece** in 1833 and who had lately put out a six-volume edition of Wordsworth, as well as the famous illustrated issue of Samuel Rogers' *Poems* and a reprint of his *Italy* with the Turner plates. Milnes sent copies to all his friends and most of his acquaintances, and received in return compliments which ranged from the vociferous and exaggerated enthusiasm of Landor to the restrained and frosty congratulations of Lord Jeffrey and Sir Robert Peel. One admirer whom he did not know, and whose opinion is thus entirely unbiassed, was very much 'affected' (as she put it in the jargon of the day) by his poem **"The Lay of the Humble":** as she lay on her couch in Wimpole Street, Miss Elizabeth Barrett read it and thought it 'exquisite.' In 1843 she confessed to R. H. Horne that she was disap-

pointed by Milnes' later poetry. This seemed by comparison with his earlier work to lack fire and imagination. He had become 'didactic.' Someone had told her, too, that **"The Lay of the Humble"** was not original. 'Taken from the German, I think they said it was. Do you know? I wish I knew. It is very beautiful in any case.'

Between them the two volumes contained nearly everything that Milnes had so far written. All the Greek poems reappeared in **Memorials of Many Scenes,** together with a set of mellifluous, nostalgic sonnets and other poems written during the years in Italy, and recalling the halcyon days at Venice and Naples, at Florence and Rome. The weeks at Bonn University also found their memorial amongst the many scenes, as well as poems written during his Irish journeys, a meditation on the Madeleine which Arthur Hallam had admired, and some rather tasteless jingles about Frome and other places in England. **Poems of Many Years** were arranged sectionally: *The Book of Youth, The Book of Friendship, The Book of Love, The Book of Reflection* and *The Book of Sorrow.* Amongst these *Books* were several poems which were especially admired: **"The Flight of Youth,"** in particular, **"The Lay of the Humble," "Shadows," "The Long Ago."** Scattered throughout the two volumes there are passages showing real sensibility. These lie embedded in much that is stilted, conventional and commonplace. Milnes' lyrical gift faded as he grew older. He was never a hard worker and it is likely that he did little polishing of his poems when he had got them down on paper. In his old age Lord Houghton once said that a few of the things he had written deserved to live. That estimate is about right. . . .

. . . . .

By the end of the eighteen-forties Milnes' ambitions as a poet had withered away. His interest in the poetry of others flourished still. In 1846 he had seriously told Panizzi that young Coventry Patmore might 'really come to a Chatterton's fate' if he was not given employment at the British Museum; he was even more ready to attack English apathy over poets than over foreign revolutionaries. *A Letter to the Marquis of Lansdowne* was not the only protest that Milnes made against the public's prejudices at this time, for it is in this light that his single celebrated and enduring work must be regarded—**The Life, Letters and Literary Remains of John Keats,** which Moxon published in the summer of 1848.

The two neat volumes of this first available biography of Keats were modestly described as 'Edited by Richard Monckton Milnes.' They contained sixty-seven of Keats' poems, together with as many of his letters as Milnes could lay his hands on. The poems and the letters were riveted together by a framework of simple

Annabel Crewe, whom Milnes married in 1851.

narrative prose, into which Milnes had inlaid the anecdotes and recollections he had picked up from John Keats' surviving friends. His stock source for the chronology of the poet's life was the unprinted memoir[1] by Charles Armitage Brown, which had been left in Milnes' care in 1841 when its author and his son Carlino had emigrated to New Zealand. Milnes had been assembling Keats material for many years[2] and Moxon had advertised the book early in 1845, though he did not sign an agreement purchasing the Keats copyrights from Keats' first publisher, Taylor, until September of that year.[3] The delay in the appearance of the *Life and Letters* was not solely due to Milnes' indolence but to certain external factors as well—the quarrel, for instance, between Brown and George Keats, the poet's brother who lived in the United States. This quarrel had prevented Brown from getting access to a major collection of John Keats' letters and poems; and it was only in 1845 that John Jeffrey, the American second husband of George Keats' widow, sent Milnes transcripts of the papers in his wife's possession.[4] Then Keats' early friend, John Hamilton Reynolds, had been touchy and difficult at first, refusing to allow publication of any of Keats' letters to

himself. Reynolds was finally won over by a letter from Milnes, and wrote 'all the papers I possess—all the information I can render—whatever I can do to aid your kind and judiciously intended work—are at your service.' By the time Milnes embarked for Spain, in September 1847, Reynolds had become restless at the long delay.

Dear Rich [ran a letter from Mr. Pemberton Milnes to his son, dated 14 September and addressed to Lisbon], There are only two letters for you at Bawtry—one from the Horse Guards refusing to exchange Wharlton into another regiment—the other signed J. H. Reynolds & only this—'My dear Sir—Elections over—Autumnal quiet on—what of Keats? Yours faithfully JHR.'

There was a brevity about the note that Mr. Milnes would have relished, but he can otherwise have cared little for the progress of Richard's work on Keats. He would certainly not have understood or even wished to understand that the issue of his son's book of Keats' manuscripts was not only far more important than the letter on *The Events of 1848* but even, in the long view, more important than any of those political events themselves.

Two volumes of Keats' verse had been re-issued in 1841. They had aroused so little interest that both Rossetti and Holman Hunt, youths who discovered his poetry in that decade, thought that they had come upon an entirely unknown poet. 'No other copies of his work than those published in his lifetime had yet appeared,' Hunt wrote of the year 1848 in *Pre-Raphaelitism and the Pre-Raphaelite Brotherhood*.[5] 'These were in mill-board covers and I had found mine in book-bins labelled "this lot 4d." ' In the 1848 Academy Hunt had exhibited a picture—*The Eve of St. Agnes*—with a subject taken from Keats, and when Milnes' book appeared that summer both he and his new friend Rossetti seized it eagerly, reading it all through an August day upon the Thames as they floated down the summer water to Greenwich and the Isle of Dogs. Few young men of their generation had even heard of John Keats; to a limited public the appearance of Milnes' volumes was almost as revolutionary as Bridges' publication of Gerard Manley Hopkins in our own century. The taut and eager face of Keats, gazing with impassioned eyes from the engraved frontispiece of Milnes' first volume,[6] is now as familiar to us, as much a part of our lives as the strange, egg-shell countenance of Shakespeare from the First Folio. In 1848 in England that face was still unknown.

The genesis of Milnes' biography lay far back in his Cambridge period. To write it was to pay an obligation to his lost youth—to those now distant days when Arthur Hallam had come bounding back from Pisa with a copy of Shelley's *Adonais* under his arm, when he and Milnes and the Tennyson brothers would read and discuss and worship the poetry of John Keats. Later, in Rome, Milnes' admiration for Keats had been strengthened and confirmed by his friendship with Severn, whom he had commissioned to copy the head of Keats for Harriette. In the summer of 1831 he had been laid up with malaria at Landor's villa at Fiesole, and had there made friends with Charles Armitage Brown. When Brown left for New Zealand he sent Milnes his Keats papers, with the request that he should publish a book of them as soon as he could. Brown did not make the choice of Milnes suddenly or idly, for he told Severn that in his opinion Milnes was better able to make a selection for publication than any man he knew. Severn, who painted Milnes in London in 1847,[7] was as anxious for the book to be published as were Brown and Reynolds, but though he volunteered to help he did not wish Milnes to print any part of Brown's memoir of Keats.

> While you are sitting [he wrote, after expostulating with Milnes for missing some appointment] I could tell you some of the many interesting things *not* in Brown's life of Keats and also explain my serious objections to its being published in any way. As I was in doubt & did not like that my individual opinion should influence you I have consulted Dilke, who more than confirms it—I have lots of beautiful things about Keats which may inspire you to begin.

Severn, like Charles Dilke, Charles Cowden Clarke, Reynolds, Haslam and other of Keats' surviving friends supplied Milnes with a great quantity of reminiscence. The usual jealousies cropped up—Severn, for instance, declaring that Brown had never been as intimate with Keats as he pretended. Benjamin Haydon also sent information, and some faulty transcripts of sonnets; his last letter, containing further recollections, was written four weeks before he cut his throat. Help of another sort (no doubt well-paid, for Milnes was always generous) was given him by the impoverished young Patmore, who acted as amanuensis during the compilation of the work. In those days Coventry Patmore was rather shocked by Keats: 'Keats' poems collectively are, I should say, a very *splendid* piece of paganism. *I have a volume of Keats' manuscript letters by me.* They do not increase my attachment to him.'[8]

Patmore was not alone in being shocked by Keats' paganism, and some people were anxious to attribute Keats' beliefs to his biographer.

> I hope Mrs. Nightingale does not bother her daughter to accept of Monckton Milnes [wrote a gossiping female in February 1849[9]]. He is not worthy of her. Have you seen his life of Keats? T. Macaulay says he never knew what religion he was of till he read his book. He expects to find an altar to Jupiter somewhere in his house.

As a biographer, indeed, Milnes was singularly forthright, for though he omitted a few personal references—notably any references to Fanny Brawne—he did not conceal anything about Keats' life. The object for which he wrote the book was simple and very characteristic. He defined it in the preface:

> I saw how grievously (Keats) was misapprehended [he wrote], even by many who wished to see in him only what was best. I perceived that many, who heartily admired his poetry, looked on it as the product of a wayward, erratic genius, self-indulgent in conceits, disrespectful of the rules and limitations of Art, not only unlearned but careless of knowledge, not only exaggerated but despising proportion. I knew that his moral disposition was assumed to be weak, gluttonous of sensual excitement, querulous of severe judgement, fantastical in its tastes and lackadaisical in its sentiments. He was all but universally believed to have been killed by a stupid, savage article in a review, and to the compassion generated by his untoward fate he was held to owe a certain personal interest, which his poetic reputation hardly justified.

Milnes' reward was the eager, emotional gratitude of Keats' friends, who wrote to him one after another to thank and to congratulate him. In other quarters, too, the book served its purpose. It was given high praise in the *Westminster,* the *Quarterly* and other reviews, and was enthusiastically admired by men of letters like Landor, Lord Jeffrey (to whom it was dedicated) and John Forster. But several very intelligent people reacted against it, adopting Macaulay's views or at any rate arriving at not dissimilar conclusions.

> Milnes has written this year a book on *Keats* [wrote Carlyle in his journal[10] for December 1848]. This remark to make on it: 'An attempt to make us eat dead dog by exquisite currying and cooking.'[11] Won't eat it. A truly unwise little book. The kind of man Keats was gets ever more horrible to me. Force of hunger for pleasure of every kind, and want of all other force—that is a combination!

Although Milnes had done his best to show that Keats was not the 'unmanly,' weak and self-indulgent character that the few people who had read his poetry still thought him, many readers would have compared *The Life, Letters and Literary Remains of John Keats* with its predecessor by four years, Dean Stanley's *Life of Arnold,* an oddly popular work which became a best-seller, whereas it took three years to exhaust the first edition of Monckton Milnes' *Keats.* Yet all through the 'fifties and 'sixties and 'seventies Keats was more and more widely read and loved in England and America. Severn said that by 1863 his grave in Rome had become a point of pilgrimage for visitors from every part of the world. Much of this strong and steady surge of recognition must be attributed to Milnes' small book.

A good biography reveals almost as much about its writer as about its subject. The very fact that Milnes' *Life of Keats* contained so many of Keats' letters was in itself revealing, for Milnes had a definite theory about biography, which may have been the result of original thought or may have been derived from Mason and Tom Moore. His preface makes the same points that William Mason made when he introduced into English literature the new biographical form of *Life and Letters* with his work on Gray, published in 1774. Milnes seems to have been more conscious of what he was doing than Mason had been, for he began by stating the case against his chosen biographical technique. For this he turned to a turgid passage from William Wordsworth. Wordsworth had declared that, in biography, truth 'is not to be sought without scruple and promulgated for its own sake.'

> The general obligation upon which I have insisted [he continued] is especially binding upon those who undertake the biography of *authors*. Assuredly there is no cause why the lives of that class of men should be pried into with diligent curiosity and laid open with the same disregard of reserve which may sometimes be expedient in composing the history of men who have borne an active part in the world.

In a long quotation Milnes reproduced Wordsworth's case for *suppressio veri,* calling it a 'grave warning.' He then set out to explain why he intended to turn his back upon these theories. He said he had not wished to construct a eulogistic monument to Keats, easy though that would have been. He proposed, instead, to let Keats speak for himself and to print as many of his actual words as he was able. It was a bold and typical decision. Had Milnes known Keats as Mason had known Gray, his book would now rank alongside that calm and vivid tribute to eighteenth-century friendship. As it is, Milnes' book remains one of the most readable and impartial biographies in English. Like most of his speeches on foreign affairs, Milnes' *Life of Keats* contained errors, a few of them flagrant. He had, for instance, relied on Mrs. Procter's recollections of Keats' appearance as against those of Keats' real friends. Mrs. Procter, who had scarcely known him, distinctly remembered that Keats' eyes were blue, and his hair auburn; neither statement was true. Then Milnes had confused the ages of the Keats brothers, and had 'killed off' Keats' friend Bailey, who he said had also died in 1821. As a matter of fact, Bailey was alive and resident in Ceylon as an archdeacon. He gravely wrote to rectify the mistake, which caused Milnes' friends some merriment, and inspired one of them to rhyme:

> Dicky Milnes—Dicky Milnes! why what the deuce could ail ye When you wrote the life of Keats— to write the death of Bailey—The poet sleeps— oh! let him sleep—within the silent tomb-o But Parson Bailey lives, and kicks—Archdeacon of Colombo—[12]

Milnes' versions of Keats' letters were not always faultless, but the essential fact about Milnes' book was its warmth, its courage and its objectivity. These were qualities which no errors of detail could impair, and here at last was an achievement Milnes could be proud of, and one which placed future generations in his debt. In a letter to Varnhagen dated August 1848 he told him that he had just

> published a life and some remains of a remarkable young poet of the name of Keats, little known even in this country. It is the biography of a mere boy. . . . I cannot expect any reputation for the book, when the merits of the subject of it are so little known.

Yet Milnes' speeches and pamphlets and verse are now utterly forgotten, and it is by virtue of his publication of Keats' poems and letters—by virtue, in fact, of his most disinterested literary action—that Milnes' name survives. Here is a thorough 'Milnesian paradox' indeed.

Milnes received many letters of congratulation from his own friends. He could feel that at least some of the people who read the book in that summer of 1848 had understood what he was trying to do. Wordsworth was not among them. 'What a pity you and Keats did not see more of one another when he expresses himself as he does about you!' Miss Martineau remarked to him at Ambleside.[13] 'Yes,' replied Wordsworth. 'It was so. If I had seen more of him, it might have done him good.'

Notes

[1] The memoir was published by the Oxford University Press in 1937. It was then in the possession of Lord Crewe, but now forms part of the Keats collections in the Houghton Library of Harvard University.

[2] The material used by Milnes for this work is now in the Houghton Library of Harvard University. This important collection of Keatsiana has lately been published in *The Keats Circle: Letters and Papers 1816-1878* (Harvard University Press, 1949) under the expert editorship of Professor Hyder E. Rollins, author of the study, *Keats' Reputation in America to 1848.*

[3] Rollins, *op. cit.*

[4] Rollins, *op. cit.*

⁵ Two vols., 1905.

⁶ Joseph Severn had lent Milnes a portrait of Keats for this engraving.

⁷ This portrait is probably that now at Madeley Manor, Staffordshire.

⁸ Letter to H. S. Sutton, dated 26 February, 1847, kindly communicated to me by the poet's great-grand-son, Mr. Derek Patmore.

⁹ Fanny Allen to her niece Emma Darwin in *A Century of Family Letters*.

¹⁰ J. A. Froude, *Thomas Carlyle, A History of His Life in London (1834-81)*, 1884, vol. i, p. 450.

¹¹ 'Carlyle of my Life of Keats—"Whatever made Milnes so waste his time—making curry of a dead dog" ': Milnes' commonplace book, 1848-9.

¹² Rollins, *op. cit.*, vol. ii, 259.

¹³ Story in commonplace book, 1848-9.

James Pope-Hennessy (essay date 1951)

SOURCE: "1858-1861" and "1861-1866 (I)," in *Monckton Milnes: The Flight of Youth, 1851-1885*, Constable, 1951, pp. 108-26, 127-60.

[*In the following excerpt, Pope-Hennessy discusses the controversy over Milnes' collection of literary erotica and his influence on the poet Algernon Charles Swinburne.*]

In scope, Milnes' library was representative of European literature in the widest sense. Round a core of the great as well as the curious classics of the past, Milnes built up a collection of contemporary poetry, fiction, biography, history, memoirs and works of criticism in four languages. Aside from his big collection of seventeenth and eighteenth century autographs, Milnes formed the admirable practice of binding holograph letters, or fragments of manuscript verse, into the relevant books of his contemporaries. Thus we find a few lines in John Keats' handwriting bound into Milnes' *Life, Letters and Literary Remains* of that poet; some of Landor's letters bound into the first editions of his various works; a copy of Prosper Mérimée's anonymous memoir of Stendhal,¹ with a wittily disingenuous note from the author denying that he had ever written this short book; there are the earliest editions of Shelley, a presentation copy (though not to Milnes) from Goethe, a piece of Voltaire's dressing-gown folded into a fine edition of *La Pucelle*;

there is Richard Burton's passport to Mecca and the visitors' book from Burns' cottage at Alloway. There are also a great number of 'association copies,' and fine bindings from celebrated royal and other libraries. Pamphlets on cognate subjects were bound together to form volumes for which Milnes invented the titles—Mrs. Norton's spate of passionate appeals for married women's rights, for example, being labelled *The Wrongs of Women*. The modern books were all rebound for Milnes by Leightons of Brewer Street, mostly in half-calf and boards with his gilt wheat-sheaf crest stamped on the side. Some of the bindings were more ambitious however—a part of the vast collection of books on the history of the French Revolution, one of Milnes' favourite subjects, was bound in red, white and blue leather, while those on the United States were stamped with gilded stars and stripes. All his friends testify to the fact that Milnes was an omnivorous reader, even by the exacting standards of those days. The remnants of the Fryston library bear witness to a culture that would have been exceptional even in a less sociable or more reclusive man.

Naturally enough, the library reflected Milnes' particular interests, and there were many thousand more books on some subjects than on others. English poetry of his own century was one of these. The French Revolution was another. A third, as we might expect in that age of doctrinal dispute and religious doubt, was theology. Magic and witchcraft were a fourth, and crime, both its execution and its punishment, formed a fifth. A sixth was Milnes' important collection of French and Italian *erotica*, some examples of which were almost as choice as anything owned by Monsieur de la Popelinière or the other amateurs of the Régence. There was also a series of books on school punishments, and all the available printed works, as well as some fragmentary manuscript ones, of a man to whom Milnes would refer as the 'odiously famous' Marquis de Sade.

'He is *the* Sadique collector of European fame,' wrote Swinburne to Rossetti in an enthusiastic letter of July 1869, which Monsieur Lafourcade first published in 1927.²

> His erotic collection of books, engravings etc. is unrivalled upon earth—unequalled I should imagine in heaven. Nothing low, nothing that is not good and genuine in the way of art and literature is admitted. There is every edition of every work of our dear and honoured Marquis.

Milnes' position as the first serious English amateur of the writings of Sade, and the alleged influence on Swinburne of the sadic collections at Fryston, have been given considerable publicity in the last thirty years, till most people who know Lord Houghton's name know it only in this context. To Milnes the works of Sade were interesting curiosities: he is unlikely to have

Some sayings of Milnes':

It is not the amount of genius or moral power expended, but concentrated, that makes what the world calls a great man; the world never sees a man but in *one* capacity.

Life may be but too long for any motions of confusion and ambition, but it is very short for the enjoyment of tranquil happiness and elevated repose; it is for these things only one wishes to have it prolonged into heaven.

We do not know how essential an ingredient even of our best pleasures their transitoriness may be; everything delightful is perhaps, *ipsa natura, too short*—regret is a continual symptom of the natural death of every gratification—if it perish not thus, it only lingers on to be killed by Time at last.

It is perhaps impossible for any truth to make its way to the general human heart, unless winged or pointed with more or less of lie.

What a rare thing is a grown-up mind!

The worst part of affectation is that there is generally so little art in it.

A man's thought is always better than his act—*i.e.,* his book than his life.

There are many men who have a sort of lyrical facility in their youth, which makes and proves them to be poets, who in manhood become utterly prosaic, and even incapable of poetical susceptibilities.

Richard Monckton Milnes, in The Life, Letters, and Friendships of Richard Monckton Milnes, First Lord Houghton, *vol. 2, by T. Wemyss Reid, Cassell and Company, 1890.*

recognised in him, as Sainte-Beuve was then doing, 'one of the greatest inspirers of the moderns.' *Justine* and *Juliette* found their natural place amongst the *erotica* at Fryston, for Milnes' collection is only interesting for having been so comprehensive and complete. The collection itself has long since disappeared: but by means of bills from Paris book-sellers, notes from Brussels, and the detailed letters of Milnes' Parisian adviser Frederick Hankey, it is not difficult to form some notion of the character of this all-too-celebrated section of his library. Examined critically, these lists of Milnes' erotic books show that his collection chiefly consisted of superlative copies of all the best-known works of this nature of the French eighteenth century. An examination of examples of these books themselves leads one to suspect that the patience with which he collected them, and the ingenuity expended in try-ing to get them into England, were seldom commensurate with the innate interest of the volumes acquired.

The conversational freedom which is one of the distinguishing marks of our present epoch makes it extremely hard to reconstruct the attitude towards sexual matters and 'loose books' prevalent among English people living a hundred years ago. In some circles the very idea of a novel in French was anathema. In 1860 Sir Walter Trevelyan obliged the young Swinburne to leave the house after having lent Lady Trevelyan a volume of the *Comédie Humaine*: 'he was a rash man who in those days recommended a French book to an English lady,' writes Gosse in reference to this incident. 'Even if she made no objection, her male relations were sure to take umbrage. Sir Walter Trevelyan threw the book on the fire with a very rough remark.'[3] In one of Milnes' later commonplace-books he records an incident told him by a friend of having met, in the Burlington Arcade, at an unusually early hour, a young man whom they both knew. Asked what he was doing, he explained that he was hurrying to a bookshop—'I have just brought a charming girl within one French novel of being seduced and now I am off to Bentleys to choose the finisher.' 'Have you read Mlle de Maupin which the Parisian ladies rave about?' wrote another friend of Milnes in a postscript to a salacious letter describing the habits of an hermaphrodite, 'It was recommended to me by quite a young woman—It is beautiful French, but a perfectly bawdy book, I cannot conceive how the censorship has allowed it to appear.'[4] In a society which judged Gautier indecent and Balzac corrupting, it is easy to see why the *chefs-d'œuvre* of Nerciat and of Restif de la Bretonne, with their *gravures libres* and frank descriptions seemed more forbidden and enticing than they can ever be to us to-day.

Swinburne's emphasis upon the quality of the component volumes of this library was evidently justified, for Milnes owned *exemplaires* of many famous illustrated books then considered suspect—*La Pucelle* with Fragonard's engravings, the illustrated *Religieuse* of Diderot, and *Les Liaisons Dangereuses* of Choderlos de Laclos. One book for which he had searched in Paris, and which was finally bought for him in 1859 and sent to London with the pages gummed together in case of discovery at the customs, was the big edition of the alleged Caracci illustrations to Aretino's sonnets. This large quarto, *L'Arétin d'Augustin Carrache ou Recueil de Postures Erotiques . . . avec texte explicatif des sujets,* contains a number of engravings after water-colours supposed to be by Agostino Caracci and to have been discovered in Italy during Napoleon's first Italian campaign, and representing classical personages making love in ways as inconvenient as they are gymnastic. Milnes also obtained with some difficulty a good copy of Louvet de Couvray's four-volume serial, *Les Amours du Chevalier de Faublas,* and of La Riche de la Popelinière's *Tableaux de Mœurs*. Other books in his possession included Nerciat's *Monrose*, *L'Etourdie* and *Félicia*, *L'Anti-justine* and the other works of Restif, *Le Joy-jou des Demoiselles* of Jouffreau de Lazarin, *L'Histoire des Flagellants*, *Venus en Rut*, Lalmond's *Pot-Pourri de Loth*, the French translation of Cleland published in 1751 as *La Fille de Joie*, *La Saladière*, an unidentifiable volume entitled *Les Yeux, le Nez et les Tetons*, *Le Soupé de Julie*, the *Bibliothèque des Amants*, *La Victime de l'amour*, *La Nouvelle Sapho*, Mirabeau's *Libertin de Qualité*, *Les Travaux d'Hercule* and *Le Petit-fils d'Hercule*, and books of elegant erotic verse such as *Le Petit-Neveu de Grècourt* printed in 1782, and its companion volume *Le Petit-Neveu de Boccace*. These, with innumerable other works of an equally resolute impropriety, went to make up the erotic library of Richard Monckton Milnes.

. . . . .

Fifty-seven letters, or fragments of letters, from Swinburne to Milnes have been preserved: an early gap in this correspondence makes clear that there must once have been more. These letters, last examined by Gosse, who printed some of them, and tactfully defined the tone of others as 'high facetious familiarity,' deal partly with Swinburne's own poetry, with the contributions which Milnes arranged for him to make to *The Spectator* (at that time, under Hutton's editorship, the most eminent of our weeklies) and with the writings of the Marquis de Sade, which Swinburne read under Milnes' auspices though against his advice. These letters scintillate with examples of Swinburne's special brand of burlesque humour which it has long been the convention to suppress as 'puerile' and 'obscene.' Blithely begun in 1861, this set of letters spans a period of twenty years, though the most interesting belong to the decade of the 'sixties, when Milnes was of real value to Swinburne and before the poet's regard for him had dwindled, as in the 'seventies it did. The last letter in the bundle has an almost symbolic significance:

> I see there is a letter from you lying here for Swinburne [wrote Theodore Watts to Lord Houghton, from The Pines, Putney Hill, probably in 1882]. I thought it might, perhaps, be an invitation which required answering. . . . Swinburne enjoyed the little luncheon the other day. But what a joke it was Lord Lytton (whom he didn't in the least know) being there!

But in 1861, before either celebrity or Watts had come his way, Swinburne found in Richard Monckton Milnes a benevolent and very painstaking friend.

The strange young gentleman whom the Milnes' butler ushered up the staircase of the Upper Brook Street house that spring evening of 1861 looked, at first go, preposterous. His head was crowned with frantic scarlet hair, his little face was white and pointed, his eyes were green and fringed with dark brown lashes. In stature he was even shorter than Monckton Milnes himself. He had a girlish figure, bottle shoulders and a dainty skipping walk: a wraith-like darting creature, comparable to the marshland *fourolle* of the Amiens folk-tales, and forming a definite contrast to his plump, red-faced, gouty host, whom George Smythe had called 'Sancho Panza' and 'Bozzy to the life' and whose features—'a countenance cut out of an orange' with a mouth that 'was one long slit'—must have seemed coarse beside Swinburne's pallid, well-bred face. Nor did the contrast stop at physical appearances. Milnes was a travelled cosmopolitan with a spacious arc of acquaintances across the map of Europe: Swinburne had been little abroad, had met few people, hated the Mediterranean, and had lately fled in disgrace from the third of three discontented years spent cooped-up in Oxford University, a place which he found depressing, amid companions whom he had despised. His genius went still unrecognised—in 1862, he said that *The Queen Mother and Rosamond* had sold seven copies— and his only real friends were the 'poet-painters,' a circle with which, as it happened, Monckton Milnes was not then familiar. Swinburne's evenings in London were spent either with his hero Rossetti, who was on the point of marrying Lizzie Siddall, or with Burne-Jones, also to be married that June. His family life formed no acceptable alternative to his lonely, somewhat baffled existence, for though his parents were affectionate, solicitous and well-disposed, he found their atmosphere oppressive:

> They doctor me with tonics & champagne [he wrote to Lord Houghton during a sojourn at their house at Henley-on-Thames in August 1867], & I thrive so well that having no one to speak to & nothing to do beyond the family wall I shall end by writing something which will make the author 'du hideux roman de J—'turn enviously in his grave. One always writes des horreurs when one is en famille.

From the outset Milnes' attitude to Swinburne was helpful and avuncular. His influence was a constructive one, 'for' (in the words of M. Lafourcade) 'he would have no more Border Ballads or translations from Boccaccio, and the result was that Swinburne wrote *Faustine*'[5]; Milnes also arranged for him to publish signed poems and unsigned reviews in *The Spectator*. Milnes was the first man of letters to recognise the immense potential importance of Swinburne's work, but it is quite apparent that he never really grasped its purport. In an article on *Atalanta in Calydon* which he concocted for *The Edinburgh* in 1865 (and of which Swinburne wrote that 'nothing yet said or written about the book has given me nearly as much pleasure')[6] Milnes praised the poet's gifts, but attacked him for his 'anti-theism,' warned him against his 'insolence of originality' and his 'obscurity,' and declared that there was 'even serious difficulty of comprehension' in many passages. For though, as Froude has remarked in his *Life of Thomas Carlyle,* Milnes had 'open eyes for genius, and reverence for it, truer and deeper than most of his contemporaries' he did not always understand its achievements. For example, Milnes was one of the only Englishmen of his day to recognise the overpowering brilliance of Alexis de Tocqueville; but the article which he published in an 1861 *Quarterly,* after this friend's death, clearly reveals that he had no conception whatever of Tocqueville's position as an historian, and no understanding of his political theory. Milnes' own most vital gift was a flair for detecting genius or originality. He had a sense for quality in human beings of any calibre, and he allowed this sense to guide him even into regions in which he felt intellectually bewildered, morally disapproving or simply at a loss. His unerring instinct led him to realise that the astonishing, voluble, red-haired boy who called on him in May 1861 was potentially one of the greatest poets England had produced; but whereas Coventry Patmore, whom Milnes had befriended in 1846, wrote verse which Milnes could admire without effort, Swinburne was at times too revolutionary, too modern, too 'obscure.' In this context an astute comment by Henry Adams is apposite: that although Milnes was 'regarded as an eccentric,' he was really only a man with 'ideas a little in advance of his time.' 'His manner,' adds Adams, 'was eccentric but not his mind, as any one could see who read a page of his poetry.'[7] There is indeed a considerable difference between **"The Beating of my own Heart"** or **"Strangers Yet"** and the first series of Swinburne's *Poems and Ballads* which appeared in 1866. Yet, blindly, by instinct, Milnes helped create the conditions in which *Poems and Ballads* were composed. By giving Swinburne needed self-confidence, by introducing him to books and people he did not know, by freeing his mind and by sympathizing with the sadistic inspiration of his verse, Milnes cleared the way for the great upsurge of lyrical poetry which produced *Laus Veneris,* the *Hymn to Proserpine, Ilicet, A Match,* the *Ballad of Burdens, Les Noyades, Faustine,* and *The Triumph of Time,* poems which, together with several critical essays and *A Year's Letters,* mark 1862 as 'the crucial year of Swinburne's early life.'[8] It is also possible that Milnes, realising 'with his great experience, that the curb of a classical form was exactly what Swinburne's genius required at the moment in order to produce a work which would be acceptable to the public,'[9] suggested to him that he should write the Greek tragedy that became *Atalanta.*

In the spring of 1861, when he first made Milnes' acquaintance, Algernon Swinburne had just succeeded in getting his father's agreement to his taking up writing as a career. It must have been a hard tussle, for after his failure at Oxford he was for some time faced with the fear of having to enter some profession:

> What *is* one to do? [he had written to his friend Lady Trevelyan from Mentone, in January 1861].[10] I can't go to the bar: and much good I shd do if I did. You know there is really no profession one can take up and go on working. Item—poetry is quite enough work for any one man. Item—who is there that is anything *besides* a poet at this day except Hugo?

That spring he met a living proof of his theory in the busy, sociable person of Richard Monckton Milnes. It is instructive to think how incredulous and irreverent Swinburne would have been had he learned that his idol, Walter Savage Landor, had once sincerely hailed the young Milnes as 'the greatest poet now living in England.' Those days were long ago.

In May 1861 Swinburne was newly returned to England from a first view of the Mediterranean. It is likely that his ready hatred for this region surprised Richard Monckton Milnes, who had often expressed his own youthful passion for it in verse, comparing

> The bland outbreathings of the midland sea,
> The aloe-fringed and myrtle-shadowed shore,

with the 'cold ground' of his native country.

> Whatever you or anyone may say [wrote Swinburne to him, in a letter of March 1868],[11] I maintain that the Nizza-Mentone province is unpleasant, angular, arid, sharp-edged, stony, *frowzy*—neither grand nor sweet—& landscape must be one or the other, if it is not to be (as Shelley says) 'damnable—and damned.'

But the more singular the impression Swinburne created the more fascinated Milnes would have been. A month later, on 5 June 1861, Swinburne was one of the eight guests at a bachelor breakfast-party given by Milnes, whose wife had taken the children down to stay at Tunbridge Wells. The other guests were Coventry Patmore, Aubrey de Vere, Arthur Russell, three gentlemen named Stigant, Cartwright and Mansfield respectively—and Captain Richard Burton, who had come back from a swift tour of North America earlier in the year and was now due to take up his new appointment as Consul at Fernando Po. This was Burton's first encounter with Swinburne, who seems to have fallen immediately under his spell. We may suppose, though we do not know for certain, that they saw each other again during that summer in London, but it is established that Swinburne was at Fryston in August when Richard Burton and his bride visited there for four days. From the entries in Mrs. Milnes' pocket diaries it is not clear whether Swinburne arrived with the Burtons on August 12, or was already in the house. When they left on August 16, Swinburne remained there, going over to luncheon at Temple Newsam on the 23rd in a carriage party consisting of his host and hostess, the painter Holman Hunt, Francis Turner Palgrave, a friend of Mrs. Milnes' named Minnie Clive, and that downright Parisian Englishwoman Madame Mohl. These details are worth recording because of the melodramatic light in which Milnes' introduction of Burton to Swinburne has been placed by the imaginative biographers of the poet.

The most recent English writer on Algernon Swinburne has used the phrase 'a piece of calculated corruption' to describe Milnes' part in initiating the passionate friendship of Burton and the young poet.[12] Like other Swinburne students he supposes the first meeting to have taken place at Fryston, a house which Monsieur Lafourcade, in his otherwise penetrating study *La Feunesse de Swinburne,* dramatises as 'l'auberge des rencontres étranges,' a sinister Yorkshire mansion filled with sadic literature and presided over by a 'feline' and malicious host. Although Monsieur Lafourcade somewhat modifies this Latin view of Monckton Milnes' character in his excellent *Swinburne: A Literary Biography,* published here in 1932, in which he chides 'ill-advised reviewers' of his earlier book for calling Milnes a 'villainous tempter,' his first interpretation of Milnes' character has persisted with all the deathless vitality of ill repute. In that useful work, *The Romantic Agony,* Professor Mario Praz goes farther. Embroidering on Monsieur Lafourcade's theme, he writes of Monckton Milnes as a man of 'Mephistophelean malice,' a sinister Virgil 'guiding Swinburne through the Inferno of his library,' a man of the world crouching spider-like at Fryston to watch the counter-play of his guests' characters with evil pleasure, and using his friends 'as instruments in order to put together some strange cruel comedy.'[13] These writers, and their followers, have succeeded in lending Milnes a baleful attraction to which, alas for his biographer, he has no real claim. In at least two recent works of American scholarship we find the tag 'unedifying' attached to Monckton Milnes and his interest in erotica.[14] To prudish and illiberal persons his name has become a bogey, to the prurient a decoy.

Truth alone is interesting in biography. I have neither the wish nor the ambition to 'whitewash' Monckton Milnes. It is however only just to point out that this apocryphal version of his character does not stand up to any commonsense investigation, and is not supported by contemporary evidence.[15] Some of the people who knew Milnes did not like him at all—finding him, as Disraeli found him, vain, envious, trivial and con-

ceited, or as Lady John Russell did, gross, and, in the words of the first secretary at the American Legation, 'smutty.'[16] None of them thought of this bluff, good talker as Mephistophelean or regarded the somewhat haphazard parties at Fryston Hall as incidents in 'some strange cruel comedy.' 'Oh how wide is the diapason of my mind! From what a height to what a depth!' Milnes had once written elegantly in an early commonplace-book. He was flattering himself. Incapable of passionate love, lacking poetic or political genius, Milnes was also incapable of real evil. He collected erotic books; he shared with Thackeray, with Burton, with Swinburne, the specially English interest in flagellation; but his attitude to these things was an extraverted, sensual attitude. In the calm words of the *Dictionary of National Biography,* Milnes was a man with 'many fine tastes and some coarse ones.'

The story of Lord Houghton's genially pointing out the choicest corner of the erotic library to his guests before setting out with Lady Houghton for Ferry Fryston church on Sunday morning has an authentic ring about it. There was the same casual, beneficent atmosphere about the two actions of Monckton Milnes for which he has chiefly been condemned—his introduction of Swinburne to Burton in the summer of 1861 and to the writings of the Marquis de Sade the year after. Milnes later became much concerned at the effects of both these introductions—for he found that Burton made Swinburne drink and he feared that Sade was becoming an obsession. The necessity to Swinburne's work of the twin stimuli of alcohol and a sadistic fancy seems never to have dawned upon Milnes' kindly mind.

Notes

[1] Milnes bought one of the twenty-five copies of the original edition of this extremely important anonymous pamphlet by Mérimée, which Firmin-Didot had printed privately in 1850. The '*H.B.*' in which Mérimée describes Stendhal's private opinions—his contempt for Christianity, his belief that most of the remarkable men of history have been sexual inverts— has only lately been reprinted, under Mérimée's name, (*Les Maîtres,* Jacques Haumont, Paris 1935). 'Cher Mr. Milnes,' Prosper Mérimée wrote from the British Museum one May evening, without date. ' . . . Je n'ai jamais rien écrit sur Beyle que la préface de l'édition complète de ses æuvres. Il y a des gens mal-intentionnés à mon égard qui m'attribuent une brochure, non pas in-4°, mais in-8°. Elle est immorale, et cela doit vous prouver qu'elle n'est pas de moi.' Milnes knew him well enough to understand what he meant.

[2] Lafourcade's *Jeunesse de Swinburne* (Oxford Press 1927) vol. I.

³ Gosse's *Swinburne* (Macmillan 1917) pp. 71-72.

⁴ Undated letter from Colonel Studholme Hodgson. *Mademoiselle de Maupin* had been first published in 1835.

⁵ Lafourcade: *Swinburne, A Literary Biography* (1932), p.97.

⁶ Swinburne to Lord Houghton, 'Friday,' August 1865 Gosse and Wise, letter XVI.

⁷ *The Education of Henry Adams,* ed. H. C. Lodge (Boston 1918).

⁸ Lafourcade, *op. cit.,* p. 96.

⁹ Lafourcade, *op. cit.,* p. 113.

¹⁰ Gosse and Wise, Letter IV.

¹¹ Unpublished letter to Lord Houghton, headed Arts Club, Hanover Square, March 28, no year.

¹² Humphrey Hare: *Swinburne: A Biographical Approach* (H. F. & G. Witherby 1949).

¹³ Mario Praz, *The Romantic Agony,* trans. Angus Davidson, 1933, pp. 215-216.

¹⁴ See Professor Hyder E. Rollins' *The Keats Circle* (Harvard University Press 1949) and the equally impressive monument of American scholarship, Dr. Gordon N. Ray's *Letters & Private Papers of W. M. Thackeray* (Oxford 1945).

¹⁵ In this context an unpublished letter from Robert Buchanan to Lord Houghton, written after a visit to Fryston in November 1868, during which he had borrowed one hundred pounds from his host, is relevant. 'I far too thoroughly disagree with you in matters of taste to feel with you on literary questions or to be influenced by your dictum,' wrote Buchanan; 'I think it has been a dictum for evil in Swinburne's case. You will not misconceive me! I regard you with admiration and even affection, and shall be grieved if you felt hurt by my word; but I cannot in honesty conceal my feeling that many of your views would be fatal were they not counteracted in your case by a heart so infinitely more noble than themselves . . . Regret nothing that you did for David Gray! God will remember that.' Buchanan (1841-1901), a Scots poet and novelist of notoriously combative temperament, who attacked and satirised the Pre-Raphelites and in particular Swinburne with great ferocity, wrote to Houghton in a later letter, dated April 1871, of the 'vile set' which Swinburne had 'got among': 'slaves who flatter and pollute him' wrote Buchanan of the Pre-Raphaelite Brotherhood, 'mean crawlers on the skirts of literature.'

¹⁶ 'Houghton as usual told some smutty stories but I shan't repeat them,' Moran wrote in his journal for 22 February 1864, of Mrs. Adams' first reception at the Legation (*The Journal of Benjamin Moran* (1857-1865), ed. Wallace & Gillespie, University of Chicago Press, 1949).

Lionel Trilling (essay date 1955)

SOURCE: "Profession: Man of the World," in *A Gathering of Fugitives*, Harcourt Brace Jovanovich, 1955, pp. 115-25.

[*In the following essay, written in 1955, Trilling remarks on Milnes' character and the reactions of his contemporaries and his biographer, James Pope-Hennessy, to it.*]

I

The addicted reader of Victorian memoirs and biographies knows them to be haunted by a presence which appears sometimes as "Mr. Monckton Milnes (now Lord Houghton)," and sometimes as "Lord Houghton (then Mr. Monckton Milnes)." To our dim sight this ubiquitous being seems to have accomplished only one thing in his lifetime that makes him worthy of recollection—he wrote a biography of Keats before anyone quite knew who Keats was. But we naturally assume that this work has been superseded, that modern scholarship has made it as ghostly as its author, and we rest content with this knowledge of Monckton Milnes: that he spent his life knowing everyone who was likely to make an item in any biographical dictionary, that he introduced everyone to everyone else at his breakfast parties, his dinner parties, his house parties.

If we look a little more particularly into the circumstances of his life, we find Milnes to have been a dilettante poet who achieved a considerable reputation for his sentimental verse but who had no great opinion of his powers in poetry and sensibly gave it up at forty. (He is, however, to be remembered as the author of the nursery classic **"Lady Moon, Lady Moon."**) He was an ambitious but quite unsuccessful political personage during his many years in the House of Commons, an inveterate traveler, a notorious gossip, something of a wit, something of a glutton—"My exit," he said, "will be the result of too many entrées."

Of the innumerable contemporary references that are made to Monckton Milnes, not a few are of a condescending sort. Disraeli despised him and left an extensive memorandum of his low opinion of Milnes; and Milnes, having had the foolhardiness to reproach Disraeli for not having included him among the characters to be recognized in *Coningsby,* found himself depicted as the Mr. Vavasour of *Tancred,* a satirical portrait which is not as destructive as it was intended to be, for Disraeli, noting the flibbertigibbet quality of Milnes, his love of celebrated people and his social busyness, could yet not bring himself to conceal his subject's genuine sweetness and powers of sympathy, or even the charm of the gusto with which he pursued his social enterprises. The point of condescension, when it was expressed, was that Milnes was a fribble. He was known to have talent, and it was believed that he had sacrificed it to vanity. His wit was not of a malicious kind and so it was not feared; it was therefore despised, as was his pleasure in talk and his insatiable social curiosity.

Sometimes the references to Milnes are charged with moral disapproval. The collections of his notable library were devoted to several interesting subjects, of which one was erotica; he had a particular interest in the works of the Marquis de Sade, who at that time was not the respectable philosophical figure he has since become, a sort of erogenous Spinoza. Swinburne browsed through this collection with delight, and it helped him to realize and encouraged him to express his already developed perversity. The French biographer of Swinburne, Georges Lafourcade, and the Italian chronicler of Romantic sadism, Mario Praz, have therefore represented Lord Houghton (formerly Mr. Monckton Milnes) as a sinister figure, one of those Milords whose devotion to the whip and the birch was understood on the Continent to be a characteristic trait of the English aristocracy, and they have written of Fryston, his country house, as a seat of iniquity.

The moral condemnation can be dismissed—the interest of Milnes in Sadic erotica was apparently not much more perverse than that of any of my readers whose eye has quickened at the sight of the phrase; and Milnes did nothing to corrupt Swinburne and much to help him.

As for the tone of condescension, this must be accepted as an essential part of the legend of Monckton Milnes. It is what gives a special meaning to the affection which many people felt for him and to the admiration for him which they expressed in language of a peculiar eloquence. It must surely have been a very rare kind of social butterfly that could have won from Carlyle the particular grace and simplicity of love and respect which he gave to Dickie Milnes. Someone once said that Lord Houghton was a good man to go to in trouble, and W. E. Forster, Matthew Arnold's brother-in-law, a Quaker of considerable austerity, capped this praise by saying in reply, "Yes, but more than that, he is a good man to go to in disgrace." People of high principle and fine sensitivity were moved to speak of him with a curious profundity of feeling, as if they saw his extravagant sociability, his mildly snobbish aspirations, his gossip, his self-indulgence,

not merely as the mask of a peculiar benevolence but as in some way its natural ground. It is as if, when they tried to praise him, they were confronted with a new possibility of human nature. They seem to have felt a gush of astonishment and relief that goodness should come out of "the world" and out of worldliness, that virtue should be of the world worldly.

In middle life Milnes thought he ought to marry, and he did marry, very suitably and happily. But before he met the lady who was to be his wife, he was drawn to a strange and very charming young woman who was, of all women, Florence Nightingale. He proposed marriage and was gently rejected. This seems expectable enough, considering the enormous disparity between the two temperaments; what we do not expect is that Florence Nightingale should have recorded in her diary how deeply involved with Milnes she felt herself to be, and her indications that she did not quite forgive him for having accepted his *congé* so easily. After his death she wrote of him to his sister:

> He had the same voice and manner for a dirty brat as for a duchess—the same desire to give pleasure and good. . . . He had I believe the genius of friendship in philanthropy—not philanthropy—but treating *all* his fellow mortals as if they were his brothers and sisters.

For Americans it is Henry Adams's estimate of Milnes that is likely to be the most memorable and telling. One of the remarkable things about Milnes was that at a time when London society was being as intensely anti-American as if it had been reading *The New Statesman* of our present day and made a point of being openly rude to American visitors, Milnes was firm in his pro-American feelings. It was to him that all distinguished Americans came, and he introduced them to his wide circle, and saw to it that they saw what they wanted to see. When the Civil War broke out and British society sided solidly with the South and discovered that there really were American gentlemen after all, Milnes stood fast in his Northern sympathies. Henry Adams, remembering the first dark days of his father's ministry to England, kept fresh Milnes's great kindness to him. At the Fryston house party to which Milnes invited him, he not only had his first tremendous sight of Swinburne, the first poet he had ever seen, but also his first experience of the pleasure of *talk.* Of Milnes, Adams wrote in the *Education:*

> Monckton Milnes was a social power in London, possibly greater than Londoners themselves quite understood, for in London Society as elsewhere, the dull and ignorant made a majority, and dull men always laughed at Monckton Milnes. . . . He himself affected social eccentricity, challenging ridicule with the indifference of one who knew himself to be the first wit in London and a maker of men—of a great many men. A word from him

went far. An invitation to his breakfast table went farther. Behind his almost Falstaffian mask and laugh of Silenus, he carried a fine, broad and high intelligence which no one questioned. As a young man he had written verses which some readers thought poetry and which were certainly not altogether prose. Later in Parliament he made speeches chiefly criticized as too good for the place and too high for the audience. Socially, he was one of the two or three men who went everywhere, knew everybody, talked of everything and had the ear of Ministers. . . . He was a voracious reader, a strong critic, an art connoisseur in certain directions, but above all he was a man of the world by profession and loved the contacts—and perhaps the collisions—of society. Milnes was the good nature of London; the Gargantuan type of its refinement and coarseness; the most universal figure of Mayfair.

II

Richard Monckton Milnes was the son of a country gentleman, Robert Pemberton Milnes, who was descended from a manufacturing family; his mother was a daughter of Lord Galway, a notorious drunkard. The elder Milnes was a man sufficiently remarkable in himself. He had greater natural force than his son, and the son was a disappointment to the father. Richard Monckton Milnes was able to win influence, but not power. Henry Adams is right in saying he had the ear of Ministers; but he had it only in certain matters—when it came to a question of a literary pension or a post in the British Museum or an Abbey burial, Milnes could get his way, but he had no credit in weightier matters. He was not a strong man in debate; but beyond that, all the Prime Ministers in his lifetime seem to have known by their animal faculty of apperception that he was not the sort of man to whom power is given—Prime Ministers know such things by sniffing. But so strong had been his father's political scent that in 1809, at the age of twenty-six, Pemberton Milnes was offered a seat in the Cabinet, either as Chancellor of the Exchequer or Secretary of War. But he said, "Oh, no. I will not accept either. With my temperament I should be dead in a year." He did not specify what element of his temperament would have made his acceptance fatal. His wife begged him on her knees to reconsider (for the sake of the children), but he would not, and retired to the country as a private gentleman.

"My father," Monckton Milnes wrote in his commonplace-book, "was always trying to give me two educations at once, one an education of ambition, vanity, emulation and progress . . . the other of independence, self-abnegation and the highest repose. He thus failed in making me either a successful politician or a contented philosopher." The relation between the father and the son was affectionate but antagonistic, and touched with a rather wry comedy. Pemberton Milnes was a Tory; his son, as he matured, took the liberal, and on the whole the intelligent, side of every public question, and he disliked country sports. The father was of the eighteenth century, and he thought the son soft, especially in his prose style, and commented frequently on his looseness of diction. He was outraged that Richard should use the phrase "balance the plain reasonableness"—"You balance probabilities—not reasonableness." And why should reasonableness be called *plain* reasonableness? Again: "p. 18—*sodden ruins*—what are *sodden* ruins?" The comedy of the relationship reached its high point when the son managed to snag a peerage for his aged father, which, of course, he looked to inherit, and the father coolly replied to the Prime Minister that on grounds of principle he could not accept what had been offered.

In 1823 Monckton Milnes went to Trinity College, Cambridge, where his talent and charm soon involved him in that world of sentimental and more-or-less erotic friendship which marked the life of the upper-class young Englishman at school and college, of which the relationship of Tennyson and Hallam is the best-known instance. Milnes, indeed, was a member of the famous "Apostles" group of Tennyson and Hallam. "That is a man I should like to know," Tennyson said to himself when, entering Trinity for the first time, he passed Milnes: "he looks like the best-tempered fellow in the world." Between Tennyson and Milnes there was a long and comfortable regard. Hallam was less responsive and there is an interesting letter in which Hallam says that he can give Milnes sympathy but not friendship in the true, high sense of that sacred word.

After leaving Trinity, Milnes went for a time to the university at Bonn, and there began his knowledge and love of German literature. His family having taken up residence in Italy, he spent a considerable time with them and then went on a tour of Greece, which was at that time a sufficiently venturesome enterprise. He made friends wherever he went, seeming to suppose that it was his clear business in life to know whoever was distinguished and interesting. His Boswellian acquisitiveness went with a tendency to a Boswellian failure of tact, and the report he received of his extended visit to Scotland indicated that he had left behind him a long trail of offense. He could make dreadful *gaffes* even in later life, when his social experience was enormous, as witness the awful dinner he gave in Paris, which appalled his friend Tocqueville and offended Prosper Mérimée. Tocqueville thought the company *"fort peu homogène"*—so badly assorted, indeed, as to constitute either a scandalous lapse of taste or a bad joke; Mérimée could not understand why, among the lesser social discomforts of the evening, he had been required to confront George Sand, whom he loathed after his brief affair with her.

The same failure of tact that could now and then overtake Milnes in his social life—it was a sort of blundering innocence—marks his whole life as a political figure. He entered the House of Commons as a member from Pontrefact, of which his father had become the squire, and he seems to have blundered at every turn. He was by no means stupid *about* politics, only *in* politics. He might have made a perfectly good political historian, but he was not meant for caucuses and committees. His political life was all bitterness to him, yet he loved it, and he could not imagine giving up his membership in the "best club in London." Social life became his chief interest, but we do not understand what Milnes felt about social life if we do not see that the only society that could interest him was one in which power of some kind, either intellectual or political, was to be seen at its work.

It is at this point that we must speak of the excellence of Mr. Pope-Hennessy's biography of Milnes. Mr. Pope-Hennessy has clearly perceived that the first virtue of the biography of such a man as Monckton Milnes is a quantitative virtue. The mass of detail of which Milnes's life was made up is of its very essence. A great novelist—Henry James, of course—might have conveyed the moral interest of Monckton Milnes's life, that of the worldling endowed with an unlooked-for moral grace which depends for its existence upon the very worldliness that makes its existence surprising. But we should always be called upon to substantiate the ideas from the good will of our imaginations; we should have been deprived of the pleasure of having the unlikely truth *demonstrated* to us, of having the moral interest unfolded in slow, uneconomical specificity, in friendship after friendship, party after party, journey after journey, vanity after vanity, benevolence after benevolence. In the management of detail Mr. Pope-Hennessy cannot be bettered. No event or circumstance is too small for him to note, no character whose path crosses Milnes's is too obscure for him to portray. At first we may wonder what we have let ourselves in for in the way of heaped-up minutiae, but very soon, as Mr. Pope-Hennessy proceeds at his equable, leisurely pace, the peculiar aesthetic of detail asserts itself. And, aesthetics apart, we begin to understand how rich a perception of an era and a society we are being given. The two volumes of Mr. Pope-Hennessy's life make a conspectus of the intellectual and social life of the nineteenth century which is not surpassed in fullness and liveliness by any other work I can call to mind.[1]

A gifted young woman, Julia Wedgwood, who knew Milnes when he was getting on in years, said this of him:

> I have a weakness for Lord Houghton; there seems to me something manqué about him, which always draws me toward people. I think in those odd

omnium gatherum collections of his there is such a curious kind of aspiration after excellence in one walk or another, and then he is content to be 2nd rate himself, which very few people are.

There is a kind of wry delicacy in this characterization of Milnes, and it really does constitute a tribute. Yet it misses the one quality of Milnes that makes it wrong for anyone to condescend to him, however affectionately. That quality is his intelligence. Milnes was a man of high, if not intense, intelligence. It required intelligence—not merely taste—and it required the courage of intelligence to value Keats when Keats's admirers could be counted on the fingers of one's hands and when he was thought of, by those who knew him at all, as a corrupt sensualist; and to value Blake when scarcely anyone else did; and to see Tocqueville's genius at first glimpse; and to be the friend of Heine and Bettina von Arnim. We jib, of course, at Milnes's friendship with Louis Napoleon, and royal princesses, and queens, at his happiness in attending openings and inaugurations and official junkets. But none of his liking for the official and the grand ever qualified his feeling for the personal, the talented, the unsuccessful. In the help of men of letters that he either extorted from the government or gave himself, he constitutes a kind of forerunner of the modern Foundation, except that he had three qualities that no Foundation is likely to have in relation to literature—courage, intelligence, and sincerity.

How very widely assorted were the traits that make up Milnes's curious personal distinction and how simply and frankly his biographer has confronted them may be suggested by the characteristics of Milnes which are listed in the admirable index to the first of Mr. Pope-Hennessy's volumes. They make an irresistible human being:

> Ambition
> Beauty, quick response to
> Boisterous high spirits
> Charm of personality
> Contrariness
> Disinterestedness
> Easy manner
> Eccentricity and love of sensation
> Emotionalism
> Enthusiasm, capacity for
> Flippancy
> Friendship, genius for
> Gaiety
> Generosity
> Genius, affinity to
> Good nature and easy-going
>   temperament
> Good temper
> Gossip, love of
> Hospitable instincts

Humour, sense of
Imagination
Indolence
Kindheartedness and sympathetic
   helpfulness
Liberalism of mind
Magpie mind
Moodiness
Music, boredom with
Nervousness as a speaker
Notoriety, passion for
Open-mindedness
Originality of minid
Paradox, love of
Passionate love, incapacity for
Persistence
Pessimism
Pomposity in public speaking
Radicalism in literary judgment
Restlessness
Romanticism
Self-confidence
Sensitiveness and vulnerability
Sensuality
Sociability
Tact
Tactlessness
Tolerance
Touchiness
Toughness
Urbanism
Vivacity
Volatility
Volubility
Wit

Notes

[1] There are one or two objections to be made of a minor, or carping, kind. I do not know who it was who instructed the English writers of nineteenth-century biographies that Wordsworth is the very type of sentimentality and taught them that whenever they refer to sentimentality they should call it "Wordsworthian sentimentality." Mr. Pope-Hennessy has not freed himself of this bad practice. Then one could wish (especially since Sir Edward Marsh is thanked for his advice on style) that Mr. Pope-Hennessy had not exemplified the tendency of English writers to follow us Americans in the use of certain slovenly neologisms. The verb *enthuse,* a "back-formation" from *enthusiasm* which implies an ignorance of the meaning of the original word, ought not to be used by a thoughtful writer. Nor should a nineteenth-century character (or anybody) be spoken of as "getting his personality across." Then on two pages (34 and 35 of the second volume) Mr. Pope-Hennessy falls prey to a sort of buck-fever as he undertakes to deal with an American

aspect of his subject. He begins by telling us that a certain Mrs. Twistleton had been born Ellen Dwight, "the daughter of a member for the Province of Massachusetts in the House of Representatives." The best opinion holds that by the nineteenth century Massachusetts was already what in this country we call a Commonwealth. Then, going on to speak of Hawthorne, Mr. Pope-Hennessy refers to him as the author of a work called *The House With the Seven Gables,* which is not unlike referring to *The Mill Upon the Floss,* or *A Tale About Two Cities,* or *Much Ado Concerning Nothing.* Having mentioned Hawthorne as the author also of *The Scarlet Letter* and *The Blithedale Romance,* he tells us that "his name more happily survives" by the *Tanglewood Tales,* which is as if he had said that Dickens's name is most happily kept in memory by *A Child's History of England.* Having occasion to refer to *The English Notebooks of Hawthorne,* he speaks of them as having been "very sanely edited" by Professor Randall Stewart, as if the *Notebooks* were a natural temptation to editorial frenzy, an impression which he confirms by speaking of them as having been "sponsored" in England by the Oxford University Press; in my experience, the O.U.P. publishes rather than sponsors books, and I cannot understand why it should have changed its practice on this one occasion.

FURTHER READING

Campbell, Ian. "Conversations with Carlyle: The Monckton Milnes Diaries." *Prose Studies* 8, No. 1 (May 1985): 48-57.
    Recounts Milnes' discussions with Carlyle, as recorded in his commonplace books.

——. "More Conversations with Carlyle: The Monckton Milnes Diaries: Part II." *Prose Studies* 9, No. 1 (May 1986): 22-9.
    Continuation of the article cited above.

Lafourcade, Georges. "Ballads and Poems (1860–1866)." In *Swinburne: A Literary Biography,* pp. 84-144. London: G. Bell and Sons, 1932.
    Briefly investigates Milnes' artistic influence on Swinburne, especially through his introduction of the poet to the works of the Marquis de Sade.

"Mr. Milnes's *Palm-Leaves.*" *Dublin University Magazine* 29, No. 169 (January 1847): 98-111.
    Review of Milnes' collection of poetry, in which the critic muses on the images of Middle-Eastern culture, politics, and religion it evokes.

West, Anthony. "Monckton Milnes." In *Principles and Persuasions: The Literary Essays of Anthony West,* pp. 77-85. New York: Harcourt, Brace and Co., 1951.

A largely anecdotal recollection of Milnes' social
gatherings at Fryston, his country house in Yorkshire.

**Additional coverage of Milnes' life and career is contained in the following source
published by Gale Research:** *Dictionary of Literary Biography,* **Vol. 32.**

Margaret (Oliphant Wilson) Oliphant

1828-1897

(Born Margaret Oliphant Wilson) Scottish novelist, biographer, short story writer, translator, and critic.

For additional information on Oliphant's life and works, see *NCLC,* Volume 11.

INTRODUCTION

A prolific writer who was extremely popular in her day, Oliphant is now remembered primarily for her novels depicting English and Scottish provincial life, for her inventive narrative style, and for her independent and resourceful female characters. Of her large body of works, the *Chronicles of Carlingford,* a series of five novels that records life in a small English town, is perhaps her best known.

Biographical Information

Born in Wallyford, Scotland, to a customs officer and his wife, Oliphant was the youngest of three children. Her mother was the dominant figure in the Wilson household; she taught Margaret to read and write and instilled in her an appreciation for Scottish lore that is evident in many of Oliphant's early works. Her later writings often reflect the contrasting personalities of her parents: her female characters tend to be strong and determined, while many of her male characters appear weak and indecisive.

In 1849, Oliphant and her brother William moved to London, where she anonymously published her first three novels, *Passages in the Life of Mrs. Margaret Maitland of Sunnyside* (1849), *Caleb Field* (1851), and *Merkland* (1851). All three were immensely popular portrayals of early nineteenth-century Scottish history, provincial life, and culture. In 1852, she married her cousin Francis Oliphant, a prominent artist. The first years of Oliphant's marriage were clouded with misfortune: she nursed her mother during a fatal illness, and two of her children died in early infancy. In addition, her husband's stained glass business faltered, and in 1859 he contracted tuberculosis. In a futile attempt to forestall the disease, he moved the family to Rome; he died, however, within several months. Oliphant, the mother of two young children and pregnant with a third, waited until the birth of her child and then, already heavily in debt, borrowed money from her publisher, William Blackwood, for her return to England.

In the early years of her marriage and during her stay in Italy, Oliphant wrote prolifically, contributing historical, biographical, and critical essays to *Blackwood's Edinburgh Magazine.* Upon her return to England, however, she found that much of her output was rejected by the periodical. Struggling to support her family and repay Blackwood for advances on her unwritten work, Oliphant conceived the plan for the *Chronicles of Carlingford.* The series was a popular and financial success, yet Oliphant's lifestyle was extravagant, and her expenses continued to exceed her income. She returned to Italy in 1864 and continued to write despite continuing personal tragedy, including the deaths of her daughter, two sons, and one of her nephews. In the last years of her life, she began writing stories that dealt with the supernatural. Among the most popular of these works were *A Beleaguered City* (1880) and *A Little Pilgrim in the Unseen* (1882). Oliphant also produced several historical studies, including *The Literary History of England in the End of the Eighteenth and Beginning of the Nineteenth Century* (1882) and *Annals of a Publishing House: Will-*

iam Blackwood and His Sons, Their Magazine and Friends (1897). In a preface to her last work, *The Ways of Life: Two Stories* (1897), Oliphant commented that she had lost much of her early enthusiasm and had little interest in presenting a positive, romantic view of life to her readers. Although she continued to write prolifically until her death in 1897, her last works, which reflect this change in outlook, are not considered among her best productions.

Major Works

As the author of numerous contributions to nineteenth-century periodicals and nearly one hundred novels, Oliphant enjoyed popular success throughout her career. She is remembered primarily for her novels, which contain realistic characters, imaginative depictions of Scottish life, and a blend of humor and pathos. *Mrs. Margaret Maitland*, *Katie Stewart* (1853), and *Kirsteen* (1890), perhaps the best examples of Oliphant's Scottish stories, are especially praised for their female characters, who are resourceful, intelligent, and determined. Some critics now regard *Kirsteen* as one of her best works, depicting as it does an unmarried woman who, driven from home by her domineering father, successfully establishes herself in a profitable and independent career. In the *Chronicles of Carlingford*, the five-novel series that is her best-known work, Oliphant sympathetically portrayed the nineteenth-century conflict between the Protestant Church of England and the re-emerging Roman Catholic Church. In the first two novels, she examined the internal conflicts of Carlingford's young clergy, while in the final two volumes of the series, *Miss Marjoribanks* and *Phoebe Junior* (1876), Oliphant concentrated more extensively on the townspeople.

Critical Reception

While many of her works enjoyed popularity during her lifetime, Oliphant's reputation diminished dramatically early in the twentieth century. Although her fiction was praised for its realistic and memorable characters, many critics suggested that, despite her wide popularity in the nineteenth century, the rapid production and sheer volume of Oliphant's writings prevented her from composing any work of lasting literary distinction. However, this judgment is being revised. Most readers now suggest that those who criticize her for creating heroines that do not take a stronger stand on women's issues have misunderstood her careful use of irony. Critics have pointed out, too, her profound understanding of gender roles and her skillful subversion of Victorian literary conventions, abilities which are employed in varying degrees of expertise in her vast literary output. Commentators have also praised her skill in the genres of biography and literary historical criticism, noting her accuracy in revealing the practices and values of Victorian culture and suggesting

that the total impact of her writings had the effect of helping to educate the expanding English readership. While Oliphant may not have achieved the enduring fame enjoyed by some of her contemporaries, her reputation as a skillful story teller who created memorable portraits of strong, capable women can now be augmented by the growing recognition of her technical and critical abilities.

*PRINCIPAL WORKS

Passages in the Life of Mrs. Margaret Maitland of Sunnyside (novel) 1849

Caleb Field: A Tale of the Puritans (novel) 1851

Merkland: A Story of Scottish Life (novel) 1851

Katie Stewart: A True Story (novel) 1853

Magdalen Hepburn: A Story of the Scottish Reformation (novel) 1854

Lilliesleaf: Being a Concluding Series of Passages in the Life of Mrs. Margaret Maitland (novel) 1855

The Athelings: Or, The Three Gifts (novel) 1857

The Days of My Life (autobiography) 1857

The Life of Edward Irving, Minister of the National Scotch Church (biography) 1862

**The Rector, and the Doctor's Family* (novel) 1863

**Salem Chapel* (novel) 1863

**The Perpetual Curate* (novel) 1864

**Miss Marjoribanks* (novel) 1866

Madonna Mary (novel) 1867

Francis of Assisi (biography) 1868

Historical Sketches of the Reign of George Second (biography) 1869

The Minister's Wife (novel) 1869

Memoirs of the Count de Montalembert: A Chapter of Recent French History (biography) 1872

**Phoebe, Junior: A Last Chronicle of Carlingford* (novel) 1876

A Beleaguered City (novel) 1880

The Literary History of England in the End of the Eighteenth and Beginning of the Nineteenth Century (history and criticism) 1882

A Little Pilgrim in the Unseen (novel) 1882

Hester (novel) 1883

The Ladies Lindores (novel) 1883

The Wizard's Son (novel) 1884

Lady Car: The Sequel of a Life (novel) 1889

Kirsteen: A Story of a Scottish Family Seventy Years Ago (novel) 1890

A Memoir of the Life of Laurence Oliphant and of Alice Oliphant, His Wife (biography) 1891

The Victorian Age of English Literature [with Francis Roman Oliphant] (history and criticism) 1892

***Annals of a Publishing House: William Blackwood and His Sons, Their Magazine and Friends* 2 vols. (history) 1897

The Ways of Life: Two Stories ["Mr. Sandford"; "Mr. Robert Dalyell"] (short stories) 1897

That Little Cutty, and Two Other Stories ["Dr. Barrère"; "Isabel Dysart"] (short stories) 1898

A Widow's Tale, and other Stories With an Introductory Note by J. M. Barrie (short stories) 1898

The Autobiography and Letters of Mrs. M.O.W. Oliphant Arranged and Edited by Mrs. Harry Coghill (autobiography and letters) 1899

Stories of the Seen and the Unseen ["The Open Door"; "Old Lady Mary"; "The Portrait"; "The Library Window"] (short stories) 1902

The Autobiography of Margaret Oliphant: The Complete Text [edited by Elisabeth Jay] (autobiography) 1990

*Many of Oliphant's works were first published serially in periodicals.

**These works are collectively referred to as the *Chronicles of Carlingford.*

***The third and final volume of this work was completed by Mary Porter in 1898.

CRITICISM

Valentine Cunningham (essay date 1975)

SOURCE: "Mrs. Oliphant and the Tradition," in *Everywhere Spoken Against: Dissent in the Victorian Novel,* Clarendon Press, 1975, pp. 231-48.

[*In the following essay, Cunningham surveys Oliphant's treatment of Scottish and English dissent. Although the critic finds Oliphant better able to present the situation in her homeland than in England, she argues that, overall, Oliphant's work suffers from a lack of "originality and imaginative engagement," and calls her fiction "simplified" and "trivial."*]

> Are you, then, so eager to return to Scott, who never seems to have suffered from writer's cramp?
> George Moore to Edmund Gosse,
> in George Moore, *Avowals.*

New Grub Street was a world away from George Eliot, but Mrs. Oliphant was often confused with her major rival.[1] Joseph Langford suspected Mrs. Oliphant of having written 'Amos Barton'.[2] George Eliot resented the imputation that *Salem Chapel* was a novel of hers: 'I am NOT the author of the *Chronicles of Carlingford.* They are written by Mrs. Oliphant. . . .' She had not read the instalments in *Blackwood's,* 'but from what Mr. Lewes tells me, they must represent the Dissenters in a very different spirit from anything that has appeared in my books'.[3] The *Spectator* thought *Salem Chapel* 'could take its place besides George Eliot's "Scenes from Clerical Life", without being hurt by the comparison'.[4] And George Eliot suspected poaching: 'Of course every writer who produces an effect on the public suggests to others a choice of subjects or of manner which is more or less conscious imitation and in some cases the inevitable result of a certain affinity.'[5]

It seems perhaps hardly coincidental that *Salem Chapel* (1862-3) follows *Adam Bede* (1859), and that *Phoebe, Junior* (1876) follows *Felix Holt* (1866).[6] But if the general similarity of subject-matter recruited George Eliot's readers for *Salem Chapel,* in the end Mrs. Oliphant could only lose by any comparison.

To Henry James Mrs. Oliphant's fecundity was 'extraordinary': 'no woman had ever, for half a century, had her personal "say" so publicly and irresponsibly.'[7] In her hey-day (the 1860s-80s) she continually rivalled the exemplary day's toil Gissing's Jasper Milvain puts in (*New Grub Street,* Ch. 14): 'there is so much of me!' she justifiably exclaimed.[8] James dubbed her 'a great *improvisatrice,* a night-working spinner of long, loose, vivid yarns, numberless, pauseless' (Trollope was 'the great *improvisatore . . .*'). He admired reluctantly, but was puzzled by

> . . . a love of letters that could be so great without ever, on a single occasion even, being greater. It was of course not a matter of mere love; it was a part of her volume and abundance that she understood life itself in a fine freehanded manner, and, I imagine, seldom refused to risk a push at a subject, however it might have given pause, that would help to turn her wide wheel.[9]

Mrs. Oliphant marshalls her thin resources to the best advantage, works over the same ground a second and third time, tackles a subject in *Blackwood's,* in a biography, in a novel. Novels are followed by sequels, sequels become a sequence; no possibility of restating a theme is lightly waived. An article on Irving (1858) becomes a fully fledged biography (1862); and with this material, plus an interest in revivalism stimulated by work on Wesley,[10] she produces a novel about charismatic revivalism, *The Minister's Wife* (1869). Admiration for Wilkie Collins, which provided material for an article (May 1862),[11] and her notion of how inferior deacons and elders could blunt the genius of a preacher (theme of the Irving article and *Life*), helped to shape the sensationalist plot and the religious matter of *Salem Chapel* (February 1862 to January 1863). Tozer of *Salem Chapel* was too profitable a seam to leave unworked, so he reappears, with his granddaughter, in *Phoebe, Junior: A Last Chronicle of Carlingford* (1876): the parting note of the title not unconnected with Trollope's *Last Chronicle of Barset* (1867).

At least some of Mrs. Oliphant's badness, the resort to popular sentiments about mothers and religion, conventionally plotted intrigue, and sensationalism, can be put down to financial calculation. There is a distinct gap between her cheaply melodramatic novels and the critical voice which deplores Bulwer's 'sham and cheap melodrama' and Charles Reade's theatricality and melodrama, which withstands the shallowness with which female novelists 'discussed and settled' the 'vexed questions of social morality, the grand problems of human experience', and which rejects the 'froth of flirtation and folly which has lately invaded like a destroying flood the realms of fiction', the books 'by millions, which . . . depreciate instead of elevating the intellectual taste of the multitude'.[12] As anonymous critic Mrs. Oliphant scorns precisely those strategies she deploys as novelist:

> Out of the mild female undergrowth, variety demands the frequent production of a sensational monster to stimulate the languid life. . . . Murder, conspiracy, robbery, fraud, are the strong colours upon the national palette. Even when we try to be Arcadian, it is Arcadia '*plus* a street-constable', as Carlyle says; and over that ideal world Mr. Justice Somebody looms supreme upon the bench, and the jurymen are always within call. . . .[13]

To attempt a popular success she crosses to the side of popular taste, and her fiction quite knowingly exploits the vices of Charles Reade and Mrs. Henry Wood that she attacks in Maga.[14] And this resort to the *kitsch* factors of sensationalism, conventional plotting, and so on, as guarantors of popular esteem, comes with curious readiness. Given the leisure she occasionally regretted not having, Mrs. Oliphant might have ironed out minor inaccuracies (Beecher of **Salem Chapel** becomes Beecham in **Phoebe Junior**; a few pages of **The Minister's Wife** after Horace Stapylton had 'begun to glide out of the habits of a lover' he is described as 'still so lover-like'; at the beginning of **Phoebe**, Vol. II, Horace Northcote's white tie is said to be always 'of the stiffest' as a sort of clerical uniform: at the end of Vol. I he had, however, appeared with white cravat 'carelessly tied').[15] But more worrying, though the lapses of memory about what she has written are symptomatic of the serious fault, is the consistent evasion of close imaginative engagement, what James called a 'full, pleasant, reckless rustle over depths and difficulties'.

Revealingly, she was 'astonished beyond measure' at the 'established intimacy' with his characters that Trollope claimed, and advocated, in his *Autobiography*: 'I am totally incapable of talking about anything I have ever done in that way.'[16] This self-confessed failure is not insignificant: it underlies the hand-me-down air of parts of her account of Dissent, the reworking of novels on other novels. Honest toil at the

anvil of fiction ('. . . this does not mean that I was indifferent to the work as work, or did not beat it out with interest and pleasure . . .') would be no substitute for originality and imaginative engagement.

Mrs. Oliphant's novels about Scottish Nonconformity— *Margaret Maitland, Magdalen Hepburn, Lilliesleaf, The Minister's Wife*—are noticeably different in spirit and tone from her novels about English Dissent, *Salem Chapel* and **Phoebe, Junior**.[17] Scottish Nonconformity is more congenial to her than English; she knows more about it. The Scottish novels were all written early (except for **The Minister's Wife**, which however stems from the early interest in Irving), generated in the period when Mrs. Oliphant's sympathies for the Scottish Free Church cause were at their strongest.

Henry James discerningly spotted where her strength lay:

> She showed in no literary relation more acuteness than in the relation—so profitable a one as it has always been—to the inexhaustible little country which has given so much, yet has ever so much more to give, and all the romance and reality of which she had at the end of her pen. Her Scotch folk have a wealth of life, and I think no Scotch talk in fiction less of a strain to the patience of the profane.[18]

Margaret Maitland is little more than a ramblingly pious tale of love and intrigue. And the treatment it incidentally affords the 1843 Disruption of the Church of Scotland, out of which emerged the (technically Nonconformist) Free Church of Scotland in which Mrs. Oliphant grew up, consists of scarcely more than sympathetic noises and a sketchy map of the dispute. But even that little does bring to the novel a bit of sociological muscle, some saving realism. It is a recruited strength that helps specify the dimensions of a world of religious experience that Mrs. Oliphant had herself inhabited, and could move freely about in, and through it the novel impinges, however slightly, on a world of real moral conflict and decision that considerably stiffens its backbone.

This reinforcement is found again in **The Minister's Wife** (1869): its engagement with the charismatic revivalism associated with Edward Irving redeems a little its trivialities of plot, its tired story-lines, and weakness of invention. But this novel, based on 'the religious movement in the West of Scotland about the year 1830',[19] one of Mrs. Oliphant's best fictions, a serious attempt to enter the revivalist mind, to penetrate the heart of a revival, comes characteristically near to shipwreck because of the banality and conventionalism with which it is associated. Once again Mrs. Oliphant had failed to perceive where her best interests might lie; the melodrama, the mysteriousness where (as in *Salem Chapel*) there is really no mystery, are allowed to undermine the religious theme. In Book III she is not content with a sometimes very moving account of the prophetess who feels left derelict by God: she must draw out the flagging Stapylton case to its bitter end, with Isabel's struggles over the baby he wants her to leave behind in Scotland when they emigrate to America, tedious maternal delight over baby's perambulatory efforts, a secret drawer's contents exposing Stapylton as murderer, murder threats, a loaded pistol, grinding and gnashing of teeth. The unimaginative ordinariness of this lifeless third volume almost completely obscures Ailie Macfarlane's reconciliation to her God.

Mrs. Oliphant professed her incapacity for assessing her material's worth ('Sometimes I find it totally impossible to form any opinion of what I have done, and send it off in hopeless perplexity, not knowing whether it is good or bad . . .'),[20] but one suspects the financial calculation all the time, a recipe for fiction that would inevitably try granting a novel as many various appeals as possible. And in striving to manage several jobs at once *The Minister's Wife* fails to do itself justice: it ends up satisfying neither as a tale of mystery and horror, nor as a religious novel.

Doubtless, one of the better-done things in the novel is the prophet John's blackmailing the prophetess Ailie into marrying him by means of religious shibboleths ('. . . hear the Word of the Lord! and see that ye sin not against the Holy Ghost'). But, characteristically, the strength of the account undoubtedly derives from St. John Rivers's pressures on Jane Eyre—pressures that are also professedly religious but are really purely sexual—to become a missionary. And any insight into the ambivalent mixture of nature and grace in these cases is weakened in the conventionalized passion— usual with Mrs. Oliphant—of Black John ('his great, heavy, passionate eyes').

Mrs. Oliphant's accounts of English Dissent lack first-hand experience. Of *Salem Chapel* she wrote:

> As a matter of fact I knew nothing about chapels, but took the sentiment and a few details from our old church in Liverpool, which was Free Church of Scotland, and where there were a few grocers and other such good folk whose ways with the minister were wonderful to behold. The saving grace of their Scotchness being withdrawn, they became still more wonderful as Dissenting deacons, and the truth of the picture was applauded to the Echoes.[21]

Her love for the English Establishment had grown, and acquaintance with the French monastic revival and with the Montalambert family helped shape her into a High Churchwoman.[22] The drift away from Free Church sympathies paralleled her social and political progress. The girl who collected signatures in Liverpool against the Corn Laws, worshipped at the Presbyterian church with 'the engineers and their families who worked in the great foundries', never went to dances, theatres, or art galleries, and who was therefore at one, culturally, socially, and politically, with the mass of Dissenters in her novels, grew up to abhor second-class rail travel and cheap clothes ('not fit for any gentlewoman to wear'), sent her sons to Eton and Balliol, and 'could say more easily than most people the things that stab and blister' about persons whose cultural position she had once shared.[23] Her strenuous scorn for provincial vulgarity is a repudiation of the Liverpool childhood (and in fact Copperhead's view of his Turner as an investment, his equation of aesthetic and monetary value, is uncomfortably close to Mrs. Oliphant's treatment of her own art as commodity). The *British Weekly* writer (presumably Nicoll) had 'often been surprised that her hard experience never seemed to school her into charity and restraint'. Her sons lacked charity too, in their priggish Toryism. Frank (Cecco), namesake of his uncle Frank who had been, like Mrs. Oliphant's mother, 'tremendously political and Radical', could class demonstrations of 'young roughs, *soi-disant* the unemployed' among the London amusements of 1887: 'Many people think that the unemployed are not bad fellows on the whole, as long as you don't ask them to work, but they are certainly an abominable nuisance.'[24]

The Free Church of Scotland had a comparatively short history of protest against the Established Church, and though its membership was to some extent socially inferior, the difference was less marked than in England: research has merely shown that the eldership of the 'Frees' (in Aberdeen) tended to be drawn from the lower middle class and that of the Establishment from the upper middle class.[25] In England, of course, Dissent's social inferiority was marked and long-entrenched, and by her shift towards Anglicanism Mrs. Oliphant was precluding very much chance of learning the English situation. In general terms she understands, and presents, the caste difference between Anglicans and Dissenters, but she is quite capable of effectively negating the barriers she points to by putting a Dissenter on the kind of socially equal footing with the Establishment he might easily have enjoyed in Scotland. Only one chapter of *Salem Chapel* after Vincent's firm impression that 'society' in Carlingford is closed to 'a poor Dissenting minister' (Ch. 5) he gets his wished-for entrée to that 'society' through meeting Lady Western in Master's bookshop. The improbability here was protested against by George Eliot: 'And certainly no dissenting life I ever came in contact with in the provinces, could furnish an example of a dissenting minister being invited to visit her by a lady of title on a first interview in a shop.'[26]

Vincent's love for Lady Western was, according to the *Nonconformist,* 'infatuation, not to say madness'.[27] There is more of this sort of madness in *Phoebe, Junior,* where Mrs. Oliphant is less interested in analysing seriously the social problems of Dissent than in developing the ironies of the fictional situation she has designed. Her ironic interest in caste concentrates on the margins where genteel poor (the May family, whose father is a Carlingford clergyman) and rising middle class (the exshopocracy as presented by Phoebe) overlap, and Dissenting railway magnates brush against third-rate peers. Phoebe feels inferior as a Dissenter to Ursula May; Ursula for her part feels inferior to Phoebe because she has shone in 'grand society'—the Copperheads' ball, grand only to Ursula. The Rev. Mr. May forges a bill drawn on Tozer, a socially despised, but nevertheless prosperous Dissenting grocer. Northcote, sometime missionary of the Liberation Society, and Anti-State-Church lecturer, is introduced into the May family, where Clarence Copperhead, son of the Dissenting millionaire, is being coached for Oxford examinations, and where Reginald May has just accepted a sinecure chaplaincy to an almshouse (shades of Trollope!). Northcote had attacked May at an Anti-State-Church meeting attended by Carlingford's enthusiastic Dissenters (Vol. II, Chs. 1 and 2). May's dismissiveness towards the Liberation Society ('A parcel of trumpery agitators, speechifiers, little petty demagogues, whom nobody ever heard of before'; 'Shopkeepers', Vol. II, Ch. 5) confronts Northcote's virulent political Dissent, but the party allegiances of both are softened over tea at Tozer's, where the butterman and leading elder is moved (unrealistically, objected the *Nonconformist*) to declare that there is no need to perpetuate public stances in private.[28] The two young men recognize mutual problems of faith and doubt in the nineteenth century, and of irksome authority (the congregation and elders in one case, and May's Dissent-abhorring, duty-shirking Rector in the other). The 'old faith' represented by the fifteenth-century Chapel of the Charity Foundation is a rebuke to Northcote's unlovely 'new agitations', and May perceives how immoral the Rector must look to Dissenting eyes. The two young, hopeful ministers turn out to be only factitiously opponents (both are 'foolish, wrong and right'), and realize their true *rapport* in the Mays' drawing-room where Northcote woos Ursula and May yearns after Phoebe. Copperhead plays his fiddle while Churchman and Dissenter burn with passion for girls of the opposite parties.[29]

The ludicrous inadequacy of this as a solution to the differences between Church and Dissent is abundantly clear, and equally clearly this simplistic but confident resolution is based on ignorance of the problem and the issues. The ease with which Dissenters are made to abandon their opposition to the Church reflects Mrs. Oliphant's simplified view of the quarrel: for her, Dissenting antagonism is simply a matter of inverted snobbery, Arnold's 'jealousy of the Establishment'. Snubbed, as he thinks, by Lady Western, Vincent delivers his sensational 'course' on Establishment evils: his passion, Mrs. Oliphant says, simply an underdog's reaction against the privileged class (*Salem Chapel,* Ch. 8). Acceptance by Lady Western dampens Vincent's ardour against the Church; friendship with Reginald May makes Northcote embarrassed by his own early antagonism; 'social elevation' modifies Phoebe's 'sectarian zeal' as it had toned down her parents' sense of social inferiority and of spiritual superiority to the Establishment (*Phoebe,* I, Ch. 2). Mrs. Oliphant hardly touches on the details of Dissenters' social and political deprivation and displays her usual lack of interest in the detailed theological differences between the parties. Northcote's speech against the Establishment is, she claims, no routine agitation, but she evades telling us what he said, coyly adding that it would be dangerous to do so.[30] Mrs. Oliphant's mentions of the Liberation Society, the 'Dis-Establishment Society', the *Nonconformist* and the *Patriot,* convey a superficial impression of knowledge. But these details were widely available, especially in and about 1862, Bicentenary of the Great Ejection (when *Salem Chapel* began to be published). The *Nonconformist* pointed out that Congregational Dissenters did not, as they do in *Salem Chapel* and *Phoebe,* talk of the 'connexion': that was Methodist jargon. Nor were the students at Homerton College, as the first chapter of *Salem Chapel* asserts, 'brought up upon the *Nonconformist* and *Eclectic Review*': 'this journal [*sic*] had the distinction of being tabooed by the quasi-Conservative alumni of that venerable institution'. The author of *Salem Chapel* was obviously 'not personally familiar with the life that he has undertaken to depict'; 'absence of that special and minute knowledge which intimate acquaintance confers' was noticeable: *Phoebe, Junior* 'could only have been written by one who knows little really of Dissent'.[31]

According to the Colbys, *Salem Chapel* has the

> . . . ring of truth and of originality—an inside view of an independent congregation presented with candor and humor and with just enough snobbish condescension to appeal to a predominantly Church of England reading public for whom the popular image of the Dissenter was still a vulgar, hymn-singing tradesman.[32]

But *Salem Chapel* is clearly deficient in truth, not entirely satisfactory as an inside view, less original than compounded of popular notions, and calqued on fictional accounts.

The sensation of 'horror', lightly dismissed by Mrs. Oliphant in *Blackwood's* in May 1855 as a mere stimulant to the jaded palates of novel-readers, was embraced as a profitable gambit in *Salem Chapel.*[33] The novel's melodramatic 'machinery'—the mysterious Mrs. 'Hilyard'; Susan Vincent's abduction; the abductor Colonel Mildmay's being shot; Susan accused of the crime; an atmosphere of murkily rainy evenings; fleeting glimpses of the avenging Mrs. Mildmay's hauntingly white face (shades of *The Woman in White*); overheard conversation; appropriately inflated rhetoric—fulfils Mrs. Oliphant's prediction that 'What Mr. Wilkie Collins has done with delicate care and laborious reticence, his followers will attempt without any such discretion. . . .'[34] The only discretion Mrs. Oliphant allowed herself, remembering her fear that Collins's imitators would glorify vice, and her rebuking *East Lynne* for representing 'the flames of vice as a purifying, fiery ordeal, through which the penitent is to come elevated and sublime', was to guarantee that the abducted Susan Vincent passed through no real 'flames of vice', had no need of penitence. She remains unscorched, if rather flushed. Mrs. Oliphant did not, however, eschew borrowing from *East Lynne*: Mildmay changes his name, calling himself Fordham, as Levison took the alias Captain Thorn; Tozer, like Mr. Joe Jiffin, owns a shop in 'the cheese and ham and butter line', with a comfortable parlour behind, and a well-furnished drawing-room upstairs.[35]

The 'sensation' element, aimed to appeal to the large audience of *The Woman in White* and *East Lynne*, constantly diverts attention from the chapel. From the vestry (Ch. 10) Vincent overhears an argument between Mrs. 'Hilyard' and Colonel Mildmay (' "She-wolf!" cried the man, grinding his teeth'). Vincent has just made a tea-meeting speech which invoked melodramatic circumstance ('the dark streets which thrilled round' his congregation). We are invited to agree that the banal events of the Hilyard-Mildmay melodrama are weightier than the interests of a Dissenting community or the preoccupations of a Dissenting pastor.

> What, then, were the poor dialectics of Church and State controversy, or the fluctuations of an uncertain young mind feeling itself superior to its work, to such a spectacle of passionate life, full of evil and of noble qualities—of guilt and suffering more intense than philosophy dreams of? (Ch. 11)

Reviewers recognized that this rejection was ill-judged: ' . . . almost any novelist could do as well or better' than the 'Mildmay melodrama'; and the *Spectator* wished ' . . . that in some new edition the Mildmay film might be skilfully removed from the book, by some neat surgical operation, and the simple squabbles of the Salem Independents left in all their purity and majesty'.[36] But while the plot advanced, the Dissenting life was treated mostly as backcloth and kept static, limited to a few basic propositions about narrowness and the congregation's power over its minister. Once

stated, these are simply repeated; and they are almost all Mrs. Oliphant has further to add in *Phoebe, Junior*.

Not surprisingly, given *Salem Chapel*'s abundant literary indebtedness and Mrs. Oliphant's ignorance, Dickens's influence is strong. Mrs. Oliphant, using her familiar smokescreen device, was publicly cool about Dickens.[37] As we have seen, she rebuked his contempt for the 'preachers of the poor'. Andrew White, a character in *The Minister's Wife*, is said to look, in funeral garb, '. . . like the conventional type (often very far from the reality), which the public accepts as that of a Dissenting pastor. It was not Chadband, benign and oily, but a more melancholy and meagre specimen' (Vol. III, Ch. 1). This double-edged rebuttal—conventional public images are often untrue, and Chadband does not represent the conventional type (a rebuke to Dickens for selecting badly)—hardly prepares the reader for Mrs. Oliphant's trading in stereotypes, and Dickensian ones at that.

Old Mr. Tufton's 'large soft flabby ministerial hand' (*Salem*, Ch. 3), and Tozer's unction, blending with grease from the bacon and butter, are by no means distant from Chadband. In *Phoebe*, Tozer has become more completely the greasy shopkeeper, the unctuous Dissenter: by the time he turns stagily on Mr. May demanding his pound of flesh ('I'll have him rot in prison for it') his sturdy support of his sect and class has been swamped by the author's satiric intent. His final speech rejecting 'clever young men' and advocating 'strong opinions' and 'no Charity' towards other denominations, was, observed the *Nonconformist*, 'not so much humorous as funny, after the manner of many of the extravagant dramatic attitudinisings of Charles Dickens'.[38]

The Salem womenfolk are cruelly pilloried: their complacent ignorance of social and cultural barrenness, their love of tea-parties ('the urns . . . well filled, the cake abundant'), their meagre ambitions and petty jealousies—just tolerable, and sometimes finely drawn in *Salem Chapel*—become tedious and simply unkind when insisted on again in *Phoebe*.

The familiarity of this fictional zone is signalled by jokes about the 'flock' (Salem matrons are no 'lambs', even if 'of the flock'), and by Mr. Morgan, the Rector in *The Perpetual Curate*, thinking that Wentworth's 'impromptu chapel' by the canal is 'a little Bethel'.[39] Salem Chapel, seedy, sombre, red-brick, is a familiar fictional property; Dissenting commercialism—Tozer's concern not to 'let the steam go down' (Ch. 4)—had been done before. Vincent's impression of the 'miserable scene of trade . . . a preaching shop, where his success was to be measured by the seat-letting, and his soul decanted out into periodical issue under the seal of Tozer & Co.,' is a colourfully extravagant version of the usual kind of changes. At his most Shylockian, Tozer becomes a Gradgrind ('the Good Samaritan was a Bad Economist'): the Gospel cannot dictate charity in a business situation, business must not be interfered with. Copperhead senior is made abruptly to conform to utilitarian type (a patent device for extending **Phoebe**'s third volume); and his liking only industrial towns like Manchester, his notion that women should be exported like other surplus raw materials, his preference for railway stations against fifteenth-century chapels, his advocacy of political economy against the unwisdom of large clerical families, are stereotyped enough. (And his sinister 'we've had enough of Christianity' is curiously at odds with his faithful Dissent.)

The spirit of Matthew Arnold imbues Mrs. Oliphant's scorn for bacon and cheese merchants, for Copperhead's interest in his Turner only as an investment, for Clarence Copperhead's 'tendency towards those demonstrative and offensive whiskers which are the special inheritance of the British Philistine' (**Phoebe**, Vol. I, Ch. 2). The *Nonconformist* suspected animus, from the 'conspicuous absence of any attempt or desire to find a reality of religious conviction or feeling underlying the supposed defects of the system or the vulgar prejudices of its adherents. . . .' It recognized an old story: this was 'the aspect in which Dissent presents itself to a large class of minds possessing considerable influence in our day'.[40]

Salem Chapel and **Phoebe, Junior** outline the stock case against the Voluntary System: it enslaves its ministers, makes them men-pleasers, panderers in the pulpit and on pastoral visits to the congregation which pays them. The commonplace nature of the argument, which had, as the *Nonconformist* reviewer conceded, elements of truth in it,[41] can be gauged by noting the similarities between Mrs. Oliphant's charges and William Pitt Scargill's *Autobiography of a Dissenting Minister* (anonymously published, 1834), a bitter novel, posing as non-fiction, by an ex-Unitarian minister.[42] Scargill quotes from William Hull a passage which might serve epigraphically for Northcote and Vincent, describing the necessity for congregation-pleasing, and the possibility of maintaining greatest popularity only by being most anti-Establishment: the minister 'maintains his ascendancy . . . by cherishing the passions of sectarian bigotry and hate. . . .'[43] The decline of Northcote's and Vincent's popularity coincides with their waning sectarian fervour.

Mrs. Oliphant, like Scargill, notes the difference between country-town and metropolitan Dissent. In the small town the chapel's social range is limited: no upper-class members (Mrs. Hilyard is a freak member, imposed on Salem by the demands of the melodrama), the poor 'don't count', and the major-

ity is 'in the way of business'. The minister's style is cramped by the constricting demands and surveillance of the small-town shopocracy. Like Vincent, Scargill's narrator, a Dissenting minister, finds irksome the teas, the pastoral visits for little but gossip, the congregation's familiarity, inevitably breeding contempt. The congregation seeks to monopolize the pastor's time, interest, presence, to dictate his life-style, his choice of wife: friendships—particularly with gentry and Anglicans—and loves are closely supervised. Any aloofness from the congregation generates disfavour ('To have people turn up their noses at you ain't pleasant . . .', 'And them getting their livin' off you all the time . . .' **Salem Chapel,** Ch. 1).

There are other pastures however. In 'the great towns of the North', ' . . . Dissent attains its highest social elevation, and Chapel people are no longer to be distinguished from Church people except by the fact that they go to Chapel instead of Church.' Beecham (**Salem**'s Beecher) graduates from Carlingford, via northern pastorates, to a prosperous metropolitan congregation. Crescent Chapel people read newspapers, and sometimes magazines, and 'knew what was going on'; old Tozer reads only old sermons, the *Congregational Magazine*, and the *Carlingford Weekly Gazette*. His wife can only offer her granddaughter Phoebe (a new women who knows her John Stuart Mill) gossip about the chapel and her daughter-in-law. Anglicans are tolerated at Crescent Chapel; Copperhead's son is at Oxford; only a few members are 'hot Voluntaries'.[44] Scargill's narrator points to the same social gulf within Dissent: one night dining with a radical Houndsditch hardwareman, leader of his Chapel's democratic faction (opponent of Test and Corporation Acts), another night with a rich dry-salter in Portman Square, where the talk was of 'the price of stocks, Beethoven's music, forced strawberries, and Russian ambition. . . . I never saw such elegant people in my life, and I did not think that there had been such among the dissenters.'

But, whether in Crescent Park or Carlingford, the Voluntary System is equally tyrannous, the leading member equally to be feared. Phoebe's 'love' for Clarence Copperhead jeopardizes her father's position as a dependent on his father's goodwill. Tozer, the senior elder, must not be upset. A 'great deal', as Scargill claims (Ch. 3), 'depends on the influence of the leading people, who govern not by any express law, but by the mere force of circumstances, and the power of wealth'. Beecher and Vincent are in the pocket of their paymasters. Mrs. Oliphant, like Scargill, derides: 'An additional fifty pounds of "salary"—a piece of plate—a congregational ovation—was it to be supposed that any Dissenting minister bred at Homerton could withstand such conciliatory overtures as these?' (**Salem Chapel**, Ch. 42.)

Political Dissent is regarded as irreligious (the *Nonconformist,* 'organ of the political Dissenter . . . can hardly be called a religious paper at all').[45] Mrs. Oliphant seems to approach, certainly in *Phoebe, Junior,* the Anglican fears of William Hull: if Congregationalists had their way, 'Radicalism would triumph; everything would be cut down to the level of republican meanness, and all that we love and revere as monuments of the ancient grandeur of our country would be disposed of by the voice of popular clamour.'[46]

Mrs. Oliphant's earlier sympathy for the 'preachers of the poor', shown in her rebuke to Dickens, has been eroded. She still talks, in *Phoebe,* of 'the little Salems and Bethesdas, with their humble flocks', a different species from Crescent Chapel, but we are never actually shown any of them. Salem Chapel certainly does not qualify: there the poor 'don't count'. We are told, indeed, that it is the parish churches that 'are like the nets in the Gospel, and take in all kinds of fish, bad and good'. But Dissenters who happen not to share the snobberies of Regent's Park and Mrs. Brown are actually discounted by the novelist: she referred contemptuously to the 'conversion of the heroes of the coal-pits and slums . . . chronicled in the literature presided over by General Booth', and to the bad English and impoliteness of the *War Cry.* Like Salem Chapel's, the life of the Salvation Army is deemed merely narrow and uncharitable.[47]

Mrs. Oliphant concentrates on the anomalies and difficulties on the surface of English Dissenting life, but fails to take account of 'the religious element', which might redeem and mellow the otherwise mean, harsh, and ungenial.[48] As her case stands, she has failed to explain Tozer's sturdy loyalty to Salem, or Copperhead's dogged allegiance ('obstinate as an old pig', according to his son; *Phoebe,* Vol. II, Ch. 11). She supports Dissenters in revolt, like Phoebe and Vincent, not realizing that they are unsympathetically disloyal. Vincent's instant feeling of 'dwindlement' in Carlingford makes one wonder why he ever went into the ministry, and his willingness to confess to Mrs. Hilyard, a fringe member, how burdensome his officers were, is at least curious.[49] And Phoebe could hardly have been 'so ready to tell strangers the quiet contempt with which she viewed her own people, and yet have preserved their entire liking and respect'.[50] Support for Vincent leads to absurdity: even if Mrs. Oliphant approved Vincent's shaking off the congregational yoke ('I am either your servant, responsible to you, or God's servant, responsible to Him' Ch. 42) it is unlikely that Homerton College would endorse this rejection of Congregational polity as 'a demonstration of the rightful claims of the preacher' (Ch. 43).

Mrs. Oliphant's acquaintance with Irving's life was clearly seminal. Irving's long-faithful *aide,* William Hamilton, was, like Tozer, a chapel-manager who loved

to have the building full.[51] His final reluctant opposition to Irving over the *charismata* is, as it were, the substance, of which Tozer's rejection of Northcote and bright young ministers is a vulgarized shadow. The Colbys have pointed out general similarities between Vincent and Irving.[52] Both men achieve their most striking effects in the pulpit by sincerity and truth to deep feelings. Vincent's sermons on the Sunday when Susan's danger has brought him to question Providence affect his audience, and revivalistically (there are sobs, screams, fainting), because they have a relation to deeply felt experience, as Irving's did: the heart is speaking. It was not, as Mrs. Oliphant wrote of Irving,

> . . . mere genius or eloquence, great as their magic is, but something infinitely greater—a man, all visible in those hours of revelation, striving mightily with every man he met, in an entire personal unity which is possible to very few, and which never fails, where it appears, to exercise an influence superior to any merely intellectual endowment.[53]

Both Vincent and Irving are challenged by lesser men, and both resist the sanction of men as being less than God's. But Irving's principled invoking of the Headship of Christ works in just that area of spirituality that *Salem Chapel* avoids. Vincent's novelistic *crise* scarcely approximates to the reality of Irving's spiritual struggles that Mrs. Oliphant conveys in her *Life* of the preacher. Vincent's resistance to the regimen of Independency on grounds vitiated by pride and his sense of 'dwindlement' is a long way from Irving's choosing to obey God rather than man. Vincent is scarcely an Irving: his treatment at the hands of his congregation does not raise the same questions about the power of the congregation as Irving's treatment by the presbytery raised about the function of presbyterian justice. Mrs. Oliphant seems, however, to think that it does, and *Salem Chapel* gloats excessively: Vincent 'took his way out of Salem with a sense of freedom, and a thrill of new power and vigour in his heart' (Ch. 42). But that echo of *Paradise Lost* ('They . . . through Eden took their solitary way') ironically serves rather to underline the reader's sense of something missing than to endorse the author's claim for a new freedom gained.

But then, she was never the best locater of the pluses and minuses in her work. Her indictment of the trade-spirit, of shopocratic scorn for the poor, of diaconal tyranny—the standard case against Dissent, the stereotyped points—in so far as it contacted the reality, could be taken, as the *Nonconformist* did take it.[54] But the most telling parts of *Salem Chapel* and *Phoebe, Junior* are where something of what Dissent meant to the chapel-member breaks through, despite the author. Mrs. Oliphant may find the odour of bacon and cheese uncongenial, even distasteful, but it claims and achieves for itself a certain validity in the novel. The tea-meetings, the congregation's relish for sitting in judgement on its pastors, Tozer's loyalty to his class and his chapel, may be from stock, a thin enough gruel, diluted further by repetition and dispensed with smug superiority (the mock heroic of 'fragrant lymph' locates Mrs. Oliphant's socially secured distance from a tea-meeting), but their value cannot be entirely suppressed. Vincent feels his ambition thwarted in a tea-meeting; the author notes that the enjoyment is that of 'humble girls and womankind who knew no pleasure more exciting'; but 'the schoolroom, with its blazing gas, its festoons, and its mottoes, its tables groaning with dark-complexioned plumcake and heavy buns' asserts its own warmth and attraction and brings home the legitimate role of a tea-meeting in the fellowship of a chapel community (**Salem Chapel**, Ch. 10). Such glimpses of the Dissenters' communal life from the inside, once admitted, effectively challenge any amount of outsiders' scorn:

> The widow looked through her veil at the butterman and the poulterer with one keen pang of resentment, of which she repented instantly. She did not despise them as another might have done. They were the constituted authorities of the place, and her son's fate, his reputation, his young life, all that he had or could hope for in the world, was in their hands. The decision of the highest authorities in the land was not so important to Arthur as that of the poulterer and butterman. . . . (Ch. 35)

> Mr. Pigeon was a heavy orator; he was a tall man, badly put together, with a hollow crease across his waistcoat, which looked very much as if he might be folded in two, and so laid away out of mischief. His arms moved foolishly about in the agonies of oratory, as if they did not belong to him; but he did not look absurd through Mrs. Vincent's crape veil. . . . (Ch. 36)

Notes

[1] Mrs. Kathleen Watson thinks there is much more to this muddled assimilation than I think viable. See 'George Eliot and Mrs. Oliphant: A Comparison in Social Attitudes', *Essays in Criticism* 19 (1969), 410-19. For discussion of contrasts see, Review of M.O.W.O's *Autobiography and Letters*, *Quarterly Review*, 190 (July 1899), 256.

[2] *GE Letters*, II. 435, footnote 5.

[3] GE to S. S. Hennell (23 Apr. [1862]), *GE Letters*, IV. 25.

[4] *Spectator*, 36 (14 Feb. 1863), 1639.

[5] GE to S. S. Hennell (1 May [1862]), *GE Letters*, IV. 28.

[6] Cf. M.O.W.O. to Blackwood (1862): ' . . . the faintest idea of imitating or attempting to rival the author of "Adam Bede", never entered my mind.' *Autobiography and Letters*, 185-6.

[7] 'London Notes', *Harper's Weekly* (Aug. 1897): *Notes on Novelists with some Other Notes* (1914), 358.

[8] *Autobiography and Letters*, 258 (20 Apr. 1876).

[9] *Notes on Novelists*, 358-9; 'Anthony Trollope', *Century Magazine* (July 1883), reprinted in *Partial Portraits: The House of Fiction*, ed. Leon Edel (paperback edn., 1962), 90.

[10] 'Historical Sketches of the Reign of George II. No. VII.—The Reformer', *Blackwood's*, 104 (Oct. 1868), 428-56.

[11] 'Sensation Novels', *Blackwood's*, 91 (May 1862), 564-84.

[12] '*Autobiography and Letters*', 434 (30 Apr. 1897); 'Charles Reade's Novels', *Blackwood's*, 106 (Oct. 1869), 510; 'Modern Novelists—Great and Small', *Blackwood's*, 77 (May 1855), 555; M. O. and F. R. Oliphant, *The Victorian Age of English Literature* (1892), II. 200; M.O.W.O., ' 'Tis Sixty Years Since', *Blackwood's*, 161 (May 1897), 619.

[13] 'Novels', *Blackwood's*, 94 (Aug. 1863), 168-9.

[14] See R. D. Altick, *The English Common Reader* (Chicago, 1957), Appendix B. Charles Reade's *It is Never Too Late to Mend* (1856) sold 65,000 in seven years, and was attacked for melodrama, which Mrs. Oliphant's novels are not exactly free of (*Blackwood's*, 106 (Oct. 1869), 510). Mrs. Henry Wood's *East Lynne* (1861) sold 430,000 up to 1898; it was charged with glorifying vice as a purifier (*Blackwood's*, 91 (May 1862), 567) but imitated in *Salem Chapel* (see Vineta and Robert A. Colby, *The Equivocal Virtue: Mrs. Oliphant and the Victorian Literary Market Place* (Hamden,, Conn., 1966), 51-2).

[15] *The Minister's Wife* (3 Vols., 1869), III. 257 and 269; *Phoebe, Junior* (3 Vols., 1876), I. 280, II. 3. Cf. M.O.W.O.: 'I don't remember much one year what I wrote the year before . . .', *Autobiography and Letters*, 241.

[16] *Autobiography and Letters*, 4; Trollope, *An Autobiography*, II. 49-51.

[17] *Passages in the Life of Mrs. Margaret Maitland*, by Herself (Henry Colburn, 3 Vols., 1849); *Magdalen*

Hepburn: A Story of the Scottish Reformation (Hurst and Blackett, 3 Vols., 1854); *Lilliesleaf . . .*, written by Herself (Hurst and Blackett, 3 Vols., 1855); *The Minister's Wife* (Hurst and Blackett, 3 Vols., 1869); *Salem Chapel* (Blackwood, 2 Vols., 1863); *Phoebe, Junior* (Hurst and Blackett, 3 Vols., 1876).

[18] *Notes on Novelists* (1914), 350 (London Notes, Aug. 1897).

[19] Preface to *The Minister's Wife*.

[20] *Autobiography and Letters,* 178.

[21] Ibid., 84.

[22] *Blackwood's,* 92 (Aug. 1862), 215. W. W. Tulloch, 'Mrs. Oliphant', *Bookman,* 12 (Aug. 1897), 115. She translated Count Charles Forbes René de Montalembert's *The Monks of the West from St. Benedict to St. Bernard* (7 Vols., 1861-79) and wrote *Memoirs of the Count de Montalembert: A Chapter of Recent French History* (2 Vols., 1872). Both were published by Blackwood.

[23] *Academy* (3 July 1897), 15-16, quoted by V. and R. A. Colby, op. cit., 237; 'Mrs. Oliphant', *British Weekly* 22 (1 July 1897), 177; *Autobiography and Letters, passim*.

[24] *Autobiography and Letters,* 10, 348.

[25] See A. A. Maclaren, 'Presbyterianism and the working class in a mid-nineteenth century city', *Scottish Historical Review,* 46 (1967), 115-39, and Geoffrey Best, *Mid-Victorian Britain 1851-1875* (1971), 185. The secession had included all classes, 'even nobles and gentry and eminent professional men'; and it set out absolutely to replicate the Establishment, on the basis of the claim to be the 'true' Church of Scotland. J. H. S. Burleigh, *A Church History of Scotland* (1960), 352, 354.

[26] (23 Apr. [1862]), *GE Letters,* IV. 25-6.

[27] 'Salem Chapel', *Nonconformist,* 23 (25 Feb. 1863), 158.

[28] *Phoebe Junior,* Vol. II, Ch. 10. 'Dissent in Fiction', *Nonconformist,* 37 (5 July 1876), 675.

[29] *Phoebe,* Vol. II, Chs. 12 and 15. Cf. Mrs. Oliphant's account of Church-Dissent relations in [Frederick William Robinson's] *Church and Chapel* (1863): 'The object of the book, as it lies on the surface, is to show how entirely external are the disagreements between the good Churchman and the good Dissenter; and how the require only to be brought together and see each other's hearts, to secure their entire brotherhood and

cooperation in all good works'. 'Novels', *Blackwood's,* 94 (1863), 179.

[30] *Phoebe,* II, Ch. 2. Cf. a similar evasion in her novel *A Son of the Soil* (1866), in reference to Colin's first Scottish *Tracts for the Times:* 'It would be doing Colin injustice to reproduce here this revolutionary document . . .' (Vol. II, Ch. 21).

[31] 'Salem Chapel', *Nonconformist,* 23 (25 Feb. 1863), 157; 'Dissent in Fiction', *Nonconformist,* 37 (5 July 1876), 675.

[32] V. and R. A. Colby, op. cit., 46.

[33] 'Modern Novelists—Great and Small', *Blackwood's,* 77 (May 1855), 566.

[34] 'Sensation Novels', *Blackwood's* 91 (May 1862), 567, 568. 'Machinery' was Mrs. Oliphant's word, *Autobiography and Letters,* 187; *Victorian Age of English Literature,* II. 186.

[35] See V. and R. A. Colby, op. cit., 51-2.

[36] *Spectator,* 36 (14 Feb. 1863), 1639. Sensation 'marred the effect' of *Salem* and *The Perpetual Curate* ('The Brownlows', *The Literary World: A Monthly Supplement to the Christian World,* 1 (14 Mar. 1878), 18); it was 'quite out of place' in *Salem* (*Nonconformist,* 23 (25 Feb. 1863), 157), and happily was absent from 'The Rector' and 'The Doctor's Family' (*Nonconformist,* 23 (17 June 1863), 494). 'The plot may be dismissed as not only bad but unnecessary' (*National Review* (1863), quoted by V. and R. A. Colby, op. cit., 49).

[37] 'Sensation Novels', *Blackwood's* (May 1862), 564-84, compares him adversely with Wilkie Collins.

[38] *Nonconformist,* 37 (5 July 1876), 675.

[39] *Salem,* Ch. 8; *The Perpetual Curate* (3 Vols., Edinburgh, 1864), Vol. I, Ch. 1.

[40] *Nonconformist* (25 Feb. 1863), 157.

[41] Ibid., 158.

[42] There is no indication that Mrs. Oliphant read this book, and indeed, if my case that she is dealing merely in conventional ideas is true, it rather helps if she did not read it. But there is an odd resemblance between *Salem Chapel*'s Adelaide Tufton and the daughter of one of the grocer-draper members of Scargill's narrator's chapel: both are unmarried, sharp-eyed, quick-witted, outspoken girls of about thirty. Scargill, op. cit. (5th edn., 1835), Chs. 4 and 6; *Salem Chapel,* Chs. 3 and 41.

[43] Scargill, op. cit., Ch. 7. He is quoting Wm. Hull, *Ecclesiastical Establishments Not Inconsistent with Christianity: With a Particular View to some Leading Objections of Modern Dissenters* (1834), 58-9.

[44] *Phoebe,* Vol. I, Chs. 1, 5, 12.

[45] *Victorian Age of English Literature,* II. 339.

[46] William Hull, *Ecclesiastical Establishments . . . Second Part; Including Remarks on the Voluntary System, and, on the Baronial Functions of the Bishops* (1834), 7.

[47] 'The Sons of the Prophets: Two Representatives of the Catholic Faith', *Blackwood's* 135 (1884), 531.

[48] *Nonconformist* (25 Feb. 1863), 158.

[49] Even the *Spectator* thought his mind disagreeable, *Spectator,* 36 (14 Feb. 1863), 1640.

[50] *Nonconformist* (5 July 1876), 675.

[51] *Life of Irving,* I. 399-400; and cf. 356.

[52] See V. and R. A. Colby, op. cit., 46-7.

[53] *Life of Irving,* I. 161.

[54] *Nonconformist* (25 Feb. 1863), 158.

R. C. Terry (essay date 1983)

SOURCE: "Queen of Popular Fiction: Mrs. Oliphant and the *Chronicles of Carlingford,*" in *Victorian Popular Fiction, 1860-80,* Macmillan Press, 1983, pp. 68-101.

[*In the following overview of the* Chronicles of Carlingford, *Terry discusses Oliphant as a "striking example" of the Victorian popular novelist—based on her talent and enormous output—and asserts that the* Carlingford *novels comprise her best work, without which readers would have an incomplete record of mid-Victorian fiction.*]

> I might have done better work. . . . Who can tell? I did with much labour what I thought the best, and there is only a might have been on the other side.
>
> Mrs Oliphant, *Autobiography and Letters* (1899)

Mrs Oliphant is a striking example of the professional woman of letters in the mid-Victorian period. Henry James, always notable for exquisitely ambiguous judgements on his fellow-writers, called her 'a gallant woman', praising her 'heroic production' (quantity uppermost in his mind rather than quality) but expressing admiration for her perception and subtlety.[1] Queen Victoria read and admired her novels, several times calling her to audience, and at her funeral in 1897 a wreath bore a message of respect and farewell from the monarch. She was a queenly personage herself in many respects. J. M. Barrie amusingly describes his first meeting with her, in 1886, when he was 'ordered' to Windsor where she was then living. He bought his first umbrella for the occasion, but it was of little avail. The regal presence unnerved him.[2] In her obituary William Blackwood wrote, 'Mrs Oliphant has been to the England of letters what the Queen has been to society as a whole. She, too, was crowned with age and honour in her own empire; widow and mother, she has tasted the triumph of life as well as the bitterness.'[3]

I chose Mrs Oliphant as the first of my middlebrow authors simply because her natural gifts of storytelling and amazing industry perfectly represent the popular novelist's approach. She was supremely one of the 'race of middlemen'.[4] More significantly, her slavery to her pen (though she enjoyed it, and wrote as spontaneously as she talked) and the compromises forced upon her for the market very well reflect the circumstances of minor writers at this time. Her output was prodigious and it is possible only to consider the best work—the *Chronicles of Carlingford*—of this 'considerable and original novelist'.[5] In a career spanning fifty years she produced almost a hundred novels, plus biographies of Edward Irving, Principal (John) Tulloch, Montalembert and Laurence Oliphant. She wrote over 200 articles and essays for *Blackwood's Edinburgh Magazine,* reviewing current books in 'Our Library Table' and earning distinction as a critic. As editor of Blackwood's Foreign Classics she steeped herself in European literature and herself contributed the volumes on Dante and Cervantes. She wrote a *Literary History of England* and a splendid labour of love, *Annals of the House of Blackwood*. Her energy and effort were phenomenal. As a young girl she worked, as Jane Austen had done, amidst the hurly-burly of the parlour. Later, as family tragedies threatened to engulf her, she wrote her way out of ruin and depression, as Mrs Trollope did, by working far into the night. 'As a breadwinner she began and as a breadwinner she was to end.'[6] This indomitable woman is an example of unmerited oblivion among lesser writers of the age, in many ways an unlucky victim of the publishing-system and of the vagaries of fortune that attend those who fail to reach the pinnacle of critical recognition rather than popular acclaim.

One of three surviving children, her two brothers, Frank and Willie, both proved weak characters who sooner or later depended on her for support.[7] When Willie failed as a minister of the English Presbyterian

Church, it was the strong resourceful Margaret who rescued him from his London lodgings, insisting with typical spirit that they go without dinner for a week to pay off one importunate creditor. 'Mrs Oliphant could never believe in a hero',[8] remarked L. P. Stebbins. The behaviour of brothers and later sons no doubt contributed to her disillusion, although there was also a young man to whom she was passionately attached as a girl, who emigrated to America and promptly dropped her. She tells the story with wry humour, but the painful incident may well have contributed to her heroines' unsentimental attitude to love: her depiction of marriage is decidedly frosty; the men in her novels decidedly weak.

In 1852 she married her cousin, Frank Oliphant, an artist in stained glass with a small business in London, but within a few years a succession of tragic events overtook her. Prospects were bright enough at first: her husband's business went well and her early literary successes brought contact with Frank Smedley, the S. C. Halls and the Howitts. Writing in her steady, carefree way she could expect about £400 for a novel—'already, of course, being told that I was working too fast, and producing too much'.[9] By 1856, when her first son, Cyril, was born, she had already lost two infants. Then in 1859 her husband died of tuberculosis in Italy, where the family had moved in hope of a cure. Mrs Oliphant had now to begin literary drudgery that lasted until her death in 1897. She recalled in 1885, 'When I thus began the world anew I had for all my fortune about £1,000 of debt, a small insurance of, I think £200 on Frank's life, our furniture laid up in a warehouse, and my own faculties, such as they were, to make our living and pay off our burdens by.'[10] She moved to London and, with three young children to care for, set herself doggedly to her nightly stint, often working until two or three in the morning, and producing sometimes two novels a year. But from this struggle emerged her best work, **Chronicles of Carlingford,** about which she said in 1894: 'The series is pretty well forgotten now, which made a considerable stir at the time, and *almost* made me one of the popularities of literature. *Almost,* never quite, though **Salem Chapel** went very near it, I believe.'[11]

At the busiest time in her career, during the early sixties, domestic burdens and sorrows accumulated. Her only daughter, Maggie, caught gastric fever and died in 1864 in Rome. She returned hurriedly to England and by the following year settled in Windsor, for she was determined that both sons should attend Eton. There was a brief period when things went well, but then in 1868 came news of her brother Frank's ruin in Canada. Now there was Frank junior to see through Eton and university. But she kept up a cheerful countenance, living for the day in extravagant style (she was not, she once said, attracted to travel second-class), and made a cosy home where all the boys'

friends were welcome. Reading her autobiography, we realise what it cost to maintain both social life and her colossal work schedule. She often pauses wistfully to wonder whether her work might have been better. And, with a strong sense of puritan guilt, whether her sons might have learned habits of work 'which now seem beyond recall' (this is in 1885), had she not so pampered them.[12]

Cyril and Francis (known as 'Cecco'), who was born in that terrible year in Italy in 1859, were, she said, 'my all in this world'.[13] To provide for them was a central concern of her life and they are a focus of her autobiography and intimately bound up with the major concerns of her fiction—the intricacies of marital adjustments (usually the woman's sacrifices to the Victorian male ego), conflicts between parents and children, the pains of motherhood. Her love for her boys, A. C. Benson believed, 'had something almost morbidly passionate about it'.[14] Even her open-handedness haunted her in respect of their characters. In a pathetic footnote in the autobiography she reproaches herself for hiding her anxieties from them and thereby encouraging their idleness and extravagance. For they proved unalterably feckless. Cyril had little capacity for work and, while his mother moved to Oxford to provide him with the creature comforts to which he was accustomed, frittered away his time. Typically, she blamed herself: 'My dearest, bright, delightful boy missed somehow his footing, how can I tell how? I often think that I had to do with it, as well as what people call inherited tendencies, and, alas! the perversity of youth, which he never outgrew.'[15]

At fifty-six, Mrs Oliphant looked back on 'a laborious life, incessant work, incessant anxiety', and, although she insisted it had not been unhappy, there is undoubtedly a sense of servitude in the way she described it. She recalled that when family responsibilities piled up on her, 'I said to myself having then perhaps a little stirring of ambition, that I must make up my mind to think no more of that, and that to bring up the boys for the service of God was better than to write a fine novel, supposing even that it was in me to do so.'[16] Doubtless such thinking coloured her attitude to her contemporaries and to literary values in general. She harps on George Eliot's example with a guilty sense of her own compromises and at the same time a half-envying disdain for her protected life: 'Should I have done better if I had been kept, like her, in a mental greenhouse and taken care of?'[17] Beside Eliot and George Sand Mrs Oliphant feels 'a fat, little, commonplace woman, rather tongue-tied . . . there is a sort of whimsical injury in it which makes me sorry for myself'.[18] Anne Thackeray, far from finding her tongue-tied, said of her, 'She was one of those people whose presence is even more than a *pleasure,* it was stimulus; she was kindly, sympathetic, and yet answering with that chord of intelligent antagonism which is so suggestive and makes for such good talk.'[19] A life of suffering etched character into her features. Observing her in the chapel of Eton College in 1874, A. C. Benson noted she had an expression of endurance 'more of repression than of suppression, as if a naturally expansive and genial nature had been thwarted and baffled'.[20]

In the eighties both sons fell ill; Cyril died in 1890 aged thirty-four, and 'Cecco' four years later. Her nephew had already succumbed in India to typhoid in 1879. 'And now I am alone', she wrote, ending her fragment of autobiography, 'I cannot write any more.' Yet she had to keep on writing, partly out of habit, partly still out of need. Nine days before her death she corrected the first volume of the **Blackwood** history, and apologised that she could not correct the second: 'I am now lying, all possibility of work over, awaiting a very speedy end', she wrote to William Blackwood. She died on 25 June 1897, the names of her sons, it is said, continually on her lips. Anne Thackeray wrote to Rhoda Broughton, 'I have lost a life-long friend, and the world too, in that wise, tender and humorous woman whom all delighted to love and appreciate. She was to me one of those people who *make* life—so many unmake it'.[21]

The reason Mrs Oliphant caught and held her public takes us to the very heart of this study, for she is a true representative of mid-Victorian minor fiction, commercial without pandering to the market; professional without being slipshod or cynical; morally straight without being mealy-mouthed or censorious; full of feeling without being gushy; stylish without being vulgar or affected. If Trollope is, as Alexander Innes Shand claimed, 'more distinctly the family novelist than anyone who has gone before him', then Mrs Oliphant comes close behind.[22] But she is not a lesser Trollope. She has her own voice and writes unique novels. If she represents what Alfred Austin in 1870 labelled the Simple School, she wears her simplicity with a difference. Austin defines the type as

> the school whose domain is the hearth, whose machinery the affections,—the school which talks to the heart without quickening its beat, yet not without moistening the eye,—the school to which home is sacred, all bad things are available only as contrasts—this we have always with us.[23]

But in Mrs Oliphant it is often a troubled hearth and an unquiet heart. Her novels have far more astringent touches than Mrs Craik's or Anne Thackeray's, for example. Shand in 1879 called her 'the salt of the contemporary generation of novelists', and it is easy to see why.[24] Justly admired for her Scottish landscapes, and winning heroines in novels such as **Katie Stewart** (1853), she returned often to Scottish characters and backgrounds, notably in **The Minister's Wife**

(1869) and **Kirsteen** (1890). A more important element in her appeal is her commonsense, realistic approach that caught, as the *Spectator* said of **A Rose in June** (1874), the beauty in the essentially commonplace. In particular she tapped a vein women could respond to, reversing Jane Austen's equation of salvation with matrimony. Unlike Trollope and other male novelists, she can see that staying single—or being widowed—has distinct advantages. The jolly spinster aunts that crop up in her novels have the best of it after all.

She is questioning women's role and in her own way getting back at sexual inequality, not by showing the sensation novel's drunkards, tyrants and boors (although they are sometimes part of the picture), but by tracing the remorseless sorrows, humiliations, envies about which women were supposed to be silent.[25] She was in some respects ahead of her time, showing a disquieting scepticism in both the consolations of faith and domestic felicity. Her menfolk are often ninnies who have given up on life, as in **May** (1873), or failures in their work, as in **At His Gates** (1872). Fruits of her own disappointed life can, of course, be discerned in all this. Robert Drummond in the latter novel is an unsuccessful artist (like Frank Oliphant), and the thrust of the novel lies with the wife's combined scorn, sympathy and guilt for not being patient about it. 'When a man must not be disturbed about bills his wife must be', she writes in **A Rose in June** (1874). Heroines frequently orphaned or prematurely widowed shoulder the burden, and do so with a healthy resentment, groaning at the unfairness of it all—the social system, husbands, brothers and sons who flopped or floundered, and even protesting God's mockery of innocent women, as in **Agnes** (1866) or **Madonna Mary** (1867). Mrs Oliphant's resentment plays quietly but no doubt to sympathetic listeners at the time, and the tune is that women's life is hard. Had she had the time, or been free of the need for cash—I do not think she lacked the courage—she had it in her to come close to tragedy like Hardy's.

This is not to deny that she wrote pot-boilers with perfunctory plots and cobbled-up endings; with such an output that is hardly surprising. Nor did she escape the more baneful influences of sensation, often marring a sensible domestic study with the apparatus of ruined heiresses, impossible wills, damning letters, skeletons in cupboards, misappropriated legacies and the like, but her novels often generate genuine feelings and not the cardboard emotions of the sensationists. It was said that there were two Mrs Oliphants: the shrewd painter of domestic realities and the more lurid storyteller who in **Carita** (1877) has a sophisticated and atheistically inclined lady suffering from cancer so revolted by her condition that she commits suicide with laudanum unwittingly supplied by her ten-year-old daughter. Lurid perhaps, but as a fictional device not entirely without significance from a psychological viewpoint.

Another Mrs Oliphant emerges in a later phase of her career and deserves brief comment. Partly because of her fascination with and proximity to death, and partly in response to a vogue for tales of the occult, Mrs Oliphant produced several striking fantasies, notably *The Beleaguered City* (1880) and *Two Stories of the Seen and Unseen* (1885). In the only full-length study of the author in modern times, V. and R. A. Colby claim that the former is one of the minor classics of Victorian literature.

The Carlingford novels, however, represent the peak of her achievement. When the first appeared there was speculation that George Eliot was the anonymous author. Eliot may have flared a nostril at the comparison, but Mr Mudie's patrons perceived similarities, and it is certainly possible that Mrs Oliphant was drawn to her subject by the popularity of *Scenes of Clerical Life*.[26] Mrs Oliphant follows Trollope in creating a rural southern county, probably Berkshire-*cum*-Hampshire, with a town, not as grand as Barchester (there is no cathedral), and characters who reappear in the series, changing with the interval of years. The town of Carlingford makes its first appearance in **'The Executor',** a short story in *Blackwood's* for May 1861, but the Dissenting community which made the series famous did not appear until the novels: *The Rector and The Doctor's Family* (3 vols, 1863), *Salem Chapel* (2 vols, 1863), *The Perpetual Curate* (3 vols, 1864), *Miss Marjoribanks* (3 vols, 1866), and *Phoebe Junior: A Last Chronicle of Carlingford* (3 vols, 1876).[27] Although geographical locations are obscurer than in Trollope's Barsetshire, it is possible to place the main spheres of action: the Dissenting chapel on the edge of town, the Anglican chapel of St Roque just half a mile from Carlingford, the parish church and, nearby, the best residential quarter. There is a canal, a railway, and a new suburb representing social changes the establishment resents and within which the young clergy and doctors carry out their progressive ideas. Whereas Barchester, however, is endangered by modernism, Carlingford is still a rural backwater: 'There are no alien activities to disturb the place—no manufactures, and not much trade'.[28]

The thirty-four pages of *The Rector* make an admirable introduction to the series, its plot involving a clash between the Revd Frank Wentworth, curate in charge of St Roque's, and the new Rector of Carlingford, Morley Proctor. Mrs Oliphant establishes convincingly the predicament of the withdrawn, studious Proctor forced to compete with the sociable Wentworth, who has the goodwill of the community to sustain him as well as natural endowments as a clergyman, and when Proctor is called in off the street

to minister to a dying woman and finds himself unable to make any effective speeches either to bring her peace of mind or to prepare her for the end he feels he has forfeited the right to remain in Carlingford. He resigns his pulpit and scuttles back to Oxford, a defeated man, but one who is beginning to confront his spiritual and temperamental inadequacies. Proctor's academic life can no longer shield him, and he must endure the guilt of knowing that something was demanded of him that he failed to give. The story ends with the assumption that eventually he did take on another parish, having married the elder Miss Wodehouse, and found his way out of a sterile existence.

Such a synopsis might suggest merely another dreary exercise in improving fiction, but *The Rector* is no tract in the Martineau tradition, and its merit arises from the malice and pettiness glimpsed within the individual and the family. The Rector's shyness, long a source of amusement to his aged mother, complicates his wooing. With awful skittishness Mrs Proctor teases him about bringing home a bride, and her supposition that it is the older, plainer daughter, Mary Wodehouse, rather than her sister, Lucy—'twenty, pretty, blue-eyed, and full of dimples'—adds to his discomfiture:

> When Mr Proctor saw his mother again at dinner, she was evidently full of some subject which would not bear talking of before the servants. The old lady looked at her son's troubled apprehensive face with smiles and nods and gay hints, which he was much too preoccupied to understand, and which only increased his bewilderment. When the good man was left alone over his glass of wine, he drank it slowly, in funereal silence, with profoundly serious looks; and what between eagerness to understand what the old lady meant, and reluctance to show the extent of his curiosity, had a very heavy half-hour of it in that grave solitary dining-room. He roused himself with an effort from this dismal state into which he was falling. He recalled with a sigh the classic board of All-Souls. Woe for the day when he was seduced to forsake that dear retirement! (ch.2)

This admirable prose reads well aloud and the cadence of the sentences and good plain diction are well directed to show Proctor's prim nature, afraid of commitment either as priest or lover. The images are not striking—bordering on cliché even—but, as with Trollope, a second reading fires the imagination: phrases such as 'funereal silence' and 'grave solitary dining-room' have a special resonance and irony in a story which is about a man being brought back to life, and there is a nice contrast between his aggravated melancholy, expressed in that splendidly rhetorical 'Woe for the day . . .', and her 'smiles and nods and gay hints'.

The art of the domestic realist is to infuse plain, ordinary, commonplace routine with dramatic intensity; as Trollope was always saying, the cardinal sin was to bore the reader. Mrs Oliphant is adept at creating conflict within the domestic circle. Here, the mutual tension is low-key and comic, but it is tension none the less. Mrs Proctor uses her deafness as a weapon, forcing her son to shout his confidences into her ear, so that the servants *will* overhear. 'His dismay and perplexity amused this wicked old woman beyond measure' (ch.2). But she loves him dearly, that is plain, and the bond between them is always clear to the reader without sentimentality.

Enmity between parents and children and sibling rivalry are frequently subjects of Mrs Oliphant's fiction. There is no malice in Mrs Proctor, but one feels there is more to Mr Wodehouse's baiting of his two girls than meets the eye. Indeed his humiliation of his elder daughter touches a darker vein of parental psychology than one might expect for so tranquil a story. He is slightly caricatured in a Dickensian manner: 'Mr Wodehouse was a man who creaked universally'; 'As he came along the garden path, the gravel started all round his unmusical foot' (ch.1), but Mrs Oliphant weaves insensitivity and coarseness into the character with more subtlety than is apparent from this metaphoric insistence. His teasing is totally different in quality from Mrs Proctor's; he seems resentful of his daughter's dependence, and is rude about Mr Wentworth behind his back. In *The Doctor's Family* he is still more cynical. Mr Wodehouse has some of the unpleasant underside Jane Austen gives several of her elderly male characters.

The charm of this prelude to the Chronicles rests on the contrast pointed out between the tranquillity of the rural scene and sleepy old town with its dusty roads, walled gardens and apple blossoms and the agitated hearts and minds of its inhabitants old and young. Its skill lies in the way Mrs Oliphant evokes comedy from the plight of her central character with his 'walled up' spirit. He is a ludicrously ancient young man, as his mother recognises, she being 'let us say, a hundred years or so younger than the Rector' (ch.2). The improvement in his temper and spirits at the end of the story has a beneficent effect on the town itself, for in *The Doctor's Family* we learn that Miss Lucy Wodehouse has learned from the former Rector's example and begun to exert herself with parish visiting.

The Doctor's Family is a longer but slighter tale with a conventional love plot. Edward Rider is a young doctor who has set up in practice in the unfashionable quarter of Carlingford—'a region of half-built streets, vulgar new roads, and heaps of desolate brick and mortar' (ch.18). Secretly he is caring for his wastrel brother, Fred, who has returned from Australia and sits in an upper room all day, smoking coarse tobacco and reading even coarser novels from the circulating library. Fred's wife, Susan, then appears, together with several infants, and her sister, Nettie Underwood, 'all action and haste' and 'not only slender, but *thin,* dark, eager, impetuous, with blazing black eyes and red lips' (ch.2). Nettie is one of those masterful young heroines Mrs Oliphant draws better than anyone since Jane Austen, and naturally she and Edward are destined for one another, after some stock misapprehensions.

Given the rather improbable extent of Nettie's self-imposed martyrdom (she is, at the crisis of the story, prepared to accompany her sister Susan and the children back to Australia) and the even more unlikely *deus ex machina* of an Australian who appears with a proposal of marriage to Susan, now widowed (Fred having fallen into the river while drunk), the story moves briskly and turns out to be fairly entertaining. Indeed its farcical elements are perhaps the most engaging, especially when amidst shouting and disturbance Edward arrives as Nettie is packing and preparing to leave England for ever. A reckless ride through the respectable streets of Carlingford in pursuit of Nettie makes plain all misunderstandings and offers the prospect of lifelong felicity, though as Miss Lucy Wodehouse perceives it would have been a neater ending if Dr Rider could instead have fallen in love with Miss Marjoribanks, daughter of the town's leading practitioner:

> If Miss Marjoribanks had only been Nettie, or Nettie Miss Marjoribanks! If not only love and happiness, but the old doctor's practice and savings, could but have been brought to heap up the measure of the young doctor's good fortune! What a pity that one cannot have everything! (ch.18)

With such gentle Trollopian irony does the story exert its charm, although its chief interest is undoubtedly the character of Nettie Underwood. One can even believe, because of her impetuousness, that she *will* go to Australia, but what is more interesting is the degree to which Mrs Oliphant undercuts Nettie's self-imposed duty, her determination to provide for her sister and family, by showing just how much it cloaks managerial pride, and how much it is her defence against becoming dependent. In Nettie we have an inspiration which flowered in a splendid portrayal in *Miss Marjoribanks*.

The appearance of *Salem Chapel* in 1863[29] was greeted with justifiable enthusiasm. The narrative is brisk and assured, moving immediately into a rapid tour of a more geographically certain Carlingford than we have seen before, and a subject is announced without loss of time: the gulf between Carlingford society and its Dissenting community. This is a novel about English social snobbery as a Scotswoman can enjoy it. The centre of action, Salem Chapel, is at the west end of Grove Street, where the houses are 'little detached boxes, each two storeys high, each fronted by a little flower-plot—clean, respectable, meagre, little habitations' (ch.1). Greengrocers, dealers in cheese and bacon, milkmen, teachers of day schools, form the élite of this cheerful congregation. The cream of society, on the other hand, is centred on the parish church and the chapel of St Roque's, and the big houses of Grange Lane, where the Wodehouses and the Marjoribanks live.

The new minister of Salem Chapel, Arthur Vincent, fresh from Homerton, and aflame with both social and professional ambitions, quickly feels the limitations of his flock and begins to hanker after Grange Lane. Almost as particular about the cut of his coat as Mr Wentworth, the perpetual curate of St Roque's, 'he came to Carlingford with elevated expectations' and was rapidly enamoured of the young dowager, Lady Western. But Vincent, not being a Christ Church man, or even a fellow of Trinity, feels at a disadvantage. He gazes on the curate with some wistfulness. 'A poor widow's son, educated at Homerton, and an English squire's son, public school, and university bred, cannot begin on the same level' (ch.2). Mrs Oliphant thus poses her hero in a beautifully ambiguous position; even his lodgings are at what the Grange Lane people call *the other end* of George Street (ch.1). Brought up in 'painful gentility' by his mother, Vincent is between two worlds, and the early chapters make a good deal of comic mileage out of Vincent's mistaken notions of himself and those around him, from the time his ego is punctured by the well-meant gift of a left-over jelly from Mrs Tozer's welcoming-party to his mortification at being tongue-tied at Lady Western's breakfast. Bitterly resentful at being adopted by the Tozers and their daughter Phoebe, who is 'pink all over', and recoiling from the smugness of Salem, Vincent antagonises his flock.

The chapel people are as realistic as though Mrs Oliphant had lived among them all her life, especially old Mr Tufton, his crippled daughter, the admirable Mr Tozer, the butterman, and his buxom daughter, Phoebe. Indeed, much of the zest of the novel comes from scenes involving these good folk and their surroundings. The tea meeting (ch.10), is full of fascinating detail, the blazing gas of the schoolroom, the decorations, the tables 'groaning with dark-complexioned plumcake and heavy buns', the urns, the ladies' bonnets, the fulsome speeches, and 'the triumphant face of Tozer at the end of the room, jammed against the wall, drinking tea out of an empty sugar-basin'—another jar to the sensibilities of the young Nonconformist.

Besides satirising the English preoccupation with class, birth and social mobility, *Salem Chapel* is also a growing-up story, explaining the constricting pressures of the social group against which the individual must struggle. Arthur Vincent, though naïve and self-satisfied, has many admirable qualities and gradually grows in maturity and self-confidence. This progress is underlined by the role of the butterman, Tozer, who sees himself as the minister's mentor and tries to manage his protégé's career. Vincent begins by hating his domination, but a bond grows between them as Tozer reveals a simple good nature that earns the minister's respect. Tozer is that rarity in a mid-Victorian novel, a tradesman drawn convincingly and without caricature. As principal deacon he obtrudes his opinions about the good of the chapel and meddles with Vincent's private life, but when troubles gather he grows stronger in his loyalty to the young minister, though Mrs Oliphant is careful not to lose sight of that proprietorial smugness in his attitude. 'I'll stand by you, sir, for one whatever happens', he declares when Vincent's fortunes are at their blackest, his face 'radiant with conscious bounty and patronage' (ch.25). But his counsel is sound, and when scandal breaks his advice is go into the pulpit as usual and face the flock; 'It's next Sunday is all the battle' (ch.27), and he grows in the reader's estimation. When Vincent most needs help he makes an oration worthy of Mark Antony to prevent the flock from repudiating its pastor.

The course of the solemn tribunal covers two splendid chapters of mingled pathos and comedy. Vincent's mother, disguised in her black shawl at the back of the Salem schoolroom, is the anguished witness, as Pigeon, the poulterer, declares that Vincent must go. Old Mr Tufton, the former minister, well-meaning but over-apologetic, only makes matters worse. Then Tozer rises and with his vigorous, ungrammatical, plain speaking both extols the minister's example and annihilates his enemies for their vindictiveness. His speech, some four pages long, is masterly characterisation, but it also expresses issues implicit in the whole novel: the tendency of the Dissenting community—of any social grouping—to cabal and conspire against its leader, and out of personal ambition to produce anarchy. Just as Tozer in his clumsy way had tried to show Vincent that he must conciliate his congregation without sacrificing his principles, he now makes a case against the tyranny exercised by the Salem people and calls for tolerance and understanding. When Vincent declares his intention of resigning, Tozer again enlists the reader's sympathy, groaning in his sleep with anxiety at the new cloud over Salem and poignantly expressing his vision of the ideal (far from Vincent's own imagining) of a friendly tea—'pleasant looks and the urns a-smoking, and a bit of green on the wall . . . a bit of an anecdote, or poetry about friends as is better friends after they've spoke their minds and had it out' (ch.40).

But the maturing of Vincent cannot reside in the kind of comfortable reconciliation that would have been accepted by his predecessor, Tufton. In a passage of Lawrencean rhetoric, Mrs Oliphant has her hero take his wounded sensibility into the countryside around Carlingford: 'Here were the hedgerows stirring, the secret grain beginning to throb conscious in the old furrows' (ch.40) and Vincent decides what to do. Once more he faces the flock in the decorated schoolroom, under the text 'Love one another' amid cheers and applause, but, 'angry, displeased, humbled in his own estimation', he discourses quietly until 'the very gaslights seem to darken in the air in the silence', and with new-found spiritual authority he leaves Salem.

Salem Chapel also contains crudely sensational plot elements, however, involving a mystery surrounding Mrs Hilyard, whose husband has for many years kept her from her own child, and for good measure almost seduces Vincent's sister, Susan. The ramifications, involving abduction, attempted murder, and ear-splittingly falsetto dialogue—'"She-wolf!" cried the man, grinding his teeth' (ch.9)—sit very uneasily with the dominant domestic realism, although the sensationalism can be defended in one important respect: it throws ironical light on the theme of irrationality in human affairs. People are subject to dark forces from within. Vincent's well-ordered life is suddenly overthrown by his infatuation with Lady Western; he is 'rapt out of himself' (ch.7). His sister's near ruin and madness, and the passionate hatred of Mrs Hilyard for her husband, are, like the violence and mystery, manifestations of the irregularity that threatens Salem, and they force Vincent into knowledge of the real evil and pain in the world that it is his business as minister to attend to. His journey to Northumberland illustrates well the relation between theme and sensational plot. The search for 'the lost creature', his sister, has the usual melodramatic ingredients, but the narrative makes thematic sense: the church bell's jangling reinforces the idea of the chaos into which Vincent has fallen—'life all disordered'—and as a minister of religion he is painfully conscious of his imperilled position among the flock (whom he has temporarily abandoned) and of his responsibilities:

> As they drove along the bleak moorland road, an early church-bell tingled into the silence, and struck, with horrible iron echoes, upon the heart of the minister of Salem. Sunday morning! Life all disordered, incoherent, desperate—all its usages set at nought and duties left behind. Nothing could have added the final touch of derangement and desperation like the sound of that bell. . . . (ch.20)

Mrs Oliphant also shows herself adept at the kind of mounting suspense that Wilkie Collins or Miss Braddon could create. At one point Vincent is idly gazing at a train just beginning to move out of the station:

> Now the tedious line glides into gradual motion. Good Heaven! what was that? the flash of a match, a sudden gleam upon vacant cushions, the profile of a face, high-featured, with the thin light locks and shadowy moustache he knew so well, standing out for a moment in aquiline distinctness against the moving space.

It is the man he is pursuing, and as the train gathers speed Vincent struggles to open a door, until several porters seize him. Passengers stare out of windows, and in one of the end compartments he sees another familiar face, that of Mrs Hilyard, 'who looked out with no surprise, but with a horrible composure in her white face, and recognized him with a look which chilled to stone'. Over-emphatic, perhaps, but full of imaginative detail and the sudden impact one associates with a Hitchcock film.

The physical reality of a community and its environment is brought to life by a host of homely touches: Tufton's neat little house with its cabbages and huge geraniums, the green door leading to the Wodehouse villa, the cheering fire in a station waiting-room. Physical actions are highly suggestive: Mrs Vincent attending to the lamps and taking comfort from this routine activity; Tozer's hand over his empty cup and saucer eloquently conveying displeasure. Domestic details are equally exact. With Mrs Oliphant we know there is even 'Wooster sauce' on the dinner table and that beds must be well aired in January. Atmosphere is her strong card: you can smell the ham and cheeses in Tozer's shop; and, even where sensational effects are uppermost, they are often underpinned and given credibility by atmospheric touches, as when Mrs Hilyard takes her long lonely walk in the dark, rainy street.

Salem Chapel is the livelier novel, but *The Perpetual Curate* the more ambitious development of Mrs Oliphant's intentions with the series.[30] This was the novel for which John Blackwood risked £1500 to his associate's wonderment, and cheered by his encouragement Mrs Oliphant declared, '*The Perpetual Curate* is the sharer of my inmost thoughts'. The hero, she said, 'is a favourite of mine, and I mean to bestow the very greatest care upon him'.[31]

Care was also given to plotting a more complex work, even though the spontaneous way she wrote was not conducive to adequate anticipation of climaxes. In chapter 37 she declares her anxiety about which of her many threads of narrative shall be taken up first, and a joke about events ending for the hero 'like a trashy novel' (ch. 48) perhaps betrays a certain unease about not having quite brought it off. It was apparent in her correspondence with Blackwood that the original intention was 'a little exhibition of all the three parties in the Church',[32] to be achieved by making her hero, Frank Wentworth, a Puseyite confronting the newly installed, rather old-fashioned 'high and dry' Rector, William Morgan. At the same time, Frank is badgered by his Low Church aunt, Leonora, who has the power of securing a living for him in Skelmersdale, and engaged in an unsuccessful struggle to prevent his brother going over to Rome.

The Perpetual Curate has much to recommend it. The larger framework enables Mrs Oliphant to have her fling at several touchy subjects: doctrinal squabbles of High, Low and Roman Church, particularly the still fascinating topic of Catholic conversion, rivalries of parents and children, prickly marital relationships, class antagonism, and that abiding Victorian preoccupation with good name. What gives it unity is the way the author shows a well-governed world turned upside down, and normally sensible, respectable and sober members of the community squabbling like pettish children. ' . . . this strange, wayward, fantastical humanity which is never to be calculated upon' (ch. 24)—the phrase takes on a special resonance as the epicentre of the novel. The opening prepares us for trouble by insisting that Carlingford is a place where nothing happens. 'It is the boast of the place that it has no particular interest' (ch.1). The rule of the clergy is emphasised:

> But in every community some centre of life is necessary. This point, round which everything circles, is, in Carlingford, found in the clergy. They are the administrators of the commonwealth, the only people who have defined and compulsory duties to give a sharp outline to life.

It is the book's business to show how this order is turned upside down and how the state totters.

At first reading the novel invites comparison with one of the Barsetshire series, not least in its title, which adopts the conveniently independent though ambiguous post Trollope chose in *Framley Parsonage* (1861) for Mr Crawley, perpetual curate of Hogglestock. That element of independence is vital for Mrs Oliphant's hero, who is also of higher social standing than the new Rector, his father being the squire of another parish. So long as Frank stays within his own segment of the parish at St Roque's Chapel he is unassailable, but he has carried his muscular Christianity to the new housing-estate and the canal, forming an impromptu chapel among the brickmakers and bargemen. Pride, breeding, youth and a certain resentment at a newcomer's authority spark off an immediate clash, when Frank deliberately insults Mr Morgan by mocking the hideous architecture of the parish church, which the Rector is planning to improve. Thus a very Trollopian conflict of opposites is initiated: old ways and new, the invasion of territory, clashes of temperament and ideology, all promising a good fight. Moreover, there is enough ambiguity in both characters for the reader to sympathise at points with each. What loads public opinion against Frank is that he is suspected of having toyed with a young girl's feelings, a moral delinquency similar to that of Mr Crawley in *The Last Chronicle of Barset* (published three years after Mrs Oliphant's novel), who is suspected of misdemeanour over a cheque. In both unlikely circumstances some kind of public tribunal is involved, and it is an unfortunate sensational element in *The Perpetual Curate* that Wentworth could actually be suspected of abduction and end up before a kangaroo court of local worthies.

That dimension of clergymen in their ministry which Trollope studiously avoids is never shirked by Mrs Oliphant. Frank Wentworth gains in depth by being shown about his active ministry; he visits the sick, baptises (a flagrant invasion of his rector's parish, which adds fuel to the row), organises a Sisterhood and a Provident Society, and hears confession too. Mrs Oliphant shows him not only preparing his sermon, but also delivering it—at the Wharfside service, for example, when his text has more fervour and effectiveness than his preaching at St Roque's. Much later in the novel, when his personal troubles are at their worst, he visits the dying Mr Wodehouse and is seen to be increasing in spiritual maturity:

> Mr Wentworth came into the silent chamber with all his anxieties throbbing in his heart, bringing life at its very height of agitation and tumult into the presence of death. He went forward to the bed, and tried for an instant to call up any spark of intelligence that might yet exist within the mind of the dying man; but Mr Wodehouse was beyond the voice of any priest. The Curate said the prayers for the dying at the bedside, suddenly filled with a great pity for the man who was thus taking leave unawares of all this mournful splendid world. (ch.27)

The mixture of emotions, the recognition of human responses getting in the way of priestly ones, the gulf between the vital young man and the dying old one, and the juxtaposition of 'mournful splendid' in that last sentence convey forcefully the ambiguity of human experience.

The characterisation of the little Welsh Rector, Mr Morgan, is equally substantial. His fundamental pleasantness, resentment at having a subordinate flout his authority, uncomfortable feelings of social inferiority, and most of all his rancour towards a young, attractive man, arising from sexual envy, are all well rendered. That the quarrel has its roots in psychological causes is understated and adds to the subtlety of characterisation, for the Rector's wife from the start shows sympathy for the curate and impatience with her husband's point of view. Indeed, the Morgans' marriage is the major achievement of the novel.[33] Some perceptive and touching comment is made upon deferred 'prudent' marriages practised among the clergy.[34] Mrs Morgan reflects drily at one point, 'how much better one knows a man after being married to him three months than after being engaged to him for ten years' (ch.5); and looking at her—'She was a good woman, but she was not fair to look upon' (ch.20)—Frank wonders what Lucy would be like if she had to wait ten years for him. The whole problem of lost years and disenchantment is beautifully rendered in chapter 28, demonstrating what insight and restraint Mrs Oliphant was capable of at her best. The scene begins with some mild skirmishes over trivia. Mrs Oliphant, true to most domestic imbroglios, notches up a list of petty irritations between both husband and wife: the Rector is late for dinner; Mrs Morgan has already changed her dress; anxious about the fish, she wonders how cook will get her own back next morning if the food is spoiled. It is a very hot day, and Mr Morgan is somewhat put about by his wife's tranquil coolness in her muslin dress. All this is a prelude to a tantalising verbal game in which the Rector, dying to impart the latest gossip concerning his curate, is held back by a mixture of propriety and pique at his wife's command of the situation. Even the sight of his favourite All-Souls pudding fails to unlock the tongue of this righteous man, while the peaches—a special care of Mrs Morgan's—are entirely overlooked in the Rector's agitation.

> She put away her peach in her resentment, and went to a side-table for her work, which she always kept handy for emergencies. Like her husband, Mrs Morgan had acquired some little 'ways' in the long ten years of their engagement, one of which was a confirmed habit of needle-work at all kinds of unnecessary moments, which much disturbed the Rector when he had anything particular to say.

Unwisely, Mr Morgan decides it is time to administer a gentle reproof about patience: ' "I am not patient," said the Rector's wife: "it never was my nature. I can't help thinking sometimes that our long experiences have done us more harm than good". . . .'

Next, arrival of the unpleasant curate, Leeson, drives Mrs Morgan out on a charitable errand. Her thoughts as she walks down Grove Street continually return to the old sadness:

> She never could help imagining what she might have been had she married ten years before at the natural period. 'And even then not a girl', she said to herself in her sensible way, as she carried this habitual thread of thought with her along the

street, past the little front gardens, where there were so many mothers with their children. On the other side of the way the genteel houses frowned darkly with their staircase windows upon the humility of Grove Street; and Mrs Morgan began to think within herself of the Misses Hemmings and other spinsters, and how they got along upon this path of life, which, after all, is never very lightsome to behold, except in the future or the past. It was dead present with the Rector's wife just then, and many speculations were in her mind, as was natural. 'Not that I could not have lived unmarried', she continued within herself, with a woman's pride; 'but things looked so different at five-and-twenty!' and in her heart she grudged the cares she had lost, and sighed over this wasting of her years.

Whenever she wrote a particular fine passage like this one, Mrs Oliphant would laughingly describe it as 'having a trot'. Here, the self-admonitory 'even then not a girl', the understated yearning for children, the oblique references to a sense of social inadequacy among the parishioners, and then the spurt of pride at the end cloaking a momentary regret for the single life, create a vivid, many-layered, sympathetic character. Soon after this Mrs Morgan meets Frank Wentworth, and her clumsy expression of sympathy, meeting with a rebuff, provokes a retort that tells the reader more about her unfulfilled longings:

> 'I don't think you would risk your prospects, and get yourself into trouble, and damage your entire life, for the sake of any girl, however pretty she might be. Men don't do such things for women nowadays, even when it is a worthy object', said the disappointed optimist.

Friendship or enmity hangs by a hair in this brief encounter.

The same tension now spills over into the Morgans' marriage, as Mrs Morgan is ashamed and angry at her husband's animosity towards his curate; he is lessened in her eyes, and it pains her deeply. The reconciliation is therefore especially touching. Mrs Oliphant, you might say, pulls off a corny trick with style. After the tribunal at which Frank Wentworth has been exonerated, Mr Morgan returns sheepishly to his wife, consumed with guilt and shame, and tells her it is time to leave Carlingford and start afresh in another living. Retiring behind her darning, Mrs Morgan senses their failure with mortification. Then he reveals that his departure will leave the Carlingford place open for Wentworth, and at once she melts, drops the stocking she was mending and begs forgiveness for her crossness: 'The excellent man was as entirely unconscious that he was being put up again at that moment with acclamations upon his pedestal, as that he had at a former time been violently displaced from it, and thrown into the category of broken idols' (ch. 45). While satisfying the romantic demands of the Mudie reader, Mrs Oliphant does not sacrifice her ironical tone; Mrs Morgan falls back into the adoring posture, flattering her husband's vanity, and he kisses her, smooths her brown hair 'with a touch which made her feel like a girl again' and goes contentedly downstairs:

> Had Mr Morgan been a Frenchman, he probably would have imagined his wife's heart to be touched by the graces of the Perpetual Curate; but, being an Englishman, and rather more certain, on the whole, of her than of himself, it did not occur to him to speculate on the subject. He was quite able to content himself with the thought that women are incomprehensible, as he went back to his study.

The gulf between male and female points of view remains, and so does Mrs Morgan's wistful longing for romance.

Both *Salem Chapel* and *The Perpetual Curate* add sensational elements to what are realistic domestic studies; *Miss Marjoribanks* on the other hand is wholly in the tradition of Jane Austen and Mrs Gaskell,[35] the story nothing more extraordinary than Lucilla Marjoribanks's 'grand design of turning the chaotic elements of society into one grand unity' (ch. 18), which also turns out to be her quest for a husband. It is, then, both romantic fairytale and comedy of manners, the most sophisticated and charming of the series, and a novel that can stand comparison with the best contemporary novels of its kind.

Gentility, breeding, and 'the painful pride of poverty' (ch. 10) are its serious topics, and upon these matters Mrs Oliphant descants with an ironic gravity worthy of comparison with Jane Austen's. The novel moves briskly, but dramatic action centres around the commotion over who will become the next member of parliament and the death of Dr Marjoribanks, events which can be accepted as part of the everyday life of Carlingford. In fact the novel sets out deliberately to mock the breathless style of the sensationists: 'the danger came sudden, appalling, and unlooked for' (ch. 14), but it is only the possibility that Mr Cavendish flirting with Barbara Lake will complicate Lucilla's plans for reforming Carlingford. And, when a more serious crisis looms, 'It was not a narrative of robbery or murder, or anything very alarming' (ch. 18), but Archdeacon Beverley recognising Cavendish, one of the pillars of Lucilla's drawing-room, as the son of a trainer or 'something about Newmarket', and the possibility that he will reveal it. At one point Cavendish's sister, Mrs Woodburn, a long-time resident of Carlingford, catching his panic at social ruin, dreads that 'there might be, for anything she could tell, a little bottle of

prussic acid in his waistcoat pocket' (ch. 30). Thus the apparatus of sensation fiction is exploited for social comedy.

Lucilla is an outsize character, 'large in all particulars', with tawny hair 'curly to exasperation' (ch. 1). In other words, she is fat and has unmanageable hair—an unusual heroine for a romantic novel. She has, however, energy and generous spirit, and has sought to compensate for her physical disadvantages by developing her intellect. One psychological insight both humorously and sympathetically conveyed is that Lucilla's self-consciousness prevents real understanding of others' needs; it is sensitivity gone inwards, with results akin to selfishness. At fifteen, she returns home after her mother's death:

> In the course of her rapid journey she had already settled upon everything that had to be done; or rather, to speak more truly, had rehearsed everything, according to the habit already acquired by a quick mind, a good deal occupied with itself. First, she meant to fall into her father's arms—forgetting with that singular facility for overlooking the peculiarities of others which belongs to such a character, that Dr Marjoribanks was very little given to embracing, and that a hasty kiss on her forehead was the warmest caress he had ever given his daughter—and then to rush up to the chamber of death and weep over dear mamma. (ch. 1)

Lucilla's sorrow is genuine, but it cannot subdue her sense of the dramatic. Later in the story a character says that she is an actress, and so she is, but at the same time she is never merely playing a part. She is utterly sincere and that is the danger. She is devoted to a heroic image of herself that makes her a mixture of bullying sweetness, queenly modesty and selfish benevolence. 'I will give up everything in the world to be a comfort to you!' she vows to her father, at which Dr Marjoribanks recoils, seeing in her the qualities of his late wife 'which had wearied his life out' (ch. 1). From finishing-school some four years later Lucilla returns, determined to show her devotion by making Grange Lane the focus of Carlingford society. Her first triumph is winning over the cook and taking her father's place at the head of the table: 'the reins of state had been smilingly withdrawn from his unconscious hands', while the drawing-room which is to be the 'inner court and centre of her kingdom' is transformed, according to her taste, from a 'waste and howling wilderness' (ch. 4).

Thus, in the first half-dozen chapters intriguing conflict extends from home into social sphere as Lucinda pursues her masterplan to rescue Carlingford from its social torpor. Lucinda combines Dorothea Brooke's idealism with Emma's egotism and there are reminders of Jane Austen in her 'well-regulated mind' (ch. 14) and that 'sublime confidence in herself which is the first necessity to a woman with a mission' (ch. 5).

Aphoristic sharpness enlivens the novel throughout. Carlingford's is 'the old fashioned orthodox way of having a great respect for religion, and as little to do with it as possible' (ch. 17). Lucilla herself keeps up 'civilities with heaven' (ch. 2) and observes of the clergy, 'A nice clergyman is almost as useful to the lady of the house as a man who can flirt' (ch. 15). Everything is for the best she reasons 'with that beautiful confidence which is common to people who have things their own way' (ch. 9). 'Lucilla had all that regard for constituted rights which is so necessary to a revolutionary of the highest class' (ch. 10). Much use is made of antithesis and hyperbole, particularly as regards Lucilla's character and attitudes. She is a 'distinguished revolutionary' (ch. 3), a 'gentle martyr' (ch. 16); she shows 'artless gratitude' (ch. 13), and possesses 'that serene self-consciousness which places the spirit above the passing vexations of the world' (ch. 23). Hyperbole is applied to Dr Marjoribanks, with his great watch 'by which all the pulses of Grange Lane considered it their duty to keep time'. The novel sparkles more than others in the Carlingford series by virtue of such linguistic exuberance.

Lucilla's mission is matrimony, although she may not realise it, and that she misses the suitor right under her nose, her cousin Tom Marjoribanks, and thereafter attracts a succession of men—all of whom she high-mindedly rejects in noble self-sacrifice both to her father and to society—becomes the essential comic point of the novel. Lucilla's belief in her altruism remains unshaken in the weeks that follow the successful receptions in her newly decorated drawing-room and her confidence grows; even religion sanctifies her mission to be a comfort to her papa. She is 'superior to earthly delight' (ch. 12), and when people fail to appreciate her sacrifices she can sigh and stand bravely to her post: 'a great soul, whose motives must always remain to some extent unappreciated' (ch. 9). Providence is definitely on her side. By such rhetoric Mrs Oliphant makes Lucilla outsize, outrageous, yet thoroughly real and lovable. For, like all good comic creations, Lucilla has the trick of remaking the world to her own specifications; against all evidence of her bulldozing, she sees herself as modest, gentle, tactful, 'fluttering her maiden plumes' (ch. 13), full of 'maiden candour and unsuspecting innocence' (ch. 27), always 'in harmony with *herself*' (ch. 28).

Even as she stands by her resolution to put off marriage for ten years, by which time she says ruefully she will be 'going off', she has moments speculating about a succession of suitors. She is a Rosalind, enjoying her freedom for the present, but looking toward matrimony. This romantic quality of the novel is seen most obviously in chapter 16, in which the motif of

the garden party is that of fairyland: the night air, moonlight, twin nightingales, all indicate that, although she is no Titania, Lucilla is a creator of magic. She behaves with the serenity that makes her superior to all vexations of this world, greeting her subjects with 'sweet humility'. The garden scene is a delicately painted idyll which ironically deploys Lucilla's coronation and the now acknowledged truth that her drawing-room is 'the seventh heaven of terrestrial harmony'.

Lucilla's pursuit of power makes *Miss Marjoribanks* a feminist novel as well as popular romance, and it is interesting to speculate how many girls relished its subversive delights. Lucilla yearns for the kind of power men have and, indeed, often exercises it. She overrules her father, she bosses Tom Marjoribanks, she scorns Mr Cavendish, and even General Travers on one occasion is cut down to his proper level. She runs rings around men, two at a time if necessary, as she proves when the rival parliamentary candidates confront each other in her drawing-room, and she is patently more capable, efficient and resourceful than anyone around her. Calling on Mr Lake the drawing-master, she knows she could give him his tea as he liked it:

> And when the tea came it was all she could do to keep herself quiet, and remember that she was a visitor, and not take it out of the incapable hands of Barbara, who never gave her father the right amount of sugar in his tea. . . . She sat with her very fingers itching to cut the bread and butter for him, and give him a cup of tea as he liked it. . . . (ch. 28)

But it is not solely a matter of the domestic capabilities of women Mrs Oliphant is extolling. A serious point is being made here about the waste of womanly potential:

> Miss Marjoribanks had her own ideas in respect to charity, and never went upon ladies' committees, nor took any further share than what was proper and necessary in parish work; and when a woman has an active mind, and still does not care for parish work, it is a little hard for her to find a 'sphere'. And Lucilla, though she said nothing about a sphere, was still more or less in that condition of mind which has been so often and so fully described to the British public— when the ripe female intelligence, not having the natural resource of a nursery and a husband to manage, turns inwards, and begins to 'make a protest' against the existing order of society, and to call the world to account for giving it no due occupation—and to consume itself. (ch. 42)

Lucilla therefore goes into politics, in the only way a woman can, by making campaign favours and electioneering for Mr Ashburton. Complementing this quiet comment on the subordinate role enforced upon women, is sympathy for the difficulties of running a household. As Mrs Centum puts it,

> ' . . . men are *so* unreasonable. I should like to know what *they* would do if they had what we have to go through: to look after all the servants— and they are always out of their senses at Christmas—and to see that the children don't have too much pudding, and to support all the noise. The holidays are the hardest work a poor woman can have', she concluded, with a sigh. . . . (ch. 10)

There is much understanding of the stresses and strains too for Mrs Woodburn, who had 'two men to carry on her shoulders' (ch. 39).

In the latter part of the novel Mrs Oliphant boldly leaps ten years. Lucilla is twenty-nine and a new crusade to get Ashburton elevated MP for Carlingford gives her abundant energy a fresh outlet, but there is a suggestion of greater maturity and yearning for happiness. The narrative has added pathos; life has gone on, people have aged. This is beautifully captured in the Chileys, on whom Lucilla calls seeking support for her candidate. Colonel Chiley expresses his impatience with the rival, Cavendish, by poking the fire vigorously, a habit that over the years has irritated, now frightens, his wife:

> She gave a little start among her cushions, and stopped down to look over the floor. 'He will never learn that he is old', she said in Lucilla's ear, who instantly came to her side to see what she wanted; and thus the two old people kept watch upon each other, and noted, with a curious mixture of vexation and sympathy, each other's declining strength. (ch.39)

Change is conveyed also by the town itself, in the new people and the expanding housing-estate. The novel takes on an evening air, rather like that of the closing stages of *As You Like It* or *The Tempest*. This is particularly noticeable when Dr Marjoribanks pats Lucilla's shoulder as he says goodnight—a rare physical gesture which causes her to look at him almost in alarm. The narrative is muted:

> Meantime the snow fell heavily outside, and wrapped everything in a soft and secret whiteness. And amid the whiteness and darkness, the lamp burned steadily outside at the garden-gate, which pointed out the Doctor's door amid all the closed houses and dark garden-walls in Grange Lane— a kind of visible succour and help always at hand for those who were suffering. (ch.42)

Despite this atmospheric anticipation, the news of the doctor's death next morning is shocking to the reader as well as to old Mrs Chiley, sobbing in her bed it was all a mistake, that it was she who ought to have died.

In the third volume, the discovery that Lucilla is not an heiress but must face a life of 'genteel economy' (ch.44) gives impetus to the plot, and the climax has appropriately romantic hyperbole as Lucilla faces the expected proposal from Ashburton and wonders about her absent cousin Tom: the 'very soul of good sense all her days, but now her ruling quality seemed to forsake her' (ch.49). Just as Ashburton starts his speech there is the sound of a coach rattling down the street, a door flung open, the crash of a china bowl, and Tom bursts into the house. The fairytale ending is assured: 'Fate and honest love had been waiting all the time till their moment came; and now it was not even necessary to say anything about it. The fact was so clear that it did not require stating. It was to be Tom after all' (ch.50).

The final touch is appropriate to Lucilla's character: having persuaded Tom to buy an estate near Carlingford she looks forward delightedly to work: 'It gave her the liveliest satisfaction to think of all the disorder and disarray of the Marchbank village. Her fingers itched to be at it—to set all the crooked things straight, and clean away the rubbish, and set everything, as she said, on a sound foundation' (ch.51). Thus Lucilla remains consistent, reconciles that heroic self-image with worthier objects, and to the end proves to Carlingford society that she is an exceptional young woman. What is more she succeeds in getting her own way, and can say to herself with secret delight that having married Tom she is Lucilla Marjoribanks still.

Ernest Baker described Mrs Oliphant as a 'Mrs Gaskell who has learned a good deal from Dickens and still more from Trollope'.[36] Of none of her novels is this more true than of *Phoebe Junior*.[37] It presents a more tranquil view of a society than any of its predecessors in the series, and perhaps for this reason has been underestimated. Echoes of Dickens occur in the caricature of the self-made man Copperhead, another Bounderby, a great unfeeling brute boasting of his struggle for success and bullying his genteel wife and nincompoop of a son, Clarence. But by far the greatest resemblance—or debt—is to Trollope. The subtitle, 'A last Chronicle' immediately brings to mind its Barset predecessor. Similarly its major episode, concerning a forged bill by the incumbent of St Roque's Chapel, Mr May, and, to an even greater degree the minor occurrence of May's son, Reginald, being offered a sinecure as warden of Carlingford Hospital for the aged, are distinctly Trollopian.

This is not to say that *Phoebe Junior* is a hotchpotch of other writers' ideas. The heroine has qualities of independence that Trollope would not quite countenance, and the milieu of chapel and tradesmen's houses, the minute observation of domestic economy, are all Mrs Oliphant's own. Ursula May's awareness of the cost of an *entrée* for a special dinner party and her anxiety all the way from purchasing to cooking and eating is a case in point, and when Ursula is taunted by her father about reading novels and not her cookery book, the reader is made to feel the frustration acutely:

> Made dishes are the most expensive things! A leg of mutton, for instance; there it is, and when one weighs it, one knows what it costs; but there is not one of those *entrées* but costs *shillings* for herbs and truffles and gravy and forcemeat, and a glass of white wine here, and a half pint of claret there. It is all very well to talk of dishes made out of nothing. The meat may not be very much—and men never think of other things, I suppose. (I, ch.13)

'Ursula's entrées' play their part in the next chapter when father's unkind remarks about the food cause Nonconformist politician Mr Northcote to fall in love with her on the spot.

Progress has begun to affect Carlingford: the Wentworths and the Wodehouses have gone away, and the Tozers have moved into Lady Weston's old house in Grange Lane.[38] For Mrs Tozer 'the increase in gentility was questionable' (I, ch.12). For Copperhead, on the other hand, rise in status, by marrying a relative of Sir Robert Dorset, has been equally unsettling: 'Mr Copperhead felt the increase in gentility as well as the failure in jollity' (I, ch.2). Throughout the story people feel the strain of keeping up appearances or striving to maintain their superiority. Mrs Tozer secretly laments the old life over the shop in the High Street, and some of Mr Tozer's irascibility stems from his awkward social position, which makes him by turns sycophantic and belligerent towards the quality. As always in Mrs Oliphant's religious groups there is discomfort among the Nonconformists who feel their inferiority to the Anglican clergy. Not only clashes over status make Horace Northcote and Reginald May ill at ease with one another, but deep-seated divisions in religious attitudes.

Other kinds of change and displacement add to the groundswell of tension. These particularly concern the careers of the two heroines, Phoebe Beecham and Ursula May, both of whom are returned from London and experiencing the constrictions of rural Carlingford. Mr May is the voice of reaction, and both of his children are blamed, Ursula for demanding recognition as a woman and Reginald for daring to exercise his ministry in a more evangelical spirit. Reginald's opposition to his father's wish that he accept a sinecure is based on a modern radicalism challenging Victorian

orthodoxies. In Ursula's case it is radicalism in the home. This is how Mr May sees the situation when Ursula wishes she could earn money:

> 'Do a little more in the house, and nobody will ask you to earn money. Yes, this is the shape things are taking nowadays,' said Mr May, 'the girls are mad to earn anyhow, and the boys, forsooth, have a hundred scruples. If women would hold their tongues and attend to their own business, I have no doubt we should have less of the other nonsense. The fact is everything is getting into an unnatural state.' (I, ch.10)

The question of women's status is thus implicit but unfortunately never debated; it was far too contentious for the popular market.

The roles of the novel's two heroines, however, are skilfully counterpointed to achieve greater depth and balance in the plot.

Both are intelligent and superior to the men around them, both affected in different ways by social pressures. Ursula, the clergyman's daughter, is one of the genteel poor, and at first regards the fashionably dressed and gracious Phoebe as an enviable model. Phoebe, however, has acquired her gentility by education and study, and is still the butterman's granddaughter. Her own mother, having risen in society, is painfully aware too of her past: 'the shop was still there, greasy and buttery as ever' (I, ch.5), and the reader who recalls that Phoebe of long ago (in *Salem Chapel*) appreciates the irony of the transformation. Sending young Phoebe back to relive her mother's social experience from a totally different position provides a splendid opportunity for social comment of which Mrs Oliphant takes full advantage.

Phoebe, armed with her finest wardrobe to meet Grange Lane society, is determined to be frank about the 'shop', but her first meeting with her grandparents is a shock:

> Yes, there could be no doubt about it; there he was, he whom she was going to visit, under whose auspices she was about to appear in Carlingford. He was not even like an old Dissenting minister, which had been her childish notion of him. He looked neither more nor less than what he was, an old shopkeeper, very decent and respectable, but a little shabby and greasy, like the men whose weekly bills she had been accustomed to pay for her mother. She felt an instant conviction that he would call her 'Ma'am', if she went up to him, and think her one of the quality. (I, ch.12)

Mrs Tozer, her grandmother, has put on her best cap, but, despite the sustaining power of this gorgeous creation, a huge brooch and a dress of copper-coloured silk which rustled a good deal as she came downstairs, is as apprehensive as Phoebe, feeling a thrill of excitement and 'sense of the difference which could not but be felt on one side as well as the other'. Emotion tells through the polite exchanges:

> 'We thought', said Mrs Tozer, 'as perhaps you mightn't be used to tea at this time of day.'

> 'Oh, it is the right time; it is the fashionable hour', said Phoebe; 'everybody has tea at five. I will run upstairs first, and take off my hat, and make myself tidy. . . .'

> 'Well?' said Mr Tozer to Mrs Tozer, as Phoebe disappeared. The two old people looked at each other with a little awe; but she, as was her nature, took the most depressing view. She shook her head. 'She's a deal too fine for us, Tozer', she said . . .

Tozer takes a more hopeful view:

> 'She came up and give me a kiss in the station, as affectionate as possible. All I can say for her is as she ain't proud.'

> Mrs Tozer shook her head; but even while she did so, pleasanter dreams stole into her soul.

> 'I hope I'll be well enough to get to chapel on Sunday,' she said, 'just to see the folks' looks. The minister needn't expect much attention to his sermon. "There's Phoebe Tozer's daughter!" they'll all be saying, and a-staring, and a-whispering.'

Phoebe, meanwhile, contemplating her grandmother's amazing cap and her grandfather's greasy coat, and facing the vast tent bed, moreen curtains and gigantic flowers of the carpet, bursts into tears:

> But her temperament did not favour panics, and giving in was not in her. . . . Now was the time to put her principles to the test; and the tears relieved her, and gave her something of the feeling of a martyr, which is always consolatory and sweet; so she dried her eyes, and bathed her face, and went downstairs cheerful and smiling, resolved that at all costs, her duty should be done, however disagreeable it might be.

Doing her duty embraces being frank about her origin, and by this Mrs Oliphant not only makes Phoebe more attractive to the reader, but also exploits further the burdens of class feeling. Ursula May, for example, is acutely embarrassed at finding out that her friend is the granddaughter of a Carlingford shopkeeper; Phoebe, though mortified by her lowly origins, faces up to the Mays and Horace Northcote with 'masterly candour'

(II, ch.6) and captivates Reginald May. She teases both him and Mr Northcote with assumed fears that two rival clergymen will quarrel, and then invites both to tea: 'She carried in her two young men as naughty boys carry stag-beetles or other such small deer. If they would fight it would be fun; and if they would not fight, why it might be fun still, and more amusing than grandmamma' (II, ch.10). This happy-go-lucky quality in Phoebe seems to promise an outcome in which the heroine of humble background marries the prince, but Mrs Oliphant varies the convention. Phoebe is presented more ambiguously as the story develops. The freedom with which she brings men to her side ('in the Tozer world, who knew anything of chaperons?'—III, ch.10) provides a clue to a character not only socially but morally ambiguous.

As reviewers recognised, Phoebe was 'not quite a lady', and while disapproving of the moral tone of the novel they had to admit that Phoebe's unconventional behaviour certainly made her interesting.[39] Her independent ways become the focus of a dramatic climax when she defies her grandfather and comes to the rescue of the curate of St Roque's after he has forged Tozer's name to a bill. With great impropriety Phoebe comes into possession of the incriminating document and withholds it from her distracted grandfather, a circumstance which led the *Saturday Review* to criticise Mrs Oliphant for preaching that a pretty girl could gain any end she set before her.[40] It is precisely this realism in her portrayal that is likely to appeal to the reader. When it comes to her dealings with suitors she is ready enough to flirt with Reginald May, but knowing full well which side her bread is buttered choose Clarence Copperhead and his fortune. This is a much bolder conclusion to a romance than Trollope permits himself.

Ursula, on the other hand, remains much closer to Trollopian type, and responds to the attentions of Mr Northcote with conventional reticence. The difference between Mrs Oliphant's two heroines is ably captured in the garden scene early in the last volume, where Janey, Ursula's sixteen-year-old sister, is the innocent observer of events under the stars, her naïveté an effective prelude to the scene—'was this how it was managed?' she wonders, as the figures move into the shadows of the laurels. Ursula feels 'a confusion strange but sweet' (III, ch.6) in the attentions of Mr Northcote, but Phoebe has no such problems when confronted by her suitors. She knows that proposals are imminent and weighs up the possibilities, concluding that she will make Clarence her career:

> Yes; she could put him into parliament, and keep him there. She could thrust him forward (she believed) to the front of affairs. He would be as good as a profession, a position, a great work to Phoebe. He meant wealth (which she dismissed.

in its superficial aspect as something meaningless and vulgar, but accepted in its higher aspect as an almost necessary condition of influence), and he meant all the possibilities of future power. Who can say that she was not as romantic as any girl of twenty could be? only her romance took an unusual form. It was her head that was full of throbbings and pulses, not her heart.

Mrs Oliphant handles the convention with some originality, hinting at the constrictions of being the angel in the house and rightly suggesting Phoebe's need for a more active role which she will take in the only form readily available, by proxy through a malleable husband. For a while, however, it seems that Phoebe will be punished for breaking with orthodoxy and accepting Clarence with reasons other than love in mind, because Copperhead says he will disown his son.[41] Clarence speaks up with primitive eloquence for the first time; Phoebe feels proud of him and, although she shivers at the prospect of his being disowned, is prepared to accept the consequences of her decision and stand by him. Such an action reassures the reader that Phoebe is, underneath it all, the regular loving and self-sacrificing female, although Mrs Oliphant does not quite capitulate, since she has the old man repent and Clarence inheriting after all. Phoebe will have her career.

In the presentation of the Mays Mrs Oliphant is at her best, depicting the endlessly interesting complex of relationships within the family. Reginald indulges in outbursts similar to his father's and exerts his authority over the girls. Likewise Ursula is inclined to patronise Janey. All the children notch up on a mental slate their father's injustices and pay him back with spurts of malice. May himself, unlike the caricatured Copperhead, is splendidly realised.[42] Indolent and self-centred—'He had never forgiven Providence for leaving him with his motherless family upon his hands' (I, ch.10)—he has turned in on himself, venting his subconscious resentments in spiteful attacks on the children. The girls for their part, 'having no softening medium of a mother's eyes to look at their father through', are harsher in their judgements than they should be; 'and he did not take pains to fascinate his children or throw the glamour of love into their eyes.' 'Both looked selfish to the other, and Mr May, no doubt, could have made out quite as good a case as the children did.' Quiet analysis of this kind shows once more Mrs Oliphant as a delicate student of character.

If the greatness of Archdeacon Grantly and Mr Harding in *Barchester Towers* or the Proudies and Mr Crawley in *The Last Chronicle of Barset* does not come quite within Mrs Oliphant's grasp, there is no denying the quality of her Chronicles of Carlingford and her moments of glory within the series. Vincent, Tozer, Lucilla

Marjoribanks and Phoebe display the angularities and inconsistencies of superior creative imagination; they are capable of surprising, like other memorable characters of fiction. She deserves better from posterity than to be so unregarded as she has been since her death. At the very least the pattern of mid-Victorian fiction is incomplete without a readily available edition of the Chronicles of Carlingford.

That she wrote too much and too quickly remains for her as for others of her kind the penalty of commercial fiction; that she recognised how much better her work might have been was her personal anguish, as her autobiography clearly shows. What remains remarkable is what she did achieve within those limitations. 'Few writers in any age', said Herbert Paul, 'have maintained so high a level over so large a surface.'[43]

Notes

[1] Quoted in Q. D. Leavis, Introduction to *Autobiography and Letters* p. 10. See also [Lady Ritchie, *From the Porch* (London, 1913)], p. 13; and A. C. Benson, *Memories and Friends* (London, 1924) p. 79.

[2] Introduction to *A Widow's Tale, and Other Stories* (Edinburgh and London, 1898). See also L. P. Stebbins, *A Victorian Album* (London, 1946) p. 189.

[3] [F. D. Tredrey, *The House of Blackwood 1804-1954* (Edinburgh, 1954)], p. 179.

[4] [V. and R. A. Colby, *The Equivocal Virtue: Mrs. Oliphant and the Literary Market Place* (New York, 1966)], p. 199.

[5] Leavis, Introduction to *Autobiography and Letters*, p. 10.

[6] Isabel Clarke, *Six Portraits* (London, 1935) p. 197. See also Tredrey, *The House of Blackwood*, p. 136. Mrs Oliphant was awarded a Civil List pension of £100 in 1868, some small reward for her labours. As she observed, 'I have worked a hole in my right forefinger' (*Autobiography and Letters*, p. 427).

[7] *Dictionary of National Biography*, XXII (Supplement) 1102-6.

[8] Stebbins, *A Victorian Album*, p. 160.

[9] *Autobiography and Letters*, p. 44.

[10] Ibid., p. 64.

[11] Ibid., p. 78.

[12] Ibid., p. 6.

[13] Ibid., p. 141.

[14] Benson, *Memories and Friends,* p. 79.

[15] *Autobiography and Letters,* p. 147.

[16] Ibid., p. 6.

[17] Ibid., p. 5.

[18] Ibid., p. 8.

[19] Ritchie, *From the Porch,* p. 23.

[20] Benson, *Memories and Friends,* p. 74.

[21] Ritchie, *From the Porch,* p. 24.

[22] Alexander Innes Shand, 'Contemporary Literature', *Blackwood's Magazine,* CXXV (Mar 1879) 338.

[23] Austin, in *Temple Bar,* XXIX (July 1870) 489.

[24] Shand, in *Blackwood's Magazine,* CXXV (Mar 1879) 337.

[25] Today's feminist criticism is giving long overdue attention to this aspect of Victorian fiction. See Françoise Basch, *Relative Creatures: Victorian Women in Society and the Novel, 1837-67* (London, 1974); Ellen Moers, *Literary Women* (New York, 1977).

[26] Trollope had begun to find fame with *The Warden* (1855) and *Barchester Towers* (1857), while Mrs Gaskell had already succeeded with *Cranford* (1853). A ready market existed for stories in rural communities. Anne Thackeray was one of several readers who made the comparison with George Eliot: see Ritchie, *From the Porch,* pp. 6, 13. Mrs Oliphant had no illusions: 'No one even will mention me in the same breath' (*Autobiography and Letters,* p. 7).

[27] For discussions on religious issues relating to these novels, see M. Maison, *Search Your Soul Eustace: A Survey of the Religious Novel in the Victorian Age* (London, 1961); V. Cunningham, *Everywhere Spoken Against: Dissent in the Victorian Novel* (Oxford, 1975); and Robert Lee Wolff, *Gains and Losses: Novels of Faith and Doubt in Victorian England* (New York, 1977).

[28] *The Rector,* ch. 1. Serialisation of *The Rector* and *The Doctor's Family* was in *Blackwood's Magazine,* Oct 1861-Jan 1862.

[29] *Salem Chapel* was first serialised in *Blackwood's Magazine,* Feb 1862-Jan 1863.

[30] *The Perpetual Curate* appeared in *Blackwood's Magazine,* June 1863-Sep 1864.

[31] *Autobiography and Letters,* p. 191.

[32] Ibid.

[33] An instance of Mrs Oliphant's shrewd observation of the strategies forced upon wives to placate male ego concerns her friend Ellen Blackett, wife of the publisher. See *Autobiography and Letters,* p. 82.

[34] A pictorial treatment is to be found in Arthur Hughes's painting *The Long Engagement* (1859), Birmingham City Museum and Art Gallery. See W. R. Greg, 'Why Are Women Redundant?', *National Review,* XIV (Apr 1862), which, among several suggestions concerning the surplus female population, argues that encouraging men to marry late incites cads to commit immoral acts.

[35] *Miss Marjoribanks* was serialised in *Blackwood's Magazine,* Feb 1865-May 1866.

[36] [Ernest Baker, *The History of the English Novel* (London, 1924-39)], X, 200.

[37] *Phoebe Junior, a Last Chronicle of Carlingford* was not serialised, but appeared in three volumes under Hurst and Blackett's imprint, 1876.

[38] A discrepancy; in *Salem Chapel* she was Lady Western.

[39] See the *Athenaeum,* no. 2539 (24 June 1876) 851.

[40] *Saturday Review,* XLII (22 July 1876) 113.

[41] The brazen Copperhead bears a resemblance to Trollope's Melmotte: *The Way We Live Now* had appeared the previous year.

[42] The *Athenaeum* found him repulsive, declaring that he should have been killed off early in the story—no. 2539 (24 June 1876) 851.

[43] Herbert Paul, *Men and Letters* (London, 1901) p. 154.

Jennifer Uglow (essay date 1984)

SOURCE: Introduction to *Hester: A Story of Contemporary Life* by Mrs. Oliphant, Virago, 1984, pp. ix-xxi.

[*In the following introduction to* Hester (1883), *Uglow discusses the novel's themes of loneliness, employment, finances, and male-female relationships, and how these motifs reflect the realities of Oliphant's own life and the values of the Victorian era.*]

Hester is a witty, ironic, forceful tale of women who run their lives either by choice or by necessity without the support of men—fatherless girls, old maids, widows, domineering sisters. But being alone, as its author knew, is not the same as being independent, and all the women in the book are presented in different ways as being entangled in complicated nets which hamper their freedom of action; almost invisible chains woven of family duty, financial need and the unspoken codes which governed "correct behaviour" for their sex and class. The main narrative traces the struggles of Hester Vernon between the ages of fourteen and twenty-three. She cannot expect a "good marriage" and her temperament, in any case, drives her to want an independent career, but at every attempt to create her own destiny she encounters the strength of these hidden bonds. Despite the title the novel has two heroines, Hester and her elderly second cousin Catherine, who seems at first to be the spider sitting in the centre of the web in which the girl is caught. The book's real romance, although Hester has a succession of suitors, is between these two women, a version of *Pride and Prejudice* in which misunderstanding, resentment and jealous independence mask similarity and attraction; "I think you and I have hated each other because we were meant to love each other, child."

They are opposed in age and youth, wealth and poverty, cynicism and idealism, but are united in their pride, their abundant energy, their emotional fervour and their desire to work, to be of use in the world. In the end, despite appearances, both are equally constrained. Catherine is head of the Vernon family, running the family bank for thirty years after saving it from near ruin precipitated by mismanagement on the part of Hester's father John. She fills a local house with her pensioners including the widowed "Mrs John" and daughter; she settles her nephews in the bank to ensure the future of the dynasty; she dominates local society. She seems free and rational but she too is presented as vulnerable, enmeshed and blinded by her emotions, her loneliness and craving for love.

The main elements in this powerful story—loneliness, family ties, money, work, strong women dictating to weak men—were all constant themes of Mrs Oliphant's novels and of her own life. As a child, she felt that the "dim figure" of her father was completely overshadowed by her mother Margaret, sharp-tongued, energetic, overseer of the family finances and a natural story teller who filled her with a romantic idea of her own side of the family, the Oliphants, "an old, chivalrous, impoverished race". She herself clung to this heritage, as Catherine does to the Vernon name, signing her name with a flourish after she married her cousin Francis as Margaret Oliphant W. Oliphant. She also always retained her tart Scottish accent, cherishing her outsider's claim to a clearer view of English manners.

As a young wife in the 1850s she was clearly disappointed by the lack of success of her unbusinesslike husband, whose craft of glass painting was rendered unfashionable by the decline of Gothic Revival architecture. Like many other professional women writers whose family depended largely on their earnings (the widowed Mary Shelley, Mrs Beeton, Mary Braddon), she worked incessantly, pausing only briefly for births or for bereavements (her mother and two of her babies), an existence vividly conjured up by Frank's note to Blackwoods in February 1855, "Our poor little darling left us as we feared, about half past three yesterday afternoon. Mrs Oliphant would beg as a favour that her article on Charles Dickens which was to have appeared in the Magazine for March, might now be arranged for April."

Frank's own health failed in 1858 and after suffering through a dank Florentine winter with their two small children, and a summer in Rome, he died in November 1859. He never told his wife that even before their disastrous Italian trip he knew his illness was terminal, a "cruel deception" she never entirely forgave. Her son Cecco (Francis) was born in December and she returned to England the following February. "When I thus began the world anew," she wrote, "I had for all my fortune about £1000 of debt, a small insurance of, I think, £200 on Frank's life, our furniture laid up in a warehouse, and my own faculties, such as they were, to make our living and pay off all our burdens by." Her loneliness was intensified by the sudden death of ten-year-old Maggie, also in Rome, in 1864. "Here is an end of all. I am alone, I am a woman. I have nobody to stand between me and the roughest edge of grief." And her burdens were increased by her brother Willie, an alcoholic, who after an initial attempt to become a Presbyterian minister, drifted into an indigent life at home and then in Italy. Ten years later she also undertook to support her widowed brother Frank, a failed businessman, and his four children.

Her novels, not surprisingly, are full of strong efficient women, who carry the loads placed on them by ineffectual men, many of whom "go to the bad" and in *Hester* she links the plight of her fictional heroines with memories "deep down in the recollection of many a woman of whom the world knows no history". Her autobiography is a short, heartrending document, but one of her most extraordinary features was her resilient spirit, "almost criminally elastic" as she herself said, a quality defined in *Hester* as "that heroism of necessity which is more effective than mere will". In the 1860s, the first decade of her widowhood, she established her reputation with the *Carlingford Chronicles* and immediately after Maggie's death wrote

Miss Marjoribanks, one of the funniest novels of the day. Contemporaries and juniors, like J. M. Barrie, remembered her not as a tight-lipped martyr but as an opinionated, entertaining woman, "In talk she was tremendously witty without trying to be so . . . and she was of an intellect so alert that one wondered she ever fell asleep."

Surveying her enormous output we too may wonder if she ever had time to sleep, for in addition to her novels, biographies, travel books and critical works she maintained "a lightly flowing stream of magazine articles, and refused no work that was offered to me". A great deal of her criticism and fiction endures remarkably well, but her best works have been forgotten along with those which she admitted were written for the "boiling of the family pot". In the mid 1870s, determined to live in style and to send her boys to Eton and Oxford, she frankly decided "with a metaphorical toss of my head", to put aside dreams of producing a masterpiece and "to set myself steadily to make as much money as I could . . . it had to be done, and that was enough".

Although her books sold well and her name was widely respected, she was not a consistently best-selling writer except for a brief period in the 1860s. Indeed professional jealousy as well as concern for "respectability" in literature may explain the vehemence of her attack in *Black-woods* in 1867 on "sensuality" in the works of women writers such as the romantic Rhoda Broughton and the outstandingly successful sensation novelist Mary Braddon. For despite her "toss of the head", she was very sensitive about her popularity and literary reputation, and at the end of her life suffered from the feeling that her talents had been largely wasted; "No one even will mention me in the same breath as George Eliot. And that is just." In fact she underestimated herself; at her death Henry James in his *London Notes,* evoked her inimitable quality, "She was really a great improvisatrice, a night working spinner of long, loose, vivid yarns, numberless, pauseless, admirable repeatedly, for their full, pleasant, reckless rustle over depths and difficulties." Several later critics have compared her analysis of provincial life with that of Eliot and Trollope.

The tension behind the preoccupation with work in *Hester* may come from the way her own writing was never considered "real work" in the same way that a man's occupation or profession would be, no matter how solid her reputation, or how many people depended on her earnings. Instead a fiction remained that her writing was an amateur activity, done in her "spare time". She wrote her early novels while her mother did needlework at the family table, and she maintained the habit in later life, always making herself available during the day for her family and friends, working in "the little second drawing room where all

the (feminine) life of the house goes on; and I don't think I have ever had two hours uninterrupted (except at night, with everybody in bed) during the whole of my literary life".

By the 1880s however, the pretence had begun to pall. She thought up schemes for journals she could edit, appealed to her editor George Craik at Macmillan to look out for something of "a permanent character, which would relieve me a little from the necessity of perpetual writing" and lamented the advantage which most literary men had of a regular salary in addition to their freelance earnings. I think it was her experience of never being taken seriously as a professional writer which swayed her feelings more and more in support of the feminist cause. In her *Blackwoods* articles of the 1850s and 60s, although she showed sympathy for the *actual* oppression of women and acknowledged the logic of demanding the vote for women householders, she defended the notion of separate spheres with defiant pride: "we are women, not lesser men. We are content with the place in the world's economy which God has given us."

But while the explicit arguments of her articles upheld the status quo, the implicit arguments of her novels were beginning to challenge it. In 1865 *Miss Marjoribanks* provided a graphic and very funny illustration of the waste which resulted from confining a woman of immense capabilities to using her talents solely in the domestic and social spheres, and in 1866 *Agnes* offered a tragic (autobiographical) vision of a disillusioned wife. These themes are repeated again and again and gradually the hidden anger found its way into her articles. At the end of a wide-ranging piece in *Fraser's Magazine* in 1880 she cried out openly against the "ungenerous" attitude of men towards women; "whatever women do, in the general, is undervalued by men in the general, because . . . it is done by women", and she declared that legal disabilities are "mere evidences of a sentiment which is more inexplicable than any other by which the human race has been actuated, a sentiment against which the most of us, at one period or another of our lives, have to struggle blindly, not knowing whence it originates, or how it is to be overcome."

Hester, written in 1883, may surprise readers today by its overtly feminist tone, since if they have any preconceived image of its author, it is likely to be the anti-feminist of the 1850s or the upholder of moral purity revealed in the attack on *Tess of the D'Urberville's* in the 1890s. But while Mrs Oliphant always retained conservative views on female sexuality she became increasingly radical in her perception of the widespread and disabling sexism rooted in the consciousness of both men and women. It is this prejudice, rather than legal or social institutions, which she attacks in *Hester.* If we read the novel as a polemic, then the crucial passage must surely be that where Hester presses Edward, her declared lover, to explain his business transactions to her, begging,

> "But tell me, only tell me a little more."

> He shook his head, "Hester," he said, "that is not what a man wants in a woman; not to go and explain it all to her with pen and ink, and tables and figures, to make her understand as he would have to do with a man. What he wants, dear, is very different—just to lean upon you—to know that you sympathise, and think of me, and feel for me, and believe in me, and that you will share whatever comes".

> Hester said nothing, but her countenance grew very grave.

She is shaken still further by her own mother's agreement that for a man to discuss business with a woman shows a lack of respect.

> There was indeed a sort of awe in the girl's perception of her mother's perfectly innocent, perfectly assured theory of what was right in women. What wonder that a man should think so, when women themselves thought so?

By 1883 not only had Mrs Oliphant changed her personal views about the rightness of the dictum "men must work, women must weep", but concrete gains had been won which, superficially, indicated an improvement in the status of women; access to higher education, the Married Women's Property acts, the extension of the municipal franchise and involvement of women in local government. But the ridicule which every campaign aroused made her painfully aware of the deep-seated resistance to change and of the underlying belief in the weakness and inferiority of the female sex. *Hester* has an ironic subtitle "A Story of Contemporary Life", for the main action is not contemporary, but begins at the end of the 1860s when the first shock of widespread assaults on traditional attitudes were still reverberating through the country. The implication is that little had really changed in the fundamental attitudes of men to women in the intervening decade.

As an indictment of social attitudes *Hester* is all the more effective because it makes no mention of violent public debates. Everything is on a small scale; the scene is not London, but Redborough, and the emotional and moral boundaries of the heroine's world are equally limited, by family ties and monetary obligations, while her possibilities of action are firmly controlled by Catherine, head of the family and of the bank. (In this version one cannot talk glibly about patriarchal institutions). The way Catherine exerts her authority constantly, cynically and in the only way open to her, through "womanly charity" is a telling comment on the delicate subject of Victorian philanthropy as an expression of power. In the town she becomes a kind of provincial Angela Burdett-Coutts, a local saint, but in the family she is seen as a none-too-benevolent despot; "she is more than the Queen; the house belongs to her, and the furniture, and everything". There is a constant conflict between dependence and dignity, gratitude and rebellion. Her personal tragedy is that, despite her keen intelligence, she is blind to the existence of this conflict in her adored protégé Edward, which drives him to hypocrisy, furtiveness and rejection. At the time of writing Mrs Oliphant was experiencing a growing estrangement from her eldest son and in the relationship of aunt and nephew she provides a bitter, ironic picture of a passion and betrayal which can be just as much part of parental and filial as of romantic love.

Catherine's public prestige and control, which endow her with an illusion of invulnerability, derive from her tight hold on the purse strings. Almost everyone in *Hester* is obsessed by money, with the exception of the Morgans, Catherine's maternal relations, who provide a counter image to her paternal family, the Vernons. In Redborough a social hierarchy based on land and birth is gradually being superseded by one dictated by wealth. The old order is overtly respected, for example in the seating arrangements at a grand Christmas party, but it is quite clear that even genteel poverty now equals powerlessness. Edward is therefore right in a sense when he forces Hester to ask "Does it all come down to money?" But Mrs Oliphant's analysis goes further. What really counts in the eyes of society is the appearance of wealth or rather the sheer *belief* in the existence of wealth, just as it is the appearance of unity which is important for a family, and the public observation of the rules of correct behaviour which define "a lady". The two central institutions of Victorian society—capitalism and the family—(how brilliant to make Vernon's a family bank) are shown to be fictions supported by faith. Vernons seems "solid as the Bank of England", yet within pages mere rumours and doubts threaten a run on the bank which would leave a whole neighbourhood ruined. The disaster is stemmed not by hard evidence of cash in the vaults but by the appearance of a Vernon (Catherine) smiling in the doorway. Private bankers depended entirely on reputation and Catherine, incidentally, provides a perfect model of the behaviour recommended in such a crisis by George Rae in his classic *The Country Banker* (1885). It is credibility, not money, which must be restored.

Yet the vision of *Hester* is not simply an easy exposé of the hollowness and hypocrisy of Victorian life. Rather it is a recognition that all relationships are analogous with financial ones, systems of debt and obligation. And that social institutions, commercial or domestic, do have value if governed by disinterested, trusting, watchful people. The delicate systems of agreement and accepted custom are in fact necessary to hold these institutions together when they are threatened, and extreme individualism, whether it takes the form of "male" capitalism (Edward's speculation) or "female" romance (Hester's longing to elope) can destroy society. Both characters envisage freedom in the same terms, as a fierce wind, exhilarating and terrifying, "the strong gale of revolution". One of the things which makes this novel exciting and uncomfortable is the tension the reader experiences between the sad loss of hopes of personal freedom and the recognition of the importance of maintaining the fabric of social life. Edward measures his "slavery" by cups of tea and Hester is held back from flight by the most slender of barriers, her mother's pleasure that they will be able to make strawberry jam in a fortnight.

It is entirely appropriate that such a momentous decision should hang on such a trivial remark. For Mrs Oliphant suggests that for most people, especially women, time is measured chiefly in terms of personal experience and daily life. The novel contains no dates; Captain Morgan, who is over eighty, remembers the Battle of Trafalgar, but Mrs John dates her youth by the songs of Mrs Haynes Bayley and the fashion for ringlets and spotted muslin. The mood of the late 1860s and early 1870s is evoked, not by mention of appropriate public events such as the 1866 collapse of Overend and Gurney which ruined thousands of small investors, but by the decline in fashion of large crinolines, by the craze for *Thé Dansants*. The point is not the "realism" of her details, but their value, as expressions of the possibilities of women's lives; Mrs John's repeated references back to "when I was young" within the novel, and the way in which the younger generation laugh at the fashions and furniture of their elders are echoed by the narrator's voice referring back from the 1880s to attitudes "in those days", reminding us constantly that all social norms are products of particular historical conditions.

It is on this level that the social comedy is most effective. Several women characters, like Hester's mother, function both as quite complex individual portraits and as types of womanhood of the period. Ellen Vernon is a fairly mild provincial copy of the fast young woman caricatured in late 60s journals as having "an inordinate love of gaiety, a bold determined manner, a total absence of respect towards her parents . . . Her conversation is full of slang—so repulsive in a feminine mouth", while Emma Ashton, the Morgan's granddaughter with her total lack of imagination and self-consciousness and constant reference to "my chance" is a ludicrous illustration of the mercenary attitude to marriage. The men too are recognisable comic types: Vernon Ridgeway, the fussy,

bitchy bachelor worried about his heating bills; Roland Ashton, the romantic outsider with melting eyes; and Harry Vernon, the upright, manly, honest Dobbin figure who seems to offer Hester the promise of a married life spent in endlessly scoring at village cricket matches.

Another of the reasons why *Hester* is disconcerting to readers familiar with the self-consistent worlds of most Victorian novels, is that Hester and Catherine seem so out of place in this nicely realised semi-comic realm. They fit no stereotypes, a fact which is made clear on Hester's first introduction, "she was not what people call unselfish—the one quality which is supposed to be appropriate to feminine natures. She was kind and warm-hearted and affectionate, but she was not without thought of herself." It is also a fact which grates on other characters in the book, "Ladies in this country have nothing to do with business—by the way, I am forgetting Aunt Catherine."

Catherine should be "a type" because she is an "old maid", as Hester's father had joked that she would be, with "one of those laughs with which a coarse-minded man waves the banner of his sex over an unmarried woman". But she is credited with neither the embittered frustration nor the sentimental gentleness associated with the opposing clichés of spinsterhood. Because she has wealth and opportunity, Mrs Oliphant is able to present her independence as a boon rather than an impediment. The situation of the growing numbers of single women was a much discussed issue in the nineteenth century, and this portrait illustrates two interesting aspects of the discussion. The first was the insistence that it was not just material dependency but internalisation of the ideal of marriage which made spinsterhood a "problem", as Josephine Butler had maintained, "There is abundance of work to be done which needs men and women detached from domestic ties; our unmarried women will be the greatest blessing to the community when they cease to be soured by disappointment or driven by destitution to despair." Again it is a problem of consciousness, or "sentiment". The second is that by the 1880s spinsterhood was beginning to be seen as a positive condition, allowing freedom of action often denied to married women, a point noted in an article on "The Future of Single Women" in the *Westminster Review* in 1884 which declared "The unmarried woman of today is a new, sturdy and vigorous type . . . The world is before her in a freer, truer and better sense than it is before any individual, male or female."

There is a sense of excitement about the presentation of Hester and Catherine, which we remember almost more than the pessimism of their story. They are large, hungry, healthy, restless, associated with words like "triumph", "energy", "pride" and they seem always to be bursting out of the domestic interiors which confine them. Catherine paces up and down, sweeping majestically from room to room, and in all formal scenes, whether frozen in humiliation at Catherine's evening parties or waltzing feverishly at Ellen's balls, Hester is uncomfortable and constrained. The central image is of her walking, alone, as in Lamb's poem, with "springy gait", or escaping to walk on the common with the old Captain, whose memories offered her access to a larger world where "there were great storms and fights, there were dangers and struggles and death lurking round every corner . . . Why was not Hester born in that day! Why was she not a man!" Neither woman can be contained in the inner world appropriate to their sex. All the emotional crises take place outside, on the porch, at the gate, beneath the trees, and above all on the road which links their two houses and which gives a kind of symbolic axis to the novel. And these scenes of excitement or decision also invariably take place at night as if Hester's intensity does not belong to mundane behaviour of everyday life.

Towards the end of the book, the plot is forced to a denouement by conventions of betrayal and revelation which belong more to sensation novels than to ironic comedies. The action is halted at crucial moments, reminding one of tableaux from melodramas or the dramatic composition of popular paintings and increasingly the characters themselves are made to sense their own symbolic power, as when Hester, full of premonitions, finds herself remembering the snaky locks and petrifying glance of Medusa. Almost every description attains the quality of metaphor, referring not only to Hester's situation but to that of so many passionate, intelligent women whose dreams of change seemed doomed to disillusionment:

> "I think—I had better go home—to my mother" the girl said, looking along the road with a dreamy terror. She was afraid of the dark, the solitude, the distance—and yet what was there left for her but to go home, which she seemed to have quitted, to have fled from, with the idea of never returning, years ago. Catherine put out her hand and grasped her. She was by far the most vigorous of the two.

It is Catherine, the old maid, who is the embodiment of strength for the future and who points the way forward, not only for Hester, but for the new breed of "odd women", the solitary heroines of the 1890s.

Elisabeth Jay (essay date 1990)

SOURCE: Introduction to *The Autobiography of Margaret Oliphant: The Complete Text*, edited and introduced by Elisabeth Jay, Oxford University Press, 1990, pp. vii-xvii.

[*In the following introduction to a new edition of Oliphant's* Autobiography *(based on the original manuscript), Jay suggests that this new work allows modern readers the chance to understand the intense relationship Oliphant felt between the act of writing and the personal and financial needs that inspired it.*]

Margaret Oliphant Wilson Oliphant, whose curious name derived from marrying a cousin on her mother's side of the family, was born on 4 April 1828 in Wallyford, Midlothian, and died in Wimbledon on 25 June 1897. Her first attempt at writing took the form of a novel written in her teens to secure 'some amusement and occupation for myself' while striving to overcome depression after a broken engagement and acting as the silent nurse and attendant her mother's serious illness required. The image is prophetic. Over the next fifty years Oliphant was to write some ninety-eight novels, fifty or more short stories, more than four hundred articles, numerous travel books and several biographies, while functioning as the mainstay of a family whose ever-widening circle and increasingly importunate demands she satisfied and, on occasion, distanced by means of her literary career. The final lines of her autobiographical manuscript, written after the death in adulthood of her two remaining children, also focus attention upon the intimate and complex relationship between the writing and the need that generated it.

> And now here I am all alone.
> I cannot write any more.

Experience had discouraged her from seeking support and solace from men. Her father seems to have been a detached, uncompanionable figure, totally overshadowed by her capable mother, to whom she was devoted. Despite being nine years younger than either of her two brothers, Oliphant provided for her elder brother Frank and his children upon his bankruptcy and subsequent mental collapse, and for the exiled life of the younger brother 'Willie' who declined into chronic alcoholism. Her husband's death after only seven years of marriage left her abroad, in debt, and with the three of her six children who had survived infancy to support. It is difficult, even with the full text of her autobiography, to construct a full picture of her marriage to her cousin Frank, which had so brief a span to survive many of the strains normal to the early years of married life, when money was short, childbearing an almost annual event, and the new relationship had to be negotiated in a strange environment under the additional strain of her parents coming to London with the sole aim of being near her. The strong emotional tie that existed between mother and daughter seems to have been a source of irritation and jealousy to Frank, especially since the bond seemed to have been cemented by a sense of the inadequacy of all the male figures in the Wilson family. Frank had therefore to carve out for himself the roles of husband and father while also trying to establish himself in business as a stained-glass window artist. Frank's naïvety in business affairs was something Oliphant could probably have forgiven, but the wound that never completely healed was Frank's failure to share with her his medical specialist's grim diagnosis of advanced tuberculosis. In retrospect she blamed herself for lack of sympathy, but also contrasted his petulant self-absorption with the heroic fortitude of her mother during her final illness. Above all the lack of trust and concern hurt, and many an apparently happily married couple in Oliphant's novels is resolved into two individuals harbouring thoughts that would astound or grieve the other. Though she set her face firmly against remarriage, partly on account of her conviction of reunion in heaven, it is remarkable that in her moments of deepest grief she seems only to think of the children already taken from her and her mother's welcoming presence, not of her husband. As the years passed and friends and dependants unknown to Frank came into being it is scarcely to be wondered at that the tenth of her life spent in marriage receded in importance.

When two of Oliphant's former dependants, her niece Denny, and her distant cousin Annie Coghill, came to publish her autobiographical manuscript in 1899, they had become so accustomed to her shaping powers as family provider, professional writer and businesswoman that they were astonished and disappointed, for 'it had no beginning: scraps had been written at long intervals and by no means consecutively'. So they attempted to redeem their relative's startling lapse by assembling the 'bits' and 'fragments' of which Oliphant herself spoke, into the narrative line they believed would prove acceptable to the market.

Yet they could not escape the anxiety 'that the needful fitting together has not been quite smoothly done', that the manuscript displayed a certain obstinate resistance to the literary template they wished to impose upon it. The reordering and suppressions involved in their editorial process wrenched the form a step away from the autobiographical impulse that had engendered it and a step nearer to the biographical record expressly forbidden by Oliphant upon her death-bed. Moreover, in their desire to 'gratify the many readers who have for so long a stretch of years regarded her as a friend', these two women in effect colluded with the constraints imposed upon women and women writers by the cultural assumptions enshrined in the market. Such a generalized accusation requires more specific illustration. Here then is the portrait of Oliphant that Annie Coghill offered to readers before they embarked upon the truncated autobiography.

> [W]hatever sufferings might be lying in wait to seize upon her solitary hours, there was almost always a pleasant welcome and talk of the very best to be found in her modest drawing-room. If the visitors were congenial, her charm of manner awoke, her simple fitness of speech clothed every subject with life and grace, her beautiful eyes shone (they never sparkled), and the spell of her exquisite womanliness made a charmed circle around her.

This blueprint for feminine behaviour stresses decorum and restraint, the ability to give life to the charmed circle without insisting upon her own presence as its creative force. The passage, with its culminating tribute to 'the very atmosphere about her which was "pure womanly",' constitutes the editors' hidden agenda. If Oliphant is to be presented as a social creature brought to life by her response to the needs of others, then the inner voice heard during those solitary hours, especially when raised against the demands imposed upon her by others, will have to be muted or altogether stifled.

The cuts that her editors made, which amounted to well over a quarter of the original manuscript, were of two sorts, though both might be seen to have their origin in their concern for this womanly image. There were small excisions of barbed comments, potentially embarrassing to the living, that seemed at odds with the qualities of charm and grace privileged in the prefatory account. The major and continuous portions of unpublished material, however, were all of a piece and written in each case immediately after the deaths in 1864, 1890 and 1864 of her three surviving children at the ages of 10, 33 and 34 respectively. These outpourings of grief, written in her 'solitary hours', form a painfully direct attempt to log the daily agony of recollection, desolation and theological speculation. They have no immediately imagined audience beyond God or her own consciousness; none the less they attain a literary stature beyond the purely personal. However intense the grief the cadences of her lucid style never deserted her and these *journal intime* passages share with the more public recollections the mark of the self-consciously professional writer feeling her way to appropriate form. At every stage of this diverse enterprise Oliphant compared her venture with the matter and mode revealed in the autobiographical literature that she read and reviewed. The process of recording her reactions to her daughter Maggie's death in the opening pages of the journal opened her eyes to the innovative nature of Tennyson's *In Memoriam*, which she had previously been inclined to judge harshly as a vehicle for philosophy rather than a spontaneous and bitter cry of pain (*Blackwood's Magazine*, February 1856). Now she recognized it as a model enabling the complex intertwining of reflection and emotion. Tennyson 'has done it already far better than I can', she wrote a few weeks after her daughter's death; nevertheless he had taught her how to 'put the long musings of my agony into words', and as she reread this section toward the end of her life she wondered whether it might not have its own place in the literature of bereavement.

It is important to make this point about the literariness of the *Autobiography* if only to dispel the long-held notion that this fragmented self-disclosure is merely a naïve compilation of diary, chronicle and anecdote, eliciting compassion for a series of personal tragedies. Even those among Oliphant's readers who had been comparably schooled in grief were impressed by the poignance with which this particular story was told. Virginia Woolf in the course of a polemical dismissal of Oliphant's novels as a kind of literary prostitution which 'smeared your mind and dejected your imagination' found herself surprised into the admission that the autobiography was, on the other hand, 'a most genuine and moving piece of work' (*Three Guineas,* 1938). Woolf had herself experienced the profoundly disturbing effects of the shockingly premature deaths of a mother, a step-sister and a brother. Moreover she had a standard of literary comparison in her father Leslie Stephen's intimate memoir of two marriages, compiled as a record for his children and known in the family as the Mausoleum Book. Although the praise 'most genuine' might seem to come uncomfortably close to the accusation of ingenuousness, the *Autobiography* is, after all, remembered as 'a piece of work', a literary artefact.

For the self that Oliphant presents in the *Autobiography* is a deliberate creation; accustomed as a novelist to examining her characters as they appeared both to themselves and to the outside world, this dual perspective emerges in the half-mocking way in which she views her relations with the world around her. Indeed one critic has sardonically described her picture of herself as a woman whose talent had been circumscribed by the demands of her family as 'one of her better fictional efforts', seeing in it a desire to disguise the fact that she was a competent professional writer who had achieved the limited best of which she was capable (W. Evans Mosier, Mosier, 'Mrs Oliphant's Literary Criticism', Ph.D. thesis, Northwestern University, 1967). The criticism misfires in confusing fiction with falsehood. There is a degree of deliberate self-marginalization in Oliphant's picture of herself as 'a fat, little commonplace woman, rather tongue-tied', living, half by choice and half by force of circumstance, a life remote from the literary coteries of London. This account ignores her friendship and acquaintance with many of the literary giants of her day, the fact that she frequented, if less frequently, the salons that were a source of inspiration to that intrepid social investigator, Henry James, and the type of wry confession found in a letter to her nephew Frank, telling him that although she did not particularly care for the way in which she had been 'made much

of' at a Balliol College ball, doubtless she would have cared had she not received this attention (27 June 1879, National Library of Scotland Acc. 5793/2). Her repeated assertions of social awkwardness neglect her considerable gifts as a hostess capable, for instance, of organizing an open-air party on the island of Runnymede on 19 June 1877 to celebrate the twenty-fifth anniversary of her connection with the publishing firm of Blackwoods, an event which in itself suggests a sense of her own worth in the creative partnership.

Her own concept of her self-effacing manner was markedly at odds with other people's assessments. James spoke of 'her sharp and handsome physiognomy'. Annie Thackeray, one of her closest friends, was forced to admit that she could be 'cold in manner and tart in speech', while J. M. Barrie, searching for the words in which to convey her combined simplicity and hauteur, described her as 'the *grande dame* at one moment, almost a girl, it might be, the next'.

Barrie's appreciation of the apparently contradictory elements in her nature may help us to appreciate the problems Oliphant encountered in her autobiographical writing. As she sought to transcribe her mother's character she realized the inadequacy of fictional tools for such a purpose.

> How little one realises the character or individuality of those who are most near and dear. It is with difficulty even now that I can analyse or make a character of her. She herself is there, not any type or variety of humankind. (p. 21)

The ensuing picture of her mother does, in part, rely upon her novelist's sense of physical presence, setting and illustrative anecdote to illuminate a psychological portraiture, but there are abundant qualifications and a sense of the inefficacy of the many superlatives she employs to convey 'this varying, this unknown and uncircumscribed spirit' (V. Woolf, 'Modern Fiction', *The Common Reader,* 1925).

One reason for Woolf's involuntary praise of the *Autobiography* may have been that it most nearly approached the condition to which she believed that fiction should aspire, 'so that, if a writer were a free man and not a slave, if he could write what he chose not what he must, if he could base his work upon his own feeling and not upon convention, there would be no plot, no comedy, no tragedy, no love interest or catastrophe in the accepted style'. Considered in the light of this paradigm it becomes possible to see the fragmentary dislocations of the *Autobiography* not merely as accidents of protracted composition, but as an experiment in narrative strategy.

While writing the first portion of the *Autobiography* in 1864 Oliphant had been reading Elizabeth Gaskell's

Life of Charlotte Brontë and had concluded that, although her own novels might not have the emotional strength of Brontë's, yet she knew herself to have a 'fuller conception of life'. She recognized that 'the love between men and women, the marrying and giving in marriage, occupy in fact, so small a portion of either existence or thought', but market forces and crushing domestic financial problems contrived to prevent her fully exploiting this vision in her fiction. In her personal writing, however, she was free to strive for a mode compatible with the sense that her life did not fall into conventional rhetorical patterns. An innate elasticity of temperament, she ruefully lamented, meant that her life must always fall short of the dignity of tragedy. As a professional critic she became increasingly interested in the autobiographical and biographical genres (biography was to become her own preferred literary mode) and her second major bout of self-inscription was prompted by her dissatisfaction with two accounts of the lives of fellow writers that had recently appeared: J. W. Cross's *Life of George Eliot* (1883) and Anthony Trollope's posthumously published *Autobiography* (1883). Both records shocked her by the way in which the animus of the life had been, or was represented as having been, committed to or shaped by the demands of the writer's art. Her own energies, she felt, as she deconstructed her life, had been more widely dispersed.

Read against recent scholarship on the autobiographical genre prompted by gender studies, Oliphant's case is peculiarly interesting. She felt herself precluded from the domestic and professional advantages accorded to male writers, whose sense of progress and achievement could be measured in attaining such public goals as secure editorial positions. Yet when she compared herself with women writers she constantly stressed the burden of business and domestic decisions, traditionally assumed to be male prerogatives, that had been forced upon her. In her case the confusion of gender-defined roles intensified the anxiety of authorship experienced by so many nineteenth-century women writers, who experienced the need to justify their public persona against the traditional expectations of female behaviour and practice fostered by their upbringing. Although the pressing financial needs consequent upon early widowhood had served to legitimate the pleasure she took in writing, she began to perceive that a sanction derived from external circumstances did not speak to her inner sense of failure. By 1885, indeed, insisting upon the claims of motherhood as paramount began to be an index of failure: her sons, now twenty-four and twenty-eight, had not been coaxed from the nest and lived a life of indolent parasitism. Forced, therefore, into the acknowledgement that 'at the end of all things the work is almost the only thing—is it not?—in which there is satisfaction' (**Autobiography and Letters**, p. 360), she found, when she examined her writing without the benefit of her accustomed alibi, that she could

not be sure her work would have been of a higher standard if she had been free of family responsibilities.

Stung by her sons' indifference and her sense of the inadequacy of either motherhood or literary reputation as a self-defining image, Oliphant resorted to writing as the epistemological tool she knew best to discover 'the thread' lying hidden 'below the surface' events of her life. The strong private need to assert her sense of self as more than a product of arbitrary external forces is, in part, suggested by the choice of Sunday evenings for this activity. Her religious upbringing would have accustomed her to the weekly opportunity provided by a private journal for self-assessment and detecting God's guiding hand in the course of daily life. Once again, however, Oliphant's desire to be true to her perception of life's apparent plotlessness led her to push against the limiting structures provided by providential explanations. Here, as in her novels, she cries out against a God whose dispositions are harsh and unfathomable and against simpleminded tracing of the ways of Providence. Increasingly she was inclined to postpone the divine revelation of purpose and meaning to the after-life—a belief which in her novels led to a marked repudiation of that favourite Victorian device, the final chapter in which order and happiness are reimposed. Bringing 'unconsidered moments of happiness' to consciousness, re-creating the impulses and needs that had driven her life, was all that remained possible in the way of self-definition, and it was in this deliberate privileging of small domestic memories and intimate friendships, over against the myths of progress achieved in a public arena often favoured by male autobiographies of the period, that constituted the poignant originality of the work. The fragments, this autobiography asserts, are the meaning and the pattern of a woman's life.

The deaths of her two sons deprived Oliphant of the will to live and consequently of her interest in the experimental process of self-re-creation. The closing portion, begun in 1894, deliberately returns us to the formula of the more public memoir designed to secure an inheritance for her unmarried niece. Nevertheless the attempt to concentrate upon 'making pennyworths of myself' sometimes defeated her, and she would find herself drifting back into the old habit of musing, pointless and painful though she now found it, or into the more subtle process of refracted autobiography observable in anecdotes and portraits that present her own case obliquely. The tenor of her life, moreover, obstinately refused to conform to the popular demand she perceived for tales of happy and successful lives, and her artistic instinct revolted against the shapeless proliferation she condemned in so many contemporary memoirs. It is perhaps unsurprising that Oliphant's editors failed to recognize the broken cadence with which the **Autobiography** ends as its wholly appropriate conclusion, expressing the agony of a continued physical existence severed from all that had made her life of interest to her. It may be easier for a later generation accustomed to the disjunctive modes of modernism to appreciate the narrative strategy of this experimental text.

The pious but misguided efforts made to rearrange her fractured narrative into the cleaner lines of a conventional memoir resulted, however, in the erection of a desolate Victorian folly. Shorn of its more incisive pieces and deprived of its more personal passages the edifice swiftly achieved the status of a period piece, a self-confirming monument to the courageous struggles of a woman who had chosen writing as the only means available to her of earning the family living. Oliphant undoubtedly played her own part in her rapid fall from critical favour. Like Trollope she probably suffered from her own self-depreciation in a posthumously published autobiography, but literary politics too contributed. Her stock-in-trade, the three-volume novel, was as she was aware, fast being superseded by the single volume, whose form invited a different style and may even have produced a different readership. Whereas three-deckers made ideal family entertainment, allowing serial reading and subsequent discussion by parents and children, the single volume might well accommodate material not considered suitable for adolescent perusal. In 1898, the year after her death, Mudie's circulating library still carried eighty-nine of her titles in its annual catalogue, but Mudie's no longer called the tune with publishers, nor did their expensive subscription any longer attract the ever-expanding and more diverse market of readers. Cheap editions of Oliphant's novels continued to appear in the early years of the new century, but neither the format nor the concerns of her fiction appealed to a post-war generation. The general reader had always formed her assumed audience and so it is less surprising that the tide of literary fashion turned more swiftly against her work than against that of less 'popular' authors. The fact that several of her obituary notices made the point that her appeal as a novelist had been as great to men as it was to women may indicate sensitivity to a new critical landscape dominated by male clubland. Liberated from the towering shadow thrown by George Eliot's long domination of the literary scene, a distinctly misogynistic tone was emerging and could be clearly detected in the remarks of male novelists who had recently suffered at the hands of Oliphant, who, as regular reviewer for *Blackwood's Magazine,* had enjoyed uninterrupted power in the critical establishment. Henry James remarked in his obituary: 'I should almost suppose in fact that no woman had ever, for half a century, had her personal "say" so publicly and irresponsibly' (*Notes and Novelists,* 1914, p. 358) and Thomas Hardy, who in 1882 had welcomed 'direct communication with a writer I have known in spirit so long' felt free by 1912 to dismiss her criticisms as 'the screaming of a poor lady in *Blackwood*' (*Collected Letters,* ed. R. L. Purdy and M. Millgate, i. 107, and Postscript to the Preface of *Jude the Obscure*).

Oliphant's own sense that she had taken 'a fuller conception of life' than many women writers may have militated against her as an early candidate for resurrection by the feminist presses of our own day. Within the last two or three years there has been a flurry of interest in her work, but because it is difficult to obtain access to her entire *œuvre* (most of her novels seem to have been pulped) and even more time-consuming to read every title, publishers have for the most part relied upon reprinting the **Chronicles of Carlingford** series in which she recognized that she had exploited a best-selling formula, or those novels such as **Kirsteen** (1890) which retained critical favour among the obituarists of the 1890s. It is still difficult for the general reader to obtain a clear picture of the professional acumen with which she responded to the changing market in her fifty years as a novelist, or of the range of her work and interests which embraced both the supernatural and the quietly traced tale of domestic suffering or triumph. Throughout her work Oliphant cast a wry eye upon the comparative lots of men and women and the subtleties of the human temperament, which often submits against its own better judgement to the orthodoxies society imposes. For society, as she often remarked, looked after its own, and virtue all too frequently had a way of becoming its own reward in the socially inferior position of the single woman. Such a view of life was not without its consequences for her writing and some of those novels which appear most completely to collude with the moral and stylistic conventions of the day do so only after a subtly subversive examination of many of the age's most treasured assumptions. The way in which her worthy but blinkered executors felt free to reshape her remains according to their own conventional pieties is merely one indicator of how easily much of her writing could be misconstrued as hack work produced in response to the prevailing fashions. Restoring the full text of her autobiography provides one way for the modern reader to catch more easily the distinctive timbre of the individual voice which ran through so much of her work.

Joseph H. O'Mealy (essay date 1992)

SOURCE: "Mrs. Oliphant, *Miss Marjoribanks,* and the Victorian Canon," in *The Victorian Newsletter*, No. 82, Fall, 1992, pp. 44-49.

[*In the essay that follows, O'Mealy argues in favor of placing Oliphant within the Victorian literary canon. As evidence, the critic focuses on the novel* Miss Marjoribanks *(1866), claiming that "its ambivalent ironies, beautifully controlled and surprisingly directed, demonstrate a high degree of literary sophistication."*]

John Sutherland's magisterial *Companion to Victorian Fiction* (which synopsizes 554 novels and gives brief notes on 878 novelists) warns against accepting the "Lilliputian dimensions" (1) of our current sense of the Victorian novel. It is a monument to his belief that the dozen or so novelists who regularly dominate bibliographies of Victorian fiction need some fresh companions, lest late twentieth-century readers never learn "what the Victorian novel actually meant to the Victorians" (1). Since Sutherland does not put forth any particular candidate for an expanded canon, the task of partisan promotion falls to others. In the spirit of what I hope is enlightened partisanship, I would like to advance the claims for Mrs. Margaret Oliphant, who, as the so-called "Queen of Popular Fiction" (Terry Ch. 4), has as great a historical claim as any to reconsideration, revaluation, and, I would argue, ultimate recovery as an important Victorian novelist.

Consider her curious case. During Margaret Oliphant's life one critic called her "the most remarkable woman of her time" (Skelton 80); at her death William Blackwood the publisher wrote, "Mrs. Oliphant has been to the England of letters what the Queen has been to society as a whole. She, too, was crowned with age and honour in her own empire" (Terry 68). But, today, when many women's literary reputations are being recovered and their works are finding a place in either the traditional canon or an all-female counter canon, this prolific and once admired Victorian novelist is still largely overlooked. Lillian Robinson's question, "Is the canon . . . to be regarded as the compendium of excellence or the record of cultural history?" (112), instead of laying out the possible strategies for Oliphant's achievement of canonical status, points out the precise nature of the dilemma. In either direction Oliphant's progress to canonical status is thwarted since she pleases neither the old guardians of the canon nor the new revisionists. To some traditionalists, the quality of Oliphant's work is questionable; to some feminists her political conservatism is an insuperable barrier. However, a close look at *Miss Marjoribanks* (1866)—arguably her best novel—reveals qualities that should please both camps. Its ambivalent ironies, beautifully controlled and surprisingly directed, demonstrate a high degree of literary sophistication, while its subtly crafted feminism points out Oliphant's sympathetic understanding of the limitations placed on the talented Victorian woman. In recovering the best of Oliphant it's possible to recover not only a fine and satisfying novel but also, more importantly, a truer sense of the immense range of quality Victorian fiction.

As the author of ninety-two novels, scores of essays, and over two dozen non-fiction works, Oliphant could once lay claim to a degree of productivity unrivaled by any serious contemporary. She could also measure her success in the distinction of being Queen Victoria's favorite novelist (Colby xiii, Sutherland 477), as well as in the large audiences many of her books attracted: "Just think of the millions she has made happy" (Skelton 76). Yet, even during her lifetime, Oliphant's future oblivion seemed inevitable. This same critic, John Skelton, introduced a caveat about Oliphant's abilities that has hung over her reputation ever since—she wrote too much, too fast. Comparing her output of two or three novels a year to Charlotte Brontë's and George Eliot's more modest production levels, Skelton admitted their greater "imaginative force," and asked, "Had Mrs. Oliphant concentrated her powers, what might she not have done? We might have had another Charlotte Brontë or another George Eliot" (80). Laying aside the question of whether a facsimile of a literary genius is ever desirable, Skelton's point about overproduction carries even more weight with a modern audience. Steeped as we are in the late twentieth-century belief that less is more, and conditioned by the modernist examples of lapidary and/or slowly gestated novels, the knowledge that the Oliphant canon contains nearly one hundred novels not only discourages the modern reader but probably gives rise to a mild contempt for the author of such excess. Even Robert and Vineta Colby, whose 1966 study of Oliphant was the first serious attempt at a revaluation, temper their advocacy with disapproval of the sheer quantity of her output. "Mrs. Oliphant predicted that she would be forgotten by the next generation, and perhaps her eclipse is a Dantean justice for one who wrote too fast and too much" (xiv).

Henry James's 1897 obituary notice of Oliphant shares a similar tone of apparent praise that, under further examination, sounds like damning.

> Her success had been in its day as great as her activity, yet it was always present to me that her singular gift was less recognised, or at any rate less reflected, less reported upon, than it deserved: unless indeed she may have been one of those difficult cases for criticism, an energy of which the spirit and the form, straggling apart, never join hands with that effect of union which in literature more than anywhere else is strength. (1411)

Again there is the reference to her great activity (he earlier refers to her "copious tribute" to the "great contemporary flood" of literature). More damaging is the orotund suggestion that perhaps Oliphant falls short of the Jamesian ideal of literary artistry; "the spirit and the form," the subject and the technique, are not in harmony. James hints at what Oliphant would never have denied. She was not an "artist" in the Jamesian sense. In her *Autobiography*, published posthumously, she refused to analyze her work, claiming that she wrote "because it gave me pleasure, because it came natural to me, because it was like talking or breathing, besides the big fact that it was necessary for me to work for my children" (4). Trollope's **Autobiography**, which James found distressingly nonchalant about the novelist's elevated calling, astonished Oliphant with its analytical comments on fictional creations: "I am totally incapable of talking about anything I have done in that way" (4), she averred.

Her male contemporaries did little to keep the memory of her novels alive, and early twentieth-century literary historians like Ernest Baker followed their lead. In his ten volume *History of the English Novel* (1924-1939) Baker found room for only a few sentences about Oliphant, dismissing her as a "domestic novelist" (8:111), that hoary euphemism for "damned scribbling woman." Once the novels fell out of print (for the longest time only **Salem Chapel,** 1863, not her finest work, was available in the Everyman Library series), Oliphant's reputation rested increasingly on her literary criticism. As recently as 1977, Elaine Showalter, in a pioneering study of the female tradition in the novel—*A Literature of Their Own*—based most of her discussion of Oliphant, not on her novels, but on quotations from her literary criticism (*passim*). Not surprisingly, it proved a somewhat unsteady prop. For more than forty years the virtual house critic of *Blackwood's,* Oliphant was conservative in her taste. She preferred the traditional English novel of Scott and Trollope, "not so much perhaps for what critics would call the highest development of art, as for a certain sanity, wholesomeness, and cleanness unknown to other literature of the same class" (102: 257). She was no stranger to skepticism, but she didn't like to see it in other people's books. *Vanity Fair,* for example, offended her sense of fairness in its satire against Amelia and Dobbin (77: 89); Chadband in *Bleak House* she regarded as a cynical and unrepresentative portrait of an evangelical clergyman (77: 463). She hated the "nasty sentiments and equivocal heroines" of sensation novels with their often glamorous depictions of female villainy (102: 280), and, even though she admired the revolutionary passions and vitality of *Jane Eyre,* she thought Charlotte Brontë skirted too close to indelicacy in her subject matter, and she worried that Brontë's legions of imitators, lacking her skills, would only debase the novel (77: 557-59).

The review that has made her appear most out of touch with modern sensibilities (Stubbs 141-42) was written the year before her death when she locked horns with Hardy over *Jude the Obscure.* She decried the novel's depiction of marriage as "shameful," reviled the creation of the openly sexual Arabella ("a human pig"), and characterized the whole enterprise as a product of "grossness, indecency, and horror" (159:138). Finally, she accused Hardy of hypocrisy for profiting twice from the novel, once in a "clean" version for serial publication, and again in the unexpurgated book edition. Her heavy-handed indignation

did not sit easily with Hardy. His contemptuous dismissal of her as "propriety and primness incarnate" (Page 24) summed up the way many modernists saw her: an Eminent Victorian relic whose very name—MRS. Oliphant—reeked of the respectability of antimacassars, horse-hair sofas, and whale-bone corsets.

For many feminists interested in recovering lost women's voices, Oliphant has been, to use James's phrase, "one of those difficult cases for criticism." Virginia Woolf, in *Three Guineas,* established one approach to her, which is to regard her as a cautionary example. She asks whether a look at Oliphant's **Autobiography** does not lead the reader "to deplore the fact that Mrs. Oliphant sold her brain, her very admirable brain, prostituted her culture and enslaved her intellectual liberty in order that she might earn her living and educate her children" (91-92). It's not that Oliphant couldn't do better, Woolf implies; it's just that she was not allowed to. Oliphant, to Woolf, is an exemplary victim of a patriarchal system that forces women to worry first about the bare mechanics of scraping a living together and then, much later and further down the line, the claims of "disinterested culture and intellectual liberty." Woolf is quick to admire Oliphant's courage and her compassion in putting her family first, but she is even quicker to emphasize the short circuiting of her literary abilities. Like Skelton, Woolf prefers to think more of what Oliphant might have been than look closely at what she was.

Later feminists have not been even so equivocally generous. Sandra Gilbert and Susan Gubar's twenty-five hundred page *Norton Anthology of Literature by Women* (1985), for example, does not mention Oliphant at all. Novelists admittedly are not allowed much space in traditional anthologies, but Gilbert and Gubar, realizing the centrality of the novel to women's writing, have broken with tradition and included three complete novels: *Jane Eyre, The Awakening,* and *The Bluest Eye.* Excerpts from Maria Edgeworth, Jane Austen, Mary Shelley, Elizabeth Gaskell, Emily Brontë, and George Eliot, and summary references to Rhoda Broughton and Mary Elizabeth Braddon constitute their canon of nineteenth-century fiction. To exclude Oliphant from a survey of women's literature, "designed to serve as a core curriculum text" (xxvii), crammed with works whose "historical, intellectual, or aesthetic significance seems clearly to merit inclusion" (xxx) is to make her doubly marginal—neither part of the woman's tradition nor the man's.

Perhaps Gilbert and Gubar do not place Oliphant in their "great tradition" of women's writing because her novels do not question or challenge the prevailing patriarchy, nor does she treat her women characters as the repressed "other." (Oliphant does not privilege alterity.) In a similar way other feminists have faulted Oliphant for her political timidity: her "superficially emancipated heroines . . . remain well within the limits of moral and social convention" and are "in no way a serious challenge to patriarchal stereotypes of feminine character and behaviour" (Stubbs 39). Perhaps it is difficult for some critics to forgive Oliphant's opposition to what she once called "the mad notion of the franchise for women" (*Autobiography* 211). Yet, as Merryn Williams reminds us in her recent biography, Oliphant made that remark in 1866, and during the remaining thirty years of her life she altered her views considerably. "She believed in a Married Women's Property Act, a mother's right to the custody of her children, women doctors, and University education for girls. . . . By 1880 she was prepared to say in public, 'I think it is highly absurd that I should not have a vote, if I want one'" (108). Oliphant apparently did not want the vote herself, but then neither did George Eliot, Christina Rossetti, nor Elizabeth Barrett Browning.

Nevertheless, Oliphant has her modern advocates. They admit without hesitation that not all her work is first-rate, but, rather than dismiss her because of it, they single out those works that represent her best efforts. They look beyond the limitations imposed on her by the need to write fast and publish frequently and emphasize their belief that "what remains remarkable is what she did achieve within those limitations" (Terry 101).

The greatest amount of positive critical attention so far has been given to Oliphant's five volume *Chronicles of Carlingford: The Rector and The Doctor's Family* (1863); *Salem Chapel* (1863); *The Perpetual Curate* (1864); *Miss Marjoribanks* (1866); and *Phoebe Junior: A Last Chronicle of Carlingford* (1876). Among them the most consistent praise has been directed at *Miss Marjoribanks*. Q. D. Leavis, who wrote an Introduction to a 1969 reprint of the novel, deserves credit for beginning the modern recovery of *Miss Marjoribanks*. She places Oliphant in the same company as Jane Austen and George Eliot as novelists of manners, and assigns Lucilla Marjoribanks, the title character, a prominent position in the Pantheon of strong women characters, somewhere between Emma Woodhouse and Dorothea Brooke, judging Lucilla "more entertaining, more impressive, and more likable than either" (1). She concludes with the hope that "perhaps our age will at last do justice to this wise and witty novel in which every sentence is exactly right and every word apt and adroitly placed" (23). While more temperate minds might balk at claims of perfection, a few other critics of the novel do share Mrs. Leavis's enthusiasm. Merryn Williams has asserted that "it is hardly possible to overpraise *Miss Marjoribanks,* which grows more impressive every time it is read" (84), and R. C. Terry has called it "a novel that can stand comparison with the best contemporary novels of its kind" (89).

Miss Marjoribanks is an ironic comedy about power, the story of a young unmarried woman's efforts to achieve power within the narrow confines allowed to daughters of the genteel classes. Lucilla Marjoribanks returns home from school at the beginning of the novel to her widowed father, a prosperous physician in the quiet Tory town of Carlingford, and to a traditional patriarchal society. It's a man's world, where the major social event is Dr. Marjoribanks's weekly all-male dinner, "to which naturally, as there was no lady in the house, ladies could not be invited" (42). To make matters worse for the wives left at home, Dr. Marjoribank's cook is so skillful at creating exquisite sauces that she spoils the men for their wives' plainer fare. For the unmarried young woman, like Lucilla, the only respectable option is to become the socially unimportant wife of such a spoiled man.

Lucilla, however, has decided during her years of exile at the Mt. Pleasant girls' school that her mission upon return will go beyond looking on at her father's festive table. Her real ambition is "the reorganization of society in Carlingford" (40). She plans to create a coherent social life for all members of the genteel classes, male and female, and to make herself the central point around which their activities revolve. The other women of the town are not up to the task, disqualified as they are by virtue of age, circumstance, or disposition from doing "anything in the way of knitting people together, and making a harmonious whole out of the scraps and fragments of society" (43). Lucilla deems herself perfect for the job: she has a passion for organization, she is unattached, and she has her father's large house and not inconsiderable income at her disposal. The first thing she does to build public confidence in her resolve to reshape Carlingford is to dispel rumors that she might marry at any time. She makes it clear to her father, to her cousin Tom, who loves her, and to anyone who asks, that she intends to devote herself to Carlingford for at least ten years. Lucilla hangs out her shingle, so to speak, and commences her "career" when she establishes her "Thursday nights." When her cousin Tom tries to impress her by declaring "I am called to the bar, and I have begun my Career" (96), Lucilla solemnly ignores him. She knows that her own "Career" as the social doyenne of Carlingford, which is as close to a public career as a Victorian young lady could hope for, is so much more real and active than a fledgling barrister's.

Lucilla is much smarter and abler than any of the men in her world. She becomes thereby Oliphant's emblem of the unfair limitations placed on Victorian women. In a world where female imagination has no real outlet, and female ability can gain no real power, Lucilla make impressive use of the meager resources at her disposal. She takes the Victorian home, which was supposed to be the realm of the private, and turns it into the public, subverting the Victorian "ideology of home and family [which] was consistently employed to oppose emergent feminism" (Stubbs 7). Her Thursday nights create a community where there was alienation and separation. The genteel classes of Carlingford gather once a week for dinner, gossip, and light entertainment. And a woman's hand guides it all. Lucilla of course performs the time-honored feminine tasks of harmonizing and unifying that Virginia Woolf recognized as Mrs. Ramsay's greatest gift and limitation. It's an ambivalence that Oliphant shares. When Oliphant refers ironically to Lucilla's Thursdays as her "great work" (122), the double-edge of that phrase is unmistakable: ordinarily a genteel Victorian woman's "work" meant her needlework or embroidery, symbols of the limits placed on female productivity. Even her father recognizes the waste inherent in Lucilla's "Thursdays." He had often complained that his sister-in-law had the son, Tom, that he had wanted, yet he has to admit "how great a loss it was to society and to herself that Lucilla was not 'the boy'" (400).

Despite gender restrictions, Lucilla's brilliance cannot be completely dimmed, only somewhat contained. Her ability to exploit convention, even to subvert it when necessary, is revealed clearly in three masterful scenes. In each of them, Lucilla demonstrates her will to power, and her skill at controlling circumstances so that a weak strategic position is converted into a commanding triumph.

When she first arrives in Carlingford the initial obstacles to Lucilla's empire-building are her father and his housekeeper, Nancy. Only nineteen, Lucilla has to establish early on her determination to run the house. Since she's a rank outsider, having been away a decade at school, and since the current inhabitants of the house are content doing things their own way, Lucilla must begin swiftly but subtly. She amuses her father with stories about her Grand Tour of the continent, and while he compounds his good mood with a glass of claret, she, "as she herself expressed it, harmonised the rooms, by the simple method of rearranging half the chairs and covering the tables with trifles of her own" (50). When her father sees her handiwork he is restrained by his usual Scottish phlegm from saying anything. The next morning, however, Lucilla "unfolded her standard" (50). She arises before he does and when he enters the breakfast room discovers her seated in his usual place blithely offering him a cup of coffee. "Dr. Marjoribanks hesitated for one momentous instant, stricken dumb by this unparalleled audacity; but so great was the effect of his daughter's courage and steadiness, that after that moment of fate he accepted the seat by the side where everything was arranged for him and to which Lucilla invited him sweetly" (50). Lucilla acts not without trepidation, but her firm belief in the wisdom of seizing opportunity by the forelock sustains her. She apologizes for taking her father's place and explains that otherwise she

"should have had to move the urn, and all the things, and I thought you would not mind" (50). Her father grumbles quietly and then submits, aware that "the reins of state had been smilingly withdrawn from his unconscious hands" (50).

Oliphant pointedly concedes that "it is no great credit to a woman of nineteen to make a man of any age throw down his arms; but to conquer a woman is a different matter" (52). To win over Nancy is the real challenge. And Lucilla does it through a confident sweetness that encourages Nancy to consider Lucilla her ally in upholding the great tradition of Marjoribanks dinners: "I have heard of papa's dinners . . . and I don't mean to let down your reputation. Now we are two women to manage everything, we ought to do still better" (52). Nancy, who had been prepared to resist any high-handed attempts to wrest control from her, is completely disarmed by Lucilla's conciliatory tactics, and "gave in like her master" (52).

Lucilla's home triumph is not yet secure, however. Her free hand at home raises the eyebrows of at least one townsperson, the evangelical rector, Mr. Bury. He considers it irregular, if not improper, for Lucilla to mix in male society without an older woman as her chaperone. Since her mother is dead, he decides to provide her with a live-in companion. Lucilla plays a little fast and loose, but all is fair, as she sees it, in her war for an independent dominion. She reads Bury's candidate, Mrs. Mortimer, quickly—"a deprecating woman, with a faint sort of pleading smile on her face" (85)—and parries Bury's pious declaration that he has found someone to take her mother's place with the disingenuous question, "Do you mean you have found some one for him [her father] to marry?" (86). The introduction of a sexual perspective completely unnerves Mrs. Mortimer, as Lucilla knew it would, and she collapses in a faint. Lucilla takes control by nearly carrying her to the sofa, and ministers to her. So much for Mrs. Mortimer as her protector. After the disgusted Bury washes his hands of Mrs. Mortimer, Lucilla candidly apologizes to her, "I knew it would hurt your feelings . . . but I could not do anything else" (89).

In these two scenes Lucilla has appropriated the conventional image of the innocent young woman whose blundering intrusions and indelicacies are well-meaning but unconscious errors at worst. Because no one can imagine her real motives (except her father who is soon amused by them), she can subvert convention and have things her own way by appearing to personify conventionality itself. As she admits: "'I always make it a point to give in to the prejudices of society. That is how I have always been so successful'" (72). She serves up revolution with a smile, founded as it is on a paradoxical adherence to the hoariest Victorian standards of decorum.

Lucilla most brilliantly manipulates the conventional code of conduct when she must save the integrity of her Thursday evenings. She learns that Mr. Cavendish, who has long been a prized jewel in her social crown, is about to be dethroned as an impostor by a visiting prelate, Archdeacon Beverley. Lucilla knows that the exposure of Cavendish, who is not a member of that illustrious family but merely a Kavan, would rend the fabric of her carefully created society, throwing everything in doubt. If Cavendish is Kavan, then who is Cavendish's sister, Mrs. Woodburn? And what status can Mr. Woodburn claim now that he is no longer married to a Cavendish? And so on. For the elite of Carlingford to discover that they have nourished an upstart in their bosoms would mean admitting that they cannot distinguish between a gentleman and a pretender. To save the status quo, Lucilla is willing to lie and risk embarrassment. At the moment the Archdeacon recognizes Cavendish at the table, Lucilla silences him by coyly confessing that "he is one of my—very particular friends" (308), in other words, that she is engaged to him, and that "he has no secrets from me" (308). The Archdeacon is confounded: "What was he to do? He could not publicly expose the man who had just received this mark of confidence from his young hostess, who knew everything" (309). Lucilla has counted on the conventional code of decorum to prevail; no one would embarrass a young lady in her own house about a suitor and expect to be considered a gentleman. Archdeacon Beverley is no cad, so Lucilla is safe. Once again, her utter confidence in her own peculiar genius and her profound understanding of the conventional minds surrounding her have turned a near disaster into a personal triumph.

No reader can fail to detect the irony in Oliphant's treatment of Lucilla's aspirations. She is fond of referring to Lucilla as "the young sovereign" (49) or as a "distinguished revolutionary" (41), eager to begin "her campaign" (98) to bring Carlingford under her sway and establish "her throne" (65) where "her subjects" (266) can pay homage to her. Some critics have worried about this irony, judging the tone "bitter" and "cold": "The portrait of Miss Marjoribanks has wit, freshness, and originality, but it lacks humanity" (Colby 63, 67). Another agrees that there is "a hardness of tone," but adds that "the wit and irony never falter; from the first page to the last it is extremely funny" (Williams 81). Oliphant's mock heroic language, laced with imperial and military tropes, can be withering, but its consistent use forces the reader to see the other side of the deflationary mock-heroic. Even as it supposedly diminishes, the comparison of Lucilla's domestic battles with the Napoleonic campaigns paradoxically elevates. We soon see that in Lucilla's milieu her ambitions do set her above the conventionality of her peers. She is both deluded to think of herself as Queen Lucilla and yet perfectly right in assuming that she is a superior being.

Perhaps it is true, as Chesterton said of Dickens's creation of Pickwick—he came to scoff but stayed to pray (70)—that Oliphant's attitude toward Lucilla changes in the course of the novel. Certainly the irony softens in the last third. And perhaps it is also fair to say that Oliphant feels some affection for her own creation, although certainly not to the uncritical degree that Stubbs suggests: "she . . . approves of both Lucilla and her activities" (41). Part of Oliphant is horrified by Lucilla's shallowness, part of her admires her spunk, and the rest admits that Lucilla is the inevitable product of a world that circumscribes talented and ambitious women so narrowly.

At the end of the novel, for example, Lucilla is ten years older, a little stouter, a little less satisfied with the regular round to Thursday evenings, and conscious of her precarious position as a woman reaching thirty without a husband. Mrs. Oliphant reminds her readers of the paradoxical Victorian usage of the word "independent" to denote both the freedom from being encumbered and the status of a married woman, no longer dependent on her parents or family.

> She was very comfortable, no doubt in every way, and met with little opposition to speak of, and had things a great deal more in her own hands than she might have had, had there been a husband in the case to satisfy; but notwithstanding, she had come to an age when most people have husbands, and when an independent position in the world becomes necessary to self-respect. To be sure Lucilla *was* independent; but then—there is a difference, as everybody knows. (342)

Like Oliphant, Lucilla is a realist and has not ignored the social advantages of marriage. She has always kept her eye out for the appropriate fellow, preferably someone, like an M. P., with access to power. Since "she had come to an age at which she might have gone into Parliament herself had there been no disqualification of sex" (394), and since "when a woman has an active mind, and still does not care for parish work, it is a little hard for her to find a sphere" (395), Lucilla faces a life crisis. Simply put, "her capabilities were greater than her work" (395). When she does marry, Lucilla chooses her cousin Tom, who has no professional standing in England, having been a barrister in India for ten years, and who cannot offer her a conventional position in society. This only gives Lucilla the chance to create a fresh mission: "the thing we both want is something to do" (483). To all Tom's protests that he hopes eventually to take care of her so she can remain idle, Lucilla turns a deaf and mildly contemptuous ear: "What was to be done with a man who had so little understanding of her, and of himself, and of the eternal fitness of things?" (484). Lucilla's view of the "eternal fitness of things" is certainly not that of the typical Victorian male. She finds a country estate for sale, fittingly named Marchbank (her name is pronounced the same), which needs a great deal of work. The tenants lead wretched, disorderly lives, much in need of a strong organizing hand. Tom, she decides, can "improve" the land, while she "improves" the people. Perhaps in a few years Tom, who has "a perfect genius for carrying out a suggestion" (496), will stand for Parliament. "Then there rose up before her a vision of a parish saved, a village reformed, a county reorganised, and a triumphant election at the end, the recompense and crown of all, which should put the government of the country itself, to a certain extent, into competent hands" (497).

Lucilla's horizons grow absurdly large at the end, her Carlingford fiefdom gladly exchanged for the prospect of a national domain. Yet underneath our amusement at her grandiose ambitions lies our realization, thanks to Oliphant, that the irony is not directed only at Lucilla. It's directed also at the world that has made Lucilla. Six years before *Middlemarch* we meet in Lucilla a comic Dorothea, also "foundress of nothing," but one who is too bustling, too bourgeois, and too bullheaded to care that her life "spent itself in channels which had no great name on earth" (Eliot 4, 613).

Perhaps our unsentimental age has finally caught up with Lucilla and with Oliphant's ironic genius. *Miss Marjoribanks* is permeated with a sense that underneath Lucilla's grand schemes and ambitions lies compromise. Since she cannot partake in the imperial public life open to young men like her cousin Tom, who goes to India, she will create her own private empire in Carlingford; since she cannot stand for Parliament herself, she will look for a mate whom she can maneuver into a seat; since she cannot remain single forever, and share in the world's power, she will marry someone she can control. In Oliphant's world everyone has to settle for the best she can get. Men and women do not necessarily understand one another, nor do they expect to. Romance and sexual attractiveness do not last long; only the foolish think so. Religion, which might be expected to answer the big questions, doesn't, nor does anyone ask them of it. Marriage does not by some immutable law bestow eternal happiness; women are not always content to be only wives and mothers, and so on. We see our disillusioned selves in the mirror that Oliphant holds up. As Q. D. Leavis pointed out, *Miss Marjoribanks* lacks the "infusion of warm feeling" that Victorian readers had come to expect: "it is not simple-minded or self-indulgent. . . . [Lucilla] had neither the Victorian sentimentality nor even the necessary reticence and sense of propriety" (23) to achieve mass popularity. We who do not demand warm feelings or propriety in our favorite characters do not miss their absence in Lucilla. In fact we delight in the wit and hard good sense that leaves them out.

Yet this is not a bitter or cynical novel. Oliphant's ironic narrative voice keeps reminding the reader of the folly in all human endeavor, yet accepts the absolute fitness, in a disappointing world, of striking the best bargain you can for yourself. Lucilla maintains a cheerful determination throughout her campaigns, occasionally disappointed but never discouraged. She doesn't analyze the unfairness of her disabilities, sometimes isn't even aware of them, but Oliphant recognizes them and prepares the reader to do likewise. The sustained artistry of Oliphant's ironic technique, poised delicately between scorn and sympathy, recognizing that Lucilla's personal shortcomings are directly related to Victorian society's narrow definition of what was an appropriate ambition for a woman, may be *Miss Marjoribanks*'s greatest strength.

If it's true, as I believe and as Margarete Holubetz asserts in her excellent but little known essay, that "there is [not] another novel of the period which dissects the Victorian conventions of feeling and behavior with such subversive irony" (42), then it is also appropriately ironic that a novel so subversive should remind us that the "Queen of Popular Fiction" can offer as complex a response to society and literature as her more canonical fellows.

Works Cited

Baker, Ernest. *History of the English Novel*. 1924-1939. New York: Barnes and Noble, 1957.

Chesterton, Gilbert Keith. *Charles Dickens*. 1906. New York: Press of the Reader's Club, 1942.

Colby, Vineta and Robert A. *The Equivocal Virtue: Mrs. Oliphant and the Victorian Literary Market Place*. New York: Archon Books, 1966.

Eliot, George. *Middlemarch*. 1871-72. Boston: Houghton Mifflin, 1956.

Gilbert, Sandra and Susan Gubar. *The Norton Anthology of Literature by Women*. New York: Norton, 1985.

Holubetz, Margarete. "The Triumph of the Gifted Woman: The Comic Manipulation of Cliché in Mrs. Oliphant's *Miss Marjoribanks*." *Zeszyty Naukowe Uniwersytetu Jagiellonskieco*. 690 (1981): 41-56.

James, Henry. "London Notes." 1897. *Henry James: Literary Criticism*. Ed. Leon Edel and Mark Wilson. New York: The Library of America, 1984.

Leavis, Q. D. "Introduction." *Miss Marjoribanks*: By Margaret Oliphant. London: Zodiac P, 1969.

Oliphant, Margaret. *Autobiography and Letters of Mrs. Margaret Oliphant*. 1899. Leicester: Leicester UP, 1974.

————. "Charles Dickens." *Blackwood's* 77 (1855): 451-66.

————. *Miss Marjoribanks*. 1866. London: Virago, 1988.

————. "Modern Novelists—Great and Small." *Blackwood's* 77 (1855): 554-68.

————. "Mr. Thackeray and His Novels." *Blackwood's* 77 (1855): 86-96

————. "Novels." *Blackwood's* 102 (1867): 257-80.

————. "The Anti-Marriage League." *Blackwood's* 159 (1896): 135-49.

Page, Norman. "Hardy, Mrs. Oliphant, and *Jude the Obscure. Victorian Newsletter* No. 46 (Fall 1974): 22-24.

Robinson, Lillian. "Treason Our Text: Feminist Challenges to the Literary Canon." *The New Feminist Criticism*. Ed. Elaine Showalter. New York: Pantheon, 1985.

Showalter, Elaine. *A Literature of Their Own*. London: Virago, 1978.

Skelton, John. "A Little Chat about Mrs. Oliphant." *Blackwood's* 133 (1883): 73-91.

Stubbs, Patricia. *Women and Fiction*. Sussex: Harvester, 1979.

Sutherland, John. *The Stanford Companion to Victorian Fiction*. Stanford: Stanford UP, 1989.

[Terry, R. C. *Victorian Popular Fiction, 1860-80*. London: Macmillan, 1983.]

Williams, Merryn. *Margaret Oliphant: A Critical Biography*. London: Macmillan, 1986.

Woolf, Virginia. *Three Guineas*. 1938. San Diego: Harcourt Brace Jovanovich, 1966.

Margarete Rubik (essay date 1994)

SOURCE: "Marriage," in *The Novels of Mrs. Oliphant: A Subversive View of Traditional Themes,* Peter Lang Publishing, 1994, pp. 169-95.

[*In the following essay, Rubik discusses Oliphant's treatment of marriage in her novels, finding her skeptical of marital happiness and often presenting an unromantic and unsentimental view of married life.*]

1) Oliphant's Fundamental Attitude

The traditional happy ending to the Victorian novel consists of the lovers' marriage, after which the course of their lives no longer needs to be related since, it is at least implied, they live happy ever after. Oliphant, who, as we have seen, appreciated the advantages of a free and independent life, comments on her contemporaries' idealisation of wedlock in a half-ironic, half-bemused tone.

> It is curious how determined the mind of the English public at least is on this subject—that the man or woman who does not marry (especially the woman, by-the-bye) has an unhappy life, and that a story which does not end in a wedding is no story at all, or at least ends badly, as people say. It happened to myself on one occasion to put together in a book the story of some friends of mine, in which this was the case. They were young, they were hopeful, they had all life before them, but they did not marry. And when the last chapter came to the consciousness of the publisher he . . . refused to pay. He said it was no story at all. (*The Marriage of Elinor*, II,30,83)

Admittedly, Oliphant, who always had an eye to the literary market, is frequently prepared to yield to her publishers' pressure and, like Trollope, to serve the popular "sweetmeats and sugar plums"[1] at the end of a novel by making the wedding bells ring. The overwhelming majority of her stories indeed end with a marriage, once the usual obstacles have been overcome. Even for the elderly Rector Proctor in "The Rector" there is the prospect of future nuptial happiness with Mary Wodehouse, an event that actually occurs in the sequel, *The Perpetual Curate. Salem Chapel* also does not leave the disappointed Vincent without hopes of finding new love. At times such a conventional happy ending seems decidedly suspect. In *Lady William*, for instance, the reader will hardly regard the dipsomaniac son of the clergyman as a suitable match for the protagonist's daughter, and in *Who Was Lost and Is Found* we may well ask how the virtuous rector's daughter is to find happiness with the good-for-nothing hero.

It is only seldom that the author frustrates the sentimental hopes that the heroine will find the love of her life in the course of the novel so blatantly and uncompromisingly as in *Joyce*, where the fanciful protagonist renounces love and flees to a remote island. In *Kirsteen*, too, the heroine remains faithful to her betrothed beyond the grave and is content with her lot as an independent, ageing spinster, much to the dismay of her relatives. In *Diana Trelawny*, sentimental souls likewise do not get their money's worth, as the heroine would not dream of accepting Count Pandolfini.

Although such an "unromantic" denouement is the exception rather than the rule in Oliphant's stories, she views the hopes of never-ending wedded bliss with the greatest scepticism and, as has been seen, frequently debunks the stock happy ending, even when she seems to be catering to the taste of the public. Occasionally, Oliphant's comments on the typical finale with bride and groom are decidedly caustic, as in *A Son of the Soil*, where, faced with the readers' clear-cut expectations of what the ending of a novel should be, she pokes fun at human preconceptions,

> which require a distinct conclusion of one kind or another. Until a man is dead, it is impossible to say what he has done, or to make any real estimate of his work. . . . There is only one other ending in life, which is equally satisfactory, and, at least on the face of it, more cheerful than dying; and that, we need not say, is marriage. (*A Son of the Soil*, III,20,221)

Marriage is here cynically equated with death; by wedding a girl he does not love, Colin metaphorically inters his ideals and plans of reform.

At the end of the novel *John* the customary marriage of the lovers is deprived of its romantic glamour by the sardonic remark that the rich suitor would have been a much better match for the spoilt girl.

> And I hope they will be very happy, now all their troubles (as people say) are over. But it is very hard to make any prediction on such a subject, and one cannot help feeling as Mr. Crediton felt, and as Kate herself even was so candid as to allow, that but for that very confusing condition called Love, which puts out so many calculations, Fred Huntley would have been a much more suitable match for her after all. (*John*, III,30,324)

Behind these humorous, but not entirely unfounded, reservations we can sense Oliphant's mistrust of the romantic love idealised by her contemporaries, which she considers a shaky foundation for married life. She sees not merely maudlin sentimentality, which many other authors warn against, but also the genuine love so highly esteemed in Victorian fiction as being too little to ensure felicitous companionship. In opposition to the spirit of the age, she rejects passionate love.

> But love, which makes labour sweet and life pleasant, does not answer for daily bread—never does, let the romancers say what they will; no— not even to women. (*Heart and Cross*, 1,7)

Oliphant frequently emphasises that romantic love is only one component of married life, which is made up of countless duties, duties which the heroine of *The Railwayman and his Children* wisely takes into account.

> It was not merely an emotional matter, but full of practical necessities and exertions. To be a true and helpful companion through all the chances of life: to govern a household: to secure comfort and peace of mind and consolation in all circumstances and occurrences for the partner of life: to care for him and his interests as nobody else could: to adopt his obligations and help him to serve God and to serve men. (*The Railwayman and his Children*, 1,8)

In the early *Lilliesleaf*, the young author already attacks the unrealistic picture of passionate intimacy so popular in contemporary literature. The match between the obstinate Rhoda and her arrogant suitor Austen is thoroughly promising, although we cannot expect a domestic idyll; even pious Mrs. Maitland has to admit that the girl is not astray with her pragmatic outlook.

> "We are not like the lovers in books, Austen and I. . . . however sentimental people are before, it is not sympathy and support, and all that stuff, but what is it to be for dinner, and how the bills are to be paid, after they are married." (*Lilliesleaf*, III,21,277f.)

Happy is the woman who embarks on such a relationship with open eyes and not in the miasma of romantic reveries. Figures like Mrs. May in *The Son of his Father*, Lily in *Sir Robert's Fortune* or the heroine of *The Marriage of Elinor* find themselves chained to inconstant, irresponsible, indeed even criminal partners after a so-called marriage of love.

Oliphant sees social compatibility, even economic interests, considerations frequently rejected as undignified calculation in contemporary fiction, as a far more permanent basis for marriage than the much-famed notion of true love. Common duties and interests ultimately guarantee that the heroine of *In Trust* will be happier with her upright cousin than with the flashy and unreliable suitor she originally adored. The marriage of a young aristocrat to a tax-collector's daughter in *Mrs. Arthur*, on the other hand, runs into unforeseen difficulties due to their completely different outlook, class affiliation and interests. Nancy's gaudy clothing, her lack of interest in French culture and her vulgar behaviour in public turn the honeymoon in Paris into one long nightmare for the bridegroom, who learns to his bewilderment that love alone will not suffice to avoid every pitfall.

> People do not marry their wives or their husbands because they understand Molière, and love the Great Masters, and know Continental history; but it is bewildering to be in Paris, or anywhere else

for that matter, with a new companion who has no associations with anything, and is at once indifferent and ignorant of all that is in the past. (*Mrs. Arthur*, II,17,213f.)

In Oliphant's novels sober deliberation in the choice of spouse, indeed even the consideration of material concerns, by no means leads to misfortune and life-long regret, the standard penalties for betraying the ideal of true love. In *Sir Tom*, the pragmatic Bice, who takes the dull Marquis Montjoie only for his property and title, will get on well with her husband all the same and make his life pleasant and amusing—something not always applicable to more romantic unions, as Oliphant maliciously adds.

> According to her code no professions of attachment or pretence of feeling were necessary. She had indeed no theories in her mind about being a good wife; but she would not be a bad one. She would keep her part of the compact; there should be nothing to complain of, nothing to object to. She would do her best to amuse the man she had to live with and make his life agreeable to him, which is a thing not always taken into consideration in marriage-contracts much more ideal in character. (*Sir Tom*, 34,344)

On the issue of mercenary marriages, branded as immoral in Victorian fiction, Oliphant assumes a stance opposed to the spirit of the age. She goes far beyond her admired predecessor Jane Austen, who also recommended prudent reflection on the choice of one's partner, but who strictly rejected the transaction Charlotte Lucas concludes. Thackeray, whose spiteful humour Oliphant also appreciated, admits that the much-maligned marriage of convenience may at times be more satisfactory than the most ardent marriage of the heart, and makes Lord Kew poke fun at old maids who believe in amorous bliss à la Philemon and Baucis.[2] Nevertheless, Thackeray is far less consistent than Mrs. Oliphant, as, on the other hand, he frequently pillories the deceitfulness and dishonesty of venal marriages, and considers the materialistic Ethel Newcome an inappropriate heroine until she is "converted" to true love.[3]

Of course, Oliphant is quite aware of the potential drawbacks of such loveless marriages. In *A House Divided Against Itself*, the parents' love match founders on insurmountable human differences, yet the repulsiveness of a venal marriage is illustrated in Nelly Winterbourn's fate, who has "sold" herself to an elderly husband and now yearns for him to die. The complete frigidity with which she is reluctantly prepared to meet a minimum of her obligations and the revulsion she feels for the dying man, whom she is expected to kiss farewell, provide the kind of horrifying insight into the nature of such a marriage expected by the reading public. In *The Ladies Lindores*, Lady

Car's despair at being forced by her father to enter into a rich marriage similarly conforms to Victorian assumptions of where such unscrupulous bartering leads.

However, far more typical of Oliphant's attitude are the successful relationships so diametrically opposed to Victorian ideals. What many writers criticised as "hypocrisy" before the altar never bothered the more religious Oliphant. Her heroines experience no qualms of conscience at the discrepancy between the romantic ideal of love and social reality. In the rare instances that Oliphant tries to present moral scruples against such economically beneficial matches, as in *The Heir Presumptive and the Heir Apparent*, or "**Mademoiselle**", her objections unwittingly seem ludicrous and irrelevant, as the author is basically convinced of the superfluity of such spurious arguments compared with more earthy and practical considerations. The marriage of convenience between the forty-year-old Evelyn and the railway millionaire in *The Railwayman and his Children* is one of the most felicitous relationships in Oliphant's oeuvre, although Evelyn only accepts her husband to escape from her humiliating position in her friend's house—she is half a guest and half a governess. In the same novel the marriage between the good-for-nothing Eddy and the grasping Marion, both of whom have no illusions as to the characters of their spouses, will never meet the disaster that befalls the romantic marriage of a Lady Car, an Elinor or a Lily, who have utterly wayward expectations of their partners.

> "I will always maintain," said Eddy, "that there never were two people so fit to go together as you and I. We haven't any wild admiration of each other; we know each other's deficiencies exactly; we don't go in for perfection, do we? But we suit . . . down to the ground. You would know what you had to expect in me, and I could keep you in order." (*The Railwayman and his Children*, 68,397)

In *For Love and Life*, Oliphant cynically asks whether it would not have been better for Margaret to take a rich husband, instead of waiting faithfully for her erstwhile sweetheart, who jilts her upon his return, condemning her to a dreary life in her brother's household. Measured against the ideal of romantic love, the marriage of convenience of the impoverished Lottie, turned out of her parental home by her stepmother, to an unloved minor canon may seem a sad lot in *Within the Precincts*; yet it is far better than the alternative of a conventional marriage of the heart to the aristocrat Rollo, who would have disavowed his middle-class wife and exploited her as a professional singer. Lottie's marriage should not be seen as an unhappy ending, merely as the necessary accommodation of a daydreamer to human and social reality.

All of this testifies to a very un-Victorian outlook on life, but, on the other hand, as is Oliphant's wont, it also has a conventional facet, namely Oliphant's negative attitude towards the problem of sexuality. In her shame-faced rejection of sexuality Oliphant was ultra-conservative and even more uncompromising than her notoriously prudish contemporaries. Of course, the nineteenth-century novel was usually very reticent on this issue, yet writers like Thackeray, who lamented the taboo preventing a more detailed treatment of the subject, were at least aware of the importance of erotic attraction. Even if most authors never made this attraction as palpable as the Bronte sisters and remained within the narrow confines of convention, this magnetism can be sensed in a number of novels. Oliphant, however, was not merely "inhibited" about speaking about the problem, she also displayed no understanding of it. She sees sexuality as something repulsive, as an act reducing human beings to the level of animals. In **"The Anti-Marriage League"** she vented her wrath on writers who interpret the relationship between man and woman only in terms of physical passion. Sexual intercourse in marriage is irrelevant, "the mere fact which is its seal, one incident in life, but no more."[4] Figures such as Evelyn in *The Railwayman and his Children* or the elderly Mary in *The Heir Presumptive and the Heir Apparent* hence recoil from the physical aspect.

> Love was not a thing to be thought of, it was out of date, it was scarcely modest to suggest it; . . . [but she] did feel affectionately towards Lord Frogmore. (*The Heir Presumptive and the Heir Apparent*, I,14,148)

For the very reason that Oliphant abhors sexuality, she views romantic love with scepticism, showing understanding for women who are primarily concerned with the social status afforded by a marriage. In this respect it is characteristic that she usually avoids presenting day-to-day life in such marriages of convenience, which would have compelled her to confront the issue. Instead, she restricts herself to giving a positive forecast of the unromantic couple's life together. And because her heroines, too, feel that sexuality is unimportant, a Phoebe can be happy with the unattractive millionaire Copperhead, jun., and an Eleanor only needs to heed financial considerations on her separation from her bigamist husband, without feeling any jealousy for her rival. For women in Oliphant's stories the relationship with a man is not an end in itself-how should it be considering the men Oliphant describes? At the same time it can be argued that Oliphant describes such contemptuous men for the very reason that she does not believe in the powers of erotic attraction. Q. D. Leavis contends that Oliphant *is* able to convey sexual magnetism:

> Oliphant is rare among Victorian novelists in being one who accepts and can establish the existence of passion and the miseries of the thwarted.[5]

However, this applies to only few of the author's stories, e.g., to **"A Widow's Tale"** or to the description of Isabel's passionate love in *The Minister's Wife*. In *Miss Marjoribanks*, which Leavis refers to, Lucilla's preference for Tom, whom she had no qualms about dispatching to India ten years previously, is only sketched in one scene; on the other hand, the sensuous Barbara's enticement of Cavendish is presented as ridiculous and unworthy of a gentleman.

In most of Oliphant's novels the relationship between two lovers is strangely unsensual, platonic and anaemic, even in the cases when girls fall in love with a man their parents object to. In *The Marriage of Elinor*, for instance, the heroine is treated with indifference by her ostensibly infatuated lover, even before their wedding. *In Trust* never succeeds in creating the impression that Anne and Douglas have a truly passionate relationship. As will be seen later, even when Oliphant sensitively sounds out the discrepancy between a rational assessment of a man and an emotional bond to him, this alleged passion is hardly sensed in the concrete description of the union.

Oliphant can only deal with the issue of sexuality plausibly by casting it in a negative light; symptomatically, her presentation of aversion to physical contact is an impressive one. Carry Lindores' disgust at her brutal husband, the horror felt by the prophetess Ailie in *The Minister's Wife* at the prospect of marrying John Diarmid, Mrs. May's remorseless hatred of her criminal husband in *The Son of his Father*, the nausea with which the protagonist of **"A Story of a Wedding Tour"** views her repugnant husband, and the physical revulsion felt by Nelly Winterbourn in *A House Divided Against Itself* against her dying husband, are all portrayed so vividly and frighteningly that they are etched on the reader's mind. On the other hand, Edith Lindores' affection for the colourless and bloodless John Erskine, young May's attachment to a clergyman's daughter, or Frances Waring's anaemic relationship to a naive suitor, all portrayed in the books just mentioned, are hardly memorable.

Although blind to the significance of sexual attraction, Oliphant can nonetheless write good novels about marriage as she displays a keen eye for the many other problems of partnership, a fine feeling for emotional fluctuations and the unsentimental insight that, in the course of time, every relationship calls on the partners to make painful compromises.

2) Novels of Marriage

> When a pair of lovers is finally delivered from all those terrible obstacles that fret the current of true love, and are at last married and settled, what more is there to be said about them? (*The Ladies Lindores*, III,16,274)

Like Trollope, of whose tongue-in-cheek commentaries this ironical affirmation of stock prejudices reminds us, Oliphant has a great deal to say about married life, so often omitted by the writers of romances.[6]

Occasionally critics have lamented the superficiality with which Victorian fiction sketched life after the honeymoon. They contend that popular literature tended to idealise wedlock or exaggerate its strife and meanness.[7] Nevertheless, the English novel of the nineteenth century is not lacking in serious descriptions of marital problems. Couples such as Rosamond and Lydgate, Glencora and Palliser, or the Gibsons, are convincing examples of a subtle and differentiated treatment of the subject.

> How did the belief grow up that the Victorian novelists could not portray marriage? It is true that their books often end with wedding bells, but the heroine with the happy ending is not the only character in them. . . . It is surprising how little the conventions of sexual reticence seem to matter when it comes to describing the considerable part of marriage that takes place out of bed.[8]

Oliphant's best novels of marriage can rank beside those of Gaskell, Eliot and Trollope, whereby Oliphant, as J. S. Clarke argues,[9] shows less tendency to exaggerate and over-dramatise. Like her more famous colleagues, she also manages to convey what Cockshut misses in so many Victorian portrayals of marriage, i.e., "a sense of causation, a regard for probability, and a subtle awareness of the slow erosion of time."[10] With empathy and humour she depicts the apparently trivial squabbles in run-of-the-mill marriages, which are not rocked by major conflicts, but jolted by trivial tribulations.

Like Trollope, however, Mrs. Oliphant also knows that minor squabbles can, at times, be escalated by emotional over-reactions into major differences, and she can capture the destructive dynamism of such quarrels. In *The Days of My Life*, published more than ten years before Trollope's *He Knew He Was Right*, she describes such a petty row, which is inflated into an obsession, and in which both partners, against all reason, refuse to give way. Oliphant convincingly describes the neurotic fascination the conflict exerts on both partners; they can neither stand meeting one another nor being ignored by one another. In the reconciliation she engineers between the couple at the end

she is less consistent than Trollope; yet despite this conventional ending the novel impresses the reader with the intensity and candour with which we are given insight into the emotional life of the female narrator, in particular.

However, most marriages Oliphant describes are not shaken by such crises. Nonetheless, a certain sense of frustration and disillusionment is felt by the women, who feel abandoned to their problems and, like Mrs. Morgan in the citation below, cannot make their sentiments known to their insensitive husbands.

> Her compunctions, her longings after the lost life which they might have lived together, her wistful womanish sense of the impoverished existence, deprived of so many experiences, on which they had entered in the dry maturity of their middle age, remained for ever a mystery to her faithful husband. (*The Perpetual Curate*, 12,119)

Instead of sharing their afflictions, husbands frequently try to shield their wives from important issues out of pure male arrogance and a misconceived notion of honour. The painter Drummond, for instance, would not dare to burden his wife with his financial straits, although she is really much more practical than he is.

> He did as so many men do, thinking it kindness; and thus left her with a host of horrible surmises to fight against, any one of which was [to her] harder than the truth. There is no way in which men, in their ignorance, inflict more harm upon women than this way. (*At His Gates*, 9,118)

The scatter-brained Major Ochterlony, the perpetrator of numerous embarrassing situations, advises his more prudent wife to read novels rather than worry her little head.

> Whether such a speech was aggravating or not to a woman who knew it was her brain which had all the real weight of family affairs to bear, may be conjectured by wives in general who know the sort of thing. (*Madonna Mary*, 1,2,24)

Whereas women are excluded from essential decisions, many husbands like to devolve unpleasant mundane worries on their spouses, who in turn react with a blend of bitterness, loving indulgence and feminine resignation,

> a tenderness in which there was a mixture of amusement and partial irritation and fun and sympathy, all mingled together. (*Joyce*, 6,25)

Such a marriage in which the wife patiently bears the everyday burdens is splendidly described in *A Rose in June*. The leisure-loving clergyman is amazed at his wife's "ignorance", who has neither the time nor the patience to share his aesthetic interests, but whom he immediately reprimands when the clamour of children disturbs his contemplation. He lives far beyond his means, but does not bother about paying his debts, expecting his wife to shield him from creditors and supplicants, at the same time ridiculing her trite worries.

> That she was careful and troubled about many things was the Rector's favourite joke. "My careful wife—my anxious wife," he called her, and, poor soul, not without cause. For it stands to reason that when a man must not be disturbed about bills, for example, his wife must be, and doubly; and when a clergyman dislikes poverty, and unlovely cottages, and poor rooms, which are less sweet than the lawn and the roses, why his wife must [sic!], and make up for his fastidiousness. (*A Rose in June*, 1,10)

In the novel Oliphant basically describes the very situation later voiced by Shaw's Candida.

> "Ask me what it costs to be James's mother and three sisters and wife and mother to his children all in one. . . . Ask the tradesmen who want to worry James and spoil his beautiful sermons who it is that puts them off. When there is money to give, he gives it: when there is money to refuse, I refuse it. I build a castle of comfort and indulgence and love for him, and stand sentinel always to keep little vulgar cares out."[11]

Such mothering is something completely different to the "discreet" support a Victorian husband was entitled to expect from his obedient spouse, and has little to do with the honour a wife owed her husband as her guide and mentor.

> It is . . . the privilege of a married woman to be able to show, by the most delicate attentions, how much she feels her husband's superiority to herself.

Oliphant's women usually lack the "pretty air of trust and dependence which charms most men" (*Diana Trelawny*, 6, 101), a prerequisite for domestic bliss. However, not all of them embark on marriage with the sang-froid of a Phoebe, a Bice or a Marian Rowland, and they do not find it easy to step down from the pinnacle of an idealised relationship, to accept the partner's inadequacies, and to make the compromises required by a marriage. Oliphant knows that disillusionment is inevitable in married life.

Like many of Oliphant's heroines, the wife of rector Morgan in *The Perpetual Curate*, who has waited for ten years to become married, is made painfully aware of his innate flaws.

The real rector to whom she was married was so different from the ideal one who courted her. (*The Perpetual Curate*, 12,115)

The Morgans' marriage, with their humdrum squabbles and makings-up, is considered one of Oliphant's most effective comedies. Frustrated by her husband's petty-mindedness and jealousy, Mrs. Morgan vents her annoyance by resorting to ostensibly innocuous female activities, such as needlework, at the very moment he would like to speak to her.

> [Her] confirmed habit of needlework at all kinds of unnecessary moments . . . much disturbed the Rector when he had anything particular to say. (*The Perpetual Curate*, 28,269)

That this domestic pastime is not quite as innocuous as would meet the eye is shown by the following metaphor:

> She . . . drove her needle so fast through the muslin she was at work upon, that it glimmered and sparkled like summer lightning before the spectator's dazzled eyes. (*The Perpetual Curate*, 28,270)

But when Morgan decides to withdraw to a parish in the country and to nominate his erstwhile antagonist Wentworth as his successor, his wife replaces him on the pedestal of her adoration with tears of joy. Ironically, the rector has no inkling of his wife's true feelings; he is equally unaware of her scant regard and of his subsequent rehabilitation in her eyes. Despite the happy ending, husband and wife ultimately remain a mystery to each other.

> The excellent man was entirely unconscious that he was being put up again at that moment with acclamations upon his pedestal, as that he had at a former time been violently displaced from it, and thrown into the category of broken idols. All this would have been as Sanscrit to the Rector of Carlingford; and the only resource he had was to make in his own mind certain half-pitying, half-affectionate remarks upon the inexplicable weakness of women. . . . Had Mr. Morgan been a Frenchman, he probably would have imagined his wife's heart to be touched by the graces of the Perpetual Curate; but being an Englishman, and rather more certain, on the whole, of her than of himself, it did not occur to him to speculate on the subject. He was quite able to content himself with the thought that women were incomprehensible, as he went back to his study. (*The Perpetual Curate*, 45,492-94)

Although the Morgans' marital ups and downs are here solved in a fashion in keeping with the comic plot, it is never doubted that a married couple must face the painful side of reality.

> She had found out the wonderful difference between anticipation and reality; and that life, even to a happy woman married after long patience to the man of her choice, was not the smooth road it looked, but a rough path cut into dangerous ruts, through which generations of men and women followed each other without ever being able to mend the way. She was not so sure as she used to be of a great many important matters which it is a wonderful consolation to be certain of—but, notwithstanding, had to go on as if she had no doubts, though the clouds of defeat, in which, certainly, no honour, though a great deal of the prestige of inexperience, had been lost, were still looming behind. (*The Perpetual Curate*, 48,538)[12]

Most couples learn to get on passably, even once, as Oliphant cynically remarks, the ardour of first love has been cooled off by the years.

> Perhaps neither husband nor wife could have explained ten years after how it was that they were so idiotic as to think that they could not live without each other; but they got on together very comfortably all the same. (*The Mystery of Mrs. Blencarrow*, 10,186)

Only wishful thinkers refuse to accept the unpleasant insight that even the beloved is a simple person with warts. Wherever idealists are not willing to cut their dreams down to size and accommodate themselves to all too human flaws, marriages end tragically, as in the case of Lady Car, whose career Oliphant pursues through two novels—*The Ladies Lindores* and *Lady Car*—and two unhappy marriages.

Unlike the docile things whom time teaches to cherish the "proper" feelings for their husbands,[13] Lady Car continues to view her brutal first husband with unabated repugnance. Her feelings of nausea and sexual violation, as she had to comply with her repulsive husband's desires at his bidding, are illustrated by her overt jubilation at his death and symbolised in the image of his trespassing into her room.[14]

> "To think I shall never be subject to all *that* any more—that he can never come in here again—that I am free—that I can be alone. Oh mother, how can you tell what it is? Never to be alone: never to have a corner in the world where— some one else has not a right to come, a better right than yourself. I don't know how I have borne it. I don't know how I can have lived, disgusted, loathing myself." (*The Ladies Lindores*, II,14,232f.)

In her second marriage to her childhood sweetheart Car does not find the hoped-for happiness either. She secretly blames Beaufort for letting her marry someone else first; for allowing her to be forced to perform sexual acts with a man she hated and for allowing her children to be fathered by a brute. All of these humiliations are so completely beyond a man's scope of perception that he cannot understand them.

> "Why expose me to all the degradations which nobody could impose on you?" (*Lady Car*, 7,123)

Beaufort cannot grasp the horror she feels at any association with her prior life, and thoughtlessly relishes his deceased rival's luxury.

However, it is bitterest for Car to share the insight typical of Oliphant's heroines that Beaufort is not the epitome of the crusader and social reformer she first fell in love with. She, who, like Dorothea Brooke, wanted to act as a muse for her husband's *magnum opus,* attempts desperately, but in vain, to reawaken his enthusiasm for the visions he has lost all interest in.

> Don Quixote disenchanted, ready to burn all his chevalier books, and see the fun of his misadventures, but urged to take the field by some delicate Dulcinea, could not have been more embarrassed and disturbed. (*Lady Car*, 4,74)

Car is one of those dreamers who seek perfection and do not content themselves with less than the absolute. In her analysis of the novel, Showalter reproaches Oliphant for identifying with Car's disappointment at her indolent husband and her dull children, and for wanting to solicit pity for a passive, indeed even parasitic form of life.

> Mrs. Oliphant never faced the dangers of a social myth that places the whole weight of feminine fulfilment on husband and children.[15]

The tone of the book is certainly pathetic at times. However, it would be erroneous to believe that Oliphant sees her heroine uncritically or fails to recognise the fallacy of the domestic myth. On the contrary, she realises the problematic nature of Car's immature idealism, and in many other novels she draws women who are not dependent on marriage and the family for their self-esteem. Car, on the other hand, must fail in her attempt to achieve the Victorian ideal that expects a woman to find complete fulfilment in marriage and her children.

The question as to how a relationship can work without admiration or even respect for one's partner is posed time and again in Oliphant's novels because of her unconventional view of gender roles.

Could Alcestis have the same respect for the man who could let her die for him? Could she go on living by his side and think just the same of him as if he had borne his own burden instead of shuffling it off upon her shoulders? The ancients did not trouble themselves with such questions, but it is a peculiarity of the modern mind that it does. (*Within the Precincts*, I,3,56)

Many of Oliphant's heroines are confronted with this issue, and usually it turns out that lack of respect is not incompatible with love, but that conflicting emotions can be painfully and inextricably intertwined. Just as the naive dreamer Lady Car represents an antithesis to the typical Oliphant heroine, her inability to come to terms with reality and her broken-hearted pining away are similarly at odds with the usual reactions evinced by Oliphant's women. The first rapture of married life may soon yield to disillusionment, yet Oliphant's protagonists continue to love their husbands, despite all their frustrations, toil and lost illusions,

in frequent disagreements, in occasional angers and impatiences, and much disappointment. What would become of the world if love did not manage to hold its footing through all these? The boys and girls of the high-flown kind are of opinion that love is too feeble to bear the destruction of the ideal. But that is all these young persons know. Love has the most robust vitality in the world—it outlives anything. (*The Ladies Lindores*, III,15,254)

Lady Lindores stands by her husband, although he disappoints and hurts her. In *The Quiet Heart*, Menie cannot bury her affections for her unworthy fiancé, just as Isabel in *The Minister's Wife* cannot stifle her passion for the criminal Stapylton, or Nelly in **"A Widow's Tale"** cannot overcome her love for her caddish suitor. Agnes in the novel of the same name may well lose the respect and trust she feels for her selfish husband, but never her love.

It is true that a wonderful disenchantment had already come to Agnes,—such a disenchantment as any sentimental young woman, brought up upon novels and fine feelings, would regard either as the occasion of utter despair, and the most summary death by heartbreak which was possible, or else as a release from all obligations towards the man who had disappointed her so sorely. She was no longer able to admire Roger, however much she tried, nor to look up to him, nor even trust him much. . . . and yet, withal, she had not ceased to love him, and stand by him with all her might, which wonderful problem of humanity is one very little discussed in works of imagination. (*Agnes*, 20,189)

In this respect, too, Oliphant's attitude is a-typical of the age, for many Victorian writers shared Charlotte Bronte's view that there is no true affection without respect and that "meanness"[16] suffocates love. Oliphant, on the other hand, seems to regard the painful and irrational tenacity of emotion as more realistic than the sudden recession of love. When George Eliot's Romola simply cuts all emotional ties to her unfaithful husband, this is seen by Oliphant as too facile a solution to the problem.

In a great many histories of human experience it is taken for granted—and indeed, perhaps, before the reign of analysis began it was almost always taken for granted—that when man and woman of the nobler kind found that a lover was unworthy, their love died along with respect. It has simplified matters in many a story. It is such a good way out of it, and saves so much trouble! The last instance I can remember is that of the noble Romola and Tito her husband, whom, though he gives her endless trouble, she is able to drop out of her stronghold of love as soon as she knows how little worthy of it is the fascinating, delightful, false Greek. My own experience is all the other way. Life, I think, is not so easy as that comes to. (**"A Widow's Tale"**, 9,49)

Of course, when she refers to the irrational persistency of feelings even following frustration and disillusionment, Oliphant is not up-holding the romantic commonplace of eternal love. In several novels she shows how married life is ultimately rendered unbearable for a woman by the constant bickering it involves. In her articles Oliphant defends the indissolubility of marriage and only reluctantly accepts divorce as the last terrible alternative to unbearable suffering.[17] Nonetheless, the question as to whether and under what circumstances a wife may leave her husband recurs time and again in Oliphant's fiction.

In accordance with accepted morality, a wife's separation from her husband is condemned in *The Days of My Life* and *Mrs. Arthur*, albeit Oliphant shows understanding for her motives and demonstrates a certain sympathy for her. However, a prerequisite for the couple's reconciliation is that the wife see reason and display remorse. In *Madonna Mary*, even Winnie's return to her worthless husband is welcomed, as, by leaving him, she had violated the social norms and abandoned her ordained guardian.

Of course, no justification is required when Isabel in *The Minister's Wife* leaves her second husband on learning that he murdered her first one. In **"A Widow's Tale"**, Oliphant also approves of Nelly's separation from her amoral husband and her return to her children, not least because Nelly, like Isabel, does not relinquish all her duties towards her husband, but supports him financially until he dies. It would also go without saying that Eleanor in **"Queen Eleanor and Fair Rosamond"** enforces a separation from her bigamous husband. What seems exceptional, however, is the cold-bloodedness with which she goes about it. Even more uncharacteristic of the age is Oliphant's challenging of sacrosanct wifely duties in *The Son of his Father*, where the wife disavows the ex-convict. The sympathy Oliphant displays in **"A Story of a Wedding Tour"** for a young bride's spontaneous flight from her odious husband is equally astonishing.

Like Anne Bronte in *The Tenant of Wildfell Hall*, in *The Marriage of Elinor* Oliphant also accepts a mother's concern for a child's moral welfare, no longer guaranteed in the circles of the immoral father, as a legitimate reason to break her marriage vows and to desert the child's father. All the same, at the end of the novel concessions are made to the tastes of the reading public by constructing a kind of reconciliation. Outwardly, judgement on Elinor's decision to leave her husband is left to the reader.

> Had Elinor fulfilled what would appear to many her first duty, and stood by Phil through neglect, ill-treatment, and misery, as she had vowed, for better, for worse, she would by this time have been not only a wretched but a deteriorated woman, and her son most probably would have been injured both in his moral and intellectual being. What she had done was not the abstract duty of her marriage vow, but it had been better— had it not been better for them both? (*The Marriage of Elinor*, II,37,169)

Elinor is fortunate in that her husband has no interest in the child and is glad to be rid of the burden of his wife, for by law he could force her to return to him or remove the child from her custody. But Elinor loses her wealth, for, although the marriage contract bars her spendthrift husband from her property, the wife willingly renounces her rights for the sake of peace.[18] Legislation and legal contracts are just as unable to protect the wife's rights as they are incapable of guaranteeing the husband's authority over his recalcitrant wife in *Mrs. Arthur*. Throughout her life Oliphant was convinced that legal provisions were ineffective in such cases.

> Let everything possible be done to protect the property of the wife. Let the law ordain her fortune and her earnings as exclusively her own as if she were unmarried. What then? . . . If the man is a brute, he may *take* his wife's money, rudely, by force of cruelty, physical or mental. . . . But in reality it is quite foolish, and a waste of strength, to be a brute for such a purpose. If he does it lovingly, all the laws in the world, all the friends in the world, all the panoply of right and personal possession, will not save the woman's fortune. Why, men of all complexions . . . become poor men at the pleasure of a young wife's caprices.

> Are women more able to resist persuasion? less likely to be "tender-hearted"? . . . This is one great thing the law cannot do—it cannot defend married people from each other.[19]

Although Oliphant doubted the effectiveness of legislation in married life, as she grew older she became more and more aware that the controversial legal reforms of the century had had a beneficial impact on women. In one of her last novels, *Sir Robert's Fortune*, she describes the terrible consequences of the rigid marriage laws at the beginning of the nineteenth century, laws fettering the heroine and showing her, "how much the property of her husband she was" (*Sir Robert's Fortune*, 44,369). Understandably, Lily would like to leave her husband, who has abducted their child and kept their marriage a secret for years. However, despite the complete break-up of the marriage, the unscrupulous man forces Lily to continue living with him by exploiting his legal rights to the full.

> Do you know . . . that you can do nothing but what I permit? You are my wife, you have nothing, your uncle's money or any other but what I give you. You're not your own to do what you like with yourself, as you seem to think—but mine to do what I like and nothing else. (*Sir Robert's Fortune*, 44,383)

The wife is completely at her hated husband's mercy and must yield, like it or not. But Oliphant spares her heroine the humiliation of such a *ménage a deux* by hurtling him down the stairs.

The break-up of a relationship is treated less melodramatically and with less clear an apportionment of guilt in *A Country Gentleman and his Family*, one of her best novels about marriage. Superficially, the quarrel between Theo Warrender and Lady Markland is sparked off by her decision to retain her first husband's title and to live in the mansion she has inherited. But his sense of offended male pride merely conceals jealousy and Theo's attempt to subjugate his independent-minded wife. He naively expects total consent from her,

> the perfect agreement of a nature which arrived at the same conclusions as his by the same means, which responded before he spoke, which was always ready to anticipate, to give him the exquisite sanction of feeling he was right by a perpetual seconding of all his decisions and anticipation of his thoughts. (*A Country Gentleman and his Family*, 47,416)

He sees his step-son as a rival and urges his wife to choose between him and the boy—a choice Lady Markland finds monstrous. She appeals to the biblical passage where it is stated that it is unthinkable for a mother to forget her child.

Is there any higher claim? Every other is at our own choice, but this is nature. God made it. It cannot change. There may be other—other . . . but only one mother. (*A Country Gentleman and his Family*, 51,456)

In vain her husband resorts to the letter of the law and to biblical commandments calling on wives to be submissive to their husbands.

"Can any one doubt what is your first duty? It is to me. It is I that must settle what our life is to be. It is you who must yield and obey. Are you not my wife?" (*A Country Gentleman and his Family*, 51,456f.)

Instead of allowing herself to be cowed, Lady Markland rebels against this "unlovely duty"; when he threatens to leave her, she will not retain him.

"You prefer Geoff to me?" "There is no preferring; it is altogether different. I will not give up my child." "Then you give up your husband?" They looked at each other again,—she deadly pale, he crimson with passion, both quivering with the strain of this struggle; her eyes mutely refusing to yield, accepting the alternative, though she said no more. And not another word was said. He turned on his heel and walked down the avenue, with quick swinging steps, without ever turning his head. She watched him till he was out of sight, till he was out of hearing, till the gate swung behind him, and he was gone. She did not know how she was to get back to the house, over that long stretch of road, without any one to help her, and thought with a sickening and failing of the long way. But in this great, sudden, unlooked-for revolution of her life she felt no weakness nor failing. The revulsion was all the greater after the long self-restraint. For the first time after so long an interval she was herself again. (*A Country Gentleman and his Family*, 51,458)

Such an emancipation from the rigid Victorian family hierarchy, which defines the husband as the head of the family and concedes him power of discretion, may have dismayed conservative readers. Yet, in this conflict Oliphant's sympathies ultimately go to Lady Markland. However, as in *The Marriage of Elinor*, in this delicate issue she prudently leaves final judgement to the reader.

She had chosen, who could say wrongly?—and yet in a way which set wrong all the circumstances of her life. (*A Country Gentleman and his Family*, 52,462)

Oliphant always resisted interpreting a wife's subordination to her husband as mindless subservience.[20] The commandment of absolute obedience would degrade a woman to the role of a slave. Oliphant constantly

stresses the responsibility of the individual, who may not delegate moral decisions to others, even if the law grants the husband sole authority. In this respect the worldly-wise Lady Randalph in *Sir Tom* acts as Oliphant's mouthpiece.

"I never was one that was very strong upon a husband's rights, I always thought that to obey meant something different from the common meaning of the word. A child must obey; but even a grown-up child's obedience is very different from what is natural and proper in a youth; and a full-grown woman never could be supposed to obey like a child." (*Sir Tom*, 14,131)

Despite her sympathy for emancipated and self-reliant women, Oliphant as a rule endeavours not to offend her readers by ending her stories with an irreconcilable separation. Preferable to such an "unhappy" ending is usually a half-hearted appeasement, unless, as in *Sir Robert's Fortune*, "A Widow's Tale", "A Story of a Wedding Tour" or *The Minister's Wife*, the husband's felicitous demise happens to liberate the wife from her hopeless predicament.

In *A House Divided Against Itself*, the sequel to *A Country Gentleman and his Family*, the reconciliation between Theo Warrender and Lady Markland—here called Waring and Markham[21]—is such a concession to public taste. Nonetheless, the children's marriages would seem to make the parents' reunion plausible. Oliphant avoids any touch of sentimentality by making it clear that such a restoration of the common household after so many years of separation would be fraught with problems. Lady Markham views reunion with her estranged husband with very mixed feelings.

When such a tie as marriage is severed, if by death or by any other separation, it is not a light thing to renew it. The thought of that possibility . . . sent the blood back to Lady Markham's heart. It was not that she was unforgiving, or even that she had not a certain remainder of love for her husband. But to resume those habits of close companionship after so many years—to give up her own individuality, in part at least, and live a dual life—this thought startled her. (*A House Divided Against Itself*, II,29,241)

How very different does this sound from the wise counsel drummed into girls that "a female's real existence only begins when she has a husband."[22]

In *At His Gates*, too, Oliphant nourishes legitimate doubts as to whether the return of the resurrected painter, which would seem to augur a soppy happy-ending, is really welcome to his widow, who has become accustomed to a life alone, in independence and with the freedom to make her own decisions.[23]

If I were to reproduce all the thoughts that coursed through Helen's mind, I should do her injury with the reader, who, no doubt, believes that the feelings in a wife's mind, when such a hope entered it, could only be those of a half-delirious joy. But Helen's thoughts were not wildly joyful. She had been hardly and painfully trained to do without him, to put him out of her life. Her soul had slid into new ways, changed meanings; and in that time what change of meaning, what difference of nature might have come to a man who had returned from death and the grave? Could it all be undone? Could it float away like a tale that is told, that tale of seven long years? Could the old assimilate with the new, and the widow become a wife again without some wrench, some convulsion of nature? (*At His Gates,* II,36,255f.)

Marriage, it is made clear, demands that women especially renounce their own personalities and make compromises they resent. Only widows and moneyed spinsters are the masters of their own lives. It is not for nothing that Mrs. Woodburn envies Miss Marjoribanks her independence and freedom, while she herself is dependent on the benevolence of her irascible husband, whom she has long ceased to love, yet whose whims she has to cater to. The psychological strain on this woman, who hourly expects Miss Marjoribanks might reveal her lowly origins to her conceited husband, is evident in the following passage, one in which Oliphant draws a particularly sarcastic picture of marriage.

But when Lucilla . . . was gone, the mimic, with her nerves strung to desperation, burst into the wildest travesty of Miss Marjoribanks's looks and manners, . . . and sent her unsuspicious husband into convulsions of laughter. He laughed until the tears ran down his cheeks—the unconscious simpleton; and all the time his wife could have liked to throw him down and trample on him, or put pins into him, or scratch his beaming, jovial countenance. (*Miss Marjoribanks,* 25,244)

In the light of such a sceptical view of marriage it is hardly surprising that Oliphant usually shows little understanding for widows who remarry. The relinquishment of the freedom and independence otherwise granted solely to men for the sake of sexual passion is incomprehensible in her eyes and leads to no good, even when Oliphant, as in the case of Nelly in **"A Widow's Tale"**, shows tolerance for a woman's delight in life. Widowers may be forgiven for remarrying but, as she argues in **Whiteladies** with a strange blend of stock expectation and feminine self-assurance, it would be an odd world if more could not be expected from a woman than a man.

Much in Oliphant's vision of marriage evidently results from her conception of the roles of man and woman. A partnership between weak and irresponsible men and dynamic and intelligent women automatically leads to the very problems and conflicts she takes up in her novels. It would not be unreasonable to assume that she knew some of these crises from personal experience. Above and beyond this, her unromantic insight that there is no such thing as perfection in life colours both her presentation and evaluation of marriage. She avoids idealisation and extreme pessimism. In many instances she distances herself from popular stereotypes and writes against stock clichés. However, not all in her picture of marriage is unconventional; on the question of sexuality, particularly, she remains the prisoner of her age. Nonetheless, her unsentimental depictions of the petty conflicts of humdrum married life, of disillusionment and compromise, are an interesting and important contribution to the novel of an age claimed not to have devoted enough attention in literature to marital problems.

Notes

[1] Anthony Trollope, *Barchester Towers,* Harmondsworth 1968, 53, 459.

[2] W. M. Thackeray, *The Newcomes,* 2 vols., London 1878, I, 30, 344f. and I, 28, 319.

[3] Jenni Calder, *Women and Marriage in Victorian Fiction,* London 1976, 30. [Calder] contends that Thackeray really believed in the true love so many Victorian novels extol.

[4] "The Anti-Marriage League", *Blackwood's,* 159 (1896), 135-49.

[5] Q. D. Leavis, "Introduction" to Margaret Oliphant, *Miss Marjoribanks,* London 1966, 7.

[6] Like Oliphant, Thackeray also pleads for literature's right to go beyond a presentation of teeny crushes and to draw a comprehensive and realistic reproduction of life when he makes Mrs. Mackenzie in *The Newcomes* voice the following criticism: "You gentlemen who write books, Mr. Pendennis, and stop at the third volume, know very well that the real story often begins afterwards. My third volume ended when I was sixteen, and was married to my poor husband. Do you think that all our adventures ended then, and that we lived happy ever after?" (*The Newcomes,* I, 23, 255).

[7] Cf. John R. Reed, *Victorian Conventions,* Athens, Ohio 1975, 105: "Popular fiction presupposed marriage as the happiest state of life." In *Victorian Women's Fiction* [Shirley Foster, *Victorian Women's Fiction: Marriage, Freedom and the Individual,* London 1985] Foster demonstrates how women writers of the time often presented marriage as the source of frustration for women. In an early pamphlet, "The

Laws Concerning Women", *Blackwood's,* 79 (1856), 379, Oliphant already castigated such sensationalist presentations of the injustice done to women in marriage: "Women's wrongs are always picturesque and attractive. They are indeed so good to make novels and poems about, so telling as illustrations of patience and gentleness, that we fear any real redress of grievances would do more harm to the literary world than it would do good to the feminine."

[8] Laurence Lerner, "Introduction" to Elizabeth Gaskell, *Wives and Daughters,* Harmondsworth 1983, 26. The problem, as Lerner recognises in *Love and Marriage* [Laurence Lerner, *Love and Marriage: Literature and Its Social Context,* London 1979], 35, is not caused by the presentation of marital conflicts itself, but by the romantic cliché of finding the ideal partner, a cliché that tempts even realists to resort to rose colours and fairy-tale stereotypes.

[9] John Stock Clarke, "Mrs. Oliphant: A Case for Reconsideration", *English,* 27 (1979), 126.

[10] A. O. J. Cockshut, *Man and Woman: A Study of Love and the Novel 1740-1940,* London 1977, 92f.

[11] G. B. Shaw, "Candida", *Plays Pleasant,* Harmondsworth 1984, 158.

[12] In its imagery this passage is reminiscent of Mrs. Pryor's warning in *Shirley* [Charlotte Brontë, *Shirley,* Oxford 1979] that the portrayal of marriage in literature is unrealistic: "They show you only the green tempting surface of the marsh, and give not one faithful or truthful hint at the slough underneath. . . . [Marriage] is never wholly happy" (*Shirley,* 21, 300).

[13] Cf. Craik's *Agatha's Husband,* where the wife learns to overcome her dislike and to love her husband. On this issue see also Calder, 33, who asserts that showing aversion to an unsympathetic husband was considered unacceptable; instead, the wife had to learn to love him.

[14] Showalter [Elaine Showalter, *A Literature of Their Own: British Women Novelists from Brontë to Lessing,* Princeton 1977], 179, refers to the metaphor of the room as a symbol of feminine sexual integrity. Such allusions are very rare in the Victorian novel, as they were considered inappropriate for the female reading public.

[15] Showalter, 179.

[16] *Shirley,* 8, 103.

[17] "The business of a righteous and rational law is not to provide facilities for escaping, but to rivet and enforce the claims of that relationship upon which all society is founded" ("The Laws Concerning Women", *Blackwood's,* 79 [1856], 382). A hesitant acceptance of divorce can be found in "The Condition of Women" [*Blackwood's* 83 (1858), 139-54]. In Oliphant's novels women are always content with separation and never seek a divorce, as they have no desire to marry once more.

[18] The novel is set before the Married Women's Property Act was passed, but even this change in the law would hardly have affected the crux of the problem. In *The Marriage of Elinor* [2 vols., Leipzig (Tauchnitz) 1892] Oliphant's attitude has clearly changed in favour of women, whereas in earlier articles, such as "The Laws Concerning Women" and "The Condition of Women" she had argued that a separation and any settlement as regards the children were bound to be unfair to one of the partners.

[19] "The Laws Concerning Women", 385.

[20] Williams [Merryn Williams, *Women in the English Novel, 1800-1900,* London 1984], 26, refers to the fact that Victorian champions of women's rights emphasised the obligation not to obey husbands in questions of conscience. On the other hand, Mrs. Craik, in a novel like *Agatha's Husband,* proves, by manipulating the plot in a complicated manner, that a wife must blindly trust her husband even in apparently debatable decisions, since she is not clever enough to understand his reasoning.

[21] [Merryn Williams, *Margaret Oliphant. A Critical Biography,* London 1986], 197, note 3, says that *A House Divided Against Itself* was really written prior to *A Country Gentleman and His Family.* Both plots roughly correspond to each other, although there are major differences in the characterisation of the parents. Lady Markham is a lady of the world, Waring a misanthropic academic. Responsibility for the failure of the marriage must be put on the shoulders of both partners, who have separated due to insurmountable differences.

[22] Janet Dunbar, *The Early Victorian Woman. Some Aspects of Her Life (1837-57),* London 1953, 17.

[23] In the story *Two Strangers* [London (Fisher Unwin) 1894] it also remains a moot point as to whether the long-separated couple really entertain the wish to live under the same roof again.

Elisabeth Jay (essay date 1995)

SOURCE: "The Woman and Her Art: An Assessment," in *Mrs. Oliphant: 'A Fiction to Herself'; A Literary Life,* Clarendon Press, 1995, pp. 289-307.

[*In the essay below, Jay, while presenting the history of Oliphant's literary reputation, outlines and comments on her various writing skills.*]

I have so far discussed the particularities of Mrs Oliphant's life and work, rather in the manner she herself suggested when sketching the outlines of one of her own female characters:

> Mrs Everard also was a widow. This fact acts upon the character like other great facts in life. It makes many and important modifications in the aspect of affairs. Life *à deux* (I don't know any English phrase which quite expresses this) is scarcely more different from the primitive and original single life than is the life which, after having been *à deux,* becomes single, without the possibility of going back to the original standing ground. That curious mingling of a man's position and responsibilities, cannot possibly fail to mould a type of character in many respects individual. A man who is widowed is not similarly affected, partly because in most cases he throws the responsibility from him, and either marries again or places some woman in the deputy position of governess or housekeeper to represent the feminine side of life, which he does not choose to take upon himself. Women, however, abandon their post much less frequently, and sometimes, I suspect get quite reconciled to the double burden . . . Sometimes they attempt too much, and often enough they fail; but so does everybody in everything, and widows' sons have not shown badly in general life.[1]

The novel in which this remark occurs was written in 1872, before her sons were old enough to be judged to have made a lamentable failure 'in general life', but Mrs Oliphant was in no doubt that it was in this wider arena that they must make their mark. She was similarly aware that her other creations, her fiction and non-fiction, would achieve a valuation in the general market-place, irrespective of the special circumstances of her own life. Feminist studies have often been accused of evading critical responsibility, either in the interests of the prior task of reclaiming neglected voices, or from a desire to resist the contamination of the male values so firmly imprinted on the traditional tests of literary greatness. Unfortunately, neither of these positions do much credit to their women subjects or to literary studies: rather they imply a view that reduces literature, of whatever calibre, to the status of a useful historical source; and the refusal to engage in critical dialogue only reinforces the suspicions indulged in by those outside the ghetto thus created.

Mrs Oliphant herself would have been irritated by any reluctance to apply the contemporary critical standards used to judge male writing to her work. As she grew older and more certain of her professional status, she became increasingly irritated by various positions which seemed to undermine or threaten a woman's right to enter the literary market-place and aim for its top prizes. The hordes of new authors who apparently regarded writing as 'the easiest trade, requiring no training at all'[2] offered an implicit attack upon her hard-won professional status and seemed to reinforce the previously fashionable thesis that, since genius was unlikely to occur in a woman, different standards of judgement were appropriate. In this respect, she felt, women artists had been their own worst enemies. They had been so anxious to avoid the stigma of abnormality or deviance from conventional notions of female propriety that they had vied with each other 'in denying all eccentricity and claiming the reputation of good housekeepers, good economists, seamstresses, and all that goes with these famous domestic qualities'. Reviewing *The Life of Harriet Beecher Stowe,* she registered her annoyance with a passage that evaluated the art in terms of the author's ability to earn mattresses for her family.

> This admirable confession of poverty and virtuous striving and the prosaic uses of the literary gift, was considered engaging and delightful to the highest degree in those days. But it has been repeated a great many times since: and we are not sure that it would not please us more now to hear that our poet authoress was a little out of the common way, that there was a touch of frenzy in her poetic eye, and that she did not think of feather-beds, but let her money drop through her fingers, and knew nothing of business.[3]

It might at first sight seem as if Mrs Oliphant's *Autobiography* was itself responsible for encouraging the application of exactly those different standards for female achievements that her criticism so strenuously repudiated. In one respect that work follows a well-documented tendency for the autobiographies of nineteenth-century women to display a degree of self-denigration wholly at odds with the evidence and spirit of either their letters or their less personal public writings.[4] Though she was inclined to minimize the quality of her achievements, she did not fall into the other well-established trait of making gestures to woman's essentially passive role as a channel through which external inspiration and energies might flow. She was not in the habit of attributing her success to good luck or the generosity of others, but stressed her own unremitting labours and the conscious choices she had made in what to us might seem fairly constricted circumstances. Nor is the passage where she asserts that her status as mother and friend was always more important than her reputation at the circulating library a plea for critical leniency on grounds of gender. Bereavement had made her sharply aware how little human consolation literary reputation could offer and, *sub specie aeternitatis,* any artistic achievement seemed both trivial and evanescent:

And now that there are no children to whom to leave any memory; and the friends drop day by day, what is the reputation of a circulating library to me? Nothing, and less than nothing—a thing the thought of which now makes me angry, that any one should for a moment imagine I cared for that, or that it made up for any loss. I am perhaps angry, less reasonably, when well-intentioned people tell me I have done good, or pious ones console me for being left behind by thoughts of the good I must yet be intended to do. God help us all! what is the good done by any such work as mine, or even better than mine.[5]

By the time that she wrote this final part of her autobiographical account she was an old woman and had been deprived of the goal and purpose which had served to legitimate her work as a female writer. She therefore felt entitled to speak out about the hollowness she had discovered behind that ideal of women as patient sufferers and inspirers of virtue. Silent suffering, or the ironic displacement of grievance, has here been replaced by the energy of openly expressed anger. It was this anger that fuelled the powerful work which was still to come in such pieces as **'The Anti-Marriage League'**, *The Makers of Modern Rome,* or *Old Mr. Tredgold*. The passage which had begun in apparent nihilism went on to arrive at an expression of the transcendent value of art.

'if any man build upon this foundation . . . wood, hay, stubble . . . if the work shall be burned, he shall suffer loss; but he himself shall be saved; yet so as by fire'. An infinitude of pains and labour, and all to disappear like the stubble and hay. Yet who knows? The little faculty may grow a bigger one in the more genial land to come, where one will have no need to think of the boiling of the daily pot.

In the depression she experienced in the early months after Cecco's death she felt that she had lost on all fronts: her children were dead and all she had to show for a life of toil was a collection of pot-boilers. 'I pay the penalty in that I shall not leave anything behind me that will live.'[6] The obituaries that immediately followed her death were by and large respectful in tone, but a series of longer, more magisterial assessments of Mrs Oliphant's achievements were to follow consequent upon the publication of her *Autobiography* in 1899. These were inclined to take her own dispiriting self-evaluation of 1894 as the definitive account, and she was laid to rest as a dreary survival of antiquated Victorian values by those anxious to embrace the artistic preoccupations of the new century. The coincidence of her death with that of the century metamorphosed her career into a symbolic watershed: the point can be conveniently illustrated by comparing Leslie Stephen's evaluation of her with that of his daughter, Virginia Woolf.[7] He presented her as a test case in considering the problem of morality versus art. At one end of the spectrum he placed Southey, who had been prepared to sacrifice all else for the chance of a seat beside Milton or Spenser; at the other he placed Mrs Oliphant, who, on the evidence of 'that most pathetic autobiography', resigned her chance of writing a novel 'to stand on the same shelf as *Adam Bede* . . . because she wished to send her boys to Eton'. Dismissing the thought that she could perhaps have sent them to 'some humbler school and have kept her family without sacrificing her talents to over-production', as not germane to his argument, he concluded that he honoured and respected her decision. His daughter, on the other hand, produced the autobiography as 'a most genuine and indeed moving piece of work' in which she found all the evidence she wanted to convince herself that in her fiction, her 'innumerable faded articles, reviews [and] sketches of one kind and another', she had 'sold her brain, her very admirable brain, prostituted her culture and enslaved her intellectual liberty in order that she might earn her living and educate her children'. Neither of them saw good reason to challenge Mrs Oliphant's own evaluation of her writings, but each confidently claimed her as a trophy for diametrically opposed prejudices, Leslie Stephen being perhaps the more open in his admission, 'I have a low opinion of the intrinsic value of artistic masterpieces.'

And there matters stood until very recently. Robert and Vineta Colby's very thorough study, *The Equivocal Virtue: Mrs Oliphant and the Victorian Literary Market Place* (1966), presented an advance in scholarship, but, as the title's reference to her unflagging industry and eye to the market indicates, did little to change her reputation. The slow change that occurred as women critics, in particular, began to recognize that her anti-feminist conclusions were predicated upon a thoroughly feminist analysis, can be gauged by the way in which the Colbys' assessment of her *Autobiography* changed from their 1966 opinion that 'Her life records are a dreary chronicle', to their description of it in 1979 as 'the most beautiful and moving of all her works'.[8] The title of Merryn Williams's very serviceable study, to which all recent researchers are indebted, *Margaret Oliphant: A Critical Biography* (1986), asserts that its subject merits critical attention, but the effect is slightly undermined by taking so many chapter-headings from Mrs Oliphant's own self-marginalizing remarks: 'General Utility Woman', 'Never Penetrating Beyond the Threshold', and 'On the Ebb Tide'. Once again, too, a slight hesitancy manifests itself as to the nature of Mrs Oliphant's true significance for twentieth-century readers: a book that 'began as a study of her major novels' reached the book-buying public as 'the first full biography'.[9]

The old tug-of-war between the life and the art as evaluative guidelines, lent heavyweight leadership by

Leslie Stephen and his daughter at the turn of the century, has become yet more intense in the late twentieth century when biographies have gained in bestseller appeal in almost direct correlation to literary criticism's increasing scepticism as to the validity and ideological respectability of using such extra-textual material.

Even were it possible or desirable to jettison the biographical dimension from the discussion, it is still not easy to assess the history of the reputation of Mrs Oliphant's writings. There has never been an informed consensus as to which works best show off her characteristic virtues. Many of her early works were out of print long before she died and, since the obituaries were often written by a later generation, one cannot but suspect that the praise meted out to her early Scottish novels was often the effect of reading *Kirsteen* (1890) rather than *Passages in the Life of Margaret Maitland,* which had last been republished in the Parlour Library in 1876, or its immediate successors, or of their gaining a reflected glory from the sudden vogue for kailyard novels at the time of her death.[10] *The Chronicles of Carlingford,* which had secured her claim to be considered in the major league of Victorian novelists, offered an easy peg upon which those with a slim acquaintance with her work could hang her reputation. Given the vagaries of republication this proved a mixed blessing: *Salem Chapel* happened to be the representative volume from this series to enter Everyman's Classics, and this encouraged many twentieth-century readers to regard her genius as irretrievably flawed by a penchant for succumbing to the 1860s fashion for the melodramatic appeal of the 'sensation novel'. In her own lifetime it would seem that the 'Little Pilgrim' series, for which she had not initially 'thought of pay at all', was to prove the best seller. She was herself amazed to discover that Macmillans had printed their twenty-first thousand of this within five years of its initial publication. She enquired whether this was 'to be received as genuine? or does the trade add on a little'. A pencilled note in the margin of this letter mentioned that the twenty-second thousand was already in print.[11] The popularity of this work was again to prove counterproductive to her reputation, since these religious allegories and fables belonged to a genre which was to fall wholly outside the boundaries of serious twentieth-century literature. The only other work to survive the almost total oblivion into which her work fell for some sixty years was *A Beleaguered City:* this was kept alive by the continuing market for tales of the supernatural. Even this may have skewed her reputation, allowing her to appear as a writer who had accidentally produced one or two worthwhile stories of the supernatural in the midst of piles of eminently forgettable three-deckers. Among her non-fiction, *The Life of Edward Irving* and her *Annals of a Publishing House* were to remain the standard works for many years; but the romantic bias

of the former and the anecdotal style of the latter, both aimed at pleasing a general readership, were to attract the criticism of an unscholarly disregard for accurate detail from the very different type of reader who had reason to consult them in the following century. Yet the fact that the major reputable publishing houses went on publishing her work for over half a century bespeaks an achievement greater than the production of formula best-sellers, which might have found their niche with second-rank publishers like the Tinsley Brothers. Nor was her appeal solely to the middle-brow English tastes of the readers whose daily lives her work might be thought to have reflected. She had a considerable following in America, was swiftly made available to English-speakers on the Continent by the Tauchnitz editions, and some of her fiction was certainly translated into French and Russian.[12]

On the face of it, her popularity abroad, with a readership remote from the domestic concerns her novels depicted, seems surprising. *The Second Son* (1888), for instance, was written specifically for the American market, and Mrs Oliphant empowered T. B. Aldrich, editor of Boston's *Atlantic Monthly,* to make any changes he deemed necessary; but the plot, with its complicated use of English laws of primogeniture and entailment of estates, made no concessions to a transatlantic readership.[13] Mrs Oliphant, it seems, was right to identify her strength as her ability for character depiction and to assume that a 'novelist working on the basis of humanity, which though varying in its modes, is practically the same among all people and in all ages', has advantages over every other writer attempting to interest readers in the reconstruction of the circumstances of a particular society.[14] From her very first short story, 'John Rintoul', it is easy to see that she compensated for her self-acknowledged limitations at plot invention and structure by relying on closely delineated character.[15] This sometimes led to problems in her longer fiction. in Occasionally, as in *Squire Arden,* it seems that, starting with only the most basic outlines of the plot in her mind, she only discovered the incumbent complications as she wrote. Sometimes Mrs Oliphant's interest in the plot from which the novel's action arises is simply superseded, as in *Madam,* by the interest she develops in a new generation of characters, who take centre-stage to the detriment of the novel's advertised centre of interest. On the other hand, habits encouraged by three-volume novels, such as following the fortune of *two* sets of characters, or moving the characters from one place to another, could sometimes be made to work to her benefit, as in *Phoebe Junior* or *The Wizard's Son,* where a clash of cultures, or the provision of an alternative world of opportunities, proves vital to the novels' thematic interests.

It was also her very strength as a character painter that threw the remaining weakness in her plots into high relief. Morally reprobate male characters occasionally disappear from her novels in a flurry of melodramatic villainy, killing any man they fear will expose them or, at the very least, indulging in hoarse curses or bitter laughter. These sudden denouements clashed crudely with her bent for meticulously tracing the after-effects of these characters' actions upon those remaining, and, however long she managed to delay such crises, they always produce a disappointing sense of being returned to the stereotypical world of sensationalism after the promise afforded by glimpses into these characters' inner self-justifications. For the ability to show both men and women in highly wrought states from which there is no obvious or immediate release was one of her most striking talents. Since the effect of her style so often relies upon a cumulative sense of image, rhythm, and cadence it is difficult to illustrate this briefly, but the capacity to allow her style to respond to the changing exigencies of plot and character is rarely shown to better effect than in ***The Second Son*** (1888), which contains two chapters focusing on different levels of emotional desperation. In the first, chapter 28, 'A Night in the Streets', we see a country girl taking panicky flight from her would-be seducer in London. Gradually her anger, self-pity, and shame subside into a desperate weariness as she finds herself alone and not knowing which way to turn in her predicament. The landscape of the suburbs in the small hours provides the perfect complement to her situation: the endless labyrinth of Roads, Gardens, and Places through which she walks coalesces into 'an awful desert of houses'. Each new turning offers simultaneously the hope of a new direction and the conviction of being utterly lost. Row upon row of doors, remaining firmly closed, mock her desire for comfort and solace. Worse still, despite her inner turmoil, she is forced to maintain an even pace throughout the small hours so as not to attract attention to herself and feels obliged to shun even those figures who might have been able to set her right upon her path.

The second chapter, 44, 'The Squire Goes Home', depicts an irascible, unpleasant old man, who has been used to imposing his own will on others through a combination of bullying and intimidation. Thwarted by a mere bunch of women, and shaking with impotent rage and shame at the revelation that his youngest son's failed seduction is well known in the neighbourhood, he decides to make his way home in the heat of the midday sun. His anger and perturbation make themselves felt in the raised beat of his pulse, which is in turn reflected in the insistence of the short clauses and phrases that describe his long and arduous walk home. The domestic turmoil that has already struck the traditional life of this very conservative squirearchy, and will result in the Squire dying of a stroke before he rescinds the will unjustly debarring his second son from the inheritance, is neatly encap-

sulated in the Squire's sudden eruption into the house during the afternoon period when the butler is 'dozing pleasantly'. Wanting to block out the penetrating sun and the 'derisive laughter of the country' that echoes in his ears, the Squire demands that the shutters be closed. The narrative focus then slides to the butler, who makes his ponderous preparations with a marked deliberation, where the various hiatuses and the syntactical inversion give pride of place to the butler's sense of grievance, and the reader's anxiety as to how long the Squire will be able to contain the temper that has nowhere to put itself is heightened by the premonitory release in the opening of the bottles: 'He sent for the various bottles, there was a popping of corks which occupied some time: and finally he took in himself to the library a tray, which the footman carried to the door.'

It was Mrs Oliphant's choice of narrative stance that allowed her to move in and out of her various characters at will, offering them up to the reader at their own evaluation, as other characters saw them, and brooded over by the narrator's voice. Her first published novel had employed a first-person narrator, an elderly single woman whose relative freedom from ties, financial and emotional, allowed her to move between and comment upon the rest of the cast. This voice blended easily with Mrs Oliphant's own authorial persona and came into its own again in the short-story cycle **'Neighbours on the Green'**. She was to find the narrative voice of female characters whose opinions diverged from her own less useful, or perhaps less appealing.[16] It was one thing to comment ironically, at times even fondly, upon the foibles of her own sex, and another to serve up their weaknesses naked, without the benefit of authorial protection, to the general reader's eye. A long career in learning to use the male voice against itself as *Maga*'s literary critic had freed her from any such reservations in disclosing male vanities. The distinction is illuminatingly and fruitfully deployed in *A Beleaguered City,* where the main narrative thrust is carried by the pompously authoritative tones of the Mayor and the female point of view separated between two versions of Mrs Oliphant, the wifely advocate of female self-sacrifice, and the slightly querulous mother whose pride in her son's achievement is almost matched by her resentment of his adult autonomy.

In the majority of her fictions an impersonal voice carries the overview, lending a characteristically ironic tone by exploiting the gaps between the characters' perception of their own and each other's lives. This does not necessarily reduce all the characters within a particular tale to peep-show dimensions, but offers the reader the kind of pleasure that one might derive from being unexpectedly offered a new and privileged view of a well-known building. The point can be briefly illustrated. In an unremarkable short story, **'A Party**

of Travellers', we are speedily introduced to one of their number as 'one of those quiet women who, without any unkindness in them, nay, with the most devoted and true affection, yet cannot help seeing the foibles of their belongings, and get a gentle fun from out of them in spite of themselves'. Such characteristics might well have qualified this woman as a narrator for a tale by Mrs Oliphant, so it comes as a surprise, which is germane to the tale's outcome, when the narrator draws us back apace to see the character from a different angle. She is observed walking on the beach, unconscious of the incongruous picture her silken dress creates there. The narrator pauses to remark what a good thing it is that few of us recognize our own distinguishing idiosyncrasies, 'for what would become of all our little individualities, our angles, the rough places which distinguish us one from another, if we could see how droll we appear—just as droll, or more so, than the other people are?'[17] As Mrs Oliphant recognized, she had to nourish this skill for sustaining an illusion of an ever-receding series of perspectives, to fight off the opposing temptation of reductionism, of which the *Saturday Review* held her guilty.

> Mrs Oliphant, in her long observation of mankind and her abundant practice in giving it to the world, seems to have come to the conclusion that—vulgarly speaking—men are much of a muchness, and that if you represent one and all as influenced by other motives than those they acknowledge, you can never be far wrong . . . She finds an easy amusement in bringing together by the ears men of different religious creeds and professions, and subduing them to uniformity by their weaknesses. A sort of unity indeed is established by this means; if people do not think all alike, at the end of the book they are all alike, which comes to much the same thing.[18]

This reviewer seems to have mistaken a strongly held philosophical conviction for artistic laziness. The circumstances of her own life, from which she drew her creative sustenance, had done much to convince her of an obstinately repetitive disposition in human affairs. Try though she might to provide different conditions for her sons' upbringing, their adult lives replicated almost exactly the depressing decline into indolent dependence that her own brothers' lives had each, very separately, taken. Place as well as character conspired to give this dreary impression of circularity: it was to be 'rotting Rome' that twice bereaved her.

Deployed at its best, this conviction that human nature is 'practically the same in all times and in all ages', but has an almost infinite capacity for discovering individually quirky variations, gave rise to a delicate capacity to hover on the borders of tragicomic irony. There are a series of family confrontations between the thrice-married Squire Wentworth and his very disparate progeny in *The Perpetual Curate* that measure up to the finest of Trollope's comic scenes. In this scene the irascible Squire, a well-intentioned father, holding the traditional views of the English squirearchy, is discussing with the son of his middle wife, the perpetual curate of the novel's title, the plight of the second son of his first wife, Gerald, whose excessively refined conscience has led him to believe he must abandon the family living and his wife and family, to become a Roman Catholic priest,

> 'There never was any evil in him, that I could see, from a child; but crotchety, always crotchety, Frank. I can see it now. It must have been their mother,' said the Squire, meditatively; 'she died young, poor girl! her character was not formed. As for *your* dear mother, my boy, she was always equal to an emergency; she would have given us the best of advice, had she been spared to us this day. Mrs Wentworth is absorbed in her nursery, as is natural, and I should not care to consult her much on such a subject . . . I consider you very like your mother, Frank. If anybody can help Gerald, it will be you . . . You have only to talk to him, and clear up the whole affair', said the Squire, recovering himself a little. He believed in 'talking to', like Louisa [Gerald's pathetic wife], and like most people who are utterly incapable of talking to any purpose . . . 'There is the bell for luncheon, and I am very glad of it', he said; 'a glass of sherry will set me all right . . . If the worst should come to the worst, as you seem to think', he said, with a kind of sigh, 'I should at least be able to provide for you, Frank. Of course, the Rectory would go to you . . .'

> So saying, the Squire led the way into the house; he had been much appalled by the first hint of this threatened calamity, and was seriously distressed and anxious still; but he was the father of many sons, and the misfortunes or blunders of one could not occupy all his heart. And even the Curate, as he followed his father into the house, felt that Louisa's words, so calmly repeated, 'Of course the Rectory will go to you', went tingling to his heart like an arrow, painfully recalling him in the midst of his anxiety, to a sense of his own interests and cares. Gerald was coming up the avenue at the moment slowly, with all the feelings of a man going to the stake . . . He thought nothing less than that his father and brother were discussing him with hearts as heavy and clouded as his own; for even he, in all his tolerance and impartiality, did not make due account of the fact, that every man has his own concerns next to him, close enough to ameliorate and lighten the weight of his anxieties for others.[19]

While the last remark from the narrator draws attention to the common denominator in human behaviour, it in no way diminishes the oddity of such a blunt, and naïvely transparent, man as the Squire having fathered two men of such refined conscience as Frank and

Undated photograph by H. L. Mendelssohn.

Gerald. While counting entirely upon the principle that 'breeding will out', the proud patriarch fails to perceive the part his own obstinate, if simple-minded, convictions have played in giving his sons a similarly blinkered view of their own rightness. Conscious of his duties and responsibilities as head of this long-established family, he has deployed money, land, livings, and wives to secure the succession, without any real glimmer of the individual susceptibilities standing in his way. The benevolent but incompetent authoritarianism that shines through his ramblings inclines us to sympathize with the sons whose life of intellectual and spiritual agonizings have so repeatedly had to encounter this brick wall. Frank and Gerald, however, are then disclosed to us as being not only motivated by equally rigid, though different, agenda, but also as more or less locked into the egocentricity of the human condition. Readers familiar with Mrs Oliphant's point of view will appreciate the unwitting accuracy with which the Squire has pinpointed Frank's good sense and willingness to make an effort on the family's behalf as proof of his strong maternal inheritance. It is a mark of Frank's 'female' sensitivity of conscience that the arrow of his selfish concerns goes 'painfully' to its mark, whereas his brother Gerald approaches the house, to which he has been invited for lunch, unshaken in his ability to transform the scene into a

martyrdom which will secure him the unchallenged central role. The passage is rich both in humour and pathos, for the occasion of this gathering, the crisis of conscience that threatens to wrench the family asunder, would have tapped deeper wells of suffering in many Victorian families, where differing religious conviction had caused separation. One phrase in this passage may have caused surprise. We are told not that Gerald, '*despite* all his tolerance and impartiality', did not take account of the absolute egocentricity of every man's view of life, but that '*in* all his tolerance and impartiality' he failed to recognize this fact. As so often, Mrs Oliphant hides within her narrative a figure who serves as a reminder to her of the temptation she had most to guard against. It is because Gerald's estimation of life is conducted from a grandly Olympian viewpoint that he can recognize neither the deep-seated selfishness of his own position nor that others, however feeble or muddle-headed they may seem, are demonstrating their humanity by the tenacity with which they cling to other viewpoints. Of his wife's to us entirely understandable, objections to the step he is proposing, all he can say is, 'It is a strange view of life, to look at it from Louisa's point.'[20] Mrs Oliphant recognized that if she confined herself to the impartial tolerance of others' 'peccadilloes' adopted by a Gerald Wentworth or a Catherine Vernon, this would reduce her writing to a uniformly cold cynicism and forfeit the ability to offer pleasure through her sense of her characters' widely differing 'views of life'. It was her greatest reservation about Jane Austen that her 'involuntary training' in silent observation and a tolerance devoid of moral anger or 'human charity' had made her slow to see 'that even the most stupid and arrogant of mortals has his rights'.[21]

Her ability to give individuality to her characters, while at the same time making us conscious of a consistent line of authorial point of view, was related to her style. She had both the mimic's ability to capture individual turns of phrase and nuance and a very sure sense of her own cadences. Her first novel, **Christian Melville,** is flawed by the over-use of rhetorical questions, pretentious phraseology, arch descriptions, and the resort to the graphic present to provide dramatic intensity; but this was the novel of a 17-year-old, and George Eliot was almost 40 when she wrote *Scenes of Clerical Life,* which manifested each of these stylistic flaws. A couple of early historical novels she wrote early in her career, **Caleb Field** and **Magdalen Hepburn: The Story of the Reformation,** though more competent pieces of work, bear the sign of the labour they cost, because both of them resort to stylistic devices alien to her normal mode: the former in 'taking a great deal of trouble about a Nonconformist minister who spoke in antitheses very carefully constructed',[22] and the latter in her endeavours to reproduce an authentic dialect regardless of its comprehensibility. Honing and polishing were wholly alien to her talent; her poetry was utterly unmemorable because the constraints of conventional metrical discipline never allowed her to do more than imitate other poets' rhythms or pad out her verses with line-fillers.

As with other very prolific artists who have been quick to discover their own voices, yet have been capable throughout their careers of curious lapses of tone and control, it has seemed most profitable to attempt to identify the constituent parts of her writing which from time to time coalesced in such a way that she hit her truest vein. We have her own authority for this approach in the story of Mr Sandford, the elderly and much respected painter, who learns to see that his finest work has always arisen 'out of the jogtrot' of his ordinary work, not from conscious attempts to change artistic direction.[23]

One of the most impressive aspects of Mrs Oliphant's achievements as a writer was the speed with which she used her prolific output to cast her juvenilia behind her, find her own voice, and achieve a resistance to the infection of other styles. Her early reviews give some indication that this was at least a semi-conscious process for they were particularly strong in noting such weaknesses in others' writing. Mrs Gore's artificiality was in part a product of 'her regular sentences . . . the dialogue which chimes in exactly the same measure, whether the speakers speak in a club, or in the dowager duchess's sombre and pious boudoir';[24] those prominent non-fiction writers Macaulay and Ruskin were judged to have developed style at the expense of content.[25] Similarly towards the end of her career she noted an attentiveness to style, bordering upon obsessiveness, as characterizing the work of Henry James or George Meredith, both of whom she felt were writing with an eye to the critics rather than the general reader.[26] Mrs Oliphant's *Autobiography* is notably free from the desire to respond to professional criticisms of her work. Fifty years of literary journalism had taught her how ephemeral such judgements were and reaffirmed her conviction that the general reader, at whom she aimed, valued the reassurance of a distinctively individual style.

She had not long been launched in her career by the time that she found the self-confidence to dismiss the comments of a certain Ann Mozley (a fellow essayist), reported to her by John Blackwood.

> As to your courteous critic's remarks, I am quite conscious of the 'to be sure's' and the 'naturally', but then a faultless style is like a faultless person, highly exasperating, and if one did not leave those little things to be taken hold of perhaps one might fare worse.[27]

She recognized these phrases, which have been interestingly linked both to the conditions under which her

mother had allowed her to legitimate her writing and to the appeal to experience that constitutes the realist writer's claim to authority, as absolutely characteristic of her style.[28] Taken together, these desires to imply inspiration rather than careful craftsmanship, and a simplicity which bespoke its origins in the truth of experience, were the hallmarks of a female tradition that had long found its natural medium in realist fiction, within whose elastic form it might also enjoy the freedom to employ, more or less covertly, the authorities and professional rhetoric marked out by education and cultural prejudice as male territory. In Mrs Oliphant's case it was the very flexibility of the realist domestic fiction, acknowledged as an appropriate sphere for women writers, that permitted the characteristic intrusions of her very personal observations into the narrator's otherwise distanced tones. She was astute enough to recognize that, given the fluctuations in narratorial distance, her 'readability' relied heavily upon a fluent style. Her chosen medium imitated and exploited all the parenthetical tricks of the colloquial register, but this, in turn, encouraged mannerisms that she dared not iron out for fear of losing 'my singsong, guided by no sort of law, but by my ear, which was in its way fastidious to the cadence and measure that pleased me'.[29]

Despite the rebuff she offered, via John Blackwood, to Ann Mozley, she had occasionally been prepared to accept criticisms of her own style from people whose opinion she respected. In 1862 she had told Blackwood that she agreed with the strictures of the Reverend Lucas Collins, a respected clerical scholar who marched under the Blackwoods' banner, about 'her tricks of style': they were 'not conscious but natural', she claimed, and, now that they had been brought to her attention, she would try and iron them out.[30] Blackwood did not think she had tried hard enough. After receiving an instalment of *The Perpetual Curate,* he wrote, 'Observe the repetition of your favourite words, "perplexed", "troubled", "little", "poor" . . . and *strike* them out as often as you can.'[31] It seems possible that the title of the 1883 *Maga* article about her work, 'A Little Chat about Mrs Oliphant' concealed an affectionate joke, rather than being offensively patronizing. The writer referred to the 'air of almost garrulous ease about her best work', noting that she did not trouble like Matthew Arnold or Thackeray to polish her periods, but went on to remark that, 'like Scott', the novelist so long acknowledged as without peer in the nineteenth century, she had 'something better than style'.[32] It was this 'something' that fascinated many of her obituarists writing in the more literary journals. As Stephen Gwyn of the *Edinburgh Review* expressed it,

> As for her style, it certainly does not conform to the prevailing standards. It does not keep one on

the stretch with continual expectation of the unexpected word: it is never contorted or tormented, never emphatic, never affected. The words flow simply and smoothly, like the utterance of a perfectly well-bred woman.

Then, perhaps aware of the note of condescension that had crept in, he tried to capture the flavour of her syntax, which had 'always . . . a certain looseness of texture', and yet never lost control of its long sentences. Speaking of **Miss Marjoribanks,** he also commended 'the neatly turned sentences which round off each chapter clearly, as if with the crack of a whip'.[33]

This chapter contains two quite lengthy quotations, chosen for other reasons than the stylistic, which, nevertheless, serve quite well to show something of her manner. The first on p. 289, takes the occasion of introducing a minor character, Mrs Everard, for launching into a disquisition on widowhood. Its tone is conversational: the narrator appears parenthetically, ostensibly admitting a degree of ignorance, while actually introducing a hint of worldly experience. The passage builds upon repetition and qualification, in a way that contrives to suggest an intimate, spoken aside to 'the gentle reader', but the sentences themselves display a far more certain sense of balance than they would normally enjoy in spoken discourse. The long, convoluted sentence beginning 'Life *à deux*' is carefully hedged about with three short emphatic sentences, all of which make much the same point, though the third ('That curious mingling . . .') serves to advance the argument by introducing the notion of role and gender. The long, intervening sentence, that manages to take us from the single life, through marriage, to a recognition of a new quality of singleness, offers us perches from which to recover our balance, before taking flight again, but avoids the monotony of mere repetition. The second use of 'original', earlier defined as a synonym for 'primitive', reminds us that we are being returned to a contemplation of 'single life', but one that has been dislocated from its previous semantic partner. By the end of the sentence we are brought to 'standing ground', while simultaneously having that security denied. The next two sentences clearly signal their related positions in the argument as a whole by locating their subjects firmly at the beginning of the sentence, before embarking upon more complicated syntactical games. Men's moral inferiority is underlined by means of twice repeating the allegation that remarriage is tantamount to a denial of duty, which then becomes women's 'burden'. The final sentence begins well, with a nicely graduated decline and fall achieved by depriving the key word 'fail' of the qualifier the previous parallel phrase enjoyed; the afterthought ('but so does . . .') perhaps shows something of the naïve charm, verging on clumsiness, of a conversational style attempting to wrench the tone back

from elegiac reverie to the exigencies of the particular occasion for this digression.

So little manuscript material remains that it is difficult to get a clear picture of Mrs Oliphant's proof revision procedures: the speed of their turnaround would suggest, however, that she had no time for polishing the individual sentence. Although one might allow for the lassitude of her final year, this response to William Blackwood's request for the tidying of a manuscript was not atypical: 'As for the mingling of *I* and *we* in the narrative: I see no objection to retaining it as it is natural to me to use the pronouns indifferently and would be troublesome and unnecessary to change.'[34]

The second lengthy passage quoted (pp. 296-7) demonstrates her ability to use dialogue imaginatively. It was no less true in her fiction than in her everyday life that she had the gift 'of making people talk': 'like the art of driving a hoop . . . I give a little touch now and then, and my victim rolls on and on.'[35] Squire Wentworth is neither an important figure in the plot, nor an intrinsically interesting character, yet his almost uninterrupted monologue manages to convey the calibre of the man, ponderous, well-meaning, and insensitive. Like Jane Austen, Mrs Oliphant had learned that bores are best left to convey their weakness directly to the reader. Though the mode of his speech to Frank is described as meditative, his thought processes, nudged slowly forward by repetition and digression, are not. And yet these characteristics are swiftly and economically established. Although the Squire talks to no purpose in terms of the particular problem he is addressing, the reader is not left to flounder amongst a heap of irrelevancies and meaningless platitudes. As in her use of dialect, Mrs Oliphant soon discovered that the secret of verisimilitude lay not in reproducing obscure vocabulary, but in using the occasional appropriate idiom and catching the particular rhythm of sentence construction. The Squire provides an exemplary illustration of the rule that Mrs Oliphant herself expounded in her article **'Success in Fiction'**, where she said that dialogue should be 'an ideal representation of what people in certain circumstances would be likely to say, leaving out the repetition, the pointless remarks, the meaningless digressions with which most of us actually dilute our conversation'.[36] Moreover, the flexibility of her impersonal narrator's medium, varying, as Gwyn put it, from 'the utterance of a perfectly well-bred woman' to the whiplash crack of a well-turned epigram, was particularly adept at gliding smoothly from a character's questions or self-communings, to the observations of a sharper, overarching intelligence. The habit of using an ironically distanced narrator could be put to good effect in passages such as this where the individual characters are so self-absorbed that we might become uncomfortably conscious of their conversational partners as frozen into a series of Browningesque 'listeners'.

Sometimes her characters are inarticulate, or reluctant to commit themselves for fear of being misunderstood, and on these occasions her power to weave back and forth between the inconsequential surface of their conversation and the thread of their inner thoughts bears comparison with such famous scenes as Virginia Woolf's Mr and Mrs Ramsay discussing whether the stocking she is knitting will be finished in time to take to the lighthouse.

It is perhaps in her use of imagery that Mrs Oliphant is most markedly in the female tradition. Although the mock-heroic metaphors and that pervade *Miss Marjoribanks* show her to have been capable of the consistent application and development of a particular trope, this is not her most characteristic mode. More frequently everyday objects and pastimes become briefly invested with a significance that transcends their literal status. This happens in much the same way that Mrs Ramsay's knitting vouches for the insistent practicality of the bounty she bestows upon all with whom she is connected, measures time passing, and can be used to convey her emotional response to the conversation flowing around her, yet obstinately refuses symbolic status. *The Perpetual Curate* supplies several examples of this process at work. Mrs Morgan, the rector of Carlingford's wife, finds that her dissatisfaction with the marriage that she and her husband have so long and so prudently deferred becomes, albeit unconsciously, almost entirely expressed in a series of trivial domestic preoccupations. The large floral pattern of the drawing-room carpet, left by a predecessor, serves as a constant reminder of the continued need for irksome frugality; her husband's tolerance of the curate's intrusions when he realizes a particular pudding is in the offing, speaks of that male collegiate world that takes servants and women for granted, and from which it is her business to wean her husband; her endless replanning of the garden and her obsessive tending of her favourite 'maidenhair fern' suggest a woman desperate to enjoy the fruits of an establishment of her own, together with her habit of resorting to memories of her single life to comfort herself for the disappointments of the married state. Mrs Morgan's expression of her anxieties and ambitions through the daily routine of managing her household is replicated time and again in Mrs Oliphant's fiction, where the pleasures and responsibilities of furnishing a house enjoy both actual and metaphorical significance for women. By such means as buying a new carpet, or repapering a room, women demonstrate their power to impose their will, and show the extent to which all but the most independent were hedged about, even in this confined sphere of operations, by the capacity or desire of their menfolk to provide the wherewithal to realize their dreams.

The psychological habit of investing objects with emotional significance is not limited to women. Gerald Wentworth, the apostate clergyman of the same novel, finds that inner struggles have become 'twined in the most inextricable way' into the form of the majestic cedar tree outside his library window. The cedar's solid shadow, untroubled by any passing breeze, recalls his ever-present trouble and reminds him that he stands to lose all that is most familiar to him. Its very passive immobility serves to reveal the intensity of inarticulate need that leads even men and women surrounded by loving families to the desperate, and to an extent risible, device of using objects as recipients and expressions of their innermost emotions.[37]

Besides the homes and feminine activities, such as sewing, discussed elsewhere in this book, two other facets of daily life seem, in Mrs Oliphant's fiction, to be capable of carrying a significance beyond the merely practical: food and dress. The capacity to provide good food for one's family or guests demonstrated, in measurable form, a woman's quality as a carer, and her wider abilities as a woman capable of organizing a household. The grandeur of Lucilla Marjoribanks' first victory is demonstrated by the manner in which she outflanks her father's housekeeper, not by imposing her own recipes, but by occupying the higher moral ground. Cutlets, gravy-beef, and the accuracy of the household accounts are as nothing in comparison to the underlying purpose they serve:

> 'Now we are two women to manage everything, we ought to do still better. I have two or three things in my head that I will tell you after; but in the meantime I want you to know that the object of my life is to be a comfort to my poor papa; and now let us think what we had better have for dinner', said the new sovereign.[38]

A late tale, **'Who Was Lost and Is Found'**, presents, as its title suggests, a muted retelling of the tale of the Prodigal Son, seen from the mother's point of view. The killing of the fatted calf, which celebrated the repentant homecoming, is here rewritten as a series of daily meals by which this anxious mother can judge her son's mood. She learns to take pleasure from the occasions when, despite his continual drinking and smoking, her son is capable of consuming the enormous meals she lays before him: 'It is a kind of certificate of morality which many a poor woman has hailed with delight.'[39] The pathos of this remark lies not only in the recognition that the mother is forced to use such trivial methods of assessing her own 'morality' as well as that of her son but in its patent reference to Mrs Oliphant's anxious supervision of her grown sons' meals. Her earliest memory of maternal love featured just such a scene of her own mother, 'who never seemed to sit down in the strange, little, warm bright picture, but to hover about the table pouring out tea, supplying everything he wanted to her boy (how proud, how fond of him!—her eyes liquid and bright with love as she hovered about)'.[40] The arbitrary particularity with which, in her *Autobiography,* Mrs Oliphant recalls the menus of meals she had provided did not spring from their being grand set-pieces, but because they were recollected in loving detail as examples of her ability to provide in maternal fashion for her party when travelling, or to create happy, informal supper parties for the young. By contrast, to the end of her life Mrs Oliphant remembered 'with a shudder a certain dish of chicken cutlets intended to be particularly delicate and dainty' that she had prepared for a dinner party with her own hands, the cook being indisposed, at the start of her association with the Blackwood family.[41] Even when her income enabled her to employ adequate domestic help, she still imaged her role as provider and carer in terms of the practical expression of domestic love. The phrase she chose, 'the boiling of the daily pot', has most often been read as a straightforward admission that she wrote 'pot-boilers', but far more illuminating is the way in which she recaptured the phrase from the language of cliché to reinvest her writing with the trappings of maternal solicitude: 'it was good to have kept the pot boiling and maintained the cheerful household fire, though it is smouldering out in darkness now.'[42]

Food might be the most basic commodity through which to express female values, but clothing ran it a close second. Again, childhood memories of her mother played their part:

> My clothes were all made by her tender hands, finer and more beautifully worked than ever child's clothes were; my under garments fine linen and trimmed with little delicate laces, to the end that there might be nothing coarse, nothing less than exquisite, about me; that I might grow up with all the delicacies of a woman's ideal child.[43]

One of the Tulloch boys claimed in his obituary that 'She wished every girl about her to be dressed as nicely as possible', and 'never thought money was thrown away on dress'.[44] She was sufficiently interested in 'dress' to contribute a book on the subject to Macmillans' Art in the Home series and to welcome the proliferation of women's fashion magazines at the end of the century.[45] The book remains of more than period interest because she sees dress as more than either merely functional or wholly superficial adornment. Carlyle's *Sartor Resartus* had alerted her to the subject's metaphorical application, but whereas Carlyle had used clothes as a means of investigating his philosophy of life, Mrs Oliphant used them as a mode of discussing art. The following passage, discussing the rules of good dress sense, could have served equally well as a guide to her position as literary critic:

> Reformation without revolution, reasonable conservatism without obstinacy, a certain reserve in respect to the new, a certain reverence for the old, combined with candour and generous appreciation of what is best in both, form the ideal temper . . .[46]

She develops the subject's moral aspect and its gender implications, dismissing those who would see it as vanity and rebutting those who see it as trivial and therefore an exclusively feminine preoccupation. Critical attention to the changing conventions of fashion is recommended, rather than slavish pursuit or arrogant dismissal. In her fiction this area of a woman's life receives attention because it shows up so clearly the strait-jacket of convention from which women sometimes yearn to escape, tempered by the realization that, like most conventions, the rituals of dress have their use, not merely to provide a social grammar but to give disciplined expression to intense emotions. Many of her fictional families find themselves simultaneously irritated and soothed by the incongruous juxtaposition of the grave and the trivial brought about by the effort to assemble mourning clothes. As a writer she was fascinated by the contrast between the intransigent materialism of clothes themselves and the subtle gradations of inner feelings they could disguise or reveal. Those novels, such as *At His Gates, Hester,* and *Kirsteen,* where money and integrity of character are drawn into a complex web of relationship, also make notable use of dress as a mirror for this curious matrix. Other values often lurked behind the simple figures of a cash transaction, as they might in the decision of what to wear. A woman could manage to subvert her husband's vulgar intention of displaying her as a clothes-horse tribute to his own earning power, by privately regarding the very frequency with which she sports these trophies as a sign of her contempt for them. 'Dressing down', on the other hand, could express sulky aggression, or an act of kindly condescension.[47]

Mrs Oliphant's use of metaphor is less dramatically signposted than it is in the writings of a Charlotte Brontë or a George Eliot, but it is none the less certainly part of that female tradition of quasi-metaphorical writing which, drawing upon women's intimacy with the deepest emotions and the daily drudge of household responsibilities, was able to establish in domestic fiction a path back and forth between the two by using familiar objects as both material setting and emotional reference points. In Mrs Oliphant's case the use of material objects provides one other dimension to her writing: their very solidity serves as an ironic contrast with the sense of life's arbitrariness, and its potential at any given moment for tragic or comic development. Her account of the time when she heard of the first ominous signs of her husband's fatal disease offers a fine illustration.

In the early summer one evening after dinner (we dined, I think, at half-past six in those days) I went out to buy some dessert-knives on which I had set my heart—they were only plated, but I had long wanted them, and by some chance was able to give myself that gratification. I had marked them in a shop not far off, and was pleased to get them, and specially happy. Some one had dined with us, either Sebastian Evans or my brother-in-law Tom,—some one familiar and intimate who was with Frank. When I came back again there was a little agitation, a slight commotion which I could not understand; and then I was told that it was nothing—the merest slight matter, nothing to be frightened at. Frank had, in coughing, brought up a little blood.

The dessert-knives and the dinner hour provide that sense of the commonplace necessary to domestic realism's verisimilitude; their very ordinariness is then used as a reliable marker in the shifting fragments of experience and sensation that make up human life. The dessert-knives remain sharply etched while the people involved in the episode have sunk into shadowy oblivion. This episode, constituting another of those 'turning-points' by which she marked her life, provides a convenient halting place in the process of making the case for Mrs Oliphant as 'worth reading'. It offers evidence of an artistry, so 'natural' as to be overlooked, in the ease with which she brings us from the loose, conversational structure of that long opening sentence to the carefully controlled *frisson* in which the passage finds its temporary resting-place. The shaping and selective powers that separate art from reportage are there in the initial decision to feature the dessert-knives, the careful isolation of the reader's naïve expectation of happiness from the narrator's tragic hindsight, and finally in the writer's ability to preside over and maintain a distance from the figures within her tale, so that the drama of the particular moment is uncontaminated by sympathetic identification. This small vignette constitutes a compelling example of the experimental egos with which the autobiographer and novelist plays, and of Mrs Oliphant's professionally astute recognition that her *métier* lay in exploiting a woman's sense of the artificiality of all attempts to draw boundaries between the life and the writing, between experience and its various representational forms. Perhaps the chief reason that she was to remain such a baffling enigma to Henry James was his conviction that he had always, unlike her, striven to ensure that his fiction should 'be in some direct relation to life'.[48]

It is, however, with the immediately preceding passage from her *Autobiography* that I should like to end my study; for in it I think we catch a glimpse of that process by which the life became transmuted into the characteristic modes of her fiction. From the 'common and homely origins', apparently containing nothing of note, and in the interstices of her roles as mother and writer, came those moments of 'fantasticating' where she saw the silhouetted figures that were her various selves—now 'eight-and-twenty, going down stairs as light as a feather', now an elderly, rheumaticky widow—so separated by 'the salt and bitter waves' of experience that only the imagination could give them the transient illusion of unity. In such a passage we see how she became 'a fiction to herself'.

> When I look back on my life, among the happy moments which I can recollect is one which is so curiously common and homely, with nothing in it, that it is strange even to record such a recollection, and yet it embodied more happiness to me than almost any real occasion as might be supposed for happiness. It was the moment after dinner when I used to run upstairs to see that all was well in the nursery, and then to turn into my room on my way down again to wash my hands, as I had a way of doing before I took up my evening work, which was generally needlework, something to make for the children. My bedroom had three windows in it, one looking out upon the gardens I have mentioned, the other two into the road. It was light enough with the lamplight outside for all I wanted. I can see it now, the glimmer of the outside lights, the room dark, the faint reflection in the glasses, and my heart full of joy and peace—for what?—for nothing—that there was no harm anywhere, the children well above stairs and their father below. I had few of the pleasures of society, no gaiety at all. I was eight-and-twenty, going down-stairs as light as a feather, to the little frock I was making. My husband also gone back for an hour or two after dinner to his work, and well—and the bairns well. I can feel now the sensation of that sweet calm and ease and peace.[49]

List of Abbreviations Used in the Notes

Annals—M. O. W. Oliphant, *Annals of a Publishing House: William Blackwood and His Sons: Their Magazine and Friends* (2 vols., 1897; the first volume was proofread by the author before her death, the second by William Blackwood). Volume iii, *The Life of John Blackwood* (1898), is by Mrs Gerald Porter, John Blackwood's daughter

Blackwood's—*Blackwood's Edinburgh Magazine*

Blackwood MS—Mrs Oliphant's letters to the Blackwoods, lodged in the National Library of Scotland. Unless otherwise stated, all letters indicated under this heading are to John Blackwood, until his death on 29 Oct. 1879. Thereafter they are to his nephew, William Blackwood

JAL—*The Autobiography of Margaret Oliphant: The Complete Text,* ed. Elisabeth Jay (Oxford and New York, 1990)

Macmillan MS—Mrs Oliphant's letters to Macmillan, lodged in the BL Macmillan Archive 54919

NLS—National Library of Scotland

Williams—Merryn Williams, *Margaret Oliphant: A Critical Biography* (London, 1986)

Notes

[1] *Innocent,* ch. 9.

[2] *Blackwood's* (Feb. 1886), 258.

[3] *Blackwood's* (Mar. 1890), 409-10.

[4] e.g. in M. G. Mason, 'The Other Voice: Autobiographies of Women Writers', in J. Olney (ed.), *Autobiography: Essays Theoretical and Critical* (Princeton, NJ, 1980), 207-35; and P. Spacks, 'Selves in Hiding', in E. C. Jelinek (ed.), *Women's Autobiography,* (Bloomington, Ind., 1980), 112-32.

[5] *JAL* 136.

[6] Ibid.

[7] L. Stephen, *National Review* (July 1899), 740-57; V. Woolf, *The Three Guineas* (1938; Oxford, 1992), 287.

[8] V. and R. A. Colby, *The Equivocal Virtue* (New York, 1966), 208; R. A. and V. Colby, 'Mrs Oliphant's Scotland: The Romance of Reality', in I. Campbell (ed.), *Nineteenth Century Scottish Fiction,* ed. I. Campbell (Manchester, 1979), 89-104.

[9] Williams, p. xi.

[10] A vogue that Mrs Oliphant herself deplored; see *Blackwood's* (Aug. 1889), 265-6.

[11] Macmillan MS, 19 Apr. 1882, 5 Dec. 1887.

[12] See above, ch. 7, n. 80. *A Rose in June* appeared in Russian in 1875, *He That Will Not When He May* in 1881, and *Lady Car* in 1893. For this information I am indebted to Mr Paul Foote of Queen's College, Oxford.

[13] Macmillan MS, 26 July 1887.

[14] *Blackwood's* (June 1888), 850-2.

[15] 'John Rintoul; or, the Fragment of a Wreck', *Blackwood's* (Mar. 1853), 329-47; (Apr. 1853), 410-30.

[16] As in *The Days of My Life* or one of the narrators in *The Last of the Mortimers: A Story in Two Voices.*

[17] 'A Party of Travellers', *Good Words* (Mar.), 211-6; (June), 423-9; (Oct. 1879), 698-705.

[18] *Saturday Review* (22 July 1876), 112-13.

[19] *The Perpetual Curate,* ch. 17.

[20] Ibid., ch. 16.

[21] *Blackwood's* (Mar. 1870), 294-6.

[22] *JAL* 30.

[23] 'Mr. Sandford', *The Ways of Life,* ch. 4.

[24] *Blackwood's* (May 1855), 555.

[25] *Blackwood's* (Aug. 1856), 128-9.

[26] *Blackwood's* (Sept. 1880), 401; (Oct. 1896), 503.

[27] Quoted in a letter from J. Blackwood to A. Mozley, 31 Mar. 1865; *Annals,* iii. 338.

[28] P. M. Davis, *Memory and Writing: From Wordsworth to Lawrence* (Liverpool, 1983), 316-17.

[29] *JAL* 104.

[30] Blackwood MS, n.d. 1862.

[31] NLS, Blackwood Letter Books. Acc. 5643, D5, 3 May 1864. In the margin of the copy of her 1858 novel, *Orphans,* held by the London Library, a reader has noted a page where 'little' occurs nine times.

[32] [John Skelton], *Blackwood's* (Jan. 1883), 73-91.

[33] *Edinburgh Review* (July 1899), 26-47.

[34] Blackwood MS, 15 Feb. 1897.

[35] *JAL* 98.

[36] *Forum* (New York, 1887-91), Aug. 1889, p. 321.

[37] *Perpetual Curate,* ch. 16.

[38] *Miss Marjoribanks,* ch. 4.

[39] *Who Was Lost and Is Found,* ch. 7.

[40] *JAL* 18-19.

[41] *Annals,* ii. 477.

[42] *JAL* 136-7.

[43] *JAL* 20.

[44] *The Bookman* (Aug. 1897), 114.

[45] *Blackwood's* (June 1895), 907.

[46] *Dress,* ch. 1.

[47] *At His Gates,* ch. 14; 'A Maiden's Mind', *Atalanta* (Dec. 1895), ch. 5; *Miss Marjoribanks,* ch. 10; *Hester,* ch. 4.

[48] *Notes on Novelists,* 358; 'Greville Fane', *The Complete Tales,* 438-9.

[49] *JAL* 63-4.

Linda Peterson (essay date 1995)

SOURCE: "The Female *Bildungsroman:* Tradition and Revision in Oliphant's Fiction," in *Margaret Oliphant: Critical Essays on a Gentle Subversive,* edited by D. J. Trela, Associated University Presses, 1995, pp. 66-89.

[*In the following essay, Peterson examines Oliphant's experimentation with the form and content of the Victorian* bildungsroman, *focusing in particular on the Carlingford novels (1861-76), on* Hester *(1883), and on* Kirsteen *(1890).*]

Modern critical discussions of Victorian *bildungsroman* distinguish sharply between male and female versions of the form. The male version, so standard distinctions suggest, uses a vocational crisis as its central dilemma, tracing the development of its hero as he seeks to find his place in the world, whether that be through accommodation, rebellion, or withdrawal; the female *bildungsroman,* in contrast, traces "a voyage in," substituting an intense self-consciousness or the psychological development of its heroine for the more active engagement with society of her male counterpart.[1] The male *bildungsroman* locates its action in the public realm; the female, in the domestic—often with marriage as the source of the heroine's dilemma.[2] As Susan J. Rosowski sums it up, the male *bildungsroman* focuses on "apprenticeship," the female on "awakening."[3]

No definition of a genre can encompass all examples— and, inevitably, dichotomies as sharp as Rosowski's leave themselves open to quibbles and exceptions. Indeed, if we follow Franco Moretti's suggestion that the *bildungsroman* as the "symbolic form of modernity" embodies cultural tensions between individuality and socialization, autonomy and normality, interiority and objectification,[4] then we might conclude that sharp gender dichotomies oversimplify an extremely complex form; traditionally, the *bildungsroman* has had to

contend with both halves of the dilemma, the professional and the domestic, the social and the psychological, the public and the interior. Perhaps, if our current understanding of the Victorian female *bildungsroman* errs, if we have narrowed its focus and concerns more than is necessary, it is because we have based our criticism on too few novels—usually on Charlotte Bronte's *Jane Eyre* and *Villette,* sometimes on George Eliot's *Mill on the Floss, Middlemarch,* and *Romola,* novels that reinscribe Victorian ideologies of gender and domesticity even as they protest against them.

As a corrective, then, and as an act of literary recovery, I examine in this essay the practice of Margaret Oliphant who, as a novelist and reviewer, produced and analyzed forms of the *bildungsroman* and whose work provides an alternative view of Victorian versions of this form (as well as some of the best examples from the period). Oliphant was a master of the genre's conventions. Because her mind was essentially critical, because she questioned conventional assumptions about "masculine" and "feminine," "male" plots and "female" plots, her novels are an important antidote to too narrow accounts of this female literary tradition.[5] I thus explore Oliphant's approach to the *bildungsroman,* focusing on four examples that span the latter half of the nineteenth century. In the novels of the Carlingford series (1861-76), I argue, Oliphant employs conventional plots of the *bildungsroman,* counterpointing male and female versions of the form; her intention is not to accept or valorize these plots but instead to subvert the conventions, often through parodying the male and ironizing the female versions. Later, in such novels as **Hester** (1883) and **Kirsteen** (1890), Oliphant becomes more critical of distinctions between "masculine" and "feminine" narratives, and she experiments with conventions of the *bildungsroman,* her female heroines often carrying out actions associated with masculine behavior. These later novels test whether the male novel of "apprenticeship" is a gender-restricted genre and what is lost (or gained) when women adopt patterns traditionally associated with men. More fundamentally, the later novels test whether marriage, the traditional site of female development, can remain at the center of a fictional form that is about *bildung,* development, growth, self-formation.

I. *Miss Marjoribanks: (Re) Writing the Female Bildungsroman*

All the novels of Oliphant's Carlingford series are, in one sense or another, versions of the *bildungsroman.* **The Rector** (1861) deals with the suitability of the vocation its hero, Mr. Proctor, has chosen. **Salem Chapel** (1863) follows the career of Arthur Vincent, a zealous Nonconformist clergyman who, with high ideals, confronts the reality of ministering to a lower-middle-class congregation. **The Perpetual Curate**

(1864) traces the progress of a high Anglican clergyman, Frank Wentworth, as he learns to minister successfully to the poor of Carlingford and, less easily, finds economic security without compromising his religious convictions. The latter two novels include subplots common for the genre, *The Perpetual Curate* in the conversion of Frank's brother Gerald to Roman Catholicism, *Salem Chapel* in the romantic adventures that tempt Arthur Vincent and force him to reevaluate his social and religious assumptions.

It is in *Miss Marjoribanks* (1865-66), however, that Oliphant takes up the question of the female *bildungsroman*—and the implications of its conventions. From the first chapter Oliphant makes it clear that her heroine will fulfill the socially accepted patterns of feminine development, which she has learned from ladies' guidebooks and novels. When Lucilla Marjoribanks hears that her invalid mother has died, she resolves to leave school and do her duty by "poor papa":

> All the way home she revolved the situation in her mind, which was considerably enlightened by novels and popular philosophy. . . . She made up her mind on her journey to a great many virtuous resolutions; for, in such a case as hers, it was evidently the duty of an only child to devote herself to her father's comfort, and become the sunshine of his life, as so many young persons of her age have been known to become in literature. (25-26)

As the allusion to literary influence hints, this novel abounds in the motifs and sentiments of Victorian domestic fiction and conduct manuals, including the best-selling *Friends in Council;* according to their dictates, Lucilla acts.[6] The plot Lucilla follows is unabashedly conventional: she remains in school to study domestic management and political economy; then she returns home to "be a comfort to dear papa"; she fulfills her responsibility to Carlingford society with great success; she is wooed by several suitors, one her dull, if devoted cousin Tom, another the more polished, if also more dangerous Mr. Cavendish; she is deserted by Cavendish (and at least two other beaux) and so must face society according to the best principles of her feminine "philosophy"; in the end, after considerable trials, Lucilla marries the appropriate man and finds her place in the world. Structurally, Oliphant even divides Lucilla's progress into two phases characteristic of the *bildungsroman* plot, the first one of "youthful confidence and undaunted trust in her own resources," the second marked by "that sense of failure which is inevitable to every high intelligence after a little intercourse with the world" (338).

Yet if the structure and episodic details of *Miss Marjoribanks* are conventional, Oliphant's treatment is

not. Everything is shot through with irony, from the little *bon mots* Lucilla utters to the major episodes of female development she must undergo. The irony makes the reader suspect the motives of Lucilla, whom some critics have called a "female egoist" hiding beneath conventional sentiments,[7] but it should also make us suspect the conventions of the female *bildungsroman* itself, which Lucilla seems so intent on fulfilling. Oliphant's publisher John Blackwood noticed a certain "hardness of tone" in the novel as if he somehow intuited that the irony was not meant simply as a display of wit. Blackwood was a shrewd reader. In *Miss Marjoribanks* the irony directs itself repeatedly against the assumptions of the fictional genre Oliphant ostensibly imitates.

As a means of locating that irony and its effects, we might focus on a crucial, if conventional episode in Lucilla's progress and the language Oliphant chooses to present it. The episode is the one in which Mr. Cavendish begins to propose marriage but, inadvertently interrupted, deserts Lucilla for Barbara Lake. This desertion parodies the "trial" that the heroine of the *bildungsroman* must invariably face—as Jane Eyre is tested by Rochester's apparent engagement to Blanche Ingram; Caroline Helstone laid low by Robert Moore's proposal to Shirley Keeldar; or, later in the century, Dorothea Brooke shocked by her discovery of Will Ladislaw and Rosamund Vincy tete-a-tete. Lucilla faces the trial but without the usual reaction. When Mr. Cavendish fails to complete his proposal, she does not weep or bemoan her state, but writes a note to Mrs. Chilley, thereby feeling "her mind relieved." "Not that it had been much distressed before," the narrator comments.

> But when she had put it in black and white, and concluded upon it, her satisfaction was more complete; and no such troublous thoughts as those which disturbed the hero of this day's transactions—no such tears as poured forth from the eyes of Barbara Lake—interfered with the maidenly composure of Lucilla's meditations. Notwithstanding all that people say to the contrary, there is a power in virtue which makes itself felt in such an emergency. Miss Marjoribanks could turn from Mr. Cavendish, who had thus failed to fulfill the demands of his position, to the serene idea of the Archdeacon, with that delightful consciousness of having nothing to reproach herself with, which is balm to a well-regulated mind. She had done her duty, whatever happened. (201)

The commentary directs itself overtly against Barbara Lake, the poor, artistic young woman who—like Jane Eyre, Lucy Snowe, and heroines of their ilk—falls in love above her station and gives way to her emotions. Barbara has, as her sister Rose laments, "no proper pride." On this level Oliphant's treatment ironizes the female *bildungsroman* in which the central crisis is invariably an intense romantic involvement, and self-development emerges from the emotional and moral testing that accompany it. The irony also directs itself, however, against Lucilla Marjoribanks who, according to philosophical "principles," has not engaged her affections. The product of Victorian guides to self-conduct, Lucilla is a little too well-regulated, a little too delighted with her behavior to serve as a counter-example to Barbara.

The effect of this complex irony is to undercut both the central assumption of the traditional female *bildungsroman* (that moral growth results from romantic or emotional trials) and the philosophy of the heroine whom Oliphant offers in contrast (that young women do best avoiding such trials). One senses that Oliphant, like her contemporary Harriet Martineau, found the female *bildungsroman* too obsessively focused on love, as if that were the only important aspect of a woman's existence. In a *Blackwood's* article published just after *Miss Marjoribanks,* Oliphant criticized modern fiction that offered as heroines "women driven wild with love for the man who leads them on to desperation . . . ; women who pray their lovers to carry them off from husbands and homes they hate; women, at the very least of it, who give and receive frantic embraces, and live in a voluptuous dream, either waiting for or brooding over the inevitable lover."[8] Yet Oliphant seems uneasy about offering an alternative to romance and marriage. Lucilla's commitment to duty—"I have always been brought up to believe that duty was happiness" (93)—threatens to empty her life of adequate shape or depth (a threat evidenced in Victorian domestic memoirs, which depended on plots external to the self). Years after her admirable behavior in the face of Cavendish's desertion, she realizes that she has found no proper sphere, "that her capabilities were greater than her work" (395). Her only real option is to accept a proposal of marriage.

That proposals of marriage determine the shape of a woman's life, and thus the shape of the female *bildungsroman,* the novel ruefully accedes. Summing up the first, not-quite-successful phase of Lucilla's development, the narrator admits "there can be little doubt that the chief way in which society is supposed to signify its approval and admiration and enthusiasm for a lady, is by making dozens of proposals to her, as may be ascertained from all the best-informed sources" (339). The narrator's irony, enveloped in the certainty of the "best-informed sources," hides a lament that this should be so. But the novel, like society, finally signifies its approval of Lucilla by granting her two proposals, both from honorable men—thus anticipating (or reinforcing) the modern critical view that "the feminine *bildungs* takes place in or on the periphery of marriage."[9] The only female character who

imagines a pattern of self-development independent of marriage proposals—Rose Lake—faces a far worse fate: the loss of her artistic career. For all its irony, for all its probing and satirizing of conventions, then, *Miss Marjoribanks* attempts no alternative structure for the female *bildungsroman*.

The limitation of Oliphant's irony reveals itself also in the language that both heroine and narrator use: in the "principles" that motivate Lucilla's actions and the mock heroic with which Oliphant describes them. Lucilla's principles are either conventional Victorian sentiments or, paradoxically, little *bon mots* that seem to defy convention. On the one hand, Lucilla justifies her behavior by repeating conventional wisdom: "I have always been brought up to believe that duty is happiness" or "It is one of my principles never to laugh about anything that has to do with religion." On the other, Lucilla amuses her listeners by uttering what seem to be shocking sentiments: "It is one of my principles always to flirt in the middle of company" (119) or, to Mr. Cavendish, "I have always reckoned upon you as such a valuable assistant. It is always an advantage to have a man who flirts" (105) or, to her father, "I am not going to swindle you, after you have had the drawing room done up, and everything" (202).

The power of the "principles" is that they allow Lucilla independence of action under the cover of conventional behavior (after all, she worries very little about the *real* comfort of her father, who often escapes to his library during her "evenings"). Further, the *bon mots* give her social control under the cover of innocent wit (in fact, Lucilla knows quite well that flirtatious men add the sexual excitement necessary for a successful social gathering). But neither conventional sentiments nor ironic witticisms have power enough to alter Lucilla's predicament. Whether conventional or anticonventional, they never allow Lucilla to escape the framework of convention. Her language lacks the power to create new patterns of action. Irony allows her only to negate, not to construct.

And the same holds true for the figurative language Oliphant uses to describe Lucilla's actions. Like Thackeray's *Vanity Fair, Miss Marjoribanks* uses the mock heroic as a major linguistic and structural device. Lucilla's social plans are described as a "campaign"; "like other conquerors," she is "destined to build her victory upon sacrifice" (109); her enemies, "like the Tuscan chivalry in the ballad," can "scarce forbear a cheer at the sight of their opponent's prowess" (121-22); when she scores a victory over Barbara Lake, her "formerly triumphant rival," the narrator comments that "she drove her chariot over Barbara" (175); and so on throughout the novel. As a complement to such military language, the language of social politics is also employed. When Mr. Cavendish wishes to praise Lucilla's social "statesmanship," for instance, he says: "I think you ought to be Prime Minister" (111).

Margarete Rubik-Holubetz has argued that "the mock heroic tone lends" a "certain heroic grandeur" to Lucilla's actions—and, indeed, Lucilla *is* larger than life.[10] Despite the apparent praise of Lucilla's abilities, the mock-heroic language tends ultimately, I believe, to diminish feminine action in the social sphere. Lucilla is a superb strategist, with brains and poise enough to earn a place in Parliament. But the mock-heroic continually reminds us how serious real warfare is deemed in the world outside the novel and how trivial Lucilla's skirmishes seem by comparison. We have not escaped the social framework of *The Rape of the Lock,* where young girls may play at epic heroism—but only until it is time for them to assume the responsibilities of marriage and motherhood in the "real" world.

In the end Lucilla puts her play aside and assumes those "real" responsibilities. The novel thus acquiesces in the convention that marriage and family will be the means by which a woman finds her place in, and leaves her mark on, the world. But even as **Miss Marjoribanks** acquiesces, there is a hint of what lies ahead in other Oliphant novels. For, if Lucilla's actions take the form of mock heroic, so too do the actions of the male characters in the novel. Mr. Cavendish, after disgracing himself by flirting with Barbara Lake, must face something worse than "the Balaclava charge itself" (150); later, in preparing for his confrontation with Archdeacon Beverly, he dresses "like Nelson going into gala uniform for a battle" (289). So, too, General Travers, mistaking Rose Lake for Lucilla, begins "in the most cruel and uncomfortable way his campaign in Carlingford" (258). Even Tom and Mr. Ashburton are made into social warriors, called "rivals" in the same "field" (477). These descriptions of male behavior as mock heroic have the effect of diminishing, too, the "careers" of men in the "real" world. And such diminishment of male patterns will be a strategy Oliphant develops in the last *bildungsroman* of the Carlingford series.

II. *Phoebe, Junior: Counterpointing Male and Female Forms*

Like its predecessors in the Carlingford series, **Phoebe, Junior** traces the development—moral, psychological, intellectual, vocational—of young persons of both sexes, in this case counter-pointing assumptions of the male and female *bildungsroman.* Phoebe Beecham, the heroine of this second-generation novel, must find her way in the well-to-do society of London Dissenters, where finding one's way means, for her as for Miss Marjoribanks, finding the right husband through whom she can work her will on the world. A girl with brains,

style, and wit, Phoebe begins by doing her duty—not to her father, as Miss Marjoribanks had, but to her sickly grandmother, the now old, still buttery Mrs. Tozer. Doing her duty leads Phoebe from London to Carlingford and, once there, into encounters with two suitors. As in conventional domestic fiction, Phoebe must choose between the two men: between the sensitive, refined (and Anglican) Reginald May and the rougher, duller, richer (and Dissenting) Clarence Copperhead. Phoebe finally chooses Clarence, but not until she has been led to examine her moral positions on love, money, religion, social status, and the family.

The novel focuses, in other words, on Phoebe's self-development, and the major details of her plot reenact common features of the female *bildungsroman:* a domestic duty initiating the action, two lovers representing different sets of values, the "right" marital choice epitomizing the heroine's moral progress.[11] Many of the assumptions about female development are conventional, too: that domestic (not religious or intellectual) crises provide the testing grounds for women's development; that this development occurs inwardly, as women sort through their feelings about love and marriage; and, most Victorian of all, that women affect society not directly but through male agents, their husbands, brothers, or sons.

For all its traces of conventionality, however, **Phoebe, Junior** has a highly unconventional effect and moves beyond Oliphant's ironic vision in **Miss Marjoribanks**. Here Oliphant plays off plots and counterplots to challenge assumptions about the differences between male and female development. Within the experiences of Phoebe, Oliphant juxtaposes a romantic feminine plot against a more hardheaded feminist one to undermine the former. Further, she sets off her heroine's complex development against the more superficial plot of Clarence, Phoebe's lover, to challenge the presumed superiority of the masculine *bildung.*

Within the heroine's experience, for instance, the romantic plot associated with Reginald May is allowed to give Phoebe an erotic thrill, those "warmer" and "more delightful" feelings (268) that other Victorian novelists reveled in.[12] Oliphant's Phoebe has the sense to see where this plot will lead: to a domestic situation, not unlike the household of the elder Mr. May, where women are adored but subservient, where women feel but do not think, where women decorate but do not shape or lead. The novel hints early on that Reginald is a chip off the old block: "how like Reginald is to papa!" his sister declares when father and son battle over the sinecure. Phoebe comprehends the danger when Reginald talks about this sister's romance with Northcote; he speaks of it as something that "would never do," as if he, the masculine authority, has the power to decide female fates.

Knowing this, and knowing also the difficulties of marrying into an Anglican family, Phoebe relegates the romantic plot to the world of fantasy (which is where Oliphant suggests such plots belong). Sometimes Phoebe retreats there to enjoy it, "to expend a little tender regret and gratitude upon poor Reginald" (268). But she does not allow foolish romance to obstruct her progress in the real world. Rather, Phoebe chooses to marry Clarence—not because of his money (though she admits it is no small advantage), but because with him she will have the power to teach and to lead, intellectually and socially. Oliphant reverses, in other words, what Elaine Baruch has identified as a common pattern in the nineteenth-century *bildungsroman:* that of a woman's education through marriage to an older, wiser man.[13] As Phoebe reasons it, "He was not very wise, nor a man to be enthusiastic about, but he would be a career. . . . She did not think of it humbly like this, but with a big capital—a Career" (234). That Oliphant imagines Phoebe's marital choice as a Career—and the term recurs throughout the novel—suggests her intention to revise and recreate the novel of female vocation, with the exploration of marriage as its focus.

It suggests, too, that Oliphant means to ironize male and female versions of the form through her treatment of the hero's and heroine's plots. In Oliphant, there are few cases in which women are not smarter or wiser than men. No Emmas recognizing the superior virtues of Mr. Knightleys, not even an Elizabeth Bennet balancing the qualities of Mr. Darcy—in Oliphant's fiction, women hold most of the (intellectual) cards. Even beyond this reversal of conventional male and female abilities, **Phoebe, Junior** undermines the assumptions of the masculine *bildungsroman,* for Clarence Copperhead's "career" is a parody of that form.

In this novel all of the young characters are seeking their place in the world, and Clarence *should* undergo at least some of the conventional episodes of a novel of development. He should, in response to some repressive or hostile force, "attempt to learn the nature of the world, discover its meaning and pattern, and acquire a philosophy of life and 'the art of living.'"[14] But Clarence does nothing of the sort. He gets sent down from Oxford, then sent away to Carlingford to study with a tutor. There, in recurring scenes that emblematize his relation to Phoebe and the world around him, he spends his evenings fiddling, while Phoebe "accompanies" him:

> He was serenely happy, caressing his fiddle between his cheek and his shoulder, and raising his pale eyes to the ceiling in an ecstasy. The music, and the audience, and the accompanyist all together were delightful to him. He could have gone on, he felt, [*sic*] not only till midnight, but till morning, and so on to midnight again. (221)

Though these scenes are "the crown of Clarence Copperhead's content and conscious success" and though the formal arrangement of player and accompanist seems to put Clarence in control, Oliphant makes it clear that Phoebe directs the action. Phoebe helps Clarence through the difficult music, keeping "time with her head, and with her hand when she could take it from the piano, until she had triumphantly tided him over the bad passage, or they had come to the point of shipwreck again" (221-22). This reversal of masculine and feminine roles, with Phoebe directing and Clarence following her lead, holds in their lives as in their music. In the finale, the narrator reports the success of Phoebe's career, telling of the latest speech that she has composed for Clarence to read in Parliament (339).

Such role reversal might be dismissed as merely humorous, the satiric play of a female novelist who thought herself more competent than the men around her. But the novel repeats, more seriously, the counterpointing of male and female plots in the lives of Ursula and Reginald May. When Ursula and Reginald first appear, they seem to fit the stereotypes of a serious young clergyman facing a vocational crisis and a silly younger sister dreaming of romance. We find Ursula thinking of "the pretty dress" she wore to the Copperhead ball, while Reginald is described as "very clever," a young man "making his own way at the university by means of scholarships . . . and to hear him talk with his father about Greek poetry and philosophy was a very fine thing indeed" (30). Yet when Ursula and Reginald reappear at home, Oliphant redefines what a "serious" vocation might mean. Reginald, in a quandary about the chaplaincy he has been offered, sits "with a candle all to himself, at writing-table in the corner" (105). Ursula works at the center-table, darning the stockings that have piled up during her holiday in London. Masculine brain work seems more significant than mindless domestic drudgery. Yet, in the narrator's commentary, the relative value of the work is challenged:

> What Reginald was doing at the writing-table was probably a great deal less useful; but the girls respected his occupation as not one ever thought of respecting theirs, and carried on their conversation under their breath, not to interrupt him. (105)

The public valuing of masculine work, and undervaluing of feminine, is one of the novel's central concerns—not only in such explicit commentary, but also in the construction of this subplot.

The plots of **Phoebe, Junior** suggest that neither masculine nor feminine patterns of self-development are intrinsically "better." Though the two Mays's lives seem to take such different courses—with Reginald devoting himself to a serious vocation and Ursula merely marrying and becoming a footnote to Northcote's career—in fact the plot emphasizes similar causes and patterns of growth in both male and female characters. Both Mays are initially obstructed (or prodded) by their father, Reginald about the chaplaincy, Ursula about domestic management; both their lives change course dramatically when Northcote appears, Reginald's after Northcote's speech against sinecures, Ursula's after Northcote's kindness at dinner; and both find their vocations simply by doing the duty near at hand, Reginald as college chaplain, Ursula as housewife. It is true that, despite the parallels, Reginald's *bildung* receives greater recognition than Ursula's. In the finale, those characters with public careers, like Reginald and Northcote, get a full paragraph of wrap-up, while Ursula becomes only a detail in the story of Northcote's self-development.

But Phoebe gets full treatment in the finale, too, with her husband Clarence functioning only as a detail. By constructing the last chapter to focus on Reginald, Northcote, *and* Phoebe, Oliphant challenges the assumption that only the male *bildungsroman* can trace a pattern of achievement and growth. Phoebe's "Career" gets the equal treatment it deserves.

Oliphant is shrewd enough to realize, however, that in the world outside the one she constructs, Phoebe's experiences may not be recognized as a pattern of self-development and public achievement. After Phoebe announces her engagement to Clarence, and just as she wages moral battle with her grandfather over Mr. May's debt, the men begin to tell their version of Phoebe's story. "She's a good girl," Tozer tells Clarence, "you'll never regret it, sir. . . . She'll do you credit, however grand you may make her" (314). And Clarence, relishing the homage, talks about her as "a clever one," in approximately the same language he uses to describe his new mare that "the governor gave a cool hundred and fifty for" (316). Phoebe, the narrator reminds us, "had more brains than both of her interlocutors put together," but despite her superiority, she is "put down and silenced by the talk" (316). Whether or not a story is perceived as a *bildungsroman* depends, this passage suggests, on the narrator and the audience. A male narrator and male audience are unlikely to tell a woman's story as one of growth or achievement. The most Oliphant can do, in 1876, is construct her heroine's tale as if it did belong within that literary tradition. Beyond that, she can only show, through irony and parody, that our assumptions about male and female development (or lack thereof) depend on the narrative conventions that novelists choose.

*III. **Hester:** Testing the Masculine Heroine*

After working out the limitations of the female *bildungsroman* in the Carlingford series, Oliphant later experimented with what might be called a "masculine heroine"—the female protagonist who adopts masculine patterns of action. Thus in **Hester** (1883) Oliphant turns away from a *bildungsroman* that locates a woman's career within the domestic sphere and toward a masculine narrative that propels the heroine into the public realm. Hester, the heroine, never quite makes it into that realm. Like Lucilla Marjoribanks and Phoebe Beecham before her, she must remain a lady and "consent," as the narrator puts it, "to be bound by other people's rules, and to put her hand to nothing that was unbecoming" (77). The frustration that ensues from such consenting—especially if a girl has, like Hester, a capacity for business—preoccupies Oliphant for much of the novel. Yet despite her attack on social conventions that restrict women's actions, Oliphant seems unable (or unwilling) to devise a literary solution that would break with the traditional focus of the female *bildungsroman* and move her heroine into the world of work.

The novel begins as if it intends to create a new kind of heroine, Oliphant's version of the New Woman of the 1880s.[15] As background to the primary plot, chapters 1-6 contrast Hester's mother, a delicate, "unpractical" figure out of an early Victorian drawing room (6), with Hester's Aunt Catherine, a strong woman who inherits the paternal "genius for business" (20) and, in a financial panic, saves the Vernon bank. This contrast seems to establish Catherine Vernon as the role model for Hester. Early scenes show Hester helping schoolboys with their lessons, figuring out their sums, and wishing "Why was not she a man?" (82). More explicitly, various characters point out the parallels between her and her competent Aunt Catherine.

Despite the parallels, Hester does not take Catherine Vernon as her model but instead sets herself against her aunt. Oliphant makes the rationale for this opposition—and the motivation for much of the plot—the natural antipathy of two strong, like-minded women, both "very sure that her own way was the right one" (89).[16] The novel betrays, however, Oliphant's deep ambivalence about the strong female character she had created and her hesitation to make Catherine a role model for the female *bildungsroman*. Her hesitation hinges on Catherine's assumption of "masculine" patterns and the loss of "feminine" values that results.

Catherine Vernon's life represents a pattern of male success. Although she initially takes over the bank to prevent a crisis and later tells Hester that women should intervene only "to save the family" (76), in fact Catherine lives out the plot of a masculine *bildungsroman*. Deserted (or neglected) by the man she loves, she moves into the male world of work, then into a male version of public philanthropy, putting her name on streets, squares, almshouses, and other public buildings. That this is "masculine" achievement the narrator makes explicit: "The people spoke of her, as they sometimes do of a very popular man, by her Christian name" (20).

Catherine's achievement is masculine in a more subtle sense, moreover. It deals with power, power that originates in money and extends its grasp over the lives of other characters. That the male *bildungsroman* deals in money and power is no new insight—as Dickens registered in *Great Expectations*. What Oliphant seems to fear is the introduction of these terms into the female *bildungsroman*. Catherine is philanthropic, generous, even benevolent, but her knowledge of power seems to result in a loss of feminine virtues. Characters critical of her public achievements voice their criticism in terms of this loss. Mrs. Merridew notes that Catherine's business engagements have given her "an unfeminine turn of mind" (313). Hester interprets Catherine's manipulation of Edward as an unfortunate example of what happens when woman attains power: "Oh, how true it must be after all," she thinks, "the picture of the tyrannical, narrow despot, exacting, remorseless, descending to the lowest details, which a woman, when endued with irresponsible power, was understood to make" (303-304). Captain Morgan, a gentler and more subtle judge, discusses Catherine's loss in terms of "innocence."

In a speech to Hester about the importance of "soft, innocent creatures" like his wife and Mrs. John, the Captain articulates what I take to be Oliphant's fear:

> You are tempted to despise [them], you clever ones, but it is a great mistake. . . . It is such souls as these that keep the world steady. We should all tumble to pieces if the race was made up of people like Catherine Vernon and you. (93)

The danger of the masculine heroine, this passage implies, is that she threatens the extinction of the race—not simply because she remains single and produces no children, but because she fails to reproduce the values associated with the feminine: kindness, faithfulness, patience, forgiveness. A modern psychologist like Nancy Chodorow would call this "the reproduction of mothering." In *Hester* it is Mrs. Morgan who expresses these feminine values most concretely when she argues for a continuing relationship with her children and grandchildren, even though it means the end of "peace and quiet"; "I like to see the children come and go—one here, one there. One in need of your sympathy, another of your help, another . . . of your pardon" (169). Hers are selfless values, rooted in the woman's "relational" understanding of her place in the community.[17]

By presenting Catherine's plot as a possible model and then preventing Hester from following it fully, Oliphant is able to experiment with a mixture of masculine and feminine values. Catherine's values are predominately masculine: public achievement, family (paternal) name, self-respect. But, exposed to masculine knowledge, she loses feminine innocence and becomes "cynical," laughing at human foibles that a woman might better weep over or try to reform (184). This cynicism has devastating effects on Edward's life and, almost, on Hester's. Oliphant intends, I think, for Hester to witness the defects of Catherine's life but avoid its extremes, to balance masculine and feminine. And the novel succeeds in that it shows Hester gaining a masculine knowledge of the self and others, while maintaining certain feminine values associated with the family. (Hester can reason out, for example, the psychological motivations of male characters like Roland and Edward, but she is appalled when Captain Morgan uses reason to argue for breaking ties with his adult children.)

Despite this success, the narrative structure of *Hester* shows the strains of trying to coordinate elements of both the male and female *bildungsroman*. From the female *bildungsroman* Oliphant takes the main plot, the story of courtship and romance that puts forward Harry first, then Roland, then Edward as possible suitors. From the male *bildungsroman* Oliphant takes the subplot in which Hester searches for her paternal heritage; this quest for knowledge leads Hester to fall from innocence, just as "the guilty pair in Paradise, in the morning of the world, must have woke out of their sleep, and felt . . . the sense of ill" (462). Both plots come skillfully together as Hester discovers her father's perfidy and Edward's at the same moment. But neither plot nor subplot takes Hester very far toward resolving the dilemma of her life: what to do with herself. The romance plot seems repetitive and inconclusive, first with its multiple chapters (10-16) giving various characters' speculations on Harry's proposal, then with similar treatments of Roland and Edward. In the subplot, Edward is quite right (in this, if in nothing else) to ridicule Hester for not knowing her father's history; surely chapter 39 is too late for an intelligent heroine to discover what everyone else has known all along.

Beyond difficulties with plot and subplot, however, the novel never resolves whether Hester—or her real-world counterparts—should follow a masculine or feminine pattern in the future. In the final chapter, having discovered the faithlessness of man, Hester insists, "I will never marry" (493) and asks Catherine to train her in the business. This decision seems sensible, given Hester's experiences and abilities. Yet Catherine insists that Hester should marry and thus forget Edward, and the novel concludes by noting "that there are two men whom she may choose between, and marry either if she pleases. . . . What can a young woman desire more than to have such a possibility of choice?" (495). What more indeed! A great deal more, the novel has implied. But Oliphant seems to have abandoned these implications, unable to imagine closure without marriage. Perhaps she felt neither satisfied with the traditional feminine plot of marriage and motherhood, nor comfortable with the masculine pattern of quest and self-fulfillment, and so ended in the only way possible—with a question.

IV. *Kirsteen: Appropriating the Male Bildungsroman*

In *Kirsteen,* Oliphant explores less ambivalently the implications of a female heroine following male life patterns—almost as if, in the decade of the 1880s, she had imagined a way to reconcile the masculine and feminine opposition that had stymied her in *Hester*. The primary plot of *Kirsteen* is, with slight variations, the plot of a male *bildungsroman*. A spirited young Scotswoman, Kirsteen leaves her Highland home to escape a marriage and future life she dreads; she flees to London to make her name and fortune. Once in the metropolis she learns the dressmaker's trade; raises the business she has entered to a flourishing, fashionable establishment; and returns to her family as its "standby" and, in economic terms, its most successful member. The novel reenacts, in other words, a classic Victorian tale of self-help: of country to city, rags to riches, obscurity to fame, insignificance to public importance (though with a variation on the heroine's status, which is aristocratic—Kirsteen is the daughter of a Highland laird—rather than middle or working class).

That Oliphant means to invoke masculine patterns of self-development and social achievement is evident from Kirsteen's articulate statement of her plans for life in London. When she explains that she has come "not to see the world, but to make my fortune," her mentor Miss Jean expresses dismay:

> That's all very well in a lad,—and there's just quantities of them goes into the city without a penny and comes out like nabobs in their carriages—but not women, my dear, let along young lassies like you. (157)

Kirsteen proves that anything lads can do lassies can do better. She not only makes her fortune but also rebuilds the family estate that her forefathers lost and her brothers have failed to buy back. This plot of female competence versus male impotence continues Oliphant's strategy of depicting strong women and thus countering fictional conventions. As with *Hester,* it may also represent Oliphant's response to the "New Woman" novel of the '80s and '90s, which featured highly competent women with (in Oliphant's view) highly undesirable sexual conduct. Oliphant creates a heroine who is competent but utterly pure.

While making Kirsteen a masculine heroine, Oliphant exposes the limitations of the conventional feminine

bildungsroman to an extent unparalleled in *Hester*. The opening chapter of *Kirsteen* presents two images of Victorian womanhood: Mrs. Douglas, Kirsteen's mother, a powerless feminine figure reduced to silence and tears; and Marg'ret, the old servant, powerful but single and virtually sexless. (We were never ones "that had much to do with the men" (157), Miss Jean says of herself and her sister Marg'ret.) These older women represent the limited possibilities for Kirsteen: marriage or spinsterhood, social position with the burdens of being a wife or personal freedom without the benefits of being a mother. Both are more extreme than the contrasting women in *Hester*. Neither appeals fully to the reader, who sees Kirsteen falling in love and, perhaps, into the trap of romance that leads to the bonds of marriage.

Subsequently, the novel develops even more images of womanhood that become warnings to Kirsteen of how effectively feminine life patterns can subdue a strong woman. Kirsteen's elder sister Anne, initially a rebel against her father's will, reappears happy in Glasgow with her husband and bairns; in an emergency, however, Anne cannot rouse herself to face the darkness of a Highland night or the danger of her father's wrath. Another sister Mary hopes, as her name hints, to marry the elderly suitor Kirsteen has refused, primarily for the wealth and social position he offers. As in Jane Austen's novels, such minor female figures represent paths the heroine must avoid. Kirsteen shows contempt for both. When Mary weds Glendochart, Kirsteen mentally echoes her father's contempt for a girl who would take her sister's "leavings." When Anne trembles, Kirsteen thinks:

> Was this the effect of marrying and being happy as people say? The little plump mother with her rosy face no longer capable of responding to any call outside her own circle of existence, the babies delving with their spoons into the porridge, covering their faces and pinafores, or holding up little gaping mouths to be fed. It had been a delightful picture which she had come in upon before at an earlier stage . . . but now it was sweet no longer. The prosaic interior, the bondage of all these little necessities, the loosening of all other bonds of older date or wider reach, was this what happiness meant? (254)

The criticism of marriage and motherhood is more probing here than in earlier Oliphant novels—and it is particularly startling given Oliphant's lifelong criticism of books that depicted motherhood as anything less than "sacred."

In 1863 Oliphant had criticized Anne Thackeray Ritchie's novel, *The Story of Elizabeth,* for its depiction of a mother-daughter rivalry in romance, a subject she considered wholly unsuitable for fiction.[18] In 1877 she had chastised Harriet Martineau for publishing an "unfavorable estimate" of her mother in the *Autobiography:* "When it [autobiography] leads to the desecration of the home, and the holding up of the chief figure in it to deliberate blame and insult, what can anyone say?"[19] Yet the dual depiction of Ann—first as a happy mother surrounded by cherubic faces, then as a quailing female afraid to leave the safety of hearth and home—shows that Oliphant could recognize the hellish bondage that even a "sacred" role might impose. If Kirsteen remains respectful of her mother, even more so than Hester does of Mrs. John, the novel's representation of marriage and motherhood make it impossible that *Kirsteen* should end with Hester's choice of "two good men."

The burden of *Kirsteen,* however, is not simply to prove that marriage constrains women (a point many a Victorian novel had made before), but more radically that marriage limits self-development—that it is essentially alien to the concept of *bildung*. That the female *bildungsroman* must abandon its obsession with marriage as the focus of its plot—whether marriage as a reward for the heroine's development or marriage as the site of the heroine's growth—is the insight that Oliphant reaches in this late work. *Kirsteen* thus challenges the tradition of Bronte, Gaskell, and Eliot in which Jane Eyre wins Rochester, Margaret Hale wins Thornton, and Dorothea Brooke wins Will Ladislaw—all after suitable bouts with the "wrong" man. Expecting the heroine to discover the "right" man and grow in the process is, to mix metaphors, barking up the wrong tree. In *Kirsteen* growth is dissociated from marriage, self-development occurs in the public realm, not in the domestic.

Despite this challenge to the dominant tradition of the female *bildungsroman,* Oliphant finds it difficult to give up the romantic plot. The novel begins as a romantic tale, when Ronald Drummond asks Kirsteen, "Will ye wait for me till I come back?" and she answers, "That I will" (17). It is true that Oliphant quickly sets this plot aside as she sends Ronald off to India and Kirsteen to London—just as, in *Great Expectations,* Dickens sends Estella off to France so that Pip can proceed with his intellectual and moral development in London. It is also true that Kirsteen must face the limitations of the romantic plot she initiates—just as Pip, in *Great Expectations,* must learn the limitations of the fairy tales he projects for himself. Yet the romantic plot retains a centrality in *Kirsteen* that it lacks in *Great Expectations* or other male *bildungsromane.*

This centrality is emblematized by the testament and the bloodstained handkerchief that Kirsteen enshrines in "a little silver casket" as "her sacred things." We are told that "the silver casket stood in Kirsteen's room during her whole life within reach of her hand"

(241). The testament and handkerchief—in effect, a book and an art object containing the record of romantic love—represent the feminine tale that can no longer be told. We might assume that Oliphant here recognizes the death of the traditional heroine's life-pattern. Yet these romantic emblems are also the basis of—perhaps even the source of—the masculine plot that Kirsteen assumes. With them succouring her in private, she can go forth into the public realm. With "no one to object any more than to praise," she is "independent" (241), free to pursue her career as an "artist"—which she does with a passion.

"Thus life was over for Kirsteen; and life began," Oliphant writes (241), as if to suggest that the two plots—the "old" feminine plot of romance, the "new" masculine plot of public achievement—are intertwined. By linking the two plots, she is, I suggest, both indulging in personal sentiment and anticipating a development in modern psychology. Personally, Oliphant had a predilection for secret romances kept well hidden from public view. In an 1870 review essay, **"Miss Austen and Miss Mitford,"** she wondered at the absence of romance in the lives of these two prominent authors:

> Had they been married women whose romance ended naturally in the commonplace way, the omission would have been less noteworthy; but there is a charm in the love which has never come to anything—the tender, pathetic, sweet recollection laid up in a virgin life, amid the faded rose-leaves and fallen flowers of youth—which is infinitely sweet and touching,—more touching than the successful and prosperous can ever be.[20]

Oliphant sentimentally gives Kirsteen that "tender, pathetic, sweet recollection" as the inspiration for her "career." The reader thus sees her as romantic heroine and New Woman both. After Ronald's death, Kirsteen "t[akes] up her work with fresh vigour" (241) and creates genuinely artistic fashions.

Psychologically, Kirsteen's approach to her 'career' anticipates the analyses of modern theorists like Chodorow, who note that women define their identity "relationally" (i.e., in relation to other people, especially family members) rather than "positionally" as men do (i.e., according to the status they have achieved in the world).[21] Kirsteen's initial motive for working in London emphasizes family contribution; she imagines providing for her mother, making Jeanie an heiress, "'Oh, that I may make my fortune and help them all,' was the real petition of her heart" (158-59). After Ronald's death, this sense of contribution is even stronger, as her mother calls on her to be the "standby" of the family and her father asks that she buy back a portion of their ancient estate.

Oliphant's insight into female development is more than psychological. It is also narrative. It shapes the plot of *Kirsteen,* as it was unable to do in *Hester.* Technically, Kirsteen's *bildung* ends with chapter 33, with the death of Ronald Drummond, her success in the professional realm, and her acceptance of a life different from the one she had planned. Yet the novel continues for another thirteen chapters, narrating the death of Mrs. Douglas and the romance of Kirsteen's younger sister Jeanie. These addenda are significant because they show Kirsteen's personal growth spreading its influence in communal service—a modification of the traditional closure in the female *bildungsroman,* where marriage signifies the heroine's successful (re)integration into the community. Here, family service signals that (re)integration.

> Her Carlingford novels parody the
> traditions of male and female
> *bildungsromane* alike, thus
> challenging values sacred to the
> Victorian ideology of separate spheres
> and testing the limits of the
> feminine.
>
> —*Linda Peterson*

Nonetheless, the reintroduction of Jeanie and the romance plot, the traditional site of female self-development, has seemed to many readers regressive, given what Oliphant has already accomplished within Kirsteen's.[22] The reintroduction of the romance plot occurs, perhaps, because Oliphant remained ambivalent about women's appropriation of masculine life-patterns. On the one hand, we see the personal and familial gain that results from Kirsteen's "masculine" career; on the other, we sense the emotional loss, and through Jeanie's plot, the unsuitability of Kirsteen's actions for all women. Thus *Kirsteen* ends with the same ambivalence we found in *Hester,* though with a more positive view of the "masculine heroine."

That an individual woman can—and has the right to—model her life on the male *bildungsroman,* the novel asserts without apology. That her version of her life-story will be comprehended, let alone accepted by others, the novel ruefully disclaims. The final chapter makes it clear that Kirsteen's story will not be read by all as a successful *bildungsroman.* Her eldest brother, who has profited by her fortune, expresses his shock at having "a London mantuamaker" for a sister, "sewing for her bread." Other characters simply interpret her experiences as a failed feminine plot, "deplor[ing] the miserable way of life she had chosen, and that she had no man" (341).

With *Kirsteen* Oliphant completes the exploration of a genre that occupied her attention from the 1860s through 1890s. Though she is often considered conservative on social issues involving women, in her fiction she was genuinely revisionary. Her Carlingford novels parody the traditions of male and female *bildungsromane* alike, thus challenging values sacred to the Victorian ideology of separate spheres and testing the limits of the feminine. In *Hester* and *Kirsteen* she is more directly subversive. Not only does she abandon a feminine tradition that makes marriage the crux of women's self-development, but she also appropriates male forms of action for her heroines and, simultaneously, anticipates a fictional tradition that will define the female self relationally, as part of a community of women rather than as an entity separate and distinct from the world.[23] If her *bildungsromane* were not canonized, as were novels like *Jane Eyre* and *The Mill on the Floss,* it may not be just that Oliphant wrote too many, too quickly. It may also be that she refused to do the cultural work of Victorian patriarchy by keeping love and marriage at the center of fictions of female development.

Notes

[1] Elizabeth Abel, Marianne Hirsch, and Elizabeth Langland summarize these critical discussions in their introduction to *The Voyage In: Fictions of Female Development* (Hanover, New Hampshire: University Press of New England, 1983) 3-14, though they take issue with overly sharp distinctions between male and female forms of the *bildungsroman.* They argue— correctly, I believe—that women writers have also developed an "apprenticeship" tradition that intersects in many significant ways with the male tradition, and their argument is implicitly supported by Rita Felski's discussion of national differences in "The Novel of Self-Discovery: A Necessary Fiction?" *Southern Review* 19 (1986) 131-48, and Annis Pratt's *Archetypal Patterns in Women's Fiction* (Bloomington: Indiana University Press, 1981). The standard history of the English *bildungsroman,* on which many subsequent discussions have been based, is Jerome Hamilton Buckley's *Season of Youth: The Bildungsroman from Dickens to Golding* (Cambridge: Harvard University Press, 1974); Buckley defines the form simply as a "novel of youth or apprenticeship" and, except in his treatment of *The Mill on the Floss,* does not concern himself with gender.

[2] See Elaine Hoffman Baruch's discussion of this feature in "The Feminine *Bildungsroman:* Education through Marriage," *Massachusetts Review* 22 (1981) 335-37, which treats late-eighteenth through early twentieth-century English and European novels.

[3] "The Novel of Awakening," in Abel, Hirsch, and Landland, eds., p. 49; originally published in *Genre* 12

(1979) 313-32. For a similar view of the European female *bildungsroman,* which emphasizes "awakening" and "autonomy" rather than "social integration," see Elaine Martin, "Theoretical Soundings: The Female Archetypal Quest in Contemporary French and German Women's Fiction," *Perspectives on Contemporary Literature* 8 (1983) 48-57.

⁴ "The Comfort of Civilization," *Representations* 12 (1985) 115-16; this essay became the introduction to *The Way of the World: The Bildungsroman in European Culture* (London: Verso, 1987).

⁵ Throughout I use "male" and "female" to refer to the sex of the author or protagonist, "masculine" and "feminine" to refer to attributes or attitudes culturally associated with men and women. Although these distinctions are modern ones, I believe Oliphant's fiction and literary criticism show her to be sensitive to the associations of certain genres or modes with women and the 'feminine,' and thus to anticipate modern discussions of gender and genre.

⁶ [Robert and Vineta Colby, *The Equivocal Virtue: Margaret Oliphant and the Victorian Literary Marketplace.* Hamden: Conn., Archon, 1966], 65-66, point out that much of Lucilla's behavior derives from *Friends in Council,* which the headmistriss of Lucilla's school gives as a prize to superior students.

⁷ Colby, 65.

⁸ "Novels," *Blackwood's Edinburgh Magazine* 102 (1867) 259.

⁹ Felski, p. 335.

¹⁰ "The Triumph of the Gifted Woman: The Comic Manipulation of Cliche in Mrs. Oliphant's *Miss Majoribanks* [sic]," *Zesszyty Naukowe Uniwersytetu Jagiellonskirco* 51 (1981) 45.

¹¹ Merryn Williams. *Margaret Oliphant: A Critical Biography.* New York: St. Martin's, 1986, 85-86, criticizes *Phoebe, Junior* for its lack of a "central theme." Though the notion of "theme" can be misleading, I believe the novel does in fact pursue the theme of moral and vocational development quite consistently.

¹² Oliphant's dislike of heroines who, like Bronte's Shirley, passionately bewail their, plight or novelists who, like Mary Elizabeth Braddon, revel in the erotic adventures of their heroines is evident from her literary reviews. See, for example, "Novels," 257-80.

¹³ Baruch, 335-39.

¹⁴ C. Hugh Holman, *A Handbook to Literature,* 3d. ed. (New York: Odyssey Press, 1972) s.v. bildungsroman.

One might argue that Clarence does learn "the nature of the world" and acquire "a philosophy of life" in that he discovers his limitations and learns that he is better off with Phoebe directing his life for him. But this self-knowledge only parodies what is expected in the male *bildungsroman.*

¹⁵ Discussion of the "New Woman" novels of the 1880s and 1890s tends to stress Oliphant's antagonism, especially her attack on Hardy's *Tess of the d'Urbervilles* and *Jude the Obscure* in reviews for *Blackwood's* (see Gail Cunningham, *The New Woman and the Victorian Novel* [London: Macmillan, 1978] 45-50, 115-117, and Lloyd Fernando, *"New Women" in the Late Victorian Novel* [University Park: Pennsylvania State University Press, 1977] 141-46). Despite her dislike of the New Woman's sexual attitudes, Oliphant was sympathetic—as Uglow points out in her edition of *Hester,* xiii-xiv—to the New Woman's desire for "real work" and for an end to being "undervalued by men."

¹⁶ Some critics believe that, when this antipathy is overcome in the final scenes, Oliphant signals her approval of Catherine as "the embodiment of strength for the future"; according to Uglow, Catherine points the way to a "new breed of 'odd women,' the solitary heroines of the 1890s" (xxi). While Catherine does anticipate certain features of the New Woman, Oliphant remained ambivalent, I believe, about the combination of strengths *and* weaknesses that this new heroine embodied. Hester is rather the inheritor of two female traditions, the female represented by Mrs. John and the feminist embodied in Catherine.

¹⁷ See Nancy Chodorow, *The Reproduction of Mothering: Psychoanalysis and the Sociology of Gender* (Berkeley: University of California Press, 1978) 126-27, 179, passim.

¹⁸ See "Novels," *Blackwood's Edinburgh Magazine* 94 (1863) 173-74. The novel was published anonymously; hence Oliphant may not have known the identity of its author when she wrote the review.

¹⁹ See "Harriet Martineau," *Blackwood's Edinburgh Magazine* 121 (1877) 476.

²⁰ "Miss Austen and Miss Mitford," *Blackwood's Edinburgh Magazine* 107 (1870) 298.

²¹ Chodorow, 126-27, 169 ff.

²² I base this statement about readers' response on the comments of participants in an NEH Institute, "The Victorian Age," held at Yale University, July 1988. I wish to thank various participants in this and the 1991 NEH Institute for their assistance with my work on *Miss Marjoribanks* and *Kirsteen.*

[23] For a discussion of this tradition, see Nina Auerbach's *Communities of Women: An Idea in Fiction* (Cambridge: Harvard University Press, 1978) that, unfortunately, excludes Oliphant.

Merryn Williams (essay date 1995)

SOURCE: "Feminist or Antifeminist? Oliphant and the Woman Question," in *Margaret Oliphant: Critical Essays on a Gentle Subversive,* edited by D. J. Trela, Associated University Presses, 1995, pp. 165-79.

[*In the essay below, Williams explores Oliphant's views on the women's movement of the mid-1860s, finding the author "a complex figure, typecast as antifeminist, yet concerned throughout her life with the problems of women."*]

On 16 August 1866 Margaret Oliphant wrote to her publisher John Blackwood:

> I send you a little paper I have just finished about Stuart Mill and his mad notion of the franchise for women. . . . Probably you will find it too respectful to Mr Mill, but I can't for my part find any satisfaction in simply jeering at a man who may do a foolish thing in his life but yet is a great philosopher. (*A&L* 211)

This has often been used against her by people who have read neither the article nor much else she wrote. Until quite recently, when her novels began to come into print again, most knowledge of her was based on the *Autobiography and Letters* from which this quotation is taken. The "fact" that she thought women's suffrage a "mad notion" has passed into literary history, and she has not been admired by feminist critics, one of whom, Patricia Stubbs, writes:

> The superficially emancipated heroines of novelists like . . . Mrs Oliphant . . . remain well within the limits of moral and social convention. Their independent-minded young ladies have shed the fragility and insipidity so admired by Wilkie Collins, but they are in no way a serious challenge to patriarchal stereotypes of feminine character or behaviour. . . . She maintained a consistently conservative attitude towards the emancipation movement.[1]

The truth is, though, that her views were neither conservative nor, over a career of nearly fifty years, consistent. "I suppose the ideas of the time do get into one's head," she wrote privately in 1895, "however much one may disapprove of them."[2]

The *Autobiography and Letters,* published in 1899 and reprinted without corrections four times, most recently in 1974 and 1988, is a flawed text. The Colbys and I discovered this in research on our respective biographies. As Elisabeth Jay noted in preparing her recently published scholarly edition, several passages in Oliphant's record of her life were struck out by the original editor, her cousin Annie Coghill. Mrs. Coghill was basically a stupid woman who presented the novelist as much more conformist than she really was. Out of thousands of letters she selected only a few, and these not always interesting or representative. The antisuffrage letter of 1866 went in, but not one of ten years later that shows that her views had changed. It refers to a story, "The Lady Candidate," which had been appearing in *Blackwood's* and that made fun of the suffragists: "This sort of glib nonsense has by degrees brought me round to the conviction that however indifferent I may be personally to political privileges the system which supposes me incapable of forming a reasonable opinion on public matters is very far from a perfect one."[3]

If we read more letters and articles, and especially her novels, a more complex picture emerges. Oliphant was not reactionary; she had much to say about the condition of women in her time. Yet it would be a mistake to typecast her as a forerunner of present-day Women's Liberationists.

"The woman question" was debated with great intensity during the second half of the nineteenth century. Briefly, in the years while Oliphant was growing up, women had no votes and few rights. Their education was poor (except in her birthplace Scotland); the professions were closed to them; married women could not own property or claim custody of children. It was almost impossible to leave a bad husband or father. A double standard of morality existed. Women were trained to think that their aim in life was to get a husband, and be despised if they did not.

Several things changed in her lifetime. The Infants' Custody and Married Women's Property Acts passed; some women got the municipal vote and others succeeded in becoming doctors; good schools for girls opened as did women's colleges at Oxford and Cambridge. The demand for the vote, which would not succeed until after World War I, was heard more often in respectable circles. The "women's movement" became a real force.

Yet not all women were struggling against the system. If we look only at novelists, who had greater opportunities than most of their sex to speak their minds, we find Charlotte Yonge declaring her "full belief in the inferiority of woman,"[4] Charlotte Bronte and George Eliot refusing to identify with the suffrage movement, and Mrs. Humphrey Ward and Eliza Lynn Linton signing the well-known "Appeal Against Female Suffrage" of 1889. This last group believed women should be educated, and should be encouraged to be responsible citizens, but were not competent to risk their lives in war or be politically active.

Oliphant took an interest in women's issues from an early stage—indeed, before most English people could have heard of it. Writing in *Merkland* (1850), only two years after the Women's Rights Association was founded in the United States, the twenty-two year old author made her heroine say: "We are one-half the world—we have our work to do, like the other half—let us do our work as honourably and wisely as we can, but for pity's sake, do not let us make this mighty bustle and noise about it . . . no one gains respect by claiming it" (2:40).

The three articles that she wrote on this subject for *Blackwood's* during the 1850s and 1860s are all critical of the women's movement, although she made it clear that she did not want to defend injustice or thwart anyone's aspirations. "This idea, that the two portions of humankind are natural antagonists to each other, is, to our thinking . . . a monstrous and unnatural idea."[5] Yet only a few pages later she refers ironically to the cherished belief that men had better brains. "Let us not enter upon the tender question of mental inferiority. Every individual woman, we presume, is perfectly easy on her own account that she at least is not remarkably behind her masculine companions."[6]

Her best-known statement is **"The Great Unrepresented,"** the 1866 article in which she took issue with Mill. He had presented a petition to Parliament, signed by several eminent women, which demanded the vote for female householders, "lone women who pay their own rent and taxes,"[7] like Margaret herself. She admitted that this was logical, but claimed that ordinary women did not want the vote and felt rather insulted when it was thrust at them. Indeed, she was somewhat critical of the "exceptional women" who had proved that they could do good work in "masculine" spheres. "By chance now and then a woman may be found who is capable of any or all these things; but if she gives up her own existence to it, then God's purpose is defeated in her . . . and she is of no more use than if she were a man."[8]

There is some ironic ambiguity in this last clause, as there is in the letter to her publisher that acknowledged that Mill was a great thinker. However, she concluded:

> Twenty literary and other exceptional women in London may speak for a hundred or two more of their like, scattered over the kingdom; but we speak for the mass, which is not exceptional, which writes no books, and paints no pictures, and wants no votes. . . . We decline Mr Mill's proposal totally, and without equivocation.[9]

This article appeared anonymously; if her readers had known that she was a literary woman who had written thirty books they might have thought the article a piece of breathtaking hypocrisy. Yet she was often diffident about her talent and level of achievement, noting in one letter that she was "a poor soul who is concerned about nothing except the most domestic and limited concerns."[10]

The tension between her role as a self-supporting writer, and what she felt to be her more important role as the mother of a family continued. Three years later we find her again writing about Mill, in a review of his *Subjection of Women*. Here, although she does not accept his picture of one sex cruelly oppressing the other, she does agree with many of the reforms he suggests. She concedes that if female householders really want the vote, they should have it. She says that the marriage law conveys "a stinging sense of humiliation and insult," and that while the average wife is not mistreated, a Married Women's Property Act is necessary to prevent a husband taking "the bread out of her mouth and the children out of her arms."[11] She now believed that women were quite capable of doing men's work, and was especially sympathetic to the campaign for women doctors.

Yet she doubted whether, in the end, changes in the law would make much difference. Women who chose to be celibate might indeed compete on equal terms with men, but she pointed out that no man was asked to make that kind of sacrifice. Those who married and had children would always fall behind their male contemporaries.

> This is the inevitable course, known only too well to every woman who has endeavoured to combine professional exertions with the ordinary duties of a man's wife. . . . Her children born amid these cares, and injured before their birth by the undue activity of brain which weakens their mother's physical powers, come into the world feeble or die in her arms, quenching out her courage in the bitterest waves of personal suffering. This is no fancy picture.[12]

So far as she was concerned, it certainly was not. During her marriage when she was writing continuously, two of her babies died of heart problems, which she believed were "connected with too much mental work" (*A* 40).

The Minister's Wife (1869), a minor but interesting novel, sheds more light on her attitudes. She did not wish, like some feminists, to be liberated from children; on the contrary, she said that the ordinary woman found, in looking after her baby, "a delight more exquisite than can be given her by all the arts and all the pleasures of the world" (3:41). The heroine becomes deeply disillusioned with her husband, who does not believe in her love for her child and expects her to think only of him:

> What he exacted was that she should have no rights, no independence of action, but should flatter him into granting all her desires . . . making herself sweet for his eyes, and submissive for his pleasure, looking up to him with anxious desire to please him, with wistful waiting upon his looks, as a slave to a Sultan. . . . Was this what she was reduced to? (3:238-39)

This women ends up, like Margaret herself, with a child but no husband. In her **Autobiography,** recalling her own seven years' marriage that had been faithful and affectionate, but perhaps not really happy, she wrote that "the love between men and women, the marrying and giving in marriage, occupy in fact so small a portion of either existence or thought" (*A* 10). Claims such as these make all the more extraordinary Patricia Stubbs's observation that "In [Oliphant's] novels the relationship between hero and heroine adheres strictly to the conventions which impose dominance on the man and submission on the woman."[13] For, as other critics have noted, Oliphant's work is full of strong, responsible women and men good for very little. We see this pattern clearly in the two best of the Carlingford novels, **The Doctor's Family** and **Miss Marjoribanks,** which were written not long before her critique of Mill.

The "hero" of **The Doctor's Family** is a weak and selfish man (whose brother is an alcoholic and dead weight), who is outclassed by the tough young heroine, Nettie. Although she marries him in the end, she is aware that she will have to make allowances:

> Nettie looked at him with a certain careless scorn of the inferior creature—"Ah, yes, I daresay, but then you are only a man," said Nettie. (116)

Patricia Stubbs has read **Miss Marjoribanks** but does not seem to have grasped its point. Here again the heroine is superior to the men she meets, most of whom are frightened by her and prefer more conventional women. When she eventually marries her kind, but not very intelligent cousin Tom, she has no intention of retreating into domesticity because "I have always been doing something, and responsible for something, all my life" (484). Yet Stubbs asserts that "Ultimately the novel still implies that the proper place for a talented young woman is in queening it over the dinner or tea table and in gracefully dispensing charity to the agricultural poor. There is no suggestion that Lucilla is in any way wasted, or that she could become bored or frustrated with the social whirl."[14] This really is perverse. Although the novel is a comedy, the author makes the serious point that no talented young woman can go on amusing herself with dinner parties forever:

> she had come to an age at which she might have gone into Parliament herself had there been no disqualification of sex, and when it was almost a necessity for her to make some use of her social influence. . . . When a woman has an active mind, and still does not care for parish work, it is a little hard for her to find a "sphere." And Lucilla, though she said nothing about a sphere, was still more or less in that condition of mind which has been so often and so fully described to the British public—when the ripe female intelligence, not having the natural resource of a nursery and a husband to manage, turns inwards, and begins to "make a protest" against the existing order of society, and to call the world to account for giving it no due occupation—and to consume itself. . . . Lucilla had become conscious that her capabilities were greater than her work. (394-95)

It is clear from this and other passages that Oliphant was well aware of the raging argument about the "woman question." Lucilla *is* wasted; there can be no question of her going into Parliament, nor will she be allowed to take over her father's medical practice as a young man could do:

> But somehow it struck the Doctor more than ever how great a loss it was to society and to herself that Lucilla was not "the boy." She could have continued, and perhaps extended, the practice, whereas just now it was quite possible that she might drop down into worsted-work and tea-parties like any other single woman. (400)

At the same time, her cousin Tom is not half so gifted. Life for a spinster without money seems likely to be "limited and unsatisfactory" (435). The other single woman in the book, the artist Rose who has given up her cherished career, suggests that Lucilla found a House of Mercy, and although this is inappropriate Lucilla has "no intention of sinking into a nobody, and giving up all power of acting upon her fellow-creatures" (435). Marriage, children, active philanthropic work, and thorough management of her husband's career offer her by far the best chance of a happy and useful life, as Linda Peterson discusses in her essay.

Although she ended most of her novels with a marriage, Oliphant herself never remarried. For most of her adult life she saw herself primarily as a mother, and noted rather sadly in **Madonna Mary** (1866) that she had little to look forward to:

> The boys *must* go away and would probably marry . . . and the mother who had given up the best part of her life to them *must* remain alone . . . her occupation over, her personal history at an end. (2:184)

She identified with older women, and noted men's scornful attitude to them. (An original objection of hers to early feminists was that they exposed other women to ridicule.) While she insisted she did not regard men as the enemy, and that most of them meant well, she bitterly resented the "ungenerous sentiment" of men toward women, and "the strong sense of superiority which exists in the male bosom from the age of two upwards."[15] These words are from the most overtly feminist piece of nonfiction she wrote, **"The Grievances of Women,"** which appeared in 1880. There is a strong undertow of deep personal feeling here. She did not go to feminist meetings, she said, but

> We are so weak as to be offended deeply and wounded by the ridicule which has not yet ceased to be poured upon every such manifestation. We shrink from the laugh of rude friends, the smile of the gentler ones. . . . Fair and honourable criticism is a thing which no accustomed writer will shrink from . . . but to be met with an insolent laugh, a storm of ridiculous epithets, and that coarse superiority of sex which a great many men think it not unbecoming to exhibit to women is a mode of treatment which affects our temper.[16]

She stated that widows like herself who brought up families and paid taxes, ought to be allowed a vote, and that women who wished to enter the professions were entitled to do so. But she felt that the real grievance was men's basic attitude, which was beyond the reach of legislation.

> Whatever women do, in the general, is undervalued by men in the general, because it is done by women. How this impairs the comfort of women, how it shakes the authority of mothers, injures the self-respect of wives, and gives a general soreness of feeling everywhere, I will not attempt to tell.[17]

That "soreness of feeling" is evident in many apparently casual remarks scattered through her novels and other works. It comes out in her comment on Mary Wollstonecraft, that the demand for women's rights has "risen almost invariably from women compelled by hard stress of circumstances to despise the men about them"; in **Within the Precincts,** where the heroine's male relatives want to make money from her singing; in her comment to Principal Tulloch who had been suffering from depression and was unable to work that she would have no wife to look after her if she became ill.[18] Yet one reason she kept away from reform movements was that she did not believe they would achieve anything.

> I admit for my part the superiority of sex. It is not a pretty subject, nor one for my handling. Yet it is a fact. As belonging to the physical part of our nature, which is universal—whereas the mental and moral part is not so—that superiority must always tell. It will keep women in subjection as long as the race endures.[19]

This is the main conclusion of **"The Grievances of Women,"** and it is this essentially tragic view that colors her great novels of the 1880s.

Even these works contain uninteresting young couples who have no problems, who are only there to pad the story or provide the happy endings that Victorians liked. Indeed, Oliphant had written, "I believe nothing can be more certain than the large predominance of happiness over unhappiness in married life."[20] Yet it is the tragic or imperfect marriages that she describes with most conviction.

The Ladies Lindores (1883) gives a haunting picture of marriage based on mental cruelty. It is a novel about male domination. Lady Caroline (a natural victim, who will rush into another unsuitable marriage at the end of the book) is compelled by her father to marry the rich but boorish Pat Torrance. Both are excellent character studies. He is a brutal man who sees her as his "proudest and finest possession" (2:188) and a "servant whom he need not fear bullying" (1:182); she an overrefined woman whose nerves are worn to shreds by his "rude fury, and ruder affection." She has "nothing but a little discussion about Wordsworth or Shelley to stand in place of happiness to her heart" (2:144). Yet it is noted other women would marry him because he is "such a cluster of worldly advantages" (1:91). Her sister believes that she should leave him rather than submit to what is virtually rape, but she will never have the strength to take such an unconventional step. She prefers to think of herself as a martyr to "duty." Yet when her husband is killed, she feels no sympathy, but cries out in a powerful and disturbing scene:

> To think I shall never be subject to all *that* anymore—that he can never come in here again— that I am free—that I can be alone. Oh, mother, how can you tell what it is? Never to be alone: never to have a corner in the world where—some one else has not a right to come, a better right than yourself. . . . It is so sweet to sit still and know that no one will burst the door open and come in. (2:265)

But Caroline is obviously not fated to be happy, partly because of her weakness, partly because she has two children who do not take after her family and are "pieces of Torrance" (3:171) who will be with her for life. Even motherhood cannot be a full consolation. Her own mother, Lady Lindores, has to watch her daughter suffer and is disenchanted with the men of her family. "Her husband was not a perfect mate for her—her son had failed to her hopes" (3:333). She must accept that "with all the relationships of life still round her, mother and wife, she, for all solace and support, was like most of us virtually alone" (3:50).

A similar type of older woman appears in another remarkable and neglected novel, *A Country Gentleman and His Family* (1886). Mrs. Warrender, mother of the "hero," has no real role in the plot but impresses one as a woman more perceptive than those around her and who has accepted that "her own being was an undiscovered country for her children" (2:218). Oliphant had much the same feeling in the 1880s, as she watched her own sons turn out so different from herself.

Theo Warrender, a depressingly convincing young man with an "extremely impatient temper and fastidious, almost capricious temperament" (2:79), becomes head of the family over his mother and older sisters after his father dies. Having been unsuccessful in the larger world, because others will not put up with his whims, he is determined that he will at best dominate his own household. He can turn his sisters out, they discover because "we are only daughters, and you are the boy" (1:96). Soon he falls in love with an older widow Frances, who with her son is in a much higher social position than he is. Theo bears down her opposition and marries her although she warns him she is "not only older in years, but so much older in life" (2:111). "I am a woman who have had to act for myself. I am Geoff's mother. I must think of him and what has to be done for him" (2:130).

The author is sympathetic to Frances's natural longings. "A woman in the flower of her life does not necessarily centre every wish in the progress of a little boy" (2:142). Yet the marriage is doomed because Theo will never accept his wife's child (and Oliphant seems to feel this is not only because he is an intolerant man but also because the situation is unnatural), and because she is not a pliable young girl but a woman of more experience than himself. She does not take his name or live in his house when they are married—more wounds to his self-esteem. Indeed, the whole novel could be called a study of "the wounds which people closely connected in life so often give to each other" (1:231). Theo not surprisingly becomes miserable.

> He was jealous of his wife, not in the ordinary vulgar way, for which there was no possibility, but for every year of additional age, and every experience, and all the life she had led apart from him. He could not endure to think that she had formed the most of her ideas before she knew him; the thought of her past was horrible to him. (3:152)

Frances attempts to make herself a lesser person for his sake. "She seemed to have one eye upon Theo always, whatever she was doing, to see that he was pleased, or at least not displeased" (3:141). But in the end, when he orders her to give up her child and seeks to enforce the conventional Victorian view of the man-woman relationship, saying "Can any one doubt what is your first duty? It is to me. It is I that must settle what our life is to be. It is you who must yield and obey" (3:216), she rebels and breaks with him. Her marriage—which has brought her two more children—becomes "a strange dream, a dream full of fever and unrest, of fugitive happiness but lasting trouble" (3:225).

Oliphant suggests in this novel that marriage "almost always makes trouble; it breaks as well as unites" (2:194). Her fine short story, **"Queen Eleanor and Fair Rosamond,"** first published in 1886, also shows a marriage that breaks down because of the man's conduct. A middle-aged couple appears to be contentedly married; when the husband goes away his wife cannot guess the real reason. "How could it mean anything except business, or the good of the children, or some other perfectly legitimate desire?"[21] In fact, he has illegitimate desires and has "married" a young girl in another town. The wife copes without self-pity, indeed with some heroism, while her husband is eventually seen as a commonplace and rather silly man, points Margarete Rubik makes in her discussion of this story in her essay.

Kirsteen is probably Oliphant's masterpiece. Here, most unusually, the heroine remains a spinster, although that does not free her from family ties. She has a fiance who dies in India; her feeling for him is the "golden thread" running through her life. But this relationship is not studied in detail. Her real links are with her sisters and the women who help her break away from home and become independent; her real fulfillment is in being a dressmaker and creating "beautiful manufactured things . . . with much of the genuine enjoyment which attends an artist in all crafts" (165). When the author looks closely at marriage relationships, her picture is much darker. Kirsteen's father, a former slave trader and future murderer treats his wife and daughters with thorough contempt, which proves intolerable for Kirsteen with her "quick temper and high spirit and lively imagination." She will "make a story for" herself (36).

It is Kirsteen who makes the family's fortune, fulfilling the pattern of success normally reserved for men, as Linda Peterson demonstrates. Yet it is done at a price, and, like her creator, she ends up a breadwinner, but also celibate with many poor relations needing her help and others upset with her because she has worked for a living. Thus Oliphant treats, not only Kirsteen, but the several spinsters in the novel, with respect and dignity.

Another novel that shows a husband as less than a great prize is *The Marriage of Elinor* (1892), in which the heroine has too much spirit to put up with her husband's infidelity, but makes a fairly happy alternative home with her mother and child. Although Oliphant's tone is cautious, she distances herself from the view that a woman should hang on to her marriage at any price:

> Had Elinor fulfilled what would appear to many her first duty, and stood by Phil through neglect, ill-treatment, and misery, as she had vowed, for better, for worse, she would by this time have been not only a wretched but a deteriorated woman, and her son most probably would have been injured both in his moral and intellectual being. What she had done was not the abstract duty of her marriage vow, but it had been better— had it not been better for them both? In such a question who is to be the judge? (3:70-71)

In this novel, the relationship between mother and adult daughter is a deep one that lasts throughout their lives, while men come and go.

During the 1880s and 1890s, while Oliphant wrote these remarkable works, a "singular and scarcely recognised revolution" had "taken place in the position and aspirations of women." These are her own words, from an article of 1889 in which she noted that many young girls were now trying to work out "their own career and destiny."[22] She sympathized, taking great trouble with the education of her two nieces so they could eventually get suitable work. Emancipated young women come into her novels too, usually in small parts like the girl in *The Railwayman and His Children* who says that "work is not the thing to make a fortune by. But I am of opinion that it is the first thing in the world" (397). *The Marriage of Elinor* contains girls who play music seriously, climb mountains and do social work in hospitals and the East End of London.

> I do not for a moment mean to imply that the Miss Gaythornes did their good work because it was the fashion: but the fact that it is the fashion has liberated many girls, and allowed them to carry out their natural wishes in that way, who otherwise would have been restrained and hampered by parents and friends, who would have upbraided them with making themselves remarkable, if in a former generation they had attempted to go to Whitechapel or St Thomas's with any active intentions. (2:230)

More women now wanted votes, held responsible jobs, and perhaps did not wish to live as their mothers had. New novels by Olive Schreiner, James, Moore, Hardy, and Gissing among others examined the position of women and the ideal relationship between the sexes. On the whole Oliphant was not impressed. In a review

of *Tess of the d'Urbervilles* she acknowledged the book's greatness, and showed sympathy for the central character, but still preferred to read about "a world which is round and contains everything, not 'the relations between the sexes' alone."[23] In an article of 1894 she sensed a certain narcissism in "the much talk about women, and their rights and disabilities, with which the air is full":

> Whether they agree or disagree, women, in this generation at least, love to read about themselves; and the subject, though beginning, we hope, to pall upon the better intellects, is always attractive to the mass which . . . is more than anything else drawn to the consideration of its own gifts and graces, as specially seen in its attitudes towards its partner in life. All this is no doubt part of the defective education of the past, and of the fact that a generation or two ago women had many real and galling disabilities, and were held under an actual subjection (by law, if only now and then in fact) which was sometimes very cruel and unjust, and always highly offensive to feminine pride.

Yet some writers, she thought, had gone too far. "They grow hot over wrongs that have long ceased to be, and argue as they might have done before there was any Married Women's Property Act or other amelioration."[24]

She returned to this subject in 1895, arguing as she had done years before that feminists had not fully addressed their minds to the question of children.

> The women who work should be . . . celibates, who make up their minds to the other line of life, and do not marry. The functions, especially of a mother, are not easily combined with any other trade or profession. We have seen very melancholy spectacles in the attempt to carry out both well. . . . But work of itself is really at bottom often more agreeable to women than it is to men.[25]

It is likely that among the "melancholy spectacles" she had seen were her own life and career. She had tried to be a good mother as well as an artist, but she knew that she had been forced to write a great deal of rubbish to get an income, and her last child had died only a few months before. It would have been simpler—she may have felt—if she had had a clearer, easier choice.

She might seem extremely hostile to the "New Woman" in her now infamous review of *Jude the Obscure,* which Hardy called "the screaming of a poor lady in *Blackwood* that there was an unholy anti-marriage league afoot."[26] Titled **"The Anti-Marriage League,"** the review discussed *Jude* and Grant Allen's *The Woman*

Who Did, both of which were hostile to marriage and featured sexually emancipated heroines.

Aware of the novels' popularity, Oliphant nonetheless protested against the tendency "to place what is called the Sex-question above all others as the theme of fiction":

> Its result is to select, as the most important thing in existence, one small (though no doubt highly important) fact of life, which natural instinct has agreed, even among savages, to keep in the background. . . . To make this the supreme incident, always in the foreground, to be discussed by young men and women, and held up before boys and girls, and intruded upon those from whom circumstances or choice have shut it off, or who have outlived the period in which it is interesting, seems to me an outrage for which there is no justification. . . . It puts life out of focus altogether, and distorts hopelessly its magnitudes and its littlenesses.

To the charge that these novelists were sex-obsessed she added that if marriage were to be downgraded, it would be women who would suffer. "It makes the woman not the helpmeet of the man according to the noble and beautiful conception of that relationship in the first description of it ever given in literature—but his accomplice . . . in a certain act common to men and beasts, and no more sacred in one case than in the other from this point of view."[27]

She had realized that men might turn certain feminist demands to their own advantage. "The desire of women for work," she had warned in **Within the Precincts,** "is apt to be supported from an undesirable side" (326). Probably most contemporary feminists shared her distrust of male novelists who, they felt, only wanted women to be sexually emancipated. The president of the National Union of Women Suffrage Societies, Millicent Fawcett, had written in her review of *The Woman Who Did* that "Mr. Grant Allen has never given help by tongue or pen to any practical effort to improve the legal or social status of women. He is not a friend but an enemy, and it is as an enemy that he endeavours to link together the claim of women to citizenship and social and industrial independence, with attacks upon marriage and the family."[28]

Oliphant also raised the "great insoluble question of what is to be the fate of children in such circumstances." Were they to be killed, as in *Jude the Obscure,* or alternatively "hang on to their mother's second honeymoon?" "Mr Hardy knows," she insisted, "that the children are a most serious part of the question of the abolition of marriage."[29] Reading this review today, one sees Oliphant overstated her case and may also have been insensitive to the quality of Hardy's

writing. Nevertheless, she raised issues that are still highly relevant.

To sum up, Margaret Oliphant is a complex figure, typecast as antifeminist, yet concerned throughout her life with the problems of women and the author of several novels that are rooted in this concern. Some of her opinions have dated; much of worth remains.

She would not have liked modern feminists. Their attitudes to sex and children would have been deeply alien to her, as would be their stridency and frequent self-pity. It is more helpful and fairer to see her as one of a long and honorable line of women who were known in England between the wars as the Old Feminists. They did not concentrate on women's "special" or biological problems, although of course they were aware of them (and might even write about them as Margaret did). Ultimately all they asked was that men and women be equal before the law and that no persons should be forbidden to make their contribution because they were the "wrong" sex. Above all, they were aware, as was Oliphant, that the world "is round, and contains everything."

Frequently Cited Sources and Abbreviations

NLS—National Library of Scotland

Colby—Robert and Vineta Colby, *The Equivocal Virtue: Margaret Oliphant and the Victorian Literary Marketplace.* Hamden, CT: Archon, 1966.

A&L—The Autobiography and Letters of Mrs. M. O. W. Oliphant. Mrs. Harry Coghill, ed. Edinburgh: Blackwood, 1898. The volume was reprinted with an introduction by Q. D. Leavis in 1974 by Leicester University Press while only the autobiography with an introductory essay by Laurie Langbauer was reprinted in 1988 by the University of Chicago Press. These editions are photographic reproductions; pagination of the autobiography and letters is the same.

A—The Autobiography of Margaret Oliphant: The Complete Text, ed. Elisabeth Jay. Oxford University Press, 1990.

Notes

[1] *Women and Fiction: Feminism and the Novel 1880-1920* (Brighton: Harvester, 1979) 39-40.

[2] Oliphant-Madge Valentine, 2 December 1895, NLS Acc.5678/4.

[3] Oliphant-JB, n.d. 1876, NLS Blackwood MS 4349.

[4] In *Womankind* (London, 1876) 1.

5 "The Laws Concerning Women," *Blackwood's* 79 (April 1856) 379.

6 "Laws" 381.

7 "The Great Unrepresented," *Blackwood's* 100 (September 1866) 369.

8 "Great," 376.

9 "Great," 379.

10 Oliphant-JB, 8 March 1865, NLS Blackwoods MS 4202.

11 [Review of Mill and Josephine Butler], *Edinburgh Review* 130 (October 1869) 580.

12 [Review] 597.

13 Stubbs, 43.

14 Stubbs, 42.

15 "The Grievances of Women," *Fraser's,* 21 (May 1880) 707.

16 "Grievances," 698.

17 "Grievances," 710.

18 *The Literary History of England in the End of the Eighteenth Century and the Beginning of the Nineteenth Century* (London: Macmillan, 1882) 2:248; Oliphant-John Tulloch, September 1881, A&L 300.

19 "Grievances," 698.

20 "Grievances," 705.

21 In *A Widow's Tale and Other Stories* (London: Blackwood, 1898) 67.

22 "The Old Saloon," *Blackwood's* 146 (August 1889) 257.

23 "The Old Saloon," *Blackwood's* 151 (March 1892) 465.

24 "The Looker-On," *Blackwood's* 156 (August 1894) 289-90.

25 "The Looker-On," *Blackwood's* 159 (January 1896) 137.

26 See Hardy's postscripts in the New Wessex Edition (London: Macmillan, 1975) 30.

27 *Blackwood's* 159 (January 1896) 137, 144-45.

28 "The Woman Who Did," *Contemporary Review* 67 (May 1895) 630.

29 "Anti-Marriage," 141, 147, 142.

FURTHER READING

Biography

Colby, Vineta, and Robert A. Colby. *The Equivocal Virtue: Mrs. Oliphant and the Victorian Literary Marketplace.* Hamden, Conn.: Archon Books, 1966, 281 p.
　　Detailed biography culled from Oliphant's *Autobiography,* her published works, and her numerous unpublished letters.

Williams, Merryn. *Margaret Oliphant: A Critical Biography,* London: Macmillan, 1986, 217 p.
　　The first full-length study of Oliphant's life.

Criticism

Clarke, John Stock. "Mrs. Oliphant's Unacknowledged Social Novels." *Notes and Queries* n.s. 28, No. 5 (October 1981): 408-13.
　　Argues from evidence in letters and her *Autobiography* for Oliphant's authorship of four novels previously attributed to her brother William Wilson.

———. "The 'Rival Novelist'—Hardy and Mrs. Oliphant." *The Thomas Hardy Journal* V, No. 3 (October 1989): 51-61.
　　Chronicles Oliphant's relationship with Hardy—particularly in light of Oliphant's less-than-laudatory reviews of Hardy's *Jude the Obscure, Tess,* and *The Woodlanders.*

Colby, Robert, and Vineta Colby. "*A Beleaguered City*: A Fable for the Victorian Age." *Nineteenth-Century Fiction* 16, No. 4 (March 1962): 283-301.
　　Claims that Oliphant's novel *A Beleaguered City* is her "finest" and should be placed among the secondary classics of literature.

———. "Mrs. Oliphant's Scotland: The Romance of Reality." In *Nineteenth-Century Scottish Fiction: Critical Essays.* Ed. Ian Campbell, pp. 89-104. New York: Barnes and Noble, 1979.
　　Suggests that Oliphant, who "retained a lingering love for the romance of Scotland," found inspiration in her native country's history, folklore, culture, people, and landscapes, and exploited this interest as "marketable literary material."

Conrad, Joseph. "Letter to William Blackwood." 4 September 1897. In *The Collected Letters of Joseph*

Conrad. Vol. 1, 1861-1897. Ed. Frederick R. Karl and Laurence Davies, pp. 379-80. London: Cambridge University Press, 1983.

> Corresponding with Oliphant's publisher, Conrad states that "she wrote too much," but he praises her work as "better . . . than George Eliot" and "*immensely superior* to any living woman novelist" he can remember.

Haythornthwaite, J. A. "A Victorian Novelist and Her Publisher: Margaret Oliphant and the House of Blackwood." *The Bibliotheck* 15, No. 1 (1988): 37-50.

> Surveys Oliphant's relationship with her most prominent publisher.

————. "The Wages of Success: *Miss Marjoribanks,* Margaret Oliphant and the House of Blackwood." *Publishing History* XV (1984): 91-107.

> Claiming that as a successful but not great author Oliphant occupies "the Victorian literary middle ground," argues that her relationship with her publisher is therefore representative of Victorian publishing practices.

Leavis, Q. D. "Introduction." In *Chronicles of Carlingford: Miss Marjoribanks, by Mrs. Oliphant,* pp. 1-24. London: Zodiac Press, 1969.

> Contends that Oliphant—and in particular *Miss Marjoribanks*—forms a link between the writings of Jane Austen and George Eliot.

O'Mealy, Joseph H. "Scenes of Professional Life: Mrs. Oliphant and the New Victorian Clergyman." *Studies in the Novel* XXIII, No. 2 (Summer 1991): 245-61.

> Observes that Oliphant worked with a historian's care in her novels of manners, creating psychologically powerful pictures of clerics in her Carlingford novels: she was "able to depict with humor and with sympathy the changing nature of the mid-Victorian clergyman's dual roles as spiritual guide and professional aspirant."

Showalter, Elaine. "Subverting the Feminine Novel: Sensationalism and Feminine Protest." In her *A Literature of Their Own: British Women Novelists from Brontë to Lessing,* pp. 153-81. Princeton, N. J.: Princeton University Press, 1977.

> Focuses on the weak-willed heroine of Oliphant's *The Ladies Lindore* (1883) and *Lady Car* (1889), suggesting that the author identified with the main character's state of "passive suffering."

Stubbs, Patricia. "The Well-Regulated Heroine." In her *Women and Fiction: Feminism and the Novel; 1880-1920,* pp. 26-50. Sussex: Harvester Press, 1979.

> Proposes that the heroine of *Miss Marjoribanks*—an independent-minded as well as manipulative character who ultimately resigns herself to dependence after marriage—typifies the traditional female Oliphant portrayed in most of her novels. According to the critic, this heroine was "in no way a serious challenge to patriarchal stereotypes of feminine character or behaviour."

Trela, D. J., ed. *Margaret Oliphant: Critical Essays on a Gentle Subversive.* Selinsgrove, Penn.: Susquehanna University Press, 1995, 190 p.

> In addition to the essays excerpted here, the fiction section of this collection includes articles on Oliphant's subversion of literary cliches, her literary reputation, and her supernatural stories; the nonfiction section includes essays that treat the editing of Oliphant's autobiography, her theory of autobiography, her theory of domestic tragedy, and her relationship with editor John Blackwood.

Additional coverage of Oliphant's life and career is contained in the following source published by Gale Research: *Dictionary of Literary Biography,* Volumes 18 and 159.

Erik Johan Stagnelius

1793-1823

Swedish poet and dramatist.

INTRODUCTION

Stagnelius wrote lyric poetry, an epic, several dramas, and an opera in a fervent, ornate style that expressed an ascetic spiritualism in terms of highly sensual imagery. Although he was virtually unknown to his contemporaries during his eleven-year career, today he is widely regarded as one of the most influential writers of the Swedish Romantic movement.

Biographical Information

Stagnelius was born on the island of Öland, off the southeastern coast of Sweden. His father, a local vicar, later became bishop of Kalmar. A solitary child, Stagnelius read widely in the classics and in Norse mythology. In 1811 he attended the University of Lund briefly as a student of theology, but soon left to pursue his studies at the University of Uppsala. There he became acquainted with the writings of contemporary European authors of the Romantic movement and began writing verses of his own. After passing a civil service exam in 1814, he accepted a junior government post at the Department of Church and Education. Around this time he was diagnosed with a severe heart ailment. His subsequent abuse of alcohol and possibly drugs is often attributed to attempts to relieve the physical suffering and mental anguish caused by his deteriorating health. Around 1817, a spiritual crisis appears to have drawn him to a mystical and fervent Christianity inspired by the writings of Gnostic and Pythagorean philosophers, who saw the soul as engaged in a constant struggle to transcend the limits of its physical prison. Although Stagnelius appears to have written steadily throughout his adult life in a number of poetic and dramatic genres, he did not mix in Swedish literary circles, and relatively little of his work was published before his death. He was found dead in bed in 1823.

Major Works

Many of Stagnelius's mature works center on the conflict between a sensual attachment to the world and a spiritual yearning for transcendence. In many of his lyric poems, spiritual aspirations are expressed metaphorically in terms of sexual desire.

His first major poem, *Vladimir den Store* (*Vladimir the Great*; 1817), has been described by Leif Sjöberg as "the first great Swedish hexameter poem"; it recounts the conversion to Christianity of a pagan warrior through his love for a Christian woman whom he has taken captive. *Liljor i Saron* (*Lilies in Sharon*), a collection of religious poems, was published with *Martyrerna* (*The Martyrs*), a verse drama expressing an ascetic Christianity, in 1821. His tragedy *Bacchanterna eller Fanatismen* (*The Bacchantes, or Fanaticism*; 1822) was his last work to be published during his lifetime. Many of the works published posthumously in his *Samlade skrifter* (*Collected Works*; 1824-26) are in the form of fragments. These include the unfinished epic poems *Blenda*, which celebrates the vigor and manly virtues of Viking days, and *Gunlög*, which affirms the divine origin of poetry.

Critical Reception

Stagnelius is seen as one of the leading representatives of the Romantic movement in Sweden. His work is often associated with that of the Swedish "Phosphorists," who valued emotion over intellect and idealized beauty as the highest expression of divinity. British and American critics have likened his work to that of the English poets William Wordsworth and Percy Bysshe Shelley. Critics often discuss Stagnelius' work in terms of contradictions. While his style is described as almost Byzantine in its rich, ornate complexity, he is also praised for the clarity of his language and the lucidity of his ideas. Both in his lyric poetry and in his dramas, a transcendent and ascetic spirituality is generally expressed in terms of highly sensual imagery, and motifs drawn from classical and Norse mythology are pressed into service to convey Christian ideals.

PRINCIPAL WORKS

Vladimir den Store [*Vladimir the Great*] (poetry) 1817
Liljor i Saron och Martyrerna [*Lilies in Sharon and The Martyrs*] (poetry and drama) 1821
Bacchanterna eller Fanatismen [*The Bacchantes, or Fanaticism*] (drama) 1822
Thorsten Fiskare [*The Fisherman Thorsten*] (drama) 1823
Samlade skrifter [*Collected Works*] 3 vols. (poetry, drama, and opera) 1824-26
Samlade skrifter [*Collected Works*] 5 vols. (poetry, drama, and opera) 1911-19
Samlade skrifter [*Collected Works*] 4 vols. (poetry, drama, and opera) 1957

CRITICISM

William and Mary Howitt (essay date 1852)

SOURCE: "Poets Belonging Generally to the New School," in *The Literature and Romance of Northern Europe: Constituting a Complete History of the Literature of Sweden, Denmark, Norway and Iceland*, Vol. II, Colburn and Co., 1852, pp. 405-26.

[*In the following excerpt, the authors characterize Stagnelius as a "gnostic" poet and cite resemblances between his work and that of English Romantic poets William Wordsworth and Percy Bysshe Shelley.*]

The most prominent poets of [the "New School"] are Stagnelius, Almquist, Livijn, Dahlgren and Fahlcrantz. It would be incorrect to allocate them with Phosphorists or Goths, for they differ both from these schools and from each other so decidedly, that they can only be styled writers of modern power, tendencies and spirit. They possess much of that independent and individual character which should be the result of the doctrine of

every man endeavouring to develop his own genius according to his own inner impulses, and the perception of his own natural organization and endowments. The greatest of these poets is unquestionably—

Erik Johan Stagnelius

Stagnelius is a genuine modern gnostic. His poetry is as fully and as positively the enunciation of gnosticism as ever were the preachings of the old Syrian and Egyptian speculative Christians. Himself a physically suffering creature, with passions at war in his body with the intense heavenward longings of his soul, he was deeply impressed with the philosophy which the gnostic sect of the early Christians inherited from Plato and Pythagoras, that our souls were once in a higher state of existence, and that, in the words of Byron, we all live in a place of penance:

> Where for our sins to sorrow we are cast.

It was the doctrine which Wordsworth drew from Plato in his noble Ode, "Intimations of Immortality from Recollections of Early Childhood."

> Our birth is but a sleep and a forgetting:
> The soul that rises with us, our life's star,
>   Hath had elsewhere its setting,
>   And cometh from afar.
>   Not in entire forgetfulness,
>   And not in utter nakedness,
> But trailing clouds of glory do we come
>   From God, who is our home:
> Heaven lies about us in our infancy!
> Shades of the prison-house being to close
>   Upon the growing boy.

The farther he goes, the more the heavenly inborn light "fades into the light of common day."

> Earth fills her lap with pleasures of her own;
> Yearnings she hath in her own natural kind,
> And, even with something of a mother's mind,
>   And no unworthy aim;
>   The homely nurse doth all she can
> To make her foster-child, her inmate man,
>   Forget the glories he hath known,
> And the imperial palace whence he came.

This is the gnosticism of a man comfortably wandering amid the lakes and mountains of Cumberland, with a good old clerk issuing stamps to the counties of Cumberland and Westmoreland, and leaving him no care except that of receiving the rich percentage. But the gnosticism of Stagnelius was held under different circumstances. Cooped in a sickly body, contending with the higher instincts of the soul, "the homely nurse," old mother earth, did seem to him to have an "unworthy aim." Psyche, in his eyes, was in bondage to Hyle; the soul was in a stern prison to matter, which was constantly endeavouring to make her,

> Forget the glories she had known,
> And the imperial palace whence she came.

Stagnelius did not, like Wordsworth, live out a serene life of upwards of seventy years, but his tried and conflicting existence terminated at the age of thirty. Therefore, we have no remoulding of his youthful doctrines, no calmer views evolved through the experience of longer and more tranquil years, but his thoughts and feelings stand before us, thrown off in the fire of youth, and the gloomy fervour with which the upward and the downward tendencies of complicated human nature inspired him.

The Swedish critics see a strong resemblance between Stagnelius and Wordsworth: we see more between him and Shelley. With the exception of the differing faiths, there is the same early fate, the same speculative spirit, the same attachment to Greek philosophy and Greek poetic forms. No one can read the **Cydippe,** the **Narcissus,** the **Bacchantes,** **"Proserpina,"** nor even his **"Svedger,"** without being struck with this. There is the same yearning after the unknown, the same tendency to the mythic and speculative, the same constant warring of oppressed nature, which Shelley has expressed in his *Prometheus Unbound,* against some overbearing power or element, and the same wonderful power of language and affluence of inspired phrase. In the very choice of the subject of the **Riddertornet** and the *Cenci* we see a resemblance. But far more lies this kinship of spirit in the spirit itself, in those longings, despairings, those far flights into the ideal world and those sufferings from the real one, which marked them both.

Stagnelius was the son of a clergyman, afterwards Bishop of Kalmar. He was born in 1793; studied in Lund, and afterwards in Upsala, and became a Clerk of Chancery in the Ecclesiastical Department in 1815, and took successive advancements in that office. He died in Stockholm in 1828. In his lifetime he published **"Women in the North,"** for which he received the prize of the Royal Academy. His **Wladimir,** a fine heroic poem in hexameters, was published in 1817; his **Lilies of Sharon,** in 1821; his **Bacchantes,** in 1822; and, after his death, his **Collected Writings** were published in three volumes by Hammarsköld.

They are his **Lilies of Sharon** which distinguish him from all other Swedish poets, and place him amongst the greatest intellectual poets of the age. Some of the critics of his native country complain of the gloom and the sorrowful tone of his poetry, and are inclined to regard it as sickly. To our fancy it is much too strong and wrestling in its nature to be sickly. That

there is a tone of suffering running through the greater part of his productions, is true; for it was the lot of Stagnelius preeminently to present an example of the truth of Shelley's declaration, that

> We learn in suffering
> What we teach in song.

We are, therefore, more pleased with the serious portions of his poetry than with the rest. The world has a superflux, and Sweden especially, of the light, the playful and the merely fanciful lyric; and we listen with a far profounder interest to the outpourings of a great and suffering soul, as it were the wail of the chained Prometheus on his midnight Caucasus, uttering his proudly sustained agonies to the stars above him. In the poem which we here quote is found the great dogma of his philosophy.

The Mystery of Sighs

> Sighs, sad sighs, they are the element
> In whose bosom breathes the Demiurgus.
> Look around thee, what makes glad thy
>   spirit?
> Does thy heart throb with a stronger
>   impulse?
> Does the rosy tint of joy empurple
> Thy cheeks' pallor only for a moment?
> Say what was it?—But a sigh of sadness,
> Which forth flowing from the fount of being
> Was bewildered in time's endless mazes.
>
> Twofold laws direct the life of mortals;
> Twofold powers divide whate'er existeth
> 'Neath the moon's for ever-changing empire.
> Hear, O mortal! Ever seeking, yearning,—
> Is the first law. Forceful separation
> Is the second. Diverse though in heaven,
> These two laws are ever undivided
> In the land where ruleth Achamot,[1]
> And in fixed duality and oneness
> Appear they in the mystery of sighs.
> 'Twixt of life and death the sigh of sorrow
> Is the human heart for ever wavering,
> And each breath it draws announces only
> Its destination in the world of thought.
>
> Lo the sea! Its waves are flowing inland,
> And will clasp with arms of earnest longing,
> 'Neath the bridal torches of the heavens,
> To its breast the earth enwreathed with
>   lilies,
> See it cometh! How its heart is throbbing
> With fierce yearning! How its arms are
>   stretched forth
> All in vain! No wishes are accomplished
> 'Neath the moon; even the fair moon's
>   waxing

Hastens its waning. Disappointed longings
Depress the sea, and all its mighty billows
Leave the shore with endless, endless
   sighing.

List the wind! how softly sweet it floateth,
'Mong the lofty poplars of the woodlands.
Hark! it sighs, and ever, ever sigheth
Like a fainting lover, and desireth
Spousal with the Flora of the summer.
Yet already die away the voices.
On the leaves' Eolian harp are sounded
Swan-like songs which fade away and
   perish.
What is spring? sighs from the green
   earth's bosom
Rising upward, and from Heaven demanding
When again begins the May of Eden?
What the butterfly in all his splendour?
What the lark that greets the light of
   morning?
What the nightingale beloved of
   shadows?
Only sighs in different forms of beauty.

Mortal! wilt thou learn of life the wisdom,
Oh, then listen! Twofold laws have guidance
Of this our life! Seeking, yearning ever
Is the first law. Forceful separation
Is the second. Consecrate to freedom
This compulsion, and thus reconciléd,
Dedicated thus, beyond the spheres,
The gates of honour will to thee be
   opened!

The same doctrine pervades the following stanzas, but accompanied by the Scripture one, that "the whole creation groaneth together for the manifestation of the sons of God."

THE SIGHS OF THE CREATURES

      What sighs the hill?
What the North wind through the pine-
   wood that blows?
      What whispers the rill,
Whilst through the valley so softly it flows?
      What says the morning,
      Golden mists born in?
What the night's moon all heaven adorning,
Silently gazing on valleys below?
What thinks the red rose? what the
   narcisse?
      Or the stern precipice,
Gloomy and threatening, what does it know?

We know, and we think, and we sigh, and
   we speak!
O man, from the trance of thy stupor awake,

And up to the primal-life's region go back!
   If thou wilt ascend to the true world ideal;
   Into light will transform all the gloomy, the
   real,
We also, transfigured, shall follow thy track.
Thou, thyself art in bonds to material
   powers.
Alas! the same terrible bondage is ours,
For lead where thou wilt we must still follow
   thee!
   One law, that is common to both, we lie
   under:
     Unfetter the creatures—thy bonds burst
     asunder;
Unfetter thyself, and thou them settest free!

Still more clearly come forth his gnostic views, in the following dialogue. It is like a painting from a pre-Raphaelite School, Italian, German, or Byzantine, with its devotional figures and golden backgrounds. Who does not see the lustrous angel, and the sorrowful soul presenting her flowers at the grating between this world and the next? They are like two figures, quaint and in white-flowing garments in the emblems of Quarles.

DIALOGUE

THE ANGEL AND THE SOUL

THE ANGEL

Come nearer the grating, O nun full of
   sorrow,
That I may give to thee the trembling
   narcissus,
The tearful white lilies, the peonies crimson,
Which Christ sendeth to thee, the King of
   the Aons,[2]
From the fair fields of heaven.

THE SOUL

How blissful thy seeming, O youth full of
   beauty!
Thy eye brightly beameth with radiance
   Olympian;
Thy countenance gloweth with health and
   with goodness,
And gracefully circle thy snowy white
   forehead
The rich curling tresses. Methinks I
   aforetime
Have heard of thy voice the low musical
   cadence;
Methinks I aforetime with rapture have
   gazed on
Thy countenance beaming; yet know I not
   where!

THE ANGEL

Thou hast seen me full oft in the All-
father's kingdom;
In the region of beauty, of spring-time
eternal,
The land of Elysium; by the eye of the
godhead
With love all eradiate, on golden clouds
borne up
In the halls of perfection thou builded thy
throne.
'Mid murmuring forests of palm-trees and
laurel,
Engirdled with azure of crystalline waters
Thy kingdom, all nature, in the light of the
May sun
Lay under thy feet. From the gates of the
morning
To shadowy sunset, when slumbers the
evening
'Mid fragrance of violets; from the home of
the North star
To the Cloud[3] which engarlands with
tremulous star-sheen
The Pole of the South, thy yearning eye
turned'st thou,
Thy eye brightly beaming, celestially filled
with
The All-father's love, with the Unity's
worship,
That infinite vastness of life universal.
Then came I with flowers from heaven
descending
To the soul in its prison. Then came I with
flowers
From the low banks of Jordan, an angel of
sacrifice
Unto the soul.

THE SOUL

How live the blessed, the hosts of immortals
Up yonder in ether? Ah! heavy my brain is
With vapours of earth. Scarce casteth one
memory
Of days quickly vanished, its pale moonlight
glimmer
Through thought's dreary night. Doth
Maria[4] encircle
With solemn star-splendour her bright
golden tresses?
Say, is not Christ throné d the King of the
Aons,
'Mid spirits beatified, suns flashing
lightning,
In the purple of love, the tiara of power?
Does the Great One remember the kiss of
the soul?

Say, has He forgotten his sad, yearning
bride?

THE ANGEL

For ever, Maria with stars brightly gleaming
Encircles her shining ambrosial tresses.
He is throné d for ever, the King of the
Aons,
In the purple of love, the tiara of power.
Thousands unnumbered, the spirits of
women,
Are crowned in His presence with roses of
spring-time,
Are clothed in the beautiful garments of
purity,
Dazzlingly snow-white. Yet doth He forget not
His first, early loved one, and ever He
hopeth
The soul is returning in splendour of
sunlight,
More glorious and reconciled to Him again.

THE SOUL

Come nearer the grating, thou youth full of
beauty!
That I may endeavour between the bars
chilly,
Between the thick bars of the damp brazen
grating,
To give thee a kiss!

THE ANGEL

Ah, snowy-pale maiden! alone lips of
crimson
And cheeks heaven-blooming may kiss an
immortal.
Once bright were thy charms, like the rose
breathing perfume
In the garden of heaven, all dewy with tear-
drops
Of feeling celestial. Now art thou, O poor
one,
Like the spring valley-lily, so wasted and
pale.
But what greeting sendest thou back unto
Christ?
Ah, answer! I like not these shadows below.

THE SOUL

Ah me! this thick grating—these cold,
brazen barriers
Exclude me from spring-time's Hesperian
valleys,
Where flowers I might gather to give to the
bridegroom.

Here I have nothing to send in return for
The gift of the bridegroom, except his own
    gift.
Take back this narcissus. Convey it, O
    angel!
Back unto Christ; say that the pearl-drops
Which tremblingly gleam in its silvery
    chalice
Are the tears of the soul. Say that for ever
Her choice she repenteth; deploreth with
    weeping
The hour when seduced by the harp-tones
    of Achamot
Downward she wandered, down unto matter.
Oh, long enough now, 'mid the Aons of
    time and space,
And with tears hotly falling, the maiden, the
    freeborn,
Has paid the high penance! Oh, long
    enough surely,
Driven from life's tree by the angel of
    vengeance
With sword fiercely flaming, hath she
    wandered, sighing
Among gloomy figures of animal being!
Is Psyche then never with Love to be
    reconciled?
Will the Phœnix not rise from its bale-fire
    more glorious?
Will the lofty blue shell of the world's egg
    break never?

In presenting copious specimens of the more characteristic poetry of Stagnelius, we have left ourselves little room to speak of its other varieties. He has written in almost every form of poetic literature—tragedy, epic, opera and psalms, ballads, dancing and drinking songs. In some of these he has not particularly succeeded. His hymns are much inferior to what might have been expected from so feeling and religious a spirit. His ballads and lyrical poems, of a more general kind, are exquisite. His *Martyrs* is a powerful and masterly performance, and unequalled in its kind by any Swedish author. The subject of it is Perpetua and her Companions, and the prayer which she teaches her little boy is one of the most touching and admirable religious effusions in any language. *Wladimir* is an equally splendid heroic poem, in vigorous hexameters. Wladimir, the yet Pagan Prince of Novogorod, is besieging the city of Theodosia, when a captive maiden is brought before him, who immediately excites a profound passion in him.

Hastily opened the doors, and into the
    monarch's proud presence
Solemnly stepped two Russians clad in their
    armour;
Between them a trembling maiden—Oh! who
    can describe her?

White as her radiant neck, her hands with
    their lily-hued fingers,
Was the veil which she wore, and on her
    chaste sorrowing bosom
Hung a cross of bright gold, the sign of the
    suffering Godhead.
Free round her shoulders her golden hair
    floated all richly,
Her cheeks were dewy with tears, and up
    towards heaven's wide empire
Beseeching she turnéd her eyes, her eyes all
    saddened with weeping.

She proves to be Anna, the sister of the Emperor Basilius. Wladimir at once releases her, and following her to Constantinople, sues for her hand, which is granted. He embraces the Christian faith, and plants it in Russia. The story is simple, but the execution is perfect.

Stagnelius was comparatively unknown during his lifetime, and many of his poems are his first sketches, as he left them, many the merest fragments; but he is now acknowledged as one of the greatest names of Sweden.

Notes

[1] Materiality;—original sin;—the mother of Demiurgus.

[2] The great intelligent powers placed by God, according to Gnostic philosophy, over the different regions of the universe. Christ, the divine Aon Logos, was over them all.

[3] The Great and Little Cloud; two constellations in the Southern hemisphere near the Pole.

[4] The Intellectual World.

Henry Wadsworth Longfellow (essay date 1870)

SOURCE: "Eric Johan Stagnelius," in *The Poets and Poetry of Europe: With Introductions and Biographical Notices*, Houghton, Mifflin and Company, 1893, p. 173.

[*In the following excerpt, originally published in 1870, the American poet comments briefly on Stagnelius's career and cites a review that typifies the Swedish lyricist as a mystical, otherworldly poet.*]

The most signal specimen of a genius at once precocious and productive, which the annals of Swedish literature afford, is Stagnelius. He died at the age of thirty, but has left behind him three epic poems,—one of which, though never completed, was written at the age of eighteen,—five tragedies, and seven other dramatic sketches, and a very large collection of elegies, sonnets, psalms, ballads, and miscellaneous lyrics; making, in all, three large octavo volumes, written in the space of twelve years, and marked with the impress of a high poetic genius.

Stagnelius was the son of a parish priest in Öland (afterwards bishop of Kalmar), and was born in 1793. He studied first at the University of Lund, and then at Upsala, where, upon passing his examination in 1814, he was made clerk in the Department of Ecclesiastical Affairs. This, or some similar office, he held until his death, in 1823. His brief existence, though completely barren of incident, was rich in intellectual achievements. "Stagnelius," says a writer in the *Foreign Review* (No. I.),

> was one of those truly poetic beings, to whom Goethe's beautiful comparison, likening the life of a poet to the gentle, everworking existence of the silkworm, may be justly applied. He was so thoroughly a poet, that all his thoughts, words, deeds, and even his errors and excesses, bore the stamp of poetic impulse. He is remarkable for a strain of deep melancholy, a profound mystical intuition of life and nature, and a longing for the moment when the imprisoned *anima* might burst its earthly tenement, and soar to the *pleroma,* as he terms it,—the purer regions of celestial air. These sentiments, cherished by the philosophy of Schelling, and the Gnostic doctrines of the Nazarenes, contained in the "Adam's Book,"[1] distinguished the poems of Stagnelius from all that we have seen of Swedish poetry. Among foreign poets, we can only compare him with the German Novalis. Both thought they saw in this visible world merely the symbolic expression of a more ecstatic order of things, and both were early summoned to those blissful regions after which they so fervently aspired,—whose bright effulgence seems to have enchanted their mental gaze, while yet inhabitants of earth.

Notes

[1] Edited by the late Dr. Norberg, the famous Swedish Orientalist, and published at Lund.

Edmund Gosse (essay date 1875)

SOURCE: "Birds of Passage," in *Cornhill Magazine,* Vol. XXXII, No. 189, September, 1875, pp. 346-53.

[In the following excerpt from an essay on several Swedish poets, Gosse praises Stagnelius' work for its spontaneity and philosophical depth.]

In presenting the reader with some specimens of Swedish poetry, and of the works of three great poets of the language, we have selected the subject of *Birds of Passage;* not because the lyrics here given exhibit these poets at their best, but because the idea is a typical one, and has been treated characteristically by each. The advent of the birds of passage is the most anxiously awaited event in the life of the North. Through the summer they bring song and love to whilom dreary silence of the woods; in autumn their flight forbodes the departure of a thousand delights and the speedy approach of a stark and cheerless torpor in nature; their return in spring is the harbinger of the realisation of the hopes and anticipations of the year. . . .

Johann Eric Stagnelius was born 1793, and died in 1823. His short life of thirty years was one of perpetual martyrdom, owing to malformation of some of his vital organs. It was, therefore, at an early period of life that he, himself of a voluptuous nature, sought to blunt the sting of bodily pain and mental agony by a frequent recourse to the Lethean draughts of the glass. In the company of gay comrades, centred round the glowing bowl, at the sight of which most northern natures will kindle up, Stagnelius was renowned for wit, wanton exuberance of spirits, and unrestrained humour. In the presence of woman his wit would sober down into sarcastic playfulness, not harsh, but pungent, and his humour sotten into genial mirth. But social indulgences belonged to the exceptions of Stagnelius' life. In general he was solitary and contemplative, and this very habit made him throw himself with all the more *abandon* into enjoyment.

With the muse his dealings were of the coyest and most unobtrusive. It is quite uncertain whether anyone, with, perhaps, the exception of a few bosom friends, knew that, during his academical residence at Lund and Upsala, he was a man of poetic gifts at all. But though he cultivated poetry in quiet, he did so none the less earnestly and devotedly. The result was a poetic creation, peculiarly Stagnelius' own, bound up with a well reasoned and deeply thought out system of philosophy. The key-note of this philosophy is *suffering.* Not only man, but all conscious nature is a world moving on an axe of pain, so to say. The sweetest manifestation of this spell-bound existence of suffering is but a sigh, an aspiration of hope for a better, freer, purer, more ideal state. In Stagnelius' philosophy these inspirations forbode the very realisation of their aim. Hence his religion is one of hope, unshaken hope, in an eternal Love, which embraces all suffering nature with a father's tenderness and affection, and leads it by long stages towards the blissful ideal for a fast flight, whither the fugitive Psyche is untiringly endeavouring to lift the fluttering dust-laden wing.

The chief peculiarity of Stagnelius' poetry is its unfettered spontaneity. He writes, as it were, despite himself. Not only is this true of his ideas, but the very melody in which they are poured forth itself gushes from an inner spring, flowing on, not through an artificially wrought channel, but in a natural stream. Stagnelius is a poet of nature, yet without the blemishes which result from want of culture. Seldom, if ever, is there found any jarring disparity between form and substance, between words and ideas. His rhymes are as correct as his rhythms are melodious, and in that respect he compares most favourably with other Swedish master-singers; and for melody it would be hard to point out any poetry, north of the Alps, to compare with that of Sweden. Stagnelius wrote utterly regardless of the world's praise or blame. He sang because it was natural necessity with him; he sang to ease his soul and lift his heart in harmonious prayer. And, singular enough, though sighing and yearning, though complaining and wailing, he never became personal, and, therefore, never bitter; his songs contain not one shrill note of despair; his sigh was on behalf of universal fallen nature, his aspiration a universal one on behalf of the fallen spirit of man.

Only six years before he died Stagnelius published his first poem, an epic on Wladimir the Great of Russia, which took the literary world of Sweden by surprise. Shortly afterwards followed a poem on *The Women of the North,* for which he carried off the prize of the Swedish Academy. By the *Lilies of Saron,* which appeared in 1821, his reputation as a poet was considered to be established, though afterwards it was still enhanced by the tragedy *Bacchanterna,* written on an antique model, the last of his greater works which appeared before his death. But his position as a poetic star of the first magnitude was first fully realised when his collected works were published after his death. . . .

Adolph Burnett Benson (essay date 1914)

SOURCE: "Erik Johan Stagnelius: The Old Norse Element as a Vehicle for Romanticism," in *The Old Norse Element in Swedish Romanticism,* Columbia University Press, 1914, pp. 125-43.

[*In the following essay, Benson examines various ways in which Stagnelius combined elements of Scandinavian mythology and ancient Hellenic drama in expressing Romantic themes.*]

The most thorough Romanticist in Sweden was the young and suffering Stagnelius. Both his life and work point him out as the natural exponent of what is deepest and most typical in Romanticism. He did not have to affiliate himself with any new school to be called Romantic. He did not have to take part in any polemics to advertise his theories. Stagnelius was something more than an obscure theorist; he was primarily a

creator. He loved to produce and what he produced came spontaneously, without undue effort or adherence to any set literary dogma. He was always independent. He educated himself by persistent browsing in his father's library, wrote independently, lived alone, and finally died alone at the age of thirty. He was an original, self-taught savant, to whom both the Northern and Southern mythologies were equally familiar. We may call him a Romantic genius. Mystical yearning, personal suffering, deep pathos, "singing eloquence," and characteristic coloring are nowhere better exemplified than in the poetry of Stagnelius. No one understood better than he the deeper significance of myth and religion, and the constant strife between matter and spirit, as pictured both in myth and religion, is a favorite theme of our poet. Sensuousness, in a carnal sense generally, is a striking quality of much of Stagnelius's poetry. Woman is the crown of nature and at the same time the most dangerous phenomenon in the universe; not even the gods can escape her artful cunning.

These are some of the characteristics noticeable in Stagnelius's treatment of Gothic themes. In other words the saga element becomes a vehicle for the Romantic, the didactic, and the autobiographical. But the vehicle itself is as important as the rest, and one is a spontaneous supplement of the other. There seems to be no militant effort to emphasize either one, and yet both are sufficiently prominent. Stagnelius's Gothicism is found in conjunction with Romanticism, then, in a more restricted sense, and Hellenism. These three the poet weaves together into a lyrical fabric of the most dazzling colors and pleasing melodies.

The saga element, though not intentionally obtrusive, is conspicuous in the very titles of Stagnelius's poems. *Gunlög, Wisbur,* and *Svegder* are recognized immediately as familiar names from the prose Edda and the Heimskringla. *Sigurd Ring* calls up the semi-historical exploits of a mighty pagan king, and *Blenda* reminds us of a period in Swedish history when harsh viking measures were not yet forgotten. Of these five works *Gunlög* is a fragmentary epic; *Blenda* is an epic, technically finished but intrinsically incomplete; *Svegder* is a dramatic fragment; and *Wisbur* and *Sigurd Ring* are short tragedies in the Greek style with choruses. In all of these we observe both a general enthusiasm for the saga age and an effort to interpret specific myths or characters. A favorite Romantic theme, like the origin of poetry in *Gunlög,* gives the author opportunity for a more lengthy discourse, and here we must study the author himself in terms of Norse mythology. But the Norse element is never a mere rhetorical ornamentation, a superficial jumble of names; it is always a thoroughly digested part of a poetic nutriment. It is a background blending harmoniously with the poet's modern reflections and feelings.

All of the above-mentioned productions were written during the last eleven years of the author's life, but none of them were published until after the author's death in 1823. In taking up his Gothic themes more in detail one need not pay much attention to chronology in composition, and but little is known about it with certainty. We shall consider *Blenda* first.

Blenda is a "Romantic Poem in Five Cantos" and is written in rimed, iambic verse of varying length. It is based on an old saga-like tradition, of which one form goes back to heathendom and the other, the one which Stagnelius used, goes back to a later narrative.[1] In it the patriotic Blenda, at the head of a band of Swedish women, attacks and slays the common enemy, the Dane. The scene is laid in the district of Wärend in the province of Småland, and the enemy comes from Skåne in the extreme southern part of Sweden, which then belonged to Denmark. In Stagnelius, also, the scene is laid right after the introduction of Christianity, and Blenda has become a demonic Judith who, for personal reasons, takes a horrible revenge on the Danes. With the Venus-girdle as an allurement, the amorous swains are enticed into camp and cruelly murdered.

Since the poet does not localize his action in the real saga age, the viking element becomes epic and general in character. Some events are given in terms of specific Norse myths, and comparative references are made to them occasionally, but otherwise it is merely a general glorification of the manly viking exploits and character. It is the effeminateness of the modern age and the sturdiness of the past that are contrasted, much as in Nicander and Beskow later. But Stagnelius makes a very ingenious plan. An unflinching bravery, like that of the heathen forefathers, is at first extolled, then aroused in the lethargic Christian warriors, who sail away at once across the Baltic to fight the pagans in Livonia. A curious put plausible plan: by pagan methods the pagans themselves are to be converted to Christianity.

The eulogy of the saga age is found in the beginning of the first canto, in Alle's rousing speech to his warriors. These have spent nineteen years in drinking, eating, hunting, and courting the favor of women. But their heathen ancestors did otherwise. In the early spring as soon as the snow had melted, they set out over the sea "to conquer or die," while "many a lonely maid stood waving a farewell with swan-white kerchief in hand." During the whole summer the viking roved about the world. He sunk fleets and broke down strongholds, rich coasts were burned and "the water-sprite blushed with blood." Scarcely had the leaves begun to fall, when the viking boats came back laden with plunder. The faithful maiden welcomed her champion, the lighted torches illumined the castle, and the drinking-horn and string-instrument contributed to the celebration. These were happy times for lovers; "there were no limits, no laws for men whose right arm was their only god," and no priest could condemn them. But since the "white Christ" came into the land, all has changed: the weapons rust, the ship decays, and ancestral manliness is buried forever in the ancestral funeral-mounds. The road to exploits and strength is closed and life has become one eternal monotony. But the viking methods must return, even if "the age of the saga is past and the heavenly kingdom has driven out the glorious Valhalla." Again swords are to flash and cloven hearts bleed, though no sacrifices glow on Odin's altar.

Thus Alle continues. Then he makes a specific appeal for vikingism to his oldest son Adolf who has fallen in love with Blenda. Alle does not blame his son for entertaining a passion for a woman, but he must win his beloved in a manly way. In olden times bravery often went hand in hand with love, but success in love could follow only as a reward of bravery and the heathen maiden often girded on her lover's sword.[2] The viking was not tormented by weak emotions; he rushed through arrows, swords, and fire to win his prize. The beauties at that time sat in high ladies'-bowers, surrounded by dragons and firm walls and could be won only by deeds and perfect manhood. Thus Ragnar Lodbrok won the hand of Herröd's daughter. And so, only when Adolf returns a victor from war, may he think of love. The joy will then be double.

In the third canto Stagnelius introduces another link which connects the modern epic with the pagan tradition. It is the inexorable Norse fate and the fulfilment of a prophecy. Eight generations back a Northern sibyl, "a century-old maid with wrinkled face and locks of snow," had appeared at Blenda's ancestral castle. To the beautiful Gerd a daughter had just been born, but the brave and stern Grim had demanded of the gods a son. Incensed, he determined to cast the child before the ravens upon the heath, and the death of the daughter seemed assured, when the sibyl appeared, drew forth a dagger, and rebuked the angry parent in the following prophetic terms: "With this dagger, a woman of this race shall save Sweden and conquer Jutland." The daughter was allowed to live, and the pagan instrument had then been handed down from mother to the oldest daughter for seven generations until now, finally, it was delivered into the hands of Blenda by her father. A miraculous power—we may call it fate—connected with a certain mechanical instrument from heathen times, was now to do its work through the agency of a Christian maid. A curious but beautiful and broad-minded thought: Norse paganism and Christianity in unison, and the latter the glorious fulfilment of the former.

Stagnelius tried his hand at humor in *Blenda,* but was not particularly successful. His expressions of humor are too realistic, often indelicate and in bad taste.

Atterbom called **Blenda** a "half-wanton Wieland epopée," due to the author's early studies of *Idris* and *Oberon*.[3]

The plan of **Blenda** was probably earlier than that of any other work of Stagnelius, but it was not finished until about 1816.[4] The first product to be finished—if we may use that term in speaking of a fragment—was the epic **Gunlög,** the greater part of which was written in 1812. Here the satirical element was present in the original source but in Stagnelius's epic it is much suppressed. The rough, grotesque, and grossly satirical gives way to a lyrico-epic "height and dignity." The pleasant Romantic elements are more prominent. Everything is colored in purple, rose, or silver, and bathed in moonlight in a "gloomy pine-forest." It is less clear and more subjective than **Blenda** but the style and form[5] are better. First a word about the original source.

The *Tales of Brage* . . . in the Snorre Edda give us two distinct parts of the original myth: (1) the origin of Suttung's mead, and (2) Odin's capture of it, signifying the origin of poetry and how it became the property of the gods. The divine Asas and the Wanes had a war with each other. They came together to make peace and spat their spittle[6] into one vessel, and out of this they created Kwasir, who was so wise that he could give advice in all things. Kwasir was killed through treachery by the dwarfs, Fjalar and Galar, His blood was collected in two pitchers and a kettle, mixed with honey, and a mead prepared from it, and he who drank thereof became a poet and a sage. Once the same dwarfs caused the death of the giant Gilling and the mead was given as indemnity to Gilling's son, Suttung, for the death of his father. Suttung had the mead brought into the mountain Hnitbjorg, where it was guarded by his daughter Gunnlod Gunlög). This is the end of the first part. Then Odin, under the name of Bolwerk, comes to Suttung's brother, Baugi. He brings about the death of his nine servants and offers to take their place in return for a drink of Kwasir's (i. e., Suttung's) mead. Odin stays through the summer but in the winter he demands his reward. Suttung refuses Odin and Baugi the coveted draught; and so Bolwerk (Odin) takes an auger, bores a hole through the Hnitbjorg mountain, changes himself to a serpent, and crawls through to Gunnold. He spends three nights with her, gets three draughts of the mead, and empties all three vessels. He then returns as he had come, assumes the shape of an eagle and flies away. He is pursued by Suttung, likewise in eagle form, but Odin arrives home in time to eject the mead into vessels stationed in the yard for the purpose, and Suttung has to be satisfied with a few drippings from behind. From now on the poet-making drink is the property of the gods alone.

We can easily see how a thorough Romanticist would revel in such a theme. Beneath the external crudeness of the Norse myth we have the profound meaning; the divine ownership of poetry. It was this theme which appealed to the young Stagnelius, as it did to so many German Romanticists. The poet was on a par with the gods and his art was a divine art and of divine origin. Consequently the humorous element in **Gunlög** is less developed, the crudeness is to a large extent removed, and the details of the original are altered[7] to suit the main purpose: the apotheosis of poetry. Then also it becomes the struggle between the powers of light and darkness, i. e., between the Asas and the dwarfs, and the former must conquer. Wickedness is punished, for the norns are ever watchful, and specific violence against the sons of poetry is eventually avenged. **Gunlög** eulogizes also the magic power of music. Music is the art, *par excellence,*—and how Romantic this is,—which can soothe the restless soul and arouse the warriors to action. Stagnelius's epic has become the carrier for expressions of tender moods and melancholy, for elegiac effusions, for didacticism, and for highly colored descriptions. Much emphasis is laid upon the history of the creation according to the Norse myth and references are made to semi-historical facts and viking customs.

The epic **Gunlög** comprises four complete cantos with fragments of a fifth and sixth. The first canto deals with Kwasir's divine calling as a poet, his war against the Asas. Kwasir has been brought up by Northern fairies "near sacred springs in the quiet grove." At seventeen he goes out to sing of the glory of the gods; to spread life and pleasure through the almighty power of song and music; and to sing of weapons and of the golden age when all was innocent.[8] He arrives at Asa-gard where he "shines like a star." Here he tells of Odin's beneficial immigration into the North and either sings mildly of death, or the strings of his harp "roar forth the thunder of war" and arouse the desire for murder. In the interim, Suttung, who reigns in the extreme North at Hnitbjorg, hears that foreign vessels have arrived on the shore of Manhem with new gods and religious services and decides to fight them. Clubs and bows and arrows are to be used "after the custom of the forefathers," "shields are cleaned with sand and bearfat," and the edges of steel sharpened on smooth rocks.

In the second canto Kwasir arrives at Suttung's court, his countenance beaming with "divine enchantment." With him is the warrior Brage who comes as a special messenger from Odin to sue for the hand of Suttung's daughter, Gunlög. The skald sings of his youth,[9] his divine gift, and of the creation of the world. But Suttung is enraged, he is only temporarily pacified by the magic power of Kwasir's music and determines "to drink intoxication out of the Asas' skulls," much as the forefathers were wont to do.[10]

The third canto is a beautiful and sublime mingling of the Romantic and the Gothic. Here we find gods and dwarfs, dreams, pathos, miracles, caves, and moonlight. Brage and Kwasir descend into a cave on a mountain to rest. Kwasir dreams. He realizes he will not live much longer, and so comes out upon a cliff near a lonely shore and sings his best songs. He tells of the dwarfs and of their partial destruction by Asa-Thor. And, alas! two dwarfs who had their forge beneath the mountain were annoyed by Kwasir's harp—"the breast where dwells the hunger for gold" is immune to the magic power of song and fraternal sympathy—and capture the minstrel. He is bound naked to a marble pillar and murdered. But the divine norn is present. She removes the corpse to save the skald from disgrace, his sacred blood is changed by a miracle to a golden yellow mead, and, together with the harp, is deposited in the lowest part of the grotto.

In the fourth canto the dwarfs are executed for not having a suit of armor ready which they were forging for Suttung, and thus the death of the skald is, in a sense, already avenged. Suttung makes further preparations to reconquer Manhem from the new gods. The army eats bear-steak prepared in copper kettles, and a mead is prepared from honey and hops. Then the dwarfs' grotto is plundered. Hjalmar, a character invented by the poet, is led by fate to Kwasir's blood or mead. He had before the making of a poet; now he becomes a real skald. His vision includes new worlds, his feelings melt together into a symphony, and everything becomes purple and gold. Through the winds of the night, among the tall pines and in a silvery moonlight the heavenly tones issue forth from his harp. The gates of heaven are now truly open to him. Suttung hears the harp and, angered, pursues the skald, but the latter is protected by the norn. It is now that Suttung procures the wonderful mead and decides to entrust it to the care of his daughter Gunlög. She is to be the custodian of it at the castle of Hnitbjorg until her father's victorious return from the war with Odin. In the meantime Brage has disappeared—the poet does not make it clear when—and returns to Odin with the tidings, while Suttung goes to sleep listening to Hjalmar's harp. Then Thor is given command of the Asa-troops, for love and longing has deprived Odin of the necessary energy to carry armor. Thus the poet:

Så stämmer kärlek hjeltars styrka ner,
Så äfven Gudar tråna för begären.[11]

The favorite thought of Stagnelius, that woman is the cause of the downfall of both men and gods, is well illustrated in the fragment of the fifth and sixth cantos. The wise Mimer points out that the Asas will never conquer Jothem unless they obtain Kwasir's golden harp to arouse the men to courage. How is this to be done? Freya's maid Lofne is selected to entice Hjalmar by womanly cunning which can do anything in the world. Hjalmar resists the temptation for a while, but finally yields passionately, Lofne obtains the harp, and

arrives at Odin's castle with it. The last part of the fragment deals with Odin's visit to Gunlög. It is extremely passionate, naïve, and suggestive. In the morning after his nocturnal sojourn, Odin drinks the mead, embraces his sweetheart again, assumes the form of an eagle (as in the original source), and flies away. In Asa-gard he ejects the mead into a beaker which "rings melodiously at every drop." Brage, who has been waiting for him, drinks it and now feels a higher divinity burning in his heart. His glance is directed toward the canopy of the stars and he is crowned king of skalds. The Jota-army is crushed and driven into the far North where they live as Lapps. Hjalmar gets a place among the skalds and Gunlög becomes the wife of Odin.

It is clear from the above analysis that in *Gunlög* Stagnelius was most interested in the purely poetic, the personal, the feminine, and the Romantic. He molds the myth to suit his will. In the next work to be considered we shall notice a somewhat different attitude.

In no production has the poet followed the original source as closely as in *Wisbur*. In this short five-act tragedy our attention is focused upon the original narrative, as given by Snorre Sturleson in the Ynglinga Saga. Fate, which played a secondary part in *Blenda* and *Gunlög*, becomes the principal motive in *Wisbur*. A curse like that upon Andvari's treasure in the Völsunga Saga rests upon our hero. It is the necessary expiation of old sins and the unavoidable repetition of the same which gives the tragic setting. It is a logical Hellenic-Gothic sequence of sin, curse, blood, and tears. Then Stagnelius weaves into his fabric the danger of ambition, the superiority of lowliness to greatness and honor, and emphasizes again the power and character of woman.

It will be remembered that Livijn had in mind a trilogy on the saga of Wisbur (Visbur), but it was never written. The main facts of the original form of the saga have, therefore, been given already.[12] We shall see that the story in the drama coincides on the whole with the original.

The enchantress Huld gives us the past history of the fatal chain, now worn by Hildur. The golden chain had once been the property of Odin's wife. It was made by the dwarf Sindre, it had the property of producing nothing but strife and war, and had been stolen by Loki for the destruction and enticement of all the gods' children. It was promised by Vaulande, Wisbur's father, to Drifva in Finland, but Vaulande was faithless, and died as a consequence, through his former sweetheart's revenge.

Now the situation becomes analogous in Wisbur's own case. His first wife Öda has been deserted. He has two sons, Gissler (Gisel) and Auder (Audur), by her and the chain and throne should belong to them. Öda appears at Wisbur's court at Uppsala to claim her just dues. A large feast is being prepared to which all are invited, including the two sons. The gods do not seem propitious but Wisbur goes blindly on. Öda's request is refused, and Wisbur declares honestly and directly that he does not love his former wife any more. Whereupon Öda becomes a raging animal, a ferocious Penthesilea, who would gladly "drink blood as she drinks the frothing mead." After a consultation with Vanlander's (Vaulande's) spirit, the reigning couple are made acquainted with the pending catastrophe. Soon crowds appear, surround the castle, and capture it. Hildur, in despair, chokes herself with the cursed chain, Wisbur falls on his sword. Auder comes on the stage with the coveted jewel, and now Öda is ready to die.

In the original the chain is mentioned only in connection with Wisbur (in Chap. 17 of the Ynglinga Saga), and the former history of the neck-ring is not mentioned at all. Stagnelius supplies the name, also, of Wisbur's second wife; the saga tells us merely that he "took to himself another wife." Likewise the details of the catastrophe have been altered to suit the dramatic situation; but the fundamental motivation of the original source has been preserved.

Wisbur is a marvelous harmony of Gothicism and Hellenism. Of course, it is primarily a lyrical reading drama; and for this reason the choruses are very prominent and contain perhaps the most beautiful poetry in the tragedy. Here the Hellenic-antique, however, overshadows the Scandinavian-antique. And what wonderful harmony here of form and content! Öda makes her awful, revengeful resolutions in ominous dactylic tetrameters;[13] when Wisbur's castle is surrounded, the chorus gives us the details in rapid dimeters, alternating with tetrameters;[14] the combat between father and son is told in exciting iambic tetrameters;[15] and a temporary calm after the storm is indicated by alternating tetrameters, and trimeters of the dactylic foot.[16] The main argument is written in the modern blank verse with little action and, like the author's other works, with much coloring of rose, lily, purple and silver. The mild sighs, moonlight and mystical yearning of a Romantic atmosphere are not wanting.

Stagnelius has put some thoughts into the minds of the characters Wisbur and Hildur which may well have an autobiographical application, especially when we know of the poet's own mental and physical suffering.

Hildur, in the first act—we may well call it a mere scene—says: "It is easy to die but cruel to tremble eternally." No doubt the poet felt the truth of this assertion. Again, in the fourth act, after Hildur has

announced the decreed doom to come, Wisbur answers with a grim humor:

> Med döden alltså endast? Goda Hildur!
> Visst skall jag dö; jag visste det förut.
> Den höga Oden före mig ju dödde,
> Han, Valhalls konung, alla diars hufvud,
> Den rika Niord, åkerbrukets Gud,
> Och Yngve Frey, den gyllne tidens drott,
> Och Fjolner, Svegder, och min far Vanlander.
> Ej annat öde kan jag vänta mig.[17]

Incidentally we get, at the same time, a good sprinkling of names from Norse mythology.

Sigurd Ring, another short tragedy in pentameters, is very much like *Wisbur.* The formal characteristics are the same; the unities are observed, the characters few, and choruses extol the heroes and heroine. There is little action; most of it is epic and lyrical. It has dramatic episodes of touching intensity, but it is too brief for a stage play. It has the usual amount of Romantic epithets and mystical longing, and evinces the most stirring pathos. No Gothic work of Stagnelius—perhaps none of his works—depicts such intensity of feeling, it seems to me, as *Sigurd Ring.* And the almost imperceptible blending of realism and lyricism in the tragedy proves unmistakably that the author is a poet of genius.

Again, "das Ewig-weibliche" plays an important rôle. In fact, it seems as if the poet at times were more interested in the heroine than in the hero. The tragedy could just as well have been called *Hilma,* the name of the heroine, as *Sigurd Ring.* How Stagnelius delights in the glorification of womanly beauty! Beauty is godlike, and the terms used in describing that of woman are frequently—and naturally—compounds of "snow" and "lily." As in *Wisbur,* there is a personal note, an evidence of the poet's own suffering. In Act III, for instance, there is much about hope, patience, and a silent resignation to whatever fate may have in store for us.

The Old Norse element in *Sigurd Ring* is different from that in *Wisbur.* In the former the original source is more truly historical and the emphasis, therefore, laid more upon viking characteristics than upon pure Norse myths. The viking qualities are idealized and accounts of them clothed in elevated language. The Northern pirate's directness of speech and uprightness is well illustrated. A promise once made is always kept. A death on the battlefield, either self-inflicted or at the hand of another, is the ideal death for an heroic viking, and the blue dwelling-place of the water-sprite is a charming grave for a Norse woman. And this has divine sanction. That Alf dies on the battlefield with Sigurd's sword, wielded by Sigurd himself, is not only desired by Alf, but decreed and fulfilled by the fate of the gods. In addition to the strictly viking element, also, we have much of the poet's reflection in "Sigurd Ring," expressed in terms of Norse myths. In illustrating the tremendous power of love (in Act II), Stagnelius introduces again—and this time he follows the original myth more closely—the story of Suttung's mead. That is, he uses that part of Norse mythology which best suits his Romantic temperament.

Sigurd Ring was one of the last kings of the mythological age of the North. He made himself the ruler of all Scandinavia by the defeat of Harald Hildetand at the memorable battle of Bråvallahed in Småland, Sweden, 730 A. D. This was the last battle in which Odin himself is said to have appeared on earth, and most of the nobles and heroes of the whole North met in combat.[18] The victory of Sigurd Ring over Harald Hildetand is mentioned in Saxo Grammaticus in the eighth book.

The scene of the original story of Stagnelius's tragedy, according to Hammarskjöld,[19] is laid in Norway, and Alf-sol (Hilma) is the daughter of a sub-king of Norway. Here Sigurd, king of Svithiod (Sweden), sues for the hand of Alf-sol but is refused by the father and brothers on the ground of old age. Then, as had been the viking custom, Sigurd resorts to force. But since Sigurd is a mighty and feared warrior, the brothers anticipate the outcome of the encounter by giving their sister poison before the fray opens. When Sigurd finds her dead he dies himself, "as he had lived, among the billows and flames."[20]

Stagnelius localizes his tragedy in Denmark in the province of Jutland, and the action which we see takes place in a colonnade-hall in Alf's castle. The name of the heroine is Hilma; Alf is her brother and guardian and under-king of Jutland; Ragnar is a hero and Hilma's accepted lover; and Sigurd, as in history, is an old man and king of Sweden, Norway and Denmark. The tragic conflict, as in the original, is between genuine love and earthly power. It is duty, sworn friendship, and honor against splendor, high position, and faithlessness. Hilma does not care for happiness in the ordinary sense; she wants a heart, and is, naturally, willing to die for her love.

The plot is very simple. Sigurd, who has always been victorious in battle, demands the hand of Hilma from her brother. The old king is straightway rejected, for Alf refuses to break his word that Ragnar shall possess her love. The refusal means war, and war under the circumstances means the defeat and probable death of Hilma's protectors. And so Hilma takes the poison prepared for her, and in the presence of her lover, Alf and Ragnar are both slain in the battle that follows, Sigurd himself commits suicide, and the bodies of Sigurd and Hilma are burned on the same funeral pyre upon the monarch's ship.

That Stagnelius had the power to create a scene of dramatic beauty is proved in the fourth act. Sigurd is just returning with the blood of Alf and Ragnar upon his conscience. He has sent thousands to Valhalla before without the slightest feeling of compunction, but the last deed worries him. In the meantime the body of Hilma has been prepared for the last rites and is lying in state. Gerda, the fostermother, tells Sigurd, who knows nothing of Hilma's death, that his bride is waiting for him in wedding array, calm, silent, and smiling. The subsequent scene, when Sigurd discovers the real state of affairs, and the heroic lamentations of the old viking king at Hilma's bier produce a dramatic situation of immense power.

The poet's own hopeful and serene view of the life to come finds a suitable expression in *Sigurd Ring* in terms of Norse mythology. The tone is that of a deep religiosity and faith in a better eternal life. The chorus in the last act sings first of the final destruction of the world. Then, last of all, it sings of the eternal bliss to come, when evil is no more; when Balder and Nanna return from the subjugated kingdom of Hel; and when the Asas discover anew in the green grass the divine runes of Allfather.

That Stagnelius knew his Norse mythology and understood its profound meaning perfectly, is nowhere better illustrated than in the interesting, seven-page dramatic fragment *Svegder*. In the original source the poet found the very essence of the moral and religious struggles of mankind. He found his own agonizing, Faustian struggle of two souls, diametrically opposed to one another, dwelling in the same breast. Here was the golden opportunity to dwell on the everlasting war between matter and spirit. Here the poet found a vehicle for symbolism and philosophy; here, again, woman becomes the only conqueror of gods; and back of it all are the blind, incomprehensible judgments of fate.

The narrative of the original Svegder (Svegde)[21] is found in the fifteenth chapter of the Ynglinga Saga by Sturleson. It deals with an Uppsala king's journey to the Black Sea to find Odin the Old. On the way he is enticed into a mountain by dwarfs and never returns. According to Sturleson, it was Svegder's second effort to reach Gudhem, i.e., "god-home," the home of Odin. "Once more Svegde set out to reach Gudhem. In the eastern part of Sweden (Svithiod) there is a large village by the name of Stone (Sten), where there is a rock as large as a big house. In the evening after sunset, when Svegde was returning from the drinking-bout to his sleeping chamber, he looked at the rock and saw that a dwarf sat beneath it. Svegde and his men were very much intoxicated and ran against the rock. The dwarf stood in the door, calling to Svegde, and bade him come in, if he wished to find Odin. Svegde hastened to come inside the rock, which closed immediately, and Svegde never came back."

Of the original dramatis personae only one character (the dwarf) appears in Stagnelius's fragment. But the poet has introduced three others: Nore, a giant; Sindre, a dwarf, servant, and watchman in the employ of Nore; and Hild, Nore's daughter, who is to entice Svegder. The hero himself does not appear, but we are acquainted with everything there is to know about him. He is the fifth grandson of Fridulf, who formerly established altars to the glory of Odin, and represents the power of light. Opposed to him are the dwarfs and the giant Nore, who represent the servants of darkness. From this list of characters the main theme may be imagined without further comment.

The dwarf has just completed a chain, the making of which has been entrusted to him by the King of the Mountain, Nore. The different links of the chain furnish material for philosophical reflections on the judgments of fate.[22] Nore tells the dwarf to keep the "new Gleipner" (the chain) which has been forged by the powers of revenge for destructive purposes against Odin's children. Then follows a brief history of the creation and of the original strife between the gods and the giants. Nore summons the sons of Ymer (here, the dwarfs), reveals to them their origin, and inspires in them a hope of future joy. The giants and dwarfs are brothers, and upon their altars the people were wont to worship, until Odin came and defeated the King of Materia, i. e., Ymer. All giants and dwarts drowned in the blood of Ymer except Bergelmer, with wife, children, and slaves, who escaped. Through these the race carried on an eternal war against the powers of light. They often forged weapons of murder for man and "by means of the alluring food of gold brought them into vice and destruction." This condition continued until Fridulf's son came and established altars to the glory of the God of Light and frightened the dwarfs back into the rivers and mountains. That is, Odin was recognized as the victor, although the divine power of darkness was still worshipped.

It is hardly necessary to observe that in the introductory epic material of the fragment we have nothing but Christian ideals in the garb of Norse mythology. Odin is virtually none other than Christ himself, or better, perhaps, the personification of what we call Christian ideals. This becomes still more evident as Nore's narrative goes on. According to a "ridiculous" saga, which originated in the "sacred palm-abode of India," Odin was to allow himself to be born of an earthly woman to redeem man. And now Svegder, who believes Odin to be his ancestor, has set out for the land of palms, olives, and sycamores to visit the God who has just been born of woman. In other words, Svegder is undertaking a pilgrimage across the Baltic to the Ori-ent, which the poet supposes to be the cradle of both the Old Norse and the Christian religions.

Then commences the real dramatic action which is very brief. Nore knows about Svegder's journey and has sent Hild to entice him. His servant, Sindre, is watching upon the top of the mountain for the approach of the victim. Sindre arrives on the scene and announces the arrival of Svegder with a band of warriors. Then Hild enters; evidently she has already laid the snare, and she sets forth how a situation of that kind must always be met. The only means for darkness to overcome light is "the haven of a maiden." A glance, a voice, will "disarm the whole power of the sun and allure the regents of the stars down from their thrones to an effeminate rest on a bed of flowers."

Here the fragment ends, and there is very little more that can be said about it. It is another illustration of a Romanticist's unsuccessful attempt to dramatize a saga theme. But this much must be said: there is a wealth of meaning hidden in the original source and it would have proved interesting to see how Stagnelius really intended to formulate the drama as a whole.

Dramatically, **Svegder** was not a success, even as far as it went; and probably could not have been, if completed. The internal meaning was more suitable for an epic than a drama, and there was not enough material in the original for a complex, well-developed plot. It was merely an episode and the hero, who is a tool of cruel fate, is practically ensnared at the beginning of the drama. There is no more to develop. Then, too, a pretentious scheme, where woman was to be the tool and unconquerable emissary of the powers of the darkness, could hardly prove an agreeable dramatic topic in this case. It was based, it seems, on personal opinions which were too severe and pessimistic.

Notes

[1] Cf. Introduction by Hammarskjöld to Stagnelius's *Samlade skrifter,* Stockholm, 1836, p. 32.

[2] Cf. the following strophe (29) from "Sång till qvinnorna i Norden" by Stagnelius:

> O sköna tid! i Sagans ljud
> Blott ännu lefvande på jorden,
> Då ynglingen i höga Norden
> Till hjelte valdes af sin brud!
> Hans dygder inga skranker funno,
> Och modet kände ingen gräns.
> O sköna tid! då kärlekens
> Och ärans eld förente brunno!

[3] See "Literära karakteristiker." Senare bandet, Örebro, 1870. Recension of Stagnelius's works, pp. 51-52.

[4] It was probably written immediately before "Wladimir den Store," which appeared in 1817.

[5] It is written in easy-flowing, regular rimed pentameters with alternating masculine and feminine rimes.

[6] The spittle of the Asas and Wanes represents the spiritual and the formal in poetry, respectively.

[7] For instance, Stagnelius uses only one vessel to collect Kwasir's blood.

[8] Cf.

> Ja, säll var jorden innan Lokes brott
> Och Höders blindhet hunnit Balder fälla, ll.
> 81-82.

[9] Cf. quotation at beginning of chapter.

[10] Cf. lines 248-49.

[11] Thus love takes away the strength of heroes; thus even the gods yearn for desires (i. e., the passion of love).

[12] Cf. Chap. I, p. 72, where the original narrative is given.

[13] Cf.

> Ormar från Nastrand! sliten mitt bröst!
> Spruten ert gift i mitt rasande hjerta!

[14] Cf.

> Ack! lössläppt är fejden;
> En rasande tiger,
> Snart fråssar den grymme på likströdda torg.

[15] Cf.

> Det vilda hafvets raseri
> Och stormens vrede tyglen I—
> Kan menskan blott ej hugnad bli?

[16] Cf.

> Stjernorna blänka så mildt i azuren
> Blommorna sofva i dalen.
> Lugn är den eviga, hulda naturen,
> Andas blott njutning och väl.

[17] [And so you come to announce] Death only? Why, my good Hildur! Of course I am to die; I knew that before. Why, the high Odin before me died, he, the king of Valhalla, the chief of all the gods. The rich Niord, the god of agriculture; and Yngve Frey, the king of the Golden Age; and Fjolner, Svegder, and my father Vanlander; no other fate may I expect.

[18] Cf. Paul C. Sinding: *The Scandinavian Races*, New York, 1875, pp. 47ff.

[19] Cf. Introduction to Stagnelius's *Samlade skrifter*, Stockholm, 1836, pp. 36-37.

[20] For his own source, Hammarskjöld refers in his Introduction to "Sveriges historia för ungdom," by M. Bruzelius. I have not seen this work myself.

[21] He was the grandfather of Wisbur, whom we have treated above.

[22] Cf. Schiller's "Das Lied von der Glocke"; the different stages in the casting of the bell and the accompanying reflections represent the different stages in the growth of an individual.

Giovanni Bach and Frederika Blankner on the style and content of Stagnelius' work:

[For Stagnelius] the opposition between ideal and real assumes tragic proportions. Such a contrast is not for him, as for others, a poetical-philosophical problem, but a problem intimately lived and never resolved, and precisely for that reason dramatic. Such inclination of his to a tragic conception of life was aggravated by the condition of his health and by an unhappy love affair.

The collection of his poems entitled: *The Lilies of Sharon* (1821-22) is full of metaphysical lucubrations, permeated by neo-Platonism, as is his play entitled, *The Bacchantes* (1822).

The Fisherman Thorsten and *The Martyrs* (found and published posthumously, 1824-26) are other plays of his, which betray, however, a marked tendency toward realism.

The principal merit of Stagnelius lies in his style, vibrant with sentiment and elevated in inspiration, but it is lacking in virility and force, poorly adapted therefore to the drama, so that the tragedies of Stagnelius have been considered by some as his most beautiful lyrics.

With Stagnelius the period of the great romanticists closes and that of their imitators begins, but in addition, across the meanderings of romanticism a new current from abroad gains power, that of realism.

Giovanni Bach and Frederika Blankner, in
The History of the Scandinavian Literature, *ed.*
Frederika Blankner, Kennikat Press, 1938.

Leif Sjöberg (essay date 1968)

SOURCE: "*Wladimir den Store:* Some Observations," in *Scandinavian Studies,* Vol. 40, No. 1, February, 1968, pp. 303-09.

[In the following essay, Sjöberg examines Stagnelius' style as well as political and religious ideas expressed in his epic poem Wladimir den Store.*]*

Wladimir den Store, the first great Swedish hexameter poem, is also the first poem which Stagnelius allowed himself to publish (1817). The reasons for this may have been many, but the main one is presumably that he had a specific poetical method—Chateaubriand's theory in *Le Génie du Christianisme*—which is almost consistently applied, and used *Les Martyrs* as a pattern. The purpose was to glorify Christianity. But perhaps there were other purposes as well. ***Wladimir den Store*** is the first poem in which Stagnelius presented his political views—which he does explicitly. He was very pro-Russian and swore allegiance to The Holy Alliance (part III, verses 180 following, are a panegyric for Czar Alexander). Olle Holmberg has found a couple of letters from which it is evident that Stagnelius was occupied with plans to marry and to take a position in the Finnish army. The poem is then to be considered a typical specimen for an officer's commission. Fredrik Böök has repudiated this view with more determination than ability to convince in *Bonniers Litterära Magasin*, 1942. It has been noted that the poem point by point follows the Russian minister Magnitzski's cultural program. The actual theme Stagnelius found in the Medieval Russian *Nestor Chronicle*, but he treated the theme in a fairly free manner. The form of the poem is Homeric; there are, for instance, a large number of compound epithets, such as "guldkedsmyckade skaran" and "mannamördande järnet."

We know from Stagnelius' own statement that he was a theater habitué, and ***Wladimir den Store*** also shows obvious theatrical impressions, above all in the visionary scenes of the first song, which are reminiscent of the effect scenes of contemporary, theater. In Part I, line 10, there appears a ballet; and Wladimir promises the goddess Lada a ballet, "en tropp af blomstrande gossar," who will "sväfva i dans med smyckade hår och retande later" as Oscar Wieselgren says in "Stagnelius, Endymion och mamsell Ginetti" (*Svenska Dagbladet, July 25, 1946*). Sven Cederblad has emphasized the importance of spectacular scenes of the theater in *Stagnelius och hans omgivning* (1936, p. 133).

The poem was published as a separate little book (without the author's name on it!) at the end of 1817, which is about the time when Byron's name was receiving attention in Swedish literary magazines (cf. G. Biller's "Byron i den svenska litteraturen före Strandberg." *Samlaren* 1912, pp. 123 ff). The poem deals with a princely person, Wladimir, whose destinies are told in three songs: the number three is essential to the composition, because it is a matter of drawing a contrast and its resolution. The poem thus is built up on the technique of opposition, which gives sharpness and liveliness. The first song juxtaposes Wladimir's melancholy and his previous achievements. The second song concerns an outward victory and an inner defeat, and in the third song the contrasts are united.

In the first two songs Wladimir's feelings describe a roller-coasterlike curve, and in the third song they have reached a measure of stability. In keeping with romantic practice, a night scene, complete with full moon, begins the poem. The Prince's *Weltschmerz* is close to paralysis; he is so caught up in himself and his brooding over the transience of things that he is blind to the allurements of the dancing girls and deaf to the music. Ivan's eulogy to his former industriousness and present felicity arouses him and he protests in an open confession and perhaps with something of a pose:

> Ack J ej kännen de qval, som under den
>   yppiga skruden
> Fräta mitt bröst: J kunnen ej se den hemliga
>   oro,
> Hvilken till Konungens innersta rum, till
>   Konungens hjärta
> Banar sig väg, genom härarnas vakt, genom
>   riglade portar,
> Och vid yppiga bord, på elastiskt svällande
>   bäddar
> Griper med armar af jern det aldrig förfelade
>   rofvet.

He knows, however, one way out of his melancholy—war; and he decides that the war trumpets shall resound early the next morning. The reader cannot help asking himself: Why was this medicine not used earlier? For the sake of the exposition or as motivation for the building up of tension, which leads to the act of aggression: the massacre? The war is the feigned solution which first occurs to him, but his subconscious also suggests other solutions to him. His dreams follow each other in rapid succession. First, the heavenly host: let yourself be converted; let war alone! Then Olga: The monastery gives peace! and finally Satan: exterminate the Christian dwarfs; cultivate the orgy! In Satan's speech there are possible reminiscenses of the rhetoric of the French revolution. A strongly visionary motif runs through the whole poem but most strikingly in Wladimir himself and as such is characteristic of him. Anna appears to him hardly different from Olga and Satan. Ivan's and Wladimir's dialog and the visions together depict Wladimir's situation and conflict. He is a man with periods of depression who seeks cheerfulness through drinking but finds only torpor and emptiness: Woman and wine no longer stimulate him, only war can renew him, and the alternative—to become a Christian, especially a monk—does not suit Wladimir.

The second song tells about the bloody attack on the city of Theodosia. When the sun has set and the battle is over, Wladimir, the victor, takes a rest, on a silken bed. He lets a young man ply him with Lesbian wine, and simultaneously the doors are opened and Anna, his captive, is brought before him. Now a change of parts takes place which is as quick as it is amazing. Conflict flares up anew—on a different level. Beauty is one of Anna's weapons and it is complemented with sighs and tears. Like so many real or fictitious heroes Wladimir is allergic to beauty in tears. He explains himself:

> Männer jag kallt ser lida och dö, men
> skönhet i tårar
> Härdar min blick ej ut

and he asks her to dry "den sorgliga daggen" and smile a little, so that he can enjoy his victory. The prisoner has vanquished the victor.

Anna exploits her advantage: Wladimir's curiosity about who she is, she satisfies only after she has uttered a prayer (or prophecy) which later is fulfilled, i.e. that Wladimir shall come to her city with the olive branch of peace in his hand. She reveals her royal lineage, further intensifies his love, and tells about her friend Eudoxia's tragic fate, which elucidates the Christian soul's way of living in unconditioned devotion:

> Du allt nu, o Wladimir! känner
> Öfver mitt öde bestäm. Dock vet att Basilii
> syster
> Mellan träldom och död ej nedrigt tvekar i
> valet.

He answers chivalrously:

> O Sköna Prinsessa! Min fånge
> Icke Du är. Befall. Den kufvade borgen Dig
> lyder . . .
> I morgon jag skall . . . sända Dig tryggad
> till kejsarestaden tillbaka.

In the third song—the next morning—Wladimir goes in to Anna hoping for some commiseration:

> Sköna Prinsessa! förgäfves min kropp var
> tröttad af striden;
> Själen tänkte på dig. I himmelsk, strålande
> fägring
> Stod för min tanke din bild och fördref den
> gyldene sömnen.

What he is in fact stating is that the kind of love he has experienced before was low instinctual desire and an intoxication of short duration.

> Tusende känslor, ej anade förr, nu mitt
> hjerta bestorma,

> Nya Solar gå opp för min blick: jag trånar,
> jag söker
> Likt en förlorad hälft, dig, Hulda! med
> darrande längtan.

In this Wladimir takes up Aristophanes' beautiful thought from Plato's Symposium. He asks for her heart and hand and offers in return half of his dominion. The dynastic problem can be solved "mellan Greklands ätter och Rysslands" (cf. Böök in his Stagnelius monograph). The suitor then comes with an unhappy turn of expression by promising Anna the people's steady worship of her as a patroness saint.

Wladimir is in a glow awaiting her answer, and the princess grows pale, but then she recovers:

> . . . Gå, krigiske furste, och aftvå
> Först dina händer från grekernas blod; först,
> Wladimir, afsvär
> Evigt de spökens tjenst, dem med rysliga
> offer du dyrkar,
> Innan om kärlek till mig, till Basilii syster, du
> talar.

Wladimir stands there irresolute, while Anna, weeping, repeats that she wants to return home. *Ett moln seglar upp på Wladimirs panna,* and his stature takes on something cosmic through this *moln.* As in Part I, 18, 31, and 302, he becomes a giant, who still is insufficient, a Morolf before an Isolde. He composes himself but reproaches her:

> Hårda Christinna! res, och le åt hedningens
> tårar.

And Anna takes him at his word. But her rejection is in reality an incentive to Wladimir's conversion, since it runs side by side with his love for her. On her way back home Anna meets Antonius, the recluse in the cave, who convinces her of her high destiny as Wladimir's spouse and as progenitor of a mighty dynasty.

Wladimir shuts himself in for three days and three nights, after which he calls together his boyars and informs them that his tentative thought had ripened into a resolve: He is ready to abandon power and battle to follow his destiny,

> att på ångerns och reningens bana

to turn to heaven, and he appeals to his warriors to receive baptism. At first he is apparently met with lack of sympathy.

> Sorgligt J tveken! Välan! sitt beslut har
> Wladimir fattat.

Then a miracle comes to his assistance, a shimmering cross appears, and the boyars are all at once ready to go to Constantinople.

While Wladimir with his boyars wanders towards the city—it is described as the pilgrimage of the blessed ones straight to the kingdom of heaven—Anna is torn between *agape* and *eros,* and it is obvious that the erotic pressure is very strong. She is no longer capable of praying for herself but shows an unselfish quality by asking Mary to save at least Wladimir's soul; she breaks out in bitter tears and is bedazzled by a vision: a heavenly, prospering youth waving a palm branch—the peace symbol—and a harp, appears before her urging:

Dröj icke längre här! Din brudgum, Wladimir,
   väntar.
Gack och i festens purpur Dig kläd.

Anna continues to pray yet a while, then stands up and walks away.

   Betjenande Tärnor
Mötte vid dörren ren. Med Syriens doftande
   oljor
Stänkte den höga sitt hår, med Indiens
   gemmer det krönte
Och kring de veka höfterna göt en slöja af
   purpur.

On this note the poem ends, so it does not actually deal with Anna's and Wladimir's union.

It is obvious that Wladimir embodies a great deal of Stagnelius' own life questioning. The oscillation between intoxication with life and satiety with life, the attempts to get past his instability, to organize his vital force into something more meaningful, the choice of philosophy or religion as diversion.

Wladimir here presumably reaches a certain equilibrium. Is this the alleged peace of the Christian believer? No, Stagnelius has not experienced it himself, and he makes no attempt to portray Anna's and Wladimir's union. From the thesis and its antithesis he has not been able to reach a synthesis; he only suggests a faint idea of it. Wladimir's change of character in the middle of the second song is, moreover, artistically unconvincing. But perhaps it reveals something of the dreamer and recluse Stagnelius and his own difficulties in making contact on a deeper level. His own love probably lacked a decisive element, a phase of change, the development into the friendship of souls, which could have been explained by means of a dialog between the main protagonists; but it is not there.

When Cederblad speaks of the development toward asceticism which the story of Wladimir's conversion reflects in him, it seems incorrect to stress its theoretical art too much. According to the prophecy Wladimir will not become an ascetic, only his vitality is channeled into the framework of marriage. Wladimir often acts in protest; he constantly finds himself in opposition to his environment: he does whatever enters his head, most often what we do not expect from him. In the middle of the festivities he is melancholy. He approves of war but does not take part in the massacre. He surrenders to Anna instead of violating her. After the victory over the Christians he himself turns Christian to the astonishment of his boyars.

Holmberg conveniently skips discussion of **Wladimir den Store** with an appreciative turn of phrase to Böök "som så genomkommenterat dikten," that there is nothing to add. My impressions and examination of Böök's commentary generally verify Holmberg's views, but a few more observations can be made. In the Stagnelius edition of 1919, which I have used, Böök refers to Scherer's 1779 version of the *Nestor Chronicle*. In the same year as Böök's commentary appeared, Norrback's translation of the *Nestor Chronicle* was published. Böök later admitted that at the time of the first edition he had insufficient knowledge of the chronicle. That explains why he mistook the many celestial visions in **Wladimir den Store** as inventions by Stagnelius, which they are not. In several chapters of the chronicle angels, apparitions, and ghosts are mentioned—the poem is clearly medieval in its receptiveness to these occult phenomena—Stagnelius was most likely influenced by them.

In Part II, 89, *Dmitri,* according to Böök, is a free invention. In the *Nestor Chronicle* (Norrback, 1919) a Dimitrius is mentioned twice in connection with *den Helige Antonius.*

In the list of names a certain Nordic tone is heard. Norrback's Rogowolod thus in Stagnelius has become Rognvald. The names which Böök has been unable to check show this even more clearly. *Mading* is alien to Russian, since the *-ng*-sound does not exist in Russian (*-nk* would be substituted for it). On the other hand *-ing* is a Nordic ending, cf. *viking, väring,* etc. *Konek* is not Russian, but is not entirely un-Nordic.

Part III, 28-29, "jag söker, / likt en förlorad hälft, dig, Hulda." Cf. Aristophanes' speech in Plato's *Symposium.*

Part III, 332 ff. mentions a two-headed eagle which flew around the cross. According to Böök Stagnelius got the image from A. W. Schlegel's poem "Der Bund der Kirche mit den Künsten," which he translated. Böök says nothing about the meaning of this symbolism. The eagle was early considered a symbol of strength and power. In *Novum* the eagle is emblematic of St. John the Evangelist and is also a symbol of the baptism, a fact which is pertinent here (cf. Helander: *Kristna symboler.* pp. 114-15). In Stagnelius' poem we have the two-headed eagle, which is a common occurrence in hearaldry. The two heads according to Brewer's *Dictionary of Phrase and Fable,* p. 319, symbolize the Eastern or Byzantine Empire and the Western or Roman Empire. It is perhaps most in keeping with the spirit of the poem to interpret the symbol as a prophecy about the emergence of the Russian Empire under the sign of the Cross—especially as Olga (Part I, 289) already has spoken about the Russian eagles.

Part III, 341, mentions maidens, "som tvagit / kläderna hvite i Lammets blod." This shows a verbal connection with John 7:14 (The Bible translation of 1917): "Dessa äro de som komma ur den stora bedrövelsen, och som hava tvagit sina kläder och gjort dem rena i Lammets blod." The expressions *Det nya Jerusalem* and *den nya födelsens vågbad* are also biblical in tone, cf. Tit. 3:5.

Wladimir's conversion, I suppose, has at least a vague point of contact with the story of Saul in the Acts of the Apostles, 9. In the *Nestor Chronicle* it says, furthermore, about Wladimir: "Till följd av en Guds skickelse hade Wladimir vid denna tid blivit angripen av en ögonsjukdom, så att han ingenting kunde se. . . ." When the bishop put his hand on him, his sight suddenly returned. Something similar, as we know, happens to Saul, too. One can also note a certain correspondence between person and thing, i.e. in Part I, 145: "Wladimir ensam låg . . . med vemod tittade Månen in."

Karl Toepfer (essay date 1992)

SOURCE: "Orfeus and the Maenads: Two Modes of Ecstatic Discourse in Stagnelius's *Bacchanterna,*" in *Scandinavian Studies,* Vol. 64, No. 1, Winter, 1992, pp. 26-52.

[*In the following essay discussing Stagnelius'* Bacchanterna, *Toepfer suggests that the poet used tensions between Classicism and Romanticism to probe the relationship between feeling and language.*]

In 1822, a year before his death, Erik Johan Stagnelius (1793-1823) completed a fascinating one-act tragedy, ***Bacchanterna eller Fanatismen***.[1] But despite the beauty of its language, the complexity of its thematic concerns, the intensity of its dramatic effects, and the bizarre grandeur of its ambitions, the play hardly enjoys the acknowledgement it deserves in discussions of the romantic contribution to drama and theater. That Stagnelius wrote in Swedish may explain in part the lack of international appreciation for his achievement. If this explanation is not entirely convincing, it

is because one can always point to Strindberg, Ingmar Bergman, or Pär Lagerqvist as producers of Swedish dramatic texts which speak in other languages. A more satisfying explanation lies in ***Bacchanterna*** itself, in its relation, not to the Swedish language as such, but to Language—or more precisely, poetic speech—as a sign of cosmic intelligence.

However, the national identity of the text looms over much of the published commentary on Stagnelius, which manages to enhance his significance by subduing his strangeness. Such commentary stresses the poet's connection to large international cultural currents but avoids focusing attention on his otherness in relation to what he perceived as a tradition or the dominant set of values defining the reality in which he lived. The emphasis is on identifying the unifying principles in the poet's works; these principles then unite him to a European rather than to an obscure, isolated, or provincial tradition.[2] It is evident, however, that ***Bacchanterna*** complicates positioning Stagnelius within various supralinguistic, transhistorical, or transnational contexts. Although no one dismisses the play as a lesser achievement, discussion of the text appears muted in relation to other works by Stagnelius.[3]

Fredrik Böök, the major commentator on the play and a very prominent and cosmopolitan figure in Swedish literary criticism, could perhaps accommodate the perversities of ***Bacchanterna*** without worrying about the provinciality of the national literature. In his three books on Stagnelius, Böök devoted entire chapters to this drama. He did not repudiate any previous interpretation, nor did he treat the text as a problem in establishing a unity for the poet's work as a whole. On the contrary, over a period of four decades, he refined and elaborated an initial perception of ***Bacchanterna*** as a major work because Stagnelius has developed a poetic language (symbolik) for embodying a diverse range of seemingly contradictory versions of reality: paganism and Christianity, Greek radiance and Nordic shadows, romantic symbolism and classical form, and archaic mythology and ascetic idealism (*Stagnelius* 454-84).[4] But in order to grasp the power of this language to complicate cultural difference, it is necessary to examine the text from a psychological, psychoanalytical perspective, which means considering the text not only in relation to the life of its author and the specific cultural milieu in which he lived but in relation to recurrent sets of motifs and images which do not seem bound to a particular time and culture (*Stagnelius än en gang* 87-116). Böök's perspective perceives poetry as the materialization of an intelligence that seeks to transcend the constraints imposed upon it by historical consciousness. Yet in the end the power of language to blur distinctions between humans and the gods is a philosophical problem which compels us to see the text as a "kritik av Martyerna," and, by implication, as the encoding of a mysterious (Platonic) logic (sällsam fantasiens logik) by which speech simultaneously manifests God and destroys the Orfic poet (*Stagnelius liv och dikt* 219-36).

In 1962, Staffan Bergsten reprinted Hammarsköld's 1824 edition of the play and published a brief afterword which focuses more narrowly than Böök on the text's sophisticated relation to classical mythology and classical models ("antika forbilderna"), presumably in order to situate Stagnelius within a more enlightened or Apollonian attitude toward religious fanaticism than reference to motifs and obsessions defining the worldview of romantic mysticism would encourage. In distancing Stagnelius from the romantic impulses ascribed to him by other commentators, Bergsten links *Bacchanterna* to the poet's other theater projects in a classical vein, such as the opera *Cydippe* and the ballet *Narcissus,* as well as to his cosmopolitan awareness of classical literature. But this strategy is not much different from others in that it stresses the text's relation to other texts rather than to language itself, rather than to a unique or strange perception of language embodied by the text.

The chief concern of previous commentary, with its emphasis on influences on Stagnelius, has been to situate this mysterious play in relation to mainstream European cultural history, whereas the objective in this essay is to situate the text in relation to ideological structures embedded in rhetorical choices and signifying practices, which control the production of historical modes of discourse. The unique value of the text, then, depends less upon its affiliation with mainstream cultural modes of discourse (classicism, romanticism) than upon its use of tensions between these modes to expose a tragic relation between language and feeling which neither discourse in itself can disclose. *Bacchanterna* dramatizes conditions under which speech moves its speakers toward ecstasy. But focusing on tensions between classical and romantic modes of discourse may conceal a deeper, more significant tension within the text. Focusing on the language of the text reveals a profound sexual difference controlling relations between speech and ecstasy. Stagnelius introduces a complex web of rhetorical devices which indicates that ecstasy emerges differently in response to two distinct modes of discourse, male and female, each of which, however, subsumes both classical and romantic modes of discourse.

Stagnelius dramatizes the romantic theme of the stigmatized individual in conflict with the homogeneous community. The text imbues this political and very conventional problem with an erotic aura, so that the principle of individuality, in the persons of Orfeus and his adept, Gorgias, appears as a masculine phenomenon, while communal identity, represented by the nameless chorus of bacchantes, implies a feminine

quality of being. The male/female polarity evolves out of a cosmic polarity of sky and earth:

Orfeus:
Mig tyctes att på spetsen af Olympus
Jag ensam stod och lät mitt fria öga
Kring verlden irra.

(172-74)

(It seemed to me that on the summit of
   Olympus
I stood alone and my eyes wandered freely
Around the world.)

Chorforeskan:
En grotta der mig vinkar i sin tysta famn.
Narciss-omblomstrad öppnar sig dess
   dunkla port.

(312-13)

(*Chorus Leader:*
One cave beckoned me into its silent
   embrace.
Narcissus blossoms opened wide round its
   dark door.)

The Olympian/chthonic conflict also entails a conflict between two modes of ecstatic discourse. The text, however, dramatizes a perception of ecstasy that is unconstrained by the pressures of family feeling. In spite of its determination to treat ecstasy as above all an erotic experience, the drama avoids any distinct reference to family life or even marriage. Instead, the play shows how ecstasy, for either sex, arises from attitudes toward language which subvert, or at least inhibit, that unity between the sexes for which marriage and the family are dominant signs.

The poetic voice of Orfeus is seductive without his wanting it to be so. The bacchantes hunt him down and destroy him because his song threatens the communal-building power of Dionysos, "verldens Gud" [1009] (the world god), even though he does not sing for the purpose of communicating with anyone but himself. Dionysus never appears, but the Chorus Leader quotes him at length (491-527). His voice,

[. . .] *var som källans sorl,*
Som i cypresselundar vindens midnatts-sus.

(486-87)

([. . .] was like a murmuring spring,
Like the midnight sigh of the wind in the
   cypress groves.)

His voice is, thus, not only an impersonation or an echo of a male voice, is not only male power transformed and manifested through a female voice, but is the transmission of a message heard only in a dream: "Systrar, hören dock min dröm" [474] (Sisters, hear my dream). For the bacchantes, ecstasy means unity with God, with a superhuman identity, and such unity signifies itself when language unfolds through an orgiastic, anonymous, and choral voice. For Orfeus, ecstasy means a supreme detachment from the world, an unbound relationship to any mythic spot of earth, and such detachment results when language manifests itself through a meditative, lyric, solo voice. The Orfic poet, perceiving language as a source of ecstasy rather than an apparatus of seduction, is indifferent to whether his voice communicates or has an audience. The ambiguity of his language is so great that it prevents any stable understanding from taking place; indeed, his language reveals a profound skepticism regarding the permanence or even the reality of human feelings. That skepticism prevented Euridyce (who here is only a name on Orfeus's lips) from accompanying him out of the underworld and motivates the bacchantes to return him forever to the cave. Yet the enigmatic beauty of his voice is seductive insofar as it awakens in the anonymous, bacchantic listener a desire for unity with a human (i.e., real) rather than divine (dreamt) identity.[5]

But the desire of the mass to absorb and consume the individual results in violence, a frenzied tearing apart of the detached poet, and so it is not surprising that Orfeus links the sound of song with the image of sacrificial blood (offerblod och sång [1111]), as if the sound and the image had a common node of origin in the human emotional system. In this text, the relation between seduction and ecstasy is very strange and complex. The language which brings ecstasy to the Orfic speaker is merely and unintentionally seductive to the bacchantic listener, who fears, all the same, that a real male voice, however enchanting, will only bring disillusionment to the (female) listener, for the singer remains loftily detached from any sense of community, communication, or unity with a (female) listener who dares to explore the possibility that a greater source of ecstasy lies in a real male than in a god she has imagined. But the ecstatic speech of the bacchantes has no seductive purpose or effect (at least for the male figures in the text), even though the seductive voice of the god, Dionysus, is embedded within their language. Making no appearance on the stage and speaking entirely through the voice of the Chorus Leader, Dionysus is the creation of a female ecstatic discourse. He signifies the perception that ecstasy is a response to an illusion, a myth, a dream, an imaginary identity which language constructs when the speaker regards ecstasy as a sign of communal understanding and communication.

The central scene in this huge one-act drama is the vast, ecstatic dialogue between the Chorus Leader and the chorus of Bacchantes (284-637). Though he makes no explicit acknowledgement in his preface to the play, Stagnelius (**"Om Bacchanterna"** [221-22]) here seems to have been inspired by the wild chorus scene near the opening of Euripides's *The Bacchae* (407 B.C.) with its turbulent, irregular speech rhythms, its hymnic reiterations of praise for Dionysus and the mythic images attached to him, and its descriptions of his divine powers. But by introducing the ecstatic chorus so early in the drama, Euripides discloses a vaguely satiric purpose. Actions which culminate in ecstasy are of less interest to him than actions which are a consequence of ecstasy. Since for Euripides, ecstasy of any sort is synonymous with hallucination, with a complete submission to illusions, the actions which result from the ecstatic state of misperception are by turns grotesque, barbaric, morbid, and, ultimately, tragic.[6] Euripides links ecstasy with a punishment inflicted upon humans by the god for a trivial insult to his honor. His motive is petty, vindictive, and never higher than human motives; indeed, he is easily mistaken for a mortal, in spite of the early grandiose glamorization of him by the chorus.

But Stagnelius, by situating the ecstatic scene in the center of the play, avoids linking ecstasy with an initiating or culminating locus of action. His strategy makes it difficult to establish a clear cause-and-effect relationship between the ecstatic state and the actions which occur either before or after it. Ecstasy obviously appears as a central force in human experience, giving meaning to the past and the future; but that means it is, in effect, a condition of being in the midst of time itself. It is not merely a transformative point in time but a point between the beginning and ending of powerful desires. Ecstatic speech emerges a kind of substrate out of which other, less central forms of experience are descended.

The scene opens with a twenty-line speech by the chorus; the lines vary in length from nine to twelve syllables. Figure 1 diagrams the diversity of verse forms and meters throughout the scene to show how radically Stagnelius departs from the classical dramatic conventions, particularly the alexandrine, followed by neo-classical or quasi-classical writers like Racine, Alfieri, and Grillparzer, even though his subject matter is perfectly classical. From a formal perspective, Stagnelius's play represents a more powerful deviation from classical dramatic form than Byron's extravagant *Manfred* (1817) or Hugo's widely influential *Hernani* (1830).

The chorus gives a luminous panoramic description of the Thracian landscape, linking the pervasive but hidden presence of Dionysos to "Guldvingade fjärilar paras" [305] (gold-sparkling couplings of butterflies).

The Chorus Leader continues the hymnic cataloguing of nature, through which the gods manifest themselves but observes that it is song which purifies her soul and transports it "till salighetens öar hän" [316] (to holy isles far away). The chorus asks, "Hvad will du höra?" [317] (What will you hear?) and proceeds to list all the gods and mythic figures for whom it has songs. The Chorus Leader responds that she would prefer to think of Bacchus (Dionysos), the "tiger-tamer" (tiger-tämjarn): "för sömnens makt / Mitt öga domnar, vakna vid hans lofsång opp" [336-39] (to seal the eyes with sleep, waken wide the song of praise for him). This instruction is curious because it seems to imply a lullaby such as she mentions in her previous speech. But what follows is an enormous eruption of language in a turbulent, epic mode. The chorus abandons the previous verse pattern: the first nineteen lines, which set the scene of Dionysos's Aegean realm as a luxuriant garden or festooned monument, are all seven syllables long. The following 110 lines are broken up into twenty-two stanzas, each four lines long. The first three lines of every stanza have eleven syllables, while the fourth line is always five syllables. Here, as elsewhere, no rhyming occurs. The chorus shifts into the past tense as it narrates the rescue by Dionysos of the love-tortured Ariadne from her abandonment by Theseus. But in telling the story, the chorus quotes the speech of Ariadne and Dionysos, so that the past becomes present through the impersonation of mythic voices. Dionysos, for example, transports Ariadne out of the chthonic prison into a celestial paradise with these words:

> *"I en guldvagn, dragen af Leoparder,*
> *Vid min sida skall du till hemlen åka.*
> *Flicka, hvad? Du tvekar. Välan! ett under*
> *Tyde min allmakt."*

(432-35)

(In a gold chariot, drawn by leopards,
Shall you ascend at my side to heaven.
What's this, girl? You tremble. Repose thou
   embraced
by all my power.)

The chorus concludes the tale with a stanza of praise for Dionysos, for "Karlekens plågor stillar/Bacchus allena" [446-47] (Love's torments Bacchus alone subdues). The Chorus Leader awakens from her dream, and the meter returns to alexandrines. Her five-line speech is a set of four questions about the power of a dream to transport one to another reality. The chorus assures her that she remains an idol of purity, a white "Venushärmande gestalt" [463] (Venus-like form); they await her command to begin the celebration of Dionysos, which means exhausting "Den långa natt i bacchisk stjernomtindrad dans" [472] (the long night in Bacchic star-speckled dance).

The Chorus Leader then delivers a long (129 lines) speech in which, slipping again into past tense, she describes her dream. In other words, the language covers the same time which the chorus devoted to the Ariadne-Dionysos story. Stagnelius wants to dramatize how the same points in time and space can encompass more than one level of consciousness or reality. These levels include more than those embodied by the chorus and Chorus Leader: they include that present-tense level of mythic consciousness embodied by Ariadne, Dionysos, and the Chorus Leader herself when the narrators impersonate their voices. She discloses that in her dream she stood atop ice-clad Mt. Rhodope when Dionysos, a figure of gold and scarlet radiance, appears before her. He speaks at length (over forty lines) through her voice. He addresses her, describes for her the manifold movements in nature and life related to his pervasive spirit, and invites her, "jordens sorgsna barn" [527] (earth's mournful child), to share with him the "orgisk" (orgiastic) experience of olympisk salighet (Olympian bliss). The next thirty lines describe her luxuriant, worshipful response to the idyllic world created by the god's aura. She calls out: " 'Låt mig bland rosenhyddor evigt här få bo' " [556] (Let me live here among rose boweries forever). Dionysos reminds her that one must fight for the rewards of heaven: " 'Mot Orfeus lyfta hämndens fruktansvärda tyrs!' " [564] (The wand of destruction must be lifted toward Orfeus). He then disappears, and she suddenly finds herself, in "namnlös fasa" (nameless terror) deep within the earth, Pluto's realm. Her language becomes increasingly excited as she beckons the invisible god and then her sisters (the chorus) for relief from torments which vaguely resemble symptoms of a powerful erotic agitation. Indeed, when she moves out of the dream itself to address the chorus directly, her speech adopts a complicated rhyme scheme, which, though intricately structured, is the wildest language in the play. She asks if the chorus hears wedding music, then compares herself, as one who seeks God in unknown realms, with a timid bride:

> *Hvad mäktar mot Guden*
> *Den skälfvande Bruden?*

(589-90)

(What power against God
Has the trembling Bride?)

It is "en jättelik bragd" [398] (a gigantic deed), this power of the god to carry away a woman's passion. She then falls to the earth in orgasmic convulsions at the conclusion of these lines:

> *Ack! phallus mig bränner,*
> *Ack! tyrsen mig rör.*
> *Mig sjelf jag ej känner.*
> *Jag dör! Jag dör!*

(599-602)

(Ah! the phallus burns me,
Ah! wands that shake me.
I know myself no more.
I die! I die!)

The chorus, though not nearly so violently aroused, pursues a minor variation of the rhyme scheme, giving an elaborate description of the radiance exuded by the exhausted, resting body of the Chorus Leader. When she awakens, the Chorus Leader shifts to a ten/eleven syllable meter to declare that she awakens to take revenge against Orfeus. She exhorts her sister to rise up and destroy his song. The scene concludes with the chorus repeating the last two lines of her eight-line speech:

> *Ja, upp till hämd! må Hebri silfverflod*
> *Förgyllas skönt af Orfei gjutna blod.*

> (636-37)

(Now to revenge! Hell's silver river shall be
Gilded rich with Orfeus's spurting blood).

Though it contains large passages spoken by a single speaker, the ecstatic rhetoric of the bacchantes is actually a complex form of dialogue. Stagnelius perceives the centrality of ecstasy in human experience as the result of a particular exchange of language between more than one speaker or voice, and for this reason, his work, in spite of the romantic instability of its structure and rhythm, remains aligned with the classical ideological perception of ecstasy as a dramatic phenomenon which is not beyond language, not ineffable, but controlled above all by language. The feminine discourse of ecstasy involves an intersection of speakers. Intersection of speakers or voices refers not only to dialogue between separate speaking bodies on the stage but to other speakers or voices contained within a single speaker or voice, a phenomenon dramatized by considerable quotation of imaginary persons and by shifting rhythms and metrical structures within speeches. In **Bacchanterna,** the intersection defining feminine ecstatic discourse thus occurs at several levels. The voice of the Chorus Leader intersects the communal voice so that her orgasmic convulsions arise concurrently with language that she addresses directly to the chorus. The feminine discourse of ecstasy also entails a dialogue between present and past, between real and imaginary voices: mythic or dreamt voices are in dialogue within and with the narrative voice, implying that ecstatic speech is to a large extent a condition of speaking for someone else, for an imagined, mythic person. A larger implication is that feminine ecstatic speech involves impersonation within extensive narration. The communal voice of rapture appears to be one that tells a story (of a solitary woman who inspires the love of a god rather than a man) which occurs outside of the conscious reality of the speakers, in either an archaic, timeless, mythic age or a dream. The narrative language itself, the description of the past event, is extravagantly sensuous, permeated with adjectives that link rarified images of nature with qualities of erotic feeling or perception: pearl-castle flesh, star-speckled dance, and the leopard-drawn gold chariot. Images drawn from mineral and floral colors predominate so that, for the speakers, a mood intensifies by the naming of a rare color in nature, in contrast to the characters in neoclassical tragedy, who tend to intensify an emotion by ascribing an allegorical or abstract value to the bodies of speaker and listener.[7]

Even more interesting is the attempt of the speakers to describe simultaneity of action at a single point in time: talking about Dionysos means talking about events happening in various places within Dionysos's realm at the same time. The description assumes the qualities of a panoramic vision. The panoramic effect also includes Stagnelius's desire to represent reality as a dialogue between two levels of consciousness. Thus, the Chorus Leader tells what happened to her while she was asleep, while we were listening to the chorus describe the Ariadne-Dionysos story. Reality consists of parallel levels of language and speech which the listener can only hear (process) one level at a time. Presumably, however, ecstasy arises precisely from an elaborate, intricate construction of simultaneous levels of language, a parallel unfolding of narratives, and intersection of voices. Stagnelius is able to dramatize that perception only by representing the levels in a linear, sequential fashion: the voice of the dream, which is the dreamer's; the woman's, which occurs after the voice in the dream, which is Dionysos's; the man's without anyone awake hearing him during the moment when the choral voice of the community speaks of him. Obviously Stagnelius has disclosed an extraordinarily complex perception of voice: voices not only speak through other voices, they speak when no one can hear them, for while no one hears the voice of Dionysos in the dream, the dreamer herself does not hear the turbulent choral voice of the community. It is possible that a collage-like dramatic technique exists for allowing the voice of the unconscious, the voice in the dream, to be heard at the same moment the spectator hears the great voice of the community, although I am not aware of any drama which applies such a technique or achieves the complexity characterizing Stagnelius's perception of voice. By having the male voice in the dream be heard through the female voice of the dream and after the dreamer has dreamt it as well as after the communal voice has spoken, the text dramatizes very effectively the perception that repression, that the voice of the unconscious, is not so much unspoken as unheard.[8]

Finally, a more abstractly formal dialogue occurs when different rhythmic and stanzaic patterns of language represent different voices within and between speakers. Ecstatic speech by no means implies a release from conventional formal constraints; rather, the language linked to ecstasy involves a dialogue of established forms, of shifting metrical structures. Indeed, the closer the language brings the speaker to orgasm, the more complex are the formal constraints on speech. At the point of convulsion, the language adopts a narrower, more intricate rhyme scheme than is to be found in all but a handful of dramas. This feature of the text contrasts significantly with the practice of strictly neo-classical drama, where the alexandrine signifies an insurmountable barrier between the speaker and ecstasy; but even in a romantic or certainly modernist context, it is very strange indeed to find the speech of a person experiencing orgasmic convulsions portraying wildness through much more complicated rhyme and metrical patterns, through a much more dense calculation of utterance, than is ever the case with the alexandrine. The chorus replicates this complicated signification of wildness in its speech immediately following the Chorus Leader's convulsion. The feminine signification of ecstasy thus becomes synonymous, not with any primal cry of release, but with elaborately intricate patterns of speech.

An equally strange element in Stagnelius's text emerges chiefly from his efforts to construct an ecstatic discourse that complicates relations between innocence and seduction. It is true that in the great speech of the Chorus Leader, Dionysos speaks with a voice that can be termed seductive:

> *"Kom! skåda sjelf till hvad olympisk salighet*
> *Jag kallar Hades fångar, jordens sorgsna barn."*

(526-27)[9]

("Come, behold yourself in that olympic bliss
I call Hades' prisoner, earth's mournful child.")

But that voice belongs as much to the Chorus Leader as to Dionysos. By impersonating the voice of Dionysos, however, the Chorus Leader distances herself from complete responsibility for her emotional condition: this other voice within her is what motivates her actions as leader of the Bacchantic community. The voice of Dionysos is seductive only as long as she is unconscious, in the world of a dream. Awake and speaking to the chorus, she has no seductive purpose, for her purpose is not to rouse the chorus to ecstasy but to justify the destruction of Orfeus, who, from the perspective of the chorus, most definitely has a seductive voice, even if, from the spectators' perspective, he has no desire at all to seduce. Stagnelius

has attempted to dramatize a more complex perception of innocence than prevails in conventional views of ecstasy, for he shows:

1. that ecstasy is a reality, not the mere promise or illusion of a seduction;

2. that ecstasy achieves powerful reality through the phenomenon of voice, not something seen;

3. that the ecstatic voice constitutes an intersection, not so much between speakers, but between levels of consciousness, narrative, linguistic form; and

4. that the voice achieves convulsive power when it becomes highly and intricately constrained in a formal sense while intersecting more than one level of consciousness.[10]

The text avoids binding an expanding state of consciousness to a consequent loss of innocence. But this perception implies that ecstasy appears as an unintended though not accidental consequence of something said with another object in mind. It is thus not really speakers (visible identities, specific bodies) who prod listeners to ecstasy; rather, it is the ecstatic energy of language itself which excites speakers. The speaker retains her innocence as long as the source of ecstasy is language, the intersection of voices within speakers, rather than speakers themselves, rather than the motives for speech. We may translate ecstatic energy to mean degree of ambiguity, as exemplified in large part by the phenomenon of intersection. Whereas normal ecstatic discourse perceives consciousness of ambiguity as dependent on loss of innocence, thus, preventing language from becoming a source of ecstasy and requiring that it remain only a means of seduction, Stagnelius perceives consciousness of ambiguity as evidence of innocence. That which is ambiguous is unintended and is the presence of another voice within a voice. Discourses of seduction assume that consciousness of ambiguity entails disguising one meaning within another; Stagnelius does not: the speaker saturates her speech with other voices, with otherness, and this otherness functions simultaneously, ambiguously, as a sign of communal anonymity and ecstatic self-abandonment. Stagnelius's perception of the speech controlled relation between ambiguity, innocence, and ecstasy is yet more mysterious. On the one hand, the referents of the female ecstatic discourse, obsessively focused on the invisible, imaginary figure of Dionysos, suggest that female ecstasy is a response to a myth or illusion. On the other hand, the signifying practice of this discourse, the relations between signifiers, suggest that the reality of ecstasy is the construction of a voice which signifies something other than its referents, signifies, indeed, the otherness of the speaker. Within this perception of ambiguity, the referent does not conceal or disguise its signifier; the ambiguity defining the feminine ecstatic discourse entails a convulsive intersection of referent and signifier.

The utopian aspect of Stagnelius's mood arises when he envisions ecstatic experience as something integrated or absorbed into a community (the chorus), if not an entire society. The Chorus Leader sinks to the earth in convulsions (*Hon nederfaller till jorden under konvulsioner* [603]) before the chorus, and the chorus, speaking in the same rhyme scheme as the orgasmic speaker, treats her action as an abstract of its own apotheosis. Classical ecstatic discourse regards the pursuit of ecstasy as a movement in tension with societal norms, which signify themselves through a code of appearances that embodies a single, shared, universal level of perception. A great distinction between catharsis and ecstasy prevails because the classical discourse, which assumes that ecstasy is beyond the power of language to construct, contain, or represent it, makes no precise distinction between society and community: ecstasy is invariably a condition of supreme fearlessness which estranges a person from the world, from the other, from people. Individuals achieve ecstasy, in which being outside oneself is synonymous with being outside all norms; societies achieve catharsis, the purgation of impulses and desires which threaten social unity. Ecstasy estranges; catharsis normalizes.

Stagnelius, however, dramatizes the complex conditions of language which permit ecstasy to assimilate a speaker into a group and, indeed, to constitute the phenomenon which bonds masses of people together. Yet he qualifies this utopian possibility by stressing in a sense the over-homogeneity of the ecstatic community. The ecstatic community exists only because a further powerful distinction prevails between male and female modes of communication. The ecstatic community is completely female. According to the logic of the text, the sexual homogeneity of the ecstatic community exists because of a feminine perception of a cosmic tension between two manifestations of maleness: the invisible god and the corporeal man. Communal ecstasy rests upon the desire for unity with a god rather than a man; the voice of a man may be overwhelmingly seductive, but it is essentially a voice of skepticism, doubt, and distrust. It is the voice of one who achieves his identity through solitude, through an attachment, not to a timeless and undying myth, but to death, to an intense awareness of the body's transitoriness and vulnerability. And the monumental signifier of this dualism defining the feminine ecstatic discourse is dialogue itself. From the feminine perspective, as embodied by the voluptuous exchanges of speech between the chorus and the Chorus Leader, dialogue is central in creating an ecstatic community, a rapturously unified body of speakers. But from the masculine perspective, as embodied by the solo figure of Orfeus, dialogue is that language, that reality, between speakers. At this point, where sexual difference becomes the central embodiment of cosmic dualities of energy, it appears that ecstatic discourse arises logically (and tragically) out of biology, a perception which classical aesthetics, with its deterministic rhetoric of fate, always embeds within its signification system.[11]

But then Stagnelius complicates this anxiety-ridden, almost desperate concern for order and constraint in female speech by contrasting the ecstatic discourse of the bacchantes with that of the solitary, fugitive male, Orfeus. Unable to escape the bacchantes, Orfeus appears stoically before them (936) and requests that he be allowed to sing a final song. His petition is not an attempt to seduce the bacchantes, for he stands ready to die by their swords (*Här står jag färdig att för edra glafvar dö* [941]). Indeed, for him, a song is the perfect emblem of a heroic death, the ideal art for eternalizing the memory of the dead, and the aesthetic complement to the sound of battle, when a man is in the midst of death. The chorus grants the request but remarks that it no longer fears the power and "veka toner" (gentle tones) of Orfeus's lyre. Though his voice may stir animals and stones, it is not appropriate that it possess "Bacchi Tärna" (bacchic maidens) who are more accustomed to the metallic sound of cymbals, pipes, and horns (952).

Orfeus then sings a brief song. Here, too, the voice accommodates very intricate formal constraints. Orfeus sings six stanzas of four lines each. The first two lines of each stanza are eleven syllables long; the second two lines are seven. The first two lines always form a rhymed couplet, but the second two lines never rhyme with each other. Instead, they rhyme respectively with the second two lines of the preceding stanza. Thus, for eleven-syllable lines, a new rhyme emerges with each stanza, while for seven-syllable lines a new rhyme emerges only in the first, third, and fifth stanzas. Though it is brief, Orfeus's song is, from a formal perspective, perhaps even more complex than the monumental dialogue between the Chorus Leader and the bacchantes.

With this intensification of formal complexity, ecstacy becomes more distinctly linked to melancholy. Each stanza seems nothing less than an elaborate metaphor describing the power of death to fracture human vanity and ambition. Orfeus compares human time to the disintegration of clouds and waves by wind and earth (stanza 1); he compares the movement of "sckickelsens lagar" (destiny's laws) to the fall of a rose, (stanza 2). In stanza 3, he addresses an obscurely identified listener (du), who is more likely the singer himself than one of the bacchantes. He sits innocently (menlos sitter) eating within the ancient, traditional community but can only slake his hunger, his burning desire (törstande brand) among the waves—the home of phantoms, frail illusions, and Acheron's sighing (stanza 4). In stanza 5, he speaks of himself as one who, in the fire of youth, celebrated life but who now warns that he, through his voice, his song, punishes vanity: "Jorden ej hyser ett väl" [978] (Earth hath not one glory). In the final stanza, an astonishingly compressed tension between bright, encouraging commands and a dark, undercutting image of a tragic sound is encountered:

> Klinga, helga terob, för sista gången!
> Höj, o bleknande mund! den sista sången.
> Svanen, gungad i säfven,
> Uppger i toner sin själ.

> (979-82)

(Resound, golden lute, for the final time!
Raise, o pallid mouth, this final melody.
The swan, swaying in the reeds,
Dissolves into tones his soul.)

The metaphorical tension between images is reinforced by the tension between eleven- and seven-syllable lines. Whereas the chorus tends to produce descriptions of a symbolic nature, in which, for example, "Glänsande armen" [415] (radiant arms) and "rosenläppar" [424] (rose lips) signify the luminous, real, material consequence of Dionysos-worship on the bodies of maenads, the monologic Orfic speaker produces metaphoric descriptions in which, for example, the listener sees the speaker's body as a swan's, sees the speaker's soul as a tone. In him, we find a fusion of metaphor, monologue, and very precise control over language.

With the Orfic discourse of ecstasy, drama almost ceases to imply a dialogue between a speaking self and an other outside the self; the "du" includes the voice that speaks it. The Orfic song is the otherworldly abstract of the voice; it is that tonality, that signification, that death-suffused finality of utterance which is other than the language which makes dialogue and the intersection of voices possible. For the bacchantes, ecstasy results from finding another voice within the speaking self; for Orfeus, ecstasy results from making the voice other than the self which speaks it. Through song, the voice becomes a metaphor, not for the power of language or its referents to contain the self, but for the power of voiced language and its signifiers to dissolve the self into tones, into something other than an image, a body, human flesh. The last stanza of the song objectifies the ideology of masculine ecstatic discourse: ecstatic self-abandonment is a final (sista) mode of dissolving into an invisible otherness (toner). The finality of ecstatic dissolution means that no one has anything more to say, the speaker has no need for another voice, dialogue comes to an end. But this finality of the lyric rather than dramatic voice also means that the masculine perspective understands ecstasy, the dissolving of the self into tones, as a supremely fearless encounter with death, not with a mythic eternity signified by a figure such as Dionysos.

The formal organization of the stanza indicates that a condition of ecstatic self-dissolution is an extreme condition of thinking and speaking metaphorically, of seeing the self in a strange other, of seeing one identity as another. The listener perceives the Orfic speaker as a swan; the soul as a tone. The sign of death manifests itself as a final melody (sista sången); the tension between I and You manifests itself as a tension between eleven- and seven-syllable lines, as a tension between rhymed couplet (eleven-syllable lines) and rhymes which complete themselves in the following stanza (seven-syllable lines). Ecstatic self-abandonment (or self-dissolution) operates as a mode of heightened, ultimate (or final) self-metaphorization and capacity to construct metaphor. Masculine ecstatic discourse manifests itself as (or like) a transfiguring voice of death, it is so completely other than the monumental intersection of voices, the turbulent surge of life, which creates the great communal I of the chorus. It is this detachment from dialogue which links the masculine ecstatic discourse to melancholy, to an intense, heroic pressure for an abstract, inhuman (though not divine) otherness: in the end, the image of the Orfic swan-male dissolved, through song, into an invisible tone awakens in the listener a more mysterious current of feeling than the mythic image of Dionysos dominating the communal unconscious.

The chorus seems deeply moved by Orfeus's song, and responds with a speech (984-95) rich in negatives: it does not know (Jag vet ej) what reward to bestow, what power resides in the lute. Though it acknowledges his innocence, it cannot endure his radiant brow nor gaze into his ancient eyes, it cannot behold his extreme struggle nor hear the surge of his death-scream (Ej hans dödsskrän vågar jag höra [995]). The bacchantes appear shocked or numbed by Orfeus's voice; their encounter with male ecstasy has a paralysing effect or, as they put it, his voice fills them with an impotent (vanmäktig) feeling. What indeed is there to give him, even in the way of pain, when he wants nothing of life or the world? Orfeus says (998) that he worships the same god as they do, but that the god assumes different names. The chorus replies that a world-god (verldens Gud) has only one name (Dionysos). Nevertheless, Orfeus asserts that he is willing to honor Dionysos "med offerblod och sång" [1012] (with sacrificial blood and song). The bacchantes then advise him to lead the procession to the dark, rural temple and sacrificial altar they have built for Dionysos. Orfeus and the bacchantes disappear after he congenially announces that he will sing a hymn to Dionysos, but, of course, such a hymn is also the voice proclaiming his own doom. The spectator never hears this hymn. Now completely captive within the female community, the voice of the living Orfeus becomes as invisible as the god Dionysos: within the female community, maleness in either its human or divine manifestations loses its body and becomes something spoken of and spoken for, rather than speaking.

The following scene (1026-80) presents a dialogue between the shepherd Hermas and the shepherdess Polydora, the only named female in the text. It was Hermas who betrayed the hiding place of Orfeus when Polydora, his bride-to-be, threatened to abandon him if he did not disclose the secret grotto to the bacchantes, of whom she is one. But now having witnessed the melancholy, solitary ecstasy of Orfeus and having assumed responsibility for his destruction, she understands the impossibility of love between the sexes:

> *Ej mannen älska kan, ej qvinnan sjelf*
> *Kan älska, nej! Farväl för evigt, Hermas!*

> (1063-64)

> (Man cannot love, nor can woman herself
> Even love, no! Farewell forever, Hermas!)

The ecstatic unity of the couple is an illusion; only the gender exclusive Bacchic community can experience ecstasy as a unity of speakers. The drama concludes with the two shepherds, Lycis and Timon, giving an account of their secret observation of the mysterious and rather morbid Bacchic ritual in which Orfeus was the object of sacrifice. The spectator does not see the ritual itself, for its ecstatic power depends upon its secrecy—it exists for the audience, for the public, for society, only as a detached male commentary, a female notion of orgy rendered public through a speculative and uninvited male intelligence. In a silver cloud, almost the image of a saint, the ghost of Orfeus appears before the men and announces his liberation from the tortures of the earth. He condemns Hermas to perpetual wandering for his cowardice before the "qvinno-hären" (woman army) and observes to Lycis that "I andars verld ock kärlek enda budet är" [1207] (in the other world, love, too, is only a word). Thus to Timon he remarks that only "högt på jorden skall man sjunga mitt beröm" [1211] (high above the earth can one sing my glory). The stage scenery presents a vast image of the Lyre and Swan constellations, and this image, aligned with the nocturnal glow of the poet's description of it and his final evocation of Hermes, "Majas vingtbeklädda Son" [1219] (Maya's wing-clad son), links the solitary Orfic voice of ecstasy to a cosmic order of signs, to celestial patterns of movement which point to an inscrutably divine order of consciousness but produce no intense sense of unity between the stars scattered across the void. For the bacchantes, ecstasy is possible only under conditions of utmost secrecy and cultic exclusivity, for it is bound up with ritual violence, with frenzied acts of sacrifice, with intoxicated submission to a god, with some invisible power that is greater than any human presence. Ecstasy does not emerge from a transgression of taboo; ecstasy unfolds within a myth-saturated rhetoric of mystery involving the authority of language in dreams and the motivating pressure of another voice within the speaker's.

This emphasis on mystification rather than transgression means that, from the feminine perspective, ecstatic experience is due to the inclination of the Bacchic community to create an atmosphere of secrecy, to forbid, to enclose, to return to the cave and contain the secrets of life within the womb of the earth. The magnitude of communal ecstatic unity remains tied to the magnitude of repression, sacrifice, and anonymity (namelessness) experienced within the community. The atmosphere of secrecy and exclusivity intensifies through dialogic and choral deployment of language, for it is through dialogue, as well as through the intersection of voices, that the speaker achieves a sense of exclusivity in relation to all that language, as an intricate and autonomous form, organism or body in itself, speaks independently of the meanings speakers consciously ascribe. The value of a secret lies in its power to bond people together at the same time that it amplifies the exclusivity of their identity. The medium by which the female ecstatic discourse exchanges secrets for supreme feelings of trust and unity is dialogue controlled by complicated, esoteric rules that allow each voice to intersect with the other.

By contrast, the Orfic (masculine) discourse of ecstasy belongs to an identity formed out of solitude, formed indeed outside of society. The discourse constructs a different, ironic mode of exclusivity: the speaker transgresses the values of the Bacchic community without desiring to do so, his speech seduces inadvertently and uncontrollably. It is a fugitive discourse: the representation of Orfeus in the text suggests that, for Stagnelius, the author's marginal, alienated status in modern as well as archaic society is due to the essentially agrarian, chthonic influence of a feminine concept of communal unity which equates erotic desire with mysterious, religious sentiment, with a cavernous hunger for an invisible, metaphysical savior, and with the myth of earth and fertility. The Orfic discourse is monologic, not because the speaker hopes to achieve greater exclusivity, but because his speech is based on the perception of language as a cosmic power which always separates speakers. From the masculine perspective, ecstasy is possible only by plunging into the universe, an immense void, in which tensions between words are as complex as tensions between stars. The Orfic voice discloses no secrets, no other voice within itself, no voice of the unconscious, for language manifests itself everywhere around us, like the sky. Language itself is the sign of otherness in the sense that the dead Orfeus can still speak high above the earth; from the masculine perspective, the supreme state of otherness is death. The ecstatic condition of being other than oneself, thus, depends on a powerful, metaphorical awareness of language itself as the voice of death. Yet the Orfic rhetoric of ecstasy is mysterious, filled with mathematical precision and semantic obscurity, indifferent to illusions of communication and unity, indifferent to motives for speech and assertions of power. Because this discourse, which resists the capacity of language to remain invisible to its speakers, is so enigmatic that it becomes unintentionally seductive, it emanates secrets that not even the gods can know. Ecstasy is this heroic state of supreme fearlessness before language, of supreme trust in language but not in speakers.

In perceiving language, and especially speech, as a kind of organism or body, as the real manifestation of the other, Stagnelius anticipates a particular vein in modernist philosophy. Heidegger, for example, in a cryptic 1950 essay, introduces and repeats, rather obsessively, the notion that "Language speaks" (198): "Man speaks in that he responds to language," which "speaks for us in what has been spoken" (210). But the phenomenon of speech, of voice, is difficult, if not impossible, to detach from the manifestation of a living form. Lacan is more explicit: "The word is in fact the gift of Language, and Language is not immaterial. It is a subtle body, but body it is" (*Speech and Language* 64). Lacan's famous statement, that "the unconscious is structured like a language" (*Fundamental Concepts* 20), suggests we should perceive language as the materialization of the unconscious, which Lacan considers the primal manifestation of otherness in relation to the self or speaking subject. Elsewhere, Lacan asserts that the unconscious, "the libido is to be conceived as an organ, in both senses of the term, as an organ-part of the organism and as an organ-instrument" (*Fundamental Concepts* 187). However, I do not want to suggest that Stagnelius perceives the otherness of language in the same way that either Heidegger or Lacan does; rather, I would suggest that one begins to contemplate language as a body, as the form of the other, when, as Stagnelius, Heidegger, and Lacan do, one begins to contemplate the relation between language and ecstasy, speech and desire. Put differently, it is when language, as in Stagnelius's text and in psychoanalysis, structures the relation between the speaking subject and the other in intensely sexual or sexualized categories that language begins to project the attributes of a body, something living, which intervenes between the speaker and the other and establishes a condition of untranscendable difference that marks a limit to the capacity of any speaker to feel unity with another. Heidegger's concept of Being supposedly transcends sexual difference, even though the dominant signifier of Being is "language which speaks"

and which, therefore, entails life and a body of it own. The monumental sexualization of ecstatic discourse in Stagnelius's play urges us to believe that the question of Being remains obscurely answered when one ignores the question of sexual difference in language, as Heidegger does when he repeats, with increasing opacity, that "language speaks."

Bacchanterna applies the emotionally turbulent logic of romanticism in defining the speech-ideological conditions, the attitudes toward language, under which ecstasy emerges but remains respectful of classicism in its choice of subject matter and extravagant concern for monumentality of form. Just as the text embodies a formal conflict between romantic (esoteric) and classical (universal) signifying practices, so the attitudes toward language embedded in the text separate themselves into masculine and feminine discourses of ecstasy, which neither romantic nor classical signifying practices can unite, even though both codes operate in conjunction to produce each discourse. The text represents the feminine notion of communal ecstasy as dependent on a mysterious or religious atmosphere of ritual violence. Insofar as ecstasy achieves reality through violent acts of sacrifice, through the exclusion/repression of the utterly other, heroic, male voice from the community, the feminine speaker will perceive language as a system for storing secrets, for saying only what the one god and his community of worshippers may hear, for saying that which no other may say alone except for the one god and the one choral voice defining the community. This attitude, when operating as dialogue, as an intersection of voices within speakers, binds speakers together into an orgiastic, utopian unity, which, however, the non-utopian, sexually-integrated public can know only through the detached, unintoxicated speech of spying male reporters (Lycis and Timon): as long as the orgy is as invisible as the god it celebrates, such ecstasy is unspeakable, remains yet another secret which simultaneously seduces and excludes the listener by being spoken.

As the work of a male author, the text constitutes a male construction of the feminine concept of ecstasy in much the same way that the Chorus Leader speaks for Dionysos. Each discourse, masculine and feminine, speaks through and for the other. Lycis's account of the Bacchic ritual, despite its voyeuristic aspect, inhibits spectator identification with the Bacchic discourse of ecstasy: the speech places the orgy at a distance in time as well as space and prepares its listeners for a far greater manifestation of cosmic being than any image of the secret, subterranean excesses of the Bacchantes: the ghost of Orfeus utterly alone among the stars, the voice of death signifying, merely by being heard within this image, that ecstasy is a transcendence of the world through poetic speech, through the stellar luminosity of language itself. No doubt concerns about censorship and decorum in premodernist culture contributed to Stagnelius's decision to contain the Bacchic orgy within the speech of a second-hand messenger. But these concerns are subordinate to the acknowledgement that drama—as discussed in those twentieth century writings about Stagnelius's play which analyze the problem of influences upon it rather than the disturbing language within it—tends to preserve a mood of secrecy in regard to relations between language and the most pervasively and intensely desired emotion: ecstasy. [Table deleted.]

Notes

[1] The edition of *Bacchanterna* cited in this essay is that which appears in volume 4 of Böök's edition of Stagnelius's, *Samlade Skrifter* (235-80). Line numbers are cited instead of pages. All translations are mine. The most recent edition of the play, with commentary by Holger Frykenstedt, is in volume 6 of *Sveriges litteratur* edited by Carl Ivar Ståhle and E. N. Tigersted. That edition contains no line numbers.

[2] For example, Benson (1-143), an American, examines Stagnelius's historical dramas in relation to Old Norse mythology in order to show how a romantic preoccupation with the origin of poetry blends harmoniously with the poet's modern reflections and feelings. A French Scandinavist, Bachelin, presents Stagnelius as a precursor of the Baudelairean romantic mood of critical detachment from modern reality. Widegren identifies gnostic components in Stagnelius's poetry which parallel motifs in the *auto sacramentales* of Calderón de la Barca. An implication of Widegren's article is that gnosticism connects poetry to a mystical ideology which transcends a specific language, culture, or historical period such as romanticism. However, neither Benson, Bachelin, nor Widegren even deals with *Bacchanterna*.

[3] Thus, Cedarblad (*Stagnelius*) merely mentions *Bacchanterna* in a large effort to link Stagnelius to a distinctly romantic aesthetic rather than religion derived from a multitude of sources which include Novalis, Böhme, Atterbom, classical mythology, esoteric Christian doctrine, and so forth (303). In an earlier book (*Studier*), Cedarblad expanded his study of influences upon the poet to include locally unique historical variables but made even fewer references to *Bacchanterna*, whose Orfeus is now understood to embody the Socratic spirit (223). Holmberg devotes only four pages (230-34) to the play, which, he proposes, dramatizes the belief that it is not sacrifice (the price paid for Dionysian release) that produces world affirmation, but death itself, the condition of being the object of sacrifice (234), and in this sense, the text is a Nietzschean critique of religious values (233). Just as brief is Andreae (82-86), who sees the text as an example of a romantic ambition to make troll music

out of language, to use poetry as the means for representing the reality of dreams.

[4] I do not disagree with Böök's interpretations of *Bacchanterna;* rather, I feel that his focus on defining the historical context for the text diverts attention from the text itself; all three of his interpretations seem provocatively incomplete, and indeed his shifting, scholarly preoccupation with Stagnelius over four decades does suggest that he was persistently haunted by the sense of having left something important about Stagnelius unsaid. But perhaps this incompleteness is due to an extravagant concern for what Stagnelius left unsaid rather than for what the commentator has left unsaid about what the text does say. In his 1919 "Kommentar" to his edition of *Bacchanterna*, Böök's exclusive purpose is to identify a vast network of influences upon Stagnelius: Euripides, Ovid, Virgil, Plutarch, Plato, among many others. In subsequent works, Böök moved toward interpreting the text in relation to these and other influences, but the effect is always to historicize the text in such a way as to diminish the significance of Stagnelius's language for a non-Swedish audience.

[5] The text suggests that the effect of a real male voice is to urge the bacchantic listener to lose the anonymity she shares with everyone else in the bacchantic community. The text emphasizes this point through the character of Polydora, a bacchant and the only named female in the text; she and Hermas anticipate marriage, but in the end, his voice is not strong enough to overcome her devotion to the Dionysos and the bacchantes, who are determined to destroy a voice that is, the voice of Orfeus. The real male voice has the power to construct a sense of difference between female listeners, and this difference threatens the communal unity of the bacchantes. The communal unity and anonymity of the bacchantes is a response to the imaginary, dreamt male voice of the god, who speaks through the voice of the woman dreamer. All the male speakers in the text have individual names, but they do not form a community. They form pairs or trios of speakers created and dissolved by conflicting desires. In the final scene, four male figures appear: the ghost of Orfeus, Timon, Lycis, and Hermas. But the ghost urges them to separate and pursue different courses of action alone.

[6] Böök (*Kommentar* 439-45) provides several examples of where Euripides' play has influenced Stagnelius. Stagnelius is close to Euripides insofar as he equates female ecstasy with a response to an illusion, a severe disorder of perception. Pentheus in Euripides's play mistakes Dionysos for an ordinary mortal and the bacchantes mistake Pentheus for a lion, whom they tear apart when he spies upon their orgiastic rites. But these misperceptions, which afflict both sexes and both ecstatic and non-ecstatic persons, derive from a

larger problem of perceiving differences between gods and humans. As Cadmus reproachfully remarks to Dionysos: Gods should be exempt from human passions (1. 1348), but they are not, and because they are not, because Dionysos acts so humanly by acting so spitefully, so vindictively, humans can feel the presence of a god only by entering into a state of delirium or grotesque masquerade as when Cadmus, Teiresias, and later Pentheus disguise themselves as bacchantes. But for Dionysos, the stimulation of ecstasy in the bacchantes is not an end in itself but a means to a dreadful end: revenge for the slander that he was of mortal rather than divine birth. "When you had time, you did not know me," he tells the men of Thebes (1. 1345). Ecstasy therefore appears as part of an unjust punishment inflicted upon human beings for their limitations of perception. But this point becomes clear when we perceive ecstasy as an initial, rather than central or culminating, experience, and for that reason, Euripides places his ecstatic chorus near the beginning of the play. What follows this ecstatic eruption is the gradual revelation of a huge, tragic error of perception which has as its consequence the destruction of an entire society. This consequence involves perceptual and emotional complexities which do not interest Stagnelius as much as those relating to the sexualization of language. Euripides's play contains grotesque comic elements, startling emotional contrasts, which are completing missing from Stagnelius's play.

[7] Consider, for example, lines 679-83 of Racine's *Phèdre*, which we may regard as a model of classical allegorization through adjectival construction.

> *Les Dieux m'en sont témoins, ces Dieux qui dans mon flanc*
> *Ont allumé le feu fatal à tout mon sang;*
> *Ces Dieux qui se sont fait une gloire cruelle*
> *De séduire le cocur d'une faible mortelle.*

> (The gods are my witness, those gods who inside me
> Have ignited the fatal fire in all my blood;
> Those gods who have made a cruel glory
> Of seducing the heart of a feeble mortal.)

The speaker uses adjectives to abstract her own identity as well as the identity of that power ("the gods") controlling her condition. "Fatal fire" and "cruel glory" do not construct a clear image of either identity; instead, they produce a more precise description of the speaker's mood. The speaker compounds the allegorization process by ascribing metaphorical actions (igniting, seducing) to the abstract identities which have the effect of turning seemingly non-abstract identities (blood, heart) into abstractions. The listener does not see the speaker's body or mood more vividly;

rather, the speaker analyzes relations between essentially invisible aspects of her identity: the listener tends to see the speaker rather than what she is talking about. Racine employs this strategy, which in this instance he actually borrows from Seneca, throughout this text and his other tragedies. By contrast, the bacchantes, in Stagnelius's text, delight in adjectival constructions which allow the listener to see the dream-like image of the invisible as an intensely sensuous phenomenon: "rosenröda peplum" (347), "Ariadne, dyster och blek" [362] (Ariadne, melancholy and pale), "med snöhvit panna och purpurkinder" [418] (with snow white forehead and scarlet cheeks), and "Kring hans gyllne hår/En purpurklasig ranka" [481] (Around his golden hair/a purple cluster of grapes) are but a few typical examples. Occasionally, however, a speaker does shift to a more allegorical mode of adjectivization: "Karlekens plågor stillar" [446] (Love's quiet torment).

[8] I am assuming, of course, that whatever is unconscious is by definition repressed and that the unconscious speaks only in a manner detached from the intentionality normally ascribed to a speech-act. What gives the voice of the unconscious a repressed status is the fact that one cannot hear it directly. Dionysos signifies the unconscious insofar as he has no voice or body, no existence, in the play, except as someone spoken of or spoken for by a female speaker. Dionysos is in the female speaker and in no way external to her. Whatever he says to her in a dream can only be heard by others when it is spoken again by the voice of the dreamer herself. In this instance, the sign of repression is language, a voice, within the speaker which can be heard, not at the moment it speaks for itself, but at the moment the speaker impersonates it and constructs the illusion that it belongs to someone else. Stagnelius's complex scene implies that the voice of the unconscious speaks to the female speaker while the female community speaks of something else, but that voice is heard only when it is spoken of or spoken again by a speaker who does not recognize the voice as her own.

[9] In her dream, she appears alone before the god, and he speaks only to her; the bacchantes do not appear in the dream. Thus, it is ironic that only one person hears the voice which creates communal unity; or rather, the voice which creates communal unity is an impersonation of a voice which one can only hear alone. Classical or conventional consciousness tends to treat seduction as a highly calculated mode of action, which occurs when one tries to satisfy a particular, problematic desire by appearing to satisfy another shared by the Other. This matter of concealing a real desire from the Other means that seduction entails a loss of innocence in the seducer. But Stagnelius links seduction to ecstasy in the sense that Orfeus' voice,

his ecstasy, is unintentionally seductive to the bacchantes. His voice does not make the bacchantes ecstatic; instead, it awakens in them the desire for an ecstasy which is greater than that which they actually experience through their own complicated mode of speech. His voice is seductive, rather than merely attractive, not because the speaker intends to undermine the unity of the bacchantes, but because the bacchantic listener perceives such disunity as the effect of the voice. The voices, the ecstasies of the bacchantes have no seductive effect upon Orfeus; they neither awaken nor satisfy any desire for unity within him. For both Orfeus and the bacchantes, ecstasy is in speaking, not listening, but each cultivates a different mode of ecstatic speech. An implication of this observation is that ecstatic unity of feeling does not depend on unity of feeling between the speaker and the Other; one's ecstasy does not depend on another's. This implication is clear in the case of Orfeus, but even the communal ecstasy of the bacchantes depends on offering to the god a sacrifice, a victim, whose otherness is such that he cannot feel what they feel. Ecstasy remains a sign of difference and differentiation; the power of this most pervasively and intensely desired emotion to create social unity is merely cultic and not universal.

[10] If we accept that language is a sign of consciousness, then levels of consciousness implies levels of knowing something or knowledge of how to use language. The play not only suggests that such knowledge is different for each sex and therefore constitutes a separate male or female discourse; it also suggests that within each discourse, especially the female discourse, different types of knowledge require the use of different voices within the speaker. A voice refers to a unique set of rhythms and rhetorical voices which embed knowledge that is not spoken of or about, and it is this knowledge, manifested through intricate intersections and formal constraints, which bestows convulsive power on the speaker.

[11] For this reason, too, classical drama, which in general values technical competence within intricate formal constraints over originality of subject matter, tends to create more complex representations of female identity than drama which strives to establish its value by resisting anonymously defined rules assigned to its genre, as if the liberation from a genre also constituted an escape from the fateful pressures of gender. And Stagnelius, by linking ecstatic discourse to fantastically elaborate manipulations, formalities, and intersections of language and voice, discloses his inclination toward that classical obsession with order which produced the complicated female protagonists of Racine's *Phèdre* (1677), Alfieri's *Mirra* (1786), Schiller's *Die Braut von Messina* (1803), Kleist's *Penthesilea* (1808), and Grillparzer's *Des Meeres und der Liebe Wellen* (1829).

Works Cited

Andreae, Daniel. *Erik Johan Stagnelius*. Stockholm: Nature och Kultur, 1955.

Bachelin, Pierre. *Les Influences françaises dans l'oeuvre de E. J. Stagnelius*. Lyon: IAC, 1952.

Benson, Adolph Burnett. *The Old Norse Elements in Swedish Romanticism*. New York: Columbia UP, 1914.

Bergsten, Staffan. "Efterskrift." See Stagnelius. *Bacchanterna*. 55-59.

Böök, Fredrik. *Erik Johan Stagnelius*. Stockholm: Bonniers, 1919.

———. "Kommentar." Stagnelius. *Samlade Skrifter*. 5: 427-48.

———. *Stagnelius än en gang*. Stockholm: Bonniers, 1942.

———. *Stagnelius liv och dikt*. Stockholm: Bonniers, 1954.

Cedarblad, Sven. *Stagnelius och hans omgivning*. Stockholm: Bonniers, 1936.

———. *Studier in Stagnelli Romantik*. Uppsala and Stockholm: Almquist and Wicksells, 1923.

Euripides. *The Bacchae*. Trans. William Arrowsmith. *The Complete Greek Tragedies*. Eds. David Grene and Richmond Lattimore. Vol. 4. Chicago: U of Chicago P, 1959-1960. 529-608. 4 vols.

Heidegger, Martin. "Language." *Poetry, Language, Thought*. Trans. Albert Hofstadter. New York: Harper and Row, 1971. 189-210.

Holmberg, Olle. *Sex Kapitel om Stagnelius*. Stockholm: Bonniers, 1941.

Lacan, Jacques. *The Four Fundamental Concepts of Psychoanalysis*. Trans. Alan Sheridan. New York: Norton, 1981.

———. *Speech and Language in Psychoanalysis*. Trans. Anthony Wilden. Baltimore: Johns Hopkins UP, 1968.

Racine, Jean. *Phèdre*. Paris: Larousse, 1933.

Stagnelius, Erik Johan. *Bacchanterna*. Stockholm: Gebers, 1962. Reprint from Stagnelius. *Samlade Skrifter*. Ed. Lorenzo Hammarsköld. Vol. 2. Stockholm: Wiborg, 1824.

———. *Bacchanterna eller fanatismen*. Ed. Holger Frykenstedt. Ståhle and Tigerstedt. 223-63.

———. "*Om Bacchanterna.*" Ståhle and Tigerstedt. 221-22.

———. *Samlade Skrifter.* Ed. Fredrik Böök. Stockholm: Bonniers, 1914-1919. 5 vols.

Ståhle, Carl Ivar and E. N. Tigerstedt, eds. *Sveriges Litteratur.* Vol. 6. Stockholm: Bonniers, 1968.

Widegren, Geo. "Gnostikern Stagnelius." *Samlaren* (1944): 115-78.

Walden; or, Life in the Woods

Henry David Thoreau

The following entry presents criticism of Thoreau's essay collection *Walden; or, Life in the Woods* (1854). For information on Thoreau's complete career, see *NCLC,* Volume 7; for a discussion of the essay "Civil Disobedience" (1849), see *NCLC,* Volume 21.

INTRODUCTION

On July 4, 1845, Thoreau took up residence at Walden Pond, two miles south of Concord, Massachusetts, on property belonging to his friend and sometime-mentor Ralph Waldo Emerson. He remained there for two years, two months, and two days, and spent his time reading, thinking, writing, observing nature, and living a simple, solitary, and fairly self-sufficient existence. Although in the popular imagination Thoreau is cast as a hermit in his woodland retreat, in truth, he was in constant communication with friends and family; he walked into town fairly regularly and he received numerous visitors at Walden. During this period, Thoreau produced a draft of *A Week on the Concord and Merrimack Rivers*, an essay collection based on an 1839 expedition with his brother John, and kept a journal of his activities which provided the source material for *Walden*. But the real inspiration for the work that would become his masterpiece was apparently provided by the many queries from curious and skeptical neighbors about his experiment in the woods, queries Thoreau initially attempted to answer in two lectures delivered at the Concord Lyceum in 1847 and entitled "The History of Myself" and "Same as Last Week." Although a revised draft of *Walden* had been completed by 1849, at the time *A Week* was published, the final version did not appear until 1854. A highly original work, *Walden* defies easy categorization; it is at once an autobiography, a nature book, social criticism, and a handbook for simple living. Popular interest and critical acclaim continue to accrue almost a century and a half after *Walden*'s publication.

Biographical Information

Born in Concord to a family of modest means, Thoreau, the only member of his family to attend college, graduated from Harvard in 1837. His early career as an educator was cut short by his opposition to corporal punishment, which resulted in his dismissal from his first teaching post. Thoreau's famous friendship with Emerson led him to take up residence

in the latter's household as a handyman, gaining access to the most prominent figures of American Transcendentalism, among them Margaret Fuller and Bronson Alcott. During this period he helped edit *The Dial*, the magazine of the New England Transcendentalists, and was a regular contributor of both poems and essays. More than one critic has suggested that Thoreau attempted to put into practice the Transcendentalists' emphasis on the spiritual over the material to a greater degree than others associated with the movement. His devotion to principle was most famously illustrated by his single night's imprisonment for failure to pay his taxes—a protest against the Mexican War and Massachusetts' endorsement of slavery. This difference between the abstract principles held by his contemporaries and the concrete actions of Thoreau is captured in the story, largely apocryphal, of that imprisonment. According to the tale, Emerson visited Thoreau in jail and asked "Why are you here?", while Thoreau allegedly replied "Why are you not here?" His incarceration became the basis for his 1849 essay "Resistance to Civil Government," popularly known as

"Civil Disobedience," and he remained committed to the abolition of slavery, speaking out against the Fugitive Slave Law of 1850.

Major Themes

The many themes of *Walden* reflect the various literary genres with which the work has been associated. As a collection of nature essays, the most common way in which the text has been read, *Walden* provides few solid contributions to the world of natural science since the focus is not so much on nature itself as on the individual's relationship to it. Thoreau stresses nature's power to renew and restore the human spirit rather than a strictly scientific appreciation of nature on its own terms. Although Thoreau was at Walden Pond more than two years, his experiences are condensed into a single year's cycle, enabling the structure of *Walden* to correspond to the changing seasons. Images of renewal, resurrection, and rebirth abound, and for this reason, the work has been as often read as a spiritual guidebook as a nature text. Although occasionally considered an autobiography, *Walden* only barely qualifies for inclusion in that genre, considering the fictional aspect of much of Thoreau's account, the limited time period covered, and his legendary reticence in revealing much about his inner life. The original impetus for *Walden* was allegedly to satisfy the curiosity of his fellow citizens at Concord, but Thoreau accommodated their interest only so far, focusing on the experiences of daily life at Walden Pond—on *how* he lived, rather than *why* he lived as he did, a topic still being debated by critics today. The details of daily living provided in *Walden* account for its reception as a guide for frugal living and self-sufficiency. The author shares practical information on securing food and shelter, albeit at a level most would hardly consider subsistence, at very little cost. This simple life—plain clothes, few furnishings, a vegetarian diet—is embraced not out of necessity but by choice, as a conscious rejection of materialism, and constitutes a major theme of the work. Reducing life's necessities to a bare minimum enabled Thoreau to earn a living by performing odd jobs approximately six months a year. The rest of his time could then be spent reading—he was considered one of the most well-read men of his time—and writing. The rejection of materialism forms the basis for a reading of *Walden* as social criticism. Thoreau despised the way his neighbors lived and compared their state to that of slaves. "The mass of men lead lives of quiet desperation," he wrote, perhaps the most famous, most quoted line of the book. But the tone of his attack on the institutions of modern society is satiric, a fact that has often been overlooked and has led to the unfair characterization of Thoreau as a humorless writer.

Critical Reception

The early reception of *Walden* was less than spectacular: the first edition of 2,000 copies did not sell out for five years. Contemporary critics were divided, some praising its originality, others worrying about the consequences for civilization if everyone were to retreat to the forest in imitation of Thoreau. Despite the slow start, however, *Walden* is now considered one of the best-selling books in the history of American literature, and its critical reputation continues to grow as much as its popular acceptance. Early critics claimed to know what the text was about, often focusing on the essays on nature while ignoring or disparaging the sections on economy, simplicity, and anti-materialism. Twentieth-century commentators, however, have emphasized the text's complexity and the many possible interpretations yielded by it. Ironically, the text whose author advocated simplicity and clarity is now often regarded as difficult, inaccessible, even "bottomless." Several versions of the *Walden* manuscript exist, given the lengthy period during which Thoreau wrote and rewrote the work, and much twentieth-century criticism centers on this process. The work has enjoyed a number of revivals as its themes have been found freshly relevant to specific periods in American history. Readers and critics in the 1930s, for example, embraced Thoreau's prescription for simple, frugal, living and often took comfort from the author's decided preference for a way of life forced on them by economic necessity. In the 1960s, Thoreau's attacks on societal institutions that demand conformity at the price of individuality found a new audience in the generation fighting for free speech and civil rights. The author's unconventional way of life, his quest for spiritual renewal and perfection, and his rejection of material possessions continue to appeal to readers and critics. Although *Walden* has long been a staple of the American literature curriculum at universities around the country, its most recent use is as a rhetoric text. Appreciated for its tight construction, impressive vocabulary, and the richness of its many allusions, *Walden* is finding new life as an example of good writing.

CRITICISM

John Sullivan Dwight (review date 1854)

SOURCE: A review of *Walden,* in *Critical Essays on Henry David Thoreau's "Walden,"* edited by Joel Myerson, G. K. Hall & Co., 1988, pp. 19-20.

[*In this review, originally published in* Dwight's Journal of Music, *the critic praises* Walden *for its originality and common-sense approach to life and nature.*]

For indoor reading, in the interims of physical fatigue and the lull of social excitement, say, for a few minutes after the evening company have dispersed and left us to our thoughts which will not sleep without some soothing efficacy of thoughts printed and impersonal, we have another book:—kindly placed in our hands upon the eve of starting on our journey, and with a delicate instinct of what was fitting, by our friend Fields, the poet partner in the firm of Ticknor and Co., the publishers,—a copy in advance of publication. In such hours one retires from Nature only to live her over in dreams and by whatever rush-light of his own reflections; and for such hours no truer friend and text book have we ever found than this wonderful new book called *Walden, or Life in the Woods,* by Henry D. Thoreau, the young Concord hermit, as he has sometimes been called. Thoreau is one of those men who has put such a determined trust in the simple dictates of common sense, as to earn the vulgar title of "transcendentalist" from his sophisticated neighbors. He is one of the few who really thinks and acts and tries life for himself, honestly weighing and reporting thereof, and in his own way (which he cares not should be others' ways) enjoying. Of course, they find him strange, fantastical, a humorist, a theorist, a dreamer. It may be or may not. One thing is certain, that his humor has led him into a life experiment, and that into a literary report or book, that is full of information, full of wisdom, full of wholesome, bracing moral atmosphere, full of beauty, poetry and entertainment for all who have the power to relish a good book. He built himself a house in the woods by Walden pond, in Concord, where he lived alone for more than two years, thinking it false economy to eat so that life must be spent in procuring what to eat, but cultivating sober, simple, philosophic habits, and daily studying the lesson which nature and the soul of nature are perpetually teaching to the individual soul, would that but listen. Every chapter of the book is redolent of pine and hemlock. With a keen eye and love for nature, many are the rare and curious facts which he reports for us. He has become the confidant of all plants and animals, and writes the poem of their lives for us. Read that chapter upon sounds, that of the owl, the bull-frog, &c.; or that in which he commemorates the battle of the red and black ants, "red-republicans and black imperialists," which "took place in the Presidency of Polk, five years before the passage of Webster's Fugitive Slave Bill." Truer touches of humor and quaint, genuine, first-hand observation you will seldom find. And then his vegetable planting—read how he was "determined to know beans!" And his shrewd criticisms, from his woodland seclusion, upon his village neighbors and upon civilized life generally, in which men are slaves to their own thrift, are worthy of a philosophic, though by no means a "melancholy, Jacques." It is the most thoroughly original book that has been produced these many days. Its literary style is admirably clear and terse and elegant;

the pictures wonderfully graphic; for the writer is a poet and a scholar as well as a tough wrestler with the first economical problems of nature, and a winner of good cheer and of free glorious leisure out of what men call the "hard realities" of life. Walden pond, a half mile in diameter, in Concord town, becomes henceforth as classical as any lake of Windermere. And we doubt not, men are beginning to look to transcendentalists for the soberest reports of good hard commonsense, as well as for the models of the clearest writing. . . .

The Albion (review date 1854)

SOURCE: A review of *Walden,* in *Albion,* Vol. 13, No. 36, September 9, 1854, p. 429.

[*This review's anonymous author recommends* Walden *as an entertaining work.*]

One of those rare books that stand a part from the herd of new publications under which the press absolutely groans; moderate in compass but eminently suggestive, being a compound of thought, feeling, and observation. Its author, it seems, during 1845, 6, and 7, played the philosophic hermit in a wood that overlooks Walden Pond, in the neighbourhood of Concord, Massachusetts. Here he tested at how cheap a rate physical existence may healthfully be maintained, and how, apart from the factitious excitement of society and the communion of mind with mind, he could cultivate a tranquil and contemplative spirit, yet resolute withal. This experiment was undeniably successful; and he has here set forth the record of his sylvan life and the musings of his happy solitude. He probably errs in believing, that life in an isolated shanty, and the strict vegetarian system, could be made profitable or pleasant to the men and women of this age. But we shall not discuss the question with this voluntary and most practical hermit. We can admire, without wishing to imitate him; and we can thank him cordially for hints on many topics that interest humanity at large, as well as for page upon page of research and anecdote, showing how lovingly he studied the instincts and the habits of the dumb associates by whom he was surrounded. The choicest and most popular works on natural history contain no descriptions more charming than those that abound in this volume. A little humour and a little satire are the pepper and salt to this part of the entertainment that Mr. Thoreau serves up. Into it we advise the reader—of unvitiated taste and unpalled appetite—to dip deeply. We at least do not come across a Walden, every day.

Possibly our strong commendation may be borne out by the [following excerpt] that we quote. [It] may well be called the "The Battle of the Ants."

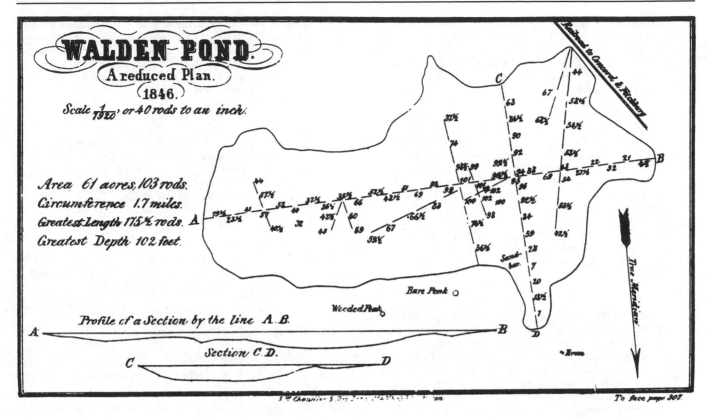

Map of Walden Pond.

I was witness to events of a less peaceful character. One day when I went out to my wood-pile, or rather my pile of stumps, I observed two large ants, the one red, the other much larger, nearly half an inch long, and black, fiercely contending with one another. Having once got hold they never let go, but struggled and wrestled and rolled on the chips incessantly. Looking farther, I was surprised to find that the chips were covered with such combatants, that it was not a *duellum,* but a *bellum,* a war between two races of ants, the red always pitted against the black, and frequently two red ones to one black. The legions of these myrmidons covered all the hills and vales in my wood-yard, and the ground was already strewed with the dead and dying, both red and black. It was the only battle which I have ever witnessed, the only battle-field I ever trod while the battle was raging; internecine war; the red republicans on the one hand, and the black imperialists on the other. On every side they were engaged in deadly combat, yet without any noise that I could hear, and human soldiers never fought so resolutely. I watched a couple that were fast locked in each other's embraces, in a little sunny valley amid the chips, now at noon-day prepared to fight till the sun went down, or life went out. The smaller red champion had fastened himself like a vice to his adversary's front, and through all the tumblings on that field never for an instant ceased to gnaw at one of his feelers near the root,

having already caused the other to go by the board; while the stronger black one dashed him from side to side, and, as I saw on looking nearer, had already divested him of several of his members. They fought with more pertinacity than bull-dogs. Neither manifested the least disposition to retreat. It was evident that their battle-cry was conquer or die. In the mean while, there came along a single red ant on the hill-side of this valley, evidently full of excitement, who either had despatched his foe, or had not yet taken part in the battle; probably the latter, for he had lost none of his limbs; whose mother had charged him to return with his shield or upon it. Or perchance he was some Achilles, who had nourished his wrath apart, and had now come to avenge or rescue his Patroclus. He saw this unequal combat from afar,—for the blacks were nearly twice the size of the red—he drew near with rapid pace until he stood on his guard within half an inch of the combatants; then, watching his opportunity, he sprang upon the black warrior, and commenced his operations near the root of his right fore-leg, leaving the foe to select among his own members; and so there were three united for life, as if a new kind of attraction had been invented which put all other locks and cements to shame. I should not have wondered by this time to find that they had their respective musical bands stationed on some eminent chip, and playing their national airs the while, to excite the slow and cheer the dying combatants. I was myself excited somewhat as if they had been men. The more you think of it the less the difference. And certainly there is not the fight recorded in Concord history, at least, if in the history of America, that will bear a moment's comparison with this, whether for the numbers engaged in it, or for the patriotism and heroism displayed. For numbers and for carnage it was an Austerlitz or Dresden. Concord fight! Two killed on the patriot's side, and Luther Blanchard wounded! Why here every ant was a Buttrick,— "Fire! for God's sake fire!"—and thousands shared the fate of Davis and Hoemer. There was not one hireling there. I have no doubt that it was a principle they fought for, as much as our ancestors, and not to avoid a three-penny tax on their tea; and the results of this battle will be as important and memorable to those whom it concerns as those of the battle of Bunker Hill, at least.

I took up the chip on which the three I have particularly described were struggling, carried it into my house, and placed it under a tumbler on my window-sill, in order to see the issue. Holding a microscope to the first-mentioned red ant, I saw that, though he was assiduously gnawing at the near fore-leg of his enemy, having severed his remaining feeler, his own breast was all torn away, exposing what vitals he had there to the jaws of the black warrior, whose breast plate was apparently too thick for him to pierce; and the dark carbuncles of the sufferer's eyes shone with ferocity such as war only could excite. They struggled half an hour longer under the tumbler, and when I looked again the black soldier had severed the heads of his foes from their bodies, and the still living heads were hanging on either side of him like ghastly trophies at his saddle-bow, still apparently as firmly fastened as ever, and he was endeavoring with feeble struggles, being without feelers and with only the remnant of a leg, and I know not how many other wounds, to divest himself of them; which at length, after half an hour more, he accomplished. I raised the glass, and he went over the window sill in that crippled state. Whether he finally survived that combat, and spent the remainder of his days in some Hotel des Invalides, I do not know; but I thought that his industry would not be worth much thereafter. I never learned which party was victorious, nor the cause of the war; but I felt for the rest of that day as if I had my feelings excited and harrowed by witnessing the struggle, the ferocity and carnage, of a human battle before my door.

Kirby and Spence tells us that the battles of ants have long been celebrated and the date of them recorded, though they say that Huber is the only modern author who appears to have witnessed them. "Æneas Sylvius," say they, "after giving a very circumstantial account of one contested with

great obstinacy by a great and small species on the trunk of a pear tree," adds that "'This action was fought in the pontificate of Eugenius the Fourth, in the presence of Nicholas Pistoriensis, an eminent lawyer, who related the whole history of the battle with the greatest fidelity. A similar engagement between great and small ants is recorded by Olans Magnus, in which the small ones, being victorious, are said to have buried the bodies of their own soldiers, but left those of their giant enemies a prey to the birds. This event happened previous to the expulsion of the tyrant Christiern the Second from Sweden." The battle which I witnessed took place in the Presidency of Polk, five years before the passage of Webster's Fugitive-Slave Bill.

We might have found something writ in gentler strain; but there is a point and a quaintness in the above warlike episode, that catches our fancy. . . .

The National Era (review date 1854)

SOURCE: A review of *Walden,* in *The National Era,* Vol. 8, No. 404, September 28, 1854, p. 155.

[*In this anonymous review, the author is concerned about the consequences for civilization if every man were to follow Thoreau's example and live a simple solitary life.*]

In its narrative, this book [*Walden*] is unique, in its philosophy quite Emersonian. It is marked by genius of a certain order, but just as strongly, by pride of intellect. It contains many acute observations on the follies of mankind, but enough of such follies to show that its author has his full share of the infirmities of human nature, without being conscious of it. By precept and example he clearly shows how very little is absolutely necessary to the subsistence of a man, what a Robinson Crusoe life he may lead in Massachusetts, how little labor he need perform, if he will but reduce his wants to the philosophical standard, and how much time he may then have for meditation and study. To go out and squat, all alone, by a pretty pond in the woods, dig, lay the foundation of a little cabin, and put it up, with borrowed tools, furnish it, raise corn, beans, and potatoes, and do one's own cooking, hermit like, so that the total cost of the whole building, furnishing, purchasing necessaries, and living for eight months, shall not exceed forty or fifty dollars, may do for an experiment, by a highly civilized man, with Yankee versatility, who has had the full benefit of the best civilization of the age. All men are not "up to" everything. But, if they were, if they all had the universal genius of the "Yankee nation," how long would they remain civilized, by squatting upon solitary duck-ponds, eschewing matrimony, casting off all ties of family, each one setting his wits to work to see how little he could do with, and how much of that little he could himself accomplish? At the end of eight months, Mr. Thoreau might remain a ruminating philosopher, but he would have few but ruminating animals to write books for.

But, with all its extravagances, its sophisms, and its intellectual pride, the book is acute and suggestive, and contains passages of great beauty.

An excerpt from *Walden*:

When I wrote the following pages, or rather the bulk of them, I lived alone, in the woods, a mile from any neighbor, in a house which I had built myself, on the shore of Walden Pond, in Concord, Massachusetts, and earned my living by the labor of my hands only. I lived there two years and two months. At present I am a sojourner in civilized life again.

I should not obtrude my affairs so much on the notice of my readers if very particular inquiries had not been made by my townsmen concerning my mode of life, which some would call impertinent, though they do not appear to me at all impertinent, but, considering the circumstances, very natural and pertinent. Some have asked what I got to eat; if I did not feel lonesome; if I was not afraid; and the like. Others have been curious to learn what portion of my income I devoted to charitable purposes; and some, who have large families, how many poor children I maintained. I will therefore ask those of my readers who feel no particular interest in me to pardon me if I undertake to answer some of these questions in this book. In most books, the *I*, or first person, is omitted; in this it will be retained; that, in respect to egotism, is the main difference. We commonly do not remember that it is, after all, always the first person that is speaking. I should not talk so much about myself if there were any body else whom I knew as well. Unfortunately, I am confined to this theme by the narrowness of my experience. Moreover, I, on my side, require of every writer, first or last, a simple and sincere account of his own life, and not merely what he has heard of other men's lives; some such account as he would send to his kindred from a distant land; for if he has lived sincerely, it must have been in a distant land to me. . . .

Henry David Thoreau, in Walden, *edited by J. Lyndon Shanley, Princeton University Press, 1971.*

National Anti-Slavery Standard (review date 1854)

SOURCE: "Thoreau's *Walden*," in *Thoreau: A Century of Criticism,* edited by Walter Harding, Southern Methodist University Press, 1954, pp. 8-11.

[*This anonymous reviewer answers* Walden's *earlier critics by suggesting that Thoreau's example provides an appealing alternative to the widespread pursuit of material gain.*]

These books [*Walden* and *A Week on the Concord and Merrimack Rivers*] spring from a depth of thought which will not suffer them to be put by, and are written in a spirit in striking contrast with that which is uppermost in our time and country. Out of the heart of practical, hard-working, progressive New England come these Oriental utterances. The life exhibited in them teaches us, much more impressively than any number of sermons could, that this Western activity of which we are so proud, these material improvements, this commercial enterprise, this rapid accumulation of wealth, even our external, associated philanthropic action, are very easily overrated. The true glory of the human soul is not to be reached by the most rapid travelling in car or steamboat, by the instant transmission of intelligence however far, by the most speedy accumulation of a fortune, and however efficient measures we may adopt for the reform of the intemperate, the emancipation of the enslaved, &c., it will avail little unless we are ourselves essentially noble enough to inspire those whom we would so benefit with nobleness. External bondage is trifling compared with the bondage of an ignoble soul. Such things are often said, doubtless, in pulpits and elsewhere, but the men who say them are too apt to live just with the crowd, and so their words come more and more to ring with a hollow sound.

It is refreshing to find in these books the sentiments of one man whose aim manifestly is to *live,* and not to waste his time upon the externals of living. Educated at Cambridge, in the way called liberal, he seems determined to make a liberal life of it, and not to become the slave of any calling, for the sake of earning a reputable livelihood or of being regarded as a useful member of society. He evidently considers it his first business to become more and more a living, advancing soul, knowing that thus alone (though he desires to think as little as possible about that) can he be, in any proper sense, useful to others. Mr. Thoreau's view of life has been called selfish. His own words, under the head of "Philanthropy" in *Walden,* are the amplest defense against this charge, to those who can appreciate them. In a deeper sense than we commonly think, charity begins at home. The man who, with any fidelity, obeys his own genius, serves men infinitely more by so doing, becoming an encouragement, a strengthener, a fountain of inspiration to them, than if he were to turn aside from his path and exhaust his energies in striving to meet their superficial needs. As a thing by the way, aside from our proper work, we may seek to remove external obstacles from the path of our neighbours, but no man can help them much who makes that his main business, instead of seeking evermore, with all his energies, to reach the loftiest point which his imagination sets before him, thus adding to the stock of true nobleness in the world.

But suppose all men should pursue Mr. Thoreau's course, it is asked triumphantly, as though, then, we should be sure to go back to barbarism. Let it be considered, in the first place, that no man could pursue his course who was a mere superficial imitator, any more than it would be a real imitation of Christ if all men were to make it their main business to go about preaching the Gospel to each other. Is it progress toward barbarism to simplify one's outward life for the sake of coming closer to Nature and to the realm of ideas? Is it civilization and refinement to be occupied evermore with adding to our material conveniences, comforts and luxuries, to make ourselves not so much living members as dead tools of society, in some bank, shop, office, pulpit or kitchen? If men were to follow in Mr. Thoreau's steps, by being more obedient to their loftiest instincts, there would, indeed, be a falling off in the splendor of our houses, in the richness of our furniture and dress, in the luxury of our tables, but how poor are these things in comparison with the new grandeur and beauty which would appear in the souls of men. What fresh and inspiring conversation should we have, instead of the wearisome gossip, which now meets us at every turn. Men toil on, wearing out body or soul, or both, that they may accumulate a needless amount of the externals of living; that they may win the regard of those no wiser than themselves; their natures become warped and hardened to their pursuits; they get fainter and fainter glimpses of the glory of the world, and, by and by, comes into their richly-adorned parlours some wise and beautiful soul, like the writer of these books, who, speaking from the fullness of his inward life, makes their luxuries appear vulgar, showing that, in a direct way, he has obtained the essence of that which his entertainers have been vainly seeking for at such a terrible expense.

It seems remarkable that these books have received no more adequate notice in our Literary Journals. But the class of scholars are often as blind as others to any new elevation of soul. In *Putnam's Magazine,* Mr. Thoreau is spoken of as an oddity, as the Yankee Diogenes, as though the really ridiculous oddity were not in us of the "starched shirt-collar" rather than in this devotee of Nature and Thought. Some have praised the originality and profound sympathy with which he views natural objects. We might as well stop with praising Jesus for the happy use he has made of the lilies of the field. The fact of surpassing interest for us is the simple grandeur of Mr. Thoreau's position—a position open to us all, and of which this sympathy with Nature is but a single result. This is seen in the less descriptive, more purely thoughtful passages, such as that upon Friendship in the "Wednesday" of the

"Week," and in those upon "Solitude," "What I Lived for," and "Higher Laws," in *Walden,* as well as in many others in both books. We do not believe that, in the whole course of literature, ancient and modern, so noble a discourse upon Friendship can be produced as that which Mr. Thoreau has given us. It points to a relation, to be sure, which, from the ordinary level of our lives, may seem remote and dreamy. But it is our thirst for, and glimpses of, such things which indicate the greatness of our nature, which give the purest charm and colouring to our lives. The striking peculiarity of Mr. Thoreau's attitude is, that while he is no religionist, and while he is eminently practical in regard to the material economics of life, he yet manifestly feels, through and through, that the loftiest dreams of the imagination are the solidest realities, and so the only foundation for us to build upon, while the affairs in which men are everywhere busying themselves so intensely are comparatively the merest froth and foam.

R. W. B. Lewis (essay date 1955)

SOURCE: "The Case against the Past," in *The American Adam: Innocence, Tragedy and Tradition in the Nineteenth Century,* The University of Chicago Press, 1955, pp. 13-27.

[*In this excerpt, Lewis discusses Thoreau's prescription for casting off tradition and convention and immersing oneself in the world of nature. Only those footnotes pertaining to the excerpt below have been reprinted.*]

"We have the Saint Vitus dance." This was Thoreau's view of the diversion of energies to material expansion and of the enthusiastic arithmetic by which expansion was constantly being measured. Miles of post roads and millions of tons of domestic export did not convince Thoreau that first principles ought to be overhauled; but a close interest in these matters did convince him that first principles had been abandoned. Probably nobody of his generation had a richer sense of the potentiality for a fresh, free, and uncluttered existence; certainly no one projected the need for the ritual burning of the past in more varied and captivating metaphors. This is what *Walden* is about; it is the most searching contemporary account of the desire for a new kind of life. But Thoreau's announcement of a spiritual molting season (one of his favorite images) did not arise from a belief that the building of railroads was proof of the irrelevance of too-well-remembered doctrines. Long before Whitman, himself a devotee of the dazzling sum, attacked the extremes of commercialism in *Democratic Vistas,* Thoreau was insisting that the obsession with railroads did not demonstrate the hope for humanity, but tended to smother it. "Men think it is essential that the *Nation* have commerce, and export ice, and talk through a telegraph and ride thirty miles an hour, without a doubt, whether *they* do or not; but whether we should live like baboons or men is a little uncertain."

Watching the local railroad train as it passed near Walden Pond on the recently laid track between Fitchburg and Boston, Thoreau noticed that while the narrow little cars moved eastward along the ground, the engine smoke drifted skyward, broadening out as it rose. The picture (it occurs in the chapter called "Sounds") provided him with a meaningful glimpse of that wholeness, of interrelated doubleness, which was for Thoreau the required shape of the life that was genuinely lived. The trouble with railroads—he said it, in fancy, to the scores of workmen he saw starting up in protest against him—was that so few persons who rode on them were heading in any definite direction or were aware of a better direction than Boston; quite a few persons were simply run over, while the building of railroads crushed the heart and life out of the builders. The trouble, in general, with expending one's strength on "internal improvements" was that the achievement, like the aim, was partial: there was nothing internal about them. The opportunity that Thoreau looked out upon from his hut at Walden was for no such superficial accomplishment, but for a wholeness of spirit realized in a direct experience of the whole of nature. The words "nature" and "wholeness" have been overworked and devitalized (Thoreau and Emerson are partly to blame), and now they are suspect; but they glow with health in the imaginatively ordered prose of Henry Thoreau.

The narrator of *Walden* is a witness to a truly new world which the speaker alone has visited, from which he has just returned, and which he is sure every individual ought to visit at least once—not the visible world around Walden Pond, but an inner world which the Walden experience allowed him to explore. Thoreau liked to pretend that his book was a purely personal act of private communion. But that was part of his rhetoric, and *Walden* is a profoundly rhetorical book, emerging unmistakably from the long New England preaching tradition; though here the trumpet call announces the best imaginable news rather than apocalyptic warnings. Thoreau, in *Walden,* is a man who has come back down into the cave to tell the residents there that they are really in chains, suffering fantastic punishments they have imposed on themselves, seeing by a light that is reflected and derivative. A major test of the visionary hero must always be the way he can put his experience to work for the benefit of mankind; he demonstrates his freedom in the liberation of others. Thoreau prescribes the following cure: the total renunciation of the traditional, the conventional, the socially acceptable, the well-worn paths of conduct, and the total immersion in nature.

Everything associated with the past should be burned away. The past should be cast off like dead skin. Thoreau remembered with sympathetic humor the pitiful efforts of one John Field, an Irishman living at near-by Baker Farm, to catch perch with shiners: "thinking to live by some derivative old-country mode in this primitive new country." "I look on England today," he wrote, "as an old gentleman who is travelling with a great deal of baggage, trumpery which has accumulated from long housekeeping, which he has not the courage to burn." Thoreau recorded with approval and some envy a Mexican purification rite practiced every fifty-two years; and he added, "I have scarcely heard of a truer sacrament." These periodic symbolic acts of refreshment, which whole societies ought to perform in each generation ("One generation abandons the enterprises of another like stranded vessels"), were valid exactly because they were images of fundamental reality itself. Individuals and groups should enact the rhythmic death and rebirth reflected in the change of season from winter to spring, in the sequence of night and day. "The phenomena of the year take place every day in a pond on a small scale." These were some of the essential facts discovered by Thoreau when he fronted them at Walden; and the experience to which he was to become a witness took its shape, in act and in description, from a desire to live in accordance with these facts. So it was that he refused the offer of a door-mat, lest he should form the habit of shaking it every morning; and, instead, every morning "I got up early and bathed in the pond; that was a religious exercise, and one of the best things which I did."

The language tells us everything, as Thoreau meant it to. He had his own sacramental system, his own rite of baptism. But his use of the word "nature" indicates that the function of sacraments was to expose the individual again to the currents flowing through nature, rather than to the grace flowing down from supernature. The ritual of purification was no less for Thoreau than for St. Paul a dying into life; but Thoreau marched to the music he heard; it was the music of the age; and he marched in a direction *opposite* to St. Paul. His familiar witticism, "One world at a time" (made on his deathbed to an eager abolitionist named Pillsbury, who looked for some illumination of the future life from the dying seer) was a fair summary of his position: with this addition, that poetry traditionally taken as hints about what could be seen through a glass darkly about the next world was taken by Thoreau as what had been seen by genius, face to face with this one. He was among the first to see Christian literature as only the purest and most inspiring of the fables about the relation of man to nature and about the infinite capacities of the unaided human spirit. The Bible (Thoreau referred to it simply as "an old book") was the finest poem which had ever been written; it was the same in substance as Homeric or Hindu mythology, but it was richer in metaphor. The Bible spoke more sharply to the human condition. This was why Thoreau, like Whitman, could employ the most traditional of religious phrases and invest them with an unexpected and dynamic new life.

It is not surprising that transcendentalism was Puritanism turned upside down, as a number of critics have pointed out; historically, it could hardly have been anything else. Transcendentalism drew on the vocabularies of European romanticism and Oriental mysticism; but the only available local vocabulary was the one that the hopeful were so anxious to escape from, and a very effective way to discredit its inherited meaning was to serve it up in an unfamiliar context. There was something gratifyingly shocking in such a use of words: "What demon possessed me that I behaved so well?" Thoreau spoke as frequently as he could, therefore, about a *sacrament,* a sacred mystery, such as baptism: in order to define the cleaning, not of St. Paul's natural man, but of the conventional or traditional man; in order, precisely, to bring into being the natural man. For the new tensions out of which insights were drawn and moral choices provoked were no longer the relation of nature and grace, of man and God, but of the natural and the artificial, the new and the old, the individual and the social or conventional. Thoreau had, as he remarked in his other deathbed witticism, no quarrel with God; his concern was simply other.

His concern was with the strangulation of nature by convention. The trouble with conventions and traditions in the New World was that they had come first; they had come from abroad and from a very long way back; and they had been superimposed upon nature. They had to be washed away, like sin, so that the natural could reveal itself again and could be permitted to create its own organic conventions. They had to be renounced, as the first phase of the ritual; and if renunciation was, as Emily Dickinson thought, a piercing virtue, it was not because it made possible an experience of God in an infusion of grace, but because it made possible an experience of self in a bath of nature.

Thoreau had, of course, learned a good deal from Emerson, whose early energy was largely directed toward constructing "an original relation with the universe" and who reverted time and again to the same theme: "beware of tradition"; "forget historical Christianity"; "lop off all superfluity and tradition, and fall back on the nature of things." And what was this nature of things which men were enjoined to fall back on? Lowell understood some of it, in one of the better sentences of his querulous and uneven essay on Thoreau (1865): "There is only one thing better than tradition, and that is the original and eternal life out of which all tradition takes its rise. It was this life which

the reformers demanded, with more or less clearness of consciousness and expression, life in politics, life in literature, life in religion." But even in this moment of qualified approval, Lowell makes it sound too pallid, soft, and ethereal. Nature was not merely the mountains and the prairie, any more than it was merely the bees and the flowers; but it was all of those things too, and it must always include them. If nature was partly represented by "Higher Laws," as the title of one chapter in *Walden* tells us, it was represented also by "Brute Neighbors," "Winter Animals," and a "Bean-Field," as we know from the titles of other chapters. Thoreau's nature is bounded by an irony which applies the phrase "Higher Laws" to a chapter that, for all its idealism, talks at some length about fried rats.

Irony too—the doubleness of things—Thoreau could learn from Emerson, as each of them had learned from Coleridge and Plato. "All the universe over," Emerson wrote in his journal (1842), "there is just one thing, this old double." The old double, the ideal and the actual, the higher law and the fried rat, required a double consciousness and found expression in a double criticism; nature could be satisfied with nothing else. Emerson tramped in mud puddles, and Thoreau, more adventurously, swam in Walden Pond; the puddle and the pond were instances of unimpeded nature; but both men searched, in their separate ways, for the spiritual analogues which completed the doubleness of nature. Their ability to address themselves with very nearly equal fluency to both dimensions of consciousness gave later comfort to idealists and nominalists alike, though neither group understood the Emersonian principle that only the whole truth could be true at all. Bronson Alcott was the most high-minded of the contemporary idealists, but Emerson chided him for neglecting the value of the many in his rapture for the one, and thought he had genius but not talent. "The philosophers of Fruitlands," Emerson said in 1843, naming Alcott's experimental community, "have such an image of virtue before their eyes, that the poetry of man and nature they never see; the poetry that is man's life, the poorest pastoral clownish life; the light that shines on a man's hat, in a child's spoon." He was harder, of course, on those who saw only the hat and the spoon: the materialists and the tradesmen whom he excoriated in many essays, and writers who stuck too obstinately to the ordinary (Emerson would say, the "vulgar") aspects of the visible world.

Thoreau's personal purification rite began with the renunciation of old hats and old spoons and went forward to the moment—as he describes himself in the opening paragraph of "Higher Laws"—when the initiate stood fully alive in the midst of nature, eating a woodchuck with his fingers, and supremely aware, at the same instant, of the higher law of virtue. "I love the wild not less than the good," Thoreau admitted, announcing duplicity in his own peculiar accent. The structure of *Walden* has a similar beginning and a similar motion forward. The book starts amid the punishing conventions of Concord, departs from them to the pond and the forest, explores the natural surroundings, and exposes the natural myth of the yearly cycle, to conclude with the arrival of spring, the full possession of life, and a representative anecdote about the sudden bursting into life of a winged insect long buried in an old table of apple-tree wood.[3]

Individual chapters are sometimes carried along to the same rhythm. "Sounds," for example, starts with conventional signs and then looks to nature for more authentic ones; it picks up the cycle of the day, as Thoreau listens to sounds around the clock; and it concludes with a total surrender to the vitalizing power of unbounded nature. Thoreau had been talking about his reading in the previous chapter; now he reminds us: "While we are confined to books . . . we are in danger of forgetting the language which all things and events speak without metaphor." Sounds are elements of this natural language: the sound of the trains passing in the morning; the church bells from Lincoln, Bedford, or Concord; the lowing of cows in the evening; "regularly at half-past seven," the vesper chant of the whip-poor-wills; the "maniacal hooting of owls," which "represent the stark twilight and unsatisfied thoughts which all have"; "late in the evening . . . the distant rumbling of wagons over bridges,—a sound heard farther than almost any other at night,—the baying of dogs . . . the trump of bullfrogs"; and then at dawn the morning song of the cockerel, the lusty call to awaken of the chanticleer which Thoreau offered on the title-page as the symbol of the book. "To walk in a winter morning, in a wood where these birds abounded . . . think of it! It would put nations on the alert." Finally, in a morning mood, Thoreau closes his chapter rejoicing that his hut has no yard, no fence, but is part of unfenced nature itself.

It was with the ultimate aim of making such an experience possible—a life determined by nature and enriched by a total awareness—that Thoreau insisted so eloquently upon the baptismal or rebirth rite. What he was demanding was that individuals start life all over again, and that in the new world a fresh start was literally and immediately possible to anyone wide enough awake to attempt it. It was in this way that the experience could also appear as a return to childhood, to the scenes and the wonder of that time. In a particularly revealing moment, Thoreau reflected, while adrift on the lake in the moonlight and playing the flute for the fishes, on a boyhood adventure at that very place. "But now," he said, "I made my home by the shore." Thoreau reflected the curious but logical reverence of his age for children: "Children, who play life, discern its true law and relations more clearly than men, who fail to live it worthily." Children seemed for Thoreau to possess some secret which had been lost in the deadening process of growing up, some intimation (like Wordsworth's child) which had faded under the routine pressure of everyday life. Emerson found the new attitude of adults toward children the appropriate symbol with which to introduce his retrospective summary of the times (1867): "Children had been repressed and kept in the background; now they were considered, cosseted and pampered." Thoreau thought he knew why: because "every child begins the world again"; every child managed to achieve without conscious effort what the adult could achieve only by the strenuous, periodic act of refreshment. In this sense, the renewal of life was a kind of homecoming; the busks and the burnings were preparatory to recapturing the outlook of children.

Psychologists who have followed Jung's poetic elaboration and doctrinaire schematizing of the guarded suggestions of Freud could make a good deal of the impulse. They might describe it as an impulse to return to the womb; and some support could doubtless be found in the image-clusters of Walden: water, caves, shipwrecks, and the like. This approach might persuasively maintain that the end of the experience narrated by Thoreau was the reintegration of the personality. And since, according to Jung, "the lake in the valley is the unconscious," it is possible to hold that *Walden* enacts and urges the escape from the convention-ridden conscious and the release of the spontaneous energies of personality lying beneath the surface, toward a reuniting of the psychic "old double." An analysis of this sort can be helpful and even illuminating, and it could be applied to the entire program of the party of Hope, substituting terms associated with the unconscious for all the terms associated with Emerson's "Reason." A certain warrant for the psychological interpretation can be found in the novels of Dr. Holmes, and the methodological issue arises more sharply in that discussion. But we may also remind ourselves that the psychological vocabulary simply manipulates a set of metaphors other than those we normally use. Probably we do not need to go so far afield to grasp what Thoreau was seeking to explain; we may even suspect that he meant what he said. And what he said was that he went to the woods in order to live deliberately, "to front only the essential facts of life"; because human life and human expression were so burdened with unexamined habits, the voice of experience so muffled by an uninvestigated inheritance, that only by a total rejection of those habits and that inheritance and by a recovery of a childlike wonder and directness could anyone find out whether life were worth living at all.

Thoreau, like most other members of the hopeful party, understood dawn and birth better than he did night and death. He responded at once to the cockerel in the morning; the screech owls at night made him bookish and sentimental. And though their wailing spoke to him about "the low spirits and melancholy forebodings of fallen souls," the whole dark side of the world was no more than another guaranty of the inexhaustible variety of nature.[4] Thoreau knew not evil; his American busk would have fallen short, like the bonfire in Hawthorne's fantasy, of the profounder need for the purification of the human heart. He would have burned away the past as the accumulation of artifice, in the name of the natural and the essential. But if the natural looked to him so much more wholesome and so much more dependable than others have since thought it, his account of the recovery of nature was never less than noble: the noblest expression, in fact and in language, of the first great aspiration of the age.

Notes

[3] I am indebted here to the analysis of *Walden* as a rebirth ritual by Stanley Hyman, "Henry Thoreau in Our Time," *Atlantic Monthly,* CLXXVIII (November, 1946), 137-46. Mr. Hyman acknowledges his own debt, which I share, to F. O. Matthiessen's treatment of Thoreau in *American Renaissance* (New York, 1941).

[4] Thoreau goes on to say that the hooting of owls "is a sound admirably suited to swamps and twilight woods which no day illustrates, suggesting a vast and undeveloped nature which men have not yet recognized." The figurative language here is suggestive and may be surprising to anyone who supposes Thoreau unaware of the very existence of the cloacal regions of mind and nature.

J. Lyndon Shanley (essay date 1957)

SOURCE: "Developing the Structure," in *The Making of Walden with the Text from the First Version,* The University of Chicago Press, 1957, pp. 74-91.

[*In this excerpt, Shanley examines the successive versions of the* Walden *manuscript to determine the development of the work's structure.*]

In some respects the most valuable insight we gain from the manuscript is that which it gives us into the structure of *Walden*. We would know something of Thoreau's revising and adding to his material simply from a comparison of his journals with the published text, but without the manuscript we would know nothing of the way in which he found out how he could best organize his material.

Furthermore, although I do not believe that we must have the information that the manuscript gives us in order to recognize the nice disposition and relations of the parts of *Walden* or that this information proves that the final structure of *Walden* is satisfying, the changes the manuscript reveals often emphasize important points in the organization of the book, and thus they may help to show the whole design to some who might not otherwise see it. This is important, for many critics have denied Thoreau's success in achieving an artistically satisfying organization of his material. James Russell Lowell, for example, declared that Thoreau "had no artistic power such as controls a great work to the serene balance of completeness, but exquisite mechanical skill in the shaping of sentences and paragraphs."[1] Sanborn presumed to "improve" the order of *Walden* in the preposterous edition of the Bibliophile Society; and even a judicious critic and editor commented in 1934 that in "the matter of organization in its larger aspects, one may concede Thoreau's weakness yet offer in extenuation the desultory and casual nature of the author's own plan."[2]

These critics might point for support to Thoreau's judgment on his writing when he was working on *A Week* at the pond: "From all points of the compass, from the earth beneath and the heavens above, have come these inspirations and been entered daily in the order of their arrival in the journal. Thereafter, when the time arrived, they were winnowed into lectures, and again, in due time, from lectures into essays. And at last they stand, like the cubes of Pythagoras, firmly on either basis; like statues on their pedestals, but the statues rarely take hold of their hands. There is only such connection and series as is attainable in galleries. And this affects their immediate practical and popular influence."[3] This describes his characteristic progress from journal notes to publication, and it is a fair comment on the lack of coherence of *A Week,* but it is far from an adequate judgment on the unity of *Walden,* as the appreciation and analyses of F. O. Matthiessen and J. W. Krutch have more recently begun to make clear.[4]

Many readers have failed to appreciate the structure of *Walden,* possibly because they looked for something different from what is there, something at once more simple and more obvious. *Walden* is not a dated chronicle of Thoreau's two years in the woods; nor is it a handbook on how to live alone at little expense, organized according to sharply defined and separated topics; nor a rigorously constructed argument designed to prove that he was right and others wrong. It is rather a unique combination of all three kinds— chronicle, topical essay, and persuasive argument.

To understand how Thoreau put these together, it is necessary first to see in some detail what the final structure of *Walden* is in the order and the relation of its parts. This structure was determined for the most part by the fact that the book was an autobiographical narrative that Thoreau wrote to answer those who had asked him what his life in the woods was like and what he did there. It was also determined, however, by the fact that in addition to answering his townsmen's question, Thoreau wanted to point out how wrong were their assumptions about living and, as a result, how poor their lives were. This second theme provided the frame in which he set his story.

He began *Walden* with his argument, saying, in effect, in "Economy": "Your lives are mean because you do not know what is worth having in life, or how to get it. I have better notions of how to live and I have tried them out. Let me tell you what I did." Then, from the beginning of "Where I Lived" through "Spring" he described his experience in such a way as to show how satisfying and joyful it was. But as he did this, he frequently reverted to his criticism of the life of most people and to his own ideals, and thus kept his argument up, not in such a manner as to prove it logically, but rather to keep reminding his readers of the contrast between their sorry pleasures and the profoundly rewarding ones he had had. For example, in "Solitude" he compared the companionship he found in the things around him with his contemporaries' loneliness in crowds; in "Baker Farm," he portrayed John Field as an example of their slavery to things and set this off against his sense of freedom; in "Brute Neighbors" he showed that the hunters of the loon did not enjoy their short-lived sport as he enjoyed his pursuit of the bird; in "House-Warming" he compared the pleasures of his simple house with the lack of real pleasure in more elegant ones. When he had finished his story, he added in "Conclusion": "Now this shows you what can be done. You don't have to waste your lives and cower despairingly before what you think are the facts of life. You too can live freely and richly; everything lies before you if you will only have faith." With "Conclusion" Thoreau rounded out Walden most fittingly: it completed his argument, and in it he returned to speaking directly to the condition of his readers just as he had done at the beginning.

Within this frame, Thoreau ordered the story of his experiment in three ways: by topics, describing various qualities and aspects of his life; by the cycle of the day, telling of the events and occupations of typical days; and by the cycle of the year, narrating the changes in his surroundings and his doings that the progress of the seasons brought about. These factors do not operate separately, but together or in turns. Thoreau's transitions from part to part are deliberately casual; the movement is not rigorous. It is conceivable that he might have arranged some of his topics in different order, but their order and relations as they stand raise no questions, cause no jars, but create the sense of an easy and natural progress through his experiences. The order Thoreau established is absolutely proper to his aim. The proof of the excellence of his life in the woods and the strength of his answers to the incredulous and the scornful did not depend on some particular predetermined scheme or on irrefutable logic but on the creation of

a living sense of what his days and months had been like.

At the start he ordered and related his material primarily by topics. First he had to describe his house and its location; in "Economy" he had told only of building it. He began "Where I Lived" with an anecdote that emphasized his uncommon taste for retired and unimproved property and also restated his very uncommon attitude toward possessions. Then he launched into the description of living in his simple, unfinished hut and of the pleasures of its site and its distance from the rest of the world. Since he went to live where he did in order to live as he wanted to, he continued in this chapter by setting forth the qualities he sought in his life.

These implied study and contemplation as opposed to hurry and acquisition, and Thoreau therefore next wrote "Reading," in which he extolled the riches to be gained from the study of the classics of all peoples and contrasted the nourishment to be had from them with the thin fare with which most of his contemporaries were content. "Reading" has a place in his story on other grounds too, for Thoreau went to the pond to write and study, and he wrote *Walden* in part at least for others who wanted to do the same. It is the one part of the book, however, that may be criticized for not being completely of a piece with the rest. Not because it is not fitted in properly, for it is, but because its material seems to have a slightly different flavor from that of the other parts; it does not appear to depend directly on his days and nights at the pond; it does not smell of the woods, as does everything else in his story.

Of course, as he pointed out in both "Reading" and "Sounds," Thoreau spent much of his time in his first summer hoeing beans. But he did not tell about that at the very beginning; from "Where I Lived" through "Visitors" he was primarily concerned with describing certain general aspects of his life before telling what he did in the different seasons as they followed one another. After "Reading," then, he wrote in "Sounds" of his study of and absorption in the sights and sounds around him. Sometimes he did nothing but sit "rapt in a revery"; at other times he watched the life about the pond, or the trains on the Fitchburg Railroad, or listened to everything that spoke around him, the bells of Acton and Bedford, the cows in distant pastures, and the whippoorwills and owls and frogs. We should note, too, that Thoreau placed and ordered this material by more than its topical relations. He carefully marked the time as summer when he sat on his doorstep or swept his house or listened to the sounds of the day and night. This is important in the total effect of summer which the early chapters develop. In addition, he took great pains to arrange the cycle of the day from morning to afternoon to evening to night throughout the chapter. . . .

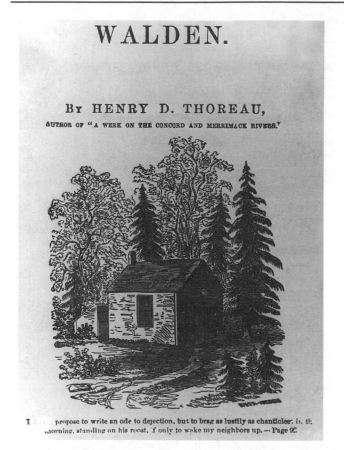

WALDEN.

By HENRY D. THOREAU,

AUTHOR OF "A WEEK ON THE CONCORD AND MERRIMACK RIVERS."

I ... propose to write an ode to dejection, but to brag as lustily as chanticleer in the morning, standing on his roost, if only to wake my neighbors up. — Page 92.

In "Solitude" he further described his enjoyment of and sympathy with his surroundings and answered directly the questions about the loneliness of his life, as well as emphasizing again how he gained the things he wanted. The answer was that he wasn't lonely even when alone. Moreover, not being a hermit in fact or in taste, he did see people; he had visitors, and in the next chapter, "Visitors," he told of his simple provisions for hospitality and described with charitable humor the pleasure he took in the simple and sometimes simple-minded company he found in the woods.

Through "Visitors" Thoreau had been answering primarily the question of what it was like to live as he had. With "The Bean-Field" he turned to answering "But what do you do there?" (This distinction is, of course, one of emphasis; he was answering both questions in all parts.) From the beginning of this chapter to the end of "Baker Farm," Thoreau ordered his material to show how he spent his summer days—morning, afternoon, and evening—at the pond. He began "The Bean-Field," "Meanwhile my beans . . . were impatient to be hoed," and thereby related his culture of beans to all that he had already written of; he had been caring for his beans ever since, and even before, he had moved into his hut in July. After describing the major morning task of his first summer in this chapter, he turned to telling of his afternoons and evenings

in "The Village," "The Ponds," and "Baker Farm." He began "The Village," "After hoeing, or perhaps reading and writing, in the forenoon, I usually bathed . . . and for the afternoon was absolutely free" and continued, "Every day or two I strolled to the village . . . it was very pleasant, when I stayed late in town, to launch myself into the night. . . . One afternoon, near the end of the first summer"; and in "The Ponds," "Sometimes . . . I rambled still farther westward [to gather berries on the hills]. . . . Occasionally, after my hoeing . . . I joined [a fisherman] . . . in warm evenings I frequently sat in the boat playing the flute. . . . Sometimes, after staying [late] in a village parlor I . . . spent the hours of midnight fishing . . . a walk through the woods [to other ponds] was often my recreation"; and in "Baker Farm," "Sometimes I rambled to pine groves . . . to particular trees. . . . I set out one afternoon to go a-fishing to Fair Haven." The long description of Walden Pond and the shorter ones of Flint's and White Pond break into the recital of his doings; but, as Thoreau said, they were his "lake country," and the wealth of details he supplied about it suggested the many afternoons he spent in it.

When he had finished telling what he did in his summer days, Thoreau was led on from the account of his fishing in "Baker Farm" to reflect, in "Higher Laws," on the conflict between his theories and practices in regard to fishing and eating and then to the never-ending conflict in all life between virtue and vice. At first glance this chapter might seem a serious break in his story, but the reflections in it are an important part of Thoreau's comment on life and his description of the qualities he sought in living; and in addition these reflections recall and pick up not only "What I Lived For" but also the argument he began in "Economy." Moreover, the pause here in his story is rhetorically sound; with "Baker Farm" Thoreau had finished one part, the account of his daily occupations in the summer, and he started afresh with new interest for his reader in "Brute Neighbors."

He used the comic interlude of the Hermit and the Poet to begin "Brute Neighbors," probably because he felt the need of some such descent from the level of "Higher Laws." In telling of the animals who were the neighbors he saw all the time, he took up again both the description of what living in the woods was like and the recital of what he did. But the major factor in organizing and relating the material from here to end of "Spring" is the passage of the months and seasons. Thoreau arranged "Brute Neighbors" with great care to run from the time when he was building his house, to June, through summer, and on to October. Thus he made the transition from the summer months of the earlier chapters and began to stress the cycle of the year. "Brute Neighbors" and "House-Warming" carry him from summer to the fall and early winter; "Former Inhabitants; and Winter Visitors" and "Winter Animals" are the deep middle of winter; "The Pond in Winter" takes him almost to the end of winter; finally there is "Spring."

But Thoreau also treated his material topically in these later chapters, and there is an interesting repetition with variation of earlier topics: parts of "House-Warming" recall the description of his hut in "Economy" and "Where I Lived"; "Former Inhabitants; and Winter Visitors" reminds us of "Solitude" and "Visitors"; in "Winter Animals" we have the "Sounds" and "Brute Neighbors" of winter; and "The Pond in Winter" recalls the earlier observations on "The Ponds."

At the beginning of "House-Warming," Thoreau returned to telling of his daily occupations, going a-graping and gathering wild apples and nuts for the winter. He noted very specially that he did these things in October, and in the rest of the chapter he noted the time of year at every point. He marked the passage of fall in the succession of September foliage, the numbed wasps of October, and the last warmth of the sun in November; and then, as he told of sitting before his fire and plastering his house and gathering wood, he marked the advance of winter: "the north wind had already begun to cool the pond. . . . I did not begin to plaster until it was freezing weather. . . . The pond had in the meanwhile skimmed over . . . at length the winter set in in good earnest." In "Former Inhabitants; and Winter Visitors" he told more of "cheerful winter evenings" by the fire when the snows were deep and the village farther away than ever; at such times he had to conjure up the former inhabitants of the neighboring woods for company. But he added that even "in the deepest snows" of winter he walked about the countryside, and from time to time three or four choice friends made their way to visit him "through snow and rain and dark."

He began "Winter Animals" with "When the ponds were firmly frozen," and described the changes in his surroundings that deep winter brought: new paths across country, new sights, new sounds, and new aspects of his animal neighbors. The activities and events of "The Pond in Winter"—cutting the ice to get water, ice-fishing, the survey of the pond through the ice, and the tale of the great ice harvest—these quite naturally followed the firm freezing of the ponds. And although robbing Walden of its coat of ice did not cause the spring breakup to come any earlier than usual, it did suggest the day when the pond would once more be a clear mirror; and so Thoreau went on to his delighted description of the coming and flourishing of spring and the advance of the year to summer again, when his first year in the woods was completed. Then, he turned back to speak directly to his readers in "Conclusion," and the gay and triumphant tone of "Spring" is continued in Thoreau's challenge to others to live with the faith his experience justified.

Much of this organization of the published *Walden* is discernible in the first version. The sequence and relations of topics, the scheme of describing his typical summer occupations, and the chronology beginning with the summer and ending with the spring—all three factors helped to organize the first version. But *Walden* was very incomplete and uncertain at many points in the first version, and it did not have the careful order and the nice articulation of parts that give the final text its complete and satisfying structure.

The changes Thoreau made in reshaping *Walden* can best be dealt with according to whether he made them to gain clarity and coherence of topics or to establish the cycle of the day or the cycle of the year. Sometimes more than one consideration dictated a change, since at a number of points the organization of the material depended upon more than one of the factors that determined the order of his story. Examples of minor changes in organization that resulted from the revisions of single paragraphs or of passages such as the sketch of Therien have already been considered. They will not be repeated here, for, although very important in the whole effect of *Walden,* they were not controlled by the demands of the over-all structure.

The first considerable change by which Thoreau achieved greater topical unity was taking the material of "Where I Lived, and What I Lived For," 18, 19, 21, and 22,[5] from its position in the first version (after "Sounds," 1, 2, and 3) and putting it, in version II, where it is in the final text. Since the passage asserts the value of living quietly and deliberately, it was not completely out of place when it followed the account of his morning meditation in "Sounds"; but Thoreau saw at his first rewriting that it was essentially an extension of his remarks on the qualities that he lived for. He gained in a second respect too, for, by removing this passage from its original place within "Sounds," he brought together the passages in "Sounds" that describe his morning meditation as he sat on his doorstep and his afternoon enjoyment of sights and sounds while he sat at his window. There is no evidence to prove that Thoreau thought of one of these improvements before the other, except that he wrote the new version of "Where I Lived, and What I Lived For" before he wrote the new one of "Sounds"; he may well have seen both improvements at once.

Thoreau did not always solve the problem of the proper place for many items so soon or so directly. In version I he had introduced his boasting of his lack of window curtains, "Economy," 89, in the middle of "The Village," 1, with: "I would observe, in a parenthesis." When he wrote version III, he decided that the passage was too parenthetical, and so he canceled it in I and copied it on a new leaf. But he does not seem to have found the place for it until version VII, when he saw that he could use it to contrast his attitude toward furniture with that of those who were trapped by theirs (see p. 63).

He was still later in settling on the right place for some of the material in "The Bean-Field." Not until he wrote the copy for the printer did he take the material on the sounds of the guns on gala days and the hum of the "trainers" out of "Sounds" and make them paragraph 7 of "The Bean-Field." They belong there rather than in "Sounds" because they were not regular daily sounds that he heard as he sat at his hut, but ones that he heard only a few times when he was "away there" in his beanfield. And not until the copy for the printer did he put his detailed farm accounts in "The Bean-Field," 12 and 13. In the first version and again in version V he wrote them out in "Economy" with his other accounts; later in V he penciled this note: "Here or under beans." In the end he transferred them to "The Bean-Field" where they belong, for they are an important item in the description of his cash-crop venture; furthermore, when they were with his other accounts in "Economy," there were too many figures together.

Even these few examples suggest that no matter where in *Walden* Thoreau might be working at any time, he strove to keep the whole piece in mind. The shift of one small item at three different times adds further evidence of this. In version II in a paragraph following "Economy," 21, he added the anecdote of the ragged Irishman who fell into the pond while cutting ice, by way of proof that the rich do not know how to use their money: he pointed out that the poor ice-cutter was more warmly dressed than his readers would be in their "fashionable garments." In version III he used the anecdote following "Economy," 37, as evidence that adequate clothing is not expensive. In V he put it in "The Pond in Winter," 18, which was at that time a more elaborate description of the ice-cutters at work than it is in the final text. In version VII and the final text, the anecdote is in "Economy," 105, where it serves as an illustration of how people often err in the pity and help that they extend to others who are supposedly worse off than themselves.

Besides the moving of items from one chapter to another, the manuscript also shows how Thoreau reorganized material within chapters and how he changed the chapter divisions themselves in order to make his topics clear and coherent. The first of these points can be illustrated only briefly here, for the changes in most chapters are too complicated to be described. The simple case of "Visitors" will have to serve. The transcription of version I shows the order of the chapter at the beginning (see pp. 169-77). Here and in version II the transition from the material of "Soli-tude" was: "As for men, they will hardly fail one anywhere," and then the description of Therien and the other individuals whom Thoreau talked with preceded the general remarks on his domestic arrangements for hospitality. But when he wrote version IV, he took from amid the material of "Solitude" the paragraph that serves as the introduction of "Visitors" in the final text: "I think that I love society as much as most. . . ." Sometime later (there is no evidence as to exactly when), he put the rest of his general remarks on visiting here at the beginning of the chapter in order to make his topic clear and to provide a better contrast to the preceding account of the pleasures of living alone in his house in the woods.

In two other cases he gained greatly by changing the points at which he had made chapter divisions. He first wrote the title of "Baker Farm" at the end of what is paragraph 2; the chapter then included only the story of his afternoon visit to Baker Farm and Fair Haven Bay. But he soon saw that "The Ponds" must end with the tribute to Walden and White ponds in paragraph 34; anything added after "Talk of heaven! ye disgrace the earth" would have been a hopeless anticlimax, and, besides, the beginning of "Baker Farm" serves to introduce the third in a series about his afternoon walks: "Sometimes I rambled to pine groves . . . or to the cedar wood . . . or to swamps. . . ."[6] He shifted the title of "House-Warming" in much the same way and for similar reasons. At first, in version V, he entitled the chapter "Fire," which he wrote at the top of a blank page, the fourth of a folio; the immediately preceding paragraph told of his sitting in the November sunshine, "House-Warming," 4. Later he wrote "House-Warming" above what is paragraph 1; the last paragraph of "Brute Neighbors" is clearly the end of the account of the animals, and "House-Warming," 1, "In October, I went a-graping . . . ," begins the description of his fall occupations.[7]

The change of name here is one of a number that Thoreau made; they too reflect his care in defining his topics. He originally wrote "Society" before the first paragraph of "Visitors," in contrast, of course, to the preceding title "Solitude." But "Visitors" is more concrete and indicates the nature of the content of the chapter more accurately. He changed "Beans" to "The Bean-Field," "Animal Food" to "Higher Laws," and "Fire" to "House-Warming" because in each case the first title was too narrow. "Fire," for example, did not cover the chimney-building, plastering, wood-gathering, and other items as does "House-Warming." "Brute Neighbors" was first entitled "Fall Animals"; since the chapter includes animals of the spring and summer, Thoreau later struck out "Fall." Finally, he wrote "Brute Neighbors," which is better than "Animals" because it suggests Thoreau's attitude toward the animals around him. "Winter Animals" was originally "Animals"; when "Fall Animals" was changed to "Animals," Thoreau added "Winter" to the title of the later chapter to distinguish it; it is a better title because more specific, and it is in keeping with "Winter Visitors" and "The Pond in Winter."

The changes Thoreau had to make in order to maintain the cycle of the day were few. As he put new material in "The Village," "The Ponds," and "Baker Farm," he did so in such a way as to keep the sequences of afternoon and evening and night with which he began. But the way in which he reordered "Sounds," 14 to 22, is a good example of his careful reworking. By the shift in version II of material from between "Sounds," 3 and 4, to "Where I Lived" (see p. 82), he had brought together in "Sounds" the events of a summer morning and a summer afternoon. But the order of the last part of the chapter was poor: the sound of cockcrow preceded the bells, and the frogs came between the whippoorwills and the screech owls. He did not work out the firm but unobtrusive progress of the final text—from afternoon through evening and finally to dawn of the next day—until the copy for the printer (or possibly version VI; the manuscript evidence is incomplete). In place of the scattered order of the earlier versions, the final text has: the rattle of a carriage or team in the afternoon, or the bells on Sundays; then at evening the distant lowing of some cow still in pasture; at "half-past seven" came the whippoorwills; later, "when other birds are still" he heard the owls; and also "late in the evening" he might hear wagons again or a cow now in a distant barnyard; "in the meanwhile" the frogs had begun their revels, which they kept up until the sun dispersed the morning mist. And so the night ended with dawn, and Thoreau went on to his remarks on cockcrowing; these led to others on his lack of the usual domestic sounds and surroundings, and so on to "Solitude."

The most extensive changes that Thoreau made in the order and relations of his material were those by which he completed the cycle of the seasons. These changes were essentially of two sorts. The first were directed to filling out the account of the seasons; they depended upon great additions, especially in version V and to a lesser extent in IV and VI. The second were directed to recording the individual events in the proper months and seasons; these depended for the most part on shifts of material that Thoreau made in the versions after V. The general effect of the changes can best be seen from a summary comparison of the contents and the order of the contents in the later parts of *Walden* in versions I and V and the published text (there were no chapter titles, of course, in I):

VERSION I
Brute Neighbors
Winter Animals
Former Inhabitants
The Pond in Winter
Spring

VERSION V
Brute Neighbors
House-Warming
Winter Animals
Former Inhabitants
Winter Visitors
The Pond in Winter
Spring

PUBLISHED TEXT
Brute Neighbors
House-Warming
Former Inhabitants; and Winter Visitors
Winter Animals
The Pond in Winter
Spring
Conclusion

In the early versions the months of fall and early winter were treated very briefly, and deep winter followed close upon the summer; it was as if Thoreau had been carried hastily into winter as he told the whole story of the animals in the woods in one long section. Details of his winter life were also missing.

Between versions IV and V, he wrote out much of the section on winter visitors. Perhaps he had not thought to include any account of his particular friends when he was preparing for lectures; but as he later reconstructed his life in the woods, he would have remembered his talks with those who were especially important as visitors when casual passers-by were few. When he wrote version V, he developed these notes into a separate whole piece, "Winter Visitors."

He made an even greater change by filling in the hitherto neglected season between the hunting of the loon and the ice-and-snow-bound world of mid-winter. He began by adding the pursuit of the loon and the flight of the ducks at the end of "Brute Neighbors"; he then made the great addition of almost all of "House-Warming" in versions V, VI, and VII. He told of his varied activities in late fall and early winter: going a-graping and nutting, building his chimney, plastering his house, gathering wood for fuel; and he described the changes in his surroundings as winter closed in. He also added a few details and comments to complete the picture of winter in "Winter Animals" and "The Pond in Winter."

When he had added the material that was necessary to fill out the cycle of the seasons, Thoreau had also to make sure that the various parts were related properly and that events of each season were in their right places. This involved the shift of material at a number of points. The major change of this sort was the reversal of the order of "Winter Animals" and "Former Inhabitants; and Winter Visitors"; he made it as he wrote the copy for the printer. The changing relations of the material in this part of *Walden* reemphasize the fact that the topical and the cyclic organizations are interwoven in the book and also that, while Thoreau's progress to his final form was constant in force, it was often tentative and complicated. In version I the sequence had been from all the material on the animals to "Former Inhabitants" to "The Pond in Winter." Topical considerations apparently influenced the placing of the material on the animals, and the cycle of the day influenced the relation of the material that followed: before Thoreau added "Winter Visitors" and "The Pond in Winter," 1 and 2, the transition was from "And with such thoughts as these I lulled myself asleep" ("Former Inhabitants," 16) to "Early in the morning" ("The Pond in Winter," 3).

After the additions, there was only a verbal transition from the allusion to "eventide" in the quotation from the Vishnu Purana ("Former Inhabitants; and Winter Visitors," 24) to the new beginning of "The Pond in Winter": "After a still winter night I awoke." But with "Winter Animals" placed after "Former Inhabitants; and Winter Visitors," there is a new transition from evening to morning, since at the end of "Winter Animals" Thoreau describes how he watched the rabbits in the evening, and then comes the morning at the beginning of "The Pond in Winter." This, however, would not have been the only or the major reason for the change; there were several others. First, the description of his cheery winter evenings by the fire in "Former Inhabitants" follows the talk of chimney, fuel, and fire in "House-Warming" better than did the beginning of "Winter Animals": "When the ponds were firmly frozen." Second, the change brought this freezing of the ponds in "Winter Animals" immediately before the ice-bound world of "The Pond in Winter." Finally, by separating "Brute Neighbors" and "Winter Animals" more widely, it produced a better distribution of the material on the animals.

At no other point did Thoreau shift or change so extensive a piece; but the very briefness of some items indicates the care with which he worked to arrange the details as well as to construct the outline of the seasons. Changes were necessary in every season. In versions I and II in "Sounds," 2, he wrote, "Sometimes in a spring morning . . . or later in the summer." In version VI and possibly in IV on a missing page, he dropped the reference to "spring," and the final text reads: "Sometimes, in a summer morning." He undoubtedly did sit on his doorstep in the spring too, but at this point he wanted to establish the fact that he was beginning his story with summer.

For the fall and winter he had a number of changes to make, and, as was the case with several "topical" items, he did not always find the right answer at once. Sometime after writing version IV, he wrote nine or ten lines on the beauty of the turning maples in September and inserted them in a blank space after the

first part of "The Ponds," 18, which is a description of the surface of Walden Pond on a calm September afternoon. They were not relevant at this point, and in version V Thoreau moved these lines on September foliage to "The Ponds," 16, in which he comments on the happy juxtaposition of water and wooded hills. But once again these new lines broke the unity of the passage to which they had been added; the emphasis on the fact that it was "September" and that there was daily changing foliage was out of place here.

When he wrote version VI, however, Thoreau was exquisitely successful in his search for the right place. In "House-Warming," 3, he had already described the numbed wasps that gathered in his house in October, and in paragraph 4 he had told how he sought the late sunshine of November on the northeast shore of the pond. Now he saw that the lines on the beauty of the September foliage would serve perfectly as the first of a three-part ode on autumn and the dying of the year, and he made them paragraph 2 of "House-Warming."

There is another interesting series of shifts of material for "House-Warming." In version VI Thoreau took the accounts of building his chimney and plastering his house from "Economy" and put them in "House-Warming" as a consecutive piece. In the copy for the printer, however, he separated them, using the passage on the chimney in "House-Warming," 5, and that on plastering in paragraph 10. He thus brought the building of the chimney into the story when he "began to have a fire at evening" in the fall, but he did not plaster his house "till it was freezing weather" in November.

It is impossible to know all the changes he made in some of the "winter" chapters and in "Spring" because of the leaves missing from version I. Certainly he moved material on the freezing and thawing of the ponds and rivers, but most details are lost. There are also a number of complicated moves of material on animals that are not fully describable. But the general nature and effect of what Thoreau did can be adequately seen from a few more items. He transferred the mice's girdling of the pitch pines from "Brute Neighbors" to "Winter Animals," 13, since they did this in the winter at the same time as they raided his store of nuts.[8] And, to put the events of spring in their proper places, he moved the spring racketing of the squirrels under his house from "Winter Animals" to "Spring," 12, and details on the breaking-up of the ice on Walden Pond from both "The Ponds," 13, and "The Pond in Winter," 16, to "Spring," 1.

As a last example, there is the change Thoreau made to mark the end of the cycle of the seasons. In version I he had described in "Brute Neighbors" how a phoebe had sometimes come and looked in at his house while he was building it in the spring months (see p. 191). Quite late in all his rewriting he wrote a revision of the passage on the last page of version I and marked it for insertion in "Spring," 25, leaving only the mere mention of the phoebe in "Brute Neighbors," 10.[9] In its new position at the end of "Spring" the passage begins: "The phoebe had already come once more and looked in at my door and window." The "once more" marks the full turn of the seasons, and thus Thoreau completed the story of his first year's life in the woods.

Notes

[1] *My Study Windows* (Boston: J. R. Osgood & Co., 1871), p. 200.

[2] Bartholow V. Crawford (ed.), *Henry David Thoreau: Representative Selections* (New York: American Book Co., 1934), p. 1.

[3] *The Writings of Henry David Thoreau* (20 vols.; Boston: Houghton Miffin Co., 1906), *Journal*, I, 413; entry is undated. Unless otherwise indicated, all references to Thoreau's published writings are to this edition.

[4] Matthiessen, *The American Renaissance* (New York: Oxford University Press, 1946), pp. 166-75; Krutch, *Thoreau*, pp. 95 ff. See also Sherman Paul, "Resolution at *Walden*," *Accent*, XII (1953), 101-13, and John C. Broderick, "Imagery in *Walden*," *University of Texas Studies in English*, XXXIII (1954), 80-89.

[5] They were not in this order in I, but when Thoreau moved them, he added paragraph 20 and ordered all the material essentially as it is in the final text: the questions of hurry and waste, with the excuse of work to be done, led to Thoreau's satire on men's desire for news and on the post office and newspapers. Following the suggestion that the preacher should cry out to men to slow down, he proposed that men should live more deliberately so that they might observe realities steadily and see things as they are.

[6] Originally there was a brief paragraph (canceled in the manuscript) preceding what is now paragraph 1 of "Baker Farm." The manuscript does not reveal for certain whether Thoreau canceled this paragraph before or after he moved the title "Baker Farm." The paragraph would have served the same function as the present first paragraph, but not so well; it began: "I also visited many a nameless little rill. . . ."

[7] He also effected a change when he made one chapter of "Former Inhabitants" and "Winter Visitors." At first they were separate. Perhaps they seemed too short to stand separately, but the main reason for bringing them together could well have been that they both dealt with people as compared with "Winter Animals" and "The Pond in Winter" which preceded and followed them until Thoreau reordered his chapters at the very last. . . .

[8] He also moved the paragraph on the moles from "Winter Animals" to "House Warming," 18, and the passage on "Bose" and the cats to "Brute Neighbors," 15, for "topical" reasons.

[9] The manuscript offers no evidence as to the exact time of this change; it was certainly after version V.

Sherman Paul (essay date 1958)

SOURCE: "*Walden*: Or, the Metamorphoses," in *The Shores of America: Thoreau's Inward Exploration*, University of Illinois Press, 1958, pp. 293-353.

[*In this excerpt, Paul examines* Walden's *numerous images of renewal and transformation.*]

My mind is bent to tell of bodies changed into new forms. Ye gods, for you yourselves have wrought the changes, breathe on these my undertakings, and bring down my song in unbroken strains from the world's very beginning even unto the present time.

—Ovid, *Metamorphoses*, I, 1-4

. . . there is but one great poetic idea possible to man—the progress of a soul through the various forms of existence.

—Margaret Fuller, "Goethe," *The Dial*, 1841

Some men's lives are but an aspiration, a yearning toward a higher state, and they are wholly misapprehended, until they are referred to, or traced through, all their metamorphoses.

—Thoreau, *Journal*, 1851

I

What Thoreau finally published on August 9, 1854, some seven years after his experiment at the Pond, was a fable of the renewal of life. The intervening years had given him much to say; he wanted, among other things, to provide a guide for students and a manual for self-reform, to record his actual experience in the woods and to defend his vocation, and to write a modern epic of farming. But most of all he wanted to set to rights again all his relations with men, society, and nature, to create again out of the chaos of his life a cosmos, to bring in again the eternal spring of the Golden Age. Written in the years of his decay, in the realization that "spring will not last forever," **Walden** was Thoreau's attempt to "drain the cup of inspiration to its last dregs."[1] Whatever its public intention, its personal intention was therapeutic: if it was his attempt to say his say once and for all, to give the world, as he said when he contemplated the unspoken wisdom of Bill Wheeler's life, "the benefit of his long trial," it was also his attempt, in Schiller's phrase, to "keep true to the dream of thy youth."[2] By enacting his aspiration in words, he was trying to sustain himself against loss. "What can be expressed in words," he told Blake, "can be expressed in life."[3] He was still haunted by the stirring injunctions of Emerson's *Nature:* idea alters circumstance, and by conforming one's life to the idea in one's mind, one builds his own world. That, indeed, was the dream of his youth, and as he looked back over the years of trial the benefit he felt he had to give the world was not the present fact of his inability to express it in life, but rather the glorious fact that he once had, and that he might again by resolution, discipline, and heroic hope. "Did you ever hear of a man," he asked Blake, "who had striven all his life faithfully and singly toward an object and in no measure obtained it? If a man constantly aspires, is he not elevated?"[4] *Walden* was a fable for renewal, a book of metamorphoses, a record of earning one's life, simply because what Thoreau was actually expressing in words he was expressing in his life. In fact, *Walden* was not so much an account of a past ecstasy—though of course it was that—as it was an account, actualized in terms of his former life in the woods, of his aspirations, of his desire for self-transcendence and self-union.

The book that finally appeared was obviously not the book that had been announced for publication earlier.[5] For as a work of recollected experience (and not recollected in tranquillity) it had a second growth, germinating slowly in the journals of the years following his experiment. New material, of course, had been added, but something more important had happened: the original Walden experience had become a symbol, an experiment, an action, that he could use to bind together the many things he had to say. The value of keeping a journal, its function for the writer, was that it helped him perform this symbolizing process—as the critic who sorts the entries in Thoreau's fashion discovers. "Each thought that is welcomed and recorded," Thoreau said, "is a nest egg, by the side of which more will be laid. Thoughts accidentally thrown together become a frame in which more may be developed and exhibited. . . . Having by chance recorded a few disconnected thoughts and then brought them into juxtaposition, they suggest a whole new field in which it was possible to labor and to think." In this way, he found, "my own writings may inspire me and at last I may make wholes of parts."[6] We have already seen the new fields that the journals of the years following Walden opened to him; they suggest that the original *Walden* might only have been another more elaborate excursion, faithful, as all his writing was, to his own experience and to his belief that the themes of literature are always

close by, but not that greatest literature which records "the world of thought and of the soul"—the "permanent" literature that all transcendentalists hoped to write.[7] At most, it would have been another *Week,* which belongs in the "permanent" class, but which is too much a static ecstasy, a trip to heaven without the tickets to limbo, purgatory, and hell, a book that speaks almost directly from the soul and that does not carry the soul through its various forms of existence. Indeed, it was out of his knowledge of these forms of existence that *Walden* took its final form.

Though Thoreau was always "sincere"—his test of a writer—he did mislead many readers by adhering to another rule for writing: that the hero hide his struggles.[8] He criticized reformers for not opening the prospects of hope, and he said that he did "not propose to write an ode to dejection. . . ."[9] But this did not mean, as many still infer, that he could not have written such an ode, that he did not have the materials for one in his life. We are inclined today to make much of the metaphysical principle of evil, even to use it as a critical measure of writing—to say that an Emerson or Thoreau did not know evil, as if this evil came in a shape other than lapse, inadequacy, or vastation, to say nothing of what Emerson called the Whiggish facts; as if anyone, especially men of such acute sensibility, could avoid it, could mount their hope on any less substantial foundation. How could we read them at all, if we thought that they did not speak to our condition, and out of the inevitable human condition? Now if he had wanted only to report his ecstasy, Thoreau might have given, as he proposed many times, an account of one day well spent in nature. But he was more concerned with telling how ecstasy was earned, how life was got, how, in the *absence* of these necessities, one deliberately remade his life. The loss behind *Walden* could only be inferred in this change from having to getting, in the pitch of resolution, in "Higher Laws," in his attribution of desperation to his neighbors (he remarked at the end of "Spring" that "through our own recovered innocence we discern the innocence of our neighbors"),[10] and, most of all, in the structure of the year.

It was, of course, a book of hope, of seasoned hope, and for his purposes the year provided a better structural pattern because it was larger and included, in a way impossible to the day, the actual details of the seasons of man, all sorts of details of growth and development and striving, the metamorphoses which now seemed to him the most important fact of life, the new basis of hope. He could have all the symbolic equivalents of the day—and, indeed, he made as much of the morning as he had in the *Week,* the significant difference now being his insistence on wakefulness. At the same time he could be true to his new knowledge of trial and discipline and seasonal weather by using symbols of gradual transformation: ice-thaw-flux; seed-flower-fruit; grub-chrysalis-butterfly; symbols, too, that in every case carried the change from lower to higher forms, from fixity to fluidity, from innocence to ripeness, from larval sensuality to aerial purity. He could spend a day in rapt contemplation as Whitman did in "Song of Myself"—"Sounds" was his record of such a day—but, what was more important, he could actually participate in the processes of building and renewing his world. Planting his seeds and harvesting his crop, clearing his land and building his hut—these were the solid activities of renewal, a history in brief of the course of agriculture from "a state of nature to the highest state of cultivation," and a literal foundation on which a number of spiritual truths could be raised.[11] A day was sufficient, of course, as a symbol of the experience of possessing the world, but now that he had to make a new world, a day was not long enough. *Walden* was written in the awareness that eternity is purchased in time, that, as Emerson said, "the years teach much which the days never know."[12]

When Thoreau, "for convenience," put the experience of two years into one, when he saw that his experience was "a fable" with a moral and that such a fable would make wholes of parts, the *Walden* we now have was finally under way.[13] Making wholes of parts had always been the most difficult thing for the transcendental writer who obeyed his genius rather than his talent, and Thoreau saw his own problem magnified in 1852—the year in which he seemed most preoccupied with the problems of composition—when he heard his friend Channing deliver "the most original lecture I ever heard," a lecture, however, that desperately needed some controlling idea. "How much more glorious if talent were added to genius," he remarked of the lecture, "if there [were] a just arrangement and development of thought, and each step were not a leap, but he ran a space to take a yet higher leap!"[14] Only the day before he had pondered on the need for "the true cement" for his thoughts and had concluded that the best solution was a fable with a moral. "The truth so told," he explained, "has the best advantages of the most abstract statement, for it is not the less universally applicable."[15] He was thinking, as he had during the composition of the *Week,* of the much-needed "myth," of that action which would give his thought concreteness as well as universality and at the same time make the thoughts of different periods in his life cohere. He had succeeded relatively well in finding one for the *Week,* and he was to do even better in *Walden,* for the myth he used not only served as the frame and foundation of truth, but put his thoughts in those natural relations in which he had found them.[16] One compensation of his years of decay was that he was forced to rely more on his talent, and his talent, as Channing justly recognized, was architectural. "The impression of the *Week* and *Walden* is single, as of a living product, a perfectly jointed build-

ing," Channing wrote; "yet no more composite productions could be cited." Both books, and later writing like "Wild Apples" and "Autumnal Tints," possessed "this unity of treatment," were products of his "constructing, combining talent."[17] For unlike most of the earlier work and the excursions, where the unity was provided by the experience itself, the later and major writing had an imaginative unity; they were the only works in which Thoreau took the liberty to alter the experience to suit his convenience, the only works in which symbol was below as well as above the texture, the very structure itself.

As a lecturer and a writer, Thoreau's experience had been similar to Channing's: he had never found an audience willing to give the needed close attention or to follow him on his own ground. He had only scorn in the *Week* and *Walden* for easy books, and in his exasperation he said that his generation hated "any direct revelation, any original thought," as "it hates virtue."[18] Prophets or transcendentalists were not wanted by the lyceums. He found, however, that his facts, if not his allegory, were often welcome, and he learned by the time he was writing *Walden* that the facts that flowered in the field would flower in books. But although he recognized the importance of the fable and admitted the need for a more orderly presentation, he did not intend to meet his audience by descending to partial truths—things "said with references to certain conventions or existing institutions, not absolutely." Instead, he said that he would speak with still "deeper references" and that to understand his words the reader himself would have to be "translated."[19]

The problem here, of course, was at the very heart of the transcendentalist's vocation as writer: how to get the reader to take the spiritual view. In the concluding pages of *Walden* Thoreau remarked that "in this part of the world it is considered a ground for complaint if a man's writings admit of more than one interpretation."[20] At the very beginning he had teased the curiosity of his neighbors (and has since teased many scholars) by telling them in allegory and whimsey something of how he had spent his life. But he teased with a purpose: he was instructing them in how to read his book, in how to cure their "brain-rot"; for the truth he wanted to express, "his facts," would be "falsehoods to the common sense." "I would so state facts," he said, "that they shall be significant, shall be myths or mythologic."[21] This is what he meant in *Walden* when he wrote that "I fear chiefly lest my expression may not be *extra-vagant* enough. . . ."[22] Extravagance, or exaggeration as he sometimes called it, was his way to truth. "It is only by emphasis and exaggeration," he wrote in his criticism of Gilpin, "that real effects are described"—and the kind of exaggeration he was considering here he employed in his description of the pond in "Where I Lived, and What I Lived For."[23] In a letter to Blake he warned, "I trust that you realize what an exaggerator I am,—that I lay myself out to exaggerate whenever I have an opportunity,—pile Pelion upon Ossa, to reach heaven so."[24] His most difficult problem in *Walden* was to get the reader above the level of common sense, that is, to see from the inside rather than the outside, to get beyond his frame of reference. To do this, he did indeed lay himself out, not only by creating a structural perspective by incongruity in the opposition of civilization and nature, but by his use of history, anthropology, and reading, by paradox, humor, irony, ridicule, and scorn, by philological puns, by parables, by dramatization, by utopian prospects, by emphatic polarities, by every variety of symbolic statement.

All this was merely to say that fact alone was not truth but the means to truth, and that, like his contemporaries Emerson, Hawthorne, Melville, and Whitman, he wanted the "volatile truth" that betrayed "the inadequacy of the residual statement."[25] He would have considered *Walden* a failure if it served only to communicate an eccentric's refusal to go along with society, as it did to most reviewers in his day, or if his "faith and piety," the fragrance of his words, were reduced to pap, as in our day, for tired businessmen long since beyond the point of no return. He told his readers not to look into the ashes for the sublimates, he reminded them that the verses of Kabir had four levels of meaning, and, like Whitman, who compared the untranslatable natural expression of his barbaric yawp to that of the hawk, Thoreau said that it was a "ridiculous demand . . . that you shall speak so that they can understand you," that "neither men nor toadstools grow so."[26] His protestation was defensible because, symbolist though he was, his symbols were not private: mystery, not mystification, was his goal. He wanted his residual statement to be natural, to translate itself and the reader as easily as any natural fact. Even his "deeper references" were natural—the reality in nature—and he was justified in believing that his residual statement, the actual record, would translate itself because nature was a universal language whose correspondences were guaranteed by the very structure of the universe. If his fable, as he claimed, was not obscure ("my shallow meaning is but too clear"),[27] its deeper meanings were; and not because he did not do everything he could, but because, as all symbolist writers discover, his readers had to be taught to read. To read *Walden* the reader had to learn how to read nature, as Thoreau pointed out in the chapters on "Reading" and "Sounds." He had little sympathy for mass culture: "Why level downward to our dullest perceptions always," he wrote, "and praise that as common sense?" He intended to speak "like a man in a waking moment, to men in their waking moments"[28]—though he did his best to use *Walden* to awaken his readers. And had he taught them to read he would have taught them as well all that he was attempting to do in *Walden*—and what Emerson had

tried to do in *Nature* and Whitman would try to do in "Song of Myself"—to stand in an original relation to the universe and to read its meanings for themselves: "How to live. How to get the most life. . . . [How to] go in search of the springs of life. . . ."[29]

II

In *Walden* Thoreau followed his advice to Channing: he ran a space in order to take the higher leap. He began with surface before he spoke of depth, with the transient rather than the permanent, with complexity before simplicity, disease before health, tradition and routine before the free, uncommitted life—with society and commodity before self and spirit. He wrote Blake that "to set about living a true life is to journey to a distant country, gradually to find ourselves surrounded by new scenes and men"; but before he told of the new country he had discovered, he described the old.[30] Like Emerson in *Nature* he began with the prudential, rising through the progressive uses of nature to spirit. Indeed, most of Emerson's treatise was embodied in *Walden:* "Commodity" in "Economy"; "Nature" and "Beauty" in "Sounds" and "Solitude"; "Language" in "Brute Neighbors"; "Discipline" in "Reading," "The Beanfield," and "Higher Laws"; "Idealism," "Spirit," and "Prospects" in "The Pond in Winter," "Spring," and "Conclusion." For that matter, Emerson's "Experience," which accounted for the philosophy of *Nature* in psychological terms, as a dialectic of spirit, was also embodied: Illusion, Temperament, Succession, Surface, Surprise, Reality, Subjectiveness—all the "lords of life" were there, as well as a similar progression from spiritual emptiness and that suspicion of "our instruments" which Emerson attributed to the fall of man, to that miraculous moment, born of engaging in actual everyday life, when life again revealed "its inscrutable possibilities."[31]

Thoreau began *Walden* on the familiar ground of "Economy," at the actual point at which he found his neighbors and himself. Here he rehearsed his own history, both past and present, of getting a living. He began his book with a genuine, practical, Yankee problem; but his concern with economy, though Yankee in its means, was spiritual in its ends. The problem, he told Blake, "is not merely to get life for our bodies, but by this or a similar discipline to get life for our souls; by cultivating the lowland farm on right principles, that is, with this view, to turn it into an upland farm."[32] Indeed, the sting in his whole treatment of economy was the determination not to get a living in the accepted but rather in the spiritual sense, with its assumption that there were necessities of the soul that were not being satisfied by the instituted ways of life, that "the country is not yet adapted to *human* culture, and we are still forced to cut our *spiritual* bread far thinner than our forefathers did their wheaten."[33] He had found, he wrote Greeley, that to have time for writing he did not need to earn his bread by the sweat of his brow, that six weeks of manual labor would support him in his simple life for a year.[34] He had also found that one need not accept the servitudes of economy any more than the servitudes of politics, that one could be free, if daring and hardy enough, to use society rather than be used by it.[35] And he had found— and this was perhaps an even more direct blow—that work itself, even the discipline of cultivating his beans, was not a duty, the penalty of man's fall, as the Puritans supposed, but a form of joy, a way to personal growth. "There is no play in them," he said of the desperate, "for this comes after work."[36]

Thoreau was assailed by reviewers in his day not only for his withdrawal from society and for making work a pastime but for his doctrine of simplicity, which seemed to them a renunciation of all the goods of a civilization whose progress was measured by the increasing flow of things. In our time, however, we have almost made the virtue of simplicity *the* moral of *Walden,* accepting it, at least when goods are scarce, in the narrowest sense Thoreau had in mind when he wrote: "The unlimited anxiety, strain, and care of some persons is one very incurable form of disease; simple arithmetic might have corrected it. . . ."[37] The economic anxiety for which he prescribed simplicity, however, was merely the most obvious symptom of still deeper anxieties, of the fact that life had lost its savor and purpose, had become fixed and external; and he himself had simplified his life, not in the spirit of denial but because he valued human life and its richer possibilities. "One's life, the enterprise he is here upon," he said, "should certainly be a grand fact to consider, not a mean or insignificant one. A man should not live without a purpose, and that purpose must surely be a grand one. But is this fact of 'our life' commonly a puff of air, a flash in the pan, a smoke, a nothing?"[38] It is true, of course, that much of "Economy" told how he had gone without, and that he made the most of the bravery of his renunciations; but what was really central was that he had experimented to find out just how important the commodities of life were. Simplifying was not so much doing without as seeing what was essential, that is, whether or not things served the grand ends of human life, if possessions helped one possess life; and that was why, in order to make his point, his strategy was so reductive. He had learned from the economy of nature that "the grand necessary of life for the brute creation is food; next, perhaps, shelter, *i.e.* a suitable climate; thirdly, perhaps, security from foes."[39] These were the essentials on the commodity level of life, necessary to any higher life, and he did not deny them. But in the business metaphors that ruled the chapter he wanted to see how far one needed to be *mortgaged* to them. His conclusion (actually the belief he used "Economy" to prove) was that they were not so important as society—materialistic society—assumed, that

they were, as they seemed on the level of brute creation, the means, not the ends of life. Like Emerson in "Commodity" he indicated the mediate uses of nature: " . . . this mercenary benefit," Emerson said, "is one which has respect to a farther good. A man is fed, not that he may be fed, but that he may work"—or, as Thoreau put it when he returned to the subject in "Conclusion," "Were preserved meats invented to preserve meat merely?"[40] Nature, in all her bounty, could be cruel, if man made commodities, the goods of life, his final good: she could put a house and barn on one's back, and make anxiety out of one's necessities.

Thoreau did not consider simplicity a palliative, as the way to make the best of an abhorrent condition. Indeed, his own example showed that he had adopted it to be rid of the condition, to seek his freedom from society, to clear away inessentials, the "trifles," to use Emerson's word, that frittered away one's life. "To the rarest genius it is most expensive," he wrote in the *Week,* "to succumb and conform to the ways of the world."[41] Simplicity was but the first requirement of perceiving the "grand fact," of preserving the "vital heat" without being "cooked *à la mode*";[42] to simplify was to make significant, to discover principles, and in his own economy it served this end. He had always lived a simple life, partly because he was not an economic man, but also because he had accepted Emerson's view that "the poet's habit of living should be set on a key so low that common influences should delight him," and because, in his role of social critic, he found that one could only speak truly (absolutely) from the vantage of "voluntary poverty."[43] In terms of his own immediate desire for renewal, however, simplification (and "Economy") became a representative anecdote of *Walden,* for he went to the Pond to recover the reality he had lost, to find it again by reducing the problem of perception to its simplest terms— man and nature. Simplification, in this sense, was his ascetic, the severe discipline by which he hoped to concentrate his forces and purify the channels of perception; and because of this he often substituted "poverty" for "simplicity," thereby hallowing the process with religious associations of renunciation and higher dedication. In 1857, bringing to the surface the submerged imagery of *Walden,* he wrote,

> By poverty, *i.e.* simplicity of life and fewness of incidents, I am solidified and crystallized, as a vapor or liquid by cold. It is a singular concentration of strength and energy and flavor. Chastity is perceptual acquaintance with the All. My diffuse and vaporous life becomes as the frost leaves and spiculae radiant as gems on the weeds and stubble in a winter morning. You think that I am impoverishing myself by withdrawing from men, but in my solitude I have woven for myself a silken web or *chrysalis,* and nymph-like, shall ere long burst forth a more perfect creature, fitted for a higher society. By simplicity, commonly

called poverty, my life is concentrated and so becomes organized, . . . which before was inorganic and lumpish.[44]

Society as Thoreau found it, however, was the cause of his diffuse and vaporous life—that "false society of men," in the lines he quoted from Chapman, that "for earthly greatness / All heavenly comforts rarefies to air."[45] Society and its economy were but the symbol of his own external or empirical self. Society was not only the grubbing of a John Field but the grublike condition, as he implied in "Higher Laws," when he compared the gross-feeding man to the larva, and said that "there are whole nations in that condition . . . whose vast abdomens betray them."[46] The kind of simplicity he had in mind, accordingly, could hardly be practiced *in* society, for, as the above passage indicated, simplicity was a simplification *from* society, a withdrawal from its larval state to nature, where the transformation he sought could take place. And that transformation would be a purification because Thoreau heaped on society all the associations of his lapse: the slimy, bestial, torpid, reptilian life; coarseness, sloth, and sensuality; rot and stench. Nature, therefore, became the crucial term, the place of spiritual alchemy, and, as the dramatic action of *Walden* suggested, the symbol of his rejection of society. But it was also only the middle term in the progression from a lower to a higher society: nature was not Thoreau's final goal, but rather the place of renewal, and out of it, as his own utopian descriptions of ideal human relations and communities revealed, he hoped would come a higher, a spiritually or inwardly formed—that is, an organic—society.[47] He did not propose nature as a permanent mode of life, any more than Emerson did in his treatise; he proposed it rather as a re-creative process of spiritualization, whereby one sharpened his sight and discovered again, in an organic world so unlike society, the possibilities and the principles of a new life. One went to nature to lose society, to die out of the old world, to find oneself and the foundations of a new world.

He went to the woods, therefore, to try this experiment, with no intention of abandoning society or of going primitive. Instead, by beginning from scratch, he would relive all human life and history and test the achievement of civilization by what he found, hoping, of course, to demonstrate that choice was still possible and to reorient society by showing what had been lost on the way.[48] What he had done for himself he wanted above all to do for society: to join the primitive virtues—whether of the American Indian or the Homeric Greek—to the genuine virtues of civilization; to join country and city, nature and society, sense and thought; to make the organic communion and harmony and joy of the one the foundation of the other. "It is surprising," he remarked, as if discovering it anew, "how much room there is in nature. . . . I enjoy the retirement and

solitude of an early settler." But he went on to say: "and yet there may be a lyceum in the evening, and there is a book-shop and library in the village, and five times a day I can be whirled to Boston within an hour."[49] It is too easy to forget in Thoreau's description of the ecstasy of the wild that he would have missed the advantages of civilization, that his problem of doing without society would have been simple if his problem had not been doing with it. After all, he read Homer and wrote a book in the woods, and, except for his retired situation, he lived a remarkably civilized and social life. Indeed, this had been part of his satisfaction: he had gone to nature because, among other reasons, it permitted an uncluttered and simple life, giving him time to be truly civilized.[50] And one of the paradoxes he exploited in making this point was that society did not civilize men, but barbarized them; reduced them, in fact, to a level of want below that of the savage. It was the simple self-sufficiency and adjustment to environment of the Indians (and of the woodchopper, too) that appealed to him, not their elementary demands on life, and had he gone to Typee he would have been as impatient to leave as Melville had been. Primitivism, he learned with some disenchantment on his trips to the forests of Maine, was at best only tonic. And in his *Journal* he wrote that "the savage lives simply through ignorance and idleness or laziness, but the philosopher lives simply through wisdom. In the case of the savage, the accompaniment of simplicity is idleness with its attendant vices, but in the case of the philosopher, it is the highest employment and development. The fact for the savage, and for the mass of mankind, is that it is better to plant, weave, and build than do nothing or worse; but the fact for the philosopher, or a nation loving wisdom, is that it is most important to cultivate the highest faculties and spend as little time as possible in planting, weaving, building, etc." In developing this thought, he came to the conclusion that his own stance as philosopher in *Walden* should have made clear: "There are two kinds of simplicity,—one that is akin to foolishness, the other to wisdom. The philosopher's style of living is only outwardly simple, but inwardly complex. The savage's style is both outwardly and inwardly simple." What he disapproved of was "their limited view, not in respect to *style,* but to the *object* of living," pointing out that the "view" was everything, that "a man who has equally limited views with respect to the end of living will not be helped by the most complex and refined style. . . ."[51] It was the primitive style, therefore, that attracted him, not the "barren simplicity of the savage," and this is what he meant when he said that "the civilized man is a more experienced and wiser savage."[52]

He simplified not to economize time but to spend it, to shed the burdens of planting, weaving, and building; and after the novelty of his account of his life wore off and the sense of freedom it created faded away, his audience still measured him by the limited view, and considered him, as his neighbors always had, a spendthrift. He was aware of this, of course, for it was the atmosphere in which he lived his life.[53] That was reason enough for trying to meet his audience with "Economy," rather than with a truer title such as "The Art of Life"—and that was why he employed humor rather than contempt, which would have been so easy for him. "Economy" had a serious, weighty, utilitarian significance for his audience; they may have wondered what the village saunterer could say on so grave a subject; but it was also a word of many meanings which Thoreau could exploit to reverse the judgment of his neighbors on his own perverse way of living. Their interest had been caught, of course, by the curiosity they had for his unusual life in the woods, but he kept it by speaking of what he had done in the current coin: in dollars, cents, and half cents. He calculated his life for them, reducing it to a pittance; but the irony, of course, was that on so little he had got so much *life* that he did not carry a house on his back (though in the case of the Hollowell farm he was tempted), or possess a corner of the world, but had all the landscape for his own, time (which Franklin said was money) to read, to sit idle all day, to walk, boat, fish, to saunter at his ease and enjoy those bounties of nature that society had not yet, nor ever would, package and sell. "Give me the poverty," he exclaimed triumphantly when cursing Flint, "that enjoys true wealth."[54] He had a self, too, that he could hug, one that was not at the beck and call of others, twisted and thwarted by innumerable demands and responsibilities which were customary but not essential. Though he figured everything closely and knew the value of means, he was hardly a good bourgeois, neither a Robinson Crusoe nor a Benjamin Franklin. He was, of course, a plebeian himself, who, schooled in economies, kept strict accounts and paid his debts, and where he could tried to get the best price for his wares, but he abjured getting and spending. His economy was spiritual: to get and spend one's life. Thus, though *Walden* was as autobiographical as Franklin's story of his youth and middle years and in its way a model for success (Thoreau told Blake, however, that he had "no designs on men at all"),[55] it undermined the Franklinian virtues and the goal of comfort they served. Bookkeeping left off with the means of life; there was no schedule for spending a day—how different Thoreau's day in "Sounds," where even the train provided a contrast to his own timekeeping—and no instrumental method of earning virtue. There were none of Franklin's social virtues and only scorn for his do-goodism. And the way to wealth, Thoreau might have said (for behind his remarks he was poking fun at the patron saint of State Street and Main Street), was not the way to health. When he wrote Blake, who was trying to use *Walden* for his guide, he gave the spirit of his economy: "It is surprising how contented one can be with nothing

definite,—only a sense of existence. . . . O how I laugh when I think of my vague, indefinite riches. No run on my bank can drain it, for my wealth is not possession but enjoyment."[56]

Indeed, the way to wealth was the way to lives of quiet desperation. That was what he wanted to tell his neighbors, and that their mean and sneaking lives were not of the nature of things—that, as he had discovered in his own case, meanness robbed one of his birthright. Had he not learned from his own experience that economy was only the first chapter of life (as it was of his book)? And had he not learned that the cure, like the anxiety if not the disease, was individual? That self-reliance was the only remedy? He spoke in the first person, then, not only because he felt that it was more honest, but in order to emphasize the individual, to show that "life" is an individual affair with unlimited possibilities of choice, and that however much one lived in society, the balance, the experience, was finally reckoned in the soul, Having already witnessed the fate of Fruitlands and Brook Farm, he entered on his own experiment alone, knowing, as he said in his review of Etzler's book, that "we must first succeed alone, that we may enjoy our success together."[57] In his equation for life, the self, as much as nature, was a permanent factor; and, like Whitman, he wanted to proclaim the "simple separate person." But although he used the "I," like Whitman, he spoke representatively. "If I seem to boast more than is becoming," he said in *Walden,* "my excuse is that I brag for humanity rather than for myself. . . ."[58] He omitted to say, however, that "I can well afford the tone of braggart there is so much truth in what I say."[59]

Before he bragged, however, he analyzed the "outward condition or circumstances"[60] of men, building up the contrast with his own life, with his inner condition, his freedom and joy. He worked from the outside and surface of life to its center: the book turned inward, going deeper and deeper, exploring the folds of nature and being. And what was true for the entire book was true of the chapter on "Economy," producing a similar perspective by incongruity. From this perspective (it was the result of the double universe of Transcendentalism, with its prudential and spiritual levels, levels which made possible a comic treatment),[61] men seemed everywhere to be "doing penance," working, as the Protestant ethic instructed them, in order to expiate their guilt. "There are some," Thoreau said in the list of those to whom he directed his book, "who complain most energetically and inconsolably of any, because they are, as they say, doing their duty."[62] But even here, he suggested, they had misread the "old book" [the Bible], had sold their souls for a mess of pottage, forgetting the injunction against "laying up treasures which moth and rust will corrupt. . . ."[63] From this insinuated religious perspective it was a "misfortune . . . to have inherited farms, houses, barns, cattle, and farming tools," for these were "inherited encumbrances," a convenient example of enslavement to the past, to tradition—obstacles which prevented a man from following his own calling, binding him with "the factitious cares and superfluously coarse labors of life," stealing his leisure (he would have said that an empty bag can stand straight), robbing him of his own "bloom" and disabling him for the "finer fruits" of life. The end product, of course, was not a man but a "machine," a man who would never grow, as Thoreau had, "like corn in the night. . . ."[64]

Having himself, he admitted, led a mean and sneaking life, he gave a bill of particulars that is still convincing and downright shameful:

> I have no doubt that some of you who read this book are unable to pay for all the dinners you have actually eaten, or for the coats and shoes which are fast wearing out or are already worn out, and have come to this page to spend borrowed or stolen time, robbing your creditors of an hour. It is evident what mean and sneaking lives many of you live, for my sight has been whetted by experience; always on the limits, trying to get into business and trying to get out of debt, a very ancient slough, called by the Latins *aes alienum,* another's brass, for some of their coins were made of brass; still living, and dying, and buried by this other's brass; always promising to pay, promising to pay, tomorrow, and dying to-day, insolvent; seeking to curry favor, to get custom, by how many modes, only not state-prison offences; lying, flattering, voting, contracting yourself into a nutshell of civility, or dilating into an atmosphere of thin and vaporous generosity, that you may persuade your neighbor to let you make his shoes, or his hat, or his coat, or his carriage, or import his groceries for him; making yourself sick, that you may lay up something against a sick day, something to be tucked away in an old chest, or in a stocking behind the plastering, or, more safely, in a brick bank; no matter where, no matter how much or how little.[65]

He compared this servitude to Negro slavery, finding this northern variety even worse, and the servitude of opinion that made it possible, that made a man the slave driver of himself, still worse. Society, of course, gave this servitude a form and rationale and made it appear to be necessary; and it was for this reason that Thoreau began the defense of his own life by preaching self-emancipation, by asking men, if only in the pages of his book, to see how differently things might be from the vantage of self-reliance. For self-reliance, as Emerson had shown in his *Essays* (*First Series*), was the first condition of entering on the new life: with man at the center, instead of at the circumference, perspectives altered radically; all things served him, old fetters snapped, blindness fell away, and he

discovered a new world where he was able to form his relations anew. Nothing less than this abrupt shift seemed the sufficient cure, nothing less would take one out of the machine of society into the organic world, or transform the inorganic and lumpish into a cosmos.

Walden dramatized this shift: unlike the *Week,* it put society fully on record and forced Thoreau to recover all the positions of his life, to enact the doctrine of self-reliance by withdrawing from his old relations (appropriately on Independence Day) and forming the new. Inevitably this self-reliance, with its repudiation of society, brought—as it also had in the case of Emerson and Whitman—the charge of egotism. But one need only consider the conditions of desperation, of waste, hurry, and restlessness that Thoreau had relentlessly described, to see that self-reliance (and the pride in self that goes with it) might even be a virtue. Observing the American of Emerson's manhood and Thoreau's youth, de Tocqueville, for example, distinguished between the pride that "cannot endure subordination" and that led the individual to take up "with low desires without daring to embark on lofty enterprises, of which he scarcely dreams," and the pride born of genuine self-assurance. "Thus," he said, "far from thinking that humility ought to be preached to our contemporaries, I would have endeavors made to give them a more enlarged idea of themselves and of their kind. Humility is unwholesome to them; what they want most is, in my opinion, pride."[66] An enlarged idea of man and lofty enterprises—these were the essence of the pride that Thoreau also preached. "To devote your life to the discovery of the divinity in nature—or to the eating of oysters! Would they not," he wrote, "be attended with very different results!"[67]

Desperation and conformity were the keynote of his social analysis; joy and freedom the alternatives he proposed. He built his chapter on "Economy" on a series of juxtapositions, all of which were based on the difference between the outer and the inner life: social servitude *vs.* self-reliance; fashions in clothing, shelter, furniture, education, and reform *vs.* his own experiments in these matters; and the old life *vs.* his aspirations for the new. On one side there were circumstances, the past, tradition and routine—his "scurvy" self,[68] his social or empirical self—and on the other, hopes for the real self, for that inner expansion that would cast the old skin and prepare the conditions for creating a new organic world (a cosmos) in terms of his inner necessities. The change he desired was not so much a rejection of all that was represented by society as it was a transformation out of it, an organic change; for between the levels of prudence and spirit, society and nature, he recognized organic continuities. *Walden* may have seemed a rejection because of the radical withdrawal it dramatized, but its natural images suggested gradual transformation through growth, withdrawal being only the symbolic equivalent of the purification that was necessary when the old life had become fixed beyond growth. He did not deny those necessities represented by society; but he wanted them to be used to liberate rather than to enslave man. "The soil, it appears, is suited to the seed," he wrote, "for it has sent its radical downward, and it may now [once the necessities had been secured] send its shoot upward also with confidence. Why has man rooted himself thus firmly in the earth, but that he may rise in the same proportion into the heavens above?—for the nobler plants are valued for the fruit they bear at last in the air and light, far from the ground, and are not treated like the humbler esculents, which, though they may be biennials, are cultivated only till they have perfected their root, and often cut down at top for this purpose, so that most would not know them in their flowering season."[69] To the ends of flower and fruit, he preached economy and tried his experiment.

Originally he had used the passage beginning with "the mass of men lead lives of quiet desperation" to introduce and organize the opening pages; now he used it to summarize and for transition to fundamental questions about "the chief end of man" and "the true necessaries and means of life."[70] Such questions implied a choice, but he pointed out that the common mode of life was actually accepted without making any. The value of nature, however, which he now introduced for the first time as a symbol of change in the images of sun and morning, was that it renewed the opportunity for choice and offered the occasion of the eternal now, the present, living experience by which the past could always be tested. With Whitman, Thoreau believed that

> There was never any more inception than
>   there is now
> Nor any more youth or age than there is
>   now,[71]

and one of the major articles of his faith in organicism, accordingly, was that everything is possible, that the past is a kind of death, forms out of which life had passed.

He was not so unmindful of history as one might assume from his views of the past. For the issue was not, as has often been supposed, a repudiation of all history, but rather a refusal to serve the authority of the past. Thoreau appropriated the wisdom of the past, even corroborated his own experience by that of history, and tried his experiment with book in hand—in "Reading" he extolled the spiritual uses of the past. He rejected only the prudential failures of history, what Parker had called the "transient," those institutional compromises and expediencies that were used by the passing generation to limit the enterprises of the new,

that, as he himself had known, were forced on the young by the position and power of the old, and which had stood in the way of his calling. In fact, Thoreau's argument for the open future was expressed in the language of the psychology of experience and was very much like that used later by Randolph Bourne in his battle with the elders: that age is hardening, a loss of "life," a living on past experiences (as Thoreau himself knew only too well); that youth, facing the world anew, in its fresh experience, is more sensitive to the needs of present "life"; that youth, therefore, is better qualified to give advice, or rather that the advice of the elders is not fitting; and that "life" is always novel, an untried experiment which the elders try to contain in an old morality, when what is needed is a morality formed by actual choice, a morality of experience. The common notion that "the whole ground of human life"[72] has been gone over—here was the cynicism of age and the seduction of history, a notion born of weariness and faithlessness that did not speak, as Thoreau believed nature did, to the inexhaustible possibilities of joy.

He was reacting, therefore, not so much against history as against the decay and lapse of which devotion to history was the outward sign. History itself was a record of lapse, at least if one read it as Emerson taught his generation to, psychologically, as the exponent of states of mind. This was also the way in which he suggested that nature be read; but where history was linear and could be read in terms of the stages of man, from youth to age, from unconscious, sensuous joy to self-consciousness, from the springtime of Greece (which Thoreau wanted to restore) to the autumn of New England, nature could be read cyclically, as a forever renewing spirit, as the force of life itself, the eternal harbinger of spring and youth. History was but the record of one impulse of nature; whenever one returned to the living foundations, history itself had a new birth. From this point of view, history was the crust of human experience; like society and the empirical self, it was the fixed form of past experience; beneath this surface, however, in nature and the real self, there was a living force, older than history but eternally young, always there to break through and to bestow an unformed future.

The possibility of choice, therefore, was as close as nature and the real self. Outer necessity could be replaced with inner freedom by self-reliance, by establishing, as "Song of Myself" also demonstrated, a primary relation with the cosmos. And as Whitman would show, only less emphatically, the means was simplification or the lessening of one's dependence on society, which for both was the outward or empirical self. "I will go to the bank by the wood and become undisguised and naked"—these are Whitman's words, but Thoreau in "Economy" was enacting a similar withdrawal and divestment. Judged by such primary relationships, the essential function of economy, of food, shelter, and clothing, was to preserve the "vital heat"—the heat of life and spirit; luxuries and comforts were "positive hindrances."[73] When he anatomized them in long sections of the chapter, they became the source of a considerable Veblenesque humor, except that for Thoreau life itself was being conspicuously consumed.

One must always take Thoreau's argument for minimums in the context of the point he is making: that we waste our lives securing more than we need, that we overdo fundamentals and reserve nothing for the true ends of life. One must remember, too, that Thoreau had a Spartan (or Puritan?) contempt for luxury, that he believed that "it does not cost much for . . . heroes to live; they do not want much furniture. . . ."[74] For, if taken literally, his Spartanism would diminish most of the beauty of life, would reduce all economy to physiological necessity on the material level and would leave beauty on the spiritual level. In his reductiveness it might even seem that he had forgotten that culture and civilization are themselves the result of a symbolizing process in which essentials acquire more than their minimum value—that they serve the ends of life by satisfying intangible wants and by expressing the personality. His critics had felt this even though they had never articulated it. But what they had failed to see in his treatment of clothing and shelter and furniture, indeed in the entire experiment at Walden Pond, was that he was not only testing civilization in terms of necessities but creating a life organically—by extension, a culture, a society, and a civilization—that he was divesting himself only to the end of clothing himself anew in garments better fitted to his inner needs. There was, in fact, no other reason for preaching self-reliance—his individualism and functionalism went together; and he wisely chose clothing and shelter for his examples because they were outward forms that intimately touched the individual and that the individual believed he could alter.

His remarks on clothing had their origin, perhaps, in the fact that he had gone to Harvard College in an unfashionable green coat and that his own rugged and still unfashionable garments, which he described with evident pride, were those of Irish laborers. His perceptions concerning their social use, however, were as sharp as Lear's, and his working-class dress as much the sign of his equalitarian sympathies as Whitman's. Clothing, he pointed out with reference to the organic fitness of the bark of a tree, did not fit the wearer like his skin, nor fit his character, nor did it even, in many cases, serve its true utility of keeping the vital heat. Instead, it disguised the self, "cloaked" it, as he wrote Blake, in the seeming of novelty, fashion, and opinion, adding a cover of respectability and pretension that denied human equality. Prompted by the occasion of getting a new coat, he told Blake that

"our garments are typical of our conformity to the ways of the world. . . ."[75] When he first canvassed this subject in a passage on the costume of Swiss singers, he said that fashionable dress was "*exo*strious, building without."[76] And in his humorous account of being fitted for a coat he wrote a parable on the difficulty of retaining one's individuality in society. All this was to be expected, fashion being open game to any critic; but the meaning of this clothes philosophy suddenly emerged in a series of images of discovery and retirement and internal growth, images of inward rather than outward change radiant with Thoreau's purpose of shedding the old by radical inner transformation: "Perhaps we should never procure a new suit . . . until we have so conducted, so enterprised or sailed in some way, that we feel like new men in the old. . . . Our moulting season, like that of the fowls, must be a crisis in our lives. The loon retires to solitary ponds to spend it. Thus also the snake casts its slough, and the caterpillar its wormy coat, by an internal industry and expansion. . . ."[77]

Houses, too, were *exo*strious (a pun on *indu*strious), a kind of outward garment, more costly, more encumbering, and more confining. These unwiedly clothes—he told the myth of Momus in the original version—took most men half their lives to purchase outright, destroyed their leisure to loaf and invite their souls, made property owners of them and tied them to institutions, and, in the end, only enclosed them in a narrow space. It was when Thoreau considered all this, especially the fact that houses kept one out of the open air, that he praised the convenient shelter of the Indians and said that the unencumbered life was a divine gift. For here again he conceived of life as a journey jeopardized by fixity: the primitive man, at least, was a "sojourner in nature," who had not yet undergone the civilizing process that made men "the tools of their tools," that turned the wayfaring man into a farmer, the tent into a house, and the house into the "tomb" of the next generation. "We now no longer camp as for a night," he said, "but have settled down on earth and forgotten heaven."[78] And even fine houses, as in the case of fashionable clothes, were generally an outward show rather than the expression or function of the indweller—houses whose foundations he distrusted because they had no basis in "beautiful housekeeping and beautiful living," houses which had not been, like those of the Puritans, built from the foundations up.[79] "Let our houses first be lined with beauty," he advised, using an image of organic functionalism, "where they come in contact with our lives, like the tenement of the shellfish, and not overlaid with it."[80]

This advice was addressed specifically to the problem of architectural ornament, and, after a brief section on building his own house, Thoreau returned to it with considerable vehemence because he had misunderstood

Horatio Greenough's theory of functionalism. He had learned of Greenough's ideas from a letter that Greenough had sent to Emerson, and though his own belief—"It would be worth the while to build still more deliberately than I did, considering, for instance, what foundation a door, a window, a cellar, a garret, have in the nature of man, and perchance never raising any superstructure until we found a better reason for it than our temporal necessities even"[81]—was everything Greenough desired, it seems that Thoreau had to call Greenough's theory "dilettantism" because Emerson approved of it. "Greenough's idea," he said, "was to make architectural ornaments have a core of truth, a necessity, and hence a beauty."[82] He objected because he thought that Greenough had begun "at the cornice, not at the foundation," that he had only "put a core of truth within the ornaments," instead of beginning with the "indweller" and the human problem of building truly "within and without."[83] He was probably misled because architecture was a fine art ("They can do without *architecture* who have no olives nor wines in the cellar")[84] whose styles were as offensive to him as the styles of literature, offensive because they were lacking in sincerity. "What of architectural beauty I now see," he said, "I know has gradually grown from within outward, out of the necessities and character of the indweller, who is the only builder,—out of some unconscious truthfulness, and nobleness, without even a thought for the appearance ["mere ornament" in the original]; and whatever additional beauty of this kind is destined to be produced will be preceded by a like unconscious beauty of life."[85] The house was the man as the style was the man: so he built his hut and his book. "Grow your own house, I say," he wrote in the *Journal*. "Build it after an Orphean fashion. When R.W.E. and Greenough have got a few blocks finished and advertized, I will look at them. When they have got my ornaments ready I will wear them."[86]

He acknowledged that "I built too heedlessly to build well,"[87] but when he described his ideal house in "House-Warming" he had grown a house, at least in his imagination, that expressed the man. His description, like that of the house in "The Landlord," was set in the context of friendship and society; he was more concerned with using the house to symbolize human qualities than with architecture proper; and yet nowhere else did he show what he meant when he demanded that a door, a window, a cellar, etc. have their foundation in the nature of man.

I sometimes dream of a larger and more populous house, standing in a golden age ["not a gilded one"], of enduring materials, and without gingerbreadwork, which shall still consist of only one room, a vast, rude, substantial, primitive hall, without ceiling or plastering, with bare rafters and purlins supporting a sort of lower heaven over one's head . . . where the king and queen posts stand out to receive your homage . . . a cavernous house, wherein you must reach up a torch upon a pole to see the roof . . . a house which you have got into when you have opened the outside door, and the ceremony is over . . . containing all the essentials of a house, and nothing for house-keeping, where you can see all the treasures of the house at one view, and everything hangs upon its peg that a man should use; at once kitchen, pantry, parlor, chamber, store-house, and garret; where you can see so necessary a thing as a barrel or a ladder, so convenient a thing as a cupboard, and hear the pot boil ["instead of a tinkling piano"] and pay your respects to the fire that cooks your dinner and the oven that bakes your bread ["bread, I say, not biscuit"], and the necessary furniture and utensils are the chief ornaments. . . .[88]

Here indeed the house was all inside and architecture had become the indweller. "This frame, so slightly clad," he said when he had his hut under way, "was a sort of crystallization around me, and reacted on the builder."[89]

If clothing and shelter were a kind of skin, furniture was "our *exuviae*"[90]—the cast skins of others and of ourselves. Furniture, of course, was a fine symbol of the burden of tradition, and Thoreau exploited nationalist sentiment to make his point—and imagery, too, that recalled a line of thought beginning with Crèvecoeur: "I look upon England to-day," Thoreau wrote, "as an old gentleman who is travelling with a great deal of baggage, trumpery which has accumulated from long housekeeping. . . . When I have met an immigrant tottering under a bundle . . . I have pitied him, not because that was his all, but because he had all *that* he could carry." Furniture was baggage and a trap, however, because Thoreau was working from the assumption of freedom to move and change—"My gay butterfly," he said, "is entangled in a spider's web then."[91] His image of the trap turned the problem into one of life and death, and he advised the remedy of burning or "purifying destruction."[92] The remedy was drastic, but once more it was not so much a simple rejection of tradition as a transformation out of it—an impulse in the affirmative spirit of Emerson's remark, "Digest and correct past experience; and blend it with the new and divine life."[93] The emphasis was on purification (inner change) rather than destruction (outer change), for the "busk" or ritual burning practiced by the Mucclasse Indians, which Thoreau cited, was only one part of a vegetation ritual, a dying out of the old into the new that also required fasting, abstinence, and purification. The busk was properly sacramental, the symbol of inner purity, of the desire for renewal from within. Rejection itself was not the guarantee of such a change, indeed belied the organic possibilities of growth. To move out of one condition into another, to cast one's slough, to stir into wakefulness—these, like the mystery of life-from-death behind the feast of the new corn, were transformations, the kind of change *Walden* so effectively dramatized because its natural symbols recaptured the deepest mysteries of vegetation myth.

In the intervals between his account of society, Thoreau placed a record of his hopes and of the initial stages of his experiment. Thus he made explicit the contrast between low and high views of life and between restlessness and purposive self-reliance. He hinted at how he desired to live and what enterprises he cherished, providing a prospectus, somewhat like Whitman's "Inscriptions," of what was to follow.[94] He began with his desire to live in the eternal present, and "Where I Lived, and What I Lived For" and the concluding fable of the artist of the city of Kouroo described his success. Then in the celebrated passage of the hound, bay horse, and turtledove, he represented, as he explained to an inquisitive correspondent, his "losses"—though even in his reply he was evasive, saying that the "hound and horse may *perhaps* be the symbols of some of them," and indicating that he had lost "a far finer and more ethereal treasure, which commonly no loss of . . . will symbolize."[95] Many have tried to determine what his losses were and the source of his symbols; even Emerson suggested that the hound was the book he would have liked to have written, the bay horse his desire for property, and the turtledove the wife of his dream.[96] But Emerson never recognized that Thoreau had lost reality, and he seems to have forgotten that Thoreau had selected for *The Dial* this passage from Mencius: "If a man lose his fowls or his dogs, he knows how to seek them. There are those who lose their hearts and know not how to seek them. The duty of the student is no other than to seek his lost heart."[97] Next—and this was not a part of his original *Journal* entry, but an addition that expressed the enterprise of his years of decay—"To anticipate, not the sunrise and the dawn merely, but, if possible, Nature herself!"—to pierce to the heart of things, to discover the laws of the seasons and of inspiration, growth, and maturity, and, as he had set down as an afterthought in the *Journal,* "To find the bottom of Walden Pond. . . ."[98] His entire experiment was dedicated to the former, and achieved in "Spring"; and in "The Pond in Winter" he succeeded in the latter. Finally, he tried "to hear what was in the wind . . . and carry it express"—to express the spirit—a vocation as unrewarded and unrecognized (never "audited," he punned) by his neighbors as his "self-appointed" superintendence of nature and the wild.

One of his losses, apparently, was his failure to fulfill his desire for social influence, to turn his private good to public account. In the thinly veiled anecdote of the Indian basket weaver, who thought that he had only to make his baskets in order to sell them, he told of the failure of the *Week.* "I too had woven a kind of basket of a delicate texture," he confessed, "but I had not

made it worthy any one's while to buy them." He had learned, however, to make it worth some one's while to buy them by the time he wrote *Walden:* "Economy" was his come-on. And yet he put most of the blame for his failure to win social acceptance in his calling on society itself. He said that he studied how "to avoid the necessity of selling them"; he asserted that "the life which men praise and regard as successful is but one kind"; and he explained that, unsuccessful in this venture, "I turned my face more exclusively than ever to the woods"—all of which was as true of his present intentions as of those of the Walden period. Whether society bought his wares or not, he said that he would continue to make them, like Hawthorne's artist of the beautiful and his own artist of the city of Kouroo, finding the value of his work in the work itself: in the spiritual transformation of the artist. *Walden,* then, was a defense of his vocation and of any independent undertaking, and in the framework of "Economy," a defense of intrinsic rather than extrinsic reward. For Thoreau was not unaware of the costs of the self-reliance he was preaching. He knew it required a determined heroism, what David Riesman calls "the nerve of failure"—the strength "to defend an independent view of the self and of what life holds," the courage "to face aloneness and the possibility of defeat in one's personal life or one's work without being morally destroyed. . . . simply the nerve to be oneself when that self is not approved of by the dominant ethic of a society."[99]

With these losses for his background, he described for the first time his purpose in going to Walden in a passage that brilliantly fused the imagery of self-reliance and spiritual discovery with that of commerce:

> If your trade is with the Celestial Empire [the contemporary China trade and his own commerce with the heavens, with reality], then some small counting house on the coast [his hut at Walden Pond] in some Salem harbor, will be fixture enough. You will export such articles as the country affords, purely native products, much ice and pine timber and a little granite, always in native bottoms [his theory of native, organic literature]. These will be good ventures. To oversee all the details yourself in person; to be at once pilot and captain, and owner and underwriter [self-reliance; firsthand experience]; to buy and sell and keep accounts; to read every letter received, and write or read every letter sent; to superintend the discharge of imports night and day; to be upon many parts of the coast almost at the same time . . . to be your own telegraph, unweariedly sweeping the horizon, speaking all passing vessels bound coastwise; to keep up a steady despatch of commodities, for the supply of such a distant and exhorbitant market; to keep yourself informed of the state of markets, prospects of war and peace everywhere, and anticipate the tendencies of trade and civilization [the seer],—taking

advantage of the results of all exploring expeditions, using new passages and all improvements in navigation;—charts to be studied, the position of reefs and new lights and buoys to be ascertained, and ever, and ever, the logarithmic tables to be corrected, for by the error of some calculator the vessel often splits upon a rock [the use and revision of history] . . . universal science to be kept pace with, studying the lives of all great discoverers and navigators, great adventurers and merchants, from Hanno and the Phoenicians down to our day; in fine, account of stock to be taken from time to time, to know how you stand. It is a labor to task the faculties of a man,—such problems of profit and loss, of interest, of tare and tret, and gauging of all kinds in it, as demand a universal knowledge.

And Walden, he said, forcing the reader to grasp his meaning or to anticipate it, was "a good place for business," "a good post and a good foundation."[100]

III

He began his trade with the Celestial Empire in March, 1845—in spring, in the season of renewal itself—by withdrawing himself from society, by casting his skin. Like the "torpid" earth and the "torpid" snake he had responded to the influence of the spring sun, had felt "the influence of the spring of springs," and had been aroused to seek "a higher and more ethereal life."[101] In effect, he had been reborn, as Emerson had said in *Nature:* "In the woods . . . a man casts off his skin, as a snake his slough, and at what period soever of life is always a child."[102] The first spring made it possible for Thoreau to recapitulate the entire history of his life from youth to maturity and made the second and dramatic rebirth of the chapter on "Spring," which was here prefigured in the same symbols of the melting pond, the returning birds, and the stray goose, the earned reward of his conscious endeavor and faith, a more eternal one because he had penetrated to the spring of springs itself. The change that had taken place in entering on his new life was now reflected in the easy and open exposition—direct prose that gave the feeling of relaxed leisureliness and yet of crisp, purposeful work that had acquainted him with his materials and that had stirred his sympathies and his senses. And the change was rhapsodized in "Where I Lived, and What I Lived For" in the ecstasy of discovering a new world, in the imperatives, ringing with his own success, on wakefulness and the morning life and on deliberate living. He had found a world that was agreeable to his imagination. "Both place and time were changed," he said, "and I dwelt nearer to those parts of the universe and to those eras in history which had most attracted me ["lived," he had said in the manuscript, "in a more primitive and absolute time"]."[103] When he described his situation at the Pond and the hut he had recently framed, he established

their values in terms of the mountain imagery that had always signified for him the dewy, pure, and auroral life. His hut was "clean" and "airy," reminding him of a hut he had seen on his trip to the mountains in 1844; a house, he said, that was fit for the gods, where one might hear celestial music. Here, he wrote, "the morning wind forever blows, the poem of creation is uninterrupted. . . ."[104] Here, indeed, was Olympus; and the pond reminded him of a mountain tarn, whose calm surface, "full of light and reflections," like the pond in "Spring," was "a lower heaven."[105] He explained these impressions in the original version by saying that "my thoughts were so leavened with expectation that the whole region where I lived seemed more elevated than it actually was"; and he admitted that "when there was no elevation in my spirits the pond did not seem elevated like a mountain tarn, but a low pool, a silent muddy water and place for fishermen."[106] In this way he acknowledged the old problem of the two selves, the task he had set himself when he wrote, "Every man is tasked to make his life, even in its details, worthy of the contemplation of his most elevated and critical hour."[107] And yet, in his attempt to renew the real self, his description of a "new and unprophaned" universe was accurate. He was, as he wrote in the quatrain on the shepherd, striving to live high, to pluck the life everlasting, the edelweiss that Emerson said signified noble purity. In the manuscript of this passage he gave the key to his mountain and morning imagery: "On the tops of mountains, as everywhere to hopeful souls, it is always morning."[108]

He did not find himself in this auroral and olympian world as he had in his youth, for he now "wished to live deliberately," to find a *point d'appui* beneath the "illusory foundations" of habit and routine.[109] Now he had to maintain his elevation by discipline, by consciously reworking the materials of his life. Thus, when he built his hut, the container of his vital heat, he did not reject the old—did not forgo the materials, tools, or wisdom of the past, or of his old self—but dismantled it, purified it, and rebuilt it anew, and with different purposes in mind. He purchased his boards from James Collins, an Irish laborer on the Fitchburg railroad, whose "dark, clammy, and aguish" shanty could well represent the lives of quiet desperation he was leaving behind and with which he wanted to contrast his own life. The essential frame of his house came directly from nature, as did the stones and sand of his chimney. The boards were a kind of skin or clothing (like the plaster he later applied, but which he disliked), and these were purified—bleached and warped back by the sun.[110] When he occupied his house in July, therefore, it was "merely a defence against the rain, without plastering or chimney, the walls being of rough weather-stained boards, with wide chinks, which made it cool at night." He had a clean and airy dwelling, open to all the influences of nature. "I did not need to go out doors to take the air," he said, "for the atmosphere within had lost none of its freshness."[111]

Thoreau did not build his hut outright, any more than one builds the self; he built his hut as he needed it, to meet the developing seasons of man, and he used it as a symbol of the growth of consciousness. If in times of ecstasy he used the cycle of day and night as the symbol of the ebb and flow of inspiration ("Sounds" is such a day), he had now learned to extend the analogy to the year. "The day is an epitome of the year," he wrote. "The night is winter, the morning and evening are the spring and fall, and the noon is the summer."[112] These seasons also followed the development of consciousness as Emerson had read them in history: "The Greek was the age of observation; the Middle Age, that of fact and thought; ours, that of reflection and ideas."[113] This explains, perhaps, why the first springtime period of **Walden** was so full of allusions to Greece ("Morning brings back the heroic ages"—"It [the hum of a mosquito] was Homer's requiem; itself an Iliad and Odyssey in the air . . ."— "Olympus is but the outside of the Earth everywhere"— "With unrelaxed nerves, with morning vigor, sail by it [the whirlpool of dinner], looking another way, tied to the mast like Ulysses"); why "Reading" turned back to the classics of antiquity; why the second spring ushers in the Golden Age—why Miss Ethel Seybold, who has studied Thoreau's use of the classics, called **Walden** "the Homeric experiment."[114]

Thoreau's development in **Walden** began in the summer, a kind of extended spring, for, as he said, "There is more day to dawn";[115] it was characterized by nooning or contemplation, by the rapt reverie of "Sounds," in which he sat in his "sunny doorway from sunrise till noon . . . amidst the pines and hickories and sumachs, in undisturbed solitude and stillness, while the birds sang around or flitted noiseless through the house, until by the sun falling in at [his] west window . . . [he] was reminded of the lapse of time."[116] Summer, therefore, was the season in which his senses were all alive, the season of external and outdoor life, when there were no barriers to communion, when he enjoyed "the bloom of the present moment."[117] It was that period of his life which he commemorated in "Solitude," where, in trying to explain to his neighbors why he was not lonely, he glorified "the friendship of the seasons," the "sweet and beneficent society in Nature," the sympathy and kindredness of things—the "infinite and unaccountable friendliness . . . like an atmosphere sustaining me . . ."[118] He said, much as Emerson had in *Nature,* that "there can be no very black melancholy to him who lives in the midst of Nature and has his senses still," that to a "healthy and innocent ear" even the storm was "Aeolian music"; and his senses, as he demonstrated in these chapters, "were as acute as Indians . . ."[119] He redefined solitude in terms of nearness, just as he had redefined economy

in terms of essentials; he was not alone because he was closer to the circulations of being, because, like Whitman realizing himself in nature, he found that "God is my father & friend, men are my brothers, and nature is my mother and my sister."[120] "Solitude," therefore, like the first chapter of *Nature* was praise to sympathy, to the conditions of the ecstasy that underlay the transcendentalist's faith: "This is a delicious evening, when the whole body is one sense, and imbibes delight through every pore. I go and come with a strange liberty in Nature, a part of herself . . . Sympathy with the fluttering alder and poplar leaves almost takes my breath away. . . ." Beginning "Solitude" with these lines, Thoreau used the more effective present tense; but, in fact, as his allusion to Hebe indicated, he was advising a cure for himself as well as his neighbors. Open all your pores to nature, live in all the seasons—these had been the injunctions of his years of decay. He invoked the goddess Hebe because she had "the power of restoring gods and men to the vigor of youth," because "wherever she came it was spring."[121] His hut, open to nature, almost one with nature like the woodman's hut in "A Winter Walk," he now used as the symbol of his attempt to renew this sympathy.

As long as possible he preferred to remain outdoors and to be warmed by the sun. But toward the end of summer he began to build his chimney and fireplace— "the most vital part ["the nucleus and heart"] of the house."[122] Again he used secondhand materials, this time striking the bricks clean with a trowel. He had already laid the foundation in the spring, and now slowly, a course of bricks at a time, he deliberately built his chimney—the symbol of the self. He said that he "proceeded slowly" because his chimney "was calculated to indure for a long time"; and he made the symbol explicit by saying that "the chimney is to some extent an independent structure, standing on the ground and rising through the house to the heavens; even after the house is burned it still stands sometimes, and its importance and independence are apparent."[123] The chimney, appropriately, was finished by November, and when "the north wind had already begun to cool the pond," he began to have a fire. "I now first began to inhabit my house," he said, "when I began to use it for warmth as well as shelter."[124] Finally, before winter, he shingled and plastered, completely closing himself off from the elements—internalizing his life. "I withdrew yet farther into my shell," he wrote, "and endeavored to keep a bright fire both within my house and within my breast."[125]

As this process makes clear, selfhood was the final fruit of maturity. But the process also brought a change from outer to inner, from unconsciousness to consciousness; and though consciousness was undoubtedly a gain, the imagery of winter and self-containment suggests that it also was a loss, the reason for

Thoreau's sense of otherness. He spoke of the change as a kind of hibernation; indeed the hut was a kind of cocoon. Though he did other things, at least in "House-Warming," which covered the transition from autumn to winter and whose theme was keeping the vital heat, he said that gathering wood for his fire was his chief employment. There is an emphasis on keeping alive, on maintaining "a kind of summer in the midst of winter";[126] he speaks of lamps used to prolong the "day." There is a thickening of his outer garments, an apparently necessary coarsening and hardening. Even certain functions, like cooking, now take place indoors. Nature does not sustain him now as it did in the earlier chapters; there is no identity between the Me and Not-me. Instead, exposed to the weather, he said that "my whole body began to grow torpid" and that he recovered his faculties and prolonged his life only when he reached "the genial atmosphere of my house. . . ." For there he had left "a cheerful housekeeper," the fire, his own "clear flame";[127] and the fire was a captive spirit, somewhat like the air bubbles in the first ice on the pond, which, he explained, eventually created the breakup and booming of spring by acting as a lens, focusing the heat of the sun and melting the ice.

The hut was perhaps the most obvious symbol of building his life, but his occupations in the woods also followed the cycle of the seasons, the growth of consciousness, and the increasing need to penetrate to the spring of springs. The first major symbol of this was the beanfield. After the earlier chapters on "Sounds" and "Solitude" (and the companion chapter on "Visitors," originally called "Society"), chapters of leisure, he turned to work, to what Emerson called discipline in *Nature.* Originally, Thoreau had introduced his own example of labor with a passage on the nobility of the common workingman, but he probably omitted it because, as in every example from building his hut to gathering wood, he wanted to affirm that the value of work was the work itself. He had worked in the beanfield, moreover, not so much for the sake of beans (reviewers made much of this diet, though Thoreau, following Pythagoras, did not eat beans) as for the sake of participating in the natural processes, for intimacy with nature, because he believed that farming was a natural and unspecialized vocation, a primitive and universal one, that men were cultivators, as Varro said, before they were citizens.[128] "They attached me to the earth," he said of his beans, "and so I got strength ["and health"] like Anteus."[129] Undoubtedly this chapter was a part of his modern epic on farming, for he was instructing his neighbors, as he had in his remarks on forests in "House-Warming," on the uses of the wild; his field, he pointed out, "was, as it were, the connecting link between wild and cultivated fields. . . ."[130]

The beanfield, however, served other purposes still more significant. In this chapter he was able to raise up the imagery of seeds that he had already planted—"The soil, it appears, is suited to the seed . . ."—". . . we will not forget that some Egyptian wheat was handed down to us by a mummy"—"Leaven, which some deem the soul of bread, the *spiritus* which fills its cellular tissue . . . first brought over in the Mayflower, did the business for America . . . this seed I regularly and faithfully procured . . ."—"All that I could say, then, with respect to farming on a large scale [apropos the Hollowell farm] . . . was that I had my seeds ready."[131] He was able to prepare for the imagery of fruit and ripening—the woodchopper's thoughts "rarely ripened"; Flint's fields bore no crops, his meadows no flowers, his trees no fruit, only dollars; "the ambrosial and essential part of the fruit is lost with the bloom which is rubbed off in the market cart . . ."; "In October I went a-graping. . . ."[132] And finally, he could prepare for the chapter on "Spring," where he referred to "the divine seed" of man and the "'germs of virtue,'" by the explicit analogy of the seeds of virtue.[133]

For what he was planting were the seeds of "sincerity, truth, simplicity, faith, innocence, and the like," and his harvest, he hoped, would be "a new generation of men."[134] The soil unfortunately was "lean and effete," exhausted by the Indians who had grown beans centuries before, but by drawing "fresher soil" around his plants, which he preferred to manure and whose freshness Evelyn said had a power of attracting "virtue," he was able to get a crop.[135] The entire process dramatized the idea of renewal, and the constant vigilance and weeding the necessity of discipline, a discipline he made heroic by translating into military terms. On the social level he was farming "the dust of my ancestors . . . to redeem the meadows they have become,"[136] or, as he said in the *Week,* planting the seeds of institutions. "He who eats the fruit, should at least plant the seed," he said; "aye, if possible a better seed than that whose fruit he has enjoyed. . . . Defray thy debt to the world; eat not the seed of institutions, as the luxurious do, but plant it rather . . . that so, perchance, one variety may at last be found worthy of preservation."[137] "The Beanfield" was an example of Thoreau's idea of organic social reform, of the reform that returned to the economy of nature rather than to the economy, and whose seeds, therefore—as he indicated in his philological pun on "spica" and "spe" and "gerendo"—were hope-bearing.[138]

This labor, of course, was also an example of self-reform; and the fact that it was now his summer and early-morning work makes it especially interesting. Had he followed the seasons faithfully, summer would not have been devoted to such laborious discipline, and he did try to suggest in the earlier chapters that it was a period of leisure and communion. He had, in fact, raised beans during the summer at the pond—primarily for economic reasons; now, however, he used this work as a symbol of his own need in these later years to make contact with nature. It might have stood for the arduous scientific discipline he had imposed on himself (he said that he was determined to know beans), although, at the same time, it stood for the more casual (or Emerson's "genial") participation in nature that helped him see nature out of the side of his eye. His work also became an example of the kind of labor Emerson required of the American scholar, labor, as Thoreau had said in "Raleigh," that removes the palaver from one's style; and it was an example of the value of staying at home, of working one's native soil. Planting and hoeing beans, indeed any organic process, could easily represent the creative process of the romantic artist; and anticipating the Artist of the railroad cut in "Spring," Thoreau said that he dabbled "like a plastic artist in the dewy and crumbling sand. . . ."[139] He was working to the end of expression, and his "instant and immeasurable crop" was inspiration and "tropes and expression"[140]—not only the correspondence of hawk-wave-thought, but the parable of the chapter itself. Here was an example of reasoning from one's hand to one's head. "It was a singular experience," he wrote in the original version, "that long acquaintance of cultivator with beans. . . ."[141]

What made it so unique? Certainly any other activity would have yielded similar truths. But in the only passage which seems to break the continuity (both the narrative sequence and sense of the present) of the chapter, Thoreau recalled his first visit to the pond, blending his memory of past satisfactions with those of the present and turning nostalgia into hope, when he wrote in the last of several versions:

> When I was four years old, as I well remember, I was brought from Boston ["the city"] to this my native town, through these very woods and this field, to the pond. It is one of the oldest scenes stamped on my memory. ["The country then was the world—the city only the gate to it."] And now to-night my flute has waked the echoes over that very water. The pines still stand here older than I; or, if some have fallen, I have cooked my supper with their stumps, and a new growth is rising all around, preparing another aspect ["a wilder and worthier"] for new infant eyes. Almost the same johnswort springs from the same perennial root in this pasture, and even I have at length helped to clothe that fabulous landscape of my infant ["youthful"] dreams ["imagination"], and one of the results of my presence and influence is seen in these bean leaves, corn blades, and potato vines.[142]

Permanence and change, and a sense that at last the change is consonant with his childhood dreams—this is the meaning the passage conveys. In "The Ponds,"

where he returned again to his youth, he told of his former ecstasy, how he had floated over the surface as the zephyrs willed, "dreaming awake"; but he went on to say that "since I left those shores the woodchoppers have still further laid them waste" and to add that "my Muse may be excused if she is silent henceforth. How can you expect the birds to sing when their groves are cut down?"[143] But he discovered that in spite of all the ravages of woodchoppers and railroads and ice cutters the pond was itself unchanged, "the same water which my youthful eyes fell on," and that, as he confessed, "all the change is in me."[144] He had discovered his own pristine eternal self, and by cultivating beans, by discipline, he was changing the aspect of the pond, that is, the shore, making it—his life—more agreeable to his imagination. "Why, here is Walden," he wrote, "the same woodland lake that I discovered so many years ago; where a forest was cut down last winter another is springing up by its shore as lustily as ever; the same thought is welling up to its surface that was then; it is the same liquid joy and happiness to itself and its Maker, ay, and it *may* be to me."[145]

That the pond was the real self and the shore the empirical self was made clear in the chapter on "The Ponds." Indeed, Thoreau dramatized in brief what the entire book dramatized in the sequence of chapters on "The Beanfield," "The Village," and "The Ponds." For he turned from his private discipline in the field to the village, where everything he had said in "Economy" was given actuality, and then to the pond. The chapter on the village ran over into that on the ponds, the significant link being these lines: " . . . not till we have lost the world, do we begin to find ourselves, and realize where we are and the infinite extent of our relations."[146] Just as he had left the city and had come to the pond in his recollection, so now he had left the village, and in both instances he had found his real self. As for his empirical self, the self he wanted to purify, it was symbolized by the stony shore:

> It is no dream of mine,
> To ornament a line;
> I cannot come nearer to God and Heaven
> Than I live to Walden even.
> I am its stony shore,
> And the breeze that passes o'er;
> In the hollow of my hand
> Are its water and its sand,
> And its deepest resort
> Lies highest in my thought.[147]

And in a variant of the poem:

> It is a part of me which I have not prophaned
> I live by the shore of me detained.
> Laden with my dregs

I stand on my legs,
While all my pure wine
I to nature consign.[148]

He even punned on its name: *"Walled-in* Pond."[149]

Thoreau used the pond, of course, as a symbol; it was
not simply the well or fountain, say, of Hawthorne.
Instead it became a symbol of all his cherished values—of eternity, of the past, of spring and morning,
of the Indian, of the Golden Age, of purity, and of the
ecstasies he had known. "I thank God," he wrote in
the *Journal,* "that he made this pond deep and pure
for a symbol."[150] The most remarkable characteristics
of the pond were its purity, depth, and transparency,
its coolness and constancy, and its lack of inlet or
outlet. "Walden plainly can never be spoiled by the
woodchopper," he remarked in the *Journal,* "for, do
what you will to the shore, there will still remain this
crystal well."[151] Thoreau described it patiently, lovingly, and at great length. Speaking of the colors it
reflected, he transformed it into the soul: "Lying between the earth and the heavens, it partakes of the
color of both."[152] Sometimes it was "more cerulean
than the sky itself"; he called it "Sky water," identifying it with the heavens because of its nature and color,
and because he found depth and height symbolic equivalents.[153] "Water, which is more fluid and like the sky
in its nature," he noted, "is still more like it in color."[154]
He spoke of the color of its "iris," of the earth as a
face and the pond as the "earth's eye; looking into
which the beholder measures the depth of his own
nature"—the very window of the soul.[155] It was the
"distiller of celestial dews," and its surface betrayed
the "spirit" in the air: "It is continually receiving new
life and motion from above"—its ripples were the
equivalents of the vibrating wire, and the pond was
the harp.[156] Though some thought it bottomless, it was
not, and its bottom was "pure sand," with only a little
sediment (the accumulation of fallen leaves, that is, of
Thoreau's seasons) in the deeper parts, but no mud,
and even in winter "a bright green weed" could be
found growing there.[157] Its surface, moreover, was "a
perfect forest mirror," reflecting all phenomena perfectly as the untarnished mind should, indeed blindingly
reflecting light.[158] Even its fish ("Ideas,—are they not
the fishes of thought?") were "cleaner, handsomer,
and firmer" because of the coldness and purity of the
water—he called them "ascetic fish"; the frogs, so
humorously treated in "Sounds," were "clean"; and
there were no suckers.[159]

Having already prepared for this symbolic use of the
pond, he even gave a mythical account of its origin;
how a hill, "which rose as high into the heavens as the
pond now sinks deep into the earth," shook and suddenly sank—a version (or an inversion) of the Fall.
And then he returned to his own fable of the old
settler, which he had used to explain why he was not

lonely at the pond and which he referred to again in
"Former Inhabitants; And Winter Visitors" to explain
his notion of society: " . . . that ancient settler [God]
. . . came here with his divining-rod [pun], saw a thin
vapor rising from the sward, and the hazel pointed
steadily downward, and he concluded to dig a well
here."[160] He called the pond "'God's Drop.'"[161] And
later, in "Former Inhabitants," he explained the failure
of those who had been before him by saying that they
had not used their water privilege—"Ay, the deep
Walden Pond and cool Brister's Spring,—privilege to
drink long and healthy draughts at these, all unimproved by these men but to dilute their glass." And
even now he was disturbed by the villagers who forgot the sacred purposes of bathing and drinking, and
thought "to bring its water, which should be as sacred
as the Ganges at least, to the village in a pipe, to wash
their dishes with!—to earn their Walden by the turning
of a cock or drawing of a plug!"[162]

He also used the pond as a symbol of his own spiritual
history. In "Higher Laws" he defended hunting and
fishing because they were "the young man's introduction to the forest, and the most original part of himself." He said that "he goes thither at first as a hunter
and fisher, until at last, if he has the seeds of a better
life in him, he distinguishes his proper objects, as a
poet or naturalist it may be. . . ."[163] In "The Ponds"
Thoreau described these summer or youthful pursuits;
it was only in "The Pond in Winter" that he had found
his proper object, had gone beneath the surface of the
pond and angled "for the pond itself. . . ."[164] He told
how in his youth he had fished the pond, how he had
floated passively on its surface, how at that time he
was rich "in sunny hours and summer days, and spent
them lavishly. . . ."[165] Now, however, he had made his
"home by the shore"[166] and his purposes were deep-
ening, and though he placed the chapter in the summer
period of the book, he could not help seeing it in the
light of his mature experience. Thus his description of
midnight fishing, one of the most brilliant passages in
the book, perfectly conveyed the sense of communion
(as did the passage on floating) as well as a sense of
the mystery of the depths:[167]

> These experiences were very memorable and
> valuable to me,—anchored in forty feet of water,
> and twenty or thirty rods from the shore,
> surrounded sometimes by thousands of small
> perch and shiners, dimpling the surface with their
> tails in the moonlight, and communicating by a
> long flaxen line with mysterious nocturnal fishes
> which had their dwelling forty feet below, or
> sometimes dragging sixty feet of line about the
> pond as I drifted in the gentle night breeze, now
> and then feeling a slight vibration along it,
> indicative of some life prowling about its extremity,
> of dull uncertain blundering purpose there, and
> slow to make up its mind. At length you slowly
> raise, pulling hand over hand, some horned pout
> squeaking and squirming to the upper air. It was

very queer, especially in dark nights, when your thoughts had wandered to vast and cosmogonal themes in other spheres, to feel this faint jerk, which came to interrupt your dreams and link you to Nature again. It seemed as if I might next cast my line upward into the air, as well as downward into this element which was scarcely more dense. Thus I caught two fishes as it were with one hook.[168]

This passage bears comparison with Melville's "The Mast-Head" and with the fishing in Hemingway's "Big Two-Hearted River," and although Thoreau never suggested that his later fishing for the pond might be "tragic," what had made that fishing necessary was.

Besides its seasonal change, its freezing and breaking up, and the fact that it was "commonly higher in the winter and lower in the summer," the pond fluctuated over the years in response to "the deep springs."[169] These "tides," as Thoreau called the rise and fall of the pond, represented the over-all movement of his life, those unaccountable rhythms and pulses of inspiration.[170] Although he reported that the pond was five feet higher than when he had lived there and as high as it had been thirty years before—measurements that did not correspond to the facts of his life—his remark that "I have observed one rise and a part of two falls, and I expect that a dozen or fifteen years hence the water will again be as low as I have ever known it" did seem to fit his experience.[171] The significant facts, however, were that these changes required many years and that the rising waters, killing the shrubs and trees at the edge of the pond, left "an unobstructed shore."[172] Like the rising waters at the end of the book, these were purificatory, one more example of the renewal of the natural processes already symbolized in the pond which the sun dusted and in which "all impurity presented to it sinks. . . ."[173]

If Thoreau had not memorialized Walden and so made its name imperishable, it should, by rights, have been called "Thoreau's Pond." For as he said of Flint's Pond, "let it be named from . . . [some] child the thread of whose history is interwoven with its own. . . ."[174] It was clearly his own self-image: "Many men have been likened to it, but few deserve that honor," he wrote. "It is the work of a brave man, surely, in whom there was no guile!" He compared it to himself, "living thus reserved and austere, like a hermit in the woods"—acquiring purity.[175] And like his own life, which was "too pure to have a market value," he, "rounded this water with his hand, deepened and clarified it in his thought, and in his will bequeathed it to Concord."[176] He wanted it to serve society as he believed the reformer should, by the example of his "greater steadfastness," like the sun in its orbit, and he said that "this vision of serenity and purity . . . seen but once . . . helps to wash out State Street and the

engine's soot."[177] And he wanted it to remind his readers of the permanent springs beneath their lives. In a passage prefiguring his own rebirth in "Spring" he wrote: "Perhaps on that spring morning when Adam and Eve were driven out of Eden Walden Pond was already in existence, and even then breaking up in a gentle spring rain accompanied with mist and a southerly wind, and covered with myriads of ducks and geese, which had not heard of the fall, when still such pure lakes sufficed them. Even then it had commenced to rise and fall, and had clarified its waters, and colored them of the hue they now wear, and obtained a patent of heaven to be the only Walden Pond in the world. . . . Who knows in how many unremembered nations' literatures this has been the Castalian Fountain? or what nymphs presided over it in the Golden Age?"[178]

Having established the pond as the soul, Thoreau also made it, in the closing paragraphs on Flint's, Goose, and White ponds, a symbol of retired and forever pure nature. And in turning to "Baker Farm," where he worked hard to make the transition, he set the chapter on "The Ponds" in the context of his summer ramblings in nature. With "Baker Farm," the next two chapters, "Higher Laws" and "Brute Neighbors," belonged to his summer experience, all bound together, superficially at least, by the common theme of fishing. Setting out to go fishing "to eke out my scanty fare of vegetables" (a hint of the problem of "Higher Laws"), he came to Baker Farm and John Field; and contrasting his leisure with Field's bogging—he told Field that although he "looked like a loafer" he was actually getting his living in the woods—he used the chapter to express his faith in the uncommitted life.[179] In the manuscript version he wrote, "Lead such a life as the children that chase butterflies in a meadow. . . . live free and persevere as you were planted. Grow wild according to thy nature. . . ."[180] But coming home with his string of fish, he made the transition to "Higher Laws," where the crucial issue was this hunger for the wild and his mature concern with ascetic discipline.[181]

We have already seen why this chapter was the confession of his resolution for purity in his later years and why the beanfield had become his discipline in summer. In it, as in "The Ponds," however, he told the history of his life in nature, a history of growing self-consciousness and coarsening, but also a history of finding his proper objects. He could no longer live like the child, for his instinct toward the wild had been replaced by "an instinct toward a higher, or . . . spiritual life. . . ."[182] He added in the manuscript that "some would say that the one impulse was directly from God, the other through nature"[183]—a remark he wisely omitted because it revealed the actual disharmony he now experienced in nature. This chapter, nevertheless, told that story, and because of its unusual tone and theme, Thoreau followed it in "Brute

Neighbors" with his humorous dialogue between the Poet (the younger Channing) and the Hermit (himself). The dialogue did the work of the transitional sentence he omitted: "But practically I was only half converted to my own arguments, for I still found myself fishing at rare intervals."[184] And the humor was self-protective: though the dialogue helped him make the point of "Economy" once more, it was a mock pastoral in which poet and hermit alike were playing at their serious vocations, and in which the obvious breach in discipline destroyed the hermit's "budding ecstasy."[185] But having treated his most important concerns sportively and thus having brought his narrative back to its summer level—and this seems the only excuse for the dialogue—Thoreau returned, in the remainder of "Brute Neighbors," to the higher uses of nature for which he was purifying himself, to the correspondences or spiritual meanings it had for him.

"Why," he asked, "do precisely these objects which we behold make a world?" And he answered that "they are all beasts of burden . . . made to carry some portion of our thoughts."[186] Mouse, phoebe, robin, partridge, otter, raccoon, woodcock, ant, stray dog or cat, loon and duck—all bore a meaning, from that of the simple friendliness of the mouse to that of the serenity and wisdom in the eye of the infant partridge with which he identified himself.[187] The ant war he described made it possible for him to show the strife in nature and in civilization, and to trace war from Homer's time through Concord Fight and Bunker Hill to Austerlitz and Dresden and the Mexican war ("red republicans" vs. "black imperialists")—even, perhaps, in its internecine character and inconclusiveness, to suggest his premonition of the Civil War.[188] And the loon, whose autumn return he described, not only helped him make the transition to autumn, as did the ducks, but enabled him to enact the play of inspiration itself. Indeed, chasing the loon—a bird he compared to a fish and said visited the deepest part of the pond— became the symbol of his search for inspiration. Consciously trying to pursue it ("While he was thinking one thing in his brain, I was endeavoring to divine his thought in mine"), he was balked; and he found that passivity was necessary, that "it was as well for me to rest on my oars and wait his reappearing as to endeavor to calculate where he would rise. . . ." That he did not succeed even then, that the loon always raised his "demoniac" laugh "in derision of my efforts," and, finally, that an east wind came "and filled the whole air with misty rain, and I was impressed as if it were the prayer of the loon answered, and his god was angry with me"—these were signs, like the "tumultuous surface" of the pond, that the serene communion of summer was gone.[189]

If the pond was the soul, then what Thoreau did there was also the record of his inner life. In "House-Warming," where he gathered the autumn fruits and built his

chimney and winter finally set in, his life began to turn inward. To keep his vital heat—his faith—was now his problem. Winter, as he depicted it in "Former Inhabitants; And Winter Visitors," was the period of his greatest solitude, when visitors were fewest, when his life was reduced to routine, when even though "the master of the house was at home," the "Visitor" never came—at least not from the town.[190] It was the time of thought and memory, of his communion with the former inhabitants of the pond whose lives introduced the possibility of failure. It was a sleepy time, reminding him of "that winter that I labored with a lethargy," falling asleep over *Gondibert,* a time when he lulled himself to sleep with reminiscences, when, like the owl, he awaited "the dawning of his day."[191] And it was the proper time for considering friendship as a spiritual necessity—not those friendships of his youth, those companions of his external life, but those companions of his thoughts whose discourse summoned "the old settler" and "expanded and racked my little house. . . ."[192]

This and the succeeding chapters recapitulated the spring and summer chapters, taking up solitude, the resources of the natural scene, sounds, and the pond, only in a different mood. In "Winter Animals" the catalog of sounds and animals conveyed a sense of impoverishment—the wilder animals hunted in former times were gone; of spiritual restlessness—the whooping pond turned in its sleep, the fox sought "expression" and struggled for "light," the bustle of squirrels and mice wakened him; and of bravery under duress—there were still the hardy jays and chickadees, the lean but vigorous and elastic hares, and the "brave bird," the partridge, "not to be scared by winter," which, like Thoreau, was "Nature's own bird," living "on buds and diet drink."[193] "Every winter," Thoreau said in "The Pond in Winter," "the liquid and trembling surface of the pond, which was so sensitive to every breath, and reflected every light and shadow, becomes solid to the depth of a foot or a foot and a half. . . . it closes its eyelids and becomes dormant for three months or more. . . . After a cold and snowy night it needed a divining rod to find it."[194]

In "The Pond in Winter," however, Thoreau did not fully develop, as one might expect, the theme of loss. He did indeed suggest his discontent and spiritual uneasiness: "After a still winter night I awoke with the impression that some question had been put to me, which I had been endeavoring in vain to answer in my sleep, as what—how—when—where?" Of course he could not answer this question in his sleep, for it was the question of life itself which only waking would answer. And therefore he went on: "But there was dawning Nature, in whom all creatures live, looking in at my broad windows with serene and satisfied face, and no question on *her* lips. I awoke to an answered question, to Nature and daylight."[195] This awakening was the beginning of his rebirth, a process that began in the conscious endeavor to find the bottom of the pond, that reached a crescendo in "Spring," and that served as the living testimony of his conclusion— "Only that day dawns to which we are awake. There is more day to dawn. The sun is but a morning star."[196] "Moral reform," he said when he first fixed the meanings of morning and awakening, "is the effort to throw off sleep. . . . To be awake is to be alive."[197]

He began "The Pond in Winter," therefore, with his morning work or ritual, going in search of water. Like the winter fishermen, who were wise in natural lore, men of "real faith" (he punned) who knew where summer had retreated and whose life was passed "deeper in Nature than the studies of the naturalist penetrate," Thoreau also cut his hole in the ice; and if he was no longer a fisherman himself, he could still glory in the fabulous pickerel of Walden, and find what was more important to him, that "its bright sanded floor [was] the same as in summer."[198] He was now penetrating the deeps to find his faith, fathoming "unceasingly," as he wrote in his youth, "for a bottom that will hold an anchor, that it may not drag."[199] He said he "was desirous to recover the long-lost bottom of Walden Pond," and he made it clear, by his verbal play on "bottom" and "foundation," that he was seeking his foundation.[200] The foundation of his faith, as his survey of the pond indicated, was the doctrine of correspondence; and what he needed to prove again was the law that guaranteed that the actual corresponded to the unseen reality. He discovered the "general regularity" of the bottom and, what was more surprising to him, "its conformity to the shores," a conformity "so perfect that a distant promontory betrayed itself in the soundings quite across the pond, and its direction could be determined by observing the opposite shore."[201] He also found to his surprise that "the line of greatest length intersected the line of greatest breadth *exactly* at the point of greatest depth. . . ." This, he wrote in the manuscript version, pointed "to a general law"; it applied to oceans (the exploration of the Over-Soul) as well as ponds, to mountains and valleys, to capes and bars—"This rule . . . is universal."[202] Thus he discovered law and harmony in nature, at the same time that he realized anew that truth was perspectival. "If we knew all the laws of Nature," he wrote, "we should need only one fact . . . to infer all the particular results at that point." But because "we know only a few laws ["the particular laws are as our points of view"] . . . our result is vitiated, not, of course, by any confusion or irregularity in Nature, but by our ignorance of essential elements in the calculation. Our notions of law and harmony are commonly confined to those instances which we detect; but the harmony which results from a far greater number of seemingly conflicting, but really concurring, laws, which we have not detected, is still more wonderful."[203]

This law also applied to man, for "as there is no exclusively physical nor exclusively moral law, this is as true in ethics as in physics. . . ."[204] "Draw lines through the length and breadth of the aggregate of a man's particular daily behaviors and waves of life into his coves and inlets," he suggested, "and where they intersect will be the height or depth of his character. Perhaps we need only to know how his shores trend and his adjacent country or circumstances, to infer his depth and concealed bottom."[205] This was the kind of character analysis Thoreau wanted applied to himself, a kind of superb topographical phrenology, which he carried out in terms of low, smooth, and Achillean shores, and projecting brows. Applied to himself, of course, it would have revealed "a corresponding depth in him"[206]—the hero whose center would have been Walden Pond itself. And once the pond was the soul, coves, inlets, and shores, the sea and navigation, provided the imagery for a conceit that seemed irresistible:

> . . . there is a bar across the entrance of our every cove, or particular inclination; each is our harbor for a season, in which we are detained and partially land-locked. These inclinations are not whimsical usually, but their form, size, and direction are determined by the promontories of the shore, the ancient axes of elevation. When this bar is gradually increased by storms, tides, or currents, or there is a subsidence of the waters, so that it reaches to the surface, that which was at first but an inclination in the shore in which a thought was harbored becomes an individual lake, cut off from the ocean, wherein the thought secures its own conditions, changes, perhaps, from salt to fresh, becomes a sweet sea, dead sea, or a marsh. At the advent of each individual into this life [he made the moral clear], may we not suppose that such a bar has risen to the surface somewhere? It is true, we are such poor navigators that our thoughts, for the most part, stand off and on upon some harborless coast, are conversant only with the bights of the bays of poesy, or steer for the public ports of entry, and go into the dry docks of science, where they merely refit for this world, and no natural currents concur to individualize them.

Walden Pond, obviously, was such an individual lake, a sweet sea, that "private sea" of thought, the self that Thoreau in "Conclusion" advised his contemporaries to explore.[207]

Exploring the pond, finally, was a contemplative labor to be contrasted with the utilitarian skimming of the pond by the ice cutters, and a conscious endeavor to be contrasted with the ecstasies of his youth. Plumbing the depths he found "a bright green weed," the symbol of organic life and soul, which, he said, "was very agreeable to behold in mid-winter";[208] and while surveying the pond he discovered the manifestation of the same organic law in the undulation of its apparently rigid surface. And the ice, which others were harvesting, was now for him the sign of his own purity rather than dormant state, the sign of that "new austerity" he spoke of in "Higher Laws" which permitted the "mind [to] descend into his body and redeem it. . . ."[209] In reading *The Harivansa* he had noted that "'the heart filled with strange affections is to be here below purified by wisdom,'" and that "'the operation which conducts the pious and penitent Brahman to the knowledge of the truth, is all interior, intellectual, mental. They are not ordinary practices which can bring light into the soul.'"[210] The pure Walden water mingled with the sacred waters of the Ganges, in the famous conclusion of this chapter, because Thoreau had translated the ice, a commodity exported to all parts of the world, into "solidified azure," a symbol of purity and spirit.[211] So also, "Higher Laws" and "The Pond in Winter" were joined together by the ascetic disciplines of Oriental philosophy—by that morning philosophy which he was now performing.

Rebirth came with spring. It was anticipated toward the end of "The Pond in Winter" when Thoreau wrote that "in thirty days more, probably, I shall look from the same window on the pure sea-green Walden water there, reflecting the clouds and the trees, and sending up its evaporations in solitude, and no traces will appear that a man has ever stood there."[212] And it was announced at the beginning of "Spring," in a passage Thoreau apparently added on the booming and breaking up of the pond in obedience to the "absolute progress of the season"—"its law to which it thunders obedience . . . as surely as the buds expand in the spring."[213] The booming, moreover, was due to "the influence of the sun's rays," a morning phenomenon chiefly, when the pond "stretched itself and yawned like a waking man. . . ."[214] "Who shall resist the thaw?" he wrote in the winter of 1852. "Let all things give way to the impulse of expression. It is the bud unfolding, the perennial spring. As well stay the spring."[215]

Gradually the weather grew warmer, the snow and ice began to melt, the "circulations" began in the rills and rivulets, purging "the blood of winter," and Thoreau no longer needed to gather wood for his fire, assured now that nature would keep his vital heat.[216] In the thawing clay of the railroad cut he saw "the Artist who made the world and me" give way to the impulse of expression.[217] Indeed, his description of the thaw, one of the most brilliant and best sustained analogies in transcendental writing, was a myth of creation *as expression,* an elaborate metaphor of the organic process of art and nature and self-reform, of the creative and shaping power of Idea, and the renewal that proceeds from the inside out. And it was more than that: a metaphor of birth, and a metaphor of purification.

The thaw was first of all a flowing, a "bursting out" of the "insides of the earth," the unfolding of "the piled-up history" of geology.[218] The thawing obeyed the law of currents and the law of vegetation, a stream that took the form of leaves and vegetation. Thoreau called it a "grotesque or mythological vegetation," and it reminded him not only of foliage, but of "brains or lungs or bowels, and excrements of all kinds." "I feel," he wrote, "as if I were nearer to the vitals of the globe. . . ."[219] This excremental character suggested "that Nature has some bowels, and . . . is mother of humanity. . . ." For the frost coming out of the ground was Spring, a newly-delivered child, "Earth . . . in her swaddling clothes" stretching forth "baby fingers on every side." In an image of life-from-decay that would have pleased Whitman, he wrote: "Fresh curls spring from the baldest brow."[220] He saw in the thaw not only the birth but the development of man: in the streams of clay the formation of blood vessels, in sand the bony matter, in finer soil the flesh—in fact, the process by which rivers were formed and valleys created served as an analogy for the creation of the human face. "What is man," he wrote, "but a mass of thawing clay? . . . Who knows what the human body would expand and flow out to under a more genial heaven?" For "more heat or other genial influences," he hinted, "would have caused it to flow yet farther."[221] Melting was self-transcendence.

In the *Week* he had written that "Nature is a greater and more perfect art, the art of God" and that "man's art has wisely imitated those forms into which all matter is most inclined to run, as foliage and fruit."[222] Now he elaborated this idea. Watching the sudden creation of the sand foliage, he said that "I am affected as if in a peculiar sense I stood in the laboratory of the Artist . . . had come to where he was still at work, sporting on this bank, and with excess of energy strewing his fresh designs about." He saw the earth laboring with "the idea inwardly" and expressing itself "outwardly in leaves. . . ."[223] At first he explained this process philologically, suggesting in the radical meanings of lobe, leaf, and globe not only the uniformity of law in rivers, ice, trees, and the globe itself, but the stages of evolutionary growth and purification. Having shown the leaflike character of liver and lungs and feathers and wings, he concluded: "You pass from the lumpish grub in the earth to the airy and fluttering butterfly. The very globe continually transcends and translates itself, and becomes winged in its orbit."[224] Then he wrote that "this one hill side illustrated the principle of all the operations of Nature. The Maker of this earth but patented a leaf." He had read Goethe seriously, and having tried to illustrate the principle himself, he omitted, as he so often did on revision, the explicit statement of his intention: "Show me how to make a leaf: and I will make you a world, and beings like you to inhabit it."[225]

The moral Thoreau drew from the process of the thaw was the central law of his life: "There is nothing inorganic." He now affirmed: "The earth is not a mere fragment of dead history, stratum upon stratum like the leaves of a book, to be studied by geologists and antiquaries chiefly, but living poetry like the leaves of a tree, which precede flowers and fruit,—not a fossil earth ["The earth is not a graveyard full of skeletons," he said in the manuscript, "but a granary full of seeds"], but a living earth; compared with whose central life all animal and vegetable life is merely parasitic. Its throes will heave our exuviae from their graves." And this law applied to man and the higher society he needed: " . . . the institutions upon it," he wrote, "are plastic like clay in the hands of the potter."[226] Hoeing beans, he had himself been a plastic artist making the soil express itself in leaves; and in "Former Inhabitants" he had identified himself with Wyman the potter, who lived deepest in the woods and who did not pay his taxes. "I had read of the potter's clay and the wheel in Scripture," he remarked, stating his theme in brief, "but it had never occurred to me that the pots we use were not such as had come down unbroken from those days . . . and I was pleased to hear that so fictile an art was even practised in my neighborhood."[227] It had not occurred to his neighbors either that at Walden he had been practicing this fictile art, that he was a reformer who likened his work to that of the thaw with its "gentle persuasion" and who did not break but melted things; whose work was an example of the symbolic imagination, of conforming his life to the idea in his mind, and who, as Emerson wrote in *Nature,* having started "in his slumber," awakes to find that "Nature is not fixed but fluid. Spirit alters, moulds, makes it."[228] At Walden he was creating such an organic life for himself, and ultimately for society. "Again, perhaps, Nature will try," he wrote, "with me for a first settler. . . ." He was the "Champollion" deciphering the hieroglyphic [the leaf] of nature, "that we may turn over a new leaf at last."[229]

In Thoreau's experience the thawing at the railroad cut was always associated with the ecstasy of the resounding telegraph wire, an ecstasy comparable to the thawing only in its suddenness. The harp analogy, however, did not afford the possibilities of symbolic richness, nor would it have so grandly pulled together the themes of **Walden**. But in omitting it Thoreau tried to make the many **Journal** observations of the later years that composed the passage the vehicle for ecstasy, and he succeeded in conveying something more and something less than the harp conveyed. The ecstasy was not spontaneous or unconscious, but intellectual; it followed from his mature study of nature and his perception of law, an ecstatic praise of this guarantee in nature but not the former ecstasy he was seeking. It was an example of his belief that "the intellect is a cleaver; it discerns and rifts its way into the secret of things."[230] But as an example of his

conscious endeavor in nature it represented the intellectual basis from which the more successful symbols of ecstasy—the melting pond and the soaring hawk—were struck.

Thoreau began to build toward ecstasy by mentioning the irrepressible joy of the squirrels, the "carols and glees" of the brooks, the first sparrows and bluebirds, with their songs of "younger hope than ever," and the green grass, "the symbol of perpetual youth," which like "human life but dies down to its root, and still puts forth its green blade to eternity." "What at such a time," he asked, "are histories, chronologies, traditions, and all written revelations?"[231] For Walden, too, had begun to melt and sparkle in the sun, its "bare face . . . full of glee and youth, as if it spoke the joy of the fishes within it, and of the sands on its shore. . . ." "Such is the contrast," he wrote, "between winter and spring. Walden was dead and is alive again."[232] The change he had sought by the discipline of purity had come with "the change from storm and winter to serene and mild weather, from dark and sluggish hours to bright and elastic ones"; and like the dawning of inspiration this "memorable crisis" was "seemingly instantaneous at last." "Suddenly," he wrote, sharpening the contrasts of the original passage—

> Suddenly an influx of light filled my house, though the evening was at hand, and the clouds of winter still overhung it, and the eaves were dripping with sleety rain. I looked out of the window, and lo! where yesterday was cold gray ice there lay the transparent pond already calm and full of hope as in a summer evening, reflecting a summer evening sky in its bosom, though none was visible overhead, as if it had intelligence with some remote horizon. I heard a robin in the distance, the first I had heard for many a thousand years . . . the same sweet and powerful song as of yore . . . the pitch-pines and shrub-oaks about my house, which had so long drooped, suddenly resumed their several characters, looked brighter, greener, and more erect and alive, as if effectually cleansed and restored by the rain ["and fitted once more to express immortal beauty and make a part of this world which is called Κόσμος or beauty"]. . . . As it grew darker, I was startled by the *honking* of geese. . . . Standing at my door, I could hear the rush of their wings. . . . So I came in, and shut the door, and passed my first spring night in the woods.[233]

With the coming of his spring had come "the creation of Cosmos out of Chaos and the realization of the Golden Age." And with creation, which he supported with citations from Ovid's *Metamorphoses,* a host of images of new birth, infancy, and innocence; a sense of new freedom, release, hope, and pardon. The world into which he had been reborn was the eternal present, that golden age, before the fall of man, when man "'cherished fidelity and rectitude'" and was sufficient in his virtue, a time when "'Punishment and fear were not,'" the trees had not been felled, and "'mortals knew no shores but their own.'"[234] And for Thoreau, finally, the symbol of this transformation was not the butterfly which the logic of his metaphors demanded, but the hawk, which sported alone in the morning air with "proud reliance"—the bird he associated with falconry, nobleness, and poetry, and with his own lonely heroism; the bird, he wrote, "that soars so loftily and circles so steadily and apparently without effort [because it] has earned this power by faithfully creeping on the ground as a reptile in a former state of existence."[235] The hawk symbolized his ultimate liberation from the senses, the final emancipation of Oriental discipline. At last, as he noted in *The Harivansa,* he was "'free in this world, as birds in the air, disengaged from every kind of chain.'"[236]

Thoreau, of course, closed his book with the fable of the beautiful bug that had come out of the dry leaf of an old table of apple-tree wood. In fact, he made this fable recapitulate his themes: "Who knows what beautiful and winged life, whose egg has been buried for ages under many concentric layers of woodenness in the dead dry life of society, deposited at the first in the alburnum of the green and living tree, which has been gradually converted into the semblance of its well-seasoned tomb . . . may unexpectedly come forth from amidst society's most trivial and handselled furniture, to enjoy its perfect summer life at last!"[237] In the manuscript of "Spring," where he proposed the tonic of wildness, he had written that "he [God] is a very *present* help in trouble, but the chief trouble is that we live in the past and in tradition, where he is not."[238] The contrast was implicit in "Spring," but Thoreau made it explicit in "Conclusion," by returning to the issues of economy and society, self-reform and discovery. And there his biting and forceful remarks on restlessness and desperation, and his injunctions to find a foundation to live in the truth and to make one's relations, were crystallized in a parable of his own life and vocation. For in order to affirm the open prospects of the eternal present, he had fashioned *Walden,* as he himself had lived, after the example of the artist of the city of Kouroo.

> There was an artist in the city of Kouroo who was disposed to strive after perfection. One day it came into his mind to make a staff. Having considered that in an imperfect work time is an ingredient, but into a perfect work time does not enter, he said to himself, It shall be perfect in all respects, though I should do nothing else in my life. He proceeded instantly to the forest for wood, being resolved that it should not be made of unsuitable material; and as he searched for and rejected stick after stick, his friends gradually deserted him, for they grew old in their works and died, but he grew not older by a moment. His singleness of purpose and resolution, and his

elevated piety, endowed him, without his knowledge, with perennial youth. As he made no compromise with Time, Time kept out of his way, and only sighed at a distance because he could not overcome him. Before he had found a stock in all respects suitable the city of Kouroo was a hoary ruin, and he sat on one of its mounds to peel the stick. Before he had given it the proper shape the dynasty of the Candahars was at an end, and with the point of the stick he wrote the name of the last of that race in the sand, and then resumed his work. By the time he had smoothed and polished the staff Kalpa was no longer the pole-star; and ere he had put on the ferule and the head adorned with precious stones, Brahma had awoke and slumbered many times. But why do I stay to mention these things? When the finishing stroke was put to his work, it suddenly expanded before the eyes of the astonished artist into the fairest of all the creations of Brahma. He had made a new system in making a staff, a world with full and fair proportions; in which, though the old cities and dynasties had passed away, fairer and more glorious ones had taken their places. And now he saw by the heap of shavings still fresh at his feet, that, for him and his work, the former lapse of time had been an illusion, and that no more time had elapsed than is required for a single scintillation from the brain of Brahma to fall on and inflame the tinder of a mortal brain. The material was pure, and his art was pure; how could the result be other than wonderful?[239]

Abbreviations

For convenience, the titles of the following standard works have been abbreviated:

W—*The Writings of Henry David Thoreau,* 20 vols., Walden edition, Boston and New York, 1906. W is used here, however, to designate only the first six volumes, which include the published writings, letters, and poems.

J—*The Journal,* vols. VII-XX of the above edition, edited by Bradford Torrey and Francis H. Allen. Since *The Journal* is also numbered from I-XIV, I have adopted this numbering.

C—*The Complete Works of Ralph Waldo Emerson,* 12 vols., Centenary edition, Boston and New York, 1903.

Emerson, J—*Journals of Ralph Waldo Emerson,* edited by Edward Waldo Emerson and Waldo Emerson Forbes, 10 vols., Boston and New York, 1909-14.

Manuscript holdings, unless specified, are identified as follows:

MA—The Pierpont Morgan Library

HM—The Huntington Library

Notes

[1] J, III, 221.

[2] J, III, 195-98.

[3] W, VI, 163.

[4] W, VI, 162.

[5] In the preface to the manuscript version (HM 924) Thoreau wrote: "Nearly all of this volume was written eight or nine years ago in the scenery & under the circumstances it describes, and a considerable part was read (at that time as lectures) before the Concord Lyceum. In what is now added the object has been chiefly to make it a completer & truer account of that portion of the author's life." According to the records of the Concord Lyceum, however, Thoreau lectured twice, in February, 1847, on the "History of Himself" (Emerson noted that he spoke about his housekeeping at the Pond), and in January, 1849, on "White Beans and Walden Pond" (see Hoeltje, "Thoreau as Lecturer," p. 491; Rusk, ed., *The Letters of Ralph Waldo Emerson,* III, 377-78). In the interest of establishing the truth of his narrative, Thoreau, of course, claimed more than a close study of the book will bear. Much was added after his experiment, not only completing but transforming the book.

[6] J, III, 217.

[7] J, III, 212.

[8] He admitted that he could tell a tale of failure but that he put a brave face on things.

[9] W, II, 94.

[10] W, II, 346-47.

[11] J, III, 328.

[12] C, III, 69.

[13] W, II, 93-94; J, III, 239.

[14] J, III, 249. See J, III, 108.

[15] J, III, 239.

[16] On the need for a "rounded" truth see J, III, 465.

[17] *Thoreau: The Poet-Naturalist* (1902), p. 39.

[18] J, III, 119.

[19] J, III, 85-86.

[20] W, II, 358. See Canby, *Thoreau,* p. 243, where Thoreau's Aunt Maria is quoted as saying: "I do love to hear things call'd by their right names, and these *Transcendentalists* do so transmogrophy . . . so transmogrophy their words and pervert common sense that I have no patience with them."

[21] J, III, 99. See also W, VI, 94 on levels of meaning.

[22] W, II, 357.

[23] J, IV, 339.

[24] W, VI, 220. See also J, I, 411-12; J, VI, 100.

[25] W, II, 357.

[26] W, II, 356, 358; HM 924.

[27] HM 924.

[28] W, II, 357.

[29] J, II, 470, 472.

[30] W, VI, 160.

[31] C, III, 75, 53.

[32] W, VI, 212.

[33] W, II, 44.

[34] W, VI, 170-71.

[35] In "Civil Disobedience" (W, IV, 381) he said: "I will still make what use and get what advantage of her [the state] I can, as is usual in such cases."

[36] W, II, 9.

[37] J, I, 436. One is reminded of Carlyle's remark: "The Fraction of Life can be increased in value not so much by increasing your Numerator as by lessening your Denominator."

[38] J, IV, 430.

[39] J, III, 459.

[40] C, I, 14; W, II, 353.

[41] W, I, 362.

[42] W, II, 14-15.

[43] C, III, 29; W, II, 16. See Shepard, ed., *The Journals of Bronson Alcott,* p. 261: "Emerson said fine

things last night [January 5, 1852] about 'Wealth,' but there are finer things far to be said in praise of Poverty, which it takes a person superior to Emerson even to say worthily. Thoreau is the better man, perhaps, to celebrate that estate, about which he knows much, and which he wears as an ornament about himself. . . ." Van Wyck Brooks pointed out in "The Literary Life in America" (1921) that in America there was no alternative—no aristocratic tradition and no tradition of voluntary poverty—to the bourgeois life (*Three Essays on America,* New York, 1934, p. 203). Both Alcott and Thoreau might be used in the creation of a tradition of voluntary poverty.

44 J, IX, 246-47.

45 W, II, 37.

46 W, II, 238.

47 In "Literary Ethics" (C, I, 175) Emerson wrote: "The reason why an ingenious soul shuns society, is to the end of finding society."

48 In a narrower sense Thoreau also relived the history of Concord. His aim was well described in 1856 when he wrote: "Human life may be transitory and full of trouble, but the perennial mind, whose survey extends from that spring to this, from Columella to Hosmer [a Concord farmer and friend of Thoreau], is superior to change. I will identify myself with that which did not die with Columella, and will not die with Hosmer" (J, VIII, 245).

49 J, IV, 478-79.

50 Undoubtedly he had been influenced by Pythagoras and by the Hindu scriptures. In 1841 he had written of the latter: "The simple life herein described confers on us a degree of freedom even in the perusal. . . . Wants so easily and gracefully satisfied that they seem more like a refined pleasure and repleteness" (J, I, 277-78).

51 J, V, 410-12.

52 J, VI, 336; W, II, 44.

53 He was the idler who had once set fire to the woods. In the opening remarks of the manuscript of *Walden* (HM 924) he joked about the owl and the cock lecturing on astronomy when they should have been asleep.

54 W, II, 218.

55 W, VI, 259. In this letter Thoreau also wrote: "To what end do I lead a simple life at all, pray? That I

may teach others to simplify their lives?—and so all our lives be *simplified* merely, like an algebraic formula? Or not, rather, that I may make use of the ground I have cleared, to live more worthily and profitably? I would fain lay the most stress forever on that which is the most important,—imports the most to me. . . . As a preacher, I should be prompted to tell men, not so much how to get their wheat bread cheaper, as of the bread of life compared with which *that* is bran. Let a man only taste these loaves, and he becomes a skillful economist at once." That is why Thoreau said that he would tempt men with "the fruit, not with the manure." The letters to Blake and Ricketson, which forced Thoreau to explain himself to his disciples, are an excellent gloss on *Walden.*

56 W, VI, 294.

57 W, IV, 299.

58 W, II, 55.

59 HM 924.

60 W, II, 4.

61 It was comic, however, only when one viewed the prudential from the spiritual level. When these levels, as we shall see, were translated into the empirical and real selves, and the spiritual was viewed from the prudential, it was tragic.

62 W, II, 4, 18.

63 W, II, 6.

64 W, II, 5-7, 124.

65 W, II, 7-8.

66 *Democracy in America,* ed. by Phillips Bradley, New York, 1945, II, 248.

67 Houghton. MS AM 278.5.

68 W, II, 37.

69 W, II, 17.

70 W, II, 9.

71 Section 3, "Song of Myself."

72 W, II, 10.

73 W, II, 15.

74 W, I, 367.

[75] W, VI, 226. The entire letter develops this theme.

[76] J, I, 199.

[77] W, II, 26.

[78] W, II, 41. He said later (p. 53) that "'carpenter' is but another name for 'coffin-maker.'"

[79] W, II, 42-43.

[80] W, II, 44. See also pp. 51-52 for Thoreau's use of the shell image.

[81] W, II, 50.

[82] J, III, 181 (January 11, 1852). Emerson received Greenough's letter on January 5, 1852. See Rusk, ed., *The Letters of Ralph Waldo Emerson*, IV, 271-72.

[83] W, II, 51.

[84] W, II, 52. He approved of the humble dwellings of the poor. And he was angered by the luxuries that were purchased at the expense of the poor, especially the Irish who were degraded by labor. See W, II, 38.

[85] W, II, 52; HM 924.

[86] J, III, 183.

[87] HM 924.

[88] W, II, 268-70; HM 924.

[89] W, II, 95.

[90] W, II, 73.

[91] W, II, 73-74.

[92] W, II, 75.

[93] C, I, 175.

[94] W, II, 18ff.

[95] W, VI, 301-2.

[96] Cited by Vivian C. Hopkins, *Spires of Form: A Study of Emerson's Aesthetic Theory*, Cambridge, 1951, p. 243n.

[97] *The Dial*, IV (Oct., 1843), 206. The other selections define superiority in terms especially applicable to Thoreau, and are a gloss perhaps on what Thoreau meant when he told of the man who had lost his hound, and in seeking it had found a man—Thoreau himself (W, II, 306). By "heart" Mencius meant man's innate goodness, which was lost by his contact with the world. See especially Mencius' allegory of the Bull Mountain, which was once covered with trees but was despoiled by woodchoppers—perhaps Thoreau's lament for the shores of Walden Pond, similarly despoiled and conveying the same kind of loss, is an echo of this famous story.

[98] J, I, 435.

[99] *Individualism Reconsidered*, pp. 66, 48.

[100] W, II, 22-23.

[101] W, II, 45-46.

[102] C, I, 9.

[103] W, II, 97; HM 924. See also W, II, 144.

[104] W, II, 94.

[105] W, II, 96.

[106] HM 924.

[107] W, II, 100.

[108] HM 924.

[109] W, II, 100, 106, 108-9.

[110] W, II, 47-48.

[111] W, II, 94-95.

[112] W, II, 332.

[113] Emerson, J, IV, 110. See also C, I, 109.

[114] "Where I Lived, and What I Lived For"; Seybold, *Thoreau: The Quest and The Classics*, Chap. III. The allusions to Greece, however, were balanced by allusions to Oriental scripture: he could only regain his Greece by purification.

[115] W, II, 367.

[116] W, II, 123-24.

[117] W, II, 123.

[118] W, II, 145-46. Thoreau was describing that "greatest delight" of which Emerson spoke in referring to the "occult relation between man and the vegetable" (C, I, 10). "Shall I not have intelligence with the earth? Am I not partly leaves and veg-

etable mould myself?" Thoreau echoed at the close of "Solitude." The whole chapter, in fact, amplifies Emerson's single line: "I am not alone and unacknowledged."

119 W, II, 145; HM 924.

120 HM 924. Thoreau was trying to make clear that the physical isolation which Lane and many others protested was not the equivalent of spiritual isolation.

121 W, II, 154.

122 W, II, 266-67; HM 924.

123 W, II, 267.

124 W, II, 267-68.

125 W, II, 275.

126 W, II, 280.

127 W, II, 279-80.

128 J, VI, 107.

129 W, II, 171; HM 924.

130 W, II, 174.

131 W, II, 17, 28, 69, 93.

132 W, II, 166, 218, 192, 263.

133 W, II, 346-47.

134 W, II, 181.

135 W, II, 171, 175, 179.

136 J, III, 334.

137 W, I, 129-30.

138 W, II, 184.

139 W, II, 173.

140 W, II, 175, 179.

141 HM 924.

142 W, II, 172; HM 924. For another and fuller version see J, I, 380-81. In HM 924 he said that the pond was his "proper nursery." In J, I, 158 he wrote: "Do not thoughts and men's lives enrich the earth and change the aspect of things as much as a new growth of wood?"

143 W, II, 213.

144 W, II, 214. On p. 361 he wrote: "Things do not change; we change."

145 W, II, 214.
146 W, II, 190.

147 W, II, 215.

148 HM 924. See Bode, ed., *Collected Poems of Henry Thoreau,* p. 288.

149 W, II, 203.

150 J, III, 232; W, II, 316. The pond was obviously the center, the focal point of the book; in this respect he had good reason to drop the subtitle.

151 J, III, 35.

152 W, II, 196.

153 W, II, 196, 209. In HM 924 he added: " . . . our imaginations require a depth in the earth beneath corresponding to the visible height of the heavens above."

154 J, IV, 134. See W, II, 210-11, where he described floating on the pond in terms of floating in the air, and where the fish reminded him of birds.

155 W, II, 196, 206.

156 W, II, 199, 209. In J, II, 57-58, the source of this line, Thoreau wrote another version of the poem cited above.

157 W, II, 198-99. In W, I, 250 Thoreau wrote: "Methinks my soul must be a bright invisible green."

158 W, II, 209, 207.

159 J, III, 232; W, II, 204-5, 197, 206. See also J, XI, 351. On November 14, 1836, Thoreau entered the following in his first notebook: "'From the primitive word Ver, signifying water . . . is derived the word verité; for as water, by reason of its transparency and limpidness, is the mirror of bodies—of physical êtres, so also is truth equally the mirror of ideas—of intellectual êtres, representing them in a manner as faithful and and [sic] clear, as the water does a physical body.' Gebelin.—Monde Primitif.—Dictionnaire Etymol. Francoise" (MA 594).

160 W, II, 202-3. For the divining rod see also W, II, 109, 312. Thoreau prepared for this chapter by speaking of fishing in "the Walden Pond of their own na-

tures" (p. 145), of "an old settler and original proprietor, who is reported to have dug Walden Pond, and stoned it, and fringed it with pine woods; who tells me stories of old time and of new eternity" (p. 152), of the woodchopper who was an example of genius in the lower grades of life, "who are as bottomless even as Walden Pond was thought to be, though they may be dark and muddy" (p. 166). The darkness and muddiness were the signs of physicality—of torpidity and sleep. Thoreau acknowledged: "My nature may be as still as this water, but it is not so pure, and its reflections are not so distinct" (J, III, 404).

161 W, II, 215.

162 W, II, 291, 213.

163 W, II, 235.

164 W, II, 236. In HM 924 he remarked: "I angled for Walden two years and upward and had a glorious [?]."

165 W, II, 213.

166 W, II, 194.

167 He also used the unknown nests (W, II, 205-6) to suggest mystery and prepare for his discoveries in "The Pond in Winter."

168 W, II, 194-95.

169 W, II, 200-201.

170 HM 924.

171 W, II, 201. See J, VI, 226-27 (April 27, 1854).

172 W, II, 201.

173 W, II, 209.

174 W, II, 217-18.

175 W, II, 214-15.

176 W, II, 221, 214-15.

177 W, II, 81, 215.

178 W, II, 199.

179 W, II, 225, 227.

180 HM 924.

181 His problem now was posed by the question, "How shall a man continue his culture after manhood?" "All

wisdom," he answered, echoing Oriental scripture, "is the reward of discipline conscious or unconscious" (Houghton. MS AM 278.5). In HM 924 there was an epigraph from Saadi on the title page on the need for obedience to law.

182 W, II, 232. This problem emerged again in "Walking," a defense of the wild in which the key metaphor was religious—*"Sainte-Terrer."* By means of this metaphor the actual wild was subtly spiritualized. See J, XI, 450 for a similar transformation of the wild.

183 HM 924.

184 HM 924.

185 W, II, 249.

186 W, II, 249.

187 W, II, 251. "Such an eye," he said, "is coeval with the sky it reflects. The woods do not yield another such gem. The traveller does not often look into such a limpid well." He also spoke of the pond as an eye and as a jewel.

188 In "My Books I'd Fain Cast-Off, I Cannot Read" (1842), he had already mentioned the ant war.

189 W, II, 259-62. Thoreau copied from *The Harivansa:* "Thought tormented by desires, is like the sea agitated by the wind" (J, II, 190).

190 W, II, 292, 298.

191 W, II, 285-86, 291, 293-94.

192 W, II, 297.

193 W, II, 301, 305.

194 W, II, 312-13.

195 W, II, 312.

196 W, II, 367.

197 W, II, 100.

198 HM 924; W, II, 313-14.

199 J, I, 54.

200 W, II, 315. Waking and sleeping merge with foundation and surface in this chapter.

201 W, II, 318.

[202] HM 924. The transcendentalists, of course, made much of correspondences and analogies. But they went further than most who read the symbolism of nature, attempting, in fact, to create a science of correspondence. Analogy for them was not a game in which one sought for resemblances, but a study of real relationships, a way of expressing law. Here Thoreau *verified* that law; here one sees that he had gone beyond the literary correspondences of "Sounds"—correspondences expressing chiefly the subjective play of his mind—to correspondences founded on the nature of fact. His whole life moved in this direction, and he was true to it in *Walden* by speaking of his early ecstasy in terms of sound and his later ecstasy in terms of sight. For sight, as Emerson wrote, was the condition of self-consciousness (C, I, 109).

[203] W, II, 320.

[204] HM 924.

[205] W, II, 321.

[206] W, II, 321.

[207] W, II, 321-22, 354.

[208] HM 924.

[209] W, II, 246.

[210] J, II, 190-91.

[211] W, II, 324.

[212] W, II, 328.

[213] W, II, 330, 333.

[214] W, II, 332.

[215] J, III, 232.

[216] W, II, 336.

[217] W, II, 338.

[218] HM 924; J, IV, 383.

[219] HM 924; W, II, 337-38.

[220] W, II, 340.

[221] W, II, 339-40. In HM 924 he indicated what he meant by adding the following: " . . . stretched on a bank in paradise. Have we not unsatisfied instincts?"

It is interesting to compare Thoreau's conscious use of the imagery of the sand bank with his personal responses. When he saw "the naked flesh of New England" in the sands of Lake Cochituate, he wrote: " . . . this is my home, my native soil; and I am a New-Englander. Of thee, O Earth, are my bone and sinew made. . . . To this dust my body will gladly return as to its origin. Here have I my habitat. I am of Thee" (J, III, 95; see also J, III, 97). These passages and his personal response to the genial influence of the thaw (J, V, 34-35) add one more meaning perhaps to his intention of redeeming the dust of his ancestors.

[222] W, I, 339-40. See also W, I, 167. In HM 956 he wrote: "The leaf is her [nature's] constant cypher [*sic*]." In a draft of "Autumnal Tints" he wrote: "I remember one who proposed to write an epic poem to be called The Leaf. This would be a sufficiently broad and fertile theme, considering the origin and end of the leaf, and that botanists regard all the parts of a plant as modified leaves merely. . . . A leaf might be taken for [the] emblem of Nature" (Houghton, MS AM 278.5).

[223] W, II, 337-38.

[224] W, II, 338.

[225] W, II, 340; HM 924.

[226] W, II, 340-41.

[227] W, II, 288.

[228] W, II, 341; C, I, 72, 76.

[229] W, II, 291, 340. Apropos of wells, he also socialized his own experience: "I trust that in this new country many wells are yet to be dug" (HM 924). He socialized his life in the spirit of a remark by Charles Emerson, whose "Notes from the Journal of a Scholar" he admired: "If to need least, is nighest to God, so also is it to impart most. There is no soundness in any philosophy short of that unlimited debt" (*The Dial,* IV [July, 1843], 91).

[230] W, II, 109. This remark was made in the context of Thoreau's desire to work through the surface to reality.

[231] W, II, 342-43.

[232] W, II, 344.

[233] W, II, 344-45; HM 924. The original passage of March 26, 1846 (J, I, 400-401), was reordered and heightened. The most significant phenomenon was the pond reflecting a summer sky. Thoreau knew from Humboldt that water is sometimes blue when the sky is overcast—that water is self-reflective (J, V, 121). Thoreau spoke of the pond as "a lower heaven" (W, II, 96) and said that the sky underlay the earth (J, III,

100). Reflection also indicated the intimacy of heaven and earth (J, II, 438) and was the first promise of summer (J, IV, 147). The passage might be compared with Rousseau's first night at the Hermitage.

[234] W, II, 348.

[235] W, II, 349; J, III, 108. In HM 924 he crossed out the fact that "it had no mate in the world." The hawk symbolized soaring thought (J, III, 143), and it was compared with the poet—"A hawk's ragged wing will grow whole again, but so will not a poet's" (J, IV, 103).

[236] J, II, 191. See J, XI, 305, 450-51.

[237] W, II, 366-67.

[238] HM 924.

[239] W, II, 359-60. Thoreau frequently used a parable to end a chapter, as in "Economy" and "Higher Laws." The parable of the artist was obviously his own work, full of revisions, with his characteristic pun ["lapse" and "elapsed"], with transparent personal allusions such as the desertion of his friends. Nor did he, always scrupulous in the matter of borrowing, use quotation marks. Though he spelled it in his own way, Kouroo was clearly Kuru, Kooroo, or Curu, the nation that fought the Pandoos in the *Mahabharata,* the sacred land that Arjuna was assigned to protect in the *Bhagavad-Gita.* Thoreau may have first come across it in the *Laws of Menu,* where it is referred to as the country of Brahmanical sages (see *The Dial,* III [Jan., 1843], 332). These Brahmins also carried staves. In writing this passage Thoreau may also have recalled Menu's saying that "from a Brâhmana, born in that country, let all men on earth learn their several usages." In *The Dial* (III, 332) he cited Menu's "The hand of an artist employed in his art is always pure." The section on time and inspiration recalls stanza 11 of his poem on "Inspiration" and a passage in J, III, 279; his remarks on redemption through art recall passages on the art of the American Indians (J, V, 526) and the morality of art (J, III, 30-31). The lesson of the *Bhagavad-Gita*—not the lesson of passivity, but of dis-interested work and contemplation—was already a part of his thought. In a letter to Blake he cited: "'Free in this world as the birds in the air, disengaged from every kind of chains, those who have practiced the *yoga* gather in Brahma the certain fruit of their works. . . . The yogi, absorbed in contemplation, contributes in his degree to creation. . . . Divine forms traverse him . . . and, united to the nature which is proper to him, he goes, he acts as animating original matter.'" In another, he advised work as a higher discipline, "the means by which we are translated." Again he told Blake, "How admirably the artist is made to accom-plish his self-culture by devotion to his art!" And finally, in a letter in which Brahmanical abstraction and work were joined, he advised Blake, "Make your failure tragical by the earnestness and steadfastness of your endeavor, and then it will not differ from success (W, VI, 175, 222, 235). See also J, XII, 344.

Walter Harding (essay date 1962)

SOURCE: "Five Ways of Looking at *Walden,*" in *The Massachusetts Review,* Vol. IV, No. 1, Autumn, 1962, pp. 149-62.

[*In this excerpt, Harding reflects on the variety of reasons why readers enjoy* Walden *and considers five possible ways of reading it; as a nature book, as a practical guide, as satire, as philosophy, and as a model of good prose.*]

Although **Walden** was not exactly a roaring success when it was published in 1854—it took five years to sell out the first edition of only two thousand copies—it has become, in the century since, one of the all-time best sellers of American literature. It has been issued in more than one hundred and fifty different editions—with a number of these editions having sold more than half a million copies each. At this moment it is in print in at least twenty-four different editions in this country alone as well as in English language editions in England, India, and Japan and in translations into French, Spanish, Portuguese, Italian, German, Dutch, Norwegian, Finnish, Swedish, Danish, Czechoslovakian, Japanese, and Sanskrit. What are the causes of this phenomenal popularity?

For the past twenty-one years I have had the good fortune to be the secretary of the Thoreau Society—one of the most unpredictable groups of individualists that has ever united itself around a common enthusiasm. It is the only literary society I know of where the professional teachers of literature are vastly outnumbered by the non-professionals. Among the regular attenders of our annual meetings are a stockbroker, a retired letter carrier, a clergyman, an outspoken atheist, an entomologist, an ornithologist, a music teacher, an archeologist, a poet, a publishing company executive, a printer, a druggist, a socialist organizer, a hardware store owner, a church organist, the author of a book entitled *Why Work?* (each year he gets permission from the local police to sleep on the front porch of the Concord High School), a telephone company executive, a novelist, a conservationist, an exponent of subsistence farming, a women who announces that she "covers the culture front in Brooklyn," a professional mountain climber, a crime expert—the list could go on almost indefinitely. What is even more interesting is that when these people have been asked to state

Photo of Walden Pond, from the site of Thoreau's hut, c. 1908.

why they are sufficiently interested in Thoreau to make the annual journey to Concord—and some of our most regular attenders come from as far away as Quebec, Illinois, North Carolina, and Texas—it is very rarely that two give the same reason. They are interested in his natural history, his politics, his economics, his prose style, his anarchism, his theology, and so on. The most phenomenal facet of Thoreau's appeal—and the appeal of his masterpiece, *Walden*—is its tremendous breadth. *Walden* is read, not for just one reason, but for many.

To most people, I suppose, *Walden* is a nature book. Certainly back at the time of its appearance it was almost universally considered to be a book about natural history, and some of Thoreau's contemporaries were annoyed that he allowed anything but nature to have a part in the book. The lengthy opening chapter on "Economy," they fussed, was a waste of time and should be skipped by the average reader. They also suggested the reader skip over such philosophical chapters as "Where I Lived and What I Lived For," "Higher Laws" and "Conclusion." When Thoreau wrote about ants or loons or muskrats or pickerel or squir-

rels or snow or ice, they argued, he was superb. But, unfortunately, he was all too ready to go off into transcendental nonsense comprehensible only to such "tedious archangels" as Amos Bronson Alcott or to such radical corrupters of idealistic American youth as Ralph Waldo Emerson. But on the birds, the bees, the flowers, and the weather Thoreau could write—and did write superbly. The late 19th Century anthologies of American literature, when Thoreau is included, almost invariably print "The Battle of the Ants" from the "Brute Neighbors" chapter of *Walden* or "The Pond in Winter."

I am not at all trying to belittle Thoreau as a nature writer. I am simply stating that that was his first and widest appeal—and in fact, still is. In the second-hand book stores of our country the dealers more often than not categorize him as a nature writer rather than as a literary figure or a philosopher.

It has been claimed—and I think quite rightfully—that he invented the natural history essay—and certainly his writings are the standard by which all nature writers since his time have been judged. He has successfully avoided the traps so many nature writers fall into of being too cute, too sentimental, too technical, or just plain dull. He never indulges in the pathetic fallacy of attributing human characteristics to the lower classes of animals. Yet neither does he write down to them. He accepts them for what they are and writes about them on their own terms. He writes about them with wit and humor—but the humor is as often at the expense of himself and his fellow man as at the expense of the animal. Take for example that passage near the end of his chapter on "Brute Neighbors" in which he talks about his checker game with the loon on Walden Pond:

As I was paddling along the north shore one very calm October afternoon, for such days especially they settle on to the lakes, like the milkweed down, having looked in vain over the pond for a loon, suddenly one, sailing out from shore toward the middle a few rods in front of me, set up his wild laugh and betrayed himself. I pursued with a paddle and he dived again, but I miscalculated the direction he would take, and we were fifty rods apart when he came to the surface this time, for I had helped to widen the interval; and again he laughed long and loud, and with more reason than before. He manoeuvered so cunningly that I could not get within half a dozen rods of him. Each time, when he came to the surface, turning his head this way and that he coolly surveyed the water and the land, and apparently chose his course so that he might come up where there was the widest expanse of water and at the greatest distance from the boat. It was surprising how quickly he made up his mind and put his resolve into execution. He led me at once to the widest part of the pond, and could not be driven from it. While he was thinking one thing in his brain, I was endeavoring to divine his thought in mine. It was a pretty game, played on the smooth surface of the pond, a man against a loon. Suddenly your adversary's checker disappears beneath the board, and the problem is to place yours nearest to where his will appear again. Sometimes he would come up unexpectedly on the opposite side of me, having apparently passed directly under the boat. . . . Once or twice I saw a ripple where he approached the surface, just put his head out to reconnoitre, and instantly dived again. I found that it was as well for me to rest on my oars and wait his reappearing as to endeavor to calculate where he would rise; for again and again, when I was straining my eyes over the surface one way, I would suddenly be startled by his unearthly laugh behind me. But why, after displaying so much cunning, did he invariably betray himself the moment he came up by that loud laugh? Did not his white breast enough betray him? He was indeed a silly loon, I thought. I could commonly hear the plash of the water when he came up, and so also detected him. But after an hour he seemed as fresh as ever, dived as willingly, and swam yet further than at first.

But so much for Thoreau as a nature writer.

A second appeal of *Walden* is as a do-it-yourself guide to the simple life. I think it highly significant that the first real surge of interest in Thoreau in the twentieth century came during the depression years of the nineteen-thirties when large masses of people—indeed almost all of us—were required willy-nilly by the press of circumstances to adopt the simple life. We had no choice in the matter, but Thoreau was one of the very few authors who not only made this simple life bearable—he even made it appealing. A friend of mine said to me back in the thirties, "You know, Thoreau is the only author you can read without a nickel in your pocket and not be insulted."

What is perhaps more phenomenal than his appeal during the depression years is the fact that in our present era of super-materialism and status-seeking he still continues to make the simple life appealing. Now I am not one who advocates that we all, literally, go out and find our own Walden Ponds, build our own cabins, and ignore civilization. It was only through a profound misunderstanding of the book *Walden* that the idea that such an abandonment of civilization was Thoreau's aim ever got into circulation. He was very careful to say in the first chapter of *Walden*:

I would not have any one adopt *my* mode of living on any account; for, beside that before he has fairly learned it I may have found out another for myself, I desire that there may be as many different persons in the world as possible; but I would have each one be very careful to find out and pursue *his own way,* and not his father's or his mother's or his neighbor's instead.

He himself lived at Walden only two of the forty-four years of his life—roughly about four per cent of his life. He went to Walden Pond to live because he had a specific purpose in mind—the writing of a book that he had found he did not have time to write if he spent his time keeping up with the proverbial Joneses. And when he had finished writing that book (incidentally that book was not *Walden* but its predecessor, *A Week on the Concord and Merrimack Rivers*), he left the pond as freely and as happily as he had gone there.

Thoreau's philosophy of the simple life does not advocate the abandonment of civilized life or a return to the jungle. He simply points out that modern life is so complex that it is impossible for each one of us to embrace all of it. We must of necessity be selective. But unfortunately our standards of selection tend to be imposed upon us by the society we live in rather than based on our own personal interests and desires. We live not our own lives but the lives imposed on us by those who surround us. We keep up with the Joneses instead of ourselves. And when we come to die, we discover that we have not lived. How many of us will be able to say as Thoreau did on his death-bed:

> I *suppose* that I have not many months to live; but, of course, I know nothing about it. I may add that I am enjoying existence as much as ever, and regret nothing.

"And regret nothing." Those are the key words. Are we able to say that honestly of our own lives? Thoreau, when he went to Walden Pond, said that he "wished to live deliberately, to front only the essential facts of life." And because he determined what was the essence of life—not for his parents, nor for his neighbors—but for himself, he was able to say at the end of his life that he regretted nothing.

How then does one get at the essence of life? All of *Walden* is devoted to answering that question. But perhaps we can find it epitomized in a brief quotation from his chapter entitled "Where I Lived and What I Lived For":

> Our life is frittered away by detail. An honest man has hardly need to count more than his ten fingers, or in extreme cases he may add his ten toes, and lump the rest. Simplicity, simplicity, simplicity! I say, let your affairs be as two or three, and not a hundred or a thousand; instead of a million count half a dozen, and keep your accounts on your thumb-nail. In the midst of this chopping sea of civilized life, such are the clouds and storms and quicksands and thousand-and-one items to be allowed for, that a man has to live, if he would not founder and go to the bottom and not make his port at all, by dead reckoning, and he must be a great calculator indeed who succeeds. Simplify, simplify. Instead of three meals a day, if it be necessary eat but one; instead of a hundred dishes, five; and reduce other things in proportion.

> Let us spend one day as deliberately as Nature, and not be thrown off the track by every nutshell and mosquito's wing that falls on the rails. Let us rise early and fast, or break fast, gently and without perturbation; let company come and let company go, let the bells ring and the children cry,—determined to make a day of it. . . . Why should we knock under and go with the stream? . . . Let us settle ourselves, and work and wedge our feet downward through the mud and slush of opinion, and prejudice, and tradition, and delusion, and appearance, that alluvion which covers the globe, through Paris and London, through New York and Boston and Concord, through Church and State, through poetry and philosophy and religion, till we come to a hard bottom and rocks in place, which we can call reality, and say, This is, and no mistake; and then begin, having a point d'appui, below freshet and frost and fire a place where you might found a wall or a state, or set a lamp-post safely, or perhaps a gauge, not a

Nilometer, but a Realometer, that future ages might know how deep a freshet of shams and appearances had gathered from time to time. . . . Be it life or death, we crave only reality. If we are really dying, let us hear the rattle in our throats and feel cold in the extremities; if we are alive, let us go about our business.

A third facet of *Walden* is its satirical criticism of modern life and living. Strangely enough this is one side of Thoreau that is sometimes misunderstood by the reader. Some take everything Thoreau says literally and seriously, ignoring the fact that the book's epigraph reads:

> I do not propose to write an ode to dejection, but to brag as lustily as chanticleer in the morning, standing on his roost, if only to wake my neighbors up.

Even as astute a critic as James Russell Lowell made the rather astounding statement that Thoreau had no sense of humor. And if one does not see Thoreau's humor, he can be assured that he is missing—or worse, mis-reading a major portion of *Walden*.

A large portion of *Walden* cannot—or at least should not—be read literally. Thoreau had a rollicking, witty sense of humor and used it extensively throughout the pages of his masterpiece. He used just about every humorous literary device on record—puns, hyperbole, slapstick, mockery, parody, burlesque, and so on. And just about every one of these devices was used with satirical intent. It is true that now and then he gets off a pun just for the pun's sake—such as that worst—or best—of all puns in the chapter on "The Ponds" where he speaks of the patient but unlucky fishermen at Walden Pond being members of the ancient sect of "Coenobites." (At least one scholarly edition of *Walden* points out in a footnote that a Coenobite is "a member of a religious community," and ignores the pun about the fishermen—"See, no bites.") But such pure puns—if I may call them "pure"—are comparatively rare. Most of Thoreau's humor, as I have said, is directed at the foibles of contemporary society—and is not only directed at them, but hits with a wallop.

Unfortunately humor is almost impossible to demonstrate by excerpts. One of its essentials is that it be seen in context, for it is often its very context that makes it humorous. But let me try a few samples:

> The head monkey at Paris puts on a traveller's cap, and all the monkeys in American do the same.

> One farmer says to me, "You cannot live on vegetable food solely, for it furnishes nothing to make bones with"; and so he religiously devotes

a part of his day to supplying his system with the raw material of bones; walking all the while he talks behind his oxen, which, with vegetable-made bones, jerk him and his lumbering plow along in spite of every obstacle.

I observed that the vitals of the village were the grocery, the bar-room, the post-office, and the bank; and, as a necessary part of the machinery, they kept a bell, a big gun, and a fire-engine, at convenient places; and the houses were so arranged as to make the most of mankind, in lanes and fronting one another, so that every traveller had to run the gauntlet, and every man, woman, and child might get a lick at him. Of course, those who were stationed nearest to the head of the line, where they could most see and be seen, and have the first blow at him, paid the highest prices for their places; and the few straggling inhabitants in the outskirts, where long gaps in the line began to occur, and the traveller could get over walls or turn aside into cow-paths, and so escape, paid a very slight ground or window tax.

If I should only give a few pulls at the parish bell-rope, as for a fire, that is, without setting the bell, there is hardly a man on his farm in the outskirts of Concord, notwithstanding that press of engagements which was his excuse so many times this morning, nor a boy, nor a woman, I might almost say, but would forsake all and follow that sound, not mainly to save property from the flames, but, if we will confess the truth, much more to see it burn.

We are eager to tunnel under the Atlantic and bring the Old World some weeks nearer to the New; but perchance the first news that will leak through into the broad, flapping American ear will be that the Princess Adelaide has the whooping cough.

If excerpting humor is dangerous, analyzing humor is even more so. Humor should stand on its own two legs—or it will fall flat on its face. But I wish to point out once again that Thoreau's humor is not used for its own sake. It is satirical humor and aimed at the reform of existing institutions and customs that Thoreau feels need the reform. And although we laugh at it—or with it—down deep underneath we realize there is often more validity to Thoreau's suggested reforms than to the customs of the society in which we live.

A fourth approach to *Walden* is the belletristic. From a purely technical standpoint, *Walden* is good writing and is worth examining as such. It has been frequently—and quite rightfully—said that Thoreau wrote the first modern American prose. One has only to compare a passage from *Walden* with one from almost any one of its contemporaries to see the differ-

ence. It was the vogue at the time to be abstract, circumlocutory, periphrastic, euphemistic, and euphuistic. *Walden* in contrast is clear, concrete, precise, and to the point. Emerson made the point a century ago when he said:

> In reading Henry Thoreau's journal [and the same can be said of *Walden*], I am very sensible of the vigour of his constitution. That oaken strength which I noted whenever he walked, or worked, or surveyed wood-lots, the same unhesitating hand with which a field-labourer accosts a piece of work, which I should shun as a waste of strength, Henry shows in his literary task. He has muscle, and ventures on and performs feats which I am forced to decline. In reading him, I find the same thought, the same spirit that is in me, but he takes a step beyond, and illustrates by excellent images that which I should have conveyed in a sleepy generality. 'Tis as if I went into a gymnasium, and saw youths leap, climb, and swing with a force unapproachable,—though their feats are only continuations of my initial grapplings and jumps.

Walden, like Thoreau's cabin, is tightly constructed. Each sentence, each paragraph, and each chapter is in its carefully chosen niche and cannot be moved or removed without severe damage to the artistry of the whole. The basic unifying device of the book is the year. Although Thoreau spent two years, two months, and two days at Walden Pond, in writing the book he compressed his adventures into the cycle of one year. *Walden* opens with the cutting down of the pine trees in March and the construction of the cabin through the spring. In summer he moves into the cabin and tends his beanfield. In the autumn he builds his fireplace and warms his house. In the winter he observes his neighbors—human, animal, and inanimate. Then with the breaking up of the ice on the pond and the renascence of spring he brings his book to a close. One of the most interesting facets of Lyndon Shanley's *The Making of Walden* is his revelation of how carefully Thoreau reworked and transposed his sentences to better carry out this theme of the cycle of the year.

Each individual chapter in the book has its set place in the book as a whole. There is a careful alternation of the spiritual and the mundane ("Higher Laws" is followed by "Brute Neighbors"), the practical and the philosophical ("Economy" is followed by "Where I Lived and What I Lived For"), the human and the animal ("Winter Visitors" is followed by "Winter Animals"). Adjacent chapters are tied together by contrast (as "Solitude" and "Visitors"), by chronology (as "The Pond in Winter" and "Spring"), or by carefully worded connective phrases (as after "Reading" he begins "Sounds" with: "But while we are confined to books . . ." Or after "The Bean-Field" he begins "The Village" with: "After hoeing . . ."). And the three major expository chapters ("Economy," "Higher Laws," and

"Conclusion") are placed strategically at the beginning, middle, and end of the book.

Within the individual chapters the details of construction are just as carefully worked out. In "The Ponds" he starts with Walden and then takes a southwestern sweep (his favorite direction for hiking according to his essay on "Walking") across Concord from Flint's Pond to Goose Pond to Fairhaven Bay, to White Pond. In "Former Inhabitants; and Winter Visitors," he starts with the residents of the days of the Revolution, works up through the most recent resident of the area—Hugh Quoil, who died the first autumn Thoreau was at the pond—and ends with those who visited him throughout his stay at the pond. Similar patterns can be worked out for each chapter.

Carefulness of construction continues into the individual paragraph. Although the average reader is not usually aware of it, Thoreau's paragraphs are unusually long. Walden contains only 423 paragraphs, an average of only slightly more than one page in the typical edition. But so carefully developed are they that one does not ordinarily notice their length. Their structure is so varied that there is little point in attempting to pick out typical examples. However, one of his favorite devices is at least worth mentioning—his use of the climax ending. Notice how frequently the final sentence in his paragraphs not only neatly sums up the paragraph as a whole, but usually carries it one step beyond, with an added thrust if the paragraph is satirical, with a broader concept if the paragraph is philosophical. Just as with his chapters, many of Thoreau's paragraphs are independent essays in themselves and can stand alone. But they cannot be moved from their specific niche within the book as a whole without damage to its structure.

Thoreau's sentences too are often unusually long. It takes very little search to find one half a page in length and more than one runs on for a full page and more. But again so carefully constructed are they that the average reader has no difficulty with their syntax and is hardly aware of their complexity. Let me take just one serpentine example from "House-Warming":

> I sometimes dream of a larger and more populous house, standing in a golden age, of enduring materials, and without gingerbread work, which shall still consist of only one room, a vast, rude, substantial, primitive hall, without ceiling or plastering, with bare rafters and purlins supporting a sort of lower heaven over one's head,—useful to keep off rain and snow, where the king and queen posts stand out to receive your homage, when you have done reverence to the prostrate Saturn of an older dynasty on stepping over the sill; a cavernous house, wherein you must reach up a torch upon a pole to see the roof; where some may live in the fireplace, some in the recess of a window, and some on settles, some at one end of the hall, some at another, and some aloft on rafters with the spiders, if they choose; a house which you have got into when you have opened the outside door, and the ceremony is over; where the weary traveler may wash, and eat, and converse, and sleep, without further journey; such a shelter as you would be glad to reach in a tempestuous night, containing all the essentials of a house, and nothing for housekeeping; where you can see all the treasures of the house at one view, and everything hangs upon its peg that a man should use; at once kitchen, pantry, parlor, chamber, storehouse, and garret; where you can see so necessary a thing as a barrel or a ladder, so convenient a thing as a cupboard, and hear the pot boil, and pay your respects to the fire that cooks your dinner, and the oven that bakes your bread, and the necessary furniture and utensils are the chief ornament where the washing is not put out, nor the fire, nor the mistress, and perhaps you are sometimes requested to move from off the trapdoor, when the cook would descend into the cellar, and so learn whether the ground is solid or hollow beneath without stamping.

Three hundred and fifty-one words—and yet I doubt if any attentive student has any difficulty with its meaning. I do not, however, want to give the impression that all of Thoreau's sentences are grammatical leviathans. There are sentences in *Walden* only five words in length. One extreme is as frequent as the other and the majority are of more moderate length. Thoreau understood fully the necessity of variety in sentence structure and length. The point is that he could handle the sentence well no matter what its length.

Perhaps the most noticeable characteristic of Thoreau's word choice is the size of his vocabulary. *Walden* is guaranteed to send the conscientious student to the dictionary. In a random sampling we find such words as *integument, umbrageous, deliquium, aliment, fluviatile,* and *periplus.* Yet Thoreau cannot be termed ostentatious in his word-usage. He simply searches for and uses the best possible word for each situation.

A second characteristic is his allusiveness. On a typical page he may echo a Biblical phrase, quote from a metaphysical poet, translate a few words from an ancient classic, make an allusion to a Greek god, cite an authority on early American history, and toss in a metaphor from a Hindu "Bible." It is true that he is usually careful to make his allusions in such a way that knowledge of the work alluded to is not essential to an understanding of Thoreau's meaning. But the serious reader has his curiosity aroused and wants his questions answered. To satisfy my own curiosity I once took a list of more than fifty different types of figures of speech—allusions, metaphors, rhetorical questions, alliteration, analogy, puns, epanorthosis, parables, similes, meiosis, anti-strophe, oxymoron, epizeuxis, anaphora, litotes, anti-thesis, portmanteau words, metonomy, contrast, personification, epistrophe, synecdoche, irony, apostrophe, hyperbole, and so on— and with no difficulty at all found excellent examples of each one in *Walden*. There is hardly a trick of the trade that Thoreau does not make use of. I think it significant that one of the most recent editions of *Walden*—one in fact published just this past year—is aimed for use as a textbook in college classes in rhetoric and grammar.

A fifth level on which to read *Walden* is the spiritual level. And I would not be exaggerating in the least to say that *Walden* has become veritably a bible—a guidebook to the higher life—for many, many people. In his chapter on "Reading," Thoreau says, "How many a man has dated a new era in his life from the reading of a book!" And *Walden* has been just such a book for many people. I spoke earlier of the fact that many of Thoreau's contemporaries went out of their way to skip over such chapters as "Economy," "Where I Lived, and What I Lived For," "Higher Laws," and "Conclusion." Ironically it is just those chapters which are most essential to *Walden* as a spiritual guidebook. And it is interesting to note that our contemporary anthologies of American literature are tending to print excerpts from those chapters rather than from the natural history chapters that I spoke of earlier.

It is a major thesis of *Walden* that the time has come for a spiritual rebirth—a renewal and rededication of our lives to higher things. It is true that we have progressed a long way from the status of the caveman. But our progress has been for the most part material rather than spiritual. We have improved our means, but not our ends. We can unquestionably travel faster than our ancestors, but we continue to waste our time in trivial pursuits when we get there. We have cut down on the number of hours of labor required to keep ourselves alive, but we have not learned what to do with the time thus saved. We devote the major part of our national energy to devising new means of blowing up the rest of the world and ignore attempts to make better men of ourselves.

Thoreau could hardly be called orthodox from a religious standpoint (or, as a matter of fact, from any standpoint at all), but it is significant to note that one of his favorite texts was "What shall it profit a man if he gain the whole world but lose his own soul?" And *Walden,* on its highest level is a guide to the saving of your own soul, to a spiritual rebirth.

As many recent critics, from F. O. Matthiessen onward, have pointed out, the most frequently recurring symbol in *Walden* from the beginning of the book to the very end is the symbol of rebirth and renewal. The book as a whole, as I have said, is based on the cycle of the seasons ending with the renewal of the earth and its life with the coming of spring. The chapter on "Sounds" follows the same pattern for the day, beginning with the sounds of morning, continuing on through the afternoon, the evening, and the night, and ending with the renewal of the world from its sleep with the crowing of the cock in the morning. Thoreau speaks of the purification ceremonies of the Indians and of the Mexicans. He tells us of the strange and wonderful insect that was reborn out of the apple-tree table after sixty years of dormancy. The very closing words of the book are a promise of a newer and better life that can be achieved if we but strive for it:

> I do not say that John or Jonathan will realize all this; but such is the character of that morrow which mere lapse of time can never make to dawn. The light which puts out our eyes is darkness to us. Only that day dawns to which we are awake. There is more day to dawn. The sun is but a morning star.

How can we approach, how can we achieve such a life? We will find one answer in "Higher Laws":

> If one listens to the faintest but constant suggestions of his genius, which are certainly true, he sees not to what extremes, or even insanity, it may lead him; and yet that way, as he grows more resolute and faithful, his road lies. The faintest assured objection which one healthy man feels will at length prevail over the arguments and customs of mankind. No man ever followed his genius till it misled him. Though the result were bodily weakness, yet perhaps no one can say that the consequences are to be regretted, for these were a life in conformity to higher principles. If the day and the night are such that you greet them with joy, and life emits a fragrance like flowers and sweet-scented herbs, is more elastic, more starry, more immortal,—that is your success. All nature is your congratulation, and you have cause momentarily to bless yourself.

And the second is from his "Conclusion":

> I learned this, at least, by my experiment: that if one advances confidently in the direction of his dreams, and endeavors to live the life which he has imagined, he will meet with a success unexpected in common hours. He will put some things behind, will pass an invisible boundary; new, universal, and more liberal laws will begin to establish themselves around and within him; or the old laws be expanded, and interpreted in his favor in a more liberal sense, and he will live with the license of a higher order of beings. In proportion as he simplifies his life, the laws of the universe will appear less complex, and solitude will not be solitude, nor poverty, nor weakness. If you have built castles in the air, your work

need not be lost; that is where they should be. Now put the foundations under them.

Thoreau is sometimes dismissed as a misanthrope or a skulker, one who devoted himself to carping and criticism. But note that when *Walden* is approached on this spiritual level, it is not negative, it is positive. Thoreau is not so much complaining about the way things are but rather showing the way things might be. He is firmly convinced that the sun *is* but a morning star.

I have approached *Walden* from five different angles. But I have by no means exhausted the number of such approaches. *Walden* can and does mean all things to all men. Therein lies its very strength. It has been tested by time and not found wanting. In its first hundred years it has grown, not diminished in stature. I have no fear as to its being lost sight of in one more century—or two—or three—or four. It will endure.

Thomas Woodson (essay date 1968)

SOURCE: "The Two Beginnings of *Walden:* A Distinction of Styles," in *ELH*, Vol. 35, No. 3, September, 1968, pp. 440-73.

[*In this excerpt, Woodson discusses* Walden *as a dialectical work with beginnings in both the private journal entries for July, 1845, and the public lecture delivered at the Concord Lyceum in February, 1847.*]

> *July 5. Saturday.* Walden—Yesterday I came here to live. My house makes me think of some mountain homes I have seen, which seemed to have a fresher auroral atmosphere about them, as I fancy of the halls of Olympus. I lodged at the house of a saw-miller last summer, on the Caatskill Mountains, high up as Pine Orchard, in the blueberry and raspberry region, where the quiet and cleanliness and coolness seemed to be all one,—which had their ambrosial character. He was the miller of the Kaaterskill Falls. . . .
>
> *July 6.* I wish to meet the facts of life—the vital facts, which are the phenomena or actuality the gods meant to show us—face to face, and so I came down here. Life! who knows what it is, what it does? If I am not quite right here, I am less wrong than before; and now let us see what they will have. . . . (*J* I. 361, 362)[1]

This is the beginning of *Walden,* in that it is the first writing Henry Thoreau did after moving on Independence Day 1845 from his parents' house in Concord, Massachusetts, into the hut he had built during the spring of that year at the side of Walden Pond. In the published *Journal,* it makes an abrupt beginning, because the records of the last three years, since 3 April

1842, are missing.[2] But to the reader of the *Journal* it is perhaps more effective thus, because the entries of 5 and 6 July 1845 so clearly begin a new life, a declaration of independence for the imagination.[3]

These passages have their places in the book Thoreau eventually published in 1854 as *Walden; or, Life in the Woods*. There they are not at the beginning, but embedded in the second chapter, "Where I Lived and What I Lived For." These memories and impressions—this manifesto of integrity and intensity—reappear in new contexts, their primacy submerged.

During his first winter at Walden Thoreau composed a lecture on Carlyle which he read at the Concord Lyceum on 4 February 1846, and published the next year in *Graham's Magazine* of Philadelphia.[4] The audience at the lyceum seemed more interested in his own eccentric behavior—staying the winter out at the pond—than in his comments on an eccentric English writer, and asked for a new and more personal lecture. Probably some time before 13 March 1846 Thoreau confided to his *Journal*: "After I lectured here before, this winter, I heard that some of my townsmen had expected of me some account of my life at the pond. This I will endeavor to give tonight" (*J* I. 485).[5] There is, however, no evidence that he delivered this lecture in 1846, except perhaps a passage in the *Journal* written after 23 December 1845 beginning, "I wish to say something to-night not of and concerning the Chinese and Sandwich Islanders, but *to* and concerning you who hear me, who are said to live in New England; . . ." (*J* I. 395).[6] But there are definite records of a lecture on 10 February 1847, entitled "The History of Myself." While only a fragment of this remains, it is substantially identical with the beginning of the first manuscript version of *Walden,* as identified by J. Lyndon Shanley.[7] The lecture began:

> I should not presume to talk so much about myself and my affairs as I shall in this lecture if very particular and personal inquiries had not been made concerning my mode of life,—what some would call impertinent, but they are by no means impertinent to me, but on the contrary very natural and pertinent considering the circumstances. Some have wished to know what I got to eat—If I didn't feel kind o' lonesome—If I wasn't afraid—What I should do if I were taken sick—and the like. Others have been inquisitive to know what portion of my income I devoted to charitable purposes,—some who have large families, how many poor children I maintained. Some have not come to my house because I lived *there*—Others have come because *I lived* there—and others again, because *I* lived there. (FV, pp. 105-106)

The lecturer assumes that his audience knows where he lived. "Walden," in other contexts a magic word, does not appear. He is more concerned with characterizing his questioners than himself, in spite of his initial modest "presumption" on them. His attitude is confidently retrospective: during the year and a half he had by them spent at Walden he had found answers to their questions, and a strategy through which to express his answers. The apparently casual reference to "income" and "charitable purposes" introduces the real subject of what is to follow: the analysis of "Economy," rather than the promised "The History of Myself."

These, then, are the two beginnings of **Walden:** the journal notes of July 1845 and the lecture of February 1847. There are, of course, earlier scraps of journal which eventually made their way into the book, and there are other indications—a revealing poem of 1838 entitled "Walden," a passage in the early essay "A Winter Walk" using observations from the **Journal** of 1840-1841—of the special importance the pond had held for Thoreau long before he went there to live.[8] In fact, he indicated later in **Walden,** in a rather Wordsworthian reminiscence, the pond had been a "fabulous landscape" for him from early childhood (**W** II. 172; **J** I. 380-381). But the passages I have quoted are the initiation of his literary commitment to the experience which was to become **Walden.**

Critics have called attention with increasing frequency in recent years to what Shanley has called "the two major elements in **Walden:** the story of how [Thoreau] lived at the pond, and the comparison of what he lived for with what many people of New England lived for."[9] Most of the story Thoreau deferred until he had fully established the comparison through the long first chapter, "Economy," one-quarter of the book's bulk. The story therefore really begins in "Where I Lived and What I Lived For." Sherman Paul has explained this structural peculiarity by comparing the sequence from "Economy" to "Spring" and "Conclusion" to that from "Commodity" to "Spirit" and "Prospects" in Emerson's *Nature,* suggesting that Thoreau's dialectic strategy in "Economy" led naturally towards a more direct presentation in later chapters: "He began with surface before he spoke of depth, with the transient rather than the permanent, with complexity before simplicity, disease before health, tradition and routine before the free, uncommitted life—with society and commodity before self and spirit."[10] Joseph Moldenhauer has taken this argument further, contrasting a negative rhetoric and satirical paradoxes in the early chapters to a positive rhetoric and "transcendental" paradoxes later, so that "as the book proceeds, the attack becomes the dance," as the style transforms a corrupt actual society to an ideal purified social harmony.[11] Sharpening the stylistic distinction yet further, Charles Anderson speaks of "two strategies of language, wit and metaphor," which "serve Thoreau as the negative and positive means of his quest." The devices of wit are directed toward cutting

through "the jungle of the world," while Thoreau's "goals themselves and the journey toward them are rendered in an intricate series of image clusters."[12]

Through these critical approaches we begin to see **Walden** as a dialectical work, a typically Romantic nineteenth-century attempt to give form and substance to differing creative impulses within the writer's consciousness. Study of the two beginnings will, I believe, help to refine this view, since the two beginnings exemplify the two basic configurations of style in Thoreau's writing. Through them I shall distinguish a number of relevant polarities: private and public, personal and social, narrative and expository, Walden-directed and Concord-directed, synthetic and analytic, mythopoeic and rhetorical.

I suppose we could call the tone of the private beginning musing or meditative. On 5 July 1845 Thoreau's mind works excursively, from the scene before his eyes to one he remembers from a long walking tour of July and August 1844.[13] His memory of his own experience merges with a literary experience, the halls of Olympus, the mountain residence of the Greek gods. On 6 July his thoughts return to the myth of Olympus, but with both greater generality and greater immediacy. He uses high, philosophical diction ("phenomena or actuality"), concrete visual imagery ("face to face"), and a casually colloquial turn of phrase ("and so I came down here"). In harmonizing these differing stylistic materials he is perhaps most peculiarly American and most particularly himself. (So Melville's Ishmael will expound on the "image of the ungraspable phantom of life," and then abruptly ask: "Who aint a slave?") In the first paragraph of his final version of **Walden,** Thoreau says he is "at present . . . a sojourner in civilized life again." But on 6 July 1845, he asks for an unqualified, absolute "Life!" which is also an unformed, tentative condition, a question mark. His attitude is prospective—he sees himself as about to re-enact the process of mythology, to participate in a story which will both explain and create his life and his world. "Down here," the shores of Walden Pond, is both offhand in manner and portentous in potential meaning, for his deepest intention is to overcome, not merely the "civilized" surrounding world, but the limiting fact of time.[14] At the end of his description of the Catskill farmhouse he says: "It was the very light and atmosphere in which the works of Grecian art were composed, and in which they rest . . . so equable and calm was the season there that you could not tell whether it was morning or noon or evening. Always there was the sound of the morning cricket." In the more generalizing manner of 6 July he says: "Even time has a depth, and below its surface the waves do not lapse and roar." This evocation of an absolute timelessness returns in the next day's entry, as does the sense of participation in a living mythology:

July 7. I am glad to remember tonight, as I sit by my door, that I too am at least a remote descendant of that heroic race of men of whom there is tradition. I too sit here on the shore of my Ithaca, a fellow wanderer and survivor of Ulysses. How symbolical, significant of I know not what, the pitch pine stands here before my door! Unlike any graph I have seen sculptured or painted yet, one of Nature's later designs, but perfect as her Grecian art. There it is, a done tree. Who can mend it? And now, where is the generation of heroes whose lives are to pass amid these our northern pines, whose exploits shall appear to posterity pictured amid these strong and shaggy forms? . . . (*J* I. 363)

A day or so later, he returns more explicitly to the theme of time: "The Great Spirit makes indifferent all times and places" (*J* I. 363).

Thoreau's immediate purpose in living at Walden was, to judge from this evidence, to unite in a single vision the example and the spirit of Greek mythology with images of his own experience—the miller's house on the mountain side, the pitch pine before his own door—and so create the "vital facts" of a new mythology, that of "heroes whose lives are to pass amid these our northern pines." He had much to say elsewhere to confirm this view of his purpose,[15] but I shall limit myself here to a description of the style through which he wished to express this mythopoeic vision.

Here is one sentence from the reminiscence of the Catskill excursion, graphically arranged so as to suggest its developing syntactic and rhythmic patterns.

> I lodged
> 　at the house
> 　　of a saw-miller
> 　　　last summer,
> 　　　　on the Catskill Mountains,
> 　high up as Pine Orchard,
> 　　　　blueberry and
> 　　in the　　　　region,
> 　　　raspberry
> 　　　quiet and
> 　where the　cleanliness and
> 　coolness　　seemed to be all one,—
> 　　which had their ambrosial character.

Quickly subject and verb place the action, anchor it to actual experience; then the series of adverbial modifiers flows forward without interruption, leading the thought forward, like climbing a mountain. Thoreau compares the place he is describing to a local spot (Pine Orchard is probably on Pine Hill, a half-mile southeast of Walden Pond), but the effect is not to return home, but through "high up" to assimilate Pine Orchard to the remoter mountain. The later modifiers spread out, doubling and tripling descriptive adjectives and nouns, reaching out to surround and complete the description, but end with a greater indefiniteness: "seemed to be all one." Finally this sense of unity, only postulated and evoked, becomes "ambrosial," taking the thought back to the "fresher auroral atmosphere" of the previous sentences; Thoreau has illustrated his "fancy" of mythic vitality and eternality through purely naturalistic language, and through a rhythmic syntax which continually rises and enriches itself. The repetitions of sound in parallel descriptive words, "blueberry and raspberry," "quiet and cleanliness and coolness," show no contrivance or calculation—the words follow the thought so naturally and spontaneously that their cumulative poetic effect is noticeable only after the sentence is ended. But most important is the open-endedness of the style; it establishes a direction—towards Olympus—but does not round off or explain the experience it creates. If the "all one" summarizes and centers the style in "ambrosial," it is a momentary centering. Like the pitch pine, the house is there, a "done" house, "a vital fact," but symbolically it is both perfectly calm and finally unknowable.

This style—loose, paratactic, developing, searching, maturing metaphoric identifications out of the organic creativity of an acute, solitary imagination—appears constantly throughout **Walden** (and in everything else Thoreau wrote), but it appears with special importance in the second chapter, "Where I Lived and What I Lived For." This chapter is, as several critics have noted, a second beginning, more explicit than "Economy" about "the ecstasy of discovering a new world,"[16] "preparation for mythic adventure" where Thoreau "begins, in some small ways, to expose his central subject."[17] The journal passages I have been discussing contribute to the preparation; it will be interesting now to see how.

The chapter consists of two parts, an introductory reminiscence of Thoreau's dealings for the Hollowell Farm (the first six paragraphs), and a longer, more complex discussion of what is promised in the chapter title (the following seventeen paragraphs). The Hollowell episode was a late addition, dating from 1852 to 1854,[18] except for its key myth-making idea, for which Thoreau reached back to the Journal of 1840 and 1841: "Wherever I sat, there I might live, and the landscape radiated from me accordingly. What is a house but a *sedes,* a seat?" (*W* II. 90).[19] To a considerable extent the style of the chapter radiates outward from this statement, extending the local and literal into expanding metaphorical suggestions. But the body of the

Hollowell episode delays, wittily and amusingly enough, this generation of symbols. The First Version of 1846-1847, reconstructed by Shanley, helps to reveal how Thoreau wanted to lead from "where" he lived to "what" he lived "for." In it the chapter (as yet untitled and unseparated from the remainder of **Walden**) begins with a brief description of the hut, which soon leads to the miller's house in the Catskills (FV, pp. 137-138). Thoreau cut part of the *Journal* sentence I have analyzed, condensing and tightening it for a more narrative function, but added another comparison to the 1844 excursion written in the same style:

> . . . The pond was like a mountain lake I had seen in the grey of the morning draped with mist, suspended in low weather from the dead willows and bare firs that stood here and there in the water. As the sun arose I saw it throwing off its nightly clothing of mist—and here and there by degrees its soft ripples or its smooth reflecting surface [was revealed]. The mists, like ghosts, were stealthily withdrawing in every direction into the woods, as if from the breaking up of some nocturnal conventicle.—Both place and time had undergone a revolution and I dwelt nearer to those eras in history which had attracted me, and as I had no clock nor watch, but the sun & moon, I also lived in primitive time . . . (FV, pp. 138-139)

This passage is in a somewhat higher key than the one about the miller's house—the fancy of the ghosts and the "conventicle" is more "literary," closer to the American Gothic of Hawthorne's night-time forest scenes—but the emphasis is again on the gradual rhythm of natural unfolding. As in the clause which concluded the earlier sentence ("which had their ambrosial character"), Thoreau's grammar is loose in reference; the flowing parataxis of " . . . and . . . or . . ." takes control; the passive verb ("was revealed") which completes the thought he had to add later when revising.[20] But most important is the sense of auroral revelation as mythical and timeless, absorbing the primitive past into the present moment.

As the chapter proceeds in this first version the theme of auroral timelessness becomes more and more central; more clearly than in the final version, the atmosphere of "quiet and cleanliness and coolness" pervades the writing. For example, here is the first version of the passage on the mosquito, which in the final version is more wittily described as "itself an Iliad and Odyssey in the air, singing its own wrath and wanderings" (*W* II. 98-99):

> In some unrecorded hours of solitude, sitting with door and windows open at very early dawn when the stillness was audible, and the atmosphere contained the auroral perfume I have mentioned, the faint hum of a mosquito, making its invisible

and unimaginable tour through the loaded and drowsy air toward elysian realms, was a trumpet that recalled what I had read of most ancient history and heroic ages. There was somewhat of that I fancy the Greeks meant by ambrosial about it—more than Sybilline or Delphic. It expressed the infinite and everlasting fertility of the . . . world. It was . . . divine. Only Homer could have named it. (FV, pp. 139-140)

Perhaps too much of this "fancy" was lost in the final pruning.

The stylistic emphasis of the July 1845 *Journal* is also confirmed by the placement within the first version of "Where I Lived and What I Lived For" of most of what became "Reading," describing the creative presence of early Greek and Oriental classics, and the first three paragraphs of "Sounds," evoking mornings at the pond "where the atmosphere was perfume & incense, and every sound the key to unheard harmonies" (FV, p. 152). At the end of "Where I Lived" in this first version stands the passage from 7 July 1845: "a fellow wanderer and survivor of Ulysses" (FV, p. 157), revised to contribute to the auroral theme of the whole.

In the published text of "Where I Lived" the journal passages with which I began and the style I have found in them are less immediately prominent. As Thoreau rewrote he made the chapter less personal, less particularized in incident and diction, less explicitly mythological in emphasis. In the later revisions he introduced snatches of quotation from the Chinese and Indian classics and fragments from a couple of earlier English poems, in order to broaden the effect. But more important, he gradually added the public dimension, contrasting his life with more conventional lives, carrying forward the theme of "Economy" into this new context: "That man who does not believe that each day contains an earlier, more sacred and auroral hour than he has yet profaned, has despaired of life, and is pursuing a descending and darkening way" (*W* II. 99). This sentence is a negative counterpart of those I have been examining, in that the "sacred and auroral hour" is passed over, subordinated, to an opposing excursive movement towards "a descending and darkening way." Rather than ascending to the mountain of Olympus at dawn the style descends to the cavern of Hades at evening. Thoreau is quite traditional (even within the epic ambiance of Homer and Milton) through the rest of the chapter in contrasting the "sacred" to the "profane" through the imagery of light and darkness and the rhythm of rising and falling.[21] Similarly the timeless world he found at the pond opposes the demythologized present condition of the town, symbolized by the newspaper, the railroad, the post office. The same style which revealed the infinite fertility of

Walden can also expose the shadowy flimsiness of Concord's prospects in time.

We can see how Thoreau has adjusted the style of the July 1845 journal to the purposes of **Walden** by looking at the famous passage which uses the manifesto of 6 July. Then he exclaimed prospectively: "I wish to meet the facts of life—the vital facts, which are the phenomena or actuality the gods meant to show us—face to face, and so I came down here. Life! . . ." Now he looks backward, but only to move forward again through the whole experience to the present moment:

> I went to the woods because I wished to live deliberately, to front only the essential facts of life, and see if I could not learn what it had to teach, and not, when I came to die, discover that I had not lived. I did not wish to live what was not life, living is so dear; nor did I wish to practise resignation, unless it was quite necessary. I wanted to live deep and suck out all the marrow of life, to live so sturdily and Spartan-like as to put to rout all that was not life, to cut a broad swath and shave close, to drive life into a corner, and reduce it to its lowest terms, and if it proved to be mean, why then to get the whole and genuine meanness of it, and publish its meanness to the world; or if it were sublime, to know it by experience, and be able to give a true account of it in my next excursion. (*W* II. 101)

The first and third of these sentences are syntactically like those of the private beginning: loose, serial, and coordinate, building up parallel clauses and phrases ("to live . . . , to front . . . , and see . . . , and not . . . discover"; "to live . . . , to live . . . , to cut . . . , to drive . . . , and reduce . . ."). The second sentence, and negative aspects of the others, develop the comparison between sacred and profane, ascent and descent. The hesitancy, the teetering effect of combining the rhythms, was already potential in the *Journal,* where Thoreau expressed sober honesty after his initial exclamation, "If I am not right here, I am less wrong than before; and now let us see what they will have." The last sentence begins with a vigorous profusion of concrete, monosyllabic actions (*deep, suck, sturdily, rout, swath, shave*), then descends, only to rise immediately to give a "true account" of itself. This "true account" of "my next excursion" is, as Edwin Fussell argues, "my next book after the *Week*"—**Walden** itself.[22] In this more philosophical, abstract publication of the private beginning, Thoreau fuses the experience of living—simply seeing what the gods meant to show him—with the experience of writing. To write **Walden** is here as prospective and open-ended as to live it.

"Where I Lived" makes the private style into a fuller expression of Thoreau, assimilating his doubts and fears to the ecstasy of his confident quest. But the chapter's purpose is not primarily to make public a private revelation, in spite of abundant indication of rhetoric at work: *I* becomes *we* or a generalized *you*; rhetorical questions lead to extended exhortations ("Let us . . . , Let us . . . , Let us . . ."); these devices engage an apparently broader audience, the citizenry of Concord or the American common reader. Yet Thoreau talks of another audience, an idealized heroic friend with whom he can be completely open: "To be awake is to be alive. I have never yet met a man who was quite awake. How could I have looked him in the face?" (*W* II. 100). Perhaps he is thinking of the gods of Walden. Can he be really talking to himself? The last two paragraphs suggest this. They begin with exhortation, but *we* and *you* give way to a final *I*. The long, sinuous sentence beginning "Let us settle ourselves, and work and wedge our feet downward . . ." finally penetrates the mud and slush of "civilization" to "a hard bottom and rocks in place, which we can call *reality,* and say, This is, and no mistake; and then begin . . ." At the bottom of this descending curve is the simplest statement of truth possible ("This is"); this ending is a new beginning, and leads to a new confrontation: "If you stand right fronting and face to face with a fact, you will see the sun glimmer on both its surfaces, as if it were a cimiter, and feel its sweet edge dividing you through the heart and marrow, and so you will happily conclude your mortal career" (*W* II. 109). Thus the entry of 6 July 1845, its expanded version earlier in the chapter, and the desire to find an awakened friend—all instances of "fronting," of meeting "facts" and "life" directly, "face to face"—all point to a final, essential beginning, which is the last paragraph of the chapter.

This last beginning culminates the series of tentative *essais,* probings of language, which I have been exploring. It begins with "Time" and ends with "here I will begin"; it brings together again the metaphysical problem and the concrete imagery; it combines the descending and ascending rhythms in a tone which is both urgent and oracular:

> Time is but the stream I go a-fishing in. I drink at it; but while I drink I see the sandy bottom and detect how shallow it is. Its thin current slides away, but eternity remains. I would drink deeper; fish in the sky, whose bottom is pebbly with stars. I cannot count one. I have always been regretting that I was not as wise as the day I was born. The intellect is a cleaver; it discerns and rifts its way into the secret of things. I do not wish to be any more busy with my hands than is necessary. My head is hands and feet. I feel all my best faculties concentrated in it. My instinct tells me that my head is an organ for burrowing, as some creatures use their snout and fore paws, and with it I would mine and burrow my way through these hills. I think that the richest vein is

somewhere hereabouts; so by the divining-rod and thin rising vapors I judge; and here I will begin to mine. (*W* II. 109)

These sentences are shorter, but hardly less coordinate and progressive than those we have examined. The flow of thought pauses momentarily at the end of each sentence, the periods slowing the process to a more condensed, momentous measure. There are thirteen sentences; in the first seven a series of *but's* and *not's* create a sense of tension and doubt, the downward rhythm, but with "The intellect is a cleaver" we begin to rise: the copular *is,* used three more times after this, makes the metaphorical identifications the style needs, and mixes beautifully with the other loaded, concentrated verbs—*discerns, rifts, mine, burrow*—to complete the rhythm of ascent.

Most remarkable and daring is how Thoreau's image of burrowing, apparently inappropriate to a "transcendental" paean, contributes to the expansive style of the last four sentences. In adapting the *Journal* passage on the Catskill miller's house he added: "Olympus is but the outside of the earth everywhere" (W. II. 94). That earthiness is as essential as the infinite mystery of the starry sky. Like Keats, who exalted the poetry of earth while he read in the heavens "huge cloudy symbols of a high romance," Thoreau, an Antaeus of poets, searches for the "alphabet" of primal being in the microcosmic world of Walden. As he carries through his symbolic fusion of intellect and instinct he seeks the richest "vein" of earth, suggesting both the body of the wonderfully fertile goddess celebrated in innumerable myths of creation, and the geologically factual world where men use divining-rods to hunt for subterranean water. Divining-rods and "thin rising vapors," moreover, take us beyond the digging of wells and the mist rising from the pond on a summer morning to evoke a magical place, an oracle perhaps—but "more than Sybilline or Delphic"—Olympus itself, where the gods of fact speak directly to him, and he, responding to the sweet edge dividing him through heart and marrow, rifts and cleaves the secret of things to the very center. And so Thoreau arrives "here," at the infinite moment and the infinite place—he announces to himself that his writing has at this point in *Walden* opened the moment of beginning. From "here" on he will open himself to tell of his mythical adventures at the pond. The reader may listen, and overhearing the poet's voice, participate imaginatively in the story.

The public beginning—the lecture of February 1847—presents a quite different style. As I noted earlier, Thoreau there begins by talking about talking about himself: "In most lectures and stories the I, or first person is omitted; in this it will be inserted, that is the main difference" (FV, p. 106); but he keeps his ex-

perience at Walden at a distance, directing his attention to the audience in front of him, putting into his own words their attitudes toward himself. It is clear from what we have seen of the private beginning that the lecture starts indirectly, hiding or at least deferring "life" at Walden. It would be natural for any orator to lead his audience gradually from the familiar to the unfamiliar. Thoreau dwells, as many readers have noticed, with great relish on the familiar, forcing his audience to see themselves through his eyes before he will raise the veil to his private world.

In syntax and rhythm, as well as in substance and diction, there are important differences. Here is the first sentence of the lecture arranged graphically:

I should not presume to talk   about myself

        so much   in this lecture

   particular and

if very   inquiries had not been made

   personal

       concerning my mode of life,—

what some would call impertinent,

but they are   impertinent to me,

     by no means

      natural and

but   very

  on the contrary   pertinent

     considering the circumstances.

There is apparent immediately a dry defensive tone, signaled first by the opening negative clause. This first clause hints, and the rest bears out, that the speaker is choosing his words carefully—perhaps even that he has been backed into a corner and must now coolly talk his way out. The sentence breaks into two main parts, separated by the dash, and each of these in turn into two parts. Each clause is controlled by a key word: *presume, inquiries, impertinent, pertinent;* successively they clarify, with almost syllogistic neatness, the theme of the main clause, Thoreau's talking about himself. To appreciate how the sentence develops we must be unusually sensitive to the meanings of the key words; this is the self-conscious style of a man educated in classical philology, a man who enjoys words and requires that they work effectively for him. This interest in manipulating words is most obvious when the style shocks or jars meanings by stretching words out of their conventional uses; Thoreau is recognized as a master of paradox and pun, as his handling of "impertinent" in this sentence shows. But the pun is not simply a means of keeping the audience's attention, nor a humorous gimmick, as it might be for some platform entertainers. By appealing to the Latin root-meanings of his key words, Thoreau creates his meaning. *Presume* means "to take a position in advance of opposition" (he later revised the first clause to: "I should not obtrude my affairs so much on the notice of my readers . . . ," increasing the formality of the diction, and making the verb mean "to thrust upon unasked"). *Inquiries,* "searchings into," is less aggressive, but is qualified by "particular and personal," balancing *presume* and likening, almost identifying, those who inquire with him who presumes. The first half of the sentence thus shows both sides of a relationship. The second half goes on to explain and justify this social aggressiveness. *Pertinent* means "held firm," and *impertinent,* "not held within the limits of propriety." The sentence becomes a debate between *I* and *some; I* impertinently redefines *impertinent* actions, "considering the circumstances," that is, "what is standing around" (the environment of Walden: another pun), to point wryly to the potential importance of both "inquiries" and "my mode of life." Every word works to reorient the casual curiosity his neighbors had shown into an aspect of his private, mythological adventure. The second half of the sentence thus argues the same balance and harmony as the first. The sentence arrives (more clearly in the final published version) at *pertinent:* it brings us back to a sense of verbal and social propriety, assuaging the audience's fears that they will be led to an immoral end. It suggests the same creative values about Walden as did the private style, but rather than opening a new perspective, it returns to the best social values, closing a superficial and erroneous perspective. This style is as contrived and artful as the other is natural and spontaneous. This style is Thoreau's weapon for conquering the opposition the Concord middle class raised to his "mode of life" at Walden.

The proprieties of public performance made Thoreau more self-conscious than he was in his *Journal*. He had grown up in a quite formal oratorical tradition, and his own personal reserve and shyness increased his need to use language to control his relationship to the audience. His public style lends itself to a variety of implied self-characterizations, or *personae;* in this one he acts as judge, logically discriminating truth from falsehood, interpreting conflicting attitudes according to apparently firmly established rules. Furthermore, he judges an ethical problem through rhetorical analysis: he defends inquiries which "some would *call* impertinent." Thoreau's public style continually looks at words as words, whether directly through defini-

tion (" . . . the cost of a thing is the amount of what I will *call* life which is required to be exchanged for it . . ." [*W* II. 34, my italics]), or indirectly through pun and paradox and the appropriation of the whole vocabulary of "economy" to describe his mythopoeic adventures at the pond.

One of Thoreau's most effective ways of opening an argument forcefully is to redefine familiar words so as to add a new dimension of meaning. **"Civil Disobedience,"** for example, opens with the motto, "That government is best which governs least"; Thoreau restates it: "That government is best which governs not at all," and explains: "Government is at best but an expedient; but most governments are usually, and all governments are sometimes, inexpedient" (*W* IV. 356). Here is the same rhythm, antithesis, balance, and periodic suspension that we have just seen in the movement from *impertinent* to *pertinent;* in **"Civil Disobedience,"** however, the logic moves from positive to negative, leaving behind a dissected sham rather than a restored harmony.

The public style dominates "Economy" and appears constantly throughout **Walden;** there is evidence of it in almost all the essays Thoreau prepared for publication, and frequently in his correspondence and **Journal** as well. Its nimble wit and sharp turns of thought have made him one of the most quotable of American writers. Perhaps his most famous aphorism is the first sentence of the ninth paragraph of "Economy," a passage as representative stylistically as "Time is but the stream I go a-fishing in":

> The mass of men lead lives of quiet desperation. What is called resignation is confirmed desperation. From the desperate city you go into the desperate country, and have to console yourself with the bravery of minks and muskrats. A stereotyped but unconscious despair is concealed even under what are called the games and amusements of mankind. There is no play in them, for this comes after work. But it is a characteristic of wisdom not to do desperate things. (*W* II. 8-9)

The first sentence has gained a fame independent of its context, and such proverbial power that it is familiar to many people who have never read **Walden**. But in the context it is the starting-point of an argument, and "quiet desperation," however brilliant a phrase, serves to lead to "confirmed desperation," "desperate city," "desperate country," "unconscious despair," and, finally, "desperate things." "Quiet desperation" is almost an oxymoron, since *desperation,* a more completed loss of hope than *despair,* implies violent, reckless action. The paragraph repeats this idea five times, as I have listed, but with decreasing intensity. As argument the paragraph develops from "mass of men" to "characteristic of wisdom," overcoming despair finally and restoring the control of common sense and of judicious, temperate awareness. Thoreau anatomizes the psychology of "desperation," penetrating the quiet surface twice by redefinition ("what is *called* resignation . . . ," "what are *called* the games . . ."), and by building toward the pun on "play": true play is true "amusement," and as well "flexibility" or "adaptability" (the "play" of a tree or of a rope), and finally "freedom or room for action"—Walden—which is even synonymous in Thoreau's implied positive context with "drama," his mythological adventure. Games conceal a stereotyped despair, when they might reveal godlike economy. Again the private vision flickers through the wit of the public style.

There is another way the two styles connect here. The third sentence parodies the excursive syntax of the private style, even to the point of hinting that Thoreau's own journey from Concord to Walden is "desperate." Within the total plot of **Walden** "the bravery of minks and muskrats" could anticipate mockingly Thoreau's encounters with woodchuck, loon, pickerel, and hawk—and perhaps it does. Thoreau reminds himself here that "wisdom" comes from the consciousness within (and even from a personal acquaintance with quiet desperation) rather than simply from favorable "circumstances." Dedication must replace "resignation." Hence the need in "Where I Lived" to recreate the atmosphere of myth.

Another instance of Thoreau's public handling of the materials of private myth is the first paragraph of the published **Walden**. This general statement he placed before the revised first sentence of the lecture:

> When I wrote the following pages, or rather the bulk of them, I lived alone, in the woods, a mile from any neighbor, in a house which I had built myself, on the shore of Walden Pond, in Concord, Massachusetts, and earned my living by the labor of my hands only. I lived there two years and two months. At present I am a sojourner in civilized life again.

The first sentence here has the syntactic form of the private style, and, to an extent, it does make an excursion, anchored by the opening subordinate clause, to the solitary achievement at Walden, thus summarizing the theme of the book. But despite the rhythmic expansion from the main clause, "I lived alone . . . ," we arrive at nothing like the ambrosial, Olympian paradise of the private beginning. Even here the mythopoeic syntax is adapted to the theme of "Economy": the sentence ends with "the labor of my hands only," rather than with the burrowing imagination. Even as small a detail as the qualification "or rather the bulk of them" reveals Thoreau's careful, analytic public voice. It is not simply a matter of diction: the "economic" vocabulary is no more concrete or "plain" than that

which aims to "meet the vital facts of life"; it is the direction of thought within sentences and paragraphs that matters most. Here the direction is toward society, a return from the woods to the town: "At present I am a sojourner in civilized life again." He mentions his return because he is now addressing a larger audience than at the Concord Lyceum; he seems to want to assure his readers, as he will do shortly through the pun on "impertinent," that he is now back where a respectable writer belongs. If the reader is satisfied to be reassured . . . fine. But of course "sojourner" and "civilized" are ironic terms. The public style allows Thoreau to play with his tone, to project various *personae*. Here his attitude toward the idea of returning is closer to Poe's extravagant duplicity in *Arthur Gordon Pym* and "Ms. Found in a Bottle" than to, say, what we would find in Washington Irving. As a "sojourner" he is only visiting, passing through town.[23] After lecturing at the Concord Lyceum on the evening of 10 February 1847 he presumably the next morning went back to his cabin at the pond. Likewise, as an essayist on "Economy" he speaks as one more deeply committed to another kind of writing, his private style. That the public style should only indirectly and gradually redefine "civilized life" as the reader knows it is consistent with the rhetorical devices it uses.

This opening paragraph only hints at the spiritual distance between Walden and Concord. Thoreau soon begins to exploit the satiric possibilities of this spatial metaphor. In the second paragraph he makes his famous appeal from "every writer, first or last, a simple and sincere account of his own life." (He slyly follows his own advice not "first" but "last.") He asks for "some such account as he would send to his kindred from a distant land; for if he has lived sincerely, it must be in a distant land to me." In the next paragraph the metaphor reaches full development:

> I would fain say something, not so much concerning the Chinese and Sandwich Islanders as you who read these pages, who are said to live in New England; something about your condition, especially your outward condition or circumstances in this world, in this town, what it is, whether it is necessary that it be as bad as it is, whether it cannot be improved as well as not. I have travelled a good deal in Concord; and everywhere, in shops, and offices, and fields, the inhabitants have appeared to me to be doing penance in a thousand remarkable ways.

This statement combines the moral tone of a Calvinist preacher with a parody of the style the contemporary reader would find in a book of travels to remote nations of the world; Thoreau observes the people of Concord as if they were the "inhabitants" of the Sandwich Islands, applying the self-righteous scorn of a pious missionary who has "travelled a good deal" and seen the pointless "penance" done by superstitious followers of unreasonable religions. He goes on to describe some extreme methods of Oriental self-torturing worship, playing on the Yankee reader's disdain for mystical mumbo-jumbo, but that long sentence of quotation brings him back to the American scene, "which I daily witness." He evokes satirically through the comparison a nightmarish panorama of bodies distorted, cramped into unnatural postures, bent over desks, machines, and plows in the "shops, and offices, and fields" of Concord.[24]

Within this satiric perspective (which continues with rich inventiveness through several more paragraphs) Thoreau's more sober personal tone is still to be detected. When he refers to "you who are *said* to live in New England," his strategy demands a redefinition of "live" and "New" towards the values of Walden. "I have travelled a good deal in Concord" is of course literally true, and suggests a more significant journey than that it parodies. In the rhythm of "what it is, whether it is necessary that it be as bad as it is, whether it cannot be improved as well as not," there is the same posture as in "I did not wish to live what was not life, living is so dear; nor did I wish to practice resignation, unless it was quite necessary." Thoreau applies the same ethical and aesthetic standards to himself and to his private experience that he does to his Concord audience. In this, as in other respects, "Economy" follows the Augustan tradition of satiric honesty. Towards the end of the chapter, he says: "I never dreamed of any enormity greater than I have committed. I never knew, and never shall know, a worse man than myself" (*W* II. 86). This is reminiscent of Pope's verse epistles and moral essays as well as of Huck Finn's reflections on murderers.

But the satirist's interest is not primarily in himself; rather he focuses his vision on the attitudes of men around him, and by dissecting their manners and motives, establishes a means of communicating his sense of a deeper reality to them. This is the function of Thoreau's public style in "Economy," and throughout *Walden*. Later, from the sane and stable voice of the "sojourner in civilized life" he will frequently modulate to the private voice that needs no audience, and no subject but the imagination's contact with the magic solitude of Walden.

In attempting to describe the characteristics of Thoreau's two styles, and of their interaction, I have worked from the most basic critical view of his writing: his two favorite subjects were "Nature" and "Society"; he is remembered as a "poet-naturalist" and as a "social critic"—thus the two legendary acts of his life are his retirement to Walden and his night in Concord jail for refusing to pay a tax. His first editors, his sister Sophia and his friend Ellery Channing, put to-

gether posthumous volumes entitled *Excursions* (1863) and *A Yankee in Canada, with Anti-Slavery and Reform Papers* (1866). Horace E. Scudder, the editor of the first collected edition (Riverside Edition, 1894), placed papers on "aspects of nature" in *Excursions,* and those which showed Thoreau to be "a student of human life, of literature and religion," in *Miscellanies,* adding that *A Week* and *Walden* demonstrate "both sides of his nature."[25] In *Walden* the pairing of chapters illustrates the point simply: "Solitude" and "Visitors"; "The Bean-Field" and "The Village"; "Brute Neighbors" and "House-Warming"; "Winter Visitors" and "Winter Animals."

As Thoreau's stature in American cultural history has steadily increased in recent years, much credit should go to non-literary reasons: he was a pioneer in advocating conservation of natural resources; he was the first to dramatize effectively civil disobedience of unjust laws. Walter Harding has aptly dedicated his biography of Thoreau to Martin Luther King, Jr. and to Edwin Way Teale. But the danger in such affiliations, however justly they honor Thoreau as a great American, is that they divert attention from his greatest accomplishment, his contribution to American literature.[26] Thoreau's truest heirs in twentieth-century America are the poets—Frost, Stevens, W. C. Williams, Robert Lowell—just as his real place in nineteenth-century history is with Wordsworth, Melville, Whitman, and Hopkins, rather than with William Lloyd Garrison and John James Audubon. In his writing what matter most are the creative relationships he elicited between "nature" and "society," and the roles of his two styles in bringing all his experience to a high degree of unity and completeness. And in this, of course, *Walden* is his greatest achievement.

The title page of the First Version reads: "Where I have been / There was none seen . . . Walden or Life in / the woods by Henry Thoreau / Addressed to my Townsmen."[27] The couplet motto, written in cramped pencil, comes from the *Journal,* where it is the terse and cryptic entry for 12 September 1841 (*J* I. 285); now it introduces the book's private theme. The title itself, in ink, clearly looks toward the public beginning in the lecture. The title page of the last manuscript version, some seven years later, drops the couplet and the phrase "Addressed to my Townsmen," but adds two new mottos or epigraphs:

> I do not propose to write an ode to dejection, but to brag as lustily as chanticlere in the morning, standing on his roost, if only to wake my neighbors up. 'The clouds, wind, moon, sun, and sky, act in cooperation, that thou might get thy daily bread, and not eat it with indifference; all revolve for thy sake, and are obedient to command; it must be an equitable condition, that thou shalt be obedient also.' Sadi.[28]

The first motto, which is repeated in "Where I Lived and What I Lived For" (*W* II. 94), announces Thoreau's public purpose on the title page of the first edition. The second was not used there, but is equally appropriate to announce his private purpose; it is quoted from the prefatory prayer in Sheik Saadi of Shiraz's *Gulistan,* a Medieval Persian collection of poetry and prose proverbs and fables.[29]

These two tones, Chanticleer's brag and Saadi's reverent obedience, epitomize Thoreau's two styles, and suggest their origins in ancient literature; Chanticleer gives the common-sense wisdom of proverbs and beast-fables through the voice of the *Eiron,* the witty ironist of classical comedy;[30] Saadi's advice is that appropriate to the mythological hero, centered in a sacred place, whether he be Hercules in the Garden of Hesperides, Adam in Eden, or Thoreau cultivating his imagination at Walden.[31]

Within the closer perspective of nineteenth-century literature, Thoreau's two styles are closely analogous to the two stylistic directions of Wordsworth's *Prelude,* as defined by Herbert Lindenberger: "the poem as personal history and as prophetic utterance." Lindenberger distinguishes at length between the poem's "public voice," which asserts "publicly communicable and valid truths" through "the older rhetoric" (with the Augustan emphasis on decorum and hierarchy in genre, diction and structure), and the poem "as a record of personal, private vision," using a new "rhetoric of interaction" to "reenact the processes of private experience"; this private style creates a sense of "hovering at the edge of something new and unpredictable," as its images of interaction synthesize experience rather than categorizing it according to accepted rules.[32] *The Prelude* differs from **Walden,** in that its public style is "constantly trying to emerge" out of Wordsworth's subjective autobiographical ground-rhythm, while in **Walden** Thoreau's external structure is objective, and moments of private vision emerge out of it. Perhaps we can account simply for this difference from the effect on both writers of their respective initial choices of poetry and prose. Or perhaps the difference indicates a more extreme isolation of Wordsworth from English culture in the 1790's than of Thoreau from American culture in the 1840's. In any case, the similar doubleness of purpose is more important. Although Thoreau could not have read *The Prelude* (published in 1850) until the method of **Walden** had already been formed, he had been familiar with Wordsworth's style in "Tintern Abbey" and *The Excursion* since his college years.

There are interesting analogues also in writers immediately contemporary to Thoreau. In Carlyle's *Sartor Resartus* G. B. Tennyson has found a stylistic "double vision" "in the interchange and struggle of the commonsense Editor with the life and mind of the mystical Teufelsdrökh." He compares Teufelsdrökh's style with "the exploded period of the baroque" "the loose sentence, the outward-flowing infinite a statement"; the Editor, more conservative, writes a sentence "that approaches the classic style" in periodic rhythm, "always tantalizing the reader, leading him on through thicket and byway, so that the reader is both participant and pursuer."[33] Similarly, Jonathan Bishop, in his discussion of Emerson's style, uses a distinction between the moral and aesthetic dimensions of Emerson's concept of the Soul: Emerson's diction and tone deal with an audience, "a world containing at least [a speaker and his] listener, a world of moral behavior," proper to the prophet, preacher, or reformer. Rhythm and metaphor, however, are more "primitive, . . . [reflecting] most directly the fundamental mode of action . . . of the organic faculty," and of the poetic imagination and isolated intellect, "purified by separation from society and contact with nature."[34] It would distort Bishop's argument to see distinctly two styles, though there are places, such as the final section of *Nature,* where Emerson calls on the voice of an "Orphic poet" to express what his usual lecturing voice cannot express. Further, Howard J. Waskow, exploring Whitman's "habit of mind," discovers "indirection" and "direction" as dialectical counterparts within the "bipolar unity" of Whitman's poetic theory. A poem of pure indirection "would represent the poet as careless of the reader, turned neither toward him nor away from him . . . And this poem would have as its focus a list of things: the poet would concentrate on the teeming life of the universe, his subject requiring no pointing to hidden meanings because meanings are in the things, and will be spontaneously sensed by the reader." Such a poem, "in its search to reach the unknown world from the perspective of the material world, . . . would focus upon action, motion, the development of things." The contrasting style, "direction," Waskow continues, leads toward "two radically different forms—toward didacticism, the issuance of verdicts, and description, the making of observations." Since these are tendencies rather than set verbal patterns or models, a single work may contain both: "Out of the Cradle Endlessly Rocking" lies "between suggestion and statement, indirection and direction": it is a narrative in which the poet's stance "describes an action but is at the same time turned toward the reader."[35] Waskow thus accounts for the central position this poem, along with **Walden,** occupies within the development of American and nineteenth-century literary history.

It seems likely that the source of these stylistic distinctions in all these writers is a sense of cleavage between private and social imaginations inherent in the Romantic cast of mind and announced first by Jean-Jacques Rousseau in the 1750's. Rousseau evolved the theory, from his *Discourse on Inequality* onward, of a conflict between man's absolute being, natural and innocently animated by *amour de soi,* and man's being relative to others, conditioned and corrupted by society and an invidious *amour-propre.*[36] By implication the highest and purest literary style is free of social ties; Rousseau contributes a seminal motive to Romantic style when he says, in the first of the *Rêveries d'un Promeneur Solitaire,* that while Montaigne wrote personal essays to be read only by others, he has written his *Rêveries* only for himself.[37] To conceive of style thus as a reflexive process rather than as transitive to other participants in language is heresy to eighteenth-century thinking about rhetoric, and also to most of those reviving the study of rhetoric in our time; we can accuse Rousseau of disingenuousness in this, but his experiment in isolating style from audience has become a fascinating and compelling ideal to many Romantic and modern writers, Henry Thoreau not the least among them. It seems fair to see the pressure of this ideal behind Sir Herbert Read's distinction of styles according to "the two directions of psychic energy which Jung has called 'extraversion' and 'introversion.'"[38] Rousseau may even be the ultimate cause of Kenneth Burke's definition of the "New Rhetoric" as one of "identification" rather than persuasion, though of course the main direction of Burke's thinking insists on the social dimension of all language.[39]

Among Thoreau's contemporaries the most outspoken proponent of distinguishing reflexive from transitive styles is John Stuart Mill. In an essay called "What is Poetry?," published in 1833, Mill extends some aesthetic ideas of Wordsworth and Coleridge to make clear, if extreme, distinctions between poetic, narrative, descriptive, and eloquent writing. These distinctions are not grammatical or formal, but intuitive and psychological, as befits Romantic assumptions. Mill's definitions of poetry and eloquence are particularly relevant to Thoreau:

> Poetry and eloquence are both alike the expression or uttering forth of feeling. But . . . eloquence is *heard*, poetry is *over*heard. Eloquence supposes an audience; the peculiarity of poetry appears to us to lie in the poet's utter unconsciousness of a listener. Poetry is feeling confessing itself to itself, in moments of solitude, and bodying itself forth in symbols which are the nearest representations of the feeling in the exact shape in which it exists in the poet's mind. Eloquence is feeling pouring itself forth to other minds, courting their sympathy, or endeavoring to influence their belief, or move them to passion or to action . . .[40]

Although these ideas may be eccentric to the Anglo-American critical tradition, they are related to DeQuincey's later theory of the literatures of knowledge and power, and to Pater's literatures of fact and of the sense of fact.[41] They are also supported by W. B. Yeats and T. S. Eliot.[42]

More immediately important for my purpose is an observation by Edward Tyrell Channing, Boylston Professor of Rhetoric at Harvard from 1819 to 1851, and Thoreau's instructor from 1835 to 1837. In his lecture "Literary Tribunals," read to Seniors at Harvard over many years, Channing takes a strikingly "modern" view (considering the American cultural lag) of the "causes of obscure communication of thought." Granting the persuasiveness of Dr. Johnson's faith in the common sense of the common reader as the best criterion for judging literature, Channing nevertheless defends the writer who appears obscure to the multitude:

> Let us suppose a retired, abstracted person, ever pondering remote truths, and fond of studying man in general by profound and severe researches into his own mind. Perhaps he lights suddenly upon principles and, in his happy contemplation of them, he does not dream how hard it may be to bring them within the comprehension of minds that have not his activity and grasp, or that quick sensibility which makes hints luminous and expands them readily into full dimension . . . Of one thing we may be very sure, that a writer of this character little troubles himself to learn whether he shall have an audience. It is enough for him that he has thoughts which must be followed out and in some ways recorded, though the toil be solitary and his conceptions be doomed to a long obscurity. Possibly the interpretation may come, and he can wait as patiently for it as the world.[43]

Channing is as responsive to Coleridge's view of literature as to Johnson's. But he is not a radical. In his lecture "A Writer's Preparation" he counsels against the notion that a young writer can attain originality by becoming a hermit and isolating himself completely from books and men: "There is good reason to think that the mind may be made as feeble in its whole character by turning perpetually upon itself and refusing help or impulse from abroad, as by immersing itself in books and resting in the thoughts and reports of other men."[44] Thoreau's public style shows his acceptance of this advice, and his private style must have been encouraged by Channing's liberal and eclectic views on evaluation. If Channing's attitude had been shared by the American literary establishment and reading public in the 1850's, neither **Walden** nor *Moby-Dick* would have suffered from popular neglect.

But environment and temperament did conspire to make Thoreau a lonely writer: those critics who emphasize the extreme intensity of his private quest and the extreme aggressiveness of his public stance certainly speak for the majority of his readers.[45] Early in his **Journal** he copied his own laborious translation of selections from Goethe's *Torquato Tasso,* a portrait of the archetypal Romantic poet:

He seems to avoid—even to flee from us,—
To seek something which we know not,
And perhaps he himself after all knows
  not . . .
His eye hardly rests upon the earth;
His ear hears the one-clang of nature; . . .
His mind collects the widely dispersed,
And his feeling animates the inanimate . . .
He seems to draw near to us, and remains
  afar from us:
He seems to be looking at us, and spirits,
  forsooth,
Appear to him strangely in our places. (J I.
  4-5)

He rarely wavered from this characterization in his many comments on poetry and style throughout his career. It is, moreover, remarkable to notice in surveying Thoreau's comments how much he says about private style and how little about public style. Conversely, a survey of criticism reveals that the public style has absorbed his readers' interest (*qua* style, and not symbolism, which is another thing), and the private style is hardly recognized. Some of his best readers have collapsed the distinction, arguing that his extreme Romantic idealization of style evaporates its substance, while his practice shows a frustrated attack on and exhortation of the reader because of his inadequacy to his own ideals.[46] This explanation is psychologically plausible, perhaps, but I hope to have shown that the stylistic facts give Thoreau more credit.

Thoreau's comments on his private style emphasize its expansive movement, the internal energy by which it transforms the language of men into a new expressive perspective. Here is a provocative early definition from the *Journal* of 1841: "We should offer up our *perfect* thoughts to the gods daily—our writing should be hymns and psalms. Who keeps a journal is purveyor for the Gods. There are two sides to every sentence; the one is contiguous to me, but the other faces the gods, and no man ever fronted it. When I utter a thought I launch a vessel which never sails in my haven more, but goes sheer off into the deep."[47] This is in the same vein as the manifesto of 6 July 1845: "I wish to meet the facts of life—the vital facts, which are the phenomena of actuality the gods meant to show us—face to face, and so I came down here." Thus Walden Pond becomes the concrete symbolic realization of Thoreau's desire every time he puts pencil to paper. Similarly, in *A Week* he speaks of moments when "the common train of my thoughts" gives way to a more creative process: "But a steep, and sudden, and by these means unaccountable transition is that from a comparatively narrow and partial, what is called common-sense view of things, to an infinitely expanded and liberating one, from seeing things as men describe them, to seeing them as men cannot describe them" (*W* I. 412-413).

This passage occurs toward the end of the *Week,* and is part of an effort both to summarize and to elevate the themes of that book. The same effort occurs in *Walden,* in the last two chapters, "Spring" and "Conclusion." In "Conclusion" Thoreau comes again to the question of the ideal style. This is the well-known paragraph on "extra-vagance," which has been read as his explanation of his rhetorical aggressiveness—his desire to exaggerate satirically in order to wake up his complacent neighbors[48]—but is essentially an invocation of his personal "genius," another pledging of his imagination to the infinite expectation of the dawn, directed first to an ideal, god-like companion and only secondarily to the men of Concord. This is the paragraph:

> It is a ridiculous demand which England and America make, that you shall speak so that they can understand you. Neither men nor toadstools grow so. As if that were important, and there were not enough to understand you without them. As if Nature could support but one order of understandings, could not sustain birds as well as quadrupeds, flying as well as creeping things, and *hush* and *whoa,* which Bright can understand, were the best English. As if there were safety in stupidity alone. I fear chiefly lest my expression may not be *extra-vagant* enough, may not wander far enough beyond the narrow limits of my daily experience, so as to be adequate to the truth of which I have been convinced. *Extra vagance!* it depends on how you are yarded. The migrating buffalo, which seeks new pastures in another latitude, is not extravagant like the cow which kicks over the pail, leaps the cowyard fence, and runs after her calf, in milking time. I desire to speak somewhere *without* bounds; like a man in a waking moment, to men in their waking moments; for I am convinced that I cannot exaggerate enough even to lay the foundation of a true expression. Who that has heard a strain of music feared then lest he should speak extravagantly any more forever? In view of the future or possible, we should live quite laxly and undefined in front, our outlines dim and misty on that side; as our shadows reveal an insensible perspiration toward the sun. The volatile truth of our words should continually betray the inadequacy of the residual statement. Their truth is instantly translated; its literal monument alone remains. The words which express our faith and piety are not definite; yet they are significant and fragrant like frankincense to superior natures. (*W* II. 356-357)

Much in the style of this passage is rhetorical and public: the opening sentences are undeniably contentious, through their punning repetition of "under-standing"; the references to natural objects and creatures are aphoristic, generalized, and exemplary; the word "extra-vagance" is an etymological redefinition, as is "exaggerate" (to "heap up" a number of facts in order "to lay the foundation of a true expression").[49] But the subject is experience and truth, not opinion and persuasion. At its conclusion the paragraph reaches out, in the manner of Thoreau's first writing at Walden, in pious prayer to the gods ("superior natures"), to create the ambrosial character, "significant and fragrant like frankincense," proper to the timelessness of myth. Thus the paragraph uses both styles to provide a rationale for the whole book's personal and mythic foundation.[50]

Most recent criticism has agreed that *Walden's* structure is controlled by the cycle of the seasons, and rounded off complete by "Spring" and "Conclusion." The cycle is thus a circle, the argument runs, and the mental excursion to "The Ponds" returns symmetrically to its rhetorical starting-point. "Conclusion," then, is most like "Economy" in openly addressing the townsmen of Concord and their fellows throughout mid-nineteenth-century America.[51] But I contend that the extra-vagant mythopoetic style, wandering far beyond the narrow limits of daily experience, is still working at the end, making "Conclusion" a sly misnomer for a new beginning. In his essay "Walking" Thoreau explicitly dismisses the circle as the right symbol to express his experience: "The outline which would bound my walks would be, not a circle, but a parabola, or rather like one of those cometary orbits which have been thought to be non-returning curves, in this case opening westward, in which my house occupies the place of the sun" (*W* V. 217). In "Conclusion" a similar geometric image of the infinite appears, in a sentence which starts rhetorically but rises to the expansive rhythm of the private style: "Start now on that farthest western way, which does not pause at the Mississippi or the Pacific, nor conduct toward a worn-out China or Japan, but leads on direct, a tangent to this sphere, summer and winter, day and night, sun down, moon down, and at last earth down too" (*W* II. 354-355). And at a similar moment in "Spring" Thoreau makes clear that in spite of his plumbings and mappings the real bottom of Walden Pond is still a mystery: "At the same time that we are earnest to explore and learn all things, we require that all things be mysterious and unexplorable, that land and sea be infinitely wild, unsurveyed and unfathomed by us because unfathomable" (*W* II. 350). Thoreau is no Oriental mystic with a Yankee accent. As a modern western man he requires both the rational impulse to analyze and communicate knowledge to other rational beings, and the poetic impulse to free himself from the limitations of rationality, to create and express an "infinitely wild" world out of the spacious resources of his imagination.

Thus "Conclusion" both concludes and begins. *A Week* lost coherence because Thoreau allowed his fascination with style as mythopoeic exploration too large a role; in Walden Pond he found a centering symbol, but one whose fluid nature allowed an open-ended struc-

ture in sentence, paragraph, chapter, and whole. In the last pages of both *A Week* and *Walden* Thoreau alludes to rising, flooding waters, an apocalyptic hint that the writer as myth-maker must always "make it new" (*W* I. 413-414, *W* II. 366). In the last sentences of *Walden* paradox gives way to mythic suggestiveness, to the same tone and style, now on a cosmic scale, that Thoreau needed on 5 July 1845 to express the "fresh auroral atmosphere" of Walden Pond: "The light that puts out our eyes is darkness to us. Only that day dawns to which we are awake. There is more day to dawn. The sun is but a morning star" (*W* II. 367).

These are sentences "launched sheer off into the deep," facing the gods. *Walden* ends with the rebirth of "Spring," the restoration of natural process, but it also begins a supernatural birth which is at once as frequent as the sunrise and as precious and essential as the Myth of Creation. Like Whitman Thoreau opens himself to the unrealized future of his people and his land, and *Walden* stands as an archetypal American book. The audience at the Concord Lyceum on a February night in 1847 heard part of the story, but only part; the whole story includes the solitary drench of light Thoreau felt early on a July morning at the pond. He finally won the struggle to make the hidden side of that prospective sentence take form in words.

Notes

[1] Citations from Thoreau's *Writings* are from the Walden Edition (20 vols.; Boston, 1906), cited as W; the *Journal,* eds. Bradford Torrey and Francis H. Allen (14 vols; Boston, 1906), is cited as J.

[2] What remains of this part of the Journal is in manuscript in the Houghton Library, Harvard, and the Huntington Library; fragments were published by F. B. Sanbors in *The First and Last Journeys of Thoreau* (Boston, 1905). See Ethel Seybold. *Thoreau: The Quest and the Classics* (New Haven, 1951), pp. 44-45, and Perry Miller, *Consciousness in Concord: The Text of Thoreau's Hitherto "Lost Journal" (1840-1841), with Notes and a Commentary* (Boston, 1958), pp. 19-20.

[3] The first manuscript page of the 5 July 1845 entry is photographically reproduced in "A Centenary Gathering for Henry David Thoreau," *Massachusetts Review,* VI (1962), 153, and in the expanded republication of the "Centenary Gathering," John H. Hicks, ed., *Thoreau in Our Season* (Amherst, Mass., 1966), p. 49. The entry's heading has been normalized in the published *Journal;* it reads *literatim:* "Walden Sat. July 5th—45." The first word, "Walden," is larger than the others; it dominates the page.

[4] "Thomas Carlyle and His Works," *Graham's Magazine,* XXX (March 1847), 145-152, and (April 1847),

238-245; revised version, W IV. 316-355. Walter Harding, "A Check List of Thoreau's Lectures," *Bulletin of the New York Public Library,* LII (1948), 80.

[5] See J. Lyndon Shanley, *The Making of Walden with the Text of the First Version* (Chicago, 1957), pp. 18-19. Shanley's text is cited as FV.

[6] This passage was not added to *Walden* until the Third Version, composed in 1848-1849; see Shanley, p. 72.

[7] F. B. Sanborn's two-page typewritten transcript of the beginning of the lecture, entitled by him "Thoreau at the Concord Lyceum," is published in Harding, "A Check List of Thoreau's Lectures," 80. This text is identical with FV, pp. 105-106, from "I should not presume . . ." through "If I wasn't afraid?" The Sanborn typescript is noted by Viola C. White, "A Check List of Thoreau Items in the Abernathy Library of Middlebury College," Reginald L. Cook, *The Concord Saunterer* (Middlebury, Vt., 1940), p. 76. See also Walter Harding, *The Days of Henry Thoreau* (New York, 1965), pp. 187-188.

[8] J I. 50-51; W V. 174-176; Miller, *Consciousness,* pp. 185-186, 194-198.

[9] Shanley, p. 19.

[10] Sherman Paul, *The Shores of America: Thoreau's Inward Exploration* (Urbana, Ill., 1958), p. 301.

[11] Joseph J. Moldenhauer, "*Walden:* The Strategy of Paradox," *The Thoreau Centennial* ed. Walter Harding (Albany, N. Y., 1965), pp. 26-27.

[12] Charles R. Anderson, "Introduction" to *Walden* in *American Literary Masters,* eds. Charles R. Anderson et al. (New York, 1965), I. 628. Another way of developing this line of argument would be to suggest that Thoreau's two strategies make *Walden* a mixture of "anatomy" and "confession," two genres of imaginative prose described by Northrop Frye, *Anatomy of Criticism* (Princeton, 1957), pp. 307-314.

[13] Although Thoreau's journal of this excursion seems not to have survived, he used another incident from it, his account of climbing Mt. Greylock in western Massachusetts, in *A Week on the Concord and Merrimack Rivers* (W I. 189-200). His companion in the Catskills, William Ellery Channing the younger, apparently left some records; see Harding, *The Days of Henry Thoreau,* pp. 171-172.

[14] Georges Poulet summarizes incisively Thoreau's attempt to "transmit an eternal richness" to the present moment by making memory a "prospective motion" from past to present, in "Time and American Writers,"

an Appendix to *Studies in Human Time* (Baltimore, 1956), pp. 334-337. See also a more general statement of Poulet's argument in his "Timelessness and Romanticism," *Journal of the History of Ideas,* XV (1954), 3-22.

[15] Thoreau is perhaps most explicit about his intentions as a maker of myths in his *Journal* (esp. J III. 85-86, 98-99; J. V. 135), although there are also important statements in *A Week* (W I. 58-61), and "Walking" (W V. 232-236), and elsewhere. F. O. Matthiessen uses the "fellow-wanderer and survivor of Ulysses" passage in his seminal discussion of Thoreau as mythmaker in *American Renaissance* (New York, 1941), p. 647.

[16] Paul, *The Shores of America,* p. 324.

[17] Lauriat Lane, Jr., "On the Organic Structure of *Walden,*" *College English,* XXI (1960), 197.

[18] Shanley, pp. 72-73.

[19] See J I. 244 and Miller, *Consciousness,* p. 151.

[20] In Shanley's text bracketed words indicate later revisions of the First Version: Shanley, p. 105.

[21] On the distinction of "sacred" and "profane," see Jonathan Bishop, "The Experience of the Sacred in Thoreau's *Week,*" *ELH,* XXXIII (1966), 66-91.

[22] Edwin Fussell, *Frontier: American Literature and the American West* (Princeton, 1965), p. 218.

[23] The ironic meaning of "sojourner" has been noticed by Fussell, *Frontier,* p. 198; by John C. Broderick, "The Movement of Thoreau's Prose," *American Literature,* XXXIII (1961), 136; and by D. Gordon Rohman, "An Annotated Edition of Henry David Thoreau's *Walden,*" unpubl. diss. (Syracuse, 1960), p. 63; Rohman suggests that the word has "the most direct connection (however ironic its usage) with the Puritan and Biblical senses of contingency . . . still thoroughly alive in the orthodox churches and evangelists' vocabulary." It thus introduces the parody of a missionary preacher's report which follows in the next paragraph. Thoreau uses "sojourner" without irony later in "Economy": "The very simplicity and nakedness of man's life in the primitive ages imply this advantage, at least, that they left him but a sojourner in nature. When he was refreshed with food and sleep, he contemplated his journey again" (W II. 41).

[24] There is a remarkably similar image in the third paragraph of the first chapter of Melville's *Moby-Dick:* " . . . But these are all landsmen; of week days pent up in lath and plaster—tied to counters, nailed to benches, clinched to desks . . ." In reaction to this

cultural paralaysis, Thoreau's sojourner, like Melville's Ishmael, feels "an everlasting itch for things remote."

25 Horace E. Scudder, "Introductory Note," to Henry David Thoreau, *Miscellanies* (Boston and New York, 1894), p. vii.

26 In 1856 Thoreau wrote: "My work is writing, and I do not hesitate, though I know that no subject is too trivial for me, tried by ordinary standards; for, ye fools, the theme is nothing, the life is everything" (J IX. 121). In 1873 Ellery Channing wrote: "No writer more demands that his reader, his critic, should look at his writing as a work of art . . . Thoreau considered his profession to be literature, and his business the building up of books out of the right material . . ." (*Thoreau the Poet-Naturalist,* ed. F. B. Sanborn [Boston, 1902], pp. 30, 49).

27 Shanley, p. 11; also in Sanborn's typescript of the lecture MS quoted by Harding, "A Check List of Thoreau's Lectures," 80.

28 Shanley, p. 13.

29 Thoreau quotes Saadi again at the end of "Economy" (W II. 87-88). These two quotations are among the transcriptions from James Ross's translation of the *Gulistan* (London, 1823) which he copied into his "Literary Notebook" during the mid-1840's. See *Thoreau's Literary Notebook in the Library of Congress: Facsimile Text,* ed. Kenneth Walter Cameron (Hartford, Conn., 1964), pp. 344-347. Emerson apparently introduced Thoreau to the *Gulistan* in 1843; see *The Correspondence of Henry David Thoreau,* eds. Walter Harding and Carl Bode (New York, 1958), p. 149. Emerson later wrote a preface to the first American edition of the *Gulistan,* published in Boston by Ticknor and Fields in 1865.

30 Thoreau's role as *Eiron* is noticed by Moldenhauer, "*Walden:* the Strategy of Paradox," p. 23.

31 Emerson wrote in *The Conduct of Life,* "The hero is he who is immovably centered" (*Complete Works,* ed. Edward Waldo Emerson [Boston, 1903], VI. 277); in an unpublished note for his essay "Thoreau," he identified Thoreau with this quality (*Complete Works,* X. 617). Karl Kerenyi, introducing the "archetypal character" of the mythological hero, quotes Emerson's dictum approvingly (*The Heroes of the Greeks* [New York, 1960], p. 3). This is one of many instances where Thoreau and Emerson, through their study of classical and Oriental literatures, anticipate twentieth-century attitudes toward the nature and function of myth.

32 Herbert Lindenberger, *On Wordsworth's Prelude* (Princeton, 1963), "Foreword" and Chapters I-III, esp.

pp. xiii, 3-5, 43. On Wordsworth's public and private voices in *The Prelude,* and Thoreau's intuitive discovery of "the Wordsworthian relation of poet and nature," see Geoffrey H. Hartman, *Wordsworth's Poetry, 1787-1814* (New Haven, 1964), pp. 168-170.

33 G. B. Tennyson, *Sartor Called Resartus: The Genesis, Structure, and Style of Thomas Carlyle's First Major Work* (Princeton, 1965), pp. 284-285, 247-249.

34 Jonathan Bishop, *Emerson on the Soul* (Cambridge, Mass., 1964), pp. 78, [108], 112, 117. All of Part II, "The Soul's Emphasis," is relevant.

35 Howard J. Waskow, *Whitman: Explorations in Form* (Chicago, 1966), pp. 63-67. All of Part I, "Whitman's Habit of Mind," is relevant.

36 See Henri Peyre, *Literature and Sincerity* (New Haven, 1963), pp. 85-86, 108-109, and J. H. Broome, *Rousseau: A Study of His Thought* (New York, 1963), pp. 39-40, 49.

37 Jean-Jacques Rousseau, *Oeuvres Complètes* eds. Bernard Gagnebin and Marcel Raymond (Paris, 1959-), I. 1001. On Rousseau's private and public styles, see Broome, pp. 183-207, esp. the analysis of two contrasting passages in the fifth *Rêverie,* pp. 205-207. Rousseau's stylistic fusing of his consciousness with the waters of the Lac de Bienne is remarkably like some of Thoreau's passages on his life at Walden. On Rousseau's fifth *Rêverie* see also Poulet, *Studies in Human Time,* pp. 169-170.

38 Herbert Read, *English Prose Style,* rev. ed. (Boston, 1952), p. 84, and Part II *passim.* Read is referring to C. G. Jung's *Psychological Types* (London, 1938).

39 Kenneth Burke, "Rhetoric—Old and New," in *New Rhetorics* ed. Martin Steinmann, Jr. (New York, 1967), p. 63. Burke's early thinking, following Marxist assumptions, insisted that "effective literature could be nothing but rhetoric," that is, manipulation of an audience (*Counter-Statement,* 2nd ed. [Chicago, 1957], p. 210), but later he announced that his *Rhetoric of Motives* would be followed by *A Symbolic of Motives,* in which a thing's "identity" would be studied as "its uniqueness as an entity in itself and by itself," presumably isolated from its effect on an audience or observer (*A Grammar of Motives and A Rhetoric of Motives* [Cleveland, 1962], p. 545). But Burke's *Language as Symbolic Action: Essays on Life, Literature, and Method* (Berkeley and Los Angeles, 1966) is not at all what he proposed as *A Symbolic of Motives:* he has made an important shift of terminology, arguing now that "viewed from the standpoint of 'symbolicity' in general, Poetics is but one of the four primary linguistic dimensions. The others are: logic, or grammer; rhetoric, the *hortatory* use of language, to induce

cooperation by persuasion and dissuasion; and ethics" (p. 28). Burke's essay "I, Eye, Ay—Concerning Emerson's Early Essay on 'Nature' and the Machinery of Transcendence" (pp. 186-200) is a good example of how the rhetorical dimension continues to dominate his thinking. (This essay is also published in *Transcendentalism and Its Legacy,* eds. Myron Simon and Thornton H. Parsons [Ann Arbor, 1966], pp. 3-24.)

Historians of rhetoric such as Hoyt H. Hudson and Wilbur Samuel Howell have argued for the continuing validity of Aristotle's distinction of rhetoric from poetics, a distinction which Burke and the "new" rhetoricians have effectively collapsed. Hudson states the claims of the tradition succinctly: "The writer in pure literature has his eye on his subject; his subject has filled his mind and engaged his interest, and he must tell about it; his task is expression; his form and style are organic with his subject. The writer of rhetorical discourse has his eye upon the audience and occasion; his task is persuasive; his form and style are organic with the occasion" ("The Field of Rhetoric," *Historical Studies of Rhetoric and Rhetoricians,* ed. Raymond F. Howes [Ithaca, N.Y., 1961], p. 13). Howell criticizes Burke from the perspective of the history of theory in "Rhetoric and Poetics: A Plea for the Recognition of the Two Literatures," *The Classical Tradition: Literary and Historical Studies in Honor of Harry Caplan,* ed. Luitpold Wallach (Ithaca, N.Y., 1966), pp. 374-390. Burke's reply to Howell, "Rhetoric and Poetics" (*Language as Symbolic Action,* pp. 295-307), is revealing.

[40] [John Stuart Mill], "What is Poetry?," *The Monthly Repository* (January, 1833), reprinted in *Mill's Essays on Literature and Society,* ed. J. B. Schneewind (New York, 1965), pp. 109-110.

[41] Wilbur Howell argues this development from Mill to DeQuincey to Pater in "Rhetoric and Poetics: A Plea for the Recognition of the Two Literatures."

[42] "We make out of the quarrel with others, rhetoric, but of the quarrel with ourselves, poetry" (W. B. Yeats, "Per Amica Silentia Lunae," *Mythologies* [London, 1959], p. 331. "The first voice is the voice of the poet talking to himself—or to nobody. The second is the voice of the poet addressing an audience, whether large or small . . ." (T. S. Eliot, "The Three Voices of Poetry," *On Poetry and Poets* [New York, 1957], p. 96).

[43] Edward T. Channing, *Lectures Read to the Seniors in Harvard College* (Boston, 1856), pp. 157-159. For an account of Thoreau's rhetorical training, see Christian P. Gruber, "The Education of Henry David Thoreau, Harvard, 1833-1837," unpubl. diss. (Princeton, 1953), Chapter VIII, "Thoreau under Channing: An Author's Apprenticeship."

[44] Edward T. Channing, *Lectures,* p. 196.

[45] On private intensity, see esp. Perry Miller, "Thoreau in the Context of International Romanticism," *New England Quarterly,* XXXIV (1961), 147-159; on public aggressiveness, see esp. Albert Gilman and Roger Brown, "Personality and Style in Concord," *Transcendentalism and its Legacy,* pp. 87-122.

[46] Charles Feidelson, Jr., *Symbolism and American Literature* (Chicago, 1953), p. 137: "This hostility [to "men of science"] affects [Thoreau]; his writing, explicitly or by implication, is always polemic and never, as he doubtless would wish, blandly indifferent to the assumptions of the enemy." Walter J. Ong, "Personalism and the Wilderness," *Kenyon Review,* XXI (1959), 299: "Thoreau withdrew into himself (or into the *Journals,* which was the same thing), only in order surreptitiously to communicate his isolation to others . . . the two-year 'isolation' at Walden turned out to be no less than a public address to the entire world."

Walter Harding claims that "constant critical analysis" of his lectures by "keen-minded audiences" made Thoreau's prose style "less pedantic and more human," leading him away from introverted writing and obscurity like that of such later writers as James Joyce: "The Influence of Thoreau's Lecturing upon His Writing," *Bull. New York Pub. Lib.,* LX (1956), 79; see also Harding, *The Days of Henry Thoreau,* e. g., pp. 211, 228, 236. But lyceum audiences were typically interested only in light and uplifting lectures, and were hardly "keen-minded"; Thoreau's comments on his audiences do not indicate that he learned much from their criticism; see, for example, J VII. 79-80, J XI. 327-328, and Vern Wagner, "The Lecture Lyceum and the Problem of Controversy," *Jour. Hist. of Ideas,* XV (1954), 119-135.

[47] Miller, *Consciousness,* p. 212; see also pp. 151, 153.

[48] See, for example, Joseph Wood Krutch, *Henry David Thoreau* (New York, 1948), pp. 274-276, and Moldenhauer, "*Walden*: The Strategy of Paradox," pp. 16-20.

[49] Of course Thoreau also uses frequently another, more conventional and purely rhetorical kind of exaggeration; for example, this from "Economy": "There is a certain class of unbelievers who sometimes ask me such questions as, if I think that I can live on vegetable food alone; and to strike at the root of the matter at once,—for the root is faith,—I am accustomed to answer such that I can live on board nails. If they cannot understand that, they cannot understand much that I have to say" (W II. 72).

[50] Compare to Thoreau's concept of extra-vagance this theory of Philip Wheelwright: "In regard to all

really important affairs where some degree of valuation and emotional commentary enters, we instinctively recognize the inadequacy of strictly logical forms of speech to do justice to our full intended meanings; and we endeavor by tone of voice, facial expression, and gesture, as well as by choice and arrangement of words, to break through the barriers of prescribed definition and express, no doubt inadequately, the more elusive elements in the situation and in our attitude towards it . . . I am suggesting that in this occasionally spontaneous out-reach beyond the conventional and formal properties of language we are perhaps coming somewhat closer to the conditions of primitive utterance (how close we cannot know) than in our more logical declarations and inquiries" ("The Semantic Approach to Myth," *Myth: A Symposium,* ed. Thomas A. Sebeok [Bloomington, Ind., 1958], p. 100).

[51] Krutch, p. 117; Broderick, "The Movement of Thoreau's Prose," 133-142; Moldenhauer, "Images of Circularity in Thoreau's Prose," *Texas Studies in Literature and Language,* I (1959), 245-263, esp. 261-263; Melvin E. Lyon, "Walden Pond as Symbol," *PMLA,* LXXXII (1967), 289-300, esp. 299-300.

Charles R. Anderson (essay date 1968)

SOURCE: "The Web," in *The Magic Circle of Walden,* Holt, Rinehart and Winston, 1968, pp. 13-92.

[*This excerpt deals with* Walden's *style and structure, which Anderson claims is both circular and web-like.*]

Walden is a unique book. There is nothing quite like it in literature. Though it made its way slowly at first, after publication in 1854, by the turn of our century it had found a small but ardent audience. This has been steadily increasing and will probably continue to do so in the future because, once "discovered," it has proved to be a book with unusual drawing power. It may never be widely popular, but it attracts devotees of many kinds in addition to those with a zeal for literature. Reading it is always an unforgettable experience, and what is chiefly remembered is its uniqueness.

Readers of the general sort, as well as more specialized students and critics, have difficulty in deciding exactly what type of book it is. One reason is that Thoreau's masterpiece does not fit easily into any standard literary genre—novel, drama, poem, or lesser categories like autobiography and informal essay. This has been both a curse and a boon. For many years the problem of identification kept *Walden* hovering outside the great house of world literature, a sort of country cousin. Now, at last admitted, there is still some apprehension about where it fits in. But, as ample

compensation for this lack of definition, every reader faces a fresh challenge: to define the quality of its greatness without benefit of a label. As a result *Walden* will undoubtedly remain a controversial book, constantly subjected to reinterpretation—a fate Thoreau would have welcomed.

It has already been approached from a variety of angles, with a resulting enrichment of its meaning. But each of them has tended to be partial, that is, incomplete, for the very reason that it reflects the specific slant of the critic instead of taking the book on its own terms. Those who read it as social criticism find the last half largely irrelevant. Those who assume it to be a book about nature find little in the first half to hold their interest. If one takes it as autobiography, he is constantly losing track of the story line. If it was the program for a new and better economy of living, why did Thoreau give up his experiment after two years and return to civilization?

The one point common to all these divergent approaches has been their concern with style, an agreement that the distinction of *Walden* may lie more in its manner than its matter. But this concern has not usually been pursued beyond a general eulogy. Perhaps it is through language that all the seemingly disparate subjects of this book are integrated into wholeness. Commenting in "Higher Laws" on the limited success of literal fishermen at Walden Pond who are content with a mere string of fish, Thoreau says they have not yet found "the hook of hooks with which to angle for the pond itself." (236) Would style be the hook of hooks, or rather the net with which to catch the whole book? Why not try an entirely new approach and read *Walden* as a poem—the transformation of a vision into words, designed so as to contain and reveal it?

That Thoreau thought of himself primarily as a poet is clear from many comments in his *Journal*. One of his first entries, just four days after he began keeping it in 1837, strikes this keynote:

> In his own magic circle wanders
> The wonderful man, and draws us
> With him to wander, and take part in it. . . .[1]

These are Goethe's lines in praise of Tasso as the representative poet. Copied down in the *Journal* that was to become the record of Thoreau's quest for truth and for a way of life, they stand as the dedication of his career and a prophetic description of his one great book. If communication can be achieved without losing integrity, Goethe seemed to promise, the problem of the self and society, the poet and his audience, can be resolved. The artist's magic circle is both the inviolable privacy of his creative life and the enchanted world he creates in his art.

Ambrotype of Thoreau at age forty-four.

Walden was to be such a "world," foreign to normal eyes until the reader is drawn into its circle by the poet's magic language to wander with him and take part in his wonderful experience. Thoreau did care deeply about reaching an audience, despite his protests to the contrary and his strict refusal to compromise with the public. His mode of communication was decided on early, as recorded in the quotation from Goethe's definition of the poet. Fifteen years later in this same **Journal,** just a month after he had taken up again the manuscript of **Walden** and was driving it through to completion, he expressed concern that his writing was becoming too factual and commonplace. Then he concluded, rounding out the quotation from Goethe: "I see that if my facts were . . . transmuted more into the substance of the human mind,—I should need but one book of poetry to contain them all."[2]

The years in between, 1837-1852, comprise the main period of Thoreau's creative life. And of all his writings his "one book of poetry" can only be **Walden** (1854). He composed a good deal of verse, mostly in the early years, but no one, the author included, would offer this as his claim to distinction. The only other book published during his lifetime, **A Week on the Concord and Merrimack Rivers** (1849), is generally

considered a trial run. During his last decade, a period of diminished creativity, his sole productions were those miscellaneous essays later to be collected and issued as **Cape Cod, The Maine Woods,** and other posthumous volumes, distinguished only in flashes. Thoreau's present high literary reputation, if it is to be sustained, must be pinned on a single book—plus the extraordinary **Journal.**

Yet the question as to whether **Walden** is a created work of art—the central one if he is to be ranked with authors like Melville and Dickinson—has with few exceptions been approached gingerly, then quickly dropped. It has style, all agree, then they rest content with quoting a few aphorisms and an occasional sentence that gleams like an Emersonian nugget. And it does have a kind of structure, some have claimed less confidently: the chapters swing loosely around the cycle of the seasons—surely not a very original or impressive unifying device. Or, as others have pointed out, the sequence of essays may seem casual but it is knit together by transitional sentences and paragraphs— that is to say, the Harvard freshman has passed his rhetoric and composition course. After such perfunctory gestures in the direction of literature, the whole question has usually been left hanging in the air while admirers of **Walden** turn to other matters which they consider more important. It was the prime American protest against materialism; it has been the bible of poor scholars and a handbook for prophets of freedom; it furnishes a calendar of the rural year for nature lovers. This is all well and good, but how does it bring the author into the circle of literary immortals any more than do Caesar's *Commentaries* or Lincoln's *Gettysburg Address?*

To call **Walden** a poem is not to say that its best passages should be extracted and rearranged as free verse, or to suggest the flowery vagueness associated with the hybrid term "prose-poem." What is needed is not a vocabulary for praising Thoreau's style but a technique for reading his masterpiece. To discover a way into the heart of **Walden** one should begin by trying for a new definition that will justify the analogy with poetry. What fittest name can be found for a book which is this, that, or the other thing, yet none of them exactly? It can be likened to a work of fiction, since it is an imaginative projection of setting, characters, and "action," although from known bases in fact. But how does this make it a poem when most fiction is prose, in essence as well as in form? The great majority of novels, such as *Vanity Fair* and *The Deerslayer,* are simply straightforward narratives whose meanings are made manifest in the resolution of their plots, though as created works of art even these rise above the prosaic level of exposition. But there are some fictions of a very different sort, much closer to the mode of poetry, like *The Scarlet Letter.* Hawthorne's meanings are revealed by indirection and irony, by dramatic scenes and ambiguous symbols. Melville, after adapting all these techniques to his own purposes, adds yet another dimension. Starting from personal experiences, he transforms them into mythical quests (in lieu of conventional plots)—simply in *Typee,* more complexly in *Moby-Dick.* Finally, the autobiographical story can find expression in outright poetry, like the blank verse of Wordsworth's *Prelude,* when inward exploration instead of outward narrative is the author's real subject.

These analogues, drawn from the writings of Thoreau's contemporaries, suggest ways in which his masterpiece also can be thought of as poetry rather than prose, if one does not insist on the mechanical distinction of verse as opposed to paragraph form. *Walden* employs all the above techniques and more besides. To read it as a poem is to assume that its meaning resides not in its logic but in its language, its structure of images, its symbolism—and is inseparable from them. Exploring it in these terms, one finds that the social satire and the naturalist's observations are literary counters, just as "autobiography" is the author's effective mask. In this way the reader can avoid being taken in by the pretended subjects (like the argument against railroads) and so discover the true poetic subjects (like the meaning of solitude). The book has long been recognized as both a negative and an affirmative one, but the definition of these two aspects and the emphasis accorded them depend on the approach. Its dual purpose has generally been taken to be merely the rejection of an economy of abundance in favor of a simple natural life. Viewed instead as a poem, *Walden* reveals itself as an experience recreated in words for the purpose of routing the World altogether and discovering the Self. Its real theme is the search for perfection, for a life of holiness, though it is certainly not rendered in Christian terms. Thoreau's own words state the paradox. In a letter of December 1852, at the very period when major revisions were transforming *Walden* from a factual to a symbolic book, he said: "My writing at present is profane, yet in a good sense, and, as it were, sacredly, I may say; for, finding the air of the temple too close, I sat outside."[3]

Two modes of language, wit and metaphor, serve Thoreau as the negative and positive means of his quest. These set up the direction of the book and open out its multiple contrasts. Not only are society and solitude juxtaposed but the civilized and the primitive, complexity and simplicity; also matter and spirit, animal faculties and the higher laws, earth and heaven, nature and God. Man cannot achieve his high aims by rejecting the one and leaping into the other, but must work his way up from the sty of materialism to the perfection he seeks. His weapons for cutting through the jungle of the world include the whole arsenal of wit: puns, understatement, extravagance, irony, verbal surprise, parody, satire, and paradox. The goals themselves and the journey toward them are rendered in an intricate series of image-clusters: animal, leaf, food and shelter, the imagery of time, the quest or journey, the cocoon, the circle, and so on.

The overall structure of *Walden* may be likened to that of both a circle and a web. The spider's web is too geometric, but it will serve as a useful analogy to begin with. Walden Pond lies at the center as a symbol of the purity and harmony yearned for by man, though unattainable. Radial lines of wit run out from this, cutting across the attractions of the purely pragmatic or sensual life. And these radials are looped with circle after concentric circle of aspiration toward the ideal life of heaven—which is also mirrored in the central pond. But Thoreau was too much a poet to be content with a mechanical design. These figures—the spider's web and the formal Euclidian circle—are suggestive merely. Like the orientals he sought an asymmetrical pattern that would satisfy the esthetic sense of form and still remain true to the nature of experience, art without the appearance of artifice.

The circle in *Walden* is less the obvious cycle of the seasons than a number of subtly suggested circular figures, overlapping as well as concentric. (This design is treated fully in a later chapter.) The web is but another name for the intricate lines of relationship that shape the total structure. But all are so woven together that the whole vibrates when any part is touched, and the ultimate motion is toward circumference. Few works of the creative imagination are more successfully unified. Few have their meaning more embedded in a complex pattern of words. *Walden* is a poem, though rendered in the guise of prose.

The interweaving of wit and metaphor in Thoreau's introductory chapters, "Economy" and "Where I Lived," is the subject of the ensuing pages.

Wit

No book aimed at heaven ever took its start more humbly from the earth than this one. It begins with a seemingly prosaic essay on the basic necessities for maintaining physical life. Instead of considering this irrelevant, Thoreau knows it is the only way to jolt his contemporaries out of the conviction that the affairs of this world leave no time for the other. Without establishing the contrary he cannot possibly expect a hearing for his own story, whether his audience consists of men who lead lives of economic desperation or lives of complacent prosperity in the best of all possible worlds. (The early 1850's was the period of greatest prosperity in America prior to the Civil War.) So his first gambit is to slay the dragon Materialism. After feinting a head-on encounter, his actual mode of assault is a series of skirmishes to prove that the monster of mid-century is a chimera, a product of the sociological imagination, and so to rout it with laughter.

The opening gun in his battle of wit is fired in the very title of his long introductory chapter, "Economy." Readers a century ago knew what to expect, or thought they did. Either the latest defense of the capitalistic system, according to such a book as John Stuart Mill's compendious *Political Economy;* or the newest revolt against it, advocating a communal sharing of profits, for the alert few who had read Karl Marx's *Manifesto.* Both were published in 1848. Both were rationalistic schemes based on faith in materialism as the only way to achieve the greatest happiness of the greatest number, opposed as their solutions were. But Thoreau's "Economy" takes Communists as well as Utilitarians by surprise, attacking where they think themselves least vulnerable. He undermines their assumption that abundance for all is the only goal and substitutes his own program for reducing the necessaries of life to a minimum. He replaces their panaceas for the common man with a Spartan discipline for the uncommon man. His is no treatise on how to acquire possessions but a sprightly fable on how to do without them. Since the age had been filled with solemn discussions of the economic problems facing an over-populated world, what Carlyle called the "dismal science," Thoreau also pretends to adopt the logical form of an expository essay with beginning, middle, and end. But this is merely an outward show of "argument."

Feeling the need to condition his audience before unleashing his novel attack, he allows himself a few preliminary pages of wit to accomplish this. In a first brief paragraph setting forth the purpose of his book, to recount his experience in living apart from the world, he employs a deliberate confounding of scale. Here is no long self-exile in the desert to commune with God, like that of Elijah, nor even a modern Crusoe retiring to an exotic island half a world away in the South Seas. Instead, like a straightfaced Yankee, he tells how he walked a mile and a half out of his native village, squatted in a friend's woods, and lived there alone for two years. Having returned home satisfied with his experiment, he concludes abruptly: "At present I am a sojourner in civilized life again." Such is the laconic summary of the central drama in his life, the autobiographical core of his masterpiece.

Next, in explaining why he obtrudes his private affairs on the public, he indulges in his first pun, a learned one. It is in answer to persistent inquiries by the villagers as to his mode of life, he says, "which some would call impertinent." (3) By bringing into play the Latin root of this adjective, he complicates its meaning: to be impertinent is to be rude only because it is

not pertinent, that is, not relevant. But the desire of normal men to understand abnormal behavior seems to him "very natural and pertinent." This leads to his ironic understatement in apologizing for the autobiographical cast of what is to follow: "In most books, the *I*, or first person, is omitted; in this it will be retained; that, in respect to egotism, is the main difference." Such is his justification for the most self-obsessed book in the history of American literature. But the third paragraph extends this "I" to global dimensions by the language of surprise: "I have travelled a good deal in Concord." (4) And his fellow townsmen become universal men by shock metaphors, compared in their unending labors to the Greek Hercules and in their penitential lives to Brahmans. By the end of page two the reader has been launched from the simple to the complex, from local and particular to archetypal experience.

The rest of the introductory pages of "Economy" crackle with word play, aphorisms, and satirical anecdotes—the weapons of his negative mode of attack. Things are encumbrances; wage-earners are worse off than southern Negroes because self-enslaved: "The better part of the man is soon plowed into the soil for compost." (6) Since the old are no good as mentors, each man must start from scratch: "One generation abandons the enterprises of another like stranded vessels." (12) And occasionally his affirmative goal shines through in a witty image: "As if you could kill time without injuring eternity." (8) At the end of nine or ten pages the reader is presumably convinced that he has not been on the road to the good life, in any sense, and has been joked out of his resignation to his present desperate status as something inescapable. He is now ready for a serious discussion of economy. Instead, the author first gives him a low-comedy pun. One advantage of his withdrawal from the civilized way of life, he says, has been to learn what are the "grossest groceries." (13)

With such a starter, only the dullest reader would expect a treatise on the dismal science when Thoreau at last gets down to business with the basic necessaries of life: "Food, Shelter, Clothing, and Fuel." These are quickly reduced to two, since food is only internal fuel and shelter an extension of clothing; then to one, since the purpose of all is to retain vital heat, that is, life. Yet these are the necessaries men devote their whole lives to acquiring in order that they may begin to "live." The magnitude of the problem is deflated by two kinds of wit: comic exaggeration of the folly of abundance, ironic reduction of man's actual needs to a minimum. The latter is used for the more basic matters of food and shelter, the former for the lesser items of fuel and clothing.

A few striking examples will indicate the manner of his argument. "The luxuriously rich are not simply kept comfortably warm, but unnaturally hot," he says; "they are cooked, of course, *à la mode*". (15) The costly new-fangled furnace for central heating, here alluded to, would naturally be a subject for travesty by the man whose advice to anyone shivering from cold was to take a brisk walk. Again, the old adage that clothes make the man offered an easy target for caricature: "Dress a scarecrow in your last shift, you standing shiftless by, who would not soonest salute the scarecrow?" (24) The pun on "shiftless" is obvious, but the more subtle one in the previous sally should not be missed either; "cooked" originally meant simply baked at a high temperature (as in terra cotta), then was later applied to the preparation of food (à la mode). The surface reader of *Walden* will miss much of the humor of its word play.

Even when Thoreau begins his discussion with apparent seriousness he invariably ends with a fillip. For example, after equating "animal life" with "animal heat," by showing scientifically that both are maintained by a kind of slow internal combustion, he concludes: "disease and death take place when this is too rapid; or [when] for want of fuel, or from some defect in the draught, the fire goes out." (14) Again, in the midst of six pages of satire on clothes as false symbols of status, ransacking history and ethnology for outrageous examples, he interrupts himself with what pretends to be a sensible solution, but is swiftly turned into a paradox: "It is desirable that a man be clad so simply that he can lay his hands on himself in the dark." (26-27)

Shelter is a more serious problem. But the idea that it is just a roomier kind of overcoat gave him a chance to ring a new change on the fig-leaf origin of clothing in relation to the primal "tree house," both of which man found ready-made in Eden: "Adam and Eve, according to the fable, wore the bower before other clothes." (30) Next, alluding to the New Testament, he indulges in a mild bit of blasphemy. "I think that I speak within bounds when I say that, though the birds of the air have their nests, and the foxes their holes, and the savages their wigwams," he begins; then, as a substitute for the promised subversion of "the Son of Man hath not where to lay his head,"[4] he concludes with housing statistics of a sort familiar today: "in modern civilized society not more than one half the families own a shelter." (33)

Next, on the assumption that he has been too extravagant in building himself a whole cabin, one room ten by fifteen feet, he invents a classic example of *reductio ad absurdum:* "I used to see a large box by the railroad, six feet long by three wide, in which the laborers locked up their tools at night; and it suggested to me that every man who was hard pushed [for a house] might get such a one for a dollar." This is Thoreau's solution for the staggering problem of housing man-

kind. Of course, it is just a ruse for playing off one extreme against another. In acquiring a dwelling one must exercise a little Yankee shrewdness, he says, "lest after all he find himself in a workhouse, a labyrinth without a clue, a museum, an almshouse, a prison, or a splendid mausoleum instead." Then after an amusing elaboration of the tool-box shelter, which he decides not to buy, he brings himself up with a halt: "I am far from jesting. Economy is a subject which admits of being treated with levity, but it cannot so be disposed of." (31-32) This likewise is a dodge. What follows merely substitutes for the raillery applied to lighter matters, such as fuel and clothing, a devastating satire on men as housebuilders, with a running comparison of wigwam and mansion. Here he calls on the whole range of modes from parody to invective, then concludes on a more serious note. Primitive man, as a tent-dweller, had the advantage of being a "sojourner in nature," he says: "We . . . have settled down on earth and forgotten heaven." (41) Wit blends into metaphor as his theme shifts from negative to positive.

Food, on the other hand, is rarely subjected to Thoreau's artillery, whether light or heavy, perhaps because he thought of it as the one indispensable necessity, many animals maintaining life by this alone. And if food is the basic tie of man to his mortal life, it has also been made paradoxically a symbol of his hope for immortality. The normal use of food in *Walden* is for images that approach the sacramental, the finest example being subtly compounded with wit. As he sits down to his elemental meal during house building, he pushes his economy to the last detail and with unanswerable consistency. "I usually carried my dinner of bread and butter," he says, "and read the newspaper in which it was wrapped, at noon, sitting amid the green pine boughs which I had cut off, and to my bread was imparted some of their fragrance, for my hands were covered with a thick coat of pitch." (46-47) With water from the pond, which he drank almost ritualistically, this would suggest a kind of outdoor Eucharist, but he contents himself here with a suggestion of incense from nature's resin.

An advocate of vegetarianism, though not a fanatic on the subject, he rebukes the meat-eaters with a parable:

> One farmer says to me, "You cannot live on vegetable food solely, for it furnishes nothing to make bones with"; and so he religiously devotes a part of his day to supplying his system with the raw material of bones; walking all the while he talks behind his oxen, which, with vegetable-made bones, jerk him and his lumbering plow along in spite of every obstacle. (10)

But Thoreau goes a long step beyond vegetarianism. After reducing his regular diet by wit to the barest minimum, he answers unbelievers by declaring: "I can live on board nails. If they cannot understand that, they cannot understand much that I have to say." (72) Readers expecting a plausible essay on food economy will be certain to call this exaggerated. He meets the objection by saying that he is only afraid he "cannot exaggerate enough," that being the very style he is aiming at. "I fear chiefly lest my expression may not be *extra-vagant* enough, may not wander far enough beyond the narrow limits of my daily experience, so as to be adequate to the truth of which I have been convinced." (357) This truth is the central quest of *Walden,* the vision of which forced him into the license of poetry in order to be able to express it. To clarify, he divides the word into its two Latin components: *Extra vagance!* "Going beyond" is one of the chief stylistic devices of both the wit and the poet. And for expressing his aspiration to live in the spirit alone, "board nails" is an appropriately extravagant term for total fasting.

The long discussion of basic economies, which forms the ostensible core of his introductory chapter, is broken right in the middle by what any economist would brand as a digression—a shower of images for his own "enterprises" after the minimum necessities have been obtained. This deliberate breaking of the rational order is proof enough that his "argument" is really an antistructure, and it points up the essentially negative purpose of the whole chapter on "Economy." There is an alternative to materialism, he says. Instead of becoming a slave to the acquisition of superfluities, it is time for man "to adventure on life now, his vacation from humbler toil having commenced." (17) At this first sounding of the affirmative note he shifts from wit to metaphor as his principal mode, though the dozen rockets that are shot off in rapid succession are an ingenious fusion of the two. All are images of the poet's vocation, in contrast to the normal trades and professions: "self-appointed inspector of snow storms," "surveyor of forest paths," "reporter to a journal of no very wide circulation" (his own *Journal,* circulated only to intimates, eventually filled fourteen volumes), and so on. (19-20)

The cluster of images begins with a cryptic symbol of what he is still in quest of: "a hound, a bay horse, and a turtle-dove," (18) which has baffled critics so far in spite of numerous attempts to explicate it. (Thoreau's own commentary, in a letter, scarcely clarifies it.)[5] He ends with an extended conceit for authorship, as a commerce with the "Celestial Empire," (22-23) developing his analogy from the contemporary China trade by an elaborate system of word play that leads from earth to heaven. This is the organizing pun of the whole chapter, suggesting the need of a spiritual economy. The passage comes to focus in a statement that flatly denies he was making an economic experiment in the normal sense of that term: "My purpose

in going to Walden Pond was not to live cheaply nor to live dearly there, but to transact some private business with the fewest obstacles." (21)

This private business, as planned in advance, was to write his first book, *A Week on the Concord and Merrimack Rivers.* Then, as he wandered in that magic circle, came the impulse to create another book, his masterpiece, which would record the actual experience of living the poet's life. The practical lesson he wanted to learn from economy was how to be a nonselling author and survive. This central "enterprise" is rendered in *Walden* by the fable of an Indian basketweaver who came to town to sell his creations and was dismayed to find that he would have to create a market for them also, or else make something that white men already wanted to buy. Thoreau, remembering the failure of *A Week,* learns from the Indian's experience by extending the metaphor to his own productions:

> I too had woven a kind of basket of a delicate texture, but I had not made it worth any one's while to buy them. Yet not the less, in my case, did I think it worth my while to weave them, and instead of studying how to make it worth men's while to buy my baskets, I studied rather how to avoid the necessity of selling them. (21)[6]

The spiritual lesson to be learned from his residence at the pond was even more important: how "to entertain the true problems of life," (13) that is, how to seek perfection. Since his previous enterprises can be described only in metaphors, this is ample evidence that his present enterprise, the Walden experiment, is symbolic also.

With these images of the quest in mind, one returns from Thoreau's strategic digression to follow through to the end his diverting escapes from the trap of materialism. By this time the reader has been properly educated, both affirmatively and negatively, to understand the author's answers to those queries by Concord villagers concerning his mode of life with which the book began. On page forty-five Thoreau takes up again where he left off at the end of the first paragraph. "Near the end of March, 1845," his story continues with the air of straightforward autobiography, "I borrowed an axe and went down to the woods by Walden Pond." (45) His concern once more is with the basic economies, now concentrated on food and shelter as he himself sought to provide them, a shift from generalized discussion to concrete narrative. His method is still that of wit, but the best of it now takes the novel form of statistics on the expense of his house and what he ate. With a bookkeeper's flourish he lists everything that went into the cost of his house down to the least item (a penny for chalk) and to the last half-cent, coming up with $28.12 1/2 for the grand total. (53-54) His next house will surpass the mansions of Concord in "grandeur and luxury," he boasts—as soon as he learns how to build it for the price of the present one.

The account of expenses for food is similarly detailed. After itemizing everything he spent during a period of eight months, he confesses unblushingly, "Yes, I did eat $8.74, all told," but adds that his readers' guilty deeds would look no better in print. (66) It is probably not a coincidence that this figure tallies with the one claimed as a possible food budget by the leader of a gastronomic reform group in New England during the 1830's and 1840's. There is every reason to believe that his book, *The Young Housekeeper* (Boston, 1838),[7] would have come under Thoreau's eye. The author was a cousin of Bronson Alcott's, and in addition to advocating simple food, natural preparation, and abstinence from meat for moral and psychological reasons, he buttressed his program with economic arguments. The vegetable and cereal diet he outlined as ample to sustain one person added up to twenty-five cents a week—less than one-fifth the usual cost, and exactly equivalent to the **Walden** total of $8.74 for eight months.

Similarly, Thoreau himself gives some comparative figures for contemporary housing that dramatize his $28.12 1/2. The rent of a dormitory room at Harvard came to a little more than that sum, $30, for just one year; an average house in Concord cost $800, about thirty times what he paid for his own. (55,34) Even if his figures for expenses were multiplied by ten, to arrive at some sort of modern currency equivalent, they would still be ludicrously low, as any economist today would testify—about $10 a month for food and less than $300 for a house. But such literal analyses are beside the point. The relation of Thoreau's statistics in **Walden** to the actual expenses of his experiment would be irrelevant even if they could be checked. (The **Journal** for this period was largely stripped for use in the book, and so contains no data of this sort.) They are part of his wit. Spread out in his book, like pages from a ledger, they are a shriveling satire on economic man's biggest bugbear, the high cost of living.

After this, abandoning the materialist's method of reckoning altogether, Thoreau pushes his economy to its ultimate definition: "The cost of a thing is the amount of what I will call life which is required to be exchanged for it, immediately or in the long run." (34) This is the basis of his most significant conclusion, in the final casting up of accounts to arrive at a time budget also: "I found that, by working about six weeks in a year, I could meet all the expenses of living." (76) (Two pages later he reduces the work period to "thirty or forty days.") The great merit of this is that it leaves the other forty-six weeks "free and clear." And the great advantage of these figures is that they reverse the average man's vacation and work periods. On the next page this is turned into a memorable parody of Adam's curse: "It is not necessary that a man should earn his living by the sweat of his brow, unless he sweats easier than I do."[8]

With so much leisure and with the perspective offered by his "primitive and frontier life, though in the midst of an outward civilization," it was inevitable that he should crow over his escape from some of the absurdities that he had left behind. He satirizes the railroad, telegraph, and other recent inventions as "improved means to an unimproved end." He indulges in a tirade against philanthropists and reformers of all kinds, including utopian experiments in communal living, such as nearby Brook Farm. These attacks grew naturally enough out of his answers to quips by his townsmen: Didn't he miss the advantages of civilization? Didn't he admit that his solitary way of life was selfish? And so on. If Walden really digresses from its theme anywhere it is in passages like these.[9] But they do not prove that its purpose was social criticism, a subject tangential to the book's chief aim. Thoreau makes himself very clear on this point. "I desire to speak," he says in disavowing the reformer's role, "as one not interested in the success or failure of the present economical and social arrangements." (62) Nor is he writing even a handbook for the individualist: "I would not have any one adopt *my* mode of living on any account . . . I would have each one be very careful to find out and pursue *his own* way." (78,79) As for his new-found independence at Walden, it enables him to follow the "bent" of his own genius, "which is a very crooked one."

Much more pertinent to Thoreau's way is his running commentary on furniture, though it begins in the lightest vein of banter. "I would rather sit on a pumpkin and have it all to myself than be crowded on a velvet cushion," he said earlier; his later revision of this epigram merely substitutes the wit of understatement: "None is so poor that he need sit on a pumpkin. That is shiftlessness." (41,72) But the accompanying inventory of his own possessions would make an Irishman's shack seem over-furnished. When a friend offered him a door mat he declined it, "preferring to wipe my feet on the sod before my door." Similarly he dispensed with curtains, having "no gazers to shut out but the sun and moon." (74) All of this leads to an aphorism that furnishes a key to the first third of **Walden:** "A man is rich in proportion to the number of things which he can afford to let alone." (91)

The opposite—an accumulation of superfluities—is exemplified in his amusing anecdote describing the auction of a local deacon's effects, "for his life had not been ineffectual." All the furnishings and the trumpery of two generations, including a dried tapeworm preserved in a bottle, were put up for sale instead of being subjected to the "purifying destruction" of fire. The neighbors eagerly bought everything and took it home to their garrets, where it would lie until their estates were settled. "When a man dies he kicks the dust," is Thoreau's dry comment. (75) But none of this is mere nonsense for its own sake. It all prepares the way for a conclusion pertinent to his central thesis, illustrated with a ritual practised by the Mucclasse Indians. Once a year all their old possessions were gathered in a common heap and consumed with fire, he records. This was followed by three days of fasting, then three days of feasting, as they prepared themselves for a new life. Of this purification by fire Thoreau declares: "I have scarcely heard of a truer sacrament, that is, as the dictionary defines it, 'outward and visible sign of an inward and spiritual grace.'" (76)

Metaphor

"Economy" is a witty fable on how to get rid of the material world, enriched with a few metaphorical hints of the quest that lies beyond.[10] It is strung on a slender chronicle of his life at Walden Pond, which makes the second chapter by its very title, "Where I Lived, and What I Lived For," seem to promise only a repetition of the first. But, in addition to its intrinsic merit, this section forms an indispensable transition from the negative approach of the introduction to the positive theme of the body of his book, and a subtle shift from wit to metaphor as the dominant style. It opens with his finest display of the former skill in a classic skit on how not to buy a farm. Over the years Thoreau had been developing in his *Journal* an elaborate conceit about the ownership of property, poetic "ownership" as opposed to legal. In an entry for 25 May 1851 one may find the germ of the well-known *Walden* anecdote. During a walk he stopped to admire the view across a valley to far away hills. "I wonder that houses are not oftener located mainly that they may command particular rare prospects," he commented: "A vista where you have the near green horizon contrasted with the distant blue one, terrestrial with celestial earth." (J, II, 215-216) Then, comparing the art of nature with the art of man (as described in various books on landscape gardening he had read), he added:

> The farmer would never suspect what it was you were buying, and such sites would be the cheapest of any. . . . a noble inheritance for your children. The true sites for human dwellings are unimproved. They command no price in the market. . . . An unchangeable kind of wealth, a *real* estate. (*J*, II, 215-216)

The turn of wit in this final phrase provided the clue for development in the *Walden* anecdote. There the whole passage is an intricate web of puns and word play, so tightly woven the reader must be on his toes to catch them. They subvert all the terminology of property ownership, *survey, deed, price,* and so on:

> At a certain season of our life we are accustomed to consider every spot as the possible site of a house. I have thus surveyed the country on every side within a dozen miles of where I live. In imagination I have bought all the farms in succession, for all were to be bought, and I knew their price. I walked over each farmer's premises, tasted his wild apples, discoursed on husbandry with him, took his farm at his price, at any price, mortgaging it to him in my mind; even put a higher price on it,—took everything but a deed of it,—took his word for his deed, for I dearly love to talk,—cultivated it, and him too to some extent, I trust. (90)

Such is the ingenuity of his satire on the real-estate business as to leave not only agents but all buyers and sellers of property feeling a little foolish. In this way Thoreau "owned" the Hollowell place during the term of his refusal—"the refusal was all I wanted." Before the farmer made out a deed his wife changed her mind, and he offered ten dollars to be released from his contract. This leads Thoreau to indulge in some paradoxical expense accounting:

> Now, to speak the truth, I had but ten cents in the world, and it surpassed my arithmetic to tell, if I was that man who had ten cents, or who had a farm, or ten dollars, or all together. However, I let him keep the ten dollars and the farm too, for I had carried it far enough; or rather, to be generous, I sold him the farm for just what I gave for it. . . . I found thus that I had been a rich man without any damage to my poverty. (91)

After the fun is over he winds up with a shining double metaphor. Ever since deciding not to buy he has annually carried off its best crop, the landscape, without need of even a wheel-barrow. Better still, the whole farm is finally put into a poem, "the most admirable kind of invisible fence," he says, leaving the owner toiling as a serf on the land Thoreau has bought with his imagination. (92)

"The present was my next experiment of this kind," he continues, in reference to his squatting on Emerson's acres and putting together his own cabin out of a dismantled railroad shanty. (93) That is, the first was an experiment in how to own a farm without buying it, the second how to build a house not so much to live in as to grow out of. So he returns yet once again to his central autobiographical experience; but most myths come to us in several versions, as in the four Gospels. At each retelling of his own story he drops back into a simple relaxed style, as if allowing the reader to catch his breath after the elaborate displays of wit and the complexity of occasional metaphorical passages. But this third style also plays a positive role in his overall language pattern. An unadorned factual narrative is ideal to begin with when one wants to put the reader in a mood for accepting the fabulous, and it has been the traditional mode for writers of scriptures and recorders of miracles. The previous versions of his Walden story have been exactly that, apparently straight-forward accounts of how he built his shelter and supplied himself with food, but with a few threads woven in that give it the strange air of a "natural" rather than a man-made house. He dug his cellar where a woodchuck formerly had its burrow, he left the bark on three sides of the studs and rafters, thus keeping them as much like trees as possible, and so on. (46, 49)

These prepare the way for stronger suggestions of the miraculous, which appear in the third and last retelling. Since he did not plaster until autumn, the walls of rough weather-stained boards were left all summer with wide chinks in them, so that "I did not need to go outdoors to take the air." (95) Then, after alluding to a passage in the Hindu scriptures praising the life of nature, he adds: "I found myself suddenly neighbor to the birds; not by having imprisoned one, but having caged myself near them." (95) The sequence reaches a climax when his own dwelling, with its "clean and airy look, especially in the morning," brings back a vision: "To my imagination it retained throughout the day more or less of this auroral character, reminding me of a certain house on a mountain which I had visited a year before. This was an airy and unplastered cabin, fit to entertain a travelling god, and where a goddess might trail her garments." (94)

The memory was of a trip to the Catskill Mountains in the summer of 1844; but it was not recorded in the *Journal,* interestingly enough, until the day after he took up residence at the pond in 1845. "*July 5. Saturday.* Walden. Yesterday I came here to live," he wrote: "My house makes me think of some mountain houses I have seen." Then he described the cabin of the miller of Kaaterskill Falls, a fascinating model for the more famous cabin of the hermit of Walden:

> The house seemed high-placed, airy, and perfumed, fit to entertain a travelling god. It was so high, indeed, that all the music, the broken strains, the waifs and accompaniments of tunes, that swept over the ridge of the Caatskills, passed through its aisles. Could not man be man in such an abode? And would he ever find out this groveling life? It was the very light and atmosphere in which the works of Grecian art were composed, and in which they rest. They have appropriated to themselves a loftier hall than mortals ever occupy, at least on a level with the mountain-brows of the world. There was wanting a little of the glare of the lower vales, and in its

place a pure twilight as became the precincts of heaven. (*J,* I, 361-362)

It is hard to say which of two facts is more interesting: that it took Walden cabin as a catalyst to precipitate the mountain cabin into Thoreau's recorded memory or that the *Journal* draft was so magically transformed when it was incorporated in the book.[11] The *Walden* version concludes:

> The winds which passed over my dwelling were such as sweep over the ridges of mountains, bearing the broken strains, or celestial parts only, of terrestrial music. The morning wind forever blows, the poem of creation is uninterrupted; but few are the ears that hear it. Olympus is but the outside of the earth everywhere. (94)

In such a dwelling anything could happen. Similar hints and gleams recur throughout the book, keeping the reader in a state of expectant wonder as he shares the narrator's anticipation of "the Visitor who never comes." (298) So he is ready to accept the advent of Thoreau's gods on their own terms when they finally do arrive, deep in the chapter on "Solitude."

Chapter 2 furnishes the transition to this spiritual life, the quest for which gradually comes to dominate the book. It does so in the first half by reversing the author's previous techniques. Instead of defending the economy of his own way of life by wit, he uses metaphor, allusion, and fable to glorify it. The factual promise of his title, "Where I Lived and What I Lived For," is part of the game by which the literal setting is subtly transmuted into the imaginary "world" of *Walden.* First the house is fit for a traveling god. Then the pond serves "to float the earth"; and its water, "full of light and reflections, becomes a lower heaven." (96) Glancing up to the galaxy, he can say that where he lives is as far off as "some remote and more celestial corner" of the system: "Both place and time were changed, and I dwelt nearer to those parts of the universe and to those eras in history which had most attracted me." (97) Best of all, the ecstasy of his life makes each morning an invitation to renewal. A sincere worshiper of Aurora, he rises early and bathes in the pond as "a religious exercise." (98) All poets make their music like Memnon at sunrise, he says: "That man who does not believe that each day contains an earlier, more sacred, and auroral hour than he has yet profaned, has despaired of life, and is pursuing a descending and darkening way." (99) Millions wake up every day to physical labor, but only one in a hundred millions "to a poetic or divine life." (100) The Walden experience, for Thoreau, is the dawn of a new life.

In a similar way the second half of this chapter prepares for his quest by using a poetic mode to define the good life that lies beyond the basic economies. Instead of occasional denials of this and that as his purpose in withdrawing from the world, he now attempts to portray it affirmatively by multiple hints and suggestions. These radiate from a key paragraph, buried in the center of the chapter, that will repay close reading. It is a series of metaphors framed by wit:

> I went to the woods because I wished to live deliberately, to front only the essential facts of life, and see if I could not learn what it had to teach, and not, when I came to die, discover that I had not lived. I did not wish to live what was not life, living is so dear; nor did I wish to practice resignation, unless it was quite necessary. I wanted to live deep and suck out all the marrow of life, to live so sturdily and Spartan-like as to put to rout all that was not life, to cut a broad swath and shave close, to drive life into a corner, and reduce it to its lowest terms, and, if it proved to be mean, why then to get the whole and genuine meanness of it, and publish its meanness to the world; or if it were sublime, to know it by experience, and be able to give a true account of it in my next excursion. For most men, it appears to me, are in a strange uncertainty about it, whether it is of the devil or of God, and have *somewhat hastily* concluded that it is the chief end of man here to "glorify God and enjoy him forever." (100-101)

The elaborate play on live and die comes to focus in the learned pun, "I wished to live deliberately"—not only unhurriedly but with deliberation. "Deliberately" is his first polysyllable, followed by a marked pause. This is skillful rhetoric, compelling the reader to speak the word slowly in order to take in its full weight (*de + librare* = to weigh). As one critic has summed up the sound effects of this passage: "The measured pace seems in exact correspondence with his carefully measured thoughts, and serves, as effective rhythm always does, to direct the fullest attention to the most important words."[12] The only way to experience life to the full is by meditating on its true values.

At the end of the paragraph, referring to the other meaning of "deliberately," Thoreau says most men have missed the way because they have "*somewhat hastily* concluded" (the italics are his) that it is the chief purpose of man here to "glorify God and enjoy him forever." This seems on the surface to advocate glorifying man, a subversion of the Shorter Catechism. But a closer look shows his purpose to be a reinterpretation of doctrine rather than blasphemy. In the first version of **Walden** this paragraph ended by saying that it is a mistake "to glorify God and Him only."[13] This merely implies that the transcendental chief-end-of-man—to worship the indwelling god—should be grafted on the Christian. But in the finished book he added a clarifying passage at the end of his first chapter: "Our hymn-books resound with a melodious curs-

ing of God and enduring Him forever. . . . There is nowhere recorded a simple and irrepressible satisfaction with the gift of life, any memorable praise of God." (87) After such preparation there was no further need in his second chapter to specify the error men fall into about the purpose of life when they jump to conclusions hastily instead of arriving at them by living deliberately. The only true way to glorify God is to enjoy the gift of life.

In between lie the images that suggest how one can "live deep" enough to experience this joy, and if they seem stern they are lifted up by the hope that life may be "sublime." They are drawn from some of the chief clusters of imagery used throughout the book: food, the military life, farming, hunting, mathematics. The verbs of action are his chief source of power. Sucking marrow is a primitive act, compatible with the life of a soldier. The range of Thoreau's desire to live fully is widened by the image of harvesting and intensified by the image of closing in on his quarry. This paragraph also provides the substance of the rest of the chapter. There the same images reappear, turned into word play, and the framing wit is expanded into metaphors. Even the phrasing is echoed, but with this novel transposing of styles.

Two examples will illustrate Thoreau's ingenuity. Advocating a "more than Spartan simplicity," he introduces a rapid fire of puns with the epigram: "Keep you accounts on your thumbnail." (102, 101) Such is the lively rebirth of his statistical figure for reducing life "to its lowest terms." Again, the witty initial sentence, "I wished to live deliberately," is developed into a series of metaphors. "Let us spend one day as deliberately as Nature," he begins, and then elaborates a dozen images of haste and distraction to be avoided, of peace and reality to be sought. (108-109) "Simplicity, simplicity, simplicity!" he urges. A late **Journal** entry defines the term: "By simplicity, commonly called poverty, my life is concentrated and so becomes organized, . . . which before was inorganic and lumpish." (**J**, IX, 246) To return to the focal paragraph, the sternness of its regimen is mitigated by the phrase with which it ends, "my next excursion," suggesting the relaxed pleasure of his life at Walden.

The purpose of Thoreau's experiment is clearer now in one sense: to withdraw from the life of civilization so that he can merge with the life of nature, to leave the artificial for the real. But this was a means rather than an end. The true quest is still withheld, only hinted at in two metaphors that bring Chapter 2 to a conclusion. "Time is but the stream I go a-fishing in," he says: "I see the sandy bottom and detect how shallow it is. Its thin current slides away, but eternity remains." (109) How to cast his line for that is the theme explored in the rest of the book. For the moment he pulls himself back to earth, where he knows he must make his start, but not by working with his hands any more than is necessary. His second metaphor forms the immediate link to the chapters that follow: "My instinct tells me that my head is an organ for burrowing, . . . and with it I would mine and burrow my way through these hills. I think that the richest vein is somewhere hereabouts." (109) The way must be through nature, though the goal is heaven. *Walden* is not the diary of a day laborer who supported himself on six weeks' work and spent the other forty-six loafing on the grass. It is a manual of stern discipline, the record of a search for the buried life of the soul.

The stage has at last been set for the revolutionary alternative Thoreau has to offer as a program for living, once the problems of economy have been met: "to adventure on life now." (17) The two opening chapters, taking up nearly a third of the book, might seem unduly long for a mere introduction. But he knew there was no other way to break down the resistance of readers, then as now, to any celebration of the life of the spirit. Though challenging in their own right as sort of modern *De Contemptu Mundi,* these attacks on worldliness are actually just a prelude to the main theme contained in the body of the book, his transcendent experience at Walden Pond. The surface disparity between the two parts has led anthologists to print "Economy" and "Where I Lived" as separable essays, but this amputation is fatal because their real goal is not social criticism. The shift from counter theme to dominant theme called for a shift in technique so radical as to threaten the unity of the whole, seemingly. The pretended expository style, so well suited as a mode of argument for proving that materialism is an encumbrance to the spirit, would not serve at all as the vehicle for a quest that could be suggested only by indirection. For the body of the book he substitutes the mode of poetry, though masked as autobiography. At the very beginning of *Walden* he had said: "I should not talk so much about myself if there were anybody else whom I knew as well. Unfortunately, I am confined to this theme by the narrowness of my experience." All he required of any writer was "a simple and sincere account of his own life." (4) Having delivered himself of this chesty dictum, he proceeds to ignore it. What he gives instead is the merest thread of an autobiographical story on which to hang his images.

But the shift in styles is more a gradual movement from one to the other than a sudden break. Several times in the introductory chapters he drops into the autobiographical vein when giving a preview of the quest to come. Occasionally, in the later chapters he returns to exposition when there is some fragment of the material world remaining to be disposed of. And both styles—expository and narrative—are really only anti-structures, as has been shown. The true stylistic mode of *Walden* is the interplay of wit and metaphor,

used respectively for his negative and affirmative purposes. The fusion of the two into an intricate counterpoint is made easy by their close kinship. Many metaphors are witty and much wit tends to be metaphorical, in both the derived meaning of that term and its seventeenth-century meaning (Wit as the power of joining thought and expression with an aptness calculated to delight by its novelty).[14] So the shift from one to the other is largely a matter of emphasis, the elaborate display of pun, irony, and satire giving way as imagery and symbolism come to dominate. The pivotal chapter, "Where I Lived, and What I Lived For," blending all these modes, forms a smooth transition between the introduction and the body of the book. With his economic needs now reduced to a minimum, he can begin to "entertain the true problems of life with freedom and a prospect of success." (13)

Patterns

What really happened at Walden Pond from 1845 to 1847 will never be known. Readers of the book are excluded from the author's outward life and given instead an inward journey or exploration. This is lightly framed in a pseudo-narrative that is made to serve his real purpose by invoking the over-image of life as a pilgrimage. It begins with Chapter 3, "Reading," and continues through Chapter 17, "Spring"—leaving the "Conclusion" as a kind of epilogue in which he allows himself to savor the fruits of his experiment. These fifteen chapters are arranged in a seemingly casual sequence in order to suggest the leisurely unfolding of experience during a year spent in the woods—the transcendental ideal of organic form. But the chronicle aspect, as indeed the whole mode of autobiography, is more a device for maneuvering than a strict form. The author himself confesses that he reduced the two years and more of his actual residence to one, "for convenience." (93-94) It can also be shown from the *Journal* that he expanded it to more than fifteen years by levying on experiences ranging from 1837 to 1854. The choice of a single year was part of the artist's search for a form he could use at least as a point of departure and return. The full unfolding of Thoreau's new structure, sprung from the circular calendar, can only come much later with an examination of the elaborate image clusters that make up the book's true form. But first there are some simpler techniques for dealing with time.

The annual cycle is an important part of the total design of Walden, but it is no mere mechanical formula of seasonal progression. True, the first ten chapters of the body of the book deal in general with summer activities, and the last five spin through the other three seasons. But just as the titles of some of the latter contain the word "Winter" or "Spring" (Chapters 14-17), the titles of some of the former, such as "Higher Laws" (Chapter 11), suggest excursions out of this time scheme and out of time itself into the Eternal Now. Besides, there are intricate interweavings of the seasons in all of the chapters. For example, Chapter 3, "Reading," is ostensibly set in summer. But Thoreau begins by leaping out of the seasonal boundary: "I kept Homer's Iliad on my table through the summer, though I looked at his page only now and then. . . . Yet I sustained myself by the prospect of such reading in future" (111)—that is, when winter would drive him indoors.

It soon becomes apparent that he is concerned with something more complex than a chronological narrative. Books, he says, are for our "*morning* hours"; they are more salutary than "the spring to our lives." (111, 119-120) The next chapter begins with a literal seasonal reference in the past tense: "I did not read books the first summer; I hoed beans." (123) Then shifting quickly to the present—"I sit at my window this summer *afternoon* . . ." (127)—it moves into his real subject: the "Sounds" (Chapter 4) that come to him from the natural world. This is followed by "Solitude" (Chapter 5), which reaches its climax of spiritual communion in "the long winter *evenings*" (152); then by its sequel "Visitors" (Chapter 6), which ranges over the whole period of his residence. All this before his actual summer activity in "The Bean-Field" (Chapter 7) brings him back to the calendar year. Clearly, spring, summer, and winter, as well as morning, afternoon, and evening are the terms of an inner timetable rather than an outer one. Similarly, in the last half of the book, where Thoreau's handling of time becomes ever more complex and significant, leading at last to his circular images for renewal and rebirth. . . .

Beneath such natural orderings of his story—the annual cycle and the autobiographical chronicle—there are two structures of much greater subtlety and significance. The one nearer the surface is a set of patterns in the chapter groupings, beginning with the dualities that plagued all transcendentalists in their search for unity. Thoreau had never forgotten the Phi Beta Kappa address at Harvard in 1837 when Emerson laid down his novel curriculum for the American Scholar. After challenging the young graduates to shake off their bondage to Europe, he announced his radical program for the true scholar's education: He is nourished and formed by nature, and though influenced by his cultural heritage as embodied in books, he should turn to them only when the original source of inspiration flags, and even then not as their slave. The one student who fully responded to Emerson's passion to "set the hearts of youth on flame" was Thoreau. He had read the master's famous little booklet entitled *Nature* the year before and understood that his call for a return to nature really meant a return through Nature to Spirit.

Ten to fifteen years later, when he was putting this theory of education to the test of actual experience in the residence at Walden Pond and the book that embodied it, he opened his own transcendental "essay" by coming to grips with the same twofold curriculum. But he reversed the emphasis and the order of treatment. Emerson, after a brief rhapsody on Nature as spiritual teacher, had placed his chief emphasis on the proper and improper use of books, as appropriate to an academic audience. But Thoreau, with his apprenticeship to institutional learning well in the past, first disposes of "Reading" as the lesser source of truth, to be consulted only in the scholar's idle times, then turns his present attention to the Book of Nature that speaks to him in the language of "Sounds" (Chapters 3 and 4). This leads directly into another pair of opposites, "Solitude" and "Visitors" (Chapters 5 and 6).

In spite of their search for unity, or more properly because of it, transcendentalists constantly found themselves confronted with a succession of dualities. This particular one had long been a concern of Emerson's poetry and prose though the volume using it as a title, *Society and Solitude,* came late in his career. Thoreau patterned "Solitude" and "Visitors" on such a duality. The next two chapters (7 and 8) are concrete illustrations of these concepts: the record of his solitary labors in "The Bean-Field" and a typical sally into "The Village" to report on the communal life of his neighbors. The two preceding chapters are part of this same dualism: "Reading," in books which are the records of civilization; "Sounds," which are best heard in his woodland retreat.

In this way the first six chapters of **Walden** (after the long introductory sections) are woven into a design of contrasting threads of society and solitude but with the latter dominant, for the society portrayed is largely make-believe or comic. The world of others as found in books consists of those companions from the past that can best be known in the solitude of one's study. The chief visitors to his woods are witty figments of his imagination or figures out of legend and fable, hence not representatives of actual society. On his trips to Concord the villagers are turned into caricatures lining the main street down which he runs the gauntlet to escape the clutches of merchants and bankers and then bolts into the woods, only to lose himself on the way back to his cabin. Scarcely a likelihood for such an experienced woodsman, this is instead a dramatic device constructed solely for the purpose of supporting his conclusion. "Not till we are lost," he says in parody of New Testament doctrine, "not till we have lost the world, do we begin to find ourselves."[15] (190) All these paths, including those that pretend to be directed toward society, lead to the world of the Self.

Thoreau's goal was solitude, with an exclusiveness that dismayed and all but alienated Emerson. It is one of their main lines of divergence. For example, there was actually a threefold program laid down in his famous address to the American Scholar: he is fashioned by nature; he is indebted to the culture of the past only as its master; and finally he expresses himself in action in order to influence society. But this last point finds no echo in *Walden*. Thoreau turned a deaf ear to Emerson's closing exhortation: "Action is with the scholar subordinate, but it is essential. Without it he is not yet man." Rejecting the popular notion that the scholar should be a recluse, Emerson had declared: "I run eagerly into this resounding tumult. I grasp the hands of those next me, and take my place in the ring to suffer and to work."[16] It is absurd, of course, to picture the sage of Concord literally in this role. The very extravagance of his language came from the pressure of his need to find a vocation for himself, now that he had stepped down from the pulpit. Though he remained a man of the study, he gradually found a way to express his thought in action by becoming the mover of other men through his lectures and essays.

The real point is that Emerson felt it to be of the first importance for the scholar to have a relation with society and to influence it. There is some irony in his envy of Thoreau who, in spite of being self-engrossed, was so useful to the community as surveyor and pencil-maker (in contrast with his own ineptness); and in his troubled admiration over an occasional bold public action by such a confirmed recluse (as in Thoreau's going to jail to protest unjust taxes). The heroic role Emerson had in mind was something quite different. His disappointment, revealing his fundamental misunderstanding of Thoreau, is clearly voiced in the funeral address over the man who had refused to become his disciple: "I so much regret the loss of his rare powers of action, that I cannot help counting it a fault in him that he had no ambition. Wanting this, instead of engineering for all America, he was the captain of a huckleberry-party."[17]

Thoreau's purpose, at least in *Walden,* was inaction rather than action—to "spend one day as deliberately as Nature." For him, the activity of men in nearby Concord was only a subject for satire. His own work in "The Bean-Field" (Chapter 7) is anything but a eulogy of the farmer, whose labors are ridiculed throughout the book as much as those of the mechanic or businessman. Instead, the key passages in this chapter deal with his joy in walking the rows barefooted, "dabbling like a plastic artist in the dewy and crumbling sand" (173); turning up Indian relics, "an instant and immeasurable crop" (175), with his hoe; or leaning on it while listening to the sounds of nature and those from the town, the latter being diminished by distance to "popguns." (176) Though his labor had the practical end of earning a living, he reduced it to a

minimum. And he is emphatic about its not being his vocation. Another summer, he vows, he will not devote so much industry to beans and corn, but will plant "such seeds, if the seed is not lost, as sincerity, truth, simplicity, faith, innocence, and the like." (181) The bean field was not his arena any more than the village was.

Perhaps as near as the scholar of *Walden* comes to expressing himself in action is in "Reading" and the related area of writing, which constituted the "private business" he had come to the woods to transact. But these were subordinate to his main purpose and so may account for this chapter's being the least satisfactory of all in terms of integration with the major theme of quest. Besides, unless books are written for some recognizable social aim, they do not measure up to Emerson's final requirement for the American Scholar. However much these chapters may owe to his writings for their pattern of polarities, they are not truly Emersonian, nor is the book as a whole. It is transcendental, but only in a special sense, as symbolized in the central chapter on the magic circle of "The Ponds." Thoreau's purpose was to express himself not in action but in words—in the poem that he wrote to himself and for himself, to illuminate the quest of a life lived deliberately in accordance with nature and the spirit.

The first half of *Walden* comes to an end with his visit to and return from the village (Chapter 8). This journey, repeated "every day or two," he says, is a kind of continuous re-enactment of his original withdrawal from the world. And just as he lost his way in the woods during this ritual flight from society, so on his return to Walden Pond he found his "Way," symbolically. It is at one and the same time the goal of his quest and the path to that goal. The stance he takes there is the epitome of inaction, meditating in his boat as it drifts in the middle of the pond, occasionally engaging in that solitary and most passive of actions as a fisherman, and a transcendental one at that, as will be seen. This is what makes "The Ponds" (Chapter 9) so important to the meaning of the whole book. Yet the focus on it is not logical but symbolic. As one goes back over the preceding chapters he is surprised to recall how casually and infrequently the pond has been mentioned until now, and it is not treated in detail again until the very end of the book. It is as if Thoreau has chosen to unveil it once at the center, then draw the curtain until he is reborn with it at spring thawing. But there is no extravagance of ritual or language attending this revelation. As he approaches it, the elaborate display of wit and metaphor subsides into simple description of its purity and serenity. At this point so successfully has the world been lost and his goal found that his former modes of rejection and seeking can be dispensed with. Walden Pond is its own sufficient symbol.[18]

In like manner, the second half of **Walden** can be shown to follow transcendental patterns. It begins with a group of chapters that form a triad centered on "Higher Laws" (Chapter 11), Thoreau's impossibly lofty aspiration for becoming divine. Those who insist on treating him as a social critic or a nature essayist have simply skipped this chapter, yet it is as integral to the book as any other. In fact, it is the exact complement to the long introductory chapter on the lower laws of economic man and fulfills its meaning by being the polar opposite. Taken together the two chapters illustrate the "two laws discrete" defined by Emerson: "Law for man and law for thing."[19] In **Walden,** Thoreau deals with them in reverse order. "Economy" attacks the luxury of a materialistic society as a way of life enslaved by things; "Higher Laws" espouses the ascetic life as man's highest aspiration. The latter (like the former) is deliberately extravagant, not to be taken literally as the program he set himself to live by, but it must be taken seriously if the reader is to grasp the true meaning of the Walden experiment. The "Higher Laws" are those principles one should follow in order to achieve perfection, and for a saint they might be feasible. For the author of **Walden** they point to a goal which, though impossible of achievement, is something more than a simple return to nature. They define his "Way" as a stern and Spartan discipline for approaching as near as possible to his ideal self.

Preceding this is "Baker Farm" (Chapter 10), named for a place where Thoreau once thought of living before he went to Walden. Now, John Field's way of life there is pictured as a travesty in miniature of "Where I Lived, and What I Lived For." This bog-trotter has sunk as near as man can to the level of non-being. If Thoreau's satire of the very rich was devastating in the introduction, his satire of the very poor in this chapter is equally so. Both are caught in the same trap of a false economy. For the seeker of perfection, civilization seems to by-pass the true problems of life. He can never find the proper path of his development by starting from it—whether as one of the complacent rich, the enslaved poor, or those in between who lead lives of quiet desperation. Instead of trying to reform civilized society, he must go back to nature and work his way up from there toward the life of the spirit. But there is a linking sentence in "Higher Laws" that warns the reader not to think that Thoreau is substituting the code of naturalism for that of humanism: "We are conscious of an animal in us, which awakens in proportion as our higher nature slumbers." (242) So, by the time he arrives at the last of the triad, "Brute Neighbors" (Chapter 12), the reader knows he is not going to be advised to "turn and live with the animals" even in Whitman's sense. Instead, he is given a modern bestiary, but with the notations more precisely scientific than in the medieval ones and with the meanings arrived at by wit and metaphor rather than moral

allegory. It is a celebration of the virtues of sheer being in the animal world.

In these three chapters, starting from bases on earth, Thoreau has triangulated toward the divine. Taken in sequence with "The Ponds" they also faintly continue the alternating pattern from solitude to society, back and forth again, though his brief visit to the shanty Irishman and his preferred companionship with his brute neighbors mark the last fading out of the social world he has renounced. The summer chapters of **Walden** have now come to an end, and with the arrival of cold weather solitude dominates the rest of the book. It does so thematically as well as literally, solitude being the inescapable condition of a life lived in the woods during the restrictive months of fall and winter. Though the last five chapters seem to follow the seasonal cycle more closely than the first ten, they also break out of the calendar quite as often, to open up new meanings. For Thoreau's is not a mere hibernation, like nature's, waiting for resurgent spring. These are the months of his greatest travail, husbanding his energies less to keep the spark of physical life glowing at his hearthside than to kindle his spirit for the new life that will be born when the old one dies. The direction of his journey is out of time into a renewal of that immortality whose intimations he had strained to hear in his lost youth.

The Weaver

Thoreau makes use of one more unifying device in the "character" of the narrator and the "voice" in which he speaks to us, for it is he who weaves the "plot" of **Walden**. A recent critic has identified him as a modern variant of the *eiron* of traditional comedy, who confronts and outwits the *alazons* of this world. Joseph Moldenhauer's idea is so ingenious and so pertinent to an understanding of the book that it deserves elaboration here. But first a full description of the types, as defined by Northrop Frye. *Alazon* is the Greek word meaning impostor, one who pretends to be something more than he is. Sometimes actual hypocrisy makes him so, but usually it is lack of self-knowledge; hence the term includes the stupid conformist, the stolid citizen, the kill-joy, and the churl. The *eiron*, on the other hand, is the man who deprecates himself, irony being a technique of appearing to be less than one is. But he is really sophisticated and immensely clever, the predestined artist, just as the *alazon* is his predestined victim. In Elizabethan plays he was the trickster (derived from the "vice" of medieval moralities), often setting actions in motion from pure love of mischief. But he goes through a great deal of disguising and many metamorphoses. He is even combined with the hero, according to Frye, "whenever the latter is a cheeky, improvident young man who hatches his own schemes."[20] Puck and Ariel are the highest examples of the type, both spiritual beings. *Alazon* and *eiron* exist in their purest form in the standard comic skit where the former complacently soliloquizes while the latter makes sarcastic asides to the audience, confident of its sympathy. Much of this is surprisingly applicable to the narrator of *Walden* and the antagonists he does battle with.

Thoreau was well acquainted with classical and renaissance drama and certainly knew these comic types from reading Aristophanes, Terence, and Shakespeare. In creating his own, he did not need to copy or invent, for he could draw from life at least as a starting point. He clearly thought many of his fellow townsmen to be *alazons* of one sort or another, and he modeled his *eiron*-narrator on himself, though so heightened as to constitute an original fictive character. The popular notion of Thoreau's being solemn as a crow, and as ungainly, needs drastic revising. He was aware of the figure he cut in the world and made comic capital out of it. The *Journal* offers many amusing examples. Once, his anecdote takes on the full flavor of comedy:

> Trying the other day to imitate the honking of geese, I found myself flapping my sides with my elbows, as with wings, and uttering something like the syllables *mow-ack* with a nasal twang and twist in my head; and I produced their note so perfectly in the opinion of the hearers that I thought I might possibly draw a flock down. (*J*, VII, 258)

Again, he has left a bizarre glimpse of himself as a lecturer, "grasping at, or even standing and reclining upon, the serene and everlasting truths." On such occasions "I have seen my auditors," he says, "compassionately or timidly watching my motions as if they were the antics of a rope-dancer or mountebank pretending to walk on air." (*J*, IX, 237-238) There can be no doubt that some of this was conscious histrionic posing. He was even striking an attitude when he chose July 4th, "Independence Day," to leave Concord and take up residence at Walden, his special kind of firecracker calculated to startle the villagers. (94) An early *Journal* entry makes an explicit justification for his posturings:

> By spells seriousness will be forced to cut capers, and drink a deep and refreshing draught of silliness; to turn this sedate day of Lucifer's and Apollo's, into an all fools' day for Harlequin and Cornwallis . . . Like overtasked schoolboys, all my members and nerves and sinews petition Thought for a recess, and my very thigh-bones itch to slip away from under me, and run and join the mêlée. I exult in stark inanity, leering on nature and the soul. We think the gods reveal themselves only to sedate and musing gentlemen. But not so; the buffoon in the midst of his antics catches unobserved glimpses, which he treasures for the lonely hour. When I have been playing tomfool,

I have been driven to exchange the old for a more liberal and catholic philosophy. (*J*, I, 175-176)

Contemporaries have left many testimonials to such a Puckish figure. Once when visiting friends in New Bedford, Thoreau was asked to sing. At first he demurred—"Oh, I fear, if I do, I shall take the roof of the house off!"—but, urged again, he delivered his favorite "Tom Bowline" with such spirit that the Quaker father of the family retired from the room. Again, at his own home in Concord on a day too stormy for his usual walk, he suddenly appeared in the parlor and amazed the company by breaking into a solo dance, "spinning airily around, displaying most remarkable litheness and agility and . . . finally [springing] over the center-table, alighting like a feather on the other side—then, not in the least out of breath [continuing] his waltz until his enthusiasm abated."[21] It was probably feats like this that made Alcott call Thoreau the "ruddiest and nimblest genius that has trodden our woods."[22] Perhaps the most charming vignette that has survived from Concord during the fabulous forties is the one sketched by the wife of Nathaniel Hawthorne, clearly designed to glorify her husband but incidentally setting Thoreau apart from his sedate literary friends most engagingly:

> One afternoon, Mr. Emerson and Mr. Thoreau went with him down the river. Henry Thoreau is an experienced skater, and was figuring dithyrambic dances and Bacchic leaps on the ice— very remarkable, but very ugly, methought. Next him followed Mr. Hawthorne who, wrapped in his cloak, moved like a self-impelled Greek statue, stately and grave. Mr. Emerson closed the line, evidently too weary to hold himself erect, pitching headforemost, half lying on the air.[23]

The *eiron* figure of Thoreau as a man has now been sufficiently established by reference to his *Journal* and by the evidence of friends. It remains only to point out how the author as a personality in life is transformed into the leading "character" in his book. He appears in the *eiron* role on the first page and continuously thereafter through the first half of *Walden,* less so in the second half. But to make sure that no one missed the pose, Thoreau scooped a choice sentence from his second chapter and used it on the title page as an epigraph: "I do not propose to write an ode to dejection, but to brag as lustily as chanticleer in the morning, standing on his roost, if only to wake my neighbors up." (94) This swaggering is countered by disarming self-deprecation at the end of the first chapter: "I never knew, and never shall know, a worse man than myself." (86) But one of the most attractive aspects of the *eiron* is his shape-shifting skill, most remarkably illustrated in the series of metaphors for the narrator's previous "enterprises," mentioned before, that form a brilliant digression early in "Economy."

In a country of self-made men, like America, where great emphasis is put on one's occupation, it is particularly effective satire for the vocationless Thoreau to take on this Protean guise, slipping into and out of fanciful versions of all the trades and professions. In addition to those enterprises already cited in other connections, two of the dozen paragraphs may be quoted here as samples of how he answered the question, What do you do?

> So many autumn, ay, and winter days, spent outside the town, trying to hear what was in the wind, to hear and carry it express! I well nigh sunk all my capital in it, and lost my own breath into the bargain, running in the face of it. . . . At other times watching from the observatory of some cliff or tree, to telegraph any new arrival; or waiting at evening on the hill-tops for the sky to fall, that I might catch something. (19)

Then in addition to being reporter to a journal "of no very wide circulation," weaver of non-selling baskets, trader with the Celestial Empire:

> I have looked after the wild stock of the town, which give a faithful herdsman a good deal of trouble by leaping fences; and . . . I have watered the red huckleberry, the sand cherry and the nettletree, the red pine and the black ash, the white grape and the yellow violet, which might have withered else in dry seasons. (20)

This same nimble and slippery fellow reappears throughout the book—evading visitors to his woodland retreat (143-144), running down hill "with the rainbow over my shoulder" to go fishing at Fair Haven (230), rushing past the crowd to a fire at Breed's hut, "I among the foremost, for I had leaped the brook." (286)

Similarly the *alazon* appears in many forms. He may be only the generalized laboring man, timorous or time-serving, so often the butt of ridicule in "Economy":

> It is very evident what mean and sneaking lives many of you live, . . . always on the limits, trying to get into business and trying to get out of debt; . . . seeking to curry favor, to get custom, by how many modes; lying, flattering, voting, contracting yourselves into a nutshell of civility, or dilating into an atmosphere of thin and vaporous generosity, that you may persuade your neighbor to let you make his shoes, or his hat, or his coat, or his carriage, or import his groceries for him. (7)

Professional reformers were more formidable antagonists, a special breed of the nineteenth century, and Thoreau devotes many pages to attacking them—all by raillery and caricature:

> As for Doing-good, that is one of the professions which are full. Moreover, I have tried it fairly, and, strange as it may seem, am satisfied that it does not agree with my constitution. . . . If anything ail a man, so that he does not perform his functions, if he have a pain in his bowels even,—for that is the seat of sympathy,—he forthwith sets about reforming,—the world. . . . And straightway his drastic philanthropy seeks out the Esquimau and the Patagonian, and embraces the populous Indian and Chinese villages; and thus, by a few years of philanthropic activity, the powers in the meanwhile using him for their own ends, no doubt, he cures himself of his dyspepsia. (81, 85-86)

Sometimes the *alazon* is only a nuisance, like the busybodies who paid visits to Walden cabin out of sheer curiosity and deserved only mild castigation: "uneasy housekeepers, who pried into my cupboard and bed when I was out,—how came Mrs.———to know that my sheets were not as clean as hers?" (169) It is for the mercenary and grasping that he saves his invective:

> *Flint's Pond!* Such is the poverty of our nomenclature. What right had the unclean and stupid farmer, whose farm abutted on this sky water, whose shores he has ruthlessly laid bare, to give his name to it? Some skin-flint, who loved better the reflecting surface of a dollar, or a bright cent, in which he could see his own brazen face; who regarded even the wild ducks which settled in it as trespassers; his fingers grown into crooked and horny talons from the long habit of grasping harpy-like. . . . I respect not his labors, his farm where everything has its price, who would carry the landscape, who would carry his God, to market, if he could get anything for him. (217-218)

It is the actual contests between *eiron* and *alazon,* of course, that provide the action in traditional comedy. In **Walden** they are usually presented in the indirect way shown above, since its mode is narrative, or poetic, rather than dramatic. But occasionally the encounter approaches a little nearer to the latter. The **Journal** itself is full of sparring with imaginary enemies. For example: "Men even think me odd and perverse because I do not prefer their society to this nymph or wood-god rather." (J, IX, 215-216) Sometimes Thoreau addresses them directly, as if present: "You think that I am impoverishing myself by withdrawing from men," and so on. (J, IX, 246) Many of the "antagonists" in **Walden** are such straw men, caught by the heel or forelock and dragged into the narrative purely for the purpose of being knocked down. But the memorable ones are sufficiently developed to pass for real "characters" and the confrontations with them have enough "action" to become miniature comic skits. Such are the scenes with the Canadian woodchopper, a natural man whom the narrator tries in vain to interest in ideas, and the meeting with the impoverished John Field, to whom he tries to give a lesson in economics—both to be treated fully in later chapters.

Two similar anecdotes will serve to illustrate the *alazon* here. The first is a simple bout with a mindless conformist, whom he mystifies with double talk:

> When I ask for a garment of a particular form, my tailoress tells me gravely, "They do not make them so now," not emphasizing the "They" at all, as if she quoted an authority as impersonal as the Fates, and I find it difficult to get made what I want, simply because she cannot believe that I mean what I say, that I am so rash. When I hear this oracular sentence, I am for a moment absorbed in thought, emphasizing to myself each word separately that I may come at the meaning of it, that I may find out by what degree of consanguinity *They* are related to *me,* and what authority they may have in an affair that affects me so nearly; and, finally, I am inclined to answer her with equal mystery, and without any more emphasis of the "they,"—"It is true, they did not make them so recently, but they do now." (27)

The second one turns from clothes to shelter, another necessity of life. To simplify the building of his own cabin he bought for $4.25 the tumbled-down shanty of James Collins, a railroad worker, in order to dismantle it and make use of its materials:

> I took down this dwelling the same morning, drawing the nails, and removed it to the pond-side by small cartloads, spreading the boards on the grass there to bleach and warp back again in the sun. . . . I was informed treacherously by a young Patrick that neighbor Seeley, an Irishman, in the intervals of the carting, transferred the still tolerable, straight, and drivable nails, staples, and spikes to his pocket, and then stood when I came back to pass the time of day, and look freshly up, unconcerned, with spring thoughts, at the devastation; there being a dearth of work, as he said. He was there to represent spectatordom, and help make this seemingly insignificant event one with the removal of the gods of Troy. (48-49)

The *alazon* here is merely a rascal, but since the *eiron* himself is a clever fellow too (though never dishonest) the rascality is winked at in the name of a larger fellowship.

Thoreau was fully aware of the role he was playing in life, as has been shown, and he confesses once outright in *Walden* to the same histrionic role there. "I had this advantage, at least, in my mode of life, over those who were obliged to look abroad for amusement, to society and the theatre, that my life itself was become my amusement and never ceased to be novel," he remarks in a casual aside: "It was a drama of many

scenes and without an end." (125) Even so, the traditional comedy structured by contests between *eiron* and *alazon* is not a model for *Walden,* only an instructive analogue. Since the argument for this influence has been put most convincingly by Professor Moldenhauer, he should be heard fully at this point. The narrator of *Walden* is the *eiron,* the witty and virtuous character whose actions are directed ultimately toward the establishment of an ideal order; the *alazons* are the hecklers and impostors, those who stand in the way of this fulfillment.[24]

In Chapter 1, "Economy" (according to this critic), Thoreau assumes a hostile audience, creates stylized individual figures who complain and try to block the action, and then "destroys" them with every kind of wit. The "plot" of *Walden* is similar to that of traditional comedy, as defined by Professor Frye. The action is a rising movement from a world ruled by conventions and the arbitrary laws of the elders to a world made free by youth, the awakened man of Thoreau's "Conclusion." The narrating "I" performs this ascent, prefiguring the spiritual transformation of the audience also. The pattern of development is a comic one, Moldenhauer sums up, contrasting two worlds: the private paradise of the narrator and the social wasteland of the audience he has left behind, inhabited respectively by happy youth and misanthropic old age. And Thoreau's rhetoric is a direct result of this debate—the dramatic status of the speaker with respect to his hostile fictive audience.

The narrator changes shapes many times. He is by turns "a severe moralist, a genial companion, a bemused 'hermit,' and a whimsical trickster," as this critic aptly puts it, at times treating the Walden experiment itself as a sly joke on solid citizens. Similarly, Thoreau uses many voices—persuasive, mocking, scolding, ecstatic. But his really distinctive voice speaks to us in paradoxes. Emerson objected to this quality in Thoreau's style. Once, in accepting an essay of his for publication in the *Dial* (1843), Emerson wrote to say that he had made numerous omissions in order to remove this "*mannerism.*" In the privacy of his *Journals* he was more outspokenly critical:

> Henry Thoreau sends me a paper with the old fault of unlimited contradiction. The trick of his rhetoric is soon learned: it consists in substituting for the obvious word and thought its diametrical antagonist. He praises wild mountains and winter forests for their domestic air; snow and ice for their warmth; villagers and woodchoppers for their urbanity, and the wilderness for resembling Rome and Paris. . . . It makes me nervous and wretched to read it.[25]

A decade later Emerson was still complaining of his friend: "Always some weary captious paradox to fight you with . . . all his resources of wit and invention are lost to me." When he read **Walden** he probably squirmed at one sentence in the "Conclusion," realizing that the author's finger was pointed at him: "In this part of the world it is considered a ground for complaint if a man's writings admit of more than one interpretation." (358) But when Thoreau himself reread his book shortly after publication, interestingly enough, he entered in his **Journal** a list of his faults, headed by: "Paradoxes,—saying just the opposite,—a style which may be imitated." (J. VII, 7-8) And yet, paradoxically, he kept on using them.

The truth of the matter is quite simple. Paradoxes, when indulged in indiscriminately, become a perverse and exasperating mannerism. Yet they can be very effective when made a disciplined and meaningful part of an author's style, as they are in **Walden**. There the first use of paradox is satirical, making the audience doubt the values of its own world, item by item, as Moldenhauer suggests; its second use is to make the narrator's world transcend the conventional world by subverting key terms in its language to new meanings. The *eiron* properly talks in riddles. He uses paradoxical language combined with verbal play to point up an actual paradox in life: that man is richest (in spiritual things) who is poorest (in material wealth). With it he can turn a cliché into an original aphorism: "How can you kill time without injuring eternity?" He can undermine what are presumed to be basic principles, such as man's need for human society: "I was no more lonely than the first spider in a new house."

For a book written in praise of the solitary life, **Walden** contains a surprising number of encounters between the narrator and representatives of society, sketched either with pretended realism or in undisguised caricature. These enliven the narrative and keep the presentation of its message from becoming solemn or didactic. They also provide one of the best ways of defining a concept such as solitude, so foreign to ordinary men as to seem an abstraction, by showing first of all what it is not. Once this has been accomplished in the first part of **Walden,** by showing the narrator participating to a limited extent in the gregarious life of men, Thoreau feels prepared to launch his quest for perfection. This is rendered largely by metaphors drawn from his experience of living alone in the woods.

Several unifying devices in **Walden** have now been pointed out: the character and speaking voice of the narrator, the transcendental patterns that give sequence to the chapters, the web of language woven by the two modes of wit and metaphor. Finally, there is an overall structure by which Thoreau achieves poetic unity: an intricate system of image-clusters that contains the book's inner meaning. Interpretation of the most significant of these will be undertaken in the chapters that follow.

Abbreviations

Alcott—*The Journals of Bronson Alcott,* ed. Odell Shepard (1938)

Cameron, *Minerva*—K. W. Cameron, ed., *The Transcendentalists and Minerva* (1958), 3 vols.

Correspondence—*The Correspondence of Henry David Thoreau,* ed. Walter Harding and Carl Bode (1958)

Emerson, *Journals—The Journals of Ralph Waldo Emerson,* eds. E. W. Emerson and W. E. Forbes (1909-14), 10 vols.

Emerson, *Works—The Complete Works of Ralph Waldo Emerson,* ed. E. W. Emerson (1903-04), 12 vols.

Harding—Walter Harding, *The Days of Henry Thoreau* (1965)

LJ—Perry Miller, *Consciousness in Concord* [Thoreau's "Lost Journal"] (1958)

Shanley—J. L. Shanley, *The Making of Walden* (1957)

Notes

[1] *"take part in it"* The translation is Thoreau's. J. I, 4-5. Cameron, *Minerva,* I, 237, says that Thoreau read Goethe's *Torquato Tasso* in German in Emerson's set of the *Werke* (Stuttgart, 1828-33). Leonora's description of the poet can be found in Vol. IX, pp. 107-108, lines 167-169:

> In diesem eignen Zauberkreise wandelt Der wunderbare Mann und zieht uns an, Mit ihm zu wandeln, teil an ihm zu nehmen . . .

[2] *"contain them all"* J, III, 311 (18 Feb. 1852). Version IV, the first significant re-writing of *Walden,* was begun about the middle of January 1852. (Shanley, 30-31)

[3] *"I sat outside"* See Thoreau's *Correspondence,* 290.

[4] *"where to lay his head"* Matthew 8.20.

[5] *letter scarcely clarifies it* In a letter of 1857, replying to a friend's inquiry as to the meaning of "a hound, a bay horse, and a turtle-dove," Thoreau said: "How shall we account for our pursuits if they are original? We get our language with which to describe our various lives out of a common mint. If others have their losses, which they are busy repairing, so have I *mine,* & their hound & horse may *perhaps* be the symbol of some of them. But also I have lost, or am in danger of losing, a far finer & more ethereal treasure, which commonly no loss of which they are conscious will

symbolize—this I answer hastily & with some hesitation, according as I now understand my own words." (*Correspondence,* 478)

[6] *"necessity of selling them"* This fable of the Indian baskets was not added to *Walden* until Version IV, summer 1852, after Thoreau knew of the failure of *A Week.* (Shanley, 31, 72)

[7] *book on food reform* William Alcott, *The Young Housekeeper* (1838), 362. See the discussion by Joseph Jones, "Transcendental Grocery Bills," UTSE, XXXVI (1957), 141-154.

[8] *"sweats easier than I do" Cf.* Genesis 3. 19. It is interesting to compare at this point one of the very earliest known writings of Thoreau, his part in a "Conference" at the time of his graduation from Harvard, August 1837, under the title of "The Commercial Spirit of Modern Times." One paragraph of it reads: "This curious world which we inhabit is more wonderful than it is convenient, more beautiful than it is useful— it is more to be admired and enjoyed then, than used. The order of things should be somewhat reversed.— the seventh should be man's day of toil, wherein to earn his living by the sweat of his brow, and the other six his sabbath of the affections and the soul, in which to range this widespread garden, and drink in the soft influences and sublime revelations of nature." (Reprinted in Cameron, *Minerva,* I, 234.)

[9] *Walden digresses See* pp. 50-53, 55-60, 62-65, 79-87. Thoreau admits his digressive tendency by reminding himself in the midst of these criticisms of society, "But to proceed with my statistics." (65)

[10] *"Economy" is a witty fable* The great difference made by the mode of wit in the presentation of the Walden experiment in economy may be illustrated by comparing the more serious treatment of such matters in the *Journal.* Thoreau's discussion of the problem ranges over a period of twenty years, from 1841 (LJ, 214) to 1861 (J, XIV, 306-307). There is a long recapitulation in the *Journal* for 1855, probably inspired by the publication of *Walden* the year before. A sample will suffice: "The world will never find out why you don't love to have your bed tucked up for you—why you will be so perverse. I enjoy more drinking water at a clear spring than out of a goblet at a gentleman's table. I like best the bread which I have baked, the garment which I have made, the shelter which I have constructed, the fuel which I have gathered," (J, VII, 502-503. See also VII, 519-520; VIII, 7-8, 18-19, 30-31—all in 1855). If *Walden* were written like this, readers might indeed think it perverse.

[11] *"the mountain cabin transformed"* In Version I of *Walden* (Shanley, 138), written in 1847 presumably,

the passage is closer to the *Journal* than to the book text. When the final revisions were made is not known.

[12] *"most important words"* F. O. Matthiessen, *American Renaissance* (1941), 95-96. Several of the points in my explication are indebted to him.

[13] *"God and Him only" See* Shanley, 141.

[14] *seventeenth-century meaning of wit* John Locke, *Essay Concerning the Human Understanding,* Chap. XI, 2. See J, V, 242, for an excellent example: "Murder will out. I find, in the dry excrement of a fox left on a rock, the vertebrae and talons of a partridge (?) which he has consumed. They are *memoires pour servir."*

[15] *parody of the New Testament* "For what shall it profit a man, if he shall gain the whole world, and lose his own soul?" (Mark 8.36)

"For whosoever . . . will lose his life for my sake shall find it." (Matthew 16.25)

"He that loveth his life shall lose it; and he that hateth his life in this world shall keep it unto life eternal." (John 12.25)

[16] *"to suffer and to work" See* Emerson, *Works,* I, 95.

[17] *"a huckleberry-party" See* Emerson's "Biographical Sketch," *The Writings of Thoreau,* I, xxxvii.

[18] *Walden Pond a symbol* There are a dozen brief but brilliant circle images in this chapter . . . , it is true, but most of its thirty pages are unadorned and factual. Another matter of special interest is the curious fact that only two or three pages of "The Ponds" are included in Version I of *Walden,* written during the actual residence there. All the rest was first drafted in the *Journal* during the summer and fall of 1852, based on trips back to the pond for this particular purpose, and then included in Versions IV-VI, 1852-1853. (See J, IV, 320-21, 335-41, 357-58, 387, 406-08, 411, 423-25, 447; V, 260, 265.) There are other symbolic passages on Walden in the *Journal,* ranging all the way from 1840 to 1860 (LJ, 185; J, XIV, 60-61).

[19] *"law for thing"* Emerson, "Ode Inscribed to W. H. Channing." Transcendentalists would probably have interpreted Thoreau's triad of being-nonbeing-becoming as an example of the Hegelian triad of thesis-antithesis-synthesis.

[20] *"hatches his own schemes"* Northrop Frye, *Anatomy of Criticism* (1957), 174; 39-40, 172-176.

[21] *"his enthusiasm abated" See* Harding, 362, 265-266.

22 *"has trodden our woods"* Alcott, 193.

23 *"lying on the air" Quoted* by Rose Hawthorne Lathrop, *Memories of Hawthorne* (1897), 53.

24 *analogue of eiron-alazon* J. J. Moldenhauer, "Paradox in *Walden,*" *Graduate Journal,* VI (1964), 132-46. I am indebted to him for the basic idea of *eiron-alazon* and the summary on this page and the following.

25 *"wretched to read it"* Emerson, *Journals,* VI, 440; the quotation in the next sentence is from IX, 15. In submitting the essay, "A Winter Walk," Thoreau had defended his style indirectly by saying: "In writing, conversation should be folded many times thick. It is the height of art that on the first perusal plain common sense should appear—on the second severe truth— and on a third beauty." *Correspondence,* 125; Emerson's reply, cited above, is printed on p. 137.

Walter Benn Michaels (essay date 1977)

SOURCE: "*Walden*'s False Bottoms," in *GLYPH,* Vol. 1, 1977, pp. 132-49.

[*In this excerpt, Michaels explores the strategies employed by* Walden'*s readers in order to deal with the text's many contradictions.*]

Walden has traditionally been regarded as both a simple and a difficult text, simple in that readers have achieved a remarkable unanimity in identifying the values Thoreau is understood to urge upon them, difficult in that they have been persistently perplexed and occasionally even annoyed by the form his exhortations take. Thoreau's Aunt Maria (the one who bailed him out of jail in the poll tax controversy) understood this as a problem in intellectual history and blamed it all on the Transcendental *Zeitgeist:* "I do love to hear things called by their right names," she said, "and these *Transcendentalists* do so transmogrophy . . . their words and pervert common sense that I have no patience with them."¹ Thoreau's Transcendentalist mentor, Emerson, found, naturally enough, another explanation, blaming instead what he called Henry's "old fault of unlimited contradiction. The trick of his rhetoric is soon learned: it consists in substituting for the obvious word and thought its diametrical antagonist. . . . It makes me," he concluded, "nervous and wretched to read it."² That old fault of contradiction is in one sense the subject of this essay, so is wretchedness and especially nervousness, so, in some degree, are the strategies readers have devised for feeling neither wretched nor nervous.

The primary strategy, it seems to me, has been to follow a policy of benign neglect in regard to the question of what *Walden* means; thus, as Charles Anderson noted some ten years ago, critics have concerned themselves largely with "style," agreeing from the start that the book's distinction lies "more in its manner than its matter."³ Anderson was referring mainly to the tradition of essentially formalist studies ushered in by F.O. Matthiessen's monumental *American Renaissance* in 1941, in which Thoreau is assimilated to the American tradition of the "native craftsman," and *Walden* itself is compared to the "artifacts of the cabinet maker, the potter and the founder."⁴ Anderson himself has no real quarrel with this procedure; his chief complaint is that Matthiessen's successors have not taken their enterprise seriously enough. The concern with *Walden*'s style, he says, "has not usually been pursued beyond a general eulogy. Perhaps it is through language that all the seemingly disparate subjects of this book are integrated into wholeness." "Why not try an entirely new approach," he suggests, "and read *Walden* as a poem?"⁵

From our present perspective, of course, it is hard to see how reading *Walden* "as a poem" constitutes an entirely new approach; it seems, if anything, a refinement of the old approaches, a way of continuing to bracket the question of *Walden*'s meaning in at least two different ways. The first is by introducing a distinction between form and content which simultaneously focuses attention on the question of form and reduces content to little more than a banality, typically, in the case of *Walden,* a statement to the effect that the book is fundamentally "a fable of the renewal of life."⁶ But from this first move follows a second, more interesting and more pervasive: the preoccupation with *Walden*'s formal qualities turns out to involve a more than tacit collaboration with the assumption that *Walden*'s meaning (what Anderson might call its content and what Stanley Cavell will explicitly call its "doctrine") is in a certain sense simple and univocal. The assertion implicit in this approach is that to examine the form of any literary "artifact" (in fact, even to define the artifact) is precisely to identify its essential unity, thus the continuity between Matthiessen's concern with *Walden*'s "structural wholeness" and Anderson's project of showing how well "integrated" the book is. Where nineteenth-century critics tended to regard *Walden* as an anthology of spectacular fragments and to explain it in terms of the brilliant but disordered personality of its author (his "critical power," wrote James Russell Lowell, was "from want of continuity of mind, very limited and inadequate"),⁷ more recent criticism, by focusing directly on the art of *Walden,* has tended to emphasize the rhetorical power of its "paradoxes," finding elegant formal patterns in what were once thought to be mere haphazard blunders. Thus, in accepting unity and coherence not simply as *desiderata* but as the characteristic identifying marks of the work of art, these critics have begun by answering the question I should like to begin by asking, the question of *Walden*'s contradictions.

Thoreau himself might well have been skeptical of some of the claims made on behalf of *Walden*'s aesthetic integrity. He imagined himself addressing "poor students," leading "mean and sneaking lives," "lying, flattering, voting."[8] "The best works of art," he said, "are the expression of man's struggle to free himself from this condition, but the effect of our art is merely to make this low state comfortable and that higher state to be forgotten" (p. 25). In this context, what we might begin to see emerging as the central problem of reading *Walden* is the persistence of our own attempts to identify and understand its unity, to dispel our nervousness by resolving or at least containing the contradictions which create it. It is just this temptation, Thoreau seems to suggest, which must be refused. And in this respect, the naïve perspective of someone like Lowell, who saw in Thoreau the absolute lack of any "artistic mastery" and in his works the total absence of any "mutual relation" between one part and another, may still be of some provisional use, not as a point of view to be reclaimed but as a reminder that resolution need not be inevitable, that we need not read to make ourselves more comfortable.

One way to begin nurturing discomfort is to focus on some of the tasks Thoreau set himself as part of his program for living a life of what he called "epic integrity." There were, of course, a good many of them, mostly along the lines of his own advice to the unhappily symbolic farmer John Field—"Grow wild according to thy nature," Thoreau urged him, "Rise free from care before the dawn. Let the noon find thee by other lakes and the night overtake thee everywhere at home" (p. 138). Some other projects, however, were conceived in less hortatory terms and the possibility of their completion was more explicitly imaginable. One, "To find the bottom of Walden Pond and what inlet and outlet it might have,"[9] worked its way eventually out of Thoreau's *Journal* and into a central position in the experiment of *Walden* itself. What gave this quest a certain piquancy were the rumours that the pond had no bottom, that, as some said, "it reached quite through to the other side of the globe." "These many stories about the bottom, or rather no bottom, of this Pond," had, Thoreau said, "no foundation for themselves." In fact, the pond was "exactly one hundred and two feet deep," his own "soundings" proved it. This is, he admits, "a remarkable depth for so small an area; yet not an inch of it can be spared by the imagination. What if all ponds were shallow? Would it not react on the minds of men? While men believe in the infinite some ponds will be thought to be bottomless" (p. 189).

If Thoreau's final position on bottoms seems to come out a little blurred here, this has an interest of its own which may be worth pursuing. On the one hand, the passage seems to be asserting that a belief in the potential bottomlessness of ponds is a Bad Thing. The villagers predisposed in this direction who set out to measure Walden with a fifty-six-pound weight and a wagon load of rope were already entrapped by their own delusions, for "while the fifty-six was resting by the way," Thoreau says, "they were paying out the rope in the vain attempt to fathom their truly immeasurable capacity for marvellousness" (p. 189). On the other hand, it isn't enough that the pond is revealed to have a "tight bottom," or even that it turns out symbolically "deep and pure"; it must be imagined bottomless to encourage men's belief in the "infinite." Thus, the passage introduces two not entirely complementary sets of dichotomies. In the first, the virtues of a pond with a "tight bottom" are contrasted with the folly of believing in bottomless ponds. But then the terms shift: the tight bottom metamorphoses into the merely "shallow" and the bottomless becomes the "infinite." The hierarchies are inverted here: on the one hand, a "tight bottom" is clearly preferable to delusory bottomlessness, on the other hand, the merely "shallow" is clearly not so good as the symbolically suggestive "infinite." Finally, the narrator is thankful that the pond was made deep, but "deep" is a little ambiguous: is he glad that the pond is *only* deep so that tough-minded men like himself can sound it and discover its hard bottom, or is he glad that the pond is so deep that it deceives men into thinking of it as bottomless and so leads them into meditations on the infinite? This second explanation seems more convincing, but then the account of the experiment seems to end with a gesture which undermines the logic according to which it was undertaken in the first place.

Sounding the depths of the pond, however, is by no means the only experimental excavation in *Walden*. There is perhaps a better-known passage near the end of the chapter called "Where I Lived and What I Lived For" which helps to clarify what is at stake in the whole bottom-hunting enterprise. "Let us settle ourselves," Thoreau says, "and work and wedge our feet downward through the mud and slush of opinion, and prejudice, and tradition, and delusion, and appearance . . . through church and state, through poetry and philosophy and religion, till we come to a hard bottom and rocks in place which we can call *reality,* and say This is, and no mistake; and then begin, having a *point d'appui* . . . a place where you might found a wall or a state" (p. 66). Measurement here is irrelevant—the issue is solidity, not depth, and the metaphysical status of hard bottoms seems a good deal less problematic. They are real, and "Be it life or death," Thoreau says, "we crave only reality." It is only when we have put ourselves in touch with such a *point d'appui* that we really begin to lead our lives and not be led by them, and the analogy with the *Walden* experiment itself is obvious—it becomes a kind of ontological scavenger-hunt—the prize is reality.

But there is at least one more hard bottom story which unhappily complicates things again. It comes several hundred pages later in the "Conclusion," and tucked in as it is between the flashier and more portentous parables of the artist from Kouroo and of the "strong and beautiful bug," it has been more or less ignored by critics. "It affords me no satisfaction to commence to spring an arch before I have got a solid foundation," Thoreau begins in the now familiar rhetoric of the moral imperative to get to the bottom of things. "Let us not play at kittlybenders," he says, "There is a solid bottom everywhere." But now the story proper gets underway and things begin to go a little haywire. "We read that the traveller asked the boy if the swamp before him had a hard bottom. The boy replied that it had. But presently the traveller's horse sank in up to the girths, and he observed to the boy, 'I thought you said that this bog had a hard bottom.' 'So it has,' answered the latter, 'but you have not got half way to it yet.'" And "so it is with the bogs and quicksands of society," Thoreau piously concludes, "but he is an old boy that knows it" (p. 219).

This puts the earlier story in a somewhat different light, I think, and for several reasons. For one thing, the tone is so different; the exalted rhetoric of the evangelist has been replaced by the fireside manner of the teller of tall tales. But more fundamentally, although the theme of the two stories has remained the same—the explorer in search of the solid foundation—the point has been rather dramatically changed. The exhortation has become a warning. The exemplary figure of the heroic traveller, "tied to his mast like Ulysses," Thoreau says, who accepts no substitutes in his quest for the real, has been replaced by the equally exemplary but much less heroic figure of the suppositious traveller drowned in his own pretension. In the first version, Thoreau recognized death as a possibility, but it was a suitably heroic one: "If you stand right fronting and face to face to a fact," he wrote in a justly famous passage, "you will see the sun glimmer on both its surfaces, as if it were a cimeter, and feel its sweet edge dividing you through the heart and marrow, and so you will happily conclude your mortal career" (p. 66). The vanishing traveller of the "conclusion" knows no such happy ending, when he hits the hard bottom he will just be dead, his only claim to immortality his skill in the art of sinking, dispiritedly, in prose.

The juxtaposition of these three passages does not in itself prove anything very startling but it does suggest what may be a useful line of inquiry. What, after all, is at stake in the search for a solid bottom? Why is the concept or the project of foundation so central to *Walden* and at the same time so problematic? At least

a preliminary answer would seem justified in focusing on the almost Cartesian process of peeling away until we reach that point of ontological certainty where we can say "This is, and no mistake." The peeling away is itself a kind of questioning: what justification do we have for our opinions, for our traditions? What authorizes church and state, poetry, philosophy, religion? The *point d'appui* has been reached only when we have asked all the questions we know how to ask and so at last have the sense of an answer we are unable ourselves to give. "After a still winter night," Thoreau says, "I awoke with the impression that some question had been put to me, which I had been endeavouring in vain to answer in my sleep, as what—how—when—where? But there was dawning Nature in whom all creatures live . . . and no question on *her* lips. I awoke to an answered question, to Nature . . ." (p. 187). The *point d'appui* then, is a place we locate by asking questions. We know that we've found it when one of our questions is answered. The name we give to this place is Nature. The search for the solid bottom is a search for justification in Nature, wedging our way through "appearance," that is to say human institutions, like church and state and philosophy, until we hit what is real, that is, natural, and not human.

That nature in its purest form should exclude humanity is perhaps a somewhat peculiar doctrine, and one which runs counter to much of what Thoreau often says, and to much of what we think about him and his enterprise. But the logic and the desires which generate this conception are made clear in **"Civil Disobedience"** when Thoreau attacks the "statesmen and legislators" who, "standing so completely within the institution, never distinctly and nakedly behold it" (p. 241). In an essay called "What Is Authority?" Hannah Arendt has described what she calls "the dichotomy between seeing truth in solitude and remoteness and being caught in the relationships and relativities of human affairs" as "authoritative for the (Western) tradition of political thought,"[10] and it is precisely this privilege of distance and detachment to which Thoreau seems to be appealing in **"Civil Disobedience"**. He goes on, however, to diagnose more specifically what is wrong with the legislators: "They speak of moving society, but have no resting-place without it." Webster, for instance, "never goes behind government and so cannot speak with authority about it." The appeal here is to the example of Archimedes—"Give me a place to stand and I will move the earth"—and the suggestion in *Walden* is that nature must be much more than a place of retreat. She is a "resting-place" only in the sense of the *"point d'appui,"* the place to stand, and she is an authoritative *point d'appui* only insofar as she is truly "behind," first, separate, and other. Thus, through most of *Walden,* when Thoreau is addressing himself to the problem of his search for a *cogito,* a political and philosophical hard bottom, the human and the natural are conceived as standing in implicit opposition to each other. Nature has a kind of literal authority precisely because she is not one of men's institutions. She serves as the location of values which are real insofar as they are not human creations. She is exemplary. "If we would restore mankind," Thoreau says, "let us first be as simple and as well as Nature ourselves" (p. 53). The force of this conception is expressed most directly, perhaps, in the short essay "Slavery in Massachusetts," written to protest the state's cooperation with the Fugitive Slave Law of 1850. The image of Nature here is a white water-lily, an emblem, like Walden Pond itself, of "purity." "It suggests what kind of laws have prevailed longest," Thoreau writes, " . . . and that there is virtue even in man, too, who is fitted to perceive and love it."[11] And, he goes on to say, "It reminds me that Nature has been partner to no Missouri Compromise. I scent no compromise in the fragrance of the water-lily." The point again is that it is Nature's independence which makes her exemplary, which, from this standpoint, justifies the retreat to Walden and authorizes the hope that something of real value may be found and hence founded there.

But this conception of nature, as attractive and useful as it is, turns out to be in some ways a misleading one. In "Slavery in Massachusetts," the encomium on the lily is preceded by a brief excursion in search of solace to "one of our ponds" (it might as well be Walden). But there is no solace to be found there. "We walk to lakes to see our serenity reflected in them," Thoreau says, "when we are not serene we go not to them."[12] For "what signifies the beauty of nature when men are base?" If the water-lily is a symbol of nature free and clear, sufficient unto itself, the pond in its role as reflector symbolizes a nature implicated in human affairs. It fails as a source of consolation because, unlike the water-lily, it participates in the world of Missouri Compromises and Fugitive Slave Laws. And this vision of nature compromised finds a significant position in *Walden* as well. In the chapter called "Sounds," Thoreau devotes the beginning of one paragraph to a sound he claims he never heard, the sound of the cock crowing. This is no doubt a kind of back-handed reference to his own declaration at the beginning of the book: "I do not propose to write an ode to dejection, but to brag as lustily as chanticleer in the morning . . . if only to wake my neighbors up" (p. 1). The writing of *Walden* makes up for the absent cock-crow. But he goes on to speak of the cock as a "once wild Indian pheasant" and to wonder if it could ever be "naturalized without being domesticated" (pp. 85-86). Here *Walden*'s customary opposition between nature and civilization turns into an opposition between wilderness and civilization, and nature ("naturalized") appears as a third term, at one remove from "wild" and in constant danger of being domesticated and so rendered useless. Furthermore, this danger appears most pronounced at a moment which has been defined as that of writing, the cock-

crow. The dismay at seeing only one's face reflected in the pond repeats itself here for a moment as the text imagines itself as a once wild voice now tamed and defused.

These two accounts suggest, then, the kind of problem that is being defined. The attraction of Nature as a bottom line is precisely its otherness—"Nature puts no question and answers none which we mortals ask" (p. 187)—and touching bottom is thus (paradoxically) a moment of recognition; we see what "really is" and our relation to it is basically one of appreciation (and perhaps emulation). The paradox, of course, is our ability to recognize something which is defined precisely by its strangeness to us, a difficulty Thoreau urges upon us when he insists that "Nature has no human inhabitant who appreciates her" (p. 134), and that "she flourishes most alone." But, as I have said, this aloneness is the chief guarantee of authenticity—when we have reached the bottom, we know at least that what we are seeing is not just ourselves. And yet this is also what is most problematic in the symbolic character of Walden Pond itself; looking into it, we find ourselves sounding the depths of our own "nature," and so the reflection makes a mockery of our enterprise. "For his genius to be effective," one critic has written, Thoreau recognized that he "had to slough off his civilized self and regain his natural self,"[13] and this seems innocuous enough. But the cosmological continuity which would authorize a notion like the "natural self" is exactly what is being questioned here. For us to recognize ourselves in Nature, Nature must be no longer herself, no longer the *point d'appui* we were looking for when we started.

But even if Nature proves inadequate as a final category, an absolute, *Walden*'s response is not to repudiate the notion of intrinsic value. The pond remains a precious stone, "too pure," he says, to have "a market value" (p. 134), and so it provides at least a symbolic alternative to the commercial values of the first chapter, "Economy." "Economy" has usually been read as a witty and bitter attack on materialism, perhaps undertaken, as Charles Anderson has suggested,[14] in response to Mill's *Political Economy* and/or Marx's *Manifesto* (both published in 1848), motivated, in any event, by a New Testament perception: "Men labor under a mistake. . . . They are employed . . . laying up treasures which moth and rust will corrupt and thieves break through and steal" (p. 3). But it isn't simply a mistake in emphasis—too much on the material and not enough on the spiritual—that Thoreau is concerned with here, for the focal point of "Economy's" attack is not wealth *per se* but "exchange," the principle of the marketplace. Thus, he questions not merely the value of material goods but the process through which the values are determined; "trade curses everything it handles," he says, "and though you trade in messages from heaven, the whole curse of trade attaches to the business" (p. 47). In some degree this can be explained as a nineteenth-century expression of a long-standing ideological debate between the political conceptions of virtue and commerce, which depended in turn upon an opposition between what J.G.A. Pocock has called "real, inheritable, and, so to speak, natural property in land,"[15] and property understood to have only what Pocock calls a "symbolic value, expressed in coin or in credit." One of the phenomena Pocock describes is the persistence with which various social groups attempted to convince themselves that their credit economies were "based on the exchange of real goods and the perception of real values." Failing this, he says, "the individual could exist, even in his own sight, only at the fluctuating value imposed upon him by his fellows."[16]

Thoreau was obviously one of those unconvinced and unhappy about it. Not only did he repudiate what he perceived as false methods of determining value, not only did he rail against the maintenance of a standing army and even reject at times the validity of the entire concept of representative government (all these, as Pocock depicts them, classical political positions); he also attacked real, so-called natural property as well, and precisely at the point which was intended to provide its justification, its inheritability. "I see young men," he says at the very beginning of *Walden,* "my townsmen, whose misfortune it is to have inherited farms, houses . . . for these are more easily acquired than got rid of" (p. 2). Here he blurs the customary distinction between real or natural and symbolic or artificial property, insisting that all property is artificial and so exposing laws of inheritance as mere fictions of continuity, designed to naturalize values which in themselves are purely arbitrary.

This points toward a rather peculiar dilemma—Thoreau's doggedly ascetic insistence on distinguishing natural values from artificial ones leads him to reject the tokens of natural value which his society provides, and so the category of the natural becomes an empty one. But this doesn't mean that the natural/arbitrary distinction breaks down. Quite the contrary: the more difficult that it becomes to identify natural principles, the more privilege attaches to a position which can be defined only in theoretical opposition to the conventional or institutional. The "resting-place without" society that Thoreau speaks of in **"Civil Disobedience"** now turns out to be located neither in nature nor in culture but in that empty space he sometimes calls "wilderness." This is perhaps what he means when he describes himself once as a "sojourner in civilized life" and another time as a "sojourner in nature." To be a sojourner everywhere is by one account (Thoreau's own in "Walking") to be "at home everywhere." In *Walden,* however, this vision of man at home in the world is undermined by the Prophetic voice which proclaims it. He denounces his contemporaries who "no longer camp as for a night but have settled down on earth and forgotten heaven" by comparing them unfavorably to the primitive nomads who "dwelt . . . in a tent in this world" (p. 25), thus invoking one of the oldest of western topoi, the moral authority of the already atavistic Hebrew nomads, the Rechabites, relating the commandments of their father to the prophet Jeremiah: "Neither shall ye build house, nor sow seed, nor plant vineyard, nor have any: but all your days ye shall dwell in tents; that ye may live many days in the land where ye be strangers" (*Jeremiah* 35:7). The Rechabites were at home nowhere, not everywhere. Jeremiah cites them as exemplars not of a healthy rusticity but of a deep-seated and devout alienation which understands every experience except that of Yahweh as empty and meaningless.[17] Thus, to be, like Thoreau, a self-appointed stranger in the land is to repudiate the values of a domesticated pastoral by recognizing the need for a resting-place beyond culture and nature both, and to accept the figurative necessity of living always in one's tent is to recognize the impossibility of ever actually locating that resting-place.

Another way to deal with this search for authority is to imagine it emanating not only from a place but from a time. In *Walden,* the notion of foundation brings these two categories uneasily together. The solid bottom is a place where you might "found a wall or a state," but the foundation of a state is perhaps more appropriately conceived as a time—July 4, for example, the day Thoreau says he moved to the woods. This constitutes an appeal to the authority of precedent which would justify also the exemplary claims *Walden* makes on behalf of itself. The precedent has force as the record of a previous "experiment," and since "No way of thinking or doing, however ancient, can be trusted without proof" (p. 5), the "experiment" of *Walden* can apparently be understood as an attempt to repeat the results originally achieved by the Founding Fathers. But the scientific term "experiment," precisely because it relies on the notion of repeatability, that is, on an unchanging natural order, turns out to work much less well in the historical context of human events. "Here is life," Thoreau says, "an experiment to a great extent untried by me; but it does not avail me that they have tried it" (p. 5). This now is a peculiar kind of empiricism which stresses not only the primacy of experience but its unrepeatability, its uniqueness. (What good is *Walden* if not as a precedent?) The revolutionary appeal to foundation as a new beginning seems to be incompatible with the empiricist notion of foundation as the experience of an immediate but principled (i.e., repeatable) reality. The historical and the scientific ideas of foundation are clearly at odds here, and Thoreau seems to recognize this when he speaks of his desire "to anticipate not the sunrise and the dawn merely, but if possible Nature herself," that is, to achieve a priority which belongs to the historical but not the natural world. Coleridge had written some twenty years before that "No natural thing or act can be called an originate" since "the moment we assume an origin in nature, a true beginning, that moment we rise above nature."[18] Thoreau speaks of coming before rather than rising above, but the sense of incompatibility is the same. Once again the desire for the solid bottom is made clear, but the attempt to locate it or specify its characteristics involves the writer in a tangle of contradictions.

What I have tried to describe thus far is a series of relationships in the text of *Walden*—between nature and culture, the finite and the infinite, and (still to come) literal and figurative language—each of which is imagined at all times hierarchically, that is, the terms don't simply coexist, one is always thought of as more basic or more important than the other. The catch is that the hierarchies are always breaking down. Sometimes nature is the ground which authorizes culture, sometimes it is merely another of culture's creations. Sometimes the search for a hard bottom is presented as the central activity of a moral life, sometimes that same search will only make a Keystone-cop martyr out of the searcher. These unresolved contradictions are, I think, what makes us nervous reading *Walden,* and the urge to resolve them seems to me a major motivating factor in most *Walden* criticism. Early, more or less explicitly biographical criticism tended to understand the inconsistencies as personal ones, stemming, in Lowell's words, from Thoreau's "want of continuity of mind." But as the history of literary criticism began to deflect its attention from authors to texts, this type of explanation naturally began to seem unsatisfactory. Allusions to Thoreau's psychological instability were now replaced by references to *Walden*'s "literary design," and paradox, hitherto understood as a more or less technical device, was now seen to lie near the very center of *Walden*'s "literariness." In one essay, by Joseph Moldenhauer,[19] Thoreau's techniques are seen in easy analogy to those of Sir Thomas Browne, Donne, and the other English Metaphysicals, and generally the "presentation of truth through paradox" is identified as Thoreau's characteristic goal, although sometimes the truth is mythical, sometimes psychological, sometimes a little of both. In any event, the formalist demand that the text be understood as a unified whole (mechanical or organic) is normative; what Moldenhauer calls the "heightened language of paradox" is seen as shocking the reader into new perceptions of ancient truths.

More recently, the question of *Walden*'s hierarchies has been raised again by Stanley Cavell in a new and interesting way. Cavell recounts what he calls the "low myth of the reader" in *Walden.* "It may be thought of," he says, as a one-sentence fabliau:

The writer has been describing the early spring days in which he went down to the woods to cut down timber for his intended house; he depicts himself carrying along his dinner of bread and butter wrapped in a newspaper which while he was resting he read. A little later, he says: "In those days when my hands were much employed, I read but little, but the least scraps of paper which lay on the ground . . . afforded me as much entertainment, in fact answered the same purpose as the *Iliad*."

If you do not know what reading can be, you might as well use the pages of the *Iliad* for the purpose for which newspaper is used after a meal in the woods. If, however, you are prepared to read, then a fragment of newspaper, discovered words, are sufficient promptings . . . The events in a newspaper, our current lives are epic, and point morals, if we know how to interpret them.[20]

The moral of this interpretation, as I understand it, is that just as the hierarchical relation between nature and culture is uncertain and problematic, so there is no necessary hierarchy among texts—a Baltimore *Morning Sun* is as good as an *Iliad* if you know how to read it. But it is interesting that one of the passages Cavell elsewhere refers to (from *Walden*'s chapter on "Reading") is concerned precisely to specify a hierarchy of texts. "I kept Homer's *Iliad* on my table through the summer," Thoreau writes, "though I looked at his page only now and then. . . . Yet I sustained myself by the prospect of such reading in the future. I read one or two shallow books of travel in the intervals of my work, till that employment made me ashamed of myself, and I asked where it was then that *I* lived" (p. 67). The contrast here is between the epic and the travelogue, and for Thoreau the latter was a particularly vexing genre. "I would fain say something, not so much concerning the Chinese and Sandwich Islanders as you who read these pages, who are said to live in New England" (p. 2), he proclaims in *Walden*'s first chapter, and in its last chapter he renounces any "exploration" beyond one's "private sea, the Atlantic and Pacific Ocean of one's being alone" (p. 212). In his personal life, too, he shied away from voyages; until his last years, he never got any farther from Concord than Staten Island, and it took only several youthful weeks on that barbaric shore to send him scurrying for home. But he was at the same time inordinately fond of travel books; one scholar's account has him reading a certifiable minimum of 172 of them,[21] and as any reader of *Walden* knows, these accounts make frequent appearances there. In fact, in "Economy," no sooner has Thoreau announced his intention to ignore the lure of Oriental exoticisms than he plunges into a series of stories about the miraculous exploits of certain heroic "Bramins." *Walden* is, in fact, chock full of the wisdom of the mysterious East. The epics which Thoreau opposes to "shallow books of travel" are, in almost the same breath, described as "books which circulate around the world," that is, they are themselves travelling books.

All this serves mainly to reinforce Cavell's point; judging by subject matter at least, epics and travelogues turn out to look pretty much the same—the significant distinctions must then be not so much in the books themselves as in the way we read them. And along these lines, Thoreau suggests in "Reading" another, perhaps more pertinent way of distinguishing between the two genres: travel books are "shallow," epics presumably are not, which is to say that in reading epics, we must be prepared to conjecture "a larger sense than common use permits" (pp. 67-68). The mark of the epic is thus that it can be, indeed must be, read figuratively, whereas the travel book lends itself only to a shallow or literal reading. Thoreau goes on to imagine the contrast between classical literature and what he calls a "cheap, contemporary literature" (p. 68) as a contrast between the eloquence of the writer who "speaks to the intellect and heart of mankind, to all in any age who can *understand* him" and the lesser eloquence of the orator who "yields to the inspiration of a transient occasion, and speaks to the mob before him, to those who can *hear* him" (p. 69). Thus the opposition between the epic and travelogue has modulated into an opposition between the figurative and the literal and then between the written and the oral. In each case, the first term of the opposition is privileged, and if we turn again to the attempt to sound the depths of Walden Pond, we can see that these are all values of what I have called 'bottomlessness'. A shallow pond would be like a shallow book, that is, a travel book one meant to be read literally. *Walden* is written "deep and pure for a symbol."

But this pattern of valorization, although convincing, is by no means ubiquitous or final. The chapter on "Reading" is followed by one called "Sounds," which systematically reconsiders the categories already introduced and which reasserts the values of the hard bottom. Here the written word is contrasted unfavorably with the magical "noise" of nature. The 'intimacy' and 'universality' for which Thoreau had praised it in the first chapter are now metamorphosed into 'confinement' and a new kind of 'provincialism.' But not only is the hierarchical relation between the written and the oral inverted, so is what we have seen to be the corresponding relation between the figurative and the literal. What in the chapter on "Reading" was seen to be the greatest virtue of the classic texts, their susceptibility to interpretation, to the conjecturing of a larger sense "too significant," Thoreau says, "to be heard by the ear," a sense which "we must be born again to speak" (p. 68), all this is set aside in favor of the "one articulation of Nature" (p. 83), the "language which all things and events speak without metaphor"

(p. 75). In "Sounds," Nature's voice is known precisely because it resists interpretation. The polysemous becomes perverse; the models of communication are the Puri Indians who, having only one word for yesterday, today, and tomorrow, "express the variety of meaning by pointing backward for yesterday, forward for tomorrow, and overhead for the passing day" (p. 75). Where the classic texts were distinguished by their underdetermined quality—since the language they were written in was "dead," their "sense" was generated only by the reader's own interpretive "wisdom," "valor," and "generosity"—nature's language in "Sounds," the song of the birds, the stirring of the trees, is eminently alive and, as the example of the Indians shows, correspondingly overdetermined. Theirs is a system of words modified only by gestures and so devised that they will allow only a single meaning. No room is left for the reader's conjectures; the goal is rather a kind of indigenous and monosyllabic literalism, so many words for so many things by the shores of Gitcheegoomee. This means, of course, that the values of bottomlessness are all drained away. The deep is replaced by the shallow, the symbolic by the actual—what we need now, Thoreau says, are "tales of real life, high and low, and founded on fact" (p. 81).

This particular set of inversions helps us to relocate, I think, the problem of reading *Walden,* which we have already defined as the problem of resolving, or at least containing, its contradictions, of establishing a certain unity. Critics like Lowell domesticated the contradictions by understanding them as personal ones; to point out Thoreau's (no doubt lamentable) inconsistencies was not, after all, to accuse him of schizophrenia—the parts where he seemed to forget himself or ignore what he had said before were evidence only of certain lapses of attention. The formalists, turning their attention from the author to the text, transformed Thoreau's faults into *Walden*'s virtues; theirs was already the language of paradox, apparent inconsistencies pointing toward final literary (i.e., not necessarily logical) truths. Now Cavell takes this process of resolution, of replacement, as far, in one direction, as it can go; the unity which was claimed first for the personality of the author, then for the formal structure of the text itself, now devolves upon the reader. *Walden*'s contradictions are resolved, he says, "if you know how to interpret them." The reader who knows how, it turns out, can discern in *Walden* "a revelation in which the paradoxes and ambiguities of its doctrine achieve a visionary union."[22] And more recent writers like Lawrence Buell have extended this principle to others among the Transcendentalists. "Emerson's contribution," Buell writes, "is to show through his paradoxical style the inoperability of doctrine, to force the auditor to read him figuratively, as he believes that scriptures should be read."[23]

But Cavell's position has its own peculiarity, for while it recognizes and even insists upon the difficulty of maintaining hierarchies in the text of *Walden,* it goes on simply to reinscribe those hierarchies in *Walden*'s readers. Knowing how to read for Cavell and for Buell is knowing how to read figuratively, and this is one of the things, Cavell says, that *Walden* teaches us. Thus the coherence that the formalists understood as the defining characteristic of the text becomes instead the defining characteristic of the reader, and the unity which was once claimed for the object itself is now claimed for the reader's experience of it. But, as we have just seen, the power of figurative reading is not the only thing *Walden* teaches us; it also urges upon us the necessity of reading literally, not so much in addition to reading figuratively as *instead* of reading figuratively. In the movement from "Reading" to "Sounds," the figurative and the literal do not coexist, they are not seen as complementary; rather the arguments Thoreau gives in support of the one take the form of attacks on the other. If, following Thoreau's guide, we conceive the literal as a meaning available to us without interpretation (i.e., the unmediated language of nature) and the figurative as a meaning generated by our own interpretive "wisdom," we find that the very act of reading commits us to a choice, not simply between different meanings, but between different stances toward reality, different versions of the self. Thus books must inevitably be "read as deliberately and reservedly as they were written" because to read *is* to deliberate, to consider and decide. "Our whole life is startlingly moral," Thoreau says, "There is never an instant's truce between virtue and vice" (p. 145). This is a call to action in the most direct sense, and the action it imagines is reading, conceived as an explicitly moral activity. Elsewhere he writes, "it appears as if men had deliberately chosen the common mode of living because they preferred it to others. Yet they honestly think there is no choice left" (p. 5). Thoreau's concern in *Walden* is, of course, to show us that we do have choices left and, by breaking down hierarchies into contradictory alternatives, to insist upon our making them. But this breakdown, which creates the opportunity, or rather the necessity for choosing, serves at the same time to undermine the rationale we might give for any particular choice. If there is no hierarchy of values, what authority can we appeal to in accounting for our decisions? What makes one choice better than another?

This is what the search for a solid bottom is all about, a location for authority, a ground upon which we can make a decision. *Walden* insists upon the necessity for such a search at the same time that it dramatizes the theoretical impossibility of succeeding in it. In this sense, the category of the bottomless is like the category of the natural, final but empty, and when Cavell urges upon us the desirability of a figurative reading, he is just removing the hard bottom from the text and relocating it in the reader. The concept remains equally problematic, our choices equally unmotivated. The result is what has been described in a different context, precisely and pejoratively, as "literary anarchy,"[24] a complaint which serves, like Emerson's attack of nerves, as a record of the response *Walden* seems to me to demand. In a political context, of course, the question of authority is an old one. Thoreau raises it himself in **"Civil Disobedience."** "One would think," he writes, "that a deliberate and practical denial of its authority was the only offence never contemplated by a government" (p. 231). The form this denial takes in **"Civil Disobedience"** is "action from principle—the perception and the performance of right," but the perception of right is exactly what *Walden* makes most equivocal, and the possibility of action from principle is exactly what *Walden* denies, since the principles it identifies are always competing ones and hence inevitably inadequate as guidelines.

To be a citizen or to be a reader of *Walden* is to participate always in an act of foundation or interpretation which is inevitably arbitrary—there is as much to be said against it as there is for it. The role of the citizen/reader then, as Thoreau said in **"Civil Disobedience,"** is "essentially wholly with anything that was." But not only is it revolutionary, it is divisive: it "divides states and churches, it divides families," it even "divides the *individual*" that is, it divides the reader himself—he is repeatedly confronted with interpretive decisions which call into question both his notion of the coherence of the text and of himself. In **"Civil Disobedience,"** however, as in most of the explicitly political texts, Thoreau professes no difficulty in locating and identifying legitimate principles of action. It is only in *Walden* itself that the principle of uncertainty is built in. "Let us not play at kittlybenders," he wrote in *Walden*'s "Conclusion," "There is a solid bottom everywhere." Kittlybenders is a children's game; it involves running or skating on thin ice as quickly as you can so that you don't fall through. If the ice breaks, of course, you're liable to find the solid bottom and so, like the traveller in the story, "conclude your mortal career." The traveller is an image of the writer and, as we can now see, of the reader too. *Walden,* as it has been all along, is a book. To read it, as Thoreau suggested some hundred pages earlier, you "lie at your length on ice only an inch thick, like a skater insect on the surface of the water, and study the bottom at your leisure" (p. 163). But, he goes on to say, "the ice itself is the object of most interest." To read *Walden,* then, is precisely to play at kittlybenders, to run the simultaneous risks of touching and not touching bottom. If our reading claims to find a solid bottom, it can only do so according to principles which the text has both authorized and repudiated; thus we run the risk of drowning in our own certainties. If it doesn't, if we embrace the idea of bottomlessness and the interest of the ice itself, we've failed *Walden*'s first test, the acceptance of our moral responsibility as deliberate readers. It's heads I win, tails you lose. No wonder the game makes us nervous.

Notes

[1] Quoted in H. S. Canby, *Thoreau* (Boston: Houghton Mifflin, 1939), p. 243.

[2] Quoted in Charles R. Anderson, *The Magic Circle of Walden* (New York: Holt, Rinehart, and Winston, 1968), p. 55.

[3] Anderson, *The Magic Circle of Walden*, p. 14.

[4] F. O. Matthiessen, *American Renaissance* (New York: Oxford University Press, 1968), p. 172.

[5] Anderson, *The Magic Circle of Walden*, p. 14.

[6] This particular quotation is from Sherman Paul, *The Shores of America* (Urbana: University of Illinois Press, 1958, 1972), p. 293, but the sentiment is almost unanimous, and it is perhaps a little misleading to single out Paul, whose book is probably the single most important work of Thoreau scholarship and whose assumptions are in many ways different from those of Matthiessen, Moldenhauer, Broderick, Anderson, *et al.*

[7] James Russell Lowell, "Thoreau," reprinted in *Walden and Civil Disobedience*, ed. Owen Thomas (New York: W. W. Norton, 1966), p. 286.

[8] Henry David Thoreau, *Walden and Civil Disobedience*, ed. Owen Thomas (New York: W. W. Norton, 1966), p. 4. All future references to *Walden* are to this edition and are included in parentheses in the text.

[9] H. D. Thoreau, *Journal*, eds. Bradford Torrey and Francis H. Allen (New York: Dover, 1962), p. 127, entry 435.

[10] Hannah Arendt, *Between Past and Future* (New York: Viking, 1961), p. 115.

[11] H. D. Thoreau, "Slavery in Massachusetts," reprinted in *Thoreau: The Major Essays* ed. with an introduction by Jeffrey L. Duncan (New York: E. P. Dutton, 1972), p. 144.

[12] Ibid.

[13] Melvin E. Lyon, "Walden Pond as Symbol," *PMLA* 82 (1967): 289.

[14] Anderson, *The Magic Circle of Walden*, p. 19.

[15] J. G. A. Pocock, *The Machiavellian Moment* (Princeton: Princeton University Press, 1975), p. 463.

[16] Ibid., p. 464.

[17] On this point, see Herbert N. Schneidau, *Sacred Discontent*, forthcoming from Louisiana State University Press.

[18] Quoted in Geoffrey Hartman, *The Fate of Reading* (Chicago: University of Chicago Press, 1975), p. 259.

[19] Joseph J. Moldenhauer, "Paradox in *Walden*, in *Twentieth Century Interpretations of Walden*, ed. with an introduction by Richard Ruland (Englewood Cliffs, N. J.,: Prentice-Hall, 1968), pp. 73-84.

[20] Stanley Cavell, *The Senses of Walden* (New York: Viking 1972), p. 67.

[21] John Aldrich Christie, *Thoreau as World Traveller* (New York: Columbia University Press, 1965), p. 44.

[22] Cavell, *The Senses of Walden*, p. 109.

[23] Lawrence Buell, *Literary Transcendentalism* (Ithaca: Cornell University Press, 1973), pp. 118-19.

[24] Charles Feidelson, Jr., *Symbolism and American Literature* (Chicago: University of Chicago Press, 1953, 1966), p. 149. Feidelson is actually discussing Emerson's own "literary doctrines."

William Gleason (essay date 1993)

SOURCE: "Re-Creating *Walden*: Thoreau's Economy of Work and Play," in *American Literature*, Vol. 65, No. 4, December, 1993, pp. 673-701.

[*In this article, Gleason looks at Thoreau's treatment of leisure, labor, and self-culture within the social and cultural context of wide-spread industrialization and Irish immigration.*]

> It is in obedience to an uninterrupted usage in our community that, on this Sabbath of the Nation, we have all put aside the common cares of life, and seized respite from the never-ending toils of labour.... —Charles Sumner, *The True Grandeur of Nations*

On 4 July 1845, as Thoreau ("by accident") "took up [his] abode in the woods,"[1] Charles Sumner exhorted Sabbath-seizing Bostonians to honor the "venerable forms" of the "Fathers of the Republic" in his Independence Day oration. "Let us imitate what in them was lofty, pure and good," declared Sumner. "Let us from them learn to bear hardship and privation."[2] Although in one sense Thoreau was engaged in precisely the opposite project—rejecting the "wisdom" of his "Mentors" (*W,* 9) by beginning (on the national day of rest) his own "experiment" (*W,* 84) in living "sturdily and Spartan-like" (*W,* 91)—he might have approved Sumner's subsequent call for national introspection: "It becomes us, on this ocasion, . . . to turn our thoughts inward, as the good man dedicates his birthday, to the consideration of his character and the mode in which its vices may be corrected and its virtues strengthened. Avoiding, then, all exultation in the prosperity that has enriched our land, . . . let us consider what we can do to elevate our character . . . and to attain to that righteousness which exalteth a nation."[3] How to "elevate our character" had become a national preoccupation for 1840s America. Thoreau biographer Robert Richardson suggests that Longfellow's Harvard lectures on Goethe and William Ellery Channing's 1838 speech on "Self-Culture" helped spur this concern in New England. Critics have long read *Walden* as a record of Thoreau's attempt at self-cultivation. Richardson, echoing Sherman Paul, asserted in 1986 that "self-culture became a major concern, perhaps the major concern of [Thoreau's] life, and increasingly he tried to reach behind the metaphor of cultivation to the reality."[4]

What Thoreau critics insufficiently acknowledge, however, is *Walden*'s more complex social and cultural heritage.[5] For Thoreau's ostensibly private retreat involved him in a series of very public debates over the cultivation of not only the individual self but also the "self" of the nation. At midcentury the United States was struggling to cope with profound changes in traditional economic and social arrangements brought on by the shift from an agricultural to an industrial economy. Along with other cultural critics such as Channing and Catharine Beecher—although typically in opposition to them—Thoreau was trying to articulate a new conception of the relationship between labor, leisure, and self-culture in the face of this emergent industrial society. We can see this attempt even in the earliest draft of *Walden,* begun at the pond late in 1846. But after 1846 the pace of change quickened dramatically, and a crucial accelerating factor was the massive influx of cheap farm and factory labor in the form of destitute Irish immigrants. In the eyes of many "native" Americans, these immigrants were welcome as useful hands but considerably more suspect as whole bodies. Seen as a demoralizing influence on the health and the very self or character of the nation, the Irish were simultaneously ignored and exploited, and sometimes even deported.

However much we tend to think of Thoreau as transcending the petty prejudices of his neighbors, the final version of *Walden* betrays a considerable anxiety about the Irish, particularly about their impact on Thoreau's reconception of the relationship between work and play. That economic pressures of another sort (namely, the poor sales of *A Week on the Concord and Merrimack Rivers*) forced Thoreau to revise *Walden* several times between 1847 and 1854—the peak years of Irish immigration and nativist anxiety—is in this instance fortunate, for it makes *Walden* an excellent test case for measuring the strain that midcentury Irish immigration could put not merely on social critics but on their very texts. Anxiety about the Irish might manifest itself in unusual ways; for Thoreau, it meant that while on the one hand (or, we might say, with one hand) he could in private write a letter for an Irishman "sending for his wife in Ireland to come to this country,"[6] on (or with) the other he could later that year publish as a central chapter in *Walden* the distressingly nativist-sounding "Baker Farm." What follows is an exploration of the social and rhetorical tensions that surround Thoreau's careful reshaping of the mature but undeniably troubled text of *Walden*.

Early in Channing's 1838 speech he defines self-culture as "the care which every man owes to himself, to the unfolding and perfecting of his nature." This linking of economic ("owes") and organic ("unfolding") metaphors recurs throughout the talk. Every man must "cultivate himself," Channing says, to discover "within him capacities of growth which deserve and will reward intense, unrelaxing toil."[7] Despite the physical and financial resonance of "growth," this self-development for Channing is principally intellectual, moral, and religious. Thoreau himself had worked similar tropes into his Harvard commencement address a year earlier to caution against the rising spirit of business in the United States: "Let men, true to their natures, cultivate the moral affections, lead manly and independent lives; let them make riches the means and not the end of existence, and we shall hear no more of the commercial spirit."[8]

Although both Channing and Thoreau encourage a "manliness" that seems metaphorically grounded in physical strength—Channing urges his audience to "build up" their "strength of mind" and "enlarge" themselves through "vigorous purpose" (*WEC,* 17, 20)—each man at first resists making actual physical development a meaningful component of self-culture. Yet in the 1840s Thoreau began to expand his earlier notion of a "manly" and "independent" life to include a healthy body. "I never feel that I am inspired," he punned on 21 June 1840, "unless my body is also—It too spurns a tame and commonplace life. . . . The body is the first proselyte the Soul makes" (*PJ,* 1:137-38). Six months later, near the end of January 1841, Thoreau turns this feeling into a directive: "We should strengthen, and beautify, and industriously mould our bodies to be fit companions of the soul.—Assist them to grow up like trees, and be agreeable and wholesome objects in nature" (*PJ,* 1:232). "Industriously mould our bodies" explicitly transforms Channing's earlier exhortation in "Self-Culture" to "strenuously . . . form and elevate our own minds" (*WEC,* 14), with Thoreau's bodies/trees subtly "elevated" by growing "up." Thoreau was

A drawing of the essayist and poet.

gradually coming to insist in his *Journal* that physical culture was a vital element of self-culture. By February 1841 he could further pun, "The care of the body is the highest exercise of prudence" (*PJ,* 1:272).

Thoreau's growing appreciation for bodily health mirrors the efforts of avant-garde educators who had been supplementing their otherwise traditionally intellectual and theological curricula with new forms of exercise and physical activity since the 1820s. In the *Prospectus* for the progressive Round Hill School in Northampton, Massachusetts, for example, founders George Bancroft and Joseph Cogswell announced that they were "deeply impressed with the necessity of uniting physical with moral education," and they incorporated calisthenics, tumbling, and long walking trips into the daily schedule of the academy. Reform-minded scholars, especially emigrés familiar with the latest European educational practices, gradually established gymnasia and exercise programs in other schools and communities. The gym at Harvard, for example, was founded in 1826 by German scholar Charles Follen, a professor of literature and close friend of Channing. The German gymnastic method was particularly hailed as an appropriate model for an American educational system already devoted to the study of classical literature and showing the influence of German idealism.

"Look at Germany," one 1830s educator urged. "The same necessity which sent Plato and Aristotle to the gymnasium after severe mental labor, still exists with the hard students of our day."[9]

Although the formalized physical training associated with German gymnastics was waning in popularity when Thoreau attended Harvard in the mid-1830s,[10] taking its place were the nascent forms of more playful, game-oriented sports such as football, baseball, and cricket. And while Thoreau not surprisingly preferred the more solitary pursuit of energetic walking to the team sports breaking out at places like Harvard, his early writings show an enthusiasm for play that matches his growing interest in physical culture. Indeed, of all the Transcendentalists, Thoreau seems most concerned with play. Orestes Brownson, with whom Thoreau lived for a short time, did lecture on the "Necessity and Means of Physical Education" in the 1830s. And Emerson frequently incorporates metaphors of sport and gaming into his writing. "Be a football to time and chance," he exhorts in his journal in 1837; "the world-spirit is a good swimmer, and storms and waves cannot drown him," he writes at the end of "Montaigne." But even Emerson acknowledged that Thoreau put into more vigorous and playful action what the senior writer of Concord thought and felt: "In reading him," Emerson notes, "I find the same thought, the same spirit that is in me, but he takes a step beyond, and illustrates by excellent images that which I should have conveyed in a sleepy generality. 'Tis as if I went into a gymnasium, and saw youths leap, climb, and swing with a force unapproachable,— though their feats are only continuations of my initial grapplings and jumps."[11]

One of Thoreau's "initial grapplings" with the relationship between work and play came during his 1837 commencement speech. After voicing somewhat commonplace phrases about the "commercial spirit" in America, Thoreau described his ideal inversion of the weekly calendar: "The order of things should be somewhat reversed,—the seventh should be man's day of toil, wherein to earn his living by the sweat of his brow, and the other six his sabbath of the affections and the soul" (*EEM,* 117). Not quite Sabbaths of the body—but just as Thoreau explored metaphors of physical culture in the early 1840s, so too did he begin to cultivate tropes of play. "Like overtasked schoolboys," he wrote in January 1841, "all my members, and nerves and sinews, petition thought for a recess,— and my very thigh bones itch to slip away from under me, and run and join the meleè—I exult in stark inanity, leering in nature and the soul" (*PJ,* 1:231). The image here is less childlike (or schoolboyish) than madly (and lasciviously) adolescent. The sly and almost sacrilegious malice of Thoreau's leer, however, yields at year's end to a decidedly less inane but still quite vigorous observation: "These motions every where in nature must surely [be] the circulations of God. The flowing sail—the running stream—the waving tree—the roving wind—whence else their infinite health and freedom—I can see nothing so holy as unrelaxed play and frolic in this bower God has built for us" (*PJ,* 1:350). In this last sentence Thoreau specifically challenges Channing's pronouncement in "Self-Culture" that it is "intense, unrelaxing toil" which deserves reward. Through his seeming oxymoron, "unrelaxed play," Thoreau defends unceasing play as infintely more rewarding—because sanctioned by God—than unceasing labor. "The suspicion of sin," Thoreau explains, "never comes to this thought" (*PJ,* 1:350).

In one sense, Thoreau's linkage of the physical and ludic dimensions of self-culture recalls the metaphoric thrust of Longfellow's lectures on Goethe to Harvard undergraduates. According to Longfellow, Goethe's pursuit of self-culture made him "like the athlete of ancient story, drawing all his strength from earth. His model was the perfect man, as man; living, moving, laboring upon earth in the sweat of his brow."[12] And yet Thoreau, who even published his own translation of Pindar's *Olympic Odes* in the *Dial* in 1844, would soon challenge Longfellow's tropes—much as he challenged Channing's—as part of *Walden*'s fundamental reconception of the relationship between work and play. "It is not necessary that a man should earn his living by the sweat of his brow," Thoreau will declare in "Economy," "unless he sweats easier than I do" (*W,* 71).

Most Americans probably did sweat more easily than Thoreau, if contemporary reports about the general fitness of the population are reliable. Americans have "spare forms and pallid complexions," Harriet Martineau observed with alarm in *Society in America,* written during her 1834-1836 tour of the States. "The feeling of vigorous health is almost unknown. Invalids are remarkably uncomplaining and unalarmed; and their friends talk of their having 'a weak breast,' and 'delicate lungs,' with little more seriousness than the English use in speaking of a common cold." In 1855 Catharine Beecher lamented that American children had become "feeble, sickly, and ugly." She also claimed that of all the married women she knew in America—and she had been to "all portions of the Free States"—only ten could be considered healthy. The "active and industrious" Americans of Jefferson's first administration, as praised by Henry Adams in his *History of the United States of America,* had degenerated into consumptive weaklings.[13]

Although both Beecher and Martineau offered more complex analyses of America's ill health, most commentators blamed an increasingly excessive devotion to business as the chief cause. "Americans work too much and play too little," complained *Harper's New Monthly Magazine,* "and would that it were only with

the usual effect of making Jonathan a dull boy. The result, however, is worse than this, for it tells very seriously against his health and vigor." "Look at our young men of fortune," *Harper's* continued. "Were there ever such weaklings? An apathetic-brained, a pale pasty-faced, narrow-chested, spindle-shanked, dwarfed race—mere walking manikins to advertise the last cut of the fashionable tailor!" "We are fast becoming," *Harper's* warned, "a nation of invalids."[14]

Certainly the quickened pace of urbanization after 1830, which brought more and more men and women into the burgeoning cities seeking employment, contributed to what the *Harper's* columnist assailed as the growth-stunting devitalization of American bodies. And although Bruce Laurie usefully reminds us that the monumental shift from rural to urban forms of labor in the mid-nineteenth century did not empty America's farms overnight—as late as 1860 eight out of ten people still lived on the land and "more wage earners worked in farmhouses and small workshops than in factories"—we cannot downplay the impact on American labor of what Daniel Rodgers has rightly called the "startling transformation" between 1815 and 1850 from "an essentially agricultural to a commercial economy."[15] As both Rodgers and Laurie report, the "expansive energy" of the antebellum economy increased production primarily in what Thoreau's contemporaries called the "household factory."[16] Families in country, town, and city spaces became increasingly enmeshed in the world of the market, and often with zeal, not regret. As one immigrant to America concluded in 1837 after ten years in Boston: "Business is the very soul of an American: he pursues it, not as a means of procuring for himself and his family the necessary comforts of life, but as the fountain of all human felicity . . . it is as if all America were but one gigantic workshop, over the entrance of which there is the blazing inscription, '*No admission here, except on business.*'"[17]

Of course American cities *were* growing apace; urban population increased by more than sixty percent in the 1830s and more than ninety percent in the 1840s. And urban workers, particularly in northeastern cities like Boston, were increasingly offered alternative "fountains" of "felicity" to occupy their nonwork hours. Market forces cousin to those revolutionizing American labor nurtured in urban centers "a booming enterprise in commercial amusement," as evidenced not only by "the tremendous growth of the theater, the music hall, the dance hall, [and] the museum, . . . but also by the stunning popularity of amusement apostles such as P. T. Barnum."[18] Midcentury moralists like Channing and Catharine Beecher's younger brother Henry denounced many of the proliferating forms of urban leisure (especially such lower-class amusements as cockfights, rat pits, and gambling tables) as desperate dissipations, more harmful to the body and the soul than chronic overwork. Channing, whose original

"Self-Culture" lecture was written for and designed to uplift a working-class audience of Boston's manual laborers, particularly inveighed against intemperance, which he felt "prostrates" the drunkard's "rational and moral powers" as thoroughly as it bloats his face and palsies his limbs (*WEC,* 100). Thoreau's pronouncements in **Walden** that the common American is neither "alert" nor "healthy" and that an "unconscious despair is concealed even under what are called the games and amusements of mankind" (*W,* 8) echo Channing's concern that play could be as dispiriting an indulgence as work for many Americans.

By contrast, Americans visiting Canada or Europe were surprised by how much more healthy their citizens seemed. "Certainly no one can visit Canada," declared Thomas Wentworth Higginson in his vituperative 1858 essay "Saints, and their Bodies," "without being struck with the spectacle of a more athletic race of people than our own. On every side one sees rosy female faces and noble manly figures." Emerson was similarly struck by the virility of the English. They are "the best stock in the world, broad-fronted, broad-bottomed," he wrote in *English Traits*. "Round, ruddy, and handsome," the men in particular partake of "vigorous health." "It was an odd proof of this impressive energy," Emerson remarked, "that in my lectures I hesitated to read and threw out for its impertinence many a disparaging phrase which I had been accustomed to spin, about poor, thin, unable mortals;—so much had the fine physique and the personal vigor of this robust race worked on my imagination." At times Emerson was almost wistful: "Other countrymen look slight and undersized beside them, and invalids. They are bigger men than the Americans."[19]

At home, personal and national anxiety about the soundness of the "American" body moved in two related yet distinct directions. On the one hand, health and fitness reformers such as Sylvester Graham and William Alcott campaigned broadly to encourage people to eat more healthful foods (more bran bread and less salt pork), get more fresh air (through better ventilation and increased exercise), and drink more pure water. On the other hand, native alarmists sought and found a more human culprit, targeting America's own "foreign" population, particularly the Irish immigrant laborers who came to the United States in record numbers in the 1840s and 1850s, as lazy and sinful breeders of disease and vice which threatened the larger population. If Americans were slow to follow Graham's and Alcott's advice (and evidence suggests that this was the case),[20] they were even slower to recognize that ill health was as much a labor issue for the working poor, whose abysmally low wages prevented them from moving out of the pestilent slums, as it was for the "young men of fortune" growing pale in the nation's counting houses. Few citizens were ready to acknowl-

edge with Boston census interpreter Lemuel Shattuck that health care was a social and not merely personal responsibility and that as much attention had to be paid to systematic improvements in building construction, street maintenance, sewage systems, cesspools, and privies as to diet and exercise.

If one book can be said to have shaped most strongly the course and discourse of health-related reform movements during the period, however, that text would be Catharine Beecher's *A Treatise on Domestic Economy*. The *Treatise* struck a responsive chord in 1840s America, offering a comprehensive program to restore national fitness and—importantly—national pride through both a systematic reorganization of domestic space and a complex of new attitudes toward domestic labor. First published in Boston in 1841, by 1843 the *Treatise* was in its fourth printing, had been adopted by Massachusetts for use in the public schools, and was being distributed nationally by Harper and Brothers. In all, the *Treatise* went through three editions and fifteen reprintings between 1841 and 1856. Beecher biographer Kathryn Kish Sklar notes that the *Treatise* established Beecher "as a national authority on the psychological state and the physical well-being of the American home."[21] Intended primarily, according to its title page, "for the use of Young Ladies At Home and At School" but articulating concepts that affected both genders, all ages, and all parts of the country, the *Treatise*'s forty chapters comprise an exhaustive reference book on nearly every aspect of domestic life, from food, clothing, and shelter to charitable giving, exercise, and first aid.

The lengthy first four chapters (almost fifty pages) justify to Beecher's audience both the writing and reading of the book as well as speak to Beecher's recognition of not only the difficulty but also the necessity of her project. The first chapter, "Peculiar Responsibilities of American Women," offers a sustained explanation of women's "exalted privilege of extending over the world those blessed influences, that are to renovate degraded man, and 'clothe all climes with beauty.'"[22] Beecher draws heavily from Tocqueville's *Democracy in America* to support her two main contentions. First, much as Channing had claimed in 1838 that self-culture would mitigate (though not materially alter) the social subordination of the working-class poor, Beecher argues that a strikingly similar process has already mitigated women's social subordination to men. For, she notes (quoting Tocqueville), "while [Americans] have allowed the social inferiority of woman to subsist, they have done all they could to raise her, morally and intellectually, to the level of man; and, in this respect, they appear . . . to have excellently understood the true principle of democratic improvement." In no other country do women occupy "a loftier position" (*T,* 8).

Second, Beecher claims an exemplary status for America: "for ages, there has been a constant progress, in all civilized nations, towards the democratic equality attained in this country" (*T,* 10). "Already," she continues, "the light is streaming into the dark prison-house of despotic lands" (*T,* 12). Thus "no American woman . . . has any occasion for feeling that hers is an humble or insignificant lot," because American women's labor, properly imitated, amounts to no less than the "regeneration of the Earth" (*T,* 13-14). Beecher closes her exuberant opening chapter by declaring—in metaphoric language echoed in the "Conclusion" to *Walden*—that any woman, working at any labor, aids the greatest work ever committed to human responsibility: "It is the building of a glorious temple, whose base shall be coextensive with the bounds of the earth, whose summit shall pierce the skies, whose splendor shall beam on all lands, and those who hew the lowliest stone, as much as those who carve the highest capital, will be equally honored when its top-stone shall be laid, with new rejoicings of the morning stars, and shoutings of the sons of God" (*T,* 14).

In chapter two, "Difficulties Peculiar to American Women," Beecher cites as impediments to the building of this temple both the lack of a ready class of domestic servants, who would not arrive in sufficient numbers until after 1845, and the susceptibility of American women to disease. The first difficulty, Beecher suggests in chapter three, "Remedy for These Difficulties," is actually a disguised blessing. If American women have to do their own housework, they will eventually—unlike the "frivolous" and dangerously idle ladies of aristocratic countries—come to revalue labor as lady-like, not vulgar (*T,* 39). This becomes Beecher's chief goal in the *Treatise:* to redefine domestic labor as "refined and genteel" (*T,* 40). The stakes as she saw them were very high. If American women continue to view housework as drudgery, they will fail to elevate themselves, their husbands, and their families— thus also failing not only their own country but (according to her premises in the first chapter) all the civilized nations of the world. Beecher also works hard to persuade women of the magnitude of both their duties and their capabilities so that they will value their labor as much as men do. She continually figures women's work in the language of American economics. In her preface she refers to women's duties as their "business" (*T,* ix); elsewhere these tasks become "domestic employments" (*T,* 26). Compared with aristocratic ladies—who don't labor at all—American women have paradoxically not only "a loftier position" but "a more elevated object of enterprise" (*T,* 15). Thus Beecher not only explicitly rehabilitates domestic labor as at once genteel, democratic, and Christian but also implicitly endorses the midcentury, middle-class ethic of enterprise.

It is against Beecher's complicated position that I would like to consider *Walden,* although not before I have detailed more carefully the affinities of Thoreau's text with the *Treatise.* "Our lives are domestic in more senses than we think," Thoreau suggests sarcastically in "Economy" (*W,* 28); yet *Walden* endorses or extends many of Beecher's views, particularly on the proper care of the body. Except for their rhetorical style, several of the *Treatise*'s pronouncements on health would not seem out of place in Thoreau's work. "Medical men . . . all agree," Beecher asserts in "On Healthful Food," "that, in America, far too large a portion of the diet consists of animal food. As a nation, the Americans are proverbial for the gross and luxurious diet with which they load their tables" (*T,* 77).[23] Not only does *Walden*'s narrator—except for "a very little salt pork" and an occasional woodchuck— eschew animal food, in "Economy" he criticizes men who starve "for want of luxuries" (*W,* 61) and twice puns on the "gross[ness]" of American "groceries" (*W,* 12, 64). Thoreau would also likely applaud Beecher's plea for simple cooking; at one point she seems even to yearn for the ultimate in simplicity: "only one article of food, and only water to drink" (*T,* 71). And he, too, rejects what she terms "stimulating drinks," such as coffee and tea (*T,* 85).

Like Beecher, Thoreau also saw no more need for clothing than to "cover nakedness" and "retain the vital heat" (*W,* 21). Beecher warns strongly against over-clothing the body, just as *Walden*'s speaker derides the "luxuriously rich" who are "not simply kept comfortably warm, but unnaturally hot" (*W,* 14). Thoreau's own morning baths and habit of early rising follow Beecher's example, although he attributes his regimen to more distant inspirations: "I have been as sincere a worshipper of Aurora as the Greeks. I got up early and bathed in the pond; that was a religious exercise, and one of the best things which I did" (*W,* 88). What for Beecher was a prudent matter of cleanliness became in *Walden* ritual and spiritual renewal. Yet a daily full-body bath was something very few Americans took.

Finally, an intriguing connection between *Walden* and the *Treatise* is the correlation between Thoreau's description of building his shelter and the detailed floor plans Beecher provides in chapter 25, "On the Construction of Houses." In some ways this is an odd chapter in the *Treatise.* In mid-nineteenth-century America, generally speaking, "Young Ladies At Home and At School" did not build houses. But their husbands did. And so Beecher explains to women how to explain to their husbands what kinds of houses best suit American families. She lists "five particulars, to which attention should be given, in building a house" (*T,* 268). First, strive for "economy of labor": your house should fit your needs. "If a man is uncertain as to his means," Beecher suggests, "it is poor economy to build a large house" (*T,* 269). For Thoreau, a ten-by-fifteen-foot house of old board sufficed, and if a man were "hard pushed," he could as well take up residence in a railroad laborer's tool box (*W,* 29). Second, writes Beecher, seek "economy of money": prefer simplicity over ornamentation; avoid what Thoreau called "the gewgaws upon the mantel-piece" (*W,* 38). Third, attain "economy of health," which to Beecher primarily meant proper "ventilation of sleeping-rooms" (*T,* 273). Thoreau, too, bragged (like a chanticleer) that the wide chinks in his boards made his house "airy" and "auroral" (*W,* 85). Fourth, provide for "economy of comfort," by using the biggest rooms for common use. Large kitchens, for Beecher, were especially desirable. Thoreau liked to cook in the biggest room of all—outdoors. Last, show good taste. There is propriety, Beecher noted, in proportion.

The foregoing is not meant to suggest that Thoreau threw in his lot with the reformers whose disparate positions Beecher collates and systematizes. On the contrary, he often ridiculed their projects. Though in demonstrable ways *Walden* adopts a reformist posture, particularly in "Economy," Thoreau perceived the lameness that too often afflicts reform. As David Reynolds has shrewdly argued, Thoreau "became the most compelling reform writer of nineteenth-century America" precisely because he "recognized *both* the promise and the perils of contemporary reform movements."[24] I won't reassemble here *Walden*'s invective against "half-witted" reformers (*W,* 151); instead I will return to the implicit question deferred at the beginning of the last section: how does *Walden* challenge Beecher's rehabilitation of American labor?

First, Thoreau would have been highly skeptical of several of Beecher's positions. He would have rejected, for example, her uncritical endorsement of the ethic of enterprise. As Leonard Neufeldt has shown, "the speaker of *Walden* manipulates the language of enterprise so as to acknowledge, parody, and counter the current language and behavior of America, to define his vocation with a logic of opposition, and to justify his art and life with the principle of *'extravagance'* (standing outside the circle of extravagant enterprise)." Although one might hesitate to see Catharine Beecher within this "circle of extravagant enterprise," Sklar notes that despite Beecher's emphasis on domestic thriftiness, the *Treatise* actually encourages "the consumption of goods as a means of promoting the national economy."[25] In "On Giving in Charity," for example, Beecher defends the use of "superfluities" in distinctly un-Thoreauvian terms:

> Suppose that two millions of the people in the United States were conscientious persons, and relinquished the use of every thing not absolutely necessary to life and health. It would instantly throw out of employment one half of the whole community. The manufacturers, mechanics, merchants, agriculturists, and all the agencies they employ, would be beggared, and one half of the community not reduced to poverty, would be obliged to spend all their extra means in simply supplying necessaries to the other half. The use of superfluities, therefore, to a certain extent, is as indispensable to promote industry, virtue, and religion, as any direct giving of money or time. (*T,* 161)

Walden's speaker, then, who wished "to front only the essential facts of life" (*W,* 90)—and who charged that "there is another alternative than to obtain the superfluities" (*W,* 15)—would have been glad to know he was threatening the national enterprise.

Second, Thoreau would likely have ridiculed Beecher's jingoistic designation of America as "the cynosúre of nations" (*T,* 12). *Walden*'s narrator notes with dismay the "popgun" echoes of gala day guns and the "distant hum" of martial music urging Americans to a war with Mexico he does not support (*W,* 160). In the "Conclusion" Thoreau flatly dismisses such mindless champions of country: "Patriotism," he says, "is a maggot in their heads" (*W,* 321). To Thoreau, who had used the same image in "Economy" to describe heedless (headless?) followers of Fashion, the "ruts of tradition and conformity" are to be avoided at all costs (*W,* 323). Thus where Thoreau's "essential" narrator threatens the enterprise of the nation, Beecher threatens what Neufeldt has aptly called Thoreau's more individualistic "enterprise of self-culture."

Third, Thoreau would probably have blanched at the twinned ideologies of deference and standardization underlying much of the *Treatise.* As I suggested earlier, Beecher accepts social subordination on the grounds that women are potentially equal to men intellectually and morally. In a sense, however, Beecher urges women to give up their claim to social power as a prerequisite for obtaining it. For not only would each woman, by assuming responsibility for raising her family the proper way, surreptitiously gain social authority within her immediate household, all American women—acting independently, but in ideological concert—would exert a massive social influence. Beecher's book became quite literally a textbook, a blueprint for an insistent systemization of American domestic practice. No longer would each housewife need to discover for herself the most expedient, productive, or frugal methods of household management. Transcending region and class, Beecher's rules would provide authoritative and programmatic responses to foreseeable events.

In a sense, by turning his back on Concord and heading for the pond, Thoreau, too, divested himself of social authority in order later to claim that authority in

Walden, which is both an exuberant record of his story and an urgent wake-up call for his neighbors/readers. And yet Beecher's goal of subsuming "individual diversity in order to build a commonality of culture"[26]—of forging, that is, an American identity by promoting nationally homogenous cultural forms—was no doubt a frightening prospect to the Thoreau who hoped that there might be "as many different persons in the world as possible" (*W,* 71), who insisted that each of his readers pursue "*his own* way" (*W,* 71; original emphasis), and who reveled in the "myriad" of forms created by the branching streams on the thawing banks of the railroad's deep cut (*W,* 307).

Finally, where Beecher seeks to transform "vulgar" labor into "noble" work and "aristocratic" leisure into "democratic" industry, Thoreau attempts a fundamentally more radical reconception of the relationship between labor and leisure. Throughout *Walden* he insists that the healthiest approach to life is to make one's work and one's play as alike as possible. To Thoreau this did not mean sacrificing either the rigor of work or the spontaneity of play but rather combining them. This prescription flew in the face of midcentury warnings against idleness; but for Thoreau leisure was anything but idle. "Men labor under a mistake," he asserts at the beginning of "Economy" (*W,* 5). And the mistake is that they don't take leisure seriously enough. The midcentury laboring man, toiling six days a week to earn his daily salt pork, molasses, and coffee, has neither time for leisure nor "leisure for a true integrity" (*W,* 6). What Thoreau attempts in *Walden* is to show each of his readers how to turn the waste of "idle work" (*W,* 57) into the profit of "free labor" (*W,* 78), how, in other words, to convert life's "hardship" into its "pastime" (*W,* 70).

These are no mean feats. But there is a significant pattern of just such reconfigurations beneath the surface of *Walden.* Thoreau rehearses over and over in this text a whole series of unexpected transformations of work into play not merely to demonstrate that in his own life labor and leisure were undifferentiated but expressly to counter the standardized, collective model of "regeneration" offered by popular writers like Catharine Beecher. Consider again, for example, the image of the thawing sandbank in "Spring." The activity Thoreau describes on the bank represents not only a myriad of forms but a process of creation—of work—that is at its heart play: "When I see on the one side the inert bank,—for the sun acts on one side first,—and on the other this luxuriant foliage, the creation of an hour, I am affected as if in a peculiar sense I stood in the laboratory of the Artist who made the world and me,—had come to where he was still at work, sporting on this bank, and with excess of energy strewing his fresh designs about. I feel as if I were nearer to the vitals of the globe" (*W,* 306). The

deliberate juxtaposition of God's "work" and his "sporting," separated by only a tenuous comma, represents Thoreau's narrowing of the semantic gap between the two activities. In the next few paragraphs, in fact, the very word "labor" itself nearly dissolves, much like the famous sandbank itself. Thoreau deftly exposes the multiple meanings of "labor," stopping just short of revealing that the word actually conceals its opposite meaning (*W,* 306). For in Latin the noun *"labor, laboris,"* means "work, labor, toil, effort." But the verb *"labor, labi, lapsus sum"* means literally "to glide, slide, fall down, slip" and figuratively "to glide by, fall away, decline, make a mistake." Thus "labor" means work, but it also means play or glide—just as Thoreau playfully skates across the pond gathering firewood in "House-Warming." And Thoreau's unmasking of "labor" also makes us see that assertion from "Economy"—"men labor under a mistake"—a little differently. Men have labored under a mistake; men have played under a mistake; men have mistaken both labor and play.

But Thoreau's linguistic sleight of hand can conceal neither his anxious desire that his project succeed nor the fact that he is trying to dissolve the distinctions between work and play at precisely the moment in American history when these activities were becoming more, not less, rigidly demarcated. One of the most striking results of the midcentury shift from the more seasonal work rhythms of pre-industrial agricultural toil to the day-in, day-out wage-driven shifts of American industrial society was the stricter and stricter separation of "work" and "play" hours. I don't mean to idealize—as Thoreau often did—the preindustrial laborer as a self-sufficient worker entirely in control of his or her own time. As Robert Gross has carefully shown, only the very wealthiest of antebellum farmers in Concord (and by extension in most of America) were able to achieve the sort of independence we have come to assume characterized every yeoman landowner.[27] I do mean to suggest that *Walden* betrays its anxiety about the obstacles to its project even more than we have recognized. More specifically, we can locate the source of this anxiety at the very human nexus—in midcentury American culture and in *Walden*—of the troubling issues of labor, leisure, health, and national identity that I have been tracing: the sudden and overwhelming rush of impoverished Irish immigrants to the shores of America.

The period during which Thoreau experienced life at the pond and then recreated that life in *Walden* covers exactly the years when the Irish presence in America triggered national concern. Between 1846 and 1855, the unprecedented years of famine emigration, at least 1.6 million Irish immigrants came to the United States. An overwhelming number of these settled in Boston; by 1855 between one-third and one-half of all Bostonians were Irish immigrants.[28] Without adequate means or labor skills, the Irish were routinely exploited by employers. To survive, the new arrivals took backbreaking jobs digging ditches, laying railroad track, running spinning mules in textile mills, or cleaning the homes of Boston's middle and upper classes. Even in Thoreau's Concord, the Irish who weren't grading railroad beds were, like John Field in "Baker Farm," spading up boggy meadow land for local native farmers who wanted to grow English hay for the market.[29]

One aspect of the massive Irish immigration which might have alarmed Thoreau was the defining role played by the Irish in accelerating the separation of work time from play time, which Thoreau was so anxious to undo. The sudden availability of cheap unskilled labor was the crucial goad to Boston's urban and industrial growth. Before the arrival of the Irish, Boston's "rigid labor supply had made industrialization impossible," argues Oscar Handlin. "It was the vital function of the Irish to thaw out the rigidity of the system. Their labor achieved the transition from the earlier commercial to the later industrial organization of the city." The presence of the Irish also helped bring to pass what Gross has called "the revolution in the countryside": the ascendancy in places like Concord of modern agricultural capitalism—the large scale production of agricultural commodities for city markets—without which "the creation of an urban-industrial society would have been impossible."[30] Each year between Thoreau's departure from the pond to become a "sojourner in civilized life again" (*W,* 3) and the publication of *Walden,* more and more Irish laborers accepted jobs antithetical to Thoreau's idiosyncratic vision of "free labor."

Thoreau's neighbors, too, were alarmed, if for somewhat less noble reasons. Not only were the Irish believed to be physically unsound—threatening the native population with vice, disease, and ignorance (particularly, Protestants felt, in the form of Catholic doctrine)—they were seen as fiscally unfit as well, an unwelcome drain on the public charities.[31] Anti-Irish sentiment escalated as "prejudice, discrimination, and explosive collisions" became "the order of the day" in midcentury America. In 1851, the peak antebellum year for Irish immigration, the General Court of Massachusetts passed aggressive legislation creating in effect a "frontier guard" against emigrants who might enter the state by land, thereby avoiding the services tax levied at the docks; those who "appeared likely candidates for public support" were denied admission and eventually deported. In the words of Boston mayor Theodore Lyman, the Irish were "a race that will never be infused into our own, but on the contrary will always remain distinct and hostile."[32]

To what degree did Thoreau share the nativist sentiments of his neighbors? Did his desire for "as many different persons in the world as possible" include the midcentury Irish? The few critics who have looked in any detail at Thoreau and the Irish differ in their assessments of his attitude toward them. Frank Buckley concluded some years back that while Thoreau's portrayal of the immigrants in his journal, letters, and published writings is free "from religious and political bias," Thoreau himself could not be considered "a consistent friend and defender of the Irish." George Ryan, on the other hand, has asserted more recently that, despite Thoreau's frequently derisive commentary, "time and increased exposure . . . improved Thoreau's attitude toward the Irish, an ethnic group he could not, at first, quite fully understand." Particularly after 1850, Ryan argues, Thoreau—who not only "performed works of charity among the immigrants" but wrote letters for them and solicited funds "with which to bring family members out to America"—was, as Walter Harding put it, "one Yankee" that the Irish "could depend on."[33]

Rather than retry Thoreau here in an effort to settle the debate between Ryan and Buckley, I will focus on the historical and literary circumstances which seem to allow each critic to be, in a sense, correct. Granting Ryan's conclusions about the post-1850 Thoreau (ninety percent of all Thoreau's "propitious remarks" about the Irish occur between 1850 and 1857),[34] doesn't *Walden*—taken by itself—support Buckley's position? In other words, if we know that Thoreau's attitude toward the Irish changed significantly for the better after 1850—during precisely the years in which he was dramatically revising the text of *Walden*—why does *Walden*'s attitude toward the Irish remain at best inconsistent? If the longest "Irish" entries in Thoreau's *Journal* after 1850 concern young Johnny Riordan, whom Thoreau not only observed with sensitivity and respect but helped clothe during the chill winter of 1851-52, why doesn't Johnny seem to make any impression on the multiple drafts of *Walden?* Why are James Collins (in his dank shanty), John Field (and his boggy ways), and Hugh Quoil (with his DTs) the text's most prominent Irish figures? Why, to paraphrase Thoreau's famous query near the beginning of "Brute Neighbors," do precisely these objects make *Walden*'s world? Or to put it another way: why does Thoreau make *Walden* say John Field instead of Johnny Riordan?[35]

The answers to these questions take us to the heart of both the larger project of *Walden* and the construction of Thoreau's rhetorical identity within the text. We need first to consider the nature of the additions and revisions which Thoreau made with respect both to the Irish and to relevant questions of labor and leisure during what Robert Sattelmeyer has classified as the second major phase of the composition of *Walden,* namely the four successive drafts written between 1852 and 1854.[36] In general, Thoreau's changes during this period work in two directions at once. To "Economy," whose initial Irish references are generally derisive, Thoreau added several passages which more thoughtfully critique the contemporary practices responsible for the conditions his first draft had mocked. For example, as though to mitigate the 1847 manuscript's description of Collins's "uncommonly fine" shanty—which was "dark, . . . dank, clammy, and aguish," reminding Thoreau of a "compost heap" (*W,* 43)—and its brief anecdote of the treacherous neighbor/nail thief Seeley, "an Irishman" (*W,* 44), Thoreau added in 1852 this lengthy passage:

> It is a mistake to suppose that, in a country where the usual evidences of civilization exist, the condition of a very large body of the inhabitants may not be as degraded as that of savages. I refer to the degraded poor, not now to the degraded rich. To know this I should not need to look farther than to the shanties which every where border our railroads, that last improvement in civilization; where I see in my daily walks human beings living in sties, and all winter with an open door, for the sake of light, without any visible, often imaginable, wood pile, and the forms of both old and young are permanently contracted by the long habit of shrinking from cold and misery, and the development of all their limbs and faculties is checked. It certainly is fair to look at that class by whose labor the works which distinguish this generation are accomplished. (*W,* 34-35)

Here Thoreau indicts the exploitive labor practices that create shanties like the one whose boards he had condescendingly purchased from James Collins. Playing somewhat on the false hierarchy of terms like "civilized" and "savage," Thoreau more explicitly puns on the passage's two central descriptive terms. First, the Irish are "degraded," shaved ruthlessly down, just as they themselves grade the slopes for the railroad; second, they are "permanently contracted," not merely shrunken by cold and want but locked into rapacious labor agreements.[37] These are the other "works" that "distinguish" Thoreau's "generation," which, he will remind us in another 1852 addition to "Economy," has witnessed "the fall from the farmer to the operative," a fall as "great and memorable as that from the man to the farmer" (*W,* 64).

It is fitting that Thoreau's observations of the Irish laborers take place during his daily exercise, for *Walden*'s attitude toward contemporary leisure also comes into focus during these years. For example, 1852 marks the first appearance in *Walden* of Thoreau's indictment of the "unconscious despair" beneath the so-called games of mankind (*W,* 8). And in 1853 he introduces into "Higher Laws" his preference for "the more primitive but solitary amusements of hunting fishing and the like" (*W,* 211). But between 1852 and

1854 Thoreau also added to *Walden* some of the more objectionable assertions about immigrants in general and the Irish in particular. In 1852, for example, the same year Thoreau critiqued the degradation inflicted on the poor, he added a fairly uncomplimentary passage about the Irish who "have built their sties" by the pond (*W,* 192), seeming to blame them along with the railroad instead of distinguishing them from it. And in 1852 and 1853 Thoreau worked into the text his largely unflattering description of Quoil—the prototypical Irish ditchdigger and drunk, with his "carmine" face and his tick-ridden garden (*W,* 262)—as well as the potentially offensive naturalist/nativist reflections in the opening to "Baker Farm" about the "halo of light" that after a rain appears around the shadows of everyone except "some Irishmen" (*W,* 202).

"Baker Farm," in fact, is a crucial chapter to decipher in regard to the Irish, for the passages on John Field and his seemingly hopeless family constitute the most detailed and most negative treatment of immigrants in *Walden.* This chapter is also a vexing one: nearly every leaf on which these specific passages probably appeared is missing from the original 1847 manuscript. Yet we can make some judgments of Thoreau's probable development of and plans for the chapter by consulting the 23 August 1845 *Journal* entry recording his original encounter with the Fields. In that entry, Thoreau's description roughly matches the published text of *Walden,* from his seeking fish and getting caught in a downpour to his taking refuge in the Fields' hut and hearing John's naively cheerful "story" of hard labor for subsistence wages (*PJ,* 2:176). While the largely negative descriptions of Field as "shiftless," his wife as "greasy," and their infant as "wrinkled" and "sibyl-like" do appear in the *Journal,* one significant addition to that record (which may or may not have been made in the 1847 text) reads: "There we sat together under that part of the roof which leaked the least, while it showered and thundered without. I had sat there many times of old before the ship was built that floated this family to America" (*W,* 204). This addition is telling because it epitomizes the recurrent tension between proximity and distance which structures the chapter. The first sentence suggests a certain closeness engendered by shared adverse circumstances: Thoreau sits within the hut, huddled "together" with the Fields, trying to stay dry. But the second sentence, its accents falling on "*many* times of old" and "*this* family," seems suspiciously proto-nativist, metaphorically separating Thoreau from the Fields, almost imaginatively returning them to Ireland.

Then, in a long section also added to the *Journal,* Thoreau tries to collapse what he perceives as the source of the gap between himself and the Fields by narrating his own "experience." If the Fields could only approach life more like Thoreau himself, they would become his "nearest neighbors" in the most

welcome sense (*W,* 205). But after the lengthy enu-
meration of what food and drink to exclude from their
diet and why—an able critique of the complicity between market economies and political economies that
reintroduces an insistent theme from "Economy"—
Thoreau snidely despairs of ever communicating the
fundamental assumptions of his project to such men
as John Field. "But alas!" he exclaims. "The culture of
an Irishman is an enterprise to be undertaken with a
sort of moral bog hoe" (*W,* 205-06). Even though
such a remark effectively stiff-arms Field as a would-
be convert to or reader of Thoreau's program—a few
pages later Thoreau "trust[s]" that Field "does not
read this" (*W,* 208)—this sentence, like the one about
the ship, begins in sympathy ("But alas!") before retreating into sarcastic remoteness. After one more brief
run at the family's methods of getting, Thoreau fairly
runs from the hut itself back into the woods.

It is during this retreat from the Fields that Thoreau
experiences a brief but intense moment of doubt as to
the wisdom of his chosen course of life. For an "instant" his own boggy ways appear "trivial" for someone "who had been sent to school and college." But
Thoreau, "with the rainbow over [his] shoulder, and
some faint tinkling sounds borne to [his] ear through
the cleansed air," overcomes this doubt precisely by
putting as much distance between himself and John
Field as possible. Go "farther and wider," Thoreau's
"Good Genius" tells him. "Take shelter under the cloud,
while they [presumably people like John Field, or even
Thoreau at the beginning of the chapter] flee to carts
and sheds. Let not to get a living be thy trade, but thy
sport" (*W,* 207). Even when John Field rematerializes
at the end of the chapter, having decided to join Thoreau
and fish instead of bog, Thoreau emphasizes the irre-
ducible gap between them. They angle from the same
boat but not the same philosophy; thus Thoreau catches
"a fair string" while Field only a "couple of fins"—
even when they swap seats—as though they were in
separate boats or on separate ponds (*W,* 208). And
that mid-expedition seat-switching, which closes the
chapter, mocks in its ineffectiveness not only Field's
attempt to get closer to Thoreau but also the very
careful, cooperative effort that an exchange of places
in a small boat inevitably requires.[38]

Why indeed would the Thoreau whose attitudes toward the Irish were broadening in the 1850s not only
retain passages like these but intensify them? At a
minimum, Field's persistent presence in the text—from
the *Journal* to the 1847 manuscript to the final edition—suggests that Thoreau saw the bog farmer from
the start as something of an emblematic foil, someone
against whom to construct his narrator's identity as,
in the words of his Good Genius, a "free" person
bound to "seek adventures," not markets (*W,* 207).
The decision to intensify the encounter—to turn a
single *Journal* entry into an elaborate set piece in which

the narrator invests so much of himself in attempting
to aid the Fields that his failure occasions serious self-
doubt—was probably made as early as 1847. We know,
for example, that Thoreau added to that manuscript
the sentences which describe the narrator's doubt and
link the Good Genius's instructions explicitly to that
sudden sense of failure. We can then surmise that
Thoreau simultaneously expanded the encounter with
the Fields to include the lengthy (yet vain) account of
his own life in order to justify through narrative his
subsequent doubt.[39]

What may have prevented Thoreau from modifying
his portrayal of the Fields after 1850 was his decision
during the second major phase of revision to make
"Baker Farm" a more structurally pivotal chapter. While
the Fields material which appears in the 1847 draft, in
which there were no chapter divisions, comes very
late in the manuscript, in the 1854 *Walden* "Baker
Farm" is considerably more central: it is the tenth
chapter out of eighteen, the first chapter of the second
half of the book. In the revised text the Good Genius's
urgings represent a renewed call to commitment, resolving whatever doubt the first half of the book may
have engendered and moving forthrightly ahead toward "Spring" and the "Conclusion." Thoreau could
thus hardly de-intensify the exasperating encounter that
crystallized this doubt, which in its turn occasioned
the introspective reaffirmation. In the revised version,
then, the narrator's identity is even more sharply tied
to John Field's and even more strongly requires Field's
obtuseness.

And yet, while in an odd sense "Baker Farm" holds the
two halves of *Walden* together largely by depicting
John Field as an Irishman apart, by the 1850s Thoreau
seems uncomfortable enough with his characterization
of Field to have tried, with mixed results, to soften its
edges. In "Spring," for example, when the narrator
declares that "in a pleasant spring morning all men's
sins are forgiven" and that "through our *own* recovered innocence we discern the innocence of our neighbors" (*W,* 314; emphasis added), he seems almost to
acknowledge Thoreau's guilt over the earlier portrayal
of his "nearest neighbor" and figuratively, though at
best obscurely, to welcome John Field back into the
book.

At about the same time that Thoreau placed this near-
apology in "Spring," he also tinkered with the immediate frame of "Baker Farm" itself. First, although he
added the seeming slur about the unworthiness of
"some Irishmen" whose shadows "had no halo," he
made a point of putting that comment in the mouth of
a visitor to Walden ("One who visited me declared
that . . .") and then followed it with a long digression
which seems to challenge the whole idea of shadow-
election as the "superstition" of "an excitable imagination" (*W,* 202). Second, after leaving Baker Farm to

explore in "Higher Laws" the competing claims of sensuality and purity, Thoreau suddenly introduces the enigmatic figure of John Farmer, who, though not identified as Irish, seems symbolically kin to John Field. Farmer, however, experiences an awakening to—or more accurately, toward—self-culture which is explicitly denied Field:

> John Farmer sat at his door one September evening, after a hard day's work, his mind still running on his labor more or less. Having bathed he sat down to recreate his intellectual man. . . . He had not attended to the train of his thoughts long when he heard some one playing on a flute, and that sound harmonized with his mood. Still he thought of his work. . . . But the notes of the flute came home to his ears out of a different sphere from that he worked in, and suggested work for certain faculties which slumbered in him. They gently did away with the street, and the village, and the state in which he lived. (*W*, 221-22)

Much like Thoreau washed by the rain before the advent of his Good Genius in "Baker Farm," the cleansed Farmer hears music in the air which prepares him to receive a new message: "Why do you stay here and live this mean moiling life, when a glorious existence is possible for you?" Unlike Thoreau, Farmer is unable "actually [to] migrate thither"; but the chapter ends with the possibility of redemptive self-cultivation still thick in the air, as Farmer "practise[s] some new austerity," letting "his mind descend into his body and redeem it, and treat[ing] himself with ever increasing respect" (*W*, 222). Through the symbolic redemption of John Farmer, Thoreau may subtly extend the same possibility to John Field—albeit without his wife and children—a possibility which the rhetorical requirements of "Baker Farm" itself refused to allow.

For all its revisions, however, *Walden* still doesn't welcome little Johnny Riordan into its pages. Even though the longest of Thoreau's several *Journal* entries on Johnny occurs precisely when Thoreau was "engrossed" in the first revisions of the second phase of *Walden* (including the revisions just detailed above),[40] even though Thoreau was pulling considerable material from the *Journal* pages around Johnny into the text, and even though Johnny "dares to live" (*J*, 3:149) and his "greater independence" and "closeness to nature" (*J*, 2:116-17) square exactly with Thoreau's larger project, Johnny cannot wedge his way into *Walden* to displace or at least comment upon Thoreau's treatment of John Field. If Sattelmeyer is correct in arguing that Thoreau's decision to let stand certain inconsistencies created by his revisions to *Walden* is "a mark of [his] maturity as a writer,"[41] then what do these apparent evasions mark?

To a certain extent they indicate that the same issues of self-identity which so strongly shaped "Baker Farm" are still at work at the end of *Walden*. From one angle the story of Johnny, as Thoreau was shaping it in the *Journal*, threatens to undo too much of the crucial rhetorical work accomplished by the treatment of John Field in "Baker Farm." For by emphasizing Johnny's determination to educate himself—he goes to school no matter how cold it is—and in general to meet the world as bravely as possible, Thoreau was in the early 1850s specifically rewriting the pessimistic ending to that chapter, in which the narrator asserts that Field, "with his inherited Irish poverty or poor life, his Adam's grandmother and boggy ways, [will] not . . . rise in this world, he nor his posterity, till their wading webbed bog-trotting feet get *talaria* to their heels" (*W*, 209). In the *Journal*, Johnny figuratively becomes John Field's posterity; as a four-year-old in 1850, Johnny represents Field's "poor starveling brat" coming of age. And, far from wading web-footed through the bogs, Johnny, "lively as a cricket," scampers past the wealthier and more duck-like Concordians who "waddle about cased in furs" (*J*, 3:150).

In another sense, the remarkable extent to which Thoreau himself was coming to identify with Johnny in the *Journal* equally threatens to undermine the mature autonomy toward which Thoreau's narrator was struggling. Not only does Johnny receive a winter coat from Thoreau, but the *Journal* records that the "countless patches" on Johnny's other clothes—and perhaps the clothes themselves—"hailed from, claimed descent from, were originally identical with pantaloons of mine" (*J*, 3:241). Even in this brief description Thoreau modulates from kinship ("hailed from") toward paternity ("claimed descent from") to an anxious identity. Elsewhere in the *Journal* Thoreau imagines himself *as* Johnny, even composing a multi-stanza folk ballad— "I am the little Irish boy/That lives in the shanty./I am four years old to-day/And shall soon be one and twenty" (*J*, 2:117)—which purports to sing of life through Johnny's eyes. But while we may be tempted to see in *Walden* traces of Johnny's vivid *Journal* presence,[42] the revised text as a whole moves toward an ethic of self-exploration that—however strong Thoreau's fascination with "the little Irish boy"—could only awkwardly admit a last-minute alter ego, especially an Irish one, to its "private sea" (*W*, 321). "Let every one mind his own business," Thoreau insists in the "Conclusion," "and endeavor to be what he was made" (*W*, 326).

Of course by keeping Johnny out of *Walden* Thoreau willfully disregards one of the key lessons of his Good Genius in "Baker Farm": "We should come home from far, from adventures, and perils, and discoveries every day, with new experience and character" (*W*, 208). Whatever discoveries Thoreau was making about the Irish after 1850, he didn't bring all of them "home" to

Walden. But he did bring them to the *Journal,* and it is literally among those pages that another reason for Johnny's absence suggests itself. For "inclosed between the leaves of one of the journals," remark the editors of the 1906 *Journal* in a footnote to the 28 January 1852 entry on Johnny, lay "some loose sheets of manuscript" containing a "more complete sketch of the little Irish boy, made up, with some revision, from the original entries" (*J,* 3:242). If Thoreau had other publication plans for the Riordan material—to issue it as a separate sketch, for example, or as part of some other work—then we might see his decision to exclude Johnny from *Walden* as an attempt to exert some control over both his literary product and the market in which he had to trade it.[43] This would have been a brave attempt in midcentury America, for all around Thoreau the expanding commercial and industrial markets were systematically undermining most forms of autonomous living.[44]

As "the most powerful and articulate critic of agricultural capitalism that America produced in the decades before the Civil War,"[45] Thoreau often demonstrates an astute understanding of the effect that these changes had on individual Americans. But he could at other times appear equally insensitive, as we have seen in his treatment of the Irish in the drafts of *Walden.* However much Thoreau's more private *Journal* reflections and certain fairly subtle revisions to *Walden* protest to the contrary, the public text of *Walden* by and large bars the Irish from the new ideology of work and play that Thoreau was attempting to formulate. Although Thoreau hoped to live outside the "restless, nervous, bustling, trivial Nineteenth Century" (*W,* 329) and to "speak somewhere *without* bounds" (*W,* 324; original emphasis), the *Walden* which he reshaped in the 1850s did not, in the end, fully accomplish those goals.

Notes

[1] Henry David Thoreau, *Walden,* ed. J. Lyndon Shanley (Princeton: Princeton Univ. Press, 1971), 84. Subsequent quotations from *Walden* are from this edition and are cited parenthetically as *W.*

[2] Charles Sumner, *The True Grandeur of Nations: An Oration Delivered Before the Authorities of the City of Boston, July 4, 1845* (Philadelphia: Henry Longstreth, 1846), 5-6.

[3] Sumner, 6.

[4] Robert D. Richardson, *Henry Thoreau: A Life of the Mind* (Berkeley: Univ. of California Press, 1986), 55, 57.

[5] Exceptions here are Leonard N. Neufeldt's "Thoreau's Enterprise of Self-Culture in a Culture of Enterprise,"

American Quarterly 39 (Summer 1987): 231-51; and Linck C. Johnson's "Revolution and Renewal: The Genres of *Walden,*" in *Critical Essays on Henry David Thoreau's "Walden",* ed. Joel Myerson (Boston: G. K. Hall, 1988), 215-35.

[6] *The Journal of Henry David Thoreau,* ed. Bradford Torrey and Francis H. Allen, 14 vols. (Boston: Houghton Mifflin, 1906), 6:158. *Journal* passages written after Spring 1848 are quoted from the twenty-volume 1906 edition of Thoreau's complete works (in which the fourteen *Journal* volumes are numbered independently) and cited parenthetically as *J,* followed by appropriate volume and page numbers. Passages written before Spring 1848 are quoted from the first two volumes of the Princeton University Press edition of Thoreau's *Journal* (*Journal 1: 1837-1844,* ed. Elizabeth Hall Witherell et al. [1981]; *Journal 2: 1842-1848,* ed. Robert Sattelmeyer [1984]) and cited parenthetically as *PJ,* followed by volume and page numbers.

[7] William Ellery Channing, "Self-Culture," in *The Works of William E. Channing, D. D.* (Boston: American Unitarian Assoc., 1877), 14, 21, 19. Subsequent quotations from this and other selections in Channing's *Works* will appear parenthetically as *WEC.*

[8] Henry D. Thoreau, *Early Essays and Miscellanies,* ed. Joseph J. Moldenhauer and Edwin Moser, with Alexander C. Kern (Princeton: Princeton Univ. Press, 1975), 117; hereafter cited as *EEM.*

[9] Quoted in John R. Betts, "Mind and Body in Early American Thought," *Journal of American History* 54 (March 1968): 793, 794, 799. Bancroft and Cogswell further claimed that they were "the first in the new continent to connect gymnastics with a purely literary establishment" (793).

[10] Guy Lewis, "The Beginning of Organized Collegiate Sport," *American Quarterly* 22 (Summer 1970): 223.

[11] Betts, "Mind and Body," 800; Ralph Waldo Emerson, *Selections from Ralph Waldo Emerson: An Organic Anthology,* ed. Stephen E. Whicher (Boston: Houghton Mifflin, 1957), 81, 301, 402.

[12] Quoted in Richardson, 55.

[13] Harriet Martineau, *Society in America,* 3 vols. (London: Saunders and Otley, 1837), 3:156; Catharine E. Beecher, *Letters to the People on Health and Happiness* (1855; rpt., New York: Arno, 1972), 8, 121; Henry Adams, *History of the United States of America During the Administrations of Thomas Jefferson and James Madison,* ed. Earl N. Harbert, 2 vols. (New York: Library of America, 1986), 1:42.

[14] "Why We Get Sick," *Harper's New Monthly Magazine,* October 1856, 642, 646, 643.

[15] Bruce Laurie, *Artisans into Workers: Labor in Nineteenth-Century America* (New York: Hill and Wang, 1989), 16; Daniel T. Rodgers, *The Work Ethic in Industrial America, 1850-1920* (Chicago: Univ. of Chicago Press, 1974), 19.

[16] Rodgers, 19; Laurie, 16.

[17] Quoted in Rodgers, 5-6 (original ellipsis and emphasis).

[18] Steven A. Riess, *City Games: The Evolution of American Urban Society and the Rise of Sports* (Urbana: Univ. of Illinois Press, 1989), 13; Stephen Hardy, *How Boston Played: Sport, Recreation, and Community, 1865-1915* (Boston: Northeastern Univ. Press, 1982), 43.

[19] Thomas Wentworth Higginson, "Saints, and Their Bodies," *Atlantic Monthly,* March 1858, 586; Ralph Waldo Emerson, *The Complete Works of Ralph Waldo Emerson,* Centenary Edition, ed. Edward Waldo Emerson, 12 vols. (Boston: Houghton Mifflin, 1876), 5:134, 65, 69, 106, 65.

[20] Lemuel Shattuck, *Report to the Committee of the City Council Appointed to Obtain the Census of Boston for the Year 1845* (1846; rpt., New York: Arno, 1976), 146-47. Shattuck acknowledges a decrease in cholera in 1845, but notes with alarm a rise in diseases of the respiratory and digestive organs. He meticulously documents, for example, "a decided increase" in deaths due to "*Enteritis,* or inflammation of the bowels," in "Bowel Complaints," and in "Diseases of the Stomach and Bowels" (147).

[21] Kathryn Kish Sklar, *Catharine Beecher: A Study in American Domesticity* (New Haven: Yale Univ. Press, 1973), 151.

[22] Catharine E. Beecher, *A Treatise on Domestic Economy* (1841; rpt., New York: Source Book, 1970), 13; hereafter cited as *T.*

[23] According to Waverly Root and Richard de Rochemont's *Eating in America: A History* (New York: William Morrow, 1976), American per capita consumption of meat was a whopping 178 pounds per year during the 1830s, a total not surpassed until 1970 (139).

[24] David S. Reynolds, *Beneath the American Renaissance: The Subversive Imagination in the Age of Emerson and Melville* (Cambridge: Harvard Univ. Press, 1989), 101.

[25] Neufeldt, 239; Sklar, 307 n.

[26] Sklar, 166.

[27] Robert A. Gross, "Culture and Cultivation: Agriculture and Society in Thoreau's Concord," *Journal of American History* 69 (June 1982): 45.

[28] See Charles Fanning, *The Irish Voice in America: Irish-American Fiction from the 1760s to the 1980s* (Lexington: Univ. Press of Kentucky, 1990), 74; Hardy, 28; and Laurie, 25-26.

[29] Gross, "Culture and Cultivation," 53.

[30] Oscar Handlin, *Boston's Immigrants: A Study in Acculturation,* rev. ed. (Cambridge: Harvard Univ. Press, 1959), 82; Gross, "Culture and Cultivation," 43.

[31] Hardy, 28-29. Fears about the Irish were not new in the late 1840s—indeed, the memory of the Charlestown Convent Fire and subsequent riot in 1837 burned bright in the minds of Boston natives and immigrants alike—but it was only after the beginning of massive famine emigration that such anxieties became distinctly national concerns. See, for example, Handlin, 187-89.

[32] Fanning, 74; George Potter, *To the Golden Door: The Story of the Irish in Ireland and America* (Boston: Little, Brown, 1960), 466-67; Handlin, 185.

[33] Frank Buckley, "Thoreau and the Irish," *New England Quarterly* 13 (September 1940): 400, 397; George E. Ryan, "Shanties and Shiftlessness: The Immigrant Irish of Henry Thoreau," *Éire-Ireland: A Journal of Irish Studies* 13 (Fall 1978): 77-78.

[34] Ryan, 77.

[35] In *Dark Thoreau* (Lincoln: Univ. of Nebraska Press, 1982), Richard Bridgman poses similar questions, but ventures no answers; see 108.

[36] Robert Sattelmeyer, "The Remaking of *Walden,*" in *Writing the American Classics,* ed. James Barbour and Tom Quirk (Chapel Hill: Univ. of North Carolina Press, 1990), 58. The two indispensable sources for information about the successive drafts of *Walden* are J. Lyndon Shanley, *The Making of "Walden," with the Text of the First Version* (Chicago: Univ. of Chicago Press, 1957); and Ronald Earl Clapper, "The Development of *Walden:* A Genetic Text," (Ph.D. diss., Univ. of California, Los Angeles, 1967).

[37] See, for example, Handlin, 70-72, and Norman Ware, *The Industrial Worker, 1840-1860: The Reaction of American Industrial Society to the Advance of the Industrial Revolution* (1924; rpt., Chicago: Ivan R. Dee, 1990), 106-48.

[38] Tellingly, in the original *Journal* entry Thoreau records that *"he* [i.e., Field] changed seats" (*PJ,* 2:177), but in the final text he changes the account to read *"we* changed seats" (*W,* 208; emphases added).

[39] In *Thoreau's Wild Rhetoric* (New York: New York Univ. Press, 1990), Henry Golemba provocatively argues that Thoreau's "xenophobia" is part of a rhetorical strategy designed to give his persona sufficient "Yankee shrewdness" and unsentimental toughness in order to make *Walden* a more attractive text to its presumably xenophobic audience (176-77). I would agree that Thoreau's incipient nativism is in part a rhetorical necessity, but only as required by *Walden*'s own logic, not by any constraints posed by potential readers.

[40] Shanley, *The Making of "Walden,"* 31.

[41] Sattelmeyer, 60.

[42] In "The Bean-Field," for example, Thoreau specifies that his formative initial visit to Walden Pond occurred "when I was four years old" (*W,* 155). In "Winter Animals" Thoreau's description of the hares that visit his cabin makes them sound at first suspiciously like destitute Irish children, coming "round my door at dusk to nibble the potato parings which I had thrown out" (*W,* 280); but he then reveals that the "poor wee thing[s], lean and bony" could "scud" over the snow with remarkable "elastic[ity]," thereby (much like Johnny) "asserting [their] vigor and the dignity of Nature" (*W,* 281). And in the "Conclusion," after relating the anecdote about the little boy who tells the traveler that the swamp before him did have a hard bottom (the traveler, his horse "up to the girths" in muck, simply hadn't reached it yet), Thoreau says, "So it is with the bogs and quicksands of society; but he is an old boy that knows it" (*W,* 330)—figuring himself, in a sense, as an adult version (an "old boy") of little Johnny.

[43] For an excellent discussion of Thoreau's complicity with the market ideology that he abhorred, see Michael T. Gilmore, *American Romanticism and the Marketplace* (Chicago: Univ. of Chicago Press, 1985), 35-51.

[44] As Ware reports, "the progress of the Industrial Revolution destroyed, not only the semi-agricultural factory population, but the New England farm that made its independence real" (74). And Gross reminds us in "Transcendentalism and Urbanism: Concord, Boston, and the Wider World," (*Journal of American Studies* 18 [December 1984]) that "at the very moment Thoreau was striving to control his own life in the face of the market, the railroad was sweeping up the remaining old-time farmers on the outskirts into the triumphant new world of agricultural capitalism" (378).

[45] Gross, "Culture and Cultivation," 44.

FURTHER READING

Boone, Joseph Allen. "Delving and Diving for Truth: Breaking through to Bottom in Thoreau's *Walden.*" *ESQ* 27, No. 3 (3rd Quarter 1981): 135-46.
> Studies the numerous references to surfaces and depths in *Walden.*

Boudreau, Gordon V. *The Roots of "Walden" and the Tree of Life.* Nashville: Vanderbilt University Press, 1990, 241 p.
> Traces the roots of *Walden* and its author's "radical genius."

Brooks, Van Wyck. "Thoreau at Walden." In *The Flowering of New England, 1815-1865*, pp. 359-73. New York: E. P. Dutton, 1937.
> Suggests that Thoreau's spartan existence at Walden Pond was not terribly different from his usual way of life.

Cavell, Stanley. *The Senses of "Walden."* New York: Viking, 1972, 120 p.
> Examines Thoreau's text at the level of word, sentence, and portion, seeking common sense, truth, and beauty, respectively.

Deevey, Edward S., Jr. "A Re-Examination of Thoreau's *Walden.*" *The Quarterly Review of Biology* 17, No. 1 (March 1942): 1-11.
> Asserts that Thoreau's observations on nature at Walden Pond constituted an original and reliable contribution to the science of limnology.

Dillman, Richard H. "The Psychological Rhetoric of *Walden.*" *ESQ* 25, No. 2 (2nd Quarter 1979): 79-91.
> Situates *Walden* within the tradition of psychological rhetoric, a tradition established in 1776 with the publication of George Campbell's *Philosophy of Rhetoric.*

Drake, William. "*Walden.*" In *Thoreau: A Collection of Critical Essays.* Ed. Sherman Paul, pp. 71-91. Englewood Cliffs: Prentice-Hall, 1962.
> Discusses Thoreau's experience at Walden Pond as an experiment, the goal of which was to solve the anxieties and conflicts of his time.

Edel, Leon. "*Walden*: The Myth and the Mystery." *The American Scholar* 44, No. 2 (Spring 1975): 272-81.
> Reassesses the Thoreauvian myth as it exists at the present time.

Garber, Frederick. *Thoreau's Fable of Inscribing*. Princeton: Princeton University Press, 1991, 226 p.

Examines Thoreau's obsession with the problem of being at home in the world.

Grusin, Richard. "Thoreau, Extravagance, and the Economy of Nature." *American Literary History* 5, No. 1 (Spring 1993): 30-50.

Offers an interpretation of Thoreau's economy of nature that is an alternative to both the traditional and the revisionist approaches.

Harding, Walter, and Michael Meyer. *The New Thoreau Handbook*. New York: New York University Press, 1980, 238 p.

A selective survey of Thoreau scholarship limited to the most significant and most generally available works.

Johnson, William C., Jr. *What Thoreau Said: "Walden" and the Unsayable*. Moscow, Idaho: University of Idaho Press, 1991, 172 p.

A hermeneutic approach to *Walden* as a scripture-like text.

Jones, Samuel Arthur, ed. *Pertaining to Thoreau: A Gathering of Ten Significant Nineteenth-Century Opinions*. Reprint. Hartford: Transcendental Books, 1970, 51 p.

An anthology of Thoreau criticism compiled in the 1890s and republished on the anniversary of Thoreau's death.

Lane, Lauriat, Jr. *Approaches to "Walden."* San Francisco: Wadsworth, 1961, 135 p.

Presents six possible approaches to interpreting *Walden*.

Lewis, Jim. "Notes and Comment: A Response to *Walden*." *Journal of American Studies* 27, No. 2 (August 1993): 237-43.

Explores the responses of modern readers of *Walden* through intertextual criticism.

Masteller, Richard N., and Jean Carwile. "Rural Architecture in Andrew Jackson Downing and Henry David Thoreau: Pattern Book Parody in *Walden*." *The New England Quarterly* LVII, No. 4 (December 1984): 483-510.

Considers Thoreau's criticism of contemporary architecture and suggests that *Walden* is actually a parody of the popular house pattern books of the time.

Myerson, Joel. *Critical Essays on Henry David Thoreau's "Walden."* Boston: G. K. Hall, 1988, 254 p.

An anthology of the more famous critical essays on *Walden*, including numerous early reviews.

Oates, Joyce Carol. Introduction to *Walden*, edited by J. Lyndon Shanley. pp. ix-xviii. Princeton, N.J.: Princeton University Press, 1971.

Oates recalls *Walden*'s effect on her as a young reader and contemplates its continuing influence on her life.

Paul, Sherman. "Resolution at Walden." *Accent* XIII, No. 2 (Spring 1953): 101-13.

Claims the broadest meaning of *Walden* is found in its author's lifelong struggle for perfection.

Peck, H. Daniel. "The Crosscurrents of *Walden*'s Pastoral." In *New Essays on "Walden."* Ed. Robert F. Sayre, pp. 73-94. Cambridge: Cambridge University Press, 1992.

Contrasts the work of earlier critics, for whom *Walden*'s meaning was clear and accessible, with later readings that attest to the text's complexity and elusiveness.

Ruland, Richard, ed. *Twentieth-Century Interpretations of Walden*. Englewood Cliffs: Prentice-Hall, 1968, 119 p.

A collection of twentieth-century critical essays which the editor claims is not so much representative as complementary.

Sattelmeyer, Robert. "The Remaking of *Walden*." In *Writing the American Classics*. Eds. James Barbour and Tom Quirk, pp. 53-78. Chapel Hill: University of North Carolina Press, 1990.

Discusses Thoreau's writing process from 1849, the intended publication date of *Walden*, to 1854, the work's actual publication date.

Sayre, Robert F., ed. *New Essays on "Walden."* Cambridge: Cambridge University Press, 1992, 117 p.

A collection of essays addressing the importance of *Walden* and the difficulties facing its readers, past and present.

Taketani, Etsuko. "Thoreau's Domestic Economy: Double Accounts in *Walden*." *The Concord Saunterer* 2, No. 1 (Fall 1994): 65-76.

Examines the interplay between domestic economy and Transcendentalism in *Walden*.

Thomas, Owen, ed. *"Walden" and Civil Disobedience: Authoritative Texts, Background, Reviews, and Essays in Criticism*. New York: Norton, 1966, 424 p.

Authoritative versions of Thoreau's two most important works, along with sufficient secondary material to aid the reader's understanding and appreciation of them.

Tillman, James S. "The Transcendental Georgic in *Walden*." *ESQ* 21, No. 3 (3rd Quarter 1975): 137-41.

Discusses Thoreau's account of his farming experiences at Walden as a variation on classical Georgic themes.

Whicher, George F. *Walden Revisited*. Chicago: Packard, 1945, 93 p.

Searching for traces of Thoreau's spiritual and moral legacy, Whicher returns to Walden Pond a century after its most famous resident occupied the site.

Woodlief, Annette M. "*Walden*: A Checklist of Literary Criticism through 1973." *Resources for American Literary Study* 5, No. 1 (Spring 1975): 15-58.

An annotated bibliography that deals exclusively with the literary responses to *Walden* from its publication date through 1973.

Yannella, Philip R. "Socio-Economic Disarray and Literary Response: Concord and *Walden*." *Mosaic* 14, No. 1 (Winter 1981): 1-24.

Examines Thoreau's condemnation of the social and economic conditions of contemporary Concord.

Additional coverage of Thoreau's life and career is contained in the following sources published by Gale Research: *Nineteenth-Century Literature Criticism,* **Vols. 7 and 21;** *DISCovering Authors; DISCovering Authors Modules—Most-Studied Authors module; World Literature Criticism, 1500 to the Present; Concise Dictionary of American Literary Biography, 1640-1865;* **and** *Dictionary of Literary Biography,* **Vol. 1.**

Nineteenth-Century Literature Criticism

Cumulative Indexes
Volumes 1-61

How to Use This Index

The main references

Calvino, Italo
1923-1985.....CLC 5, 8, 11, 22, 33, 39,
73; SSC 3

---

list all author entries in the following Gale Literary Criticism series:

BLC = *Black Literature Criticism*
CLC = *Contemporary Literary Criticism*
CLR = *Children's Literature Review*
CMLC = *Classical and Medieval Literature Criticism*
DA = *DISCovering Authors*
DAB = *DISCovering Authors: British*
DAC = *DISCovering Authors: Canadian*
DAM = *DISCovering Authors Modules*
   DRAM: Dramatists module
   MST: Most-studied authors module
   MULT: Multicultural authors module
   NOV: Novelists module
   POET: Poets module
   POP: Popular/genre writers module

DC = *Drama Criticism*
HLC = *Hispanic Literature Criticism*
LC = *Literature Criticism from 1400 to 1800*
NCLC = *Nineteenth-Century Literature Criticism*
PC = *Poetry Criticism*
SSC = *Short Story Criticism*
TCLC = *Twentieth-Century Literary Criticism*
WLC = *World Literature Criticism, 1500 to the Present*

The cross-references

See also CANR 23; CA 85-88;
obituary CA 116

---

list all author entries in the following Gale biographical and literary sources:

AAYA = *Authors & Artists for Young Adults*
AITN = *Authors in the News*
BEST = *Bestsellers*
BW = *Black Writers*
CA = *Contemporary Authors*
CAAS = *Contemporary Authors Autobiography Series*
CABS = *Contemporary Authors Bibliographical Series*
CANR = *Contemporary Authors New Revision Series*
CAP = *Contemporary Authors Permanent Series*
CDALB = *Concise Dictionary of American Literary Biography*
CDBLB = *Concise Dictionary of British Literary Biography*

DLB = *Dictionary of Literary Biography*
DLBD = *Dictionary of Literary Biography Documentary Series*
DLBY = *Dictionary of Literary Biography Yearbook*
HW = *Hispanic Writers*
JRDA = *Junior DISCovering Authors*
MAICYA = *Major Authors and Illustrators for Children and Young Adults*
MTCW = *Major 20th-Century Writers*
NNAL = *Native North American Literature*
SAAS = *Something about the Author Autobiography Series*
SATA = *Something about the Author*
YABC = *Yesterday's Authors of Books for Children*

Literary Criticism Series
Cumulative Author Index

Abasiyanik, Sait Faik 1906-1954
See Sait Faik
See also CA 123

Abbey, Edward 1927-1989 ...... CLC 36, 59
See also CA 45-48; 128; CANR 2, 41

Abbott, Lee K(ittredge) 1947- ...... CLC 48
See also CA 124; CANR 51; DLB 130

Abe, Kobo
1924-1993 .... CLC 8, 22, 53, 81;
DAM NOV
See also CA 65-68; 140; CANR 24; MTCW

Abelard, Peter c. 1079-c. 1142 ... CMLC 11
See also DLB 115

Abell, Kjeld 1901-1961........... CLC 15
See also CA 111

Abish, Walter 1931- .... CLC 22
See also CA 101; CANR 37; DLB 130

Abrahams, Peter (Henry) 1919- ..... CLC 4
See also BW 1; CA 57-60; CANR 26;
DLB 117; MTCW

Abrams, M(eyer) H(oward) 1912-... CLC 24
See also CA 57-60; CANR 13, 33; DLB 67

Abse, Dannie
1923- ... CLC 7, 29; DAB; DAM POET
See also CA 53-56; CAAS 1; CANR 4, 46;
DLB 27

Achebe, (Albert) Chinua(lumogu)
1930- ..... CLC 1, 3, 5, 7, 11, 26, 51, 75;
BLC; DA; DAB; DAC; DAM MST,
MULT, NOV; WLC
See also AAYA 15; BW 2; CA 1-4R;
CANR 6, 26, 47; CLR 20; DLB 117;
MAICYA; MTCW; SATA 40;
SATA-Brief 38

Acker, Kathy 1948- .... CLC 45
See also CA 117; 122; CANR 55

Ackroyd, Peter 1949-.......... CLC 34, 52
See also CA 123; 127; CANR 51; DLB 155;
INT 127

Acorn, Milton 1923-......... CLC 15; DAC
See also CA 103; DLB 53; INT 103

Adamov, Arthur
1908-1970 .... CLC 4, 25; DAM DRAM
See also CA 17-18; 25-28R; CAP 2; MTCW

Adams, Alice (Boyd)
1926- .... CLC 6, 13, 46; SSC 24
See also CA 81-84; CANR 26, 53;
DLBY 86; INT CANR-26; MTCW

Adams, Andy 1859-1935......... TCLC 56
See also YABC 1

Adams, Douglas (Noel)
1952- .... CLC 27, 60; DAM POP
See also AAYA 4; BEST 89:3; CA 106;
CANR 34; DLBY 83; JRDA

Adams, Francis 1862-1893....... NCLC 33

Adams, Henry (Brooks)
1838-1918 ..... TCLC 4, 52; DA; DAB;
DAC; DAM MST
See also CA 104; 133; DLB 12, 47

Adams, Richard (George)
1920- .... CLC 4, 5, 18; DAM NOV
See also AAYA 16; AITN 1, 2; CA 49-52;
CANR 3, 35; CLR 20; JRDA; MAICYA;
MTCW; SATA 7, 69

Adamson, Joy(-Friederike Victoria)
1910-1980 .... CLC 17
See also CA 69-72; 93-96; CANR 22;
MTCW; SATA 11; SATA-Obit 22

Adcock, Fleur 1934-............. CLC 41
See also CA 25-28R; CAAS 23; CANR 11,
34; DLB 40

Addams, Charles (Samuel)
1912-1988 .... CLC 30
See also CA 61-64; 126; CANR 12

Addison, Joseph 1672-1719 .... LC 18
See also CDBLB 1660-1789; DLB 101

Adler, Alfred (F.) 1870-1937...... TCLC 61
See also CA 119

Adler, C(arole) S(chwerdtfeger)
1932- .... CLC 35
See also AAYA 4; CA 89-92; CANR 19,
40; JRDA; MAICYA; SAAS 15;
SATA 26, 63

Adler, Renata 1938-............. CLC 8, 31
See also CA 49-52; CANR 5, 22, 52;
MTCW

Ady, Endre 1877-1919 .... TCLC 11
See also CA 107

Aeschylus
525B.C.-456B.C........ CMLC 11; DA;
DAB; DAC; DAM DRAM, MST
See also DLB 176

Afton, Effie
See Harper, Frances Ellen Watkins

Agapida, Fray Antonio
See Irving, Washington

Agee, James (Rufus)
1909-1955 .... TCLC 1, 19; DAM NOV
See also AITN 1; CA 108; 148;
CDALB 1941-1968; DLB 2, 26, 152

Aghill, Gordon
See Silverberg, Robert

Agnon, S(hmuel) Y(osef Halevi)
1888-1970 .... CLC 4, 8, 14
See also CA 17-18; 25-28R; CAP 2; MTCW

Agrippa von Nettesheim, Henry Cornelius
1486-1535 .... LC 27

Aherne, Owen
See Cassill, R(onald) V(erlin)

Ai 1947-................... CLC 4, 14, 69
See also CA 85-88; CAAS 13; DLB 120

Aickman, Robert (Fordyce)
1914-1981 .... CLC 57
See also CA 5-8R; CANR 3

Aiken, Conrad (Potter)
1889-1973 .... CLC 1, 3, 5, 10, 52;
DAM NOV, POET; SSC 9
See also CA 5-8R; 45-48; CANR 4;
CDALB 1929-1941; DLB 9, 45, 102;
MTCW; SATA 3, 30

Aiken, Joan (Delano) 1924-........ CLC 35
See also AAYA 1; CA 9-12R; CANR 4, 23,
34; CLR 1, 19; DLB 161; JRDA;
MAICYA; MTCW; SAAS 1; SATA 2,
30, 73

Ainsworth, William Harrison
1805-1882 .... NCLC 13
See also DLB 21; SATA 24

Aitmatov, Chingiz (Torekulovich)
1928-....................... CLC 71
See also CA 103; CANR 38; MTCW;
SATA 56

Akers, Floyd
See Baum, L(yman) Frank

Akhmadulina, Bella Akhatovna
1937- .... CLC 53; DAM POET
See also CA 65-68

Akhmatova, Anna
1888-1966 .... CLC 11, 25, 64;
DAM POET; PC 2
See also CA 19-20; 25-28R; CANR 35;
CAP 1; MTCW

Aksakov, Sergei Timofeyvich
1791-1859 .... NCLC 2

Aksenov, Vassily
See Aksyonov, Vassily (Pavlovich)

Aksyonov, Vassily (Pavlovich)
1932- .... CLC 22, 37
See also CA 53-56; CANR 12, 48

Akutagawa, Ryunosuke
1892-1927 .... TCLC 16
See also CA 117; 154

Alain 1868-1951 .... TCLC 41

Alain-Fournier.................... TCLC 6
See also Fournier, Henri Alban
See also DLB 65

Alarcon, Pedro Antonio de
1833-1891 .... NCLC 1

Alas (y Urena), Leopoldo (Enrique Garcia)
1852-1901 .... TCLC 29
See also CA 113; 131; HW

Albee, Edward (Franklin III)
1928- ...... CLC 1, 2, 3, 5, 9, 11, 13, 25,
53, 86; DA; DAB; DAC; DAM DRAM,
MST; WLC
See also AITN 1; CA 5-8R;
CANR 8, 54; CDALB 1941-1968; DLB 7;
INT CANR-8; MTCW

Alberti, Rafael 1902- . . . . CLC 7
See also CA 85-88; DLB 108

Albert the Great 1200(?)-1280. . . . CMLC 16
See also DLB 115

Alcala-Galiano, Juan Valera y
See Valera y Alcala-Galiano, Juan

Alcott, Amos Bronson 1799-1888 . . NCLC 1
See also DLB 1

Alcott, Louisa May
1832-1888 . . . . . NCLC 6, 58; DA; DAB;
DAC; DAM MST, NOV; WLC
See also AAYA 20; CDALB 1865-1917;
CLR 1, 38; DLB 1, 42, 79; DLBD 14;
JRDA; MAICYA; YABC 1

Aldanov, M. A.
See Aldanov, Mark (Alexandrovich)

Aldanov, Mark (Alexandrovich)
1886(?)-1957 . . . . TCLC 23
See also CA 118

Aldington, Richard 1892-1962. . . . . . CLC 49
See also CA 85-88; CANR 45; DLB 20, 36,
100, 149

Aldiss, Brian W(ilson)
1925- . . . . CLC 5, 14, 40; DAM NOV
See also CA 5-8R; CAAS 2; CANR 5, 28;
DLB 14; MTCW; SATA 34

Alegria, Claribel
1924- . . . . CLC 75; DAM MULT
See also CA 131; CAAS 15; DLB 145; HW

Alegria, Fernando 1918- . . . . CLC 57
See also CA 9-12R; CANR 5, 32; HW

Aleichem, Sholom . . . . TCLC 1, 35
See also Rabinovitch, Sholem

Aleixandre, Vicente
1898-1984 . . . . CLC 9, 36; DAM POET;
PC 15
See also CA 85-88; 114; CANR 26;
DLB 108; HW; MTCW

Alepoudelis, Odysseus
See Elytis, Odysseus

Aleshkovsky, Joseph 1929-
See Aleshkovsky, Yuz
See also CA 121; 128

Aleshkovsky, Yuz . . . . CLC 44
See also Aleshkovsky, Joseph

Alexander, Lloyd (Chudley) 1924- . . CLC 35
See also AAYA 1; CA 1-4R; CANR 1, 24,
38, 55; CLR 1, 5; DLB 52; JRDA;
MAICYA; MTCW; SAAS 19; SATA 3,
49, 81

Alexie, Sherman (Joseph, Jr.)
1966- . . . . CLC 96; DAM MULT
See also CA 138; DLB 175; NNAL

Alfau, Felipe 1902- . . . . CLC 66
See also CA 137

Alger, Horatio, Jr. 1832-1899 . . . . . NCLC 8
See also DLB 42; SATA 16

Algren, Nelson 1909-1981 . . . . CLC 4, 10, 33
See also CA 13-16R; 103; CANR 20;
CDALB 1941-1968; DLB 9; DLBY 81,
82; MTCW

Ali, Ahmed 1910- . . . . CLC 69
See also CA 25-28R; CANR 15, 34

Alighieri, Dante 1265-1321 . . . . CMLC 3, 18

Allan, John B.
See Westlake, Donald E(dwin)

Allen, Edward 1948- . . . . CLC 59

Allen, Paula Gunn
1939- . . . . CLC 84; DAM MULT
See also CA 112; 143; DLB 175; NNAL

Allen, Roland
See Ayckbourn, Alan

Allen, Sarah A.
See Hopkins, Pauline Elizabeth

Allen, Woody
1935- . . . . CLC 16, 52; DAM POP
See also AAYA 10; CA 33-36R; CANR 27,
38; DLB 44; MTCW

Allende, Isabel
1942- . . . . CLC 39, 57, 97; DAM MULT,
NOV; HLC
See also AAYA 18; CA 125; 130;
CANR 51; DLB 145; HW; INT 130;
MTCW

Alleyn, Ellen
See Rossetti, Christina (Georgina)

Allingham, Margery (Louise)
1904-1966 . . . . CLC 19
See also CA 5-8R; 25-28R; CANR 4;
DLB 77; MTCW

Allingham, William 1824-1889 . . . NCLC 25
See also DLB 35

Allison, Dorothy E. 1949- . . . . CLC 78
See also CA 140

Allston, Washington 1779-1843. . . . NCLC 2
See also DLB 1

Almedingen, E. M. . . . . CLC 12
See also Almedingen, Martha Edith von
See also SATA 3

Almedingen, Martha Edith von 1898-1971
See Almedingen, E. M.
See also CA 1-4R; CANR 1

Almqvist, Carl Jonas Love
1793-1866 . . . . NCLC 42

Alonso, Damaso 1898-1990 . . . . CLC 14
See also CA 110; 131; 130; DLB 108; HW

Alov
See Gogol, Nikolai (Vasilyevich)

Alta 1942- . . . . CLC 19
See also CA 57-60

Alter, Robert B(ernard) 1935- . . . . . . CLC 34
See also CA 49-52; CANR 1, 47

Alther, Lisa 1944- . . . . CLC 7, 41
See also CA 65-68; CANR 12, 30, 51;
MTCW

Altman, Robert 1925- . . . . CLC 16
See also CA 73-76; CANR 43

Alvarez, A(lfred) 1929- . . . . CLC 5, 13
See also CA 1-4R; CANR 3, 33; DLB 14,
40

Alvarez, Alejandro Rodriguez 1903-1965
See Casona, Alejandro
See also CA 131; 93-96; HW

Alvarez, Julia 1950- . . . . CLC 93
See also CA 147

Alvaro, Corrado 1896-1956 . . . . TCLC 60

Amado, Jorge
1912- . . . . . . CLC 13, 40; DAM MULT,
NOV; HLC
See also CA 77-80; CANR 35; DLB 113;
MTCW

Ambler, Eric 1909- . . . . CLC 4, 6, 9
See also CA 9-12R; CANR 7, 38; DLB 77;
MTCW

Amichai, Yehuda 1924- . . . . . . CLC 9, 22, 57
See also CA 85-88; CANR 46; MTCW

Amiel, Henri Frederic 1821-1881 . . NCLC 4

Amis, Kingsley (William)
1922-1995 . . . . . CLC 1, 2, 3, 5, 8, 13, 40,
44; DA; DAB; DAC; DAM MST, NOV
See also AITN 2; CA 9-12R; 150; CANR 8,
28, 54; CDBLB 1945-1960; DLB 15, 27,
100, 139; INT CANR-8; MTCW

Amis, Martin (Louis)
1949- . . . . CLC 4, 9, 38, 62
See also BEST 90:3; CA 65-68; CANR 8,
27, 54; DLB 14; INT CANR-27

Ammons, A(rchie) R(andolph)
1926- . . . . CLC 2, 3, 5, 8, 9, 25, 57;
DAM POET; PC 16
See also AITN 1; CA 9-12R; CANR 6, 36,
51; DLB 5, 165; MTCW

Amo, Tauraatua i
See Adams, Henry (Brooks)

Anand, Mulk Raj
1905- . . . . CLC 23, 93; DAM NOV
See also CA 65-68; CANR 32; MTCW

Anatol
See Schnitzler, Arthur

Anaximander
c. 610B.C.-c. 546B.C. . . . . CMLC 22

Anaya, Rudolfo A(lfonso)
1937- . . . . CLC 23; DAM MULT, NOV;
HLC
See also AAYA 20; CA 45-48; CAAS 4;
CANR 1, 32, 51; DLB 82; HW 1; MTCW

Andersen, Hans Christian
1805-1875 . . . . NCLC 7; DA; DAB;
DAC; DAM MST, POP; SSC 6; WLC
See also CLR 6; MAICYA; YABC 1

Anderson, C. Farley
See Mencken, H(enry) L(ouis); Nathan,
George Jean

Anderson, Jessica (Margaret) Queale
. . . . CLC 37
See also CA 9-12R; CANR 4

Anderson, Jon (Victor)
1940- . . . . CLC 9; DAM POET
See also CA 25-28R; CANR 20

Anderson, Lindsay (Gordon)
1923-1994 . . . . CLC 20
See also CA 125; 128; 146

Anderson, Maxwell
1888-1959 . . . . . . TCLC 2; DAM DRAM
See also CA 105; 152; DLB 7

Anderson, Poul (William) 1926- . . . . CLC 15
See also AAYA 5; CA 1-4R; CAAS 2;
CANR 2, 15, 34; DLB 8; INT CANR-15;
MTCW; SATA 90; SATA-Brief 39

Anderson, Robert (Woodruff)
  1917- . . . . CLC 23; DAM DRAM
  See also AITN 1; CA 21-24R; CANR 32;
  DLB 7

Anderson, Sherwood
  1876-1941 . . . . TCLC 1, 10, 24; DA;
    DAB; DAC; DAM MST, NOV; SSC 1;
                                       WLC
  See also CA 104; 121; CDALB 1917-1929;
  DLB 4, 9, 86; DLBD 1; MTCW

Andier, Pierre
  See Desnos, Robert

Andouard
  See Giraudoux, (Hippolyte) Jean

Andrade, Carlos Drummond de . . . . . . CLC 18
  See also Drummond de Andrade, Carlos

Andrade, Mario de 1893-1945 . . . . . TCLC 43

Andreae, Johann V(alentin)
  1586-1654 . . . . LC 32
  See also DLB 164

Andreas-Salome, Lou 1861-1937 . . . TCLC 56
  See also DLB 66

Andrewes, Lancelot 1555-1626 . . . . LC 5
  See also DLB 151, 172

Andrews, Cicily Fairfield
  See West, Rebecca

Andrews, Elton V.
  See Pohl, Frederik

Andreyev, Leonid (Nikolaevich)
  1871-1919 . . . . TCLC 3
  See also CA 104

Andric, Ivo 1892-1975 . . . . CLC 8
  See also CA 81-84; 57-60; CANR 43;
  DLB 147; MTCW

Angelique, Pierre
  See Bataille, Georges

Angell, Roger 1920- . . . . CLC 26
  See also CA 57-60; CANR 13, 44; DLB 171

Angelou, Maya
  1928- . . . . CLC 12, 35, 64, 77; BLC; DA;
    DAB; DAC; DAM MST, MULT, POET,
                                        POP
  See also AAYA 7, 20; BW 2; CA 65-68;
  CANR 19, 42; DLB 38; MTCW;
  SATA 49

Annensky, Innokenty (Fyodorovich)
  1856-1909 . . . . TCLC 14
  See also CA 110; 155

Annunzio, Gabriele d'
  See D'Annunzio, Gabriele

Anon, Charles Robert
  See Pessoa, Fernando (Antonio Nogueira)

Anouilh, Jean (Marie Lucien Pierre)
  1910-1987 . . . . . . CLC 1, 3, 8, 13, 40, 50;
                                    DAM DRAM
  See also CA 17-20R; 123; CANR 32;
  MTCW

Anthony, Florence
  See Ai

Anthony, John
  See Ciardi, John (Anthony)

Anthony, Peter
  See Shaffer, Anthony (Joshua); Shaffer,
  Peter (Levin)

Anthony, Piers 1934- . . CLC 35; DAM POP
  See also AAYA 11; CA 21-24R; CANR 28,
  56; DLB 8; MTCW; SAAS 22; SATA 84

Antoine, Marc
  See Proust, (Valentin-Louis-George-Eugene-)
  Marcel

Antoninus, Brother
  See Everson, William (Oliver)

Antonioni, Michelangelo 1912- . . . . . CLC 20
  See also CA 73-76; CANR 45

Antschel, Paul 1920-1970
  See Celan, Paul
  See also CA 85-88; CANR 33; MTCW

Anwar, Chairil 1922-1949 . . . . TCLC 22
  See also CA 121

Apollinaire, Guillaume
  1880-1918 . . . . TCLC 3, 8, 51;
                               DAM POET; PC 7
  See also Kostrowitzki, Wilhelm Apollinaris
  de
  See also CA 152

Appelfeld, Aharon 1932- . . . . CLC 23, 47
  See also CA 112; 133

Apple, Max (Isaac) 1941- . . . . CLC 9, 33
  See also CA 81-84; CANR 19, 54; DLB 130

Appleman, Philip (Dean) 1926- . . . . . CLC 51
  See also CA 13-16R; CAAS 18; CANR 6,
  29, 56

Appleton, Lawrence
  See Lovecraft, H(oward) P(hillips)

Apteryx
  See Eliot, T(homas) S(tearns)

Apuleius, (Lucius Madaurensis)
  125(?)-175(?) . . . . CMLC 1

Aquin, Hubert 1929-1977 . . . . CLC 15
  See also CA 105; DLB 53

Aragon, Louis
  1897-1982 . . . . . CLC 3, 22; DAM NOV,
                                         POET
  See also CA 69-72; 108; CANR 28;
  DLB 72; MTCW

Arany, Janos 1817-1882 . . . . NCLC 34

Arbuthnot, John 1667-1735 . . . . LC 1
  See also DLB 101

Archer, Herbert Winslow
  See Mencken, H(enry) L(ouis)

Archer, Jeffrey (Howard)
  1940- . . . . CLC 28; DAM POP
  See also AAYA 16; BEST 89:3; CA 77-80;
  CANR 22, 52; INT CANR-22

Archer, Jules 1915- . . . . CLC 12
  See also CA 9-12R; CANR 6; SAAS 5;
  SATA 4, 85

Archer, Lee
  See Ellison, Harlan (Jay)

Arden, John
  1930- . . . . . CLC 6, 13, 15; DAM DRAM
  See also CA 13-16R; CAAS 4; CANR 31;
  DLB 13; MTCW

Arenas, Reinaldo
  1943-1990 . . . . . . CLC 41; DAM MULT;
                                          HLC
  See also CA 124; 128; 133; DLB 145; HW

Arendt, Hannah 1906-1975 . . . . . CLC 66, 98
  See also CA 17-20R; 61-64; CANR 26;
  MTCW

Aretino, Pietro 1492-1556 . . . . LC 12

Arghezi, Tudor . . . . CLC 80
  See also Theodorescu, Ion N.

Arguedas, Jose Maria
  1911-1969 . . . . CLC 10, 18
  See also CA 89-92; DLB 113; HW

Argueta, Manlio 1936- . . . . CLC 31
  See also CA 131; DLB 145; HW

Ariosto, Ludovico 1474-1533 . . . . LC 6

Aristides
  See Epstein, Joseph

Aristophanes
  450B.C.-385B.C. . . . . CMLC 4; DA;
    DAB; DAC; DAM DRAM, MST; DC 2
  See also DLB 176

Arlt, Roberto (Godofredo Christophersen)
  1900-1942 . . . . . TCLC 29; DAM MULT;
                                          HLC
  See also CA 123; 131; HW

Armah, Ayi Kwei
  1939- . . . . CLC 5, 33; BLC;
                              DAM MULT, POET
  See also BW 1; CA 61-64; CANR 21;
  DLB 117; MTCW

Armatrading, Joan 1950- . . . . CLC 17
  See also CA 114

Arnette, Robert
  See Silverberg, Robert

Arnim, Achim von (Ludwig Joachim von
  Arnim) 1781-1831 . . . . NCLC 5
  See also DLB 90

Arnim, Bettina von 1785-1859 . . . . NCLC 38
  See also DLB 90

Arnold, Matthew
  1822-1888 . . . . . NCLC 6, 29; DA; DAB;
    DAC; DAM MST, POET; PC 5; WLC
  See also CDBLB 1832-1890; DLB 32, 57

Arnold, Thomas 1795-1842 . . . . . . NCLC 18
  See also DLB 55

Arnow, Harriette (Louisa) Simpson
  1908-1986 . . . . CLC 2, 7, 18
  See also CA 9-12R; 118; CANR 14; DLB 6;
  MTCW; SATA 42; SATA-Obit 47

Arp, Hans
  See Arp, Jean

Arp, Jean 1887-1966 . . . . CLC 5
  See also CA 81-84; 25-28R; CANR 42

Arrabal
  See Arrabal, Fernando

Arrabal, Fernando 1932- . . . CLC 2, 9, 18, 58
  See also CA 9-12R; CANR 15

Arrick, Fran . . . . CLC 30
  See also Gaberman, Judie Angell

Artaud, Antonin (Marie Joseph)
  1896-1948 . . . TCLC 3, 36; DAM DRAM
  See also CA 104; 149

Arthur, Ruth M(abel) 1905-1979 . . . . CLC 12
  See also CA 9-12R; 85-88; CANR 4;
  SATA 7, 26

Artsybashev, Mikhail (Petrovich)
  1878-1927 . . . . TCLC 31

Bailey, Paul 1937- .... **CLC 45**
See also CA 21-24R; CANR 16; DLB 14

Baillie, Joanna 1762-1851 .... **NCLC 2**
See also DLB 93

Bainbridge, Beryl (Margaret)
1933- .... **CLC 4, 5, 8, 10, 14, 18, 22, 62; DAM NOV**
See also CA 21-24R; CANR 24, 55; DLB 14; MTCW

Baker, Elliott 1922- .... **CLC 8**
See also CA 45-48; CANR 2

Baker, Jean H. .... **TCLC 3, 10**
See also Russell, George William

Baker, Nicholson
1957- .... **CLC 61; DAM POP**
See also CA 135

Baker, Ray Stannard 1870-1946... **TCLC 47**
See also CA 118

Baker, Russell (Wayne) 1925-...... **CLC 31**
See also BEST 89:4; CA 57-60; CANR 11, 41; MTCW

Bakhtin, M.
See Bakhtin, Mikhail Mikhailovich

Bakhtin, M. M.
See Bakhtin, Mikhail Mikhailovich

Bakhtin, Mikhail
See Bakhtin, Mikhail Mikhailovich

Bakhtin, Mikhail Mikhailovich
1895-1975 .... **CLC 83**
See also CA 128; 113

Bakshi, Ralph 1938(?)-............ **CLC 26**
See also CA 112; 138

Bakunin, Mikhail (Alexandrovich)
1814-1876 .... **NCLC 25, 58**

Baldwin, James (Arthur)
1924-1987 ...... **CLC 1, 2, 3, 4, 5, 8, 13, 15, 17, 42, 50, 67, 90; BLC; DA; DAB; DAC; DAM MST, MULT, NOV, POP; DC 1; SSC 10; WLC**
See also AAYA 4; BW 1; CA 1-4R; 124; CABS 1; CANR 3, 24; CDALB 1941-1968; DLB 2, 7, 33; DLBY 87; MTCW; SATA 9; SATA-Obit 54

Ballard, J(ames) G(raham)
1930- .... **CLC 3, 6, 14, 36; DAM NOV, POP; SSC 1**
See also AAYA 3; CA 5-8R; CANR 15, 39; DLB 14; MTCW

Balmont, Konstantin (Dmitriyevich)
1867-1943 .... **TCLC 11**
See also CA 109; 155

Balzac, Honore de
1799-1850 .... **NCLC 5, 35, 53; DA; DAB; DAC; DAM MST, NOV; SSC 5; WLC**
See also DLB 119

Bambara, Toni Cade
1939-1995 ...... **CLC 19, 88; BLC; DA; DAC; DAM MST, MULT**
See also AAYA 5; BW 2; CA 29-32R; 150; CANR 24, 49; DLB 38; MTCW

Bamdad, A.
See Shamlu, Ahmad

Banat, D. R.
See Bradbury, Ray (Douglas)

Bancroft, Laura
See Baum, L(yman) Frank

Banim, John 1798-1842 .... **NCLC 13**
See also DLB 116, 158, 159

Banim, Michael 1796-1874 ...... **NCLC 13**
See also DLB 158, 159

Banjo, The
See Paterson, A(ndrew) B(arton)

Banks, Iain
See Banks, Iain M(enzies)

Banks, Iain M(enzies) 1954- .... **CLC 34**
See also CA 123; 128; INT 128

Banks, Lynne Reid .... **CLC 23**
See also Reid Banks, Lynne
See also AAYA 6

Banks, Russell 1940- .... **CLC 37, 72**
See also CA 65-68; CAAS 15; CANR 19, 52; DLB 130

Banville, John 1945-.............. **CLC 46**
See also CA 117; 128; DLB 14; INT 128

Banville, Theodore (Faullain) de
1832-1891 .... **NCLC 9**

Baraka, Amiri
1934- .... **CLC 1, 2, 3, 5, 10, 14, 33; BLC; DA; DAC; DAM MST, MULT, POET, POP; DC 6; PC 4**
See also Jones, LeRoi
See also BW 2; CA 21-24R; CABS 3; CANR 27, 38; CDALB 1941-1968; DLB 5, 7, 16, 38; DLBD 8; MTCW

Barbauld, Anna Laetitia
1743-1825 .... **NCLC 50**
See also DLB 107, 109, 142, 158

Barbellion, W. N. P. .... **TCLC 24**
See also Cummings, Bruce F(rederick)

Barbera, Jack (Vincent) 1945-...... **CLC 44**
See also CA 110; CANR 45

Barbey d'Aurevilly, Jules Amedee
1808-1889 .... **NCLC 1; SSC 17**
See also DLB 119

Barbusse, Henri 1873-1935 .... **TCLC 5**
See also CA 105; 154; DLB 65

Barclay, Bill
See Moorcock, Michael (John)

Barclay, William Ewert
See Moorcock, Michael (John)

Barea, Arturo 1897-1957 .... **TCLC 14**
See also CA 111

Barfoot, Joan 1946- .... **CLC 18**
See also CA 105

Baring, Maurice 1874-1945 .... **TCLC 8**
See also CA 105; DLB 34

Barker, Clive 1952- ... **CLC 52; DAM POP**
See also AAYA 10; BEST 90:3; CA 121; 129; INT 129; MTCW

Barker, George Granville
1913-1991 ..... **CLC 8, 48; DAM POET**
See also CA 9-12R; 135; CANR 7, 38; DLB 20; MTCW

Barker, Harley Granville
See Granville-Barker, Harley
See also DLB 10

Barker, Howard 1946-............ **CLC 37**
See also CA 102; DLB 13

Barker, Pat(ricia) 1943-........ **CLC 32, 94**
See also CA 117; 122; CANR 50; INT 122

Barlow, Joel 1754-1812 .... **NCLC 23**
See also DLB 37

Barnard, Mary (Ethel) 1909-....... **CLC 48**
See also CA 21-22; CAP 2

Barnes, Djuna
1892-1982 ... **CLC 3, 4, 8, 11, 29; SSC 3**
See also CA 9-12R; 107; CANR 16, 55; DLB 4, 9, 45; MTCW

Barnes, Julian (Patrick)
1946- .... **CLC 42; DAB**
See also CA 102; CANR 19, 54; DLBY 93

Barnes, Peter 1931- .... **CLC 5, 56**
See also CA 65-68; CAAS 12; CANR 33, 34; DLB 13; MTCW

Baroja (y Nessi), Pio
1872-1956 .... **TCLC 8; HLC**
See also CA 104

Baron, David
See Pinter, Harold

Baron Corvo
See Rolfe, Frederick (William Serafino Austin Lewis Mary)

Barondess, Sue K(aufman)
1926-1977 .... **CLC 8**
See also Kaufman, Sue
See also CA 1-4R; 69-72; CANR 1

Baron de Teive
See Pessoa, Fernando (Antonio Nogueira)

Barres, Maurice 1862-1923 .... **TCLC 47**
See also DLB 123

Barreto, Afonso Henrique de Lima
See Lima Barreto, Afonso Henrique de

Barrett, (Roger) Syd 1946- .... **CLC 35**

Barrett, William (Christopher)
1913-1992 .... **CLC 27**
See also CA 13-16R; 139; CANR 11; INT CANR-11

Barrie, J(ames) M(atthew)
1860-1937 .... **TCLC 2; DAB; DAM DRAM**
See also CA 104; 136; CDBLB 1890-1914; CLR 16; DLB 10, 141, 156; MAICYA; YABC 1

Barrington, Michael
See Moorcock, Michael (John)

Barrol, Grady
See Bograd, Larry

Barry, Mike
See Malzberg, Barry N(athaniel)

Barry, Philip 1896-1949.......... **TCLC 11**
See also CA 109; DLB 7

Bart, Andre Schwarz
See Schwarz-Bart, Andre

Barth, John (Simmons)
1930- ...... **CLC 1, 2, 3, 5, 7, 9, 10, 14, 27, 51, 89; DAM NOV; SSC 10**
See also AITN 1, 2; CA 1-4R; CABS 1; CANR 5, 23, 49; DLB 2; MTCW

Barthelme, Donald
1931-1989 ..... CLC 1, 2, 3, 5, 6, 8, 13,
23, 46, 59; DAM NOV; SSC 2
See also CA 21-24R; 129; CANR 20;
DLB 2; DLBY 80, 89; MTCW; SATA 7;
SATA-Obit 62

Barthelme, Frederick 1943- .... CLC 36
See also CA 114; 122; DLBY 85; INT 122

Barthes, Roland (Gerard)
1915-1980 .... CLC 24, 83
See also CA 130; 97-100; MTCW

Barzun, Jacques (Martin) 1907- .... CLC 51
See also CA 61-64; CANR 22

Bashevis, Isaac
See Singer, Isaac Bashevis

Bashkirtseff, Marie 1859-1884 ... NCLC 27

Basho
See Matsuo Basho

Bass, Kingsley B., Jr.
See Bullins, Ed

Bass, Rick 1958-................ CLC 79
See also CA 126; CANR 53

Bassani, Giorgio 1916-............. CLC 9
See also CA 65-68; CANR 33; DLB 128,
177; MTCW

Bastos, Augusto (Antonio) Roa
See Roa Bastos, Augusto (Antonio)

Bataille, Georges 1897-1962 .... CLC 29
See also CA 101; 89-92

Bates, H(erbert) E(rnest)
1905-1974 .... CLC 46; DAB;
DAM POP; SSC 10
See also CA 93-96; 45-48; CANR 34;
DLB 162; MTCW

Bauchart
See Camus, Albert

Baudelaire, Charles
1821-1867 .... NCLC 6, 29, 55; DA;
DAB; DAC; DAM MST, POET; PC 1;
SSC 18; WLC

Baudrillard, Jean 1929-........... CLC 60

Baum, L(yman) Frank 1856-1919 ... TCLC 7
See also CA 108; 133; CLR 15; DLB 22;
JRDA; MAICYA; MTCW; SATA 18

Baum, Louis F.
See Baum, L(yman) Frank

Baumbach, Jonathan 1933- ...... CLC 6, 23
See also CA 13-16R; CAAS 5; CANR 12;
DLBY 80; INT CANR-12; MTCW

Bausch, Richard (Carl) 1945- ...... CLC 51
See also CA 101; CAAS 14; CANR 43;
DLB 130

Baxter, Charles
1947- .... CLC 45, 78; DAM POP
See also CA 57-60; CANR 40; DLB 130

Baxter, George Owen
See Faust, Frederick (Schiller)

Baxter, James K(eir) 1926-1972 .... CLC 14
See also CA 77-80

Baxter, John
See Hunt, E(verette) Howard, (Jr.)

Bayer, Sylvia
See Glassco, John

Baynton, Barbara 1857-1929 ...... TCLC 57

Beagle, Peter S(oyer) 1939-........ CLC 7
See also CA 9-12R; CANR 4, 51;
DLBY 80; INT CANR-4; SATA 60

Bean, Normal
See Burroughs, Edgar Rice

Beard, Charles A(ustin)
1874-1948 .... TCLC 15
See also CA 115; DLB 17; SATA 18

Beardsley, Aubrey 1872-1898 ..... NCLC 6

Beattie, Ann
1947- .... CLC 8, 13, 18, 40, 63;
DAM NOV, POP; SSC 11
See also BEST 90:2; CA 81-84; CANR 53;
DLBY 82; MTCW

Beattie, James 1735-1803 .... NCLC 25
See also DLB 109

Beauchamp, Kathleen Mansfield 1888-1923
See Mansfield, Katherine
See also CA 104; 134; DA; DAC;
DAM MST

Beaumarchais, Pierre-Augustin Caron de
1732-1799 .... DC 4
See also DAM DRAM

Beaumont, Francis
1584(?)-1616 .... LC 33; DC 6
See also CDBLB Before 1660; DLB 58, 121

**Beauvoir, Simone (Lucie Ernestine Marie
Bertrand) de**
1908-1986 .... CLC 1, 2, 4, 8, 14, 31, 44,
50, 71; DA; DAB; DAC; DAM MST,
NOV; WLC
See also CA 9-12R; 118; CANR 28;
DLB 72; DLBY 86; MTCW

Becker, Carl 1873-1945 .... TCLC 63:
See also DLB 17

Becker, Jurek 1937-........... CLC 7, 19
See also CA 85-88; DLB 75

Becker, Walter 1950-............. CLC 26

Beckett, Samuel (Barclay)
1906-1989 ...... CLC 1, 2, 3, 4, 6, 9, 10,
11, 14, 18, 29, 57, 59, 83; DA; DAB;
DAC; DAM DRAM, MST, NOV;
SSC 16; WLC
See also CA 5-8R; 130; CANR 33;
CDBLB 1945-1960; DLB 13, 15;
DLBY 90; MTCW

Beckford, William 1760-1844 .... NCLC 16
See also DLB 39

Beckman, Gunnel 1910-........... CLC 26
See also CA 33-36R; CANR 15; CLR 25;
MAICYA; SAAS 9; SATA 6

Becque, Henri 1837-1899........ NCLC 3

Beddoes, Thomas Lovell
1803-1849 .... NCLC 3
See also DLB 96

Bede c. 673-735............... CMLC 20
See also DLB 146

Bedford, Donald F.
See Fearing, Kenneth (Flexner)

Beecher, Catharine Esther
1800-1878 .... NCLC 30
See also DLB 1

Beecher, John 1904-1980.......... CLC 6
See also AITN 1; CA 5-8R; 105; CANR 8

Beer, Johann 1655-1700............. LC 5
See also DLB 168

Beer, Patricia 1924-.............. CLC 58
See also CA 61-64; CANR 13, 46; DLB 40

Beerbohm, Max
See Beerbohm, (Henry) Max(imilian)

Beerbohm, (Henry) Max(imilian)
1872-1956 .... TCLC 1, 24
See also CA 104; 154; DLB 34, 100

Beer-Hofmann, Richard
1866-1945 .... TCLC 60
See also DLB 81

Begiebing, Robert J(ohn) 1946-..... CLC 70
See also CA 122; CANR 40

Behan, Brendan
1923-1964 .... CLC 1, 8, 11, 15, 79;
DAM DRAM
See also CA 73-76; CANR 33;
CDBLB 1945-1960; DLB 13; MTCW

Behn, Aphra
1640(?)-1689 ...... LC 1, 30; DA; DAB;
DAC; DAM DRAM, MST, NOV,
POET; DC 4; PC 13; WLC
See also DLB 39, 80, 131

Behrman, S(amuel) N(athaniel)
1893-1973 .... CLC 40
See also CA 13-16; 45-48; CAP 1; DLB 7,
44

Belasco, David 1853-1931 .... TCLC 3
See also CA 104; DLB 7

Belcheva, Elisaveta 1893- .... CLC 10
See also Bagryana, Elisaveta

Beldone, Phil "Cheech"
See Ellison, Harlan (Jay)

Beleno
See Azuela, Mariano

Belinski, Vissarion Grigoryevich
1811-1848 .... NCLC 5

Belitt, Ben 1911-................. CLC 22
See also CA 13-16R; CAAS 4; CANR 7;
DLB 5

Bell, Gertrude 1868-1926........ TCLC 67
See also DLB 174

Bell, James Madison
1826-1902 .... TCLC 43; BLC;
DAM MULT
See also BW 1; CA 122; 124; DLB 50

Bell, Madison Smartt 1957-........ CLC 41
See also CA 111; CANR 28, 54

Bell, Marvin (Hartley)
1937- .... CLC 8, 31; DAM POET
See also CA 21-24R; CAAS 14; DLB 5;
MTCW

Bell, W. L. D.
See Mencken, H(enry) L(ouis)

Bellamy, Atwood C.
See Mencken, H(enry) L(ouis)

Bellamy, Edward 1850-1898 ...... NCLC 4
See also DLB 12

Bellin, Edward J.
See Kuttner, Henry

Belloc, (Joseph) Hilaire (Pierre Sebastien Rene Swanton)
1870-1953 ... **TCLC 7, 18; DAM POET**
See also CA 106; 152; DLB 19, 100, 141, 174; YABC 1

Belloc, Joseph Peter Rene Hilaire
See Belloc, (Joseph) Hilaire (Pierre Sebastien Rene Swanton)

Belloc, Joseph Pierre Hilaire
See Belloc, (Joseph) Hilaire (Pierre Sebastien Rene Swanton)

Belloc, M. A.
See Lowndes, Marie Adelaide (Belloc)

Bellow, Saul
1915- ...... **CLC 1, 2, 3, 6, 8, 10, 13, 15, 25, 33, 34, 63, 79; DA; DAB; DAC; DAM MST, NOV, POP; SSC 14; WLC**
See also AITN 2; BEST 89:3; CA 5-8R; CABS 1; CANR 29, 53; CDALB 1941-1968; DLB 2, 28; DLBD 3; DLBY 82; MTCW

Belser, Reimond Karel Maria de 1929-
See Ruyslinck, Ward
See also CA 152

Bely, Andrey .... **TCLC 7; PC 11**
See also Bugayev, Boris Nikolayevich

Benary, Margot
See Benary-Isbert, Margot

Benary-Isbert, Margot 1889-1979... **CLC 12**
See also CA 5-8R; 89-92; CANR 4; CLR 12; MAICYA; SATA 2; SATA-Obit 21

Benavente (y Martinez), Jacinto
1866-1954 ..... **TCLC 3; DAM DRAM, MULT**
See also CA 106; 131; HW; MTCW

Benchley, Peter (Bradford)
1940- ..... **CLC 4, 8; DAM NOV, POP**
See also AAYA 14; AITN 2; CA 17-20R; CANR 12, 35; MTCW; SATA 3, 89

Benchley, Robert (Charles)
1889-1945 .... **TCLC 1, 55**
See also CA 105; 153; DLB 11

Benda, Julien 1867-1956 .... **TCLC 60**
See also CA 120; 154

Benedict, Ruth 1887-1948 .... **TCLC 60**

Benedikt, Michael 1935- .... **CLC 4, 14**
See also CA 13-16R; CANR 7; DLB 5

Benet, Juan 1927-................ **CLC 28**
See also CA 143

Benet, Stephen Vincent
1898-1943 ...... **TCLC 7; DAM POET; SSC 10**
See also CA 104; 152; DLB 4, 48, 102; YABC 1

Benet, William Rose
1886-1950 ...... **TCLC 28; DAM POET**
See also CA 118; 152; DLB 45

Benford, Gregory (Albert) 1941-.... **CLC 52**
See also CA 69-72; CANR 12, 24, 49; DLBY 82

Bengtsson, Frans (Gunnar)
1894-1954 .... **TCLC 48**

Benjamin, David
See Slavitt, David R(ytman)

Benjamin, Lois
See Gould, Lois

Benjamin, Walter 1892-1940 ...... **TCLC 39**

Benn, Gottfried 1886-1956 .... **TCLC 3**
See also CA 106; 153; DLB 56

Bennett, Alan
1934- ... **CLC 45, 77; DAB; DAM MST**
See also CA 103; CANR 35, 55; MTCW

Bennett, (Enoch) Arnold
1867-1931 .... **TCLC 5, 20**
See also CA 106; 155; CDBLB 1890-1914; DLB 10, 34, 98, 135

Bennett, Elizabeth
See Mitchell, Margaret (Munnerlyn)

Bennett, George Harold 1930-
See Bennett, Hal
See also BW 1; CA 97-100

Bennett, Hal .... **CLC 5**
See also Bennett, George Harold
See also DLB 33

Bennett, Jay 1912-................ **CLC 35**
See also AAYA 10; CA 69-72; CANR 11, 42; JRDA; SAAS 4; SATA 41, 87; SATA-Brief 27

Bennett, Louise (Simone)
1919- ..... **CLC 28; BLC; DAM MULT**
See also BW 2; CA 151; DLB 117

Benson, E(dward) F(rederic)
1867-1940 .... **TCLC 27**
See also CA 114; DLB 135, 153

Benson, Jackson J. 1930-.......... **CLC 34**
See also CA 25-28R; DLB 111

Benson, Sally 1900-1972 .... **CLC 17**
See also CA 19-20; 37-40R; CAP 1; SATA 1, 35; SATA-Obit 27

Benson, Stella 1892-1933........ **TCLC 17**
See also CA 117; 155; DLB 36, 162

Bentham, Jeremy 1748-1832 ..... **NCLC 38**
See also DLB 107, 158

Bentley, E(dmund) C(lerihew)
1875-1956 .... **TCLC 12**
See also CA 108; DLB 70

Bentley, Eric (Russell) 1916-....... **CLC 24**
See also CA 5-8R; CANR 6; INT CANR-6

Beranger, Pierre Jean de
1780-1857 .... **NCLC 34**

Berdyaev, Nicolas
See Berdyaev, Nikolai (Aleksandrovich)

Berdyaev, Nikolai (Aleksandrovich)
1874-1948 .... **TCLC 67**
See also CA 120

Berendt, John (Lawrence) 1939-.... **CLC 86**
See also CA 146

Berger, Colonel
See Malraux, (Georges-)Andre

Berger, John (Peter) 1926- ...... **CLC 2, 19**
See also CA 81-84; CANR 51; DLB 14

Berger, Melvin H. 1927-.......... **CLC 12**
See also CA 5-8R; CANR 4; CLR 32; SAAS 2; SATA 5, 88

Berger, Thomas (Louis)
1924- .... **CLC 3, 5, 8, 11, 18, 38; DAM NOV**
See also CA 1-4R; CANR 5, 28, 51; DLB 2; DLBY 80; INT CANR-28; MTCW

Bergman, (Ernst) Ingmar
1918- .... **CLC 16, 72**
See also CA 81-84; CANR 33

Bergson, Henri 1859-1941 .... **TCLC 32**

Bergstein, Eleanor 1938-.......... **CLC 4**
See also CA 53-56; CANR 5

Berkoff, Steven 1937-............. **CLC 56**
See also CA 104

Bermant, Chaim (Icyk) 1929- ...... **CLC 40**
See also CA 57-60; CANR 6, 31, 57

Bern, Victoria
See Fisher, M(ary) F(rances) K(ennedy)

Bernanos, (Paul Louis) Georges
1888-1948 .... **TCLC 3**
See also CA 104; 130; DLB 72

Bernard, April 1956- .... **CLC 59**
See also CA 131

Berne, Victoria
See Fisher, M(ary) F(rances) K(ennedy)

Bernhard, Thomas
1931-1989 .... **CLC 3, 32, 61**
See also CA 85-88; 127; CANR 32, 57; DLB 85, 124; MTCW

Berriault, Gina 1926-............. **CLC 54**
See also CA 116; 129; DLB 130

Berrigan, Daniel 1921-............ **CLC 4**
See also CA 33-36R; CAAS 1; CANR 11, 43; DLB 5

Berrigan, Edmund Joseph Michael, Jr.
1934-1983
See Berrigan, Ted
See also CA 61-64; 110; CANR 14

Berrigan, Ted.................... **CLC 37**
See also Berrigan, Edmund Joseph Michael, Jr.
See also DLB 5, 169

Berry, Charles Edward Anderson 1931-
See Berry, Chuck
See also CA 115

Berry, Chuck.................... **CLC 17**
See also Berry, Charles Edward Anderson

Berry, Jonas
See Ashbery, John (Lawrence)

Berry, Wendell (Erdman)
1934- .... **CLC 4, 6, 8, 27, 46; DAM POET**
See also AITN 1; CA 73-76; CANR 50; DLB 5, 6

Berryman, John
1914-1972 ...... **CLC 1, 2, 3, 4, 6, 8, 10, 13, 25, 62; DAM POET**
See also CA 13-16; 33-36R; CABS 2; CANR 35; CAP 1; CDALB 1941-1968; DLB 48; MTCW

Bertolucci, Bernardo 1940- .... **CLC 16**
See also CA 106

Bertrand, Aloysius 1807-1841 .... **NCLC 31**

Bertran de Born c. 1140-1215 ..... **CMLC 5**

Besant, Annie (Wood) 1847-1933 ... **TCLC 9**
See also CA 105

Bessie, Alvah 1904-1985. . . . . **CLC 23**
See also CA 5-8R; 116; CANR 2; DLB 26

Bethlen, T. D.
See Silverberg, Robert

Beti, Mongo . . . . **CLC 27; BLC; DAM MULT**
See also Biyidi, Alexandre

Betjeman, John
1906-1984 . . . . **CLC 2, 6, 10, 34, 43;**
DAB; DAM MST, POET
See also CA 9-12R; 112; CANR 33, 56;
CDBLB 1945-1960; DLB 20; DLBY 84;
MTCW

Bettelheim, Bruno 1903-1990 . . . . . . **CLC 79**
See also CA 81-84; 131; CANR 23; MTCW

Betti, Ugo 1892-1953 . . . . **TCLC 5**
See also CA 104; 155

Betts, Doris (Waugh) 1932- . . . . **CLC 3, 6, 28**
See also CA 13-16R; CANR 9; DLBY 82;
INT CANR-9

Bevan, Alistair
See Roberts, Keith (John Kingston)

Bialik, Chaim Nachman
1873-1934 . . . . **TCLC 25**

Bickerstaff, Isaac
See Swift, Jonathan

Bidart, Frank 1939- . . . . **CLC 33**
See also CA 140

Bienek, Horst 1930- . . . . **CLC 7, 11**
See also CA 73-76; DLB 75

Bierce, Ambrose (Gwinett)
1842-1914(?) . . . . **TCLC 1, 7, 44; DA;**
DAC; DAM MST; SSC 9; WLC
See also CA 104; 139; CDALB 1865-1917;
DLB 11, 12, 23, 71, 74

Biggers, Earl Derr 1884-1933 . . . . . **TCLC 65**
See also CA 108; 153

Billings, Josh
See Shaw, Henry Wheeler

Billington, (Lady) Rachel (Mary)
1942- . . . . **CLC 43**
See also AITN 2; CA 33-36R; CANR 44

Binyon, T(imothy) J(ohn) 1936- . . . . **CLC 34**
See also CA 111; CANR 28

Bioy Casares, Adolfo
1914- . . . . **CLC 4, 8, 13, 88;**
DAM MULT; HLC; SSC 17
See also CA 29-32R; CANR 19, 43;
DLB 113; HW; MTCW

Bird, Cordwainer
See Ellison, Harlan (Jay)

Bird, Robert Montgomery
1806-1854 . . . . **NCLC 1**

Birney, (Alfred) Earle
1904- . . . . **CLC 1, 4, 6, 11; DAC;**
DAM MST, POET
See also CA 1-4R; CANR 5, 20; DLB 88;
MTCW

Bishop, Elizabeth
1911-1979 . . . . . . **CLC 1, 4, 9, 13, 15, 32;**
DA; DAC; DAM MST, POET; PC 3
See also CA 5-8R; 89-92; CABS 2;
CANR 26; CDALB 1968-1988; DLB 5,
169; MTCW; SATA-Obit 24

Bishop, John 1935- . . . . **CLC 10**
See also CA 105

Bissett, Bill 1939- . . . . **CLC 18; PC 14**
See also CA 69-72; CAAS 19; CANR 15;
DLB 53; MTCW

Bitov, Andrei (Georgievich) 1937- . . . **CLC 57**
See also CA 142

Biyidi, Alexandre 1932-
See Beti, Mongo
See also BW 1; CA 114; 124; MTCW

Bjarme, Brynjolf
See Ibsen, Henrik (Johan)

Bjornson, Bjornstjerne (Martinius)
1832-1910 . . . . **TCLC 7, 37**
See also CA 104

Black, Robert
See Holdstock, Robert P.

Blackburn, Paul 1926-1971 . . . . . . **CLC 9, 43**
See also CA 81-84; 33-36R; CANR 34;
DLB 16; DLBY 81

Black Elk
1863-1950 . . . . . **TCLC 33; DAM MULT**
See also CA 144; NNAL

Black Hobart
See Sanders, (James) Ed(ward)

Blacklin, Malcolm
See Chambers, Aidan

Blackmore, R(ichard) D(oddridge)
1825-1900 . . . . **TCLC 27**
See also CA 120; DLB 18

Blackmur, R(ichard) P(almer)
1904-1965 . . . . **CLC 2, 24**
See also CA 11-12; 25-28R; CAP 1; DLB 63

Black Tarantula
See Acker, Kathy

Blackwood, Algernon (Henry)
1869-1951 . . . . **TCLC 5**
See also CA 105; 150; DLB 153, 156

Blackwood, Caroline
1931-1996 . . . . **CLC 6, 9, 100**
See also CA 85-88; 151; CANR 32;
DLB 14; MTCW

Blade, Alexander
See Hamilton, Edmond; Silverberg, Robert

Blaga, Lucian 1895-1961 . . . . **CLC 75**

Blair, Eric (Arthur) 1903-1950
See Orwell, George
See also CA 104; 132; DA; DAB; DAC;
DAM MST, NOV; MTCW; SATA 29

Blais, Marie-Claire
1939- . . . . **CLC 2, 4, 6, 13, 22; DAC;**
DAM MST
See also CA 21-24R; CAAS 4; CANR 38;
DLB 53; MTCW

Blaise, Clark 1940- . . . . **CLC 29**
See also AITN 2; CA 53-56; CAAS 3;
CANR 5; DLB 53

Blake, Nicholas
See Day Lewis, C(ecil)
See also DLB 77

Blake, William
1757-1827 . . . . **NCLC 13, 37, 57; DA;**
DAB; DAC; DAM MST, POET; PC 12;
WLC
See also CDBLB 1789-1832; DLB 93, 163;
MAICYA; SATA 30

Blake, William J(ames) 1894-1969 . . . **PC 12**
See also CA 5-8R; 25-28R

Blasco Ibanez, Vicente
1867-1928 . . . . **TCLC 12; DAM NOV**
See also CA 110; 131; HW; MTCW

Blatty, William Peter
1928- . . . . **CLC 2; DAM POP**
See also CA 5-8R; CANR 9

Bleeck, Oliver
See Thomas, Ross (Elmore)

Blessing, Lee 1949- . . . . **CLC 54**

Blish, James (Benjamin)
1921-1975 . . . . **CLC 14**
See also CA 1-4R; 57-60; CANR 3; DLB 8;
MTCW; SATA 66

Bliss, Reginald
See Wells, H(erbert) G(eorge)

Blixen, Karen (Christentze Dinesen)
1885-1962
See Dinesen, Isak
See also CA 25-28; CANR 22, 50; CAP 2;
MTCW; SATA 44

Bloch, Robert (Albert) 1917-1994 . . . **CLC 33**
See also CA 5-8R; 146; CAAS 20; CANR 5;
DLB 44; INT CANR-5; SATA 12;
SATA-Obit 82

Blok, Alexander (Alexandrovich)
1880-1921 . . . . **TCLC 5**
See also CA 104

Blom, Jan
See Breytenbach, Breyten

Bloom, Harold 1930- . . . . **CLC 24**
See also CA 13-16R; CANR 39; DLB 67

Bloomfield, Aurelius
See Bourne, Randolph S(illiman)

Blount, Roy (Alton), Jr. 1941- . . . . . **CLC 38**
See also CA 53-56; CANR 10, 28;
INT CANR-28; MTCW

Bloy, Leon 1846-1917 . . . . **TCLC 22**
See also CA 121; DLB 123

Blume, Judy (Sussman)
1938- . . . **CLC 12, 30; DAM NOV, POP**
See also AAYA 3; CA 29-32R; CANR 13,
37; CLR 2, 15; DLB 52; JRDA;
MAICYA; MTCW; SATA 2, 31, 79

Blunden, Edmund (Charles)
1896-1974 . . . . **CLC 2, 56**
See also CA 17-18; 45-48; CANR 54;
CAP 2; DLB 20, 100, 155; MTCW

Bly, Robert (Elwood)
1926- . . . . **CLC 1, 2, 5, 10, 15, 38;**
DAM POET
See also CA 5-8R; CANR 41; DLB 5;
MTCW

Boas, Franz 1858-1942 . . . . **TCLC 56**
See also CA 115

Bobette
See Simenon, Georges (Jacques Christian)

Boccaccio, Giovanni
1313-1375 . . . . **CMLC 13; SSC 10**

Bochco, Steven 1943- . . . . **CLC 35**
See also AAYA 11; CA 124; 138

Bodenheim, Maxwell 1892-1954 . . . **TCLC 44**
See also CA 110; DLB 9, 45

Bodker, Cecil 1927- . . . . CLC 21
See also CA 73-76; CANR 13, 44; CLR 23;
MAICYA; SATA 14

Boell, Heinrich (Theodor)
1917-1985 . . . . CLC 2, 3, 6, 9, 11, 15, 27,
**32, 72; DA; DAB; DAC; DAM MST,
NOV; SSC 23; WLC**
See also CA 21-24R; 116; CANR 24;
DLB 69; DLBY 85; MTCW

Boerne, Alfred
See Doeblin, Alfred

Boethius 480(?)-524(?) . . . . CMLC 15
See also DLB 115

Bogan, Louise
1897-1970 . . . . CLC 4, 39, 46, 93;
DAM POET; PC 12
See also CA 73-76; 25-28R; CANR 33;
DLB 45, 169; MTCW

Bogarde, Dirk . . . . CLC 19
See also Van Den Bogarde, Derek Jules
Gaspard Ulric Niven
See also DLB 14

Bogosian, Eric 1953- . . . . CLC 45
See also CA 138

Bograd, Larry 1953- . . . . CLC 35
See also CA 93-96; CANR 57; SAAS 21;
SATA 33, 89

Boiardo, Matteo Maria 1441-1494 . . . . LC 6

Boileau-Despreaux, Nicolas
1636-1711 . . . . LC 3

Bojer, Johan 1872-1959 . . . . TCLC 64

Boland, Eavan (Aisling)
1944- . . . . CLC 40, 67; DAM POET
See also CA 143; DLB 40

Bolt, Lee
See Faust, Frederick (Schiller)

Bolt, Robert (Oxton)
1924-1995 . . . . . . CLC 14; DAM DRAM
See also CA 17-20R; 147; CANR 35;
DLB 13; MTCW

Bombet, Louis-Alexandre-Cesar
See Stendhal

Bomkauf
See Kaufman, Bob (Garnell)

Bonaventura . . . . NCLC 35
See also DLB 90

Bond, Edward
1934- . . . CLC 4, 6, 13, 23; DAM DRAM
See also CA 25-28R; CANR 38; DLB 13;
MTCW

Bonham, Frank 1914-1989 . . . . CLC 12
See also AAYA 1; CA 9-12R; CANR 4, 36;
JRDA; MAICYA; SAAS 3; SATA 1, 49;
SATA-Obit 62

Bonnefoy, Yves
1923- . . . . . . CLC 9, 15, 58; DAM MST,
POET
See also CA 85-88; CANR 33; MTCW

Bontemps, Arna(ud Wendell)
1902-1973 . . . . CLC 1, 18; BLC;
DAM MULT, NOV, POET
See also BW 1; CA 1-4R; 41-44R; CANR 4,
35; CLR 6; DLB 48, 51; JRDA;
MAICYA; MTCW; SATA 2, 44;
SATA-Obit 24

Booth, Martin 1944- . . . . CLC 13
See also CA 93-96; CAAS 2

Booth, Philip 1925- . . . . CLC 23
See also CA 5-8R; CANR 5; DLBY 82

Booth, Wayne C(layson) 1921- . . . . . CLC 24
See also CA 1-4R; CAAS 5; CANR 3, 43;
DLB 67

Borchert, Wolfgang 1921-1947 . . . . . TCLC 5
See also CA 104; DLB 69, 124

Borel, Petrus 1809-1859 . . . . NCLC 41

Borges, Jorge Luis
1899-1986 . . . CLC 1, 2, 3, 4, 6, 8, 9, 10,
**13, 19, 44, 48, 83; DA; DAB; DAC;
DAM MST, MULT; HLC; SSC 4; WLC**
See also AAYA 19; CA 21-24R; CANR 19,
33; DLB 113; DLBY 86; HW; MTCW

Borowski, Tadeusz 1922-1951 . . . . . . TCLC 9
See also CA 106; 154

Borrow, George (Henry)
1803-1881 . . . . NCLC 9
See also DLB 21, 55, 166

Bosman, Herman Charles
1905-1951 . . . . TCLC 49

Bosschere, Jean de 1878(?)-1953 . . . TCLC 19
See also CA 115

Boswell, James
1740-1795 . . . . . . LC 4; DA; DAB; DAC;
DAM MST; WLC
See also CDBLB 1660-1789; DLB 104, 142

Bottoms, David 1949- . . . . CLC 53
See also CA 105; CANR 22; DLB 120;
DLBY 83

Boucicault, Dion 1820-1890 . . . . . . NCLC 41

Boucolon, Maryse 1937(?)-
See Conde, Maryse
See also CA 110; CANR 30, 53

Bourget, Paul (Charles Joseph)
1852-1935 . . . . TCLC 12
See also CA 107; DLB 123

Bourjaily, Vance (Nye) 1922- . . . . CLC 8, 62
See also CA 1-4R; CAAS 1; CANR 2;
DLB 2, 143

Bourne, Randolph S(illiman)
1886-1918 . . . . TCLC 16
See also CA 117; 155; DLB 63

Bova, Ben(jamin William) 1932- . . . . CLC 45
See also AAYA 16; CA 5-8R; CAAS 18;
CANR 11, 56; CLR 3; DLBY 81;
INT CANR-11; MAICYA; MTCW;
SATA 6, 68

Bowen, Elizabeth (Dorothea Cole)
1899-1973 . . . . . . CLC 1, 3, 6, 11, 15, 22;
DAM NOV; SSC 3
See also CA 17-18; 41-44R; CANR 35;
CAP 2; CDBLB 1945-1960; DLB 15, 162;
MTCW

Bowering, George 1935- . . . . CLC 15, 47
See also CA 21-24R; CAAS 16; CANR 10;
DLB 53

Bowering, Marilyn R(uthe) 1949- . . . CLC 32
See also CA 101; CANR 49

Bowers, Edgar 1924- . . . . CLC 9
See also CA 5-8R; CANR 24; DLB 5

Bowie, David . . . . CLC 17
See also Jones, David Robert

Bowles, Jane (Sydney)
1917-1973 . . . . CLC 3, 68
See also CA 19-20; 41-44R; CAP 2

Bowles, Paul (Frederick)
1910- . . . . CLC 1, 2, 19, 53; SSC 3
See also CA 1-4R; CAAS 1; CANR 1, 19,
50; DLB 5, 6; MTCW

Box, Edgar
See Vidal, Gore

Boyd, Nancy
See Millay, Edna St. Vincent

Boyd, William 1952- . . . . CLC 28, 53, 70
See also CA 114; 120; CANR 51

Boyle, Kay
1902-1992 . . . . . CLC 1, 5, 19, 58; SSC 5
See also CA 13-16R; 140; CAAS 1;
CANR 29; DLB 4, 9, 48, 86; DLBY 93;
MTCW

Boyle, Mark
See Kienzle, William X(avier)

Boyle, Patrick 1905-1982 . . . . CLC 19
See also CA 127

Boyle, T. C. 1948-
See Boyle, T(homas) Coraghessan

Boyle, T(homas) Coraghessan
1948- . . . . . CLC 36, 55, 90; DAM POP;
SSC 16
See also BEST 90:4; CA 120; CANR 44;
DLBY 86

Boz
See Dickens, Charles (John Huffam)

Brackenridge, Hugh Henry
1748-1816 . . . . NCLC 7
See also DLB 11, 37

Bradbury, Edward P.
See Moorcock, Michael (John)

Bradbury, Malcolm (Stanley)
1932- . . . . CLC 32, 61; DAM NOV
See also CA 1-4R; CANR 1, 33; DLB 14;
MTCW

Bradbury, Ray (Douglas)
1920- . . . . . CLC 1, 3, 10, 15, 42, 98; DA;
**DAB; DAC; DAM MST, NOV, POP;
WLC**
See also AAYA 15; AITN 1, 2; CA 1-4R;
CANR 2, 30; CDALB 1968-1988; DLB 2,
8; INT CANR-30; MTCW; SATA 11, 64

Bradford, Gamaliel 1863-1932 . . . . . TCLC 36
See also DLB 17

Bradley, David (Henry, Jr.)
1950- . . . . . CLC 23; BLC; DAM MULT
See also BW 1; CA 104; CANR 26; DLB 33

Bradley, John Ed(mund, Jr.)
1958- . . . . CLC 55
See also CA 139

Bradley, Marion Zimmer
1930- . . . . CLC 30; DAM POP
See also AAYA 9; CA 57-60; CAAS 10;
CANR 7, 31, 51; DLB 8; MTCW;
SATA 90

Bradstreet, Anne
1612(?)-1672 . . . . . . LC 4, 30; DA; DAC;
DAM MST, POET; PC 10
See also CDALB 1640-1865; DLB 24

Brady, Joan 1939- . . . . CLC 86
See also CA 141

Broumas, Olga 1949- . . . . CLC 10, 73
See also CA 85-88; CANR 20

Brown, Alan 1951- . . . . CLC 99

Brown, Charles Brockden
1771-1810 . . . . NCLC 22
See also CDALB 1640-1865; DLB 37, 59, 73

Brown, Christy 1932-1981 . . . . CLC 63
See also CA 105; 104; DLB 14

Brown, Claude
1937- . . . . . CLC 30; BLC; DAM MULT
See also AAYA 7; BW 1; CA 73-76

Brown, Dee (Alexander)
1908- . . . . CLC 18, 47; DAM POP
See also CA 13-16R; CAAS 6; CANR 11, 45; DLBY 80; MTCW; SATA 5

Brown, George
See Wertmueller, Lina

Brown, George Douglas
1869-1902 . . . . TCLC 28

Brown, George Mackay
1921-1996 . . . . CLC 5, 48, 100
See also CA 21-24R; 151; CAAS 6; CANR 12, 37; DLB 14, 27, 139; MTCW; SATA 35

Brown, (William) Larry 1951- . . . . . . CLC 73
See also CA 130; 134; INT 133

Brown, Moses
See Barrett, William (Christopher)

Brown, Rita Mae
1944- . . . . . CLC 18, 43, 79; DAM NOV, POP
See also CA 45-48; CANR 2, 11, 35; INT CANR-11; MTCW

Brown, Roderick (Langmere) Haig-
See Haig-Brown, Roderick (Langmere)

Brown, Rosellen 1939- . . . . CLC 32
See also CA 77-80; CAAS 10; CANR 14, 44

Brown, Sterling Allen
1901-1989 . . . . CLC 1, 23, 59; BLC; DAM MULT, POET
See also BW 1; CA 85-88; 127; CANR 26; DLB 48, 51, 63; MTCW

Brown, Will
See Ainsworth, William Harrison

Brown, William Wells
1813-1884 . . . . NCLC 2; BLC; DAM MULT; DC 1
See also DLB 3, 50

Browne, (Clyde) Jackson 1948(?)- . . . CLC 21
See also CA 120

Browning, Elizabeth Barrett
1806-1861 . . . . NCLC 1, 16, 61; DA; DAB; DAC; DAM MST, POET; PC 6; WLC
See also CDBLB 1832-1890; DLB 32

Browning, Robert
1812-1889 . . . . NCLC 19; DA; DAB; DAC; DAM MST, POET; PC 2
See also CDBLB 1832-1890; DLB 32, 163; YABC 1

Browning, Tod 1882-1962 . . . . CLC 16
See also CA 141; 117

Brownson, Orestes (Augustus)
1803-1876 . . . . NCLC 50

Bruccoli, Matthew J(oseph) 1931- . . CLC 34
See also CA 9-12R; CANR 7; DLB 103

Bruce, Lenny . . . . CLC 21
See also Schneider, Leonard Alfred

Bruin, John
See Brutus, Dennis

Brulard, Henri
See Stendhal

Brulls, Christian
See Simenon, Georges (Jacques Christian)

Brunner, John (Kilian Houston)
1934-1995 . . . . . . CLC 8, 10; DAM POP
See also CA 1-4R; 149; CAAS 8; CANR 2, 37; MTCW

Bruno, Giordano 1548-1600 . . . . LC 27

Brutus, Dennis
1924- . . . . . CLC 43; BLC; DAM MULT, POET
See also BW 2; CA 49-52; CAAS 14; CANR 2, 27, 42; DLB 117

Bryan, C(ourtlandt) D(ixon) B(arnes)
1936- . . . . CLC 29
See also CA 73-76; CANR 13; INT CANR-13

Bryan, Michael
See Moore, Brian

Bryant, William Cullen
1794-1878 . . . . . NCLC 6, 46; DA; DAB; DAC; DAM MST, POET
See also CDALB 1640-1865; DLB 3, 43, 59

Bryusov, Valery Yakovlevich
1873-1924 . . . . TCLC 10
See also CA 107; 155

Buchan, John
1875-1940 . . . . TCLC 41; DAB; DAM POP
See also CA 108; 145; DLB 34, 70, 156; YABC 2

Buchanan, George 1506-1582 . . . . LC 4

Buchheim, Lothar-Guenther 1918- . . . CLC 6
See also CA 85-88

Buchner, (Karl) Georg
1813-1837 . . . . NCLC 26

Buchwald, Art(hur) 1925- . . . . CLC 33
See also AITN 1; CA 5-8R; CANR 21; MTCW; SATA 10

Buck, Pearl S(ydenstricker)
1892-1973 . . . . CLC 7, 11, 18; DA; DAB; DAC; DAM MST, NOV
See also AITN 1; CA 1-4R; 41-44R; CANR 1, 34; DLB 9, 102; MTCW; SATA 1, 25

Buckler, Ernest
1908-1984 . . CLC 13; DAC; DAM MST
See also CA 11-12; 114; CAP 1; DLB 68; SATA 47

Buckley, Vincent (Thomas)
1925-1988 . . . . CLC 57
See also CA 101

Buckley, William F(rank), Jr.
1925- . . . . CLC 7, 18, 37; DAM POP
See also AITN 1; CA 1-4R; CANR 1, 24, 53; DLB 137; DLBY 80; INT CANR-24; MTCW

Buechner, (Carl) Frederick
1926- . . . . . . CLC 2, 4, 6, 9; DAM NOV
See also CA 13-16R; CANR 11, 39; DLBY 80; INT CANR-11; MTCW

Buell, John (Edward) 1927- . . . . CLC 10
See also CA 1-4R; DLB 53

Buero Vallejo, Antonio 1916- . . . CLC 15, 46
See also CA 106; CANR 24, 49; HW; MTCW

Bufalino, Gesualdo 1920(?)- . . . . CLC 74

Bugayev, Boris Nikolayevich 1880-1934
See Bely, Andrey
See also CA 104

Bukowski, Charles
1920-1994 . . . . CLC 2, 5, 9, 41, 82; DAM NOV, POET
See also CA 17-20R; 144; CANR 40; DLB 5, 130, 169; MTCW

Bulgakov, Mikhail (Afanas'evich)
1891-1940 . . . . TCLC 2, 16; DAM DRAM, NOV; SSC 18
See also CA 105; 152

Bulgya, Alexander Alexandrovich
1901-1956 . . . . TCLC 53
See also Fadeyev, Alexander
See also CA 117

Bullins, Ed
1935- . . . . CLC 1, 5, 7; BLC; DAM DRAM, MULT; DC 6
See also BW 2; CA 49-52; CAAS 16; CANR 24, 46; DLB 7, 38; MTCW

Bulwer-Lytton, Edward (George Earle Lytton)
1803-1873 . . . . NCLC 1, 45
See also DLB 21

Bunin, Ivan Alexeyevich
1870-1953 . . . . TCLC 6; SSC 5
See also CA 104

Bunting, Basil
1900-1985 . . . . CLC 10, 39, 47; DAM POET
See also CA 53-56; 115; CANR 7; DLB 20

Bunuel, Luis
1900-1983 . . . . CLC 16, 80; DAM MULT; HLC
See also CA 101; 110; CANR 32; HW

Bunyan, John
1628-1688 . . . . . . LC 4; DA; DAB; DAC; DAM MST; WLC
See also CDBLB 1660-1789; DLB 39

Burckhardt, Jacob (Christoph)
1818-1897 . . . . NCLC 49

Burford, Eleanor
See Hibbert, Eleanor Alice Burford

Burgess, Anthony
. CLC 1, 2, 4, 5, 8, 10, 13, 15, 22, 40, 62, 81, 94; DAB
See also Wilson, John (Anthony) Burgess
See also AITN 1; CDBLB 1960 to Present; DLB 14

Burke, Edmund
1729(?)-1797 . . . . . . LC 7, 36; DA; DAB; DAC; DAM MST; WLC
See also DLB 104

Campos, Alvaro de
See Pessoa, Fernando (Antonio Nogueira)

Camus, Albert
1913-1960 .... CLC 1, 2, 4, 9, 11, 14, 32,
63, 69; DA; DAB; DAC; DAM DRAM,
MST, NOV; DC 2; SSC 9; WLC
See also CA 89-92; DLB 72; MTCW

Canby, Vincent 1924- .... CLC 13
See also CA 81-84

Cancale
See Desnos, Robert

Canetti, Elias
1905-1994 .... CLC 3, 14, 25, 75, 86
See also CA 21-24R; 146; CANR 23;
DLB 85, 124; MTCW

Canin, Ethan 1960- .... CLC 55
See also CA 131; 135

Cannon, Curt
See Hunter, Evan

Cape, Judith
See Page, P(atricia) K(athleen)

Capek, Karel
1890-1938 ...... TCLC 6, 37; DA; DAB;
DAC; DAM DRAM, MST, NOV; DC 1;
WLC
See also CA 104; 140

Capote, Truman
1924-1984 ...... CLC 1, 3, 8, 13, 19, 34,
38, 58; DA; DAB; DAC; DAM MST,
NOV, POP; SSC 2; WLC
See also CA 5-8R; 113; CANR 18;
CDALB 1941-1968; DLB 2; DLBY 80,
84; MTCW; SATA 91

Capra, Frank 1897-1991 .... CLC 16
See also CA 61-64; 135

Caputo, Philip 1941- .... CLC 32
See also CA 73-76; CANR 40

Card, Orson Scott
1951- ...... CLC 44, 47, 50; DAM POP
See also AAYA 11; CA 102; CANR 27, 47;
INT CANR-27; MTCW; SATA 83

Cardenal, Ernesto
1925- .... CLC 31; DAM MULT,
POET; HLC
See also CA 49-52; CANR 2, 32; HW;
MTCW

Cardozo, Benjamin N(athan)
1870-1938 .... TCLC 65
See also CA 117

Carducci, Giosue 1835-1907 ...... TCLC 32

Carew, Thomas 1595(?)-1640 .... LC 13
See also DLB 126

Carey, Ernestine Gilbreth 1908- .... CLC 17
See also CA 5-8R; SATA 2

Carey, Peter 1943- .... CLC 40, 55, 96
See also CA 123; 127; CANR 53; INT 127;
MTCW

Carleton, William 1794-1869 ...... NCLC 3
See also DLB 159

Carlisle, Henry (Coffin) 1926- ...... CLC 33
See also CA 13-16R; CANR 15

Carlsen, Chris
See Holdstock, Robert P.

Carlson, Ron(ald F.) 1947- .... CLC 54
See also CA 105; CANR 27

Carlyle, Thomas
1795-1881 ...... NCLC 22; DA; DAB;
DAC; DAM MST
See also CDBLB 1789-1832; DLB 55; 144

Carman, (William) Bliss
1861-1929 .... TCLC 7; DAC
See also CA 104; 152; DLB 92

Carnegie, Dale 1888-1955 .... TCLC 53

Carossa, Hans 1878-1956 .... TCLC 48
See also DLB 66

Carpenter, Don(ald Richard)
1931-1995 .... CLC 41
See also CA 45-48; 149; CANR 1

Carpentier (y Valmont), Alejo
1904-1980 .... CLC 8, 11, 38;
DAM MULT; HLC
See also CA 65-68; 97-100; CANR 11;
DLB 113; HW

Carr, Caleb 1955(?)- .... CLC 86
See also CA 147

Carr, Emily 1871-1945 .... TCLC 32
See also DLB 68

Carr, John Dickson 1906-1977 ...... CLC 3
See also CA 49-52; 69-72; CANR 3, 33;
MTCW

Carr, Philippa
See Hibbert, Eleanor Alice Burford

Carr, Virginia Spencer 1929- .... CLC 34
See also CA 61-64; DLB 111

Carrere, Emmanuel 1957- .... CLC 89

Carrier, Roch
1937- ... CLC 13, 78; DAC; DAM MST
See also CA 130; DLB 53

Carroll, James P. 1943(?)- .... CLC 38
See also CA 81-84

Carroll, Jim 1951- .... CLC 35
See also AAYA 17; CA 45-48; CANR 42

Carroll, Lewis .... NCLC 2, 53; WLC
See also Dodgson, Charles Lutwidge
See also CDBLB 1832-1890; CLR 2, 18;
DLB 18, 163; JRDA

Carroll, Paul Vincent 1900-1968 .... CLC 10
See also CA 9-12R; 25-28R; DLB 10

Carruth, Hayden
1921- ...... CLC 4, 7, 10, 18, 84; PC 10
See also CA 9-12R; CANR 4, 38; DLB 5,
165; INT CANR-4; MTCW; SATA 47

Carson, Rachel Louise
1907-1964 .... CLC 71; DAM POP
See also CA 77-80; CANR 35; MTCW;
SATA 23

Carter, Angela (Olive)
1940-1992 ...... CLC 5, 41, 76; SSC 13
See also CA 53-56; 136; CANR 12, 36;
DLB 14; MTCW; SATA 66;
SATA-Obit 70

Carter, Nick
See Smith, Martin Cruz

Carver, Raymond
1938-1988 .... CLC 22, 36, 53, 55;
DAM NOV; SSC 8
See also CA 33-36R; 126; CANR 17, 34;
DLB 130; DLBY 84, 88; MTCW

Cary, Elizabeth, Lady Falkland
1585-1639 .... LC 30

Cary, (Arthur) Joyce (Lunel)
1888-1957 .... TCLC 1, 29
See also CA 104; CDBLB 1914-1945;
DLB 15, 100

Casanova de Seingalt, Giovanni Jacopo
1725-1798 .... LC 13

Casares, Adolfo Bioy
See Bioy Casares, Adolfo

Casely-Hayford, J(oseph) E(phraim)
1866-1930 .... TCLC 24; BLC;
DAM MULT
See also BW 2; CA 123; 152

Casey, John (Dudley) 1939- .... CLC 59
See also BEST 90:2; CA 69-72; CANR 23

Casey, Michael 1947- .... CLC 2
See also CA 65-68; DLB 5

Casey, Patrick
See Thurman, Wallace (Henry)

Casey, Warren (Peter) 1935-1988 ... CLC 12
See also CA 101; 127; INT 101

Casona, Alejandro .... CLC 49
See also Alvarez, Alejandro Rodriguez

Cassavetes, John 1929-1989 .... CLC 20
See also CA 85-88; 127

Cassian, Nina 1924- .... PC 17

Cassill, R(onald) V(erlin) 1919- ... CLC 4, 23
See also CA 9-12R; CAAS 1; CANR 7, 45;
DLB 6

Cassirer, Ernst 1874-1945 .... TCLC 61

Cassity, (Allen) Turner 1929- ... CLC 6, 42
See also CA 17-20R; CAAS 8; CANR 11;
DLB 105

Castaneda, Carlos 1931(?)- .... CLC 12
See also CA 25-28R; CANR 32; HW;
MTCW

Castedo, Elena 1937- .... CLC 65
See also CA 132

Castedo-Ellerman, Elena
See Castedo, Elena

Castellanos, Rosario
1925-1974 ...... CLC 66; DAM MULT;
HLC
See also CA 131; 53-56; DLB 113; HW

Castelvetro, Lodovico 1505-1571 ..... LC 12

Castiglione, Baldassare 1478-1529 ... LC 12

Castle, Robert
See Hamilton, Edmond

Castro, Guillen de 1569-1631 .... LC 19

Castro, Rosalia de
1837-1885 ...... NCLC 3; DAM MULT

Cather, Willa
See Cather, Willa Sibert

Cather, Willa Sibert
1873-1947 .... TCLC 1, 11, 31; DA;
DAB; DAC; DAM MST, NOV; SSC 2;
WLC
See also CA 104; 128; CDALB 1865-1917;
DLB 9, 54, 78; DLBD 1; MTCW;
SATA 30

Cato, Marcus Porcius
234B.C.-149B.C. .... CMLC 21

Chesnutt, Charles W(addell)
     1858-1932 . . . . **TCLC 5, 39; BLC;**
                              DAM MULT; SSC 7
See also BW 1; CA 106; 125; DLB 12, 50,
   78; MTCW

Chester, Alfred 1929(?)-1971 . . . . . . **CLC 49**
See also CA 33-36R; DLB 130

Chesterton, G(ilbert) K(eith)
     1874-1936 . . . . **TCLC 1, 6, 64;**
                           DAM NOV, POET; SSC 1
See also CA 104; 132; CDBLB 1914-1945;
   DLB 10, 19, 34, 70, 98, 149; MTCW;
   SATA 27

Chiang Pin-chin 1904-1986
See Ding Ling
See also CA 118

Ch'ien Chung-shu 1910- . . . . **CLC 22**
See also CA 130; MTCW

Child, L. Maria
See Child, Lydia Maria

Child, Lydia Maria 1802-1880 . . . . **NCLC 6**
See also DLB 1, 74; SATA 67

Child, Mrs.
See Child, Lydia Maria

Child, Philip 1898-1978 . . . . **CLC 19, 68**
See also CA 13-14; CAP 1; SATA 47

Childers, (Robert) Erskine
     1870-1922 . . . . **TCLC 65**
See also CA 113; 153; DLB 70

Childress, Alice
     1920-1994 . . . . **CLC 12, 15, 86, 96; BLC;**
                 DAM DRAM, MULT, NOV; DC 4
See also AAYA 8; BW 2; CA 45-48; 146;
   CANR 3, 27, 50; CLR 14; DLB 7, 38;
   JRDA; MAICYA; MTCW; SATA 7, 48,
   81

Chin, Frank (Chew, Jr.) 1940- . . . . **DC 7**
See also CA 33-36R; DAM MULT

Chislett, (Margaret) Anne 1943- . . . . **CLC 34**
See also CA 151

Chitty, Thomas Willes 1926- . . . . **CLC 11**
See also Hinde, Thomas
See also CA 5-8R

Chivers, Thomas Holley
     1809-1858 . . . . **NCLC 49**
See also DLB 3

Chomette, Rene Lucien 1898-1981
See Clair, Rene
See also CA 103

Chopin, Kate
     . . . . **TCLC 5, 14; DA; DAB; SSC 8**
See also Chopin, Katherine
See also CDALB 1865-1917; DLB 12, 78

Chopin, Katherine 1851-1904
See Chopin, Kate
See also CA 104; 122; DAC; DAM MST,
   NOV

Chretien de Troyes
     c. 12th cent. - . . . . **CMLC 10**

Christie
See Ichikawa, Kon

Christie, Agatha (Mary Clarissa)
     1890-1976 . . . . . **CLC 1, 6, 8, 12, 39, 48;**
                           DAB; DAC; DAM NOV
See also AAYA 9; AITN 1, 2; CA 17-20R;
   61-64; CANR 10, 37; CDBLB 1914-1945;
   DLB 13, 77; MTCW; SATA 36

Christie, (Ann) Philippa
See Pearce, Philippa
See also CA 5-8R; CANR 4

Christine de Pizan 1365(?)-1431(?) . . . . **LC 9**

Chubb, Elmer
See Masters, Edgar Lee

Chulkov, Mikhail Dmitrievich
     1743-1792 . . . . **LC 2**
See also DLB 150

Churchill, Caryl 1938- . . . **CLC 31, 55; DC 5**
See also CA 102; CANR 22, 46; DLB 13;
   MTCW

Churchill, Charles 1731-1764 . . . . **LC 3**
See also DLB 109

Chute, Carolyn 1947- . . . . **CLC 39**
See also CA 123

Ciardi, John (Anthony)
     1916-1986 . . . . **CLC 10, 40, 44;**
                                      DAM POET
See also CA 5-8R; 118; CAAS 2; CANR 5,
   33; CLR 19; DLB 5; DLBY 86;
   INT CANR-5; MAICYA; MTCW;
   SATA 1, 65; SATA-Obit 46

Cicero, Marcus Tullius
     106B.C.-43B.C. . . . . **CMLC 3**

Cimino, Michael 1943- . . . . **CLC 16**
See also CA 105

Cioran, E(mil) M. 1911-1995 . . . . **CLC 64**
See also CA 25-28R; 149

Cisneros, Sandra
     1954- . . . . . **CLC 69; DAM MULT; HLC**
See also AAYA 9; CA 131; DLB 122, 152;
   HW

Cixous, Helene 1937- . . . . **CLC 92**
See also CA 126; CANR 55; DLB 83;
   MTCW

Clair, Rene . . . . **CLC 20**
See also Chomette, Rene Lucien

Clampitt, Amy 1920-1994 . . . . **CLC 32**
See also CA 110; 146; CANR 29; DLB 105

Clancy, Thomas L., Jr. 1947-
See Clancy, Tom
See also CA 125; 131; INT 131; MTCW

Clancy, Tom . . . . . **CLC 45; DAM NOV, POP**
See also Clancy, Thomas L., Jr.
See also AAYA 9; BEST 89:1, 90:1

Clare, John
     1793-1864 . . . . **NCLC 9; DAB;**
                                      DAM POET
See also DLB 55, 96

Clarin
See Alas (y Urena), Leopoldo (Enrique
   Garcia)

Clark, Al C.
See Goines, Donald

Clark, (Robert) Brian 1932- . . . . **CLC 29**
See also CA 41-44R

Clark, Curt
See Westlake, Donald E(dwin)

Clark, Eleanor 1913-1996 . . . . **CLC 5, 19**
See also CA 9-12R; 151; CANR 41; DLB 6

Clark, J. P.
See Clark, John Pepper
See also DLB 117

Clark, John Pepper
     1935- . . . . **CLC 38; BLC; DAM DRAM,**
                                 MULT; DC 5
See also Clark, J. P.
See also BW 1; CA 65-68; CANR 16

Clark, M. R.
See Clark, Mavis Thorpe

Clark, Mavis Thorpe 1909- . . . . **CLC 12**
See also CA 57-60; CANR 8, 37; CLR 30;
   MAICYA; SAAS 5; SATA 8, 74

Clark, Walter Van Tilburg
     1909-1971 . . . . **CLC 28**
See also CA 9-12R; 33-36R; DLB 9;
   SATA 8

Clarke, Arthur C(harles)
     1917- . . . . **CLC 1, 4, 13, 18, 35;**
                                 DAM POP; SSC 3
See also AAYA 4; CA 1-4R; CANR 2, 28,
   55; JRDA; MAICYA; MTCW; SATA 13,
   70

Clarke, Austin
     1896-1974 . . . . . . **CLC 6, 9; DAM POET**
See also CA 29-32; 49-52; CAP 2; DLB 10,
   20

Clarke, Austin C(hesterfield)
     1934- . . . . **CLC 8, 53; BLC; DAC;**
                                      DAM MULT
See also BW 1; CA 25-28R; CAAS 16;
   CANR 14, 32; DLB 53, 125

Clarke, Gillian 1937- . . . . **CLC 61**
See also CA 106; DLB 40

Clarke, Marcus (Andrew Hislop)
     1846-1881 . . . . **NCLC 19**

Clarke, Shirley 1925- . . . . **CLC 16**

Clash, The
See Headon, (Nicky) Topper; Jones, Mick;
   Simonon, Paul; Strummer, Joe

Claudel, Paul (Louis Charles Marie)
     1868-1955 . . . . **TCLC 2, 10**
See also CA 104

Clavell, James (duMaresq)
     1925-1994 . . . . **CLC 6, 25, 87;**
                                 DAM NOV, POP
See also CA 25-28R; 146; CANR 26, 48;
   MTCW

Cleaver, (Leroy) Eldridge
     1935- . . . . . **CLC 30; BLC; DAM MULT**
See also BW 1; CA 21-24R; CANR 16

Cleese, John (Marwood) 1939- . . . . . **CLC 21**
See also Monty Python
See also CA 112; 116; CANR 35; MTCW

Cleishbotham, Jebediah
See Scott, Walter

Cleland, John 1710-1789 . . . . **LC 2**
See also DLB 39

Clemens, Samuel Langhorne 1835-1910
See Twain, Mark
See also CA 104; 135; CDALB 1865-1917;
   DA; DAB; DAC; DAM MST, NOV;
   DLB 11, 12, 23, 64, 74; JRDA;
   MAICYA; YABC 2

Cleophil
See Congreve, William

Clerihew, E.
See Bentley, E(dmund) C(lerihew)

Clerk, N. W.
See Lewis, C(live) S(taples)

Cliff, Jimmy . . . . **CLC 21**
See also Chambers, James

Clifton, (Thelma) Lucille
1936- . . . . **CLC 19, 66; BLC;**
DAM MULT, POET; PC 17
See also BW 2; CA 49-52; CANR 2, 24, 42;
CLR 5; DLB 5, 41; MAICYA; MTCW;
SATA 20, 69

Clinton, Dirk
See Silverberg, Robert

Clough, Arthur Hugh 1819-1861 . . **NCLC 27**
See also DLB 32

Clutha, Janet Paterson Frame 1924-
See Frame, Janet
See also CA 1-4R; CANR 2, 36; MTCW

Clyne, Terence
See Blatty, William Peter

Cobalt, Martin
See Mayne, William (James Carter)

Cobbett, William 1763-1835 . . . . . **NCLC 49**
See also DLB 43, 107, 158

Coburn, D(onald) L(ee) 1938- . . . . . . **CLC 10**
See also CA 89-92

Cocteau, Jean (Maurice Eugene Clement)
1889-1963 . . . . **CLC 1, 8, 15, 16, 43; DA;**
DAB; DAC; DAM DRAM, MST, NOV;
WLC
See also CA 25-28; CANR 40; CAP 2;
DLB 65; MTCW

Codrescu, Andrei
1946- . . . . **CLC 46; DAM POET**
See also CA 33-36R; CAAS 19; CANR 13,
34, 53

Coe, Max
See Bourne, Randolph S(illiman)

Coe, Tucker
See Westlake, Donald E(dwin)

Coetzee, J(ohn) M(ichael)
1940- . . . . . . **CLC 23, 33, 66; DAM NOV**
See also CA 77-80; CANR 41, 54; MTCW

Coffey, Brian
See Koontz, Dean R(ay)

Cohan, George M. 1878-1942 . . . . . **TCLC 60**

Cohen, Arthur A(llen)
1928-1986 . . . . **CLC 7, 31**
See also CA 1-4R; 120; CANR 1, 17, 42;
DLB 28

Cohen, Leonard (Norman)
1934- . . . . **CLC 3, 38; DAC; DAM MST**
See also CA 21-24R; CANR 14; DLB 53;
MTCW

Cohen, Matt 1942- . . . . **CLC 19; DAC**
See also CA 61-64; CAAS 18; CANR 40;
DLB 53

Cohen-Solal, Annie 19(?)- . . . . **CLC 50**

Colegate, Isabel 1931- . . . . **CLC 36**
See also CA 17-20R; CANR 8, 22; DLB 14;
INT CANR-22; MTCW

Coleman, Emmett
See Reed, Ishmael

Coleridge, Samuel Taylor
1772-1834 . . . . . **NCLC 9, 54; DA; DAB;**
DAC; DAM MST, POET; PC 11; WLC
See also CDBLB 1789-1832; DLB 93, 107

Coleridge, Sara 1802-1852 . . . . **NCLC 31**

Coles, Don 1928- . . . . **CLC 46**
See also CA 115; CANR 38

Colette, (Sidonie-Gabrielle)
1873-1954 . . . . **TCLC 1, 5, 16;**
DAM NOV; SSC 10
See also CA 104; 131; DLB 65; MTCW

Collett, (Jacobine) Camilla (Wergeland)
1813-1895 . . . . **NCLC 22**

Collier, Christopher 1930- . . . . **CLC 30**
See also AAYA 13; CA 33-36R; CANR 13,
33; JRDA; MAICYA; SATA 16, 70

Collier, James L(incoln)
1928- . . . . **CLC 30; DAM POP**
See also AAYA 13; CA 9-12R; CANR 4,
33; CLR 3; JRDA; MAICYA; SAAS 21;
SATA 8, 70

Collier, Jeremy 1650-1726 . . . . **LC 6**

Collier, John 1901-1980 . . . . **SSC 19**
See also CA 65-68; 97-100; CANR 10;
DLB 77

Collingwood, R(obin) G(eorge)
1889(?)-1943 . . . . **TCLC 67**
See also CA 117; 155

Collins, Hunt
See Hunter, Evan

Collins, Linda 1931- . . . . **CLC 44**
See also CA 125

Collins, (William) Wilkie
1824-1889 . . . . **NCLC 1, 18**
See also CDBLB 1832-1890; DLB 18, 70,
159

Collins, William
1721-1759 . . . . **LC 4; DAM POET**
See also DLB 109

Collodi, Carlo 1826-1890 . . . . **NCLC 54**
See also Lorenzini, Carlo
See also CLR 5

Colman, George
See Glassco, John

Colt, Winchester Remington
See Hubbard, L(afayette) Ron(ald)

Colter, Cyrus 1910- . . . . **CLC 58**
See also BW 1; CA 65-68; CANR 10;
DLB 33

Colton, James
See Hansen, Joseph

Colum, Padraic 1881-1972 . . . . **CLC 28**
See also CA 73-76; 33-36R; CANR 35;
CLR 36; MAICYA; MTCW; SATA 15

Colvin, James
See Moorcock, Michael (John)

Colwin, Laurie (E.)
1944-1992 . . . . **CLC 5, 13, 23, 84**
See also CA 89-92; 139; CANR 20, 46;
DLBY 80; MTCW

Comfort, Alex(ander)
1920- . . . . **CLC 7; DAM POP**
See also CA 1-4R; CANR 1, 45

Comfort, Montgomery
See Campbell, (John) Ramsey

Compton-Burnett, I(vy)
1884(?)-1969 . . . . . . **CLC 1, 3, 10, 15, 34;**
DAM NOV
See also CA 1-4R; 25-28R; CANR 4;
DLB 36; MTCW

Comstock, Anthony 1844-1915 . . . . **TCLC 13**
See also CA 110

Comte, Auguste 1798-1857 . . . . **NCLC 54**

Conan Doyle, Arthur
See Doyle, Arthur Conan

Conde, Maryse
1937- . . . . **CLC 52, 92; DAM MULT**
See also Boucolon, Maryse
See also BW 2

Condillac, Etienne Bonnot de
1714-1780 . . . . **LC 26**

Condon, Richard (Thomas)
1915-1996 . . . . . **CLC 4, 6, 8, 10, 45, 100;**
DAM NOV
See also BEST 90:3; CA 1-4R; 151;
CAAS 1; CANR 2, 23; INT CANR-23;
MTCW

Confucius
551B.C.-479B.C. . . . . **CMLC 19; DA;**
DAB; DAC; DAM MST

Congreve, William
1670-1729 . . . . **LC 5, 21; DA; DAB;**
DAC; DAM DRAM, MST, POET;
DC 2; WLC
See also CDBLB 1660-1789; DLB 39, 84

Connell, Evan S(helby), Jr.
1924- . . . . **CLC 4, 6, 45; DAM NOV**
See also AAYA 7; CA 1-4R; CAAS 2;
CANR 2, 39; DLB 2; DLBY 81; MTCW

Connelly, Marc(us Cook)
1890-1980 . . . . **CLC 7**
See also CA 85-88; 102; CANR 30; DLB 7;
DLBY 80; SATA-Obit 25

Connor, Ralph . . . . **TCLC 31**
See also Gordon, Charles William
See also DLB 92

Conrad, Joseph
1857-1924 . . . . **TCLC 1, 6, 13, 25, 43, 57;**
DA; DAB; DAC; DAM MST, NOV;
SSC 9; WLC
See also CA 104; 131; CDBLB 1890-1914;
DLB 10, 34, 98, 156; MTCW; SATA 27

Conrad, Robert Arnold
See Hart, Moss

Conroy, Donald Pat(rick)
1945- . . . **CLC 30, 74; DAM NOV, POP**
See also AAYA 8; AITN 1; CA 85-88;
CANR 24, 53; DLB 6; MTCW

Constant (de Rebecque), (Henri) Benjamin
1767-1830 . . . . **NCLC 6**
See also DLB 119

Conybeare, Charles Augustus
See Eliot, T(homas) S(tearns)

Cook, Michael 1933- . . . . **CLC 58**
See also CA 93-96; DLB 53

Cook, Robin 1940- . . . . . **CLC 14; DAM POP**
See also BEST 90:2; CA 108; 111;
CANR 41; INT 111

Daudet, (Louis Marie) Alphonse
    1840-1897 . . . . **NCLC 1**
    See also DLB 123

Daumal, Rene 1908-1944 . . . . **TCLC 14**
    See also CA 114

Davenport, Guy (Mattison, Jr.)
    1927- . . . . **CLC 6, 14, 38; SSC 16**
    See also CA 33-36R; CANR 23; DLB 130

Davidson, Avram 1923-
    See Queen, Ellery
    See also CA 101; CANR 26; DLB 8

Davidson, Donald (Grady)
    1893-1968 . . . . **CLC 2, 13, 19**
    See also CA 5-8R; 25-28R; CANR 4;
    DLB 45

Davidson, Hugh
    See Hamilton, Edmond

Davidson, John 1857-1909 . . . . **TCLC 24**
    See also CA 118; DLB 19

Davidson, Sara 1943- . . . . **CLC 9**
    See also CA 81-84; CANR 44

Davie, Donald (Alfred)
    1922-1995 . . . . **CLC 5, 8, 10, 31**
    See also CA 1-4R; 149; CAAS 3; CANR 1,
    44; DLB 27; MTCW

Davies, Ray(mond Douglas) 1944- . . **CLC 21**
    See also CA 116; 146

Davies, Rhys 1903-1978 . . . . **CLC 23**
    See also CA 9-12R; 81-84; CANR 4;
    DLB 139

Davies, (William) Robertson
    1913-1995 . . . . . **CLC 2, 7, 13, 25, 42, 75,
        91; DA; DAB; DAC; DAM MST, NOV,
                POP; WLC**
    See also BEST 89:2; CA 33-36R; 150;
    CANR 17, 42; DLB 68; INT CANR-17;
    MTCW

Davies, W(illiam) H(enry)
    1871-1940 . . . . **TCLC 5**
    See also CA 104; DLB 19, 174

Davies, Walter C.
    See Kornbluth, C(yril) M.

Davis, Angela (Yvonne)
    1944- . . . . **CLC 77; DAM MULT**
    See also BW 2; CA 57-60; CANR 10

Davis, B. Lynch
    See Bioy Casares, Adolfo; Borges, Jorge
    Luis

Davis, Gordon
    See Hunt, E(verette) Howard, (Jr.)

Davis, Harold Lenoir 1896-1960 . . . . **CLC 49**
    See also CA 89-92; DLB 9

Davis, Rebecca (Blaine) Harding
    1831-1910 . . . . **TCLC 6**
    See also CA 104; DLB 74

Davis, Richard Harding
    1864-1916 . . . . **TCLC 24**
    See also CA 114; DLB 12, 23, 78, 79;
    DLBD 13

Davison, Frank Dalby 1893-1970 . . . **CLC 15**
    See also CA 116

Davison, Lawrence H.
    See Lawrence, D(avid) H(erbert Richards)

Davison, Peter (Hubert) 1928- . . . . . **CLC 28**
    See also CA 9-12R; CAAS 4; CANR 3, 43;
    DLB 5

Davys, Mary 1674-1732 . . . . **LC 1**
    See also DLB 39

Dawson, Fielding 1930- . . . . **CLC 6**
    See also CA 85-88; DLB 130

Dawson, Peter
    See Faust, Frederick (Schiller)

Day, Clarence (Shepard, Jr.)
    1874-1935 . . . . **TCLC 25**
    See also CA 108; DLB 11

Day, Thomas 1748-1789 . . . . **LC 1**
    See also DLB 39; YABC 1

Day Lewis, C(ecil)
    1904-1972 . . . . **CLC 1, 6, 10;
                DAM POET; PC 11**
    See also Blake, Nicholas
    See also CA 13-16; 33-36R; CANR 34;
    CAP 1; DLB 15, 20; MTCW

Dazai, Osamu . . . . **TCLC 11**
    See also Tsushima, Shuji

de Andrade, Carlos Drummond
    See Drummond de Andrade, Carlos

Deane, Norman
    See Creasey, John

de Beauvoir, Simone (Lucie Ernestine Marie
    Bertrand)
    See Beauvoir, Simone (Lucie Ernestine
    Marie Bertrand) de

de Brissac, Malcolm
    See Dickinson, Peter (Malcolm)

de Chardin, Pierre Teilhard
    See Teilhard de Chardin, (Marie Joseph)
    Pierre

Dee, John 1527-1608 . . . . **LC 20**

Deer, Sandra 1940- . . . . **CLC 45**

De Ferrari, Gabriella 1941- . . . . **CLC 65**
    See also CA 146

Defoe, Daniel
    1660(?)-1731 . . . . **LC 1; DA; DAB; DAC;
                DAM MST, NOV; WLC**
    See also CDBLB 1660-1789; DLB 39, 95,
    101; JRDA; MAICYA; SATA 22

de Gourmont, Remy(-Marie-Charles)
    See Gourmont, Remy (-Marie-Charles) de

de Hartog, Jan 1914- . . . . **CLC 19**
    See also CA 1-4R; CANR 1

de Hostos, E. M.
    See Hostos (y Bonilla), Eugenio Maria de

de Hostos, Eugenio M.
    See Hostos (y Bonilla), Eugenio Maria de

Deighton, Len . . . . **CLC 4, 7, 22, 46**
    See also Deighton, Leonard Cyril
    See also AAYA 6; BEST 89:2;
    CDBLB 1960 to Present; DLB 87

Deighton, Leonard Cyril 1929-
    See Deighton, Len
    See also CA 9-12R; CANR 19, 33;
    DAM NOV, POP; MTCW

Dekker, Thomas
    1572(?)-1632 . . . . . **LC 22; DAM DRAM**
    See also CDBLB Before 1660; DLB 62, 172

Delafield, E. M. 1890-1943 . . . . **TCLC 61**
    See also Dashwood, Edmee Elizabeth
    Monica de la Pasture
    See also DLB 34

de la Mare, Walter (John)
    1873-1956 . . . . **TCLC 4, 53; DAB; DAC;
            DAM MST, POET; SSC 14; WLC**
    See also CDBLB 1914-1945; CLR 23;
    DLB 162; SATA 16

Delaney, Franey
    See O'Hara, John (Henry)

Delaney, Shelagh
    1939- . . . . **CLC 29; DAM DRAM**
    See also CA 17-20R; CANR 30;
    CDBLB 1960 to Present; DLB 13;
    MTCW

Delany, Mary (Granville Pendarves)
    1700-1788 . . . . **LC 12**

Delany, Samuel R(ay, Jr.)
    1942- . . . . **CLC 8, 14, 38; BLC;
                DAM MULT**
    See also BW 2; CA 81-84; CANR 27, 43;
    DLB 8, 33; MTCW

De La Ramee, (Marie) Louise 1839-1908
    See Ouida
    See also SATA 20

de la Roche, Mazo 1879-1961 . . . . . . **CLC 14**
    See also CA 85-88; CANR 30; DLB 68;
    SATA 64

Delbanco, Nicholas (Franklin)
    1942- . . . . **CLC 6, 13**
    See also CA 17-20R; CAAS 2; CANR 29,
    55; DLB 6

del Castillo, Michel 1933- . . . . **CLC 38**
    See also CA 109

Deledda, Grazia (Cosima)
    1875(?)-1936 . . . . **TCLC 23**
    See also CA 123

Delibes, Miguel . . . . **CLC 8, 18**
    See also Delibes Setien, Miguel

Delibes Setien, Miguel 1920-
    See Delibes, Miguel
    See also CA 45-48; CANR 1, 32; HW;
    MTCW

DeLillo, Don
    1936- . . . . . **CLC 8, 10, 13, 27, 39, 54, 76;
                DAM NOV, POP**
    See also BEST 89:1; CA 81-84; CANR 21;
    DLB 6, 173; MTCW

de Lisser, H. G.
    See De Lisser, H(erbert) G(eorge)
    See also DLB 117

De Lisser, H(erbert) G(eorge)
    1878-1944 . . . . **TCLC 12**
    See also de Lisser, H. G.
    See also BW 2; CA 109; 152

Deloria, Vine (Victor), Jr.
    1933- . . . . **CLC 21; DAM MULT**
    See also CA 53-56; CANR 5, 20, 48;
    DLB 175; MTCW; NNAL; SATA 21

Del Vecchio, John M(ichael)
    1947- . . . . **CLC 29**
    See also CA 110; DLBD 9

de Man, Paul (Adolph Michel)
    1919-1983 . . . . **CLC 55**
    See also CA 128; 111; DLB 67; MTCW

De Marinis, Rick 1934-.......... CLC 54
  See also CA 57-60; CAAS 24; CANR 9, 25, 50

Dembry, R. Emmet
  See Murfree, Mary Noailles

Demby, William
  1922- ..... CLC 53; BLC; DAM MULT
  See also BW 1; CA 81-84; DLB 33

de Menton, Francisco
  See Chin, Frank (Chew, Jr.)

Demijohn, Thom
  See Disch, Thomas M(ichael)

de Montherlant, Henry (Milon)
  See Montherlant, Henry (Milon) de

Demosthenes 384B.C.-322B.C. ... CMLC 13
  See also DLB 176

de Natale, Francine
  See Malzberg, Barry N(athaniel)

Denby, Edwin (Orr) 1903-1983..... CLC 48
  See also CA 138; 110

Denis, Julio
  See Cortazar, Julio

Denmark, Harrison
  See Zelazny, Roger (Joseph)

Dennis, John 1658-1734........... LC 11
  See also DLB 101

Dennis, Nigel (Forbes) 1912-1989.... CLC 8
  See also CA 25-28R; 129; DLB 13, 15;
  MTCW

De Palma, Brian (Russell) 1940-.... CLC 20
  See also CA 109

De Quincey, Thomas 1785-1859 ... NCLC 4
  See also CDBLB 1789-1832; DLB 110; 144

Deren, Eleanora 1908(?)-1961
  See Deren, Maya
  See also CA 111

Deren, Maya .... CLC 16
  See also Deren, Eleanora

Derleth, August (William)
  1909-1971 .... CLC 31
  See also CA 1-4R; 29-32R; CANR 4;
  DLB 9; SATA 5

Der Nister 1884-1950............ TCLC 56

de Routisie, Albert
  See Aragon, Louis

Derrida, Jacques 1930-......... CLC 24, 87
  See also CA 124; 127

Derry Down Derry
  See Lear, Edward

Dersonnes, Jacques
  See Simenon, Georges (Jacques Christian)

Desai, Anita
  1937- .... CLC 19, 37, 97; DAB;
                                  DAM NOV
  See also CA 81-84; CANR 33, 53; MTCW;
  SATA 63

de Saint-Luc, Jean
  See Glassco, John

de Saint Roman, Arnaud
  See Aragon, Louis

Descartes, Rene 1596-1650 ...... LC 20, 35

De Sica, Vittorio 1901(?)-1974 ..... CLC 20
  See also CA 117

Desnos, Robert 1900-1945....... TCLC 22
  See also CA 121; 151

Destouches, Louis-Ferdinand
  1894-1961 .... CLC 9, 15
  See also Celine, Louis-Ferdinand
  See also CA 85-88; CANR 28; MTCW

de Tolignac, Gaston
  See Griffith, D(avid Lewelyn) W(ark)

Deutsch, Babette 1895-1982 .... CLC 18
  See also CA 1-4R; 108; CANR 4; DLB 45;
  SATA 1; SATA-Obit 33

Devenant, William 1606-1649 .... LC 13

Devkota, Laxmiprasad
  1909-1959 .... TCLC 23
  See also CA 123

De Voto, Bernard (Augustine)
  1897-1955 .... TCLC 29
  See also CA 113; DLB 9

De Vries, Peter
  1910-1993 .... CLC 1, 2, 3, 7, 10, 28, 46;
                                  DAM NOV
  See also CA 17-20R; 142; CANR 41;
  DLB 6; DLBY 82; MTCW

Dexter, John
  See Bradley, Marion Zimmer

Dexter, Martin
  See Faust, Frederick (Schiller)

Dexter, Pete
  1943- .... CLC 34, 55; DAM POP
  See also BEST 89:2; CA 127; 131; INT 131;
  MTCW

Diamano, Silmang
  See Senghor, Leopold Sedar

Diamond, Neil 1941- .... CLC 30
  See also CA 108

Diaz del Castillo, Bernal 1496-1584.. LC 31

di Bassetto, Corno
  See Shaw, George Bernard

Dick, Philip K(indred)
  1928-1982 .... CLC 10, 30, 72;
                                  DAM NOV, POP
  See also CA 49-52; 106; CANR 2, 16;
  DLB 8; MTCW

Dickens, Charles (John Huffam)
  1812-1870 ...... NCLC 3, 8, 18, 26, 37,
  50; DA; DAB; DAC; DAM MST, NOV;
                                  SSC 17; WLC
  See also CDBLB 1832-1890; DLB 21, 55,
  70, 159, 166; JRDA; MAICYA; SATA 15

Dickey, James (Lafayette)
  1923-1997 .... CLC 1, 2, 4, 7, 10, 15, 47;
                                  DAM NOV, POET, POP
  See also AITN 1, 2; CA 9-12R; 156;
  CABS 2; CANR 10, 48;
  CDALB 1968-1988; DLB 5; DLBD 7;
  DLBY 82, 93; INT CANR-10; MTCW

Dickey, William 1928-1994 ...... CLC 3, 28
  See also CA 9-12R; 145; CANR 24; DLB 5

Dickinson, Charles 1951-.......... CLC 49
  See also CA 128

Dickinson, Emily (Elizabeth)
  1830-1886 .... NCLC 21; DA; DAB;
  DAC; DAM MST, POET; PC 1; WLC
  See also CDALB 1865-1917; DLB 1;
  SATA 29

Dickinson, Peter (Malcolm)
  1927- .... CLC 12, 35
  See also AAYA 9; CA 41-44R; CANR 31;
  CLR 29; DLB 87, 161; JRDA; MAICYA;
  SATA 5, 62

Dickson, Carr
  See Carr, John Dickson

Dickson, Carter
  See Carr, John Dickson

Diderot, Denis 1713-1784 .... LC 26

Didion, Joan
  1934- .. CLC 1, 3, 8, 14, 32; DAM NOV
  See also AITN 1; CA 5-8R; CANR 14, 52;
  CDALB 1968-1988; DLB 2, 173;
  DLBY 81, 86; MTCW

Dietrich, Robert
  See Hunt, E(verette) Howard, (Jr.)

Dillard, Annie
  1945- .... CLC 9, 60; DAM NOV
  See also AAYA 6; CA 49-52; CANR 3, 43;
  DLBY 80; MTCW; SATA 10

Dillard, R(ichard) H(enry) W(ilde)
  1937- .... CLC 5
  See also CA 21-24R; CAAS 7; CANR 10;
  DLB 5

Dillon, Eilis 1920-1994........... CLC 17
  See also CA 9-12R; 147; CAAS 3; CANR 4,
  38; CLR 26; MAICYA; SATA 2, 74;
  SATA-Obit 83

Dimont, Penelope
  See Mortimer, Penelope (Ruth)

Dinesen, Isak........ CLC 10, 29, 95; SSC 7
  See also Blixen, Karen (Christentze
  Dinesen)

Ding Ling....................... CLC 68
  See also Chiang Pin-chin

Disch, Thomas M(ichael) 1940-... CLC 7, 36
  See also AAYA 17; CA 21-24R; CAAS 4;
  CANR 17, 36, 54; CLR 18; DLB 8;
  MAICYA; MTCW; SAAS 15; SATA 92

Disch, Tom
  See Disch, Thomas M(ichael)

d'Isly, Georges
  See Simenon, Georges (Jacques Christian)

Disraeli, Benjamin 1804-1881 .. NCLC 2, 39
  See also DLB 21, 55

Ditcum, Steve
  See Crumb, R(obert)

Dixon, Paige
  See Corcoran, Barbara

Dixon, Stephen 1936-..... CLC 52; SSC 16
  See also CA 89-92; CANR 17, 40, 54;
  DLB 130

Dobell, Sydney Thompson
  1824-1874 .... NCLC 43
  See also DLB 32

Doblin, Alfred .... TCLC 13
  See also Doeblin, Alfred

Dobrolyubov, Nikolai Alexandrovich
  1836-1861 .... NCLC 5

Dobyns, Stephen 1941-............ CLC 37
  See also CA 45-48; CANR 2, 18

Doctorow, E(dgar) L(aurence)
1931- . . . . . **CLC 6, 11, 15, 18, 37, 44, 65; DAM NOV, POP**
See also AITN 2; BEST 89:3; CA 45-48; CANR 2, 33, 51; CDALB 1968-1988; DLB 2, 28, 173; DLBY 80; MTCW

Dodgson, Charles Lutwidge 1832-1898
See Carroll, Lewis
See also CLR 2; DA; DAB; DAC; DAM MST, NOV, POET; MAICYA; YABC 2

Dodson, Owen (Vincent)
1914-1983 . . . . **CLC 79; BLC; DAM MULT**
See also BW 1; CA 65-68; 110; CANR 24; DLB 76

Doeblin, Alfred 1878-1957 . . . . **TCLC 13**
See also Doblin, Alfred
See also CA 110; 141; DLB 66

Doerr, Harriet 1910- . . . . **CLC 34**
See also CA 117; 122; CANR 47; INT 122

Domecq, H(onorio) Bustos
See Bioy Casares, Adolfo; Borges, Jorge Luis

Domini, Rey
See Lorde, Audre (Geraldine)

Dominique
See Proust, (Valentin-Louis-George-Eugene-) Marcel

Don, A
See Stephen, Leslie

Donaldson, Stephen R.
1947- . . . . **CLC 46; DAM POP**
See also CA 89-92; CANR 13, 55; INT CANR-13

Donleavy, J(ames) P(atrick)
1926- . . . . **CLC 1, 4, 6, 10, 45**
See also AITN 2; CA 9-12R; CANR 24, 49; DLB 6, 173; INT CANR-24; MTCW

Donne, John
1572-1631 . . . . **LC 10, 24; DA; DAB; DAC; DAM MST, POET; PC 1**
See also CDBLB Before 1660; DLB 121, 151

Donnell, David 1939(?)- . . . . **CLC 34**

Donoghue, P. S.
See Hunt, E(verette) Howard, (Jr.)

Donoso (Yanez), Jose
1924-1996 . . . . **CLC 4, 8, 11, 32, 99; DAM MULT; HLC**
See also CA 81-84; 155; CANR 32; DLB 113; HW; MTCW

Donovan, John 1928-1992 . . . . **CLC 35**
See also AAYA 20; CA 97-100; 137; CLR 3; MAICYA; SATA 72; SATA-Brief 29

Don Roberto
See Cunninghame Graham, R(obert) B(ontine)

Doolittle, Hilda
1886-1961 . . . . . **CLC 3, 8, 14, 31, 34, 73; DA; DAC; DAM MST, POET; PC 5; WLC**
See also H. D.
See also CA 97-100; CANR 35; DLB 4, 45; MTCW

Dorfman, Ariel
1942- . . . . **CLC 48, 77; DAM MULT; HLC**
See also CA 124; 130; HW; INT 130

Dorn, Edward (Merton) 1929- . . . **CLC 10, 18**
See also CA 93-96; CANR 42; DLB 5; INT 93-96

Dorsan, Luc
See Simenon, Georges (Jacques Christian)

Dorsange, Jean
See Simenon, Georges (Jacques Christian)

Dos Passos, John (Roderigo)
1896-1970 . . . . . . **CLC 1, 4, 8, 11, 15, 25, 34, 82; DA; DAB; DAC; DAM MST, NOV; WLC**
See also CA 1-4R; 29-32R; CANR 3; CDALB 1929-1941; DLB 4, 9; DLBD 1; MTCW

Dossage, Jean
See Simenon, Georges (Jacques Christian)

Dostoevsky, Fedor Mikhailovich
1821-1881 . . . . . . **NCLC 2, 7, 21, 33, 43; DA; DAB; DAC; DAM MST, NOV; SSC 2; WLC**

Doughty, Charles M(ontagu)
1843-1926 . . . . **TCLC 27**
See also CA 115; DLB 19, 57, 174

Douglas, Ellen . . . . **CLC 73**
See also Haxton, Josephine Ayres; Williamson, Ellen Douglas

Douglas, Gavin 1475(?)-1522 . . . . **LC 20**

Douglas, Keith 1920-1944 . . . . **TCLC 40**
See also DLB 27

Douglas, Leonard
See Bradbury, Ray (Douglas)

Douglas, Michael
See Crichton, (John) Michael

Douglas, Norman 1868-1952 . . . . . . **TCLC 68**

Douglass, Frederick
1817(?)-1895 . . . . **NCLC 7, 55; BLC; DA; DAC; DAM MST, MULT; WLC**
See also CDALB 1640-1865; DLB 1, 43, 50, 79; SATA 29

Dourado, (Waldomiro Freitas) Autran
1926- . . . . **CLC 23, 60**
See also CA 25-28R; CANR 34

Dourado, Waldomiro Autran
See Dourado, (Waldomiro Freitas) Autran

Dove, Rita (Frances)
1952- . . . . **CLC 50, 81; DAM MULT, POET; PC 6**
See also BW 2; CA 109; CAAS 19; CANR 27, 42; DLB 120

Dowell, Coleman 1925-1985 . . . . **CLC 60**
See also CA 25-28R; 117; CANR 10; DLB 130

Dowson, Ernest (Christopher)
1867-1900 . . . . **TCLC 4**
See also CA 105; 150; DLB 19, 135

Doyle, A. Conan
See Doyle, Arthur Conan

Doyle, Arthur Conan
1859-1930 . . . . **TCLC 7; DA; DAB; DAC; DAM MST, NOV; SSC 12; WLC**
See also AAYA 14; CA 104; 122; CDBLB 1890-1914; DLB 18, 70, 156; MTCW; SATA 24

Doyle, Conan
See Doyle, Arthur Conan

Doyle, John
See Graves, Robert (von Ranke)

Doyle, Roddy 1958(?)- . . . . **CLC 81**
See also AAYA 14; CA 143

Doyle, Sir A. Conan
See Doyle, Arthur Conan

Doyle, Sir Arthur Conan
See Doyle, Arthur Conan

Dr. A
See Asimov, Isaac; Silverstein, Alvin

Drabble, Margaret
1939- . . . . **CLC 2, 3, 5, 8, 10, 22, 53; DAB; DAC; DAM MST, NOV, POP**
See also CA 13-16R; CANR 18, 35; CDBLB 1960 to Present; DLB 14, 155; MTCW; SATA 48

Drapier, M. B.
See Swift, Jonathan

Drayham, James
See Mencken, H(enry) L(ouis)

Drayton, Michael 1563-1631 . . . . **LC 8**

Dreadstone, Carl
See Campbell, (John) Ramsey

Dreiser, Theodore (Herman Albert)
1871-1945 . . . . **TCLC 10, 18, 35; DA; DAC; DAM MST, NOV; WLC**
See also CA 106; 132; CDALB 1865-1917; DLB 9, 12, 102, 137; DLBD 1; MTCW

Drexler, Rosalyn 1926- . . . . **CLC 2, 6**
See also CA 81-84

Dreyer, Carl Theodor 1889-1968. . . . **CLC 16**
See also CA 116

Drieu la Rochelle, Pierre(-Eugene)
1893-1945 . . . . **TCLC 21**
See also CA 117; DLB 72

Drinkwater, John 1882-1937 . . . . . . **TCLC 57**
See also CA 109; 149; DLB 10, 19, 149

Drop Shot
See Cable, George Washington

Droste-Hulshoff, Annette Freiin von
1797-1848 . . . . **NCLC 3**
See also DLB 133

Drummond, Walter
See Silverberg, Robert

Drummond, William Henry
1854-1907 . . . . **TCLC 25**
See also DLB 92

Drummond de Andrade, Carlos
1902-1987 . . . . **CLC 18**
See also Andrade, Carlos Drummond de
See also CA 132; 123

Drury, Allen (Stuart) 1918- . . . . **CLC 37**
See also CA 57-60; CANR 18, 52; INT CANR-18

Dryden, John
 1631-1700 . . . . **LC 3, 21; DA; DAB;**
 DAC; DAM DRAM, MST, POET;
 DC 3; WLC
 See also CDBLB 1660-1789; DLB 80, 101,
 131

Duberman, Martin 1930- . . . . **CLC 8**
 See also CA 1-4R; CANR 2

Dubie, Norman (Evans) 1945- . . . . . . **CLC 36**
 See also CA 69-72; CANR 12; DLB 120

Du Bois, W(illiam) E(dward) B(urghardt)
 1868-1963 . . . . **CLC 1, 2, 13, 64, 96;**
 BLC; DA; DAC; DAM MST, MULT,
 NOV; WLC
 See also BW 1; CA 85-88; CANR 34;
 CDALB 1865-1917; DLB 47, 50, 91;
 MTCW; SATA 42

Dubus, Andre
 1936- . . . . **CLC 13, 36, 97; SSC 15**
 See also CA 21-24R; CANR 17; DLB 130;
 INT CANR-17

Duca Minimo
 See D'Annunzio, Gabriele

Ducharme, Rejean 1941- . . . . **CLC 74**
 See also DLB 60

Duclos, Charles Pinot 1704-1772 . . . . . **LC 1**

Dudek, Louis 1918- . . . . **CLC 11, 19**
 See also CA 45-48; CAAS 14; CANR 1;
 DLB 88

Duerrenmatt, Friedrich
 1921-1990 . . . . . . **CLC 1, 4, 8, 11, 15, 43;**
 DAM DRAM
 See also CA 17-20R; CANR 33; DLB 69,
 124; MTCW

Duffy, Bruce (?)- . . . . **CLC 50**

Duffy, Maureen 1933- . . . . **CLC 37**
 See also CA 25-28R; CANR 33; DLB 14;
 MTCW

Dugan, Alan 1923- . . . . **CLC 2, 6**
 See also CA 81-84; DLB 5

du Gard, Roger Martin
 See Martin du Gard, Roger

Duhamel, Georges 1884-1966 . . . . **CLC 8**
 See also CA 81-84; 25-28R; CANR 35;
 DLB 65; MTCW

Dujardin, Edouard (Emile Louis)
 1861-1949 . . . . **TCLC 13**
 See also CA 109; DLB 123

Dumas, Alexandre (Davy de la Pailleterie)
 1802-1870 . . . . **NCLC 11; DA; DAB;**
 DAC; DAM MST, NOV; WLC
 See also DLB 119; SATA 18

Dumas, Alexandre
 1824-1895 . . . . **NCLC 9; DC 1**

Dumas, Claudine
 See Malzberg, Barry N(athaniel)

Dumas, Henry L. 1934-1968 . . . . . **CLC 6, 62**
 See also BW 1; CA 85-88; DLB 41

du Maurier, Daphne
 1907-1989 . . . . **CLC 6, 11, 59; DAB;**
 DAC; DAM MST, POP; SSC 18
 See also CA 5-8R; 128; CANR 6, 55;
 MTCW; SATA 27; SATA-Obit 60

Dunbar, Paul Laurence
 1872-1906 . . . . . **TCLC 2, 12; BLC; DA;**
 DAC; DAM MST, MULT, POET; PC 5;
 SSC 8; WLC
 See also BW 1; CA 104; 124;
 CDALB 1865-1917; DLB 50, 54, 78;
 SATA 34

Dunbar, William 1460(?)-1530(?) . . . . **LC 20**
 See also DLB 132, 146

Duncan, Dora Angela
 See Duncan, Isadora

Duncan, Isadora 1877(?)-1927 . . . . . **TCLC 68**
 See also CA 118; 149

Duncan, Lois 1934- . . . . **CLC 26**
 See also AAYA 4; CA 1-4R; CANR 2, 23,
 36; CLR 29; JRDA; MAICYA; SAAS 2;
 SATA 1, 36, 75

Duncan, Robert (Edward)
 1919-1988 . . . . **CLC 1, 2, 4, 7, 15, 41, 55;**
 DAM POET; PC 2
 See also CA 9-12R; 124; CANR 28; DLB 5,
 16; MTCW

Duncan, Sara Jeannette
 1861-1922 . . . . **TCLC 60**
 See also DLB 92

Dunlap, William 1766-1839 . . . . **NCLC 2**
 See also DLB 30, 37, 59

Dunn, Douglas (Eaglesham)
 1942- . . . . **CLC 6, 40**
 See also CA 45-48; CANR 2, 33; DLB 40;
 MTCW

Dunn, Katherine (Karen) 1945- . . . . . **CLC 71**
 See also CA 33-36R

Dunn, Stephen 1939- . . . . **CLC 36**
 See also CA 33-36R; CANR 12, 48, 53;
 DLB 105

Dunne, Finley Peter 1867-1936 . . . . **TCLC 28**
 See also CA 108; DLB 11, 23

Dunne, John Gregory 1932- . . . . **CLC 28**
 See also CA 25-28R; CANR 14, 50;
 DLBY 80

Dunsany, Edward John Moreton Drax
 Plunkett 1878-1957
 See Dunsany, Lord
 See also CA 104; 148; DLB 10

Dunsany, Lord . . . . **TCLC 2, 59**
 See also Dunsany, Edward John Moreton
 Drax Plunkett
 See also DLB 77, 153, 156

du Perry, Jean
 See Simenon, Georges (Jacques Christian)

Durang, Christopher (Ferdinand)
 1949- . . . . **CLC 27, 38**
 See also CA 105; CANR 50

Duras, Marguerite
 1914-1996 . . . . . **CLC 3, 6, 11, 20, 34, 40,**
 68, 100
 See also CA 25-28R; 151; CANR 50;
 DLB 83; MTCW

Durban, (Rosa) Pam 1947- . . . . **CLC 39**
 See also CA 123

Durcan, Paul
 1944- . . . . **CLC 43, 70; DAM POET**
 See also CA 134

Durkheim, Emile 1858-1917 . . . . . . **TCLC 55**

Durrell, Lawrence (George)
 1912-1990 . . . . **CLC 1, 4, 6, 8, 13, 27, 41;**
 DAM NOV
 See also CA 9-12R; 132; CANR 40;
 CDBLB 1945-1960; DLB 15, 27;
 DLBY 90; MTCW

Durrenmatt, Friedrich
 See Duerrenmatt, Friedrich

Dutt, Toru 1856-1877 . . . . **NCLC 29**

Dwight, Timothy 1752-1817 . . . . . . **NCLC 13**
 See also DLB 37

Dworkin, Andrea 1946- . . . . **CLC 43**
 See also CA 77-80; CAAS 21; CANR 16,
 39; INT CANR-16; MTCW

Dwyer, Deanna
 See Koontz, Dean R(ay)

Dwyer, K. R.
 See Koontz, Dean R(ay)

Dylan, Bob 1941- . . . . . . **CLC 3, 4, 6, 12, 77**
 See also CA 41-44R; DLB 16

Eagleton, Terence (Francis) 1943-
 See Eagleton, Terry
 See also CA 57-60; CANR 7, 23; MTCW

Eagleton, Terry . . . . **CLC 63**
 See also Eagleton, Terence (Francis)

Early, Jack
 See Scoppettone, Sandra

East, Michael
 See West, Morris L(anglo)

Eastaway, Edward
 See Thomas, (Philip) Edward

Eastlake, William (Derry) 1917- . . . . . **CLC 8**
 See also CA 5-8R; CAAS 1; CANR 5;
 DLB 6; INT CANR-5

Eastman, Charles A(lexander)
 1858-1939 . . . . . **TCLC 55; DAM MULT**
 See also DLB 175; NNAL; YABC 1

Eberhart, Richard (Ghormley)
 1904- . . **CLC 3, 11, 19, 56; DAM POET**
 See also CA 1-4R; CANR 2;
 CDALB 1941-1968; DLB 48; MTCW

Eberstadt, Fernanda 1960- . . . . **CLC 39**
 See also CA 136

Echegaray (y Eizaguirre), Jose (Maria Waldo)
 1832-1916 . . . . **TCLC 4**
 See also CA 104; CANR 32; HW; MTCW

Echeverria, (Jose) Esteban (Antonino)
 1805-1851 . . . . **NCLC 18**

Echo
 See Proust, (Valentin-Louis-George-Eugene-)
 Marcel

Eckert, Allan W. 1931- . . . . **CLC 17**
 See also AAYA 18; CA 13-16R; CANR 14,
 45; INT CANR-14; SAAS 21; SATA 29,
 91; SATA-Brief 27

Eckhart, Meister 1260(?)-1328(?) . . **CMLC 9**
 See also DLB 115

Eckmar, F. R.
 See de Hartog, Jan

Eco, Umberto
 1932- . . . **CLC 28, 60; DAM NOV, POP**
 See also BEST 90:1; CA 77-80; CANR 12,
 33, 55; MTCW

Ende, Michael (Andreas Helmuth)
    1929-1995 . . . . CLC 31
    See also CA 118; 124; 149; CANR 36;
    CLR 14; DLB 75; MAICYA; SATA 61;
    SATA-Brief 42; SATA-Obit 86

Endo, Shusaku
    1923-1996 . . . . . . CLC 7, 14, 19, 54, 99;
                                        DAM NOV
    See also CA 29-32R; 153; CANR 21, 54;
    MTCW

Engel, Marian 1933-1985 . . . . CLC 36
    See also CA 25-28R; CANR 12; DLB 53;
    INT CANR-12

Engelhardt, Frederick
    See Hubbard, L(afayette) Ron(ald)

Enright, D(ennis) J(oseph)
    1920- . . . . CLC 4, 8, 31
    See also CA 1-4R; CANR 1, 42; DLB 27;
    SATA 25

Enzensberger, Hans Magnus
    1929- . . . . CLC 43
    See also CA 116; 119

Ephron, Nora 1941- . . . . CLC 17, 31
    See also AITN 2; CA 65-68; CANR 12, 39

Epicurus 341B.C.-270B.C. . . . . CMLC 21
    See also DLB 176

Epsilon
    See Betjeman, John

Epstein, Daniel Mark 1948- . . . . CLC 7
    See also CA 49-52; CANR 2, 53

Epstein, Jacob 1956- . . . . CLC 19
    See also CA 114

Epstein, Joseph 1937- . . . . CLC 39
    See also CA 112; 119; CANR 50

Epstein, Leslie 1938- . . . . CLC 27
    See also CA 73-76; CAAS 12; CANR 23

Equiano, Olaudah
    1745(?)-1797 . . . . LC 16; BLC;
                                        DAM MULT
    See also DLB 37, 50

Erasmus, Desiderius 1469(?)-1536. . . . LC 16

Erdman, Paul E(mil) 1932- . . . . CLC 25
    See also AITN 1; CA 61-64; CANR 13, 43

Erdrich, Louise
    1954- . . . . CLC 39, 54; DAM MULT,
                                        NOV, POP
    See also AAYA 10; BEST 89:1; CA 114;
    CANR 41; DLB 152, 175; MTCW;
    NNAL

Erenburg, Ilya (Grigoryevich)
    See Ehrenburg, Ilya (Grigoryevich)

Erickson, Stephen Michael 1950-
    See Erickson, Steve
    See also CA 129

Erickson, Steve . . . . CLC 64
    See also Erickson, Stephen Michael

Ericson, Walter
    See Fast, Howard (Melvin)

Eriksson, Buntel
    See Bergman, (Ernst) Ingmar

Ernaux, Annie 1940- . . . . CLC 88
    See also CA 147

Eschenbach, Wolfram von
    See Wolfram von Eschenbach

Eseki, Bruno
    See Mphahlele, Ezekiel

Esenin, Sergei (Alexandrovich)
    1895-1925 . . . . TCLC 4
    See also CA 104

Eshleman, Clayton 1935- . . . . CLC 7
    See also CA 33-36R; CAAS 6; DLB 5

Espriella, Don Manuel Alvarez
    See Southey, Robert

Espriu, Salvador 1913-1985 . . . . CLC 9
    See also CA 154; 115; DLB 134

Espronceda, Jose de 1808-1842. . . NCLC 39

Esse, James
    See Stephens, James

Esterbrook, Tom
    See Hubbard, L(afayette) Ron(ald)

Estleman, Loren D.
    1952- . . . . . . CLC 48; DAM NOV, POP
    See also CA 85-88; CANR 27;
    INT CANR-27; MTCW

Eugenides, Jeffrey 1960(?)- . . . . CLC 81
    See also CA 144

Euripides c. 485B.C.-406B.C. . . . . DC 4
    See also DA; DAB; DAC; DAM DRAM,
    MST; DLB 176

Evan, Evin
    See Faust, Frederick (Schiller)

Evans, Evan
    See Faust, Frederick (Schiller)

Evans, Marian
    See Eliot, George

Evans, Mary Ann
    See Eliot, George

Evarts, Esther
    See Benson, Sally

Everett, Percival L. 1956- . . . . CLC 57
    See also BW 2; CA 129

Everson, R(onald) G(ilmour)
    1903- . . . . CLC 27
    See also CA 17-20R; DLB 88

Everson, William (Oliver)
    1912-1994 . . . . CLC 1, 5, 14
    See also CA 9-12R; 145; CANR 20; DLB 5,
    16; MTCW

Evtushenko, Evgenii Aleksandrovich
    See Yevtushenko, Yevgeny (Alexandrovich)

Ewart, Gavin (Buchanan)
    1916-1995 . . . . CLC 13, 46
    See also CA 89-92; 150; CANR 17, 46;
    DLB 40; MTCW

Ewers, Hanns Heinz 1871-1943 . . . TCLC 12
    See also CA 109; 149

Ewing, Frederick R.
    See Sturgeon, Theodore (Hamilton)

Exley, Frederick (Earl)
    1929-1992 . . . . CLC 6, 11
    See also AITN 2; CA 81-84; 138; DLB 143;
    DLBY 81

Eynhardt, Guillermo
    See Quiroga, Horacio (Sylvestre)

Ezekiel, Nissim 1924- . . . . CLC 61
    See also CA 61-64

Ezekiel, Tish O'Dowd 1943- . . . . CLC 34
    See also CA 129

Fadeyev, A.
    See Bulgya, Alexander Alexandrovich

Fadeyev, Alexander. . . . . TCLC 53
    See also Bulgya, Alexander Alexandrovich

Fagen, Donald 1948-. . . . . CLC 26

Fainzilberg, Ilya Arnoldovich 1897-1937
    See Ilf, Ilya
    See also CA 120

Fair, Ronald L. 1932-. . . . . CLC 18
    See also BW 1; CA 69-72; CANR 25;
    DLB 33

Fairbairns, Zoe (Ann) 1948- . . . . CLC 32
    See also CA 103; CANR 21

Falco, Gian
    See Papini, Giovanni

Falconer, James
    See Kirkup, James

Falconer, Kenneth
    See Kornbluth, C(yril) M.

Falkland, Samuel
    See Heijermans, Herman

Fallaci, Oriana 1930- . . . . CLC 11
    See also CA 77-80; CANR 15; MTCW

Faludy, George 1913-. . . . . CLC 42
    See also CA 21-24R

Faludy, Gyoergy
    See Faludy, George

Fanon, Frantz
    1925-1961 . . . . CLC 74; BLC;
                                        DAM MULT
    See also BW 1; CA 116; 89-92

Fanshawe, Ann 1625-1680 . . . . LC 11

Fante, John (Thomas) 1911-1983 . . . CLC 60
    See also CA 69-72; 109; CANR 23;
    DLB 130; DLBY 83

Farah, Nuruddin
    1945- . . . . . CLC 53; BLC; DAM MULT
    See also BW 2; CA 106; DLB 125

Fargue, Leon-Paul 1876(?)-1947 . . . TCLC 11
    See also CA 109

Farigoule, Louis
    See Romains, Jules

Farina, Richard 1936(?)-1966 . . . . CLC 9
    See also CA 81-84; 25-28R

Farley, Walter (Lorimer)
    1915-1989 . . . . CLC 17
    See also CA 17-20R; CANR 8, 29; DLB 22;
    JRDA; MAICYA; SATA 2, 43

Farmer, Philip Jose 1918-. . . . . . . CLC 1, 19
    See also CA 1-4R; CANR 4, 35; DLB 8;
    MTCW

Farquhar, George
    1677-1707 . . . . LC 21; DAM DRAM
    See also DLB 84

Farrell, J(ames) G(ordon)
    1935-1979 . . . . CLC 6
    See also CA 73-76; 89-92; CANR 36;
    DLB 14; MTCW

Farrell, James T(homas)
    1904-1979 . . . . CLC 1, 4, 8, 11, 66
    See also CA 5-8R; 89-92; CANR 9; DLB 4,
    9, 86; DLBD 2; MTCW

Farren, Richard J.
    See Betjeman, John

Farren, Richard M.
See Betjeman, John

Fassbinder, Rainer Werner
1946-1982 . . . . **CLC 20**
See also CA 93-96; 106; CANR 31

Fast, Howard (Melvin)
1914- . . . . **CLC 23; DAM NOV**
See also AAYA 16; CA 1-4R; CAAS 18;
CANR 1, 33, 54; DLB 9; INT CANR-33;
SATA 7

Faulcon, Robert
See Holdstock, Robert P.

Faulkner, William (Cuthbert)
1897-1962 . . . . . **CLC 1, 3, 6, 8, 9, 11, 14,**
18, 28, 52, 68; DA; DAB; DAC;
DAM MST, NOV; SSC 1; WLC
See also AAYA 7; CA 81-84; CANR 33;
CDALB 1929-1941; DLB 9, 11, 44, 102;
DLBD 2; DLBY 86; MTCW

Fauset, Jessie Redmon
1884(?)-1961 . . . . **CLC 19, 54; BLC;**
DAM MULT
See also BW 1; CA 109; DLB 51

Faust, Frederick (Schiller)
1892-1944(?) . . . . . **TCLC 49; DAM POP**
See also CA 108; 152

Faust, Irvin 1924- . . . . **CLC 8**
See also CA 33-36R; CANR 28; DLB 2, 28;
DLBY 80

Fawkes, Guy
See Benchley, Robert (Charles)

Fearing, Kenneth (Flexner)
1902-1961 . . . . **CLC 51**
See also CA 93-96; DLB 9

Fecamps, Elise
See Creasey, John

Federman, Raymond 1928- . . . . . . **CLC 6, 47**
See also CA 17-20R; CAAS 8; CANR 10,
43; DLBY 80

Federspiel, J(uerg) F. 1931- . . . . **CLC 42**
See also CA 146

Feiffer, Jules (Ralph)
1929- . . . . . . **CLC 2, 8, 64; DAM DRAM**
See also AAYA 3; CA 17-20R; CANR 30;
DLB 7, 44; INT CANR-30; MTCW;
SATA 8, 61

Feige, Hermann Albert Otto Maximilian
See Traven, B.

Feinberg, David B. 1956-1994 . . . . . . **CLC 59**
See also CA 135; 147

Feinstein, Elaine 1930- . . . . **CLC 36**
See also CA 69-72; CAAS 1; CANR 31;
DLB 14, 40; MTCW

Feldman, Irving (Mordecai) 1928- . . . . **CLC 7**
See also CA 1-4R; CANR 1; DLB 169

Fellini, Federico 1920-1993 . . . . . **CLC 16, 85**
See also CA 65-68; 143; CANR 33

Felsen, Henry Gregor 1916- . . . . **CLC 17**
See also CA 1-4R; CANR 1; SAAS 2;
SATA 1

Fenton, James Martin 1949- . . . . **CLC 32**
See also CA 102; DLB 40

Ferber, Edna 1887-1968 . . . . **CLC 18, 93**
See also AITN 1; CA 5-8R; 25-28R; DLB 9,
28, 86; MTCW; SATA 7

Ferguson, Helen
See Kavan, Anna

Ferguson, Samuel 1810-1886 . . . . . **NCLC 33**
See also DLB 32

Fergusson, Robert 1750-1774 . . . . **LC 29**
See also DLB 109

Ferling, Lawrence
See Ferlinghetti, Lawrence (Monsanto)

Ferlinghetti, Lawrence (Monsanto)
1919(?)- . . . . **CLC 2, 6, 10, 27;**
DAM POET; PC 1
See also CA 5-8R; CANR 3, 41;
CDALB 1941-1968; DLB 5, 16; MTCW

Fernandez, Vicente Garcia Huidobro
See Huidobro Fernandez, Vicente Garcia

Ferrer, Gabriel (Francisco Victor) Miro
See Miro (Ferrer), Gabriel (Francisco
Victor)

Ferrier, Susan (Edmonstone)
1782-1854 . . . . **NCLC 8**
See also DLB 116

Ferrigno, Robert 1948(?)- . . . . **CLC 65**
See also CA 140

Ferron, Jacques 1921-1985 . . . **CLC 94; DAC**
See also CA 117; 129; DLB 60

Feuchtwanger, Lion 1884-1958 . . . . . **TCLC 3**
See also CA 104; DLB 66

Feuillet, Octave 1821-1890 . . . . . . **NCLC 45**

Feydeau, Georges (Leon Jules Marie)
1862-1921 . . . . . **TCLC 22; DAM DRAM**
See also CA 113; 152

Ficino, Marsilio 1433-1499 . . . . **LC 12**

Fiedeler, Hans
See Doeblin, Alfred

Fiedler, Leslie A(aron)
1917- . . . . **CLC 4, 13, 24**
See also CA 9-12R; CANR 7; DLB 28, 67;
MTCW

Field, Andrew 1938- . . . . **CLC 44**
See also CA 97-100; CANR 25

Field, Eugene 1850-1895 . . . . **NCLC 3**
See also DLB 23, 42, 140; DLBD 13;
MAICYA; SATA 16

Field, Gans T.
See Wellman, Manly Wade

Field, Michael . . . . **TCLC 43**

Field, Peter
See Hobson, Laura Z(ametkin)

Fielding, Henry
1707-1754 . . . . . . **LC 1; DA; DAB; DAC;**
DAM DRAM, MST, NOV; WLC
See also CDBLB 1660-1789; DLB 39, 84,
101

Fielding, Sarah 1710-1768 . . . . **LC 1**
See also DLB 39

Fierstein, Harvey (Forbes)
1954- . . . . . **CLC 33; DAM DRAM, POP**
See also CA 123; 129

Figes, Eva 1932- . . . . **CLC 31**
See also CA 53-56; CANR 4, 44; DLB 14

Finch, Robert (Duer Claydon)
1900- . . . . **CLC 18**
See also CA 57-60; CANR 9, 24, 49;
DLB 88

Findley, Timothy
1930- . . . . . . **CLC 27; DAC; DAM MST**
See also CA 25-28R; CANR 12, 42;
DLB 53

Fink, William
See Mencken, H(enry) L(ouis)

Firbank, Louis 1942-
See Reed, Lou
See also CA 117

Firbank, (Arthur Annesley) Ronald
1886-1926 . . . . **TCLC 1**
See also CA 104; DLB 36

Fisher, M(ary) F(rances) K(ennedy)
1908-1992 . . . . **CLC 76, 87**
See also CA 77-80; 138; CANR 44

Fisher, Roy 1930- . . . . **CLC 25**
See also CA 81-84; CAAS 10; CANR 16;
DLB 40

Fisher, Rudolph
1897-1934 . . . . **TCLC 11; BLC;**
DAM MULT; SSC 25
See also BW 1; CA 107; 124; DLB 51, 102

Fisher, Vardis (Alvero) 1895-1968 . . . . **CLC 7**
See also CA 5-8R; 25-28R; DLB 9

Fiske, Tarleton
See Bloch, Robert (Albert)

Fitch, Clarke
See Sinclair, Upton (Beall)

Fitch, John IV
See Cormier, Robert (Edmund)

Fitzgerald, Captain Hugh
See Baum, L(yman) Frank

FitzGerald, Edward 1809-1883 . . . . **NCLC 9**
See also DLB 32

Fitzgerald, F(rancis) Scott (Key)
1896-1940 . . . . **TCLC 1, 6, 14, 28, 55;**
DA; DAB; DAC; DAM MST, NOV;
SSC 6; WLC
See also AITN 1; CA 110; 123;
CDALB 1917-1929; DLB 4, 9, 86;
DLBD 1; DLBY 81; MTCW

Fitzgerald, Penelope 1916- . . . **CLC 19, 51, 61**
See also CA 85-88; CAAS 10; CANR 56;
DLB 14

Fitzgerald, Robert (Stuart)
1910-1985 . . . . **CLC 39**
See also CA 1-4R; 114; CANR 1; DLBY 80

FitzGerald, Robert D(avid)
1902-1987 . . . . **CLC 19**
See also CA 17-20R

Fitzgerald, Zelda (Sayre)
1900-1948 . . . . **TCLC 52**
See also CA 117; 126; DLBY 84

Flanagan, Thomas (James Bonner)
1923- . . . . **CLC 25, 52**
See also CA 108; CANR 55; DLBY 80;
INT 108; MTCW

Flaubert, Gustave
1821-1880 . . . . **NCLC 2, 10, 19; DA;**
DAB; DAC; DAM MST, NOV; SSC 11;
WLC
See also DLB 119

Flecker, Herman Elroy
See Flecker, (Herman) James Elroy

Fredro, Aleksander 1793-1876..... NCLC 8

Freeling, Nicolas 1927-............ CLC 38
See also CA 49-52; CAAS 12; CANR 1, 17, 50; DLB 87

Freeman, Douglas Southall
1886-1953 .... TCLC 11
See also CA 109; DLB 17

Freeman, Judith 1946-............ CLC 55
See also CA 148

Freeman, Mary Eleanor Wilkins
1852-1930 .... TCLC 9; SSC 1
See also CA 106; DLB 12, 78

Freeman, R(ichard) Austin
1862-1943 .... TCLC 21
See also CA 113; DLB 70

French, Albert 1943-............ CLC 86

French, Marilyn
1929-................. CLC 10, 18, 60;
DAM DRAM, NOV, POP
See also CA 69-72; CANR 3, 31;
INT CANR-31; MTCW

French, Paul
See Asimov, Isaac

Freneau, Philip Morin 1752-1832.. NCLC 1
See also DLB 37, 43

Freud, Sigmund 1856-1939 .... TCLC 52
See also CA 115; 133; MTCW

Friedan, Betty (Naomi) 1921-...... CLC 74
See also CA 65-68; CANR 18, 45; MTCW

Friedlander, Saul 1932-........... CLC 90
See also CA 117; 130

Friedman, B(ernard) H(arper)
1926-....................... CLC 7
See also CA 1-4R; CANR 3, 48

Friedman, Bruce Jay 1930-.... CLC 3, 5, 56
See also CA 9-12R; CANR 25, 52; DLB 2, 28; INT CANR-25

Friel, Brian 1929-........... CLC 5, 42, 59
See also CA 21-24R; CANR 33; DLB 13; MTCW

Friis-Baastad, Babbis Ellinor
1921-1970 .... CLC 12
See also CA 17-20R; 134; SATA 7

Frisch, Max (Rudolf)
1911-1991 ..... CLC 3, 9, 14, 18, 32, 44;
DAM DRAM, NOV
See also CA 85-88; 134; CANR 32;
DLB 69, 124; MTCW

Fromentin, Eugene (Samuel Auguste)
1820-1876 .... NCLC 10
See also DLB 123

Frost, Frederick
See Faust, Frederick (Schiller)

Frost, Robert (Lee)
1874-1963 .... CLC 1, 3, 4, 9, 10, 13, 15,
26, 34, 44; DA; DAB; DAC; DAM MST,
POET; PC 1; WLC
See also AAYA 21; CA 89-92; CANR 33;
CDALB 1917-1929; DLB 54; DLBD 7;
MTCW; SATA 14

Froude, James Anthony
1818-1894 .... NCLC 43
See also DLB 18, 57, 144

Froy, Herald
See Waterhouse, Keith (Spencer)

Fry, Christopher
1907- ..... CLC 2, 10, 14; DAM DRAM
See also CA 17-20R; CAAS 23; CANR 9, 30; DLB 13; MTCW; SATA 66

Frye, (Herman) Northrop
1912-1991 .... CLC 24, 70
See also CA 5-8R; 133; CANR 8, 37;
DLB 67, 68; MTCW

Fuchs, Daniel 1909-1993 .... CLC 8, 22
See also CA 81-84; 142; CAAS 5;
CANR 40; DLB 9, 26, 28; DLBY 93

Fuchs, Daniel 1934-.............. CLC 34
See also CA 37-40R; CANR 14, 48

Fuentes, Carlos
1928- ...... CLC 3, 8, 10, 13, 22, 41, 60;
DA; DAB; DAC; DAM MST, MULT,
NOV; HLC; SSC 24; WLC
See also AAYA 4; AITN 2; CA 69-72;
CANR 10, 32; DLB 113; HW; MTCW

Fuentes, Gregorio Lopez y
See Lopez y Fuentes, Gregorio

Fugard, (Harold) Athol
1932- .... CLC 5, 9, 14, 25, 40, 80;
DAM DRAM; DC 3
See also AAYA 17; CA 85-88; CANR 32, 54; MTCW

Fugard, Sheila 1932-............ CLC 48
See also CA 125

Fuller, Charles (H., Jr.)
1939- .... CLC 25; BLC; DAM DRAM,
MULT; DC 1
See also BW 2; CA 108; 112; DLB 38;
INT 112; MTCW

Fuller, John (Leopold) 1937-....... CLC 62
See also CA 21-24R; CANR 9, 44; DLB 40

Fuller, Margaret .... NCLC 5, 50
See also Ossoli, Sarah Margaret (Fuller marchesa d')

Fuller, Roy (Broadbent)
1912-1991 .... CLC 4, 28
See also CA 5-8R; 135; CAAS 10;
CANR 53; DLB 15, 20; SATA 87

Fulton, Alice 1952-.............. CLC 52
See also CA 116; CANR 57

Furphy, Joseph 1843-1912....... TCLC 25

Fussell, Paul 1924-.............. CLC 74
See also BEST 90:1; CA 17-20R; CANR 8, 21, 35; INT CANR-21; MTCW

Futabatei, Shimei 1864-1909...... TCLC 44

Futrelle, Jacques 1875-1912 ...... TCLC 19
See also CA 113; 155

Gaboriau, Emile 1835-1873...... NCLC 14

Gadda, Carlo Emilio 1893-1973 .... CLC 11
See also CA 89-92; DLB 177

Gaddis, William
1922- ..... CLC 1, 3, 6, 8, 10, 19, 43, 86
See also CA 17-20R; CANR 21, 48; DLB 2; MTCW

Gage, Walter
See Inge, William (Motter)

Gaines, Ernest J(ames)
1933-......... CLC 3, 11, 18, 86; BLC;
DAM MULT
See also AAYA 18; AITN 1; BW 2;
CA 9-12R; CANR 6, 24, 42;
CDALB 1968-1988; DLB 2, 33, 152;
DLBY 80; MTCW; SATA 86

Gaitskill, Mary 1954-............ CLC 69
See also CA 128

Galdos, Benito Perez
See Perez Galdos, Benito

Gale, Zona
1874-1938 ...... TCLC 7; DAM DRAM
See also CA 105; 153; DLB 9, 78

Galeano, Eduardo (Hughes) 1940-... CLC 72
See also CA 29-32R; CANR 13, 32; HW

Galiano, Juan Valera y Alcala
See Valera y Alcala-Galiano, Juan

Gallagher, Tess
1943- .. CLC 18, 63; DAM POET; PC 9
See also CA 106; DLB 120

Gallant, Mavis
1922-............ CLC 7, 18, 38; DAC;
DAM MST; SSC 5
See also CA 69-72; CANR 29; DLB 53;
MTCW

Gallant, Roy A(rthur) 1924-....... CLC 17
See also CA 5-8R; CANR 4, 29, 54;
CLR 30; MAICYA; SATA 4, 68

Gallico, Paul (William) 1897-1976 ... CLC 2
See also AITN 1; CA 5-8R; 69-72;
CANR 23; DLB 9, 171; MAICYA;
SATA 13

Gallo, Max Louis 1932-........... CLC 95
See also CA 85-88

Gallois, Lucien
See Desnos, Robert

Gallup, Ralph
See Whitemore, Hugh (John)

Galsworthy, John
1867-1933 ...... TCLC 1, 45; DA; DAB;
DAC; DAM DRAM, MST, NOV;
SSC 22; WLC 2
See also CA 104; 141; CDBLB 1890-1914;
DLB 10, 34, 98, 162

Galt, John 1779-1839............ NCLC 1
See also DLB 99, 116, 159

Galvin, James 1951-.............. CLC 38
See also CA 108; CANR 26

Gamboa, Federico 1864-1939...... TCLC 36

Gandhi, M. K.
See Gandhi, Mohandas Karamchand

Gandhi, Mahatma
See Gandhi, Mohandas Karamchand

Gandhi, Mohandas Karamchand
1869-1948 ..... TCLC 59; DAM MULT
See also CA 121; 132; MTCW

Gann, Ernest Kellogg 1910-1991.... CLC 23
See also AITN 1; CA 1-4R; 136; CANR 1

Garcia, Cristina 1958-............ CLC 76
See also CA 141

Garcia Lorca, Federico
1898-1936 ... **TCLC 1, 7, 49; DA; DAB;**
DAC; DAM DRAM, MST, MULT,
POET; DC 2; HLC; PC 3; WLC
See also CA 104; 131; DLB 108; HW;
MTCW

Garcia Marquez, Gabriel (Jose)
1928- .... **CLC 2, 3, 8, 10, 15, 27, 47, 55,**
68; DA; DAB; DAC; DAM MST,
MULT, NOV, POP; HLC; SSC 8; WLC
See also AAYA 3; BEST 89:1, 90:4;
CA 33-36R; CANR 10, 28, 50; DLB 113;
HW; MTCW

Gard, Janice
See Latham, Jean Lee

Gard, Roger Martin du
See Martin du Gard, Roger

Gardam, Jane 1928-.............. **CLC 43**
See also CA 49-52; CANR 2, 18, 33, 54;
CLR 12; DLB 14, 161; MAICYA;
MTCW; SAAS 9; SATA 39, 76;
SATA-Brief 28

Gardner, Herb(ert) 1934-......... **CLC 44**
See also CA 149

Gardner, John (Champlin), Jr.
1933-1982 ..... **CLC 2, 3, 5, 7, 8, 10, 18,**
28, 34; DAM NOV, POP; SSC 7
See also AITN 1; CA 65-68; 107;
CANR 33; DLB 2; DLBY 82; MTCW;
SATA 40; SATA-Obit 31

Gardner, John (Edmund)
1926- .... **CLC 30; DAM POP**
See also CA 103; CANR 15; MTCW

Gardner, Miriam
See Bradley, Marion Zimmer

Gardner, Noel
See Kuttner, Henry

Gardons, S. S.
See Snodgrass, W(illiam) D(e Witt)

Garfield, Leon 1921-1996.......... **CLC 12**
See also AAYA 8; CA 17-20R; 152;
CANR 38, 41; CLR 21; DLB 161; JRDA;
MAICYA; SATA 1, 32, 76;
SATA-Obit 90

Garland, (Hannibal) Hamlin
1860-1940 .... **TCLC 3; SSC 18**
See also CA 104; DLB 12, 71, 78

Garneau, (Hector de) Saint-Denys
1912-1943 .... **TCLC 13**
See also CA 111; DLB 88

Garner, Alan
1934- .... **CLC 17; DAB; DAM POP**
See also AAYA 18; CA 73-76; CANR 15;
CLR 20; DLB 161; MAICYA; MTCW;
SATA 18, 69

Garner, Hugh 1913-1979.......... **CLC 13**
See also CA 69-72; CANR 31; DLB 68

Garnett, David 1892-1981.......... **CLC 3**
See also CA 5-8R; 103; CANR 17; DLB 34

Garos, Stephanie
See Katz, Steve

Garrett, George (Palmer)
1929- .... **CLC 3, 11, 51**
See also CA 1-4R; CAAS 5; CANR 1, 42;
DLB 2, 5, 130, 152; DLBY 83

Garrick, David
1717-1779 ...... **LC 15; DAM DRAM**
See also DLB 84

Garrigue, Jean 1914-1972 .... **CLC 2, 8**
See also CA 5-8R; 37-40R; CANR 20

Garrison, Frederick
See Sinclair, Upton (Beall)

Garth, Will
See Hamilton, Edmond; Kuttner, Henry

Garvey, Marcus (Moziah, Jr.)
1887-1940 .... **TCLC 41; BLC;**
DAM MULT
See also BW 1; CA 120; 124

Gary, Romain .... **CLC 25**
See also Kacew, Romain
See also DLB 83

Gascar, Pierre .... **CLC 11**
See also Fournier, Pierre

Gascoyne, David (Emery) 1916- .... **CLC 45**
See also CA 65-68; CANR 10, 28, 54;
DLB 20; MTCW

Gaskell, Elizabeth Cleghorn
1810-1865 .... **NCLC 5; DAB;**
DAM MST; SSC 25
See also CDBLB 1832-1890; DLB 21, 144,
159

Gass, William H(oward)
1924- ... **CLC 1, 2, 8, 11, 15, 39; SSC 12**
See also CA 17-20R; CANR 30; DLB 2;
MTCW

Gasset, Jose Ortega y
See Ortega y Gasset, Jose

Gates, Henry Louis, Jr.
1950- .... **CLC 65; DAM MULT**
See also BW 2; CA 109; CANR 25, 53;
DLB 67

Gautier, Theophile
1811-1872 .... **NCLC 1, 59;**
DAM POET; SSC 20
See also DLB 119

Gawsworth, John
See Bates, H(erbert) E(rnest)

Gay, Oliver
See Gogarty, Oliver St. John

Gaye, Marvin (Penze) 1939-1984 ... **CLC 26**
See also CA 112

Gebler, Carlo (Ernest) 1954-....... **CLC 39**
See also CA 119; 133

Gee, Maggie (Mary) 1948-........ **CLC 57**
See also CA 130

Gee, Maurice (Gough) 1931-....... **CLC 29**
See also CA 97-100; SATA 46

Gelbart, Larry (Simon) 1923- ... **CLC 21, 61**
See also CA 73-76; CANR 45

Gelber, Jack 1932-........ **CLC 1, 6, 14, 79**
See also CA 1-4R; CANR 2; DLB 7

Gellhorn, Martha (Ellis) 1908- .. **CLC 14, 60**
See also CA 77-80; CANR 44; DLBY 82

Genet, Jean
1910-1986 ...... **CLC 1, 2, 5, 10, 14, 44,**
46; DAM DRAM
See also CA 13-16R; CANR 18; DLB 72;
DLBY 86; MTCW

Gent, Peter 1942-................. **CLC 29**
See also AITN 1; CA 89-92; DLBY 82

Gentlewoman in New England, A
See Bradstreet, Anne

Gentlewoman in Those Parts, A
See Bradstreet, Anne

George, Jean Craighead 1919-...... **CLC 35**
See also AAYA 8; CA 5-8R; CANR 25;
CLR 1; DLB 52; JRDA; MAICYA;
SATA 2, 68

George, Stefan (Anton)
1868-1933 .... **TCLC 2, 14**
See also CA 104

Georges, Georges Martin
See Simenon, Georges (Jacques Christian)

Gerhardi, William Alexander
See Gerhardie, William Alexander

Gerhardie, William Alexander
1895-1977 .... **CLC 5**
See also CA 25-28R; 73-76; CANR 18;
DLB 36

Gerstler, Amy 1956-.............. **CLC 70**
See also CA 146

Gertler, T. .... **CLC 34**
See also CA 116; 121; INT 121

gfgg........................ **CLC XvXzc**

Ghalib........................ **NCLC 39**
See also Ghalib, Hsadullah Khan

Ghalib, Hsadullah Khan 1797-1869
See Ghalib
See also DAM POET

Ghelderode, Michel de
1898-1962 .... **CLC 6, 11; DAM DRAM**
See also CA 85-88; CANR 40

Ghiselin, Brewster 1903-.......... **CLC 23**
See also CA 13-16R; CAAS 10; CANR 13

Ghose, Zulfikar 1935-.............. **CLC 42**
See also CA 65-68

Ghosh, Amitav 1956- .... **CLC 44**
See also CA 147

Giacosa, Giuseppe 1847-1906 ...... **TCLC 7**
See also CA 104

Gibb, Lee
See Waterhouse, Keith (Spencer)

Gibbon, Lewis Grassic .... **TCLC 4**
See also Mitchell, James Leslie

Gibbons, Kaye
1960- .... **CLC 50, 88; DAM POP**
See also CA 151

Gibran, Kahlil
1883-1931 .... **TCLC 1, 9; DAM POET,**
POP; PC 9
See also CA 104; 150

Gibran, Khalil
See Gibran, Kahlil

Gibson, William
1914- .... **CLC 23; DA; DAB; DAC;**
DAM DRAM, MST
See also CA 9-12R; CANR 9, 42; DLB 7;
SATA 66

Gibson, William (Ford)
1948- .... **CLC 39, 63; DAM POP**
See also AAYA 12; CA 126; 133; CANR 52

Gide, Andre (Paul Guillaume)
1869-1951 .... **TCLC 5, 12, 36; DA;
DAB; DAC; DAM MST, NOV; SSC 13;
WLC**
See also CA 104; 124; DLB 65; MTCW

Gifford, Barry (Colby) 1946-....... **CLC 34**
See also CA 65-68; CANR 9, 30, 40

Gilbert, W(illiam) S(chwenck)
1836-1911 ..... **TCLC 3; DAM DRAM,
POET**
See also CA 104; SATA 36

Gilbreth, Frank B., Jr. 1911-....... **CLC 17**
See also CA 9-12R; SATA 2

Gilchrist, Ellen
1935- .... **CLC 34, 48; DAM POP;
SSC 14**
See also CA 113; 116; CANR 41; DLB 130;
MTCW

Giles, Molly 1942-............. **CLC 39**
See also CA 126

Gill, Patrick
See Creasey, John

Gilliam, Terry (Vance) 1940-....... **CLC 21**
See also Monty Python
See also AAYA 19; CA 108; 113;
CANR 35; INT 113

Gillian, Jerry
See Gilliam, Terry (Vance)

Gilliatt, Penelope (Ann Douglass)
1932-1993 .... **CLC 2, 10, 13, 53**
See also AITN 2; CA 13-16R; 141;
CANR 49; DLB 14

Gilman, Charlotte (Anna) Perkins (Stetson)
1860-1935 .... **TCLC 9, 37; SSC 13**
See also CA 106; 150

Gilmour, David 1949-............ **CLC 35**
See also CA 138, 147

Gilpin, William 1724-1804....... **NCLC 30**

Gilray, J. D.
See Mencken, H(enry) L(ouis)

Gilroy, Frank D(aniel) 1925-........ **CLC 2**
See also CA 81-84; CANR 32; DLB 7

Gilstrap, John 1957(?)-............ **CLC 99**

Ginsberg, Allen
1926-.... **CLC 1, 2, 3, 4, 6, 13, 36, 69;
DA; DAB; DAC; DAM MST, POET;
PC 4; WLC 3**
See also AITN 1; CA 1-4R; CANR 2, 41;
CDALB 1941-1968; DLB 5, 16, 169;
MTCW

Ginzburg, Natalia
1916-1991 .... **CLC 5, 11, 54, 70**
See also CA 85-88; 135; CANR 33;
DLB 177; MTCW

Giono, Jean 1895-1970......... **CLC 4, 11**
See also CA 45-48; 29-32R; CANR 2, 35;
DLB 72; MTCW

Giovanni, Nikki
1943- ...... **CLC 2, 4, 19, 64; BLC; DA;
DAB; DAC; DAM MST, MULT, POET**
See also AITN 1; BW 2; CA 29-32R;
CAAS 6; CANR 18, 41; CLR 6; DLB 5,
41; INT CANR-18; MAICYA; MTCW;
SATA 24

Giovene, Andrea 1904-............ **CLC 7**
See also CA 85-88

Gippius, Zinaida (Nikolayevna) 1869-1945
See Hippius, Zinaida
See also CA 106

Giraudoux, (Hippolyte) Jean
1882-1944 .... **TCLC 2, 7; DAM DRAM**
See also CA 104; DLB 65

Gironella, Jose Maria 1917-....... **CLC 11**
See also CA 101

Gissing, George (Robert)
1857-1903 .... **TCLC 3, 24, 47**
See also CA 105; DLB 18, 135

Giurlani, Aldo
See Palazzeschi, Aldo

Gladkov, Fyodor (Vasilyevich)
1883-1958 .... **TCLC 27**

Glanville, Brian (Lester) 1931-...... **CLC 6**
See also CA 5-8R; CAAS 9; CANR 3;
DLB 15, 139; SATA 42

Glasgow, Ellen (Anderson Gholson)
1873(?)-1945 .... **TCLC 2, 7**
See also CA 104; DLB 9, 12

Glaspell, Susan 1882(?)-1948...... **TCLC 55**
See also CA 110; 154; DLB 7, 9, 78;
YABC 2

Glassco, John 1909-1981 .... **CLC 9**
See also CA 13-16R; 102; CANR 15;
DLB 68

Glasscock, Amnesia
See Steinbeck, John (Ernst)

Glasser, Ronald J. 1940(?)-........ **CLC 37**

Glassman, Joyce
See Johnson, Joyce

Glendinning, Victoria 1937-........ **CLC 50**
See also CA 120; 127; DLB 155

Glissant, Edouard
1928- .... **CLC 10, 68; DAM MULT**
See also CA 153

Gloag, Julian 1930- .... **CLC 40**
See also AITN 1; CA 65-68; CANR 10

Glowacki, Aleksander
See Prus, Boleslaw

Gluck, Louise (Elisabeth)
1943- .... **CLC 7, 22, 44, 81;
DAM POET; PC 16**
See also CA 33-36R; CANR 40; DLB 5

Gobineau, Joseph Arthur (Comte) de
1816-1882 .... **NCLC 17**
See also DLB 123

Godard, Jean-Luc 1930-........... **CLC 20**
See also CA 93-96

Godden, (Margaret) Rumer 1907-... **CLC 53**
See also AAYA 6; CA 5-8R; CANR 4, 27,
36, 55; CLR 20; DLB 161; MAICYA;
SAAS 12; SATA 3, 36

Godoy Alcayaga, Lucila 1889-1957
See Mistral, Gabriela
See also BW 2; CA 104; 131; DAM MULT;
HW; MTCW

Godwin, Gail (Kathleen)
1937- .... **CLC 5, 8, 22, 31, 69;
DAM POP**
See also CA 29-32R; CANR 15, 43; DLB 6;
INT CANR-15; MTCW

Godwin, William 1756-1836...... **NCLC 14**
See also CDBLB 1789-1832; DLB 39, 104,
142, 158, 163

Goebbels, Josef
See Goebbels, (Paul) Joseph

Goebbels, (Paul) Joseph
1897-1945 .... **TCLC 68**
See also CA 115; 148

Goebbels, Joseph Paul
See Goebbels, (Paul) Joseph

Goethe, Johann Wolfgang von
1749-1832 .... **NCLC 4, 22, 34; DA;
DAB; DAC; DAM DRAM, MST,
POET; PC 5; WLC 3**
See also DLB 94

Gogarty, Oliver St. John
1878-1957 .... **TCLC 15**
See also CA 109; 150; DLB 15, 19

Gogol, Nikolai (Vasilyevich)
1809-1852 .... **NCLC 5, 15, 31; DA;
DAB; DAC; DAM DRAM, MST; DC 1;
SSC 4; WLC**

Goines, Donald
1937(?)-1974 .... **CLC 80; BLC;
DAM MULT, POP**
See also AITN 1; BW 1; CA 124; 114;
DLB 33

Gold, Herbert 1924-....... **CLC 4, 7, 14, 42**
See also CA 9-12R; CANR 17, 45; DLB 2;
DLBY 81

Goldbarth, Albert 1948-........ **CLC 5, 38**
See also CA 53-56; CANR 6, 40; DLB 120

Goldberg, Anatol 1910-1982 .... **CLC 34**
See also CA 131; 117

Goldemberg, Isaac 1945- .... **CLC 52**
See also CA 69-72; CAAS 12; CANR 11,
32; HW

Golding, William (Gerald)
1911-1993 .... **CLC 1, 2, 3, 8, 10, 17, 27,
58, 81; DA; DAB; DAC; DAM MST,
NOV; WLC**
See also AAYA 5; CA 5-8R; 141;
CANR 13, 33, 54; CDBLB 1945-1960;
DLB 15, 100; MTCW

Goldman, Emma 1869-1940....... **TCLC 13**
See also CA 110; 150

Goldman, Francisco 1955-......... **CLC 76**

Goldman, William (W.) 1931-.... **CLC 1, 48**
See also CA 9-12R; CANR 29; DLB 44

Goldmann, Lucien 1913-1970 ...... **CLC 24**
See also CA 25-28; CAP 2

Goldoni, Carlo
1707-1793 .... **LC 4; DAM DRAM**

Goldsberry, Steven 1949-.......... **CLC 34**
See also CA 131

Goldsmith, Oliver
1728-1774 ...... **LC 2; DA; DAB; DAC;
DAM DRAM, MST, NOV, POET;
WLC**
See also CDBLB 1660-1789; DLB 39, 89,
104, 109, 142; SATA 26

Goldsmith, Peter
See Priestley, J(ohn) B(oynton)

Green, Julian (Hartridge) 1900-
See Green, Julien
See also CA 21-24R; CANR 33; DLB 4, 72;
MTCW

Green, Julien . . . . **CLC 3, 11, 77**
See also Green, Julian (Hartridge)

Green, Paul (Eliot)
1894-1981 . . . . . . **CLC 25; DAM DRAM**
See also AITN 1; CA 5-8R; 103; CANR 3;
DLB 7, 9; DLBY 81

Greenberg, Ivan 1908-1973
See Rahv, Philip
See also CA 85-88

Greenberg, Joanne (Goldenberg)
1932- . . . . **CLC 7, 30**
See also AAYA 12; CA 5-8R; CANR 14,
32; SATA 25

Greenberg, Richard 1959(?)- . . . . **CLC 57**
See also CA 138

Greene, Bette 1934- . . . . **CLC 30**
See also AAYA 7; CA 53-56; CANR 4;
CLR 2; JRDA; MAICYA; SAAS 16;
SATA 8

Greene, Gael . . . . **CLC 8**
See also CA 13-16R; CANR 10

Greene, Graham
1904-1991 . . . . **CLC 1, 3, 6, 9, 14, 18, 27,
37, 70, 72; DA; DAB; DAC; DAM MST,
NOV; WLC**
See also AITN 2; CA 13-16R; 133;
CANR 35; CDBLB 1945-1960; DLB 13,
15, 77, 100, 162; DLBY 91; MTCW;
SATA 20

Greer, Richard
See Silverberg, Robert

Gregor, Arthur 1923- . . . . **CLC 9**
See also CA 25-28R; CAAS 10; CANR 11;
SATA 36

Gregor, Lee
See Pohl, Frederik

Gregory, Isabella Augusta (Persse)
1852-1932 . . . . **TCLC 1**
See also CA 104; DLB 10

Gregory, J. Dennis
See Williams, John A(lfred)

Grendon, Stephen
See Derleth, August (William)

Grenville, Kate 1950- . . . . **CLC 61**
See also CA 118; CANR 53

Grenville, Pelham
See Wodehouse, P(elham) G(renville)

Greve, Felix Paul (Berthold Friedrich)
1879-1948
See Grove, Frederick Philip
See also CA 104; 141; DAC; DAM MST

Grey, Zane
1872-1939 . . . . **TCLC 6; DAM POP**
See also CA 104; 132; DLB 9; MTCW

Grieg, (Johan) Nordahl (Brun)
1902-1943 . . . . **TCLC 10**
See also CA 107

Grieve, C(hristopher) M(urray)
1892-1978 . . . . **CLC 11, 19; DAM POET**
See also MacDiarmid, Hugh; Pteleon
See also CA 5-8R; 85-88; CANR 33;
MTCW

Griffin, Gerald 1803-1840 . . . . **NCLC 7**
See also DLB 159

Griffin, John Howard 1920-1980. . . . **CLC 68**
See also AITN 1; CA 1-4R; 101; CANR 2

Griffin, Peter 1942- . . . . **CLC 39**
See also CA 136

Griffith, D(avid Lewelyn) W(ark)
1875(?)-1948 . . . . **TCLC 68**
See also CA 119; 150

Griffith, Lawrence
See Griffith, D(avid Lewelyn) W(ark)

Griffiths, Trevor 1935- . . . . **CLC 13, 52**
See also CA 97-100; CANR 45; DLB 13

Grigson, Geoffrey (Edward Harvey)
1905-1985 . . . . **CLC 7, 39**
See also CA 25-28R; 118; CANR 20, 33;
DLB 27; MTCW

Grillparzer, Franz 1791-1872 . . . . . . **NCLC 1**
See also DLB 133

Grimble, Reverend Charles James
See Eliot, T(homas) S(tearns)

Grimke, Charlotte L(ottie) Forten
1837(?)-1914
See Forten, Charlotte L.
See also BW 1; CA 117; 124; DAM MULT,
POET

Grimm, Jacob Ludwig Karl
1785-1863 . . . . **NCLC 3**
See also DLB 90; MAICYA; SATA 22

Grimm, Wilhelm Karl 1786-1859 . . **NCLC 3**
See also DLB 90; MAICYA; SATA 22

**Grimmelshausen, Johann Jakob Christoffel
von** 1621-1676 . . . . **LC 6**
See also DLB 168

Grindel, Eugene 1895-1952
See Eluard, Paul
See also CA 104

Grisham, John 1955- . . **CLC 84; DAM POP**
See also AAYA 14; CA 138; CANR 47

Grossman, David 1954- . . . . **CLC 67**
See also CA 138

Grossman, Vasily (Semenovich)
1905-1964 . . . . **CLC 41**
See also CA 124; 130; MTCW

Grove, Frederick Philip . . . . **TCLC 4**
See also Greve, Felix Paul (Berthold
Friedrich)
See also DLB 92

Grubb
See Crumb, R(obert)

Grumbach, Doris (Isaac)
1918- . . . . **CLC 13, 22, 64**
See also CA 5-8R; CAAS 2; CANR 9, 42;
INT CANR-9

Grundtvig, Nicolai Frederik Severin
1783-1872 . . . . **NCLC 1**

Grunge
See Crumb, R(obert)

Grunwald, Lisa 1959- . . . . **CLC 44**
See also CA 120

Guare, John
1938- . . . . **CLC 8, 14, 29, 67;
DAM DRAM**
See also CA 73-76; CANR 21; DLB 7;
MTCW

Gudjonsson, Halldor Kiljan 1902-
See Laxness, Halldor
See also CA 103

Guenter, Erich
See Eich, Guenter

Guest, Barbara 1920- . . . . **CLC 34**
See also CA 25-28R; CANR 11, 44; DLB 5

Guest, Judith (Ann)
1936- . . . . **CLC 8, 30; DAM NOV, POP**
See also AAYA 7; CA 77-80; CANR 15;
INT CANR-15; MTCW

Guevara, Che . . . . **CLC 87; HLC**
See also Guevara (Serna), Ernesto

Guevara (Serna), Ernesto 1928-1967
See Guevara, Che
See also CA 127; 111; CANR 56;
DAM MULT; HW

Guild, Nicholas M. 1944- . . . . **CLC 33**
See also CA 93-96

Guillemin, Jacques
See Sartre, Jean-Paul

Guillen, Jorge
1893-1984 . . . . . . **CLC 11; DAM MULT,
POET**
See also CA 89-92; 112; DLB 108; HW

Guillen, Nicolas (Cristobal)
1902-1989 . . . . **CLC 48, 79; BLC;
DAM MST, MULT, POET; HLC**
See also BW 2; CA 116; 125; 129; HW

Guillevic, (Eugene) 1907- . . . . **CLC 33**
See also CA 93-96

Guillois
See Desnos, Robert

Guillois, Valentin
See Desnos, Robert

Guiney, Louise Imogen
1861-1920 . . . . **TCLC 41**
See also DLB 54

Guiraldes, Ricardo (Guillermo)
1886-1927 . . . . **TCLC 39**
See also CA 131; HW; MTCW

Gumilev, Nikolai Stephanovich
1886-1921 . . . . **TCLC 60**

Gunesekera, Romesh . . . . **CLC 91**

Gunn, Bill . . . . **CLC 5**
See also Gunn, William Harrison
See also DLB 38

Gunn, Thom(son William)
1929- . . . . **CLC 3, 6, 18, 32, 81;
DAM POET**
See also CA 17-20R; CANR 9, 33;
CDBLB 1960 to Present; DLB 27;
INT CANR-33; MTCW

Gunn, William Harrison 1934(?)-1989
See Gunn, Bill
See also AITN 1; BW 1; CA 13-16R; 128;
CANR 12, 25

Gunnars, Kristjana 1948- . . . . **CLC 69**
See also CA 113; DLB 60

Gurganus, Allan
1947- . . . . **CLC 70; DAM POP**
See also BEST 90:1; CA 135

Gurney, A(lbert) R(amsdell), Jr.
1930- . . . . **CLC 32, 50, 54; DAM DRAM**
See also CA 77-80; CANR 32

Harling, Robert 1951(?)- .... **CLC 53**
  See also CA 147

Harmon, William (Ruth) 1938-..... **CLC 38**
  See also CA 33-36R; CANR 14, 32, 35;
  SATA 65

Harper, F. E. W.
  See Harper, Frances Ellen Watkins

Harper, Frances E. W.
  See Harper, Frances Ellen Watkins

Harper, Frances E. Watkins
  See Harper, Frances Ellen Watkins

Harper, Frances Ellen
  See Harper, Frances Ellen Watkins

Harper, Frances Ellen Watkins
  1825-1911 .... **TCLC 14; BLC;**
                   DAM MULT, POET
  See also BW 1; CA 111; 125; DLB 50

Harper, Michael S(teven) 1938- .. **CLC 7, 22**
  See also BW 1; CA 33-36R; CANR 24;
  DLB 41

Harper, Mrs. F. E. W.
  See Harper, Frances Ellen Watkins

Harris, Christie (Lucy) Irwin
  1907- .... **CLC 12**
  See also CA 5-8R; CANR 6; DLB 88;
  JRDA; MAICYA; SAAS 10; SATA 6, 74

Harris, Frank 1856-1931 .... **TCLC 24**
  See also CA 109; 150; DLB 156

Harris, George Washington
  1814-1869 .... **NCLC 23**
  See also DLB 3, 11

Harris, Joel Chandler
  1848-1908 .... **TCLC 2; SSC 19**
  See also CA 104; 137; DLB 11, 23, 42, 78,
  91; MAICYA; YABC 1

Harris, John (Wyndham Parkes Lucas)
  Beynon 1903-1969
  See Wyndham, John
  See also CA 102; 89-92

Harris, MacDonald................. **CLC 9**
  See also Heiney, Donald (William)

Harris, Mark 1922- .... **CLC 19**
  See also CA 5-8R; CAAS 3; CANR 2, 55;
  DLB 2; DLBY 80

Harris, (Theodore) Wilson 1921-.... **CLC 25**
  See also BW 2; CA 65-68; CAAS 16;
  CANR 11, 27; DLB 117; MTCW

Harrison, Elizabeth Cavanna 1909-
  See Cavanna, Betty
  See also CA 9-12R; CANR 6, 27

Harrison, Harry (Max) 1925-...... **CLC 42**
  See also CA 1-4R; CANR 5, 21; DLB 8;
  SATA 4

Harrison, James (Thomas)
  1937- .... **CLC 6, 14, 33, 66; SSC 19**
  See also CA 13-16R; CANR 8, 51;
  DLBY 82; INT CANR-8

Harrison, Jim
  See Harrison, James (Thomas)

Harrison, Kathryn 1961-.......... **CLC 70**
  See also CA 144

Harrison, Tony 1937-............. **CLC 43**
  See also CA 65-68; CANR 44; DLB 40;
  MTCW

Harriss, Will(ard Irvin) 1922-...... **CLC 34**
  See also CA 111

Harson, Sley
  See Ellison, Harlan (Jay)

Hart, Ellis
  See Ellison, Harlan (Jay)

Hart, Josephine
  1942(?)- .... **CLC 70; DAM POP**
  See also CA 138

Hart, Moss
  1904-1961 ...... **CLC 66; DAM DRAM**
  See also CA 109; 89-92; DLB 7

Harte, (Francis) Bret(t)
  1836(?)-1902 .... **TCLC 1, 25; DA; DAC;**
                   DAM MST; SSC 8; WLC
  See also CA 104; 140; CDALB 1865-1917;
  DLB 12, 64, 74, 79; SATA 26

Hartley, L(eslie) P(oles)
  1895-1972 .... **CLC 2, 22**
  See also CA 45-48; 37-40R; CANR 33;
  DLB 15, 139; MTCW

Hartman, Geoffrey H. 1929-....... **CLC 27**
  See also CA 117; 125; DLB 67

Hartmann von Aue
  c. 1160-c. 1205 .... **CMLC 15**
  See also DLB 138

Hartmann von Aue 1170-1210.... **CMLC 15**

Haruf, Kent 1943- .... **CLC 34**
  See also CA 149

Harwood, Ronald
  1934- .... **CLC 32; DAM DRAM, MST**
  See also CA 1-4R; CANR 4, 55; DLB 13

Hasek, Jaroslav (Matej Frantisek)
  1883-1923 .... **TCLC 4**
  See also CA 104; 129; MTCW

Hass, Robert
  1941- .... **CLC 18, 39, 99; PC 16**
  See also CA 111; CANR 30, 50; DLB 105

Hastings, Hudson
  See Kuttner, Henry

Hastings, Selina................... **CLC 44**

Hathorne, John 1641-1717......... **LC 38**

Hatteras, Amelia
  See Mencken, H(enry) L(ouis)

Hatteras, Owen................... **TCLC 18**
  See also Mencken, H(enry) L(ouis); Nathan,
  George Jean

Hauptmann, Gerhart (Johann Robert)
  1862-1946 ...... **TCLC 4; DAM DRAM**
  See also CA 104; 153; DLB 66, 118

Havel, Vaclav
  1936-................ **CLC 25, 58, 65;**
                   DAM DRAM; DC 6
  See also CA 104; CANR 36; MTCW

Haviaras, Stratis................. **CLC 33**
  See also Chaviaras, Strates

Hawes, Stephen 1475(?)-1523(?) ..... **LC 17**

Hawkes, John (Clendennin Burne, Jr.)
  1925- ...... **CLC 1, 2, 3, 4, 7, 9, 14, 15,**
                   27, 49
  See also CA 1-4R; CANR 2, 47; DLB 2, 7;
  DLBY 80; MTCW

Hawking, S. W.
  See Hawking, Stephen W(illiam)

Hawking, Stephen W(illiam)
  1942- .... **CLC 63**
  See also AAYA 13; BEST 89:1; CA 126;
  129; CANR 48

Hawthorne, Julian 1846-1934 ..... **TCLC 25**

Hawthorne, Nathaniel
  1804-1864 .... **NCLC 39; DA; DAB;**
                   DAC; DAM MST, NOV; SSC 3; WLC
  See also AAYA 18; CDALB 1640-1865;
  DLB 1, 74; YABC 2

Haxton, Josephine Ayres 1921-
  See Douglas, Ellen
  See also CA 115; CANR 41

Hayaseca y Eizaguirre, Jorge
  See Echegaray (y Eizaguirre), Jose (Maria
  Waldo)

Hayashi Fumiko 1904-1951....... **TCLC 27**

Haycraft, Anna
  See Ellis, Alice Thomas
  See also CA 122

Hayden, Robert E(arl)
  1913-1980 ...... **CLC 5, 9, 14, 37; BLC;**
                   DA; DAC; DAM MST, MULT, POET;
                   PC 6
  See also BW 1; CA 69-72; 97-100; CABS 2;
  CANR 24; CDALB 1941-1968; DLB 5,
  76; MTCW; SATA 19; SATA-Obit 26

Hayford, J(oseph) E(phraim) Casely
  See Casely-Hayford, J(oseph) E(phraim)

Hayman, Ronald 1932-............ **CLC 44**
  See also CA 25-28R; CANR 18, 50;
  DLB 155

Haywood, Eliza (Fowler)
  1693(?)-1756 .... **LC 1**

Hazlitt, William 1778-1830...... **NCLC 29**
  See also DLB 110, 158

Hazzard, Shirley 1931- .... **CLC 18**
  See also CA 9-12R; CANR 4; DLBY 82;
  MTCW

Head, Bessie
  1937-1986 .... **CLC 25, 67; BLC;**
                   DAM MULT
  See also BW 2; CA 29-32R; 119; CANR 25;
  DLB 117; MTCW

Headon, (Nicky) Topper 1956(?)- ... **CLC 30**

Heaney, Seamus (Justin)
  1939- ...... **CLC 5, 7, 14, 25, 37, 74, 91;**
                   DAB; DAM POET
  See also CA 85-88; CANR 25, 48;
  CDBLB 1960 to Present; DLB 40;
  DLBY 95; MTCW

Hearn, (Patricio) Lafcadio (Tessima Carlos)
  1850-1904 .... **TCLC 9**
  See also CA 105; DLB 12, 78

Hearne, Vicki 1946-.............. **CLC 56**
  See also CA 139

Hearon, Shelby 1931-............. **CLC 63**
  See also AITN 2; CA 25-28R; CANR 18,
  48

Heat-Moon, William Least......... **CLC 29**
  See also Trogdon, William (Lewis)
  See also AAYA 9

Hebbel, Friedrich
  1813-1863 .... **NCLC 43; DAM DRAM**
  See also DLB 129

Hebert, Anne
  1916- .... **CLC 4, 13, 29; DAC;**
                    DAM MST, POET
  See also CA 85-88; DLB 68; MTCW

Hecht, Anthony (Evan)
  1923- ...... **CLC 8, 13, 19; DAM POET**
  See also CA 9-12R; CANR 6; DLB 5, 169

Hecht, Ben 1894-1964 .... **CLC 8**
  See also CA 85-88; DLB 7, 9, 25, 26, 28, 86

Hedayat, Sadeq 1903-1951....... **TCLC 21**
  See also CA 120

Hegel, Georg Wilhelm Friedrich
  1770-1831 .... **NCLC 46**
  See also DLB 90

Heidegger, Martin 1889-1976 ...... **CLC 24**
  See also CA 81-84; 65-68; CANR 34;
  MTCW

Heidenstam, (Carl Gustaf) Verner von
  1859-1940 .... **TCLC 5**
  See also CA 104

Heifner, Jack 1946- .... **CLC 11**
  See also CA 105; CANR 47

Heijermans, Herman 1864-1924 ... **TCLC 24**
  See also CA 123

Heilbrun, Carolyn G(old) 1926-..... **CLC 25**
  See also CA 45-48; CANR 1, 28

Heine, Heinrich 1797-1856 .... **NCLC 4, 54**
  See also DLB 90

Heinemann, Larry (Curtiss) 1944- .. **CLC 50**
  See also CA 110; CAAS 21; CANR 31;
  DLBD 9; INT CANR-31

Heiney, Donald (William) 1921-1993
  See Harris, MacDonald
  See also CA 1-4R; 142; CANR 3

Heinlein, Robert A(nson)
  1907-1988 ...... **CLC 1, 3, 8, 14, 26, 55;**
                   DAM POP
  See also AAYA 17; CA 1-4R; 125;
  CANR 1, 20, 53; DLB 8; JRDA;
  MAICYA; MTCW; SATA 9, 69;
  SATA-Obit 56

Helforth, John
  See Doolittle, Hilda

Hellenhofferu, Vojtech Kapristian z
  See Hasek, Jaroslav (Matej Frantisek)

Heller, Joseph
  1923- .... **CLC 1, 3, 5, 8, 11, 36, 63; DA;**
             DAB; DAC; DAM MST, NOV, POP;
                                        WLC
  See also AITN 1; CA 5-8R; CABS 1;
  CANR 8, 42; DLB 2, 28; DLBY 80;
  INT CANR-8; MTCW

Hellman, Lillian (Florence)
  1906-1984 ...... **CLC 2, 4, 8, 14, 18, 34,**
                   44, 52; DAM DRAM; DC 1
  See also AITN 1, 2; CA 13-16R; 112;
  CANR 33; DLB 7; DLBY 84; MTCW

Helprin, Mark
  1947- .... **CLC 7, 10, 22, 32;**
                       DAM NOV, POP
  See also CA 81-84; CANR 47; DLBY 85;
  MTCW

Helvetius, Claude-Adrien
  1715-1771 .... **LC 26**

Helyar, Jane Penelope Josephine 1933-
  See Poole, Josephine
  See also CA 21-24R; CANR 10, 26;
  SATA 82

Hemans, Felicia 1793-1835 ...... **NCLC 29**
  See also DLB 96

Hemingway, Ernest (Miller)
  1899-1961 .... **CLC 1, 3, 6, 8, 10, 13, 19,**
                30, 34, 39, 41, 44, 50, 61, 80; DA; DAB;
                DAC; DAM MST, NOV; SSC 25; WLC
  See also AAYA 19; CA 77-80; CANR 34;
  CDALB 1917-1929; DLB 4, 9, 102;
  DLBD 1; DLBY 81, 87; MTCW

Hempel, Amy 1951- .... **CLC 39**
  See also CA 118; 137

Henderson, F. C.
  See Mencken, H(enry) L(ouis)

Henderson, Sylvia
  See Ashton-Warner, Sylvia (Constance)

Henley, Beth .... **CLC 23; DC 6**
  See also Henley, Elizabeth Becker
  See also CABS 3; DLBY 86

Henley, Elizabeth Becker 1952-
  See Henley, Beth
  See also CA 107; CANR 32; DAM DRAM,
  MST; MTCW

Henley, William Ernest
  1849-1903 .... **TCLC 8**
  See also CA 105; DLB 19

Hennissart, Martha
  See Lathen, Emma
  See also CA 85-88

Henry, O. .... **TCLC 1, 19; SSC 5; WLC**
  See also Porter, William Sydney

Henry, Patrick 1736-1799 .... **LC 25**

Henryson, Robert 1430(?)-1506(?).... **LC 20**
  See also DLB 146

Henry VIII 1491-1547............. **LC 10**

Henschke, Alfred
  See Klabund

Hentoff, Nat(han Irving) 1925- ..... **CLC 26**
  See also AAYA 4; CA 1-4R; CAAS 6;
  CANR 5, 25; CLR 1; INT CANR-25;
  JRDA; MAICYA; SATA 42, 69;
  SATA-Brief 27

Heppenstall, (John) Rayner
  1911-1981 .... **CLC 10**
  See also CA 1-4R; 103; CANR 29

Heraclitus
  c. 540B.C.-c. 450B.C......... **CMLC 22**
  See also DLB 176

Herbert, Frank (Patrick)
  1920-1986 ...... **CLC 12, 23, 35, 44, 85;**
                                      DAM POP
  See also AAYA 21; CA 53-56; 118;
  CANR 5, 43; DLB 8; INT CANR-5;
  MTCW; SATA 9, 37; SATA-Obit 47

Herbert, George
  1593-1633 .... **LC 24; DAB;**
                          DAM POET; PC 4
  See also CDBLB Before 1660; DLB 126

Herbert, Zbigniew
  1924- .... **CLC 9, 43; DAM POET**
  See also CA 89-92; CANR 36; MTCW

Herbst, Josephine (Frey)
  1897-1969 .... **CLC 34**
  See also CA 5-8R; 25-28R; DLB 9

Hergesheimer, Joseph
  1880-1954 .... **TCLC 11**
  See also CA 109; DLB 102, 9

Herlihy, James Leo 1927-1993 ...... **CLC 6**
  See also CA 1-4R; 143; CANR 2

Hermogenes fl. c. 175- .... **CMLC 6**

Hernandez, Jose 1834-1886 ...... **NCLC 17**

Herodotus c. 484B.C.-429B.C..... **CMLC 17**
  See also DLB 176

Herrick, Robert
  1591-1674 ..... **LC 13; DA; DAB; DAC;**
                 DAM MST, POP; PC 9
  See also DLB 126

Herring, Guilles
  See Somerville, Edith

Herriot, James
  1916-1995 .... **CLC 12; DAM POP**
  See also Wight, James Alfred
  See also AAYA 1; CA 148; CANR 40;
  SATA 86

Herrmann, Dorothy 1941-........ **CLC 44**
  See also CA 107

Herrmann, Taffy
  See Herrmann, Dorothy

Hersey, John (Richard)
  1914-1993 .... **CLC 1, 2, 7, 9, 40, 81, 97;**
                                      DAM POP
  See also CA 17-20R; 140; CANR 33;
  DLB 6; MTCW; SATA 25;
  SATA-Obit 76

Herzen, Aleksandr Ivanovich
  1812-1870 .... **NCLC 10, 61**

Herzl, Theodor 1860-1904....... **TCLC 36**

Herzog, Werner 1942-............ **CLC 16**
  See also CA 89-92

Hesiod c. 8th cent. B.C.- .... **CMLC 5**
  See also DLB 176

Hesse, Hermann
  1877-1962 .... **CLC 1, 2, 3, 6, 11, 17, 25,**
                69; DA; DAB; DAC; DAM MST, NOV;
                                   SSC 9; WLC
  See also CA 17-18; CAP 2; DLB 66;
  MTCW; SATA 50

Hewes, Cady
  See De Voto, Bernard (Augustine)

Heyen, William 1940- .... **CLC 13, 18**
  See also CA 33-36R; CAAS 9; DLB 5

Heyerdahl, Thor 1914-............ **CLC 26**
  See also CA 5-8R; CANR 5, 22; MTCW;
  SATA 2, 52

Heym, Georg (Theodor Franz Arthur)
  1887-1912 .... **TCLC 9**
  See also CA 106

Heym, Stefan 1913-.............. **CLC 41**
  See also CA 9-12R; CANR 4; DLB 69

Heyse, Paul (Johann Ludwig von)
  1830-1914 .... **TCLC 8**
  See also CA 104; DLB 129

Heyward, (Edwin) DuBose
  1885-1940 .... **TCLC 59**
  See also CA 108; DLB 7, 9, 45; SATA 21

Hibbert, Eleanor Alice Burford
1906-1993 . . . . **CLC 7; DAM POP**
See also BEST 90:4; CA 17-20R; 140;
CANR 9, 28; SATA 2; SATA-Obit 74

Hichens, Robert S. 1864-1950 . . . . . **TCLC 64**
See also DLB 153

Higgins, George V(incent)
1939- . . . . **CLC 4, 7, 10, 18**
See also CA 77-80; CAAS 5; CANR 17, 51;
DLB 2; DLBY 81; INT CANR-17;
MTCW

Higginson, Thomas Wentworth
1823-1911 . . . . **TCLC 36**
See also DLB 1, 64

Highet, Helen
See MacInnes, Helen (Clark)

Highsmith, (Mary) Patricia
1921-1995 . . . . **CLC 2, 4, 14, 42;**
DAM NOV, POP
See also CA 1-4R; 147; CANR 1, 20, 48;
MTCW

Highwater, Jamake (Mamake)
1942(?)- . . . . **CLC 12**
See also AAYA 7; CA 65-68; CAAS 7;
CANR 10, 34; CLR 17; DLB 52;
DLBY 85; JRDA; MAICYA; SATA 32,
69; SATA-Brief 30

Highway, Tomson
1951- . . . . . **CLC 92; DAC; DAM MULT**
See also CA 151; NNAL

Higuchi, Ichiyo 1872-1896 . . . . . . **NCLC 49**

Hijuelos, Oscar
1951- . . . . **CLC 65; DAM MULT, POP;**
HLC
See also BEST 90:1; CA 123; CANR 50;
DLB 145; HW

Hikmet, Nazim 1902(?)-1963 . . . . . . **CLC 40**
See also CA 141; 93-96

Hildegard von Bingen
1098-1179 . . . . **CMLC 20**
See also DLB 148

Hildesheimer, Wolfgang
1916-1991 . . . . **CLC 49**
See also CA 101; 135; DLB 69, 124

Hill, Geoffrey (William)
1932- . . . **CLC 5, 8, 18, 45; DAM POET**
See also CA 81-84; CANR 21;
CDBLB 1960 to Present; DLB 40;
MTCW

Hill, George Roy 1921- . . . . **CLC 26**
See also CA 110; 122

Hill, John
See Koontz, Dean R(ay)

Hill, Susan (Elizabeth)
1942- . . **CLC 4; DAB; DAM MST, NOV**
See also CA 33-36R; CANR 29; DLB 14,
139; MTCW

Hillerman, Tony
1925- . . . . **CLC 62; DAM POP**
See also AAYA 6; BEST 89:1; CA 29-32R;
CANR 21, 42; SATA 6

Hillesum, Etty 1914-1943 . . . . **TCLC 49**
See also CA 137

Hilliard, Noel (Harvey) 1929- . . . . . . **CLC 15**
See also CA 9-12R; CANR 7

Hillis, Rick 1956- . . . . **CLC 66**
See also CA 134

Hilton, James 1900-1954 . . . . **TCLC 21**
See also CA 108; DLB 34, 77; SATA 34

Himes, Chester (Bomar)
1909-1984 . . . . **CLC 2, 4, 7, 18, 58; BLC;**
DAM MULT
See also BW 2; CA 25-28R; 114; CANR 22;
DLB 2, 76, 143; MTCW

Hinde, Thomas . . . . **CLC 6, 11**
See also Chitty, Thomas Willes

Hindin, Nathan
See Bloch, Robert (Albert)

Hine, (William) Daryl 1936- . . . . **CLC 15**
See also CA 1-4R; CAAS 15; CANR 1, 20;
DLB 60

Hinkson, Katharine Tynan
See Tynan, Katharine

Hinton, S(usan) E(loise)
1950- . . . . **CLC 30; DA; DAB; DAC;**
DAM MST, NOV
See also AAYA 2; CA 81-84; CANR 32;
CLR 3, 23; JRDA; MAICYA; MTCW;
SATA 19, 58

Hippius, Zinaida . . . . **TCLC 9**
See also Gippius, Zinaida (Nikolayevna)

Hiraoka, Kimitake 1925-1970
See Mishima, Yukio
See also CA 97-100; 29-32R; DAM DRAM;
MTCW

Hirsch, E(ric) D(onald), Jr. 1928- . . . **CLC 79**
See also CA 25-28R; CANR 27, 51;
DLB 67; INT CANR-27; MTCW

Hirsch, Edward 1950- . . . . **CLC 31, 50**
See also CA 104; CANR 20, 42; DLB 120

Hitchcock, Alfred (Joseph)
1899-1980 . . . . **CLC 16**
See also CA 97-100; SATA 27;
SATA-Obit 24

Hitler, Adolf 1889-1945 . . . . **TCLC 53**
See also CA 117; 147

Hoagland, Edward 1932- . . . . **CLC 28**
See also CA 1-4R; CANR 2, 31, 57; DLB 6;
SATA 51

Hoban, Russell (Conwell)
1925- . . . . **CLC 7, 25; DAM NOV**
See also CA 5-8R; CANR 23, 37; CLR 3;
DLB 52; MAICYA; MTCW; SATA 1,
40, 78

Hobbes, Thomas 1588-1679 . . . . **LC 36**
See also DLB 151

Hobbs, Perry
See Blackmur, R(ichard) P(almer)

Hobson, Laura Z(ametkin)
1900-1986 . . . . **CLC 7, 25**
See also CA 17-20R; 118; CANR 55;
DLB 28; SATA 52

Hochhuth, Rolf
1931- . . . . . . **CLC 4, 11, 18; DAM DRAM**
See also CA 5-8R; CANR 33; DLB 124;
MTCW

Hochman, Sandra 1936- . . . . **CLC 3, 8**
See also CA 5-8R; DLB 5

Hochwaelder, Fritz
1911-1986 . . . . . . **CLC 36; DAM DRAM**
See also CA 29-32R; 120; CANR 42;
MTCW

Hochwalder, Fritz
See Hochwaelder, Fritz

Hocking, Mary (Eunice) 1921- . . . . . **CLC 13**
See also CA 101; CANR 18, 40

Hodgins, Jack 1938- . . . . **CLC 23**
See also CA 93-96; DLB 60

Hodgson, William Hope
1877(?)-1918 . . . . **TCLC 13**
See also CA 111; DLB 70, 153, 156

Hoeg, Peter 1957- . . . . **CLC 95**
See also CA 151

Hoffman, Alice
1952- . . . . **CLC 51; DAM NOV**
See also CA 77-80; CANR 34; MTCW

Hoffman, Daniel (Gerard)
1923- . . . . **CLC 6, 13, 23**
See also CA 1-4R; CANR 4; DLB 5

Hoffman, Stanley 1944- . . . . **CLC 5**
See also CA 77-80

Hoffman, William M(oses) 1939- . . . **CLC 40**
See also CA 57-60; CANR 11

Hoffmann, E(rnst) T(heodor) A(madeus)
1776-1822 . . . . **NCLC 2; SSC 13**
See also DLB 90; SATA 27

Hofmann, Gert 1931- . . . . **CLC 54**
See also CA 128

Hofmannsthal, Hugo von
1874-1929 . . . . **TCLC 11; DAM DRAM;**
DC 4
See also CA 106; 153; DLB 81, 118

Hogan, Linda
1947- . . . . **CLC 73; DAM MULT**
See also CA 120; CANR 45; DLB 175;
NNAL

Hogarth, Charles
See Creasey, John

Hogarth, Emmett
See Polonsky, Abraham (Lincoln)

Hogg, James 1770-1835 . . . . **NCLC 4**
See also DLB 93, 116, 159

Holbach, Paul Henri Thiry Baron
1723-1789 . . . . **LC 14**

Holberg, Ludvig 1684-1754 . . . . **LC 6**

Holden, Ursula 1921- . . . . **CLC 18**
See also CA 101; CAAS 8; CANR 22

Holderlin, (Johann Christian) Friedrich
1770-1843 . . . . **NCLC 16; PC 4**

Holdstock, Robert
See Holdstock, Robert P.

Holdstock, Robert P. 1948- . . . . **CLC 39**
See also CA 131

Holland, Isabelle 1920- . . . . **CLC 21**
See also AAYA 11; CA 21-24R; CANR 10,
25, 47; JRDA; MAICYA; SATA 8, 70

Holland, Marcus
See Caldwell, (Janet Miriam) Taylor
(Holland)

Hollander, John 1929- . . . . . . **CLC 2, 5, 8, 14**
See also CA 1-4R; CANR 1, 52; DLB 5;
SATA 13

Hollander, Paul
See Silverberg, Robert

Holleran, Andrew 1943(?)-......... **CLC 38**
See also CA 144

Hollinghurst, Alan 1954-....... **CLC 55, 91**
See also CA 114

Hollis, Jim
See Summers, Hollis (Spurgeon, Jr.)

Holly, Buddy 1936-1959 .... **TCLC 65**

Holmes, John
See Souster, (Holmes) Raymond

Holmes, John Clellon 1926-1988.... **CLC 56**
See also CA 9-12R; 125; CANR 4; DLB 16

Holmes, Oliver Wendell
1809-1894 .... **NCLC 14**
See also CDALB 1640-1865; DLB 1;
SATA 34

Holmes, Raymond
See Souster, (Holmes) Raymond

Holt, Victoria
See Hibbert, Eleanor Alice Burford

Holub, Miroslav 1923-............. **CLC 4**
See also CA 21-24R; CANR 10

Homer
c. 8th cent. B.C.-..... **CMLC 1, 16; DA;**
DAB; DAC; DAM MST, POET
See also DLB 176

Honig, Edwin 1919-.............. **CLC 33**
See also CA 5-8R; CAAS 8; CANR 4, 45;
DLB 5

Hood, Hugh (John Blagdon)
1928-.................... **CLC 15, 28**
See also CA 49-52; CAAS 17; CANR 1, 33;
DLB 53

Hood, Thomas 1799-1845........ **NCLC 16**
See also DLB 96

Hooker, (Peter) Jeremy 1941-...... **CLC 43**
See also CA 77-80; CANR 22; DLB 40

hooks, bell .... **CLC 94**
See also Watkins, Gloria

Hope, A(lec) D(erwent) 1907-.... **CLC 3, 51**
See also CA 21-24R; CANR 33; MTCW

Hope, Brian
See Creasey, John

Hope, Christopher (David Tully)
1944-....................... **CLC 52**
See also CA 106; CANR 47; SATA 62

Hopkins, Gerard Manley
1844-1889 .... **NCLC 17; DA; DAB;**
DAC; DAM MST, POET; PC 15; WLC
See also CDBLB 1890-1914; DLB 35, 57

Hopkins, John (Richard) 1931-...... **CLC 4**
See also CA 85-88

Hopkins, Pauline Elizabeth
1859-1930 .... **TCLC 28; BLC;**
DAM MULT
See also BW 2; CA 141; DLB 50

Hopkinson, Francis 1737-1791 ...... **LC 25**
See also DLB 31

Hopley-Woolrich, Cornell George 1903-1968
See Woolrich, Cornell
See also CA 13-14; CAP 1

Horatio
See Proust, (Valentin-Louis-George-Eugene-)
Marcel

Horgan, Paul (George Vincent O'Shaughnessy)
1903-1995 ..... **CLC 9, 53; DAM NOV**
See also CA 13-16R; 147; CANR 9, 35;
DLB 102; DLBY 85; INT CANR-9;
MTCW; SATA 13; SATA-Obit 84

Horn, Peter
See Kuttner, Henry

Hornem, Horace Esq.
See Byron, George Gordon (Noel)

Hornung, E(rnest) W(illiam)
1866-1921 .... **TCLC 59**
See also CA 108; DLB 70

Horovitz, Israel (Arthur)
1939- .... **CLC 56; DAM DRAM**
See also CA 33-36R; CANR 46; DLB 7

Horvath, Odon von
See Horvath, Oedoen von
See also DLB 85, 124

Horvath, Oedoen von 1901-1938... **TCLC 45**
See also Horvath, Odon von
See also CA 118

Horwitz, Julius 1920-1986........ **CLC 14**
See also CA 9-12R; 119; CANR 12

Hospital, Janette Turner 1942-..... **CLC 42**
See also CA 108; CANR 48

Hostos, E. M. de
See Hostos (y Bonilla), Eugenio Maria de

Hostos, Eugenio M. de
See Hostos (y Bonilla), Eugenio Maria de

Hostos, Eugenio Maria
See Hostos (y Bonilla), Eugenio Maria de

Hostos (y Bonilla), Eugenio Maria de
1839-1903 .... **TCLC 24**
See also CA 123; 131; HW

Houdini
See Lovecraft, H(oward) P(hillips)

Hougan, Carolyn 1943- .... **CLC 34**
See also CA 139

Household, Geoffrey (Edward West)
1900-1988 .... **CLC 11**
See also CA 77-80; 126; DLB 87; SATA 14;
SATA-Obit 59

Housman, A(lfred) E(dward)
1859-1936 ..... **TCLC 1, 10; DA; DAB;**
DAC; DAM MST, POET; PC 2
See also CA 104; 125; DLB 19; MTCW

Housman, Laurence 1865-1959 ..... **TCLC 7**
See also CA 106; 155; DLB 10; SATA 25

Howard, Elizabeth Jane 1923- ... **CLC 7, 29**
See also CA 5-8R; CANR 8

Howard, Maureen 1930- ..... **CLC 5, 14, 46**
See also CA 53-56; CANR 31; DLBY 83;
INT CANR-31; MTCW

Howard, Richard 1929- ...... **CLC 7, 10, 47**
See also AITN 1; CA 85-88; CANR 25;
DLB 5; INT CANR-25

Howard, Robert Ervin 1906-1936... **TCLC 8**
See also CA 105

Howard, Warren F.
See Pohl, Frederik

Howe, Fanny 1940- .... **CLC 47**
See also CA 117; SATA-Brief 52

Howe, Irving 1920-1993.......... **CLC 85**
See also CA 9-12R; 141; CANR 21, 50;
DLB 67; MTCW

Howe, Julia Ward 1819-1910 ..... **TCLC 21**
See also CA 117; DLB 1

Howe, Susan 1937-.............. **CLC 72**
See also DLB 120

Howe, Tina 1937-................ **CLC 48**
See also CA 109

Howell, James 1594(?)-1666 .... **LC 13**
See also DLB 151

Howells, W. D.
See Howells, William Dean

Howells, William D.
See Howells, William Dean

Howells, William Dean
1837-1920 .... **TCLC 7, 17, 41**
See also CA 104; 134; CDALB 1865-1917;
DLB 12, 64, 74, 79

Howes, Barbara 1914-1996 .... **CLC 15**
See also CA 9-12R; 151; CAAS 3;
CANR 53; SATA 5

Hrabal, Bohumil 1914-1997..... **CLC 13, 67**
See also CA 106; 156; CAAS 12; CANR 57

Hsun, Lu
See Lu Hsun

Hubbard, L(afayette) Ron(ald)
1911-1986 .... **CLC 43; DAM POP**
See also CA 77-80; 118; CANR 52

Huch, Ricarda (Octavia)
1864-1947 .... **TCLC 13**
See also CA 111; DLB 66

Huddle, David 1942- .... **CLC 49**
See also CA 57-60; CAAS 20; DLB 130

Hudson, Jeffrey
See Crichton, (John) Michael

Hudson, W(illiam) H(enry)
1841-1922 .... **TCLC 29**
See also CA 115; DLB 98, 153, 174;
SATA 35

Hueffer, Ford Madox
See Ford, Ford Madox

Hughart, Barry 1934-.............. **CLC 39**
See also CA 137

Hughes, Colin
See Creasey, John

Hughes, David (John) 1930- .... **CLC 48**
See also CA 116; 129; DLB 14

Hughes, Edward James
See Hughes, Ted
See also DAM MST, POET

Hughes, (James) Langston
1902-1967 ..... **CLC 1, 5, 10, 15, 35, 44;**
BLC; DA; DAB; DAC; DAM DRAM,
MST, MULT, POET; DC 3; PC 1;
SSC 6; WLC
See also AAYA 12; BW 1; CA 1-4R;
25-28R; CANR 1, 34; CDALB 1929-1941;
CLR 17; DLB 4, 7, 48, 51, 86; JRDA;
MAICYA; MTCW; SATA 4, 33

Hughes, Richard (Arthur Warren)
1900-1976 ...... **CLC 1, 11; DAM NOV**
See also CA 5-8R; 65-68; CANR 4;
DLB 15, 161; MTCW; SATA 8;
SATA-Obit 25

Hughes, Ted
1930- .... **CLC 2, 4, 9, 14, 37; DAB;**
DAC; PC 7
See also Hughes, Edward James
See also CA 1-4R; CANR 1, 33; CLR 3;
DLB 40, 161; MAICYA; MTCW;
SATA 49; SATA-Brief 27

Hugo, Richard F(ranklin)
1923-1982 .... **CLC 6, 18, 32;**
DAM POET
See also CA 49-52; 108; CANR 3; DLB 5

Hugo, Victor (Marie)
1802-1885 .... **NCLC 3, 10, 21; DA;**
DAB; DAC; DAM DRAM, MST, NOV,
POET; PC 17; WLC
See also DLB 119; SATA 47

Huidobro, Vicente
See Huidobro Fernandez, Vicente Garcia

Huidobro Fernandez, Vicente Garcia
1893-1948 .... **TCLC 31**
See also CA 131; HW

Hulme, Keri 1947- .... **CLC 39**
See also CA 125; INT 125

Hulme, T(homas) E(rnest)
1883-1917 .... **TCLC 21**
See also CA 117; DLB 19

Hume, David 1711-1776............. **LC 7**
See also DLB 104

Humphrey, William 1924-......... **CLC 45**
See also CA 77-80; DLB 6

Humphreys, Emyr Owen 1919-..... **CLC 47**
See also CA 5-8R; CANR 3, 24; DLB 15

Humphreys, Josephine 1945-.... **CLC 34, 57**
See also CA 121; 127; INT 127

Huneker, James Gibbons
1857-1921 .... **TCLC 65**
See also DLB 71

Hungerford, Pixie
See Brinsmead, H(esba) F(ay)

Hunt, E(verette) Howard, (Jr.)
1918- .... **CLC 3**
See also AITN 1; CA 45-48; CANR 2, 47

Hunt, Kyle
See Creasey, John

Hunt, (James Henry) Leigh
1784-1859 ...... **NCLC 1; DAM POET**

Hunt, Marsha 1946-.............. **CLC 70**
See also BW 2; CA 143

Hunt, Violet 1866-1942 .... **TCLC 53**
See also DLB 162

Hunter, E. Waldo
See Sturgeon, Theodore (Hamilton)

Hunter, Evan
1926- .... **CLC 11, 31; DAM POP**
See also CA 5-8R; CANR 5, 38; DLBY 82;
INT CANR-5; MTCW; SATA 25

Hunter, Kristin (Eggleston) 1931-... **CLC 35**
See also AITN 1; BW 1; CA 13-16R;
CANR 13; CLR 3; DLB 33;
INT CANR-13; MAICYA; SAAS 10;
SATA 12

Hunter, Mollie 1922-............. **CLC 21**
See also McIlwraith, Maureen Mollie
Hunter
See also AAYA 13; CANR 37; CLR 25;
DLB 161; JRDA; MAICYA; SAAS 7;
SATA 54

Hunter, Robert (?)-1734............. **LC 7**

Hurston, Zora Neale
1903-1960 .... **CLC 7, 30, 61; BLC; DA;**
DAC; DAM MST, MULT, NOV; SSC 4
See also AAYA 15; BW 1; CA 85-88;
DLB 51, 86; MTCW

Huston, John (Marcellus)
1906-1987 .... **CLC 20**
See also CA 73-76; 123; CANR 34; DLB 26

Hustvedt, Siri 1955-.............. **CLC 76**
See also CA 137

Hutten, Ulrich von 1488-1523....... **LC 16**

Huxley, Aldous (Leonard)
1894-1963 ..... **CLC 1, 3, 4, 5, 8, 11, 18,**
35, 79; DA; DAB; DAC; DAM MST,
NOV; WLC
See also AAYA 11; CA 85-88; CANR 44;
CDBLB 1914-1945; DLB 36, 100, 162;
MTCW; SATA 63

Huysmans, Charles Marie Georges
1848-1907
See Huysmans, Joris-Karl
See also CA 104

Huysmans, Joris-Karl........... TCLC 7, 69
See also Huysmans, Charles Marie Georges
See also DLB 123

Hwang, David Henry
1957- .... **CLC 55; DAM DRAM; DC 4**
See also CA 127; 132; INT 132

Hyde, Anthony 1946-............. **CLC 42**
See also CA 136

Hyde, Margaret O(ldroyd) 1917-... **CLC 21**
See also CA 1-4R; CANR 1, 36; CLR 23;
JRDA; MAICYA; SAAS 8; SATA 1, 42,
76

Hynes, James 1956(?)-............ **CLC 65**

Ian, Janis 1951- .... **CLC 21**
See also CA 105

Ibanez, Vicente Blasco
See Blasco Ibanez, Vicente

Ibarguengoitia, Jorge 1928-1983.... **CLC 37**
See also CA 124; 113; HW

Ibsen, Henrik (Johan)
1828-1906 .... **TCLC 2, 8, 16, 37, 52;**
DA; DAB; DAC; DAM DRAM, MST;
DC 2; WLC
See also CA 104; 141

Ibuse Masuji 1898-1993........... **CLC 22**
See also CA 127; 141

Ichikawa, Kon 1915-.............. **CLC 20**
See also CA 121

Idle, Eric 1943-.................. **CLC 21**
See also Monty Python
See also CA 116; CANR 35

Ignatow, David 1914-...... **CLC 4, 7, 14, 40**
See also CA 9-12R; CAAS 3; CANR 31, 57;
DLB 5

Ihimaera, Witi 1944- .... **CLC 46**
See also CA 77-80

Ilf, Ilya.......................... TCLC 21
See also Fainzilberg, Ilya Arnoldovich

Illyes, Gyula 1902-1983............ **PC 16**
See also CA 114; 109

Immermann, Karl (Lebrecht)
1796-1840 .... **NCLC 4, 49**
See also DLB 133

Inclan, Ramon (Maria) del Valle
See Valle-Inclan, Ramon (Maria) del

Infante, G(uillermo) Cabrera
See Cabrera Infante, G(uillermo)

Ingalls, Rachel (Holmes) 1940-..... **CLC 42**
See also CA 123; 127

Ingamells, Rex 1913-1955 .... **TCLC 35**

Inge, William (Motter)
1913-1973 .. **CLC 1, 8, 19; DAM DRAM**
See also CA 9-12R; CDALB 1941-1968;
DLB 7; MTCW

Ingelow, Jean 1820-1897 .... **NCLC 39**
See also DLB 35, 163; SATA 33

Ingram, Willis J.
See Harris, Mark

Innaurato, Albert (F.) 1948(?)- .. **CLC 21, 60**
See also CA 115; 122; INT 122

Innes, Michael
See Stewart, J(ohn) I(nnes) M(ackintosh)

Ionesco, Eugene
1909-1994 .... **CLC 1, 4, 6, 9, 11, 15, 41,**
86; DA; DAB; DAC; DAM DRAM,
MST; WLC
See also CA 9-12R; 144; CANR 55;
MTCW; SATA 7; SATA-Obit 79

Iqbal, Muhammad 1873-1938 ..... **TCLC 28**

Ireland, Patrick
See O'Doherty, Brian

Iron, Ralph
See Schreiner, Olive (Emilie Albertina)

Irving, John (Winslow)
1942- ..... **CLC 13, 23, 38; DAM NOV,**
POP
See also AAYA 8; BEST 89:3; CA 25-28R;
CANR 28; DLB 6; DLBY 82; MTCW

Irving, Washington
1783-1859 ..... **NCLC 2, 19; DA; DAB;**
DAM MST; SSC 2; WLC
See also CDALB 1640-1865; DLB 3, 11, 30,
59, 73, 74; YABC 2

Irwin, P. K.
See Page, P(atricia) K(athleen)

Isaacs, Susan 1943- ... **CLC 32; DAM POP**
See also BEST 89:1; CA 89-92; CANR 20,
41; INT CANR-20; MTCW

Isherwood, Christopher (William Bradshaw)
1904-1986 .... **CLC 1, 9, 11, 14, 44;**
DAM DRAM, NOV
See also CA 13-16R; 117; CANR 35;
DLB 15; DLBY 86; MTCW

Jimenez Mantecon, Juan
See Jimenez (Mantecon), Juan Ramon

Joel, Billy . . . . **CLC 26**
See also Joel, William Martin

Joel, William Martin 1949-
See Joel, Billy
See also CA 108

John of the Cross, St. 1542-1591 . . . . **LC 18**

Johnson, B(ryan) S(tanley William)
1933-1973 . . . . **CLC 6, 9**
See also CA 9-12R; 53-56; CANR 9;
DLB 14, 40

Johnson, Benj. F. of Boo
See Riley, James Whitcomb

Johnson, Benjamin F. of Boo
See Riley, James Whitcomb

Johnson, Charles (Richard)
1948- . . . . **CLC 7, 51, 65; BLC;**
DAM MULT
See also BW 2; CA 116; CAAS 18;
CANR 42; DLB 33

Johnson, Denis 1949- . . . . **CLC 52**
See also CA 117; 121; DLB 120

Johnson, Diane 1934- . . . . **CLC 5, 13, 48**
See also CA 41-44R; CANR 17, 40;
DLBY 80; INT CANR-17; MTCW

Johnson, Eyvind (Olof Verner)
1900-1976 . . . . **CLC 14**
See also CA 73-76; 69-72; CANR 34

Johnson, J. R.
See James, C(yril) L(ionel) R(obert)

Johnson, James Weldon
1871-1938 . . . . **TCLC 3, 19; BLC;**
DAM MULT, POET
See also BW 1; CA 104; 125;
CDALB 1917-1929; CLR 32; DLB 51;
MTCW; SATA 31

Johnson, Joyce 1935- . . . . **CLC 58**
See also CA 125; 129

Johnson, Lionel (Pigot)
1867-1902 . . . . **TCLC 19**
See also CA 117; DLB 19

Johnson, Mel
See Malzberg, Barry N(athaniel)

Johnson, Pamela Hansford
1912-1981 . . . . **CLC 1, 7, 27**
See also CA 1-4R; 104; CANR 2, 28;
DLB 15; MTCW

Johnson, Robert 1911(?)-1938 . . . . . **TCLC 69**

Johnson, Samuel
1709-1784 . . . . . **LC 15; DA; DAB; DAC;**
DAM MST; WLC
See also CDBLB 1660-1789; DLB 39, 95,
104, 142

Johnson, Uwe
1934-1984 . . . . **CLC 5, 10, 15, 40**
See also CA 1-4R; 112; CANR 1, 39;
DLB 75; MTCW

Johnston, George (Benson) 1913- . . . **CLC 51**
See also CA 1-4R; CANR 5, 20; DLB 88

Johnston, Jennifer 1930- . . . . **CLC 7**
See also CA 85-88; DLB 14

Jolley, (Monica) Elizabeth
1923- . . . . **CLC 46; SSC 19**
See also CA 127; CAAS 13

Jones, Arthur Llewellyn 1863-1947
See Machen, Arthur
See also CA 104

Jones, D(ouglas) G(ordon) 1929- . . . . **CLC 10**
See also CA 29-32R; CANR 13; DLB 53

Jones, David (Michael)
1895-1974 . . . . **CLC 2, 4, 7, 13, 42**
See also CA 9-12R; 53-56; CANR 28;
CDBLB 1945-1960; DLB 20, 100; MTCW

Jones, David Robert 1947-
See Bowie, David
See also CA 103

Jones, Diana Wynne 1934- . . . . **CLC 26**
See also AAYA 12; CA 49-52; CANR 4,
26, 56; CLR 23; DLB 161; JRDA;
MAICYA; SAAS 7; SATA 9, 70

Jones, Edward P. 1950- . . . . **CLC 76**
See also BW 2; CA 142

Jones, Gayl
1949- . . . . **CLC 6, 9; BLC; DAM MULT**
See also BW 2; CA 77-80; CANR 27;
DLB 33; MTCW

Jones, James 1921-1977 . . . . **CLC 1, 3, 10, 39**
See also AITN 1, 2; CA 1-4R; 69-72;
CANR 6; DLB 2, 143; MTCW

Jones, John J.
See Lovecraft, H(oward) P(hillips)

Jones, LeRoi . . . . **CLC 1, 2, 3, 5, 10, 14**
See also Baraka, Amiri

Jones, Louis B. . . . . **CLC 65**
See also CA 141

Jones, Madison (Percy, Jr.) 1925- . . . **CLC 4**
See also CA 13-16R; CAAS 11; CANR 7,
54; DLB 152

Jones, Mervyn 1922- . . . . **CLC 10, 52**
See also CA 45-48; CAAS 5; CANR 1;
MTCW

Jones, Mick 1956(?)- . . . . **CLC 30**

Jones, Nettie (Pearl) 1941- . . . . **CLC 34**
See also BW 2; CA 137; CAAS 20

Jones, Preston 1936-1979 . . . . **CLC 10**
See also CA 73-76; 89-92; DLB 7

Jones, Robert F(rancis) 1934- . . . . **CLC 7**
See also CA 49-52; CANR 2

Jones, Rod 1953- . . . . **CLC 50**
See also CA 128

Jones, Terence Graham Parry
1942- . . . . **CLC 21**
See also Jones, Terry; Monty Python
See also CA 112; 116; CANR 35; INT 116

Jones, Terry
See Jones, Terence Graham Parry
See also SATA 67; SATA-Brief 51

Jones, Thom 1945(?)- . . . . **CLC 81**

Jong, Erica
1942- . . . . **CLC 4, 6, 8, 18, 83;**
DAM NOV, POP
See also AITN 1; BEST 90:2; CA 73-76;
CANR 26, 52; DLB 2, 5, 28, 152;
INT CANR-26; MTCW

Jonson, Ben(jamin)
1572(?)-1637 . . . . . . **LC 6, 33; DA; DAB;**
DAC; DAM DRAM, MST, POET;
DC 4; PC 17; WLC
See also CDBLB Before 1660; DLB 62, 121

Jordan, June
1936- . . . . . **CLC 5, 11, 23; DAM MULT,**
POET
See also AAYA 2; BW 2; CA 33-36R;
CANR 25; CLR 10; DLB 38; MAICYA;
MTCW; SATA 4

Jordan, Pat(rick M.) 1941- . . . . **CLC 37**
See also CA 33-36R

Jorgensen, Ivar
See Ellison, Harlan (Jay)

Jorgenson, Ivar
See Silverberg, Robert

Josephus, Flavius c. 37-100 . . . . . **CMLC 13**

Josipovici, Gabriel 1940- . . . . **CLC 6, 43**
See also CA 37-40R; CAAS 8; CANR 47;
DLB 14

Joubert, Joseph 1754-1824 . . . . **NCLC 9**

Jouve, Pierre Jean 1887-1976 . . . . . . **CLC 47**
See also CA 65-68

Joyce, James (Augustine Aloysius)
1882-1941 . . . . **TCLC 3, 8, 16, 35, 52;**
DA; DAB; DAC; DAM MST, NOV,
POET; SSC 3; WLC
See also CA 104; 126; CDBLB 1914-1945;
DLB 10, 19, 36, 162; MTCW

Jozsef, Attila 1905-1937 . . . . **TCLC 22**
See also CA 116

Juana Ines de la Cruz 1651(?)-1695 . . . **LC 5**

Judd, Cyril
See Kornbluth, C(yril) M.; Pohl, Frederik

Julian of Norwich 1342(?)-1416(?) . . . . **LC 6**
See also DLB 146

Juniper, Alex
See Hospital, Janette Turner

Junius
See Luxemburg, Rosa

Just, Ward (Swift) 1935- . . . . **CLC 4, 27**
See also CA 25-28R; CANR 32;
INT CANR-32

Justice, Donald (Rodney)
1925- . . . . **CLC 6, 19; DAM POET**
See also CA 5-8R; CANR 26, 54;
DLBY 83; INT CANR-26

Juvenal c. 55-c. 127 . . . . **CMLC 8**

Juvenis
See Bourne, Randolph S(illiman)

Kacew, Romain 1914-1980
See Gary, Romain
See also CA 108; 102

Kadare, Ismail 1936- . . . . **CLC 52**

Kadohata, Cynthia . . . . **CLC 59**
See also CA 140

Kafka, Franz
1883-1924 . . . . **TCLC 2, 6, 13, 29, 47, 53;**
DA; DAB; DAC; DAM MST, NOV;
SSC 5; WLC
See also CA 105; 126; DLB 81; MTCW

Kahanovitsch, Pinkhes
See Der Nister

Kahn, Roger 1927- . . . . **CLC 30**
See also CA 25-28R; CANR 44; DLB 171;
SATA 37

Kain, Saul
See Sassoon, Siegfried (Lorraine)

Author Index

Kerr, Jean 1923-................ **CLC 22**
See also CA 5-8R; CANR 7; INT CANR-7

Kerr, M. E. .... **CLC 12, 35**
See also Meaker, Marijane (Agnes)
See also AAYA 2; CLR 29; SAAS 1

Kerr, Robert .... **CLC 55**

Kerrigan, (Thomas) Anthony
1918- .... **CLC 4, 6**
See also CA 49-52; CAAS 11; CANR 4

Kerry, Lois
See Duncan, Lois

Kesey, Ken (Elton)
1935- ...... **CLC 1, 3, 6, 11, 46, 64; DA;**
DAB; DAC; DAM MST, NOV, POP;
WLC
See also CA 1-4R; CANR 22, 38;
CDALB 1968-1988; DLB 2, 16; MTCW;
SATA 66

Kesselring, Joseph (Otto)
1902-1967 ..... **CLC 45; DAM DRAM,**
MST
See also CA 150

Kessler, Jascha (Frederick) 1929-.... **CLC 4**
See also CA 17-20R; CANR 8, 48

Kettelkamp, Larry (Dale) 1933- .... **CLC 12**
See also CA 29-32R; CANR 16; SAAS 3;
SATA 2

Key, Ellen 1849-1926........... **TCLC 65**

Keyber, Conny
See Fielding, Henry

Keyes, Daniel
1927- .... **CLC 80; DA; DAC;**
DAM MST, NOV
See also CA 17-20R; CANR 10, 26, 54;
SATA 37

Keynes, John Maynard
1883-1946 .... **TCLC 64**
See also CA 114; DLBD 10

Khanshendel, Chiron
See Rose, Wendy

Khayyam, Omar
1048-1131 .... **CMLC 11; DAM POET;**
PC 8

Kherdian, David 1931-........... **CLC 6, 9**
See also CA 21-24R; CAAS 2; CANR 39;
CLR 24; JRDA; MAICYA; SATA 16, 74

Khlebnikov, Velimir .... **TCLC 20**
See also Khlebnikov, Viktor Vladimirovich

Khlebnikov, Viktor Vladimirovich 1885-1922
See Khlebnikov, Velimir
See also CA 117

Khodasevich, Vladislav (Felitsianovich)
1886-1939 .... **TCLC 15**
See also CA 115

Kielland, Alexander Lange
1849-1906 .... **TCLC 5**
See also CA 104

Kiely, Benedict 1919-.......... **CLC 23, 43**
See also CA 1-4R; CANR 2; DLB 15

Kienzle, William X(avier)
1928- .... **CLC 25; DAM POP**
See also CA 93-96; CAAS 1; CANR 9, 31;
INT CANR-31; MTCW

Kierkegaard, Soren 1813-1855.... **NCLC 34**

Killens, John Oliver 1916-1987..... **CLC 10**
See also BW 2; CA 77-80; 123; CAAS 2;
CANR 26; DLB 33

Killigrew, Anne 1660-1685.......... **LC 4**
See also DLB 131

Kim
See Simenon, Georges (Jacques Christian)

Kincaid, Jamaica
1949- .... **CLC 43, 68; BLC;**
DAM MULT, NOV
See also AAYA 13; BW 2; CA 125;
CANR 47; DLB 157

King, Francis (Henry)
1923- .... **CLC 8, 53; DAM NOV**
See also CA 1-4R; CANR 1, 33; DLB 15,
139; MTCW

King, Martin Luther, Jr.
1929-1968 .... **CLC 83; BLC; DA; DAB;**
DAC; DAM MST, MULT
See also BW 2; CA 25-28; CANR 27, 44;
CAP 2; MTCW; SATA 14

King, Stephen (Edwin)
1947- .... **CLC 12, 26, 37, 61;**
DAM NOV, POP; SSC 17
See also AAYA 1, 17; BEST 90:1;
CA 61-64; CANR 1, 30, 52; DLB 143;
DLBY 80; JRDA; MTCW; SATA 9, 55

King, Steve
See King, Stephen (Edwin)

King, Thomas
1943- ..... **CLC 89; DAC; DAM MULT**
See also CA 144; DLB 175; NNAL

Kingman, Lee.................... **CLC 17**
See also Natti, (Mary) Lee
See also SAAS 3; SATA 1, 67

Kingsley, Charles 1819-1875..... **NCLC 35**
See also DLB 21, 32, 163; YABC 2

Kingsley, Sidney 1906-1995........ **CLC 44**
See also CA 85-88; 147; DLB 7

Kingsolver, Barbara
1955- .... **CLC 55, 81; DAM POP**
See also AAYA 15; CA 129; 134; INT 134

Kingston, Maxine (Ting Ting) Hong
1940- .... **CLC 12, 19, 58; DAM MULT,**
NOV
See also AAYA 8; CA 69-72; CANR 13,
38; DLB 173; DLBY 80; INT CANR-13;
MTCW; SATA 53

Kinnell, Galway
1927- .... **CLC 1, 2, 3, 5, 13, 29**
See also CA 9-12R; CANR 10, 34; DLB 5;
DLBY 87; INT CANR-34; MTCW

Kinsella, Thomas 1928- .... **CLC 4, 19**
See also CA 17-20R; CANR 15; DLB 27;
MTCW

Kinsella, W(illiam) P(atrick)
1935- .... **CLC 27, 43; DAC;**
DAM NOV, POP
See also AAYA 7; CA 97-100; CAAS 7;
CANR 21, 35; INT CANR-21; MTCW

Kipling, (Joseph) Rudyard
1865-1936 ...... **TCLC 8, 17; DA; DAB;**
DAC; DAM MST, POET; PC 3; SSC 5;
WLC
See also CA 105; 120; CANR 33;
CDBLB 1890-1914; CLR 39; DLB 19, 34,
141, 156; MAICYA; MTCW; YABC 2

Kirkup, James 1918- .... **CLC 1**
See also CA 1-4R; CAAS 4; CANR 2;
DLB 27; SATA 12

Kirkwood, James 1930(?)-1989 ...... **CLC 9**
See also AITN 2; CA 1-4R; 128; CANR 6,
40

Kirshner, Sidney
See Kingsley, Sidney

Kis, Danilo 1935-1989 .... **CLC 57**
See also CA 109; 118; 129; MTCW

Kivi, Aleksis 1834-1872........ **NCLC 30**

Kizer, Carolyn (Ashley)
1925- ..... **CLC 15, 39, 80; DAM POET**
See also CA 65-68; CAAS 5; CANR 24;
DLB 5, 169

Klabund 1890-1928.............. **TCLC 44**
See also DLB 66

Klappert, Peter 1942-............. **CLC 57**
See also CA 33-36R; DLB 5

Klein, A(braham) M(oses)
1909-1972 .... **CLC 19; DAB; DAC;**
DAM MST
See also CA 101; 37-40R; DLB 68

Klein, Norma 1938-1989 .... **CLC 30**
See also AAYA 2; CA 41-44R; 128;
CANR 15, 37; CLR 2, 19;
INT CANR-15; JRDA; MAICYA;
SAAS 1; SATA 7, 57

Klein, T(heodore) E(ibon) D(onald)
1947- .... **CLC 34**
See also CA 119; CANR 44

Kleist, Heinrich von
1777-1811 .... **NCLC 2, 37;**
DAM DRAM; SSC 22
See also DLB 90

Klima, Ivan 1931-..... **CLC 56; DAM NOV**
See also CA 25-28R; CANR 17, 50

Klimentov, Andrei Platonovich 1899-1951
See Platonov, Andrei
See also CA 108

Klinger, Friedrich Maximilian von
1752-1831 .... **NCLC 1**
See also DLB 94

Klopstock, Friedrich Gottlieb
1724-1803 .... **NCLC 11**
See also DLB 97

Knapp, Caroline 1959-............ **CLC 99**
See also CA 154

Knebel, Fletcher 1911-1993........ **CLC 14**
See also AITN 1; CA 1-4R; 140; CAAS 3;
CANR 1, 36; SATA 36; SATA-Obit 75

Knickerbocker, Diedrich
See Irving, Washington

Knight, Etheridge
1931-1991 .... **CLC 40; BLC;**
DAM POET; PC 14
See also BW 1; CA 21-24R; 133; CANR 23;
DLB 41

Knight, Sarah Kemble 1666-1727 ..... **LC 7**
See also DLB 24

Knister, Raymond 1899-1932...... **TCLC 56**
See also DLB 68

Knowles, John
1926- ...... **CLC 1, 4, 10, 26; DA; DAC;
DAM MST, NOV**
See also AAYA 10; CA 17-20R; CANR 40;
CDALB 1968-1988; DLB 6; MTCW;
SATA 8, 89

Knox, Calvin M.
See Silverberg, Robert

Knox, John   c. 1505-1572 .... **LC 37**
See also DLB 132

Knye, Cassandra
See Disch, Thomas M(ichael)

Koch, C(hristopher) J(ohn)   1932- ... **CLC 42**
See also CA 127

Koch, Christopher
See Koch, C(hristopher) J(ohn)

Koch, Kenneth
1925- .... **CLC 5, 8, 44; DAM POET**
See also CA 1-4R; CANR 6, 36, 57; DLB 5;
INT CANR-36; SATA 65

Kochanowski, Jan   1530-1584 .... **LC 10**

Kock, Charles Paul de
1794-1871 .... **NCLC 16**

Koda Shigeyuki   1867-1947
See Rohan, Koda
See also CA 121

Koestler, Arthur
1905-1983 .... **CLC 1, 3, 6, 8, 15, 33**
See also CA 1-4R; 109; CANR 1, 33;
CDBLB 1945-1960; DLBY 83; MTCW

Kogawa, Joy Nozomi
1935- ...... **CLC 78; DAC; DAM MST,
MULT**
See also CA 101; CANR 19

Kohout, Pavel   1928- .... **CLC 13**
See also CA 45-48; CANR 3

Koizumi, Yakumo
See Hearn, (Patricio) Lafcadio (Tessima
Carlos)

Kolmar, Gertrud   1894-1943 .... **TCLC 40**

Komunyakaa, Yusef   1947- ...... **CLC 86, 94**
See also CA 147; DLB 120

Konrad, George
See Konrad, Gyoergy

Konrad, Gyoergy   1933- ...... **CLC 4, 10, 73**
See also CA 85-88

Konwicki, Tadeusz   1926- ..... **CLC 8, 28, 54**
See also CA 101; CAAS 9; CANR 39;
MTCW

Koontz, Dean R(ay)
1945- ...... **CLC 78; DAM NOV, POP**
See also AAYA 9; BEST 89:3, 90:2;
CA 108; CANR 19, 36, 52; MTCW;
SATA 92

Kopit, Arthur (Lee)
1937- ..... **CLC 1, 18, 33; DAM DRAM**
See also AITN 1; CA 81-84; CABS 3;
DLB 7; MTCW

Kops, Bernard   1926- .... **CLC 4**
See also CA 5-8R; DLB 13

Kornbluth, C(yril) M.   1923-1958 .... **TCLC 8**
See also CA 105; DLB 8

Korolenko, V. G.
See Korolenko, Vladimir Galaktionovich

Korolenko, Vladimir
See Korolenko, Vladimir Galaktionovich

Korolenko, Vladimir G.
See Korolenko, Vladimir Galaktionovich

Korolenko, Vladimir Galaktionovich
1853-1921 .... **TCLC 22**
See also CA 121

Korzybski, Alfred (Habdank Skarbek)
1879-1950 .... **TCLC 61**
See also CA 123

Kosinski, Jerzy (Nikodem)
1933-1991 .... **CLC 1, 2, 3, 6, 10, 15, 53,
70; DAM NOV**
See also CA 17-20R; 134; CANR 9, 46;
DLB 2; DLBY 82; MTCW

Kostelanetz, Richard (Cory)   1940- .. **CLC 28**
See also CA 13-16R; CAAS 8; CANR 38

Kostrowitzki, Wilhelm Apollinaris de
1880-1918
See Apollinaire, Guillaume
See also CA 104

Kotlowitz, Robert   1924- .... **CLC 4**
See also CA 33-36R; CANR 36

Kotzebue, August (Friedrich Ferdinand) von
1761-1819 .... **NCLC 25**
See also DLB 94

Kotzwinkle, William   1938- ... **CLC 5, 14, 35**
See also CA 45-48; CANR 3, 44; CLR 6;
DLB 173; MAICYA; SATA 24, 70

Kowna, Stancy
See Szymborska, Wislawa

Kozol, Jonathan   1936- .... **CLC 17**
See also CA 61-64; CANR 16, 45

Kozoll, Michael   1940(?)- .... **CLC 35**

Kramer, Kathryn   19(?)- .... **CLC 34**

Kramer, Larry   1935- .. **CLC 42; DAM POP**
See also CA 124; 126

Krasicki, Ignacy   1735-1801 .... **NCLC 8**

Krasinski, Zygmunt   1812-1859 .... **NCLC 4**

Kraus, Karl   1874-1936 .... **TCLC 5**
See also CA 104; DLB 118

Kreve (Mickevicius), Vincas
1882-1954 .... **TCLC 27**

Kristeva, Julia   1941- .... **CLC 77**
See also CA 154

Kristofferson, Kris   1936- .... **CLC 26**
See also CA 104

Krizanc, John   1956- .... **CLC 57**

Krleza, Miroslav   1893-1981 .... **CLC 8**
See also CA 97-100; 105; CANR 50;
DLB 147

Kroetsch, Robert
1927- .... **CLC 5, 23, 57; DAC;
DAM POET**
See also CA 17-20R; CANR 8, 38; DLB 53;
MTCW

Kroetz, Franz
See Kroetz, Franz Xaver

Kroetz, Franz Xaver   1946- .... **CLC 41**
See also CA 130

Kroker, Arthur   1945- .... **CLC 77**

Kropotkin, Peter (Aleksieevich)
1842-1921 .... **TCLC 36**
See also CA 119

Krotkov, Yuri   1917- .... **CLC 19**
See also CA 102

Krumb
See Crumb, R(obert)

Krumgold, Joseph (Quincy)
1908-1980 .... **CLC 12**
See also CA 9-12R; 101; CANR 7;
MAICYA; SATA 1, 48; SATA-Obit 23

Krumwitz
See Crumb, R(obert)

Krutch, Joseph Wood   1893-1970.... **CLC 24**
See also CA 1-4R; 25-28R; CANR 4;
DLB 63

Krutzch, Gus
See Eliot, T(homas) S(tearns)

Krylov, Ivan Andreevich
1768(?)-1844 .... **NCLC 1**
See also DLB 150

Kubin, Alfred (Leopold Isidor)
1877-1959 .... **TCLC 23**
See also CA 112; 149; DLB 81

Kubrick, Stanley   1928- .... **CLC 16**
See also CA 81-84; CANR 33; DLB 26

Kumin, Maxine (Winokur)
1925- ..... **CLC 5, 13, 28; DAM POET;
PC 15**
See also AITN 2; CA 1-4R; CAAS 8;
CANR 1, 21; DLB 5; MTCW; SATA 12

Kundera, Milan
1929- .... **CLC 4, 9, 19, 32, 68;
DAM NOV; SSC 24**
See also AAYA 2; CA 85-88; CANR 19,
52; MTCW

Kunene, Mazisi (Raymond)   1930-... **CLC 85**
See also BW 1; CA 125; DLB 117

Kunitz, Stanley (Jasspon)
1905- .... **CLC 6, 11, 14**
See also CA 41-44R; CANR 26, 57;
DLB 48; INT CANR-26; MTCW

Kunze, Reiner   1933- .... **CLC 10**
See also CA 93-96; DLB 75

Kuprin, Aleksandr Ivanovich
1870-1938 .... **TCLC 5**
See also CA 104

Kureishi, Hanif   1954(?)- .... **CLC 64**
See also CA 139

Kurosawa, Akira
1910- .... **CLC 16; DAM MULT**
See also AAYA 11; CA 101; CANR 46

Kushner, Tony
1957(?)- .... **CLC 81; DAM DRAM**
See also CA 144

Kuttner, Henry   1915-1958 .... **TCLC 10**
See also CA 107; DLB 8

Kuzma, Greg   1944- .... **CLC 7**
See also CA 33-36R

Kuzmin, Mikhail   1872(?)-1936 .... **TCLC 40**

Kyd, Thomas
1558-1594 .... **LC 22; DAM DRAM;
DC 3**
See also DLB 62

Kyprianos, Iossif
See Samarakis, Antonis

La Bruyere, Jean de 1645-1696...... **LC 17**

Lacan, Jacques (Marie Emile)
1901-1981 .... **CLC 75**
See also CA 121; 104

Laclos, Pierre Ambroise Francois Choderlos
de 1741-1803 .... **NCLC 4**

La Colere, Francois
See Aragon, Louis

Lacolere, Francois
See Aragon, Louis

La Deshabilleuse
See Simenon, Georges (Jacques Christian)

Lady Gregory
See Gregory, Isabella Augusta (Persse)

Lady of Quality, A
See Bagnold, Enid

La Fayette, Marie (Madelaine Pioche de la
Vergne Comtes 1634-1693....... **LC 2**

Lafayette, Rene
See Hubbard, L(afayette) Ron(ald)

Laforgue, Jules
1860-1887 .... **NCLC 5, 53; PC 14;**
SSC 20

Lagerkvist, Paer (Fabian)
1891-1974 .... **CLC 7, 10, 13, 54;**
DAM DRAM, NOV
See also Lagerkvist, Par
See also CA 85-88; 49-52; MTCW

Lagerkvist, Par .... **SSC 12**
See also Lagerkvist, Paer (Fabian)

Lagerloef, Selma (Ottiliana Lovisa)
1858-1940 .... **TCLC 4, 36**
See also Lagerlof, Selma (Ottiliana Lovisa)
See also CA 108; SATA 15

Lagerlof, Selma (Ottiliana Lovisa)
See Lagerloef, Selma (Ottiliana Lovisa)
See also CLR 7; SATA 15

La Guma, (Justin) Alex(ander)
1925-1985 .... **CLC 19; DAM NOV**
See also BW 1; CA 49-52; 118; CANR 25;
DLB 117; MTCW

Laidlaw, A. K.
See Grieve, C(hristopher) M(urray)

Lainez, Manuel Mujica
See Mujica Lainez, Manuel
See also HW

Laing, R(onald) D(avid)
1927-1989 .... **CLC 95**
See also CA 107; 129; CANR 34; MTCW

Lamartine, Alphonse (Marie Louis Prat) de
1790-1869 ..... **NCLC 11; DAM POET;**
PC 16

Lamb, Charles
1775-1834 ...... **NCLC 10; DA; DAB;**
DAC; DAM MST; WLC
See also CDBLB 1789-1832; DLB 93, 107,
163; SATA 17

Lamb, Lady Caroline 1785-1828.. **NCLC 38**
See also DLB 116

Lamming, George (William)
1927- .... **CLC 2, 4, 66; BLC;**
DAM MULT
See also BW 2; CA 85-88; CANR 26;
DLB 125; MTCW

L'Amour, Louis (Dearborn)
1908-1988 .... **CLC 25, 55; DAM NOV,**
POP
See also AAYA 16; AITN 2; BEST 89:2;
CA 1-4R; 125; CANR 3, 25, 40;
DLBY 80; MTCW

Lampedusa, Giuseppe (Tomasi) di
1896-1957 .... **TCLC 13**
See also Tomasi di Lampedusa, Giuseppe
See also DLB 177

Lampman, Archibald 1861-1899 .. **NCLC 25**
See also DLB 92

Lancaster, Bruce 1896-1963........ **CLC 36**
See also CA 9-10; CAP 1; SATA 9

Lanchester, John.................. **CLC 99**

Landau, Mark Alexandrovich
See Aldanov, Mark (Alexandrovich)

Landau-Aldanov, Mark Alexandrovich
See Aldanov, Mark (Alexandrovich)

Landis, Jerry
See Simon, Paul (Frederick)

Landis, John 1950-............... **CLC 26**
See also CA 112; 122

Landolfi, Tommaso 1908-1979... **CLC 11, 49**
See also CA 127; 117; DLB 177

Landon, Letitia Elizabeth
1802-1838 .... **NCLC 15**
See also DLB 96

Landor, Walter Savage
1775-1864 .... **NCLC 14**
See also DLB 93, 107

Landwirth, Heinz 1927-
See Lind, Jakov
See also CA 9-12R; CANR 7

Lane, Patrick
1939- .... **CLC 25; DAM POET**
See also CA 97-100; CANR 54; DLB 53;
INT 97-100

Lang, Andrew 1844-1912........ **TCLC 16**
See also CA 114; 137; DLB 98, 141;
MAICYA; SATA 16

Lang, Fritz 1890-1976 .... **CLC 20**
See also CA 77-80; 69-72; CANR 30

Lange, John
See Crichton, (John) Michael

Langer, Elinor 1939- .... **CLC 34**
See also CA 121

Langland, William
1330(?)-1400(?) ...... **LC 19; DA; DAB;**
DAC; DAM MST, POET
See also DLB 146

Langstaff, Launcelot
See Irving, Washington

Lanier, Sidney
1842-1881 ...... **NCLC 6; DAM POET**
See also DLB 64; DLBD 13; MAICYA;
SATA 18

Lanyer, Aemilia 1569-1645 ...... **LC 10, 30**
See also DLB 121

Lao Tzu .... **CMLC 7**

Lapine, James (Elliot) 1949-....... **CLC 39**
See also CA 123; 130; CANR 54; INT 130

Larbaud, Valery (Nicolas)
1881-1957 .... **TCLC 9**
See also CA 106; 152

Lardner, Ring
See Lardner, Ring(gold) W(ilmer)

Lardner, Ring W., Jr.
See Lardner, Ring(gold) W(ilmer)

Lardner, Ring(gold) W(ilmer)
1885-1933 .... **TCLC 2, 14**
See also CA 104; 131; CDALB 1917-1929;
DLB 11, 25, 86; MTCW

Laredo, Betty
See Codrescu, Andrei

Larkin, Maia
See Wojciechowska, Maia (Teresa)

Larkin, Philip (Arthur)
1922-1985 .... **CLC 3, 5, 8, 9, 13, 18, 33,**
39, 64; DAB; DAM MST, POET
See also CA 5-8R; 117; CANR 24;
CDBLB 1960 to Present; DLB 27;
MTCW

Larra (y Sanchez de Castro), Mariano Jose de
1809-1837 .... **NCLC 17**

Larsen, Eric 1941- .... **CLC 55**
See also CA 132

Larsen, Nella
1891-1964 .... **CLC 37; BLC;**
DAM MULT
See also BW 1; CA 125; DLB 51

Larson, Charles R(aymond) 1938-... **CLC 31**
See also CA 53-56; CANR 4

Larson, Jonathan 1961(?)-1996..... **CLC 99**

Las Casas, Bartolome de 1474-1566.. **LC 31**

Lasker-Schueler, Else 1869-1945 .. **TCLC 57**
See also DLB 66, 124

Latham, Jean Lee 1902-........... **CLC 12**
See also AITN 1; CA 5-8R; CANR 7;
MAICYA; SATA 2, 68

Latham, Mavis
See Clark, Mavis Thorpe

Lathen, Emma................... **CLC 2**
See also Hennissart, Martha; Latsis, Mary
J(ane)

Lathrop, Francis
See Leiber, Fritz (Reuter, Jr.)

Latsis, Mary J(ane)
See Lathen, Emma
See also CA 85-88

Lattimore, Richmond (Alexander)
1906-1984 .... **CLC 3**
See also CA 1-4R; 112; CANR 1

Laughlin, James 1914-............ **CLC 49**
See also CA 21-24R; CAAS 22; CANR 9,
47; DLB 48

Laurence, (Jean) Margaret (Wemyss)
1926-1987 .... **CLC 3, 6, 13, 50, 62;**
DAC; DAM MST; SSC 7
See also CA 5-8R; 121; CANR 33; DLB 53;
MTCW; SATA-Obit 50

Laurent, Antoine 1952- .... **CLC 50**

Lauscher, Hermann
See Hesse, Hermann

Lautreamont, Comte de
 1846-1870 . . . . **NCLC 12; SSC 14**

Laverty, Donald
 See Blish, James (Benjamin)

Lavin, Mary
 1912-1996 . . . . **CLC 4, 18, 99; SSC 4**
 See also CA 9-12R; 151; CANR 33;
 DLB 15; MTCW

Lavond, Paul Dennis
 See Kornbluth, C(yril) M.; Pohl, Frederik

Lawler, Raymond Evenor 1922- . . . . **CLC 58**
 See also CA 103

Lawrence, D(avid) H(erbert Richards)
 1885-1930 . . . . **TCLC 2, 9, 16, 33, 48, 61;**
 DA; DAB; DAC; DAM MST, NOV,
 POET; SSC 4, 19; WLC
 See also CA 104; 121; CDBLB 1914-1945;
 DLB 10, 19, 36, 98, 162; MTCW

Lawrence, T(homas) E(dward)
 1888-1935 . . . . **TCLC 18**
 See also Dale, Colin
 See also CA 115

Lawrence of Arabia
 See Lawrence, T(homas) E(dward)

Lawson, Henry (Archibald Hertzberg)
 1867-1922 . . . . **TCLC 27; SSC 18**
 See also CA 120

Lawton, Dennis
 See Faust, Frederick (Schiller)

Laxness, Halldor . . . . **CLC 25**
 See also Gudjonsson, Halldor Kiljan

Layamon fl. c. 1200- . . . . **CMLC 10**
 See also DLB 146

Laye, Camara
 1928-1980 . . . . **CLC 4, 38; BLC;**
 DAM MULT
 See also BW 1; CA 85-88; 97-100;
 CANR 25; MTCW

Layton, Irving (Peter)
 1912- . . . . **CLC 2, 15; DAC; DAM MST,**
 POET
 See also CA 1-4R; CANR 2, 33, 43;
 DLB 88; MTCW

Lazarus, Emma 1849-1887 . . . . **NCLC 8**

Lazarus, Felix
 See Cable, George Washington

Lazarus, Henry
 See Slavitt, David R(ytman)

Lea, Joan
 See Neufeld, John (Arthur)

Leacock, Stephen (Butler)
 1869-1944 . . **TCLC 2; DAC; DAM MST**
 See also CA 104; 141; DLB 92

Lear, Edward 1812-1888 . . . . **NCLC 3**
 See also CLR 1; DLB 32, 163, 166;
 MAICYA; SATA 18

Lear, Norman (Milton) 1922- . . . . . . **CLC 12**
 See also CA 73-76

Leavis, F(rank) R(aymond)
 1895-1978 . . . . **CLC 24**
 See also CA 21-24R; 77-80; CANR 44;
 MTCW

Leavitt, David 1961- . . . **CLC 34; DAM POP**
 See also CA 116; 122; CANR 50; DLB 130;
 INT 122

Leblanc, Maurice (Marie Emile)
 1864-1941 . . . . **TCLC 49**
 See also CA 110

Lebowitz, Fran(ces Ann)
 1951(?)- . . . . **CLC 11, 36**
 See also CA 81-84; CANR 14;
 INT CANR-14; MTCW

Lebrecht, Peter
 See Tieck, (Johann) Ludwig

le Carre, John . . . . **CLC 3, 5, 9, 15, 28**
 See also Cornwell, David (John Moore)
 See also BEST 89:4; CDBLB 1960 to
 Present; DLB 87

Le Clezio, J(ean) M(arie) G(ustave)
 1940- . . . . **CLC 31**
 See also CA 116; 128; DLB 83

Leconte de Lisle, Charles-Marie-Rene
 1818-1894 . . . . **NCLC 29**

Le Coq, Monsieur
 See Simenon, Georges (Jacques Christian)

Leduc, Violette 1907-1972 . . . . **CLC 22**
 See also CA 13-14; 33-36R; CAP 1

Ledwidge, Francis 1887(?)-1917 . . . **TCLC 23**
 See also CA 123; DLB 20

Lee, Andrea
 1953- . . . . . **CLC 36; BLC; DAM MULT**
 See also BW 1; CA 125

Lee, Andrew
 See Auchincloss, Louis (Stanton)

Lee, Chang-rae 1965- . . . . **CLC 91**
 See also CA 148

Lee, Don L. . . . . **CLC 2**
 See also Madhubuti, Haki R.

Lee, George W(ashington)
 1894-1976 . . . . **CLC 52; BLC;**
 DAM MULT
 See also BW 1; CA 125; DLB 51

Lee, (Nelle) Harper
 1926- . . . . **CLC 12, 60; DA; DAB; DAC;**
 DAM MST, NOV; WLC
 See also AAYA 13; CA 13-16R; CANR 51;
 CDALB 1941-1968; DLB 6; MTCW;
 SATA 11

Lee, Helen Elaine 1959(?)- . . . . **CLC 86**
 See also CA 148

Lee, Julian
 See Latham, Jean Lee

Lee, Larry
 See Lee, Lawrence

Lee, Laurie
 1914- . . . . **CLC 90; DAB; DAM POP**
 See also CA 77-80; CANR 33; DLB 27;
 MTCW

Lee, Lawrence 1941-1990 . . . . **CLC 34**
 See also CA 131; CANR 43

Lee, Manfred B(ennington)
 1905-1971 . . . . **CLC 11**
 See also Queen, Ellery
 See also CA 1-4R; 29-32R; CANR 2;
 DLB 137

Lee, Stan 1922- . . . . **CLC 17**
 See also AAYA 5; CA 108; 111; INT 111

Lee, Tanith 1947- . . . . **CLC 46**
 See also AAYA 15; CA 37-40R; CANR 53;
 SATA 8, 88

Lee, Vernon . . . . **TCLC 5**
 See also Paget, Violet
 See also DLB 57, 153, 156, 174

Lee, William
 See Burroughs, William S(eward)

Lee, Willy
 See Burroughs, William S(eward)

Lee-Hamilton, Eugene (Jacob)
 1845-1907 . . . . **TCLC 22**
 See also CA 117

Leet, Judith 1935- . . . . **CLC 11**

Le Fanu, Joseph Sheridan
 1814-1873 . . . . **NCLC 9, 58; DAM POP;**
 SSC 14
 See also DLB 21, 70, 159

Leffland, Ella 1931- . . . . **CLC 19**
 See also CA 29-32R; CANR 35; DLBY 84;
 INT CANR-35; SATA 65

Leger, Alexis
 See Leger, (Marie-Rene Auguste) Alexis
 Saint-Leger

Leger, (Marie-Rene Auguste) Alexis
 Saint-Leger
 1887-1975 . . . . **CLC 11; DAM POET**
 See also Perse, St.-John
 See also CA 13-16R; 61-64; CANR 43;
 MTCW

Leger, Saintleger
 See Leger, (Marie-Rene Auguste) Alexis
 Saint-Leger

Le Guin, Ursula K(roeber)
 1929- . . . . . . **CLC 8, 13, 22, 45, 71; DAB;**
 DAC; DAM MST, POP; SSC 12
 See also AAYA 9; AITN 1; CA 21-24R;
 CANR 9, 32, 52; CDALB 1968-1988;
 CLR 3, 28; DLB 8, 52; INT CANR-32;
 JRDA; MAICYA; MTCW; SATA 4, 52

Lehmann, Rosamond (Nina)
 1901-1990 . . . . **CLC 5**
 See also CA 77-80; 131; CANR 8; DLB 15

Leiber, Fritz (Reuter, Jr.)
 1910-1992 . . . . **CLC 25**
 See also CA 45-48; 139; CANR 2, 40;
 DLB 8; MTCW; SATA 45;
 SATA-Obit 73

Leibniz, Gottfried Wilhelm von
 1646-1716 . . . . **LC 35**
 See also DLB 168

Leimbach, Martha 1963-
 See Leimbach, Marti
 See also CA 130

Leimbach, Marti . . . . **CLC 65**
 See also Leimbach, Martha

Leino, Eino . . . . **TCLC 24**
 See also Loennbohm, Armas Eino Leopold

Leiris, Michel (Julien) 1901-1990 . . . **CLC 61**
 See also CA 119; 128; 132

Leithauser, Brad 1953- . . . . **CLC 27**
 See also CA 107; CANR 27; DLB 120

Lelchuk, Alan 1938- . . . . **CLC 5**
 See also CA 45-48; CAAS 20; CANR 1

Lem, Stanislaw 1921- . . . . **CLC 8, 15, 40**
 See also CA 105; CAAS 1; CANR 32;
 MTCW

Lemann, Nancy 1956-............ CLC 39
See also CA 118; 136

Lemonnier, (Antoine Louis) Camille
1844-1913 .... TCLC 22
See also CA 121

Lenau, Nikolaus 1802-1850...... NCLC 16

L'Engle, Madeleine (Camp Franklin)
1918- .... CLC 12; DAM POP
See also AAYA 1; AITN 2; CA 1-4R;
CANR 3, 21, 39; CLR 1, 14; DLB 52;
JRDA; MAICYA; MTCW; SAAS 15;
SATA 1, 27, 75

Lengyel, Jozsef 1896-1975......... CLC 7
See also CA 85-88; 57-60

Lenin 1870-1924
See Lenin, V. I.
See also CA 121

Lenin, V. I. .... TCLC 67
See also Lenin

Lennon, John (Ono)
1940-1980 .... CLC 12, 35
See also CA 102

Lennox, Charlotte Ramsay
1729(?)-1804 .... NCLC 23
See also DLB 39

Lentricchia, Frank (Jr.) 1940-...... CLC 34
See also CA 25-28R; CANR 19

Lenz, Siegfried 1926-............ CLC 27
See also CA 89-92; DLB 75

Leonard, Elmore (John, Jr.)
1925- ...... CLC 28, 34, 71; DAM POP
See also AITN 1; BEST 89:1, 90:4;
CA 81-84; CANR 12, 28, 53; DLB 173;
INT CANR-28; MTCW

Leonard, Hugh. .... CLC 19
See also Byrne, John Keyes
See also DLB 13

Leonov, Leonid (Maximovich)
1899-1994 .... CLC 92; DAM NOV
See also CA 129; MTCW

Leopardi, (Conte) Giacomo
1798-1837 .... NCLC 22

Le Reveler
See Artaud, Antonin (Marie Joseph)

Lerman, Eleanor 1952-............ CLC 9
See also CA 85-88

Lerman, Rhoda 1936-............ CLC 56
See also CA 49-52

Lermontov, Mikhail Yuryevich
1814-1841 .... NCLC 47

Leroux, Gaston 1868-1927........ TCLC 25
See also CA 108; 136; SATA 65

Lesage, Alain-Rene 1668-1747....... LC 28

Leskov, Nikolai (Semyonovich)
1831-1895 .... NCLC 25

Lessing, Doris (May)
1919- .... CLC 1, 2, 3, 6, 10, 15, 22, 40,
94; DA; DAB; DAC; DAM MST, NOV;
SSC 6
See also CA 9-12R; CAAS 14; CANR 33,
54; CDBLB 1960 to Present; DLB 15,
139; DLBY 85; MTCW

Lessing, Gotthold Ephraim
1729-1781 .... LC 8
See also DLB 97

Lester, Richard 1932-............ CLC 20

Lever, Charles (James)
1806-1872 .... NCLC 23
See also DLB 21

Leverson, Ada 1865(?)-1936(?) .... TCLC 18
See also Elaine
See also CA 117; DLB 153

Levertov, Denise
1923- ...... CLC 1, 2, 3, 5, 8, 15, 28, 66;
DAM POET; PC 11
See also CA 1-4R; CAAS 19; CANR 3, 29,
50; DLB 5, 165; INT CANR-29; MTCW

Levi, Jonathan..................... CLC 76

Levi, Peter (Chad Tigar) 1931-..... CLC 41
See also CA 5-8R; CANR 34; DLB 40

Levi, Primo
1919-1987 .... CLC 37, 50; SSC 12
See also CA 13-16R; 122; CANR 12, 33;
DLB 177; MTCW

Levin, Ira 1929- ..... CLC 3, 6; DAM POP
See also CA 21-24R; CANR 17, 44;
MTCW; SATA 66

Levin, Meyer
1905-1981 .... CLC 7; DAM POP
See also AITN 1; CA 9-12R; 104;
CANR 15; DLB 9, 28; DLBY 81;
SATA 21; SATA-Obit 27

Levine, Norman 1924-............ CLC 54
See also CA 73-76; CAAS 23; CANR 14;
DLB 88

Levine, Philip
1928-........... CLC 2, 4, 5, 9, 14, 33;
DAM POET
See also CA 9-12R; CANR 9, 37, 52;
DLB 5

Levinson, Deirdre 1931-........... CLC 49
See also CA 73-76

Levi-Strauss, Claude 1908- .... CLC 38
See also CA 1-4R; CANR 6, 32, 57; MTCW

Levitin, Sonia (Wolff) 1934- .... CLC 17
See also AAYA 13; CA 29-32R; CANR 14,
32; JRDA; MAICYA; SAAS 2; SATA 4,
68

Levon, O. U.
See Kesey, Ken (Elton)

Levy, Amy 1861-1889........... NCLC 59
See also DLB 156

Lewes, George Henry
1817-1878 .... NCLC 25
See also DLB 55, 144

Lewis, Alun 1915-1944........... TCLC 3
See also CA 104; DLB 20, 162

Lewis, C. Day
See Day Lewis, C(ecil)

Lewis, C(live) S(taples)
1898-1963 ..... CLC 1, 3, 6, 14, 27; DA;
DAB; DAC; DAM MST, NOV, POP;
WLC
See also AAYA 3; CA 81-84; CANR 33;
CDBLB 1945-1960; CLR 3, 27; DLB 15,
100, 160; JRDA; MAICYA; MTCW;
SATA 13

Lewis, Janet 1899-.............. CLC 41
See also Winters, Janet Lewis
See also CA 9-12R; CANR 29; CAP 1;
DLBY 87

Lewis, Matthew Gregory
1775-1818 .... NCLC 11
See also DLB 39, 158

Lewis, (Harry) Sinclair
1885-1951 ..... TCLC 4, 13, 23, 39; DA;
DAB; DAC; DAM MST, NOV; WLC
See also CA 104; 133; CDALB 1917-1929;
DLB 9, 102; DLBD 1; MTCW

Lewis, (Percy) Wyndham
1884(?)-1957 .... TCLC 2, 9
See also CA 104; DLB 15

Lewisohn, Ludwig 1883-1955..... TCLC 19
See also CA 107; DLB 4, 9, 28, 102

Leyner, Mark 1956-.............. CLC 92
See also CA 110; CANR 28, 53

Lezama Lima, Jose
1910-1976 .... CLC 4, 10; DAM MULT
See also CA 77-80; DLB 113; HW

L'Heureux, John (Clarke) 1934-.... CLC 52
See also CA 13-16R; CANR 23, 45

Liddell, C. H.
See Kuttner, Henry

Lie, Jonas (Lauritz Idemil)
1833-1908(?) .... TCLC 5
See also CA 115

Lieber, Joel 1937-1971............. CLC 6
See also CA 73-76; 29-32R

Lieber, Stanley Martin
See Lee, Stan

Lieberman, Laurence (James)
1935-...................... CLC 4, 36
See also CA 17-20R; CANR 8, 36

Lieksman, Anders
See Haavikko, Paavo Juhani

Li Fei-kan 1904-
See Pa Chin
See also CA 105

Lifton, Robert Jay 1926-.......... CLC 67
See also CA 17-20R; CANR 27;
INT CANR-27; SATA 66

Lightfoot, Gordon 1938-.......... CLC 26
See also CA 109

Lightman, Alan P. 1948-......... CLC 81
See also CA 141

Ligotti, Thomas (Robert)
1953- .... CLC 44; SSC 16
See also CA 123; CANR 49

Li Ho 791-817.................... PC 13

Liliencron, (Friedrich Adolf Axel) Detlev von
1844-1909 .... TCLC 18
See also CA 117

Lilly, William 1602-1681.......... LC 27

Lima, Jose Lezama
See Lezama Lima, Jose

Lima Barreto, Afonso Henrique de
1881-1922 .... TCLC 23
See also CA 117

Limonov, Edward 1944-.......... CLC 67
See also CA 137

Lin, Frank
See Atherton, Gertrude (Franklin Horn)

Lincoln, Abraham 1809-1865..... NCLC 18

Lowry, (Clarence) Malcolm
1909-1957 . . . . **TCLC 6, 40**
See also CA 105; 131; CDBLB 1945-1960;
DLB 15; MTCW

Lowry, Mina Gertrude 1882-1966
See Loy, Mina
See also CA 113

Loxsmith, John
See Brunner, John (Kilian Houston)

Loy, Mina . . . . **CLC 28; DAM POET; PC 16**
See also Lowry, Mina Gertrude
See also DLB 4, 54

Loyson-Bridet
See Schwob, (Mayer Andre) Marcel

Lucas, Craig 1951- . . . . **CLC 64**
See also CA 137

Lucas, George 1944- . . . . **CLC 16**
See also AAYA 1; CA 77-80; CANR 30;
SATA 56

Lucas, Hans
See Godard, Jean-Luc

Lucas, Victoria
See Plath, Sylvia

Ludlam, Charles 1943-1987 . . . . . **CLC 46, 50**
See also CA 85-88; 122

Ludlum, Robert
1927- . . . **CLC 22, 43; DAM NOV, POP**
See also AAYA 10; BEST 89:1, 90:3;
CA 33-36R; CANR 25, 41; DLBY 82;
MTCW

Ludwig, Ken . . . . **CLC 60**

Ludwig, Otto 1813-1865 . . . . **NCLC 4**
See also DLB 129

Lugones, Leopoldo 1874-1938 . . . . . **TCLC 15**
See also CA 116; 131; HW

Lu Hsun 1881-1936 . . . . . . **TCLC 3; SSC 20**
See also Shu-Jen, Chou

Lukacs, George . . . . **CLC 24**
See also Lukacs, Gyorgy (Szegeny von)

Lukacs, Gyorgy (Szegeny von) 1885-1971
See Lukacs, George
See also CA 101; 29-32R

Luke, Peter (Ambrose Cyprian)
1919-1995 . . . . **CLC 38**
See also CA 81-84; 147; DLB 13

Lunar, Dennis
See Mungo, Raymond

Lurie, Alison 1926- . . . . **CLC 4, 5, 18, 39**
See also CA 1-4R; CANR 2, 17, 50; DLB 2;
MTCW; SATA 46

Lustig, Arnost 1926- . . . . **CLC 56**
See also AAYA 3; CA 69-72; CANR 47;
SATA 56

Luther, Martin 1483-1546 . . . . **LC 9, 37**

Luxemburg, Rosa 1870(?)-1919 . . . . **TCLC 63**
See also CA 118

Luzi, Mario 1914- . . . . **CLC 13**
See also CA 61-64; CANR 9; DLB 128

Lyly, John 1554(?)-1606 . . . . **DC 7**
See also DAM DRAM; DLB 62, 167

L'Ymagier
See Gourmont, Remy (-Marie-Charles) de

Lynch, B. Suarez
See Bioy Casares, Adolfo; Borges, Jorge
Luis

Lynch, David (K.) 1946- . . . . **CLC 66**
See also CA 124; 129

Lynch, James
See Andreyev, Leonid (Nikolaevich)

Lynch Davis, B.
See Bioy Casares, Adolfo; Borges, Jorge
Luis

Lyndsay, Sir David 1490-1555 . . . . . . **LC 20**

Lynn, Kenneth S(chuyler) 1923- . . . . **CLC 50**
See also CA 1-4R; CANR 3, 27

Lynx
See West, Rebecca

Lyons, Marcus
See Blish, James (Benjamin)

Lyre, Pinchbeck
See Sassoon, Siegfried (Lorraine)

Lytle, Andrew (Nelson) 1902-1995 . . **CLC 22**
See also CA 9-12R; 150; DLB 6; DLBY 95

Lyttelton, George 1709-1773 . . . . **LC 10**

Maas, Peter 1929- . . . . **CLC 29**
See also CA 93-96; INT 93-96

Macaulay, Rose 1881-1958 . . . . . **TCLC 7, 44**
See also CA 104; DLB 36

Macaulay, Thomas Babington
1800-1859 . . . . **NCLC 42**
See also CDBLB 1832-1890; DLB 32, 55

MacBeth, George (Mann)
1932-1992 . . . . **CLC 2, 5, 9**
See also CA 25-28R; 136; DLB 40; MTCW;
SATA 4; SATA-Obit 70

MacCaig, Norman (Alexander)
1910- . . . . . **CLC 36; DAB; DAM POET**
See also CA 9-12R; CANR 3, 34; DLB 27

MacCarthy, (Sir Charles Otto) Desmond
1877-1952 . . . . **TCLC 36**

MacDiarmid, Hugh
. . . . **CLC 2, 4, 11, 19, 63; PC 9**
See also Grieve, C(hristopher) M(urray)
See also CDBLB 1945-1960; DLB 20

MacDonald, Anson
See Heinlein, Robert A(nson)

Macdonald, Cynthia 1928- . . . . . . **CLC 13, 19**
See also CA 49-52; CANR 4, 44; DLB 105

MacDonald, George 1824-1905 . . . . . **TCLC 9**
See also CA 106; 137; DLB 18, 163;
MAICYA; SATA 33

Macdonald, John
See Millar, Kenneth

MacDonald, John D(ann)
1916-1986 . . . . **CLC 3, 27, 44;**
DAM NOV, POP
See also CA 1-4R; 121; CANR 1, 19;
DLB 8; DLBY 86; MTCW

Macdonald, John Ross
See Millar, Kenneth

Macdonald, Ross . . . . . **CLC 1, 2, 3, 14, 34, 41**
See also Millar, Kenneth
See also DLBD 6

MacDougal, John
See Blish, James (Benjamin)

MacEwen, Gwendolyn (Margaret)
1941-1987 . . . . **CLC 13, 55**
See also CA 9-12R; 124; CANR 7, 22;
DLB 53; SATA 50; SATA-Obit 55

Macha, Karel Hynek 1810-1846 . . **NCLC 46**

Machado (y Ruiz), Antonio
1875-1939 . . . . **TCLC 3**
See also CA 104; DLB 108

Machado de Assis, Joaquim Maria
1839-1908 . . . . . **TCLC 10; BLC; SSC 24**
See also CA 107; 153

Machen, Arthur . . . . **TCLC 4; SSC 20**
See also Jones, Arthur Llewellyn
See also DLB 36, 156

Machiavelli, Niccolo
1469-1527 . . . . **LC 8, 36; DA; DAB;**
DAC; DAM MST

MacInnes, Colin 1914-1976 . . . . . . **CLC 4, 23**
See also CA 69-72; 65-68; CANR 21;
DLB 14; MTCW

MacInnes, Helen (Clark)
1907-1985 . . . . . **CLC 27, 39; DAM POP**
See also CA 1-4R; 117; CANR 1, 28;
DLB 87; MTCW; SATA 22;
SATA-Obit 44

Mackay, Mary 1855-1924
See Corelli, Marie
See also CA 118

Mackenzie, Compton (Edward Montague)
1883-1972 . . . . **CLC 18**
See also CA 21-22; 37-40R; CAP 2;
DLB 34, 100

Mackenzie, Henry 1745-1831 . . . . **NCLC 41**
See also DLB 39

Mackintosh, Elizabeth 1896(?)-1952
See Tey, Josephine
See also CA 110

MacLaren, James
See Grieve, C(hristopher) M(urray)

Mac Laverty, Bernard 1942- . . . . **CLC 31**
See also CA 116; 118; CANR 43; INT 118

MacLean, Alistair (Stuart)
1922-1987 . . . . **CLC 3, 13, 50, 63;**
DAM POP
See also CA 57-60; 121; CANR 28; MTCW;
SATA 23; SATA-Obit 50

Maclean, Norman (Fitzroy)
1902-1990 . . . . **CLC 78; DAM POP;**
SSC 13
See also CA 102; 132; CANR 49

MacLeish, Archibald
1892-1982 . . . . **CLC 3, 8, 14, 68;**
DAM POET
See also CA 9-12R; 106; CANR 33; DLB 4,
7, 45; DLBY 82; MTCW

MacLennan, (John) Hugh
1907-1990 . . . . **CLC 2, 14, 92; DAC;**
DAM MST
See also CA 5-8R; 142; CANR 33; DLB 68;
MTCW

MacLeod, Alistair
1936- . . . . . . **CLC 56; DAC; DAM MST**
See also CA 123; DLB 60

McInerney, Jay
1955- . . . . **CLC 34; DAM POP**
See also AAYA 18; CA 116; 123;
CANR 45; INT 123

McIntyre, Vonda N(eel) 1948- . . . . . **CLC 18**
See also CA 81-84; CANR 17, 34; MTCW

McKay, Claude
. . . . **TCLC 7, 41; BLC; DAB; PC 2**
See also McKay, Festus Claudius
See also DLB 4, 45, 51, 117

McKay, Festus Claudius 1889-1948
See McKay, Claude
See also BW 1; CA 104; 124; DA; DAC;
DAM MST, MULT, NOV, POET;
MTCW; WLC

McKuen, Rod 1933- . . . . **CLC 1, 3**
See also AITN 1; CA 41-44R; CANR 40

McLoughlin, R. B.
See Mencken, H(enry) L(ouis)

McLuhan, (Herbert) Marshall
1911-1980 . . . . **CLC 37, 83**
See also CA 9-12R; 102; CANR 12, 34;
DLB 88; INT CANR-12; MTCW

McMillan, Terry (L.)
1951- . . . . **CLC 50, 61; DAM MULT,
NOV, POP**
See also AAYA 21; BW 2; CA 140

McMurtry, Larry (Jeff)
1936- . . . . **CLC 2, 3, 7, 11, 27, 44;
DAM NOV, POP**
See also AAYA 15; AITN 2; BEST 89:2;
CA 5-8R; CANR 19, 43;
CDALB 1968-1988; DLB 2, 143;
DLBY 80, 87; MTCW

McNally, T. M. 1961- . . . . **CLC 82**

McNally, Terrence
1939- . . . **CLC 4, 7, 41, 91; DAM DRAM**
See also CA 45-48; CANR 2, 56; DLB 7

McNamer, Deirdre 1950- . . . . **CLC 70**

McNeile, Herman Cyril 1888-1937
See Sapper
See also DLB 77

McNickle, (William) D'Arcy
1904-1977 . . . . . . **CLC 89; DAM MULT**
See also CA 9-12R; 85-88; CANR 5, 45;
DLB 175; NNAL; SATA-Obit 22

McPhee, John (Angus) 1931- . . . . . . **CLC 36**
See also BEST 90:1; CA 65-68; CANR 20,
46; MTCW

McPherson, James Alan
1943- . . . . **CLC 19, 77**
See also BW 1; CA 25-28R; CAAS 17;
CANR 24; DLB 38; MTCW

McPherson, William (Alexander)
1933- . . . . **CLC 34**
See also CA 69-72; CANR 28;
INT CANR-28

Mead, Margaret 1901-1978 . . . . **CLC 37**
See also AITN 1; CA 1-4R; 81-84;
CANR 4; MTCW; SATA-Obit 20

Meaker, Marijane (Agnes) 1927-
See Kerr, M. E.
See also CA 107; CANR 37; INT 107;
JRDA; MAICYA; MTCW; SATA 20, 61

Medoff, Mark (Howard)
1940- . . . . **CLC 6, 23; DAM DRAM**
See also AITN 1; CA 53-56; CANR 5;
DLB 7; INT CANR-5

Medvedev, P. N.
See Bakhtin, Mikhail Mikhailovich

Meged, Aharon
See Megged, Aharon

Meged, Aron
See Megged, Aharon

Megged, Aharon 1920- . . . . **CLC 9**
See also CA 49-52; CAAS 13; CANR 1

Mehta, Ved (Parkash) 1934- . . . . **CLC 37**
See also CA 1-4R; CANR 2, 23; MTCW

Melanter
See Blackmore, R(ichard) D(oddridge)

Melikow, Loris
See Hofmannsthal, Hugo von

Melmoth, Sebastian
See Wilde, Oscar (Fingal O'Flahertie Wills)

Meltzer, Milton 1915- . . . . **CLC 26**
See also AAYA 8; CA 13-16R; CANR 38;
CLR 13; DLB 61; JRDA; MAICYA;
SAAS 1; SATA 1, 50, 80

Melville, Herman
1819-1891 . . . . . **NCLC 3, 12, 29, 45, 49;
DA; DAB; DAC; DAM MST, NOV;
SSC 1, 17; WLC**
See also CDALB 1640-1865; DLB 3, 74;
SATA 59

Menander
c. 342B.C.-c. 292B.C. . . . . **CMLC 9;
DAM DRAM; DC 3**
See also DLB 176

Mencken, H(enry) L(ouis)
1880-1956 . . . . **TCLC 13**
See also CA 105; 125; CDALB 1917-1929;
DLB 11, 29, 63, 137; MTCW

Mendelsohn, Jane 1965(?)- . . . . **CLC 99**
See also CA 154

Mercer, David
1928-1980 . . . . **CLC 5; DAM DRAM**
See also CA 9-12R; 102; CANR 23;
DLB 13; MTCW

Merchant, Paul
See Ellison, Harlan (Jay)

Meredith, George
1828-1909 . . **TCLC 17, 43; DAM POET**
See also CA 117; 153; CDBLB 1832-1890;
DLB 18, 35, 57, 159

Meredith, William (Morris)
1919- . . **CLC 4, 13, 22, 55; DAM POET**
See also CA 9-12R; CAAS 14; CANR 6, 40;
DLB 5

Merezhkovsky, Dmitry Sergeyevich
1865-1941 . . . . **TCLC 29**

Merimee, Prosper
1803-1870 . . . . **NCLC 6; SSC 7**
See also DLB 119

Merkin, Daphne 1954- . . . . **CLC 44**
See also CA 123

Merlin, Arthur
See Blish, James (Benjamin)

Merrill, James (Ingram)
1926-1995 . . . . **CLC 2, 3, 6, 8, 13, 18, 34,
91; DAM POET**
See also CA 13-16R; 147; CANR 10, 49;
DLB 5, 165; DLBY 85; INT CANR-10;
MTCW

Merriman, Alex
See Silverberg, Robert

Merritt, E. B.
See Waddington, Miriam

Merton, Thomas
1915-1968 . . **CLC 1, 3, 11, 34, 83; PC 10**
See also CA 5-8R; 25-28R; CANR 22, 53;
DLB 48; DLBY 81; MTCW

Merwin, W(illiam) S(tanley)
1927- . . . . . . **CLC 1, 2, 3, 5, 8, 13, 18, 45,
88; DAM POET**
See also CA 13-16R; CANR 15, 51; DLB 5,
169; INT CANR-15; MTCW

Metcalf, John 1938- . . . . **CLC 37**
See also CA 113; DLB 60

Metcalf, Suzanne
See Baum, L(yman) Frank

Mew, Charlotte (Mary)
1870-1928 . . . . **TCLC 8**
See also CA 105; DLB 19, 135

Mewshaw, Michael 1943- . . . . **CLC 9**
See also CA 53-56; CANR 7, 47; DLBY 80

Meyer, June
See Jordan, June

Meyer, Lynn
See Slavitt, David R(ytman)

Meyer-Meyrink, Gustav 1868-1932
See Meyrink, Gustav
See also CA 117

Meyers, Jeffrey 1939- . . . . **CLC 39**
See also CA 73-76; CANR 54; DLB 111

Meynell, Alice (Christina Gertrude Thompson)
1847-1922 . . . . **TCLC 6**
See also CA 104; DLB 19, 98

Meyrink, Gustav . . . . **TCLC 21**
See also Meyer-Meyrink, Gustav
See also DLB 81

Michaels, Leonard
1933- . . . . **CLC 6, 25; SSC 16**
See also CA 61-64; CANR 21; DLB 130;
MTCW

Michaux, Henri 1899-1984 . . . . . . **CLC 8, 19**
See also CA 85-88; 114

Michelangelo 1475-1564 . . . . **LC 12**

Michelet, Jules 1798-1874 . . . . **NCLC 31**

Michener, James A(lbert)
1907(?)- . . . . **CLC 1, 5, 11, 29, 60;
DAM NOV, POP**
See also AITN 1; BEST 90:1; CA 5-8R;
CANR 21, 45; DLB 6; MTCW

Mickiewicz, Adam 1798-1855 . . . . . **NCLC 3**

Middleton, Christopher 1926- . . . . . . **CLC 13**
See also CA 13-16R; CANR 29, 54;
DLB 40

Middleton, Richard (Barham)
1882-1911 . . . . **TCLC 56**
See also DLB 156

Montesquieu, Charles-Louis de Secondat
  1689-1755 . . . . LC 7

Montgomery, (Robert) Bruce   1921-1978
  See Crispin, Edmund
  See also CA 104

Montgomery, L(ucy) M(aud)
  1874-1942 . . . . TCLC 51; DAC;
                                   DAM MST
  See also AAYA 12; CA 108; 137; CLR 8;
  DLB 92; DLBD 14; JRDA; MAICYA;
  YABC 1

Montgomery, Marion H., Jr. 1925- . . CLC 7
  See also AITN 1; CA 1-4R; CANR 3, 48;
  DLB 6

Montgomery, Max
  See Davenport, Guy (Mattison, Jr.)

Montherlant, Henry (Milon) de
  1896-1972 . . . . CLC 8, 19; DAM DRAM
  See also CA 85-88; 37-40R; DLB 72;
  MTCW

Monty Python
  See Chapman, Graham; Cleese, John
  (Marwood); Gilliam, Terry (Vance); Idle,
  Eric; Jones, Terence Graham Parry; Palin,
  Michael (Edward)
  See also AAYA 7

Moodie, Susanna (Strickland)
  1803-1885 . . . . NCLC 14
  See also DLB 99

Mooney, Edward 1951-
  See Mooney, Ted
  See also CA 130

Mooney, Ted . . . . CLC 25
  See also Mooney, Edward

Moorcock, Michael (John)
  1939- . . . . CLC 5, 27, 58
  See also CA 45-48; CAAS 5; CANR 2, 17,
  38; DLB 14; MTCW

Moore, Brian
  1921- . . . . . . CLC 1, 3, 5, 7, 8, 19, 32, 90;
                                 DAB; DAC; DAM MST
  See also CA 1-4R; CANR 1, 25, 42; MTCW

Moore, Edward
  See Muir, Edwin

Moore, George Augustus
  1852-1933 . . . . TCLC 7; SSC 19
  See also CA 104; DLB 10, 18, 57, 135

Moore, Lorrie . . . . CLC 39, 45, 68
  See also Moore, Marie Lorena

Moore, Marianne (Craig)
  1887-1972 . . . . CLC 1, 2, 4, 8, 10, 13, 19,
  47; DA; DAB; DAC; DAM MST, POET;
                                                PC 4
  See also CA 1-4R; 33-36R; CANR 3;
  CDALB 1929-1941; DLB 45; DLBD 7;
  MTCW; SATA 20

Moore, Marie Lorena 1957-
  See Moore, Lorrie
  See also CA 116; CANR 39

Moore, Thomas 1779-1852 . . . . NCLC 6
  See also DLB 96, 144

Morand, Paul 1888-1976 . . CLC 41; SSC 22
  See also CA 69-72; DLB 65

Morante, Elsa 1918-1985 . . . . CLC 8, 47
  See also CA 85-88; 117; CANR 35;
  DLB 177; MTCW

Moravia, Alberto
  1907-1990 . . . . CLC 2, 7, 11, 27, 46
  See also Pincherle, Alberto
  See also DLB 177

More, Hannah 1745-1833 . . . . NCLC 27
  See also DLB 107, 109, 116, 158

More, Henry 1614-1687 . . . . LC 9
  See also DLB 126

More, Sir Thomas 1478-1535 . . . . LC 10, 32

Moreas, Jean . . . . TCLC 18
  See also Papadiamantopoulos, Johannes

Morgan, Berry 1919- . . . . CLC 6
  See also CA 49-52; DLB 6

Morgan, Claire
  See Highsmith, (Mary) Patricia

Morgan, Edwin (George) 1920- . . . . . CLC 31
  See also CA 5-8R; CANR 3, 43; DLB 27

Morgan, (George) Frederick
  1922- . . . . CLC 23
  See also CA 17-20R; CANR 21

Morgan, Harriet
  See Mencken, H(enry) L(ouis)

Morgan, Jane
  See Cooper, James Fenimore

Morgan, Janet 1945- . . . . CLC 39
  See also CA 65-68

Morgan, Lady 1776(?)-1859 . . . . . . NCLC 29
  See also DLB 116, 158

Morgan, Robin 1941- . . . . CLC 2
  See also CA 69-72; CANR 29; MTCW;
  SATA 80

Morgan, Scott
  See Kuttner, Henry

Morgan, Seth 1949(?)-1990 . . . . CLC 65
  See also CA 132

Morgenstern, Christian
  1871-1914 . . . . TCLC 8
  See also CA 105

Morgenstern, S.
  See Goldman, William (W.)

Moricz, Zsigmond 1879-1942 . . . . . TCLC 33

Morike, Eduard (Friedrich)
  1804-1875 . . . . NCLC 10
  See also DLB 133

Mori Ogai . . . . TCLC 14
  See also Mori Rintaro

Mori Rintaro 1862-1922
  See Mori Ogai
  See also CA 110

Moritz, Karl Philipp 1756-1793 . . . . . . LC 2
  See also DLB 94

Morland, Peter Henry
  See Faust, Frederick (Schiller)

Morren, Theophil
  See Hofmannsthal, Hugo von

Morris, Bill 1952- . . . . CLC 76

Morris, Julian
  See West, Morris L(anglo)

Morris, Steveland Judkins 1950(?)-
  See Wonder, Stevie
  See also CA 111

Morris, William 1834-1896 . . . . NCLC 4
  See also CDBLB 1832-1890; DLB 18, 35,
  57, 156

Morris, Wright 1910-... CLC 1, 3, 7, 18, 37
  See also CA 9-12R; CANR 21; DLB 2;
  DLBY 81; MTCW

Morrison, Chloe Anthony Wofford
  See Morrison, Toni

Morrison, James Douglas 1943-1971
  See Morrison, Jim
  See also CA 73-76; CANR 40

Morrison, Jim . . . . CLC 17
  See also Morrison, James Douglas

Morrison, Toni
  1931- . . . . CLC 4, 10, 22, 55, 81, 87;
  BLC; DA; DAB; DAC; DAM MST,
                                 MULT, NOV, POP
  See also AAYA 1; BW 2; CA 29-32R;
  CANR 27, 42; CDALB 1968-1988;
  DLB 6, 33, 143; DLBY 81; MTCW;
  SATA 57

Morrison, Van 1945- . . . . CLC 21
  See also CA 116

Morrissy, Mary 1958- . . . . CLC 99

Mortimer, John (Clifford)
  1923- . . . . . . CLC 28, 43; DAM DRAM,
                                              POP
  See also CA 13-16R; CANR 21;
  CDBLB 1960 to Present; DLB 13;
  INT CANR-21; MTCW

Mortimer, Penelope (Ruth) 1918-... CLC 5
  See also CA 57-60; CANR 45

Morton, Anthony
  See Creasey, John

Mosher, Howard Frank 1943-... CLC 62
  See also CA 139

Mosley, Nicholas 1923- . . . . CLC 43, 70
  See also CA 69-72; CANR 41; DLB 14

Mosley, Walter
  1952- . . . . . CLC 97; DAM MULT, POP
  See also AAYA 17; BW 2; CA 142;
  CANR 57

Moss, Howard
  1922-1987 . . . . CLC 7, 14, 45, 50;
                                           DAM POET
  See also CA 1-4R; 123; CANR 1, 44;
  DLB 5

Mossgiel, Rab
  See Burns, Robert

Motion, Andrew (Peter) 1952-... CLC 47
  See also CA 146; DLB 40

Motley, Willard (Francis)
  1909-1965 . . . . CLC 18
  See also BW 1; CA 117; 106; DLB 76, 143

Motoori, Norinaga 1730-1801 . . . . NCLC 45

Mott, Michael (Charles Alston)
  1930- . . . . CLC 15, 34
  See also CA 5-8R; CAAS 7; CANR 7, 29

Mountain Wolf Woman
  1884-1960 . . . . CLC 92
  See also CA 144; NNAL

Moure, Erin 1955- . . . . CLC 88
  See also CA 113; DLB 60

Nerval, Gerard de
1808-1855 . . . . . **NCLC 1; PC 13; SSC 18**

Nervo, (Jose) Amado (Ruiz de)
1870-1919 . . . . **TCLC 11**
See also CA 109; 131; HW

Nessi, Pio Baroja y
See Baroja (y Nessi), Pio

Nestroy, Johann 1801-1862 . . . . . . **NCLC 42**
See also DLB 133

Neufeld, John (Arthur) 1938- . . . . . . **CLC 17**
See also AAYA 11; CA 25-28R; CANR 11,
37, 56; MAICYA; SAAS 3; SATA 6, 81

Neville, Emily Cheney 1919- . . . . **CLC 12**
See also CA 5-8R; CANR 3, 37; JRDA;
MAICYA; SAAS 2; SATA 1

Newbound, Bernard Slade 1930-
See Slade, Bernard
See also CA 81-84; CANR 49;
DAM DRAM

Newby, P(ercy) H(oward)
1918- . . . . **CLC 2, 13; DAM NOV**
See also CA 5-8R; CANR 32; DLB 15;
MTCW

Newlove, Donald 1928- . . . . **CLC 6**
See also CA 29-32R; CANR 25

Newlove, John (Herbert) 1938- . . . . . **CLC 14**
See also CA 21-24R; CANR 9, 25

Newman, Charles 1938- . . . . **CLC 2, 8**
See also CA 21-24R

Newman, Edwin (Harold) 1919- . . . . **CLC 14**
See also AITN 1; CA 69-72; CANR 5

Newman, John Henry
1801-1890 . . . . **NCLC 38**
See also DLB 18, 32, 55

Newton, Suzanne 1936- . . . . **CLC 35**
See also CA 41-44R; CANR 14; JRDA;
SATA 5, 77

Nexo, Martin Andersen
1869-1954 . . . . **TCLC 43**

Nezval, Vitezslav 1900-1958 . . . . . . **TCLC 44**
See also CA 123

Ng, Fae Myenne 1957(?)- . . . . **CLC 81**
See also CA 146

Ngema, Mbongeni 1955- . . . . **CLC 57**
See also BW 2; CA 143

Ngugi, James T(hiong'o) . . . . **CLC 3, 7, 13**
See also Ngugi wa Thiong'o

Ngugi wa Thiong'o
1938- . . . . . **CLC 36; BLC; DAM MULT,
NOV**
See also Ngugi, James T(hiong'o)
See also BW 2; CA 81-84; CANR 27;
DLB 125; MTCW

Nichol, B(arrie) P(hillip)
1944-1988 . . . . **CLC 18**
See also CA 53-56; DLB 53; SATA 66

Nichols, John (Treadwell) 1940- . . . . **CLC 38**
See also CA 9-12R; CAAS 2; CANR 6;
DLBY 82

Nichols, Leigh
See Koontz, Dean R(ay)

Nichols, Peter (Richard)
1927- . . . . **CLC 5, 36, 65**
See also CA 104; CANR 33; DLB 13;
MTCW

Nicolas, F. R. E.
See Freeling, Nicolas

Niedecker, Lorine
1903-1970 . . . . **CLC 10, 42; DAM POET**
See also CA 25-28; CAP 2; DLB 48

Nietzsche, Friedrich (Wilhelm)
1844-1900 . . . . **TCLC 10, 18, 55**
See also CA 107; 121; DLB 129

Nievo, Ippolito 1831-1861 . . . . **NCLC 22**

Nightingale, Anne Redmon 1943-
See Redmon, Anne
See also CA 103

Nik. T. O.
See Annensky, Innokenty (Fyodorovich)

Nin, Anais
1903-1977 . . . . . . **CLC 1, 4, 8, 11, 14, 60;
DAM NOV, POP; SSC 10**
See also AITN 2; CA 13-16R; 69-72;
CANR 22, 53; DLB 2, 4, 152; MTCW

Nishiwaki, Junzaburo 1894-1982 . . . . **PC 15**
See also CA 107

Nissenson, Hugh 1933- . . . . **CLC 4, 9**
See also CA 17-20R; CANR 27; DLB 28

Niven, Larry . . . . **CLC 8**
See also Niven, Laurence Van Cott
See also DLB 8

Niven, Laurence Van Cott 1938-
See Niven, Larry
See also CA 21-24R; CAAS 12; CANR 14,
44; DAM POP; MTCW

Nixon, Agnes Eckhardt 1927- . . . . . . **CLC 21**
See also CA 110

Nizan, Paul 1905-1940 . . . . **TCLC 40**
See also DLB 72

Nkosi, Lewis
1936- . . . . . **CLC 45; BLC; DAM MULT**
See also BW 1; CA 65-68; CANR 27;
DLB 157

Nodier, (Jean) Charles (Emmanuel)
1780-1844 . . . . **NCLC 19**
See also DLB 119

Nolan, Christopher 1965- . . . . **CLC 58**
See also CA 111

Noon, Jeff 1957- . . . . **CLC 91**
See also CA 148

Norden, Charles
See Durrell, Lawrence (George)

Nordhoff, Charles (Bernard)
1887-1947 . . . . **TCLC 23**
See also CA 108; DLB 9; SATA 23

Norfolk, Lawrence 1963- . . . . **CLC 76**
See also CA 144

Norman, Marsha
1947- . . . . **CLC 28; DAM DRAM**
See also CA 105; CABS 3; CANR 41;
DLBY 84

Norris, Benjamin Franklin, Jr.
1870-1902 . . . . **TCLC 24**
See also Norris, Frank
See also CA 110

Norris, Frank
See Norris, Benjamin Franklin, Jr.
See also CDALB 1865-1917; DLB 12, 71

Norris, Leslie 1921- . . . . **CLC 14**
See also CA 11-12; CANR 14; CAP 1;
DLB 27

North, Andrew
See Norton, Andre

North, Anthony
See Koontz, Dean R(ay)

North, Captain George
See Stevenson, Robert Louis (Balfour)

North, Milou
See Erdrich, Louise

Northrup, B. A.
See Hubbard, L(afayette) Ron(ald)

North Staffs
See Hulme, T(homas) E(rnest)

Norton, Alice Mary
See Norton, Andre
See also MAICYA; SATA 1, 43

Norton, Andre 1912- . . . . **CLC 12**
See also Norton, Alice Mary
See also AAYA 14; CA 1-4R; CANR 2, 31;
DLB 8, 52; JRDA; MTCW; SATA 91

Norton, Caroline 1808-1877 . . . . . . **NCLC 47**
See also DLB 21, 159

Norway, Nevil Shute 1899-1960
See Shute, Nevil
See also CA 102; 93-96

Norwid, Cyprian Kamil
1821-1883 . . . . **NCLC 17**

Nosille, Nabrah
See Ellison, Harlan (Jay)

Nossack, Hans Erich 1901-1978 . . . . . **CLC 6**
See also CA 93-96; 85-88; DLB 69

Nostradamus 1503-1566 . . . . **LC 27**

Nosu, Chuji
See Ozu, Yasujiro

Notenburg, Eleanora (Genrikhovna) von
See Guro, Elena

Nova, Craig 1945- . . . . **CLC 7, 31**
See also CA 45-48; CANR 2, 53

Novak, Joseph
See Kosinski, Jerzy (Nikodem)

Novalis 1772-1801 . . . . **NCLC 13**
See also DLB 90

Nowlan, Alden (Albert)
1933-1983 . . **CLC 15; DAC; DAM MST**
See also CA 9-12R; CANR 5; DLB 53

Noyes, Alfred 1880-1958 . . . . **TCLC 7**
See also CA 104; DLB 20

Nunn, Kem 19(?)- . . . . **CLC 34**

Nye, Robert
1939- . . . . **CLC 13, 42; DAM NOV**
See also CA 33-36R; CANR 29; DLB 14;
MTCW; SATA 6

Nyro, Laura 1947- . . . . **CLC 17**

Oates, Joyce Carol
1938- . . . . . . **CLC 1, 2, 3, 6, 9, 11, 15, 19,
33, 52; DA; DAB; DAC; DAM MST,
NOV, POP; SSC 6; WLC**
See also AAYA 15; AITN 1; BEST 89:2;
CA 5-8R; CANR 25, 45;
CDALB 1968-1988; DLB 2, 5, 130;
DLBY 81; INT CANR-25; MTCW

O'Brien, Darcy 1939-............. CLC 11
See also CA 21-24R; CANR 8

O'Brien, E. G.
See Clarke, Arthur C(harles)

O'Brien, Edna
1936- .... CLC 3, 5, 8, 13, 36, 65;
DAM NOV; SSC 10
See also CA 1-4R; CANR 6, 41;
CDBLB 1960 to Present; DLB 14;
MTCW

O'Brien, Fitz-James 1828-1862... NCLC 21
See also DLB 74

O'Brien, Flann....... CLC 1, 4, 5, 7, 10, 47
See also O Nuallain, Brian

O'Brien, Richard 1942-........... CLC 17
See also CA 124

O'Brien, Tim
1946- ...... CLC 7, 19, 40; DAM POP
See also AAYA 16; CA 85-88; CANR 40;
DLB 152; DLBD 9; DLBY 80

Obstfelder, Sigbjoern 1866-1900... TCLC 23
See also CA 123

O'Casey, Sean
1880-1964 ...... CLC 1, 5, 9, 11, 15, 88;
DAB; DAC; DAM DRAM, MST
See also CA 89-92; CDBLB 1914-1945;
DLB 10; MTCW

O'Cathasaigh, Sean
See O'Casey, Sean

Ochs, Phil 1940-1976............. CLC 17
See also CA 65-68

O'Connor, Edwin (Greene)
1918-1968 .... CLC 14
See also CA 93-96; 25-28R

O'Connor, (Mary) Flannery
1925-1964 .... CLC 1, 2, 3, 6, 10, 13, 15,
21, 66; DA; DAB; DAC; DAM MST,
NOV; SSC 1, 23; WLC
See also AAYA 7; CA 1-4R; CANR 3, 41;
CDALB 1941-1968; DLB 2, 152;
DLBD 12; DLBY 80; MTCW

O'Connor, Frank........... CLC 23; SSC 5
See also O'Donovan, Michael John
See also DLB 162

O'Dell, Scott 1898-1989........... CLC 30
See also AAYA 3; CA 61-64; 129;
CANR 12, 30; CLR 1, 16; DLB 52;
JRDA; MAICYA; SATA 12, 60

Odets, Clifford
1906-1963 .... CLC 2, 28, 98;
DAM DRAM; DC 6
See also CA 85-88; DLB 7, 26; MTCW

O'Doherty, Brian 1934-........... CLC 76
See also CA 105

O'Donnell, K. M.
See Malzberg, Barry N(athaniel)

O'Donnell, Lawrence
See Kuttner, Henry

O'Donovan, Michael John
1903-1966 .... CLC 14
See also O'Connor, Frank
See also CA 93-96

Oe, Kenzaburo
1935- ..... CLC 10, 36, 86; DAM NOV;
SSC 20
See also CA 97-100; CANR 36, 50;
DLBY 94; MTCW

O'Faolain, Julia 1932-....... CLC 6, 19, 47
See also CA 81-84; CAAS 2; CANR 12;
DLB 14; MTCW

O'Faolain, Sean
1900-1991 .... CLC 1, 7, 14, 32, 70;
SSC 13
See also CA 61-64; 134; CANR 12;
DLB 15, 162; MTCW

O'Flaherty, Liam
1896-1984 .... CLC 5, 34; SSC 6
See also CA 101; 113; CANR 35; DLB 36,
162; DLBY 84; MTCW

Ogilvy, Gavin
See Barrie, J(ames) M(atthew)

O'Grady, Standish (James)
1846-1928 .... TCLC 5
See also CA 104

O'Grady, Timothy 1951-........... CLC 59
See also CA 138

O'Hara, Frank
1926-1966 .... CLC 2, 5, 13, 78;
DAM POET
See also CA 9-12R; 25-28R; CANR 33;
DLB 5, 16; MTCW

O'Hara, John (Henry)
1905-1970 .... CLC 1, 2, 3, 6, 11, 42;
DAM NOV; SSC 15
See also CA 5-8R; 25-28R; CANR 31;
CDALB 1929-1941; DLB 9, 86; DLBD 2;
MTCW

O Hehir, Diana 1922- .... CLC 41
See also CA 93-96

Okigbo, Christopher (Ifenayichukwu)
1932-1967 .... CLC 25, 84; BLC;
DAM MULT, POET; PC 7
See also BW 1; CA 77-80; DLB 125;
MTCW

Okri, Ben 1959- .... CLC 87
See also BW 2; CA 130; 138; DLB 157;
INT 138

Olds, Sharon
1942- ..... CLC 32, 39, 85; DAM POET
See also CA 101; CANR 18, 41; DLB 120

Oldstyle, Jonathan
See Irving, Washington

Olesha, Yuri (Karlovich)
1899-1960 .... CLC 8
See also CA 85-88

Oliphant, Laurence
1829(?)-1888 .... NCLC 47
See also DLB 18, 166

Oliphant, Margaret (Oliphant Wilson)
1828-1897 .... NCLC 11, 61; SSC 25
See also DLB 18, 159

Oliver, Mary 1935-........ CLC 19, 34, 98
See also CA 21-24R; CANR 9, 43; DLB 5

Olivier, Laurence (Kerr)
1907-1989 .... CLC 20
See also CA 111; 150; 129

Olsen, Tillie
1913- ..... CLC 4, 13; DA; DAB; DAC;
DAM MST; SSC 11
See also CA 1-4R; CANR 1, 43; DLB 28;
DLBY 80; MTCW

Olson, Charles (John)
1910-1970 ..... CLC 1, 2, 5, 6, 9, 11, 29;
DAM POET
See also CA 13-16; 25-28R; CABS 2;
CANR 35; CAP 1; DLB 5, 16; MTCW

Olson, Toby 1937- .... CLC 28
See also CA 65-68; CANR 9, 31

Olyesha, Yuri
See Olesha, Yuri (Karlovich)

Ondaatje, (Philip) Michael
1943- .... CLC 14, 29, 51, 76; DAB;
DAC; DAM MST
See also CA 77-80; CANR 42; DLB 60

Oneal, Elizabeth 1934-
See Oneal, Zibby
See also CA 106; CANR 28; MAICYA;
SATA 30, 82

Oneal, Zibby .... CLC 30
See also Oneal, Elizabeth
See also AAYA 5; CLR 13; JRDA

O'Neill, Eugene (Gladstone)
1888-1953 ...... TCLC 1, 6, 27, 49; DA;
DAB; DAC; DAM DRAM, MST; WLC
See also AITN 1; CA 110; 132;
CDALB 1929-1941; DLB 7; MTCW

Onetti, Juan Carlos
1909-1994 .... CLC 7, 10; DAM MULT,
NOV; SSC 23
See also CA 85-88; 145; CANR 32;
DLB 113; HW; MTCW

O Nuallain, Brian 1911-1966
See O'Brien, Flann
See also CA 21-22; 25-28R; CAP 2

Oppen, George 1908-1984 .... CLC 7, 13, 34
See also CA 13-16R; 113; CANR 8; DLB 5,
165

Oppenheim, E(dward) Phillips
1866-1946 .... TCLC 45
See also CA 111; DLB 70

Origen c. 185-c. 254............. CMLC 19

Orlovitz, Gil 1918-1973........... CLC 22
See also CA 77-80; 45-48; DLB 2, 5

Orris
See Ingelow, Jean

Ortega y Gasset, Jose
1883-1955 ..... TCLC 9; DAM MULT;
HLC
See also CA 106; 130; HW; MTCW

Ortese, Anna Maria 1914-........ CLC 89
See also DLB 177

Ortiz, Simon J(oseph)
1941- .... CLC 45; DAM MULT,
POET; PC 17
See also CA 134; DLB 120, 175; NNAL

Orton, Joe .... CLC 4, 13, 43; DC 3
See also Orton, John Kingsley
See also CDBLB 1960 to Present; DLB 13

Orton, John Kingsley 1933-1967
See Orton, Joe
See also CA 85-88; CANR 35;
DAM DRAM; MTCW

Orwell, George
..... TCLC 2, 6, 15, 31, 51; DAB; WLC
See also Blair, Eric (Arthur)
See also CDBLB 1945-1960; DLB 15, 98

Osborne, David
See Silverberg, Robert

Osborne, George
See Silverberg, Robert

Osborne, John (James)
1929-1994 ..... CLC 1, 2, 5, 11, 45; DA;
DAB; DAC; DAM DRAM, MST; WLC
See also CA 13-16R; 147; CANR 21, 56;
CDBLB 1945-1960; DLB 13; MTCW

Osborne, Lawrence 1958- .... CLC 50

Oshima, Nagisa 1932- .... CLC 20
See also CA 116; 121

Oskison, John Milton
1874-1947 ..... TCLC 35; DAM MULT
See also CA 144; DLB 175; NNAL

Ossoli, Sarah Margaret (Fuller marchesa d')
1810-1850
See Fuller, Margaret
See also SATA 25

Ostrovsky, Alexander
1823-1886 .... NCLC 30, 57

Otero, Blas de 1916-1979........ CLC 11
See also CA 89-92; DLB 134

Otto, Whitney 1955-.............. CLC 70
See also CA 140

Ouida .... TCLC 43
See also De La Ramee, (Marie) Louise
See also DLB 18, 156

Ousmane, Sembene 1923- .... CLC 66; BLC
See also BW 1; CA 117; 125; MTCW

Ovid
43B.C.-18(?) ... CMLC 7; DAM POET;
PC 2

Owen, Hugh
See Faust, Frederick (Schiller)

Owen, Wilfred (Edward Salter)
1893-1918 ...... TCLC 5, 27; DA; DAB;
DAC; DAM MST, POET; WLC
See also CA 104; 141; CDBLB 1914-1945;
DLB 20

Owens, Rochelle 1936-............ CLC 8
See also CA 17-20R; CAAS 2; CANR 39

Oz, Amos
1939-......... CLC 5, 8, 11, 27, 33, 54;
DAM NOV
See also CA 53-56; CANR 27, 47; MTCW

Ozick, Cynthia
1928- .... CLC 3, 7, 28, 62; DAM NOV,
POP; SSC 15
See also BEST 90:1; CA 17-20R; CANR 23;
DLB 28, 152; DLBY 82; INT CANR-23;
MTCW

Ozu, Yasujiro 1903-1963.......... CLC 16
See also CA 112

Pacheco, C.
See Pessoa, Fernando (Antonio Nogueira)

Pa Chin .... CLC 18
See also Li Fei-kan

Pack, Robert 1929-............... CLC 13
See also CA 1-4R; CANR 3, 44; DLB 5

Padgett, Lewis
See Kuttner, Henry

Padilla (Lorenzo), Heberto 1932-... CLC 38
See also AITN 1; CA 123; 131; HW

Page, Jimmy 1944-.............. CLC 12

Page, Louise 1955-.............. CLC 40
See also CA 140

Page, P(atricia) K(athleen)
1916- .... CLC 7, 18; DAC; DAM MST;
PC 12
See also CA 53-56; CANR 4, 22; DLB 68;
MTCW

Page, Thomas Nelson 1853-1922.... SSC 23
See also CA 118; DLB 12, 78; DLBD 13

Paget, Violet 1856-1935
See Lee, Vernon
See also CA 104

Paget-Lowe, Henry
See Lovecraft, H(oward) P(hillips)

Paglia, Camille (Anna) 1947-....... CLC 68
See also CA 140

Paige, Richard
See Koontz, Dean R(ay)

Pakenham, Antonia
See Fraser, (Lady) Antonia (Pakenham)

Palamas, Kostes 1859-1943 .... TCLC 5
See also CA 105

Palazzeschi, Aldo 1885-1974....... TCLC 11
See also CA 89-92; 53-56; DLB 114

Paley, Grace
1922- .... CLC 4, 6, 37; DAM POP;
SSC 8
See also CA 25-28R; CANR 13, 46;
DLB 28; INT CANR-13; MTCW

Palin, Michael (Edward) 1943-..... CLC 21
See also Monty Python
See also CA 107; CANR 35; SATA 67

Palliser, Charles 1947-............ CLC 65
See also CA 136

Palma, Ricardo 1833-1919........ TCLC 29

Pancake, Breece Dexter 1952-1979
See Pancake, Breece D'J
See also CA 123; 109

Pancake, Breece D'J............... CLC 29
See also Pancake, Breece Dexter
See also DLB 130

Panko, Rudy
See Gogol, Nikolai (Vasilyevich)

Papadiamantis, Alexandros
1851-1911 .... TCLC 29

Papadiamantopoulos, Johannes 1856-1910
See Moreas, Jean
See also CA 117

Papini, Giovanni 1881-1956....... TCLC 22
See also CA 121

Paracelsus 1493-1541.............. LC 14

Parasol, Peter
See Stevens, Wallace

Pareto, Vilfredo 1848-1923 .... TCLC 69

Parfenie, Maria
See Codrescu, Andrei

Parini, Jay (Lee) 1948- .... CLC 54
See also CA 97-100; CAAS 16; CANR 32

Park, Jordan
See Kornbluth, C(yril) M.; Pohl, Frederik

Parker, Bert
See Ellison, Harlan (Jay)

Parker, Dorothy (Rothschild)
1893-1967 .... CLC 15, 68;
DAM POET; SSC 2
See also CA 19-20; 25-28R; CAP 2;
DLB 11, 45, 86; MTCW

Parker, Robert B(rown)
1932- ...... CLC 27; DAM NOV, POP
See also BEST 89:4; CA 49-52; CANR 1,
26, 52; INT CANR-26; MTCW

Parkin, Frank 1940-.............. CLC 43
See also CA 147

Parkman, Francis, Jr.
1823-1893 .... NCLC 12
See also DLB 1, 30

Parks, Gordon (Alexander Buchanan)
1912-... CLC 1, 16; BLC; DAM MULT
See also AITN 2; BW 2; CA 41-44R;
CANR 26; DLB 33; SATA 8

Parmenides
c. 515B.C.-c. 450B.C........ CMLC 22
See also DLB 176

Parnell, Thomas 1679-1718 .... LC 3
See also DLB 94

Parra, Nicanor
1914- ...... CLC 2; DAM MULT; HLC
See also CA 85-88; CANR 32; HW; MTCW

Parrish, Mary Frances
See Fisher, M(ary) F(rances) K(ennedy)

Parson
See Coleridge, Samuel Taylor

Parson Lot
See Kingsley, Charles

Partridge, Anthony
See Oppenheim, E(dward) Phillips

Pascal, Blaise 1623-1662 .... LC 35

Pascoli, Giovanni 1855-1912 ...... TCLC 45

Pasolini, Pier Paolo
1922-1975 .... CLC 20, 37; PC 17
See also CA 93-96; 61-64; DLB 128, 177;
MTCW

Pasquini
See Silone, Ignazio

Pastan, Linda (Olenik)
1932- .... CLC 27; DAM POET
See also CA 61-64; CANR 18, 40; DLB 5

Pasternak, Boris (Leonidovich)
1890-1960 ...... CLC 7, 10, 18, 63; DA;
DAB; DAC; DAM MST, NOV, POET;
PC 6; WLC
See also CA 127; 116; MTCW

Patchen, Kenneth
1911-1972 ...CLC 1, 2, 18; DAM POET
See also CA 1-4R; 33-36R; CANR 3, 35;
DLB 16, 48; MTCW

Pater, Walter (Horatio)
1839-1894 .... NCLC 7
See also CDBLB 1832-1890; DLB 57, 156

Paterson, A(ndrew) B(arton)
1864-1941 .... TCLC 32
See also CA 155

Paterson, Katherine (Womeldorf)
    1932- .... CLC 12, 30
    See also AAYA 1; CA 21-24R; CANR 28;
    CLR 7; DLB 52; JRDA; MAICYA;
    MTCW; SATA 13, 53, 92

Patmore, Coventry Kersey Dighton
    1823-1896 .... NCLC 9
    See also DLB 35, 98

Paton, Alan (Stewart)
    1903-1988 ...... CLC 4, 10, 25, 55; DA;
        DAB; DAC; DAM MST, NOV; WLC
    See also CA 13-16; 125; CANR 22; CAP 1;
    MTCW; SATA 11; SATA-Obit 56

Paton Walsh, Gillian 1937-
    See Walsh, Jill Paton
    See also CANR 38; JRDA; MAICYA;
    SAAS 3; SATA 4, 72

Paulding, James Kirke 1778-1860.. NCLC 2
    See also DLB 3, 59, 74

Paulin, Thomas Neilson 1949-
    See Paulin, Tom
    See also CA 123; 128

Paulin, Tom .... CLC 37
    See also Paulin, Thomas Neilson
    See also DLB 40

Paustovsky, Konstantin (Georgievich)
    1892-1968 .... CLC 40
    See also CA 93-96; 25-28R

Pavese, Cesare
    1908-1950 ..... TCLC 3; PC 13; SSC 19
    See also CA 104; DLB 128, 177

Pavic, Milorad 1929- .... CLC 60
    See also CA 136

Payne, Alan
    See Jakes, John (William)

Paz, Gil
    See Lugones, Leopoldo

Paz, Octavio
    1914- .... CLC 3, 4, 6, 10, 19, 51, 65;
        DA; DAB; DAC; DAM MST, MULT,
            POET; HLC; PC 1; WLC
    See also CA 73-76; CANR 32; DLBY 90;
    HW; MTCW

p'Bitek, Okot
    1931-1982 .... CLC 96; BLC;
                    DAM MULT
    See also BW 2; CA 124; 107; DLB 125;
    MTCW

Peacock, Molly 1947- .... CLC 60
    See also CA 103; CAAS 21; CANR 52;
    DLB 120

Peacock, Thomas Love
    1785-1866 .... NCLC 22
    See also DLB 96, 116

Peake, Mervyn 1911-1968 ...... CLC 7, 54
    See also CA 5-8R; 25-28R; CANR 3;
    DLB 15, 160; MTCW; SATA 23

Pearce, Philippa .... CLC 21
    See also Christie, (Ann) Philippa
    See also CLR 9; DLB 161; MAICYA;
    SATA 1, 67

Pearl, Eric
    See Elman, Richard

Pearson, T(homas) R(eid) 1956- .... CLC 39
    See also CA 120; 130; INT 130

Peck, Dale 1967- .... CLC 81
    See also CA 146

Peck, John 1941- .... CLC 3
    See also CA 49-52; CANR 3

Peck, Richard (Wayne) 1934- ...... CLC 21
    See also AAYA 1; CA 85-88; CANR 19,
    38; CLR 15; INT CANR-19; JRDA;
    MAICYA; SAAS 2; SATA 18, 55

Peck, Robert Newton
    1928- .. CLC 17; DA; DAC; DAM MST
    See also AAYA 3; CA 81-84; CANR 31;
    CLR 45; JRDA; MAICYA; SAAS 1;
    SATA 21, 62

Peckinpah, (David) Sam(uel)
    1925-1984 .... CLC 20
    See also CA 109; 114

Pedersen, Knut 1859-1952
    See Hamsun, Knut
    See also CA 104; 119; MTCW

Peeslake, Gaffer
    See Durrell, Lawrence (George)

Peguy, Charles Pierre
    1873-1914 .... TCLC 10
    See also CA 107

Pena, Ramon del Valle y
    See Valle-Inclan, Ramon (Maria) del

Pendennis, Arthur Esquir
    See Thackeray, William Makepeace

Penn, William 1644-1718 .... LC 25
    See also DLB 24

Pepys, Samuel
    1633-1703 ..... LC 11; DA; DAB; DAC;
                    DAM MST; WLC
    See also CDBLB 1660-1789; DLB 101

Percy, Walker
    1916-1990 .... CLC 2, 3, 6, 8, 14, 18, 47,
        65; DAM NOV, POP
    See also CA 1-4R; 131; CANR 1, 23;
    DLB 2; DLBY 80, 90; MTCW

Perec, Georges 1936-1982 .... CLC 56
    See also CA 141; DLB 83

Pereda (y Sanchez de Porrua), Jose Maria de
    1833-1906 .... TCLC 16
    See also CA 117

Pereda y Porrua, Jose Maria de
    See Pereda (y Sanchez de Porrua), Jose
    Maria de

Peregoy, George Weems
    See Mencken, H(enry) L(ouis)

Perelman, S(idney) J(oseph)
    1904-1979 ...... CLC 3, 5, 9, 15, 23, 44,
        49; DAM DRAM
    See also AITN 1, 2; CA 73-76; 89-92;
    CANR 18; DLB 11, 44; MTCW

Peret, Benjamin 1899-1959 .... TCLC 20
    See also CA 117

Peretz, Isaac Loeb 1851(?)-1915... TCLC 16
    See also CA 109

Peretz, Yitzhok Leibush
    See Peretz, Isaac Loeb

Perez Galdos, Benito 1843-1920... TCLC 27
    See also CA 125; 153; HW

Perrault, Charles 1628-1703 .... LC 2
    See also MAICYA; SATA 25

Perry, Brighton
    See Sherwood, Robert E(mmet)

Perse, St.-John .... CLC 4, 11, 46
    See also Leger, (Marie-Rene Auguste) Alexis
    Saint-Leger

Perutz, Leo 1882-1957 .... TCLC 60
    See also DLB 81

Peseenz, Tulio F.
    See Lopez y Fuentes, Gregorio

Pesetsky, Bette 1932- .... CLC 28
    See also CA 133; DLB 130

Peshkov, Alexei Maximovich 1868-1936
    See Gorky, Maxim
    See also CA 105; 141; DA; DAC;
    DAM DRAM, MST, NOV

Pessoa, Fernando (Antonio Nogueira)
    1888-1935 .... TCLC 27; HLC
    See also CA 125

Peterkin, Julia Mood 1880-1961.... CLC 31
    See also CA 102; DLB 9

Peters, Joan K. 1945- .... CLC 39

Peters, Robert L(ouis) 1924- .... CLC 7
    See also CA 13-16R; CAAS 8; DLB 105

Petofi, Sandor 1823-1849 .... NCLC 21

Petrakis, Harry Mark 1923- .... CLC 3
    See also CA 9-12R; CANR 4, 30

Petrarch
    1304-1374 .... CMLC 20; DAM POET;
                    PC 8

Petrov, Evgeny .... TCLC 21
    See also Kataev, Evgeny Petrovich

Petry, Ann (Lane) 1908- ...... CLC 1, 7, 18
    See also BW 1; CA 5-8R; CAAS 6;
    CANR 4, 46; CLR 12; DLB 76; JRDA;
    MAICYA; MTCW; SATA 5

Petursson, Halligrimur 1614-1674 .... LC 8

Philips, Katherine 1632-1664 .... LC 30
    See also DLB 131

Philipson, Morris H. 1926- .... CLC 53
    See also CA 1-4R; CANR 4

Phillips, Caryl
    1958- .... CLC 96; DAM MULT
    See also BW 2; CA 141; DLB 157

Phillips, David Graham
    1867-1911 .... TCLC 44
    See also CA 108; DLB 9, 12

Phillips, Jack
    See Sandburg, Carl (August)

Phillips, Jayne Anne
    1952- .... CLC 15, 33; SSC 16
    See also CA 101; CANR 24, 50; DLBY 80;
    INT CANR-24; MTCW

Phillips, Richard
    See Dick, Philip K(indred)

Phillips, Robert (Schaeffer) 1938-... CLC 28
    See also CA 17-20R; CAAS 13; CANR 8;
    DLB 105

Phillips, Ward
    See Lovecraft, H(oward) P(hillips)

Piccolo, Lucio 1901-1969 .... CLC 13
    See also CA 97-100; DLB 114

Pickthall, Marjorie L(owry) C(hristie)
    1883-1922 .... TCLC 21
    See also CA 107; DLB 92

Pico della Mirandola, Giovanni
1463-1494 .... **LC 15**

Piercy, Marge
1936- .... **CLC 3, 6, 14, 18, 27, 62**
See also CA 21-24R; CAAS 1; CANR 13,
43; DLB 120; MTCW

Piers, Robert
See Anthony, Piers

Pieyre de Mandiargues, Andre   1909-1991
See Mandiargues, Andre Pieyre de
See also CA 103; 136; CANR 22

Pilnyak, Boris .... **TCLC 23**
See also Vogau, Boris Andreyevich

Pincherle, Alberto
1907-1990 ..... **CLC 11, 18; DAM NOV**
See also Moravia, Alberto
See also CA 25-28R; 132; CANR 33;
MTCW

Pinckney, Darryl   1953- .... **CLC 76**
See also BW 2; CA 143

Pindar   518B.C.-446B.C. .... **CMLC 12**
See also DLB 176

Pineda, Cecile   1942- .... **CLC 39**
See also CA 118

Pinero, Arthur Wing
1855-1934 ..... **TCLC 32; DAM DRAM**
See also CA 110; 153; DLB 10

Pinero, Miguel (Antonio Gomez)
1946-1988 .... **CLC 4, 55**
See also CA 61-64; 125; CANR 29; HW

Pinget, Robert   1919- .... **CLC 7, 13, 37**
See also CA 85-88; DLB 83

Pink Floyd
See Barrett, (Roger) Syd; Gilmour, David;
Mason, Nick; Waters, Roger; Wright,
Rick

Pinkney, Edward   1802-1828 ..... **NCLC 31**

Pinkwater, Daniel Manus   1941- .... **CLC 35**
See also Pinkwater, Manus
See also AAYA 1; CA 29-32R; CANR 12,
38; CLR 4; JRDA; MAICYA; SAAS 3;
SATA 46, 76

Pinkwater, Manus
See Pinkwater, Daniel Manus
See also SATA 8

Pinsky, Robert
1940- .. **CLC 9, 19, 38, 94; DAM POET**
See also CA 29-32R; CAAS 4; DLBY 82

Pinta, Harold
See Pinter, Harold

Pinter, Harold
1930- ..... **CLC 1, 3, 6, 9, 11, 15, 27, 58,
73; DA; DAB; DAC; DAM DRAM,
MST; WLC**
See also CA 5-8R; CANR 33; CDBLB 1960
to Present; DLB 13; MTCW

Piozzi, Hester Lynch (Thrale)
1741-1821 .... **NCLC 57**
See also DLB 104, 142

Pirandello, Luigi
1867-1936 ..... **TCLC 4, 29; DA; DAB;
DAC; DAM DRAM, MST; DC 5;
SSC 22; WLC**
See also CA 104; 153

Pirsig, Robert M(aynard)
1928- .... **CLC 4, 6, 73; DAM POP**
See also CA 53-56; CANR 42; MTCW;
SATA 39

Pisarev, Dmitry Ivanovich
1840-1868 .... **NCLC 25**

Pix, Mary (Griffith)   1666-1709 .... **LC 8**
See also DLB 80

Pixerecourt, Guilbert de
1773-1844 .... **NCLC 39**

Plaidy, Jean
See Hibbert, Eleanor Alice Burford

Planche, James Robinson
1796-1880 .... **NCLC 42**

Plant, Robert   1948- .... **CLC 12**

Plante, David (Robert)
1940- .... **CLC 7, 23, 38; DAM NOV**
See also CA 37-40R; CANR 12, 36;
DLBY 83; INT CANR-12; MTCW

Plath, Sylvia
1932-1963 ..... **CLC 1, 2, 3, 5, 9, 11, 14,
17, 50, 51, 62; DA; DAB; DAC;
DAM MST, POET; PC 1; WLC**
See also AAYA 13; CA 19-20; CANR 34;
CAP 2; CDALB 1941-1968; DLB 5, 6,
152; MTCW

Plato
428(?)B.C.-348(?)B.C. .... **CMLC 8; DA;
DAB; DAC; DAM MST**
See also DLB 176

Platonov, Andrei .... **TCLC 14**
See also Klimentov, Andrei Platonovich

Platt, Kin   1911- .... **CLC 26**
See also AAYA 11; CA 17-20R; CANR 11;
JRDA; SAAS 17; SATA 21, 86

Plautus   c. 251B.C.-184B.C. .... **DC 6**

Plick et Plock
See Simenon, Georges (Jacques Christian)

Plimpton, George (Ames)   1927- ..... **CLC 36**
See also AITN 1; CA 21-24R; CANR 32;
MTCW; SATA 10

Plomer, William Charles Franklin
1903-1973 .... **CLC 4, 8**
See also CA 21-22; CANR 34; CAP 2;
DLB 20, 162; MTCW; SATA 24

Plowman, Piers
See Kavanagh, Patrick (Joseph)

Plum, J.
See Wodehouse, P(elham) G(renville)

Plumly, Stanley (Ross)   1939- ...... **CLC 33**
See also CA 108; 110; DLB 5; INT 110

Plumpe, Friedrich Wilhelm
1888-1931 .... **TCLC 53**
See also CA 112

Poe, Edgar Allan
1809-1849 .... **NCLC 1, 16, 55; DA;
DAB; DAC; DAM MST, POET; PC 1;
SSC 1, 22; WLC**
See also AAYA 14; CDALB 1640-1865;
DLB 3, 59, 73, 74; SATA 23

Poet of Titchfield Street, The
See Pound, Ezra (Weston Loomis)

Pohl, Frederik   1919- ..... **CLC 18; SSC 25**
See also CA 61-64; CAAS 1; CANR 11, 37;
DLB 8; INT CANR-11; MTCW;
SATA 24

Poirier, Louis   1910-
See Gracq, Julien
See also CA 122; 126

Poitier, Sidney   1927- .... **CLC 26**
See also BW 1; CA 117

Polanski, Roman   1933- .... **CLC 16**
See also CA 77-80

Poliakoff, Stephen   1952- .... **CLC 38**
See also CA 106; DLB 13

Police, The
See Copeland, Stewart (Armstrong);
Summers, Andrew James; Sumner,
Gordon Matthew

Polidori, John William
1795-1821 .... **NCLC 51**
See also DLB 116

Pollitt, Katha   1949- .... **CLC 28**
See also CA 120; 122; MTCW

Pollock, (Mary) Sharon
1936- .... **CLC 50; DAC; DAM DRAM,
MST**
See also CA 141; DLB 60

Polo, Marco   1254-1324 .... **CMLC 15**

Polonsky, Abraham (Lincoln)
1910- .... **CLC 92**
See also CA 104; DLB 26; INT 104

Polybius   c. 200B.C.-c. 118B.C. .... **CMLC 17**
See also DLB 176

Pomerance, Bernard
1940- .... **CLC 13; DAM DRAM**
See also CA 101; CANR 49

Ponge, Francis (Jean Gaston Alfred)
1899-1988 ..... **CLC 6, 18; DAM POET**
See also CA 85-88; 126; CANR 40

Pontoppidan, Henrik   1857-1943 ... **TCLC 29**

Poole, Josephine .... **CLC 17**
See also Helyar, Jane Penelope Josephine
See also SAAS 2; SATA 5

Popa, Vasko   1922-1991 .... **CLC 19**
See also CA 112; 148

Pope, Alexander
1688-1744 ...... **LC 3; DA; DAB; DAC;
DAM MST, POET; WLC**
See also CDBLB 1660-1789; DLB 95, 101

Porter, Connie (Rose)   1959(?)- ..... **CLC 70**
See also BW 2; CA 142; SATA 81

Porter, Gene(va Grace) Stratton
1863(?)-1924 .... **TCLC 21**
See also CA 112

Porter, Katherine Anne
1890-1980 ...... **CLC 1, 3, 7, 10, 13, 15,
27; DA; DAB; DAC; DAM MST, NOV;
SSC 4**
See also AITN 2; CA 1-4R; 101; CANR 1;
DLB 4, 9, 102; DLBD 12; DLBY 80;
MTCW; SATA 39; SATA-Obit 23

Porter, Peter (Neville Frederick)
1929- .... **CLC 5, 13, 33**
See also CA 85-88; DLB 40

Porter, William Sydney   1862-1910
   See Henry, O.
   See also CA 104; 131; CDALB 1865-1917;
   DA; DAB; DAC; DAM MST; DLB 12,
   78, 79; MTCW; YABC 2

Portillo (y Pacheco), Jose Lopez
   See Lopez Portillo (y Pacheco), Jose

Post, Melville Davisson
   1869-1930 .... TCLC 39
   See also CA 110

Potok, Chaim
   1929- .... CLC 2, 7, 14, 26; DAM NOV
   See also AAYA 15; AITN 1, 2; CA 17-20R;
   CANR 19, 35; DLB 28, 152;
   INT CANR-19; MTCW; SATA 33

Potter, Beatrice
   See Webb, (Martha) Beatrice (Potter)
   See also MAICYA

Potter, Dennis (Christopher George)
   1935-1994 .... CLC 58, 86
   See also CA 107; 145; CANR 33; MTCW

Pound, Ezra (Weston Loomis)
   1885-1972 ...... CLC 1, 2, 3, 4, 5, 7, 10,
   13, 18, 34, 48, 50; DA; DAB; DAC;
   DAM MST, POET; PC 4; WLC
   See also CA 5-8R; 37-40R; CANR 40;
   CDALB 1917-1929; DLB 4, 45, 63;
   MTCW

Povod, Reinaldo   1959-1994 .... CLC 44
   See also CA 136; 146

Powell, Adam Clayton, Jr.
   1908-1972 .... CLC 89; BLC;
   DAM MULT
   See also BW 1; CA 102; 33-36R

Powell, Anthony (Dymoke)
   1905- .... CLC 1, 3, 7, 9, 10, 31
   See also CA 1-4R; CANR 1, 32;
   CDBLB 1945-1960; DLB 15; MTCW

Powell, Dawn   1897-1965 .... CLC 66
   See also CA 5-8R

Powell, Padgett   1952- .... CLC 34
   See also CA 126

Power, Susan .... CLC 91

Powers, J(ames) F(arl)
   1917- .... CLC 1, 4, 8, 57; SSC 4
   See also CA 1-4R; CANR 2; DLB 130;
   MTCW

Powers, John J(ames)   1945-
   See Powers, John R.
   See also CA 69-72

Powers, John R. .... CLC 66
   See also Powers, John J(ames)

Powers, Richard (S.)   1957- .... CLC 93
   See also CA 148

Pownall, David   1938- .... CLC 10
   See also CA 89-92; CAAS 18; CANR 49;
   DLB 14

Powys, John Cowper
   1872-1963 .... CLC 7, 9, 15, 46
   See also CA 85-88; DLB 15; MTCW

Powys, T(heodore) F(rancis)
   1875-1953 .... TCLC 9
   See also CA 106; DLB 36, 162

Prager, Emily   1952- .... CLC 56

Pratt, E(dwin) J(ohn)
   1883(?)-1964 .... CLC 19; DAC;
   DAM POET
   See also CA 141; 93-96; DLB 92

Premchand .... TCLC 21
   See also Srivastava, Dhanpat Rai

Preussler, Otfried   1923- .... CLC 17
   See also CA 77-80; SATA 24

Prevert, Jacques (Henri Marie)
   1900-1977 .... CLC 15
   See also CA 77-80; 69-72; CANR 29;
   MTCW; SATA-Obit 30

Prevost, Abbe (Antoine Francois)
   1697-1763 .... LC 1

Price, (Edward) Reynolds
   1933- .... CLC 3, 6, 13, 43, 50, 63;
   DAM NOV; SSC 22
   See also CA 1-4R; CANR 1, 37; DLB 2;
   INT CANR-37

Price, Richard   1949- .... CLC 6, 12
   See also CA 49-52; CANR 3; DLBY 81

Prichard, Katharine Susannah
   1883-1969 .... CLC 46
   See also CA 11-12; CANR 33; CAP 1;
   MTCW; SATA 66

Priestley, J(ohn) B(oynton)
   1894-1984 .... CLC 2, 5, 9, 34;
   DAM DRAM, NOV
   See also CA 9-12R; 113; CANR 33;
   CDBLB 1914-1945; DLB 10, 34, 77, 100,
   139; DLBY 84; MTCW

Prince   1958(?)- .... CLC 35

Prince, F(rank) T(empleton)   1912- .. CLC 22
   See also CA 101; CANR 43; DLB 20

Prince Kropotkin
   See Kropotkin, Peter (Alekseievich)

Prior, Matthew   1664-1721 .... LC 4
   See also DLB 95

Pritchard, William H(arrison)
   1932- .... CLC 34
   See also CA 65-68; CANR 23; DLB 111

Pritchett, V(ictor) S(awdon)
   1900- .... CLC 5, 13, 15, 41;
   DAM NOV; SSC 14
   See also CA 61-64; CANR 31; DLB 15,
   139; MTCW

Private 19022
   See Manning, Frederic

Probst, Mark   1925- .... CLC 59
   See also CA 130

Prokosch, Frederic   1908-1989 .... CLC 4, 48
   See also CA 73-76; 128; DLB 48

Prophet, The
   See Dreiser, Theodore (Herman Albert)

Prose, Francine   1947- .... CLC 45
   See also CA 109; 112; CANR 46

Proudhon
   See Cunha, Euclides (Rodrigues Pimenta) da

Proulx, E. Annie   1935- .... CLC 81

Proust, (Valentin-Louis-George-Eugene-)
   Marcel
   1871-1922 .... TCLC 7, 13, 33; DA;
   DAB; DAC; DAM MST, NOV; WLC
   See also CA 104; 120; DLB 65; MTCW

Prowler, Harley
   See Masters, Edgar Lee

Prus, Boleslaw   1845-1912 .... TCLC 48

Pryor, Richard (Franklin Lenox Thomas)
   1940- .... CLC 26
   See also CA 122

Przybyszewski, Stanislaw
   1868-1927 .... TCLC 36
   See also DLB 66

Pteleon
   See Grieve, C(hristopher) M(urray)
   See also DAM POET

Puckett, Lute
   See Masters, Edgar Lee

Puig, Manuel
   1932-1990 .... CLC 3, 5, 10, 28, 65;
   DAM MULT; HLC
   See also CA 45-48; CANR 2, 32; DLB 113;
   HW; MTCW

Purdy, Al(fred Wellington)
   1918- .... CLC 3, 6, 14, 50; DAC;
   DAM MST, POET
   See also CA 81-84; CAAS 17; CANR 42;
   DLB 88

Purdy, James (Amos)
   1923- .... CLC 2, 4, 10, 28, 52
   See also CA 33-36R; CAAS 1; CANR 19,
   51; DLB 2; INT CANR-19; MTCW

Pure, Simon
   See Swinnerton, Frank Arthur

Pushkin, Alexander (Sergeyevich)
   1799-1837 ..... NCLC 3, 27; DA; DAB;
   DAC; DAM DRAM, MST, POET;
   PC 10; WLC
   See also SATA 61

P'u Sung-ling   1640-1715 .... LC 3

Putnam, Arthur Lee
   See Alger, Horatio, Jr.

Puzo, Mario
   1920- ..... CLC 1, 2, 6, 36; DAM NOV,
   POP
   See also CA 65-68; CANR 4, 42; DLB 6;
   MTCW

Pygge, Edward
   See Barnes, Julian (Patrick)

Pym, Barbara (Mary Crampton)
   1913-1980 .... CLC 13, 19, 37
   See also CA 13-14; 97-100; CANR 13, 34;
   CAP 1; DLB 14; DLBY 87; MTCW

Pynchon, Thomas (Ruggles, Jr.)
   1937- ..... CLC 2, 3, 6, 9, 11, 18, 33, 62,
   72; DA; DAB; DAC; DAM MST, NOV,
   POP; SSC 14; WLC
   See also BEST 90:2; CA 17-20R; CANR 22,
   46; DLB 2, 173; MTCW

Pythagoras
   c. 570B.C.-c. 500B.C......... CMLC 22
   See also DLB 176

Qian Zhongshu
   See Ch'ien Chung-shu

Qroll
   See Dagerman, Stig (Halvard)

Quarrington, Paul (Lewis)   1953- .... CLC 65
   See also CA 129

Quasimodo, Salvatore 1901-1968 ... **CLC 10**
See also CA 13-16; 25-28R; CAP 1;
DLB 114; MTCW

Quay, Stephen 1947- .... **CLC 95**

Quay, The Brothers
See Quay, Stephen; Quay, Timothy

Quay, Timothy 1947-............. **CLC 95**

Queen, Ellery.................. **CLC 3, 11**
See also Dannay, Frederic; Davidson,
Avram; Lee, Manfred B(ennington);
Marlowe, Stephen; Sturgeon, Theodore
(Hamilton); Vance, John Holbrook

Queen, Ellery, Jr.
See Dannay, Frederic; Lee, Manfred
B(ennington)

Queneau, Raymond
1903-1976 ....**CLC 2, 5, 10, 42**
See also CA 77-80; 69-72; CANR 32;
DLB 72; MTCW

Quevedo, Francisco de 1580-1645.... **LC 23**

Quiller-Couch, Arthur Thomas
1863-1944 .... **TCLC 53**
See also CA 118; DLB 135, 153

Quin, Ann (Marie) 1936-1973...... **CLC 6**
See also CA 9-12R; 45-48; DLB 14

Quinn, Martin
See Smith, Martin Cruz

Quinn, Peter 1947-............... **CLC 91**

Quinn, Simon
See Smith, Martin Cruz

Quiroga, Horacio (Sylvestre)
1878-1937 ..... **TCLC 20; DAM MULT;**
HLC
See also CA 117; 131; HW; MTCW

Quoirez, Francoise 1935-........... **CLC 9**
See also Sagan, Francoise
See also CA 49-52; CANR 6, 39; MTCW

Raabe, Wilhelm 1831-1910 .... **TCLC 45**
See also DLB 129

Rabe, David (William)
1940- ...... **CLC 4, 8, 33; DAM DRAM**
See also CA 85-88; CABS 3; DLB 7

Rabelais, Francois
1483-1553 ...... **LC 5; DA; DAB; DAC;**
DAM MST; WLC

Rabinovitch, Sholem 1859-1916
See Aleichem, Sholom
See also CA 104

Rachilde 1860-1953 .... **TCLC 67**
See also DLB 123

Racine, Jean
1639-1699 .... **LC 28; DAB; DAM MST**

Radcliffe, Ann (Ward)
1764-1823 .... **NCLC 6, 55**
See also DLB 39

Radiguet, Raymond 1903-1923 .... **TCLC 29**
See also DLB 65

Radnoti, Miklos 1909-1944 .... **TCLC 16**
See also CA 118

Rado, James 1939-............... **CLC 17**
See also CA 105

Radvanyi, Netty 1900-1983
See Seghers, Anna
See also CA 85-88; 110

Rae, Ben
See Griffiths, Trevor

Raeburn, John (Hay) 1941-........ **CLC 34**
See also CA 57-60

Ragni, Gerome 1942-1991 .... **CLC 17**
See also CA 105; 134

Rahv, Philip 1908-1973 .... **CLC 24**
See also Greenberg, Ivan
See also DLB 137

Raine, Craig 1944-............... **CLC 32**
See also CA 108; CANR 29, 51; DLB 40

Raine, Kathleen (Jessie) 1908- ... **CLC 7, 45**
See also CA 85-88; CANR 46; DLB 20;
MTCW

Rainis, Janis 1865-1929 .... **TCLC 29**

Rakosi, Carl.................... **CLC 47**
See also Rawley, Callman
See also CAAS 5

Raleigh, Richard
See Lovecraft, H(oward) P(hillips)

Raleigh, Sir Walter 1554(?)-1618 .... **LC 31**
See also CDBLB Before 1660; DLB 172

Rallentando, H. P.
See Sayers, Dorothy L(eigh)

Ramal, Walter
See de la Mare, Walter (John)

Ramon, Juan
See Jimenez (Mantecon), Juan Ramon

Ramos, Graciliano 1892-1953 ..... **TCLC 32**

Rampersad, Arnold 1941-......... **CLC 44**
See also BW 2; CA 127; 133; DLB 111;
INT 133

Rampling, Anne
See Rice, Anne

Ramsay, Allan 1684(?)-1758 .... **LC 29**
See also DLB 95

Ramuz, Charles-Ferdinand
1878-1947 .... **TCLC 33**

Rand, Ayn
1905-1982 ...... **CLC 3, 30, 44, 79; DA;**
DAC; DAM MST, NOV, POP; WLC
See also AAYA 10; CA 13-16R; 105;
CANR 27; MTCW

Randall, Dudley (Felker)
1914- ...... **CLC 1; BLC; DAM MULT**
See also BW 1; CA 25-28R; CANR 23;
DLB 41

Randall, Robert
See Silverberg, Robert

Ranger, Ken
See Creasey, John

Ransom, John Crowe
1888-1974 .... **CLC 2, 4, 5, 11, 24;**
DAM POET
See also CA 5-8R; 49-52; CANR 6, 34;
DLB 45, 63; MTCW

Rao, Raja 1909- ... **CLC 25, 56; DAM NOV**
See also CA 73-76; CANR 51; MTCW

Raphael, Frederic (Michael)
1931- .... **CLC 2, 14**
See also CA 1-4R; CANR 1; DLB 14

Ratcliffe, James P.
See Mencken, H(enry) L(ouis)

Rathbone, Julian 1935- .... **CLC 41**
See also CA 101; CANR 34

Rattigan, Terence (Mervyn)
1911-1977 .... **CLC 7; DAM DRAM**
See also CA 85-88; 73-76;
CDBLB 1945-1960; DLB 13; MTCW

Ratushinskaya, Irina 1954-........ **CLC 54**
See also CA 129

Raven, Simon (Arthur Noel)
1927- .... **CLC 14**
See also CA 81-84

Rawley, Callman 1903-
See Rakosi, Carl
See also CA 21-24R; CANR 12, 32

Rawlings, Marjorie Kinnan
1896-1953 .... **TCLC 4**
See also AAYA 20; CA 104; 137; DLB 9,
22, 102; JRDA; MAICYA; YABC 1

Ray, Satyajit
1921-1992 ... **CLC 16, 76; DAM MULT**
See also CA 114; 137

Read, Herbert Edward 1893-1968.... **CLC 4**
See also CA 85-88; 25-28R; DLB 20, 149

Read, Piers Paul 1941- ...... **CLC 4, 10, 25**
See also CA 21-24R; CANR 38; DLB 14;
SATA 21

Reade, Charles 1814-1884 .... **NCLC 2**
See also DLB 21

Reade, Hamish
See Gray, Simon (James Holliday)

Reading, Peter 1946- .... **CLC 47**
See also CA 103; CANR 46; DLB 40

Reaney, James
1926- ...... **CLC 13; DAC; DAM MST**
See also CA 41-44R; CAAS 15; CANR 42;
DLB 68; SATA 43

Rebreanu, Liviu 1885-1944 .... **TCLC 28**

Rechy, John (Francisco)
1934- .... **CLC 1, 7, 14, 18;**
DAM MULT; HLC
See also CA 5-8R; CAAS 4; CANR 6, 32;
DLB 122; DLBY 82; HW; INT CANR-6

Redcam, Tom 1870-1933 .... **TCLC 25**

Reddin, Keith.................... **CLC 67**

Redgrove, Peter (William)
1932- .... **CLC 6, 41**
See also CA 1-4R; CANR 3, 39; DLB 40

Redmon, Anne.................... **CLC 22**
See also Nightingale, Anne Redmon
See also DLBY 86

Reed, Eliot
See Ambler, Eric

Reed, Ishmael
1938- .... **CLC 2, 3, 5, 6, 13, 32, 60;**
BLC; DAM MULT
See also BW 2; CA 21-24R; CANR 25, 48;
DLB 2, 5, 33, 169; DLBD 8; MTCW

Reed, John (Silas) 1887-1920 ...... **TCLC 9**
See also CA 106

Reed, Lou.................... **CLC 21**
See also Firbank, Louis

Reeve, Clara 1729-1807 .... **NCLC 19**
See also DLB 39

Reich, Wilhelm 1897-1957........ **TCLC 57**

Reid, Christopher (John) 1949- . . . . . **CLC 33**
See also CA 140; DLB 40

Reid, Desmond
See Moorcock, Michael (John)

Reid Banks, Lynne 1929-
See Banks, Lynne Reid
See also CA 1-4R; CANR 6, 22, 38;
CLR 24; JRDA; MAICYA; SATA 22, 75

Reilly, William K.
See Creasey, John

Reiner, Max
See Caldwell, (Janet Miriam) Taylor
(Holland)

Reis, Ricardo
See Pessoa, Fernando (Antonio Nogueira)

Remarque, Erich Maria
1898-1970 . . . . **CLC 21; DA; DAB; DAC;**
DAM MST, NOV
See also CA 77-80; 29-32R; DLB 56;
MTCW

Remizov, A.
See Remizov, Aleksei (Mikhailovich)

Remizov, A. M.
See Remizov, Aleksei (Mikhailovich)

Remizov, Aleksei (Mikhailovich)
1877-1957 . . . . **TCLC 27**
See also CA 125; 133

Renan, Joseph Ernest
1823-1892 . . . . **NCLC 26**

Renard, Jules 1864-1910 . . . . **TCLC 17**
See also CA 117

Renault, Mary . . . . **CLC 3, 11, 17**
See also Challans, Mary
See also DLBY 83

Rendell, Ruth (Barbara)
1930- . . . . **CLC 28, 48; DAM POP**
See also Vine, Barbara
See also CA 109; CANR 32, 52; DLB 87;
INT CANR-32; MTCW

Renoir, Jean 1894-1979 . . . . **CLC 20**
See also CA 129; 85-88

Resnais, Alain 1922- . . . . **CLC 16**

Reverdy, Pierre 1889-1960 . . . . **CLC 53**
See also CA 97-100; 89-92

Rexroth, Kenneth
1905-1982 . . . . . . **CLC 1, 2, 6, 11, 22, 49;**
DAM POET
See also CA 5-8R; 107; CANR 14, 34;
CDALB 1941-1968; DLB 16, 48, 165;
DLBY 82; INT CANR-14; MTCW

Reyes, Alfonso 1889-1959 . . . . **TCLC 33**
See also CA 131; HW

Reyes y Basoalto, Ricardo Eliecer Neftali
See Neruda, Pablo

Reymont, Wladyslaw (Stanislaw)
1868(?)-1925 . . . . **TCLC 5**
See also CA 104

Reynolds, Jonathan 1942- . . . . **CLC 6, 38**
See also CA 65-68; CANR 28

Reynolds, Joshua 1723-1792 . . . . **LC 15**
See also DLB 104

Reynolds, Michael Shane 1937- . . . . **CLC 44**
See also CA 65-68; CANR 9

Reznikoff, Charles 1894-1976 . . . . **CLC 9**
See also CA 33-36; 61-64; CAP 2; DLB 28,
45

Rezzori (d'Arezzo), Gregor von
1914- . . . . **CLC 25**
See also CA 122; 136

Rhine, Richard
See Silverstein, Alvin

Rhodes, Eugene Manlove
1869-1934 . . . . **TCLC 53**

R'hoone
See Balzac, Honore de

Rhys, Jean
1890(?)-1979 . . . . **CLC 2, 4, 6, 14, 19, 51;**
DAM NOV; SSC 21
See also CA 25-28R; 85-88; CANR 35;
CDBLB 1945-1960; DLB 36, 117, 162;
MTCW

Ribeiro, Darcy 1922-1997 . . . . **CLC 34**
See also CA 33-36R; 156

Ribeiro, Joao Ubaldo (Osorio Pimentel)
1941- . . . . **CLC 10, 67**
See also CA 81-84

Ribman, Ronald (Burt) 1932- . . . . **CLC 7**
See also CA 21-24R; CANR 46

Ricci, Nino 1959- . . . . **CLC 70**
See also CA 137

Rice, Anne 1941- . . . . . **CLC 41; DAM POP**
See also AAYA 9; BEST 89:2; CA 65-68;
CANR 12, 36, 53

Rice, Elmer (Leopold)
1892-1967 . . . . **CLC 7, 49; DAM DRAM**
See also CA 21-22; 25-28R; CAP 2; DLB 4,
7; MTCW

Rice, Tim(othy Miles Bindon)
1944- . . . . **CLC 21**
See also CA 103; CANR 46

Rich, Adrienne (Cecile)
1929- . . . . **CLC 3, 6, 7, 11, 18, 36, 73, 76;**
DAM POET; PC 5
See also CA 9-12R; CANR 20, 53; DLB 5,
67; MTCW

Rich, Barbara
See Graves, Robert (von Ranke)

Rich, Robert
See Trumbo, Dalton

Richard, Keith . . . . **CLC 17**
See also Richards, Keith

Richards, David Adams
1950- . . . . **CLC 59; DAC**
See also CA 93-96; DLB 53

Richards, I(vor) A(rmstrong)
1893-1979 . . . . **CLC 14, 24**
See also CA 41-44R; 89-92; CANR 34;
DLB 27

Richards, Keith 1943-
See Richard, Keith
See also CA 107

Richardson, Anne
See Roiphe, Anne (Richardson)

Richardson, Dorothy Miller
1873-1957 . . . . **TCLC 3**
See also CA 104; DLB 36

Richardson, Ethel Florence (Lindesay)
1870-1946
See Richardson, Henry Handel
See also CA 105

Richardson, Henry Handel . . . . **TCLC 4**
See also Richardson, Ethel Florence
(Lindesay)

Richardson, John
1796-1852 . . . . **NCLC 55; DAC**
See also DLB 99

Richardson, Samuel
1689-1761 . . . . . . **LC 1; DA; DAB; DAC;**
DAM MST, NOV; WLC
See also CDBLB 1660-1789; DLB 39

Richler, Mordecai
1931- . . . . **CLC 3, 5, 9, 13, 18, 46, 70;**
DAC; DAM MST, NOV
See also AITN 1; CA 65-68; CANR 31;
CLR 17; DLB 53; MAICYA; MTCW;
SATA 44; SATA-Brief 27

Richter, Conrad (Michael)
1890-1968 . . . . **CLC 30**
See also AAYA 21; CA 5-8R; 25-28R;
CANR 23; DLB 9; MTCW; SATA 3

Ricostranza, Tom
See Ellis, Trey

Riddell, J. H. 1832-1906 . . . . **TCLC 40**

Riding, Laura . . . . **CLC 3, 7**
See also Jackson, Laura (Riding)

Riefenstahl, Berta Helene Amalia 1902-
See Riefenstahl, Leni
See also CA 108

Riefenstahl, Leni . . . . **CLC 16**
See also Riefenstahl, Berta Helene Amalia

Riffe, Ernest
See Bergman, (Ernst) Ingmar

Riggs, (Rolla) Lynn
1899-1954 . . . . . **TCLC 56; DAM MULT**
See also CA 144; DLB 175; NNAL

Riley, James Whitcomb
1849-1916 . . . . . . **TCLC 51; DAM POET**
See also CA 118; 137; MAICYA; SATA 17

Riley, Tex
See Creasey, John

Rilke, Rainer Maria
1875-1926 . . . . **TCLC 1, 6, 19;**
DAM POET; PC 2
See also CA 104; 132; DLB 81; MTCW

Rimbaud, (Jean Nicolas) Arthur
1854-1891 . . . . . **NCLC 4, 35; DA; DAB;**
DAC; DAM MST, POET; PC 3; WLC

Rinehart, Mary Roberts
1876-1958 . . . . **TCLC 52**
See also CA 108

Ringmaster, The
See Mencken, H(enry) L(ouis)

Ringwood, Gwen(dolyn Margaret) Pharis
1910-1984 . . . . **CLC 48**
See also CA 148; 112; DLB 88

Rio, Michel 19(?)- . . . . **CLC 43**

Ritsos, Giannes
See Ritsos, Yannis

Ritsos, Yannis 1909-1990 . . . . . **CLC 6, 13, 31**
See also CA 77-80; 133; CANR 39; MTCW

Ritter, Erika 1948(?)- . . . . **CLC 52**

Rivera, Jose Eustasio 1889-1928... **TCLC 35**
See also HW

Rivers, Conrad Kent 1933-1968...... **CLC 1**
See also BW 1; CA 85-88; DLB 41

Rivers, Elfrida
See Bradley, Marion Zimmer

Riverside, John
See Heinlein, Robert A(nson)

Rizal, Jose 1861-1896.......... **NCLC 27**

Roa Bastos, Augusto (Antonio)
1917- ..... **CLC 45; DAM MULT; HLC**
See also CA 131; DLB 113; HW

Robbe-Grillet, Alain
1922- ...... **CLC 1, 2, 4, 6, 8, 10, 14, 43**
See also CA 9-12R; CANR 33; DLB 83;
MTCW

Robbins, Harold
1916- .... **CLC 5; DAM NOV**
See also CA 73-76; CANR 26, 54; MTCW

Robbins, Thomas Eugene 1936-
See Robbins, Tom
See also CA 81-84; CANR 29; DAM NOV,
POP; MTCW

Robbins, Tom............... **CLC 9, 32, 64**
See also Robbins, Thomas Eugene
See also BEST 90:3; DLBY 80

Robbins, Trina 1938- .... **CLC 21**
See also CA 128

Roberts, Charles G(eorge) D(ouglas)
1860-1943 .... **TCLC 8**
See also CA 105; CLR 33; DLB 92;
SATA 88; SATA-Brief 29

Roberts, Elizabeth Madox
1886-1941 .... **TCLC 68**
See also CA 111; DLB 9, 54, 102;
SATA 33; SATA-Brief 27

Roberts, Kate 1891-1985 .... **CLC 15**
See also CA 107; 116

Roberts, Keith (John Kingston)
1935- .... **CLC 14**
See also CA 25-28R; CANR 46

Roberts, Kenneth (Lewis)
1885-1957 .... **TCLC 23**
See also CA 109; DLB 9

Roberts, Michele (B.) 1949-........ **CLC 48**
See also CA 115

Robertson, Ellis
See Ellison, Harlan (Jay); Silverberg, Robert

Robertson, Thomas William
1829-1871 .... **NCLC 35; DAM DRAM**

Robinson, Edwin Arlington
1869-1935 .... **TCLC 5; DA; DAC;**
DAM MST, POET; PC 1
See also CA 104; 133; CDALB 1865-1917;
DLB 54; MTCW

Robinson, Henry Crabb
1775-1867 .... **NCLC 15**
See also DLB 107

Robinson, Jill 1936- .... **CLC 10**
See also CA 102; INT 102

Robinson, Kim Stanley 1952- ...... **CLC 34**
See also CA 126

Robinson, Lloyd
See Silverberg, Robert

Robinson, Marilynne 1944-........ **CLC 25**
See also CA 116

Robinson, Smokey................. **CLC 21**
See also Robinson, William, Jr.

Robinson, William, Jr. 1940-
See Robinson, Smokey
See also CA 116

Robison, Mary 1949- .... **CLC 42, 98**
See also CA 113; 116; DLB 130; INT 116

Rod, Edouard 1857-1910 .... **TCLC 52**

Roddenberry, Eugene Wesley 1921-1991
See Roddenberry, Gene
See also CA 110; 135; CANR 37; SATA 45;
SATA-Obit 69

Roddenberry, Gene................ **CLC 17**
See also Roddenberry, Eugene Wesley
See also AAYA 5; SATA-Obit 69

Rodgers, Mary 1931- .... **CLC 12**
See also CA 49-52; CANR 8, 55; CLR 20;
INT CANR-8; JRDA; MAICYA;
SATA 8

Rodgers, W(illiam) R(obert)
1909-1969 .... **CLC 7**
See also CA 85-88; DLB 20

Rodman, Eric
See Silverberg, Robert

Rodman, Howard 1920(?)-1985 ..... **CLC 65**
See also CA 118

Rodman, Maia
See Wojciechowska, Maia (Teresa)

Rodriguez, Claudio 1934-.......... **CLC 10**
See also DLB 134

Roelvaag, O(le) E(dvart)
1876-1931 .... **TCLC 17**
See also CA 117; DLB 9

Roethke, Theodore (Huebner)
1908-1963 ...... **CLC 1, 3, 8, 11, 19, 46;**
DAM POET; PC 15
See also CA 81-84; CABS 2;
CDALB 1941-1968; DLB 5; MTCW

Rogers, Thomas Hunton 1927- ..... **CLC 57**
See also CA 89-92; INT 89-92

Rogers, Will(iam Penn Adair)
1879-1935 ...... **TCLC 8; DAM MULT**
See also CA 105; 144; DLB 11; NNAL

Rogin, Gilbert 1929-.............. **CLC 18**
See also CA 65-68; CANR 15

Rohan, Koda .... **TCLC 22**
See also Koda Shigeyuki

Rohmer, Eric.................... **CLC 16**
See also Scherer, Jean-Marie Maurice

Rohmer, Sax .... **TCLC 28**
See also Ward, Arthur Henry Sarsfield
See also DLB 70

Roiphe, Anne (Richardson)
1935- .... **CLC 3, 9**
See also CA 89-92; CANR 45; DLBY 80;
INT 89-92

Rojas, Fernando de 1465-1541 ..... **LC 23**

Rolfe, Frederick (William Serafino Austin
Lewis Mary) 1860-1913...... **TCLC 12**
See also CA 107; DLB 34, 156

Rolland, Romain 1866-1944...... **TCLC 23**
See also CA 118; DLB 65

Rolle, Richard c. 1300-c. 1349 ... **CMLC 21**
See also DLB 146

Rolvaag, O(le) E(dvart)
See Roelvaag, O(le) E(dvart)

Romain Arnaud, Saint
See Aragon, Louis

Romains, Jules 1885-1972 .... **CLC 7**
See also CA 85-88; CANR 34; DLB 65;
MTCW

Romero, Jose Ruben 1890-1952 ... **TCLC 14**
See also CA 114; 131; HW

Ronsard, Pierre de
1524-1585 .... **LC 6; PC 11**

Rooke, Leon
1934- .... **CLC 25, 34; DAM POP**
See also CA 25-28R; CANR 23, 53

Roosevelt, Theodore 1858-1919.... **TCLC 69**
See also CA 115; DLB 47

Roper, William 1498-1578 .... **LC 10**

Roquelaure, A. N.
See Rice, Anne

Rosa, Joao Guimaraes 1908-1967... **CLC 23**
See also CA 89-92; DLB 113

Rose, Wendy
1948- ..... **CLC 85; DAM MULT; PC 13**
See also CA 53-56; CANR 5, 51; DLB 175;
NNAL; SATA 12

Rosen, Richard (Dean) 1949-....... **CLC 39**
See also CA 77-80; INT CANR-30

Rosenberg, Isaac 1890-1918....... **TCLC 12**
See also CA 107; DLB 20

Rosenblatt, Joe .... **CLC 15**
See also Rosenblatt, Joseph

Rosenblatt, Joseph 1933-
See Rosenblatt, Joe
See also CA 89-92; INT 89-92

Rosenfeld, Samuel 1896-1963
See Tzara, Tristan
See also CA 89-92

Rosenstock, Sami
See Tzara, Tristan

Rosenstock, Samuel
See Tzara, Tristan

Rosenthal, M(acha) L(ouis)
1917-1996 .... **CLC 28**
See also CA 1-4R; 152; CAAS 6; CANR 4,
51; DLB 5; SATA 59

Ross, Barnaby
See Dannay, Frederic

Ross, Bernard L.
See Follett, Ken(neth Martin)

Ross, J. H.
See Lawrence, T(homas) E(dward)

Ross, Martin
See Martin, Violet Florence
See also DLB 135

Ross, (James) Sinclair
1908- ...... **CLC 13; DAC; DAM MST;**
SSC 24
See also CA 73-76; DLB 88

Rossetti, Christina (Georgina)
1830-1894 ..... **NCLC 2, 50; DA; DAB;**
DAC; DAM MST, POET; PC 7; WLC
See also DLB 35, 163; MAICYA; SATA 20

Saintsbury, George (Edward Bateman)
1845-1933 .... **TCLC 31**
See also DLB 57, 149

Sait Faik .... **TCLC 23**
See also Abasiyanik, Sait Faik

Saki .... **TCLC 3; SSC 12**
See also Munro, H(ector) H(ugh)

Sala, George Augustus .... **NCLC 46**

Salama, Hannu 1936-............ **CLC 18**

Salamanca, J(ack) R(ichard)
1922- .... **CLC 4, 15**
See also CA 25-28R

Sale, J. Kirkpatrick
See Sale, Kirkpatrick

Sale, Kirkpatrick 1937- .... **CLC 68**
See also CA 13-16R; CANR 10

Salinas, Luis Omar
1937- ..... **CLC 90; DAM MULT; HLC**
See also CA 131; DLB 82; HW

Salinas (y Serrano), Pedro
1891(?)-1951 .... **TCLC 17**
See also CA 117; DLB 134

Salinger, J(erome) D(avid)
1919- ...... **CLC 1, 3, 8, 12, 55, 56; DA; DAB; DAC; DAM MST, NOV, POP; SSC 2; WLC**
See also AAYA 2; CA 5-8R; CANR 39; CDALB 1941-1968; CLR 18; DLB 2, 102, 173; MAICYA; MTCW; SATA 67

Salisbury, John
See Caute, David

Salter, James 1925- .... **CLC 7, 52, 59**
See also CA 73-76; DLB 130

Saltus, Edgar (Everton)
1855-1921 .... **TCLC 8**
See also CA 105

Saltykov, Mikhail Evgrafovich
1826-1889 .... **NCLC 16**

Samarakis, Antonis 1919- .... **CLC 5**
See also CA 25-28R; CAAS 16; CANR 36

Sanchez, Florencio 1875-1910 ..... **TCLC 37**
See also CA 153; HW

Sanchez, Luis Rafael 1936-........ **CLC 23**
See also CA 128; DLB 145; HW

Sanchez, Sonia
1934- ...... **CLC 5; BLC; DAM MULT; PC 9**
See also BW 2; CA 33-36R; CANR 24, 49; CLR 18; DLB 41; DLBD 8; MAICYA; MTCW; SATA 22

Sand, George
1804-1876 .... **NCLC 2, 42, 57; DA; DAB; DAC; DAM MST, NOV; WLC**
See also DLB 119

Sandburg, Carl (August)
1878-1967 .... **CLC 1, 4, 10, 15, 35; DA; DAB; DAC; DAM MST, POET; PC 2; WLC**
See also CA 5-8R; 25-28R; CANR 35; CDALB 1865-1917; DLB 17, 54; MAICYA; MTCW; SATA 8

Sandburg, Charles
See Sandburg, Carl (August)

Sandburg, Charles A.
See Sandburg, Carl (August)

Sanders, (James) Ed(ward) 1939- ... **CLC 53**
See also CA 13-16R; CAAS 21; CANR 13, 44; DLB 16

Sanders, Lawrence
1920- .... **CLC 41; DAM POP**
See also BEST 89:4; CA 81-84; CANR 33; MTCW

Sanders, Noah
See Blount, Roy (Alton), Jr.

Sanders, Winston P.
See Anderson, Poul (William)

Sandoz, Mari(e Susette)
1896-1966 .... **CLC 28**
See also CA 1-4R; 25-28R; CANR 17; DLB 9; MTCW; SATA 5

Saner, Reg(inald Anthony) 1931- .... **CLC 9**
See also CA 65-68

Sannazaro, Jacopo 1456(?)-1530...... **LC 8**

Sansom, William
1912-1976 ...... **CLC 2, 6; DAM NOV; SSC 21**
See also CA 5-8R; 65-68; CANR 42; DLB 139; MTCW

Santayana, George 1863-1952 ..... **TCLC 40**
See also CA 115; DLB 54, 71; DLBD 13

Santiago, Danny .... **CLC 33**
See also James, Daniel (Lewis)
See also DLB 122

Santmyer, Helen Hoover
1895-1986 .... **CLC 33**
See also CA 1-4R; 118; CANR 15, 33; DLBY 84; MTCW

Santos, Bienvenido N(uqui)
1911-1996 ...... **CLC 22; DAM MULT**
See also CA 101; 151; CANR 19, 46

Sapper .... **TCLC 44**
See also McNeile, Herman Cyril

Sapphire 1950- .... **CLC 99**

Sappho
fl. 6th cent. B.C.- .... **CMLC 3; DAM POET; PC 5**
See also DLB 176

Sarduy, Severo 1937-1993 .... **CLC 6, 97**
See also CA 89-92; 142; DLB 113; HW

Sargeson, Frank 1903-1982 .... **CLC 31**
See also CA 25-28R; 106; CANR 38

Sarmiento, Felix Ruben Garcia
See Dario, Ruben

Saroyan, William
1908-1981 ..... **CLC 1, 8, 10, 29, 34, 56; DA; DAB; DAC; DAM DRAM, MST, NOV; SSC 21; WLC**
See also CA 5-8R; 103; CANR 30; DLB 7, 9, 86; DLBY 81; MTCW; SATA 23; SATA-Obit 24

Sarraute, Nathalie
1900- .... **CLC 1, 2, 4, 8, 10, 31, 80**
See also CA 9-12R; CANR 23; DLB 83; MTCW

Sarton, (Eleanor) May
1912-1995 .... **CLC 4, 14, 49, 91; DAM POET**
See also CA 1-4R; 149; CANR 1, 34, 55; DLB 48; DLBY 81; INT CANR-34; MTCW; SATA 36; SATA-Obit 86

Sartre, Jean-Paul
1905-1980 .... **CLC 1, 4, 7, 9, 13, 18, 24, 44, 50, 52; DA; DAB; DAC; DAM DRAM, MST, NOV; DC 3; WLC**
See also CA 9-12R; 97-100; CANR 21; DLB 72; MTCW

Sassoon, Siegfried (Lorraine)
1886-1967 .... **CLC 36; DAB; DAM MST, NOV, POET; PC 12**
See also CA 104; 25-28R; CANR 36; DLB 20; MTCW

Satterfield, Charles
See Pohl, Frederik

Saul, John (W. III)
1942- ...... **CLC 46; DAM NOV, POP**
See also AAYA 10; BEST 90:4; CA 81-84; CANR 16, 40

Saunders, Caleb
See Heinlein, Robert A(nson)

Saura (Atares), Carlos 1932-....... **CLC 20**
See also CA 114; 131; HW

Sauser-Hall, Frederic 1887-1961.... **CLC 18**
See also Cendrars, Blaise
See also CA 102; 93-96; CANR 36; MTCW

Saussure, Ferdinand de
1857-1913 .... **TCLC 49**

Savage, Catharine
See Brosman, Catharine Savage

Savage, Thomas 1915- .... **CLC 40**
See also CA 126; 132; CAAS 15; INT 132

Savan, Glenn 19(?)- .... **CLC 50**

Sayers, Dorothy L(eigh)
1893-1957 ..... **TCLC 2, 15; DAM POP**
See also CA 104; 119; CDBLB 1914-1945; DLB 10, 36, 77, 100; MTCW

Sayers, Valerie 1952-............. **CLC 50**
See also CA 134

Sayles, John (Thomas)
1950- .... **CLC 7, 10, 14**
See also CA 57-60; CANR 41; DLB 44

Scammell, Michael 1935-.......... **CLC 34**
See also CA 156

Scannell, Vernon 1922- .... **CLC 49**
See also CA 5-8R; CANR 8, 24, 57; DLB 27; SATA 59

Scarlett, Susan
See Streatfeild, (Mary) Noel

Schaeffer, Susan Fromberg
1941- .... **CLC 6, 11, 22**
See also CA 49-52; CANR 18; DLB 28; MTCW; SATA 22

Schary, Jill
See Robinson, Jill

Schell, Jonathan 1943-............ **CLC 35**
See also CA 73-76; CANR 12

Schelling, Friedrich Wilhelm Joseph von
1775-1854 .... **NCLC 30**
See also DLB 90

Schendel, Arthur van 1874-1946 ... **TCLC 56**

Scherer, Jean-Marie Maurice 1920-
See Rohmer, Eric
See also CA 110

Schevill, James (Erwin) 1920-....... **CLC 7**
See also CA 5-8R; CAAS 12

Serna, Ramon Gomez de la
  See Gomez de la Serna, Ramon

Serpieres
  See Guillevic, (Eugene)

Service, Robert
  See Service, Robert W(illiam)
  See also DAB; DLB 92

Service, Robert W(illiam)
    1874(?)-1958 . . . . . . **TCLC 15; DA; DAC;**
        DAM MST, POET; WLC
  See also Service, Robert
  See also CA 115; 140; SATA 20

Seth, Vikram
    1952- . . . . **CLC 43, 90; DAM MULT**
  See also CA 121; 127; CANR 50; DLB 120;
  INT 127

Seton, Cynthia Propper
    1926-1982 . . . . **CLC 27**
  See also CA 5-8R; 108; CANR 7

Seton, Ernest (Evan) Thompson
    1860-1946 . . . . **TCLC 31**
  See also CA 109; DLB 92; DLBD 13;
  JRDA; SATA 18

Seton-Thompson, Ernest
  See Seton, Ernest (Evan) Thompson

Settle, Mary Lee 1918- . . . . **CLC 19, 61**
  See also CA 89-92; CAAS 1; CANR 44;
  DLB 6; INT 89-92

Seuphor, Michel
  See Arp, Jean

Sevigne, Marie (de Rabutin-Chantal) Marquise
    de 1626-1696 . . . . **LC 11**

Sewall, Samuel 1652-1730 . . . . **LC 38**
  See also DLB 24

Sexton, Anne (Harvey)
    1928-1974 . . . . **CLC 2, 4, 6, 8, 10, 15, 53;**
        DA; DAB; DAC; DAM MST, POET;
                                  PC 2; WLC
  See also CA 1-4R; 53-56; CABS 2;
  CANR 3, 36; CDALB 1941-1968; DLB 5,
  169; MTCW; SATA 10

Shaara, Michael (Joseph, Jr.)
    1929-1988 . . . . **CLC 15; DAM POP**
  See also AITN 1; CA 102; 125; CANR 52;
  DLBY 83

Shackleton, C. C.
  See Aldiss, Brian W(ilson)

Shacochis, Bob . . . . **CLC 39**
  See also Shacochis, Robert G.

Shacochis, Robert G. 1951-
  See Shacochis, Bob
  See also CA 119; 124; INT 124

Shaffer, Anthony (Joshua)
    1926- . . . . **CLC 19; DAM DRAM**
  See also CA 110; 116; DLB 13

Shaffer, Peter (Levin)
    1926- . . . . . . **CLC 5, 14, 18, 37, 60; DAB;**
                  DAM DRAM, MST; DC 7
  See also CA 25-28R; CANR 25, 47;
  CDBLB 1960 to Present; DLB 13;
  MTCW

Shakey, Bernard
  See Young, Neil

Shalamov, Varlam (Tikhonovich)
    1907(?)-1982 . . . . **CLC 18**
  See also CA 129; 105

Shamlu, Ahmad 1925- . . . . **CLC 10**

Shammas, Anton 1951- . . . . **CLC 55**

Shange, Ntozake
    1948- . . . . **CLC 8, 25, 38, 74; BLC;**
                  DAM DRAM, MULT; DC 3
  See also AAYA 9; BW 2; CA 85-88;
  CABS 3; CANR 27, 48; DLB 38; MTCW

Shanley, John Patrick 1950- . . . . **CLC 75**
  See also CA 128; 133

Shapcott, Thomas W(illiam) 1935- . . **CLC 38**
  See also CA 69-72; CANR 49

Shapiro, Jane . . . . **CLC 76**

Shapiro, Karl (Jay) 1913- . . **CLC 4, 8, 15, 53**
  See also CA 1-4R; CAAS 6; CANR 1, 36;
  DLB 48; MTCW

Sharp, William 1855-1905 . . . . **TCLC 39**
  See also DLB 156

Sharpe, Thomas Ridley 1928-
  See Sharpe, Tom
  See also CA 114; 122; INT 122

Sharpe, Tom . . . . **CLC 36**
  See also Sharpe, Thomas Ridley
  See also DLB 14

Shaw, Bernard . . . . **TCLC 45**
  See also Shaw, George Bernard
  See also BW 1

Shaw, G. Bernard
  See Shaw, George Bernard

Shaw, George Bernard
    1856-1950 . . . **TCLC 3, 9, 21; DA; DAB;**
        DAC; DAM DRAM, MST; WLC
  See also Shaw, Bernard
  See also CA 104; 128; CDBLB 1914-1945;
  DLB 10, 57; MTCW

Shaw, Henry Wheeler
    1818-1885 . . . . **NCLC 15**
  See also DLB 11

Shaw, Irwin
    1913-1984 . . . . **CLC 7, 23, 34;**
                              DAM DRAM, POP
  See also AITN 1; CA 13-16R; 112;
  CANR 21; CDALB 1941-1968; DLB 6,
  102; DLBY 84; MTCW

Shaw, Robert 1927-1978 . . . . **CLC 5**
  See also AITN 1; CA 1-4R; 81-84;
  CANR 4; DLB 13, 14

Shaw, T. E.
  See Lawrence, T(homas) E(dward)

Shawn, Wallace 1943- . . . . **CLC 41**
  See also CA 112

Shea, Lisa 1953- . . . . **CLC 86**
  See also CA 147

Sheed, Wilfrid (John Joseph)
    1930- . . . . **CLC 2, 4, 10, 53**
  See also CA 65-68; CANR 30; DLB 6;
  MTCW

Sheldon, Alice Hastings Bradley
    1915(?)-1987
  See Tiptree, James, Jr.
  See also CA 108; 122; CANR 34; INT 108;
  MTCW

Sheldon, John
  See Bloch, Robert (Albert)

Shelley, Mary Wollstonecraft (Godwin)
    1797-1851 . . . . **NCLC 14, 59; DA; DAB;**
        DAC; DAM MST, NOV; WLC
  See also AAYA 20; CDBLB 1789-1832;
  DLB 110, 116, 159; SATA 29

Shelley, Percy Bysshe
    1792-1822 . . . . **NCLC 18; DA; DAB;**
        DAC; DAM MST, POET; PC 14; WLC
  See also CDBLB 1789-1832; DLB 96, 110,
  158

Shepard, Jim 1956- . . . . **CLC 36**
  See also CA 137; SATA 90

Shepard, Lucius 1947- . . . . **CLC 34**
  See also CA 128; 141

Shepard, Sam
    1943- . . . . **CLC 4, 6, 17, 34, 41, 44;**
                              DAM DRAM; DC 5
  See also AAYA 1; CA 69-72; CABS 3;
  CANR 22; DLB 7; MTCW

Shepherd, Michael
  See Ludlum, Robert

Sherburne, Zoa (Morin) 1912- . . . . . . **CLC 30**
  See also AAYA 13; CA 1-4R; CANR 3, 37;
  MAICYA; SAAS 18; SATA 3

Sheridan, Frances 1724-1766 . . . . **LC 7**
  See also DLB 39, 84

Sheridan, Richard Brinsley
    1751-1816 . . . . **NCLC 5; DA; DAB;**
        DAC; DAM DRAM, MST; DC 1; WLC
  See also CDBLB 1660-1789; DLB 89

Sherman, Jonathan Marc . . . . **CLC 55**

Sherman, Martin 1941(?)- . . . . **CLC 19**
  See also CA 116; 123

Sherwin, Judith Johnson 1936- . . . **CLC 7, 15**
  See also CA 25-28R; CANR 34

Sherwood, Frances 1940- . . . . **CLC 81**
  See also CA 146

Sherwood, Robert E(mmet)
    1896-1955 . . . . . . **TCLC 3; DAM DRAM**
  See also CA 104; 153; DLB 7, 26

Shestov, Lev 1866-1938 . . . . **TCLC 56**

Shevchenko, Taras 1814-1861 . . . . **NCLC 54**

Shiel, M(atthew) P(hipps)
    1865-1947 . . . . **TCLC 8**
  See also CA 106; DLB 153

Shields, Carol 1935- . . . . **CLC 91; DAC**
  See also CA 81-84; CANR 51

Shields, David 1956- . . . . **CLC 97**
  See also CA 124; CANR 48

Shiga, Naoya 1883-1971 . . . **CLC 33; SSC 23**
  See also CA 101; 33-36R

Shilts, Randy 1951-1994 . . . . **CLC 85**
  See also AAYA 19; CA 115; 127; 144;
  CANR 45; INT 127

Shimazaki, Haruki 1872-1943
  See Shimazaki Toson
  See also CA 105; 134

Shimazaki Toson . . . . **TCLC 5**
  See also Shimazaki, Haruki

Sholokhov, Mikhail (Aleksandrovich)
    1905-1984 . . . . **CLC 7, 15**
  See also CA 101; 112; MTCW;
  SATA-Obit 36

Sjowall, Maj
See Sjoewall, Maj

Skelton, Robin 1925- . . . . CLC 13
See also AITN 2; CA 5-8R; CAAS 5;
CANR 28; DLB 27, 53

Skolimowski, Jerzy 1938- . . . . CLC 20
See also CA 128

Skram, Amalie (Bertha)
1847-1905 . . . . TCLC 25

Skvorecky, Josef (Vaclav)
1924- . . . . CLC 15, 39, 69; DAC;
DAM NOV
See also CA 61-64; CAAS 1; CANR 10, 34;
MTCW

Slade, Bernard . . . . CLC 11, 46
See also Newbound, Bernard Slade
See also CAAS 9; DLB 53

Slaughter, Carolyn 1946- . . . . CLC 56
See also CA 85-88

Slaughter, Frank G(ill) 1908- . . . . . . CLC 29
See also AITN 2; CA 5-8R; CANR 5;
INT CANR-5

Slavitt, David R(ytman) 1935- . . . . CLC 5, 14
See also CA 21-24R; CAAS 3; CANR 41;
DLB 5, 6

Slesinger, Tess 1905-1945 . . . . TCLC 10
See also CA 107; DLB 102

Slessor, Kenneth 1901-1971 . . . . CLC 14
See also CA 102; 89-92

Slowacki, Juliusz 1809-1849 . . . . . NCLC 15

Smart, Christopher
1722-1771 . . . LC 3; DAM POET; PC 13
See also DLB 109

Smart, Elizabeth 1913-1986 . . . . CLC 54
See also CA 81-84; 118; DLB 88

Smiley, Jane (Graves)
1949- . . . . CLC 53, 76; DAM POP
See also CA 104; CANR 30, 50;
INT CANR-30

Smith, A(rthur) J(ames) M(arshall)
1902-1980 . . . . CLC 15; DAC
See also CA 1-4R; 102; CANR 4; DLB 88

Smith, Adam 1723-1790 . . . . LC 36
See also DLB 104

Smith, Alexander 1829-1867 . . . . . NCLC 59
See also DLB 32, 55

Smith, Anna Deavere 1950- . . . . CLC 86
See also CA 133

Smith, Betty (Wehner) 1896-1972 . . . CLC 19
See also CA 5-8R; 33-36R; DLBY 82;
SATA 6

Smith, Charlotte (Turner)
1749-1806 . . . . NCLC 23
See also DLB 39, 109

Smith, Clark Ashton 1893-1961 . . . . CLC 43
See also CA 143

Smith, Dave . . . . CLC 22, 42
See also Smith, David (Jeddie)
See also CAAS 7; DLB 5

Smith, David (Jeddie) 1942-
See Smith, Dave
See also CA 49-52; CANR 1; DAM POET

Smith, Florence Margaret 1902-1971
See Smith, Stevie
See also CA 17-18; 29-32R; CANR 35;
CAP 2; DAM POET; MTCW

Smith, Iain Crichton 1928- . . . . CLC 64
See also CA 21-24R; DLB 40, 139

Smith, John 1580(?)-1631 . . . . LC 9

Smith, Johnston
See Crane, Stephen (Townley)

Smith, Joseph, Jr. 1805-1844 . . . . NCLC 53

Smith, Lee 1944- . . . . CLC 25, 73
See also CA 114; 119; CANR 46; DLB 143;
DLBY 83; INT 119

Smith, Martin
See Smith, Martin Cruz

Smith, Martin Cruz
1942- . . . . . CLC 25; DAM MULT, POP
See also BEST 89:4; CA 85-88; CANR 6,
23, 43; INT CANR-23; NNAL

Smith, Mary-Ann Tirone 1944- . . . . . CLC 39
See also CA 118; 136

Smith, Patti 1946- . . . . CLC 12
See also CA 93-96

Smith, Pauline (Urmson)
1882-1959 . . . . TCLC 25

Smith, Rosamond
See Oates, Joyce Carol

Smith, Sheila Kaye
See Kaye-Smith, Sheila

Smith, Stevie . . . . . . CLC 3, 8, 25, 44; PC 12
See also Smith, Florence Margaret
See also DLB 20

Smith, Wilbur (Addison) 1933- . . . . . CLC 33
See also CA 13-16R; CANR 7, 46; MTCW

Smith, William Jay 1918- . . . . CLC 6
See also CA 5-8R; CANR 44; DLB 5;
MAICYA; SAAS 22; SATA 2, 68

Smith, Woodrow Wilson
See Kuttner, Henry

Smolenskin, Peretz 1842-1885 . . . . NCLC 30

Smollett, Tobias (George) 1721-1771 . . LC 2
See also CDBLB 1660-1789; DLB 39, 104

Snodgrass, W(illiam) D(e Witt)
1926- . . . . CLC 2, 6, 10, 18, 68;
DAM POET
See also CA 1-4R; CANR 6, 36; DLB 5;
MTCW

Snow, C(harles) P(ercy)
1905-1980 . . . . CLC 1, 4, 6, 9, 13, 19;
DAM NOV
See also CA 5-8R; 101; CANR 28;
CDBLB 1945-1960; DLB 15, 77; MTCW

Snow, Frances Compton
See Adams, Henry (Brooks)

Snyder, Gary (Sherman)
1930- . . CLC 1, 2, 5, 9, 32; DAM POET
See also CA 17-20R; CANR 30; DLB 5, 16,
165

Snyder, Zilpha Keatley 1927- . . . . . . CLC 17
See also AAYA 15; CA 9-12R; CANR 38;
CLR 31; JRDA; MAICYA; SAAS 2;
SATA 1, 28, 75

Soares, Bernardo
See Pessoa, Fernando (Antonio Nogueira)

Sobh, A.
See Shamlu, Ahmad

Sobol, Joshua . . . . CLC 60

Soderberg, Hjalmar 1869-1941 . . . . TCLC 39

Sodergran, Edith (Irene)
See Soedergran, Edith (Irene)

Soedergran, Edith (Irene)
1892-1923 . . . . TCLC 31

Softly, Edgar
See Lovecraft, H(oward) P(hillips)

Softly, Edward
See Lovecraft, H(oward) P(hillips)

Sokolov, Raymond 1941- . . . . CLC 7
See also CA 85-88

Solo, Jay
See Ellison, Harlan (Jay)

Sologub, Fyodor . . . . TCLC 9
See also Teternikov, Fyodor Kuzmich

Solomons, Ikey Esquir
See Thackeray, William Makepeace

Solomos, Dionysios 1798-1857 . . . NCLC 15

Solwoska, Mara
See French, Marilyn

Solzhenitsyn, Aleksandr I(sayevich)
1918- . . . . . . CLC 1, 2, 4, 7, 9, 10, 18, 26,
34, 78; DA; DAB; DAC; DAM MST,
NOV; WLC
See also AITN 1; CA 69-72; CANR 40;
MTCW

Somers, Jane
See Lessing, Doris (May)

Somerville, Edith 1858-1949 . . . . . . TCLC 51
See also DLB 135

Somerville & Ross
See Martin, Violet Florence; Somerville,
Edith

Sommer, Scott 1951- . . . . CLC 25
See also CA 106

Sondheim, Stephen (Joshua)
1930- . . . . CLC 30, 39; DAM DRAM
See also AAYA 11; CA 103; CANR 47

Sontag, Susan
1933- . . . . CLC 1, 2, 10, 13, 31;
DAM POP
See also CA 17-20R; CANR 25, 51; DLB 2,
67; MTCW

Sophocles
496(?)B.C.-406(?)B.C. . . . . CMLC 2; DA;
DAB; DAC; DAM DRAM, MST; DC 1
See also DLB 176

Sordello 1189-1269 . . . . CMLC 15

Sorel, Julia
See Drexler, Rosalyn

Sorrentino, Gilbert
1929- . . . . CLC 3, 7, 14, 22, 40
See also CA 77-80; CANR 14, 33; DLB 5,
173; DLBY 80; INT CANR-14

Soto, Gary
1952- . . . . CLC 32, 80; DAM MULT;
HLC
See also AAYA 10; CA 119; 125;
CANR 50; CLR 38; DLB 82; HW;
INT 125; JRDA; SATA 80

Soupault, Philippe 1897-1990 ...... CLC 68
See also CA 116; 147; 131

Souster, (Holmes) Raymond
1921- ... CLC 5, 14; DAC; DAM POET
See also CA 13-16R; CAAS 14; CANR 13, 29, 53; DLB 88; SATA 63

Southern, Terry 1924(?)-1995 .... CLC 7
See also CA 1-4R; 150; CANR 1, 55; DLB 2

Southey, Robert 1774-1843 .... NCLC 8
See also DLB 93, 107, 142; SATA 54

Southworth, Emma Dorothy Eliza Nevitte
1819-1899 .... NCLC 26

Souza, Ernest
See Scott, Evelyn

Soyinka, Wole
1934- .... CLC 3, 5, 14, 36, 44; BLC;
DA; DAB; DAC; DAM DRAM, MST,
MULT; DC 2; WLC
See also BW 2; CA 13-16R; CANR 27, 39;
DLB 125; MTCW

Spackman, W(illiam) M(ode)
1905-1990 .... CLC 46
See also CA 81-84; 132

Spacks, Barry (Bernard) 1931- ..... CLC 14
See also CA 154; CANR 33; DLB 105

Spanidou, Irini 1946- .... CLC 44

Spark, Muriel (Sarah)
1918- ..... CLC 2, 3, 5, 8, 13, 18, 40, 94;
DAB; DAC; DAM MST, NOV; SSC 10
See also CA 5-8R; CANR 12, 36;
CDBLB 1945-1960; DLB 15, 139;
INT CANR-12; MTCW

Spaulding, Douglas
See Bradbury, Ray (Douglas)

Spaulding, Leonard
See Bradbury, Ray (Douglas)

Spence, J. A. D.
See Eliot, T(homas) S(tearns)

Spencer, Elizabeth 1921- .... CLC 22
See also CA 13-16R; CANR 32; DLB 6;
MTCW; SATA 14

Spencer, Leonard G.
See Silverberg, Robert

Spencer, Scott 1945- .... CLC 30
See also CA 113; CANR 51; DLBY 86

Spender, Stephen (Harold)
1909-1995 ...... CLC 1, 2, 5, 10, 41, 91;
DAM POET
See also CA 9-12R; 149; CANR 31, 54;
CDBLB 1945-1960; DLB 20; MTCW

Spengler, Oswald (Arnold Gottfried)
1880-1936 .... TCLC 25
See also CA 118

Spenser, Edmund
1552(?)-1599 .... LC 5; DA; DAB; DAC;
DAM MST, POET; PC 8; WLC
See also CDBLB Before 1660; DLB 167

Spicer, Jack
1925-1965 .... CLC 8, 18, 72;
DAM POET
See also CA 85-88; DLB 5, 16

Spiegelman, Art 1948- .... CLC 76
See also AAYA 10; CA 125; CANR 41, 55

Spielberg, Peter 1929- .... CLC 6
See also CA 5-8R; CANR 4, 48; DLBY 81

Spielberg, Steven 1947- .... CLC 20
See also AAYA 8; CA 77-80; CANR 32;
SATA 32

Spillane, Frank Morrison 1918-
See Spillane, Mickey
See also CA 25-28R; CANR 28; MTCW;
SATA 66

Spillane, Mickey .... CLC 3, 13
See also Spillane, Frank Morrison

Spinoza, Benedictus de 1632-1677 .... LC 9

Spinrad, Norman (Richard) 1940- ... CLC 46
See also CA 37-40R; CAAS 19; CANR 20;
DLB 8; INT CANR-20

Spitteler, Carl (Friedrich Georg)
1845-1924 .... TCLC 12
See also CA 109; DLB 129

Spivack, Kathleen (Romola Drucker)
1938- .... CLC 6
See also CA 49-52

Spoto, Donald 1941- .... CLC 39
See also CA 65-68; CANR 11, 57

Springsteen, Bruce (F.) 1949- ...... CLC 17
See also CA 111

Spurling, Hilary 1940- .... CLC 34
See also CA 104; CANR 25, 52

Spyker, John Howland
See Elman, Richard

Squires, (James) Radcliffe
1917-1993 .... CLC 51
See also CA 1-4R; 140; CANR 6, 21

Srivastava, Dhanpat Rai 1880(?)-1936
See Premchand
See also CA 118

Stacy, Donald
See Pohl, Frederik

Stael, Germaine de
See Stael-Holstein, Anne Louise Germaine
Necker Baronn
See also DLB 119

Stael-Holstein, Anne Louise Germaine Necker
Baronn 1766-1817 .... NCLC 3
See also Stael, Germaine de

Stafford, Jean 1915-1979 ... CLC 4, 7, 19, 68
See also CA 1-4R; 85-88; CANR 3; DLB 2,
173; MTCW; SATA-Obit 22

Stafford, William (Edgar)
1914-1993 ... CLC 4, 7, 29; DAM POET
See also CA 5-8R; 142; CAAS 3; CANR 5,
22; DLB 5; INT CANR-22

Stagnelius, Eric Johan
1793-1823 .... NCLC 61

Staines, Trevor
See Brunner, John (Kilian Houston)

Stairs, Gordon
See Austin, Mary (Hunter)

Stannard, Martin 1947- .... CLC 44
See also CA 142; DLB 155

Stanton, Maura 1946- .... CLC 9
See also CA 89-92; CANR 15; DLB 120

Stanton, Schuyler
See Baum, L(yman) Frank

Stapledon, (William) Olaf
1886-1950 .... TCLC 22
See also CA 111; DLB 15

Starbuck, George (Edwin)
1931-1996 .... CLC 53; DAM POET
See also CA 21-24R; 153; CANR 23

Stark, Richard
See Westlake, Donald E(dwin)

Staunton, Schuyler
See Baum, L(yman) Frank

Stead, Christina (Ellen)
1902-1983 .... CLC 2, 5, 8, 32, 80
See also CA 13-16R; 109; CANR 33, 40;
MTCW

Stead, William Thomas
1849-1912 .... TCLC 48

Steele, Richard 1672-1729 .... LC 18
See also CDBLB 1660-1789; DLB 84, 101

Steele, Timothy (Reid) 1948- ...... CLC 45
See also CA 93-96; CANR 16, 50; DLB 120

Steffens, (Joseph) Lincoln
1866-1936 .... TCLC 20
See also CA 117

Stegner, Wallace (Earle)
1909-1993 ... CLC 9, 49, 81; DAM NOV
See also AITN 1; BEST 90:3; CA 1-4R;
141; CAAS 9; CANR 1, 21, 46; DLB 9;
DLBY 93; MTCW

Stein, Gertrude
1874-1946 ...... TCLC 1, 6, 28, 48; DA;
DAB; DAC; DAM MST, NOV, POET;
WLC
See also CA 104; 132; CDALB 1917-1929;
DLB 4, 54, 86; MTCW

Steinbeck, John (Ernst)
1902-1968 .... CLC 1, 5, 9, 13, 21, 34,
45, 75; DA; DAB; DAC; DAM DRAM,
MST, NOV; SSC 11; WLC
See also AAYA 12; CA 1-4R; 25-28R;
CANR 1, 35; CDALB 1929-1941; DLB 7,
9; DLBD 2; MTCW; SATA 9

Steinem, Gloria 1934- .... CLC 63
See also CA 53-56; CANR 28, 51; MTCW

Steiner, George
1929- .... CLC 24; DAM NOV
See also CA 73-76; CANR 31; DLB 67;
MTCW; SATA 62

Steiner, K. Leslie
See Delany, Samuel R(ay, Jr.)

Steiner, Rudolf 1861-1925 .... TCLC 13
See also CA 107

Stendhal
1783-1842 .... NCLC 23, 46; DA; DAB;
DAC; DAM MST, NOV; WLC
See also DLB 119

Stephen, Leslie 1832-1904 .... TCLC 23
See also CA 123; DLB 57, 144

Stephen, Sir Leslie
See Stephen, Leslie

Stephen, Virginia
See Woolf, (Adeline) Virginia

Stephens, James 1882(?)-1950 ...... TCLC 4
See also CA 104; DLB 19, 153, 162

Stephens, Reed
See Donaldson, Stephen R.

Steptoe, Lydia
  See Barnes, Djuna

Sterchi, Beat 1949-.............. CLC 65

Sterling, Brett
  See Bradbury, Ray (Douglas); Hamilton,
  Edmond

Sterling, Bruce 1954-............. CLC 72
  See also CA 119; CANR 44

Sterling, George 1869-1926....... TCLC 20
  See also CA 117; DLB 54

Stern, Gerald 1925-.......... CLC 40, 100
  See also CA 81-84; CANR 28; DLB 105

Stern, Richard (Gustave) 1928-... CLC 4, 39
  See also CA 1-4R; CANR 1, 25, 52;
  DLBY 87; INT CANR-25

Sternberg, Josef von 1894-1969..... CLC 20
  See also CA 81-84

Sterne, Laurence
  1713-1768 ...... LC 2; DA; DAB; DAC;
  DAM MST, NOV; WLC
  See also CDBLB 1660-1789; DLB 39

Sternheim, (William Adolf) Carl
  1878-1942 .... TCLC 8
  See also CA 105; DLB 56, 118

Stevens, Mark 1951- .... CLC 34
  See also CA 122

Stevens, Wallace
  1879-1955 .... TCLC 3, 12, 45; DA;
  DAB; DAC; DAM MST, POET; PC 6;
  WLC
  See also CA 104; 124; CDALB 1929-1941;
  DLB 54; MTCW

Stevenson, Anne (Katharine)
  1933-...................... CLC 7, 33
  See also CA 17-20R; CAAS 9; CANR 9, 33;
  DLB 40; MTCW

Stevenson, Robert Louis (Balfour)
  1850-1894 ..... NCLC 5, 14; DA; DAB;
  DAC; DAM MST, NOV; SSC 11; WLC
  See also CDBLB 1890-1914; CLR 10, 11;
  DLB 18, 57, 141, 156, 174; DLBD 13;
  JRDA; MAICYA; YABC 2

Stewart, J(ohn) I(nnes) M(ackintosh)
  1906-1994 .... CLC 7, 14, 32
  See also CA 85-88; 147; CAAS 3;
  CANR 47; MTCW

Stewart, Mary (Florence Elinor)
  1916- .... CLC 7, 35; DAB
  See also CA 1-4R; CANR 1; SATA 12

Stewart, Mary Rainbow
  See Stewart, Mary (Florence Elinor)

Stifle, June
  See Campbell, Maria

Stifter, Adalbert 1805-1868...... NCLC 41
  See also DLB 133

Still, James 1906-................ CLC 49
  See also CA 65-68; CAAS 17; CANR 10,
  26; DLB 9; SATA 29

Sting
  See Sumner, Gordon Matthew

Stirling, Arthur
  See Sinclair, Upton (Beall)

Stitt, Milan 1941-................ CLC 29
  See also CA 69-72

Stockton, Francis Richard 1834-1902
  See Stockton, Frank R.
  See also CA 108; 137; MAICYA; SATA 44

Stockton, Frank R............... TCLC 47
  See also Stockton, Francis Richard
  See also DLB 42, 74; DLBD 13;
  SATA-Brief 32

Stoddard, Charles
  See Kuttner, Henry

Stoker, Abraham 1847-1912
  See Stoker, Bram
  See also CA 105; DA; DAC; DAM MST,
  NOV; SATA 29

Stoker, Bram
  1847-1912 .... TCLC 8; DAB; WLC
  See also Stoker, Abraham
  See also CA 150; CDBLB 1890-1914;
  DLB 36, 70

Stolz, Mary (Slattery) 1920-....... CLC 12
  See also AAYA 8; AITN 1; CA 5-8R;
  CANR 13, 41; JRDA; MAICYA;
  SAAS 3; SATA 10, 71

Stone, Irving
  1903-1989 .... CLC 7; DAM POP
  See also AITN 1; CA 1-4R; 129; CAAS 3;
  CANR 1, 23; INT CANR-23; MTCW;
  SATA 3; SATA-Obit 64

Stone, Oliver (William) 1946-...... CLC 73
  See also AAYA 15; CA 110; CANR 55

Stone, Robert (Anthony)
  1937-.................. CLC 5, 23, 42
  See also CA 85-88; CANR 23; DLB 152;
  INT CANR-23; MTCW

Stone, Zachary
  See Follett, Ken(neth Martin)

Stoppard, Tom
  1937-...... CLC 1, 3, 4, 5, 8, 15, 29, 34,
  63, 91; DA; DAB; DAC; DAM DRAM,
  MST; DC 6; WLC
  See also CA 81-84; CANR 39;
  CDBLB 1960 to Present; DLB 13;
  DLBY 85; MTCW

Storey, David (Malcolm)
  1933-..... CLC 2, 4, 5, 8; DAM DRAM
  See also CA 81-84; CANR 36; DLB 13, 14;
  MTCW

Storm, Hyemeyohsts
  1935-........... CLC 3; DAM MULT
  See also CA 81-84; CANR 45; NNAL

Storm, (Hans) Theodor (Woldsen)
  1817-1888 .... NCLC 1

Storni, Alfonsina
  1892-1938 ..... TCLC 5; DAM MULT;
  HLC
  See also CA 104; 131; HW

Stoughton, William 1631-1701....... LC 38
  See also DLB 24

Stout, Rex (Todhunter) 1886-1975 ... CLC 3
  See also AITN 2; CA 61-64

Stow, (Julian) Randolph 1935- .. CLC 23, 48
  See also CA 13-16R; CANR 33; MTCW

Stowe, Harriet (Elizabeth) Beecher
  1811-1896 ..... NCLC 3, 50; DA; DAB;
  DAC; DAM MST, NOV; WLC
  See also CDALB 1865-1917; DLB 1, 12, 42,
  74; JRDA; MAICYA; YABC 1

Strachey, (Giles) Lytton
  1880-1932 .... TCLC 12
  See also CA 110; DLB 149; DLBD 10

Strand, Mark
  1934-.. CLC 6, 18, 41, 71; DAM POET
  See also CA 21-24R; CANR 40; DLB 5;
  SATA 41

Straub, Peter (Francis)
  1943-................ CLC 28; DAM POP
  See also BEST 89:1; CA 85-88; CANR 28;
  DLBY 84; MTCW

Strauss, Botho 1944- .... CLC 22
  See also DLB 124

Streatfeild, (Mary) Noel
  1895(?)-1986 .... CLC 21
  See also CA 81-84; 120; CANR 31;
  CLR 17; DLB 160; MAICYA; SATA 20;
  SATA-Obit 48

Stribling, T(homas) S(igismund)
  1881-1965 .... CLC 23
  See also CA 107; DLB 9

Strindberg, (Johan) August
  1849-1912 ...... TCLC 1, 8, 21, 47; DA;
  DAB; DAC; DAM DRAM, MST; WLC
  See also CA 104; 135

Stringer, Arthur 1874-1950....... TCLC 37
  See also DLB 92

Stringer, David
  See Roberts, Keith (John Kingston)

Strugatskii, Arkadii (Natanovich)
  1925-1991 .... CLC 27
  See also CA 106; 135

Strugatskii, Boris (Natanovich)
  1933-...................... CLC 27
  See also CA 106

Strummer, Joe 1953(?)-........... CLC 30

Stuart, Don A.
  See Campbell, John W(ood, Jr.)

Stuart, Ian
  See MacLean, Alistair (Stuart)

Stuart, Jesse (Hilton)
  1906-1984 .... CLC 1, 8, 11, 14, 34
  See also CA 5-8R; 112; CANR 31; DLB 9,
  48, 102; DLBY 84; SATA 2;
  SATA-Obit 36

Sturgeon, Theodore (Hamilton)
  1918-1985 .... CLC 22, 39
  See also Queen, Ellery
  See also CA 81-84; 116; CANR 32; DLB 8;
  DLBY 85; MTCW

Sturges, Preston 1898-1959....... TCLC 48
  See also CA 114; 149; DLB 26

Styron, William
  1925-.......... CLC 1, 3, 5, 11, 15, 60;
  DAM NOV, POP; SSC 25
  See also BEST 90:4; CA 5-8R; CANR 6, 33;
  CDALB 1968-1988; DLB 2, 143;
  DLBY 80; INT CANR-6; MTCW

Suarez Lynch, B.
  See Bioy Casares, Adolfo; Borges, Jorge
  Luis

Su Chien 1884-1918
  See Su Man-shu
  See also CA 123

Suckow, Ruth 1892-1960.......... SSC 18
  See also CA 113; DLB 9, 102

Sudermann, Hermann 1857-1928 . . **TCLC 15**
See also CA 107; DLB 118

Sue, Eugene 1804-1857 . . . . **NCLC 1**
See also DLB 119

Sueskind, Patrick 1949- . . . . **CLC 44**
See also Suskind, Patrick

Sukenick, Ronald 1932- . . . . . **CLC 3, 4, 6, 48**
See also CA 25-28R; CAAS 8; CANR 32;
DLB 173; DLBY 81

Suknaski, Andrew 1942- . . . . **CLC 19**
See also CA 101; DLB 53

Sullivan, Vernon
See Vian, Boris

Sully Prudhomme 1839-1907 . . . . . **TCLC 31**

Su Man-shu . . . . **TCLC 24**
See also Su Chien

Summerforest, Ivy B.
See Kirkup, James

Summers, Andrew James 1942- . . . . . **CLC 26**

Summers, Andy
See Summers, Andrew James

Summers, Hollis (Spurgeon, Jr.)
1916- . . . . **CLC 10**
See also CA 5-8R; CANR 3; DLB 6

Summers, (Alphonsus Joseph-Mary Augustus)
Montague 1880-1948 . . . . **TCLC 16**
See also CA 118

Sumner, Gordon Matthew 1951- . . . . **CLC 26**

Surtees, Robert Smith
1803-1864 . . . . **NCLC 14**
See also DLB 21

Susann, Jacqueline 1921-1974 . . . . **CLC 3**
See also AITN 1; CA 65-68; 53-56; MTCW

Su Shih 1036-1101 . . . . **CMLC 15**

Suskind, Patrick
See Sueskind, Patrick
See also CA 145

Sutcliff, Rosemary
1920-1992 . . . . **CLC 26; DAB; DAC;**
DAM MST, POP
See also AAYA 10; CA 5-8R; 139;
CANR 37; CLR 1, 37; JRDA; MAICYA;
SATA 6, 44, 78; SATA-Obit 73

Sutro, Alfred 1863-1933 . . . . **TCLC 6**
See also CA 105; DLB 10

Sutton, Henry
See Slavitt, David R(ytman)

Svevo, Italo
1861-1928 . . . . **TCLC 2, 35; SSC 25**
See also Schmitz, Aron Hector

Swados, Elizabeth (A.) 1951- . . . . **CLC 12**
See also CA 97-100; CANR 49; INT 97-100

Swados, Harvey 1920-1972 . . . . **CLC 5**
See also CA 5-8R; 37-40R; CANR 6;
DLB 2

Swan, Gladys 1934- . . . . **CLC 69**
See also CA 101; CANR 17, 39

Swarthout, Glendon (Fred)
1918-1992 . . . . **CLC 35**
See also CA 1-4R; 139; CANR 1, 47;
SATA 26

Sweet, Sarah C.
See Jewett, (Theodora) Sarah Orne

Swenson, May
1919-1989 . . . . **CLC 4, 14, 61; DA; DAB;**
DAC; DAM MST, POET; PC 14
See also CA 5-8R; 130; CANR 36; DLB 5;
MTCW; SATA 15

Swift, Augustus
See Lovecraft, H(oward) P(hillips)

Swift, Graham (Colin) 1949- . . . . **CLC 41, 88**
See also CA 117; 122; CANR 46

Swift, Jonathan
1667-1745 . . . . . . **LC 1; DA; DAB; DAC;**
DAM MST, NOV, POET; PC 9; WLC
See also CDBLB 1660-1789; DLB 39, 95,
101; SATA 19

Swinburne, Algernon Charles
1837-1909 . . . . . . **TCLC 8, 36; DA; DAB;**
DAC; DAM MST, POET; WLC
See also CA 105; 140; CDBLB 1832-1890;
DLB 35, 57

Swinfen, Ann . . . . **CLC 34**

Swinnerton, Frank Arthur
1884-1982 . . . . **CLC 31**
See also CA 108; DLB 34

Swithen, John
See King, Stephen (Edwin)

Sylvia
See Ashton-Warner, Sylvia (Constance)

Symmes, Robert Edward
See Duncan, Robert (Edward)

Symonds, John Addington
1840-1893 . . . . **NCLC 34**
See also DLB 57, 144

Symons, Arthur 1865-1945 . . . . **TCLC 11**
See also CA 107; DLB 19, 57, 149

Symons, Julian (Gustave)
1912-1994 . . . . **CLC 2, 14, 32**
See also CA 49-52; 147; CAAS 3; CANR 3,
33; DLB 87, 155; DLBY 92; MTCW

Synge, (Edmund) J(ohn) M(illington)
1871-1909 . . . . **TCLC 6, 37;**
DAM DRAM; DC 2
See also CA 104; 141; CDBLB 1890-1914;
DLB 10, 19

Syruc, J.
See Milosz, Czeslaw

Szirtes, George 1948- . . . . **CLC 46**
See also CA 109; CANR 27

Szymborska, Wislawa 1923- . . . . **CLC 99**
See also CA 154

T. O., Nik
See Annensky, Innokenty (Fyodorovich)

Tabori, George 1914- . . . . **CLC 19**
See also CA 49-52; CANR 4

Tagore, Rabindranath
1861-1941 . . . . **TCLC 3, 53;**
DAM DRAM, POET; PC 8
See also CA 104; 120; MTCW

Taine, Hippolyte Adolphe
1828-1893 . . . . **NCLC 15**

Talese, Gay 1932- . . . . **CLC 37**
See also AITN 1; CA 1-4R; CANR 9;
INT CANR-9; MTCW

Tallent, Elizabeth (Ann) 1954- . . . . . **CLC 45**
See also CA 117; DLB 130

Tally, Ted 1952- . . . . **CLC 42**
See also CA 120; 124; INT 124

Tamayo y Baus, Manuel
1829-1898 . . . . **NCLC 1**

Tammsaare, A(nton) H(ansen)
1878-1940 . . . . **TCLC 27**

Tan, Amy (Ruth)
1952- . . . . **CLC 59; DAM MULT, NOV,**
POP
See also AAYA 9; BEST 89:3; CA 136;
CANR 54; DLB 173; SATA 75

Tandem, Felix
See Spitteler, Carl (Friedrich Georg)

Tanizaki, Jun'ichiro
1886-1965 . . . . . . **CLC 8, 14, 28; SSC 21**
See also CA 93-96; 25-28R

Tanner, William
See Amis, Kingsley (William)

Tao Lao
See Storni, Alfonsina

Tarassoff, Lev
See Troyat, Henri

Tarbell, Ida M(inerva)
1857-1944 . . . . **TCLC 40**
See also CA 122; DLB 47

Tarkington, (Newton) Booth
1869-1946 . . . . **TCLC 9**
See also CA 110; 143; DLB 9, 102;
SATA 17

Tarkovsky, Andrei (Arsenyevich)
1932-1986 . . . . **CLC 75**
See also CA 127

Tartt, Donna 1964(?)- . . . . **CLC 76**
See also CA 142

Tasso, Torquato 1544-1595 . . . . **LC 5**

Tate, (John Orley) Allen
1899-1979 . . . . **CLC 2, 4, 6, 9, 11, 14, 24**
See also CA 5-8R; 85-88; CANR 32;
DLB 4, 45, 63; MTCW

Tate, Ellalice
See Hibbert, Eleanor Alice Burford

Tate, James (Vincent) 1943- . . **CLC 2, 6, 25**
See also CA 21-24R; CANR 29, 57; DLB 5,
169

Tavel, Ronald 1940- . . . . **CLC 6**
See also CA 21-24R; CANR 33

Taylor, C(ecil) P(hilip) 1929-1981 . . . **CLC 27**
See also CA 25-28R; 105; CANR 47

Taylor, Edward
1642(?)-1729 . . . . **LC 11; DA; DAB;**
DAC; DAM MST, POET
See also DLB 24

Taylor, Eleanor Ross 1920- . . . . **CLC 5**
See also CA 81-84

Taylor, Elizabeth 1912-1975 . . . **CLC 2, 4, 29**
See also CA 13-16R; CANR 9; DLB 139;
MTCW; SATA 13

Taylor, Henry (Splawn) 1942- . . . . . . **CLC 44**
See also CA 33-36R; CAAS 7; CANR 31;
DLB 5

Taylor, Kamala (Purnaiya) 1924-
See Markandaya, Kamala
See also CA 77-80

Tiptree, James, Jr. . . . . CLC 48, 50
See also Sheldon, Alice Hastings Bradley
See also DLB 8

Titmarsh, Michael Angelo
See Thackeray, William Makepeace

Tocqueville, Alexis (Charles Henri Maurice
Clerel Comte) 1805-1859 . . . . . NCLC 7

Tolkien, J(ohn) R(onald) R(euel)
1892-1973 . . . . CLC 1, 2, 3, 8, 12, 38;
DA; DAB; DAC; DAM MST, NOV,
POP; WLC
See also AAYA 10; AITN 1; CA 17-18;
45-48; CANR 36; CAP 2;
CDBLB 1914-1945; DLB 15, 160; JRDA;
MAICYA; MTCW; SATA 2, 32;
SATA-Obit 24

Toller, Ernst 1893-1939 . . . . TCLC 10
See also CA 107; DLB 124

Tolson, M. B.
See Tolson, Melvin B(eaunorus)

Tolson, Melvin B(eaunorus)
1898(?)-1966 . . . . CLC 36; BLC;
DAM MULT, POET
See also BW 1; CA 124; 89-92; DLB 48, 76

Tolstoi, Aleksei Nikolaevich
See Tolstoy, Alexey Nikolaevich

Tolstoy, Alexey Nikolaevich
1882-1945 . . . . TCLC 18
See also CA 107

Tolstoy, Count Leo
See Tolstoy, Leo (Nikolaevich)

Tolstoy, Leo (Nikolaevich)
1828-1910 . . . . . . TCLC 4, 11, 17, 28, 44;
DA; DAB; DAC; DAM MST, NOV;
SSC 9; WLC
See also CA 104; 123; SATA 26

Tomasi di Lampedusa, Giuseppe 1896-1957
See Lampedusa, Giuseppe (Tomasi) di
See also CA 111

Tomlin, Lily . . . . CLC 17
See also Tomlin, Mary Jean

Tomlin, Mary Jean 1939(?)-
See Tomlin, Lily
See also CA 117

Tomlinson, (Alfred) Charles
1927- . . . . CLC 2, 4, 6, 13, 45;
DAM POET; PC 17
See also CA 5-8R; CANR 33; DLB 40

Tonson, Jacob
See Bennett, (Enoch) Arnold

Toole, John Kennedy
1937-1969 . . . . CLC 19, 64
See also CA 104; DLBY 81

Toomer, Jean
1894-1967 . . . . . . CLC 1, 4, 13, 22; BLC;
DAM MULT; PC 7; SSC 1
See also BW 1; CA 85-88;
CDALB 1917-1929; DLB 45, 51; MTCW

Torley, Luke
See Blish, James (Benjamin)

Tornimparte, Alessandra
See Ginzburg, Natalia

Torre, Raoul della
See Mencken, H(enry) L(ouis)

Torrey, E(dwin) Fuller 1937- . . . . CLC 34
See also CA 119

Torsvan, Ben Traven
See Traven, B.

Torsvan, Benno Traven
See Traven, B.

Torsvan, Berick Traven
See Traven, B.

Torsvan, Berwick Traven
See Traven, B.

Torsvan, Bruno Traven
See Traven, B.

Torsvan, Traven
See Traven, B.

Tournier, Michel (Edouard)
1924- . . . . CLC 6, 23, 36, 95
See also CA 49-52; CANR 3, 36; DLB 83;
MTCW; SATA 23

Tournimparte, Alessandra
See Ginzburg, Natalia

Towers, Ivar
See Kornbluth, C(yril) M.

Towne, Robert (Burton) 1936(?)- . . . . CLC 87
See also CA 108; DLB 44

Townsend, Sue 1946- . . CLC 61; DAB; DAC
See also CA 119; 127; INT 127; MTCW;
SATA 55; SATA-Brief 48

Townshend, Peter (Dennis Blandford)
1945- . . . . CLC 17, 42
See also CA 107

Tozzi, Federigo 1883-1920 . . . . TCLC 31

Traill, Catharine Parr
1802-1899 . . . . NCLC 31
See also DLB 99

Trakl, Georg 1887-1914 . . . . TCLC 5
See also CA 104

Transtroemer, Tomas (Goesta)
1931- . . . . CLC 52, 65; DAM POET
See also CA 117; 129; CAAS 17

Transtromer, Tomas Gosta
See Transtroemer, Tomas (Goesta)

Traven, B. (?)-1969 . . . . CLC 8, 11
See also CA 19-20; 25-28R; CAP 2; DLB 9,
56; MTCW

Treitel, Jonathan 1959- . . . . CLC 70

Tremain, Rose 1943- . . . . CLC 42
See also CA 97-100; CANR 44; DLB 14

Tremblay, Michel
1942- . . . . . . CLC 29; DAC; DAM MST
See also CA 116; 128; DLB 60; MTCW

Trevanian . . . . CLC 29
See also Whitaker, Rod(ney)

Trevor, Glen
See Hilton, James

Trevor, William
1928- . . . . . CLC 7, 9, 14, 25, 71; SSC 21
See also Cox, William Trevor
See also DLB 14, 139

Trifonov, Yuri (Valentinovich)
1925-1981 . . . . CLC 45
See also CA 126; 103; MTCW

Trilling, Lionel 1905-1975 . . . . CLC 9, 11, 24
See also CA 9-12R; 61-64; CANR 10;
DLB 28, 63; INT CANR-10; MTCW

Trimball, W. H.
See Mencken, H(enry) L(ouis)

Tristan
See Gomez de la Serna, Ramon

Tristram
See Housman, A(lfred) E(dward)

Trogdon, William (Lewis) 1939-
See Heat-Moon, William Least
See also CA 115; 119; CANR 47; INT 119

Trollope, Anthony
1815-1882 . . . . . NCLC 6, 33; DA; DAB;
DAC; DAM MST, NOV; WLC
See also CDBLB 1832-1890; DLB 21, 57,
159; SATA 22

Trollope, Frances 1779-1863 . . . . . NCLC 30
See also DLB 21, 166

Trotsky, Leon 1879-1940 . . . . TCLC 22
See also CA 118

Trotter (Cockburn), Catharine
1679-1749 . . . . LC 8
See also DLB 84

Trout, Kilgore
See Farmer, Philip Jose

Trow, George W. S. 1943- . . . . CLC 52
See also CA 126

Troyat, Henri 1911- . . . . CLC 23
See also CA 45-48; CANR 2, 33; MTCW

Trudeau, G(arretson) B(eekman) 1948-
See Trudeau, Garry B.
See also CA 81-84; CANR 31; SATA 35

Trudeau, Garry B. . . . . CLC 12
See also Trudeau, G(arretson) B(eekman)
See also AAYA 10; AITN 2

Truffaut, Francois 1932-1984 . . . . CLC 20
See also CA 81-84; 113; CANR 34

Trumbo, Dalton 1905-1976 . . . . CLC 19
See also CA 21-24R; 69-72; CANR 10;
DLB 26

Trumbull, John 1750-1831 . . . . NCLC 30
See also DLB 31

Trundlett, Helen B.
See Eliot, T(homas) S(tearns)

Tryon, Thomas
1926-1991 . . . . . . CLC 3, 11; DAM POP
See also AITN 1; CA 29-32R; 135;
CANR 32; MTCW

Tryon, Tom
See Tryon, Thomas

Ts'ao Hsueh-ch'in 1715(?)-1763 . . . . . . LC 1

Tsushima, Shuji 1909-1948
See Dazai, Osamu
See also CA 107

Tsvetaeva (Efron), Marina (Ivanovna)
1892-1941 . . . . TCLC 7, 35; PC 14
See also CA 104; 128; MTCW

Tuck, Lily 1938- . . . . CLC 70
See also CA 139

Tu Fu 712-770 . . . . PC 9
See also DAM MULT

Tunis, John R(oberts) 1889-1975 . . . CLC 12
See also CA 61-64; DLB 22, 171; JRDA;
MAICYA; SATA 37; SATA-Brief 30

Tuohy, Frank.................... CLC 37
See also Tuohy, John Francis
See also DLB 14, 139

Tuohy, John Francis 1925-
See Tuohy, Frank
See also CA 5-8R; CANR 3, 47

Turco, Lewis (Putnam) 1934- ... CLC 11, 63
See also CA 13-16R; CAAS 22; CANR 24,
51; DLBY 84

Turgenev, Ivan
1818-1883 .... NCLC 21; DA; DAB;
DAC; DAM MST, NOV; DC 7; SSC 7;
WLC

Turgot, Anne-Robert-Jacques
1727-1781 .... LC 26

Turner, Frederick 1943-.......... CLC 48
See also CA 73-76; CAAS 10; CANR 12,
30, 56; DLB 40

Tutu, Desmond M(pilo)
1931- ..... CLC 80; BLC; DAM MULT
See also BW 1; CA 125

Tutuola, Amos
1920- .... CLC 5, 14, 29; BLC;
DAM MULT
See also BW 2; CA 9-12R; CANR 27;
DLB 125; MTCW

Twain, Mark
..... TCLC 6, 12, 19, 36, 48, 59; SSC 6;
WLC
See also Clemens, Samuel Langhorne
See also AAYA 20; DLB 11, 12, 23, 64, 74

Tyler, Anne
1941- .... CLC 7, 11, 18, 28, 44, 59;
DAM NOV, POP
See also AAYA 18; BEST 89:1; CA 9-12R;
CANR 11, 33, 53; DLB 6, 143; DLBY 82;
MTCW; SATA 7, 90

Tyler, Royall 1757-1826.......... NCLC 3
See also DLB 37

Tynan, Katharine 1861-1931 .... TCLC 3
See also CA 104; DLB 153

Tyutchev, Fyodor 1803-1873 ..... NCLC 34

Tzara, Tristan
1896-1963 .... CLC 47; DAM POET
See also Rosenfeld, Samuel; Rosenstock,
Sami; Rosenstock, Samuel
See also CA 153

Uhry, Alfred
1936- ..... CLC 55; DAM DRAM, POP
See also CA 127; 133; INT 133

Ulf, Haerved
See Strindberg, (Johan) August

Ulf, Harved
See Strindberg, (Johan) August

Ulibarri, Sabine R(eyes)
1919- .... CLC 83; DAM MULT
See also CA 131; DLB 82; HW

Unamuno (y Jugo), Miguel de
1864-1936 ... TCLC 2, 9; DAM MULT,
NOV; HLC; SSC 11
See also CA 104; 131; DLB 108; HW;
MTCW

Undercliffe, Errol
See Campbell, (John) Ramsey

Underwood, Miles
See Glassco, John

Undset, Sigrid
1882-1949 .... TCLC 3; DA; DAB;
DAC; DAM MST, NOV; WLC
See also CA 104; 129; MTCW

Ungaretti, Giuseppe
1888-1970 .... CLC 7, 11, 15
See also CA 19-20; 25-28R; CAP 2;
DLB 114

Unger, Douglas 1952-............ CLC 34
See also CA 130

Unsworth, Barry (Forster) 1930-.... CLC 76
See also CA 25-28R; CANR 30, 54

Updike, John (Hoyer)
1932- ...... CLC 1, 2, 3, 5, 7, 9, 13, 15,
23, 34, 43, 70; DA; DAB; DAC;
DAM MST, NOV, POET, POP;
SSC 13; WLC
See also CA 1-4R; CABS 1; CANR 4, 33,
51; CDALB 1968-1988; DLB 2, 5, 143;
DLBD 3; DLBY 80, 82; MTCW

Upshaw, Margaret Mitchell
See Mitchell, Margaret (Munnerlyn)

Upton, Mark
See Sanders, Lawrence

Urdang, Constance (Henriette)
1922- .... CLC 47
See also CA 21-24R; CANR 9, 24

Uriel, Henry
See Faust, Frederick (Schiller)

Uris, Leon (Marcus)
1924- .... CLC 7, 32; DAM NOV, POP
See also AITN 1, 2; BEST 89:2; CA 1-4R;
CANR 1, 40; MTCW; SATA 49

Urmuz
See Codrescu, Andrei

Urquhart, Jane 1949-........ CLC 90; DAC
See also CA 113; CANR 32

Ustinov, Peter (Alexander) 1921-.... CLC 1
See also AITN 1; CA 13-16R; CANR 25,
51; DLB 13

Vaculik, Ludvik 1926-............ CLC 7
See also CA 53-56

Valdez, Luis (Miguel)
1940- ..... CLC 84; DAM MULT; HLC
See also CA 101; CANR 32; DLB 122; HW

Valenzuela, Luisa
1938- ... CLC 31; DAM MULT; SSC 14
See also CA 101; CANR 32; DLB 113; HW

Valera y Alcala-Galiano, Juan
1824-1905 .... TCLC 10
See also CA 106

Valery, (Ambroise) Paul (Toussaint Jules)
1871-1945 .... TCLC 4, 15;
DAM POET; PC 9
See also CA 104; 122; MTCW

Valle-Inclan, Ramon (Maria) del
1866-1936 ..... TCLC 5; DAM MULT;
HLC
See also CA 106; 153; DLB 134

Vallejo, Antonio Buero
See Buero Vallejo, Antonio

Vallejo, Cesar (Abraham)
1892-1938 .... TCLC 3, 56;
DAM MULT; HLC
See also CA 105; 153; HW

Vallette, Marguerite Eymery
See Rachilde

Valle Y Pena, Ramon del
See Valle-Inclan, Ramon (Maria) del

Van Ash, Cay 1918-.............. CLC 34

Vanbrugh, Sir John
1664-1726 .... LC 21; DAM DRAM
See also DLB 80

Van Campen, Karl
See Campbell, John W(ood, Jr.)

Vance, Gerald
See Silverberg, Robert

Vance, Jack...................... CLC 35
See also Vance, John Holbrook
See also DLB 8

Vance, John Holbrook 1916-
See Queen, Ellery; Vance, Jack
See also CA 29-32R; CANR 17; MTCW

**Van Den Bogarde, Derek Jules Gaspard Ulric
Niven** 1921-
See Bogarde, Dirk
See also CA 77-80

Vandenburgh, Jane .... CLC 59

Vanderhaeghe, Guy 1951- .... CLC 41
See also CA 113

van der Post, Laurens (Jan)
1906-1996 .... CLC 5
See also CA 5-8R; 155; CANR 35

van de Wetering, Janwillem 1931- ... CLC 47
See also CA 49-52; CANR 4

Van Dine, S. S. .... TCLC 23
See also Wright, Willard Huntington

Van Doren, Carl (Clinton)
1885-1950 .... TCLC 18
See also CA 111

Van Doren, Mark 1894-1972..... CLC 6, 10
See also CA 1-4R; 37-40R; CANR 3;
DLB 45; MTCW

Van Druten, John (William)
1901-1957 .... TCLC 2
See also CA 104; DLB 10

Van Duyn, Mona (Jane)
1921- .... CLC 3, 7, 63; DAM POET
See also CA 9-12R; CANR 7, 38; DLB 5

Van Dyne, Edith
See Baum, L(yman) Frank

van Itallie, Jean-Claude 1936-....... CLC 3
See also CA 45-48; CAAS 2; CANR 1, 48;
DLB 7

van Ostaijen, Paul 1896-1928 ..... TCLC 33

Van Peebles, Melvin
1932- .... CLC 2, 20; DAM MULT
See also BW 2; CA 85-88; CANR 27

Vansittart, Peter 1920-............ CLC 42
See also CA 1-4R; CANR 3, 49

Van Vechten, Carl 1880-1964 ...... CLC 33
See also CA 89-92; DLB 4, 9, 51

Van Vogt, A(lfred) E(lton) 1912-..... CLC 1
See also CA 21-24R; CANR 28; DLB 8;
SATA 14

Varda, Agnes 1928- .... CLC 16
See also CA 116; 122

Wakoski, Diane
1937- . . . . **CLC 2, 4, 7, 9, 11, 40;**
DAM POET; PC 15
See also CA 13-16R; CAAS 1; CANR 9;
DLB 5; INT CANR-9

Wakoski-Sherbell, Diane
See Wakoski, Diane

Walcott, Derek (Alton)
1930- . . . . **CLC 2, 4, 9, 14, 25, 42, 67, 76;**
BLC; DAB; DAC; DAM MST, MULT,
POET; DC 7
See also BW 2; CA 89-92; CANR 26, 47;
DLB 117; DLBY 81; MTCW

Waldman, Anne 1945- . . . . **CLC 7**
See also CA 37-40R; CAAS 17; CANR 34;
DLB 16

Waldo, E. Hunter
See Sturgeon, Theodore (Hamilton)

Waldo, Edward Hamilton
See Sturgeon, Theodore (Hamilton)

Walker, Alice (Malsenior)
1944- . . . . **CLC 5, 6, 9, 19, 27, 46, 58;**
BLC; DA; DAB; DAC; DAM MST,
MULT, NOV, POET, POP; SSC 5
See also AAYA 3; BEST 89:4; BW 2;
CA 37-40R; CANR 9, 27, 49;
CDALB 1968-1988; DLB 6, 33, 143;
INT CANR-27; MTCW; SATA 31

Walker, David Harry 1911-1992 . . . . **CLC 14**
See also CA 1-4R; 137; CANR 1; SATA 8;
SATA-Obit 71

Walker, Edward Joseph 1934-
See Walker, Ted
See also CA 21-24R; CANR 12, 28, 53

Walker, George F.
1947- . . . . **CLC 44, 61; DAB; DAC;**
DAM MST
See also CA 103; CANR 21, 43; DLB 60

Walker, Joseph A.
1935- . . . . **CLC 19; DAM DRAM, MST**
See also BW 1; CA 89-92; CANR 26;
DLB 38

Walker, Margaret (Abigail)
1915- . . . . **CLC 1, 6; BLC; DAM MULT**
See also BW 2; CA 73-76; CANR 26, 54;
DLB 76, 152; MTCW

Walker, Ted . . . . **CLC 13**
See also Walker, Edward Joseph
See also DLB 40

Wallace, David Foster 1962- . . . . **CLC 50**
See also CA 132

Wallace, Dexter
See Masters, Edgar Lee

Wallace, (Richard Horatio) Edgar
1875-1932 . . . . **TCLC 57**
See also CA 115; DLB 70

Wallace, Irving
1916-1990 . . . . . **CLC 7, 13; DAM NOV,**
POP
See also AITN 1; CA 1-4R; 132; CAAS 1;
CANR 1, 27; INT CANR-27; MTCW

Wallant, Edward Lewis
1926-1962 . . . . **CLC 5, 10**
See also CA 1-4R; CANR 22; DLB 2, 28,
143; MTCW

Walley, Byron
See Card, Orson Scott

Walpole, Horace 1717-1797 . . . . **LC 2**
See also DLB 39, 104

Walpole, Hugh (Seymour)
1884-1941 . . . . **TCLC 5**
See also CA 104; DLB 34

Walser, Martin 1927- . . . . **CLC 27**
See also CA 57-60; CANR 8, 46; DLB 75,
124

Walser, Robert
1878-1956 . . . . **TCLC 18; SSC 20**
See also CA 118; DLB 66

Walsh, Jill Paton . . . . **CLC 35**
See also Paton Walsh, Gillian
See also AAYA 11; CLR 2; DLB 161;
SAAS 3

Walter, Villiam Christian
See Andersen, Hans Christian

Wambaugh, Joseph (Aloysius, Jr.)
1937- . . . . **CLC 3, 18; DAM NOV, POP**
See also AITN 1; BEST 89:3; CA 33-36R;
CANR 42; DLB 6; DLBY 83; MTCW

Ward, Arthur Henry Sarsfield 1883-1959
See Rohmer, Sax
See also CA 108

Ward, Douglas Turner 1930- . . . . **CLC 19**
See also BW 1; CA 81-84; CANR 27;
DLB 7, 38

Ward, Mary Augusta
See Ward, Mrs. Humphry

Ward, Mrs. Humphry
1851-1920 . . . . **TCLC 55**
See also DLB 18

Ward, Peter
See Faust, Frederick (Schiller)

Warhol, Andy 1928(?)-1987 . . . . **CLC 20**
See also AAYA 12; BEST 89:4; CA 89-92;
121; CANR 34

Warner, Francis (Robert le Plastrier)
1937- . . . . **CLC 14**
See also CA 53-56; CANR 11

Warner, Marina 1946- . . . . **CLC 59**
See also CA 65-68; CANR 21, 55

Warner, Rex (Ernest) 1905-1986 . . . . **CLC 45**
See also CA 89-92; 119; DLB 15

Warner, Susan (Bogert)
1819-1885 . . . . **NCLC 31**
See also DLB 3, 42

Warner, Sylvia (Constance) Ashton
See Ashton-Warner, Sylvia (Constance)

Warner, Sylvia Townsend
1893-1978 . . . . **CLC 7, 19; SSC 23**
See also CA 61-64; 77-80; CANR 16;
DLB 34, 139; MTCW

Warren, Mercy Otis 1728-1814 . . . **NCLC 13**
See also DLB 31

Warren, Robert Penn
1905-1989 . . . . **CLC 1, 4, 6, 8, 10, 13, 18,**
39, 53, 59; DA; DAB; DAC; DAM MST,
NOV, POET; SSC 4; WLC
See also AITN 1; CA 13-16R; 129;
CANR 10, 47; CDALB 1968-1988;
DLB 2, 48, 152; DLBY 80, 89;
INT CANR-10; MTCW; SATA 46;
SATA-Obit 63

Warshofsky, Isaac
See Singer, Isaac Bashevis

Warton, Thomas
1728-1790 . . . . **LC 15; DAM POET**
See also DLB 104, 109

Waruk, Kona
See Harris, (Theodore) Wilson

Warung, Price 1855-1911 . . . . **TCLC 45**

Warwick, Jarvis
See Garner, Hugh

Washington, Alex
See Harris, Mark

Washington, Booker T(aliaferro)
1856-1915 . . . . **TCLC 10; BLC;**
DAM MULT
See also BW 1; CA 114; 125; SATA 28

Washington, George 1732-1799 . . . . . . **LC 25**
See also DLB 31

Wassermann, (Karl) Jakob
1873-1934 . . . . **TCLC 6**
See also CA 104; DLB 66

Wasserstein, Wendy
1950- . . . . **CLC 32, 59, 90;**
DAM DRAM; DC 4
See also CA 121; 129; CABS 3; CANR 53;
INT 129

Waterhouse, Keith (Spencer)
1929- . . . . **CLC 47**
See also CA 5-8R; CANR 38; DLB 13, 15;
MTCW

Waters, Frank (Joseph)
1902-1995 . . . . **CLC 88**
See also CA 5-8R; 149; CAAS 13; CANR 3,
18; DLBY 86

Waters, Roger 1944- . . . . **CLC 35**

Watkins, Frances Ellen
See Harper, Frances Ellen Watkins

Watkins, Gerrold
See Malzberg, Barry N(athaniel)

Watkins, Gloria 1955(?)-
See hooks, bell
See also BW 2; CA 143

Watkins, Paul 1964- . . . . **CLC 55**
See also CA 132

Watkins, Vernon Phillips
1906-1967 . . . . **CLC 43**
See also CA 9-10; 25-28R; CAP 1; DLB 20

Watson, Irving S.
See Mencken, H(enry) L(ouis)

Watson, John H.
See Farmer, Philip Jose

Watson, Richard F.
See Silverberg, Robert

Waugh, Auberon (Alexander) 1939- . . **CLC 7**
See also CA 45-48; CANR 6, 22; DLB 14

Wharton, James
See Mencken, H(enry) L(ouis)

Wharton, William (a pseudonym)
.... **CLC 18, 37**
See also CA 93-96; DLBY 80; INT 93-96

Wheatley (Peters), Phillis
1754(?)-1784 .... **LC 3; BLC; DA; DAC;**
DAM MST, MULT, POET; PC 3; WLC
See also CDALB 1640-1865; DLB 31, 50

Wheelock, John Hall 1886-1978.... **CLC 14**
See also CA 13-16R; 77-80; CANR 14;
DLB 45

White, E(lwyn) B(rooks)
1899-1985 .. **CLC 10, 34, 39; DAM POP**
See also AITN 2; CA 13-16R; 116;
CANR 16, 37; CLR 1, 21; DLB 11, 22;
MAICYA; MTCW; SATA 2, 29;
SATA-Obit 44

White, Edmund (Valentine III)
1940- .... **CLC 27; DAM POP**
See also AAYA 7; CA 45-48; CANR 3, 19,
36; MTCW

White, Patrick (Victor Martindale)
1912-1990 .. **CLC 3, 4, 5, 7, 9, 18, 65, 69**
See also CA 81-84; 132; CANR 43; MTCW

White, Phyllis Dorothy James 1920-
See James, P. D.
See also CA 21-24R; CANR 17, 43;
DAM POP; MTCW

White, T(erence) H(anbury)
1906-1964 .... **CLC 30**
See also CA 73-76; CANR 37; DLB 160;
JRDA; MAICYA; SATA 12

White, Terence de Vere
1912-1994 .... **CLC 49**
See also CA 49-52; 145; CANR 3

White, Walter F(rancis)
1893-1955 .... **TCLC 15**
See also White, Walter
See also BW 1; CA 115; 124; DLB 51

White, William Hale 1831-1913
See Rutherford, Mark
See also CA 121

Whitehead, E(dward) A(nthony)
1933- .... **CLC 5**
See also CA 65-68

Whitemore, Hugh (John) 1936-..... **CLC 37**
See also CA 132; INT 132

Whitman, Sarah Helen (Power)
1803-1878 .... **NCLC 19**
See also DLB 1

Whitman, Walt(er)
1819-1892 ..... **NCLC 4, 31; DA; DAB;**
DAC; DAM MST, POET; PC 3; WLC
See also CDALB 1640-1865; DLB 3, 64;
SATA 20

Whitney, Phyllis A(yame)
1903- .... **CLC 42; DAM POP**
See also AITN 2; BEST 90:3; CA 1-4R;
CANR 3, 25, 38; JRDA; MAICYA;
SATA 1, 30

Whittemore, (Edward) Reed (Jr.)
1919- .... **CLC 4**
See also CA 9-12R; CAAS 8; CANR 4;
DLB 5

Whittier, John Greenleaf
1807-1892 .... **NCLC 8, 59**
See also DLB 1

Whittlebot, Hernia
See Coward, Noel (Peirce)

Wicker, Thomas Grey 1926-
See Wicker, Tom
See also CA 65-68; CANR 21, 46

Wicker, Tom .... **CLC 7**
See also Wicker, Thomas Grey

Wideman, John Edgar
1941- .... **CLC 5, 34, 36, 67; BLC;**
DAM MULT
See also BW 2; CA 85-88; CANR 14, 42;
DLB 33, 143

Wiebe, Rudy (Henry)
1934- .... **CLC 6, 11, 14; DAC;**
DAM MST
See also CA 37-40R; CANR 42; DLB 60

Wieland, Christoph Martin
1733-1813 .... **NCLC 17**
See also DLB 97

Wiene, Robert 1881-1938........ **TCLC 56**

Wieners, John 1934-............... **CLC 7**
See also CA 13-16R; DLB 16

Wiesel, Elie(zer)
1928- ...... **CLC 3, 5, 11, 37; DA; DAB;**
DAC; DAM MST, NOV
See also AAYA 7; AITN 1; CA 5-8R;
CAAS 4; CANR 8, 40; DLB 83;
DLBY 87; INT CANR-8; MTCW;
SATA 56

Wiggins, Marianne 1947-......... **CLC 57**
See also BEST 89:3; CA 130

Wight, James Alfred 1916-
See Herriot, James
See also CA 77-80; SATA 55;
SATA-Brief 44

Wilbur, Richard (Purdy)
1921- ... **CLC 3, 6, 9, 14, 53; DA; DAB;**
DAC; DAM MST, POET
See also CA 1-4R; CABS 2; CANR 2, 29;
DLB 5, 169; INT CANR-29; MTCW;
SATA 9

Wild, Peter 1940-................ **CLC 14**
See also CA 37-40R; DLB 5

Wilde, Oscar (Fingal O'Flahertie Wills)
1854(?)-1900 .... **TCLC 1, 8, 23, 41; DA;**
DAB; DAC; DAM DRAM, MST, NOV;
SSC 11; WLC
See also CA 104; 119; CDBLB 1890-1914;
DLB 10, 19, 34, 57, 141, 156; SATA 24

Wilder, Billy .... **CLC 20**
See also Wilder, Samuel
See also DLB 26

Wilder, Samuel 1906-
See Wilder, Billy
See also CA 89-92

Wilder, Thornton (Niven)
1897-1975 ...... **CLC 1, 5, 6, 10, 15, 35,**
82; DA; DAB; DAC; DAM DRAM,
MST, NOV; DC 1; WLC
See also AITN 2; CA 13-16R; 61-64;
CANR 40; DLB 4, 7, 9; MTCW

Wilding, Michael 1942-.......... **CLC 73**
See also CA 104; CANR 24, 49

Wiley, Richard 1944-............. **CLC 44**
See also CA 121; 129

Wilhelm, Kate .... **CLC 7**
See also Wilhelm, Katie Gertrude
See also AAYA 20; CAAS 5; DLB 8;
INT CANR-17

Wilhelm, Katie Gertrude 1928-
See Wilhelm, Kate
See also CA 37-40R; CANR 17, 36; MTCW

Wilkins, Mary
See Freeman, Mary Eleanor Wilkins

Willard, Nancy 1936-........... **CLC 7, 37**
See also CA 89-92; CANR 10, 39; CLR 5;
DLB 5, 52; MAICYA; MTCW;
SATA 37, 71; SATA-Brief 30

Williams, C(harles) K(enneth)
1936- .... **CLC 33, 56; DAM POET**
See also CA 37-40R; CAAS 26; CANR 57;
DLB 5

Williams, Charles
See Collier, James L(incoln)

Williams, Charles (Walter Stansby)
1886-1945 .... **TCLC 1, 11**
See also CA 104; DLB 100, 153

Williams, (George) Emlyn
1905-1987 ...... **CLC 15; DAM DRAM**
See also CA 104; 123; CANR 36; DLB 10,
77; MTCW

Williams, Hugo 1942-............ **CLC 42**
See also CA 17-20R; CANR 45; DLB 40

Williams, J. Walker
See Wodehouse, P(elham) G(renville)

Williams, John A(lfred)
1925- ... **CLC 5, 13; BLC; DAM MULT**
See also BW 2; CA 53-56; CAAS 3;
CANR 6, 26, 51; DLB 2, 33;
INT CANR-6

Williams, Jonathan (Chamberlain)
1929- .... **CLC 13**
See also CA 9-12R; CAAS 12; CANR 8;
DLB 5

Williams, Joy 1944-.............. **CLC 31**
See also CA 41-44R; CANR 22, 48

Williams, Norman 1952- .... **CLC 39**
See also CA 118

Williams, Sherley Anne
1944- ..... **CLC 89; BLC; DAM MULT,**
POET
See also BW 2; CA 73-76; CANR 25;
DLB 41; INT CANR-25; SATA 78

Williams, Shirley
See Williams, Sherley Anne

Williams, Tennessee
1911-1983 ..... **CLC 1, 2, 5, 7, 8, 11, 15,**
19, 30, 39, 45, 71; DA; DAB; DAC;
DAM DRAM, MST; DC 4; WLC
See also AITN 1, 2; CA 5-8R; 108;
CABS 3; CANR 31; CDALB 1941-1968;
DLB 7; DLBD 4; DLBY 83; MTCW

Williams, Thomas (Alonzo)
1926-1990 .... **CLC 14**
See also CA 1-4R; 132; CANR 2

Williams, William C.
See Williams, William Carlos

Zimmerman, Robert
See Dylan, Bob

Zindel, Paul
1936- . . . . . **CLC 6, 26; DA; DAB; DAC;**
DAM DRAM, MST, NOV; DC 5
See also AAYA 2; CA 73-76; CANR 31;
CLR 3, 45; DLB 7, 52; JRDA; MAICYA;
MTCW; SATA 16, 58

Zinov'Ev, A. A.
See Zinoviev, Alexander (Aleksandrovich)

Zinoviev, Alexander (Aleksandrovich)
1922- . . . . **CLC 19**
See also CA 116; 133; CAAS 10

Zoilus
See Lovecraft, H(oward) P(hillips)

Zola, Emile (Edouard Charles Antoine)
1840-1902 . . . . . . **TCLC 1, 6, 21, 41; DA;**
DAB; DAC; DAM MST, NOV; WLC
See also CA 104; 138; DLB 123

Zoline, Pamela 1941- . . . . **CLC 62**

Zorrilla y Moral, Jose 1817-1893 . . **NCLC 6**

Zoshchenko, Mikhail (Mikhailovich)
1895-1958 . . . . **TCLC 15; SSC 15**
See also CA 115

Zuckmayer, Carl 1896-1977 . . . . **CLC 18**
See also CA 69-72; DLB 56, 124

Zuk, Georges
See Skelton, Robin

Zukofsky, Louis
1904-1978 . . . . **CLC 1, 2, 4, 7, 11, 18;**
DAM POET; PC 11
See also CA 9-12R; 77-80; CANR 39;
DLB 5, 165; MTCW

Zweig, Paul 1935-1984 . . . . **CLC 34, 42**
See also CA 85-88; 113

Zweig, Stefan 1881-1942 . . . . **TCLC 17**
See also CA 112; DLB 81, 118

Zwingli, Huldreich 1484-1531 . . . . **LC 37**

Literary Criticism Series
Cumulative Topic Index

This index lists all topic entries in Gale's *Classical and Medieval Literature Criticism, Contemporary Literary Criticism, Literature Criticism from 1400 to 1800, Nineteenth-Century Literature Criticism,* and *Twentieth-Century Literary Criticism.*

Topic Index

Topic Index

Topic Index

Young Playwrights Festival
    1988—CLC 55: 376-81
    1989—CLC 59: 398-403
    1990—CLC 65: 444-8

Topic Index

NCLC Cumulative Nationality Index

AMERICAN
Alcott, Amos Bronson **1**
Alcott, Louisa May **6, 58**
Alger, Horatio **8**
Allston, Washington **2**
Audubon, John James **47**
Barlow, Joel **23**
Beecher, Catharine Esther **30**
Bellamy, Edward **4**
Bird, Robert Montgomery **1**
Brackenridge, Hugh Henry **7**
Brentano, Clemens (Maria) **1**
Brown, Charles Brockden **22**
Brown, William Wells **2**
Brownson, Orestes **50**
Bryant, William Cullen **6, 46**
Calhoun, John Caldwell **15**
Channing, William Ellery **17**
Child, Lydia Maria **6**
Chivers, Thomas Holley **49**
Cooke, John Esten **5**
Cooper, James Fenimore **1, 27, 54**
Crockett, David **8**
Dana, Richard Henry, Sr. **53**
Dickinson, Emily (Elizabeth) **21**
Douglass, Frederick **7, 55**
Dunlap, William **2**
Dwight, Timothy **13**
Emerson, Ralph Waldo **1, 38**
Field, Eugene **3**
Foster, Stephen Collins **26**
Frederic, Harold **10**
Freneau, Philip Morin **1**
Fuller, Margaret **5, 50**
Halleck, Fitz-Greene **47**
Hamilton, Alexander **49**
Hammon, Jupiter **5**
Harris, George Washington **23**

Hawthorne, Nathaniel **2, 10, 17, 23, 39**
Holmes, Oliver Wendell **14**
Irving, Washington **2, 19**
James, Henry, Sr. **53**
Jefferson, Thomas **11**
Kennedy, John Pendleton **2**
Lanier, Sidney **6**
Lazarus, Emma **8**
Lincoln, Abraham **18**
Longfellow, Henry Wadsworth **2, 45**
Lowell, James Russell **2**
Melville, Herman **3, 12, 29, 45, 49**
Parkman, Francis **12**
Paulding, James Kirke **2**
Pinkney, Edward **31**
Poe, Edgar Allan **1, 16, 55**
Rowson, Susanna Haswell **5**
Sand, George **57**
Sedgwick, Catharine Maria **19**
Shaw, Henry Wheeler **15**
Sheridan, Richard Brinsley **5**
Signourney, Lydia Howard (Huntley) **21**
Simms, William Gilmore **3**
Smith, Joseph, Jr. **53**
Southworth, Emma Dorothy Eliza Nevitte **26**
Stowe, Harriet (Elizabeth) Beecher **3, 50**
Thoreau, Henry David **7, 21, 61**
Timrod, Henry **25**
Trumbull, John **30**
Tyler, Royall **3**
Very, Jones **9**
Warner, Susan (Bogert) **31**
Warren, Mercy Otis **13**
Webster, Noah **30**
Whitman, Sarah Helen (Power) **19**
Whitman, Walt(er) **4, 31**
Whittier, John Greenleaf **8, 59**

ARGENTINIAN
Echeverria, (Jose) Esteban (Antonino) **18**
Hernandez, Jose **17**

AUSTRALIAN
Adams, Francis **33**
Clarke, Marcus (Andrew Hislop) **19**
Gordon, Adam Lindsay **21**
Kendall, Henry **12**

AUSTRIAN
Grillparzer, Franz **1**
Lenau, Nikolaus **16**
Nestroy, Johann **42**
Sacher-Masoch, Leopold von **31**
Stifter, Adalbert **41**

CANADIAN
Crawford, Isabella Valancy **12**
Haliburton, Thomas Chandler **15**
Lampman, Archibald **25**
Moodie, Susanna (Strickland) **14**
Richardson, John **55**
Traill, Catharine Parr **31**

CZECH
Macha, Karel Hynek **46**

DANISH
Andersen, Hans Christian **7**
Grundtvig, Nicolai Frederik Severin **1**
Jacobsen, Jens Peter **34**
Kierkegaard, Soren **34**

ENGLISH
Ainsworth, William Harrison **13**
Arnold, Matthew **6, 29**
Arnold, Thomas **18**

Tieck, (Johann) Ludwig **5, 46**
Wagner, Richard **9**
Wieland, Christoph Martin **17**

GREEK
Solomos, Dionysios **15**

HUNGARIAN
Arany, Janos **34**
Madach, Imre **19**
Petofi, Sandor **21**

INDIAN
Chatterji, Bankim Chandra **19**
Dutt, Toru **29**
Ghalib **39**

IRISH
Allingham, William **25**
Banim, John **13**
Banim, Michael **13**
Boucicault, Dion **41**
Carleton, William **3**
Croker, John Wilson **10**
Darley, George **2**
Edgeworth, Maria **1, 51**
Ferguson, Samuel **33**
Griffin, Gerald **7**
Jameson, Anna **43**
Le Fanu, Joseph Sheridan **9, 58**
Lever, Charles (James) **23**
Maginn, William **8**
Mangan, James Clarence **27**
Maturin, Charles Robert **6**
Moore, Thomas **6**
Morgan, Lady **29**
O'Brien, Fitz-James **21**

ITALIAN
Collodi, Carlo (Carlo Lorenzini) **54**
Da Ponte, Lorenzo **50**
Foscolo, Ugo **8**
Gozzi, (Conte) Carlo **23**
Leopardi, (Conte) Giacomo **22**
Manzoni, Alessandro **29**
Mazzini, Guiseppe **34**
Nievo, Ippolito **22**

JAPANESE
Higuchi Ichiyo **49**
Motoori, Norinaga **45**

LITHUANIAN
Mapu, Abraham (ben Jekutiel) **18**

MEXICAN
Lizardi, Jose Joaquin Fernandez de **30**

NORWEGIAN

Collett, (Jacobine) Camilla (Wergeland) **22**
Wergeland, Henrik Arnold **5**

POLISH
Fredro, Aleksander **8**
Krasicki, Ignacy **8**
Krasinski, Zygmunt **4**
Mickiewicz, Adam **3**
Norwid, Cyprian Kamil **17**
Slowacki, Juliusz **15**

ROMANIAN
Eminescu, Mihail **33**

RUSSIAN
Aksakov, Sergei Timofeyvich **2**
Bakunin, Mikhail (Alexandrovich) **25, 58**
Bashkirtseff, Marie **27**
Belinski, Vissarion Grigoryevich **5**
Chernyshevsky, Nikolay Gavrilovich **1**
Dobrolyubov, Nikolai Alexandrovich **5**
Dostoevsky, Fedor Mikhailovich **2, 7, 21, 33, 43**
Gogol, Nikolai (Vasilyevich) **5, 15, 31**
Goncharov, Ivan Alexandrovich **1**
Herzen, Aleksandr Ivanovich **10, 61**
Karamzin, Nikolai Mikhailovich **3**
Krylov, Ivan Andreevich **1**
Lermontov, Mikhail Yuryevich **5**
Leskov, Nikolai (Semyonovich) **25**
Nekrasov, Nikolai Alekseevich **11**
Ostrovsky, Alexander **30, 57**
Pisarev, Dmitry Ivanovich **25**
Pushkin, Alexander (Sergeyevich) **3, 27**
Saltykov, Mikhail Evgrafovich **16**
Smolenskin, Peretz **30**
Turgenev, Ivan **21**
Tyutchev, Fyodor **34**
Zhukovsky, Vasily **35**

SCOTTISH
Baillie, Joanna **2**
Beattie, James **25**
Campbell, Thomas **19**
Ferrier, Susan (Edmonstone) **8**
Galt, John **1**
Hogg, James **4**
Jeffrey, Francis **33**
Lockhart, John Gibson **6**
Mackenzie, Henry **41**
Oliphant, Margaret (Oliphant Wilson) **11, 61**
Scott, Walter **15**
Smith, Alexander **59**
Stevenson, Robert Louis (Balfour) **5, 14**
Thomson, James, **18**
Wilson, John **5**

SPANISH

Alarcon, Pedro Antonio de **1**
Caballero, Fernan **10**
Castro, Rosalia de **3**
Espronceda, Jose de **39**
Larra (y Sanchez de Castro), Mariano Jose de **17**
Tamayo y Baus, Manuel **1**
Zorrilla y Moral, Jose **6**

SWEDISH
Almqvist, Carl Jonas Love **42**
Bremer, Fredrika **11**
Stagnelius, Erik Johan **61**
Tegner, Esaias **2**

SWISS
Amiel, Henri Frederic **4**
Burckhardt, Jacob **49**
Keller, Gottfried **2**
Wyss, Johann David Von **10**

UKRAINIAN
Taras Shevchenko **54**

Nationality Index

NCLC 61 Title Index

Title Index